D0187915

# COLLINS GEM

# SPANISH DICTIONARY

## SPANISH ◆ ENGLISH
## ENGLISH ◆ SPANISH

HarperCollins*Publishers*

*first published in this edition 1982*
*third edition 1993*

© William Collins Sons & Co. Ltd. 1982, 1989
© HarperCollins Publishers 1993

**first reprint 1993**

ISBN 0 00 470048-1

Mike Gonzalez
Margaret Tejerizo, John Forry,
Carmen Billinghurst, Liam Kane,
Pat Feehan, Soledad Pérez-López,
José Ramón Parrondo, Teresa Alvarez

*editorial staff / redacción*
Joyce Littlejohn, Claire Evans,
Jeremy Butterfield, Irene Lakhani,
Lesley Johnston

Ediciones Grijalbo, S.A.
Aragón 385, Barcelona 08013
ISBN 84-253-2522-6

*All rights reserved / reservados todos
los derechos para España*

*A catalogue record for this book is
available from the British Library*

*Typeset by Morton Word Processing Ltd, Scarborough*

*Printed in Great Britain by
HarperCollins Manufacturing, Glasgow*

| | | |
|---|---|---|
| ÍNDICE | | CONTENTS |

## INTRODUCCIÓN

Estamos muy satisfechos de que hayas decidido comprar el Diccionario de Inglés Collins Gem y esperamos que lo disfrutes y que te sirva de gran ayuda ya sea en el colegio, en el trabajo, en tus vacaciones o en casa.

Esta introducción pretende darte algunas indicaciones para ayudarte a sacar el mayor provecho de este diccionario; no sólo de su extenso vocabulario, sino de todo la información que te proporciona cada entrada. Esta te ayudará a leer y comprender — y también a comunicarte y a expresarte — en inglés moderno.

El Diccionario de Inglés Collins Gem comienza con una lista de abreviaturas utilizadas en el texto y con una ilustración de los sonidos representados por los símbolos fonéticos. Al final del diccionario encontrarás una tabla de los verbos irregulares del inglés, y para terminar, una sección sobre el uso de los números y de las expresiones de tiempo.

## EL MANEJO DE TU DICCIONARIO COLLINS GEM

La amplia información que te ofrece este dic̶c̶i̶o̶n̶a̶r̶i̶o̶ aparece presentada en distintas tipografías, c̶o̶n̶ ̶c̶a̶r̶á̶c̶t̶e̶res de diversos tamaños y con distintos símb̶o̶l̶o̶s̶,̶ ̶a̶b̶reviaturas y paréntesis. Los apartados siguientes̶ ̶e̶x̶p̶l̶i̶c̶a̶n̶ las reglas y símbolos utilizados.

### entradas

Las palabras que consultas en el diccionario — las "entradas" —

aparecen ordenadas alfabéticamente y en **caracteres gruesos** para
una identificación más rápida. Las dos palabras que ocupan el
margen superior de cada página indican la primera y la última
entrada de la página en cuestión.

La información sobre el uso o la forma de determinadas entradas
aparece entre paréntesis, detrás de la transcripción fonética, y
generalmente en forma abreviada y en cursiva (p.ej.: *(fam)*,
*(COM)*).

En algunos casos se ha considerado oportuno agrupar palabras de
una misma familia (**nación, nacionalismo; accept, acceptance**)
bajo una misma entrada, en caracteres gruesos de tamaño algo
más pequeño que los de la entrada principal.
Las expresiones de uso corriente en las que aparece una entrada se
dan en negrita (p.ej.: **to be in a hurry**).

### Símbolos fonéticos
La transcripción fonética de cada entrada (que indica su pronunciación) aparece entre corchetes, inmediatamente después de la entrada (p.ej.: **knead** [niːd]). En la página ix encontrarás una lista de
los símbolos fonéticos utilizados en este diccionario.

### Traducciones
Las traducciones de las entradas aparecen en caracteres normales,
y en los casos en los que existen significados o usos diferentes, éstos
aparecen separados mediante un punto y coma. A menudo encontrarás también otras palabras en cursiva y entre paréntesis antes
de las traducciones. Estas sugieren contextos en los que la entrada
podría aparecer (p.ej.: **rough** (*voice*) o (*weather*)) o proporcionan
sinónimos (p.ej.: **rough** (*violent*)).

### Palabras clave
Particular relevancia reciben ciertas palabras inglesas y españo-
las que han sido consideradas palabras ''clave'' en cada lengua.
Estas pueden, por ejemplo, ser de utilización muy corriente o tener
distintos usos (**de, haber; get, that**). La combinación de rombos y
números te permitirá distinguir las diferentes categorías gramaticales y los diferentes significados. Las indicaciones en cursiva y
entre paréntesis proporcionan además importante información
adicional.

### Información gramatical
Las categorías gramaticales aparecen en forma abreviada y en
cursiva después de la transcripción fonética de cada entrada (*vi,
adv, conj*).

También se indican la forma femenina y los plurales irregulares de
los sustantivos del inglés (**child, ~ren**).

# INTRODUCTION

We are delighted you have decided to buy the Collins Gem Spanish Dictionary and hope you will enjoy and benefit from using it at school, at home, on holiday or at work.

This introduction gives you a few tips on how to get the most out of your dictionary — not simply from its comprehensive wordlist but also from the information provided in each entry. This will help you to read and understand modern Spanish, as well as communicate and express yourself in the language.

The Collins Gem Spanish Dictionary begins by listing the abbreviations used in the text and illustrating the sounds shown by the phonetic symbols. You will find Spanish verb tables at the back, followed by a final section on numbers and time expressions.

## USING YOUR COLLINS GEM DICTIONARY

A wealth of information is presented in the dictionary, using various typefaces, sizes of type, symbols, abbreviations and brackets. The conventions and symbols used are explained in the following sections.

### Headwords

The words you look up in a dictionary — "headwords" — are listed alphabetically. They are printed in **bold type** for rapid identification. The two headwords appearing at the top of each page indicate the first and last word dealt with on the page in question.

Information about the usage or form of certain headwords is given in brackets after the phonetic spelling. This usually appears in abbreviated form and in italics (e.g. *(fam)*, *(COMM)*).

Where appropriate, words related to headwords are grouped in the same entry (**nación, nacionalismo; accept, acceptance**) in a slightly smaller bold type than the headword.

Common expressions in which the headword appears are shown in a different bold roman type (e.g. **hacer calor**).

### Phonetic spellings

The phonetic spelling of each headword (indicating its pronunciation) is given in square brackets immediately after the headword (e.g. **dónde** [ˈdonde]). A list of these symbols is given on page ix.

## Translations

Headword translations are given in ordinary type and, where more than one meaning or usage exists, these are separated by a semicolon. You will often find other words in italics in brackets before the translations. These offer suggested contexts in which the headword might appear (e.g. **grande** (*de tamaño*)) or provide synonyms (e.g. **grande** (*alto*) *o* (*distinguido*)).

## "Key" words

Special status is given to certain Spanish and English words which are considered as "key" words in each language. They may, for example, occur very frequently or have several types of usage (e.g. **de, haber**). A combination of lozenges and numbers helps you to distinguish different parts of speech and different meanings. Further helpful information is provided in brackets and in italics.

## Grammatical information

Parts of speech are given in abbreviated form in italics after the phonetic spellings of headwords (e.g. *vt, adv, conj*).

Genders of Spanish nouns are indicated as follows: nm for a masculine and nf for a feminine noun. Feminine and irregular plural forms of nouns are also shown (**irlandés, esa; luz,** (*pl* **luces**)).

# ABREVIATURAS

# ABBREVIATIONS

| | | |
|---|---|---|
| abreviatura | **ab(b)r** | abbreviation |
| adjetivo, locución adjetiva | **adj** | adjective, adjectival phrase |
| administración | **ADMIN** | administration |
| adverbio, locución adverbial | **adv** | adverb, adverbial phrase |
| agricultura | **AGR** | agriculture |
| América Latina | **AM** | Latin America |
| anatomía | **ANAT** | anatomy |
| arquitectura | **ARQ, ARCH** | architecture |
| el automóvil | **AUT(O)** | the motor car and motoring |
| aviación, viajes aéreos | **AVIAT** | flying, air travel |
| biología | **BIO(L)** | biology |
| botánica, flores | **BOT** | botany |
| inglés británico | **BRIT** | British English |
| química | **CHEM** | chemistry |
| comercio, finanzas, banca | **COM(M)** | commerce, finance, banking |
| informática | **COMPUT** | computers |
| conjunción | **conj** | conjunction |
| construcción | **CONSTR** | building |
| compuesto | **cpd** | compound element |
| cocina | **CULIN** | cookery |
| economía | **ECON** | economics |
| electricidad, electrónica | **ELEC** | electricity, electronics |
| enseñanza, sistema escolar y universitario | **ESCOL** | schooling, schools and universities |
| España | **Esp** | Spain |
| especialmente | **esp** | especially |
| exclamación, interjección | **excl** | exclamation, interjection |
| femenino | **f** | feminine |
| lengua familiar (! vulgar) | **fam (!)** | colloquial usage (! particularly offensive) |
| ferrocarril | **FERRO** | railways |
| uso figurado | **fig** | figurative use |
| fotografía | **FOTO** | photography |
| (verbo inglés) del cual la partícula es inseparable | **fus** | (phrasal verb) where the particle is inseparable |
| generalmente | **gen** | generally |
| geografía, geología | **GEO** | geography, geology |
| geometría | **GEOM** | geometry |
| uso familiar (! vulgar) | **inf (!)** | colloquial usage (! particularly offensive) |
| infinitivo | **infin** | infinitive |
| informática | **INFORM** | computers |
| invariable | **inv** | invariable |
| irregular | **irreg** | irregular |
| lo jurídico | **JUR** | law |
| América Latina | **LAM** | Latin America |
| gramática, lingüística | **LING** | grammar, linguistics |

| ABREVIATURAS | | ABBREVIATIONS |
|---|---|---|
| masculino | m | masculine |
| masculino/femenino | m/f | masculine/feminine |
| matemáticas | MATH | mathematics |
| medicina | MED | medicine |
| lo militar, ejército | MIL | military matters |
| música | MUS | music |
| sustantivo, nombre | n | noun |
| navegación, náutica | NAUT | sailing, navigation |
| sustantivo numérico | num | numeral noun |
| complemento | obj | (grammatical) object |
| | o.s. | oneself |
| peyorativo | pey, pej | derogatory, pejorative |
| fotografía | PHOT | photography |
| fisiología | PHYSIOL | physiology |
| plural | pl | plural |
| política | POL | politics |
| participio de pasado | pp | past participle |
| preposición | prep | preposition |
| pronombre | pron | pronoun |
| psicología, psiquiatría | PSICO, PSYCH | psychology, psychiatry |
| tiempo pasado | pt | past tense |
| química | QUIM | chemistry |
| ferrocarril | RAIL | railways |
| | sb | somebody |
| religión | REL | religion |
| enseñanza, sistema escolar y universitario | SCH | schooling, schools and universities |
| singular | sg | singular |
| España | SP | Spain |
| | sth | something |
| sujeto | su(bj) | (grammatical) subject |
| subjuntivo | subjun | subjunctive |
| tauromaquia | TAUR | bullfighting |
| también | tb | also |
| técnica, tecnología | TEC(H) | technical term, technology |
| telecomunicaciones | TELEC, TEL | telecommunications |
| televisión | TV | television |
| imprenta, tipografía | TIP, TYP | typography, printing |
| inglés norteamericano | US | American English |
| verbo | vb | verb |
| verbo intransitivo | vi | intransitive verb |
| verbo pronominal | vr | reflexive verb |
| verbo transitivo | vt | transitive verb |
| zoología | ZOOL | zoology |
| marca registrada | ® | registered trademark |
| indica un equivalente cultural | ≈ | introduces a cultural equivalent |

# SPANISH PRONUNCIATION

## Consonants

| | | | |
|---|---|---|---|
| c | [k] | caja | c before *a*, *o* or *u* is pronounced as in cat |
| ce, ci | [θe, θi] | cero<br>cielo | c before *e* or *i* is pronounced as in thin |
| ch | [tʃ] | chiste | ch is pronounced as ch in chair |
| d | [d, ð] | danés<br>ciudad | at the beginning of a phrase or after *l* or *n*, d is pronounced as in English. In any other position it is pronounced like th in the |
| g | [g, ɤ] | gafas<br>paga | g before *a*, *o* or *u* is pronounced as in gap, if at the beginning of a phrase or after *n*. In other positions the sound is softened |
| ge, gi | [xe, xi] | gente<br>girar | g before *e* or *i* is pronounced similar to ch in Scottish loch |
| h | | haber | h is always silent in Spanish |
| j | [x] | jugar | j is pronounced similar to ch in Scottish loch |
| ll | [ʎ] | talle | ll is pronounced like the lli in million |
| ñ | [ɲ] | niño | ñ is pronounced like the ni in onion |
| q | [k] | que | q is pronounced as k in king |
| r, rr | [r, rr] | quitar<br>garra | r is always pronounced in Spanish, unlike the silent r in dancer. rr is trilled, like a Scottish r |
| s | [s] | quizás<br>isla | s is usually pronounced as in pass, but before *b, d, g, l, m* or *n* it is pronounced as in rose |
| v | [b, ß] | vía<br>dividir | v is pronounced something like b. At the beginning of a phrase or after *m* or *n* it is pronounced as b in boy. In any other position the sound is softened |
| z | [θ] | tenaz | z is pronounced as th in thin |

b, f, k, l, m, n, p, t and x are pronounced as in English.

## Vowels

| a | [a] | pata | not as long as *a* in *far*. When followed by a consonant in the same syllable (i.e. in a closed syllable), as in *amante*, the *a* is short, as in *bat* |
|---|-----|------|---|
| e | [e] | m*e* | like *e* in *they*. In a closed syllable, as in *gente*, the *e* is short as in *pet* |
| i | [i] | p*i*no | as in m*ea*n or mach*i*ne |
| o | [o] | l*o* | as in l*o*cal. In a closed syllable, as in *control*, the *o* is short as in *cot* |
| u | [u] | l*u*nes | as in *rule*. It is silent after *q*, and in *gue*, *gui*, unless marked *güe*, *güi* e.g. antig*ü*edad |

## Diphthongs

| ai, ay | [ai] | b*ai*le | as *i* in *ride* |
|--------|------|---------|------|
| au | [au] | *au*to | as *ou* in *shout* |
| ei, ey | [ei] | b*ue*y | as *ey* in *grey* |
| eu | [eu] | d*eu*da | both elements pronounced independently [e] + [u] |
| oi, oy | [oi] | h*oy* | as *oy* in *toy* |

## Stress

The rules of stress in Spanish are as follows:
(a) when a word ends in a vowel or in *n* or *s*, the second last syllable is stressed: pa*ta*ta, pa*ta*tas, *co*me, *co*men
(b) when a word ends in a consonant other than *n* or *s*, the stress falls on the last syllable: pa*red*, ha*blar*
(c) when the rules set out in a and b are not applied, an acute accent appears over the stressed vowel: co*mún*, geogra*fía*, in*glés*

In the phonetic transcription, the symbol ['] precedes the syllable on which the stress falls.

# PRONUNCIACIÓN INGLESA

**Vocales y diptongos**

| | *Ejemplo inglés* | *Ejemplo español/explicación* |
|---|---|---|
| ɑː | f*a*ther | Entre *a* de p*a*dre y *o* de n*o*che |
| ʌ | b*u*t, c*o*me | *a* muy breve |
| æ | m*a*n, c*a*t | Se mantienen los labios en la posición de *e* en p*e*na y luego se pronuncia el sonido *a* |
| ə | f*a*ther, *a*go | Sonido indistinto parecido a una *e* u *o* casi mudas |
| əː | b*i*rd, h*ea*rd | Entre *e* abierta, y *o* cerrada, sonido alargado |
| ɛ | g*e*t, b*e*d | como en p*e*rro |
| ɪ | *i*t, b*i*g | Más breve que en s*i* |
| iː | t*ea*, s*ee* | Como en f*i*no |
| ɔ | h*o*t, w*a*sh | Como en t*o*rre |
| ɔː | s*a*w, *a*ll | Como en p*o*r |
| u | p*u*t, b*oo*k | Sonido breve, más cerrado que b*u*rro |
| uː | t*oo*, y*ou* | Sonido largo, como en *u*no |
| aɪ | fl*y*, h*i*gh | Como en fr*ai*le |
| au | h*ow*, h*ou*se | Como en p*au*sa |
| ɛə | th*ere*, b*ear* | Casi como en v*ea*, pero el sonido *a* se mezcla con el indistinto [ə] |
| eɪ | d*ay*, ob*ey* | *e* cerrada seguida por una *i* débil |
| ɪə | h*ere*, h*ear* | Como en man*ía*, mezclándose el sonido *a* con el indistinto [ə] |
| əu | g*o*, n*o*te | [ə] seguido por una breve *u* |
| ɔɪ | b*oy*, *oi*l | Como en v*oy* |
| uə | p*oor*, s*ure* | *u* bastante larga más el sonido indistinto [ə] |

# Consonantes

| | Ejemplo inglés | Ejemplo español/explicación |
|---|---|---|
| d | men*d*ed | Como en con*d*e, an*d*ar |
| g | *g*o, *g*et, bi*g* | Como en *g*rande, *g*ol |
| dʒ | *g*in, *j*udge | Como en la *ll* andaluza y en *G*enerali-tat (catalán) |
| ŋ | si*ng* | Como en ví*n*culo |
| h | *h*ouse, *h*e | Como la jota hispanoamericana |
| j | *y*oung, *y*es | Como en *y*a |
| k | *c*ome, mo*ck* | Como en *c*aña, Es*c*ocia |
| r | *r*ed, t*r*ead | Se pronuncia con la punta de la lengua hacia atrás y sin hacerla vibrar |
| s | *s*and, ye*s* | Como en *c*asa, *s*esión |
| z | ro*s*e, *z*ebra | Como en de*s*de, mi*s*mo |
| ʃ | *sh*e, ma*ch*ine | Como en *ch*ambre (francés), ro*x*o (portugués) |
| tʃ | *ch*in, ri*ch* | Como en *ch*ocolate |
| v | *v*alley | Como en f, pero se retiran los dientes superiores vibrándolos contra el labio inferior |
| w | *w*ater, *wh*ich | Como en la *u* de h*u*evo, p*u*ede |
| ʒ | vi*s*ion | Como en *j*ournal (francés) |
| θ | *th*ink, my*th* | Como en re*c*eta, *z*apato |
| ð | *th*is, *th*e | Como en la *d* de habla*d*o, verda*d* |

b, p, f, m, n, l, t iguales que en español

El signo * indica que la r final escrita apenas se pronuncia en inglés británico cuando la palabra siguiente empieza con vocal. El signo ['] indica la sílaba acentuada.

# ESPAÑOL - INGLÉS
# SPANISH - ENGLISH
## A

---

**PALABRA CLAVE**

**a** [a] *(a+ el = al)* *prep* **1** *(dirección)* to; **fueron → Madrid/Grecia** they went to Madrid/Greece; **me voy ~ casa** I'm going home

**2** *(distancia)*: **está ~ 15 km de aquí** it's 15 kms from here

**3** *(posición)*: **estar ~ la mesa** to be at table; **al lado de** next to, beside; **ver** *tb* **puerta**

**4** *(tiempo)*: **~ las 10/~ medianoche** at 10/midnight; **~ la mañana siguiente** the following morning; **~ los pocos días** after a few days; **estamos ~ 9 de julio** it's the ninth of July; **~ los 24 años** at the age of 24; **al año/~ la semana** *(AM)* a year/week later

**5** *(manera)*: **~ la francesa** the French way; **~ caballo** on horseback; **~ oscuras** in the dark

**6** *(medio, instrumento)*: **~ lápiz** in pencil; **~ mano** by hand; **cocina ~ gas** gas stove

**7** *(razón)*: **~ 30 ptas el kilo** at 30 pesetas a kilo; **~ más de 50 km/h** at more than 50 kms per hour

**8** *(dativo)*: **se lo di → él** I gave it to him; **vi al policía** I saw the policeman; **se lo compré ~ él** I bought it from him

**9** *(tras ciertos verbos)*: **voy ~ verle** I'm going to see him; **empezó ~ trabajar** he started working *o* to work

**10** *(+ infin)*: **al verle, le reconocí inmediatamente** when I saw him I recognized him at once; **el camino ~ recorrer** the distance we *(etc)* have to travel; **¡~ callar!** keep quiet!; **¡~ comer!** let's eat!

**abad, esa** [a'βað, 'ðesa] *nm/f* abbot/

abbess; **~ía** *nf* abbey

**abajo** [a'βaxo] *adv* *(situación)* (down) below, underneath; *(en edificio)* downstairs; *(dirección)* down, downwards; **el piso de ~** the downstairs flat; **la parte de ~** the lower part; **¡~ el gobierno!** down with the government!; **cuesta/río ~** downhill/downstream; **de arriba ~** from top to bottom; **el ~ firmante** the undersigned; **más ~** lower *o* further down

**abalanzarse** [aβalan'θarse] *vr*: **~ sobre** *o* **contra** to throw o.s. at

**abalorios** [aβa'lorjos] *nmpl* *(chucherías)* trinkets

**abanderado** [aβande'raðo] *nm* standardbearer

**abandonado, a** [aβando'naðo, a] *adj* derelict; *(desatendido)* abandoned; *(desierto)* deserted; *(descuidado)* neglected

**abandonar** [aβando'nar] *vt* to leave; *(persona)* to abandon, desert; *(cosa)* to abandon, leave behind; *(descuidar)* to neglect; *(renunciar a)* to give up; *(INFORM)* to quit; **~se** *vr*: **~se a** to abandon o.s. to; **abandono** *nm* *(acto)* desertion, abandonment; *(estado)* abandon, neglect; *(renuncia)* withdrawal, retirement; **ganar por abandono** to win by default

**abanicar** [aβani'kar] *vt* to fan; **abanico** *nm* fan; *(NAUT)* derrick

**abaratar** [aβara'tar] *vt* to lower the price of ♦ *vi* to go *o* come down in price; **~se** *vr* to go *o* come down in price

**abarcar** [aβar'kar] *vt* to include, embrace; *(AM)* to monopolize

**abarrotado, a** [aβarro'taðo, a] *adj* packed

**abarrotar** [aβarro'tar] *vt* *(local, estadio, teatro)* to fill, pack

**abarrotero, a** [aβarro'tero, a] (AM) nm/f grocer; **abarrotes** nmpl (AM) groceries, provisions

**abastecer** [aβaste'θer] vt: ~ (de) to supply (with); **abastecimiento** nm supply

**abasto** [a'βasto] nm supply; (abundancia) abundance; **no dar ~ a** to be unable to cope with

**abatido, a** [aβa'tiðo, a] adj dejected, downcast

**abatimiento** [aβati'mjento] nm (depresión) dejection, depression

**abatir** [aβa'tir] vt (muro) to demolish; (pájaro) to shoot o bring down; (fig) to depress; ~se vr to get depressed; ~se sobre to swoop o pounce on

**abdicación** [aβðika'θjon] nf abdication

**abdicar** [aβði'kar] vi to abdicate

**abdomen** [aβ'ðomen] nm abdomen; **abdominales** nmpl (tb: ejercicios abdominales) sit-ups

**abecedario** [aβeθe'ðarjo] nm alphabet

**abedul** [aβe'ðul] nm birch

**abeja** [a'βexa] nf bee

**abejorro** [aβe'xorro] nm bumblebee

**aberración** [aβerra'θjon] nf aberration

**abertura** [aβer'tura] nf = apertura

**abeto** [a'βeto] nm fir

**abierto, a** [a'βjerto, a] pp de abrir ♦ adj open; (AM) generous

**abigarrado, a** [aβiɣa'rraðo, a] adj multi-coloured

**abismal** [aβis'mal] adj (fig) vast, enormous

**abismar** [aβis'mar] vt to humble, cast down; ~se vr to sink; ~se en (fig) to be plunged into

**abismo** [a'βismo] nm abyss

**abjurar** [aβxu'rar] vi: ~ de to abjure, forswear

**ablandar** [aβlan'dar] vt to soften ♦ vi to get softer; ~se vr to get softer

**abnegación** [aβneɣa'θjon] nf self-denial

**abnegado, a** [aβne'ɣaðo, a] adj self-sacrificing

**abocado, a** [aβo'kaðo, a] adj: verse ~ al desastre to be heading for disaster

**abochornar** [aβotʃor'nar] vt to embarrass; ~se vr to get flustered; (BOT) to wilt

**abofetear** [aβofete'ar] vt to slap (in the face)

**abogado, a** [aβo'ɣaðo, a] nm/f lawyer; (notario) solicitor; (en tribunal) barrister (BRIT), attorney (US); ~ **defensor** defence lawyer o attorney (US)

**abogar** [aβo'ɣar] vi: ~ **por** to plead for; (fig) to advocate

**abolengo** [aβo'leŋgo] nm ancestry, lineage

**abolición** [aβoli'θjon] nf abolition

**abolir** [aβo'lir] vt to abolish; (cancelar) to cancel

**abolladura** [aβoʎa'ðura] nf dent

**abollar** [aβo'ʎar] vt to dent

**abominable** [aβomi'naβle] adj abominable

**abonado, a** [aβo'naðo, a] adj (deuda) paid(-up) ♦ nm/f subscriber

**abonar** [aβo'nar] vt (deuda) to settle; (terreno) to fertilize; (idea) to endorse; ~se vr to subscribe; **abono** nm payment; fertilizer; subscription

**abordar** [aβor'ðar] vt (barco) to board; (asunto) to broach

**aborigen** [aβo'rixen] nm/f aborigine

**aborrecer** [aβorre'θer] vt to hate, loathe

**abortar** [aβor'tar] vi (malparir) to have a miscarriage; (deliberadamente) to have an abortion; **aborto** nm miscarriage; abortion

**abotonar** [aβoto'nar] vt to button (up), do up

**abovedado, a** [aβoβe'ðaðo, a] adj vaulted, domed

**abrasar** [aβra'sar] vt to burn (up); (AGR) to dry up, parch

**abrazadera** [aβraθa'ðera] nf bracket

**abrazar** [aβra'θar] vt to embrace, hug

**abrazo** [a'βraθo] nm embrace, hug;

un ~ *(en carta)* with best wishes

**abrebotellas** [aβreβo'teʎas] *nm inv* bottle opener

**abrecartas** [aβre'kartas] *nm inv* letter opener

**abrelatas** [aβre'latas] *nm inv* tin *(BRIT)* o can opener

**abreviar** [aβre'βjar] *vt* to abbreviate; *(texto)* to abridge; *(plazo)* to reduce; **abreviatura** *nf* abbreviation

**abridor** [aβri'ðor] *nm* bottle opener; *(de latas)* tin *(BRIT)* o can opener

**abrigar** [aβri'xar] *vt (proteger)* to shelter; *(suj: ropa)* to keep warm; *(fig)* to cherish

**abrigo** [a'βriɣo] *nm (prenda)* coat, overcoat; *(lugar protegido)* shelter

**abril** [a'βril] *nm* April

**abrillantar** [aβriʎan'tar] *vt* to polish

**abrir** [a'βrir] *vt* to open (up) ♦ *vi* to open; ~se *vr* to open; *(extenderse)* to open out; *(cielo)* to clear; ~**se paso** to find o force a way through

**abrochar** [aβro'tʃar] *vt (con botones)* to button (up); *(zapato, con broche)* to do up

**abrumar** [aβru'mar] *vt* to overwhelm; *(sobrecargar)* to weigh down

**abrupto, a** [a'βrupto, a] *adj* abrupt; *(empinado)* steep

**absceso** [aβs'θeso] *nm* abscess

**absentismo** [aβsen'tismo] *nm* absenteeism

**absolución** [aβsolu'θjon] *nf (REL)* absolution; *(JUR)* acquittal

**absoluto, a** [aβso'luto, a] *adj* absolute; **en ~** *adv* not at all

**absolver** [aβsol'βer] *vt* to absolve; *(JUR)* to pardon; (: *acusado*) to acquit

**absorbente** [aβsor'βente] *adj* absorbent; *(interesante)* absorbing

**absorber** [aβsor'βer] *vt* to absorb; *(embeber)* to soak up

**absorción** [aβsor'θjon] *nf* absorption; *(COM)* takeover

**absorto, a** [aβ'sorto, a] *pp de* absorber ♦ *adj* absorbed, engrossed

**abstemio, a** [aβs'temjo, a] *adj* teeto-

**abstención** [aβsten'θjon] *nf* abstention

**abstenerse** [aβste'nerse] *vr*: ~ **(de)** to abstain o refrain (from)

**abstinencia** [aβsti'nenθja] *nf* abstinence; *(ayuno)* fasting

**abstracción** [aβstrak'θjon] *nf* abstraction

**abstracto, a** [aβs'trakto, a] *adj* abstract

**abstraer** [aβstra'er] *vt* to abstract; ~se *vr* to become absorbed

**abstraído, a** [aβstra'iðo, a] *adj* absent-minded

**absuelto** [aβ'swelto] *pp de* absolver

**absurdo, a** [aβ'surðo, a] *adj* absurd

**abuchear** [aβutʃe'ar] *vt (a actor, orador)* to boo

**abuelo, a** [a'βwelo, a] *nm/f* grandfather/mother; ~**s** *nmpl* grandparents

**abulia** [a'βulja] *nf* apathy

**abultado, a** [aβul'taðo, a] *adj* bulky

**abultar** [aβul'tar] *vt* to enlarge; *(aumentar)* to increase; *(fig)* to exaggerate ♦ *vi* to be bulky

**abundancia** [aβun'danθja] *nf*: **una ~ de** plenty of; **abundante** *adj* abundant, plentiful

**abundar** [aβun'dar] *vi* to abound, be plentiful

**aburguesarse** [aβurxe'sarse] *vr* to become middle-class

**aburrido, a** [aβu'rriðo, a] *adj (hastiado)* bored; *(que aburre)* boring; **aburrimiento** *nm* boredom, tedium

**aburrir** [aβu'rrir] *vt* to bore; ~se *vr* to be bored, get bored

**abusar** [aβu'sar] *vi* to go too far; ~ **de** to abuse

**abusivo, a** [aβu'siβo, a] *adj (precio)* exorbitant

**abuso** [a'βuso] *nm* abuse

**abyecto, a** [aβ'jekto, a] *adj* wretched, abject

**A.C.** *abr (= Año de Cristo)* A.D.

**a/c** *abr (= al cuidado de)* c/o

**acá** [a'ka] *adv (lugar)* here; ¿**de**

cuándo ~? since when?

**acabado, a** [aka'βaðo, a] *adj* finished, complete; (*perfecto*) perfect; (*agotado*) worn out; (*fig*) masterly ♦ *nm* finish

**acabar** [aka'βar] *vt* (*llevar a su fin*) to finish, complete; (*consumir*) to use up; (*rematar*) to finish off ♦ *vi* to finish, end; ~**se** *vr* to finish, stop; (*terminarse*) to be over; (*agotarse*) to run out; ~ **con** to put an end to; ~ **de llegar** to have just arrived; ~ **por hacer** to end up by doing; ¡se acabó! it's all over!; (*¡basta!*) that's enough!

**acabóse** [aka'βose] *nm*: esto es el ~ this is the last straw

**academia** [aka'ðemja] *nf* academy; **académico, a** *adj* academic

**acaecer** [akae'θer] *vi* to happen, occur

**acalorado, a** [akalo'raðo, a] *adj* (*discusión*) heated

**acalorarse** [akalo'rarse] *vr* (*fig*) to get heated

**acallar** [aka'ʎar] *vt* (*persona*) to silence; (*protestas, rumores*) to suppress

**acampar** [akam'par] *vi* to camp

**acantilado** [akanti'laðo] *nm* cliff

**acaparar** [akapa'rar] *vt* to monopolize; (*acumular*) to hoard

**acariciar** [akari'θjar] *vt* to caress; (*esperanza*) to cherish

**acarrear** [akarre'ar] *vt* to transport; (*fig*) to cause, result in

**acaso** [a'kaso] *adv* perhaps, maybe ♦ *nm* chance; (**por**) **si** ~ (just) in case

**acatamiento** [akata'mjento] *nm* respect; (*ley*) observance

**acatar** [aka'tar] *vt* to respect; (*ley*) obey

**acatarrarse** [akata'rrarse] *vr* to catch a cold

**acaudalado, a** [akauða'laðo, a] *adj* well-off

**acaudillar** [akauði'ʎar] *vt* to lead, command

**acceder** [akθe'ðer] *vi*: ~ **a** (*petición*

*etc*) to agree to; (*tener acceso a*) to have access to; (*INFORM*) to access

**accesible** [akθe'siβle] *adj* accessible

**acceso** [ak'θeso] *nm* access, entry; (*camino*) access, approach; (*MED*) attack, fit

**accesorio, a** [akθe'sorjo, a] *adj, nm* accessory

**accidentado, a** [akθiðen'taðo, a] *adj* uneven; (*montañoso*) hilly; (*azaroso*) eventful ♦ *nm/f* accident victim

**accidental** [akθiðen'tal] *adj* accidental; **accidentarse** *vr* to have an accident

**accidente** [akθi'ðente] *nm* accident; ~**s** *nmpl* (*de terreno*) unevenness *sg*

**acción** [ak'θjon] *nf* action; (*acto*) action, act; (*COM*) share; (*JUR*) action, lawsuit; ~ **ordinaria/preferente** ordinary/preference share; **accionar** *vt* to work, operate; (*INFORM*) to drive

**accionista** [akθjo'nista] *nm/f* shareholder, stockholder

**acebo** [a'θeβo] *nm* holly; (*árbol*) holly tree

**acechar** [aθe'tʃar] *vt* to spy on; (*aguardar*) to lie in wait for; **acecho** *nm*: **estar al acecho (de)** to lie in wait (for)

**aceitar** [aθei'tar] *vt* to oil, lubricate

**aceite** [a'θeite] *nm* oil; (*de oliva*) olive oil; ~**ra** *nf* oilcan; **aceitoso, a** *adj* oily

**aceituna** [aθei'tuna] *nf* olive

**acelerador** [aθelera'ðor] *nm* accelerator

**acelerar** [aθele'rar] *vt* to accelerate

**acelga** [a'θelγa] *nf* chard, beet

**acento** [a'θento] *nm* accent; (*acentuación*) stress

**acentuar** [aθen'twar] *vt* to accent; to stress; (*fig*) to accentuate

**acepción** [aθep'θjon] *nf* meaning

**aceptable** [aθep'taβle] *adj* acceptable

**aceptación** [aθepta'θjon] *nf* acceptance; (*aprobación*) approval

**aceptar** [aθep'tar] *vt* to accept;

(*aprobar*) to approve

**acequia** [a'θekja] *nf* irrigation ditch

**acera** [a'θera] *nf* pavement (*BRIT*), sidewalk (*US*)

**acerca** [a'θerka]: ~ **de** *prep* about, concerning

**acercar** [aθer'kar] *vt* to bring o move nearer; ~**se** *vr* to approach, come near

**acerico** [aθe'riko] *nm* pincushion

**acero** [a'θero] *nm* steel

**acérrimo, a** [a'θerrimo, a] *adj* (*partidario*) staunch; (*enemigo*) bitter

**acertado, a** [aθer'taðo, a] *adj* correct; (*apropiado*) apt; (*sensato*) sensible

**acertar** [aθer'tar] *vt* (*blanco*) to hit; (*solución*) to get right; (*adivinar*) to guess ♦ *vi* to get it right, be right; ~ **a** to manage to; ~ **con** to happen o hit on

**acertijo** [aθer'tixo] *nm* riddle, puzzle

**acervo** [a'θerβo] *nm* heap; ~ **común** undivided estate

**aciago, a** [a'θjavo, a] *adj* ill-fated, fateful

**acicalar** [aθika'lar] *vt* to polish; (*persona*) to dress up; ~**se** *vr* to get dressed up

**acicate** [aθi'kate] *nm* spur

**acidez** [aθi'ðeθ] *nf* acidity

**ácido, a** ['aθiðo, a] *adj* sour, acid ♦ *nm* acid

**acierto** *etc* [a'θjerto] *vb ver* **acertar** ♦ *nm* success; (*buen paso*) wise move; (*solución*) solution; (*habilidad*) skill, ability

**aclamación** [aklama'θjon] *nf* acclamation; (*aplausos*) applause

**aclamar** [akla'mar] *vt* to acclaim; (*aplaudir*) to applaud

**aclaración** [aklara'θjon] *nf* clarification, explanation

**aclarar** [akla'rar] *vt* to clarify, explain; (*ropa*) to rinse ♦ *vi* to clear up; ~**se** *vr* (*explicarse*) to understand; ~**se la garganta** to clear one's throat

**aclaratorio, a** [aklara'torjo, a] *adj* explanatory

**aclimatación** [aklimata'θjon] *nf* acclimatization

**aclimatar** [aklima'tar] *vt* to acclimatize; ~**se** *vr* to become acclimatized

**acné** [ak'ne] *nm* acne

**acobardar** [akoβar'ðar] *vt* to intimidate

**acodarse** [ako'ðarse] *vr*: ~ **en** to lean on

**acogedor, a** [akoxe'ðor, a] *adj* welcoming; (*hospitalario*) hospitable

**acoger** [ako'xer] *vt* to welcome; (*abrigar*) to shelter; ~**se** *vr* to take refuge

**acogida** [ako'xiða] *nf* reception; refuge

**acolchar** [akol'tʃar] *vt* to pad; (*fig*) to cushion

**acometer** [akome'ter] *vt* to attack; (*emprender*) to undertake; **acometida** *nf* attack, assault

**acomodado, a** [akomo'ðaðo, a] *adj* (*persona*) well-to-do

**acomodador, a** [akomoða'ðor, a] *nm/f* usher(ette)

**acomodar** [akomo'ðar] *vt* to adjust; (*alojar*) to accommodate; ~**se** *vr* to conform; (*instalarse*) to install o.s.; (*adaptarse*) ~**se (a)** to adapt (to)

**acomodaticio, a** [akomoða'tiθjo, a] *adj* (*pey*) accommodating, obliging; (*manejable*) pliable

**acompañar** [akompa'ɲar] *vt* to accompany; (*documentos*) to enclose

**acondicionar** [akondiθjo'nar] *vt* to arrange, prepare; (*pelo*) to condition

**acongojar** [akoŋgo'xar] *vt* to distress, grieve

**aconsejar** [akonse'xar] *vt* to advise, counsel; ~**se** *vr*: ~**se con** to consult

**acontecer** [akonte'θer] *vi* to happen, occur; **acontecimiento** *nm* event

**acopio** [a'kopjo] *nm* store, stock

**acoplamiento** [akopla'mjento] *nm* coupling, joint; **acoplar** *vt* to fit; (*ELEC*) to connect; (*vagones*) to couple

**acorazado, a** [akora'θaðo, a] adj armour-plated, armoured ♦ nm battleship

**acordar** [akor'ðar] vt (resolver) to agree, resolve; (recordar) to remind; ~se vr to agree; ~se (de algo) to remember (sth); **acorde** adj (MUS) harmonious; **acorde** con (medidas etc) in keeping with ♦ nm chord

**acordeón** [akorðe'on] nm accordion

**acordonado, a** [akorðo'naðo, a] adj (calle) cordoned-off

**acorralar** [akorra'lar] vt to round up, corral

**acortar** [akor'tar] vt to shorten; (duración) to cut short; (cantidad) to reduce; ~se vr to become shorter

**acosar** [ako'sar] vt to pursue relentlessly; (fig) to hound, pester

**acostar** [akos'tar] vt (en cama) to put to bed; (en suelo) to lay down; (barco) to bring alongside; ~se vr to go to bed; to lie down; ~se con algn to sleep with sb

**acostumbrado, a** [akostum'braðo, a] adj usual; ~ a used to

**acostumbrar** [akostum'brar] vt: ~ a uno a algo to get sb used to sth vi: ~ (a) hacer to be in the habit of doing; ~se vr: ~se a to get used to

**acotación** [akota'θjon] nf marginal note; (GEO) elevation mark; (de límite) boundary mark; (TEATRO) stage direction

**ácrata** ['akrata] adj, nm/f anarchist

**acre** ['akre] adj (olor) sharp, bitter; (olor) acrid; (fig) biting ♦ nm acre

**acrecentar** [akreθen'tar] vt to increase, augment

**acreditar** [akreði'tar] vt (garantizar) to vouch for, guarantee; (autorizar) to authorize; (dar prueba de) to prove; (COM: abonar) to credit; (embajador) to accredit; ~se vr to become famous

**acreedor, a** [akree'ðor, a] adj: ~ de worthy of ♦ nm/f creditor

**acribillar** [akriβi'λar] vt: ~ a balazos to riddle with bullets

**acrimonia** [akri'monja] nf acrimony

**acritud** [akri'tuð] nf = acrimonia

**acróbata** [a'kroβata] nm/f acrobat

**acta** ['akta] nf certificate; (de comisión) minutes pl, record; ~ de nacimiento/de matrimonio birth/marriage certificate; ~ notarial affidavit

**actitud** [akti'tuð] nf attitude; (postura) posture

**activar** [akti'βar] vt to activate; (acelerar) to speed up

**actividad** [aktiβi'ðað] nf activity

**activo, a** [ak'tiβo, a] adj active; (vivo) lively ♦ nm (COM) assets pl

**acto** ['akto] nm act, action; (ceremonia) ceremony, (TEATRO) act; en el ~ immediately

**actor** [ak'tor] nm actor; (JUR) plaintiff ♦ adj: parte ~ a prosecution

**actriz** [ak'triθ] nf actress

**actuación** [aktwa'θjon] nf action; (comportamiento) conduct, behaviour; (JUR) proceedings pl; (desempeño) performance

**actual** [ak'twal] adj present(-day), current; ~idad nf present; ~idades nfpl (noticias) news sg; en la ~idad at present; (hoy día) nowadays

**actualizar** [aktwali'θar] vt to update, modernize

**actualmente** [aktwal'mente] adv at present; (hoy día) nowadays

**actuar** [ak'twar] vi (obrar) to work, operate; (actor) to act, perform ♦ vt to work, operate; ~ de to act as

**acuarela** [akwa'rela] nf watercolour

**acuario** [a'kwarjo] nm aquarium; (ASTROLOGÍA): A~ Aquarius

**acuartelar** [akwarte'lar] vt (MIL: disciplinar) to confine to barracks

**acuático, a** [a'kwatiko, a] adj aquatic

**acuciante** [aku'θjante] adj urgent

**acuciar** [aku'θjar] vt to urge on

**acuclillarse** [akukλi'λarse] vr to crouch down

**acuchillar** [akutʃi'λar] vt (TEC) to plane (down), smooth

**acudir** [aku'ðir] vi (asistir) to attend; (ir) to go; ~ a (fig) to turn to; ~ en ayuda de to go to the aid of

**acuerdo** *etc* [a'kwerðo] *vb ver* **acordar ♦** *nm* agreement; **¡de ~!** agreed!; **de ~ con** (*persona*) in agreement with; (*acción, documento*) in accordance with; **estar de ~ con** to be agreed, agree

**acumular** [akumu'lar] *vt* to accumulate, collect

**acuñar** [aku'ɲar] *vt* (*moneda*) to mint; (*frase*) to coin

**acupuntura** [akusun'tura] *nf* acupuncture

**acuoso, a** [a'kwoso, a] *adj* watery

**acurrucarse** [akurru'karse] *vr* to crouch; (*ovillarse*) to curl up

**acusación** [akusa'θjon] *nf* accusation

**acusar** [aku'sar] *vt* to accuse; (*revelar*) to reveal; (*denunciar*) to denounce

**acuse** [a'kuse] *nm*: **~ de recibo** acknowledgement of receipt

**acústica** [a'kustika] *nf* acoustics *pl*

**acústico, a** [a'kustiko, a] *adj* acoustic

**achacar** [atʃa'kar] *vt* to attribute

**achacoso, a** [atʃa'koso, a] *adj* sickly

**achantar** [atʃan'tar] (*fam*) *vt* to scare, frighten; **~se** *vr* to back down

**achaque** *etc* [a'tʃake] *vb ver* **achacar ♦** *nm* ailment

**achicar** [atʃi'kar] *vt* to reduce; (*humillar*) to humiliate; (*NAUT*) to bale out

**achicoria** [atʃi'korja] *nf* chicory

**achicharrar** [atʃitʃa'rrar] *vt* to scorch, burn

**adagio** [a'ðaxjo] *nm* adage; (*MUS*) adagio

**adaptación** [aðapta'θjon] *nf* adaptation

**adaptador** [aðapta'ðor] *nm* (*ELEC*) adapter

**adaptar** [aðap'tar] *vt* to adapt; (*acomodar*) to fit

**adecuado, a** [aðe'kwaðo, a] *adj* (*apto*) suitable; (*oportuno*) appropriate

**adecuar** [aðe'kwar] *vt* to adapt; to

make suitable

**a. de J.C.** *abr* (= *antes de Jesucristo*) B.C.

**adelantado, a** [aðelan'taðo, a] *adj* advanced; (*reloj*) fast; **pagar por ~** to pay in advance

**adelantamiento** [aðelanta'mjento] *nm* advance, advancement; (*AUTO*) overtaking

**adelantar** [aðelan'tar] *vt* to move forward; (*avanzar*) to advance; (*acelerar*) to speed up; (*AUTO*) to overtake **♦** *vi* to go forward, advance; **~se** *vr* to go forward, advance

**adelante** [aðe'lante] *adv* forward(s), ahead **♦** *excl* come in!; **de hoy en ~** from now on; **más ~** later on; (*más allá*) further on

**adelanto** [aðe'lanto] *nm* advance; (*mejora*) improvement; (*progreso*) progress

**adelgazar** [aðelva'θar] *vt* to thin (down) **♦** *vi* to get thin; (*con régimen*) to slim down, lose weight

**ademán** [aðe'man] *nm* gesture; **ademanes** *nmpl* manners; **en ~ de** as if to

**además** [aðe'mas] *adv* besides; (*por otra parte*) moreover; (*también*) also; **~ de** besides, in addition to

**adentrarse** [aðen'trarse] *vr*: **~ en** to go into, get inside; (*penetrar*) to penetrate (into)

**adentro** [a'ðentro] *adv* inside, in; **mar ~** out at sea; **tierra ~** inland

**adepto, a** [a'ðepto, a] *nm/f* supporter

**aderezar** [aðere'θar] *vt* (*ensalada*) to dress; (*comida*) to season; **aderezo** *nm* dressing; seasoning

**adeudar** [aðeu'ðar] *vt* to owe; **~se** *vr* to run into debt

**adherirse** [aðe'rirse] *vr*: **~ a** to adhere to; (*partido*) to join

**adhesión** [aðe'sjon] *nf* adhesion; (*fig*) adherence

**adicción** [aðik'θjon] *nf* addiction

**adición** [aði'θjon] *nf* addition

**adicto, a** [a'ðikto, a] *adj*: **~ a** addicted to; (*dedicado*) devoted to **♦**

**adiestrar** [aðjes'trar] *vt* to train, teach; (*conducir*) to guide, lead; ~se *vr* to practise; (*enseñarse*) to train o.s.

**adinerado, a** [aðine'raðo, a] *adj* wealthy

**adiós** [a'ðjos] *excl* (*para despedirse*) goodbye!, cheerio!; (*al pasar*) hello!

**aditivo** [aði'tiβo] *nm* additive

**adivinanza** [aðiβi'nanθa] *nf* riddle

**adivinar** [aðiβi'nar] *vt* to prophesy; (*conjeturar*) to guess; **adivino, a** *nm/f* fortune-teller

**adj** *abr* ( = **adjunto**) encl.

**adjetivo** [aðxe'tiβo] *nm* adjective

**adjudicación** [aðxuðika'θjon] *nf* award; adjudication

**adjudicar** [aðxuði'kar] *vt* to award; ~se *vr*: ~se algo to appropriate sth

**adjuntar** [aðxun'tar] *vt* to attach, enclose; **adjunto, a** *adj* attached, enclosed ♦ *nm/f* assistant

**administración** [aðministra'θjon] *nf* administration; (*dirección*) management; **administrador, a** *nm/f* administrator; manager(ess)

**administrar** [aðminis'trar] *vt* to administer; **administrativo, a** *adj* administrative

**admirable** [aðmi'raβle] *adj* admirable

**admiración** [aðmira'θjon] *nf* admiration; (*asombro*) wonder; (*LING*) exclamation mark

**admirar** [aðmi'rar] *vt* to admire; (*extrañar*) to surprise; ~se *vr* to be surprised

**admisible** [aðmi'siβle] *adj* admissible

**admisión** [aðmi'sjon] *nf* admission; (*reconocimiento*) acceptance

**admitir** [aðmi'tir] *vt* to admit; (*aceptar*) to accept

**admonición** [aðmoni'θjon] *nf* warning

**adobar** [aðo'βar] *vt* (*CULIN*) to season

**adobe** [a'ðoβe] *nm* adobe, sun-dried brick

**adoctrinar** [aðoktri'nar] *vt*: ~ en to indoctrinate with

**adolecer** [aðole'θer] *vi*: ~ de to suffer from

**adolescente** [aðoles'θente] *nm/f* adolescent, teenager

**adonde** [a'ðonde] *conj* (to) where

**adónde** [a'ðonde] *adv* = **dónde**

**adopción** [aðop'θjon] *nf* adoption

**adoptar** [aðop'tar] *vt* to adopt

**adoptivo, a** [aðop'tiβo, a] *adj* (*padres*) adoptive; (*hijo*) adopted

**adoquín** [aðo'kin] *nm* paving stone

**adorar** [aðo'rar] *vt* to adore

**adormecer** [aðorme'θer] *vt* to put to sleep; ~se *vr* to become sleepy; (*dormirse*) to fall asleep

**adornar** [aðor'nar] *vt* to adorn

**adorno** [a'ðorno] *nm* adornment; (*decoración*) decoration

**adosado, a** [aðo'saðo, a] *adj*: **casa adosada** semi-detached house

**adquiero** *etc vb ver* **adquirir**

**adquirir** [aðki'rir] *vt* to acquire, obtain

**adquisición** [aðkisi'θjon] *nf* acquisition

**adrede** [a'ðreðe] *adv* on purpose

**adscribir** [aðskri'βir] *vt* to appoint

**adscrito** *pp de* **adscribir**

**aduana** [a'ðwana] *nf* customs *pl*

**aduanero, a** [aðwa'nero, a] *adj* customs *cpd* ♦ *nm/f* customs officer

**aducir** [aðu'θir] *vt* to adduce; (*dar como prueba*) to offer as proof

**adueñarse** [aðwe'narse] *vr*: ~ de to take possession of

**adulación** [aðula'θjon] *nf* flattery

**adular** [aðu'lar] *vt* to flatter

**adulterar** [aðulte'rar] *vt* to adulterate ♦ *vi* to commit adultery

**adulterio** [aðul'terjo] *nm* adultery

**adúltero, a** [a'ðultero, a] *adj* adulterous ♦ *nm/f* adulterer/adulteress

**adulto, a** [a'ðulto, a] *adj, nm/f* adult

**adusto, a** [a'ðusto, a] *adj* stern; (*austero*) austere

**advenedizo, a** [aðβene'ðiθo, a] *nm/f* upstart

**advenimiento** [aðβeni'mjento] nm arrival; (al trono) accession

**adverbio** [að'βerβjo] nm adverb

**adversario, a** [aðβer'sarjo. a] nm/f adversary

**adversidad** [aðβersi'ðað] nf adversity; (contratiempo) setback

**adverso, a** [að'βerso. a] adj adverse

**advertencia** [aðβer'tenθja] nf warning; (prefacio) preface, foreword

**advertir** [aðβer'tir] vt to notice; (avisar): ~ **a uno de** to warn sb about o of

**Adviento** [að'βjento] nm Advent

**advierto** etc vb ver **advertir**

**adyacente** [aðja'θente] adj adjacent

**aéreo, a** [a'ereo. a] adj aerial

**aerobic** [ae'roβik] nm aerobics sg

**aerodeslizador** [aeroðesliða'ðor] nm hovercraft

**aerodeslizante** [aeroðesli'θante] nm = **aerodeslizador**

**aeromozo, a** [aero'moθo. a] (AM) nm/f air steward(ess)

**aeronáutica** [aero'nautika] nf aeronautics sg

**aeronave** [aero'naβe] nm spaceship

**aeroplano** [aero'plano] nm aeroplane

**aeropuerto** [aero'pwerto] nm airport

**aerosol** [aero'sol] nm aerosol

**afabilidad** [afaβili'ðað] nf friendliness; **afable** [a'faβle] adj affable

**afamado, a** [afa'maðo. a] adj famous

**afán** [a'fan] nm hard work; (deseo) desire

**afanar** [afa'nar] vt to harass; (fam) to pinch; ~**se** vr: ~**se por hacer** to strive to do; **afanoso, a** adj (trabajo) hard; (trabajador) industrious

**afear** [afe'ar] vt to disfigure

**afección** [afek'θjon] nf (MED) disease

**afectación** [afekta'θjon] nf affectation; **afectado, a** adj affected

**afectar** [afek'tar] vt to affect

**afectísimo, a** [afek'tisimo. a] adj affectionate; ~ **suyo** yours truly

**afectivo, a** [afek'tiβo. a] adj (problema etc) emotional

**afecto** [a'fekto] nm affection; **tenerle** ~ **a uno** to be fond of sb

**afectuoso, a** [afek'twoso. a] adj affectionate

**afeitar** [afei'tar] vt to shave; ~**se** vr to shave

**afeminado, a** [afemi'naðo. a] adj effeminate

**aferrar** [afe'rrar] vt to grasp; (barco) to moor ♦ vi to moor

**Afganistán** [afvanis'tan] nm Afghanistan

**afianzamiento** [afjanθa'mjento] nm strengthening; securing

**afianzar** [afjan'θar] vt to strengthen; to secure; ~**se** vr to become established

**afición** [afi'θjon] nf fondness, liking; **la ~** the fans pl; **pinto por ~** I paint as a hobby; **aficionado, a** adj keen, enthusiastic; (no profesional) amateur ♦ nm/f enthusiast, fan; amateur; **ser aficionado a algo** to be very keen on o fond of sth

**aficionar** [afiθjo'nar] vt: ~ **a uno a algo** to make sb like sth; ~**se** vr: ~**se a algo** to grow fond of sth

**afiche** [a'fitfe] (AM) nm poster

**afilado, a** [afi'laðo. a] adj sharp

**afilar** [afi'lar] vt to sharpen

**afiliarse** [afi'ljarse] vr to affiliate

**afín** [a'fin] adj (parecido) similar; (conexo) related

**afinar** [afi'nar] vt: ~ **a uno o algo** (TEC) to refine; (MUS) to tune ♦ vi (tocar) to play in tune; (cantar) to sing in tune

**afincarse** [afin'karse] vr to settle

**afinidad** [afini'ðað] nf affinity; (parentesco) relationship; **por ~** by marriage

**afirmación** [afirma'θjon] nf affirmation

**afirmar** [afir'mar] vt to affirm, state; (reforzar) to strengthen; **afirmativo, a** adj affirmative

**aflicción** [aflik'θjon] nf affliction; (dolor) grief

**afligir** [afli'xir] vt to afflict; (apenar)

to distress; ~se vr to grieve

**aflojar** [aflo'xar] vt to slacken; (desatar) to loosen, undo; (relajar) to relax ♦ vi to drop; (bajar) to go down; ~se vr to relax

**aflorar** [aflo'rar] vi to come to the surface, emerge

**afluente** [aflu'ente] adj flowing ♦ nm tributary

**afluir** [aflu'ir] vi to flow

**afmo, a** abr (= afectísimo(a) suyo(a)) Yours

**afónico, a** [a'foniko, a] adj: estar ~ to have a sore throat; to have lost one's voice

**aforo** [a'foro] nm (de teatro etc) capacity

**afortunado, a** [afortu'naðo, a] adj fortunate, lucky

**afrancesado, a** [afranθe'saðo, a] adj francophile; (pey) Frenchified

**afrenta** [a'frenta] nf affront, insult; (deshonra) dishonour, shame

**África** ['afrika] nf Africa; ~ del Sur South Africa; ~ del Norte North Africa; **africano, a** adj, nm/f African

**afrontar** [afron'tar] vt to confront; (poner cara a cara) to bring face to face

**afuera** [a'fwera] adv out, outside; ~s nfpl outskirts

**agachar** [aga'tʃar] vt to bend, bow; ~se vr to stoop, bend

**agalla** [a'gaʎa] nf (ZOOL) gill; ~s nfpl (MED) tonsillitis sg; (ANAT) tonsils; tener ~s (fam) to have guts

**agarradera** [agarra'ðera] nf = agarradero

**agarradero** [agarra'ðero] nm handle; ~s nmpl (fig) pull sg, influence sg

**agarrado, a** [aga'rraðo, a] adj mean, stingy

**agarrar** [aga'rrar] vt to grasp, grab; (AM) to take, catch; (recoger) to pick up ♦ vi (planta) to take root; ~se vr to hold on (tightly)

**agarrotar** [agarro'tar] vt (lío) to tie tightly; (persona) to squeeze tightly; (reo) to garrotte; ~se vr (motor) to

seize up; (MED) to stiffen

**agasajar** [agasa'xar] vt to treat well, fête

**agazaparse** [agaθa'parse] vr to crouch down

**agencia** [a'xenθja] nf agency; ~ inmobiliaria estate (BRIT) o real estate (US) agent's (office); ~ de viajes travel agency

**agenciarse** [axen'θjarse] vr to obtain, procure

**agenda** [a'xenda] nf diary

**agente** [a'xente] nm/f agent; (de policía) policeman/policewoman; ~ inmobiliario estate agent (BRIT), realtor (US); ~ de seguros insurance agent

**ágil** ['axil] adj agile, nimble; **agilidad** nf agility, nimbleness

**agilizar** [axili'θar] vt (trámites) to speed up

**agitación** [axita'θjon] nf (de mano etc) shaking, waving; (de líquido etc) stirring; (fig) agitation

**agitado, a** [axi'taðo, a] adj hectic; (viaje) bumpy

**agitar** [axi'tar] vt to wave, shake; (líquido) to stir; (fig) to stir up, excite; ~se vr to get excited; (inquietarse) to get worried o upset

**aglomeración** [axlomera'θjon] nf: ~ de tráfico/gente traffic jam/mass of people

**aglomerar** [axlome'rar] vt to crowd together; ~se vr to crowd together

**agnóstico, a** [ay'nostiko, a] adj, nm/f agnostic

**agobiar** [axo'βjar] vt to weigh down; (oprimir) to oppress; (cargar) to burden

**agolparse** [axol'parse] vr to crowd together

**agonía** [axo'nia] nf death throes pl; (fig) agony, anguish

**agonizante** [axoni'θante] adj dying

**agonizar** [axoni'θar] vi (tb: estar agonizando) to be dying

**agosto** [a'yosto] nm August

**agotado, a** [axo'taðo, a] adj (persona) exhausted; (libros) out of print;

(*acabado*) finished; (*COM*) sold out

**agotador, a** [aɣota'ðor, a] *adj* exhausting

**agotamiento** [aɣota'mjento] *nm* exhaustion

**agotar** [aɣo'tar] *vt* to exhaust; (*consumir*) to drain; (*recursos*) to use up, deplete; ~**se** *vr* to be exhausted; (*acabarse*) to run out; (*libro*) to go out of print

**agraciado, a** [aɣra'θjaðo, a] *adj* (*atractivo*) attractive; (*en sorteo etc*) lucky

**agradable** [aɣra'ðaβle] *adj* pleasant, nice

**agradar** [aɣra'ðar] *vt*: él me agrada I like him

**agradecer** [aɣraðe'θer] *vt* to thank; (*favor etc*) to be grateful for; **agradecido, a** *adj* grateful; **¡muy ~!** thanks a lot!; **agradecimiento** *nm* thanks *pl*; gratitude

**agradezco** *etc vb ver* **agradecer**

**agrado** [a'ɣraðo] *nm*: **ser de tu** *etc* ~ to be to your *etc* liking

**agrandar** [aɣran'dar] *vt* to enlarge; (*fig*) to exaggerate; ~**se** *vr* to get bigger

**agrario, a** [a'ɣrarjo, a] *adj* agrarian, land *cpd*; (*política*) agricultural, farming

**agravante** [aɣra'βante] *adj* aggravating ♦ *nf*: **con la ~ de que ...** with the further difficulty that ....

**agravar** [aɣra'βar] *vt* (*pesar sobre*) to make heavier; (*irritar*) to aggravate; ~**se** *vr* to worsen, get worse

**agraviar** [aɣra'βjar] *vt* to offend; (*ser injusto con*) to wrong; ~**se** *vr* to take offence; **agravio** *nm* offence; wrong; (*JUR*) grievance

**agredir** [aɣre'ðir] *vt* to attack

**agregado, a** [aɣre'ɣaðo, a] *nm/f*: **A~** = teacher (*who is not head of department*) ♦ *nm* aggregate; (*persona*) attaché

**agregar** [aɣre'ɣar] *vt* to gather; (*añadir*) to add; (*persona*) to appoint

**agresión** [aɣre'sjon] *nf* aggression

**agresivo, a** [aɣre'siβo, a] *adj* aggressive

**agriar** [a'ɣrjar] *vt* to (turn) sour; ~**se** *vr* to turn sour

**agrícola** [a'ɣrikola] *adj* farming *cpd*, agricultural

**agricultor, a** [aɣrikul'tor, a] *nm/f* farmer

**agricultura** [aɣrikul'tura] *nf* agriculture, farming

**agridulce** [aɣri'ðulθe] *adj* bittersweet; (*CULIN*) sweet and sour

**agrietarse** [aɣrje'tarse] *vr* to crack; (*piel*) to chap

**agrimensor, a** [aɣrimen'sor, a] *nm/f* surveyor

**agrio, a** ['aɣrjo, a] *adj* bitter

**agronomía** [aɣrono'mia] *nf* agronomy, agriculture

**agropecuario, a** [aɣrope'kwarjo, a] *adj* farming *cpd*, agricultural

**agrupación** [aɣrupa'θjon] *nf* group; (*acto*) grouping

**agrupar** [aɣru'par] *vt* to group

**agua** ['aɣwa] *nf* water; (*NAUT*) wake; (*ARQ*) slope of a roof; ~**s** *nfpl* (*de piedra*) water *sg*, sparkle *sg*; (*MED*) water *sg*, urine *sg*; (*NAUT*) waters; ~**s abajo/arriba** downstream/upstream; ~ **bendita/destilada/potable** holy/distilled/drinking water; ~ **caliente** hot water; ~ **corriente** running water; ~ **de colonia** eau de cologne; ~ **mineral (con/sin gas)** (carbonated/uncarbonated) mineral water; ~ **oxigenada** hydrogen peroxide; ~**s jurisdiccionales** territorial waters

**aguacate** [aɣwa'kate] *nm* avocado (pear)

**aguacero** [aɣwa'θero] *nm* (heavy) shower, downpour

**aguada** [a'ɣwaða] *nf* (*AGR*) watering place; (*NAUT*) water supply; (*ARTE*) watercolour

**aguado, a** [a'ɣwaðo, a] *adj* watery, watered down

**aguafiestas** [aɣwa'fjestas] *nm/f inv* spoilsport, killjoy

**aguanieve** [aɣwa'njeβe] *nf* sleet

**aguantar** [aɣwan'tar] *vt* to bear, put

up with; (*sostener*) to hold up ♦ *vi* to
last; ~se *vr* to restrain o.s.; **aguante** *nm* (*paciencia*) patience; (*resistencia*) endurance

**aguar** [a'war] *vt* to water down

**aguardar** [awar'ðar] *vt* to wait for

**aguardiente** [awar'ðjente] *nm*
brandy, liquor

**aguarrás** [awa'rras] *nm* turpentine

**agudeza** [ayu'ðeθa] *nf* sharpness;
(*ingenio*) wit

**agudizar** [ayuði'θar] *vt* (*crisis*) to
make worse; ~se *vr* to get worse

**agudo, a** [a'yuðo, a] *adj* sharp;
(*voz*) high-pitched, piercing; (*dolor,
enfermedad*) acute

**agüero** [a'ɣwero] *nm*: **buen/mal** ~
good/bad omen

**aguijón** [axi'xon] *nm* sting; (*fig*)
spur

**águila** [a'xila] *nf* eagle; (*fig*) genius

**aguileño, a** [axi'leɲo, a] *adj* (*nariz*)
aquiline; (*rostro*) sharp-featured

**aguinaldo** [axi'naldo] *nm* Christmas
box

**aguja** [a'xuxa] *nf* needle; (*de reloj*)
hand; (*ARQ*) spire; (*TEC*) firing-pin;
~s *nfpl* (*ZOOL*) ribs; (*FERRO*)
points

**agujerear** [axuxere'ar] *vt* to make
holes in

**agujero** [axu'xero] *nm* hole

**agujetas** [axu'xetas] *nfpl* stitch *sg*;
(*rigidez*) stiffness *sg*

**aguzar** [axu'θar] *vt* to sharpen; (*fig*)
to incite

**ahí** [a'i] *adv* there; **de** ~ **que** so that,
with the result that; ~ **llega** here he
comes; **por** ~ that way; (*allá*) over
there; **200 o por** ~ 200 or so

**ahijado, a** [ai'xaðo, a] *nm/f* godson/
daughter

**ahínco** [a'inko] *nm* earnestness

**ahíto, a** [a'ito, a] *adj*: **estoy** ~ I'm
full up

**ahogar** [ao'yar] *vt* to drown; (*asfixiar*) to suffocate, smother; (*fuego*)
to put out; ~se *vr* (*en el agua*) to
drown; (*por asfixia*) to suffocate

**ahogo** [a'oxo] *nm* breathlessness;

(*fig*) financial difficulty

**ahondar** [aon'dar] *vt* to deepen,
make deeper; (*fig*) to study thoroughly ♦ *vi*: ~ **en** to study thoroughly

**ahora** [a'ora] *adv* now; (*hace poco*) a
moment ago, just now; (*dentro de
poco*) in a moment; ~ **voy** I'm coming; ~ **mismo** right now; ~ **bien**
now then; **por** ~ for the present

**ahorcar** [aor'kar] *vt* to hang; ~se *vr*
to hang o.s.

**ahorita** [ao'rita] (*fam: esp AM*) *adv*
right now

**ahorrar** [ao'rrar] *vt* (*dinero*) to save;
(*esfuerzos*) to save, avoid; **ahorro**
*nm* (*acto*) saving; (*frugalidad*)
thrift; **ahorros** *nmpl* (*dinero*) savings

**ahuecar** [awe'kar] *vt* to hollow (out);
(*voz*) to deepen; ~se *vr* to give o.s.
airs

**ahumar** [au'mar] *vt* to smoke, cure;
(*llenar de humo*) to fill with smoke ♦
*vi* to smoke; ~se *vr* to fill with
smoke

**ahuyentar** [aujen'tar] *vt* to drive off,
frighten off; (*fig*) to dispel

**airado, a** [ai'raðo, a] *adj* angry

**airar** [ai'rar] *vt* to anger; ~se *vr* to
get angry

**aire** ['aire] *nm* air; (*viento*) wind;
(*corriente*) draught; (*MUS*) tune; ~s
*nmpl*: **darse** ~s to give o.s. airs; **al**
~ **libre** in the open air; ~ **acondicionado** air conditioning; **airearse**
*vr* (*persona*) to go out for a breath of
fresh air; **airoso, a** *adj* windy;
draughty; (*fig*) graceful

**aislado, a** [ais'laðo, a] *adj* isolated;
(*incomunicado*) cut-off; (*ELEC*) insu-
lated

**aislar** [ais'lar] *vt* to isolate; (*ELEC*)
to insulate

**ajardinado, a** [axarði'naðo, a] *adj*
landscaped

**ajedrez** [axe'ðreθ] *nm* chess

**ajeno, a** [a'xeno, a] *adj* (*que perte-
nece a otro*) somebody else's; ~
foreign to; ~ **de** free from, devoid of

**ajetreado, a** [axetre'aðo, a] *adj* busy

**ajetreo** [axe'treo] *nm* bustle

**ají** [a'xi] *nm* chilli, red pepper; (*salsa*) chilli sauce

**ajo** ['axo] *nm* garlic

**ajuar** [a'xwar] *nm* household furnishings *pl*; (*de novia*) trousseau; (*de niño*) layette

**ajustado, a** [axus'taðo, a] *adj* (*tornillo*) tight; (*cálculo*) right; (*ropa*) tight(-fitting); (*DEPORTE: resultado*) close

**ajustar** [axus'tar] *vt* (*adaptar*) to adjust; (*encajar*) to fit; (*TEC*) to engage; (*IMPRENTA*) to make up; (*apretar*) to tighten; (*concertar*) to agree (on); (*reconciliar*) to reconcile; (*cuentas, deudas*) to settle ♦ *vi* to fit; ~se *vr*: ~se a (*precio etc*) to be in keeping with, fit in with; ~ las cuentas a uno to get even with sb

**ajuste** [a'xuste] *nm* adjustment; (*COSTURA*) fitting; (*acuerdo*) compromise; (*de cuenta*) settlement

**al** [al] (= a + el) *ver* a

**ala** ['ala] *nf* wing; (*de sombrero*) brim; (*futbolista*) winger

**alabanza** [ala'ßanθa] *nf* praise

**alabar** [ala'ßar] *vt* to praise

**alacena** [ala'θena] *nf* kitchen cupboard (*BRIT*), kitchen closet (*US*)

**alacrán** [ala'kran] *nm* scorpion

**alado, a** [a'laðo, a] *adj* winged

**alambique** [alam'bike] *nm* still

**alambrada** [alam'braða] *nf* wire fence; (*red*) wire netting

**alambrado** [alam'braðo] *nm* = alambrada

**alambre** [a'lambre] *nm* wire; ~ de púas barbed wire

**alameda** [ala'meða] *nf* (*plantío*) poplar grove; (*lugar de paseo*) avenue, boulevard

**álamo** ['alamo] *nm* poplar; ~ temblón aspen

**alarde** [a'larðe] *nm* show, display; hacer ~ de to boast of

**alargador** [alarxa'ðor] *nm* (*ELEC*) extension lead

**alargar** [alar'var] *vt* to lengthen, extend; (*paso*) to hasten; (*brazo*) to stretch out; (*cuerda*) to pay out; (*conversación*) to spin out; ~se *vr* to get longer

**alarido** [ala'riðo] *nm* shriek

**alarma** [a'larma] *nf* alarm

**alarmar** *vt* to alarm; ~se to get alarmed; **alarmante** [alar'mante] *adj* alarming

**alba** ['alßa] *nf* dawn

**albacea** [alßa'θea] *nm/f* executor/executrix

**Albania** [al'ßanja] *nf* Albania

**albañal** [alßa'nal] *nm* drain, sewer

**albañil** [alßa'nil] *nm* bricklayer; (*cantero*) mason

**albarán** [alßa'ran] *nm* (*COM*) delivery note, invoice

**albaricoque** [alßari'koke] *nm* apricot

**albedrío** [alße'ðrio] *nm*: **libre** ~ free will

**alberca** [al'ßerka] *nf* reservoir; (*AM*) swimming pool

**albergar** [alßer'var] *vt* to shelter

**albergue** *etc* [al'ßerxe] *vb ver* **albergar** ♦ *nm* shelter, refuge; ~ **juvenil** youth hostel

**albóndiga** [al'ßondiva] *nf* meatball

**albornoz** [alßor'noθ] *nm* (*de los árabes*) burnous; (*para el baño*) bathrobe

**alborotar** [alßoro'tar] *vi* to make a row ♦ *vt* to agitate, stir up; ~se *vr* to get excited; (*mar*) to get rough; **alboroto** [alßo'roto] *nm* row, uproar

**alborozar** [alßoro'θar] *vt* to gladden; ~se *vr* to rejoice

**alborozo** [alßo'roθo] *nm* joy

**álbum** ['alßum] (*pl* ~s, ~es) *nm* album; ~ **de recortes** scrapbook

**albumen** [al'ßumen] *nm* egg white, albumen

**alcachofa** [alka'tʃofa] *nf* artichoke

**alcalde, esa** [al'kalde, esa] *nm/f* mayor(ess)

**alcaldía** [alkal'dia] *nf* mayoralty; (*lugar*) mayor's office

**alcance** *etc* [al'kanθe] *vb ver* **alcan-**

zar ♦ *nm* reach; (COM) adverse balance

**alcantarilla** [alkanta'riʎa] *nf* (de aguas cloacales) sewer; (en la calle) gutter

**alcanzar** [alkan'θar] *vt* (algo: con la mano, el pie) to reach; (alguien: en el camino etc) to catch up (with); (autobús) to catch; (suj: bala) to hit, strike ♦ *vi* (ser suficiente) to be enough; ~ **a hacer** to manage to do

**alcaparra** [alka'parra] *nf* caper

**alcayata** [alka'jata] *nf* hook

**alcázar** [al'kaθar] *nm* fortress; (NAUT) quarter-deck

**alcoba** [al'koβa] *nf* bedroom

**alcohol** [al'kol] *nm* alcohol; ~ **metílico** methylated spirits *pl* (BRIT), wood alcohol (US); **alcohólico, a** *adj, nm/f* alcohólico

**alcoholímetro** [alko'limetro] *nm* Breathalyser ® (BRIT), drunkometer (US)

**alcoholismo** [alko'lismo] *nm* alcoholism

**alcornoque** [alkor'noke] *nm* cork tree; (fam) idiot

**alcurnia** [al'kurnja] *nf* lineage

**aldaba** [al'daβa] *nf* (door) knocker

**aldea** [al'dea] *nf* village; **~no, a** *adj* village *cpd* ♦ *nm/f* villager

**aleación** [alea'θjon] *nf* alloy

**aleatorio, a** [alea'torjo, a] *adj* random

**aleccionar** [alekθjo'nar] *vt* to instruct; (adiestrar) to train

**alegación** [aleɣa'θjon] *nf* allegation

**alegar** [ale'ɣar] *vt* to allege; (JUR) to plead ♦ *vi* (AM) to argue

**alegato** [ale'ɣato] *nm* (JUR) allegation; (AM) argument

**alegoría** [aleɣo'ria] *nf* allegory

**alegrar** [ale'ɣrar] *vt* (causar alegría) to cheer (up); (fuego) to poke; (fiesta) to liven up; **~se** *vr* (fam) to get merry o tight; **~se de** to be glad about

**alegre** [a'leɣre] *adj* happy, cheerful; (fam) merry, tight; (chiste) risqué, blue; **alegría** *nf* happiness; merri-

ment

**alejamiento** [alexa'mjento] *nm* removal; (distancia) remoteness

**alejar** [ale'xar] *vt* to remove; (fig) to estrange; **~se** *vr* to move away

**alemán, ana** [ale'man, ana] *adj, nm/f* German ♦ *nm* (LING) German

**Alemania** [ale'manja] *nf*: ~ **Occidental/Oriental** West/East Germany

**alentador, a** [alenta'ðor, a] *adj* encouraging

**alentar** [alen'tar] *vt* to encourage

**alergia** [a'lerxja] *nf* allergy

**alero** [a'lero] *nm* (de tejado) eaves *pl*; (de carruaje) mudguard

**alerta** [a'lerta] *adj, nm* alert

**aleta** [a'leta] *nf* (de pez) fin; (de ave) wing; (de foca, DEPORTE) flipper; (AUTO) mudguard

**aletargar** [aletar'ɣar] *vt* to make drowsy; (entumecer) to make numb; **~se** *vr* to grow drowsy; to become numb

**aletear** [alete'ar] *vi* to flutter

**alevín** [ale'βin] *nm* fry, young fish

**alevino** [ale'βino] *nm* = **alevín**

**alevosía** [aleβo'sia] *nf* treachery

**alfabeto** [alfa'βeto] *nm* alphabet

**alfalfa** [al'falfa] *nf* alfalfa, lucerne

**alfarería** [alfare'ria] *nf* pottery; (tienda) pottery shop; **alfarero, a** *nm/f* potter

**alféizar** [al'feiθar] *nm* window-sill

**alférez** [al'fereθ] *nm* (MIL) second lieutenant; (NAUT) ensign

**alfil** [al'fil] *nm* (AJEDREZ) bishop

**alfiler** [alfi'ler] *nm* pin; (broche) clip; (pinza) clothes peg

**alfiletero** [alfile'tero] *nm* needlecase

**alfombra** [al'fombra] *nf* carpet; (más pequeña) rug; **alfombrar** *vt* to carpet; **alfombrilla** *nf* rug, mat

**alforja** [al'forxa] *nf* saddlebag

**algarabía** [alɣara'βia] (fam) *nf* gibberish; (griterío) hullabaloo

**algas** [al'ɣas] *nfpl* seaweed

**álgebra** ['alxeβra] *nf* algebra

**álgido, a** ['alxiðo] *adj* icy, chilly;

(*momento etc*) crucial, decisive

**algo** [ˈalɣo] *pron* something; anything
♦ *adv* somewhat, rather; ¿~ más?
anything else?; (*en tienda*) is that
all?; **por ~ será** there must be some
reason for it

**algodón** [alɣoˈðon] *nm* cotton; (*planta*) cotton plant; ~ **de azúcar** candy
floss (*BRIT*), cotton candy (*US*); ~
**hidrófilo** cotton wool (*BRIT*), absorbent cotton (*US*)

**algodonero, a** [alɣoðoˈnero, a] *adj*
cotton *cpd* ♦ *nm/f* cotton grower ♦
*nm* cotton plant

**alguacil** [alɣwaˈθil] *nm* bailiff;
(*TAUR*) mounted official

**alguien** [ˈalɣjen] *pron* someone,
somebody; (*en frases interrogativas*)
anyone, anybody

**alguno, a** [alˈɣuno, a] *adj* (*delante
de nm*: **algún**) some; (*después de
n*): **no tiene talento alguno** he has
no talent, he doesn't have any talent
♦ *pron* (*alguien*) someone, somebody; **algún que otro libro** some
book or other; **algún día iré** I'll go
one ◊ some day; **sin interés** = without the slightest interest; ~ **que otro**
an occasional one; ~**s piensan** some
(people) think

**alhaja** [aˈlaxa] *nf* jewel; (*tesoro*) precious object, treasure

**alhelí** [aleˈli] *nm* wallflower, stock

**aliado, a** [aˈljaðo, a] *adj* allied

**alianza** [aˈljanθa] *nf* alliance; (*anillo*)
wedding ring

**aliar** [aˈljar] *vt* to ally; ~**se** *vr* to
form an alliance

**alias** [ˈaljas] *adv* alias

**alicates** [aliˈkates] *nmpl* pliers; ~ **de
uñas** nail clippers

**aliciente** [aliˈθjente] *nm* incentive;
(*atracción*) attraction

**alienación** [aljenaˈθjon] *nf* alienation

**aliento** [aˈljento] *nm* breath; (*respiración*) breathing; **sin ~** breathless

**aligerar** [alixeˈrar] *vt* to lighten; (*reducir*) to shorten; (*aliviar*) to alleviate; (*mitigar*) to ease; (*paso*) to

quicken

**alijo** [aˈlixo] *nm* consignment

**alimaña** [aliˈmaɲa] *nf* pest

**alimentación** [alimentaˈθjon] *nf* (*comida*) food; (*acción*) feeding; (*tienda*) grocer's (shop); **alimentador**
*nm*: **alimentador de papel** sheet-feeder

**alimentar** [alimenˈtar] *vt* to feed;
(*nutrir*) to nourish; ~**se** *vr* to feed

**alimenticio, a** [alimenˈtiθjo, a] *adj*
food *cpd*; (*nutritivo*) nourishing, nutritious

**alimento** [aliˈmento] *nm* food; (*nutrición*) nourishment; ~**s** *nmpl* (*JUR*) alimony *sg*

**alineación** [alineaˈθjon] *nf* alignment; (*DEPORTE*) line-up

**alinear** [alineˈar] *vt* to align; ~**se** *vr*
(*DEPORTE*) to line up; ~**se en** to
fall in with

**aliñar** [aliˈɲar] *vt* (*CULIN*) to season;
**aliño** *nm* (*CULIN*) dressing

**alioli** [aliˈoli] *nm* garlic mayonnaise

**alisar** [aliˈsar] *vt* to smooth

**aliso** [aˈliso] *nm* alder

**alistarse** [alisˈtarse] *vr* to enlist; (*inscribirse*) to enrol

**aliviar** [aliˈβjar] *vt* (*carga*) to lighten;
(*persona*) to relieve; (*dolor*) to relieve, alleviate

**alivio** [aˈliβjo] *nm* alleviation, relief

**aljibe** [alˈxiβe] *nm* cistern

**alma** [ˈalma] *nf* soul; (*persona*) person; (*TEC*) core

**almacén** [almaˈθen] *nm* (*depósito*)
warehouse, store; (*MIL*) magazine;
(*AM*) shop; (*grandes*) **almacenes**
*nmpl* department store *sg*; **almacenaje** *nm* storage; **almacenaje secundaria** (*INFORM*) backing storage

**almacenar** [almaθeˈnar] *vt* to store,
put in storage; (*proveerse*) to stock
up with; **almacenero** *nm* warehouseman; (*AM*) shopkeeper

**almanaque** [almaˈnake] *nm* almanac

**almeja** [alˈmexa] *nf* clam

**almendra** [alˈmendra] *nf* almond; **almendro** *nm* almond tree

**almíbar** [al'miβar] *nm* syrup

**almidón** [almi'ðon] *nm* starch; **almidonar** *vt* to starch

**almirante** [almi'rante] *nm* admiral

**almirez** [almi'reθ] *nm* mortar

**almizcle** [al'miθkle] *nm* musk

**almohada** [almo'aða] *nf* pillow; (*funda*) pillowcase; **almohadilla** *nf* cushion; (*TEC*) pad; (*AM*) pincushion

**almohadón** [almoa'ðon] *nm* large pillow; bolster

**almorranas** [almo'rranas] *nfpl* piles, haemorrhoids

**almorzar** [almor'θar] *vt*: ~ **una tortilla** to have an omelette for lunch ♦ *vi* to (have) lunch

**almuerzo** *etc* [al'mwerθo] *vb ver* **almorzar** ♦ *nm* lunch

**alocado, a** [alo'kaðo, a] *adj* crazy

**alojamiento** [aloxa'mjento] *nm* lodging(s) (*pl*); (*viviendas*) housing

**alojar** [alo'xar] *vt* to lodge; ~se *vr* to lodge, stay

**alondra** [a'londra] *nf* lark, skylark

**alpargata** [alpar'yata] *nf* rope-soled sandal, espadrille

**Alpes** [alpes] *nmpl*: **los** ~ the Alps

**alpinismo** [alpi'nismo] *nm* mountaineering, climbing; **alpinista** *nm/f* mountaineer, climber

**alpiste** [al'piste] *nm* birdseed

**alquería** [alke'ria] *nf* farmhouse

**alquilar** [alki'lar] *vt* (*suj: propietario: inmuebles*) to let, rent (out); (: *coche*) to hire out; (: *TV*) to rent (out); (*suj: alquilador: inmuebles, TV*) to rent; (: *coche*) to hire; **se alquila casa** "house to let (*BRIT*) o to rent (*US*)"

**alquiler** [alki'ler] *nm* renting; letting; hiring; (*arriendo*) rent; hire charge; ~ **de automóviles** car hire; **de** ~ for hire

**alquimia** [al'kimja] *nf* alchemy

**alquitrán** [alki'tran] *nm* tar

**alrededor** [alreðe'ðor] *adv* around, about; ~ **de** around, about; **mirar a su** ~ to look (round) about one; ~**es** *nmpl* surroundings

**alta** ['alta] *nf* (certificate of) discharge; **dar de** ~ to discharge

**altanería** [altane'ria] *nf* haughtiness, arrogance; **altanero, a** *adj* arrogant, haughty

**altar** [al'tar] *nm* altar

**altavoz** [alta'βoθ] *nm* loudspeaker; (*amplificador*) amplifier

**alteración** [altera'θjon] *nf* alteration; (*alboroto*) disturbance

**alterar** [alte'rar] *vt* to alter; to disturb; ~se *vr* (*persona*) to get upset

**altercado** [alter'kaðo] *nm* argument

**alternar** [alter'nar] *vt* to alternate ♦ *vi* to alternate; (*turnar*) to take turns; ~se *vr* to alternate; to take turns; ~ **con** to mix with; **alternativa** *nf* alternative; (*elección*) choice; **alternativo, a** *adj* alternative; (*alterno*) alternating; **alterno, a** *adj* alternate; (*ELEC*) alternating

**Alteza** [al'teθa] *nf* (*tratamiento*) Highness

**altibajos** [alti'βaxos] *nmpl* ups and downs

**altiplanicie** [altipla'niθje] *nf* high plateau

**altiplano** [alti'plano] *nm* = **altiplanicie**

**altisonante** [altiso'nante] *adj* highflown, high-sounding

**altitud** [alti'tuð] *nf* height; (*AVIAT, GEO*) altitude

**altivez** [alti'βeθ] *nf* haughtiness, arrogance; **altivo, a** *adj* haughty, arrogant

**alto, a** ['alto, a] *adj* high; (*persona*) tall; (*sonido*) high, sharp; (*noble*) high, lofty ♦ *nm* halt; (*MUS*) alto; (*GEO*) hill; (*AM*) pile ♦ *adv* (*de sitio*) high; (*de sonido*) loud, loudly ♦ *excl* halt!; **la pared tiene 2 metros de** ~ the wall is 2 metres high; **en alta mar** on the high seas; **en voz alta** in a loud voice; **las altas horas de la noche** the small o wee hours; **en lo** ~ **de** at the top of; **pasar por** ~ to overlook

**altoparlante** [altopar'lante] (*AM*) *nm* loudspeaker

**altruismo** [altru'ismo] *nm* altruism

**altura** [al'tura] *nf* height; (*NAUT*) depth; (*GEO*) latitude; **la pared tiene 1.80 de ~** the wall is 1 metre 80cm high; **a estas ~s** at this stage; **a estas ~s del año** at this time of the year

**alubia** [a'luβja] *nf* French bean, kidney bean

**alucinación** [aluθina'θjon] *nf* hallucination

**alucinar** [aluθi'nar] *vi* to hallucinate ♦ *vt* to deceive; (*fascinar*) to fascinate

**alud** [a'luð] *nm* avalanche; (*fig*) flood

**aludir** [alu'ðir] *vi*: **~ a** to allude to; **darse por aludido** to take the hint

**alumbrado** [alum'braðo] *nm* lighting; **alumbramiento** *nm* lighting; (*MED*) childbirth, delivery

**alumbrar** [alum'brar] *vt* to light (up) ♦ *vi* (*MED*) to give birth

**aluminio** [alu'minjo] *nm* aluminium (*BRIT*), aluminum (*US*)

**alumno, a** [a'lumno, a] *nm/f* pupil, student

**alunizar** [aluni'θar] *vi* to land on the moon

**alusión** [alu'sjon] *nf* allusion

**alusivo, a** [alu'siβo, a] *adj* allusive

**aluvión** [aluβ'jon] *nm* alluvium; (*fig*) flood

**alverja** [al'βerxa] *nf* (*AM*) pea

**alza** ['alθa] *nf* rise; (*MIL*) sight

**alzada** [al'θaða] *nf* (*de caballos*) height; (*JUR*) appeal

**alzamiento** [alθa'mjento] *nm* (*aumento*) rise, increase; (*acción*) lifting, raising; (*mejor postura*) higher bid; (*rebelión*) rising; (*COM*) fraudulent bankruptcy

**alzar** [al'θar] *vt* to lift (up); (*precio, muro*) to raise; (*cuello de abrigo*) to turn up; (*AGR*) to gather in; (*IMPRENTA*) to gather; **~se** *vr* to get up, rise; (*rebelarse*) to revolt; (*COM*) to go fraudulently bankrupt; (*JUR*) to appeal

**allá** [a'ʎa] *adv* (*lugar*) there; (*por ahí*) over there; (*tiempo*) then; **~**

**abajo** down there; **más ~** further on; **más ~ de** beyond; **¡~ tú!** that's your problem!

**allanamiento** [aʎana'mjento] *nm*: **~ de morada** burglary

**allanar** [aʎa'nar] *vt* to flatten, level (out); (*igualar*) to smooth (out); (*fig*) to subdue; (*JUR*) to burgle, break into; **~se** *vr* to fall down; **~se a** to submit to, accept

**allegado, a** [aʎe'γaðo, a] *adj* near, close ♦ *nm/f* relation

**allí** [a'ʎi] *adv* there; **~ mismo** right there; **por ~** over there; (*por ese camino*) that way

**ama** ['ama] *nf* lady of the house; (*dueña*) owner; (*institutriz*) governess; (*madre adoptiva*) foster mother; **~ de casa** housewife; **~ de llaves** housekeeper

**amabilidad** [amaβili'ðað] *nf* kindness; (*simpatía*) niceness; **amable** *adj* kind; nice; **es usted muy amable** that's very kind of you

**amaestrado, a** [amaes'traðo, a] *adj* (*animal: en circo etc*) performing

**amaestrar** [amaes'trar] *vt* to train

**amago** [a'maɣo] *nm* threat; (*gesto*) threatening gesture; (*MED*) symptom

**amainar** [amai'nar] *vi* (*viento*) to die down

**amalgama** [amal'ɣama] *nf* amalgam; **amalgamar** *vt* to amalgamate; (*combinar*) to combine, mix

**amamantar** [amaman'tar] *vt* to suckle, nurse

**amanecer** [amane'θer] *vi* to dawn ♦ *nm* dawn; **~ afiebrado** to wake up with a fever

**amanerado, a** [amane'raðo, a] *adj* affected

**amansar** [aman'sar] *vt* to tame; (*persona*) to subdue; **~se** *vr* (*persona*) to calm down

**amante** [a'mante] *adj*: **~ de** fond of ♦ *nm/f* lover

**amapola** [ama'pola] *nf* poppy

**amar** [a'mar] *vt* to love

**amarar** [ama'rar] *vi* (*avión*) to land

(on the sea)

**amargado, a** [amar'ɣaðo, a] *adj* bitter

**amargar** [amar'ɣar] *vt* to make bitter; (*fig*) to embitter; ~**se** *vr* to become embittered

**amargo, a** [a'marɣo, a] *adj* bitter; **amargura** *nf* bitterness

**amarillento, a** [amari'ʎento, a] *adj* yellowish; (*tez*) sallow; **amarillo, a** *adj, nm* yellow

**amarrar** [ama'rrar] *vt* to moor; (*sujetar*) to tie up

**amarras** [a'marras] *nfpl*: **soltar** ~ to set sail

**amartillar** [amarti'ʎar] (*fusil*) to cock

**amasar** [ama'sar] *vt* (*masa*) to knead; (*mezclar*) to mix, prepare; (*confeccionar*) to concoct; **amasijo** *nm* kneading; mixing; (*fig*) hotchpotch

**amateur** ['amatur] *nm/f* amateur

**amatista** [ama'tista] *nf* amethyst

**amazona** [a'maθona] *nf* horsewoman; **A~s** *nm*: **el A~s** the Amazon

**ambages** [am'baxes] *nmpl*: **sin** ~ in plain language

**ámbar** ['ambar] *nm* amber

**ambición** [ambi'θjon] *nf* ambition; **ambicionar** *vt* to aspire to; **ambicioso, a** *adj* ambitious

**ambidextro, a** [ambi'ðekstro, a] *adj* ambidextrous

**ambientación** [ambjenta'θjon] *nf* (*CINE, TEATRO etc*) setting; (*RADIO*) sound effects

**ambiente** [am'bjente] *nm* (*tb fig*) atmosphere; (*medio*) environment

**ambigüedad** [ambiɣwe'ðað] *nf* ambiguity; **ambiguo, a** *adj* ambiguous

**ámbito** ['ambito] *nm* (*campo*) field; (*fig*) scope

**ambos, as** ['ambos, as] *adj pl, pron pl* both

**ambulancia** [ambu'lanθja] *nf* ambulance

**ambulante** [ambu'lante] *adj* travelling *cpd*, itinerant

**ambulatorio** [ambula'torjo] *nm* state health-service clinic

**amedrentar** [ameðren'tar] *vt* to scare

**amén** [a'men] *excl* amen; ~ **de** besides

**amenaza** [ame'naθa] *nf* threat

**amenazar** [amena'θar] *vt* to threaten ♦ *vi*: ~ **con hacer** to threaten to do

**amenidad** [ameni'ðað] *nf* pleasantness

**ameno, a** [a'meno, a] *adj* pleasant

**América** [a'merika] *nf* America; ~ **del Norte/del Sur** North/South America; ~ **Central/Latina** Central/Latin America; **americana** *nf* coat, jacket; *ver tb* **americano**; **americano, a** *adj, nm/f* American

**amerizar** [ameri'θar] *vi* (*avión*) to land (on the sea)

**ametralladora** [ametraʎa'ðora] *nf* machine gun

**amianto** [a'mjanto] *nm* asbestos

**amigable** [ami'ɣaβle] *adj* friendly

**amígdala** [a'miɣðala] *nf* tonsil; **amigdalitis** *nf* tonsillitis

**amigo, a** [a'miɣo, a] *adj* friendly ♦ *nm/f* friend; (*amante*) lover; **ser** ~ **de algo** to be fond of sth; **ser muy** ~**s** to be close friends

**amilanar** [amila'nar] *vt* to scare; ~**se** *vr* to get scared

**aminorar** [amino'rar] *vt* to diminish; (*reducir*) to reduce; ~ **la marcha** to slow down

**amistad** [amis'tað] *nf* friendship; ~**es** *nfpl* (*amigos*) friends; **amistoso, a** *adj* friendly

**amnesia** [am'nesja] *nf* amnesia

**amnistía** [amnis'tia] *nf* amnesty

**amo** ['amo] *nm* owner; (*jefe*) boss

**amodorrarse** [amoðo'rrarse] *vr* to get sleepy

**amolar** [amo'lar] *vt* (*perseguir*) to annoy

**amoldar** [amol'dar] *vt* to mould; (*adaptar*) to adapt

**amonestación** [amonesta'θjon] *nf* warning; **amonestaciones** *nfpl* (*REL*) marriage banns

**amonestar** [amones'tar] vt to warn; (REL) to publish the banns of

**amontonar** [amonto'nar] vt to collect, pile up; ~se vr to crowd together; (acumularse) to pile up

**amor** [a'mor] nm love; (amante) lover; hacer el ~ to make love; ~ proprio self-respect

**amoratado, a** [amora'taðo, a] adj purple

**amordazar** [amorða'θar] vt to muzzle; (fig) to gag

**amorfo, a** [a'morfo, a] adj amorphous, shapeless

**amoroso, a** [amo'roso, a] adj affectionate, loving

**amortajar** [amorta'xar] vt to shroud

**amortiguador** [amortiɣwa'ðor] nm shock absorber; (parachoques) bumper; ~es nmpl (AUTO) suspension sg

**amortiguar** [amorti'ɣwar] vt to deaden; (ruido) to muffle; (color) to soften

**amortización** [amortiθa'θjon] nf (de deuda) repayment; (de bono) redemption

**amotinar** [amoti'nar] vt to stir up, incite to riot); ~se vr to mutiny

**amparar** [ampa'rar] vt to protect; ~se vr to seek protection; (de la lluvia etc) to shelter; **amparo** nm help, protection; al ~ de under the protection of

**amperio** [am'perjo] nm ampère, amp

**ampliación** [amplja'θjon] nf enlargement; (extensión) extension

**ampliar** [am'pljar] vt to enlarge; to extend

**amplificación** [amplifika'θjon] nf enlargement; **amplificador** nm amplifier

**amplificar** [amplifi'kar] vt to amplify

**amplio, a** [am'pljo, a] adj spacious; (de falda etc) full; (extenso) extensive; (ancho) wide; **amplitud** nf spaciousness; extent; (fig) amplitude

**ampolla** [am'poʎa] nf blister; (MED) ampoule

**ampuloso, a** [ampu'loso, a] adj bombastic, pompous

**amputar** [ampu'tar] vt to cut off, amputate

**amueblar** [amwe'βlar] vt to furnish

**amurallar** [amura'ʎar] vt to wall up o in

**anacronismo** [anakro'nismo] nm anachronism

**anadear** [anaðe'ar] vi to waddle

**anales** [a'nales] nmpl annals

**analfabetismo** [analfaβe'tismo] nm illiteracy; **analfabeto, a** adj, nm/f illiterate

**analgésico** [anal'xesiko] nm painkiller, analgesic

**análisis** [a'nalisis] nm inv analysis

**analista** [ana'lista] nm/f (gen) analyst

**analizar** [anali'θar] vt to analyse

**analogía** [analo'xia] nf analogy

**analógico, a** [ana'loxiko, a] adj (INFORM) analog; (reloj) analogue (BRIT), analog (US)

**análogo, a** [a'naloɣo, a] adj analogous, similar

**ananá(s)** [ana'na(s)] nm pineapple

**anaquel** [ana'kel] nm shelf

**anarquía** [anar'kia] nf anarchy; **anarquismo** nm anarchism; **anarquista** nm/f anarchist

**anatomía** [anato'mia] nf anatomy

**anca** ['anka] nf rump, haunch; ~s nfpl (fam) behind sg

**anciano, a** [an'θjano, a] adj old, aged ♦ nm/f old man/woman; elder

**ancla** ['ankla] nf anchor; ~dero nm anchorage; **anclar** vi to (drop) anchor

**ancho, a** ['antʃo, a] adj wide; (falda) full; (fig) liberal ♦ nm width; (FERRO) gauge; **ponerse** ~ to get conceited; **estar a sus anchas** to be at one's ease

**anchoa** [an'tʃoa] nf anchovy

**anchura** [an'tʃura] nf width; (extensión) wideness

**andadura** [anda'ðura] nf gait; (de caballo) pace

**Andalucía** [andalu'θia] nf Andalusia; **andaluz, a** adj, nm/f Andalusian

**andamiaje** [anda'mjaxe] *nm* = **andamio**

**andamio** [an'damjo] *nm* scaffold(ing)

**andar** [an'dar] *vt* to go, cover, travel ♦ *vi* to go, walk, travel; *(funcionar)* to go, work; *(estar)* to be ♦ *nm* walk, gait, pace; ~**se** *vr* to go away; ~ **a pie/a caballo/en bicicleta** to go on foot/on horseback/by bicycle; ~ **haciendo algo** to be doing sth; ¡**anda!** *(sorpresa)* go on!; **anda por o en los 40** he's about 40

**andariego** [anda'rjexo, a] *adj (itinerante)* wandering

**andén** [an'den] *nm (FERRO)* platform; *(NAUT)* quayside; *(AM: de la calle)* pavement *(BRIT)*, sidewalk *(US)*

**Andes** ['andes] *nmpl*: los ~ the Andes

**Andorra** [an'dorra] *nf* Andorra

**andrajo** [an'draxo] *nm* rag; ~**so, a** *adj* ragged

**anduve** *etc* [an'duβe] *vb ver* **andar**

**anécdota** [a'nekðota] *nf* anecdote, story

**anegar** [ane'γar] *vt* to flood; *(ahogar)* to drown; ~**se** *vr* to drown; *(hundirse)* to sink

**anejo** [a'nexo, a] *adj, nm* = **anexo**

**anemia** [a'nemja] *nf* anaemia

**anestesia** [anes'tesja] *nf* anaesthesia

**anestésico** [anes'tesiko] *nm* anaesthetic

**anexar** [anek'sar] *vt* to annex; *(documento)* to attach; **anexión** *nf* annexation; **anexionamiento** *nm* annexation; **anexo, a** *adj* attached ♦ *nm* annexe

**anfibio, a** [an'fiβjo, a] *adj* amphibious ♦ *nm* amphibian

**anfiteatro** [anfite'atro] *nm* amphitheatre; *(TEATRO)* dress circle

**anfitrión, ona** [anfi'trjon, ona] *nm/f* host(ess)

**ángel** ['anxel] *nm* angel; ~ **de la guarda** guardian angel; **tener** ~ to be charming; **angélica** *adj* an-

gelic(al); **angélico, a** *adj* angelic(al)

**angina** [an'xina] *nf (MED)* inflammation of the throat; ~ **de pecho** angina; **tener** ~**s** to have tonsillitis

**anglicano, a** [angli'kano, a] *adj, nm/f* Anglican

**anglosajón, ona** [anglosa'xon, ona] *adj* Anglo-Saxon

**angosto, a** [an'gosto, a] *adj* narrow

**anguila** [an'gila] *nf* eel; ~**s** *nfpl (NAUT)* slipway *sg*

**angula** [an'gula] *nf* elver, baby eel

**ángulo** ['angulo] *nm* angle; *(esquina)* corner; *(curva)* bend

**angustia** [an'gustja] *nf* anguish; **angustiar** *vt* to distress, grieve

**anhelar** [ane'lar] *vt* to be eager for; *(desear)* to long for, desire ♦ *vi* to pant, gasp; **anhelo** *nm* eagerness; desire

**anidar** [ani'ðar] *vi* to nest

**anillo** [a'niʎo] *nm* ring; ~ **de boda** wedding ring

**animación** [anima'θjon] *nf* liveliness; *(vitalidad)* life; *(actividad)* activity; bustle

**animado, a** [ani'maðo, a] *adj (vivaz)* animated; **animador, a** *nm/f (TV)* host(ess), compère; *(DEPORTE)* cheerleader

**animadversión** [animaðßer'sjon] *nf* ill-will, antagonism

**animal** [ani'mal] *adj* animal; *(fig)* stupid ♦ *nm* animal; *(fig)* fool; *(bestia)* brute

**animar** [ani'mar] *vt (BIO)* to animate, give life to; *(fig)* to liven up, brighten up, cheer up; *(estimular)* to stimulate; ~**se** *vr* to cheer up; to feel encouraged; *(decidirse)* to make up one's mind

**ánimo** ['animo] *nm (alma)* soul; *(mente)* mind; *(valentía)* courage ♦ *excl* cheer up!

**animoso, a** [ani'moso, a] *adj* brave; *(vivo)* lively

**aniquilar** [aniki'lar] *vt* to annihilate, destroy

**anís** [a'nis] *nm* aniseed; *(licor)* anisette

**aniversario** [aniβer'sarjo] nm anniversary

**anoche** [a'notʃe] adv last night; **antes de ~** the night before last

**anochecer** [anotʃe'θer] vi to get dark ♦ nm nightfall, dark; **al ~** at nightfall

**anodino, a** [ano'ðino, a] adj dull, anodyne

**anomalía** [anoma'lia] nf anomaly

**anonadado, a** [anona'ðaðo, a] adj: **estar/quedar/sentirse ~** to be overwhelmed o amazed

**anonimato** [anoni'mato] nm anonymity

**anónimo, a** [a'nonimo, a] adj anonymous; (COM) limited ♦ nm (carta) anonymous letter; (: maliciosa) poison-pen letter

**anormal** [anor'mal] adj abnormal

**anotación** [anota'θjon] nf note; annotation

**anotar** [ano'tar] vt to note down; (comentar) to annotate

**anquilosamiento** [ankilosa'mjento] nm (fig) paralysis; stagnation

**anquilosarse** [ankilo'sarse] vr (fig: persona) to get out of touch; (método, costumbres) to go out of date

**ansia** ['ansja] nf anxiety; (anhelo) yearning; **ansiar** vt to long for

**ansiedad** [ansje'ðað] nf anxiety

**ansioso, a** [an'sjoso, a] adj anxious; (anhelante) eager; **~ de** o **por algo** greedy for sth

**antagónico, a** [anta'γoniko, a] adj antagonistic; (opuesto) contrasting; **antagonista** nm/f antagonist

**antaño** [an'taɲo] adv long ago, formerly

**Antártico** [an'tartiko] nm: **el ~** the Antarctic

**ante** ['ante] prep before, in the presence of; (problema etc) faced with ♦ nm (piel) suede; **~ todo** above all

**anteanoche** [antea'notʃe] adv the night before last

**anteayer** [antea'jer] adv the day before yesterday

**antebrazo** [ante'βraθo] nm forearm

**antecedente** [anteθe'ðente] adj previous ♦ nm antecedent; **~s** nmpl (JUR): **~s penales** criminal record; (procedencia) background

**anteceder** [anteθe'ðer] vt to precede, go before

**antecesor, a** [anteθe'sor, a] nm/f predecessor

**antedicho, a** [ante'ðitʃo, a] adj aforementioned

**antelación** [antela'θjon] nf: **con ~** in advance

**antemano** [ante'mano]: **de ~** adv beforehand, in advance

**antena** [an'tena] nf antenna; (de televisión etc) aerial; **~ parabólica** satellite dish

**anteojo** [ante'oxo] nm eyeglass; **~s** nmpl (AM) glasses, spectacles

**antepasados** [antepa'saðos] nmpl ancestors

**antepecho** [ante'petʃo] nm guardrail, parapet; (repisa) ledge, sill

**anteponer** [antepo'ner] vt to place in front; (fig) to prefer

**anteproyecto** [antepro'jekto] nm preliminary sketch; (fig) blueprint

**anterior** [ante'rjor] adj preceding, previous; **~idad** nf: **con ~idad a** prior to, before

**antes** ['antes] adv (con prioridad) before ♦ prep: **~ de** before ♦ conj: **~ de ir/de que te vayas** before going/before you go; **~ bien** (but) rather; **dos días ~** two days before o previously; **no quiso venir ~** she didn't want to come any earlier; **tomo el avión ~ que el barco** I take the plane rather than the boat; **~ que** yo before me; **lo ~ posible** as soon as possible; **cuanto ~ mejor** the sooner the better

**antiaéreo, a** [antia'ereo, a] adj anti-aircraft

**antibalas** [anti'βalas] adj inv: **chaleco ~** bullet-proof jacket

**antibiótico** [anti'βjotiko] nm antibiotic

**anticiclón** [antiθi'klon] nm anticyclone

**anticipación** [antiθipa'θjon] *nf* anticipation; **con 10 minutos de** ~ 10 minutes early

**anticipado, a** [antiθi'paðo, a] *adj* (*pago*) advance; **por** ~ in advance

**anticipar** [antiθi'par] *vt* to anticipate; (*adelantar*) to bring forward; (*COM*) to advance; ~**se** *vr*: ~**se a su época** to be ahead of one's time

**anticipo** [anti'θipo] *nm* (*COM*) advance

**anticonceptivo, a** [antikonθep'tißo, a] *adj, nm* contraceptive

**anticongelante** [antikonxe'lante] *nm* antifreeze

**anticuado, a** [anti'kwaðo, a] *adj* out-of-date, old-fashioned; (*desusado*) obsolete

**anticuario** [anti'kwarjo] *nm* antique dealer

**anticuerpo** [anti'kwerpo] *nm* (*MED*) antibody

**antídoto** [an'tiðoto] *nm* antidote

**antiestético, a** [anties'tetiko, a] *adj* unsightly

**antifaz** [anti'faθ] *nm* mask; (*velo*) veil

**antigualla** [anti'ɣwaʎa] *nf* antique; (*reliquia*) relic

**antiguamente** [antiɣwa'mente] *adv* formerly; (*hace mucho tiempo*) long ago

**antigüedad** [antiɣwe'ðað] *nf* antiquity; (*artículo*) antique; (*rango*) seniority

**antiguo, a** [an'tiɣwo, a] *adj* old, ancient; (*que fue*) former

**antílope** [an'tilope] *nm* antelope

**Antillas** [an'tiʎas] *nfpl*: **las** ~ the West Indies

**antinatural** [antinatu'ral] *adj* unnatural

**antipatía** [antipa'tia] *nf* antipathy, dislike; **antipático, a** *adj* disagreeable, unpleasant

**antirrobo** [anti'rroßo] *adj inv* (*alarma etc*) anti-theft

**antisemita** [antise'mita] *adj* anti-Semitic ♦ *nm/f* anti-Semite

**antiséptico, a** [anti'septiko, a] *adj* antiseptic ♦ *nm* antiseptic

**antítesis** [an'titesis] *nf inv* antithesis

**antojadizo, a** [antoxa'ðiθo, a] *adj* capricious

**antojarse** [anto'xarse] *vr* (*desear*): **se me antoja comprarlo** I have a mind to buy it; (*pensar*): **se me antoja que** I have a feeling that

**antojo** [an'toxo] *nm* caprice, whim; (*rosa*) birthmark; (*lunar*) mole

**antología** [antolo'xia] *nf* anthology

**antorcha** [an'tortʃa] *nf* torch

**antro** ['antro] *nm* cavern

**antropófago, a** [antro'pofaʋo, a] *adj, nm/f* cannibal

**antropología** [antropolo'xia] *nf* anthropology

**anual** [a'nwal] *adj* annual; ~**idad** *nf* annuity

**anuario** [a'nwarjo] *nm* yearbook

**anudar** [anu'ðar] *vt* to knot, tie; (*unir*) to join; ~**se** *vr* to get tied up

**anulación** [anula'θjon] *nf* annulment; (*cancelación*) cancellation

**anular** [anu'lar] *vt* (*contrato*) to annul, cancel; (*ley*) to revoke, repeal; (*suscripción*) to cancel ♦ *nm* ring finger

**anunciación** [anunθja'θjon] *nf* announcement; (*REL*): **A**~ Annunciation

**anunciante** [anun'θjante] *nm/f* (*COM*) advertiser

**anunciar** [anun'θjar] *vt* to announce; (*proclamar*) to proclaim; (*COM*) to advertise

**anuncio** [a'nunθjo] *nm* announcement; (*señal*) sign; (*COM*) advertisement; (*cartel*) poster

**anzuelo** [an'θwelo] *nm* hook; (*para pescar*) fish hook

**añadidura** [aɲaði'ðura] *nf* addition, extra; **por** ~ besides, in addition

**añadir** [aɲa'ðir] *vt* to add

**añejo, a** [a'ɲexo, a] *adj* old; (*vino*) mellow

**añicos** [a'ɲikos] *nmpl*: **hacer** ~ to smash, shatter

**añil** [a'ɲil] *nm* (*BOT, color*) indigo

**año** ['aɲo] *nm* year; ¡**Feliz A**~ **Nue-**

vo! Happy New Year!; **tener 15 ~s** to be 15 (years old); **los ~s 90** the nineties; **~ bisiesto/escolar** leap/school year; **el ~ que viene** next year

**añoranza** [aɲo'ranθa] *nf* nostalgia; (*anhelo*) longing

**apabullar** [apaβu'ʎar] *vt* (*tb fig*) to crush, squash

**apacentar** [apaθen'tar] *vt* to pasture, graze

**apacible** [apa'θiβle] *adj* gentle, mild

**apaciguar** [apaθi'ɣwar] *vt* to pacify, calm (down)

**apadrinar** [apaðri'nar] *vt* to sponsor, support; (*REL*) to be godfather to

**apagado, a** [apa'ɣaðo, a] *adj* (*volcán*) extinct; (*color*) dull; (*voz*) quiet; (*sonido*) muted, muffled; (*persona*: *apático*) listless; **estar ~** (*fuego, luz*) to be out; (*RADIO, TV etc*) to be off

**apagar** [apa'ɣar] *vt* to put out; (*ELEC, RADIO, TV*) to turn off; (*sonido*) to silence, muffle; (*sed*) to quench

**apagón** [apa'ɣon] *nm* blackout; power cut

**apalabrar** [apala'βrar] *vt* to agree to; (*contratar*) to engage

**apalear** [apale'ar] *vt* to beat, thrash; (*AGR*) to winnow

**apañar** [apa'ɲar] *vt* to pick up; (*asir*) to take hold of, grasp; (*reparar*) to mend, patch up; **~se** *vr* to manage, get along

**aparador** [apara'ðor] *nm* sideboard; (*escaparate*) shop window

**aparato** [apa'rato] *nm* apparatus; (*máquina*) machine; (*doméstico*) appliance; (*boato*) ostentation; **~ de facsímil** facsimile (machine), fax; **~ digestivo** (*ANAT*) digestive system; **~so, a** *adj* showy, ostentatious

**aparcamiento** [aparka'mjento] *nm* car park (*BRIT*), parking lot (*US*)

**aparcar** [apar'kar] *vt, vi* to park

**aparear** [apare'ar] *vt* (*objetos*) to pair, match; (*animales*) to mate; **~se** *vr* to make a pair; to mate

**aparecer** [apare'θer] *vi* to appear; **~se** *vr* to appear

**aparejado, a** [apare'xaðo, a] *adj* fit, suitable; **llevar** *o* **traer ~** to involve; **aparejador, a** *nm/f* (*ARQ*) master builder

**aparejo** [apa'rexo] *nm* preparation; harness; rigging; (*de poleas*) block and tackle

**aparentar** [aparen'tar] *vt* (*edad*) to look; (*fingir*): **~ tristeza** to pretend to be sad

**aparente** [apa'rente] *adj* apparent; (*adecuado*) suitable

**aparezco** *etc vb ver* **aparecer**

**aparición** [apari'θjon] *nf* appearance; (*de libro*) publication; (*espectro*) apparition

**apariencia** [apa'rjenθja] *nf* (*outward*) appearance; **en ~** outwardly, seemingly

**apartado, a** [apar'taðo, a] *adj* separate; (*lejano*) remote ♦ *nm* (*tipográfico*) paragraph; **~ (de correos)** post office box

**apartamento** [aparta'mento] *nm* apartment, flat (*BRIT*)

**apartamiento** [aparta'mjento] *nm* separation; (*aislamiento*) remoteness, isolation; (*AM*) apartment, flat (*BRIT*)

**apartar** [apar'tar] *vt* to separate; (*quitar*) to remove; (*MINEROLOGIA*) to extract; **~se** *vr* to separate, part; (*irse*) to move away; to keep away

**aparte** [a'parte] *adv* (*separadamente*) separately; (*además*) besides ♦ *nm* aside; (*tipográfico*) new paragraph

**apasionado, a** [apasjo'naðo, a] *adj* passionate; biassed, prejudiced

**apasionar** [apasjo'nar] *vt* to excite; **le apasiona el fútbol** she's crazy about football; **~se** *vr* to get excited

**apatía** [apa'tia] *nf* apathy

**apático, a** [a'patiko, a] *adj* apathetic

**apátrida** [a'patriða] *adj* stateless

**Apdo** *abr* (= *Apartado (de Correos)*) PO Box

**apeadero** [apea'ðero] *nm* halt, stop, stopping place

**apearse** [ape'arse] *vr* (*jinete*) to dismount; (*bajarse*) to get down *o* out; (*AUTO, FERRO*) to get off *o* out

**apechugar** [apetʃu'ɣar] *vr*: ~ con algo to face up to sth

**apedrear** [apeðre'ar] *vt* to stone

**apegarse** [ape'ɣarse] *vr*: ~ a to become attached to; **apego** *nm* attachment, devotion

**apelación** [apela'θjon] *nf* appeal

**apelar** [ape'lar] *vi* to appeal; ~ a (*fig*) to resort to

**apelmazarse** [apelma'θarse] *vr* (*masa, arroz*) to go hard; (*prenda de tana*) to shrink

**apellidar** [apeʎi'ðar] *vt* to call, name; ~se *vr*: **se apellida Pérez** her (sur)name's Pérez

**apellido** [ape'ʎiðo] *nm* surname

**apenar** [ape'nar] *vt* to grieve, trouble; (*AM: avergonzar*) to embarrass; ~se *vr* to grieve; (*AM*) to be embarrassed

**apenas** [a'penas] *adv* scarcely, hardly ♦ *conj* as soon as, no sooner

**apéndice** [a'pendiθe] *nm* appendix; **apendicitis** *nf* appendicitis

**aperitivo** [aperi'tiβo] *nm* (*bebida*) aperitif; (*comida*) appetizer

**apero** [a'pero] *nm* (*AGR*) implement; ~s *nmpl* farm equipment *sg*

**apertura** [aper'tura] *nf* opening; (*POL*) liberalization

**apesadumbrar** [apesaðum'brar] *vt* to grieve, sadden; ~se *vr* to distress o.s

**apestar** [apes'tar] *vt* to infect ♦ *vi*: ~ (a) to stink of

**apetecer** [apete'θer] *vt*: ¿te apetece un café? do you fancy a (cup of) coffee?; **apetecible** *adj* desirable; (*comida*) appetizing

**apetito** [ape'tito] *nm* appetite; ~so, a *adj* appetizing; (*fig*) tempting

**apiadarse** [apja'ðarse] *vr*: ~ de to take pity on

**ápice** ['apiθe] *nm* apex; (*fig*) whit, iota

**apilar** [api'lar] *vt* to pile *o* heap up; ~se *vr* to pile up

**apiñarse** [api'ɲarse] *vr* to crowd *o* press together

**apio** ['apjo] *nm* celery

**apisonadora** [apisona'ðora] *nf* (*máquina*) steamroller

**aplacar** [apla'kar] *vt* to placate; ~se *vr* to calm down

**aplanar** [apla'nar] *vt* to smooth, level; (*allanar*) to roll flat, flatten

**aplastante** [aplas'tante] *adj* overwhelming; (*lógica*) compelling

**aplastar** [aplas'tar] *vt* to squash (flat); (*fig*) to crush

**aplatanarse** [aplata'narse] *vr* to get lethargic

**aplaudir** [aplau'ðir] *vt* to applaud

**aplauso** [a'plauso] *nm* applause; (*fig*) approval, acclaim

**aplazamiento** [aplaθa'mjento] *nm* postponement

**aplazar** [apla'θar] *vt* to postpone, defer

**aplicación** [aplika'θjon] *nf* application; (*esfuerzo*) effort

**aplicado, a** [apli'kaðo, a] *adj* diligent, hard-working

**aplicar** [apli'kar] *vt* (*ejecutar*) to apply; ~se *vr* to apply o.s.

**aplique** *etc* [a'plike] *vb ver* **aplicar** ♦ *nm* wall light

**aplomo** [a'plomo] *nm* aplomb, self-assurance

**apocado, a** [apo'kaðo, a] *adj* timid

**apocarse** [apo'karse] *vr* to feel small *o* humiliated

**apodar** [apo'ðar] *vt* to nickname

**apoderado** [apoðe'raðo] *nm* agent, representative

**apoderar** [apoðe'rar] *vt* to authorize, empower; (*JUR*) to grant (s.o) power of attorney to; ~se *vr*: ~se de to take possession of

**apodo** [a'poðo] *nm* nickname

**apogeo** [apo'xeo] *nm* peak, summit

**apolillarse** [apoli'ʎarse] *vr* to get moth-eaten

**apología** [apolo'xia] *nf* eulogy; (*defensa*) defence

**apoltronarse** [apoltro'narse] *vr* to get lazy

**apoplejía** [apople'xia] *nf* apoplexy, stroke

**apoquinar** [apoki'nar] (*fam*) *vt* to fork out, cough up

**aporrear** [aporre'ar] *vt* to beat (up)

**aportar** [apor'tar] *vt* to contribute ♦ *vi* to reach port; ~se *vr* (*AM*: *llegar*) to arrive, come

**aposento** [apo'sento] *nm* lodging; (*habitación*) room

**aposta** [a'posta] *adv* deliberately, on purpose

**apostar** [apos'tar] *vt* to bet, stake; (*tropas etc*) to station, post ♦ *vi* to bet

**apóstol** [a'postol] *nm* apostle

**apóstrofo** [a'postrofo] *nm* apostrophe

**apoyar** [apo'jar] *vt* to lean, rest; (*fig*) to support, back; ~se *vr*: ~se en to lean on; **apoyo** *nm* (*gen*) support; backing, help

**apreciable** [apre'θjaβle] *adj* considerable; (*fig*) esteemed

**apreciar** [apre'θjar] *vt* to evaluate, assess; (*COM*) to appreciate, value; (*persona*) to respect; (*tamaño*) to gauge, assess; (*detalles*) to notice

**aprecio** [a'preθjo] *nm* valuation, estimate; (*fig*) appreciation

**aprehender** [apreen'der] *vt* to apprehend, detain; **aprehensión** *nf* detention, capture

**apremiante** [apre'mjante] *adj* urgent, pressing

**apremiar** [apre'mjar] *vt* to compel, force ♦ *vi* to be urgent, press; **apremio** *nm* urgency

**aprender** [apren'der] *vt*, *vi* to learn

**aprendiz, a** [apren'diθ, a] *nm/f* apprentice; (*principiante*) learner; ~ **de conductor** learner driver; ~**aje** *nm* apprenticeship

**aprensión** [apren'sjon] *nm* apprehension, fear; **aprensivo, a** *adj* apprehensive

**apresar** [apre'sar] *vt* to seize; (*capturar*) to capture

**aprestar** [apres'tar] *vt* to prepare, get ready; (*TEC*) to prime, size; ~se *vr* to get ready

**apresurado, a** [apresu'raðo, a] *adj* hurried, hasty; **apresuramiento** *nm* hurry, haste

**apresurar** [apresu'rar] *vt* to hurry, accelerate; ~se *vr* to hurry, make haste

**apretado, a** [apre'taðo, a] *adj* tight; (*escritura*) cramped

**apretar** [apre'tar] *vt* to squeeze; (*TEC*) to tighten; (*presionar*) to press together, pack ♦ *vi* to be too tight

**apretón** [apre'ton] *nm* squeeze; ~ **de manos** handshake

**aprieto** [a'prjeto] *nm* squeeze; (*dificultad*) difficulty; **estar en un** ~ to be in a fix

**aprisa** [a'prisa] *adv* quickly, hurriedly

**aprisionar** [aprisjo'nar] *vt* to imprison

**aprobación** [aproβa'θjon] *nf* approval

**aprobar** [apro'βar] *vt* to approve (of); (*examen, materia*) to pass ♦ *vi* to pass

**apropiación** [apropja'θjon] *nf* appropriation

**apropiado, a** [apro'pjaðo, a] *adj* appropriate

**apropiarse** [apro'pjarse] *vr*: ~ **de** to appropriate

**aprovechado, a** [aproβe'tʃaðo, a] *adj* industrious, hard-working; (*económico*) thrifty; (*pey*) unscrupulous; **aprovechamiento** *nm* use; exploitation

**aprovechar** [aproβe'tʃar] *vt* to use; (*explotar*) to exploit; (*experiencia*) to profit from; (*oferta, oportunidad*) to take advantage of ♦ *vi* to progress, improve; ~se *vr*: ~**se de** to make use of; to take advantage of; **¡que aproveche!** enjoy your meal!

**aproximación** [aproksima'θjon] *nf* approximation; (*de lotería*) consolation prize; **aproximado, a** *adj* approximate

**aproximar** [aproksi'mar] *vt* to bring nearer; **~se** *vr* to come near, approach

**apruebo** *etc vb ver* aprobar

**aptitud** [apti'tuð] *nf* aptitude

**apto, a** ['apto, a] *adj* suitable

**apuesta** [a'pwesta] *nf* bet, wager

**apuesto, a** [a'pwesto, a] *adj* neat, elegant

**apuntador** [apunta'ðor] *nm* prompter

**apuntalar** [apunta'lar] *vt* to prop up

**apuntar** [apun'tar] *vt* (con arma) to aim at; (con dedo) to point at o to; (anotar) to note (down); (TEATRO) to prompt; **~se** *vr* (DEPORTE: tanto, victoria) to score; (ESCOL) to enrol

**apunte** [a'punte] *nm* note

**apuñalar** [apuɲa'lar] *vt* to stab

**apurado, a** [apu'raðo, a] *adj* needy; (difícil) difficult; (peligroso) dangerous; (AM) hurried, rushed

**apurar** [apu'rar] *vt* (agotar) to drain; (recursos) to use up; (molestar) to annoy; **~se** *vr* (preocuparse) to worry; (darse prisa) to hurry

**apuro** [a'puro] *nm* (aprieto) fix, jam; (escasez) want, hardship; (vergüenza) embarrassment; (AM) haste, urgency

**aquejado, a** [ake'xaðo, a] *adj:* **~ de** (MED) afflicted by

**aquel, aquella** [a'kel, a'keʎa] (pl aquellos, as) *adj* that; (pl) those

**aquél, aquélla** [a'kel, a'keʎa] (pl aquéllos, as) *pron* that (one); (pl) those (ones)

**aquello** [a'keʎo] *pron* that, that business

**aquí** [a'ki] *adv* (lugar) here; (tiempo) now; **~ arriba** up here; **~ mismo** right here; **~ yace** here lies; **de ~ a siete días** a week from now

**aquietar** [akje'tar] *vt* to quieten (down), calm (down)

**ara** ['ara] *nf:* **en ~s de** for the sake of

**árabe** ['araβe] *adj, nm/f* Arab ♦ *nm* (LING) Arabic

**Arabia** [a'raβja] *nf:* **~ Saudí** o Saudita Saudi Arabia

**arado** [a'raðo] *nm* plough

**Aragón** [ara'xon] *nm* Aragon; **aragonés, esa** *adj, nm/f* Aragonese

**arancel** [aran'θel] *nm* tariff, duty; **~ de aduanas** customs (duty)

**arandela** [aran'dela] *nf* (TEC) washer

**araña** [a'raɲa] *nf* (ZOOL) spider; (lámpara) chandelier

**arañar** [ara'ɲar] *vt* to scratch

**arañazo** [ara'ɲaθo] *nm* scratch

**arar** [a'rar] *vt* to plough, till

**arbitraje** [arβi'traxe] *nm* arbitration

**arbitrar** [arβi'trar] *vt* to arbitrate in; (DEPORTE) to referee ♦ *vi* to arbitrate

**arbitrariedad** [arβitrarje'ðað] *nf* arbitrariness; (acto) arbitrary act; **arbitrario, a** *adj* arbitrary

**arbitrio** [ar'βitrjo] *nm* free will; (JUR) adjudication, decision

**árbitro** ['arβitro] *nm* arbitrator; (DEPORTE) referee; (TENIS) umpire

**árbol** [ar'βol] *nm* (BOT) tree; (NAUT) mast; (TEC) axle, shaft; **arbolado, a** *adj* wooded; (camino etc) tree-lined ♦ *nm* woodland

**~rboleda** [arβo'leða] *nf* grove, plantation

**arbusto** [ar'βusto] *nm* bush, shrub

**arca** ['arka] *nf* chest, box

**arcada** [ar'kaða] *nf* arcade; (de puente) arch, span; **~s** *nfpl* (náuseas) retching *sg*

**arcaico, a** [ar'kaiko, a] *adj* archaic

**arce** [ar'θe] *nm* maple tree

**arcén** [ar'θen] *nm* (de autopista) hard shoulder; (de carretera) verge

**arcilla** [ar'θiʎa] *nf* clay

**arco** [ar'ko] *nm* arch; (MAT) arc; (MIL, MUS) bow; **~ iris** rainbow

**archipiélago** [artʃi'pjelaxo] *nm* archipelago

**archivador** [artʃiβa'ðor] *nm* filing cabinet

**archivar** [artʃi'βar] *vt* to file (away); **archivo** *nm* file, archive(s) (pl)

**arder** [ar'ðer] *vi* to burn; **estar que**

**arde** (*persona*) to fume

**ardid** [ar'ðið] *nm* ploy, trick

**ardiente** [ar'ðjente] *adj* burning, ardent

**ardilla** [ar'ðiʎa] *nf* squirrel

**ardor** [ar'ðor] *nm* (*calor*) heat; (*fig*) ardour; ~ **de estómago** heartburn

**arduo, a** [ar'ðwo, a] *adj* arduous

**área** ['area] *nf* area; (*DEPORTE*) penalty area

**arena** [a'rena] *nf* sand; (*de una lucha*) arena; ~ **movedizas** quicksand *sg*

**arenal** [are'nal] *nm* (*arena movediza*) quicksand

**arengar** [aren'gar] *vt* to harangue

**arenisca** [are'niska] *nf* sandstone; (*cascajo*) grit

**arenoso, a** [are'noso, a] *adj* sandy

**arenque** [a'renke] *nm* herring

**arete** [a'rete] *nm* earring

**argamasa** [arɣa'masa] *nf* mortar, plaster

**Argel** [ar'xel] *n* Algiers; ~**ia** *nf* Algeria; **argelino, a** *adj, nm/f* Algerian

**Argentina** [arxen'tina] *nf*: (**la**) A~ Argentina

**argentino, a** [arxen'tino, a] *adj* Argentinian; (*de plata*) silvery ♦ *nm/f* Argentinian

**argolla** [ar'ɣoʎa] *nf* (large) ring

**argot** [ar'ɣo] (*pl* ~**s**) *nm* slang

**argucia** [ar'ɣuθja] *nf* subtlety, sophistry

**argüir** [ar'ɣwir] *vt* to deduce; (*discutir*) to argue; (*indicar*) to indicate, imply; (*censurar*) to reproach ♦ *vi* to argue

**argumentación** [arɣumenta'θjon] *nf* (line) of argument

**argumentar** [arɣumen'tar] *vt, vi* to argue

**argumento** [arɣu'mento] *nm* argument; (*razonamiento*) reasoning; (*de novela etc*) plot; (*CINE, TV*) storyline

**aria** ['arja] *nf* aria

**aridez** [ari'ðeθ] *nf* aridity, dryness

**árido, a** ['ariðo, a] *adj* arid, dry; ~**s** *nmpl* (*COM*) dry goods

**Aries** ['arjes] *nm* Aries

**ario, a** ['arjo, a] *adj* Aryan

**arisco, a** [a'risko, a] *adj* surly; (*insociable*) unsociable

**aristócrata** [aris'tokrata] *nm/f* aristocrat

**aritmética** [arit'metika] *nf* arithmetic

**arma** ['arma] *nf* arm; ~**s** *nfpl* arms; ~ **blanca** blade, knife; (*espada*) sword; ~ **de fuego** firearm; ~**s cortas** small arms

**armada** [ar'maða] *nf* armada; (*flota*) fleet

**armadillo** [arma'ðiʎo] *nm* armadillo

**armado, a** [ar'maðo, a] *adj* armed; (*TEC*) reinforced

**armador** [arma'ðor] *nm* (*NAUT*) shipowner

**armadura** [arma'ðura] *nf* (*MIL*) armour; (*TEC*) framework; (*ZOOL*) skeleton; (*FISICA*) armature

**armamento** [arma'mento] *nm* armament; (*NAUT*) fitting-out

**armar** [ar'mar] *vt* (*soldado*) to arm; (*máquina*) to assemble; (*navio*) to fit out; ~**la**, ~ **un** lío to start a row, kick up a fuss

**armario** [ar'marjo] *nm* wardrobe; (*de cocina, baño*) cupboard

**armatoste** [arma'toste] *nm* (*mueble*) monstrosity; (*máquina*) contraption

**armazón** [arma'θon] *nf o m* body, chassis; (*de mueble etc*) frame; (*ARQ*) skeleton

**armería** [arme'ria] *nf* (*museo*) military museum; (*tienda*) gunsmith's

**armiño** [ar'miɲo] *nm* stoat; (*piel*) ermine

**armisticio** [armis'tiθjo] *nm* armistice

**armonía** [armo'nia] *nf* harmony

**armónica** [ar'monika] *nf* harmonica

**armonioso, a** [armo'njoso, a] *adj* harmonious

**armonizar** [armoni'θar] *vt* to harmonize; (*diferencias*) to reconcile ♦ *vi*: ~ **con** (*fig*) to be in keeping with; (*colores*) to tone in with, blend

**arnés** [ar'nes] *nm* armour; **arneses** *nmpl* (*de caballo etc*) harness *sg*

**aro** ['aro] nm ring; (tejo) quoit; (AM: pendiente) earring

**aroma** [a'roma] nm aroma, scent

**aromático, a** [aro'matiko, a] adj aromatic

**arpa** ['arpa] nf harp

**arpía** [ar'pia] nf shrew

**arpillera** [arpi'ʎera] nf sacking, sackcloth

**arpón** [ar'pon] nm harpoon

**arquear** [arke'ar] vt to arch, bend; ~se vr to arch, bend

**arqueología** [arkeolo'xia] nf archaeology; **arqueólogo, a** nm/f archaeologist

**arquero** [ar'kero] nm archer, bowman

**arquetipo** [arke'tipo] nm archetype

**arquitecto** [arki'tekto] nm architect; **arquitectura** nf architecture

**arrabal** [arra'βal] nm suburb; (AM) slum; ~es nmpl (afueras) outskirts

**arraigado, a** [arrai'ɣaðo, a] adj deep-rooted; (fig) established

**arraigar** [arrai'ɣar] vt to establish ♦ vi to take root; ~se vr to take root; (persona) to settle

**arrancar** [arran'kar] vt (sacar) to extract, pull out; (arrebatar) to snatch (away); (INFORM) to boot; (fig) to extract ♦ vi (AUTO, máquina) to start; (ponerse en marcha) to get going; ~ de to stem from

**arranque** etc [a'rranke] vb ver **arrancar** ♦ nm sudden start; (AUTO) start; (fig) fit, outburst

**arrasar** [arra'sar] vt (aplanar) to level, flatten; (destruir) to demolish

**arrastrado, a** [arras'traðo, a] adj poor, wretched; (AM) servile

**arrastrar** [arras'trar] vt to drag (along); (fig) to drag down, degrade; (suj: agua, viento) to carry away ♦ vi to drag, trail on the ground; ~se vr to crawl; (fig) to grovel; llevar algo arrastrado to drag sth along

**arrastre** [a'rrastre] nm drag, dragging

**arre** ['arre] excl gee up!

**arrear** [arre'ar] vt to drive on, urge on ♦ vi to hurry along

**arrebatado, a** [arreβa'taðo, a] adj rash, impetuous; (repentino) sudden, hasty

**arrebatar** [arreβa'tar] vt to snatch (away), seize; (fig) to captivate; ~se vr to get carried away, get excited

**arrebato** [arre'βato] nm fit of rage, fury; (éxtasis) rapture

**arrecife** [arre'θife] nm (tb: ~ de coral) reef

**arredrarse** [arre'ðrarse] vr: ~ (ante algo) to be intimidated (by sth)

**arreglado, a** [arre'ɣlaðo, a] adj (ordenado) neat, orderly; (moderado) moderate, reasonable

**arreglar** [arre'ɣlar] vt (poner orden) to tidy up; (algo roto) to fix, repair; (problema) to solve; ~se vr to reach an understanding; **arreglárselas** (fam) to get by, manage

**arreglo** [a'rreɣlo] nm settlement; (orden) order; (acuerdo) agreement; (MUS) arrangement, setting

**arrellanarse** [arreʎa'narse] vr: ~ en to sit back in/on

**arremangar** [arreman'gar] vt to roll up, turn up; ~se vr to roll up one's sleeves

**arremeter** [arreme'ter] vi: ~ contra to attack, rush at

**arrendamiento** [arrenda'mjento] nm letting; (alquiler) hiring; (contrato) lease; (alquiler) rent; **arrendar** vt to let, lease; to rent; **arrendatario, a** nm/f tenant

**arreo** [a'rreo] nm adornment; ~s nmpl (de caballo) harness sg, trappings

**arrepentimiento** [arrepenti'mjento] nm regret, repentance

**arrepentirse** [arrepen'tirse] vr to repent; ~ de to regret

**arrestar** [arres'tar] vt to arrest; (encarcelar) to imprison; **arresto** nm arrest; (MIL) detention; (audacia) boldness, daring; **arresto domiciliario** house arrest

**arriar** |a'rrjar| vt (velas) to haul down; (bandera) to lower, strike; (cable) to pay out

---
PALABRA CLAVE
---

**arriba** |a'rriβa| adv **1** (posición) above; desde ~ from above; ~ de todo at the very top, right on top; Juan está ~ Juan is upstairs; lo ~ mencionado the aforementioned
**2** (dirección): calle ~ up the street
**3**: de ~ abajo from top to bottom; mirar a uno de ~ abajo to look sb up and down
**4**: para ~: de 5000 pesetas para ~ from 5000 pesetas up(wards)
♦ adj: de ~: el piso de ~ the upstairs flat (BRIT) o apartment; la parte de ~ the top o upper part
♦ prep: ~ de (AM) above; ~ de 200 dólares more than 200 dollars
♦ excl: ¡~! up!; ¡manos ~! hands up!; ¡~ España! long live Spain!

**arribar** |arri'βar| vi to put into port; (llegar) to arrive

**arribista** |arri'βista| nm/f parvenu(e), upstart

**arriendo** etc |a'rrjendo| vb ver **arrendar** ♦ nm = **arrendamiento**

**arriero** |a'rrjero| nm muleteer

**arriesgado, a** |arrjes'xaðo, a| adj (peligroso) risky; (audaz) bold, daring

**arriesgar** |arrjes'xar| vt to risk; (poner en peligro) to endanger; ~se vr to take a risk

**arrimar** |arri'mar| vt (acercar) to bring close; (poner de lado) to set aside; ~se vr to come close o closer; ~se a to lean on

**arrinconar** |arrinko'nar| vt (colocar) to put in a corner; (enemigo) to corner; (fig) to put on one side; (abandonar) to push aside

**arrodillarse** |arroði'Karse| vr to kneel (down)

**arrogancia** |arro'xanθja| nf arrogance; **arrogante** adj arrogant

**arrojar** |arro'xar| vt to throw, hurl;

(humo) to emit, give out; (COM) to yield, produce; ~se vr to throw o hurl o.s

**arroyo** |a'rroxo| nm stream; (de la calle) gutter

**arroz** |a'rroθ| nm rice; ~ con leche rice pudding

**arruga** |a'rruɣa| nf fold; (de cara) wrinkle; (de vestido) crease

**arrugar** |arru'xar| vt to fold; to wrinkle; to crease; ~se vr to get creased

**arruinar** |arrwi'nar| vt to ruin, wreck; ~se vr to be ruined, go bankrupt

**arrullar** |arru'Kar| vi to coo ♦ vt to lull to sleep

**arsenal** |arse'nal| nm naval dockyard; (MIL) arsenal

**arsénico** |ar'seniko| nm arsenic

**arte** |'arte| (gen m en sg y siempre f en pl) nm art; (maña) skill, guile; ~s nfpl (bellas ~s) arts

**artefacto** |arte'fakto| nm appliance; (ARQUEOLOGIA) artefact

**arteria** |ar'terja| nf artery

**artesanía** |artesa'nia| nf craftsmanship; (artículos) handicrafts pl; **artesano, a** nm/f artisan, craftsman/woman

**ártico, a** |'artiko, a| adj Arctic ♦ nm: el A~ the Arctic

**articulación** |artikula'θjon| nf articulation; (MED, TEC) joint; **articulado, a** adj articulated; jointed

**articular** |artiku'lar| vt to articulate; to join together

**artículo** |ar'tikulo| nm article; (cosa) thing, article; ~s nmpl (COM) goods

**artífice** |ar'tifiθe| nm/f artist,

**arrollador, a** |arroʎa'ðor. a| adj overwhelming

**arrollar** |arro'ʎar| vt (AUTO etc) to run over, knock down; (DEPORTE) to crush

**arropar** |arro'par| vt to cover, wrap up; ~se vr to wrap o.s. up

**arrostrar** |arros'trar| vt to face (up to); ~se vr: ~se con uno to face up to sb

craftsman/woman; (fig) architect

**artificial** [artiˈfiθjal] adj artificial

**artificio** [artiˈfiθjo] nm art, skill; (artesanía) craftsmanship; (astucia) cunning

**artilugio** [artiˈluxjo] nm gadget

**artillería** [artiʎeˈria] nf artillery

**artillero** [artiˈʎero] nm artilleryman, gunner

**artimaña** [artiˈmaɲa] nf trap, snare; (astucia) cunning

**artista** [arˈtista] nm/f (pintor) artist, painter; (TEATRO) artist, artiste; ~ de cine film actor/actress; **artístico, a** adj artistic

**artritis** [arˈtritis] nf arthritis

**arveja** [arˈβexa] (AM) nf pea

**arzobispo** [arθoˈβispo] nm archbishop

**as** [as] nm ace

**asa** [ˈasa] nf handle; (fig) lever

**asado** [aˈsaðo] nm roast (meat); (AM: barbacoa) barbecue

**asador** [asaˈðor] nm spit

**asadura** [asaˈðura] nf entrails pl, offal

**asalariado, a** [asalaˈrjaðo, a] adj paid, salaried ♦ nm/f wage earner

**asaltador, a** [asaltaˈðor, a] nm/f assailant

**asaltante** [asalˈtante] nm/f = asaltador, a

**asaltar** [asalˈtar] vt to attack, assault; (fig) to assail; **asalto** nm attack, assault; (DEPORTE) round

**asamblea** [asamˈblea] nf assembly; (reunión) meeting

**asar** [aˈsar] vt to roast

**asbesto** [asˈβesto] nm asbestos

**ascendencia** [asθenˈdenθja] nf ancestry; (AM) ascendancy; de ~ francesa of French origin

**ascender** [asθenˈder] vi (subir) to ascend, rise; (ser promovido) to gain promotion ♦ vt to promote; ~ a to amount to; **ascendiente** nm influence ♦ nm/f ancestor

**ascensión** [asθenˈsjon] nf ascent; (REL); la A~ the Ascension

**ascenso** [asˈθenso] nm ascent; (promoción) promotion

**ascensor** [asθenˈsor] nm lift (BRIT), elevator (US)

**ascético, a** [asˈθetiko, a] adj ascetic

**asco** [ˈasko] nm: ¡qué ~! how revolting o disgusting!; el ajo me da ~ I hate o loathe garlic; **estar hecho un ~** to be filthy

**ascua** [ˈaskwa] nf ember; **estar en ~s** to be on tenterhooks

**aseado, a** [aseˈaðo, a] adj clean; (arreglado) tidy; (pulcro) smart

**asear** [aseˈar] vt to clean, wash; to tidy (up)

**asediar** [aseˈðjar] vt (MIL) to besiege, lay siege to; (fig) to chase, pester; **asedio** nm siege; (COM) run

**asegurado, a** [aseɣuˈraðo, a] adj insured; **asegurador, a** nm/f insurer

**asegurar** [aseɣuˈrar] vt (consolidar) to secure, fasten; (dar garantía de) to guarantee; (preservar) to safeguard; (afirmar, dar por cierto) to assure, affirm; (tranquilizar) to reassure; (tomar un seguro) to insure; ~se vt to assure o.s., make sure

**asemejarse** [aseme'xarse] vt to be alike; ~ a to be like, resemble

**asentado, a** [asenˈtaðo, a] adj established, settled

**asentar** [asenˈtar] vt (sentar) to seat, sit down; (poner) to place, establish; (alisar) to level, smooth down o out; (anotar) to note down ♦ vi to be suitable, suit

**asentir** [asenˈtir] vi to assent, agree; ~ con la cabeza to nod (one's head)

**aseo** [aˈseo] nm cleanliness; ~s nmpl (servicios) toilet sg (BRIT), cloakroom sg (BRIT), restroom sg (US)

**aséptico, a** [aˈseptiko, a] adj germ-free, free from infection

**asequible** [aseˈkiβle] adj (precio) reasonable; (meta) attainable; (persona) approachable

**aserradero** [aseraˈðero] nm sawmill; **aserrar** vt to saw

**asesinar** [asesiˈnar] vt to murder; (POL) to assassinate; **asesinato** nm murder; assassination

**asesino, a** [ase'sino, a] *nm/f* murderer, killer; (*POL*) assassin

**asesor, a** [ase'sor, a] *nm/f* adviser, consultant

**asesorar** [aseso'rar] *vt* (*JUR*) to advise, give legal advice to; (*COM*) to act as consultant to; ~se *vr*: ~se con *o* de to take advice from, consult; **asesoría** *nf* (*cargo*) consultancy; (*oficina*) consultant's office

**asestar** [ases'tar] *vt* (*golpe*) to deal, strike; (*arma*) to aim; (*tiro*) to fire

**asfalto** [as'falto] *nm* asphalt

**asfixia** [as'fiksja] *nf* asphyxia, suffocation

**asfixiar** [asfik'sjar] *vt* to asphyxiate, suffocate; ~se *vr* to be asphyxiated, suffocate

**asgo** *etc vb ver* **asir**

**así** [a'si] *adv* (*de esta manera*) in this way, like this, thus; (*aunque*) although; (*tan pronto como*) as soon as; ~ que so; ~ como as well as; ~ y todo even so; ¿no es ~? isn't it?, didn't you? *etc*; ~ de grande this big

**Asia** ['asja] *nf* Asia; **asiático, a** *adj, nm/f* Asian, Asiatic

**asidero** [asi'ðero] *nm* handle

**asiduidad** [asiðwi'ðað] *nf* assiduousness; **asiduo, a** *adj* assiduous; (*frecuente*) frequent ♦ *nm/f* regular (customer)

**asiento** [a'sjento] *nm* (*mueble*) seat, chair; (*de coche, en tribunal etc*) seat; (*localidad*) seat, place; (*fundamento*) site; ~ delantero/trasero front/back seat

**asignación** [asiɣna'θjon] *nf* (*atribución*) assignment; (*reparto*) allocation; (*sueldo*) salary; ~ (*semanal*) pocket money

**asignar** [asiɣ'nar] *vt* to assign, allocate

**asignatura** [asiɣna'tura] *nf* subject; course

**asilado, a** [asi'laðo, a] *nm/f* inmate; (*POL*) refugee

**asilo** [a'silo] *nm* (*refugio*) asylum, refuge; (*establecimiento*) home, insti-

tution; ~ político political asylum

**asimilación** [asimila'θjon] *nf* assimilation

**asimilar** [asimi'lar] *vt* to assimilate

**asimismo** [asi'mismo] *adv* in the same way, likewise

**asir** [a'sir] *vt* to seize, grasp

**asistencia** [asis'tenθja] *nf* audience; (*MED*) attendance; (*ayuda*) assistance; **asistente** *nm/f* assistant; los asistentes those present; ~ social social worker

**asistido, a** [asis'tiðo, a] *adj*: ~ por ordenador computer-assisted

**asistir** [asis'tir] *vt* to assist, help ♦ *vi*: ~ a to attend, be present at

**asma** ['asma] *nf* asthma

**asno** ['asno] *nm* donkey; (*fig*) ass

**asociación** [asoθja'θjon] *nf* association; (*COM*) partnership; **asociado, a** *adj* associate ♦ *nm/f* associate; (*COM*) partner

**asociar** [aso'θjar] *vt* to associate

**asolar** [aso'lar] *vt* to destroy

**asolearse** [asole'arse] *vr* to sunbathe

**asomar** [aso'mar] *vt* to show, stick out ♦ *vi* to appear; ~se *vr* to appear, show up; ~ la cabeza por la ventana to put one's head out of the window

**asombrar** [asom'brar] *vt* to amaze, astonish; ~se *vr* (*sorprenderse*) to be amazed; (*asustarse*) to get a fright; **asombro** *nm* amazement, astonishment; (*susto*) fright; **asombroso, a** *adj* astonishing, amazing

**asomo** [a'somo] *nm* hint, sign

**aspa** ['aspa] *nf* (*cruz*) cross; (*de molino*) sail; en ~ X-shaped

**aspaviento** [aspa'βjento] *nm* exaggerated display of feeling; (*fam*) fuss

**aspecto** [as'pekto] *nm* (*apariencia*) look, appearance; (*fig*) aspect

**aspereza** [aspe'reθa] *nf* roughness; (*agrura*) sourness; (*de carácter*) surliness; **áspero, a** *adj* rough; bitter, sour; harsh

**aspersión** [asper'sjon] *nf* sprinkling

**aspiración** [aspira'θjon] *nf* breath, inhalation; (*MUS*) short pause; aspi-

**raciones** nfpl (ambiciones) aspirations

**aspirador** [aspira'ðor] nm = **aspiradora**

**aspiradora** [aspira'ðora] nf vacuum cleaner, Hoover ®

**aspirante** [aspi'rante] nm/f (candidato) candidate; (DEPORTE) contender

**aspirar** [aspi'rar] vt to breathe in ♦ vi: ~ a to aspire to

**aspirina** [aspi'rina] nf aspirin

**asquear** [aske'ar] vt to sicken ♦ vi to be sickening; ~se vr to feel disgusted; **asqueroso, a** adj disgusting, sickening

**asta** ['asta] nf lance; (arpón) spear; (mango) shaft, handle; (ZOOL) horn; a media ~ at half mast

**astado, a** [as'taðo, a] adj horned ♦ nm bull

**asterisco** [aste'risko] nm asterisk

**astilla** [as'tiʎa] nf splinter; (pedacito) chip; ~s nfpl (leña) firewood sg

**astillero** [asti'ʎero] nm shipyard

**astringente** [astrin'xente] adj, nm astringent

**astro** ['astro] nm star

**astrología** [astrolo'xia] nf astrology; **astrólogo, a** nm/f astrologer

**astronauta** [astro'nauta] nm/f astronaut

**astronave** [astro'naβe] nm spaceship

**astronomía** [astrono'mia] nf astronomy; **astrónomo, a** nm/f astronomer

**astucia** [as'tuθja] nf astuteness; (ardid) clever trick; **astuto, a** adj astute; (taimado) cunning

**asueto** [a'sweto] nm holiday; (tiempo libre) time off no pl

**asumir** [asu'mir] vt to assume

**asunción** [asun'θjon] nf assumption; (REL) A~ Assumption

**asunto** [a'sunto] nm (tema) matter, subject; (negocio) business

**asustar** [asus'tar] vt to frighten; ~se vr to be o (become) frightened

**atacar** [ata'kar] vt to attack

**atadura** [ata'ðura] nf bond, tie

**atajar** [ata'xar] vt (enfermedad, mal) to stop ♦ vi (persona) to take a short cut

**atajo** [a'taxo] nm short cut; (DEPORTE) tackle

**atañer** [ata'ɲer] vi: ~ a to concern

**ataque** etc [a'take] vb ver **atacar** ♦ nm attack; ~ **cardíaco** heart attack

**atar** [a'tar] vt to tie, tie up

**atardecer** [atarðe'θer] vi to get dark ♦ nm evening; (crepusculo) dusk

**atareado, a** [atare'aðo, a] adj busy

**atascar** [atas'kar] vt to clog up; (obstruir) to jam; (fig) to hinder; ~se vr to stall; (cañeria) to get blocked up; **atasco** nm obstruction; (AUTO) traffic jam

**ataúd** [ata'uð] nm coffin

**ataviar** [ata'βjar] vt to deck, array; ~se vr to dress up

**atavío** [ata'βio] nm attire, dress; ~s nmpl finery sg

**atemorizar** [atemori'θar] vt to frighten, scare; ~se vr to get scared

**Atenas** [a'tenas] n Athens

**atención** [aten'θjon] nf attention; (bondad) kindness ♦ excl (be) careful!, look out!

**atender** [aten'der] vt to attend to, look after ♦ vi to pay attention

**atenerse** [ate'nerse] vr: ~ a to abide by, adhere to

**atentado** [aten'taðo] nm crime, illegal act; (asalto) assault; ~ **contra la vida de uno** attempt on sb's life

**atentamente** [atenta'mente] adv: **Le saluda** ~ Yours faithfully

**atentar** [aten'tar] vi: ~ a o **contra** to commit an outrage against

**atento, a** [a'tento, a] adj attentive, observant; (cortés) polite, thoughtful

**atenuante** [ate'nwante] adj extenuating

**atenuar** [ate'nwar] vt (disminuir) to lessen, minimize

**ateo, a** [a'teo, a] adj atheistic ♦ nm/f atheist

**aterciopelado, a** [aterθjope'laðo, a] adj velvety

**aterido, a** [ate'riðo, a] adj: ~ **de**

frío frozen stiff

**aterrador, a** [aterra'ðor, a] *adj* frightening

**aterrar** [ate'rrar] *vt* to frighten; to terrify; ~se *vr* to be frightened; to be terrified

**aterrizaje** [aterri'θaxe] *nm* (AVIAT) landing

**aterrizar** [aterri'θar] *vi* to land

**aterrorizar** [aterrori'θar] *vt* to terrify

**atesorar** [ateso'rar] *vt* to hoard, store up

**atestado, a** [ates'taðo, a] *adj* packed ♦ *nm* (JUR) affidavit

**atestar** [ates'tar] *vt* to pack, stuff; (JUR) to attest, testify to

**atestiguar** [atesti'vwar] *vt* to testify to, bear witness to

**atiborrar** [atiβo'rrar] *vt* to fill, stuff; ~se *vr* to stuff o.s

**ático** ['atiko] *nm* attic; ~ de lujo penthouse (flat (BRIT) o apartment)

**atildar** [atil'dar] *vt* to criticize; ~se *vr* to spruce o.s. up

**atinado, a** [ati'naðo, a] *adj* (sensato) wise; (correcto) right, correct

**atinar** [ati'nar] *vi* (al disparar): ~ al blanco to hit the target; (fig) to be right

**atisbar** [atis'βar] *vt* to spy on; (echar una ojeada) to peep at

**atizar** [ati'θar] *vt* to poke; (horno etc) to stoke; (fig) to stir up, rouse

**atlántico, a** [at'lantiko, a] *adj* Atlantic ♦ *nm*: el (océano) A~ the Atlantic (Ocean)

**atlas** ['atlas] *nm* atlas

**atleta** [at'leta] *nm* athlete; **atlético, a** *adj* athletic; **atletismo** *nm* athletics *sg*

**atmósfera** [at'mosfera] *nf* atmosphere

**atolondramiento** [atolondra'mjento] *nm* bewilderment; (insensatez) silliness

**atolladero** [atoʎa'ðero] *nm* (fig) jam, fix

**atómico, a** [a'tomiko, a] *adj* atomic

**atomizador** [atomiθa'ðor] *nm* atomizer; (de perfume) spray

**átomo** ['atomo] *nm* atom

**atónito, a** [a'tonito, a] *adj* astonished, amazed

**atontado, a** [aton'taðo, a] *adj* stunned; (bobo) silly, daft

**atontar** [aton'tar] *vt* to stun; ~se *vr* to become confused

**atormentar** [atormen'tar] *vt* to torture; (molestar) to torment; (acosar) to plague, harass

**atornillar** [atorni'ʎar] *vt* to screw on o down

**atosigar** [atosi'ðar] *vt* (fig) to harass, pester

**atracador, a** [atraka'ðor, a] *nm/f* robber

**atracar** [atra'kar] *vt* (NAUT) to moor; (robar) to hold up, rob ♦ *vi* to moor; ~se *vr*: ~se (de) to stuff o.s. (with)

**atracción** [atrak'θjon] *nf* attraction

**atraco** [a'trako] *nm* holdup, robbery

**atracón** [atra'kon] *nm*: darse o pegarse un ~ (de) (fam) to stuff o.s. (with)

**atractivo, a** [atrak'tiβo, a] *adj* attractive ♦ *nm* appeal

**atraer** [atra'er] *vt* to attract

**atragantarse** [atravan'tarse] *vr*: ~ (con) to choke (on); se me ha atragantado el chico I can't stand the boy

**atrancar** [atran'kar] *vt* (puerta) to bar, bolt

**atrapar** [atra'par] *vt* to trap; (resfriado etc) to catch

**atrás** [a'tras] *adv* (movimiento) back(wards); (lugar) behind; (tiempo) previously; **ir hacia** ~ to go back(wards); **ir a** ~ to go to the rear; **estar** ~ to be behind o at the back

**atrasado, a** [atra'saðo, a] *adj* (pago) overdue, late; (país) backward

**atrasar** [atra'sar] *vi* to be slow; ~se *vr* to remain behind; (tren) to be o run late; **atraso** *nm* slowness; lateness, delay; (de país) backwardness; **atrasos** *nmpl* (COM) arrears

**atravesar** [atraβe'sar] *vt* (cruzar) to

cross (over); (*traspasar*) to pierce; to go through; (*poner al través*) to lay o put across; ~se *vr* to come in between; (*intervenir*) to interfere

**atravieso** *etc vb ver* **atravesar**

**atrayente** [atra'jente] *adj* attractive

**atreverse** [atre'βerse] *vr* to dare; (*insolentarse*) to be insolent; **atrevido, a** *adj* daring; insolent; **atrevimiento** *nm* daring; insolence

**atribución** [atriβu'θjon] *nf*: **atribuciones** (POL) powers; (ADMIN) responsibilities

**atribuir** [atriβu'ir] *vt* to attribute; (*funciones*) to confer

**atribular** [atriβu'lar] *vt* to afflict, distress

**atributo** [atri'βuto] *nm* attribute

**atril** [a'tril] *nm* (*para libro*) lectern; (MUS) music stand

**atrocidad** [atroθi'ðað] *nf* atrocity, outrage

**atropellar** [atrope'ʎar] *vt* (*derribar*) to knock over o down; (*empujar*) to push (aside); (AUTO) to run over, run down; (*agraviar*) to insult; ~se *vr* to act hastily; **atropello** *nm* (AUTO) accident; (*empujón*) push; (*agravio*) wrong; (*atrocidad*) outrage

**atroz** [a'troθ] *adj* atrocious, awful

**atto, a** *abr* = **atento**

**atuendo** [a'twendo] *nm* attire

**atún** [a'tun] *nm* tuna

**aturdir** [atur'ðir] *vt* to stun; (*de ruido*) to deafen; (*fig*) to dumbfound, bewilder

**atusar** [atu'sar] *vt* to smooth (down)

**audacia** [au'ðaθja] *nf* boldness, audacity; **audaz** *adj* bold, audacious

**audible** [au'ðiβle] *adj* audible

**audición** [auði'θjon] *nf* hearing; (TEATRO) audition

**audiencia** [au'ðjenθja] *nf* audience; A~ (JUR) High Court

**audífono** [au'ðifono] *nm* (*para sordos*) hearing aid

**auditor** [auði'tor] *nm* (JUR) judge advocate; (COM) auditor

**auditorio** [auði'torjo] *nm* audience; (*sala*) auditorium

**auge** ['auxe] *nm* boom; (*clímax*) climax

**augurar** [auɣu'rar] *vt* to predict; (*presagiar*) to portend

**augurio** [au'ɣurjo] *nm* omen

**aula** ['aula] *nf* classroom; (*en universidad etc*) lecture room

**aullar** [au'ʎar] *vi* to howl, yell

**aullido** [au'ʎiðo] *nm* howl, yell

**aumentar** [aumen'tar] *vt* to increase; (*precios*) to put up; (*producción*) to step up; (*con microscopio, anteojos*) to magnify ♦ *vi* to increase, be on the increase; ~se *vr* to increase, be on the increase; **aumento** *nm* increase; rise

**aun** [a'un] *adv* even; ~ así even so; ~ más even o yet more

**aún** [a'un] *adv*: ~ está aquí he's still here; ~ no lo sabemos we don't know yet; ¿no ha venido ~? hasn't she come yet?

**aunque** [a'unke] *conj* though, although, even though

**aúpa** [a'upa] *excl* come on!

**aureola** [aure'ola] *nf* halo

**auricular** [auriku'lar] *nm* (TEL) earpiece, receiver; ~es *nmpl* (*para escuchar musica etc*) headphones

**aurora** [au'rora] *nf* dawn

**auscultar** [auskul'tar] *vt* (MED: *pecho*) to listen to, sound

**ausencia** [au'senθja] *nf* absence

**ausentarse** [ausen'tarse] *vr* to go away; (*por poco tiempo*) to go out

**ausente** [au'sente] *adj* absent

**auspicios** [aus'piθjos] *nmpl* auspices; (*protección*) protection *sg*

**austeridad** [austeri'ðað] *nf* austerity; **austero, a** *adj* austere

**austral** [aus'tral] *adj* southern ♦ *nm* monetary unit of Argentina

**Australia** [aus'tralja] *nf* Australia; **australiano, a** *adj, nm/f* Australian

**Austria** ['austrja] *nf* Austria; **austríaco, a** *adj, nm/f* Austrian

**auténtico, a** [au'tentiko, a] *adj* authentic

**auto** ['auto] *nm* (JUR) edict, decree; (: *orden*) writ; (AUTO) car; ~s *nmpl* (*JUR*) proceedings; (: *acta*) court record *sg*

**autoadhesivo** [autoaðe'siβo] *adj* self-adhesive; (*sobre*) self-sealing

**autobiografía** [autoβjoɣra'fia] *nf* autobiography

**autobús** [auto'βus] *nm* bus

**autocar** [auto'kar] *nm* coach (*BRIT*), (passenger) bus (*US*)

**autóctono, a** [au'toktono, a] *adj* native, indigenous

**autodefensa** [autoðe'fensa] *nf* self-defence

**autodeterminación** [autoðeterminaθjon] *nf* self-determination

**autodidacto, a** [autoði'ðakto, a] *adj* self-taught

**autoescuela** [autoes'kwela] *nf* driving school

**autógrafo** [au'toɣrafo] *nm* autograph

**automación** [automa'θjon] *nf* = automatización

**autómata** [au'tomata] *nm* automaton

**automático, a** [auto'matiko, a] *adj* automatic ♦ *nm* press stud

**automatización** [automatiθa'θjon] *nf* automation

**automotor, triz** [automo'tor, 'triθ] *adj* self-propelled ♦ *nm* diesel train

**automóvil** [auto'moβil] *nm* (motor) car (*BRIT*), automobile (*US*); **automovilismo** *nm* (*actividad*) motoring; (*DEPORTE*) motor racing; **automovilista** *nm/f* motorist, driver; **automovilístico, a** *adj* (*industria*) motor *cpd*

**autonomía** [autono'mia] *nf* autonomy; **autónomo, a** (*ESP*) *adj* (*POL*) autonomous; **autonómico, a** (*ESP*) *adj* (*POL*) autonomous

**autopista** [auto'pista] *nf* motorway (*BRIT*), freeway (*US*); ~ **de peaje** toll road (*BRIT*), turnpike road (*US*)

**autopsia** [au'topsja] *nf* autopsy, post-mortem

**autor, a** [au'tor, a] *nm/f* author

**autoridad** [autori'ðað] *nf* authority; **autoritario, a** *adj* authoritarian

**autorización** [autoriθa'θjon] *nf* authorization; **autorizado, a** *adj* authorized; (*aprobado*) approved

**autorizar** [autori'θar] *vt* to authorize; (*aprobar*) to approve

**autorretrato** [autorre'trato] *nm* self-portrait

**autoservicio** [autoser'βiθjo] *nm* (*tienda*) self-service shop (*BRIT*) o store (*US*); (*restaurante*) self-service restaurant

**autostop** [auto'stop] *nm* hitch-hiking; **hacer** ~ to hitch-hike; **~ista** *nm/f* hitch-hiker

**autosuficiencia** [autosufi'θjenθja] *nf* self-sufficiency

**autovía** [auto'βia] *nf* ≈ A-road (*BRIT*), dual carriageway (*BRIT*), ≈ state highway (*US*)

**auxiliar** [auksi'ljar] *vt* to help ♦ *nm/f* assistant; **auxilio** *nm* assistance, help; **primeros auxilios** first aid *sg*

**Av** *abr* (= **Avenida**) Av(e).

**aval** [a'βal] *nm* guarantee; (*persona*) guarantor

**avalancha** [aβa'lantʃa] *nf* avalanche

**avance** [a'βanθe] *nm* advance; (*pago*) advance payment; (*CINE*) trailer

**avanzar** [aβan'θar] *vt, vi* to advance

**avaricia** [aβa'riθja] *nf* avarice, greed; **avaricioso, a** *adj* avaricious, greedy

**avaro, a** [a'βaro, a] *adj* miserly, mean ♦ *nm/f* miser

**avasallar** [aβasa'ʎar] *vt* to subdue, subjugate

**Avda** *abr* (= **Avenida**) Av(e).

**ave** ['aβe] *nf* bird; ~ **de rapiña** bird of prey

**avecinarse** [aβeθi'narse] *vr* (*tormenta, fig*) to be on the way

**avellana** [aβe'ʎana] *nf* hazelnut; **avellano** *nm* hazel tree

**avemaría** [aβema'ria] *nm* Hail Mary, Ave Maria

**avena** [a'βena] *nf* oats *pl*

**avenida** [aβe'niða] *nf* (*calle*) avenue

**avenir** [aβe'nir] *vt* to reconcile; **~se** *vr* to come to an agreement, reach a compromise

**aventajado, a** [aβenta'xaðo, a] *adj*

outstanding

**aventajar** [aβenta'xar] vt (sobrepasar) to surpass, outstrip

**aventar** [aβen'tar] vt to fan, blow; (grano) to winnow

**aventura** [aβen'tura] nf adventure; **aventurado, a** [aβervon'θar] a adj risky; **aventurero, a** adj adventurous

**avergonzar** [aβervon'θar] vt to shame; (desconcertar) to embarrass; ~se vr to be ashamed; (turbarse) to be embarrassed

**avería** [aβe'ria] nf (TEC) breakdown, fault

**averiado, a** [aβe'rjaðo, a] adj broken down; "~" "out of order"

**averiguación** [aβeriɣwa'θjon] nf investigation; (descubrimiento) ascertainment

**averiguar** [aβeri'ɣwar] vt to investigate; (descubrir) to find out, ascertain

**aversión** [aβer'sjon] nf aversion, dislike

**avestruz** [aβes'truθ] nm ostrich

**aviación** [aβja'θjon] nf aviation; (fuerzas aéreas) air force

**aviador, a** [aβja'ðor, a] nm/f aviator, airman/woman

**avicultura** [aβikul'tura] nf poultry farming

**avidez** [aβi'ðeθ] nf avidity, eagerness; **ávido, a** adj avid, eager

**avinagrado, a** [aβina'ɣraðo, a] adj sour, acid

**avío** [a'βio] nm preparation; ~s nmpl (equipamiento) gear sg, kit sg

**avión** [a'βjon] nm aeroplane; (ave) martin; ~ **de reacción** jet (plane)

**avioneta** [aβjo'neta] nf light aircraft

**avisar** [aβi'sar] vt (advertir) to warn, notify; (informar) to tell; (aconsejar) to advise, counsel; **aviso** nm warning; (noticia) notice

**avispa** [a'βispa] nf wasp

**avispado, a** [aβis'paðo, a] adj sharp, clever

**avispero** [aβis'pero] nm wasp's nest

**avispón** [aβis'pon] nm hornet

**avistar** [aβis'tar] vt to sight, spot

**avituallar** [aβitwa'ʎar] vt to supply with food

**avivar** [aβi'βar] vt to strengthen, intensify; ~se vr to revive, acquire new life

**axila** [ak'sila] nf armpit

**axioma** [ak'sjoma] nm axiom

**ay** [ai] excl (dolor) ow!, ouch!; (aflicción) oh!, oh dear!; ¡ ~ **de mí!** poor me!

**aya** ['aja] nf governess; (niñera) nanny

**ayer** [a'jer] adv, nm yesterday; **antes de** ~ the day before yesterday

**ayote** [a'jote] (AM) nm pumpkin

**ayuda** [a'juða] nf help, assistance ♦ nm page; **ayudante, a** nm/f assistant, helper; (ESCOL) assistant; (MIL) adjutant

**ayudar** [aju'ðar] vt to help, assist

**ayunar** [aju'nar] vi to fast; **ayuna** nfpl: **estar en ayunas** (no haber comido) to be fasting; (ignorar) to be in the dark; **ayuno** nm fast; fasting

**ayuntamiento** [ajunta'mjento] nm (consejo) town (o city) council; (edificio) town (o city) hall

**azabache** [aθa'βatʃe] nm jet

**azada** [a'θaða] nf hoe

**azafata** [aθa'fata] nf air stewardess

**azafrán** [aθa'fran] nm saffron

**azahar** [aθa'ar] nm orange/lemon blossom

**azar** [a'θar] nm (casualidad) chance, fate; (desgracia) misfortune, accident; **por** ~ by chance; **al** ~ at random

**azoramiento** [aθora'mjento] nm alarm; (confusión) confusion

**azorar** [aθo'rar] vt to alarm; ~se vr to get alarmed

**Azores** [a'θores] nfpl: **las** ~ the Azores

**azotar** [aθo'tar] vt to whip, beat; (pegar) to spank; **azote** nm (látigo) whip; (latigazo) lash, stroke; (en las nalgas) spank; (calamidad) calamity

**azotea** [aθo'tea] nf (flat) roof

**azteca** [aθ'teka] adj, nm/f Aztec

**azúcar** [a'θukar] nm sugar; **azucara-**

do, a *adj* sugary, sweet

**azucarero, a** [aθuka'rero, a] *adj* sugar *cpd* ♦ *nm* sugar bowl

**azucena** [aθu'θena] *nf* white lily

**azufre** [a'θufre] *nm* sulphur

**azul** [a'θul] *adj, nm* blue; ~ **marino** navy blue

**azulejo** [aθu'lexo] *nm* tile

**azuzar** [aθu'θar] *vt* to incite, egg on

# B

**B.A.** *abr* (= Buenos Aires) B.A.

**baba** ['baβa] *nf* spittle, saliva; **babear** *vi* to drool, slaver

**babero** [ba'βero] *nm* bib

**babor** [ba'βor] *nm* port (side)

**baboso, a** [ba'βoso, a] *adj* (AM: fam) *adj* silly

**baca** ['baka] *nf* (AUTO) luggage o roof rack

**bacalao** [baka'lao] *nm* cod(fish)

**bacteria** [bak'terja] *nf* bacterium, germ

**báculo** ['bakulo] *nm* stick, staff

**bache** ['batʃe] *nm* pothole, rut; (fig) bad patch

**bagaje** [ba'vaxe] *nm* baggage, luggage

**Bahama** [ba'ama]: **las (Islas) ~** *nfpl* the Bahamas

**bahía** [ba'ia] *nf* bay

**bailar** [bai'lar] *vt, vi* to dance; **~ín, ina** *nm/f* (ballet) dancer; **baile** *nm* dance; (formal) ball

**baja** ['baxa] *nf* drop, fall; (MIL) casualty; **dar de ~** (soldado) to discharge; (empleado) to dismiss

**bajada** [ba'xaða] *nf* descent; (camino) slope; (de aguas) ebb

**bajar** [ba'xar] *vi* to go down, come down; (temperatura, precios) to drop, fall ♦ *vt* (cabeza) to bow; (escalera) to go down, come down; (precio, voz) to lower; (llevar abajo) to take down; **~se** *vr* (de coche) to get out; (de autobús, tren) to get off; **~ de** (coche) to get out of; (autobús, tren) to get off

**bajeza** [ba'xeθa] *nf* baseness *no pl*; (una ~) vile deed

**bajío** [ba'xio] *nm* shoal, sandbank; (AM) lowlands *pl*

**bajo, a** ['baxo, a] *adj* (mueble, número, precio) low; (piso) ground; (de estatura) small, short; (color) pale; (sonido) faint, soft, low; (voz: en tono) deep; (metal) base; (humilde) low, humble ♦ *adv* (hablar) softly, quietly; (volar) low ♦ *prep* under, below, underneath ♦ *nm* (MUS) bass; **~ la lluvia** in the rain

**bajón** [ba'xon] *nm* fall, drop

**bala** ['bala] *nf* bullet

**balance** [ba'lanθe] *nm* (COM) balance; (: libro) balance sheet; (: cuenta general) stocktaking

**balancear** [balanθe'ar] *vt* to balance ♦ *vi* to swing (to and fro); (vacilar) to hesitate; **~se** *vr* to swing (to and fro); to hesitate; **balanceo** *nm* swinging

**balanza** [ba'lanθa] *nf* scales *pl*, balance; (ASTROLOGÍA) B~ Libra; **~ comercial** balance of trade; **~ de pagos** balance of payments

**balar** [ba'lar] *vi* to bleat

**balaustrada** [balaus'traða] *nf* balustrade; (pasamanos) banisters *pl*

**balazo** [ba'laθo] *nm* (golpe) shot; (herida) bullet wound

**balbucear** [balβuθe'ar] *vi, vt* to stammer, stutter; **balbuceo** *nm* stammering, stuttering

**balbucir** [balβu'θir] *vi, vt* to stammer, stutter

**balcón** [bal'kon] *nm* balcony

**balde** ['balde] *nm* bucket, pail; **de ~** (for) free, for nothing; **en ~** in vain

**baldío, a** [bal'dio, a] *adj* uncultivated; (terreno) waste ♦ *nm* waste land

**baldosa** [bal'dosa] *nf* (azulejo) floor tile; (grande) flagstone; **baldosín** *nm* (small) tile

**Baleares** [bale'ares] *nfpl*: **las (Islas) ~** the Balearic Islands

**balido** [ba'liðo] *nm* bleat, bleating

**balín** [ba'lin] *nm* pellet; **balines**

*nmpl* buckshot *sg*

**baliza** [ba'liθa] *nf* (*AVIAT*) beacon; (*NAUT*) buoy

**balneario, a** [balne'arjo, a] *adj*: estación balnearia (bathing) resort ♦ *nm* spa, health resort

**balón** [ba'lon] *nm* ball

**baloncesto** [balon'θesto] *nm* basketball

**balonmano** [balom'mano] *nm* handball

**balonvolea** [balombo'lea] *nm* volleyball

**balsa** ['balsa] *nf* raft; (*BOT*) balsa wood

**bálsamo** ['balsamo] *nm* balsam, balm

**baluarte** [ba'lwarte] *nm* bastion, bulwark

**ballena** [ba'ʎena] *nf* whale

**ballesta** [ba'ʎesta] *nf* crossbow; (*AUTO*) spring

**ballet** [ba'le] (*pl* ~s) *nm* ballet

**bambolear** [bambole'ar] *vi* to swing, sway; (*silla*) to wobble; ~se *vr* to swing, sway; to wobble; **bamboleo** *nm* swinging, swaying; wobbling

**bambú** [bam'bu] *nm* bamboo

**banana** [ba'nana] (*AM*) *nf* banana; **banano** (*AM*) *nm* banana tree

**banca** ['banka] *nf* (*asiento*) bench; (*COM*) banking

**bancario, a** [ban'karjo, a] *adj* banking *cpd*, bank *cpd*

**bancarrota** [banka'rrota] *nf* bankruptcy; **hacer** ~ to go bankrupt

**banco** ['banko] *nm* bench; (*ESCOL*) desk; (*COM*) bank; (*GEO*) stratum; ~ **de crédito/de ahorros** credit/savings bank; ~ **de arena** sandbank; ~ **de datos** databank; ~ **de hielo** iceberg

**banda** ['banda] *nf* band; (*pandilla*) gang; (*NAUT*) side, edge; **la B~ Oriental** Uruguay; ~ **sonora** soundtrack

**bandada** [ban'daða] *nf* (*de pájaros*) flock; (*de peces*) shoal

**bandazo** [ban'daθo] *nm*: **dar** ~s to sway from side to side

**bandeja** [ban'dexa] *nf* tray

**bandera** [ban'dera] *nf* (*de tela*) flag; (*estandarte*) banner

**banderilla** [bande'riʎa] *nf* banderilla

**banderín** [bande'rin] *nm* pennant, small flag

**bandido** [ban'diðo] *nm* bandit

**bando** ['bando] *nm* (*edicto*) edict, proclamation; (*facción*) faction; **los** ~**s** (*REL*) the banns

**bandolera** [bando'lera] *nf*: **llevar en** ~ to wear across one's chest

**bandolero** [bando'lero] *nm* bandit, brigand

**Bangladesh** [baengla'deʃ] *nm* Bangladesh

**banquero** [ban'kero] *nm* banker

**banqueta** [ban'keta] *nf* stool; (*AM: en la calle*) pavement (*BRIT*), sidewalk (*US*)

**banquete** [ban'kete] *nm* banquet; (*para convidados*) formal dinner

**banquillo** [ban'kiʎo] *nm* (*JUR*) dock, prisoner's bench; (*banco*) bench; (*para los pies*) footstool

**bañador** [baɲa'ðor] *nm* swimming costume (*BRIT*), bathing suit (*US*)

**bañar** [ba'ɲar] *vt* to bath, bathe; (*objeto*) to dip; (*de barniz*) to coat; ~se *vr* (*en el mar*) to bathe, swim; (*en la bañera*) to have a bath

**bañera** [ba'ɲera] *nf* bath(tub)

**bañero, a** [ba'ɲero, a] *nm/f* lifeguard

**bañista** [ba'ɲista] *nm/f* bather

**baño** ['baɲo] *nm* (*en bañera*) bath; (*en río*) dip, swim; (*cuarto*) bathroom; (*bañera*) bath(tub); (*capa*) coating

**baqueta** [ba'keta] *nf* (*MUS*) drumstick

**bar** [bar] *nm* bar

**barahúnda** [bara'unda] *nf* uproar, hubbub

**baraja** [ba'raxa] *nf* pack (of cards); **barajar** *vt* (*naipes*) to shuffle; (*fig*) to jumble up

**baranda** [ba'randa] *nf* = **barandilla**

**barandilla** [baran'diʎa] *nf* rail, railing

**baratija** [bara'tixa] *nf* trinket

**baratillo** [bara'tiʎo] *nm* (*tienda*) junkshop; (*subasta*) bargain sale; (*conjunto de cosas*) secondhand goods *pl*

**barato, a** [ba'rato, a] *adj* cheap ♦ *adv* cheap, cheaply

**baraúnda** [bara'unda] *nf* = **barahúnda**

**barba** ['barβa] *nf* (*mentón*) chin; (*pelo*) beard

**barbacoa** [barβa'koa] *nf* (*parrilla*) barbecue; (*carne*) barbecued meat

**barbaridad** [barβari'ðað] *nf* barbarity; (*acto*) barbarism; (*atrocidad*) outrage; **una** ~ (*fam*) loads; **¡qué** ~! (*fam*) how awful!

**barbarie** [bar'βarje] *nf* barbarism, savagery; (*crueldad*) barbarity

**barbarismo** [barβa'rismo] *nm* = barbarie

**bárbaro, a** ['barβaro, a] *adj* barbarous, cruel; (*grosero*) rough, uncouth ♦ *nm/f* barbarian ♦ *adv*: **lo pasamos** ~ (*fam*) we had a great time; **¡qué** ~! (*fam*) how marvellous!; **un éxito** ~ (*fam*) a terrific success; **es un tipo** ~ (*fam*) he's a great bloke

**barbecho** [bar'βetʃo] *nm* fallow land

**barbero** [bar'βero] *nm* barber, hairdresser

**barbilampiño** [barβilam'piɲo] *adj* clean-shaven, smooth-faced; (*fig*) inexperienced

**barbilla** [bar'βiʎa] *nf* chin, tip of the chin

**barbo** ['barβo] *nm*: ~ **de mar** red mullet

**barbotear** [barβote'ar] *vt, vi* to mutter, mumble

**barbudo, a** [bar'βuðo, a] *adj* bearded

**barca** ['barka] *nf* (small) boat; ~ **pesquera** fishing boat; ~ **de pasaje** ferry; ~**za** *nf* barge; ~**za de desembarco** landing craft

**Barcelona** [barθe'lona] *n* Barcelona

**barcelonés, esa** [barθelo'nes, esa] *adj* of o from Barcelona

**barco** ['barko] *nm* boat; (*buque*) ship; ~ **de carga** cargo boat; ~ **de vela** sailing ship

**baremo** [ba'remo] *nm* (*MAT, fig*) scale

**barítono** [ba'ritono] *nm* baritone

**barman** [barman] *nm* barman

**Barna.** *abr* = **Barcelona**

**barniz** [bar'niθ] *nm* varnish; (*en la loza*) glaze; (*fig*) veneer; ~**ar** *vt* to varnish; (*loza*) to glaze

**barómetro** [ba'rometro] *nm* barometer

**barquero** [bar'kero] *nm* boatman

**barquillo** [bar'kiʎo] *nm* cone, cornet

**barra** ['barra] *nf* bar, rod; (*de un bar, café*) bar; (*de pan*) French stick; (*palanca*) lever; ~ **de carmín** o **de labios** lipstick; ~ **libra** free bar

**barraca** [ba'rraka] *nf* hut, cabin

**barranco** [ba'rranko] *nm* ravine; (*fig*) difficulty

**barrena** [ba'rrena] *nf* drill; **barrenar** *vt* to drill (through); bore; **barreno** *nm* large drill

**barrer** [ba'rrer] *vt* to sweep; (*quitar*) to sweep away

**barrera** [ba'rrera] *nf* barrier

**barriada** [ba'rrjaða] *nf* quarter, district

**barricada** [barri'kaða] *nf* barricade

**barrida** [ba'rriða] *nf* sweep, sweeping

**barrido** [ba'rriðo] *nm* = **barrida**

**barriga** [ba'rriɣa] *nf* belly; (*panza*) paunch; **barrigón, ona** *adj* potbellied; **barrigudo, a** *adj* potbellied

**barril** [ba'rril] *nm* barrel, cask

**barrio** [barrjo] *nm* (*vecindad*) area, neighborhood (*US*); (*en las afueras*) suburb; ~ **chino** red-light district

**barro** ['barro] *nm* (*lodo*) mud; (*objetos*) earthenware; (*MED*) pimple

**barroco, a** [ba'rroko, a] *adj, nm* baroque

**barrote** [ba'rrote] *nm* (*de ventana*) bar

**barruntar** [barrun'tar] *vt* (*conjeturar*) to guess; (*presentir*) to suspect; **barrunto** *nm* guess; suspicion

**bartola** [bar'tola]: **a la** ~ *adv*: **tirarse a la** ~ to take it easy, be lazy

**bártulos** ['bartulos] *nmpl* things, belongings

**barullo** [ba'ruʎo] *nm* row, uproar

**basar** [ba'sar] *vt* to base; ~**se** *vr*: ~**se en** to be based on

**basca** ['baska] *nf* nausea

**báscula** ['baskula] *nf* (platform) scales

**base** ['base] *nf* base; **a** ~ **de** on the basis of; (*mediante*) by means of; ~ **de datos** (*INFORM*) database

**básico, a** ['basiko, a] *adj* basic

**basílica** [ba'silika] *nf* basilica

---

PALABRA CLAVE

**bastante** [bas'tante] *adj* **1** (*suficiente*) enough; ~ **dinero** enough *o* sufficient money; ~**s libros** enough books

**2** (*valor intensivo*): ~ **gente** quite a lot of people; **tener** ~ **calor** to be rather hot

♦ *adv*: ~ **bueno/malo** quite good/ rather bad; ~ **rico** pretty rich; (*lo*) ~ **inteligente (como) para hacer algo** clever enough *o* sufficiently clever to do sth

---

**bastar** [bas'tar] *vi* to be enough *o* sufficient; ~**se** *vr* to be self-sufficient; ~ **para** to be enough to; ¡**basta!** (that's) enough!

**bastardilla** [bastar'ðiʎa] *nf* italics

**bastardo, a** [bas'tarðo, a] *adj, nm/f* bastard

**bastidor** [basti'ðor] *nm* frame; (*de coche*) chassis; (*TEATRO*) wing; **entre ~es** (*fig*) behind the scenes

**basto, a** ['basto, a] *adj* coarse, rough; ~**s** *nmpl* (*NAIPES*) ≈ clubs

**bastón** [bas'ton] *nm* stick, staff; (*para pasear*) walking stick

**bastoncillo** [baston'θiʎo] *nm* cotton bud

**bastos** ['bastos] *nmpl* (*NAIPES*) clubs

**basura** [ba'sura] *nf* rubbish (*BRIT*), garbage (*US*)

**basurero** [basu'rero] *nm* (*hombre*) dustman (*BRIT*), garbage man (*US*); (*lugar*) dump; (*cubo*) (rubbish) bin

(*BRIT*), trash can (*US*)

**bata** ['bata] *nf* (*gen*) dressing gown; (*cubretodo*) smock, overall; (*MED, TEC etc*) lab(oratory) coat

**batalla** [ba'taʎa] *nf* battle; **de** ~ (*fig*) for everyday use

**batallar** [bata'ʎar] *vi* to fight

**batallón** [bata'ʎon] *nm* battalion

**batata** [ba'tata] (*AM*) *nf* sweet potato

**batería** [bate'ria] *nf* battery; (*MUS*) drums; ~ **de cocina** kitchen utensils

**batido, a** [ba'tiðo, a] *adj* (*camino*) beaten, well-trodden ♦ *nm* (*CULIN*): ~ **(de leche)** milk shake

**batidora** [bati'ðora] *nf* beater, mixer; ~ **eléctrica** food mixer, blender

**batir** [ba'tir] *vt* to beat, strike; (*vencer*) to beat, defeat; (*revolver*) to beat, mix; ~**se** *vr* to fight; ~ **palmas** to clap, applaud

**batuta** [ba'tuta] *nf* baton; **llevar la** ~ (*fig*) to be the boss, be in charge

**baúl** [ba'ul] *nm* trunk; (*AUTO*) boot (*BRIT*), trunk (*US*)

**bautismo** [bau'tismo] *nm* baptism, christening

**bautizar** [bauti'θar] *vt* to baptize, christen; (*fam: diluir*) to water down; **bautizo** *nm* baptism, christening

**baya** ['baja] *nf* berry

**bayeta** [ba'jeta] *nf* floorcloth

**bayo, a** ['bajo, a] *adj* bay

**bayoneta** [bajo'neta] *nf* bayonet

**baza** ['baθa] *nf* trick; **meter** ~ to butt in

**bazar** [ba'θar] *nm* bazaar

**bazofia** [ba'θofja] *nf* pigswill (*BRIT*), hogwash (*US*); (*libro etc*) trash

**beato, a** [be'ato, a] *adj* blessed; (*piadoso*) pious

**bebé** [be'βe] (*pl* ~**s**) *nm* baby

**bebedero** [beβe'ðero] *nm* (*para animales*) drinking trough

**bebedor, a** [beβe'ðor, a] *adj* hard-drinking

**beber** [be'βer] *vt, vi* to drink

**bebida** [be'βiða] *nf* drink; **bebido, a** *adj* drunk

**beca** ['beka] *nf* grant, scholarship

**becario, a** [be'karjo, a] nm/f scholarship holder, grant holder

**bedel** [be'ðel] nm (ESCOL) janitor; (UNIV) porter

**béisbol** ['beisβol] nm (DEPORTE) baseball

**belén** [be'len] nm (de navidad) nativity scene, crib; B~ Bethlehem

**belga** ['belɣa] adj, nm/f Belgian

**Bélgica** ['belxika] nf Belgium

**bélico, a** ['beliko, a] adj (actitud) warlike; **belicoso, a** adj (guerrero) warlike; (agresivo) aggressive, bellicose

**beligerante** [belixe'rante] adj belligerent

**belleza** [be'ʎeθa] nf beauty

**bello, a** ['beʎo, a] adj beautiful, lovely; **Bellas Artes** Fine Art

**bellota** [be'ʎota] nf acorn

**bemol** [be'mol] nm (MUS) flat; esto tiene ~es (fam) this is a tough one

**bencina** [ben'θina] (AM) nf (gasolina) petrol (BRIT), gasoline (US)

**bendecir** [bende'θir] vt to bless

**bendición** [bendi'θjon] nf blessing

**bendito, a** [ben'dito, a] pp de **bendecir** ♦ adj holy; (afortunado) lucky; (feliz) happy; (sencillo) simple ♦ nm/f simple soul

**beneficencia** [benefi'θenθja] nf charity

**beneficiar** [benefi'θjar] vt to benefit, be of benefit to; ~se vr to benefit, profit; ~io, a nm/f beneficiary

**beneficio** [bene'fiθjo] nm (bien) benefit, advantage; (ganancia) profit, gain; ~so, a adj beneficial

**benéfico, a** [be'nefiko, a] adj charitable

**beneplácito** [bene'plaθito] nm approval, consent

**benevolencia** [beneβo'lenθja] nf benevolence, kindness; **benévolo, a** adj benevolent, kind

**benigno, a** [be'niɣno, a] adj kind; (suave) mild; (MED: tumor) benign, non-malignant

**berberecho** [berße'retʃo] nm (ZOOL, CULIN) cockle

**berenjena** [beren'xena] nf aubergine (BRIT), eggplant (US)

**Berlín** [ber'lin] n Berlin; **berlinés, esa** adj of o from Berlin ♦ nm/f Berliner

**bermudas** [ber'muðas] nfpl Bermuda shorts

**berrear** [berre'ar] vi to bellow, low

**berrido** [be'rriðo] nm bellow(ing)

**berrinche** [be'rrintʃe] (fam) nm temper, tantrum

**berro** ['berro] nm watercress

**berza** ['berθa] nf cabbage

**besamel** [besa'mel] nf (CULIN) white sauce, bechamel sauce

**besar** [be'sar] vt to kiss; (fig: tocar) to graze; ~se vr to kiss (one another); **beso** nm kiss

**bestia** ['bestja] nf beast, animal; (fig) idiot; ~ **de carga** beast of burden

**bestial** [bes'tjal] adj bestial; (fam) terrific; ~**idad** nf bestiality; (fam) stupidity

**besugo** [be'suɣo] nm sea bream; (fam) idiot

**besuquear** [besuke'ar] vt to cover with kisses; ~**se** vr to kiss and cuddle

**betún** [be'tun] nm shoe polish; (QUIMICA) bitumen

**biberón** [biße'ron] nm feeding bottle

**Biblia** ['bißlja] nf Bible

**bibliografía** [bißljoɣra'fia] nf bibliography

**biblioteca** [bißljo'teka] nf library; (mueble) bookshelves; ~ **de consulta** reference library; ~**rio, a** nm/f librarian

**bicarbonato** [bikarßo'nato] nm bicarbonate

**bici** ['biθi] (fam) nf bike

**bicicleta** [biθi'kleta] nf bicycle, cycle; **ir en** ~ to cycle

**bicho** ['bitʃo] nm (animal) small animal; (sabandija) bug, insect; (TAUR) bull

**bidé** [bi'ðe] (pl ~s) nm bidet

**bidón** [bi'ðon] nm (de aceite) drum; (de gasolina) can

PALABRA CLAVE

**bien** [bjen] *nm* **1** *(bienestar)* good; te lo digo por tu ~ I'm telling you for your own good; el ~ y el mal good and evil

**2** *(posesión)*: ~es goods; ~es de consumo consumer goods; ~es inmuebles o raíces/~es muebles real estate *sg*/personal property *sg*

♦ *adv* **1** *(de manera satisfactoria, correcta etc)* well; **trabaja/come** ~ she works/eats well; **contestó** ~ he answered correctly; **me siento** ~ I feel fine; **no me siento** ~ I don't feel very well; **se está** ~ **aquí** it's nice here

**2** *(frases)*: **hiciste** ~ **en llamarme** you were right to call me

**3** *(valor intensivo)* very; **un cuarto** ~ **caliente** a nice warm room; ~ **se ve que** ... it's quite clear that ...

**4**: **estar** ~: **estoy muy** ~ **aquí** I feel very happy here; **está** ~ **que vengan** it's all right for them to come; **¡está** ~! lo haré oh all right, I'll do it

**5** *(de buena gana)*: **yo** ~ **que iría pero** ... I'd gladly go but ...

♦ *excl*: **¡** ~! *(aprobación)* O.K.!; **¡muy** ~! well done!

♦ *adj inv (matiz despectivo)*: **niño** ~ rich kid; **gente** ~ posh people

♦ *conj* **1**: ~ ... ~ ... ~ **en coche/en tren** either by car or by train

**2**: **no** ~ *(esp AM)*: **no** ~ **llegue se llamaré** as soon as I arrive I'll call you

**3**: **si** ~ even though; *ver tb* **más**

**bienal** [bje'nal] *adj* biennial

**bienaventurado, a** [bjenaßentu'raðo, a] *adj (feliz)* happy, fortunate

**bienestar** [bjenes'tar] *nm* well-being, welfare

**bienhechor, a** [bjene'tʃor, a] *adj* beneficent ♦ *nm/f* benefactor/benefactress

**bienvenida** [bjembe'niða] *nf* welcome; **dar la** ~ **a uno** to welcome

**sb**

**bienvenido** [bjembe'niðo] *excl* welcome!

**bife** ['bife] *(AM) nm* steak

**bifurcación** [bifurka'θjon] *nf* fork

**bifurcarse** [bifur'karse] *vr (camino, carretera, río)* to fork

**bigamia** [bi'ɣamja] *nf* bigamy; **bígamo, a** *adj* bigamous ♦ *nm/f* bigamist

**bigote** [bi'ɣote] *nm* moustache; **bigotudo, a** *adj* with a big moustache

**bikini** [bi'kini] *nm* bikini; *(CULIN)* toasted ham and cheese sandwich

**bilbaíno, a** [bilßa'ino, a] *adj* from o of Bilbao

**bilingüe** [bi'liŋgwe] *adj* bilingual

**billar** [bi'ʎar] *nm* billiards *sg*; *(lugar)* billiard hall; *(mini-casino)* amusement arcade; ~ **americano** pool

**billete** [bi'ʎete] *nm* ticket; *(de banco)* (bank)note *(BRIT)*, bill *(US)*; *(carta)* note; ~ **sencillo**, ~ **de ida solamente** single *(BRIT)* o one-way *(US)* ticket; ~ **de ida y vuelta** return *(BRIT)* o round-trip *(US)* ticket; ~ **de 20 libras** £20 note

**billetera** [biʎe'tera] *nf* wallet

**billetero** [biʎe'tero] *nm* = **billetera**

**billón** [bi'ʎon] *nm* billion

**bimensual** [bimen'swal] *adj* twice monthly

**bimotor** [bimo'tor] *adj* twin-engined ♦ *nm* twin-engined plane

**bingo** ['biŋgo] *nm* bingo

**biodegradable** [bioðeɣra'ðaßle] *adj* biodegradable

**biografía** [bjoɣra'fia] *nf* biography; **biógrafo, a** *nm/f* biographer

**biología** [bjolo'xia] *nf* biology; **biológico, a** *adj* biological; **biólogo, a** *nm/f* biologist

**biombo** ['bjombo] *nm* (folding) screen

**biopsia** [bi'opsja] *nf* biopsy

**biquini** [bi'kini] *nm* bikini

**birlar** [bir'lar] *(fam) vt* to pinch

**Birmania** [bir'manja] *nf* Burma

**birria** ['birrja] *nf*: **ser una** ~ *(película, libro)* to be rubbish

**bis** [bis] *excl* encore! ♦ *adv*: **viven**

en el 27 ~ they live at 27a

**bisabuelo, a** [bisa'βwelo, a] *nm/f* great-grandfather/mother

**bisagra** [bi'sayra] *nf* hinge

**bisbisar** [bisβi'sar] *vt* to mutter, mumble

**bisbisear** [bisβise'ar] *vt* = bisbisar

**bisiesto** [bi'sjesto] *adj*: año ~ leap year

**bisnieto, a** [bis'njeto, a] *nm/f* great-grandson/daughter

**bisonte** [bi'sonte] *nm* bison

**bisté** [bis'te] *nm* = **bistec**

**bistec** [bis'tek] *nm* steak

**bisturí** [bistu'ri] *nm* scalpel

**bisutería** [bisute'ria] *nf* imitation *o* costume jewellery

**bit** [bit] *nm* (INFORM) bit

**bizco, a** [biθko, a] *adj* cross-eyed

**bizcocho** [biθ'kotʃo] *nm* (CULIN) sponge cake

**bizquear** [biθke'ar] *vi* to squint

**blanca** ['blanka] *nf* (MUS) minim; estar sin ~ to be broke; *ver tb* **blanco**

**blanco, a** ['blanko, a] *adj* white ♦ *nm/f* white man/woman, white ♦ *nm* (color) white; (en texto) blank; (MIL, fig) target; en ~ blank; noche en ~ sleepless night

**blancura** [blan'kura] *nf* whiteness

**blandir** [blan'dir] *vt* to brandish

**blando, a** ['blando, a] *adj* soft; (tierno) tender, gentle; (carácter) mild; (fam) cowardly; **blandura** *nf* softness; tenderness; mildness

**blanquear** [blanke'ar] *vt* to whiten; (fachada) to whitewash; (paño) to bleach ♦ *vi* to turn white; **blanquecino, a** *adj* whitish

**blasfemar** [blasfe'mar] *vi* to blaspheme, curse; **blasfemia** *nf* blasphemy

**blasón** [bla'son] *nm* coat of arms; (fig) honour; **blasonar** *vt* to emblazon ♦ *vi* to boast, brag

**bledo** ['bleðo] *nm*: me importa un ~ I couldn't care less

**blindado, a** [blin'daðo, a] *adj* (MIL) armour-plated; (antibala) bullet-

proof; **coche** (ESP) *o* **carro** (AM) ~ armoured car

**blindaje** [blin'daxe] *nm* armour, armour-plating

**bloc** [blok] (*pl* ~**s**) *nm* writing pad

**bloque** ['bloke] *nm* block; (POL) bloc; ~ **de cilindros** cylinder block

**bloquear** [bloke'ar] *vt* to blockade; **bloqueo** *nm* blockade; (COM) freezing, blocking

**blusa** ['blusa] *nf* blouse

**boato** [bo'ato] *nm* show, ostentation

**bobada** [bo'βaða] *nf* foolish action; foolish statement; **decir** ~**s** to talk nonsense

**bobería** [boβe'ria] *nf* = **bobada**

**bobina** [bo'βina] *nf* (TEC) bobbin; (FOTO) spool; (ELEC) coil

**bobo, a** ['boβo, a] *adj* (tonto) daft, silly; (cándido) naïve ♦ *nm/f* fool, idiot ♦ *nm* (TEATRO) clown, funny man

**boca** ['boka] *nf* mouth; (de crustáceo) pincer; (de cañón) muzzle; (entrada) mouth, entrance; ~ **abajo/arriba** face down/up; **se me hace agua la** ~ my mouth is watering

**bocacalle** [boka'kaʎe] *nf* (entrance to a) street; **la primera** ~ **the** first turning *o* street

**bocadillo** [boka'ðiʎo] *nm* sandwich

**bocado** [bo'kaðo] *nm* mouthful, bite; (de caballo) bridle; ~ **de Adán** Adam's apple

**bocajarro** [boka'xarro]: **a** ~ *adv* (disparar, preguntar) point-blank

**bocanada** [boka'naða] *nf* (de vino) mouthful, swallow; (de aire) gust, puff

**bocata** [bo'kata] (fam) *nm* sarnie

**bocazas** [bo'kaθas] (fam) *nm inv* bigmouth

**boceto** [bo'θeto] *nm* sketch, outline

**bocina** [bo'θina] *nf* (MUS) trumpet; (AUTO) horn; (para hablar) megaphone

**bochorno** [bo'tʃorno] *nm* (vergüenza) embarrassment; (calor): **hace** ~ it's very muggy; **~so, a** *adj* muggy; embarrassing

**boda** ['boða] nf (tb: ~s) wedding, marriage; (fiesta) wedding reception; ~s de plata/de oro silver/golden wedding

**bodega** [bo'ðexa] nf (de vino) (wine) cellar; (depósito) storeroom; (de barco) hold

**bodegón** [boðe'xon] nm (ARTE) still life

**bofe** ['bofe] nm (tb: ~s: de res) lights

**bofetada** [bofe'taða] nf slap (in the face)

**bofetón** [bofe'ton] nm = bofetada

**boga** ['boxa] nf: en ~ (fig) in vogue

**bogar** [bo'xar] vi (remar) to row; (navegar) to sail

**Bogotá** [boxo'ta] n Bogotá

**bohemio, a** [bo'emjo, a] adj, nm/f Bohemian

**boicot** [boi'kot] (pl ~s) nm boycott; ~ear vt to boycott; ~eo nm boycott

**boina** ['boina] nf beret

**bola** ['bola] nf ball; (canica) marble; (NAIPES) (grand) slam; (betún) shoe polish; (mentira) tale, story; ~s (AM) nfpl bolas sg; ~ de billar billiard ball; ~ de nieve snowball

**bolchevique** [boltʃe'ßike] adj, nm/f Bolshevik

**boleadoras** [bolea'ðoras] (AM) nfpl bolas sg

**bolera** [bo'lera] nf skittle o bowling alley

**boleta** [bo'leta] (AM) nf (billete) ticket; (permiso) pass, permit

**boletería** [bolete'ria] (AM) nf ticket office

**boletín** [bole'tin] nm bulletin; (periódico) journal, review; ~ de noticias news bulletin

**boleto** [bo'leto] nm ticket

**boli** ['boli] (fam) nm Biro ®, pen

**boliche** [bo'litʃe] nm (bola) jack; (juego) bowls sg; (lugar) bowling alley

**bolígrafo** [bo'lixrafo] nm ball-point pen, Biro ®

**bolívar** [bo'lißar] nm monetary unit

of Venezuela

**Bolivia** [bo'lißja] nf Bolivia; **boliviano, a** adj, nm/f Bolivian

**bolo** ['bolo] nm skittle; (píldora) (large) pill; (juego de) ~s nmpl skittles sg

**bolsa** ['bolsa] nf (cartera) purse; (saco) bag; (AM) pocket; (ANAT) cavity, sac; (COM) stock exchange; (MINERÍA) pocket; de ~ pocket cpd; ~ de agua caliente hot water bottle; ~ de aire air pocket; ~ de papel paper bag; ~ de plástico plastic bag

**bolsillo** [bol'siʎo] nm pocket; (cartera) purse; de ~ pocket(-size)

**bolsista** [bol'sista] nm/f stockbroker

**bolso** ['bolso] nm (bolsa) bag; (de mujer) handbag

**bollo** ['boʎo] nm (pan) roll; (bulto) bump, lump; (abolladura) dent

**bomba** ['bomba] nf (MIL) bomb; (TEC) pump ♦ (fam) adj: noticia ~ bombshell ♦ (fam) adv: pasarlo ~ to have a great time; ~ atómica/de humo/de retardo atomic/smoke/time bomb; ~ de gasolina petrol pump

**bombardear** [bombarðe'ar] vt to bombard; (MIL) to bomb; **bombardeo** nm bombardment; bombing

**bombardero** [bombar'ðero] nm bomber

**bombear** [bombe'ar] vt (agua) to pump (out o up); (MIL) to bomb; ~se vr to warp

**bombero** [bom'bero] nm fireman

**bombilla** [bom'biʎa] (ESP) nf (light) bulb

**bombín** [bom'bin] nm bowler hat

**bombo** ['bombo] nm (MUS) bass drum; (TEC) drum

**bombón** [bom'bon] nm chocolate

**bombona** [bom'bona] nf (de butano, oxígeno) cylinder

**bonachón, ona** [bona'tʃon, ona] adj good-natured, easy-going

**bonanza** [bo'nanθa] nf (NAUT) fair weather; (fig) bonanza; (MINERÍA) rich pocket o vein

**bondad** [bon'dað] nf goodness, kindness; **tenga la ~ de** (please) be good enough to; **~oso, a** adj good, kind

**bonificación** [bonifika'θjon] nf bonus

**bonito, a** [bo'nito, a] adj pretty; (agradable) nice ♦ nm (atún) tuna (fish)

**bono** ['bono] nm voucher; (FINANZAS) bond

**bonobús** [bono'ßus] (ESP) nm bus pass

**boquerón** [boke'ron] nm (pez) (kind of) anchovy; (agujero) large hole

**boquete** [bo'kete] nm gap, hole

**boquiabierto, a** [bokja'ßjerto, a] adj: **quedar ~** to be amazed o flabbergasted

**boquilla** [bo'kiʎa] nf (para riego) nozzle; (para cigarro) cigarette holder; (MUS) mouthpiece

**borbotón** [borßo'ton] nm: **salir a borbotones** to gush out

**borda** ['borða] nf (NAUT) (ship's) rail; **tirar algo/caerse por la ~** to throw sth/fall overboard

**bordado** [bor'ðaðo] nm embroidery

**bordar** [bor'ðar] vt to embroider

**borde** ['borðe] nm edge, border; (de camino etc) side; (en la costura) hem; **al ~ de** (fig) on the verge o brink of; **ser ~** (ESP: fam) to be a pain (in the neck); **~ar** vt to border

**bordillo** [bor'ðiʎo] nm kerb (BRIT), curb (US)

**bordo** ['borðo] nm (NAUT) side; **a ~ on board**

**borinqueño, a** [borin'keɲo, a] adj, nm/f Puerto Rican

**borla** ['borla] nf (adorno) tassel

**borra** ['borra] nf (pelusa) fluff; (sedimento) sediment

**borrachera** [borra'tʃera] nf (ebriedad) drunkenness; (orgía) spree, binge

**borracho, a** [bo'rratʃo, a] adj drunk ♦ nm/f (que bebe mucho) drunkard, drunk; (temporalmente) drunk, drunk man/woman

**borrador** [borra'ðor] nm (escritura) first draft, rough sketch; (cuaderno)

scribbling pad; (goma) rubber (BRIT), eraser

**borrar** [bo'rrar] vt to erase, rub out

**borrasca** [bo'rraska] nf storm

**borrico, a** [bo'rriko, a] nm/f donkey/she-donkey; (fig) stupid man/woman

**borrón** [bo'rron] nm (mancha) stain

**borroso, a** [bo'rroso, a] adj vague, unclear; (escritura) illegible

**bosque** ['boske] nm wood; (grande) forest

**bosquejar** [boske'xar] vt to sketch; **bosquejo** nm sketch

**bostezar** [boste'θar] vi to yawn; **bostezo** nm yawn

**bota** ['bota] nf (calzado) boot; (saco) leather wine bottle; **~s de agua, ~ de goma** Wellingtons

**botánica** [bo'tanika] nf (ciencia) botany; ver tb **botánico**

**botánico, a** [bo'taniko, a] adj botanical ♦ nm/f botanist

**botar** [bo'tar] vt to throw, hurl; (NAUT) to launch; (fam) to throw out ♦ vi to bounce

**bote** ['bote] nm (salto) bounce; (golpe) thrust; (vasija) tin, can; (embarcación) boat; **de ~ en ~** packed, jammed full; **~ de la basura** (AM) dustbin (BRIT), trashcan (US); **~ salvavidas** lifeboat

**botella** [bo'teʎa] nf bottle; **botellín** nm small bottle

**botica** [bo'tika] nf chemist's (shop) (BRIT), pharmacy; **~rio, a** nm/f chemist (BRIT), pharmacist

**botijo** [bo'tixo] nm (earthenware) jug

**botín** [bo'tin] nm (calzado) half boot; (polaina) spat; (MIL) booty

**botiquín** [boti'kin] nm (armario) medicine cabinet; (portátil) first-aid kit

**botón** [bo'ton] nm button; (BOT) bud; (de florete) tip; **~ de oro** buttercup

**botones** [bo'tones] nm inv bellboy (BRIT), bellhop (US)

**bóveda** ['boßeða] nf (ARQ) vault

**boxeador** [boksea'ðor] nm boxer

**boxear** [bokse'ar] vi to box

**boxeo** [bok'seo] nm boxing

**boya** ['boja] nf (NAUT) buoy; (flotador) float

**boyante** [bo'jante] adj prosperous

**bozal** [bo'θal] nm (de caballo) halter; (de perro) muzzle

**bracear** [braθe'ar] vi (agitar los brazos) to wave one's arms

**bracero** [bra'θero] nm labourer; (en el campo) farmhand

**braga** ['braγa] nf (cuerda) sling, rope; (de bebé) nappy (BRIT), diaper (US); ~s nfpl (de mujer) panties, knickers (BRIT)

**bragueta** [bra'γeta] nf fly, flies pl

**braille** [breil] nm braille

**bramar** [bra'mar] vi to bellow, roar; **bramido** nm bellow, roar

**brasa** ['brasa] nf live o hot coal

**brasero** [bra'sero] nm brazier

**Brasil** [bra'sil] nm: (el) ~ Brazil; **brasileño, a** adj, nm/f Brazilian

**bravata** [bra'βata] nf boast

**braveza** [bra'βeθa] nf (valor) bravery; (ferocidad) ferocity

**bravío, a** [bra'βio, a] adj wild; (feroz) fierce

**bravo, a** ['braβo, a] adj (valiente) brave; (bueno) fine, splendid; (feroz) ferocious; (salvaje) wild; (mar etc) rough, stormy ♦ excl bravo!; **bravura** nf bravery; ferocity; (pey) boast

**braza** ['braθa] nf fathom; **nadar a la ~** to swim the breast-stroke

**brazada** [bra'θaða] nf stroke

**brazado** [bra'θaðo] nm armful

**brazalete** [braθa'lete] nm (pulsera) bracelet; (banda) armband

**brazo** ['braθo] nm arm; (ZOOL) foreleg; (BOT) limb, branch; **luchar a ~ partido** to fight hand-to-hand; **ir cogidos del ~** to walk arm in arm

**brea** ['brea] nf pitch, tar

**brebaje** [bre'βaxe] nm potion

**brecha** ['bretʃa] nf (hoyo, vacío) gap, opening; (MIL, fig) breach

**brega** ['breγa] nf (lucha) struggle; (trabajo) hard work

**breve** ['breβe] adj short, brief ♦ nf

(MUS) breve; ~**dad** nf brevity, shortness

**brezo** ['breθo] nm heather

**bribón, ona** [bri'βon, ona] adj idle, lazy ♦ nm/f (vagabundo) vagabond; (pícaro) rascal, rogue

**bricolaje** [briko'laxe] nm do-it-yourself, DIY

**brida** ['briða] nf bridle, rein; (TEC) clamp; **a toda ~** at top speed

**bridge** [britʃ] nm bridge

**brigada** [bri'γaða] nf (unidad) brigade; (trabajadores) squad, gang ♦ nm = staff-sergeant, sergeant-major

**brillante** [bri'ʃante] adj brilliant ♦ nm diamond

**brillar** [bri'ʃar] vi (tb fig) to shine; (joyas) to sparkle

**brillo** ['briʃo] nm shine; (brillantez) brilliance; (fig) splendour; **sacar ~ a** to polish

**brincar** [brin'kar] vi to skip about, hop about, jump about; **está que brinca** he's hopping mad

**brinco** ['brinko] nm jump, leap

**brindar** [brin'dar] vi: **a o por** to drink (a toast) to ♦ vt to offer, present

**brindis** ['brindis] nm inv toast; (TAUR) (ceremony of) dedication

**brío** ['brio] nm spirit, dash; **brioso, a** adj spirited, dashing

**brisa** ['brisa] nf breeze

**británico, a** [bri'taniko, a] adj British ♦ nm/f Briton, British person

**brizna** ['briθna] nf (de hierba, paja) blade; (de tabaco) leaf

**broca** ['broka] nf (TEC) drill, bit

**brocal** [bro'kal] nm rim

**brocha** ['brotʃa] nf (large) paintbrush; ~ **de afeitar** shaving brush

**broche** ['brotʃe] nm brooch

**broma** ['broma] nf joke; **en** ~ in fun, as a joke; ~ **pesada** practical joke; **bromear** vi to joke

**bromista** [bro'mista] adj fond of joking ♦ nm/f joker, wag

**bronca** ['bronka] nf row; **echar una** ~ **a uno** to tick sb off

**bronce** ['bronθe] nm bronze; ~**ado,**

**a** adj bronze; (por el sol) tanned ♦ nm (sun)tan; (TEC) bronzing

**bronceador** [bronθea'ðor] nm suntan lotion

**broncearse** [bronθe'arse] vr to get a suntan

**bronco, a** ['bronko, a] adj (manera) rude, surly; (voz) harsh

**bronquio** ['bronkjo] nm (ANAT) bronchial tube

**bronquitis** [bron'kitis] nf inv bronchitis

**brotar** [bro'tar] vi (BOT) to sprout; (aguas) to gush (forth); (MED) to break out

**brote** ['brote] nm (BOT) shoot; (MED, fig) outbreak

**bruces** ['bruθes]: de ~ adv: caer o dar de ~ to fall headlong, fall flat

**bruja** ['bruxa] nf witch; **brujería** nf witchcraft

**brujo** ['bruxo] nm wizard, magician

**brújula** ['bruxula] nf compass

**bruma** ['bruma] nf mist; **brumoso, a** adj misty

**bruñir** [bru'ɲir] vt to polish

**brusco, a** ['brusko, a] adj (súbito) sudden; (áspero) brusque

**Bruselas** [bru'selas] n Brussels

**brutal** [bru'tal] adj brutal

**brutalidad** [brutali'ðað] nf brutality

**bruto, a** ['bruto, a] adj (idiota) stupid; (bestial) brutish; (peso) gross; en ~ raw, unworked

**Bs.As.** abr (= Buenos Aires) B.A.

**bucal** [bu'kal] adj oral; por vía ~ orally

**bucear** [buθe'ar] vi to dive ♦ vt to explore; **buceo** nm diving; (fig) investigation

**bucle** ['bukle] nm curl

**budismo** [bu'ðismo] nm Buddhism

**buen** [bwen] adj ver **bueno**

**buenamente** [bwena'mente] adv (fácilmente) easily; (voluntariamente) willingly

**buenaventura** [bwenaβen'tura] nf (suerte) good luck; (adivinación) fortune

**bueno, a** ['bweno, a] (antes de nmsg: **buen**) adj **1** (excelente etc) good; es un libro ~ o es un buen libro it's a good book; hace ~, hace buen tiempo the weather is fine, it is fine; el ~ de Paco good old Paco; fue muy ~ conmigo he was very nice o kind to me

**2** (apropiado): ser ~ para to be good for; creo que vamos por buen camino I think we're on the right track

**3** (irónico): le di un buen rapapolvo I gave him a good o real ticking off; ¡buen conductor estás hecho! some o a fine driver you are!; ¡estaría ~ que ...! a fine thing it would be if ...!

**4** (atractivo, sabroso): está ~ este bizcocho this sponge is delicious; Carmen está muy buena Carmen is looking good

**5** (saludos): ¡buen día!, ¡~s días! (good) morning!; ¡buenas (tardes)! (good) afternoon!; (más tarde) (good) evening!; ¡buenas noches! good night!

**6** (otras locuciones): estar de buenas to be in a good mood; por las buenas o por las malas by hook or by crook; de buenas a primeras all of a sudden

♦ excl: ¡~! all right!; ~, ¿y qué? well, so what?

**Buenos Aires** nm Buenos Aires

**buey** [bwei] nm ox

**búfalo** ['bufalo] nm buffalo

**bufanda** [bu'fanda] nf scarf

**bufar** [bu'far] vi to snort

**bufete** [bu'fete] nm (despacho de abogado) lawyer's office

**buffer** ['bufer] nm (INFORM) buffer

**bufón** [bu'fon, ona] nm clown

**buhardilla** [buar'ðiʎa] nf (desván) attic

**búho** ['buo] nm owl; (fig) hermit, recluse

**buhonero** [buo'nero] *nm* pedlar

**buitre** ['bwitre] *nm* vulture

**bujía** [bu'xia] *nf* (*vela*) candle; (*ELEC*) candle (power); (*AUTO*) spark plug

**bula** ['bula] *nf* (papal) bull

**bulbo** ['bulβo] *nm* bulb

**bulevar** [bule'βar] *nm* boulevard

**Bulgaria** [bul'xarja] *nf* Bulgaria; **búlgaro, a** *adj*, *nm/f* Bulgarian

**bulto** ['bulto] *nm* (*paquete*) package; (*fardo*) bundle; (*tamaño*) size, bulkiness; (*MED*) swelling, lump; (*silueta*) vague shape; (*estatua*) bust, statue

**bulla** ['buʎa] *nf* (*ruido*) uproar; (*de gente*) crowd

**bullicio** [bu'ʎiθjo] *nm* (*ruido*) uproar; (*movimiento*) bustle

**bullir** [bu'ʎir] *vi* (*hervir*) to boil; (*burbujear*) to bubble; (*mover*) to move, stir

**buñuelo** [bu'ɲwelo] *nm* ≈ doughnut (*BRIT*), ≈ donut (*US*); (*fruta de sartén*) fritter

**BUP** [bup] *nm abr* (*ESP*: = *Bachillerato Unificado Polivalente*) *secondary education and leaving certificate for 14-17 age group*

**buque** ['buke] *nm* ship, vessel

**burbuja** [bur'βuxa] *nf* bubble; **burbujear** *vi* to bubble

**burdel** [bur'ðel] *nm* brothel

**burdo, a** ['burðo, a] *adj* coarse, rough

**burgués, esa** [bur'xes, esa] *adj* middle-class, bourgeois; **burguesía** *nf* middle class, bourgeoisie

**burla** ['burla] *nf* (*mofa*) gibe; (*broma*) joke; (*engaño*) trick

**burladero** [burla'ðero] *nm* (bullfighter's) refuge

**burlar** [bur'lar] *vt* (*engañar*) to deceive; (*seducir*) to seduce ♦ *vi* to joke; **~se** *vr* to joke; **~se de** to make fun of

**burlesco, a** [bur'lesko, a] *adj* burlesque

**burlón, ona** [bur'lon, ona] *adj* mocking

**burocracia** [buro'kraθja] *nf* civil service; (*pey*) bureaucracy

**burócrata** [bu'rokrata] *nm/f* civil servant; (*pey*) bureaucrat

**burrada** [bu'rraða] *nf*: **decir/soltar ~s** to talk nonsense; **hacer ~s** to act stupid; **una ~ a** (hell of a) lot

**burro, a** ['burro, a] *nm/f* donkey/she-donkey; (*fig*) ass, idiot

**bursátil** [bur'satil] *adj* stock-exchange *cpd*

**bus** [bus] *nm* bus

**busca** ['buska] *nf* search, hunt ♦ *nm* (*TEL*) bleeper; **en ~ de** in search of

**buscar** [bus'kar] *vt* to look for, search for, seek ♦ *vi* to look, search, seek; **busca secretaria** secretary wanted

**busque** *etc vb ver* **buscar**

**búsqueda** ['buskeða] *nf* = **busca** *nf*

**busto** ['busto] *nm* (*ANAT*, *ARTE*) bust

**butaca** [bu'taka] *nf* armchair; (*de cine, teatro*) stall, seat

**butano** [bu'tano] *nm* butane (gas)

**buzo** ['buθo] *nm* diver

**buzón** [bu'θon] *nm* (*en puerta*) letter box; (*en la calle*) pillar box

# C

**C.** *abr* (= *centígrado*) C; (= *compañía*) Co.

**c.** *abr* (= *capítulo*) c.

**C/** *abr* (= *calle*) St

**c.a.** *abr* (= *corriente alterna*) AC

**cabal** [ka'βal] *adj* (*exacto*) exact; (*correcto*) right, proper; (*acabado*) finished, complete; **~es** *nmpl*: **estar en sus ~es** to be in one's right mind

**cábalas** ['kaβalas] *nfpl* to guess

**cabalgar** [kaβal'xar] *vt*, *vi* to ride

**cabalgata** [kaβal'yata] *nf* procession

**caballa** [ka'βaʎa] *nf* mackerel

**caballeresco, a** [kaβaʎe'resko, a] *adj* noble, chivalrous

**caballería** [kaβaʎe'ria] *nf* mount; (*MIL*) cavalry

**caballeriza** [kaβaˈʎeˈriθa] nf stable; **caballerizo** nm groom, stableman

**caballero** [kaβaˈʎero] nm (hombre galante) gentleman; (de la orden de caballería) knight; (trato directo) sir

**caballerosidad** [kaβaʎerosiˈðað] nf chivalry

**caballete** [kaβaˈʎete] nm (ARTE) easel; (TEC) trestle

**caballito** [kaβaˈʎito] nm (caballo pequeño) small horse, pony; ~s nmpl (en verbena) roundabout, merry-go-round

**caballo** [kaˈβaʎo] nm horse; (AJEDREZ) knight; (NAIPES) queen; en ~ to ride; ~ de vapor o de fuerza horsepower; ~ de carreras racehorse

**cabaña** [kaˈβaɲa] nf (casita) hut, cabin

**cabaré** [kaβaˈre] (pl ~s) nm cabaret

**cabaret** [kaβaˈre] (pl ~s) nm cabaret

**cabecear** [kaβeθeˈar] vt, vi to nod

**cabecera** [kaβeˈθera] nf head; (de distrito) chief town; (IMPRENTA) headline

**cabecilla** [kaβeˈθiʎa] nm ringleader

**cabellera** [kaβeˈʎera] nf (head of) hair; (de cometa) tail

**cabello** [kaˈβeʎo] nm (tb: ~s) hair

**caber** [kaˈβer] vi (entrar) to fit, go; **caben** 3 más there's room for 3 more

**cabestrillo** [kaβesˈtriʎo] nm sling

**cabestro** [kaˈβestro] nm halter

**cabeza** [kaˈβeθa] nf head; (POL) chief, leader; ~da nf (golpe) butt; dar ~das to nod off; **cabezón, ona** adj heady; (fam: persona) pig-headed

**cabida** [kaˈβiða] nf space

**cabildo** [kaˈβildo] nm (de iglesia) chapter; (POL) town council

**cabina** [kaˈβina] nf cabin; (de camión) cab; ~ telefónica telephone box (BRIT) o booth

**cabizbajo, a** [kaβiθˈβaxo, a] adj crestfallen, dejected

**cable** [ˈkaβle] nm cable

**cabo** [ˈkaβo] nm (de objeto) end, extremity; (MIL) corporal; (NAUT) rope, cable; (GEO) cape; al ~ de 3 días after 3 days

**cabra** [ˈkaβra] nf goat

**cabré** etc vb ver **caber**

**cabrear** [kaβreˈar] (fam) vt to bug; ~se vr (enfadarse) to fly off the handle

**cabrío, a** [kaˈβrio, a] adj goatish; **macho** ~ (he-)goat, billy goat

**cabriola** [kaˈβrjola] nf caper

**cabritilla** [kaβriˈtiʎa] nf kid, kidskin

**cabrito** [kaˈβrito] nm kid

**cabrón** [kaˈβron] nm cuckold; (fam!) bastard (!)

**caca** [ˈkaka] (fam) nf shit; (usado para/por niños) pooh

**cacahuete** [kakaˈwete] (ESP) nm peanut

**cacao** [kaˈkao] nm cocoa; (BOT) cacao

**cacarear** [kakareˈar] vi (persona) to boast; (gallina) to crow

**cacería** [kaθeˈria] nf hunt

**cacerola** [kaθeˈrola] nf pan, saucepan

**cacique** [kaˈθike] nm chief, local ruler; (POL) local party boss; **caciquismo** nm system of control by the local boss

**caco** [ˈkako] nm pickpocket

**cacto** [ˈkakto] nm cactus

**cactus** [ˈkaktus] nm inv cactus

**cachalote** [katʃaˈlote] nm (ZOOL) sperm whale

**cacharro** [kaˈtʃarro] nm earthenware pot; ~s nmpl pots and pans

**cachear** [katʃeˈar] vt to search, frisk

**cachemir** [katʃeˈmir] nm cashmere

**cacheo** [kaˈtʃeo] nm searching, frisking

**cachete** [kaˈtʃete] nm (ANAT) cheek; (bofetada) slap (in the face)

**cachiporra** [katʃiˈporra] nf truncheon

**cachivache** [katʃiˈβatʃe] nm (trasto) piece of junk; ~s nmpl junk sg

**cacho** [ˈkatʃo, a] nm (small) bit; (AM: cuerno) horn

**cachondeo** [katʃonˈdeo] (fam) nm farce, joke

**cachondo, a** [ka'tʃondo, a] adj (ZOOL) on heat; (fam) sexy; (gracioso) funny

**cachorro, a** [ka'tʃorro, a] nm/f (perro) pup, puppy; (león) cub

**cada** ['kaða] adj inv each; (antes de número) every; ~ día each day, every day; ~ **dos días** every other day; ~ **uno/a** each one, every one; ~ **vez más/menos** more and more/less and less; **uno de ~ diez** one out of every ten

**cadalso** [ka'ðalso] nm scaffold

**cadáver** [ka'ðaßer] nm (dead) body, corpse

**cadena** [ka'ðena] nf chain; (TV) channel; **trabajo en ~** assembly line work; ~ **perpetua** (JUR) life imprisonment

**cadencia** [ka'ðenθja] nf rhythm

**cadera** [ka'ðera] nf hip

**cadete** [ka'ðete] nm cadet

**caducar** [kaðu'kar] vi to expire; **caduco, a** adj expired; (persona) very old

**C.A.E.** abr (= cóbrese al entregar) C.O.D.

**caer** [ka'er] vi to fall (down); ~**se** vr to fall (down); **me cae bien/mal** I get on well with him/I can't stand him; ~ **en la cuenta** to catch on; **su cumpleaños cae en viernes** his birthday falls on a Friday

**café** [ka'fe] (pl ~s) nm (bebida, planta) coffee; (lugar) café ♦ adj (color) brown; ~ **con leche** white coffee; ~ **solo** black coffee

**cafetera** [kafe'tera] nf coffee pot

**cafetería** [kafete'ria] nf (gen) café

**cafetero, a** [kafe'tero, a] adj coffee cpd; **ser muy** ~ to be a coffee addict

**cagar** [ka'ɣar] (fam!) vt to shit (!); **to bungle, mess up** ♦ vi to have a shit (!)

**caída** [ka'iða] nf (gen) fall; (declive) slope; (disminución) fall, drop

**caído, a** [ka'iðo, a] adj drooping

**caiga** etc vb ver **caer**

**caimán** [kai'man] nm alligator

**caja** ['kaxa] nf box; (para reloj) case; (de ascensor) shaft; (COM) cashbox; (donde se hacen los pagos) cashdesk; (: en supermercado) checkout, till; ~ **de ahorros** savings bank; ~ **de cambios** gearbox; ~ **fuerte**, ~ **de caudales** safe, strongbox

**cajero, a** [ka'xero, a] nm/f cashier; ~ **automático** cash dispenser

**cajetilla** [kaxe'tiʎa] nf (de cigarrillos) packet

**cajón** [ka'xon] nm big box; (de mueble) drawer

**cal** [kal] nf lime

**cala** ['kala] nf (GEO) cove, inlet; (de barco) hold

**calabacín** [kalaßa'θin] nm (BOT) baby marrow; (: más pequeño) courgette (BRIT), zucchini (US)

**calabaza** [kala'ßaθa] nf (BOT) pumpkin

**calabozo** [kala'ßoθo] nm (cárcel) prison; (celda) cell

**calada** [ka'laða] nf (de cigarrillo) puff

**calado, a** [ka'laðo, a] adj (prenda) lace cpd ♦ nm (NAUT) draught

**calamar** [kala'mar] nm squid no pl

**calambre** [ka'lambre] nm (tb: ~s) cramp

**calamidad** [kalami'ðað] nf calamity, disaster

**calar** [ka'lar] vt to soak, drench; (penetrar) to pierce, penetrate; (comprender) to see through; (vela) to lower; ~**se** vr (AUTO) to stall; ~**se las gafas** to stick one's glasses on

**calavera** [kala'ßera] nf skull

**calcañal** [kalka'ɲal] nm = **calcañar**

**calcañar** [kalka'ɲar] nm heel

**calcaño** [kal'kaɲo] nm = **calcañar**

**calcar** [kal'kar] vt (reproducir) to trace; (imitar) to copy

**calcetín** [kalθe'tin] nm sock

**calcinar** [kalθi'nar] vt to burn, blacken

**calcio** ['kalθjo] nm calcium

**calco** ['kalko] nm tracing

**calcomanía** [kalkoma'nia] nf transfer

**calculador, a** [kalkula'ðor, a] *adj (persona)* calculating

**calculadora** [kalkula'ðora] *nf* calculator

**calcular** [kalku'lar] *vt (MAT)* to calculate, compute; ~ **que** ... to reckon that ...; **cálculo** *nm* calculation

**caldear** [kalde'ar] *vt* to warm (up), heat (up)

**caldera** [kal'dera] *nf* boiler

**calderilla** [kalde'riʎa] *nf (moneda)* small change

**caldero** [kal'dero] *nm* small boiler

**caldo** ['kaldo] *nm* stock; *(consomé)* consommé

**calefacción** [kalefak'θjon] *nf* heating; ~ **central** central heating

**calendario** [kalen'darjo] *nm* calendar

**calentador** [kalenta'ðor] *nm* heater

**calentamiento** [kalenta'mjento] *nm (DEPORTE)* warm-up

**calentar** [kalen'tar] *vt* to heat (up); ~**se** *vr* to heat up, warm up; *(fig: discusión etc)* to get heated

**calentura** [kalen'tura] *nf (MED)* fever, (high) temperature

**calibrar** [kali'βrar] *vt* to gauge, measure; **calibre** *nm (de cañón)* calibre, bore; *(diámetro)* diameter; *(fig)* calibre

**calidad** [kali'ðað] *nf* quality; **de ~** quality *cpd*; **en ~ de** in the capacity of, as

**cálido, a** ['kaliðo, a] *adj* hot; *(fig)* warm

**caliente** *etc* [ka'ljente] *vb ver* **calentar** ♦ *adj* hot; *(fig)* fiery; *(disputa)* heated; *(fam: cachondo)* randy

**calificación** [kalifika'θjon] *nf* qualification; *(de alumno)* grade, mark

**calificar** [kalifi'kar] *vt* to qualify; *(alumno)* to grade, mark; ~ **de** to describe as

**calima** [ka'lima] *nf (cerca del mar)* mist

**cáliz** [ka'liθ] *nm* chalice

**caliza** [ka'liθa] *nf* limestone

**calizo, a** [ka'liθo, a] *adj* lime *cpd*

**calma** ['kalma] *nf* calm; *(pachorra)* slowness

**calmante** [kal'mante] *nm* sedative, tranquillizer

**calmar** [kal'mar] *vt* to calm, calm down ♦ *vi (tempestad)* to abate; *(mente etc)* to become calm

**calmoso, a** [kal'moso, a] *adj* calm, quiet

**calor** [ka'lor] *nm* heat; *(~ agradable)* warmth; **hace ~** it's hot; **tener ~** to be hot

**caloría** [kalo'ria] *nf* calorie

**calumnia** [ka'lumnja] *nf* calumny, slander; **calumnioso, a** *adj* slanderous

**caluroso, a** [kalu'roso, a] *adj* hot; *(sin exceso)* warm; *(fig)* enthusiastic

**calva** ['kalβa] *nf* bald patch; *(en bosque)* clearing

**calvario** [kal'βarjo] *nm* stations *pl* of the cross

**calvicie** [kal'βiθje] *nf* baldness

**calvo, a** ['kalβo, a] *adj* bald; *(terreno)* bare, barren; *(tejido)* threadbare

**calza** ['kalθa] *nf* wedge, chock

**calzada** [kal'θaða] *nf* roadway, highway

**calzado, a** [kal'θaðo, a] *adj* shod ♦ *nm* footwear

**calzador** [kalθa'ðor] *nm* shoehorn

**calzar** [kal'θar] *vt (zapatos etc)* to wear; *(un mueble)* to put a wedge under; ~**se** *vr*: ~**se los zapatos** to put on one's shoes; **¿qué (número) calza?** what size do you take?

**calzón** [kal'θon] *nm (tb: calzones nmpl)* shorts; *(AM: de hombre)* pants; *(: de mujer)* panties

**calzoncillos** [kalθon'θiʎos] *nmpl* underpants

**callado, a** [ka'ʎaðo, a] *adj* quiet

**callar** [ka'ʎar] *vt (asunto delicado)* to keep quiet about, say nothing about; *(persona, opinión)* to silence ♦ *vi* to keep quiet, be silent; ~**se** *vr* to keep quiet, be silent; **¡cállate!** be quiet!, shut up!

**calle** ['kaʎe] *nf* street; *(DEPORTE)* lane; ~ **arriba/abajo** up/down the street; ~ **de un solo sentido** one-way street

**calleja** [ka'λexa] *nf* alley, narrow street; **callejear** *vi* to wander (about) the streets; **callejero, a** *adj* street *cpd* ♦ *nm* street map; **callejón** *nm* alley, passage; **callejón sin salida** cul-de-sac; **callejuela** *nf* side-street, alley

**callista** [ka'λista] *nm/f* chiropodist

**callo** ['kaλo] *nm* callus; (*en el pie*) corn; ~s *nmpl* (*CULIN*) tripe *sg*; ~**so, a** *adj* horny, rough

**cama** ['kama] *nf* bed; (*GEO*) stratum; ~ **individual/de matrimonio** single/double bed

**camada** [ka'maða] *nf* litter; (*de personas*) gang, band

**camafeo** [kama'feo] *nm* cameo

**camaleón** [kamale'on] *nm* (*ZOOL*) chameleon

**cámara** ['kamara] *nf* chamber; (*habitación*) room; (*sala*) hall; (*CINE*) cine camera; (*fotográfica*) camera; ~ **de aire** inner tube; ~ **de comercio** chamber of commerce; ~ **frigorífica** cold-storage room

**camarada** [kama'raða] *nm* comrade, companion

**camarera** [kama'rera] *nf* (*en restaurante*) waitress; (*en casa, hotel*) maid

**camarero** [kama'rero] *nm* waiter

**camarilla** [kama'riλa] *nf* (*clan*) clique; (*POL*) lobby

**camarón** [kama'ron] *nm* shrimp

**camarote** [kama'rote] *nm* cabin

**cambiable** [kam'bjaβle] *adj* (*variable*) changeable, variable; (*intercambiable*) interchangeable

**cambiante** [kam'bjante] *adj* variable

**cambiar** [kam'bjar] *vt* to change; (*dinero*) to exchange ♦ *vi* to change; ~**se** *vr* (*mudarse*) to move; (*de ropa*) to change; ~ **de idea** to change one's mind; ~ **de ropa** to change (one's clothes)

**cambiazo** [kam'bjaθo] *nm*: **dar el** ~ **a uno** to swindle sb

**cambio** ['kambjo] *nm* change; (*trueque*) exchange; (*COM*) rate of ex-

change; (*oficina*) bureau de change; (*dinero menudo*) small change; **en** ~ on the other hand; (*en lugar de*) instead; ~ **de divisas** foreign exchange; ~ **de velocidades** gear lever; ~ **de vía** points *pl*

**camelar** [kame'lar] *vt* (*con mujer*) to flirt with; (*persuadir*) to cajole

**camello** [ka'meλo] *nm* camel; (*fam: traficante*) pusher

**camerino** [kame'rino] *nm* (*TEATRO*) dressing room

**camilla** [ka'miλa] *nf* (*MED*) stretcher

**caminante** [kami'nante] *nm/f* traveller

**caminar** [kami'nar] *vi* (*marchar*) to walk, go; (*viajar*) to travel, journey ♦ *vt* (*recorrer*) to cover, travel

**caminata** [kami'nata] *nf* long walk; (*por el campo*) hike

**camino** [ka'mino] *nm* way, road; (*sendero*) track; **a medio** ~ halfway (there); **en el** ~ on the way, en route; ~ **de** on the way to; ~ **particular** private road

**camión** [ka'mjon] *nm* lorry (*BRIT*), truck (*US*); (: *cisterna* tanker; **camionero, a** *nm/f* lorry or truck driver

**camioneta** [kamjo'neta] *nf* van, light truck

**camisa** [ka'misa] *nf* shirt; (*BOT*) skin; ~ **de fuerza** straitjacket; **camisería** *nf* outfitter's (shop)

**camiseta** [kami'seta] *nf* (*prenda*) tee-shirt; (: *ropa interior*) vest; (*de deportista*) top

**camisón** [kami'son] *nm* nightdress, nightgown

**camorra** [ka'morra] *nf*: **armar** ~ or **buscar** ~ to look for trouble, kick up a fuss

**campamento** [kampa'mento] *nm* camp

**campana** [kam'pana] *nf* bell; ~ **de cristal** bell jar; ~**da** *nf* peal; ~**rio** *nm* belfry

**campanilla** [kampa'niλa] *nf* small

bell

**campaña** [kam'paɲa] *nf* (MIL, POL) campaign

**campechano, a** [kampe'tʃano, a] *adj* (franco) open

**campeón, ona** [kampe'on, ona] *nm/f* champion; **campeonato** *nm* championship

**campesino, a** [kampe'sino, a] *adj* country *cpd*, rural; (gente) peasant *cpd* ♦ *nm/f* countryman/woman; (agricultor) farmer

**campestre** [kam'pestre] *adj* country *cpd*, rural

**camping** ['kampin] (pl ~s) *nm* camping; (lugar) campsite; **ir de** o **hacer** ~ to go camping

**campo** ['kampo] *nm* (fuera de la ciudad) country, countryside; (AGR, ELEC) field; (de fútbol) pitch; (de golf) course; (MIL) camp; ~ **de batalla** battlefield; ~ **de deportes** sports ground, playing field

**camposanto** [kampo'santo] *nm* cemetery

**camuflaje** [kamu'flaxe] *nm* camouflage

**cana** ['kana] *nf* white o grey hair; **tener** ~**s** to be going grey

**Canadá** [kana'ða] *nm* Canada; **canadiense** *adj*, *nm/f* Canadian ♦ *nf* furlined jacket

**canal** [ka'nal] *nm* canal; (GEO) channel, strait; (de televisión) channel; (de tejado) gutter; ~ **de Panamá** Panama Canal; ~**izar** *vt* to channel

**canalón** [kana'lon] *nm* (conducto vertical) drainpipe; (del tejado) gutter

**canalla** [ka'naʎa] *nf* rabble, mob ♦ *nm* swine

**canapé** [kana'pe] (pl ~s) *nm* sofa, settee; (CULIN) canapé

**Canarias** [ka'narjas] *nfpl*: (las Islas) ~ the Canary Islands, the Canaries

**canario, a** [ka'narjo, a] *adj*, *nm/f* (native) of the Canary Isles ♦ *nm* (ZOOL) canary

**canasta** [ka'nasta] *nf* (round) basket; **canastilla** *nf* small basket; (de niño) layette

**canasto** [ka'nasto] *nm* large basket

**cancela** [kan'θela] *nf* gate

**cancelación** [kanθela'θjon] *nf* cancellation

**cancelar** [kanθe'lar] *vt* to cancel; (una deuda) to write off

**cáncer** ['kanθer] *nm* (MED) cancer; (ASTROLOGÍA): **C~** Cancer

**canciller** [kanθi'ʎer] *nm* chancellor

**canción** [kan'θjon] *nf* song; ~ **de cuna** lullaby; **cancionero** *nm* song book

**cancha** ['kantʃa] *nf* (de baloncesto, tenis etc) court; (AM: de fútbol) pitch

**candado** [kan'daðo] *nm* padlock

**candente** [kan'dente] *adj* red-hot; (fig: tema) burning

**candidato, a** [kandi'ðato, a] *nm/f* candidate

**candidez** [kandi'ðeθ] *nf* (sencillez) simplicity; (simpleza) naïveté; **cándido, a** *adj* simple; naive

**candil** [kan'dil] *nm* oil lamp; ~**ejas** *nfpl* (TEATRO) footlights

**candor** [kan'dor] *nm* (sinceridad) frankness; (inocencia) innocence

**canela** [ka'nela] *nf* cinnamon

**cangrejo** [kan'grexo] *nm* crab

**canguro** [kan'guro] *nm* kangaroo; **hacer de** ~ to babysit

**caníbal** [ka'niβal] *adj*, *nm/f* cannibal

**canica** [ka'nika] *nf* marble

**canijo, a** [ka'nixo, a] *adj* frail, sickly

**canino, a** [ka'nino, a] *adj* canine ♦ *nm* canine (tooth)

**canjear** [kanxe'ar] *vt* to exchange

**cano, a** ['kano, a] *adj* grey-haired, white-haired

**canoa** [ka'noa] *nf* canoe

**canon** ['kanon] *nm* canon; (pensión) rent; (COM) tax

**canónigo** [ka'noniχo] *nm* canon

**canonizar** [kanoni'θar] *vt* to canonize

**canoso, a** [ka'noso, a] *adj* grey-haired

**cansado, a** [kan'saðo, a] *adj* tired, weary; *(tedioso)* tedious, boring
**cansancio** [kan'sanθjo] *nm* tiredness, fatigue
**cansar** [kan'sar] *vt (fatigar)* to tire, tire out; *(aburrir)* to bore; *(fastidiar)* to bother; ~**se** *vr* to tire, get tired; *(aburrirse)* to get bored
**cantábrico, a** [kan'taβriko, a] *adj* Cantabrian; **mar** C~ Bay of Biscay
**cantante** [kan'tante] *adj* singing ♦ *nm/f* singer
**cantar** [kan'tar] *vt* to sing ♦ *vi* to sing; *(insecto)* to chirp; *(rechinar)* to squeak ♦ *nm (acción)* singing; *(canción)* song; *(poema)* poem
**cántara** [kantara] *nf* large pitcher
**cántaro** ['kantaro] *nm* pitcher, jug; **llover a** ~**s** to rain cats and dogs
**cante** ['kante] *nm*: ~ **jondo** flamenco singing
**cantera** [kan'tera] *nf* quarry
**cantidad** [kanti'ðað] *nf* quantity, amount
**cantilena** [kanti'lena] *nf* = **cantinela**
**cantimplora** [kantim'plora] *nf (frasco)* water bottle, canteen
**cantina** [kan'tina] *nf* canteen; *(de estación)* buffet
**cantinela** [kanti'nela] *nf* ballad, song
**canto** ['kanto] *nm* singing; *(canción)* song; *(borde)* edge, rim; *(de un cuchillo)* back; ~ **rodado** boulder
**cantor, a** [kan'tor, a] *nm/f* singer
**canturrear** [kanture'ar] *vi* to sing softly
**canuto** [ka'nuto] *nm (tubo)* small tube; *(fam: droga)* joint
**caña** ['kaɲa] *nf (BOT: tallo)* stem, stalk; *(carrizo)* reed; *(vaso)* tumbler; *(de cerveza)* glass of beer; *(ANAT)* shinbone; ~ **de azúcar** sugar cane; ~ **de pescar** fishing rod
**cañada** [ka'ɲaða] *nf (entre dos montañas)* gully, ravine; *(camino)* cattle track
**cáñamo** ['kaɲamo] *nm* hemp
**cañería** [kaɲe'ria] *nf (tubo)* pipe
**caño** ['kaɲo] *nm (tubo)* tube, pipe; *(de albañal)* sewer; *(MUS)* pipe; *(de* fuente) jet
**cañón** [ka'ɲon] *nm (MIL)* cannon; *(de fusil)* barrel; *(GEO)* canyon, gorge
**caoba** [ka'oβa] *nf* mahogany
**caos** ['kaos] *nm* chaos
**cap.** *abr* (= *capítulo*) ch
**capa** [ka'pa] *nf* cloak, cape; *(GEO)* layer, stratum; **so** ~ **de** under the pretext of; ~ **de ozono** ozone layer
**capacidad** [kapaθi'ðað] *nf (medida)* capacity; *(aptitud)* capacity, ability
**capacitar** [kapaθi'tar] *vt*: ~ **a algn para (hacer)** to enable sb to (do)
**capar** [ka'par] *vt* to castrate, geld
**caparazón** [kapara'θon] *nm* shell
**capataz** [kapa'taθ] *nm* foreman
**capaz** [ka'paθ] *adj* able, capable; *(amplio)* capacious, roomy
**capcioso, a** [kap'θjoso, a] *adj* wily, deceitful
**capellán** [kape'ʎan] *nm* chaplain; *(sacerdote)* priest
**caperuza** [kape'ruθa] *nf* hood
**capicúa** [kapi'kua] *adj inv (número, fecha)* reversible
**capilla** [ka'piʎa] *nf* chapel
**capital** [kapi'tal] *adj* capital ♦ *nm (COM)* capital ♦ *nf (ciudad)* capital; ~ **social** share capital
**capitalismo** [kapita'lismo] *nm* capitalism; **capitalista** *adj, nm/f* capitalist
**capitán** [kapi'tan] *nm* captain
**capitanear** [kapitane'ar] *vt* to captain
**capitulación** [kapitula'θjon] *nf (rendición)* capitulation, surrender; *(acuerdo)* agreement, pact; **capitulaciones (matrimoniales)** *nfpl* marriage contract *sg*
**capitular** [kapitu'lar] *vi* to come to terms, make an agreement
**capítulo** [ka'pitulo] *nm* chapter
**capó** [ka'po] *nm (AUTO)* bonnet
**capón** [ka'pon] *nm (gallo)* capon
**capota** [ka'pota] *nf (de mujer)* bonnet; *(AUTO)* hood *(BRIT)*, top *(US)*
**capote** [ka'pote] *nm (abrigo: de militar)* greatcoat; *(: de torero)* cloak

**Capricornio** [kapri'kornjo] *nm* Capricorn

**capricho** [ka'pritʃo] *nm* whim, caprice; **~so, a** *adj* capricious

**cápsula** ['kapsula] *nf* capsule

**captar** [kap'tar] *vt* (*comprender*) to understand; (*RADIO*) to pick up; (*atención, apoyo*) to attract

**captura** [kap'tura] *nf* capture; (*JUR*) arrest; **capturar** *vt* to capture; to arrest

**capucha** [ka'putʃa] *nf* hood, cowl

**capullo** [ka'puʎo] *nm* (*BOT*) bud; (*ZOOL*) cocoon; (*fam*) idiot

**caqui** ['kaki] *nm* khaki

**cara** ['kara] *nf* (*ANAT, de moneda*) face; (*aspecto*) appearance; (*de disco*) side; (*fig*) boldness; **~ a** facing; **de ~** opposite, facing; **dar la ~** to face the consequences; **¿~ o cruz?** heads or tails?; **¡qué ~ (más dura)!** what a nerve!

**carabina** [kara'βina] *nf* carbine, rifle; (*persona*) chaperone

**Caracas** [ka'rakas] *n* Caracas

**caracol** [kara'kol] *nm* (*ZOOL*) snail; (*concha*) (sea) shell

**carácter** [ka'rakter] (*pl* **caracteres**) *nm* character; **tener buen/mal ~** to be good natured/bad tempered

**característica** [karakte'ristika] *nf* characteristic

**característico, a** [karakte'ristiko, a] *adj* characteristic

**caracterizar** [karakteri'θar] *vt* (*distinguir*) to characterize, typify; (*honrar*) to confer (a) distinction on

**caradura** [kara'ðura] *nm/f*: **es un ~** he's got a nerve

**carajillo** [kara'xiʎo] *nm* coffee with a dash of brandy

**carajo** [ka'raxo] (*fam!*) *nm*: **¡~!** shit! (*!*)

**caramba** [ka'ramba] *excl* good gracious!

**carámbano** [ka'rambano] *nm* icicle

**caramelo** [kara'melo] *nm* (*dulce*) sweet; (*azúcar fundida*) caramel

**caravana** [kara'βana] *nf* caravan; (*fig*) group; (*AUTO*) tailback

**carbón** [kar'βon] *nm* coal; **papel ~** carbon paper; **carboncillo** *nm* (*ARTE*) charcoal; **carbonero, a** *nm/f* coal merchant; **carbonilla** [-'niʎa] *nf* coal dust

**carbonizar** [karβoni'θar] *vt* to carbonize; (*quemar*) to char

**carbono** [kar'βono] *nm* carbon

**carburador** [karβura'ðor] *nm* carburettor

**carburante** [karβu'rante] *nm* (*para motor*) fuel

**carcajada** [karka'xaða] *nf* (loud) laugh, guffaw

**cárcel** ['karθel] *nf* prison, jail; (*TEC*) clamp; **carcelero, a** *adj* prison *cpd* ♦ *nm/f* warder

**carcoma** [kar'koma] *nf* woodworm

**carcomer** [karko'mer] *vt* to bore into, eat into; (*fig*) to undermine; **~se** *vr* to become worm-eaten; (*fig*) to decay

**cardar** [kar'ðar] *vt* (*pelo*) to backcomb

**cardenal** [karðe'nal] *nm* (*REL*) cardinal; (*MED*) bruise

**cardíaco, a** [kar'ðiako, a] *adj* cardiac, heart *cpd*

**cardinal** [karði'nal] *adj* cardinal

**cardo** ['karðo] *nm* thistle

**carearse** [kare'arse] *vr* to come face to face, meet

**carecer** [kare'θer] *vi*: **~ de** to lack, be in need of

**carencia** [ka'renθja] *nf* lack; (*escasez*) shortage; (*MED*) deficiency

**carente** [ka'rente] *adj*: **~ de** lacking in, devoid of

**carestía** [kares'tia] *nf* (*escasez*) scarcity, shortage; (*COM*) high cost

**careta** [ka'reta] *nf* mask

**carga** ['karxa] *nf* (*peso, ELEC*) load; (*de barco*) cargo, freight; (*MIL*) charge; (*obligación, responsabilidad*) duty, obligation

**cargado, a** [kar'xaðo, a] *adj* loaded; (*ELEC*) live; (*café, té*) strong; (*cielo*) overcast

**cargamento** [karxa'mento] *nm* (*acción*) loading; (*mercancías*) load, cargo

**cargar** [kar'ɣar] vt (barco, arma) to load; (ELEC) to charge; (COM: algo en cuenta) to charge; (INFORM) to load ♦ vi (MIL: enemigo) to charge; (AUTO) to load up; (inclinarse) to lean; ~ **con** to pick up, carry away; (peso, fig) to shoulder, bear; **~se** (fam) vr (estropear) to break; (matar) to bump off

**cargo** ['karɣo] nm (puesto) post, office; (responsabilidad) duty, obligation; (fig) weight, burden; (JUR) charge; **hacerse ~ de** to take charge of o responsibility for

**carguero** [kar'ɣero] nm freighter, cargo boat; (avión) freight plane

**Caribe** [ka'riβe] nm: **el ~** the Caribbean; **del ~** Caribbean

**caribeño, a** [kari'βeɲo, a] adj Caribbean

**caricatura** [karika'tura] nf caricature

**caricia** [ka'riθja] nf caress

**caridad** [kari'ðað] nf charity

**caries** ['karjes] nf inv (MED) tooth decay

**cariño** [ka'riɲo] nm affection, love; (caricia) caress; (en carta) love ...; **tener ~ a** to be fond of; **~so, a** adj affectionate

**carisma** [ka'risma] nm charisma

**caritativo, a** [karita'tiβo, a] adj charitable

**cariz** [ka'riθ] nm: **tener** o **tomar buen/mal ~** to look good/bad

**carmesí** [karme'si] adj, nm crimson

**carmín** [kar'min] nm lipstick

**carnal** [kar'nal] adj carnal; **primo ~** first cousin

**carnaval** [karna'βal] nm carnival

**carne** ['karne] nf flesh; (CULIN) meat; **~ de cerdo/cordero/ternera/ vaca** pork/lamb/veal/beef; **~ de gallina** (fig): **se me pone la ~ de gallina sólo verlo** I get the creeps just seeing it

**carné** [kar'ne] (pl **~s**) nm: **~ de conducir** driving licence (BRIT), driver's license (US); **~ de identidad** identity card

**carnero** [kar'nero] nm sheep, ram; (carne) mutton

**carnet** [kar'ne] (pl **~s**) nm = **carné**

**carnicería** [karniθe'ria] nf butcher's (shop); (fig: matanza) carnage, slaughter

**carnicero, a** [karni'θero, a] adj carnivorous ♦ nm/f (tb fig) butcher; (carnívoro) carnivore

**carnívoro, a** [kar'niβoro, a] adj carnivorous

**carnoso, a** [kar'noso, a] adj beefy, fat

**caro, a** ['karo, a] adj dear; (COM) dear, expensive ♦ adv dear, dearly

**carpa** ['karpa] nf (pez) carp; (de circo) big top; (AM: de camping) tent

**carpeta** [kar'peta] nf folder, file

**carpintería** [karpinte'ria] nf carpentry, joinery; **carpintero** nm carpenter

**carraspear** [karraspe'ar] vi to clear one's throat

**carraspera** [karras'pera] nf hoarseness

**carrera** [ka'rrera] nf (acción) run(ning); (espacio recorrido) run; (certamen) race; (trayecto) course; (profesión) career; (ESCOL) course

**carreta** [ka'rreta] nf wagon, cart

**carrete** [ka'rrete] nm reel, spool; (TEC) coil

**carretera** [karre'tera] nf (main) road, highway; **~ de circunvalación** ring road; **~ nacional** ≈ A road (BRIT), ≈ state highway (US)

**carretilla** [karre'tiʎa] nf trolley; (AGR) (wheel)barrow

**carril** [ka'rril] nm furrow; (de autopista) lane; (FERRO) rail

**carrillo** [ka'rriʎo] nm (ANAT) cheek; (TEC) pulley

**carro** ['karro] nm cart, wagon; (MIL) tank; (AM: coche) car

**carrocería** [karroθe'ria] nf bodywork, coachwork

**carroña** [ka'rroɲa] nf carrion no pl

**carroza** [ka'rroθa] nf (vehículo) coach

**carrusel** [karru'sel] nm merry-go-round, roundabout

**carta** ['karta] *nf* letter; *(CULIN: menu, (naipe)* card; *(mapa)* map; *(JUR)* document; ~ **de ajuste** *(TV)* test card; ~ **de crédito** credit card; ~ **certificada** registered letter; ~ **marítima** chart; ~ **verde** *(AUTO)* green card

**cartabón** [karta'βon] *nm* set square

**cartel** [kar'tel] *nm (anuncio)* poster, placard; *(ESCOL)* wall chart; *(COM)* cartel; ~**era** *nf* hoarding, billboard; *(en periódico etc)* entertainments guide; "**en ~era**" "showing"

**cartera** [kar'tera] *nf (de bolsillo)* wallet; *(de colegial, cobrador)* satchel; *(de señora)* handbag; *(para documentos)* briefcase; *(COM)* portfolio; **ocupa la ~ de Agricultura** she is Minister of Agriculture

**carterista** [karte'rista] *nm/f* pickpocket

**cartero** [kar'tero] *nm* postman

**cartilla** [kar'tiʎa] *nf* primer, first reading book; ~ **de ahorros** savings book

**cartón** [kar'ton] *nm* cardboard; ~ **piedra** papier-maché

**cartucho** [kar'tutʃo] *nm (MIL)* cartridge

**cartulina** [kartu'lina] *nf* card

**casa** ['kasa] *nf* house; *(hogar)* home; *(edificio)* building; *(COM)* firm, company; **en ~** at home; ~ **consistorial** town hall; ~ **de huéspedes** boarding house; ~ **de socorro** first aid post

**casado, a** [ka'saðo, a] *adj* married ♦ *nm/f* married man/woman

**casamiento** [kasa'mjento] *nm* marriage, wedding

**casar** [ka'sar] *vt* to marry; *(JUR)* to quash, annul; ~**se** *vr* to marry, get married

**cascabel** [kaska'βel] *nm* (small) bell

**cascada** [kas'kaða] *nf* waterfall

**cascanueces** [kaska'nweθes] *nm inv* nutcrackers *pl*

**cascar** [kas'kar] *vt* to crack, split, break (open); ~**se** *vr* to crack, split, break (open)

**cáscara** ['kaskara] *nf (de huevo, fruta seca)* shell; *(de fruta)* skin; *(de limón)* peel

**casco** ['kasko] *nm (de bombero, soldado)* helmet; *(NAUT: de barco)* hull; *(ZOOL: de caballo)* hoof; *(botella)* empty bottle; *(de ciudad)*: **el ~ antiguo** the old part; **el ~ urbano** the town centre

**cascote** [kas'kote] *nm* rubble

**caserío** [kase'rio] *nm* hamlet; *(casa)* country house

**casero, a** [ka'sero, a] *adj (pan etc)* home-made ♦ *nm/f (propietario)* landlord/lady; *(COM)* house agent; **ser muy ~** to be home-loving; "**comida casera**" "home cooking"

**caseta** [ka'seta] *nf* hut; *(para bañista)* cubicle; *(de feria)* stall

**casete** [ka'sete] *nm o f* cassette

**casi** ['kasi] *adv* almost, nearly; ~ **nada** hardly anything; ~ **nunca** hardly ever, almost never; ~ **te caes** you almost fell

**casilla** [ka'siʎa] *nf (casita)* hut, cabin; *(TEATRO)* box office; *(AJEDREZ)* square; *(para cartas)* pigeonhole; **casillero** *nm (para cartas)* pigeonholes *pl*

**casino** [ka'sino] *nm* club; *(de juego)* casino

**caso** ['kaso] *nm* case; **en ~ de ...** in case of ...; **en ~ de que ...** in case ...; **el ~ es que** the fact is that; **en ese ~** in that case; **hacer ~ a** to pay attention to; **hacer o venir al ~** to be relevant

**caspa** ['kaspa] *nf* dandruff

**cassette** [ka'sete] *nm o f* = **casete**

**casta** ['kasta] *nf* caste; *(raza)* breed; *(linaje)* lineage

**castaña** [kas'taɲa] *nf* chestnut

**castañetear** [kastaɲete'ar] *vi (dientes)* to chatter

**castaño, a** [kas'taɲo, a] *adj* chestnut(-coloured), brown ♦ *nm* chestnut tree

**castañuelas** [kasta'ɲwelas] *nfpl* castanets

**castellano, a** [kaste'ʎano, a] *adj, nm/f* Castilian ♦ *nm (LING)* Castilian, Spanish

**castidad** [kasti'ðað] nf chastity, purity

**castigar** [kasti'ɣar] vt to punish; (DEPORTE) to penalize; (afligir) to afflict; **castigo** nm punishment; (DEPORTE) penalty

**Castilla** [kas'tiʎa] nf Castille

**castillo** [kas'tiʎo] nm castle

**castizo, a** [kas'tiθo, a] adj (LING) pure; (de buena casta) purebred, pedigree

**casto, a** ['kasto, a] adj chaste, pure

**castor** [kas'tor] nm beaver

**castrar** [kas'trar] vt to castrate

**castrense** [kas'trense] adj (disciplina, vida) military

**casual** [ka'swal] adj chance, accidental; ~**idad** nf chance, accident; (combinación de circunstancias) coincidence; ¡qué ~**idad!** what a coincidence!

**cataclismo** [kata'klismo] nm cataclysm

**catador, a** [kata'ðor, a] nm/f wine taster

**catalán, ana** [kata'lan, ana] adj, nm/f Catalan ♦ nm (LING) Catalan

**catalizador** [kataliθa'ðor] nm catalyst; (AUT) catalytic convertor

**catalogar** [katalo'ɣar] vt to catalogue; ~ **a algn(de)** (fig) to categorize sb(as)

**catálogo** [ka'taloɣo] nm catalogue

**Cataluña** [kata'luɲa] nf Catalonia

**catar** [ka'tar] vt to taste, sample

**catarata** [kata'rata] nf (GEO) waterfall; (MED) cataract

**catarro** [ka'tarro] nm catarrh; (constipado) cold

**catástrofe** [ka'tastrofe] nf catastrophe

**catear** [kate'ar] (fam) vt (examen, alumno) to fail

**cátedra** ['kateðra] nf (UNIV) chair, professorship

**catedral** [kate'ðral] nf cathedral

**catedrático, a** [kate'ðratiko, a] nm/f professor

**categoría** [kateɣo'ria] nf category;

(rango) rank, standing; (calidad) quality; **de** ~ (hotel) top-class

**categórico, a** [kate'ɣoriko, a] adj categorical

**cateto, a** ['kateto, a] (pey) nm/f peasant

**catolicismo** [katoli'θismo] nm Catholicism

**católico, a** [ka'toliko, a] adj, nm/f Catholic

**catorce** [ka'torθe] num fourteen

**cauce** ['kauθe] nm (de río) riverbed; (fig) channel

**caución** [kau'θjon] nf bail; **caucionar** vt (JUR) to bail, go bail for

**caucho** ['kautʃo] nm rubber; (AM: llanta) tyre

**caudal** [kau'ðal] nm (de río) volume, flow; (fortuna) wealth; (abundancia) abundance; ~**oso, a** adj (río) large; (persona) wealthy, rich

**caudillo** [kau'ðiʎo] nm leader, chief

**causa** ['kausa] nf cause; (razón) reason; (JUR) lawsuit, case; **a** ~ **de** because of

**causar** [kau'sar] vt to cause

**cautela** [kau'tela] nf caution, cautiousness; **cauteloso, a** adj cautious, wary

**cautivar** [kauti'βar] vt to capture; (fig) to captivate

**cautiverio** [kauti'βerjo] nm captivity

**cautividad** [kautiβi'ðað] nf = cautiverio

**cautivo, a** [kau'tiβo, a] adj, nm/f captive

**cauto, a** ['kauto, a] adj cautious, careful

**cava** ['kaβa] nm champagne-type wine

**cavar** [ka'βar] vt to dig

**caverna** [ka'βerna] nf cave, cavern

**cavidad** [kaβi'ðað] nf cavity

**cavilar** [kaβi'lar] vt to ponder

**cayado** [ka'jaðo] nm (de pastor) crook; (de obispo) crozier

**cayendo** etc vb ver **caer**

**caza** ['kaθa] nf (acción: gen) hunting; (: con fusil) shooting; (una ~) hunt, chase; (animales) game ♦ nm

(*AVIAT*) fighter

**cazador, a** [kaθa'ðor, a] *nm/f* hunter; **cazadora** *nf* jacket

**cazar** [ka'θar] *vt* to hunt; (*perseguir*) to chase; (*prender*) to catch

**cazo** ['kaθo] *nm* saucepan

**cazuela** [ka'θwela] *nf* (*vasija*) pan; (*guisado*) casserole

**CD** *abbr* (= compact disc) CD

**CD-ROM** *abbr m* CD-ROM

**cebada** [θe'βaða] *nf* barley

**cebar** [θe'βar] *vt* (*animal*) to fatten (up); (*anzuelo*) to bait; (*MIL, TEC*) to prime

**cebo** ['θeβo] *nm* (*para animales*) feed, food; (*para peces, fig*) bait; (*de arma*) charge

**cebolla** [θe'βoʎa] *nf* onion; **cebollin** *nm* spring onion

**cebra** ['θeβra] *nf* zebra

**cecear** [θeθe'ar] *vi* to lisp; **ceceo** *nm* lisp

**ceder** [θe'ðer] *vt* to hand over, give up, part with ♦ *vi* (*renunciar*) to give in, yield; (*disminuir*) to diminish, decline; (*romperse*) to give way

**cedro** ['θeðro] *nm* cedar

**cédula** ['θeðula] *nf* certificate, document

**CE** *nf abr* (= Comunidad Europea) EC

**cegar** [θe'ɣar] *vt* to blind; (*tubería etc*) to block up, stop up ♦ *vi* to go blind; **~se** *vr*: **~se (de)** to be blinded (by)

**ceguera** [θe'ɣera] *nf* blindness

**CEI** *abbr* (= Confederación de Estados Independientes) CIS

**ceja** ['θexa] *nf* eyebrow

**cejar** [θe'xar] *vi* (*fig*) to back down

**celada** [θe'laða] *nf* ambush, trap

**celador, a** [θela'ðor, a] *nm/f* (*de edificio*) watchman; (*de museo etc*) attendant

**celda** ['θelda] *nf* cell

**celebración** [θeleβra'θjon] *nf* celebration

**celebrar** [θele'βrar] *vt* to celebrate; (*alabar*) to praise ♦ *vi* to be glad; **~se** *vr* to occur, take place

**célebre** ['θelebre] *adj* famous

**celebridad** [θeleβri'ðað] *nf* fame; (*persona*) celebrity

**celeste** [θe'leste] *adj* sky-blue; celestial, heavenly

**celestial** [θeles'tjal] *adj* celestial, heavenly

**celibato** [θeli'βato] *nm* celibacy

**célibe** [θe'liβe] *adj, nm/f* celibate

**celo**[1] ['θelo] *nm* zeal; (*REL*) fervour; (*ZOOL*): **en ~** on heat; **~s** *nmpl* (*envidia*) jealousy *sg*; **tener ~s** to be jealous

**celo**[2] ['θelo] ® *nm* Sellotape ®

**celofán** [θelo'fan] *nm* cellophane

**celoso, a** [θe'loso, a] *adj* (*envidioso*) jealous; (*trabajador*) zealous; (*desconfiado*) suspicious

**celta** ['θelta] *adj* Celtic ♦ *nm/f* Celt

**célula** ['θelula] *nf* cell; **~ solar** solar cell

**celulitis** [θelu'litis] *nf* cellulite

**celuloide** [θelu'loiðe] *nm* celluloid

**cementerio** [θemen'terjo] *nm* cemetery, graveyard

**cemento** [θe'mento] *nm* cement; (*hormigón*) concrete; (*AM: cola*) glue

**cena** ['θena] *nf* evening meal, dinner

**cenagal** [θena'ɣal] *nm* bog, quagmire

**cenar** [θe'nar] *vt* to have for dinner ♦ *vi* to have dinner

**cenicero** [θeni'θero] *nm* ashtray

**cenit** [θe'nit] *nm* zenith

**ceniza** [θe'niθa] *nf* ash, ashes *pl*

**censo** ['θenso] *nm* census; **~ electoral** electoral roll

**censura** [θen'sura] *nf* (*POL*) censorship; (*moral*) censure, criticism

**censurar** [θensu'rar] *vt* (*idea*) to censure; (*cortar: película*) to censor

**centella** [θen'teʎa] *nf* spark

**centellear** [θenteʎe'ar] *vi* (*metal*) to gleam; (*estrella*) to twinkle; (*fig*) to sparkle

**centenar** [θente'nar] *nm* hundred

**centenario, a** [θente'narjo, a] *adj* centenary; hundred-year-old ♦ *nm* centenary

**centeno** [θen'teno] *nm* (*BOT*) rye

**centésimo, a** [θen'tesimo, a] *adj*
hundredth

**centigrado** [θen'tiγraðo] *adj* centigrade

**centímetro** [θen'timetro] *nm* centimetre (*BRIT*), centimeter (*US*)

**céntimo** [θentimo] *nm* cent

**centinela** [θenti'nela] *nm* sentry,
guard

**centollo** [θen'toʎo] *nm* spider crab

**central** [θen'tral] *adj* central ♦ *nf*
head office; (*TEC*) plant; (*TEL*) exchange; **~ eléctrica** power station;
**~ nuclear** nuclear power station

**centralizar** [θentrali'θar] *vt* to cen-
tralize

**centrar** [θen'trar] *vt* to centre

**céntrico, a** ['θentriko, a] *adj* central

**centrifugar** [θentrifu'γar] *vt* to spin-
dry

**centrista** [θen'trista] *adj* centre *cpd*

**centro** ['θentro] *nm* centre; **~ comercial** shopping centre; **~ juvenil**
youth club

**centroamericano, a** [θentroameri-
'kano, a] *adj, nm/f* Central American

**ceñido, a** [θe'niðo, a] *adj* (*chaqueta,
pantalón*) tight(-fitting)

**ceñir** [θe'nir] *vt* (*rodear*) to encircle,
surround; (*ajustar*) to fit (tightly);
(*apretar*) to tighten

**ceño** ['θeno] *nm* frown, scowl; **fruncir el ~** to frown, knit one's brow

**CEOE** *nf abr* (*ESP: = Confederación
Española de Organizaciones
Empresariales*) ≈ CBI (*BRIT*), em-
ployers' organization

**cepillar** [θepi'ʎar] *vt* to brush; (*madera*) to plane (down)

**cepillo** [θe'piʎo] *nm* brush; (*para
madera*) plane; **~ de dientes** tooth-
brush

**cera** ['θera] *nf* wax

**cerámica** [θe'ramika] *nf* pottery;
(*arte*) ceramics

**cerca** ['θerka] *nf* fence ♦ *adv* near,
nearby, close ♦ *nmpl*: **~s** foreground
*sg*; **~ de** near, close to

**cercanía** [θerka'nia] *nf* nearness,

closeness; **~s** *nfpl* (*afueras*) outskirts, suburbs

**cercano, a** [θer'kano, a] *adj* close,
near

**cercar** [θer'kar] *vt* to fence in; (*rodear*) to surround

**cerciorar** [θerθjo'rar] *vt* (*asegurar*)
to assure; **~se** *vr* (*descubrir*) to find
out; (*asegurarse*) to make sure

**cerco** ['θerko] *nm* (*AGR*) enclosure;
(*AM*) fence; (*MIL*) siege

**cerdo, a** ['θerðo, a] *nm/f* pig/sow

**cereal** [θere'al] *nm* cereal; **~es** *nmpl*
cereals, grain *sg*

**cerebro** [θe'reβro] *nm* brain; (*fig*)
brains *pl*

**ceremonia** [θere'monja] *nf* ceremony; **ceremonial** *adj, nm* ceremonial; **ceremonioso, a** *adj* ce-
remonious; (*cumplido*) formal

**cereza** [θe'reθa] *nf* cherry

**cerilla** [θe'riʎa] *nf* (*fósforo*) match

**cernerse** [θer'nerse] *vr* to hover

**cero** ['θero] *nm* nothing, zero

**cerrado, a** [θe'rraðo, a] *adj* closed,
shut; (*con llave*) locked; (*tiempo*)
cloudy, overcast; (*curva*) sharp;
(*acento*) thick, broad

**cerradura** [θerra'ðura] *nf* (*acción*)
closing; (*mecanismo*) lock

**cerrajero** [θerra'xero] *nm* locksmith

**cerrar** [θe'rrar] *vt* to close, shut;
(*paso, carretera*) to close; (*grifo*) to
turn off; (*cuenta, negocio*) to close ♦
*vi* to close, shut; (*la noche*) to come
down; **~se** *vr* to close, shut; **~ con
llave** to lock; **~ un trato** to strike a
bargain

**cerro** ['θerro] *nm* hill

**cerrojo** [θe'rroxo] *nm* (*herramienta*)
bolt; (*de puerta*) latch

**certamen** [θer'tamen] *nm* competition, contest

**certero, a** [θer'tero, a] *adj* (*gen*)
accurate

**certeza** [θer'teθa] *nf* certainty

**certidumbre** [θerti'ðumbre] *nf* = certeza

**certificado** [θertifi'kaðo] *nm* certificate

**certificar** [θeɾtifi'kaɾ] *vt* (*asegurar*, *atestar*) to certify

**cervatillo** [θeɾβa'tiʎo] *nm* fawn

**cervecería** [θeɾβeθe'ria] *nf* (*fábrica*) brewery; (*bar*) public house, pub

**cerveza** [θeɾ'βeθa] *nf* beer

**cesante** [θe'sante] *adj* redundant

**cesantía** [θesan'tia] *nf* unemployment

**cesar** [θe'saɾ] *vi* to cease, stop ♦ *vt* (*funcionario*) to remove from office

**cesárea** [θe'saɾea] *nf* (MED) Caesarean operation *o* section

**cese** ['θese] *nm* (*de trabajo*) dismissal; (*de pago*) suspension

**césped** ['θespeð] *nm* grass, lawn

**cesta** ['θesta] *nf* basket

**cesto** ['θesto] *nm* (large) basket, hamper

**cetro** ['θetɾo] *nm* sceptre

**cfr** *abr* (= *confróntese*) cf.

**ch...** *see under* CH, *after* C

**Cía** *abr* (= *compañía*) Co.

**cianuro** [θja'nuɾo] *nm* cyanide

**cicatriz** [θika'tɾiθ] *nf* scar; **~arse** *vr* to heal (up), form a scar

**ciclismo** [θi'klismo] *nm* cycling

**ciclista** [θi'lista] *adj* cycle *cpd* ♦ *nm/f* cyclist

**ciclo** ['θiklo] *nm* cycle

**ciclón** [θi'klon] *nm* cyclone

**ciego, a** ['θjeɣo, a] *adj* blind ♦ *nm/f* blind man/woman

**cielo** ['θjelo] *nm* sky; (REL) heaven; **¡~s!** good heavens!

**ciempiés** [θjem'pjes] *nm inv* centipede

**cien** [θjen] *num ver* ciento

**ciénaga** ['θjenaɣa] *nf* marsh, swamp

**ciencia** ['θjenθja] *nf* science; **~s** *nfpl* (ESCOL) science *sg*; **~-ficción** *nf* science fiction

**cieno** ['θjeno] *nm* mud, mire

**científico, a** [θjen'tifiko, a] *adj* scientific ♦ *nm/f* scientist

**ciento** ['θjento] (*tb*: **cien**) *num* hundred; **pagar al 10 por ~** to pay at 10 per cent

**cierne** ['θjeɾne] *nm*: **en ~** in blossom

**cierre** *etc* ['θjeɾre] *vb ver* cerrar ♦ *nm* closing, shutting; (*con llave*)

**locking**; **~ de cremallera** zip (fastener)

**cierro** *etc vb ver* cerrar

**cierto, a** ['θjeɾto, a] *adj* sure, certain; (*un tal*) a certain; (*correcto*) right, correct; **~ hombre** a certain man; **ciertas personas** a certain *o* some people; **sí, es ~** yes, that's correct

**ciervo** ['θjeɾβo] *nm* (ZOOL) deer; (: *macho*) stag

**cierzo** ['θjeɾθo] *nm* north wind

**cifra** ['θifɾa] *nf* number, numeral; (*cantidad*) number, quantity; (*secreta*) code

**cifrar** [θi'fɾaɾ] *vt* to code, write in code; (*resumir*) to abridge

**cigala** [θi'ɣala] *nf* Norway lobster

**cigarra** [θi'ɣara] *nf* cicada

**cigarrera** [θiɣa'rera] *nf* cigar case

**cigarrillo** [θiɣa'riʎo] *nm* cigarette

**cigarro** [θi'ɣaro] *nm* cigarette; (*puro*) cigar

**cigüeña** [θi'ɣweɲa] *nf* stork

**cilíndrico, a** [θi'lindɾiko, a] *adj* cylindrical

**cilindro** [θi'lindɾo] *nm* cylinder

**cima** ['θima] *nf* (*de montaña*) top, peak; (*de árbol*) top; (*fig*) height

**cimbrarse** [θim'bɾaɾse] *vr* to sway

**cimbrear** [θimbɾe'aɾ] *vt* = **cimbrar**

**cimentar** [θimen'taɾ] *vt* to lay the foundations of; (*fig*: *fundar*) to found

**cimiento** [θi'mjento] *nm* foundation

**cinc** [θink] *nm* zinc

**cincel** [θin'θel] *nm* chisel; **~ar** *vt* to chisel

**cinco** ['θinko] *num* five

**cincuenta** [θin'kwenta] *num* fifty

**cine** ['θine] *nm* cinema

**cineasta** [θine'asta] *nm/f* (*director de cine*) film director

**cinematográfico, a** [θinemato-'ɣɾafiko, a] *adj* cine-, film *cpd*

**cínico, a** ['θiniko, a] *adj* cynical ♦ *nm/f* cynic

**cinismo** [θi'nismo] *nm* cynicism

**cinta** ['θinta] *nf* band, strip; (*de tela*) ribbon; (*película*) reel; (*de máquina de escribir*) ribbon; **~ adhesiva**

sticky tape; ~ **de vídeo** videotape; ~ **magnetofónica** tape; ~ **métrica** tape measure

**cinto** [θinto] nm belt

**cintura** [θin'tura] nf waist

**cinturón** [θintu'ron] nm belt; ~ **de seguridad** safety belt

**ciprés** [θi'pres] nm cypress (tree)

**circo** ['θirko] nm circus

**circuito** [θir'kwito] nm circuit

**circulación** [θirkula'θjon] nf circulation; (AUTO) traffic

**circular** [θirku'lar] adj, nf circular ♦ vi, vt to circulate ♦ vi (AUTO) to drive; **"circule por la derecha"** "keep (to the) right"

**círculo** ['θirkulo] nm circle; ~ **vicioso** vicious circle

**circuncidar** [θirkunθi'dar] vt to circumcise

**circundar** [θirkun'dar] vt to surround

**circunferencia** [θirkunfe'renθja] nf circumference

**circunscribir** [θirkunskri'βir] vt to circumscribe; ~**se** vr to be limited

**circunscripción** [θirkunskrip'θjon] nf division; (POL) constituency

**circunspecto, a** [θirkuns'pekto, a] adj circumspect, cautious

**circunstancia** [θirkuns'tanθja] nf circumstance

**cirio** ['θirjo] nm (wax) candle

**ciruela** [θi'rwela] nf plum; ~ **pasa** prune

**cirugía** [θiru'xia] nf surgery; ~ **estética** o **plástica** plastic surgery

**cirujano** [θiru'xano] nm surgeon

**cisne** ['θisne] nm swan

**cisterna** [θis'terna] nf cistern, tank

**cita** ['θita] nf appointment, meeting; (de novios) date; (referencia) quotation

**citación** [θita'θjon] nf (JUR) summons sg

**citar** [θi'tar] vt (gen) to make an appointment with; (JUR) to summons; (un autor, texto) to quote; ~**se** vr: **se citaron en el cine** they arranged to meet at the cinema

**cítricos** ['θitrikos] nmpl citrus

fruit(s)

**ciudad** [θju'ðað] nf town; (más grande) city; ~**anía** nf citizenship; ~**ano, a** nm/f citizen

**cívico, a** ['θiβiko, a] adj civic

**civil** [θi'βil] adj civil ♦ nm (guardia) policeman

**civilización** [θiβiliθa'θjon] nf civilization

**civilizar** [θiβili'θar] vt to civilize

**civismo** [θi'βismo] nm public spirit

**cizaña** [θi'θaɲa] nf (fig) discord

**cl.** abr (= centilitro) cl.

**clamar** [kla'mar] vt to clamour for, cry out for ♦ vi to cry out, clamour

**clamor** [kla'mor] nm (grito) cry, shout; (fig) clamour, protest

**clandestino, a** [klandes'tino, a] adj clandestine; (POL) underground

**clara** ['klara] nf (de huevo) egg white

**claraboya** [klara'βoja] nf skylight

**clarear** [klare'ar] vi (el día) to dawn; (el cielo) to clear up, brighten up; ~**se** vr to be transparent

**clarete** [kla'rete] nm rosé (wine)

**claridad** [klari'ðað] nf (del día) brightness; (de estilo) clarity

**clarificar** [klarifi'kar] vt to clarify

**clarín** [kla'rin] nm bugle

**clarinete** [klari'nete] nm clarinet

**clarividencia** [klariβi'ðenθja] nf clairvoyance; (fig) far-sightedness

**claro, a** ['klaro, a] adj clear; (luminoso) bright; (color) light; (evidente) clear, evident; (poco espeso) thin ♦ nm (en bosque) clearing ♦ adv clearly ♦ excl (tb: ~ **que sí**) of course!

**clase** ['klase] nf class; ~ **alta/media/obrera** upper/middle/working class; ~**s particulares** private lessons, private tuition

**clásico, a** ['klasiko, a] adj classical; (fig) classic

**clasificación** [klasifika'θjon] nf classification; (DEPORTE) league (table)

**clasificar** [klasifi'kar] vt to classify

**claudicar** [klauði'kar] vi (fig) to back down

**claustro** ['klaustro] nm cloister

**cláusula** ['klausula] nf clause

**clausura** [klau'sura] nf closing, closure; **clausurar** vt (congreso etc) to bring to a close

**clavar** [kla'βar] vt (clavo) to hammer in; (cuchillo) to stick, thrust; (tablas etc) to nail (together)

**clave** ['klaβe] nf key; (MUS) clef

**clavel** [kla'βel] nm carnation

**clavícula** [kla'βikula] nf collar bone

**clavija** [kla'βixa] nf peg, dowel, pin; (ELEC) plug

**clavo** ['klaβo] nm (de metal) nail; (BOT) clove

**claxon** ['klakson] (pl ~s) nm horn

**clemencia** [kle'menθja] nf mercy, clemency

**cleptómano, a** [klep'tomano, a] nmf kleptomaniac

**clerical** [kleri'kal] adj clerical

**clérigo** ['klerixo] nm priest

**clero** ['klero] nm clergy

**cliché** [kli'tʃe] nm cliché; (FOTO) negative

**cliente, a** ['kljente, a] nmf client, customer

**clientela** [kljen'tela] nf clientele, customers pl

**clima** ['klima] nm climate

**climatizado, a** [klimati'θaðo, a] adj air-conditioned

**clímax** ['klimaks] nm inv climax

**clínica** ['klinika] nf clinic; (particular) private hospital

**clip** [klip] (pl ~s) nm paper clip

**clítoris** ['klitoris] nm inv (ANAT) clitoris

**cloaca** [klo'aka] nf sewer

**cloro** ['kloro] nm chlorine

**club** [klub] (pl ~s o ~es) nm club; ~ de jóvenes youth club

**cm** abr (= centímetro, centímetros) cm

**C.N.T.** (ESP) abr = Confederación Nacional de Trabajo

**coacción** [koak'θjon] nf coercion, compulsion; **coaccionar** vt to compel

**coagular** [koaxu'lar] vt (leche, sangre) to clot; ~se vr to clot; **coágulo** nm clot

**coalición** [koali'θjon] nf coalition

**coartada** [koar'taða] nf alibi

**coartar** [koar'tar] vt to limit, restrict

**coba** ['koβa] nf: dar ~ a uno to soft-soap sb

**cobarde** [ko'βarðe] adj cowardly ♦ nm coward; **cobardía** nf cowardice

**cobaya** [ko'βaja] nf guinea pig

**cobertizo** [koβer'tiθo] nm shelter

**cobertura** [koβer'tura] nf cover

**cobija** [ko'βixa] (AM) nf blanket

**cobijar** [koβi'xar] vt (cubrir) to cover; (abrigar) to shelter; **cobijo** nm shelter

**cobra** ['koβra] nf cobra

**cobrador, a** [koβra'ðor, a] nm/f (de autobús) conductor/conductress; (de impuestos, gas) collector

**cobrar** [ko'βrar] vt (cheque) to cash; (sueldo) to collect, draw; (objeto) to recover; (precio) to charge; (deuda) to collect ♦ vi to draw one's pay; ~se vr to recover, get well; **cóbrese al entregar** cash on delivery

**cobre** ['koβre] nm copper; ~s nmpl (MUS) brass instruments

**cobro** ['koβro] nm (de cheque) cashing; (pago) payment; **presentar al** ~ to cash

**Coca-Cola** ['koka'kola] ® nf Coca-Cola ®

**cocaína** [koka'ina] nf cocaine

**cocción** [kok'θjon] nf (CULIN) cooking; (: el hervir) boiling

**cocear** [koθe'ar] vi to kick

**cocer** [ko'θer] vt, vi to cook; (en agua) to boil; (en horno) to bake

**cocido** [ko'θiðo] nm stew

**cocina** [ko'θina] nf kitchen; (aparato) cooker, stove; (acto) cookery; ~ eléctrica/de gas electric/gas cooker; ~ francesa French cuisine; **cocinar** vt, vi to cook

**cocinero, a** [koθi'nero, a] nm/f cook

**coco** ['koko] nm coconut; ~tero nm coconut palm

**cocodrilo** [koko'ðrilo] nm crocodile

**cóctel** ['koktel] nm cocktail

**coche** ['kotʃe] nm (AUTO) car

(BRIT), automobile (US); (de tren, de caballos) coach, carriage; (para niños) pram (BRIT), baby carriage (US); ir en ~ to drive; ~ celular Black Maria, prison van; ~ de bomberos fire engine; ~ fúnebre hearse; **coche-cama** (pl **coches-cama**) nm (FERRO) sleeping car, sleeper

**cochera** [ko'tʃera] nf garage; (de autobuses, trenes) depot

**coche restaurante** (pl **coches restaurante**) nm (FERRO) dining car, diner

**cochino, a** [ko'tʃino, a] adj filthy, dirty ♦ nm/f pig

**codazo** [ko'ðaθo] nm: dar un ~ a uno to nudge sb

**codicia** [ko'ðiθja] nf greed; (fig) lust; **codiciar** vt to covet; **codicioso, a** adj covetous

**código** ['koðiɣo] nm code; ~ de barras bar code; ~ civil common law; ~ de (la) circulación highway code; ~ postale postcode

**codillo** [ko'ðiʎo] nm (ZOOL) knee; (TEC) elbow (joint)

**codo** ['koðo] nm (ANAT, de tubo) elbow; (ZOOL) knee

**codorniz** [koðor'niθ] nf quail

**coerción** [koer'θjon] nf coercion

**coetáneo, a** [koe'taneo, a] adj, nm/f contemporary

**coexistir** [koe(k)sis'tir] vi to coexist

**cofradía** [kofra'ðia] nf brotherhood, fraternity

**cofre** ['kofre] nm (de joyas) case; (de dinero) chest

**coger** [ko'xer] (ESP) vt to take (hold of); (objeto caído) to pick up; (frutas) to pick, harvest; (resfriado, ladrón, pelota) to catch ♦ vi: ~ por el buen camino to take the right road; ~se vr (el dedo) to catch; ~se a algo to get hold of sth

**cogollo** [ko'ɣoʎo] nm (de lechuga) heart

**cogote** [ko'ɣote] nm back o nape of the neck

**cohabitar** [koaβi'tar] vi to live to-

gether, cohabit

**cohecho** [ko'etʃo] nm (acción) bribery; (soborno) bribe

**coherente** [koe'rente] adj coherent

**cohesión** [koe'sjon] nm cohesion

**cohete** [ko'ete] nm rocket

**cohibido, a** [koi'βiðo, a] adj (PSICO) inhibited; (tímido) shy

**cohibir** [koi'βir] vt to restrain, restrict

**coincidencia** [koinθi'ðenθja] nf coincidence

**coincidir** [koinθi'ðir] vi (en idea) to coincide, agree; (en lugar) to coincide

**coito** ['koito] nm intercourse, coitus

**coja** etc vb ver **coger**

**cojear** [koxe'ar] vi (persona) to limp, hobble; (mueble) to wobble, rock

**cojera** [ko'xera] nf lameness; (andar cojo) limp

**cojín** [ko'xin] nm cushion; **cojinete** nm small cushion, pad; (TEC) ball bearing

**cojo, a** [ko'xo, a] etc vb ver **coger** ♦ adj (que no puede andar) lame, crippled; (mueble) wobbly ♦ nm/f lame person, cripple

**cojón** [ko'xon] nm (fam!): ¡cojones! shit! (!); **cojonudo, a** (fam) adj great, fantastic

**col** [kol] nf cabbage; ~es de Bruselas Brussels sprouts

**cola** ['kola] nf tail; (de gente) queue; (lugar) end, last place; (para pegar) glue, gum; hacer ~ to queue (up)

**colaborador, a** [kolaβora'ðor, a] nm/f collaborator

**colaborar** [kolaβo'rar] vi to collaborate

**colada** [ko'laða] nf: hacer la ~ to do the washing

**colador** [kola'ðor] nm (de té) strainer; (para verduras etc) colander

**colapso** [ko'lapso] nm collapse; ~ nervioso nervous breakdown

**colar** [ko'lar] vt (líquido) to strain off; (metal) to cast ♦ vi to ooze, seep (through); ~se vr to jump the queue; ~se en to get into without paying; (fiesta) to gatecrash

**colateral** [kolate'ral] nm collateral

**colcha** ['koltʃa] nf bedspread

**colchón** [kol'tʃon] nm mattress; ~ inflable o neumático air bed, air mattress

**colchoneta** [koltʃo'neta] nf (en gimnasio) mattress

**colear** [kole'ar] vi (perro) to wag its tail

**colección** [kolek'θjon] nf collection; **coleccionar** vt to collect; **coleccionista** nm/f collector

**colecta** [ko'lekta] nf collection

**colectivo, a** [kolek'tiβo, a] adj collective, joint ♦ nm (AM) (small) bus

**colector** [kolek'tor] nm collector; (sumidero) sewer

**colega** [ko'lexa] nm/f colleague

**colegial, a** [kole'xjal, a] nm/f schoolboy/girl

**colegio** [ko'lexjo] nm college; (escuela) school; (de abogados etc) association; ~ **electoral** polling station; ~ **mayor** hall of residence

**colegir** [kole'xir] vt (juntar) to collect, gather; (deducir) to infer, conclude

**cólera** ['kolera] nf (ira) anger; (MED) cholera; **colérico, a** [ko'leriko, a] adj irascible, bad-tempered

**colesterol** [koleste'rol] nm cholesterol

**coleta** [ko'leta] nf pigtail

**colgante** [kol'xante] adj hanging ♦ nm (joya) pendant

**colgar** [kol'xar] vt to hang (up); (ropa) to hang out ♦ vi to hang; (teléfono) to hang up

**cólico** ['koliko] nm colic

**coliflor** [koli'flor] nf cauliflower

**colilla** [ko'liʎa] nf cigarette end, butt

**colina** [ko'lina] nf hill

**colindante** [kolin'dante] adj adjacent, neighbouring

**colisión** [koli'sjon] nf collision; ~ **de frente** head-on crash

**colmado, a** [kol'maðo, a] adj full

**colmar** [kol'mar] vt to fill to the brim; (fig) to fulfil, realize

**colmena** [kol'mena] nf beehive

**colmillo** [kol'miʎo] nm (diente) eye tooth; (de elefante) tusk; (de perro) fang

**colmo** ['kolmo] nm height, summit; ¡es el ~! it's the limit!

**colocación** [koloka'θjon] nf (acto) placing; (empleo) job, position; (situación) place, position

**colocar** [kolo'kar] vt to place, put, position; (dinero) to invest; (poner en empleo) to find a job for; ~se vr to get a job

**Colombia** [ko'lombja] nf Colombia; **colombiano, a** adj, nm/f Colombian

**colonia** [ko'lonja] nf colony; (de casas) housing estate; (agua de ~) cologne

**colonización** [koloniθa'θjon] nf colonization; **colonizador, a** [koloniθa'ðor, a] adj colonizing ♦ nm/f colonist, settler

**colonizar** [koloni'θar] vt to colonize

**coloquio** [ko'lokjo] nm conversation; (congreso) conference

**color** [ko'lor] nm colour

**colorado, a** [kolo'raðo, a] adj (rojo) red; (LAM: chiste) rude

**colorante** [kolo'rante] nm colouring

**colorear** [kolore'ar] vt to colour

**colorete** [kolo'rete] nm blusher

**colorido** [kolo'riðo] nm colouring

**columna** [ko'lumna] nf column; (pilar) pillar; (apoyo) support

**columpiar** [kolum'pjar] vt to swing; ~se vr to swing; **columpio** nm swing

**collar** [ko'ʎar] nm necklace; (de perro) collar

**coma** ['koma] nf comma ♦ nm (MED) coma

**comadre** [ko'maðre] nf (madrina) godmother; (vecina) neighbour; (chismosa) gossip; **comadrona** nf midwife

**comandancia** [koman'danθja] nf command

**comandante** [koman'dante] nm commandant

**comarca** [ko'marka] nf region

**comba** ['komba] nf (curva) curve; (cuerda) skipping rope; **saltar a la ~** to skip

**combar** [kom'bar] vt to bend, curve

**combate** [kom'bate] nm fight; (fig) battle; **combatiente** nm combatant

**combatir** [komba'tir] vt to fight, combat

**combinación** [kombina'θjon] nf combination; (QUIMICA) compound; (bebida) cocktail; (plan) scheme, setup; (prenda) slip

**combinar** [kombi'nar] vt to combine

**combustible** [kombus'tiβle] nm fuel

**combustión** [kombus'tjon] nf combustion

**comedia** [ko'meðja] nf comedy; (TEATRO) play, drama

**comediante** [kome'ðjante] nm/f (comic) actor/actress

**comedido, a** [kome'ðiðo, a] adj moderate

**comedor, a** [kome'ðor, a] nm/f (persona) glutton ♦ nm (habitación) dining room; (restaurante) restaurant; (cantina) canteen

**comensal** [komen'sal] nm/f fellow guest o diner

**comentar** [komen'tar] vt to comment on; (fam) to discuss

**comentario** [komen'tarjo] nm comment, remark; (literario) commentary; **~s** nmpl (chismes) gossip sg

**comentarista** [komenta'rista] nm/f commentator

**comenzar** [komen'θar] vt, vi to begin, start, commence; **~ a hacer algo** to begin o start doing sth

**comer** [ko'mer] vt to eat; (DAMAS, AJEDREZ) to take, capture ♦ vi to eat; (almorzar) to have lunch; **~se** vr to eat up

**comercial** [komer'θjal] adj commercial; (relativo al negocio) business cpd; **comercializar** vt (producto) to market; (pey) to commercialize

**comerciante** [komer'θjante] nm/f trader, merchant

**comerciar** [komer'θjar] vi to trade,

do business

**comercio** [ko'merθjo] nm commerce, trade; (negocio) business; (fig) dealings pl

**comestible** [komes'tiβle] adj eatable, edible; **~s** nmpl food sg, foodstuffs

**cometa** [ko'meta] nm comet ♦ nf kite

**cometer** [kome'ter] vt to commit

**cometido** [kome'tiðo] nm (misión) task, assignment; (deber) commitment

**comezón** [kome'θon] nf itch, itching

**cómic** ['komik] nm (historieta) comic

**comicios** [ko'miθjos] nmpl elections

**cómico, a** ['komiko, a] adj comic(al) ♦ nm/f comedian; (de teatro) (comic) actor/actress

**comida** [ko'miða] nf (alimento) food; (almuerzo, cena) meal; (de mediodía) lunch

**comidilla** [komi'ðiʎa] nf: **ser la ~ de la ciudad** to be the talk of the town

**comienzo** etc [ko'mjenθo] vb ver **comenzar** ♦ nm beginning, start

**comilona** [komi'lona] nf (fam) nf blow-out

**comillas** [ko'miʎas] nfpl quotation marks

**comino** [ko'mino] nm: **(no) me importa un ~** I don't give a damn

**comisaría** [komisa'ria] nf (de policía) police station; (MIL) commissariat

**comisario** [komi'sarjo] nm (MIL etc) commissary; (POL) commissar

**comisión** [komi'sjon] nf commission

**comité** [komi'te] (pl **~s**) nm committee

**comitiva** [komi'tiβa] nf retinue

**como** ['komo] adv as; (tal ~) like; (aproximadamente) about, approximately ♦ conj (ya que, puesto que) as, since; (en cuanto) as soon as; **¡~ no!** of course!; **~ no lo haga hoy** unless he does it today; **~ si** as if; **es tan alto ~ ancho** it is as high as it is wide

**cómo** ['komo] adv how?, why? ♦ excl what?, I beg your pardon? ♦ nm: **el ~ y el porqué** the whys and wherefores

**cómoda** ['komoða] nf chest of drawers

**comodidad** [komoði'ðað] nf comfort; **venga a su ~** come at your convenience

**comodín** [komo'ðin] nm joker

**cómodo, a** ['komoðo, a] adj comfortable; (práctico, de fácil uso) convenient

**compact disc** nm compact disk player

**compacto, a** [kom'pakto, a] adj compact

**compadecer** [kompaðe'θer] vt to pity, be sorry for; **~se** vr: **~se de** to pity, be o feel sorry for

**compadre** [kom'paðre] nm (padrino) godfather; (amigo) friend, pal

**compañero, a** [kompa'ɲero, a] nm/f companion; (novio) boy/girlfriend; **~ de clase** classmate

**compañía** [kompa'ɲia] nf company

**comparación** [kompara'θjon] nf comparison; **en ~ con** in comparison with

**comparar** [kompa'rar] vt to compare

**comparativo, a** [kompara'tiβo, a] adj comparative

**comparecer** [kompare'θer] vi to appear (in court)

**comparsa** [kom'parsa] nm/f (TEATRO) extra

**compartimiento** [komparti'mjento] nm (FERRO) compartment

**compartir** [kompar'tir] vt to share; (dinero, comida etc) to divide (up), share (out)

**compás** [kom'pas] nm (MUS) beat, rhythm; (MAT) compasses pl; (NAUT etc) compass

**compasión** [kompa'sjon] nf compassion, pity

**compasivo, a** [kompa'siβo, a] adj compassionate

**compatibilidad** [kompatiβili'ðað] nf compatibility

**compatible** [kompa'tiβle] adj compatible

**compatriota** [kompa'trjota] nm/f compatriot, fellow countryman/woman

**compenetrarse** [kompene'trarse] vr (persona) to see eye to eye

**compendiar** [kompen'djar] vt to summarize; (libro) to abridge; **compendio** nm summary; abridgement

**compensación** [kompensa'θjon] nf compensation

**compensar** [kompen'sar] vt to compensate

**competencia** [kompe'tenθja] nf (incumbencia) domain, field; (JUR, habilidad) competence; (rivalidad) competition

**competente** [kompe'tente] adj (JUR, persona) competent; (conveniente) suitable

**competición** [kompeti'θjon] nf competition

**competir** [kompe'tir] vi to compete

**compilar** [kompi'lar] vt to compile

**complacencia** [kompla'θenθja] nf (placer) pleasure; (tolerancia excesiva) complacency

**complacer** [kompla'θer] vt to please; **~se** vr to be pleased

**complaciente** [kompla'θjente] adj kind, obliging, helpful

**complejo, a** [kom'plexo, a] adj, nm complex

**complementario, a** [komplemen'tarjo, a] adj complementary

**completar** [komple'tar] vt to complete

**completo, a** [kom'pleto, a] adj complete; (perfecto) perfect; (lleno) full ♦ nm full complement

**complicado, a** [kompli'kaðo, a] adj complicated; **estar ~ en** to be mixed up in

**complicar** [kompli'kar] vt to complicate

**cómplice** ['kompliθe] nm/f accomplice

**complot** [kom'plo(t)] (pl ~s) nm plot; (conspiración) conspiracy

**componer** [kompo'ner] vt to make up, put together; (MUS, LITERATURA, IMPRENTA) to compose; (algo roto) to mend, repair; (arreglar) to arrange; ~se vr: ~se de to consist of; **componérselas para hacer algo** to manage to do sth

**comportamiento** [komporta'mjento] nm behaviour, conduct

**comportarse** [kompor'tarse] vr to behave

**composición** [komposi'θjon] nf composition

**compositor, a** [komposi'tor, a] nm/f composer

**compostura** [kompos'tura] nf (composición) composition; (reparación) mending, repair; (acuerdo) agreement; (actitud) composure

**compra** [kompra] nf purchase; ~s nfpl purchases, shopping sg; **ir de ~s** to go shopping; **comprador, a** nm/f buyer, purchaser

**comprar** [kom'prar] vt to buy, purchase

**comprender** [kompren'der] vt to understand; (incluir) to comprise, include

**comprensión** [kompren'sjon] nf understanding; (totalidad) comprehensiveness; **comprensivo, a** adj comprehensive; (actitud) understanding

**compresa** [kom'presa] nf: ~ **higiénica** sanitary towel (BRIT) o napkin (US)

**comprimido, a** [kompri'miðo, a] adj compressed ♦ nm (MED) pill, tablet

**comprimir** [kompri'mir] vt to compress; (fig) to control

**comprobante** [kompro'βante] nm proof; (COM) voucher; ~ **de recibo** receipt

**comprobar** [kompro'βar] vt to check; (probar) to prove; (TEC) to check, test

**comprometer** [komprome'ter] vt to compromise; (exponer) to endanger; ~se vr to compromise o.s.; (involucrarse) to get involved

**compromiso** [kompro'miso] nm (obligación) obligation; (cometido) commitment; (convenio) agreement; (dificultad) awkward situation

**compuesto, a** [kom'pwesto, a] adj: ~ **de** composed of, made up of ♦ nm compound

**computador** [komputa'ðor] nm computer; ~ **central** mainframe computer; ~ **personal** personal computer

**computadora** [komputa'ðora] nf = **computador**

**cómputo** ['komputo] nm calculation

**comulgar** [komul'ɣar] vi to receive communion

**común** [ko'mun] adj common ♦ nm: **el** ~ the community

**comunicación** [komunika'θjon] nf communication; (informe) report

**comunicado** [komuni'kaðo] nm announcement; ~ **de prensa** press release

**comunicar** [komuni'kar] vt, vi to communicate; ~se vr to communicate; **está comunicando** (TEL) the line's engaged (BRIT) o busy (US); **comunicativo, a** adj communicative

**comunidad** [komuni'ðað] nf community; ~ **autónoma** (POL) autonomous region; C~ **Económica Europea** European Economic Community

**comunión** [komu'njon] nf communion

**comunismo** [komu'nismo] nm communism; **comunista** adj, nm/f communist

**PALABRA CLAVE**

**con** [kon] prep **1** (medio, compañía); **comer** ~ **cuchara** to eat with a spoon; **pasear** ~ **uno** to go for a walk with sb

**2** (a pesar de): ~ **todo, merece nuestros respetos** all the same, he deserves our respect

**3** (para ~): **es muy bueno para** ~ **los niños** he's very good with (the) children

**4** (+ infin): ~ **llegar tan tarde se**

**quedó sin comer** by arriving so late he missed out on eating
♦ *conj*: ~ **que: será suficiente ~ que le escribas** it will be sufficient if you write to her

**conato** [ko'nato] *nm* attempt; ~ **de robo** attempted robbery

**concebir** [konθe'βir] *vt, vi* to conceive

**conceder** [konθe'ðer] *vt* to concede

**concejal, a** [konθe'xal, a] *nm/f* town councillor

**concentración** [konθentra'θjon] *nf* concentration

**concentrar** [konθen'trar] *vt* to concentrate; ~**se** *vr* to concentrate

**concepción** [konθep'θjon] *nf* conception

**concepto** [kon'θepto] *nm* concept

**concernir** [konθer'nir] *vi* to concern; **en lo que concierne a ...** (*cosa*) as far as ... is concerned; **en lo que a mí concierne** as far as I'm concerned

**concertar** [konθer'tar] *vt* (*MUS*) to harmonize; (*acordar: precio*) to agree; (: *tratado*) to conclude; (*trato*) to arrange, fix up; (*combinar: esfuerzos*) to coordinate; (*reconciliar: personas*) to reconcile ♦ *vi* to harmonize, be in tune

**concesión** [konθe'sjon] *nf* concession

**concesionario** [konθesjo'narjo] *nm* (licensed) dealer, agent

**conciencia** [kon'θjenθja] *nf* conscience; **tener/tomar ~ de** to be/become aware of; **tener la ~ limpia/tranquila** to have a clear conscience

**concienciar** [konθjen'θjar] *vt* to make aware; ~**se** *vr* to become aware

**concienzudo, a** [konθjen'θuðo, a] *adj* conscientious

**concierto** *etc* [kon'θjerto] *vb ver* **concertar** ♦ *nm* concert; (*obra*) concerto

**conciliar** [konθi'ljar] *vt* to reconcile

**concilio** [kon'θiljo] *nm* council

**conciso, a** [kon'θiso, a] *adj* concise

**conciudadano, a** [konθjuða'ðano, a] *nm/f* fellow citizen

**concluir** [konklu'ir] *vt, vi* to conclude; ~**se** *vr* to conclude

**conclusión** [konklu'sjon] *nf* conclusion

**concluyente** [konklu'jente] *adj* (*prueba, información*) conclusive

**concordar** [konkor'ðar] *vt* to reconcile ♦ *vi* to agree, tally

**concordia** [kon'korðja] *nf* harmony

**concretar** [konkre'tar] *vt* to make concrete, make more specific; ~**se** *vr* to become more definite

**concreto, a** [kon'kreto, a] *adj, nm* (*AM*) concrete; **en ~** (*en resumen*) to sum up; (*específicamente*) specifically; **no hay nada en ~** there's nothing definite

**concurrencia** [konku'rrenθja] *nf* turnout

**concurrido, a** [konku'rriðo, a] *adj* (*calle*) busy; (*local, reunión*) crowded

**concurrir** [konku'rrir] *vi* (*juntarse: ríos*) to meet, come together; (: *personas*) to gather, meet

**concursante** [konkur'sante] *nm/f* competitor

**concurso** [kon'kurso] *nm* (*de público*) crowd; (*ESCOL, DEPORTE, competencia*) competition; (*ayuda*) help, cooperation

**concha** ['kontʃa] *nf* shell

**condal** [kon'dal] *adj*: **la Ciudad C~** Barcelona

**conde** ['konde] *nm* count

**condecoración** [kondekora'θjon] *nf* (*MIL*) medal

**condecorar** [kondeko'rar] *vt* (*MIL*) to decorate

**condena** [kon'dena] *nf* sentence

**condenación** [kondena'θjon] *nf* condemnation; (*REL*) damnation

**condenar** [konde'nar] *vt* to condemn; (*JUR*) to convict; ~**se** *vr* (*JUR*) to confess (one's guilt); (*REL*) to be damned

**condensar** [konden'sar] *vt* to condense

**condesa** [kon'desa] nf countess

**condescender** [kondesθen'der] vi to acquiesce, comply

**condición** [kondi'θjon] nf condition; **condicional** adj conditional

**condicionar** [kondiθjo'nar] vt (acondicionar) to condition; ~ **algo a** to make sth conditional on

**condimento** [kondi'mento] nm seasoning

**condolerse** [kondo'lerse] vr to sympathize

**condón** [kon'don] nm condom

**conducir** [kondu'θir] vt to take, convey; (AUTO) to drive ♦ vi to drive; (fig) to lead; ~**se** vr to behave

**conducta** [kon'dukta] nf conduct, behaviour

**conducto** [kon'dukto] nm pipe, tube; (fig) channel

**conductor, a** [konduk'tor, a] adj leading, guiding ♦ nm (FISICA) conductor; (de vehículo) driver

**conduje** etc vb ver **conducir**

**conduzco** etc vb ver **conducir**

**conectado, a** [konek'taðo, a] adj (INFORM) on-line

**conectar** [konek'tar] vt to connect (up); (enchufar) plug in

**conejillo** [kone'xiλo] nm: ~ **de Indias** (ZOOL) guinea pig

**conejo** [ko'nexo] nm rabbit

**conexión** [konek'sjon] nf connection

**confección** [confe(k)'θjon] nf preparation; (industria) clothing industry

**confeccionar** [konfekθjo'nar] vt to make (up)

**confederación** [konfeðera'θjon] nf confederation

**conferencia** [konfe'renθja] nf conference; (lección) lecture; (TEL) call

**conferir** [konfe'rir] vt to award

**confesar** [konfe'sar] vt to confess, admit

**confesión** [konfe'sjon] nf confession

**confesionario** [konfesjo'narjo] nm confessional

**confeti** [kon'feti] nm confetti

**confiado, a** [kon'fjaðo, a] adj (crédulo) trusting; (seguro) confident; (presumido) conceited, vain

**confianza** [kon'fjanθa] nf trust; (aliento, confidence) confidence; (familiaridad) intimacy, familiarity; (pey) vanity, conceit

**confiar** [kon'fjar] vt to entrust ♦ vi to trust

**confidencia** [konfi'ðenθja] nf confidence

**confidencial** [konfiðen'θjal] adj confidential

**confidente** [konfi'ðente] nmf confidant/e; (policial) informer

**configurar** [konfiγu'rar] vt to shape, form

**confín** [kon'fin] nm limit; **confines** nmpl confines, limits

**confinar** [konfi'nar] vi to confine; (desterrar) to banish

**confirmar** [konfir'mar] vt to confirm

**confiscar** [konfis'kar] vt to confiscate

**confite** [kon'fite] nm sweet (BRIT), candy (US)

**confitería** [konfite'ria] nf confectionery; (tienda) confectioner's (shop)

**confitura** [konfi'tura] nf jam

**conflictivo, a** [konflik'tiβo, a] adj (asunto, propuesta) controversial; (país, situación) troubled

**conflicto** [kon'flikto] nm conflict; (fig) clash

**confluir** [kon'flwir] vi (ríos) to meet; (gente) to gather

**conformar** [konfor'mar] vt to shape, fashion ♦ vi to agree; ~**se** vr to conform; (resignarse) to resign o.s

**conforme** [kon'forme] adj (correspondiente): ~ **con** in line with; (de acuerdo): **estar** ~**s (con algo)** to be in agreement (with sth) ♦ adv as ♦ excl agreed! ♦ prep: a in accordance with; **quedarse** ~ **(con algo)** to be satisfied (with sth)

**conformidad** [konformi'ðað] nf (semejanza) similarity; (acuerdo) agreement; (resignación) resignation; **conformista** adj, nmf conformist

**confortable** [konfor'taßle] *adj* comfortable

**confortar** [konfor'tar] *vt* to comfort

**confrontar** [konfron'tar] *vt* to confront; (*dos personas*) to bring face to face; (*cotejar*) to compare ♦ *vi* to border

**confundir** [konfun'dir] *vt* (*borrar*) to blur; (*equivocar*) to mistake, confuse; (*mezclar*) to mix; (*turbar*) to confuse; ~**se** *vr* (*hacerse borroso*) to become blurred; (*turbarse*) to get confused; (*equivocarse*) to make a mistake; (*mezclarse*) to mix

**confusión** [konfu'sjon] *nf* confusion

**confuso, a** [kon'fuso, a] *adj* confused

**congelado, a** [konxe'laðo, a] *adj* frozen; ~**s** *nmpl* frozen food(s); **congelador** *nm* (*aparato*) freezer, deep freeze; **congeladora** *nf* freezer, deep freeze

**congelar** [konxe'lar] *vt* to freeze; ~**se** *vr* (*sangre, grasa*) to congeal

**congeniar** [konxe'njar] *vi* to get on (*BRIT*) o along (*US*) well

**congestión** [konxes'tjon] *nf* congestion

**congestionar** [konxestjo'nar] *vt* to congest; ~**se** *vr*: **se le congestionó la cara** his face became flushed

**congoja** [kon'goxa] *nf* distress, grief

**congraciarse** [kongra'θjarse] *vr* to ingratiate o.s.

**congratular** [kongratu'lar] *vt* to congratulate

**congregación** [kongreɣa'θjon] *nf* congregation

**congregar** [kongre'ɣar] *vt* to gather together; ~**se** *vr* to gather together

**congresista** [kongre'sista] *nm/f* delegate, congressman/woman

**congreso** [kon'greso] *nm* congress

**conjetura** [konxe'tura] *nf* guess; **conjeturar** *vt* to guess

**conjugar** [konxu'ɣar] *vt* to combine, fit together; (*LING*) to conjugate

**conjunción** [konxun'θjon] *nf* conjunction

**conjunto, a** [kon'xunto, a] *adj* joint,

united ♦ *nm* whole; (*MUS*) band; **en ~** as a whole

**conjurar** [konxu'rar] *vt* (*REL*) to exorcise; (*fig*) to ward off ♦ *vi* to plot

**conmemoración** [konmemora'θjon] *nf* commemoration

**conmemorar** [konmemo'rar] *vt* to commemorate

**conmigo** [kon'miɣo] *pron* with me

**conminar** [konmi'nar] *vt* to threaten

**conmoción** [konmo'θjon] *nf* shock; (*fig*) upheaval; ~ **cerebral** (*MED*) concussion

**conmovedor, a** [konmoße'ðor, a] *adj* touching, moving; (*emocionante*) exciting

**conmover** [konmo'ßer] *vt* to shake, disturb; (*fig*) to move

**conmutador** [konmuta'ðor] *nm* switch; (*AM*: *TEL*: *centralita*) switchboard; (: *central*) telephone exchange

**cono** [´kono] *nm* cone

**conocedor, a** [konoθe'ðor, a] *adj* expert, knowledgeable ♦ *nm/f* expert

**conocer** [kono'θer] *vt* to know; (*por primera vez*) to meet, get to know; (*entender*) to know about; (*reconocer*) to recognize; ~**se** *vr* (*una persona*) to know o.s.; (*dos personas*) to (get to) know each other

**conocido, a** [kono'θiðo, a] *adj* (well-)known ♦ *nm/f* acquaintance

**conocimiento** [konoθi'mjento] *nm* knowledge; (*MED*) consciousness; ~**s** *nmpl* (*personas*) acquaintances; (*saber*) knowledge *sg*

**conozco** *etc vb ver* **conocer**

**conque** [´konke] *conj* and so, then

**conquista** [kon'kista] *nf* conquest; **conquistador, a** *adj* conquering ♦ *nm* conqueror

**conquistar** [konkis'tar] *vt* to conquer

**consagrar** [konsa'ɣrar] *vt* (*REL*) to consecrate; (*fig*) to devote

**consciente** [kons'θjente] *adj* conscious

**consecución** [konseku'θjon] *nf* acquisition; (*de fin*) attainment

**consecuencia** [konse'kwenθja] *nf*

consequence, outcome; *(firmeza)* consistency

**consecuente** [konse'kwente] *adj* consistent

**consecutivo, a** [konseku'tiβo, a] *adj* consecutive

**conseguir** [konse'vir] *vt* to get, obtain; *(sus fines)* to attain

**consejero, a** [konse'xero, a] *nm/f* adviser, consultant; *(POL)* councillor

**consejo** [kon'sexo] *nm* advice; *(POL)* council; ~ **de administración** *(COM)* board of directors; ~ **de guerra** court martial; ~ **de ministros** cabinet meeting

**consenso** [kon'senso] *nm* consensus

**consentimiento** [konsenti'mjento] *nm* consent

**consentir** [konsen'tir] *vt (permitir, tolerar)* to consent to; *(mimar)* to pamper, spoil; *(aguantar)* to put up with ♦ *vi* to agree, consent; ~ **que uno haga algo** to allow sb to do sth

**conserje** [kon'serxe] *nm* caretaker; *(portero)* porter

**conservación** [konserβa'θjon] *nf* conservation; *(de alimentos, vida)* preservation

**conservador, a** [konserβa'ðor, a] *adj (POL)* conservative ♦ *nm/f* conservative

**conservante** [konser'βante] *nm* preservative

**conservar** [konser'βar] *vt* to conserve, keep; *(alimentos, vida)* to preserve; ~**se** *vr* to survive

**conservas** [kon'serβas] *nfpl* canned food(s) *(pl)*

**conservatorio** [konserβa'torjo] *nm (MUS)* conservatoire, conservatory

**considerable** [konsiðe'raβle] *adj* considerable

**consideración** [konsiðera'θjon] *nf* consideration; *(estimación)* respect

**considerado, a** [konsiðe'raðo, a] *adj (atento)* considerate; *(respetado)* respected

**considerar** [konsiðe'rar] *vt* to consider

**consigna** [kon'sivna] *nf (orden)* order, instruction; *(para equipajes)* left-luggage office

**consigo** *etc* [kon'sivo] *vb ver* **conseguir** ♦ *pron (m)* with him; *(f)* with her; *(Vd)* with you; *(reflexivo)* with o.s

**consiguiendo** *etc vb ver* **conseguir**

**consiguiente** [konsi'vjente] *adj* consequent; **por** ~ **and so, therefore,** consequently

**consistente** [konsis'tente] *adj* consistent; *(sólido)* solid, firm; *(válido)* sound

**consistir** [konsis'tir] *vi*: ~ **en** *(componerse de)* to consist of; *(ser resultado de)* to be due to

**consolación** [konsola'θjon] *nf* consolation

**consolar** [konso'lar] *vt* to console

**consolidar** [konsoli'ðar] *vt* to consolidate

**consomé** [konso'me] *(pl* ~**s)** *nm* consommé, clear soup

**consonante** [konso'nante] *adj* consonant, harmonious ♦ *nf* consonant

**consorcio** [kon'sorθjo] *nm* consortium

**conspiración** [konspira'θjon] *nf* conspiracy

**conspirador, a** [konspira'ðor, a] *nm/f* conspirator

**conspirar** [konspi'rar] *vi* to conspire

**constancia** [kon'stanθja] *nf* constancy; **dejar** ~ **de** to put on record

**constante** [kons'tante] *adj, nf* constant

**constar** [kons'tar] *vi (evidenciarse)* to be clear *o* evident; ~ **de** to consist of

**constatar** [konsta'tar] *vt (controlar)* to check; *(observar)* to note

**consternación** [konsterna'θjon] *nf* consternation

**constipado, a** [konsti'paðo, a] *adj*: **estar** ~ to have a cold ♦ *nm* cold

**constitución** [konstitu'θjon] *nf* constitution; **constitucional** *adj* constitutional

**constituir** [konstitu'ir] *vt (formar, componer)* to constitute, make up;

*(fundar, erigir, ordenar)* to constitute, establish

**constituyente** [konstitu'jente] *adj* constituent

**constreñir** [konstre'ɲir] *vt (restringir)* to restrict

**construcción** [konstruk'θjon] *nf* construction, building

**constructor, a** [konstruk'tor, a] *nm/f* builder

**construir** [konstru'ir] *vt* to build, construct

**construyendo** *etc vb ver* **construir**

**consuelo** [kon'swelo] *nm* consolation, solace

**cónsul** ['konsul] *nm* consul; **consulado** [konsu'laðo] *nm* consulate

**consulta** [kon'sulta] *nf* consultation; *(MED):* **horas de ~** surgery hours

**consultar** [konsul'tar] *vt* to consult

**consultorio** [konsul'torjo] *nm (MED)* surgery

**consumar** [konsu'mar] *vt* to complete, carry out; *(crimen)* to commit; *(sentencia)* to carry out

**consumición** [konsumi'θjon] *nf* consumption; *(bebida)* drink; *(comida)* food; **~ mínima** cover charge

**consumidor, a** [konsumi'ðor, a] *nm/f* consumer

**consumir** [konsu'mir] *vt* to consume; **~se** *vr* to be consumed; *(persona)* to waste away

**consumismo** [konsu'mismo] *nm* consumerism

**consumo** [kon'sumo] *nm* consumption

**contabilidad** [kontaβili'ðað] *nf* accounting, book-keeping; *(profesión)* accountancy; **contable** *nm/f* accountant

**contacto** [kon'takto] *nm* contact; *(AUTO)* ignition

**contado, a** [kon'taðo, a] *adj:* **~s** *(escasos)* numbered, scarce, few ♦ *nm:* **pagar al ~** to pay (in) cash

**contador, a** [konta'ðor, a] *nm (aparato)* meter; *(AM: contante)* accountant

**contagiar** [konta'xjar] *vt (enfermedad)* to pass on, transmit; *(persona)*

to infect; **~se** *vr* to become infected

**contagio** [kon'taxjo] *nm* infection; **contagioso, a** *adj* infectious; *(fig)* catching

**contaminación** [kontamina'θjon] *nf* contamination; *(polución)* pollution

**contaminar** [kontami'nar] *vt* to contaminate; *(aire, agua)* to pollute

**contante** [kon'tante] *adj:* **dinero ~ (y sonante)** cash

**contar** [kon'tar] *vt (páginas, dinero)* to count; *(anécdota, chiste etc)* to tell ♦ *vi* to count; **~ con** to rely on, count on

**contemplación** [kontempla'θjon] *nf* contemplation

**contemplar** [kontem'plar] *vt* to contemplate; *(mirar)* to look at

**contemporáneo, a** [kontempo'raneo, a] *adj, nm/f* contemporary

**contendiente** [konten'djente] *nm/f* contestant

**contenedor** [kontene'ðor] *nm* container

**contener** [konte'ner] *vt* to contain, hold; *(retener)* to hold back, contain; **~se** *vr* to control o restrain o.s.

**contenido, a** [konte'niðo, a] *adj (moderado)* restrained; *(risa etc)* suppressed ♦ *nm* contents *pl*, content

**contentar** [konten'tar] *vt (satisfacer)* to satisfy; *(complacer)* to please; **~se** *vr* to be satisfied

**contento, a** [kon'tento, a] *adj* contented, content; *(alegre)* pleased; *(feliz)* happy

**contestación** [kontesta'θjon] *nf* answer, reply

**contestador** [kontesta'ðor] *nm:* **~ automático** answering machine

**contestar** [kontes'tar] *vt* to answer, reply; *(JUR)* to corroborate, confirm

**contexto** [kon'te(k)sto] *nm* context

**contienda** [kon'tjenda] *nf* contest

**contigo** [kon'tiɣo] *pron* with you

**contiguo, a** [kon'tiɣwo, a] *adj (de al lado)* next; *(vecino)* adjacent, adjoining

**continente** [konti'nente] *adj, nm* continent

**contingencia** [kontin'xenθja] *nf* contingency; (*riesgo*) risk; **contingente** *adj, nm* contingent

**continuación** [kontinwa'θjon] *nf* continuation; **a ~** then, next

**continuar** [konti'nwar] *vt* to continue, go on with ♦ *vi* to continue, go on; **~ hablando** to continue talking *o* to talk

**continuidad** [kontinwi'ðað] *nf* continuity

**continuo, a** [kon'tinwo, a] *adj* (*sin interrupción*) continuous; (*acción perseverante*) continual

**contorno** [kon'torno] *nm* outline; (*GEO*) contour; **~s** *nmpl* neighbourhood *sg*, surrounding area *sg*

**contorsión** [kontor'sjon] *nf* contortion

**contra** ['kontra] *prep, ad* against ♦ *nm inv* con ♦ *nf*: **la C~** (*de Nicaragua*) the Contras *pl*

**contraataque** [kontraa'take] *nm* counter-attack

**contrabajo** [kontra'βaxo] *nm* double bass

**contrabandista** [kontraβan'dista] *nm/f* smuggler

**contrabando** [kontra'βando] *nm* (*acción*) smuggling; (*mercancías*) contraband

**contracción** [kontrak'θjon] *nf* contraction

**contracorriente** [kontrako'rrjente]: **(a) ~** *adv* against the current

**contrachapado** [kontratʃa'paðo] *nm* plywood

**contradecir** [kontraðe'θir] *vt* to contradict

**contradicción** [kontraðik'θjon] *nf* contradiction

**contradictorio, a** [kontraðik'torjo, a] *adj* contradictory

**contraer** [kontra'er] *vt* to contract; (*limitar*) to restrict; **~se** *vr* to contract; (*limitarse*) to limit o.s.

**contraluz** [kontra'luθ] *nf*: **a ~** against the light

**contramaestre** [kontrama'estre] *nm* foreman

**contrapartida** [kontrapar'tiða] *nf*: **como ~ (de)** in return (for)

**contrapelo** [kontra'pelo]: **a ~** *adv* the wrong way

**contrapesar** [kontrape'sar] *vt* to counterbalance; (*fig*) to offset; **contrapeso** *nm* counterweight

**contraportada** [kontrapor'taða] *nf* (*de revista*) back cover

**contraproducente** [kontraproðu'θente] *adj* counterproductive

**contrariar** [kontra'rjar] *vt* (*oponerse*) to oppose; (*poner obstáculo*) to impede; (*enfadar*) to vex

**contrariedad** [kontrarje'ðað] *nf* (*oposición*) opposition; (*obstáculo*) obstacle, setback; (*disgusto*) vexation, annoyance

**contrario, a** [kon'trarjo, a] *adj* contrary; (*persona*) opposed; (*sentido, lado*) opposite ♦ *nm/f* enemy, adversary; (*DEPORTE*) opponent; **al/por el ~** on the contrary; **de lo ~** otherwise

**contrarrestar** [kontrarres'tar] *vt* to counteract

**contrasentido** [kontrasen'tiðo] *nm*: **es un ~ que él ...** it doesn't make sense for him to ...

**contraseña** [kontra'seɲa] *nf* (*INFORM*) password

**contrastar** [kontras'tar] *vt* to resist ♦ *vi* to contrast

**contraste** [kon'traste] *nm* contrast

**contratar** [kontra'tar] *vt* (*firmar un acuerdo para*) to contract for; (*empleados, obreros*) to hire, engage; **~se** *vr* to sign on

**contratiempo** [kontra'tjempo] *nm* setback

**contratista** [kontra'tista] *nm/f* contractor

**contrato** [kon'trato] *nm* contract

**contravenir** [kontraβe'nir] *vi*: **~ a** to contravene, violate

**contraventana** [kontraβen'tana] *nf* shutter

**contribución** [kontriβu'θjon] *nf* (*municipal etc*) tax; (*ayuda*) contribution

**contribuir** [kontriβu'ir] *vt*, *vi* to contribute; (*COM*) to pay (in taxes)

**contribuyente** [kontriβu'jente] *nm/f* (*COM*) taxpayer; (*que ayuda*) contributor

**contrincante** [kontrin'kante] *nm* opponent

**control** [kon'trol] *nm* control; (*inspección*) inspection, check; **~ador, a** *nm/f* controller; **~ador aéreo** air-traffic controller

**controlar** [kontro'lar] *vt* to control; (*inspeccionar*) to inspect, check

**controversia** [kontro'βersja] *nf* controversy

**contundente** [kontun'dente] *adj* (*instrumento*) blunt; (*argumento, derrota*) overwhelming

**contusión** [kontu'sjon] *nf* bruise

**convalecencia** [kombale'θenθja] *nf* convalescence

**convalecer** [kombale'θer] *vi* to convalesce, get better

**convaleciente** [kombale'θjente] *adj, nm/f* convalescent

**convalidar** [kombali'ðar] *vt* (*título*) to recognize

**convencer** [komben'θer] *vt* to convince; (*persuadir*) to persuade

**convencimiento** [kombenθi'mjento] *nm* (*acción*) convincing; (*persuasión*) persuasion; (*certidumbre*) conviction

**convención** [komben'θjon] *nf* convention

**conveniencia** [kombe'njenθja] *nf* suitability; (*conformidad*) agreement; (*utilidad, provecho*) usefulness; **~s** *nfpl* (*convenciones*) conventions; (*COM*) property *sg*

**conveniente** [kombe'njente] *adj* suitable; (*útil*) useful

**convenio** [kom'benjo] *nm* agreement, treaty

**convenir** [kombe'nir] *vi* (*estar de acuerdo*) to agree; (*ser conveniente*) to suit, be suitable

**convento** [kom'bento] *nm* convent

**convenza** *etc vb ver* **convencer**

**converger** [komber'xer] *vi* to converge

**convergir** [komber'xir] *vi* = **converger**

**conversación** [kombersa'θjon] *nf* conversation

**conversar** [komber'sar] *vi* to talk, converse

**conversión** [komber'sjon] *nf* conversion

**convertir** [komber'tir] *vt* to convert

**convicción** [kombik'θjon] *nf* conviction

**convicto, a** [kom'bikto, a] *adj* convicted, found guilty; (*condenado*) condemned

**convidado, a** [kombi'ðaðo, a] *nm/f* guest

**convidar** [kombi'ðar] *vt* to invite

**convincente** [kombin'θente] *adj* convincing

**convite** [kom'bite] *nm* invitation; (*banquete*) banquet

**convivencia** [kombi'βenθja] *nf* coexistence, living together

**convivir** [kombi'βir] *vi* to live together

**convocar** [kombo'kar] *vt* to summon, call (together)

**convocatoria** [komboka'torja] *nf* (*de oposiciones, elecciones*) notice; (*de huelga*) call

**convulsión** [kombul'sjon] *nf* convulsion

**conyugal** [konju'γal] *adj* conjugal; **cónyuge** ['konjuxe] *nm/f* spouse

**coñac** [ko'ɲa(k)] (*pl* **~s**) *nm* cognac, brandy

**coño** ['koɲo] (*fam!*) *excl* (*enfado*) shit! (!); (*sorpresa*) bloody hell! (!)

**cooperación** [koopera'θjon] *nf* cooperation

**cooperar** [koope'rar] *vi* to cooperate

**cooperativa** [koopera'tiβa] *nf* cooperative

**coordinadora** [koorðina'ðora] *nf* (*comité*) coordinating committee

**coordinar** [koorði'nar] *vt* to coordinate

**copa** ['kopa] *nf* cup; (*vaso*) glass; (*bebida*): (**tomar una**) **~** (to have a) drink; (*de árbol*) top; (*de som-

*brero*) crown; ~s *nfpl* (*NAIPES*) ≈ hearts

**copia** ['kopja] *nf* copy; ~ **de respaldo** *o* **seguridad** (*INFORM*) back-up copy; **copiar** *vt* to copy

**copioso, a** [ko'pjoso, a] *adj* copious, plentiful

**copla** ['kopla] *nf* verse; (*canción*) (popular) song

**copo** ['kopo] *nm*: ~ **de nieve** snowflake; ~s **de maíz** cornflakes

**copropietarios** [kopropje'tarjos] *nmpl* joint owners

**coqueta** [ko'keta] *adj* flirtatious, coquettish; **coquetear** *vi* to flirt

**coraje** [ko'raxe] *nm* courage; (*ánimo*) spirit; (*ira*) anger

**coral** [ko'ral] *adj* choral ♦ *nf* (*MUS*) choir ♦ *nm* (*ZOOL*) coral

**coraza** [ko'raθa] *nf* (*armadura*) armour; (*blindaje*) armour-plating

**corazón** [kora'θon] *nm* heart

**corazonada** [koraθo'naða] *nf* impulse; (*presentimiento*) hunch

**corbata** [kor'βata] *nf* tie

**corchete** [kor'tʃete] *nm* catch, clasp

**corcho** ['kortʃo] *nm* cork; (*PESCA*) float

**cordel** [kor'ðel] *nm* cord, line

**cordero** [kor'ðero] *nm* lamb

**cordial** [kor'ðjal] *adj* cordial; ~**idad** *nf* warmth, cordiality

**cordillera** [korði'ʎera] *nf* range of (mountains)

**Córdoba** ['korðoβa] *n* Cordova

**cordón** [kor'ðon] *nm* (*cuerda*) cord, string; (*de zapatos*) lace; (*MIL etc*) cordon

**cordura** [kor'ðura] *nf*: **con** ~ (*obrar, hablar*) sensibly

**corneta** [kor'neta] *nf* bugle

**cornisa** [kor'nisa] *nf* (*ARQ*) cornice

**coro** ['koro] *nm* chorus; (*conjunto de cantores*) choir

**corona** [ko'rona] *nf* crown; (*de flores*) garland; ~**ción** *nf* coronation; **coronar** *vt* to crown

**coronel** [koro'nel] *nm* colonel

**coronilla** [koro'niʎa] *nf* (*ANAT*) crown (of the head)

**corporación** [korpora'θjon] *nf* corporation

**corporal** [korpo'ral] *adj* corporal, bodily

**corpulento, a** [korpu'lento a] *adj* (*persona*) heavily-built

**corral** [ko'ral] *nm* farmyard

**correa** [ko'rrea] *nf* strap; (*cinturón*) belt; (*de perro*) lead, leash

**corrección** [korrek'θjon] *nf* correction; (*reprensión*) rebuke; **correccional** *nm* reformatory

**correcto, a** [ko'rrekto, a] *adj* correct; (*persona*) well-mannered

**corredizo, a** [korre'ðiθo, a] *adj* (*puerta etc*) sliding

**corredor, a** [korre'ðor, a] *adj* running ♦ *nm* (*pasillo*) corridor; (*balcón corrido*) gallery; (*COM*) agent, broker ♦ *nmf* (*DEPORTE*) runner

**corregir** [korre'xir] *vt* (*error*) to correct; (*amonestar, reprender*) to rebuke, reprimand; ~**se** *vr* to reform

**correo** [ko'rreo] *nm* post, mail; (*persona*) courier; **C~s** *nmpl* Post Office *sg*; ~ **aéreo** airmail

**correr** [ko'rrer] *vt* to run; (*viajar*) to cover, travel; (*cortinas*) to draw; (*cerrojo*) to shoot ♦ *vi* to run; (*liquido*) to run, flow; ~**se** *vr* to slide, move; (*colores*) to run

**correspondencia** [korrespon'denθja] *nf* correspondence; (*FERRO*) connection

**corresponder** [korrespon'der] *vi* to correspond; (*convenir*) to be suitable; (*pertenecer*) to belong; (*tocar*) to concern; ~**se** *vr* (*por escrito*) to correspond; (*amarse*) to love one another

**correspondiente** [korrespon'djente] *adj* corresponding

**corresponsal** [korrespon'sal] *nmf* correspondent

**corrida** [ko'rriða] *nf* (*de toros*) bullfight

**corrido, a** [ko'rriðo, a] *adj* (*avergonzado*) abashed; **3 noches corridas** 3 nights running; **un kilo** ~ a good kilo

**corriente** [ko'rrjente] adj (agua) running; (fig) flowing; (dinero etc) current; (común) ordinary, normal ♦ nf current ♦ nm current month; ~ eléctrica electric current

**corrija** etc vb ver **corregir**

**corrillo** [ko'rriʎo] nm ring, circle (of people); (fig) clique

**corro** ['korro] nm ring, circle (of people)

**corroborar** [korroβo'rar] vt to corroborate

**corroer** [korro'er] vt to corrode; (GEO) to erode

**corromper** [korrom'per] vt (madera) to rot; (fig) to corrupt

**corrosivo, a** [korro'siβo, a] adj corrosive

**corrupción** [korrup'θjon] nf rot, decay; (fig) corruption

**corsé** [kor'se] nm corset

**cortacésped** [korta'θespeð] nm lawn mower

**cortado, a** [kor'taðo, a] adj (gen) cut; (leche) sour; (confuso) confused; (desconcertado) embarrassed ♦ nm coffee (with a little milk)

**cortar** [kor'tar] vt to cut; (suministro) to cut off; (un pasaje) to cut out ♦ vi to cut; ~se vr (turbarse) to become embarrassed; (leche) to turn, curdle; ~se el pelo to have one's haircut

**cortauñas** [korta'uɲas] nm inv nail clippers pl

**corte** ['korte] nm cut, cutting; (de tela) piece, length ♦ nf: las C~s the Spanish Parliament; ~ y confección dressmaking; ~ de luz power cut

**cortejar** [korte'xar] vt to court

**cortejo** [kor'texo] nm entourage; ~ fúnebre funeral procession

**cortés** [kor'tes] adj courteous, polite

**cortesía** [korte'sia] nf courtesy

**corteza** [kor'teθa] nf (de árbol) bark; (de pan) crust

**cortina** [kor'tina] nf curtain

**corto, a** ['korto, a] adj (breve) short; (tímido) bashful; ~ de luces not very bright; ~ de vista short-

sighted; estar ~ de fondos to be short of funds; ~circuito nm short circuit; ~metraje nm (CINE) short

**cosa** ['kosa] nf thing; (asunto) affair; ~ de about; eso es ~ mía that's my business

**coscorrón** [kosko'rron] nm bump on the head

**cosecha** [ko'setʃa] nf (AGR) harvest; (de vino) vintage

**cosechar** [kose'tʃar] vt to harvest, gather (in)

**coser** [ko'ser] vt to sew

**cosmético, a** [kos'metiko, a] adj, nm cosmetic

**cosquillas** [kos'kiʎas] nfpl: hacer ~ to tickle; tener ~ to be ticklish

**costa** ['kosta] nf (GEO) coast; C~ Brava Costa Brava; C~ Cantábrica Cantabrian Coast; C~ del Sol Costa del Sol; a toda ~ at any price

**costado** [kos'taðo] nm side

**costar** [kos'tar] vt (valer) to cost; (necesitar) to require, need; me cuesta hablarle I find it hard to talk to him

**Costa Rica** nf Costa Rica; **costarricense** adj, nm/f Costa Rican; **costarriqueño, a** adj, nm/f Costa Rican

**coste** ['koste] nm = **costo**

**costear** [koste'ar] vt to pay for

**costero, a** [kos'tero, a] adj (pueblecito, camino) coastal

**costilla** [kos'tiʎa] nf rib; (CULIN) cutlet

**costo** ['kosto] nm cost, price; ~ de la vida cost of living; ~so, a adj costly, expensive

**costra** ['kostra] nf (corteza) crust; (MED) scab

**costumbre** [kos'tumbre] nf custom, habit

**costura** [kos'tura] nf sewing, needlework; (zurcido) seam

**costurera** [kostu'rera] nf dressmaker

**costurero** [kostu'rero] nm sewing box o case

**cotejar** [kote'xar] vt to compare

**cotidiano, a** [koti'ðjano, a] adj daily, day to day

**cotilla** [ko'tiʎa] nm/f (fam) gossip; **cotillear** vi to gossip

**cotización** [kotiθa'θjon] nf (COM) quotation, price; (de club) dues pl

**cotizar** [koti'θar] vt (COM) to quote, price; ~se vr: ~se a to sell at, fetch; (BOLSA) to stand at, be quoted at

**coto** ['koto] nm (terreno cercado) enclosure; (de caza) reserve

**cotorra** [ko'torra] nf parrot

**COU** [kou] (ESP) nm abr (= Curso de Orientación Universitaria) 1 year course leading to final school leaving certificate and university entrance examinations

**coyote** [ko'jote] nm coyote, prairie wolf

**coyuntura** [kojun'tura] nf (ANAT) joint; (fig) juncture, occasion

**crack** nm (droga) crack

**coz** [koθ] nf kick

**cráneo** ['kraneo] nm skull, cranium

**cráter** ['krater] nm crater

**creación** [krea'θjon] nf creation

**creador, a** [krea'ðor, a] adj creative ♦ nm/f creator

**crear** [kre'ar] vt to create, make

**crecer** [kre'θer] vi to grow; (precio) to rise

**creces** ['kreθes] : con ~ adv amply, fully

**crecido, a** [kre'θiðo, a] adj (persona, planta) full-grown; (cantidad) large

**creciente** [kre'θjente] adj growing; (cantidad) increasing; (luna) crescent ♦ nm crescent

**crecimiento** [kreθi'mjento] nm growth; (aumento) increase

**credenciales** [kreðen'θjales] nfpl credentials

**crédito** ['kreðito] nm credit

**credo** ['kreðo] nm creed

**crédulo, a** ['kreðula, a] adj credulous

**creencia** [kre'enθja] nf belief

**creer** [kre'er] vt, vi to think, believe; ~se vr to believe o.s. (to be); ~ en to believe in; ¡ya lo creo! I should think so!

**creíble** [kre'iβle] adj credible, believable

**creído, a** [kre'iðo, a] adj (engreído) conceited

**crema** ['krema] nf cream; (natillas) custard; ~ **pastelera** (confectioner's) custard

**cremallera** [krema'ʎera] nf zip (fastener)

**crematorio** [krema'torjo] nm (tb: horno ~) crematorium

**crepitar** [krepi'tar] vi to crackle

**crepúsculo** [kre'puskulo] nm twilight, dusk

**crespo, a** ['krespo, a] adj (pelo) curly

**cresta** ['kresta] nf (GEO, ZOOL) crest

**creyendo** etc vb ver **creer**

**creyente** [kre'jente] nm/f believer

**creyó** etc vb ver **creer**

**crezco** etc vb ver **crecer**

**cría** etc ['kria] vb ver **criar** ♦ nf (de animales) rearing, breeding; (animal) young; ver tb **crío**

**criadero** [kria'ðero] nm nursery; (ZOOL) breeding place

**criado, a** [kria'ðo, a] nm servant ♦ nf servant, maid

**criador** [kria'ðor] nm breeder

**crianza** [kri'anθa] nf rearing, breeding; (fig) breeding

**criar** [kri'ar] vt (amamantar) to suckle, feed; (educar) to bring up; (producir) to grow, produce; (animales) to breed

**criatura** [kria'tura] nf creature; (niño) baby, (small) child

**criba** ['kriβa] nf sieve; **cribar** vt to sieve

**crimen** ['krimen] nm crime

**criminal** [krimi'nal] adj, nm/f criminal

**crin** [krin] nf (tb: ~es nfpl) mane

**crío, a** ['krio, a] (fam) nm/f (niño) kid

**crisis** ['krisis] nf inv crisis; ~ **nerviosa** nervous breakdown

**crispar** [kris'par] vt (músculo) to tense (up); (nervios) to set on edge

**cristal** [kris'tal] nm crystal; (de ventana) glass, pane; (lente) lens; **~ino, a** adj crystalline; (fig) clear ♦ nm lens (of the eye); **~izar** vt, vi to crystallize

**cristiandad** [kristjan'dað] nf Christendom

**cristianismo** [kristja'nismo] nm Christianity

**cristiano, a** [kris'tjano, a] adj, nm/f Christian

**Cristo** ['kristo] nm Christ; (crucifijo) crucifix

**criterio** [kri'terjo] nm criterion; (juicio) judgement

**crítica** ['kritika] nf criticism; ver tb crítico

**criticar** [kriti'kar] vt to criticize

**crítico, a** ['kritiko, a] adj critical ♦ nm/f critic

**Croacia** nf Croatia

**croar** [kro'ar] vi to croak

**croqueta** [kro'keta] nf (CULIN) croquette

**cromo** ['kromo] nm chrome

**crónica** ['kronika] nf chronicle, account

**crónico, a** ['kroniko, a] adj chronic

**cronómetro** [kro'nometro] nm (DEPORTE) stopwatch

**cruce** etc ['kruθe] vb ver **cruzar** ♦ nm crossing; (de carreteras) crossroads

**crucificar** [kruθifi'kar] vt to crucify

**crucifijo** [kruθi'fixo] nm crucifix

**crucigrama** [kruθi'vrama] nm crossword (puzzle)

**crudo, a** ['kruðo, a] adj raw; (no maduro) unripe; (petróleo) crude; (rudo, cruel) cruel ♦ nm crude (oil)

**cruel** [krwel] adj cruel; **~dad** nf cruelty

**crujido** [kru'xiðo] nm (de madera etc) creak

**crujiente** [kru'xjente] adj (galleta etc) crunchy

**crujir** [kru'xir] vi (madera etc) to creak; (dedos) to crack; (dientes) to grind; (nieve, arena) to crunch

**cruz** [kruθ] nf cross; (de moneda) tails sg; **~ gamada** swastika

**cruzada** [kru'θaða] nf crusade

**cruzado, a** [kru'θaðo, a] adj crossed ♦ nm crusader

**cruzar** [kru'θar] vt to cross; **~se** vr (líneas etc) to cross; (personas) to pass each other

**Cruz Roja** nf Red Cross

**cuaderno** [kwa'ðerno] nm notebook; (de escuela) exercise book; (NAUT) logbook

**cuadra** ['kwaðra] nf (caballeriza) stable; (AM) block

**cuadrado, a** [kwa'ðraðo, a] adj square ♦ nm (MAT) square

**cuadrar** [kwa'ðrar] vt to square ♦ vi: **~ con** to square with, tally with; **~se** vr (soldado) to stand to attention

**cuadrilátero** [kwaðri'latero] nm (DEPORTE) boxing ring; (GEOM) quadrilateral

**cuadrilla** [kwa'ðriʎa] nf party, group

**cuadro** ['kwaðro] nm square; (ARTE) painting; (TEATRO) scene; (diagrama) chart; (DEPORTE, MED) team; (POL) executive; **tela a ~s** checked (BRIT) o chequered (US) material

**cuádruple** ['kwaðruple] adj quadruple

**cuádruplo, a** ['kwaðruplo, a] adj quadruple

**cuajar** [kwa'xar] vt to thicken; (leche) to curdle; (sangre) to congeal; (adornar) to adorn; (CULIN) to set; **~se** vr to curdle; to congeal; to set; (llenarse) to fill up

**cuajo** ['kwaxo] nm: **de ~** (arrancar) by the roots; (cortar) completely

**cual** [kwal] adv like, as ♦ pron: **el ~** etc which; (persona: sujeto) who; (: objeto) whom ♦ adj such as; **cada ~** each one; **tal ~** just as it is

**cuál** [kwal] pron interr which (one)

**cualesquier(a)** [kwales'kjer(a)] pl de **cualquier(a)**

**cualidad** [kwali'ðað] nf quality

**cualquier** [kwal'kjer] adj ver **cualquiera**

**cualquiera** [kwal'kjera] (pl **cualesquiera**) adj (delante de nm sy f: **cualquier**) any ♦ pron anybody; **un coche ~** servirá any car will do; **no es un hombre ~** he isn't just anybody; **cualquier día/libro** any day/book; **eso ~** lo sabe hacer anybody can do that; **es un ~** he's a nobody

**cuando** ['kwando] adv when; (aun si) if, even if ♦ conj (puesto que) since ♦ prep: **yo, ~ niño ... when I was a child ...; ~ no** sea así even if it is not so; **~ más** at (the) most; **~ menos** at least; **~ no** if not, otherwise; **de ~ en ~** from time to time

**cuándo** ['kwando] adv when; **¿desde ~?, ¿de ~ acá?** since when?

**cuantía** [kwan'tia] nf (importe: de pérdidas, deuda, daños) extent

**cuantioso, a** [kwan'tjoso, a] adj substantial

┌─────────────────────┐
│ *PALABRA CLAVE* │
└─────────────────────┘

**cuanto, a** ['kwanto, a] adj **1** (todo): **tiene todo ~ desea** he's got everything he wants; **le daremos ~s ejemplares necesite** we'll give him as many copies as o all the copies he needs; **~s hombres la ven** all the men who see her

**2**: **unos ~s: había unos ~s periodistas** there were (quite) a few journalists

**3** (+ más): **~ más vino bebes peor te sentirás** the more wine you drink the worse you'll feel

♦ pron: **tiene ~ desea** he has everything he wants; **tome ~/~s quiera** take as much/many as you want

♦ adv: **en ~:** en **~ profesor** as a teacher; **en ~ a mí** as for me; ver tb **antes**

♦ conj **1**: **~ más gana menos gasta** the more he earns the less he spends; **~ más joven se es más se es confiado** the younger you are the more trusting you are

**2**: **en ~:** en **~ llegue/llegué** as soon as I arrive/arrived

**cuánto, a** ['kwanto, a] adj (exclamación) what a lot of; (interr: sg) how much?; (: pl) how many? ♦ pron, adv how; (interr: sg) how much?; (: pl) how many?; **¡cuánta gente!** what a lot of people!; **¿~ cuesta?** how much does it cost?; **¿a ~ estamos?** what's the date?; **Señor no sé ~s** Mr. So-and-So

**cuarenta** [kwa'renta] num forty

**cuarentena** [kwaren'tena] nf quarantine

**cuaresma** [kwa'resma] nf Lent

**cuarta** ['kwarta] nf (MAT) quarter, fourth; (palmo) span

**cuartear** [kwarte'ar] vt to quarter; (dividir) to divide up; **~se** vr to crack, split

**cuartel** [kwar'tel] nm (de ciudad) quarter, district; (MIL) barracks pl; **~ general** headquarters pl

**cuarteto** [kwar'teto] nm quartet

**cuarto, a** ['kwarto, a] adj fourth ♦ nm (MAT) quarter, fourth; (habitación) room; **~ de baño** bathroom; **~ de estar** living room; **~ de hora** quarter (of an) hour; **~ de kilo** quarter kilo

**cuatro** ['kwatro] num four

**cuba** ['kuβa] nf cask, barrel

**Cuba** ['kuβa] nf Cuba; **cubano, a** adj, nm/f Cuban

**cúbico, a** ['kuβiko, a] adj cubic

**cubierta** [ku'βjerta] nf cover, covering; (neumático) tyre; (NAUT) deck

**cubierto, a** [ku'βjerto, a] pp de **cubrir** ♦ adj covered ♦ nm cover; (en la mesa) place; **~s** nmpl cutlery sg; **a ~ de** covered with o in

**cubil** [ku'βil] nm den; **~ete** nm (en juegos) cup

**cubito** [ku'βito] nm: **~ de hielo** ice-cube

**cubo** ['kuβo] nm cube; (balde) bucket, tub; (TEC) drum

**cubrecama** [kuβre'kama] nm bedspread

**cubrir** [ku'βrir] vt to cover; **~se** vr (cielo) to become overcast

**cucaracha** [kuka'ratʃa] nf cockroach

**cuclillas** [ku'kliʎas] *nfpl*: **en ~** squatting

**cuco, a** ['kuko, a] *adj* pretty; (*astuto*) sharp ♦ *nm* cuckoo

**cucurucho** [kuku'rutʃo] *nm* cornet

**cuchara** [ku'tʃara] *nf* spoon; (*TEC*) scoop; **~da** *nf* spoonful; **~dita** *nf* teaspoonful

**cucharilla** [kutʃa'riʎa] *nf* teaspoon

**cucharón** [kutʃa'ron] *nm* ladle

**cuchichear** [kutʃitʃe'ar] *vi* to whisper

**cuchilla** [ku'tʃiʎa] *nf* (large) knife; (*de arma blanca*) blade; **~ de afeitar** razor blade

**cuchillo** [ku'tʃiʎo] *nm* knife

**cuchitril** [kutʃi'tril] *nm* hovel; (*habitación etc*) pigsty

**cuello** ['kweʎo] *nm* (*ANAT*) neck; (*de vestido, camisa*) collar

**cuenca** ['kwenka] *nf* (*ANAT*) eye socket; (*GEO*) bowl, deep valley

**cuenco** ['kwenko] *nm* bowl

**cuenta** *etc* ['kwenta] *vb ver* **contar** ♦ *nf* (*cálculo*) count, counting; (*en café, restaurante*) bill; (*COM*) account; (*de collar*) bead; (*cálculo*) account; **a fin de ~s** in the end; **caer en la ~** to catch on; **darse ~ de** to realize; **tener en ~** to bear in mind; **echar ~s** to take stock; **~ corriente/de ahorros** current/savings account; **~ atrás** countdown; **~kilómetros** *nm inv* ≈ milometer; (*de velocidad*) speedometer

**cuento** *etc* ['kwento] *vb ver* **contar** ♦ *nm* story

**cuerda** ['kwerða] *nf* rope; (*hilo*) string; (*de reloj*) spring; **dar ~ a un reloj** to wind up a clock; **~ floja** tightrope

**cuerdo, a** ['kwerðo, a] *adj* sane; (*prudente*) wise, sensible

**cuerno** ['kwerno] *nm* horn

**cuero** ['kwero] *nm* (*ZOOL*) skin, hide; (*TEC*) leather; **en ~s** stark naked; **~ cabelludo** scalp

**cuerpo** ['kwerpo] *nm* body

**cuervo** ['kwerβo] *nm* crow

**cuesta** *etc* ['kwesta] *vb ver* **costar** ♦

**cuesta** *etc vb ver* **costar**

*nf* slope; (*en camino etc*) hill; **~ arriba/abajo** uphill/downhill; **a ~s** on one's back

**cueste** *etc vb ver* **costar**

**cuestión** [kwes'tjon] *nf* matter, question, issue; (*riña*) quarrel, dispute

**cueva** ['kweβa] *nf* cave

**cuidado** [kwi'ðaðo] *nm* care, carefulness; (*preocupación*) care, worry ♦ *excl* careful!, look out!

**cuidadoso, a** [kwiða'ðoso, a] *adj* careful; (*preocupado*) anxious

**cuidar** [kwi'ðar] *vt* (*MED*) to take care for; (*ocuparse de*) to take care of, look after ♦ *vi*: **~ de** to take care of, look after; **~se** *vr* to look after o.s.; **~se de hacer algo** to take care to do sth

**culata** [ku'lata] *nf* (*de fusil*) butt

**culebra** [ku'leβra] *nf* snake

**culebrón** [kule'βron] (*fam*) *nm* (*TV*) soap-opera

**culinario, a** [kuli'narjo, a] *adj* culinary, cooking *cpd*

**culminación** [kulmina'θjon] *nf* culmination

**culo** ['kulo] *nm* bottom, backside; (*de vaso, botella*) bottom

**culpa** ['kulpa] *nf* fault; (*JUR*) guilt; **por ~ de** because of, through; **tener la ~ (de)** to be to blame (for); **~bilidad** *nf* guilt; **~ble** *adj* guilty ♦ *nm/f* culprit

**culpar** [kul'par] *vt* to blame; (*acusar*) to accuse

**cultivar** [kulti'βar] *vt* to cultivate

**cultivo** [kul'tiβo] *nm* (*acto*) cultivation; (*plantas*) crop

**culto, a** ['kulto, a] *adj* (*cultivado*) cultivated; (*que tiene cultura*) cultured, educated ♦ *nm* (*homenaje*) worship; (*religión*) cult

**cultura** [kul'tura] *nf* culture

**culturismo** [kultu'rismo] *nm* bodybuilding

**cumbre** ['kumbre] *nf* summit, top

**cumpleaños** [kumple'aɲos] *nm inv* birthday

**cumplido, a** [kum'pliðo, a] *adj* complete, perfect; (*abundante*) plentiful;

(*cortés*) courteous ♦ *nm* compliment; **visita de ~** courtesy call

**cumplidor, a** [kumpli'ðor, a] *adj* reliable

**cumplimentar** [kumplimen'tar] *vt* to congratulate

**cumplimiento** [kumpli'mjento] *nm* (*de un deber*) fulfilment; (*acabamiento*) completion

**cumplir** [kum'plir] *vt* (*orden*) to carry out, obey; (*promesa*) to carry out, fulfil; (*condena*) to serve; (*años*) to reach, attain ♦ *vi*: **~ con** (*deberes*) to carry out, fulfil; **~se** *vr* (*plazo*) to expire; **hoy cumple dieciocho años** he is eighteen today

**cúmulo** ['kumulo] *nm* heap

**cuna** ['kuna] *nf* cradle, cot

**cundir** [kun'dir] *vi* (*noticia, rumor, pánico*) to spread; (*rendir*) to go a long way

**cuneta** [ku'neta] *nf* ditch

**cuña** ['kuɲa] *nf* wedge

**cuñado, a** [ku'ɲaðo, a] *nm/f* brother/sister-in-law

**cuota** ['kwota] *nf* (*parte proporcional*) share; (*cotización*) fee, dues *pl*

**cupe** *etc vb ver* **caber**

**cupiera** *etc vb ver* **caber**

**cupo** ['kupo] *vb ver* **caber** ♦ *nm* quota

**cupón** [ku'pon] *nm* coupon

**cúpula** ['kupula] *nf* dome

**cura** ['kura] *nf* (*curación*) cure; (*método curativo*) treatment ♦ *nm* priest

**curación** [kura'θjon] *nf* cure; (*acción*) curing

**curandero, a** [kuran'dero, a] *nm/f* quack

**curar** [ku'rar] *vt* (*MED: herida*) to treat, dress; (: *enfermo*) to cure; (*CULIN*) to cure, salt; (*cuero*) to tan ♦ *vi* to get well, recover; **~se** *vr* to get well, recover

**curiosear** [kurjose'ar] *vt* to glance at, look over ♦ *vi* to look round, wander round; (*explorar*) to poke about

**curiosidad** [kurjosi'ðað] *nf* curiosity

**curioso, a** [ku'rjoso, a] *adj* curious ♦ *nm/f* bystander, onlooker

**currante** [ku'rrante] (*fam*) *nm/f* worker

**currar** [ku'rrar] (*fam*) *vi* to work

**currelar** [kurre'lar] (*fam*) *vi* to work

**currículo** [ku'rrikulo] = **curriculum**

**curriculum** [ku'rrikulum] *nm* curriculum vitae

**curro** ['kurro] (*fam*) *nm* work, job

**cursi** ['kursi] (*fam*) *adj* pretentious; (*amanerado*) affected

**cursillo** [kur'siʎo] *nm* short course

**cursiva** [kur'siβa] *nf* italics *pl*

**curso** ['kurso] *nm* course; **en ~** (*año*) current; (*proceso*) going on, under way

**cursor** [kur'sor] *nm* (*INFORM*) cursor

**curtido, a** [kur'tiðo, a] *adj* (*cara etc*) weather-beaten; (*fig: persona*) experienced

**curtir** [kur'tir] *vt* (*cuero etc*) to tan

**curva** [kur'βa] *nf* curve, bend

**curvo, a** [kur'βo, a] *adj* (*gen*) curved; (*torcido*) bent

**cúspide** [kus'piðe] *nf* (*GEO*) peak; (*fig*) top

**custodia** [kus'toðja] *nf* safekeeping; custody; **custodiar** *vt* (*conservar*) to take care of; (*vigilar*) to guard

**cutícula** [ku'tikula] *nf* cuticle

**cutis** ['kutis] *nm inv* skin, complexion

**cutre** ['kutre] (*fam*) *adj* (*lugar*) grotty; (*persona*) naff

**cuyo, a** ['kujo, a] *pron* (*de quien*) whose; (*de que*) whose, of which; **en ~ caso** in which case

**C.V.** *abr* (= *caballos de vapor*) H.P.

## CH

**chabacano, a** [tʃaβa'kano, a] *adj* vulgar, coarse

**chabola** [tʃa'βola] *nf* shack; **~s** *nfpl* shanty town *sg*

**chacal** [tʃa'kal] *nm* jackal

**chacra** ['tʃakra] (*AM*) *nf* smallholding

**chacha** ['tʃatʃa] (*fam*) *nf* maid

**cháchara** ['tʃatʃara] *nf* chatter; estar de ~ to chatter away

**chafar** [tʃa'far] vt (aplastar) to crush; (arruinar) to ruin

**chal** [tʃal] nm shawl

**chalado, a** [tʃa'lado, a] (fam) adj crazy

**chalé** [tʃa'le] (pl ~s) nm villa; ≈ detached house

**chaleco** [tʃa'leko] nm waistcoat, vest (US); ~ **salvavidas** life jacket

**chalet** [tʃa'le] (pl ~s) nm = **chalé**

**champán** [tʃam'pan] nm champagne

**champaña** [tʃam'paɲa] nm = **champán**

**champiñón** [tʃampi'ɲon] nm mushroom

**champú** [tʃam'pu] (pl **champúes**, **champús**) nm shampoo

**chamuscar** [tʃamus'kar] vt to scorch, sear, singe

**chance** [tʃanθe] (AM) nm chance

**chancho, a** ['tʃantʃo, a] (AM) nm/f pig

**chanchullo** [tʃan'tʃuʎo] (fam) nm fiddle

**chandal** [tʃan'dal] nm tracksuit

**chantaje** [tʃan'taxe] nm blackmail

**chapa** ['tʃapa] nf (de metal) plate, sheet; (de madera) board, panel; (AM: AUTO) number (BRIT) o license (US) plate

**chaparrón** [tʃapa'rron] nm downpour, cloudburst

**chapotear** [tʃapote'ar] vi to splash about

**chapucero, a** [tʃapu'θero, a] adj rough, crude ♦ nm/f bungler

**chapurrear** [tʃapurre'ar] vt (idioma) to speak badly

**chapuza** [tʃa'puθa] nf botched job

**chapuzón** [tʃapu'θon] nm: **darse un** ~ to go for a dip

**chaqueta** [tʃa'keta] nf jacket

**chaquetón** [tʃake'ton] nm long jacket

**charca** ['tʃarka] nf pond, pool

**charco** ['tʃarko] nm pool, puddle

**charcutería** [tʃarkute'ria] nf (tienda) shop selling, chiefly pork meat products; (productos) cooked pork

meats pl

**charla** ['tʃarla] nf talk, chat; (conferencia) lecture

**charlar** [tʃar'lar] vi to talk, chat

**charlatán, ana** [tʃarla'tan, ana] nm/f chatterbox; (estafador) trickster

**charol** [tʃa'rol] nm varnish; (cuero) patent leather

**chascarrillo** [tʃaska'rriʎo] (fam) nm funny story

**chasco** ['tʃasko] nm (broma) trick, joke; (desengaño) disappointment

**chasis** ['tʃasis] nm inv chassis

**chasquear** [tʃaske'ar] vt (látigo) to crack; (lengua) to click; **chasquido** nm crack; click

**chatarra** [tʃa'tarra] nf scrap (metal)

**chato, a** ['tʃato, a] adj flat; (nariz) snub

**chaval, a** [tʃa'βal, a] nm/f kid, lad/ lass

**checo(e)slovaco, a** [tʃeko(e)slo-'βako, a] adj, nm/f Czech, Czechoslovak

**Checo(e)slovaquia** [tʃeko(e)slo-'βakja] nf Czechoslovakia

**cheque** ['tʃeke] nm cheque (BRIT), check (US); ~ **de viajero** traveller's cheque (BRIT), traveler's check (US)

**chequeo** [tʃe'keo] nm (MED) check-up; (AUTO) service

**chequera** [tʃe'kera] (AM) nf chequebook (BRIT), checkbook (US)

**chicano, a** [tʃi'kano, a] adj, nm/f chicano

**chicle** ['tʃikle] nm chewing gum

**chico, a** ['tʃiko, a] adj small, little ♦ nm/f (niño) child; (muchacho) boy/ girl

**chícharo** ['tʃitʃaro] (AM) nm pea

**chichón** [tʃi'tʃon] nm bump, lump

**chiflado, a** [tʃi'flaðo, a] adj crazy

**chiflar** [tʃi'flar] vt to hiss, boo

**chile** ['tʃile] nm chilli pepper

**Chile** ['tʃile] nm Chile; **chileno, a** adj, nm/f Chilean

**chillar** [tʃi'ʎar] vi (persona) to yell, scream; (animal salvaje) to howl;

(cerdo) to squeal; (puerta) to creak

**chillido** [tʃiˈʎiðo] nm (de persona) yell, scream; (de animal) howl; (de frenos) screech(ing)

**chillón, ona** [tʃiˈʎon, ona] adj (niño) noisy; (color) loud, gaudy

**chimenea** [tʃimeˈnea] nf chimney; (hogar) fireplace

**China** [ˈtʃina] nf: (la) ~ China

**chinche** [ˈtʃintʃe] nf (insecto) (bed)bug; (TEC) drawing pin (BRIT), thumbtack (US) ♦ nm/f nuisance, pest

**chincheta** [tʃinˈtʃeta] nf drawing pin (BRIT), thumbtack (US)

**chino, a** [ˈtʃino, a] adj, nm/f Chinese ♦ nm (LING) Chinese

**chipirón** [tʃipiˈron] nm (ZOOL, CULIN) squid

**Chipre** [ˈtʃipre] nf Cyprus; **chipriota** adj, nm/f Cypriot

**chiquillo, a** [tʃiˈkiʎo, a] nm/f (fam) kid

**chiringuito** [tʃirinˈɣito] nm small open-air bar

**chiripa** [tʃiˈripa] nf fluke

**chirriar** [tʃiˈrrjar] vi (goznes etc) to creak, squeak; (pájaros) to chirp, sing

**chirrido** [tʃiˈrriðo] nm creak(ing), squeak(ing); (de pájaro) chirp(ing)

**chis** [tʃis] excl sh!

**chisme** [ˈtʃisme] nm (habladurías) piece of gossip; (fam: objeto) thingummyjig

**chismoso, a** [tʃisˈmoso, a] adj gossiping ♦ nm/f gossip

**chispa** [ˈtʃispa] nf spark; (fig) sparkle; (ingenio) wit; (fam) drunkenness

**chispear** [tʃispeˈar] vi to spark; (lloviznar) to drizzle

**chisporrotear** [tʃisporroteˈar] vi (fuego) to throw out sparks; (leña) to crackle; (aceite) to hiss, splutter

**chiste** [ˈtʃiste] nm joke, funny story

**chistoso, a** [tʃisˈtoso, a] adj (gracioso) funny, amusing; (bromista) witty

**chivo, a** [ˈtʃißo, a] nm/f (billy-/nanny-)goat; ~ **expiatorio** scape-

goat

**chocante** [tʃoˈkante] adj startling; (extraño) odd; (ofensivo) shocking

**chocar** [tʃoˈkar] vi (coches etc) to collide, crash ♦ vt to shock; (sorprender) to startle; ~ **con** to collide with; (fig) to run into, run up against; **¡chócala!** (fam) put it there!

**chocolate** [tʃokoˈlate] adj, nm chocolate; **chocolatina** nf chocolate

**chochear** [tʃotʃeˈar] vi to dodder, be senile

**chocho, a** [ˈtʃotʃo, a] adj doddering, senile; (fig) soft, doting

**chofer** [tʃoˈfer] nm = **chófer**

**chófer** [ˈtʃofer] nm driver

**chollo** [ˈtʃoʎo] (fam) nm bargain, snip

**choque** etc [ˈtʃoke] vb ver **chocar** ♦ nm (impacto) impact; (golpe) jolt; (AUTO) crash; (fig) conflict; ~ **frontal** head-on collision

**chorizo** [tʃoˈriθo] nm hard pork sausage, (type of) salami

**chorrear** [tʃorreˈar] vi to gush (out), spout (out); (gotear) to drip, trickle

**chorro** [ˈtʃorro] nm jet; (fig) stream

**choza** [ˈtʃoθa] nf hut, shack

**chubasco** [tʃuˈßasko] nm squall

**chubasquero** nm lightweight raincoat

**chuchería** [tʃutʃeˈria] nf trinket

**chuleta** [tʃuˈleta] nf chop, cutlet

**chulo** [ˈtʃulo] nm (pícaro) rascal; (rufián) pimp

**chupar** [tʃuˈpar] vt to suck; (absorber) to absorb; ~se vr to grow thin

**chupete** [tʃuˈpete] nm dummy (BRIT), pacifier (US)

**churro, a** [ˈtʃurro, a] adj coarse ♦ nm (type of) fritter

**chusma** [ˈtʃusma] nf rabble, mob

**chutar** [tʃuˈtar] vi (DEPORTE) to shoot (at goal)

# D

**D.** abr (= Don) Esq.

**Da.** abr = Doña

**dádiva** ['daðiβa] nf (donación) donation; (regalo) gift; **dadivoso, a** adj generous

**dado, a** ['dado, a] pp de **dar** ♦ nm die; ~s nmpl dice; ~ que given that

**daltónico, a** [dal'toniko, a] adj colour-blind

**dama** ['dama] nf (gen) lady; (AJEDREZ) queen; ~s nfpl (juego) draughts sg

**damnificar** [damnifi'kar] vt to harm; (persona) to injure

**danés, esa** [da'nes, esa] adj Danish ♦ nm/f Dane

**danzar** [dan'θar] vt, vi to dance

**dañar** [da'ɲar] vt (objeto) to damage; (persona) to hurt; ~se vr (objeto) to get damaged

**dañino, a** [da'ɲino, a] adj harmful

**daño** ['daɲo] nm (a un objeto) damage; (a una persona) harm, injury; ~s y perjuicios (JUR) damages; hacer ~ a to damage; (persona) to hurt, injure; hacerse ~ to hurt o.s.

---

*PALABRA CLAVE*

**dar** [dar] vt 1 (gen) to give; (obra de teatro) to put on; (film) to show; (fiesta) to hold; ~ algo a uno to give sb sth o sth to sb; ~ de beber a uno to give sb a drink

2 (producir: intereses) to yield; (fruta) to produce

3 (locuciones +n): da gusto escucharle it's a pleasure to listen to him; ver tb paseo y otros sustantivos

4 (+n: = perífrasis de verbo): me da pena/asco it frightens/sickens me

5 (considerar): ~ algo por descontado/entendido to take sth for granted/as read; ~ algo por concluido to consider sth finished

6 (hora): el reloj dio las 6 the clock struck 6 (o'clock)

7: me da lo mismo it's all the same to me; ver tb igual, más

♦ vi 1: ~ con: dimos con él dos horas más tarde we came across him two hours later; al final di con la solución I eventually came up with the answer

2: ~ en: ~ en (blanco, suelo) to hit; el sol me da en la cara the sun is shining (right) on my face

3: ~ de sí (zapatos etc) to stretch, give

♦ ~se vr 1: ~se por vencido to give up

2 (ocurrir): se han dado muchos casos there have been a lot of cases

3: ~se a: se ha dado a la bebida he's taken to drinking

4: se me dan bien/mal las ciencias I'm good/bad at science

5: dárselas de: se las da de experto he fancies himself o poses as an expert

---

**dardo** ['darðo] nm dart

**dársena** ['darsena] nf dock

**datar** [da'tar] vi: ~ de to date from

**dátil** ['datil] nm date

**dato** ['dato] nm fact, piece of information

**DC** abbr m (= disco compacto) CD

**dcha.** abr (= derecha) r.h.

**d. de J.C.** abr (= después de Jesucristo) A.D.

---

*PALABRA CLAVE*

**de** [de] prep (de + el = del) 1 (posesión) of; la casa ~ Isabel/mis padres Isabel's/my parents' house; es ~ ellos it's theirs

2 (origen, distancia, con números) from; soy ~ Gijón I'm from Gijón; ~ 8 a 20 from 8 to 20; salir del cine to go out of o leave the cinema; ~ ... en ... from ... to ...; ~ 2 en 2 by 2, 2 at a time

3 (valor descriptivo): una copa ~ vino a glass of wine; la mesa ~ la cocina the kitchen table; un billete

~ 1000 pesetas a 1000 peseta note; un niño ~ tres años a three-year-old (child); una máquina ~ coser a sewing machine; ir vestido ~ gris to be dressed in grey; la niña del vestido azul the girl in the blue dress; trabaja ~ profesora she works as a teacher; ~ lado sideways; ~ atrás/delante rear/front

**4** (hora, tiempo): a las 8 ~ la mañana at 8 o'clock in the morning; ~ día/noche by day/night; ~ hoy en ocho días a week from now; ~ niño era gordo as a child he was fat

**5** (comparaciones): más/menos ~ cien personas more/less than a hundred people; el más caro ~ la tienda the most expensive in the shop; menos/más ~ lo pensado less/more than expected

**6** (causa): del calor from the heat; ~ puro tonto out of sheer stupidity

**7** (tema): clases ~ inglés English classes; ¿sabes algo ~ él? do you know anything about him?; un libro ~ física a physics book

**8** (adj + de + infin): fácil ~ entender easy to understand

**9** (oraciones pasivas): fue respetado ~ todos he was loved by all

**10** (condicional + infin) if: ~ ser posible if possible; ~ no terminarlo hoy if I etc don't finish it today

**dé** vb ver **dar**

**deambular** [deambu'lar] vi to stroll, wander

**debajo** [de'βaxo] adv underneath; ~ de below, under; por ~ de beneath

**debate** [de'βate] nm debate; **debatir** vt to debate

**deber** [de'βer] nm duty ♦ vt to owe ♦ vi: debe (de) it must, it should; ~es nmpl (ESCOL) homework; debo hacerlo I must do it; debe de ir he should go; ~se vr: ~se a to be owing o due to

**debido, a** [de'βiðo, a] adj proper, just; ~ a due to, because of

**débil** ['deβil] adj (persona, carácter)

weak; (luz) dim; **debilidad** nf weakness; dimness

**debilitar** [deβili'tar] vt to weaken; ~se vr to grow weak

**debutar** [deβu'tar] vi to make one's debut

**década** ['dekaða] nf decade

**decadencia** [deka'ðenθja] nf (estado) decadence; (proceso) decline, decay

**decaer** [deka'er] vi (declinar) to decline; (debilitarse) to weaken

**decaído, a** [deka'iðo, a] adj: estar ~ (abatido) to be down

**decaimiento** [dekai'mjento] nm (declinación) decline; (desaliento) discouragement; (MED: estado débil) weakness

**decano, a** [de'kano, a] nm/f (de universidad etc) dean

**decapitar** [dekapi'tar] vt to behead

**decena** [de'θena] nf: una ~ ten (or so)

**decencia** [de'θenθja] nf (modestia) modesty; (honestidad) respectability

**decente** [de'θente] adj (correcto) seemly, proper; (honesto) respectable

**decepción** [deθep'θjon] nf disappointment

**decepcionar** [deθepθjo'nar] vt to disappoint

**decidir** [deθi'ðir] vt (persuadir) to convince, persuade; (resolver) to decide ♦ vi to decide; ~se vr: ~se a to make up one's mind to

**décimo, a** ['deθimo, a] adj tenth ♦ nm tenth

**decir** [de'θir] vt (expresar) to say; (contar) to tell; (hablar) to speak ♦ nm saying; ~se vr: se dice que it is said that; ~ para o entre sí to say to o.s.; querer ~ to mean; ¡dígame! (TEL) hello!; (en tienda) can I help you?

**decisión** [deθi'sjon] nf (resolución) decision; (firmeza) decisiveness

**decisivo, a** [deθi'siβo, a] adj decisive

**declamar** [dekla'mar] vt, vi to declaim

**declaración** [deklara'θjon] nf (*manifestación*) statement; (*explicación*) explanation; ~ **de ingresos** o **de la renta** o **fiscal** income-tax return

**declarar** [dekla'rar] vt to declare ♦ vi to declare; (*JUR*) to testify; ~**se** vr to propose

**declinar** [dekli'nar] vt (*gen*) to decline; (*JUR*) to reject ♦ vi (*el día*) to draw to a close

**declive** [de'kliße] nm (*cuesta*) slope; (*fig*) decline

**decodificador** [dekoðifika'ðor] nm decoder

**decolorarse** [dekolo'rarse] vr to become discoloured

**decoración** [dekora'θjon] nf decoration

**decorado** [deko'raðo] nm (*CINE, TEATRO*) scenery, set

**decorar** [deko'rar] vt to decorate; **decorativo, a** adj ornamental, decorative

**decoro** [de'koro] nm (*respeto*) respect; (*dignidad*) decency; (*recato*) propriety; ~**so, a** adj (*decente*) decent; (*modesto*) modest; (*digno*) proper

**decrecer** [dekre'θer] vi to decrease, diminish

**decrépito, a** [de'krepito, a] adj decrepit

**decretar** [dekre'tar] vt to decree; **decreto** nm decree

**dedal** [de'ðal] nm thimble

**dedicación** [deðika'θjon] nf dedication

**dedicar** [deði'kar] vt (*libro*) to dedicate; (*tiempo, dinero*) to devote; (*palabras: decir, consagrar*) to dedicate, devote; **dedicatoria** nf (*de libro*) dedication

**dedo** ['deðo] nm finger; ~ (**del pie**) toe; ~ **pulgar** thumb; ~ **índice** index finger; ~ **mayor** o **cordial** middle finger; ~ **anular** ring finger; ~ **meñique** little finger; **hacer** ~ (*fam*) to hitch (a lift)

**deducción** [deðuk'θjon] nf deduction

**deducir** [deðu'θir] vt (*concluir*) to deduce, infer; (*COM*) to deduct

**defecto** [de'fekto] nm defect, flaw; **defectuoso, a** adj defective, faulty

**defender** [defen'der] vt to defend

**defensa** [de'fensa] nf defence ♦ nm (*DEPORTE*) defender, back; **defensiva** nf: **a la** ~ on the defensive; **defensivo, a** adj defensive

**defensor, a** [defen'sor, a] adj defending ♦ nm/f (*abogado* ~) defending counsel; (*protector*) protector

**deficiencia** [defi'θjenθja] nf deficiency

**deficiente** [defi'θjente] adj (*defectuoso*) defective; ~ **en** lacking o deficient in; **ser un** ~ **mental** to be mentally handicapped

**déficit** ['defiθit] (pl ~s) nm deficit

**definición** [defini'θjon] nf definition

**definir** [defi'nir] vt (*determinar*) to determine, establish; (*decidir*) to define; (*aclarar*) to clarify; **definitivo, a** adj definitive; **en definitiva** definitively; (*en resumen*) in short

**deformación** [deforma'θjon] nf (*alteración*) deformation; (*RADIO etc*) distortion

**deformar** [defor'mar] vt (*gen*) to deform; ~**se** vr to become deformed; **deforme** adj (*informe*) deformed; (*feo*) ugly; (*malhecho*) misshapen

**defraudar** [defrau'ðar] vt (*decepcionar*) to disappoint; (*estafar*) to cheat; to defraud

**defunción** [defun'θjon] nf death, demise

**degeneración** [dexenera'θjon] nf (*de las células*) degeneration; (*moral*) degeneracy

**degenerar** [dexene'rar] vi to degenerate

**degollar** [deɣo'ʎar] vt to behead; (*fig*) to slaughter

**degradar** [deɣra'ðar] vt to debase, degrade; ~**se** vr to demean o.s

**degustación** [deɣusta'θjon] nf sampling, tasting

**deificar** [deifi'kar] vt (*persona*) to deify

**dejadez** [dexa'ðeθ] nf (negligencia) neglect; (descuido) untidiness, carelessness

**dejar** [de'xar] vt to leave; (permitir) to allow, let; (abandonar) to abandon, forsake; (beneficios) to produce, yield ♦ vi: ~ de (parar) to stop; (no hacer) to fail to; **no dejes de comprar un billete** make sure you buy a ticket; ~ **a un lado** to leave o set aside

**dejo** ['dexo] nm (LING) accent

**del** [del] = de+el) ver de

**delantal** [delan'tal] nm apron

**delante** [de'lante] adv in front, (enfrente) opposite; (adelante) ahead; ~ de in front of, before

**delantera** [delan'tera] nf (de vestido, casa etc) front part; (DEPORTE) forward line; **llevar la ~ (a uno)** to be ahead (of sb)

**delantero, a** [delan'tero, a] adj front ♦ nm (DEPORTE) forward, striker

**delatar** [dela'tar] vt to inform on o against, betray; **delator, a** nm/f informer

**delegación** [deleɣa'θjon] nf (acción, delegados) delegation; (COM: oficina) office, branch; ~ **de policía** police station

**delegado, a** [dele'ɣaðo, a] nm/f delegate; (COM) agent

**delegar** [dele'ɣar] vt to delegate

**deletrear** [deletre'ar] vt to spell (out)

**deleznable** [deleθ'naβle] adj brittle; (excusa, idea) feeble

**delfín** [del'fin] nm dolphin

**delgadez** [delɣa'ðeθ] nf thinness, slimness

**delgado, a** [del'ɣaðo, a] adj thin; (persona) slim, thin; (tierra) poor; (tela etc) light, delicate

**deliberación** [deliβera'θjon] nf deliberation

**deliberar** [deliβe'rar] vt to debate, discuss

**delicadeza** [delika'ðeθa] nf (gen) delicacy; (refinamiento, sutileza) refinement

**delicado, a** [deli'kaðo, a] adj (gen) delicate; (sensible) sensitive; (quisquilloso) touchy

**delicia** [de'liθja] nf delight

**delicioso, a** [deli'θjoso, a] adj (gracioso) delightful; (exquisito) delicious

**delimitar** [delimi'tar] vt (funciones, responsabilidades) to define

**delincuencia** [delin'kwenθja] nf delinquency; **delincuente** nm/f delinquent; (criminal) criminal

**delineante** [deline'ante] nm/f draughtsman/woman

**delinear** [deline'ar] vt (dibujo) to draw; (fig, contornos) to outline

**delinquir** [delin'kir] vi to commit an offence

**delirante** [deli'rante] adj delirious

**delirar** [deli'rar] vi to be delirious, rave

**delirio** [de'lirjo] nm (MED) delirium; (palabras insensatas) ravings pl

**delito** [de'lito] nm (gen) crime; (infracción) offence

**delta** ['delta] nm delta

**demacrado, a** [dema'kraðo, a] adj: **estar ~** to look pale and drawn, be wasted away

**demagogo, a** [dema'ɣoɣo, a] nm/f demagogue

**demanda** [de'manda] nf (pedido, COM) demand; (petición) request; (JUR) action, lawsuit

**demandante** [deman'dante] nm/f claimant

**demandar** [deman'dar] vt (gen) to demand; (JUR) to sue, file a lawsuit against

**demarcación** [demarka'θjon] nf (de terreno) demarcation

**demás** [de'mas] adj: **los ~ niños** the other children, the remaining children ♦ pron: **los/las ~** the others, the rest (of them); **lo ~** the rest (of it)

**demasía** [dema'sia] nf (exceso) excess, surplus; **comer en ~** to eat to excess

**demasiado, a** [dema'sjaðo, a] adj: **~ vino** too much wine; **~s libros**

too many books ♦ adv (antes de adj, adv) too; **¡esto es ~!** that's the limit!; **hace ~ calor** it's too hot; **~ despacio** too slowly; **~s too** many

**demencia** [de'menθa] nf (locura) madness; **demente** nm/f lunatic ♦ adj mad, insane

**democracia** [demo'kraθja] nf democracy

**demócrata** [de'mokrata] nm/f democrat; **democrático, a** adj democratic

**demoler** [demo'ler] vt to demolish; **demolición, a** nf demolition

**demonio** [de'monjo] nm devil, demon; **¡~s!** hell!, damn!; **¿cómo ~s?** how the hell?

**demora** [de'mora] nf delay; **demorar** vt (retardar) to delay, hold back; (detener) to hold up ♦ vi to linger, stay on; **~se** vr to be delayed

**demos** vb ver **dar**

**demostración** [demostra'θjon] nf (MAT) proof; (de afecto) show, display

**demostrar** [demos'trar] vt (probar) to prove; (mostrar) to show; (manifestar) to demonstrate

**demudado, a** [demu'ðaðo, a] adj (rostro) pale

**den** vb ver **dar**

**denegar** [dene'var] vt (rechazar) to refuse; (JUR) to reject

**denigrar** [deni'xrar] vt (desacreditar, infamar) to denigrate; (injuriar) to insult

**denominación** [denomina'θjon] nf (clase) denomination

**denotar** [deno'tar] vt (indicar) to indicate; (significar) to denote

**densidad** [densi'ðað] nf (FÍSICA) density; (fig) thickness

**denso, a** [denso, a] adj (apretado) solid; (espeso, pastoso) thick; (fig) heavy

**dentadura** [denta'ðura] nf (set of) teeth pl; **~ postiza** false teeth pl

**dentera** [den'tera] nf (sensación desagradable) the shivers pl

**dentífrico, a** [den'tifriko, a] adj dental ♦ nm toothpaste

**dentista** [den'tista] nm/f dentist

**dentro** ['dentro] adv inside ♦ prep: **~ de** in, inside, within; **por ~** (on the) inside; **mirar por ~** to look inside; **~ de tres meses** within three months

**denuncia** [de'nunθja] nf (delación) denunciation; (acusación) accusation; (de accidente) report; **denunciar** vt to report; (delatar) to inform on o against

**departamento** [departa'mento] nm (sección administrativa) department, section; (AM: apartamento) flat (BRIT), apartment

**dependencia** [depen'denθja] nf dependence; (POL) dependency; (COM) office, section

**depender** [depen'der] vi: **~ de** to depend on

**dependienta** [depen'djenta] nf saleswoman, shop assistant

**dependiente** [depen'djente] adj dependent ♦ nm salesman, shop assistant

**depilar** [depi'lar] vt (con cera) to wax; (cejas) to pluck; **depilatorio** nm hair remover

**deplorable** [deplo'raβle] adj deplorable

**deplorar** [deplo'rar] vt to deplore

**deponer** [depo'ner] vt to lay down ♦ vi (JUR) to give evidence; (declarar) to make a statement

**deportar** [depor'tar] vt to deport

**deporte** [de'porte] nm sport; **hacer ~** to play sports; **deportista** adj sports cpd ♦ nm/f sportsman/woman; **deportivo, a** adj (club, periódico) sports cpd ♦ nm sports car

**depositante** [deposi'tante] nm/f depositor

**depositar** [deposi'tar] vt (dinero) to deposit; (mercancías) to put away, store; (persona) to confide; **~se** vr to settle; **~io, a** nm/f trustee

**depósito** [de'posito] nm (gen) deposit; (almacén) warehouse, store; (de agua, gasolina etc) tank; **~ de cadáveres** mortuary

**depreciar** [depre'θjar] vt to depreciate, reduce the value of; ~se vr to
depreciate, lose value

**depredador, a** [depreða'ðor, a] adj
predatory ♦ nm predator

**depresión** [depre'sjon] nf depression

**deprimido, a** [depri'miðo, a] adj depressed

**deprimir** [depri'mir] vt to depress;
~se vr (persona) to become depressed

**deprisa** [de'prisa] adv quickly, hurriedly

**depuración** [depura'θjon] nf purifi-
cation; (POL) purge

**depurar** [depu'rar] vt to purify; (purgar) to purge

**derecha** [de'retʃa] nf right(-hand)
side; (POL) right; a la ~ (estar) on
the right; (torcer etc) (to the) right

**derecho, a** [de'retʃo, a] adj right,
right-hand ♦ nm (privilegio) right;
(lado) right(-hand) side; (leyes) law
♦ adv straight, directly; ~s nmpl
(de aduana) duty sg; (de autor) roy-
alties; tener ~ a to have a right to

**deriva** [de'riβa] nf: ir o estar a la ~
to drift, be adrift

**derivado** [deri'βaðo] nm (COM) by-
product

**derivar** [deri'βar] vt to derive; (desviar) to direct ♦ vi to derive, be derived; (NAUT) to drift; ~se vr to derive, be derived; to drift

**derramamiento** [derrama'mjento]
nm (dispersión) spilling; ~ de
sangre bloodshed

**derramar** [derra'mar] vt to spill;
(verter) to pour out; (esparcir) to
scatter; ~se vr to pour out; ~ lágrimas to weep

**derrame** [de'rrame] nm (de líquido)
spilling; (de sangre) shedding; (de
tubo etc) overflow; (pérdida) leak-
age; (MED) discharge; (declive)
slope

**derredor** [derre'ðor] adv: al o en ~
de around, about

**derretido, a** [derre'tiðo, a] adj
melted; (metal) molten

**derretir** [derre'tir] vt (gen) to melt;
(nieve) to thaw; (fig) to squander;
~se vr to melt

**derribar** [derri'βar] vt to knock
down; (construcción) to demolish;
(persona, gobierno, político) to bring
down

**derrocar** [derro'kar] vt (gobierno) to
bring down, overthrow

**derrochar** [derro'tʃar] vt to squander; **derroche** nm (despilfarro)
waste, squandering

**derrota** [de'rrota] nf (NAUT) course;
(MIL, DEPORTE etc) defeat, rout;
**derrotar** vt (gen) to defeat; **derrote-
ro** nm (rumbo) course

**derruir** [derru'ir] vt (edificio) to demolish

**derrumbar** [derrum'bar] vt (edificio)
to knock down; ~se vr to collapse

**derruyendo** etc vb ver **derruir**

**des** vb ver **dar**

**desabotonar** [desaβoto'nar] vt to
unbutton, undo ♦ vi (flores) to
bloom; ~se vr to come undone

**desabrido, a** [desa'βriðo, a] adj (comida) insipid, tasteless; (persona)
rude, surly; (respuesta) sharp;
(tiempo) unpleasant

**desabrochar** [desaβro'tʃar] vt (botones, broches) to undo, unfasten;
~se vr (ropa etc) to come undone

**desacato** [desa'kato] nm (falta de
respeto) disrespect; (JUR) contempt

**desacertado, a** [desaθer'taðo, a]
adj (equivocado) mistaken; (inoportuno) unwise

**desacierto** [desa'θjerto] nm mistake,
error

**desaconsejado, a** [desakonse'xaðo,
a] adj ill-advised

**desaconsejar** [desakonse'xar] vt to
advise against

**desacreditar** [desakreði'tar] vt (desprestigiar) to discredit, bring into
disrepute; (denigrar) to run down

**desacuerdo** [desa'kwerðo] nm (conflicto) disagreement, discord; (error)
error, blunder

**desafiar** [desa'fjar] vt (retar) to chal-

lenge; (enfrentarse a) to defy
**desafilado, a** [desafi'laðo, a] adj
blunt
**desafinado, a** [desafi'naðo, a] adj:
estar ~ to be out of tune
**desafinar** [desafi'nar] vi (al cantar)
to be o go out of tune
**desafío** etc [desa'fio] vb ver **desafiar**
♦ nm (reto) challenge; (combate)
duel; (resistencia) defiance
**desaforado, a** [desafo'raðo, a] adj
(grito) ear-splitting; (comportamiento) outrageous
**desafortunadamente** [desafortu-
naða'mente] adv unfortunately
**desafortunado, a** [desafortu'naðo,
a] adj (desgraciado) unfortunate, unlucky
**desagradable** [desavra'ðaßle] adj
(fastidioso, enojoso) unpleasant;
(irritante) disagreeable
**desagradar** [desavra'ðar] vi (disgustar) to displease; (molestar) to
bother
**desagradecido, a** [desavraðe'θiðo,
a] adj ungrateful
**desagrado** [desa'vraðo] nm (disgusto) displeasure; (contrariedad)
dissatisfaction
**desagraviar** [desavra'ßjar] vt to
make amends to
**desagüe** [des'avwe] nm (de un líquido) drainage; (cañería) drainpipe;
(salida) outlet, drain
**desaguisado, a** [desavi'saðo, a] adj
illegal ♦ nm outrage
**desahogado, a** [desao'xaðo, a] adj
(holgado) comfortable; (espacioso)
roomy, large
**desahogar** [desao'xar] vt (aliviar)
to ease, relieve; (ira) to vent; ~se
vr (relajarse) to relax; (desfogarse)
to let off steam
**desahogo** [desa'oxo] nm (alivio) relief; (comodidad) comfort, ease
**desahuciar** [desau'θjar] vt (enfermo) to give up hope for; (inquilino)
to evict; **desahucio** nm eviction
**desairar** [desai'rar] vt (menospreciar) to slight, snub; (cosa) to dis-

regard
**desaire** [des'aire] nm (menosprecio)
slight; (falta de garbo) unattractive-
ness
**desajustar** [desaxus'tar] vt (desarreglar) to disarrange; (desconcertar)
to throw off balance; ~se vr to get
out of order; (aflojarse) to loosen
**desajuste** [desa'xuste] nm (de máquina) disorder; (situación) imbalance
**desalentador, a** [desalenta'ðor, a]
adj discouraging
**desalentar** [desalen'tar] vt (desanimar) to discourage
**desaliento** etc [desa'ljento] vb ver
**desalentar** ♦ nm discouragement
**desaliño** [desa'liɲo] nm (negligencia) slovenliness
**desalmado, a** [desal'maðo, a] adj
(cruel) cruel, heartless
**desalojar** [desalo'xar] vt (expulsar,
echar) to eject; (abandonar) to move
out of ♦ vi to move out
**desamor** [desa'mor] nm (frialdad)
indifference; (odio) dislike
**desamparado, a** [desampa'raðo, a]
adj (persona) helpless; (lugar: expuesto) exposed; (desierto) deserted
**desamparar** [desampa'rar] vt (abandonar) to desert, abandon; (JUR) to
leave defenceless; (barco) to abandon
**desandar** [desan'dar] vt: ~ lo andado o el camino to retrace one's
steps
**desangrar** [desan'grar] vt to bleed;
(fig: persona) to bleed dry; ~se vr
to lose a lot of blood
**desanimado, a** [desani'maðo, a]
adj (persona) downhearted; (espectáculo, fiesta) dull
**desanimar** [desani'mar] vt (desalentar) to discourage; (deprimir) to depress; ~se vr to lose heart
**desapacible** [desapa'θißle] adj (gen)
unpleasant
**desaparecer** [desapare'θer] vi (gen)
to disappear; (el sol, la luz) to vanish; **desaparecido, a** adj missing;

**desaparecidos** nmpl (en accidente) people missing; **desaparición** nf disappearance

**desapasionado, a** [desapasjo'naðo, a] adj dispassionate, impartial

**desapego** [desa'peɣo] nm (frialdad) coolness; (distancia) detachment

**desapercibido, a** [desaperθi'βiðo, a] adj (desprevenido) unprepared; pasar ~ to go unnoticed

**desaprensivo, a** [desapren'siβo, a] adj unscrupulous

**desaprobar** [desapro'βar] vt (reprobar) to disapprove of; (condenar) to condemn; (no consentir) to reject

**desaprovechado, a** [desaproβe-'tʃaðo, a] adj (oportunidad, tiempo) wasted; (estudiante) slack

**desaprovechar** [desaproβe'tʃar] vt to waste

**desarmar** [desar'mar] vt (MIL, fig) to disarm; (TEC) to take apart, dismantle; **desarme** nm disarmament

**desarraigar** [desarrai'ɣar] vt to uproot; **desarraigo** nm uprooting

**desarreglar** [desarre'ɣlar] vt (desordenar) to disarrange; (trastocar) to upset, disturb

**desarreglo** [desa'rreɣlo] nm (de casa, persona) untidiness; (desorden) disorder

**desarrollar** [desarro'ʎar] vt (gen) to develop; (extender) to unfold; ~se vr to develop; (extenderse) to open (out); (FOTO) to develop; **desarrollo** nm development

**desarticular** [desartiku'lar] vt (hueso) to dislocate; (objeto) to take apart; (fig) to break up

**desasir** [desa'sir] vt to loosen; ~se vr to extricate o.s.; ~se de to let go, give up

**desasosegar** [desasose'ɣar] vt (inquietar) to disturb, make uneasy; ~se vr to become uneasy

**desasosiego** etc [desaso'sjeɣo] vb ver desasosegar ♦ nm (intranquilidad) uneasiness, restlessness; (ansiedad) anxiety

**desastrado, a** [desas'traðo, a] adj (desaliñado) shabby; (sucio) dirty

**desastre** [de'sastre] nm disaster; **desastroso, a** adj disastrous

**desatado, a** [desa'taðo, a] adj (desligado) untied; (violento) violent, wild

**desatar** [desa'tar] vt (nudo) to untie; (paquete) to undo; (separar) to detach; ~se vr (zapatos) to come untied; (tormenta) to break

**desatascar** [desatas'kar] vt (cañería) to unblock, clear

**desatender** [desaten'der] vt (no prestar atención a) to disregard; (abandonar) to neglect

**desatento, a** [desa'tento, a] adj (distraído) inattentive; (descortés) discourteous

**desatinado, a** [desati'naðo, a] adj foolish, silly; **desatino** nm (idiotez) foolishness, folly; (error) blunder

**desatornillar** [desatorni'ʎar] vt to unscrew

**desatrancar** [desatran'kar] vt (puerta) to unbolt; (cañería) to clear, unblock

**desautorizado, a** [desautori'θaðo, a] adj unauthorized

**desautorizar** [desautori'θar] vt (oficial) to deprive of authority; (informe) to deny

**desavenencia** [desaβe'nenθja] nf (desacuerdo) disagreement; (discrepancia) quarrel

**desayunar** [desaju'nar] vi to have breakfast ♦ vt to have for breakfast; **desayuno** nm breakfast

**desazón** [desa'θon] nf (angustia) anxiety; (fig) annoyance

**desazonar** [desaθo'nar] vt (fig) to annoy, upset; ~se vr (enojarse) to be annoyed; (preocuparse) to worry, be anxious

**desbandarse** [desβan'darse] vr (MIL) to disband; (fig) to flee in disorder

**desbarajuste** [desβara'xuste] nm confusion, disorder

**desbaratar** [desβara'tar] vt (deshacer, destruir) to ruin

**desbloquear** [desβloke'ar] vt (negociaciones, tráfico) to get going again; (COM: cuenta) to unfreeze

**desbocado, a** [desβo'kaðo, a] adj (caballo) runaway

**desbordar** [desβor'ðar] vt (sobrepasar) to go beyond; (exceder) to exceed ♦ vi (río) to overflow; (entusiasmo) to overflow; ~se vr to overflow; to erupt

**descabalgar** [deskaβal'ɣar] vi to dismount

**descabellado, a** [deskaβe'ʎaðo, a] adj (disparatado) wild, crazy

**descafeinado, a** [deskafei'naðo, a] adj decaffeinated ♦ nm decaffeinated coffee

**descalabro** [deska'laβro] nm blow; (desgracia) misfortune

**descalificar** [deskalifi'kar] vt to disqualify; (desacreditar) to discredit

**descalzar** [deskal'θar] vt (zapato) to take off; **descalzo, a** adj barefoot(ed); (fig) destitute

**descambiar** [deskam'bjar] vt to exchange

**descaminado, a** [deskami'naðo, a] adj (equivocado) on the wrong road; (fig) misguided

**descampado** [deskam'paðo] nm open space

**descansado, a** [deskan'saðo, a] adj (gen) rested; (que tranquiliza) restful

**descansar** [deskan'sar] vt (gen) to rest ♦ vi to rest, have a rest; (echarse) to lie down

**descansillo** [deskan'siʎo] nm (de escalera) landing

**descanso** [des'kanso] nm (reposo) rest; (alivio) relief; (pausa) break; (DEPORTE) interval, half time

**descapotable** [deskapo'taβle] nm (tb: coche: ~) convertible

**descarado, a** [deska'raðo, a] adj shameless; (insolente) cheeky

**descarga** [des'karɣa] nf (ARQ, ELEC, MIL) discharge; (NAUT) unloading

**descargar** [deskar'ɣar] vt to unload;

(golpe) to let fly; ~se vr to unburden o.s.; **descargo** nm (COM) receipt; (JUR) evidence

**descarnado, a** [deskar'naðo, a] adj scrawny; (fig) bare

**descaro** [des'karo] nm nerve

**descarriar** [deska'rrjar] vt (descaminar) to misdirect; (fig) to lead astray; ~se vr (perderse) to lose one's way; (separarse) to stray; (pervertirse) to err, go astray

**descarrilamiento** [deskarrila'mjento] nm (de tren) derailment

**descarrilar** [deskarri'lar] vi to be derailed

**descartar** [deskar'tar] vt (rechazar) to reject; (eliminar) to rule out; ~se vr (NAIPES) to discard; ~se de to shirk

**descascarillado, a** [deskaskari'ʎaðo, a] adj (paredes) peeling

**descendencia** [desθen'denθja] nf (origen) origin, descent; (hijos) offspring

**descender** [desθen'der] vt (bajar: escalera) to go down ♦ vi to descend; (temperatura, nivel) to fall, drop; ~ de to be descended from

**descendiente** [desθen'djente] nm/f descendant

**descenso** [des'θenso] nm descent; (de temperatura) drop

**descifrar** [desθi'frar] vt to decipher; (mensaje) to decode

**descolgar** [deskol'ɣar] vt (bajar) to take down; (teléfono) to pick up; ~se vr to let o.s. down

**descolorido, a** [deskolo'riðo, a] adj faded; (pálido) pale

**descompasado, a** [deskompa'saðo, a] adj (sin proporción) out of all proportion; (excesivo) excessive

**descomponer** [deskompo'ner] vt (desordenar) to disarrange, disturb; (TEC) to put out of order; (dividir) to break down (into parts); (fig) to provoke; ~se vr (corromperse) to rot, decompose; (el tiempo) to change (for the worse); (TEC) to break down

**descomposición** [deskomposi'θjon]
nf (gen) breakdown; (de fruta etc)
decomposition; ~ **de vientre** stomach upset, diarrhoea

**descompostura** [deskompos'tura]
nf (TEC) breakdown; (desorganización) disorganization; (desorden) untidiness

**descompuesto, a** [deskom'pwesto,
a] adj (corrompido) decomposed;
(roto) broken

**descomunal** [deskomu'nal] adj
(enorme) huge

**desconcertado, a** [deskonθer'taðo,
a] adj disconcerted, bewildered

**desconcertar** [deskonθer'tar] vt
(confundir) to baffle; (incomodar) to
upset, put out; ~**se** vr (turbarse) to
be upset

**desconcierto** etc [deskon'θjerto] vb
ver **desconcertar** ♦ nm (gen) disorder; (desorientación) uncertainty;
(inquietud) uneasiness

**desconchado, a** [deskon'tʃaðo, a]
adj (pintura) peeling

**desconectar** [deskonek'tar] vt to
disconnect

**desconfianza** [deskon'fjanθa] nf distrust

**desconfiar** [deskon'fjar] vi to be distrustful; ~ **de** to distrust, suspect

**descongelar** [deskonxe'lar] vt to defrost; (COM, POL) to unfreeze

**descongestionar** [deskonxestjo'nar]
vt (cabeza, tráfico) to clear

**desconocer** [deskono'θer] vt (ignorar) not to know, be ignorant of; (no
aceptar) to deny; (repudiar) to disown

**desconocido, a** [deskono'θiðo, a]
adj unknown ♦ nmf stranger

**desconocimiento** [deskonoθi'mjen-
to] nm (falta de conocimientos) ignorance; (repudio) disregard

**desconsiderado, a** [deskonsiðe-
'raðo, a] adj inconsiderate; (insensible) thoughtless

**desconsolar** [deskonso'lar] vt to distress; ~**se** vr to despair

**desconsuelo** etc [deskon'swelo] vb

ver **desconsolar** ♦ nm (tristeza) distress; (desesperación) despair

**descontado, a** [deskon'taðo, a]
adj: **dar por** ~ (**que**) to take (it)
for granted that

**descontar** [deskon'tar] vt (deducir)
to take away, deduct; (rebajar) to
discount

**descontento, a** [deskon'tento, a]
adj dissatisfied ♦ nm dissatisfaction,
discontent

**descorazonar** [deskoraθo'nar] vt to
discourage, dishearten

**descorchar** [deskor'tʃar] vt to un-
cork

**descorrer** [desko'rrer] vt (cortinas,
cerrojo) to draw back

**descortés** [deskor'tes] adj (mal educado) discourteous; (grosero) rude

**descoser** [desko'ser] vt to unstitch;
~**se** vr to come apart (at the seams)

**descosido, a** [desko'siðo, a] adj
(COSTURA) unstitched; (desordenado) disjointed

**descrédito** [des'kreðito] nm discredit

**descreído, a** [deskre'iðo, a] adj (incrédulo) incredulous; (falto de fe)
unbelieving

**descremado, a** [deskre'maðo, a]
adj skimmed

**describir** [deskri'βir] vt to describe;
**descripción** [deskrip'θjon] nf description

**descrito** [des'krito] pp de **describir**

**descuartizar** [deskwarti'θar] vt (animal) to cut up

**descubierto, a** [desku'βjerto, a] pp
de **descubrir** ♦ adj uncovered, bare;
(persona) bareheaded ♦ nm (bancario) overdraft; **al** ~ in the open

**descubrimiento** [deskuβri'mjento]
nm (hallazgo) discovery; (revelación) revelation

**descubrir** [desku'βrir] vt to discover,
find; (inaugurar) to unveil; (vislumbrar) to detect; (revelar) to reveal,
show; (destapar) to uncover; ~**se** vr
to reveal o.s.; (quitarse sombrero) to
take off one's hat; (confesar) to con-

fess

**descuento** etc [des'kwento] vb ver descontar ♦ nm discount

**descuidado, a** [deskwi'ðaðo, a] adj (sin cuidado) careless; (desordenado) untidy; (olvidadizo) forgetful; (dejado) neglected; (desprevenido) unprepared

**descuidar** [deskwi'ðar] vt (dejar) to neglect; (olvidar) to overlook ♦ vi (distraerse) to be careless; (estar desaliñado) to let o.s. go; (desprevenirse) to drop one's guard; ~se vr to be careless; to let o.s. go; to drop one's guard; ¡descuida! don't worry!; **descuido** nm (dejadez) carelessness; (olvido) negligence

_PALABRA CLAVE_

**desde** ['desðe] prep 1 (lugar) from; ~ Burgos hasta mi casa hay 30 km it's 30 kms from Burgos to my house

2 (posición): hablaba ~ el balcón she was speaking from the balcony

3 (tiempo: + adv, n): ~ ahora from now on; ~ la boda since the wedding; ~ niño since I etc was a child; ~ 3 años atrás since 3 years ago

4 (tiempo: + vb) since; for; nos conocemos ~ 1978/ ~ hace 20 años we've known each other since 1978/for 20 years; no le veo ~ 1983/ ~ hace 5 años I haven't seen him since 1983/for 5 years

5 (gama): ~ los más lujosos hasta los más económicos from the most luxurious to the most reasonably priced

6: ~ luego (que no) of course (not) ♦ conj: ~ que: ~ que recuerdo for as long as I can remember; ~ que llegó no ha salido he hasn't been out since he arrived

**desdecirse** [desðe'θirse] vr to retract; ~ de to go back on

**desdén** [des'ðen] nm scorn

**desdeñar** [desðe'ɲar] vt (despreciar) to scorn

**desdicha** [des'ðitʃa] nf (desgracia) misfortune; (infelicidad) unhappiness; **desdichado, a** adj (sin suerte) unlucky; (infeliz) unhappy

**desdoblar** [desðo'βlar] vt (extender) to spread out; (desplegar) to unfold

**desear** [dese'ar] vt to want, desire, wish for

**desecar** [dese'kar] vt to dry up; ~se vr to dry up

**desechar** [dese'tʃar] vt (basura) to throw out o away; (ideas) to reject, discard; **desechos** nmpl rubbish sg, waste sg

**desembalar** [desemba'lar] vt to unpack

**desembarazado, a** [desembara'θaðo, a] adj (libre) clear, free; (desenvuelto) free and easy

**desembarazar** [desembara'θar] vt (desocupar) to clear; (desenredar) to free; ~se vr: ~se de to free o.s. of, get rid of

**desembarcar** [desembar'kar] vt (mercancías etc) to unload ♦ vi to disembark; ~se vr to disembark

**desembocadura** [desemboka'ðura] nf (de río) mouth; (de calle) opening

**desembocar** [desembo'kar] vi to flow into; (fig) to result in

**desembolso** [desem'bolso] nm payment

**desembragar** [desembra'ɣar] vi to declutch

**desembrollar** [desembro'ʎar] vt (madeja) to unravel; (asunto, malentendido) to sort out

**desemejanza** [deseme'xanθa] nf dissimilarity

**desempaquetar** [desempake'tar] vt (regalo) to unwrap; (mercancía) to unpack

**desempatar** [desempa'tar] vi to replay, hold a play-off; **desempate** nm (FUTBOL) replay, play-off; (TENIS) tie-break(er)

**desempeñar** [desempe'ɲar] vt (cargo) to hold; (papel) to perform; (lo empeñado) to redeem; ~se vr to get out of debt; ~ un papel (fig) to play

(a role)

**desempeño** [desem'peɲo] *nm* redeeming; *(de cargo)* occupation

**desempleado, a** [desemple'aðo, a] *nm/f* unemployed person; **desempleo** *nm* unemployment

**desempolvar** [desempol'ßar] *vt* *(muebles etc)* to dust; *(lo olvidado)* to revive

**desencadenar** [desenkaðe'nar] *vt* to unchain; *(ira)* to unleash; **~se** *vr* to break loose; *(tormenta)* to burst; *(guerra)* to break out

**desencajar** [desenka'xar] *vt* *(hueso)* to dislocate; *(mecanismo, pieza)* to disconnect, disengage

**desencanto** [desen'kanto] *nm* disillusionment

**desenchufar** [desentʃu'far] *vt* to unplug

**desenfadado, a** [desenfa'ðaðo, a] *adj* *(desenvuelto)* uninhibited; *(descarado)* forward; **desenfado** *nm* *(libertad)* freedom; *(comportamiento)* free and easy manner; *(descaro)* forwardness

**desenfocado, a** [desenfo'kaðo, a] *adj* *(FOTO)* out of focus

**desenfrenado, a** [desenfre'naðo, a] *adj* *(descontrolado)* uncontrolled; *(inmoderado)* unbridled; **desenfreno** *nm* *(vicio)* wildness; *(de las pasiones)* lack of self-control

**desenganchar** [desengan'tʃar] *vt* *(gen)* to unhook; *(FERRO)* to uncouple

**desengañar** [desenga'nar] *vt* to disillusion; **~se** *vr* to become disillusioned; **desengaño** *nm* disillusionment; *(decepción)* disappointment

**desenlace** [desen'laθe] *nm* outcome

**desenmarañar** [desenmara'nar] *vt* *(fig)* to unravel

**desenmascarar** [desenmaska'rar] *vt* to unmask

**desenredar** [desenre'ðar] *vt* *(pelo)* to untangle; *(problema)* to sort out

**desenroscar** [desenros'kar] *vt* to unscrew

**desentenderse** [desenten'derse] *vr:*

**~ de** to pretend not to know about; *(apartarse)* to have nothing to do with

**desenterrar** [desente'rrar] *vt* to exhume; *(tesoro, fig)* to unearth, dig up

**desentonar** [desento'nar] *vt* *(MUS)* to sing (o play) out of tune; *(color)* to clash

**desentrañar** [desentra'nar] *vt* *(misterio)* to unravel

**desentumecer** [desentume'θer] *vt* *(pierna etc)* to stretch; *(DEPORTE)* to loosen up

**desenvoltura** [desenßol'tura] *nf* *(libertad, gracia)* ease; *(descaro)* free and easy manner

**desenvolver** [desenßol'ßer] *vt* *(paquete)* to unwrap; *(fig)* to develop; **~se** *vr* *(desarrollarse)* to unfold, develop; *(arreglárselas)* to cope

**deseo** [de'seo] *nm* desire, wish; **~so, a** *adj:* **estar ~so de** to be anxious to

**desequilibrado, a** [desekili'ßraðo, a] *adj* unbalanced

**desertar** [deser'tar] *vi* to desert

**desértico, a** [de'sertiko, a] *adj* desert *cpd*

**desesperación** [desespera'θjon] *nf* *(impaciencia)* desperation, despair; *(irritación)* fury

**desesperar** [desespe'rar] *vt* to drive to despair; *(exasperar)* to drive to distraction ♦ *vi:* **~ de** to despair of; **~se** *vr* to despair, lose hope

**desestabilizar** [desestaßili'θar] *vt* to destabilize

**desestimar** [desesti'mar] *vt* *(menospreciar)* to have a low opinion of; *(rechazar)* to reject

**desfachatez** [desfatʃa'teθ] *nf* *(insolencia)* impudence; *(descaro)* rudeness

**desfalco** [des'falko] *nm* embezzlement

**desfallecer** [desfaʎe'θer] *vi* *(perder las fuerzas)* to become weak; *(desvanecerse)* to faint

**desfasado, a** [desfa'saðo, a] *adj* *(anticuado)* old-fashioned; **desfase** *nm* *(diferencia)* gap

**desfavorable** [desfaβo'raβle] adj unfavourable

**desfigurar** [desfixu'rar] vt (cara) to disfigure; (cuerpo) to deform

**desfiladero** [desfila'ðero] nm gorge

**desfilar** [desfi'lar] vi to parade; **desfile** nm procession

**desfogarse** [desfo'varse] vr (fig) to let off steam

**desgajar** [desva'xar] vt (arrancar) to tear off; (romper) to break off; ~se vr to come off

**desgana** [des'vana] nf (falta de apetito) loss of appetite; (renuncia) unwillingness; ~**do, a** adj: **estar** ~**do** (sin apetito) to have no appetite; (sin entusiasmo) to have lost interest

**desgarrador, a** [desvarra'ðor, a] adj (fig) heartrending

**desgarrar** [desva'rrar] vt to tear (up); (fig) to shatter; **desgarro** nm (en tela) tear; (aflicción) grief; (descaro) impudence

**desgastar** [desvas'tar] vt (deteriorar) to wear away o down; (estropear) to spoil; ~se vr to get worn out; **desgaste** nm wear (and tear)

**desglosar** [desvlo'sar] vt (factura) to break down

**desgracia** [des'vraθja] nf misfortune; (accidente) accident; (vergüenza) disgrace; (contratiempo) setback; **por** ~ unfortunately

**desgraciado, a** [desvra'θjaðo, a] adj (sin suerte) unlucky, unfortunate; (miserable) wretched; (infeliz) miserable

**desgravación** [desvraßa'θjon] nf (COM): ~ **fiscal** tax relief

**desgravar** [desvra'ßar] vt (impuestos) to reduce the tax o duty on

**desgreñado, a** [desvre'paðo, a] adj dishevelled

**deshabitado, a** [desaßi'taðo, a] adj uninhabited

**deshacer** [desa'θer] vt (casa) to break up; (TEC) to take apart; (enemigo) to defeat; (diluir) to melt; (contrato) to break; (intriga) to solve; ~se vr (disolverse) to melt;

(despedazarse) to come apart o undone; ~se de to get rid of; ~se en lágrimas to burst into tears

**desharrapado, a** [desarra'paðo, a] adj (persona) shabby

**deshecho, a** [des'etʃo, a] adj undone; (roto) smashed; (persona): **estar** ~ to be shattered

**desheredar** [desere'ðar] vt to disinherit

**deshidratar** [desiðra'tar] vt to dehydrate

**deshielo** [des'jelo] nm thaw

**deshonesto, a** [deso'nesto, a] adj indecent

**deshonra** [des'onra] nf (deshonor) dishonour; (vergüenza) shame

**deshora** [des'ora]: **a** ~ adv at the wrong time

**deshuesar** [deswe'sar] vt (carne) to bone; (fruta) to stone

**desierto, a** [de'sjerto, a] adj (casa, calle, negocio) deserted ♦ nm desert

**designar** [desiv'nar] vt (nombrar) to designate; (indicar) to fix

**designio** [de'sixnjo] nm plan

**desigual** [desi'vwal] adj (terreno) uneven; (lucha etc) unequal

**desilusión** [desilu'sjon] nf disillusionment; (decepción) disappointment; **desilusionar** vt to disillusion; to disappoint; **desilusionarse** vr to become disillusioned

**desinfectar** [desinfek'tar] vt to disinfect

**desinflar** [desin'flar] vt to deflate

**desintegración** [desintevra'θjon] nf disintegration

**desinterés** [desinte'res] nm (objetividad) disinterestedness; (altruismo) unselfishness

**desintoxicarse** [desintoksi'karse] vr (drogadicto) to undergo dextoxification

**desistir** [desis'tir] vi (renunciar) to stop, desist

**desleal** [desle'al] adj (infiel) disloyal; (COM: competencia) unfair; ~**tad** nf disloyalty

**desleír** [desle'ir] vt (líquido) to dilute; (*sólido*) to dissolve

**deslenguado, a** |deslen'gwaðo, a| *adj* (*grosero*) foul-mouthed

**desligar** |desli'var| *vt* (*desatar*) to untie, undo; (*separar*) to separate; ~**se** *vr* (*de un compromiso*) to extricate o.s.

**desliz** |des'liθ| *nm* (*fig*) lapse; ~**ar** *vt* to slip, slide

**deslucido, a** |deslu'θiðo, a| *adj* dull; (*torpe*) awkward, graceless; (*deslustrado*) tarnished

**deslumbrar** |deslum'brar| *vt* to dazzle

**desmadrarse** |desma'ðrarse| (*fam*) *vr* (*descontrolarse*) to run wild; (*divertirse*) to let one's hair down

**desmán** |des'man| *nm* (*exceso*) outrage; (*abuso de poder*) abuse

**desmandarse** |desman'darse| *vr* (*portarse mal*) to behave badly; (*excederse*) to get out of hand; (*caballo*) to bolt

**desmantelar** |desmante'lar| *vt* (*deshacer*) to dismantle; (*casa*) to strip

**desmaquillador** |desmakiʎa'ðor| *nm* make-up remover

**desmayado, a** |desma'jaðo, a| *adj* (*sin sentido*) unconscious; (*carácter*) dull; (*débil*) faint, weak

**desmayar** |desma'jar| *vi* to lose heart; ~**se** *vr* (*MED*) to faint; **desmayo** *nm* (*MED: acto*) faint; (*: estado*) unconsciousness; (*depresión*) dejection

**desmedido, a** |desme'ðiðo, a| *adj* excessive

**desmejorar** |desmexo'rar| *vt* (*dañar*) to impair, spoil; (*MED*) to weaken

**desmembrar** |desmem'brar| *vt* (*MED*) to dismember; (*fig*) to separate

**desmemoriado, a** |desmemo'rjaðo, a| *adj* forgetful

**desmentir** |desmen'tir| *vt* (*contradecir*) to contradict; (*refutar*) to deny ♦ *vi*: ~ **de** to refute; ~**se** *vr* to contradict o.s.

**desmenuzar** |desmenu'θar| *vt* (*des-*

hacer*) to crumble; (*carne*) to chop; (*examinar*) to examine closely

**desmerecer** |desmere'θer| *vt* to be unworthy of ♦ *vi* (*deteriorarse*) to deteriorate

**desmesurado, a** |desmesu'raðo, a| *adj* disproportionate

**desmontable** |desmon'taβle| *adj* (*que se quita: pieza*) detachable; (*que sa pueda plegar etc*) collapsible, folding

**desmontar** |desmon'tar| *vt* (*deshacer*) to dismantle; (*tierra*) to level ♦ *vi* to dismount

**desmoralizar** |desmorali'θar| *vt* to demoralize

**desmoronar** |desmoro'nar| *vt* to wear away, erode; ~**se** *vr* (*edificio, dique*) to fall into disrepair; (*economía*) to decline

**desnatado, a** |desna'taðo, a| *adj* skimmed

**desnivel** |desni'βel| *nm* (*de terreno*) unevenness

**desnudar** |desnu'ðar| *vt* (*desvestir*) to undress; (*despojar*) to strip; ~**se** *vr* (*desvestirse*) to get undressed; **desnudo, a** *adj* naked ♦ *nm/f* nude; **desnudo de** devoid o bereft of

**desnutrición** |desnutri'θjon| *nf* malnutrition; **desnutrido, a** *adj* undernourished

**desobedecer** |desoβeðe'θer| *vt, vi* to disobey; **desobediencia** *nf* disobedience

**desocupado, a** |desoku'paðo, a| *adj* at leisure; (*desempleado*) unemployed; (*deshabitado*) empty, vacant

**desocupar** |desoku'par| *vt* to vacate

**desodorante** |desoðo'rante| *nm* deodorant

**desolación** |desola'θjon| *nf* (*lugar*) desolation; (*fig*) grief

**desolar** |deso'lar| *vt* to ruin, lay waste

**desorbitado, a** |desorβi'taðo, a| *adj* (*excesivo: ambición*) boundless; (*deseos*) excessive; (*: precio*) exorbitant

**desorden** |des'orðen| *nm* confusion; (*político*) disorder, unrest

**desorganizar** [desorɣani'θar] *vt*
(*desordenar*) to disorganize; **desorganización** *nf* (*de persona*) disorganization; (*en empresa, oficina*) disorder, chaos

**desorientar** [desorjen'tar] *vt* (*extraviar*) to mislead; (*confundir, desconcertar*) to confuse; **~se** *vr* (*perderse*) to lose one's way

**despabilado, a** [despaβi'laðo, a] *adj* (*despierto*) wide-awake; (*fig*) alert, sharp

**despabilar** [despaβi'lar] *vt* (*el ingenio*) to sharpen ♦ *vi* to wake up; (*fig*) to get a move on; **~se** *vr* to wake up; to get a move on

**despacio** [des'paθjo] *adv* slowly

**despachar** [despa'tʃar] *vt* (*negocio*) to do, complete; (*enviar*) to send, dispatch; (*vender*) to sell, deal in; (*billete*) to issue; (*mandar ir*) to send away

**despacho** [des'patʃo] *nm* (*oficina*) office; (*de paquetes*) dispatch; (*venta*) sale; (*comunicación*) message

**desparpajo** [despar'paxo] *nm* self-confidence; (*pey*) nerve

**desparramar** [desparra'mar] *vt* (*esparcir*) to scatter; (*líquido*) to spill

**despavorido, a** [despaβo'riðo, a] *adj* terrified

**despectivo, a** [despek'tiβo, a] *adj* (*despreciativo*) derogatory; (*LING*) pejorative

**despecho** [des'petʃo] *nm* spite; a ~ de in spite of

**despedazar** [despeða'θar] *vt* to tear to pieces

**despedida** [despe'ðiða] *nf* (*adiós*) farewell; (*de obrero*) sacking

**despedir** [despe'ðir] *vt* (*visita*) to see off, show out; (*empleado*) to dismiss; (*inquilino*) to evict; (*objeto*) to hurl; (*olor etc*) to give out o off; **~se** *vr*: **~se de** to say goodbye to

**despegar** [despe'ɣar] *vt* to unstick ♦ *vi* (*avión*) to take off; **~se** *vr* to come loose, come unstuck; **despego** *nm* detachment

**despegue** *etc* [des'peɣe] *vb ver* des-

**pegar** ♦ *nm* takeoff

**despeinado, a** [despei'naðo, a] *adj* dishevelled, unkempt

**despejado, a** [despe'xaðo, a] *adj* (*lugar*) clear, free; (*cielo*) clear; (*persona*) wide-awake, bright

**despejar** [despe'xar] *vt* (*gen*) to clear; (*misterio*) to clear up ♦ *vi* (*el tiempo*) to clear; **~se** *vr* (*tiempo, cielo*) to clear (up); (*misterio*) to become clearer; (*cabeza*) to clear

**despellejar** [despeʎe'xar] *vt* (*animal*) to skin

**despensa** [des'pensa] *nf* larder

**despeñadero** [despeɲa'ðero] *nm* (*GEO*) cliff, precipice

**despeñarse** [despe'ɲarse] *vr* to hurl o.s. down; (*coche*) to tumble over

**desperdicio** [desper'ðiθjo] *nm* (*despilfarro*) squandering; **~s** *nmpl* (*basura*) rubbish *sg* (*BRIT*), garbage *sg* (*US*); (*residuos*) waste *sg*

**desperdigarse** [desperði'varse] *vr* (*rebaño, familia*) to scatter, spread out; (*granos de arroz, semillas*) to scatter

**desperezarse** [despere'θarse] *vr* to stretch

**desperfecto** [desper'fekto] *nm* (*deterioro*) slight damage; (*defecto*) flaw, imperfection

**despertador** [desperta'ðor] *nm* alarm clock

**despertar** [desper'tar] *nm* awakening ♦ *vt* (*persona*) to wake up; (*recuerdos*) to revive; (*sentimiento*) to arouse ♦ *vi* to awaken, wake up; **~se** *vr* to awaken, wake up

**despiadado, a** [despja'ðaðo, a] *adj* (*ataque*) merciless; (*persona*) heartless

**despido** *etc* [des'piðo] *vb ver* **despedir** ♦ *nm* dismissal, sacking

**despierto, a** *etc* [des'pjerto, a] *vb ver* **despertar** ♦ *adj* (*fig*) sharp, alert

**despilfarro** [despil'farro] *nm* (*derroche*) squandering; (*lujo desmedido*) extravagance

**despistar** [despis'tar] *vt* to throw off
the track *o* scent; *(fig)* to mislead,
confuse; ~**se** *vr* to take the wrong
road; *(fig)* to become confused

**despiste** [des'piste] *nm* absent-
mindedness; **un** ~ a mistake, slip

**desplazamiento** [desplaθa'mjento]
*nm* displacement

**desplazar** [despla'θar] *vt* to move;
*(NAUT)* to displace; *(INFORM)* to
scroll; *(fig)* to oust; ~**se** *vr (persona)* to travel

**desplegar** [desple'ɣar] *vt (tela, papel)* to unfold, open out; *(bandera)* to
unfurl; **despliegue** *etc* [des'pleɣe] *vb
ver* **desplegar ♦** *nm* display

**desplomarse** [desplo'marse] *vr
(edificio, gobierno, persona)* to collapse

**desplumar** [desplu'mar] *vt (ave)* to
pluck; *(fam: estafar)* to fleece

**despoblado, a** [despo'ßlaðo, a] *adj
(sin habitantes)* uninhabited

**despojar** [despo'xar] *vt (alguien: de
sus bienes)* to divest of, deprive of;
*(casa)* to strip, leave bare; *(alguien:
de su cargo)* to strip of

**despojo** [des'poxo] *nm (acto)* plundering; *(objetos)* plunder, loot; ~**s**
*nmpl (de ave, res)* offal *sg*

**desposado, a** [despo'saðo, a] *adj,
nm/f* newly-wed

**desposar** [despo'sar] *vt* to marry;
~**se** *vr* to get married

**desposeer** [despose'er] *vt:* ~ **a uno
de** *(puesto, autoridad)* to strip sb of

**déspota** [despota] *nm/f* despot

**despreciar** [despre'θjar] *vt (desdeñar)* to despise, scorn; *(afrentar)* to
slight; **desprecio** *nm* scorn, contempt; slight

**desprender** [despren'der] *vt
(broche)* to unfasten; *(olor)* to give
off; ~**se** *vr (botón: caerse)* to fall
off; *(broche)* to come unfastened;
*(olor, perfume)* to be given off; ~**se
de algo que** ... to draw from sth
that ...

**desprendimiento** [desprendi'mjen-

to] *nm (gen)* loosening; *(generosidad)* disinterestedness; *(indiferencia)* detachment; *(de gas)* leak;
*(de tierra, rocas)* landslide

**despreocupado, a** [despreoku-
'paðo, a] *adj (sin preocupación)* un-
worried, nonchalant; *(negligente)*
careless

**despreocuparse** [despreoku'parse]
*vr* not to worry; ~ **de** to have no interest in

**desprestigiar** [despresti'xjar] *vt (criticar)* to run down; *(desacreditar)* to
discredit

**desprevenido, a** [despreße'niðo, a]
*adj (no preparado)* unprepared, un-
ready

**desproporcionado, a** [despropor-
θjo'naðo, a] *adj* disproportionate, out
of proportion

**desprovisto, a** [despro'ßisto, a]
*adj:* ~ **de** devoid of

**después** [des'pwes] *adv* afterwards,
later; *(próximo paso)* next; ~ **de
comer** after lunch; **un año** ~ a year
later; ~ **se debatió el tema** next
the matter was discussed; ~ **de corregido el texto** after the text had
been corrected; ~ **de todo** after all

**desquiciado, a** [deski'θjaðo, a] *adj*
deranged

**desquite** [des'kite] *nm (satisfacción)*
satisfaction; *(venganza)* revenge

**destacar** [desta'kar] *vt* to emphasize,
point up; *(MIL)* to detach, detail **♦**
*vi (resaltarse)* to stand out; *(persona)* to be outstanding *o* exceptional;
~**se** *vr* to stand out; to be outstanding *o* exceptional

**destajo** [des'taxo] *nm:* **trabajar a** ~
to do piecework

**destapar** [desta'par] *vt (botella)* to
open; *(cacerola)* to take the lid off;
*(descubrir)* to uncover; ~**se** *vr (re-
velarse)* to reveal one's true character

**destartalado, a** [destarta'laðo, a]
*adj (desordenado)* untidy; *(ruinoso)*
tumbledown

**destello** [des'teʎo] *nm (de estrella)*

twinkle; *(de faro)* signal light

**destemplado, a** [destem'plaðo, a] *adj (MUS)* out of tune; *(voz)* harsh; *(MED)* out of sorts; *(tiempo)* unpleasant, nasty

**desteñir** [deste'nir] *vt* to fade ♦ *vi* to fade; ~se *vr* to fade; **esta tela no destiñe** this fabric will not run

**desternillarse** [desterni'ʎarse] *vr*: ~ **de risa** to split one's sides laughing

**desterrar** [deste'rrar] *vt (exilar)* to exile; *(fig)* to banish, dismiss

**destiempo** [des'tjempo]: **a** ~ *adv* out of turn

**destierro** etc [des'tjerro] *vb ver* **desterrar** ♦ *nm* exile

**destilar** [desti'lar] *vt* to distil; **destilería** *nf* distillery

**destinar** [desti'nar] *vt (funcionario)* to appoint, assign; *(fondos)*: ~ **(a)** to set aside (for)

**destinatario, a** [destina'tarjo, a] *nm/f* addressee

**destino** [des'tino] *nm (suerte)* destiny; *(de avión, viajero)* destination

**destituir** [destitu'ir] *vt* to dismiss

**destornillador** [destorniʎa'ðor] *nm* screwdriver

**destornillar** [destorni'ʎar] *vt (tornillo)* to unscrew; ~se *vr* to come unscrewed

**destreza** [des'treθa] *nf (habilidad)* skill; *(maña)* dexterity

**destrozar** [destro'θar] *vt (romper)* to smash, break (up); *(estropear)* to ruin; *(nervios)* to shatter

**destrozo** [des'troθo] *nm (acción)* destruction; *(desastre)* smashing; ~s *nmpl (pedazos)* pieces; *(daños)* havoc *sg*

**destrucción** [destruk'θjon] *nf* destruction

**destruir** [destru'ir] *vt* to destroy

**desuso** [des'uso] *nm* disuse; **caer en** ~ to become obsolete

**desvalido, a** [desβa'liðo, a] *adj (desprotegido)* destitute; *(sin fuerzas)* helpless

**desvalijar** [desβali'xar] *vt (persona)* to rob; *(casa, tienda)* to burgle; *(coche)* to break into

**desván** [des'βan] *nm* attic

**desvanecer** [desβane'θer] *vt (disipar)* to dispel; *(borrar)* to blur; ~se *vr (humo etc)* to vanish, disappear; *(color)* to fade; *(recuerdo, sonido)* to fade away; *(MED)* to pass out; *(duda)* to be dispelled

**desvanecimiento** [desβaneθi'mjento] *nm (desaparición)* disappearance; *(de colores)* fading; *(evaporación)* evaporation; *(MED)* fainting fit

**desvariar** [desβa'rjar] *vi (enfermo)* to be delirious; **desvarío** *nm* delirium

**desvelar** [desβe'lar] *vt* to keep awake; ~se *vr (no poder dormir)* to stay awake; *(vigilar)* to be vigilant o watchful

**desvelos** [des'βelos] *nmpl* worrying *sg*

**desvencijado, a** [desβenθi'xaðo, a] *adj (silla)* rickety; *(máquina)* broken-down

**desventaja** [desβen'taxa] *nf* disadvantage

**desventura** [desβen'tura] *nf* misfortune

**desvergonzado, a** [desβergon'θaðo, a] *adj* shameless

**desvergüenza** [desβer'ɣwenθa] *nf (descaro)* shamelessness; *(insolencia)* impudence; *(mala conducta)* effrontery

**desvestir** [desβes'tir] *vt* to undress; ~se *vr* to undress

**desviación** [desβja'θjon] *nf* deviation; *(AUTO)* diversion, detour

**desviar** [des'βjar] *vt* to turn aside; *(río)* to alter the course of; *(navío)* to divert, re-route; *(conversación)* to sidetrack; ~se *vr (apartarse del camino)* to turn aside; *(: barco)* to go off course

**desvío** etc [des'βio] *vb ver* **desviar** ♦ *nm (desviación)* detour, diversion; *(fig)* indifference

**desvirtuar** [desβir'twar] *vt* to spoil; ~se *vr* to spoil

**desvivirse** [desβi'βirse] *vr*: ~ **por** *(anhelar)* to long for, crave for; *(ha-*

cer lo posible por) to do one's utmost for

**detallar** [deta'ʎar] vt to detail

**detalle** [de'taʎe] nm detail; (fig) gesture, token; al ~ in detail; (COM) retail

**detallista** [deta'ʎista] nm/f retailer

**detective** [detek'tiβe] nm/f detective

**detener** [dete'ner] vt (gen) to stop; (JUR) to arrest; (objeto) to keep; ~se vr to stop; (demorarse): ~se en to delay over, linger over

**detenidamente** [deteniða'mente] adv (minuciosamente) carefully; (extensamente) at great length

**detenido, a** [dete'niðo, a] adj (arrestado) under arrest; (minucioso) detailed ♦ nm/f person under arrest, prisoner

**detenimiento** [deteni'mjento] nm: con ~ thoroughly; (observar, considerar) carefully

**detergente** [deter'xente] nm detergent

**deteriorar** [deterjo'rar] vt to spoil, damage; ~se vr to deteriorate; **deterioro** nm deterioration

**determinación** [determina'θjon] nf (empeño) determination; (decisión) decision; **determinado, a** adj specific

**determinar** [determi'nar] vt (plazo) to fix; (precio) to settle; ~se vr to decide

**detestar** [detes'tar] vt to detest

**detractor, a** [detrak'tor, a] nm/f slanderer, libeller

**detrás** [de'tras] adv behind; (atrás) at the back; ~ de behind

**detrimento** [detri'mento] nm: en ~ de to the detriment of

**deuda** [deuða] nf (condición) indebtedness, debt; (cantidad) debt

**devaluación** [deβalwa'θjon] nf devaluation

**devastar** [deβas'tar] vt (destruir) to devastate

**devoción** [deβo'θjon] nf devotion

**devolución** [deβolu'θjon] nf (reenvío) return, sending back; (reembolso) repayment; (JUR) devolution

**devolver** [deβol'βer] vt to return; (lo extraviado, lo prestado) to give back; (carta al correo) to send back; (COM) to repay, refund; (lo prestado) to give back ♦ vi (vomitar) to be sick

**devorar** [deβo'rar] vt to devour

**devoto, a** [de'βoto, a] adj devout ♦ nm/f admirer

**devuelto** pp de **devolver**

**devuelva** etc vb ver **devolver**

**di** vb ver **dar**; **decir**

**día** ['dia] nm day; ¿qué ~ es? what's the date?; estar/poner al ~ to be/keep up to date; el ~ de hoy/de mañana today/tomorrow; al ~ siguiente (on) the following day; vivir al ~ to live from hand to mouth; de ~ by day, in daylight; en pleno ~ in full daylight; D~ de Reyes Epiphany; ~ festivo (ESP) o feriado (AM) holiday; ~ libre day off

**diabetes** [dja'βetes] nf diabetes

**diablo** ['djaβlo] nm devil; **diablura** nf prank

**diadema** [dja'ðema] nf tiara

**diafragma** [dja'fraxma] nm diaphragm

**diagnosis** [djax'nosis] nf inv diagnosis

**diagnóstico** [djax'nostiko] nm = diagnosis

**diagonal** [djayo'nal] adj diagonal

**diagrama** [dja'xrama] nm diagram; ~ de flujo flowchart

**dial** ['djal] nm dial

**dialecto** [dja'lekto] nm dialect

**dialogar** [djalo'xar] vi: ~ con (POL) to hold talks with

**diálogo** ['djaloxo] nm dialogue

**diamante** [dja'mante] nm diamond

**diana** ['djana] nf (MIL) reveille; (de blanco) centre, bull's-eye

**diapositiva** [djaposi'tiβa] nf (FOTO) slide, transparency

**diario, a** [a ['djarjo, a] adj daily ♦ nm newspaper; a ~ daily; de ~ everyday

**diarrea** [dja'rrea] nf diarrhoea

**dibujar** [diβu'xar] vt to draw, sketch;

**dibujo** nm drawing; **dibujos animados** cartoons

**diccionario** [dikθjo'narjo] nm dictionary

**dice** etc vb ver **decir**

**diciembre** [di'θjembre] nm December

**dictado** [dik'taðo] nm dictation

**dictador** [dikta'ðor] nm dictator; **dictadura** nf dictatorship

**dictamen** [dik'tamen] nm (opinión) opinion; (juicio) judgment; (informe) report

**dictar** [dik'tar] vt (carta) to dictate; (JUR: sentencia) to pronounce; (decreto) to issue; (AM: clase) to give

**dicho, a** ['ditʃo, a] pp de **decir ♦** adj: en ~s países in the aforementioned countries ♦ nm saying

**dichoso, a** [di'tʃoso, a] adj happy

**didáctico, a** [di'ðaktiko, a] adj educational

**diecinueve** [djeθi'nweβe] num nineteen

**dieciocho** [djeθi'otʃo] num eighteen

**dieciséis** [djeθi'seis] num sixteen

**diecisiete** [djeθi'sjete] num seventeen

**diente** ['djente] nm (ANAT, TEC) tooth; (ZOOL) fang; (: de elefante) tusk; (de ajo) clove; **hablar entre ~s** to mutter, mumble

**diera** etc vb ver **dar**

**diesel** ['disel] adj: motor ~ diesel engine

**diestro, a** ['djestro, a] adj (derecho) right; (hábil) skilful

**dieta** ['djeta] nf diet; **dietético, a** adj diet (atr), dietary

**diez** [djeθ] num ten

**diezmar** [djeθ'mar] vt (población) to decimate

**difamar** [difa'mar] vt (JUR: hablando) to slander; (: por escrito) to libel

**diferencia** [dife'renθja] nf difference; **diferenciar** vt to differentiate between ♦ vi to differ; **diferenciarse** vr to differ, be different; (distinguirse) to distinguish o.s.

**diferente** [dife'rente] adj different

**diferido** [dife'riðo] nm: en ~ (TV etc) recorded

**difícil** [di'fiθil] adj difficult

**dificultad** [difikul'taθ] nf difficulty; (problema) trouble; (objeción) objection

**dificultar** [difikul'tar] vt (complicar) to complicate, make difficult; (estorbar) to obstruct

**difteria** [dif'terja] nf diphtheria

**difundir** [difun'dir] vt (calor, luz) to diffuse; (RADIO, TV) to broadcast; ~ **una noticia** to spread a piece of news; **~se** vr to spread (out)

**difunto, a** [di'funto, a] adj dead, deceased ♦ nm/f deceased (person)

**difusión** [difu'sjon] nf (RADIO, TV) broadcasting

**diga** etc vb ver **decir**

**digerir** [dixe'rir] vt to digest; (fig) to absorb; **digestión** nf digestion; **digestivo, a** adj digestive

**digital** [dixi'tal] adj (INFORM) digital

**dignarse** [diy'narse] vr to deign to

**dignatario, a** [diyna'tarjo, a] nm/f dignitary

**dignidad** [diyni'ðað] nf dignity

**digno, a** ['diyno, a] adj worthy

**digo** etc vb ver **decir**

**dije** etc vb ver **decir**

**dilapidar** [dilapi'ðar] vt (dinero, herencia) to squander, waste

**dilatar** [dila'tar] vt (cuerpo) to dilate; (prolongar) to prolong; (aplazar) to delay

**dilema** [di'lema] nm dilemma

**diligencia** [dili'xenθja] nf diligence; (ocupación) errand, job; **~s** nfpl (JUR) formalities; **diligente** adj diligent

**diluir** [dilu'ir] vt to dilute

**diluvio** [di'luβjo] nm deluge, flood

**dimensión** [dimen'sjon] nf dimension

**diminuto, a** [dimi'nuto, a] adj tiny, diminutive

**dimitir** [dimi'tir] vi to resign

**dimos** vb ver **dar**

**Dinamarca** [dina'marka] nf Den

mark

**dinámico, a** [di'namiko, a] *adj* dynamic

**dinamita** [dina'mita] *nf* dynamite

**dínamo** ['dinamo] *nf* dynamo

**dineral** [dine'ral] *nm* large sum of money, fortune

**dinero** [di'nero] *nm* money; ~ contante, ~ efectivo (ready) cash; ~ suelto (loose) change

**dio** *vb ver* **dar**

**dios** [djos] *nm* god; **¡D~ mío!** (oh), my God!

**diosa** ['djosa] *nf* goddess

**diploma** [di'ploma] *nm* diploma

**diplomacia** [diplo'maθja] *nf* diplomacy; (*fig*) tact

**diplomado, a** [diplo'maðo, a] *adj* qualified

**diplomático, a** [diplo'matiko, a] *adj* diplomatic ♦ *nm/f* diplomat

**diputación** [diputa'θjon] *nf* (*tb:* ~ **provincial**) = county council

**diputado, a** [dipu'taðo, a] *nm/f* delegate; (*POL*) ≈ member of parliament (*BRIT*); ≈ representative (*US*)

**dique** ['dike] *nm* dyke

**diré** *etc vb ver* **decir**

**dirección** [direk'θjon] *nf* direction; (*señas*) address; (*AUTO*) steering; (*gerencia*) management; (*POL*) leadership; ~ **única/prohibida** one-way street/no entry

**directa** [di'rekta] *nf* (*AUT*) top gear

**directiva** [direk'tiβa] *nf* (*DEP, tb: junta ~*) board of directors

**directo, a** [di'rekto, a] *adj* direct; (*RADIO, TV*) live; **transmitir en ~** to broadcast live

**director, a** [direk'tor, a] *adj* leading ♦ *nm/f* director; (*ESCOL*) head(teacher) (*BRIT*), principal (*US*); (*gerente*) manager(ess); (*PRENSA*) editor; ~ **de cine** film director; ~ **general** managing director

**dirigente** [diri'xente] *nm/f* (*POL*) leader

**dirigir** [diri'xir] *vt* to direct; (*carta*)

to address; (*obra de teatro, film*) to direct; (*MUS*) to conduct; (*comercio*) to manage; ~**se** *vr*: ~**se a** to go towards, make one's way towards; (*hablar con*) to speak to

**dirija** *etc vb ver* **dirigir**

**discernir** [disθer'nir] *vt* (*distinguir, discriminar*) to discern

**disciplina** [disθi'plina] *nf* discipline

**discípulo, a** [dis'θipulo, a] *nm/f* disciple

**disco** ['disko] *nm* disc; (*DEPORTE*) discus; (*TEL*) dial; (*AUTO: semáforo*) light; (*MUS*) record; (*INFORM*): ~ **flexible/rígido** floppy/hard disk; ~ **compacto/de larga duración** compact disc/long-playing record; ~ **de freno** brake disc

**disconforme** [diskon'forme] *adj* differing; **estar** ~ (**con**) to be in disagreement (with)

**discordia** [dis'korðja] *nf* discord

**discoteca** [disko'teka] *nf* discotheque

**discreción** [diskre'θjon] *nf* discretion; (*reserva*) prudence; **comer a** ~ to eat as much as one wishes; **discrecional** *adj* (*facultativo*) discretionary

**discrepancia** [diskre'panθja] *nf* (*diferencia*) discrepancy; (*desacuerdo*) disagreement

**discreto, a** [dis'kreto, a] *adj* (*diplomático*) discreet; (*sensato*) sensible; (*reservado*) quiet; (*sobrio*) sober

**discriminación** [diskrimina'θjon] *nf* discrimination

**disculpa** [dis'kulpa] *nf* excuse; (*pedir perdón*) apology; **pedir ~s a/por** to apologize to/for; **disculpar** *vt* to excuse, pardon; **disculparse** *vr* to excuse o.s.; to apologize

**discurrir** [disku'rrir] *vi* (*pensar, reflexionar*) to think, meditate; (*recorrer*) to roam, wander; (*el tiempo*) to pass, to go

**discurso** [dis'kurso] *nm* speech

**discusión** [disku'sjon] *nf* (*diálogo*) discussion; (*riña*) argument

**discutir** [disku'tir] *vt* (*debatir*) to discuss; (*pelear*) to argue about; (*contradecir*) to argue against ♦ *vi* to discuss; (*disputar*) to argue

**disecar** [dise'kar] *vt* (*conservar: animal*) to stuff; (: *planta*) to dry

**diseminar** [disemi'nar] *vt* to disseminate, spread

**diseño** [di'seɲo] *nm* design; (*ARTE*) drawing

**disfraz** [dis'fraθ] *nm* (*máscara*) disguise; (*excusa*) pretext; **~ar** *vt* to disguise; **~arse** *vr*: **~arse de** to disguise o.s. as

**disfrutar** [disfru'tar] *vt* to enjoy ♦ *vi* to enjoy o.s.; **~ de** to enjoy, possess

**disgregarse** [disɣre'ɣarse] *vr* (*muchedumbre*) to disperse

**disgustar** [disɣus'tar] *vt* (*no gustar*) to displease; (*contrariar, enojar*) to annoy, upset; **~se** *vr* to be annoyed; (*dos personas*) to fall out

**disgusto** [dis'ɣusto] *nm* (*repugnancia*) disgust; (*contrariedad*) annoyance; (*tristeza*) grief; (*riña*) quarrel; (*avería*) misfortune

**disidente** [disi'ðente] *nm* dissident

**disimular** [disimu'lar] *vt* (*ocultar*) to hide, conceal ♦ *vi* to dissemble

**disipar** [disi'par] *vt* to dispel; (*fortuna*) to squander; **~se** *vr* (*nubes*) to vanish; (*indisciplinarse*) to dissipate

**dislocarse** [dislo'karse] *vr* (*articulación*) to sprain, dislocate

**disminución** [disminu'θjon] *nf* decrease, reduction

**disminuir** [disminu'ir] *vt* to decrease, diminish

**disociarse** [diso'θjarse] *vr*: **~ (de)** to dissociate o.s. (from)

**disolver** [disol'ßer] *vt* (*gen*) to dissolve; **~se** *vr* to dissolve; (*COM*) to go into liquidation

**dispar** [dis'par] *adj* different

**disparar** [dispa'rar] *vt, vi* to shoot, fire

**disparate** [dispa'rate] *nm* (*tontería*) foolish remark; (*error*) blunder; **decir ~** to talk nonsense

**disparo** [dis'paro] *nm* shot

**dispensar** [dispen'sar] *vt* to dis-

pense; (*disculpar*) to excuse

**dispersar** [disper'sar] *vt* to disperse; **~se** *vr* to scatter

**disponer** [dispo'ner] *vt* (*arreglar*) to arrange; (*ordenar*) to put in order; (*preparar*) to prepare, get ready ♦ *vi*: **~ de** to have, own; **~se** *vr*: **~se a** o **para hacer** to prepare to do

**disponible** [dispo'nißle] *adj* available

**disposición** [disposi'θjon] *nf* arrangement, disposition; (*aptitud*) aptitude; (*INFORM*) layout; **a la ~ de** at the disposal of; **~ de ánimo** state of mind

**dispositivo** [disposi'tißo] *nm* device, mechanism

**dispuesto, a** [dis'pwesto, a] *pp de* **disponer** ♦ *adj* (*arreglado*) arranged; (*preparado*) disposed

**disputar** [dispu'tar] *vt* (*discutir*) to dispute, question; (*contender*) to contend for ♦ *vi* to argue

**disquete** [dis'kete] *nm* floppy disk, diskette

**distancia** [dis'tanθja] *nf* distance

**distanciar** [distan'θjar] *vt* to space out; **~se** *vr* to become estranged

**distante** [dis'tante] *adj* distant

**distar** [dis'tar] *vi*: **dista 5km de aquí** it is 5km from here

**diste** *vb ver* **dar**

**disteis** [disteis] *vb ver* **dar**

**distensión** [disten'sjon] *nf* (*en las relaciones*) relaxation; (*POL*) détente; (*muscular*) strain

**distinción** [distin'θjon] *nf* distinction; (*elegancia*) elegance; (*honor*) honour

**distinguido, a** [distin'ɡiðo, a] *adj* distinguished

**distinguir** [distin'ɡir] *vt* to distinguish; (*escoger*) to single out; **~se** *vr* to be distinguished

**distintivo** [distin'tißo] *nm* badge; (*fig*) characteristic

**distinto, a** [dis'tinto, a] *adj* different; (*claro*) clear

**distracción** [distrak'θjon] *nf* distraction; (*pasatiempo*) hobby, pastime;

(*olvido*) absent-mindedness, distraction

**distraer** [distra'er] vt (*atención*) to distract; (*divertir*) to amuse; (*fondos*) to embezzle; **~se** vr (*entretenerse*) to amuse o.s.; (*perder la concentración*) to allow one's attention to wander

**distraído, a** [distra'iðo, a] adj (*gen*) absent-minded; (*entretenido*) amusing

**distribuidor, a** [distriβui'ðor, a] nm/f distributor; (*AUT*) distributor; **distribuidora** nf (*COM*) dealer, agent; (*CINE*) distributor

**distribuir** [distriβu'ir] vt to distribute

**distrito** [dis'trito] nm (*sector, territorio*) region; (*barrio*) district

**disturbio** [dis'turβio] nm disturbance; (*desorden*) riot

**disuadir** [diswa'ðir] vt to dissuade

**disuelto** [di'swelto] pp de **disolver**

**disyuntiva** [disjun'tiβa] nf dilemma

**DIU** nm abr (= *dispositivo intrauterino*) IUD

**diurno, a** ['djurno, a] adj day cpd

**divagar** [diβa'ɣar] vi (*desviarse*) to digress

**diván** [di'βan] nm divan

**divergencia** [diβer'xenθja] nf divergence

**diversidad** [diβersi'ðað] nf diversity, variety

**diversificar** [diβersifi'kar] vt to diversify

**diversión** [diβer'sjon] nf (*gen*) entertainment; (*actividad*) hobby, pastime

**diverso, a** [di'βerso, a] adj diverse; **~s** nmpl sundries; **~s libros** several books

**divertido, a** [diβer'tiðo, a] adj (*chiste*) amusing; (*fiesta etc*) enjoyable

**divertir** [diβer'tir] vt (*entretener, recrear*) to amuse; **~se** vr (*pasarlo bien*) to have a good time; (*distraerse*) to amuse o.s

**dividir** [diβi'ðir] vt (*gen*) to divide; (*separar*) to separate; (*distribuir*) to distribute, share out

**divierta** etc vb ver **divertir**

**dividendo** [diβi'ðendo] nm (*COM*): **~s** nmpl dividends

**divino, a** [di'βino, a] adj divine

**divirtiendo** etc vb ver **divertir**

**divisa** [di'βisa] nf (*emblema, moneda*) emblem, badge; **~s** nfpl foreign exchange sg

**divisar** [diβi'sar] vt to make out, distinguish

**división** [diβi'sjon] nf (*gen*) division; (*de partido*) split; (*de país*) partition

**divorciar** [diβor'θjar] vt to divorce; **~se** vr to get divorced; **divorcio** nm divorce

**divulgar** [diβul'ɣar] vt (*desparramar*) to spread; (*hacer circular*) to divulge, circulate; **~se** vr to leak out

**DNI** (*ESP*) nm abr (= *Documento Nacional de Identidad*) national identity card

**Dña.** abr (= *doña*) Mrs

**do** [do] nm (*MUS*) do, C

**dobladillo** [doβla'ðiʎo] nm (*de vestido*) hem; (*de pantalón: vuelta*) turnup (*BRIT*), cuff (*US*)

**doblar** [do'βlar] vt to double; (*papel*) to fold; (*caño*) to bend; (*la esquina*) to turn, go round; (*film*) to dub ♦ vi to turn; (*campana*) to toll; **~se** vr (*plegarse*) to fold (up), crease; (*encorvarse*) to bend

**doble** ['doβle] adj double; (*de dos aspectos*) dual; (*fig*) two-faced ♦ nm double ♦ nm/f (*TEATRO*) double, stand-in; (*DEPORTE*) doubles sg; **con sentido ~** with a double meaning

**doblegar** [doβle'ɣar] vt to fold, crease; **~se** vr to yield

**doblez** [do'βleθ] nm double, hem ♦ nf insincerity, duplicity

**doce** ['doθe] num twelve; **~na** nf dozen

**docente** [do'θente] adj: **centro/personal ~** teaching establishment/staff

**dócil** [do'θil] adj (*pasivo*) docile; (*obediente*) obedient

**docto, a** ['dokto, a] adj: **~ en in-**

structed in

**doctor, a** [dok'tor, a] *nm/f* doctor

**doctorado** [dokto'raðo] *nm* doctorate

**doctrina** [dok'trina] *nf* doctrine, teaching

**documentación** [dokumenta'θjon] *nf* documentation, papers *pl*

**documental** [dokumen'tal] *adj, nm* documentary

**documento** [doku'mento] *nm* (*certificado*) document; ~ **national de identidad** identity card

**dólar** ['dolar] *nm* dollar

**doler** [do'ler] *vt, vi* to hurt; (*fig*) to grieve; ~**se** *vr* (*de su situación*) to grieve, feel sorry; (*de las desgracias ajenas*) to sympathize; **me duele el brazo** my arm hurts

**dolor** [do'lor] *nm* pain; (*fig*) grief, sorrow; ~ **de cabeza** headache; ~ **de estómago** stomachache

**domar** [do'mar] *vt* to tame

**domesticar** [domesti'kar] *vt* = **domar**

**doméstico, a** [do'mestiko, a] *adj* (*vida, servicio*) home; (*tareas*) household; (*animal*) tame, pet

**domiciliación** [domiθilia'θjon] *nf*: ~ **de pagos** (*COM*) standing order

**domicilio** [domi'θiljo] *nm* home; ~ **particular** private residence; ~ **social** (*COM*) head office; **sin** ~ **fijo** of no fixed abode

**dominante** [domi'nante] *adj* dominant; (*persona*) domineering

**dominar** [domi'nar] *vt* (*gen*) to dominate; (*idiomas*) to be fluent in ♦ *vi* to dominate, prevail; ~**se** *vr* to control o.s.

**domingo** [do'mingo] *nm* Sunday

**dominio** [do'minjo] *nm* (*tierras*) domain; (*autoridad*) power, authority; (*de las pasiones*) grip, hold; (*de idiomas*) command

**don** [don] *nm* (*talento*) gift; ~ **Juan Gómez** Mr Juan Gomez *o* Juan Gomez Esq

**donaire** [do'naire] *nm* charm

**donar** [do'nar] *vt* to donate

**donativo** [dona'tiβo] *nm* donation

**doncella** [don'θeλa] *nf* (*criada*) maid

**donde** ['donde] *adv* where ♦ *prep*: **el coche está allí** ~ **el farol** the car is over there by the lamppost *o* where the lamppost is; **por** ~ through which; **en** ~ where, in which

**dónde** ['donde] *adv interrogativo* where?; **¿a** ~ **vas?** where are you going (to)?; **¿de** ~ **vienes?** where have you come from?; **¿por** ~? where?, whereabouts?

**dondequiera** [donde'kjera] *adv* anywhere; **por** ~ everywhere, all over the place ♦ *conj*: ~ **que** wherever

**doña** ['doɲa] *nf*: ~ **Alicia** Alicia; ~ **Victoria Benito** Mrs Victoria Benito

**dorado, a** [do'raðo, a] *adj* (*color*) golden; (*TEC*) gilt

**dormir** [dor'mir] *vt*: ~ **la siesta por la tarde** to have an afternoon nap ♦ *vi* to sleep; ~**se** *vr* to fall asleep

**dormitar** [dormi'tar] *vi* to doze

**dormitorio** [dormi'torjo] *nm* bedroom; ~ **común** dormitory

**dorsal** [dor'sal] *nm* (*DEPORTE*) number

**dorso** ['dorso] *nm* (*de mano*) back; (*de hoja*) other side

**dos** [dos] *num* two

**dosis** ['dosis] *nf inv* dose, dosage

**dotado, a** [do'taðo, a] *adj* gifted; ~ **de** endowed with

**dotar** [do'tar] *vt* to endow; **dote** *nf* dowry; **dotes** *nfpl* (*talentos*) gifts

**doy** *vb ver* **dar**

**dragaminas** [draɣa'minas] *nm* minesweeper

**dragar** [dra'ɣar] *vt* (*río*) to dredge; (*minas*) to sweep

**drama** ['drama] *nm* drama

**dramaturgo** [drama'turɣo] *nm* dramatist, playwright

**drástico, a** [dras'tiko, a] *adj* drastic

**drenaje** [dre'naxe] *nm* drainage

**droga** ['droɣa] *nf* drug

**drogadicto, a** [droɣa'ðikto, a] *nm/f* drug addict

**droguería** [droɣe'ria] *nf* hardware shop (*BRIT*) *o* store (*US*)

**ducha** ['dutʃa] nf (baño) shower; (MED) douche; **ducharse** vr to take a shower

**duda** ['duða] nf doubt; **dudar** vt, vi to doubt; **dudoso, a** [du'ðoso, a] adj (incierto) hesitant; (sospechoso) doubtful

**duela** etc vb ver **doler**

**duelo** ['dwelo] vb ver **doler** ♦ nm (combate) duel; (luto) mourning

**duende** ['dwende] nm imp, goblin

**dueño, a** ['dweɲo, a] nm/f (propietario) owner; (de pensión, taberna) landlord/lady; (empresario) employer

**duermo** etc vb ver **dormir**

**dulce** ['dulθe] adj sweet ♦ adv gently, softly ♦ nm sweet

**dulzura** [dul'θura] nf sweetness; (ternura) gentleness

**duna** ['duna] nf (GEO) dune

**dúo** ['duo] nm duet

**duplicar** [dupli'kar] vt (hacer el doble de) to duplicate; ~**se** vr to double

**duque** ['duke] nm duke; ~**sa** nf duchess

**duración** [dura'θjon] nf (de película, disco etc) length; (de pila etc) life; (curso: de acontecimientos etc) duration

**duradero, a** [dura'ðero, a] adj (tela etc) hard-wearing; (fe, paz) lasting

**durante** [du'rante] prep during

**durar** [du'rar] vi (permanecer) to last; (recuerdo) to remain

**durazno** [du'raθno] (AM) nm (fruta) peach; (árbol) peach tree

**durex** ['dureks] (AM) nm (tira adhesiva) Sellotape ® (BRIT), Scotch tape ® (US)

**dureza** [du'reθa] nf (calidad) hardness

**duro, a** ['duro, a] adj hard; (carácter) tough ♦ adv hard ♦ nm (moneda) five peseta coin o piece

# E

**e** [e] conj and

**E** abr (= este) E

**ebanista** [eβa'nista] nm/f cabinetmaker

**ébano** ['eβano] nm ebony

**ebrio, a** ['eβrjo, a] adj drunk

**ebullición** [eβuʎi'θjon] nf boiling

**eccema** [ek'θema] nf (MED) eczema

**eclesiástico, a** [ekle'sjastiko, a] adj ecclesiastical

**eclipse** [e'klipse] nm eclipse

**eco** ['eko] nm echo; **tener ~** to catch on

**ecología** [ekolo'xia] nf ecology; **ecologista** [ekolo'xista] adj ecological, environmental ♦ nm/f environmentalist

**economato** [ekono'mato] nm cooperative store

**economía** [ekono'mia] nf (sistema) economy; (cualidad) thrift

**económico, a** [eko'nomiko, a] adj (barato) cheap, economical; (persona) thrifty; (COM: año etc) financial; (: situación) economic

**economista** [ekono'mista] nm/f economist

**ECU** [eku] nm ECU

**ecuador** [ekwa'ðor] nm equator; (el) E~ Ecuador

**ecuánime** [e'kwanime] adj (carácter) level-headed; (estado) calm

**ecuatoriano, a** [ekwato'rjano, a] adj, nm/f Ecuadorian

**ecuestre** [e'kwestre] adj equestrian

**eczema** [ek'θema] nm = **eccema**

**echar** [e'tʃar] vt to throw; (agua, vino) to pour (out); (empleado: despedir) to fire, sack; (humo) to sprout; (cartas) to post; (humo) to emit, give out ♦ vi: ~ **a correr/llorar** to run off/burst into tears; ~**se** vr to lie down; ~ **llave a** to lock (up); ~ **abajo** (gobierno) to overthrow; (edificio) to demolish; ~ **mano a** to lay hands on; ~ **una mano a uno** (ayudar) to give sb a hand; ~ **de menos** to miss

**edad** [e'ðað] *nf* age; ¿**qué ~ tienes?** how old are you?; **tiene ocho años de ~** he is eight (years old); **de ~ mediana/avanzada** middle-aged/ advanced in years; **la E~ Media** the Middle Ages

**edición** [eði'θjon] *nf* (*acto*) publication; (*ejemplar*) edition

**edicto** [e'ðikto] *nm* edict, proclamation

**edificio** [eði'fiθjo] *nm* building; (*fig*) edifice, structure

**Edimburgo** [eðim'burvo] *nm* Edinburgh

**editar** [eði'tar] *vt* (*publicar*) to publish; (*preparar textos*) to edit

**editor, a** [eði'tor, a] *nm/f* (*que publica*) publisher; (*redactor*) editor ♦ *adj*: **casa ~a** publishing house, publisher; **~ial** *adj* editorial ♦ *nm* leading article, editorial; **casa ~ial** publishing house, publisher

**edredón** [eðre'ðon] *nm* duvet

**educación** [eðuka'θjon] *nf* education; (*crianza*) upbringing; (*modales*) (good) manners *pl*

**educar** [eðu'kar] *vt* to educate; (*criar*) to bring up; (*voz*) to train

**EE. UU.** *nmpl abr* (= *Estados Unidos*) US(A)

**efectista** [efek'tista] *adj* sensationalist

**efectivamente** [efektiβa'mente] *adv* (*como respuesta*) exactly, precisely; (*verdaderamente*) really; (*de hecho*) in fact

**efectivo, a** [efek'tiβo, a] *adj* effective; (*real*) actual, real ♦ *nm*: **pagar en ~** to pay (in) cash; **hacer ~ un cheque** to cash a cheque

**efecto** [e'fekto] *nm* effect, result; **~s** *nmpl* (~**s personales**) effects; (*bienes*) goods; (*COM*) assets; **en ~** in fact; (*respuesta*) exactly, indeed; **~ invernadero** greenhouse effect

**efectuar** [efek'twar] *vt* to carry out; (*viaje*) to make

**eficacia** [efi'kaθja] *nf* (*de persona*) efficiency; (*de medicamento etc*) ef-

fectiveness

**eficaz** [efi'kaθ] *adj* (*persona*) efficient; (*acción*) effective

**eficiente** [efi'θjente] *adj* efficient

**efusivo, a** [efu'siβo, a] *adj* effusive; **mis más efusivas gracias** my warmest thanks

**EGB** (*ESP*) *nf abr* (*ESCOL*) = *Educación General Básica*

**egipcio, a** [e'xipθjo, a] *adj, nm/f* Egyptian

**Egipto** [e'xipto] *nm* Egypt

**egoísmo** [evo'ismo] *nm* egoism

**egoísta** [evo'ista] *adj* egoistical, selfish ♦ *nm/f* egoist

**egregio, a** [e'xrexjo, a] *adj* eminent, distinguished

**Eire** [eire] *nm* Eire

**ej.** *abr* (= *ejemplo*) eg

**eje** ['exe] *nm* (*GEO, MAT*) axis; (*de rueda*) axle; (*de máquina*) shaft, spindle

**ejecución** [exeku'θjon] *nf* execution; (*cumplimiento*) fulfilment; (*actuación*) performance; (*JUR*: *embargo de deudor*) attachment

**ejecutar** [exeku'tar] *vt* to execute, carry out; (*matar*) to execute; (*cumplir*) to fulfil; (*MUS*) to perform; (*JUR*: *embargar*) to attach, distrain (on)

**ejecutivo, a** [exeku'tiβo, a] *adj* executive; **el (poder) ~** the executive (power)

**ejemplar** [exem'plar] *adj* exemplary ♦ *nm* example; (*ZOOL*) specimen; (*de libro*) copy; (*de periódico*) number, issue

**ejemplo** [e'xemplo] *nm* example; **por ~** for example

**ejercer** [exer'θer] *vt* to exercise; (*influencia*) to exert; (*un oficio*) to practise ♦ *vi* (*practicar*): ~ **(de)** to practise (as); (*tener oficio*) to hold office

**ejercicio** [exer'θiθjo] *nm* exercise; (*período*) tenure; ~ **comercial** financial year

**ejército** [e'xerθito] *nm* army; **entrar en el ~** to join the army, join up

**ejote** [e'xote] (AM) nm green bean

---
**PALABRA CLAVE**
---

**el** [el] (f la, pl los, las, neutro lo) art
def **1** the; **el libro/la mesa/los estu-
diantes** the book/table/students

**2** (con n abstracto: no se traduce):
**el amor/la juventud** love/youth

**3** (posesión: se traduce a menudo por
adj posesivo): **romperse el brazo** to
break one's arm; **levantó la mano**
he put his hand up; **se puso el sombrero** she put her hat on

**4** (valor descriptivo): **tener la boca
grande/los ojos azules** to have a
big mouth/blue eyes

**5** (con días): **me iré el viernes**
I'll leave on Friday; **los domingos
suelo ir a nadar** on Sundays I generally go swimming

**6** (lo + adj): **lo difícil/caro** what is
difficult/expensive; (= cuán): **no se
da cuenta de lo pesado que es he**
doesn't realise how boring he is

♦ pron demos **1**: **mi libro y el de
usted** my book and yours; **las de
Pepe son mejores** Pepe's are better; **no la(s) blanca(s) sino la(s)
gris(es)** not the white one(s) but the
grey one(s)

**2**: **lo de: lo de ayer** what happened
yesterday; **lo de las facturas** that
business about the invoices

♦ pron relativo: **el que** etc **1** (indef): **el (los) que quiera(n) que se
vaya(n)** anyone who wants to can
leave; **llévese el que más le guste**
take the one you like best

**2** (def): **el que compré ayer** the
one I bought yesterday; **los que se
van** those who leave

**3**: **lo que: lo que pienso yo/más
me gusta** what I think/like most

♦ conj: **el que: el que lo diga** the
fact that he says so; **el que sea tan
vago me molesta** his being so lazy
bothers me

♦ excl: **¡el susto que me diste!**
what a fright you gave me!

♦ pron personal **1** (persona: m) him;

(: f) her; (: pl) them; **lo/las veo** I
can see him/them

**2** (animal, cosa: sg) it; (: pl) them;
**lo** (o **la**) **veo** I can see it; **los** (o **las**)
**veo** I can see them

**3**: **lo** (como sustituto de frase): **no
lo sabía** I didn't know; **ya lo entiendo** I understand now

**él** [el] pron (persona) he; (cosa) it;
(después de prep: persona) him; (:
cosa) it; **de ~** his

**elaborar** [elaβo'rar] vt (producto) to
make, manufacture; (preparar) to
prepare; (madera, metal etc) to
work; (proyecto etc) to work on o out

**elasticidad** [elastiθi'ðað] nf elasticity

**elástico, a** [e'lastiko, a] adj elastic;
(flexible) flexible ♦ nm elastic; (un
~) elastic band

**elección** [elek'θjon] nf election; (selección) choice, selection

**electorado** [elekto'raðo] nm electo-
rate, voters pl

**electricidad** [elektriθi'ðað] nf electricity

**electricista** [elektri'θista] nm/f electrician

**eléctrico, a** [e'lektriko, a] adj electric

**electro...** [elektro] prefijo electro...;
**~cardiograma** nm electrocardio-
gram; **~cutar** vt to electrocute; **~do**
nm electrode; **~domésticos** nmpl
(electrical) household appliances;
**~magnético, a** adj electromagnetic

**electrónica** [elek'tronika] nf elec-
tronics sg

**electrónico, a** [elek'troniko, a] adj
electronic

**electrotecnia** [elektro'teknja] nf
electrical engineering; **electrotécni-
co, a** nm/f electrical engineer

**elefante** [ele'fante] nm elephant

**elegancia** [ele'vanθja] nf elegance,
grace; (estilo) stylishness

**elegante** [ele'vante] adj elegant,
graceful; (estiloso) stylish, fashionable

**elegía** [ele'xia] nf elegy

**elegir** [ele'xir] vt (escoger) to choose,

select; (*optar*) to opt for; (*presidente*) to elect

**elemental** [elemen'tal] *adj* (*claro*, *obvio*) elementary; (*fundamental*) elemental, fundamental

**elemento** [ele'mento] *nm* element; (*fig*) ingredient; ~s *nmpl* elements, rudiments

**elenco** [e'lenko] *nm* (*TEATRO*, *CINE*) cast

**elepé** [ele'pe] (*pl*: elepés) *nm* L.P.

**elevación** [eleβa'θjon] *nf* elevation; (*acto*) raising, lifting; (*de precios*) rise; (*GEO etc*) height, altitude; (*de persona*) nobleness

**elevar** [ele'βar] *vt* to raise, lift (up); (*precio*) to put up; ~se *vr* (*edificio*) to rise; (*precios*) to go up; (*transportarse, enajenarse*) to get carried away

**eligiendo** *etc vb ver* **elegir**

**elija** *etc vb ver* **elegir**

**eliminar** [elimi'nar] *vt* to eliminate, remove

**eliminatoria** [elimina'torja] *nf* heat, preliminary (round)

**elite** [e'lite] *nf* elite

**elocuencia** [elo'kwenθja] *nf* eloquence

**elogiar** [elo'xjar] *vt* to praise, eulogize; **elogio** *nm* praise

**elote** [e'lote] (*AM*) *nm* corn on the cob

**eludir** [elu'ðir] *vt* (*evitar*) to avoid, evade; (*escapar*) to escape, elude

**ella** ['eʎa] *pron* (*persona*) she; (*cosa*) it; (*después de prep: persona*) her; (: *cosa*) it; **ello** ['eʎo] *pron* it

**ellas** ['eʎas] *pron* (*personas y cosas*) they; (*después de prep*) them; **de** ~ theirs

**ello** ['eʎo] *pron* it

**ellos** ['eʎos] *pron* they; (*después de prep*) them; **de** ~ theirs

**emanar** [ema'nar] *vi*: ~ **de** to emanate from, come from; (*derivar de*) to originate in

**emancipar** [emanθi'par] *vt* to emancipate; ~se *vr* to become emancipated, free o.s.

**embadurnar** [embaður'nar] *vt* to smear

**embajada** [emba'xaða] *nf* embassy

**embajador, a** [embaxa'ðor, a] *nm/f* ambassador/ambassadress

**embalaje** [emba'laxe] *nm* packing

**embalar** [emba'lar] *vt* (*envolver*) to parcel, wrap (up); (*envasar*) to package; ~se *vr* to go fast

**embalsamar** [embalsa'mar] *vt* to embalm

**embalse** [em'balse] *nm* (*presa*) dam; (*lago*) reservoir

**embarazada** [embara'θaða] *adj* pregnant ♦ *nf* pregnant woman

**embarazar** [embara'θar] *vt* to obstruct, hamper; ~se *vr* (*aturdirse*) to become embarrassed; (*confundirse*) to get into a mess

**embarazo** [emba'raθo] *nm* (*de mujer*) pregnancy; (*impedimento*) obstacle, obstruction; (*timidez*) embarrassment; **embarazoso, a** *adj* awkward, embarrassing

**embarcación** [embarka'θjon] *nf* (*barco*) boat, craft; (*acto*) embarkation, boarding

**embarcadero** [embarka'ðero] *nm* pier, landing stage

**embarcar** [embar'kar] *vt* (*cargamento*) to ship, stow; (*persona*) to embark, put on board; ~se *vr* to embark, go on board

**embargar** [embar'gar] *vt* (*JUR*) to seize, impound

**embargo** [em'barvo] *nm* (*JUR*) seizure; (*COM, POL*) embargo

**embargue** *etc* [em'barve] *etc vb ver* embargar

**embarque** *etc* [em'barke] *vb ver* embarcar ♦ *nm* shipment, loading

**embaucar** [embau'kar] *vt* to trick, fool

**embeber** [embe'βer] *vt* (*absorber*) to absorb, soak up; (*empapar*) to saturate ♦ *vi* to shrink; ~se *vr*: ~se **en un libro** to be engrossed *o* absorbed in a book

**embellecer** [embeʎe'θer] *vt* to embellish, beautify

**embestida** [embes'tiða] nf attack, onslaught; (carga) charge

**embestir** [embes'tir] vt to attack, assault; to charge, attack ♦ vi to attack

**emblema** [em'blema] nm emblem

**embobado, a** [embo'ßaðo, a] adj (atontado) stunned, bewildered

**embolia** [em'bolja] nf (MED) clot

**émbolo** ['embolo] nm (AUTO) piston

**embolsar** [embol'sar] vt to pocket, put in one's pocket

**emborrachar** [emborra'tʃar] vt to make drunk, intoxicate; ~se vr to get drunk

**emboscada** [embos'kaða] nf (celada) ambush

**embotar** [embo'tar] vt to blunt, dull; ~se vr (adormecerse) to go numb

**embotellamiento** [emboteʎa'mjento] nm (AUTO) traffic jam

**embotellar** [embote'ʎar] vt to bottle; ~se vr (circulación) to get into a jam

**embozo** [em'boθo] nm (de sábana) turndown

**embrague** [em'braße] nm (tb: pedal de ~) clutch

**embriagar** [embrja'ɣar] vt (emborrachar) to make drunk; (alegrar) to delight; ~se vr (emborracharse) to get drunk

**embriaguez** [embrja'ɣeθ] nf (borrachera) drunkenness

**embrión** [em'brjon] nm embryo

**embrollar** [embro'ʎar] vt (el asunto) to confuse, complicate; (persona) to involve, embroil; ~se vr (confundirse) to get into a muddle o mess

**embrollo** [em'broʎo] nm (enredo) muddle, confusion; (aprieto) fix, jam

**embrujado, a** [embru'xaðo, a] adj bewitched; **casa embrujada** haunted house

**embrutecer** [embrute'θer] vt (atontar) to stupefy; ~se vr to be stupefied

**embudo** [em'buðo] nm funnel

**embuste** [em'buste] nm trick; (mentira) lie; (hum) fib; **~ro, a** adj lying,

**embestida** 112 **empalmar**

deceitful ♦ nm/f (tramposo) cheat; (mentiroso) liar; (humorístico) fibber

**embutido** [embu'tiðo] nm (CULIN) sausage; (TEC) inlay

**embutir** [embu'tir] vt (TEC) to inlay; (llenar) to pack tight, cram

**emergencia** [emer'xenθja] nf emergency; (surgimiento) emergence

**emerger** [emer'xer] vi to emerge, appear

**emigración** [emiɣra'θjon] nf emigration; (de pájaros) migration

**emigrar** [emi'ɣrar] vi (personas) to emigrate; (pájaros) to migrate

**eminencia** [emi'nenθja] nf eminence; **eminente** adj eminent, distinguished; (elevado) high

**emisario** [emi'sarjo] nm emissary

**emisión** [emi'sjon] nf (acto) emission; (COM etc) issue; (RADIO, TV: acto) broadcasting; (: programa) broadcast, programme (BRIT) program (US)

**emisora** [emi'sora] nf radio o broadcasting station

**emitir** [emi'tir] vt (olor etc) to emit, give off; (moneda etc) to issue; (opinión) to express; (RADIO) to broadcast

**emoción** [emo'θjon] nf emotion; (excitación) excitement; (sentimiento) feeling

**emocionante** [emoθjo'nante] adj (excitante) exciting, thrilling

**emocionar** [emoθjo'nar] vt (excitar) to excite, thrill; (conmover) to move, touch; (impresionar) to impress

**emotivo, a** [emo'tißo, a] adj emotional

**empacar** [empa'kar] vt (gen) to pack; (en caja) to bale, crate

**empacho** [em'patʃo] nm (MED) indigestion; (fig) embarrassment

**empadronarse** [empaðro'narse] vr (POL: como elector) to register

**empalagoso, a** [empala'ɣoso, a] adj cloying; (fig) tiresome

**empalizada** [empali'θaða] nf (valla) fence

**empalmar** [empal'mar] vt to join,

connect ♦ vi (dos caminos) to meet, join; **empalme** nm joint, connection; junction; (de trenes) connection

**empanada** [empa'naða] nf pie, pasty

**empantanarse** [empanta'narse] vr to get swamped; (fig) to get bogged down

**empañarse** [empa'ɲarse] vr (cristales etc) to steam up

**empapar** [empa'par] vt (mojar) to soak, saturate; (absorber) to soak up, absorb; ~**se** vr: ~**se de** to soak up

**empapelar** [empape'lar] vt (paredes) to paper

**empaquetar** [empake'tar] vt to pack, parcel up

**emparedado** [empare'ðaðo] nm sandwich

**empastar** [empas'tar] vt (embadurnar) to paste; (diente) to fill

**empaste** [em'paste] nm (de diente) filling

**empatar** [empa'tar] vi to draw, tie; **empate** nm draw, tie

**empecé** etc vb ver **empezar**

**empedernido, a** [empeðer'niðo, a] adj hard, heartless; (fijado) hardened, inveterate

**empedrado, a** [empe'ðraðo, a] adj paved ♦ nm paving

**empeine** [em'peine] nm (de pie, zapato) instep

**empellón** [empe'ʎon] nm push, shove

**empeñado, a** [empe'ɲaðo, a] adj (persona) determined; (objeto) pawned

**empeñar** [empe'ɲar] vt (objeto) to pawn, pledge; (persona) to compel; ~**se** vr (obligarse) to bind o.s., pledge o.s.; (endeudarse) to get into debt; ~**se en** to be set on, be determined to

**empeño** [em'peɲo] nm (determinación, insistencia) determination, insistence; (cosa prendada) pledge; **casa de** ~**s** pawnshop

**empeorar** [empeo'rar] vt to make worse, worsen ♦ vi to get worse, de-

teriorate

**empequeñecer** [empekeɲe'θer] vt to dwarf; (fig) to belittle

**emperador** [empera'ðor] nm emperor; **emperatriz** nf empress

**empezar** [empe'θar] vt, vi to begin, start

**empiece** etc vb ver **empezar**

**empiezo** etc vb ver **empezar**

**empinar** [empi'nar] vt to raise; ~**se** vr (persona) to stand on tiptoe; (animal) to rear up; (camino) to climb steeply

**empírico, a** [em'piriko, a] adj empirical

**emplasto** [em'plasto] nm (MED) plaster

**emplazamiento** [emplaθa'mjento] nm site, location; (JUR) summons sg

**emplazar** [empla'θar] vt (ubicar) to site, place, locate; (JUR) to summons; (convocar) to summon

**empleado, a** [emple'aðo, a] nm/f (gen) employee; (de banco etc) clerk

**emplear** [emple'ar] vt (usar) to use, employ; (dar trabajo a) to employ; ~**se** vr (conseguir trabajo) to be employed; (ocuparse) to occupy o.s.

**empleo** [em'pleo] nm (puesto) job; (puestos: colectivamente) employment; (uso) use, employment

**empobrecer** [empoβre'θer] vt to impoverish; ~**se** vr to become poor o impoverished

**empolvarse** [empol'βarse] vr to powder one's face

**empollar** [empo'ʎar] (fam) vt, vi to swot (up); **empollón, ona** (fam) nm/f swot

**emporio** [em'porjo] nm emporium, trading centre; (AM: gran almacén) department store

**empotrado, a** [empo'traðo, a] adj (armario etc) built-in

**emprender** [empren'der] vt (empezar) to begin, embark on; (acometer) to tackle, take on

**empresa** [em'presa] nf (de espíritu etc) enterprise; (COM) company, firm; ~**rio, a** nm/f (COM) manager

**empréstito** [em'prestito] nm (public) loan

**empujar** [empu'xar] vt to push, shove; **empuje** nm thrust; (presión) pressure; (fig) vigour, drive

**empujón** [empu'xon] nm push, shove

**empuñar** [empu'ɲar] vt (asir) to grasp, take (firm) hold of

**emular** [emu'lar] vt to emulate; (rivalizar) to rival

---

PALABRA CLAVE

---

**en** [en] prep **1** (posición) in; (: sobre) on; **está ~ el cajón** it's in the drawer; **~ Argentina/La Paz** in Argentina/La Paz; **~ la oficina/el colegio** at the office/school; **está ~ el suelo/quinto piso** it's on the floor/the fifth floor

**2** (dirección) into; **entró ~ el aula** she went into the classroom; **meter algo ~ el bolso** to put sth into one's bag

**3** (tiempo) in; on; **~ 1605/3 semanas/invierno** in 1605/3 weeks/winter; **~ (el mes de) enero** in the month of) January; **~ aquella ocasión/época** on that occasion/at that time

**4** (precio) for; **lo vendió ~ 20 dólares** he sold it for 20 dollars

**5** (diferencia) by; **reducir/aumentar ~ una tercera parte/un 20 por ciento** to reduce/increase by a third/20 per cent

**6** (manera): **~ avión/autobús** by plane/bus; **escrito ~ inglés** written in English

**7** (después de vb que indica gastar etc) on; **han cobrado demasiado ~ dietas** they've charged too much to expenses; **se le va la mitad del sueldo ~ comida** he spends half his salary on food

**8** (tema, ocupación): **experto ~ la materia** expert on the subject; **trabaja ~ la construcción** he works in the building industry

**9** (adj + ~ + infin): **lento ~ reaccionar** slow to react

---

**enaguas** [e'naɣwas] nfpl petticoat sg, underskirt sg

**enajenación** [enaxena'θjon] nf (fig: distracción) absent-mindedness; (: embelesamiento) rapture, trance

**enajenamiento** [enaxena'mjento] nm = **enajenación**

**enajenar** [enaxe'nar] vt to alienate; (fig) to carry away

**enamorado, a** [enamo'raðo, a] adj in love ♦ nm/f lover

**enamorar** [enamo'rar] vt to win the love of; **~se vr: ~se de alguien** to fall in love with sb

**enano, a** [e'nano, a] adj tiny ♦ nm/f dwarf

**enardecer** [enarðe'θer] vt (pasiones) to fire, inflame; (persona) to fill with enthusiasm; **~se vr: ~se por** to get excited about; (entusiasmarse) to get enthusiastic about

**encabezamiento** [enkaβeθa'mjento] nm (de carta) heading; (de periódico) headline; (preámbulo) foreword, preface

**encabezar** [enkaβe'θar] vt (movimiento, revolución) to lead, head; (lista) to head, be at the top of; (carta) to put a heading to; (libro) to entitle

**encadenar** [enkaðe'nar] vt to chain (together); (poner grilletes a) to shackle

**encajar** [enka'xar] vt (ajustar): ~ (en) to fit (into); (fam: golpe) to give, deal; (entrometer) to insert ♦ vi to fit (well); (fig: corresponder a) to match; **~se vr: ~se en un sillón** to squeeze into a chair

**encaje** [en'kaxe] nm (labor) lace

**encalar** [enka'lar] vt (pared) to whitewash

**encallar** [enka'ʎar] vi (NAUT) to run aground

**encaminar** [enkami'nar] vt to direct, send; **~se vr: ~se a** to set out for

**encandilar** [enkandi'lar] vt to dazzle

**encantado, a** [enkan'taðo, a] adj (hechizado) bewitched; (muy conten-

*to)* delighted; ~! how do you do, pleased to meet you

**encantador, a** [enkanta'ðor, a] *adj* charming, lovely ♦ *nm/f* magician, enchanter/enchantress

**encantar** [enkan'tar] *vt* to charm, delight; *(hechizar)* to bewitch, cast a spell on; **encanto** *nm (magia)* spell, charm; *(fig)* charm, delight

**encarcelar** [enkarθe'lar] *vt* to imprison, jail

**encarecer** [enkare'θer] *vt* to put up the price of ♦ *vi* to get dearer; ~se *vr* to get dearer

**encarecimiento** [enkareθi'mjento] *nm* price increase

**encargado, a** [enkar'xaðo, a] *adj* in charge ♦ *nm/f* agent, representative; *(responsable)* person in charge

**encargar** [enkar'xar] *vt* to entrust; *(recomendar)* to urge, recommend; ~se *vr*: ~se de to look after, take charge of

**encargo** [en'karxo] *nm (pedido)* assignment, job; *(responsabilidad)* responsibility; *(recomendación)* recommendation; *(COM)* order

**encariñarse** [enkari'parse] *vr*: ~ con to grow fond of, get attached to

**encarnación** [enkarna'θjon] *nf* incarnation, embodiment

**encarnizado, a** [enkarni'θaðo, a] *adj (lucha)* bloody, fierce

**encarrilar** [enkarri'lar] *vt (tren)* to put back on the rails; *(fig)* to correct, put on the right track

**encasillar** [enkasi'ʎar] *vt (tb fig)* to pigeonhole; *(actor)* to typecast

**encasquetar** [enkaske'tar] *vt (gorro, sombrero)* to pull on, stick on; ~se *vr* to pull on, stick on

**encauzar** [enkau'θar] *vt* to channel

**encendedor** [enθende'ðor] *nm* lighter

**encender** [enθen'der] *vt (con fuego)* to light; *(incendiar)* to set fire to; *(luz, radio)* to put on, switch on; *(avivar: pasiones)* to inflame; ~se *vr* to catch fire; *(excitarse)* to get excited; *(de cólera)* to flare up; *(el ros-*

*tro)* to blush

**encendido** [enθen'diðo] *nm (AUTO)* ignition

**encerado** [enθe'raðo] *nm (ESCOL)* blackboard

**encerar** [enθe'rar] *vt (suelo)* to wax, polish

**encerrar** [enθe'rrar] *vt (confinar)* to shut in, shut up; *(comprender, incluir)* to include, contain

**encía** [en'θia] *nf* gum

**encienda** *etc vb ver* encender

**encierro** [en'θjerro] *etc vb ver* encerrar ♦ *nm* shutting in, shutting up; *(calabozo)* prison

**encima** [en'θima] *adv (sobre)* above, over; *(además)* besides; ~ de *(en)* on, on top of; *(sobre)* above, over; *(además de)* besides, on top of; por ~ de over; ¿llevas dinero ~? have you (got) any money on you?; se me vino ~ it took me by surprise

**encinta** [en'θinta] *adj* pregnant

**enclenque** [en'klenke] *adj* weak, sickly

**encoger** [enko'xer] *vt* to shrink, contract; *(fig: asustar)* to scare; ~se *vr* to shrink, contract; *(fig)* to cringe; ~se de hombros to shrug one's shoulders

**encolar** [enko'lar] *vt (engomar)* to glue, paste; *(pegar)* to stick down

**encolerizar** [enkoleri'θar] *vt* to anger, provoke; ~se *vr* to get angry

**encomendar** [enkomen'dar] *vt* to entrust, commend; ~se *vr*: ~se a to put one's trust in

**encomiar** [enko'mjar] *vt* to praise, pay tribute to

**encomienda** *etc* [enko'mjenda] *vb ver* encomendar ♦ *nf (encargo)* charge, commission; *(elogio)* tribute; ~ postal *(AM)* parcel post

**encontrado, a** [enkon'traðo, a] *adj (contrario)* contrary, conflicting; *(hostil)* hostile

**encontrar** [enkon'trar] *vt (hallar)* to find; *(inesperadamente)* to meet, run into; ~se *vr* to meet (each other); *(situarse)* to be (situated); *(entrar* *en conflicto*) to crash, collide; ~**se con** to meet; ~**se bien (de salud)** to feel well

**encorvar** [enkor'βar] *vt* to curve; (*inclinar*) to bend (down); ~**se** *vr* to bend down, bend over

**encrespar** [enkres'par] *vt* (*cabellos*) to curl; (*fig*) to anger, irritate; ~**se** *vr* (*el mar*) to get rough; (*fig*) to get cross, get irritated

**encrucijada** [enkruθi'xaða] *nf* crossroads *sg*; (*empalme*) junction

**encuadernación** [enkwaðerna'θjon] *nf* binding

**encuadernador, a** [enkwaðerna-'ðor, a] *nm/f* bookbinder

**encuadrar** [enkwa'ðrar] *vt* (*retrato*) to frame; (*ajustar*) to fit, insert; (*encerrar*) to contain

**encubrir** [enku'βrir] *vt* (*ocultar*) to hide, conceal; (*criminal*) to harbour, shelter

**encuentro** *etc* [en'kwentro] *vb ver* **encontrar ♦** *nm* (*de personas*) meeting; (*AUTO etc*) collision, crash; (*DEPORTE*) match, game; (*MIL*) encounter

**encuesta** [en'kwesta] *nf* inquiry, investigation; (*sondeo*) (public) opinion poll; ~ **judicial** post mortem

**encumbrar** [enkum'brar] *vt* (*persona*) to exalt; ~**se** *vr* (*fig*) to become conceited

**encharcado, a** [entʃar'kaðo, a] *adj* (*terreno*) flooded

**encharcarse** [entʃar'karse] *vr* to get flooded

**enchufado, a** [entʃu'faðo, a] (*fam*) *nm/f* well-connected person

**enchufar** [entʃu'far] *vt* (*ELEC*) to plug in; (*TEC*) to connect, fit together; **enchufe** *nm* (*ELEC: clavija*) plug; (*: toma*) socket; (*de dos tubos*) joint, connection; (*fam: influencia*) contact, connection; (*: puesto*) cushy job

**endeble** [en'deβle] *adj* (*argumento, excusa, persona*) weak

**endémico, a** [en'demiko, a] *adj* (*MED*) endemic; (*fig*) rife, chronic

**endemoniado, a** [endemo'njaðo, a] *adj* possessed (of the devil); (*travieso*) devilish

**enderezar** [endere'θar] *vt* (*poner derecho*) to straighten (out); (*: verticalmente*) to set upright; (*fig*) to straighten o sort out; (*dirigir*) to direct; ~**se** *vr* (*persona sentada*) to straighten up

**endeudarse** [endeu'ðarse] *vr* to get into debt

**endiablado, a** [endja'βlaðo, a] *adj* devilish, diabolical; (*travieso*) mischievous

**endilgar** [endil'βar] (*fam*) *vt*: ~**le algo a uno** to lumber sb with sth; ~**le un sermón a uno** to lecture sb

**endiñar** [endi'par] (*fam*) *vt* (*bofetón*) to land, belt

**endosar** [endo'sar] *vt* (*cheque etc*) to endorse

**endulzar** [endul'θar] *vt* to sweeten; (*suavizar*) to soften

**endurecer** [endure'θer] *vt* to harden; ~**se** *vr* to harden, grow hard

**enema** [e'nema] *nm* (*MED*) enema

**enemigo, a** [ene'miɣo, a] *adj* enemy, hostile **♦** *nm/f* enemy

**enemistad** [enemis'tað] *nf* enmity

**enemistar** [enemis'tar] *vt* to make enemies of, cause a rift between; ~**se** *vr* to become enemies; (*amigos*) to fall out

**energía** [ener'xia] *nf* (*vigor*) energy, drive; (*empuje*) push; (*TEC, ELEC*) energy, power; ~ **eólica** wind power; ~ **solar** solar energy/power

**enérgico, a** [e'nerxiko, a] *adj* (*gen*) energetic; (*voz, modales*) forceful

**energúmeno, a** [ener'ɣumeno, a] (*fam*) *nm/f* (*fig*) madman/woman

**enero** [e'nero] *nm* January

**enfadado, a** [enfa'ðaðo, a] *adj* angry, annoyed

**enfadar** [enfa'ðar] *vt* to anger, annoy; ~**se** *vr* to get angry o annoyed

**enfado** [en'faðo] *nm* (*enojo*) anger, annoyance; (*disgusto*) trouble, bother

**énfasis** ['enfasis] *nm* emphasis, stress

**enfático, a** [en'fatiko, a] *adj* emphatic

**enfermar** [enfer'mar] *vt* to make ill ♦ *vi* to fall ill, be taken ill

**enfermedad** [enferme'ðað] *nf* illness; ~ **venérea** venereal disease

**enfermera** [enfer'mera] *nf* nurse

**enfermería** [enferme'ria] *nf* infirmary; (*de colegio etc*) sick bay

**enfermero** [enfer'mero] *nm* (male) nurse ,

**enfermizo, a** [enfer'miθo, a] *adj* (*persona*) sickly, unhealthy; (*fig*) unhealthy

**enfermo, a** [en'fermo, a] *adj* ill, sick ♦ *nm/f* invalid, sick person; (*en hospital*) patient

**enflaquecer** [enflake'θer] *vt* (*adelgazar*) to make thin; (*debilitar*) to weaken

**enfocar** [enfo'kar] *vt* (*foto etc*) to focus; (*problema etc*) to consider, look at

**enfoque** *etc* [en'foke] *vb ver* enfocar ♦ *nm* focus.

**enfrascarse** [enfras'karse] *vr*: ~ **en algo** to bury o.s. in sth

**enfrentar** [enfren'tar] *vt* (*peligro*) to face (up to), confront; (*oponer*) to bring face to face; ~se *vr* (*dos personas*) to face o confront each other; (*DEPORTE: dos equipos*) to meet; ~se a o con to face up to, confront

**enfrente** [en'frente] *adv* opposite; **la casa de ~** the house opposite; **la casa across the street;** ~ **de** opposite, facing

**enfriamiento** [enfria'mjento] *nm* chilling, refrigeration; (*MED*) cold, chill

**enfriar** [enfri'ar] *vt* (*alimentos*) to cool, chill; (*algo caliente*) to cool down; (*habitación*) to air, freshen; ~se *vr* to cool down; (*MED*) to catch a chill; (*amistad*) to cool

**enfurecer** [enfure'θer] *vt* to enrage, madden; ~se *vr* to become furious, fly into a rage; (*mar*) to get rough

**engalanar** [engala'nar] *vt* (*adornar*) to adorn; (*ciudad*) to decorate; ~se

*vr* to get dressed up

**enganchar** [engan'tʃar] *vt* to hook; (*ropa*) to hang up; (*dos vagones*) to hitch up; (*TEC*) to couple, connect; (*MIL*) to recruit; (*fam: persona*) to rope in; ~se *vr* (*MIL*) to enlist, join up

**enganche** [en'gantʃe] *nm* hook; (*TEC*) coupling, connection; (*acto*) hooking (up); (*MIL*) recruitment, enlistment; (*AM: depósito*) deposit

**engañar** [enga'nar] *vt* to deceive; (*estafar*) to cheat, swindle; ~se *vr* (*equivocarse*) to be wrong; (*disimular la verdad*) to deceive o.s.

**engaño** [en'gano] *nm* deceit; (*estafa*) trick, swindle; (*error*) mistake, misunderstanding; (*ilusión*) delusion; ~**so, a** *adj* (*tramposo*) crooked; (*mentiroso*) dishonest, deceitful; (*aspecto*) deceptive; (*consejo*) misleading

**engarzar** [engar'θar] *vt* (*joya*) to set, mount; (*fig*) to link, connect

**engatusar** [engatu'sar] (*fam*) *vt* to coax

**engendrar** [enxen'drar] *vt* to breed; (*procrear*) to beget; (*fig*) to cause, produce; **engendro** [en'xendro] *nm* (*BIO*) foetus; (*fig*) monstrosity; (*idea*) brainchild

**englobar** [englo'βar] *vt* (*incluir*) to include, comprise

**engordar** [engor'ðar] *vt* to fatten ♦ *vi* to get fat, put on weight

**engorroso, a** [engo'rroso, a] *adj* bothersome, trying

**engranaje** [engra'naxe] *nm* (*AUTO*) gear

**engrandecer** [engrande'θer] *vt* to enlarge, magnify; (*alabar*) to praise, speak highly of; (*exagerar*) to exaggerate

**engrasar** [engra'sar] *vt* (*TEC: poner grasa*) to grease; (: *lubricar*) to lubricate, oil; (*manchar*) to make greasy

**engreído, a** [engre'iðo, a] *adj* vain, conceited

**engrosar** [engro'sar] *vt* (*ensanchar*) to enlarge; (*aumentar*) to increase;

*(hinchar)* to swell

**enhebrar** [ene'βrar] *vt* to thread

**enhorabuena** [enora'βwena] *excl:*
¡~! congratulations! ♦ *nf:* dar la ~
a to congratulate

**enigma** [e'niɣma] *nm* enigma; *(pro-blema)* puzzle; *(misterio)* mystery

**enjabonar** [enxaβo'nar] *vt* to soap;
*(fam: adular)* to soft-soap; *(: rega-ñar)* to tick off

**enjambre** [en'xambre] *nm* swarm

**enjaular** [enxau'lar] *vt* to (put in a
cage; *(fam)* to jail, lock up

**enjuagar** [enxwa'ɣar] *vt (ropa)* to
rinse (out)

**enjuague** *etc* [en'xwaɣe] *vb ver* en-
**juagar** ♦ *nm (MED)* mouthwash;
*(de ropa)* rinse, rinsing

**enjugar** [enxu'ɣar] *vt* to wipe (off);
*(lágrimas)* to dry; *(déficit)* to wipe
out

**enjuiciar** [enxwi'θjar] *vt (JUR: pro-cesar)* to prosecute, try; *(fig)* to
judge

**enjuto, a** [en'xuto, a] *adj* dry, dried
up; *(fig)* lean, skinny

**enlace** [en'laθe] *nm* link, connection;
*(relación)* relationship; *(tb:* ~ *matri-monial)* marriage; *(de carretera,
trenes)* connection; ~ **sindical** shop
steward

**enlatado, a** [enla'taðo, a] *adj (comi-da, productos)* tinned, canned

**enlazar** [enla'θar] *vt (unir con lazos)*
to bind together; *(atar)* to tie; *(conec-tar)* to link, connect; *(AM)* to lasso

**enlodar** [enlo'ðar] *vt* to cover in
mud; *(fig: manchar)* to stain; *(: re-bajar)* to debase

**enloquecer** [enloke'θer] *vt* to drive
mad ♦ *vi* to go mad; ~**se** *vr* to go
mad

**enlutado, a** [enlu'taðo, a] *adj (per-sona)* in mourning

**enmarañar** [enmara'ɲar] *vt (enre-dar)* to tangle (up), entangle; *(com-plicar)* to complicate; *(confundir)* to
confuse; ~**se** *vr (enredarse)* to be-come entangled; *(confundirse)* to get
confused

**enmarcar** [enmar'kar] *vt (cuadro)* to
frame

**enmascarar** [enmaska'rar] *vt* to
mask; ~**se** *vr* to put on a mask

**enmendar** [enmen'dar] *vt* to emend,
correct; *(constitución etc)* to amend;
*(comportamiento)* to reform; ~**se** *vr*
to reform, mend one's ways; **en-mienda** *nf* correction; amendment;
reform

**enmohecerse** [enmoe'θerse] *vr
(metal)* to rust, go rusty; *(muro,
plantas)* to get mouldy

**enmudecer** [enmuðe'θer] *vt (perder
el habla)* to fall silent; *(guardar si-lencio)* to remain silent; ~**se** *vr* to
fall silent; to remain silent

**ennegrecer** [ennɛɣre'θer] *vt (poner
negro)* to blacken; *(oscurecer)* to
darken; ~**se** *vr* to turn black; *(os-curecerse)* to get dark, darken

**ennoblecer** [ennoβle'θer] *vt* to enno-ble

**enojar** [eno'xar] *vt (encolerizar)* to
anger; *(disgustar)* to annoy, upset;
~**se** *vr* to get angry; to get annoyed

**enojo** [e'noxo] *nm (cólera)* anger;
*(irritación)* annoyance; ~**so, a** *adj*
annoying

**enorgullecerse** [enorɣuʎe'θerse] *vr*
to be proud; ~ de to pride o.s. on, be
proud of

**enorme** [e'norme] *adj* enormous,
huge; *(fig)* monstrous; **enormidad** *nf*
hugeness, immensity

**enrarecido, a** [enrare'θiðo, a] *adj
(atmósfera, aire)* rarefied

**enredadera** [enreða'ðera] *nf (BOT)*
creeper, climbing plant

**enredar** [enre'ðar] *vt (cables, hilos
etc)* to tangle (up), entangle; *(situa-ción)* to complicate, confuse; *(meter
cizaña)* to sow discord among o be-tween; *(implicar)* to embroil, impli-cate; ~**se** *vr* to get entangled; get
tangled (up); *(situación)* to get com-plicated; *(persona)* to get embroiled;
*(AM: fam)* to meddle

**enredo** [en'reðo] *nm (maraña)* tan-gle; *(confusión)* mix-up, confusion;

*(intriga)* intrigue

**enrejado** [enre'xaðo] *nm* fence, railings *pl*

**enrevesado, a** [enreβe'saðo, a] *adj* *(asunto)* complicated, involved

**enriquecer** [enrike'θer] *vt* to make rich, enrich; ~**se** *vr* to get rich

**enrojecer** [enroxe'θer] *vt* to redden ♦ *vi* *(persona)* to blush; ~**se** *vr* to blush

**enrolar** [enro'lar] *vt* *(MIL)* to enlist; *(reclutar)* to recruit; ~**se** *vr* *(MIL)* to join up; *(afiliarse)* to enrol

**enrollar** [enro'ʎar] *vt* to roll (up), wind (up)

**enroscar** [enros'kar] *vt* *(torcer, doblar)* to coil (round), wind; *(tornillo, rosca)* to screw in; ~**se** *vr* to coil, wind

**ensalada** [ensa'laða] *nf* salad; **ensaladilla (rusa)** *nf* Russian salad

**ensalzar** [ensal'θar] *vt* *(alabar)* to praise, extol; *(exaltar)* to exalt

**ensambladura** [ensambla'ðura] *nf* assembly; *(TEC)* joint

**ensamblaje** [ensam'blaxe] *nm* = **ensambladura**

**ensanchar** [ensan'tʃar] *vt* *(hacer más ancho)* to widen; *(agrandar)* to enlarge, expand; *(COSTURA)* to let out; ~**se** *vr* to get wider, expand; *(pey)* to give o.s. airs; **ensanche** *nm* *(de calle)* widening; *(de negocio)* expansion

**ensangrentar** [ensangren'tar] *vt* to stain with blood

**ensañar** [ensa'ɲar] *vt* to enrage; ~**se** *vr*: ~**se con** to treat brutally

**ensartar** [ensar'tar] *vt* *(cuentas, perlas etc)* to string (together)

**ensayar** [ensa'jar] *vt* to test, try (out); *(TEATRO)* to rehearse

**ensayista** [ensa'jista] *nm* essayist

**ensayo** [en'sajo] *nm* test, trial; *(QUIMICA)* experiment; *(TEATRO)* rehearsal; *(DEPORTE)* try; *(ESCOL, LITERATURA)* essay

**ensenada** [ense'naða] *nf* inlet, cove

**enseñanza** [ense'ɲanθa] *nf* *(educación)* education; *(acción)* teaching;

*(doctrina)* teaching, doctrine

**enseñar** [ense'ɲar] *vt* *(educar)* to teach; *(instruir)* to teach, instruct; *(mostrar, señalar)* to show

**enseres** [en'seres] *nmpl* belongings

**ensillar** [ensi'ʎar] *vt* to saddle (up)

**ensimismarse** [ensimis'marse] *vr* *(abstraerse)* to become lost in thought; *(estar absorto)* to be lost in thought; *(AM)* to become conceited

**ensombrecer** [ensombre'θer] *vt* to darken, cast a shadow over; *(fig)* to overshadow, put in the shade

**ensordecer** [ensorðe'θer] *vt* to deafen ♦ *vi* to go deaf

**ensortijado, a** [ensorti'xaðo, a] *adj* *(pelo)* curly

**ensuciar** [ensu'θjar] *vt* *(manchar)* to dirty, soil; *(fig)* to defile; ~**se** *vr* to get dirty; *(niño)* to wet o.s.

**ensueño** [en'sweɲo] *nm* *(sueño)* dream, fantasy; *(ilusión)* illusion; *(soñando despierto)* daydream

**entablar** [enta'βlar] *vt* *(recubrir)* to board (up); *(AJEDREZ, DAMAS)* to set up; *(conversación)* to strike up; *(JUR)* to file ♦ *vi* to draw

**entablillar** [entaβli'ʎar] *vt* *(MED)* to put in a) splint

**entallar** [enta'ʎar] *vt* *(traje)* to tailor ♦ *vi*: **el traje entalla bien** the suit fits well

**ente** ['ente] *nm* *(organización)* body, organization; *(fam: persona)* odd character

**entender** [enten'der] *vt* *(comprender)* to understand; *(darse cuenta)* to realize; *(querer decir)* to mean ♦ *vi* to understand; *(creer)* to think, believe; ~**se** *vr* *(comprenderse)* to be understood; *(2 personas)* to get on together; *(ponerse de acuerdo)* to agree, reach an agreement; ~ **de** to know all about; ~ **algo de** to know a little about; ~ **en** to deal with, have to do with; ~**se mal** *(2 personas)* to get on badly

**entendido, a** [enten'diðo, a] *adj* *(comprendido)* understood; *(hábil)* skilled; *(inteligente)* knowledgeable

♦ *nm/f* (*experto*) expert ♦ *excl* agreed!; **entendimiento** *nm* (*comprensión*) understanding; (*inteligencia*) mind, intellect; (*juicio*) judgement

**enterado, a** [ente'raðo, a] *adj* well-informed; **estar ~ de** to know about, be aware of

**enteramente** [entera'mente] *adv* entirely, completely

**enterar** [ente'rar] *vt* (*informar*) to inform, tell; **~se** *vr* to find out, get to know

**entereza** [ente're0a] *nf* (*totalidad*) entirety; (*fig: carácter*) strength of mind; (: *honradez*) integrity

**enternecer** [enterne'0er] *vt* (*ablandar*) to soften; (*apiadar*) to touch, move; **~se** *vr* to be touched, be moved

**entero, a** [en'tero, a] *adj* (*total*) whole, entire; (*fig: recto*) honest; (: *firme*) firm, resolute ♦ *nm* (*COM: punto*) point; (*AM: pago*) pay- ment

**enterrador** [enterra'ðor] *nm* grave-digger

**enterrar** [ente'rrar] *vt* to bury

**entibiar** [enti'ßjar] *vt* (*enfriar*) to cool; (*calentar*) to warm; **~se** *vr* (*fig*) to cool

**entidad** [enti'ðað] *nf* (*empresa*) firm, company; (*organismo*) body; (*sociedad*) society; (*FILOSOFIA*) entity

**entiendo** *etc vb ver* **entender**

**entierro** [en'tjerro] *nm* (*acción*) burial; (*funeral*) funeral

**entomología** [entomolo'xia] *nf* entomology

**entonación** [entona'0jon] *nf* (*LING*) intonation; (*fig*) conceit

**entonar** [ento'nar] *vt* (*canción*) to intone; (*colores*) to tone; (*MED*) to tone up ♦ *vi* to be in tune; **~se** *vr* (*engreírse*) to give o.s. airs

**entonces** [en'ton0es] *adv* then, at that time; **desde ~** since then; **en aquel ~** at that time; (*pues*) **~ y** so

**entornar** [entor'nar] *vt* (*puerta, ven-*

*tana*) to half close, leave ajar; (*los ojos*) to screw up

**entorpecer** [entorpe'0er] *vt* (*entendimiento*) to dull; (*impedir*) to obstruct, hinder; (: *tránsito*) to slow down, delay

**entrada** [en'traða] *nf* (*acción*) entry, access; (*sitio*) entrance, way in; (*INFORM*) input; (*COM*) receipts *pl*, takings *pl*; (*CULIN*) starter; (*DEPORTE*) innings *sg*; (*TEATRO*) house, audience; (*para el cine etc*) ticket; (*COM*): **~s y salidas** income and expenditure; (*TEC*): **~ de aire** air intake *o* inlet; **de ~** from the outset

**entrado, a** [en'traðo, a] *adj*: **~ en años** elderly; **una vez ~ el verano** in the summer(time), when summer comes

**entramparse** [entram'parse] *vr* to get into debt

**entrante** [en'trante] *adj* next, coming; **mes/año ~** next month/year

**entraña** [en'trana] *nf* (*fig: centro*) heart, core; (*raíz*) root; **~s** *nfpl* (*ANAT*) entrails; (*fig*) heart *sg*; **sin ~s** (*fig*) heartless; **entrañable** *adj* close, intimate; **entrañar** *vt* to entail

**entrar** [en'trar] *vt* (*introducir*) to bring in; (*INFORM*) to input ♦ *vi* (*meterse*) to go in, come in, enter; (*comenzar*): **~ diciendo** to begin by saying; **hacer ~** to show in; **no me entra** I can't get the hang of it

**entre** ['entre] *prep* (*dos*) between; (*más de dos*) among(st)

**entreabrir** [entrea'ßrir] *vt* to half-open, open halfway

**entrecejo** [entre'0exo] *nm*: **fruncir el ~** to frown

**entrecortado, a** [entrekor'taðo, a] *adj* (*respiración*) difficult; (*habla*) faltering

**entredicho** [entre'ðit͡ʃo] *nm* (*JUR*) injunction; **poner en ~** to cast doubt on; **estar en ~** to be banned

**entrega** [en'trexa] *nf* (*de mercancías*) delivery; (*de novela etc*) instalment

**entregar** [entre'var] *vt* (*dar*) to hand (over), deliver; ~se *vr* (*rendirse*) to surrender, give in, submit; (*dedicarse*) to devote o.s.

**entrelazar** [entrela'θar] *vt* to entwine

**entremeses** [entre'meses] *nmpl* hors d'œuvres

**entremeter** [entreme'ter] *vt* to insert, put in; ~se *vr* to meddle, interfere; **entremetido, a** *adj* meddling, interfering

**entremezclar** [entremeθ'klar] *vt* to intermingle; ~se *vr* to intermingle

**entrenador, a** [entrena'ðor, a] *nm/f* trainer, coach

**entrenarse** [entre'narse] *vr* to train

**entrepierna** [entre'pjerna] *nf* crotch

**entresacar** [entresa'kar] *vt* to pick out, select

**entresuelo** [entre'swelo] *nm* mezzanine

**entretanto** [entre'tanto] *adv* meanwhile, meantime

**entretejer** [entrete'xer] *vt* to interweave

**entretener** [entrete'ner] *vt* (*divertir*) to entertain, amuse; (*detener*) to hold up, delay; (*mantener*) to maintain; ~se *vr* (*divertirse*) to amuse o.s.; (*retrasarse*) to delay, linger; **entretenido, a** *adj* entertaining, amusing; **entretenimiento** *nm* entertainment, amusement; (*mantenimiento*) upkeep, maintenance

**entrever** [entre'βer] *vt* to glimpse, catch a glimpse of

**entrevista** [entre'βista] *nf* interview; **entrevistar** *vt* to interview; **entrevistarse** *vr* to have an interview

**entristecer** [entriste'θer] *vt* to sadden, grieve; ~se *vr* to grow sad

**entrometerse** [entrome'terse] *vr*: ~ (en) to interfere (in o with)

**entroncar** [entron'kar] *vi* to be connected o related

**entumecer** [entume'θer] *vt* to numb, benumb; ~se *vr* (*por el frío*) to go o become numb; **entumecido, a** *adj* numb, stiff

**enturbiar** [entur'βjar] *vt* (*el agua*) to make cloudy; (*fig*) to confuse; ~se *vr* (*oscurecerse*) to become cloudy; (*fig*) to get confused, become obscure

**entusiasmar** [entusjas'mar] *vt* to excite, fill with enthusiasm; (*gustar mucho*) to delight; ~se *vr*: ~se con o por to get enthusiastic o excited about

**entusiasmo** [entu'sjasmo] *nm* enthusiasm; (*excitación*) excitement

**entusiasta** [entu'sjasta] *adj* enthusiastic ♦ *nm/f* enthusiast

**enumerar** [enume'rar] *vt* to enumerate

**enunciación** [enunθja'θjon] *nf* enunciation

**enunciado** [enun'θjaðo] *nm* enunciation; (*declaración*) declaration, statement

**envainar** [embai'nar] *vt* to sheathe

**envalentonar** [embalento'nar] *vt* to give courage to; ~se *vr* (*pey: jactarse*) to boast, brag

**envanecer** [embane'θer] *vt* to make conceited; ~se *vr* to grow conceited

**envasar** [emba'sar] *vt* (*empaquetar*) to pack, wrap; (*enfrascar*) to bottle; (*enlatar*) to can; (*embolsar*) to pocket

**envase** [em'base] *nm* (*en paquete*) packing, wrapping; (*en botella*) bottling; (*en lata*) canning; (*recipiente*) container; (*paquete*) package; (*botella*) bottle; (*lata*) tin (BRIT), can

**envejecer** [embexe'θer] *vt* to make old, age ♦ *vi* (*volverse viejo*) to grow old; (*parecer viejo*) to age; ~se *vr* to grow old; to age

**envenenar** [embene'nar] *vt* to poison; (*fig*) to embitter

**envergadura** [emberxa'ðura] *nf* (*fig*) scope, compass

**envés** [em'bes] *nm* (*de tela*) back, wrong side

**enviar** [em'bjar] *vt* to send

**enviciarse** [embi'θjarse] *vr*: ~ (con) to get addicted (to)

**envidia** [em'biðja] *nf* envy; **tener** ~ a to envy, be jealous of; **envidiar** *vt* *(desear)* to envy; *(tener celos de)* to be jealous of

**envío** [em'bio] *nm (acción)* sending; *(de mercancías)* consignment; *(de dinero)* remittance

**enviudar** [embju'ðar] *vi* to be widowed

**envoltura** [embol'tura] *nf (cobertura)* cover; *(embalaje)* wrapper, wrapping; **envoltorio** *nm* package

**envolver** [embol'βer] *vt* to wrap (up); *(cubrir)* to cover; *(enemigo)* to surround; *(implicar)* to involve, implicate

**envuelto** [em'bwelto] *pp de* envolver

**enyesar** [enje'sar] *vt (pared)* to plaster; *(MED)* to put in plaster

**enzarzarse** [enθar'θarse] *vr*: ~ en *(en pelea)* to get mixed up in; *(en disputa)* to get involved in

**épica** ['epika] *nf* epic

**épico, a** ['epiko, a] *adj* epic

**epidemia** [epi'ðemja] *nf* epidemic

**epilepsia** [epi'lepsja] *nf* epilepsy

**epílogo** [e'piloxo] *nm* epilogue

**episodio** [epi'soðjo] *nm* episode

**epístola** [e'pistola] *nf* epistle

**época** ['epoka] *nf* period, time; *(HISTORIA)* age, epoch; **hacer** ~ to be epoch-making

**equidad** [eki'ðað] *nf* equity

**equilibrar** [ekili'βrar] *vt* to balance; **equilibrio** *nm* balance, equilibrium; **equilibrista** *nmf (funámbulo)* tightrope walker; *(acróbata)* acrobat

**equipaje** [eki'paxe] *nm (equipo)* equipment, kit; ~ **de mano** hand luggage

**equipar** [eki'par] *vt (proveer)* to equip

**equipararse** [ekipa'rarse] *vr*: ~ **con** to be on a level with

**equipo** [e'kipo] *nm (conjunto de cosas)* equipment; *(DEPORTE)* team; *(de obreros)* shift

**equis** ['ekis] *nf inv* (the letter) X

**equitación** [ekita'θjon] *nf (acto)* riding; *(arte)* horsemanship

**equitativo, a** [ekita'tiβo, a] *adj*

equitable, fair

**equivalente** [ekiβa'lente] *adj, nm* equivalent

**equivaler** [ekiβa'ler] *vi* to be equivalent *o* equal

**equivocación** [ekiβoka'θjon] *nf* mistake, error

**equivocado, a** [ekiβo'kaðo, a] *adj* wrong, mistaken

**equivocarse** [ekiβo'karse] *vr* to be wrong, make a mistake; ~ **de camino** to take the wrong road

**equívoco, a** [e'kiβoko, a] *adj (dudoso)* suspect; *(ambiguo)* ambiguous ♦ *nm* ambiguity; *(malentendido)* misunderstanding

**era** ['era] *vb ver* ser ♦ *nf* era, age

**erais** *vb ver* ser

**éramos** *vb ver* ser

**eran** *vb ver* ser

**erario** [e'rarjo] *nm* exchequer *(BRIT)*, treasury

**erección** [erek'θjon] *nf* erection

**eras** *vb ver* ser

**eres** *vb ver* ser

**erguir** [er'ɣir] *vt* to raise, lift; *(poner derecho)* to straighten; ~**se** *vr* to straighten up

**erigir** [eri'xir] *vt* to erect, build; ~**se** *vr*: ~**se en** to set o.s. up as

**erizarse** [eri'θarse] *vr (pelo: de perro)* to bristle; *(: de persona)* to stand on end

**erizo** [e'riθo] *nm (ZOOL)* hedgehog; ~ **de mar** sea-urchin

**ermita** [er'mita] *nf* hermitage

**ermitaño, a** [ermi'taɲo, a] *nm/f* hermit

**erosión** [ero'sjon] *nf* erosion

**erosionar** [erosjo'nar] *vt* to erode

**erótico, a** [e'rotiko, a] *adj* erotic; **erotismo** *nm* eroticism

**erradicar** [erraði'kar] *vt* to eradicate

**errante** [e'rrante] *adj* wandering, errant

**errar** [e'rrar] *vi (vagar)* to wander, roam; *(equivocarse)* to be mistaken ♦ *vt*: ~ **el camino** to take the wrong road; ~ **el tiro** to miss

**erróneo, a** [e'rroneo, a] *adj (equivo-*

*cado*) wrong, mistaken; (*falso*) false, untrue

**error** [e'rror] *nm* error, mistake; (*INFORM*) bug; ~ **de imprenta** misprint

**eructar** [eruk'tar] *vt* to belch, burp

**erudito, a** [eru'ðito, a] *adj* erudite, learned

**erupción** [erup'θjon] *nf* eruption; (*MED*) rash

**es** *vb ver* **ser**

**esa** ['esa] (*pl* **esas**) *adj demos ver* **ese**

**ésa** ['esa] (*pl* **esas**) *pron ver* **ese**

**esbelto, a** [es'Belto, a] *adj* slim, slender

**esbozo** [es'Boθo] *nm* sketch, outline

**escabeche** [eska'Betʃe] *nm* brine; (*de aceitunas etc*) pickle; **en ~** pickled

**escabroso, a** [eska'Broso, a] *adj* (*accidentado*) rough, uneven; (*fig*) tough, difficult; (: *atrevido*) risqué

**escabullirse** [eskaβu'ʎirse] *vr* to slip away, to clear out

**escafandra** [eska'fandra] *nf* (*buzo*) diving suit; (~ *espacial*) space suit

**escala** [es'kala] *nf* (*proporción, MUS*) scale; (*de mano*) ladder; (*AVIAT*) stopover; **hacer ~ en** to stop o call in at

**escalafón** [eskala'fon] *nm* (*escala de salarios*) salary scale, wage scale

**escalar** [eska'lar] *vt* to climb, scale

**escalera** [eska'lera] *nf* stairs *pl*, staircase; (*escala*) ladder; (*NAIPES*) run; ~ **mecánica** escalator; ~ **de caracol** spiral staircase

**escalfar** [eskal'far] *vt* (*huevos*) to poach

**escalinata** [eskali'nata] *nf* staircase

**escalofriante** [eskalo'frjante] *adj* chilling

**escalofrío** [eskalo'frio] *nm* (*MED*) chill; ~**s** *nmpl* (*fig*) shivers

**escalón** [eska'lon] *nm* step, stair; (*de escalera*) rung

**escalope** [eska'lope] *nm* (*CULIN*) escalope

**escama** [es'kama] *nf* (*de pez, serpiente*) scale; (*de jabón*) flake; (*fig*) resentment

**escamar** [eska'mar] *vt* (*fig*) to make wary o suspicious

**escamotear** [eskamote'ar] *vt* (*robar*) to lift, swipe; (*hacer desaparecer*) to make disappear

**escampar** [eskam'par] *vb impers* to stop raining

**escandalizar** [eskandali'θar] *vt* to scandalize, shock; ~**se** *vr* to be shocked; (*ofenderse*) to be offended

**escándalo** [es'kandalo] *nm* scandal; (*alboroto, tumulto*) row, uproar; **escandaloso, a** *adj* scandalous, shocking

**escandinavo, a** [eskandi'naβo, a] *adj, nm/f* Scandinavian

**escaño** [es'kaɲo] *nm* bench; (*POL*) seat

**escapar** [eska'par] *vi* (*gen*) to escape, run away; (*DEPORTE*) to break away; ~**se** *vr* to escape, get away; (*agua, gas*) to leak (out)

**escaparate** [eskapa'rate] *nm* shop window

**escape** [es'kape] *nm* (*de agua, gas*) leak; (*de motor*) exhaust; (*de persona*) escape

**escarabajo** [eskara'Baxo] *nm* beetle

**escaramuza** [eskara'muθa] *nf* skirmish; (*fig*) brush

**escarbar** [eskar'Bar] *vt* (*gallina*) to scratch; (*fig*) to inquire into, investigate

**escarceos** [eskar'θeos] *nmpl* (*fig*): **en mis ~ con la política ...** in my dealings with politics ...; ~ **amorosos** love affairs

**escarcha** [es'kartʃa] *nf* frost

**escarchado, a** [eskar'tʃaðo, a] *adj* (*CULIN: fruta*) crystallized

**escarlata** [eskar'lata] *adj inv* scarlet; **escarlatina** *nf* scarlet fever

**escarmentar** [eskarmen'tar] *vt* to punish severely ♦ *vi* to learn one's lesson

**escarmiento** *etc* [eskar'mjento] *vb ver* **escarmentar** ♦ *nm* (*ejemplo*) lesson; (*castigo*) punishment

**escarnio** [es'karnjo] nm mockery; (injuria) insult

**escarola** [eska'rola] nf endive

**escarpado, a** [eskar'paðo, a] adj (pendiente) sheer, steep; (rocas) craggy

**escasear** [eskase'ar] vi to be scarce

**escasez** [eska'seθ] nf (falta) shortage, scarcity; (pobreza) poverty

**escaso, a** [es'kaso, a] adj (poco) scarce; (raro) rare; (ralo) thin, sparse; (limitado) limited

**escatimar** [eskati'mar] vt (limitar) to skimp (on), be sparing with

**escayola** [eska'jola] nf plaster

**escena** [es'θena] nf scene

**escenario** [esθe'narjo] nm (TEATRO) stage; (CINE) set; (fig) scene; **escenografía** nf set design

**escepticismo** [esθepti'θismo] nm scepticism; **escéptico, a** adj sceptical ♦ nm/f sceptic

**escisión** [esθi'sjon] nf (de partido, secta) split

**esclarecer** [esklare'θer] vt (iluminar) to light up, illuminate; (misterio, problema) to shed light on

**esclavitud** [esklaβi'tuð] nf slavery

**esclavizar** [esklaβi'θar] vt to enslave

**esclavo, a** [es'klaβo, a] nm/f slave

**esclusa** [es'klusa] nf (de canal) lock; (compuerta) floodgate

**escoba** [es'koβa] nf broom

**escocer** [esko'θer] vi to burn, sting; ~se vr to chafe, get chafed

**escocés, esa** [esko'θes, esa] adj Scottish ♦ nm/f Scotsman/woman, Scot

**Escocia** [es'koθja] nf Scotland

**escoger** [esko'xer] vt to choose, pick, select; **escogido, a** adj chosen, selected; (calidad) choice, select

**escolar** [esko'lar] adj school cpd ♦ nm/f schoolboy/girl, pupil

**escolta** [es'kolta] nf escort; **escoltar** vt to escort

**escollo** [es'koʎo] nm reef

**escombros** [es'kombros] nmpl (basura) rubbish sg; (restos) debris sg

**esconder** [eskon'der] vt to hide, conceal; ~se vr to hide; **escondidas** (AM) nfpl a ~ secretly; **escondite** nm hiding place; (juego) hide-and-seek; **escondrijo** nm hiding place, hideout

**escopeta** [esko'peta] nf shotgun

**escoria** [es'korja] nf (de alto horno) slag; (fig) scum, dregs pl

**Escorpio** [es'korpjo] nm Scorpio

**escorpión** [eskor'pjon] nm scorpion

**escotado, a** [esko'taðo, a] adj low-cut

**escote** [es'kote] nm (de vestido) low neck; **pagar a ~** to share the expenses

**escotilla** [esko'tiʎa] nf (NAUT) hatch(way)

**escozor** [esko'θor] nm (dolor) sting(ing)

**escribir** [eskri'βir] vt, vi to write; ~ a máquina to type; **¿cómo se escribe?** how do you spell it?

**escrito, a** [es'krito, a] pp de **escribir** ♦ nm (documento) document; (manuscrito) text, manuscript; **por** ~ in writing

**escritor, a** [eskri'tor, a] nm/f writer

**escritorio** [eskri'torjo] nm desk; (oficina) office

**escritura** [eskri'tura] nf (acción) writing; (caligrafía) (hand)writing; (JUR: documento) deed

**escrúpulo** [es'krupulo] nm scruple; (minuciosidad) scrupulousness; **escrupuloso, a** adj scrupulous

**escrutar** [eskru'tar] vt to scrutinize, examine; (votos) to count

**escrutinio** [eskru'tinjo] nm (examen atento) scrutiny; (POL: recuento de votos) count(ing)

**escuadra** [es'kwaðra] nf (MIL etc) squad; (NAUT) squadron; (de coches etc) fleet; **escuadrilla** nf (de aviones) squadron; (AM: de obreros) gang

**escuadrón** [eskwa'ðron] nm squadron

**escuálido, a** [es'kwaliðo, a] adj skinny, scraggy; (sucio) squalid

**escuchar** [esku'tʃar] vt to listen to ♦ vi to listen

**escudilla** [esku'ðiʎa] *nf* bowl, basin

**escudo** [es'kuðo] *nm* shield

**escudriñar** [eskuðri'ɲar] *vt* (*examinar*) to investigate, scrutinize; (*mirar de lejos*) to scan

**escuela** [es'kwela] *nf* school; ~ **de artes y oficios** (*ESP*) ≈ technical college; ~ **normal** teacher training college

**escueto, a** [es'kweto, a] *adj* plain; (*estilo*) simple

**escuincle** [es'kwinkle] (*AM: fam*) *nm/f* kid

**esculpir** [eskul'pir] *vt* to sculpt; (*grabar*) to engrave; (*tallar*) to carve; **escultor, a** *nm/f* sculptor/tress; **escultura** *nf* sculpture

**escupidera** [eskupi'ðera] *nf* spittoon

**escupir** [esku'pir] *vt, vi* to spit (out)

**escurreplatos** [eskurre'platos] *nm inv* plate rack

**escurridizo, a** [eskurri'ðiθo, a] *adj* slippery

**escurridor** [eskurri'ðor] *nm* colander

**escurrir** [esku'rrir] *vt* (*ropa*) to wring out; (*verduras, platos*) to drain ♦ *vi* (*líquidos*) to drip; ~**se** *vr* (*secarse*) to drain; (*resbalarse*) to slip, slide; (*escaparse*) to slip away

**ese** ['ese] (*f* **esa**, *pl* **esos, esas**) *adj demos* (*sg*) that; (*pl*) those

**ése** ['ese] (*f* **ésa**, *pl* **ésos, ésas**) *pron* (*sg*) that (one); (*pl*) those (ones); ~ ... **éste** ... the former ... the latter ...; **no me vengas con ésas** don't give me any more of that nonsense

**esencia** [e'senθja] *nf* essence; **esencial** *adj* essential

**esfera** [es'fera] *nf* sphere; (*de reloj*) face; **esférico, a** *adj* spherical

**esforzarse** [esfor'θarse] *vr* to exert o.s., make an effort

**esfuerzo** *etc* [es'fwerθo] *vb ver* **esforzar** ♦ *nm* effort

**esfumarse** [esfu'marse] *vr* (*apoyo, esperanzas*) to fade away

**esgrima** [es'ɣrima] *nf* fencing

**esgrimir** [esɣri'mir] *vt* (*arma*) to brandish; (*argumento*) to use

**esguince** [es'ɣinθe] *nm* (*MED*)

sprain

**eslabón** [esla'βon] *nm* link

**esmaltar** [esmal'tar] *vt* to enamel; **esmalte** *nm* enamel; **esmalte de uñas** nail varnish *o* polish

**esmerado, a** [esme'raðo, a] *adj* careful, neat

**esmeralda** [esme'ralda] *nf* emerald

**esmerarse** [esme'rarse] *vr* (*aplicarse*) to take great pains, exercise great care; (*afanarse*) to work hard

**esmero** [es'mero] *nm* (great) care

**esnob** [es'nob] (*pl* ~**s**) *adj* (*persona*) snobbish; (*coche etc*) posh ♦ *nm/f* snob; ~**ismo** *nm* snobbery

**eso** ['eso] *pron* that, that thing *o* matter; ~ **de su coche** that business about his car; ~ **de ir al cine** all that about going to the cinema; ~ **a de las cinco** at about five o'clock; **en** ~ thereupon, at that point; ~**s** that's it; **¡**~ **sí que es vida!** now that is really living!; **por** ~ **te lo dije** that's why I told you; **y** ~ **que llovía** in spite of the fact it was raining

**esófago** [e'sofaxo] *nm* (*ANAT*) oesophagus

**esos** ['esos] *adj demos ver* **ese**

**ésos** ['esos] *pron ver* **ése**

**espabilar** *etc* [espaβi'lar] = **despabilar** *etc*

**espacial** [espa'θjal] *adj* (*del espacio*) space *cpd*

**espaciar** [espa'θjar] *vt* to space (out)

**espacio** [es'paθjo] *nm* space; (*MUS*) interval; (*RADIO, TV*) programme (*BRIT*), program (*US*); **el** ~ space; ~**so, a** *adj* spacious, roomy

**espada** [es'paða] *nf* sword; ~**s** *nfpl* (*NAIPES*) spades

**espaguetis** [espa'ɣetis] *nmpl* spaghetti *sg*

**espalda** [es'palda] *nf* (*gen*) back; ~**s** *nfpl* (*hombros*) shoulders; **a** ~**s de uno** behind sb's back; **tenderse de** ~**s** to lie (down) on one's back; **volver la** ~ **a alguien** to cold-shoulder sb

**espantadizo, a** [espanta'ðiθo, a]

*adj* timid, easily frightened

**espantajo** [espan'taxo] *nm* = **espantapájaros**

**espantapájaros** [espanta'paxaros] *nm inv* scarecrow

**espantar** [espan'tar] *vt* (*asustar*) to frighten, scare; (*ahuyentar*) to frighten off; (*asombrar*) to horrify, appal; ~**se** *vr* to get frightened o scared; to be appalled

**espanto** [es'panto] *nm* (*susto*) fright; (*terror*) terror; (*asombro*) astonishment; ~**so, a** *adj* frightening; terrifying; astonishing

**España** [es'paɲa] *nf* Spain; **español, a** *adj* Spanish ♦ *nm/f* Spaniard ♦ *nm* (*LING*) Spanish

**esparadrapo** [espara'ðrapo] *nm* (sticking) plaster (*BRIT*), adhesive tape (*US*)

**esparcimiento** [esparθi'mjento] *nm* (*dispersión*) spreading; (*derramamiento*) scattering; (*fig*) cheerfulness

**esparcir** [espar'θir] *vt* to spread; (*derramar*) to scatter; ~**se** *vr* to spread (out); to scatter; (*divertirse*) to enjoy o.s.

**espárrago** [es'parraɣo] *nm* asparagus

**esparto** [es'parto] *nm* esparto (grass)

**espasmo** [es'pasmo] *nm* spasm

**espátula** [es'patula] *nf* spatula

**especia** [es'peθja] *nf* spice

**especial** [espe'θjal] *adj* special; ~**idad** *nf* speciality (*BRIT*), specialty (*US*)

**especie** [es'peθje] *nf* (*BIO*) species; (*clase*) kind, sort; en ~ in kind

**especificar** [espeθifi'kar] *vt* to specify; **específico, a** *adj* specific

**espécimen** [es'peθimen] (*pl* **especímenes**) *nm* specimen

**espectáculo** [espek'takulo] *nm* (*gen*) spectacle; (*TEATRO etc*) show

**espectador, a** [espekta'ðor, a] *nm/f* spectator

**espectro** [es'pektro] *nm* ghost; (*fig*) spectre

**especular** [espeku'lar] *vt, vi* to

speculate

**espejismo** [espe'xismo] *nm* mirage

**espejo** [es'pexo] *nm* mirror; (*fig*) model; ~ **retrovisor** rear-view mirror

**espeluznante** [espeluθ'nante] *adj* horrifying, hair-raising

**espera** [es'pera] *nf* (*pausa, intervalo*) wait; (*JUR: plazo*) respite; en ~ de waiting for; (*con expectativa*) expecting

**esperanza** [espe'ranθa] *nf* (*confianza*) hope; (*expectativa*) expectation; hay pocas ~s de que venga there is little prospect of his coming

**esperar** [espe'rar] *vt* (*aguardar*) to wait for; (*tener expectativa de*) to expect; (*desear*) to hope for ♦ *vi* to wait; to expect; to hope

**esperma** [es'perma] *nf* sperm

**espesar** [espe'sar] *vt* to thicken; ~**se** *vr* to thicken, get thicker

**espeso, a** [es'peso, a] *adj* thick; **espesor** *nm* thickness

**espía** [es'pia] *nm/f* spy; **espiar** *vt* (*observar*) to spy on ♦ *vi*: ~ **para** to spy for

**espiga** [es'piɣa] *nf* (*BOT: de trigo etc*) ear

**espigón** [espi'ɣon] *nm* (*BOT*) ear; (*NAUT*) breakwater

**espina** [es'pina] *nf* thorn; (*de pez*) bone; ~ **dorsal** (*ANAT*) spine

**espinaca** [espi'naka] *nf* spinach

**espinazo** [espi'naθo] *nm* spine, backbone

**espinilla** [espi'niʎa] *nf* (*ANAT: tibia*) shin(bone); (*grano*) blackhead

**espino** [es'pino] *nm* hawthorn

**espinoso, a** [espi'noso, a] *adj* (*planta*) thorny, prickly; (*fig*) difficult

**espionaje** [espjo'naxe] *nm* spying, espionage

**espiral** [espi'ral] *adj, nf* spiral

**espirar** [espi'rar] *vt* to breathe out, exhale

**espiritista** [espiri'tista] *adj, nm/f* spiritualist

**espíritu** [es'piritu] *nm* spirit; **espiritual** *adj* spiritual

**espita** [es'pita] *nf* tap

**espléndido, a** [es'plendiðo, a] *adj* (*magnífico*) magnificent, splendid; (*generoso*) generous

**esplendor** [esplen'dor] *nm* splendour

**espolear** [espole'ar] *vt* to spur on

**espoleta** [espo'leta] *nf* (*de bomba*) fuse

**espolón** [espo'lon] *nm* sea wall

**espolvorear** [espolβore'ar] *vt* to dust, sprinkle

**esponja** [es'ponxa] *nf* sponge; (*fig*) sponger; **esponjoso, a** *adj* spongy

**espontaneidad** [espontanei'ðað] *nf* spontaneity; **espontáneo, a** *adj* spontaneous

**esposa** [es'posa] *nf* wife; **~s** *nfpl* handcuffs; **esposar** *vt* to handcuff

**esposo** [es'poso] *nm* husband

**espuela** [es'pwela] *nf* spur

**espuma** [es'puma] *nf* foam; (*de cerveza*) froth, head; (*de jabón*) lather; **espumadera** *nf* (*utensilio*) skimmer; **espumoso, a** *adj* frothy, foamy; (*vino*) sparkling

**esqueje** [es'kexe] *nm* (*de planta*) cutting

**esqueleto** [eske'leto] *nm* skeleton

**esquema** [es'kema] *nm* (*diagrama*) diagram; (*dibujo*) plan; (*plan*) scheme; (*FILOSOFIA*) schema

**esquí** [es'ki] (*pl* **~s**) *nm* (*objeto*) ski; (*DEPORTE*) skiing; **~ acuático** water-skiing; **esquiar** *vi* to ski

**esquilar** [eski'lar] *vt* to shear

**esquimal** [eski'mal] *adj, nm/f* Eskimo

**esquina** [es'kina] *nf* corner

**esquinazo** [eski'naθo] *nm*: **dar ~ a** algn to give sb the slip

**esquirol** [eski'rol] *nm* blackleg

**esquivar** [eski'βar] *vt* to avoid; (*evadir*) to dodge, elude

**esquivo, a** [es'kiβo, a] *adj* evasive; (*tímido*) reserved; (*huraño*) unsociable

**esta** ['esta] *adj demos ver* este

**ésta** ['esta] *pron ver* éste

**está** *vb ver* estar

**estabilidad** [estaβili'ðað] *nf* stabil-

ity; **estable** *adj* stable

**establecer** [estaβle'θer] *vt* to establish; **~se** *vr* to establish o.s.; (*echar raíces*) to settle (down); **establecimiento** *nm* establishment

**establo** [es'taβlo] *nm* (*AGR*) stable

**estaca** [es'taka] *nf* stake, post; (*de tienda de campaña*) peg

**estacada** [esta'kaða] *nf* (*cerca*) fence, fencing; (*palenque*) stockade

**estación** [esta'θjon] *nf* station; (*del año*) season; **~ de autobuses** bus station; **~ balnearia** seaside resort; **~ de servicio** service station

**estacionamiento** [estaθjona'mjento] *nm* (*AUTO*) parking; (*MIL*) stationing

**estacionar** [estaθjo'nar] *vt* (*AUTO*) to park; (*MIL*) to station; **~io, a** *adj* stationary; (*COM: mercado*) slack

**estadio** [es'taðjo] *nm* (*fase*) stage, phase; (*DEPORTE*) stadium

**estadista** [esta'ðista] *nm* (*POL*) statesman; (*ESTADISTICA*) statistician

**estadística** [esta'ðistika] *nf* figure, statistic; (*ciencia*) statistics *sg*

**estado** [es'taðo] *nm* (*POL*: *condición*) state; **~ de ánimo** state of mind; **~ de cuenta** bank statement; **~ de sitio** state of siege; **~ civil** marital status; **~ mayor** staff; **estar en ~** to be pregnant; **(los) E~s Unidos** *nmpl* the United States (of America) *sg*

**estadounidense** [estaðouni'ðense] *adj* United States *cpd*, American ♦ *nm/f* American

**estafa** [es'tafa] *nf* swindle, trick; **estafar** *vt* to swindle, defraud

**estafeta** [esta'feta] *nf* (*oficina de correos*) post office; **~ diplomática** diplomatic bag

**estáis** *vb ver* estar

**estallar** [esta'ʎar] *vi* to burst; (*bomba*) to explode, go off; (*epidemia, guerra, rebelión*) to break out; **~ en llanto** to burst into tears; **estallido** *nm* explosion; (*fig*) outbreak

**estampa** [es'tampa] *nf* (*impresión,*

**imprenta)** print, engraving; (*imagen, figura: de persona*) appearance

**estampado, a** [estam'paðo, a] *adj* printed ♦ *nm* (*impresión: acción*) printing; (: *efecto*) print; (*marca*) stamping

**estampar** [estam'par] *vt* (*imprimir*) to print; (*marcar*) to stamp; (*metal*) to engrave; (*poner sello en*) to stamp; (*fig*) to stamp, imprint

**estampida** [estam'piða] *nf* stampede

**estampido** [estam'piðo] *nm* bang, report

**estampilla** [estam'piʎa] *nf* stamp

**están** *vb ver* **estar**

**estancado, a** [estan'kaðo, a] *adj* stagnant

**estancar** [estan'kar] *vt* (*aguas*) to hold up, hold back; (*COM*) to monopolize; (*fig*) to block, hold up; **~se** *vr* to stagnate

**estancia** [es'tanθja] *nf* (*permanencia*) stay; (*sala*) room; (*AM*) farm, ranch; **estanciero** (*AM*) *nm* farmer, rancher

**estanco, a** [es'tanko, a] *adj* watertight ♦ *nm* tobacconist's (shop), cigar store (US)

**estándar** [es'tandar] *adj, nm* standard; **estandarizar** *vt* to standardize

**estandarte** [estan'darte] *nm* banner, standard

**estanque** [es'tanke] *nm* (*lago*) pool, pond; (*AGR*) reservoir

**estanquero, a** [estan'kero, a] *nm/f* tobacconist

**estante** [es'tante] *nm* (*armario*) rack, stand; (*biblioteca*) bookcase; (*anaquel*) shelf; (*AM*) prop; **estantería** *nf* shelving, shelves *pl*

**estaño** [es'taɲo] *nm* tin

---

PALABRA CLAVE

**estar** [es'tar] *vi* **1** (*posición*) to be; **está en la plaza** it's in the square; **¿está Juan?** is Juan in?; **estamos a 30 km de Junín** we're 30 kms from Junín

**2** (+ *adj: estado*) to be; **~ enfermo** to be ill; **está muy elegante** he's

looking very smart; **¿cómo estás?** how are you keeping?

**3** (+ *gerundio*) to be; **estoy leyendo** I'm reading

**4** (*uso pasivo*): **está condenado a muerte** he's been condemned to death; **está envasado en ...** it's packed in ...

**5** (*con fechas*): **¿a cuántos estamos?** what's the date today?; **estamos a 5 de mayo** it's the 5th of May

**6** (*locuciones*): **¿estamos?** (*¿de acuerdo?*) okay?; (*¿listo?*) ready?; **¡ya está bien!** that's enough!

**7**: **~ de**: **~ de vacaciones/viaje** to be on holiday/away o on a trip; **está de camarero** he's working as a waiter

**8**: **~ para**: **está para salir** he's about to leave; **no estoy para bromas** I'm not in the mood for jokes

**9**: **~ por** (*propuesta etc*) to be in favour of; (*persona etc*) to support, side with; **está por limpiar** it still has to be cleaned

**10**: **~ sin**: **~ sin dinero** to have no money; **está sin terminar** it isn't finished yet

♦ **~se** *vr*: **se estuvo en la cama toda la tarde** he stayed in bed all afternoon

---

**estas** ['estas] *adj demos ver* **este**

**éstas** ['estas] *pron ver* **éste**

**estatal** [esta'tal] *adj* state *cpd*

**estático, a** [es'tatiko, a] *adj* static

**estatua** [es'tatwa] *nf* statue

**estatura** [esta'tura] *nf* stature, height

**estatuto** [esta'tuto] *nm* (*JUR*) statute; (*de ciudad*) bye-law; (*de comité*) rule

**este¹** ['este] *nm* east

**este²** ['este] (*f* **esta**, *pl* **estos**, **estas**) *adj demos* (*sg*) this; (*pl*) these

**éste** ['este] (*f* **ésta**, *pl* **éstos**, **éstas**) *pron* (*sg*) this (one); (*pl*) these (ones); **ése ... ~ ...** the former ... the latter ...

**esté** *etc vb ver* **estar**

**estela** [es'tela] nf wash; (fig) trail

**estelar** [este'lar] adj (ASTRO) stellar; (actuación, reparto) star (atr)

**estén** etc vb ver **estar**

**estenografía** [estenoɣra'fia] nf shorthand (BRIT), stenography (US)

**estepa** [es'tepa] nf (GEO) steppe

**estera** [es'tera] nf mat(ting)

**estéreo** [es'tereo] adj inv, nm stereo; **estereotipo** nm stereotype

**estéril** [es'teril] adj sterile, barren; (fig) vain, futile; **esterilizar** vt to sterilize

**esterlina** [ester'lina] adj: **libra ~** pound sterling

**estés** etc vb ver **estar**

**estética** [es'tetika] nf aesthetics sg

**estético, a** [es'tetiko, a] adj aesthetic

**estibador** [estiβa'ðor] nm stevedore, docker

**estiércol** [es'tjerkol] nm dung, manure

**estigma** [es'tiɣma] nm stigma

**estilarse** [esti'larse] vr to be in fashion

**estilo** [es'tilo] nm style; (TEC) stylus; (NATACION) stroke; **algo por el ~** something along those lines

**estima** [es'tima] nf esteem, respect

**estimación** [estima'θjon] nf (evaluación) estimation; (aprecio, afecto) esteem, regard

**estimar** [esti'mar] vt (evaluar) to estimate; (valorar) to value; (apreciar) to esteem, respect; (pensar, considerar) to think, reckon

**estimulante** [estimu'lante] adj stimulating ♦ nm stimulant

**estimular** [estimu'lar] vt to stimulate; (excitar) to excite

**estímulo** [es'timulo] nm stimulus; (ánimo) encouragement

**estío** [es'tio] nm summer

**estipulación** [estipula'θjon] nf stipulation, condition

**estipular** [estipu'lar] vt to stipulate

**estirado, a** [esti'raðo, a] adj (lenso) (stretched o drawn) tight; (fig: persona) stiff, pompous

**estirar** [esti'rar] vt to stretch; (dinero, suma etc) to stretch out; **~se** vr to stretch

**estirón** [esti'ron] nm pull, tug; (crecimiento) spurt, sudden growth; **dar un ~** (niño) to shoot up

**estirpe** [es'tirpe] nf stock, lineage

**estival** [esti'βal] adj summer cpd

**esto** ['esto] pron this, this thing o matter; **~ de la boda** this business about the wedding

**Estocolmo** [esto'kolmo] nm Stockholm

**estofado** [esto'faðo] nm (CULIN) stew

**estofar** [esto'far] vt (CULIN) to stew

**estómago** [es'tomaɣo] nm stomach; **tener ~** to be thick-skinned

**estorbar** [estor'βar] vt to hinder, obstruct; (fig) to bother, disturb ♦ vi to be in the way; **estorbo** nm (molestia) bother, nuisance; (obstáculo) hindrance, obstacle

**estornudar** [estornu'ðar] vi to sneeze

**estos** ['estos] adj demos ver **este**

**éstos** ['estos] pron ver **éste**

**estoy** vb ver **estar**

**estrado** [es'traðo] nm platform

**estrafalario, a** [estrafa'larjo, a] adj odd, eccentric; (desarreglado) slovenly, sloppy

**estrago** [es'traɣo] nm ruin, destruction; **hacer ~s en** to wreak havoc among

**estragón** [estra'ɣon] nm tarragon

**estrambótico, a** [estram'botiko, a] adj (persona) eccentric; (peinado, ropa) outlandish

**estrangulador, a** [estrangula'ðor, a] nm/f strangler ♦ nm (TEC) throttle; (AUTO) choke

**estrangular** [estrangu'lar] vt (persona) to strangle; (MED) to strangulate

**estraperlo** [estra'perlo] nm black market

**estratagema** [estrata'xema] nf (MIL) stratagem; (astucia) cunning

**estrategia** [estra'texja] nf strategy;

**estratégico, a** adj strategic

**estrato** [es'trato] nm stratum, layer

**estrechamente** [es'tretʃamente] adv (intimamente) closely, intimately; (pobremente: vivir) poorly

**estrechar** [estre'tʃar] vt (reducir) to narrow; (COSTURA) to take in; (persona) to hug, embrace; ~se vr (reducirse) to narrow, grow narrow; (2 personas) to embrace; ~ **la mano** to shake hands

**estrechez** [estre'tʃeθ] nf narrowness; (de ropa) tightness; (intimidad) intimacy; (COM) want o shortage of money; **estrecheces** nfpl (dificultades económicas) financial difficulties

**estrecho, a** [es'tretʃo, a] adj narrow; (apretado) tight; (íntimo) close, intimate; (miserable) mean ◊ nm strait; ~ **de miras** narrow-minded

**estrella** [es'treʎa] nf star; ~ **de mar** (ZOOL) starfish; ~ **fugaz** shooting star; **estrellado, a** adj (forma) starshaped; (cielo) starry

**estrellar** [estre'ʎar] vt (hacer añicos) to smash (to pieces); (huevos) to fry; ~se vr to smash; (chocarse) to crash; (fracasar) to fail

**estremecer** [estreme'θer] vt to shake; ~se vr to shake, tremble; **estremecimiento** nm (temblor) trembling, shaking

**estrenar** [estre'nar] vt (vestido) to wear for the first time; (casa) to move into; (película, obra de teatro) to premiere; ~se vr (persona) to make one's début; **estreno** nm (primer uso) first use; (CINE etc) première

**estreñido, a** [estre'niðo, a] adj constipated

**estreñimiento** [estreni'mjento] nm constipation

**estrépito** [es'trepito] nm noise, racket; (fig) fuss; **estrepitoso, a** adj noisy; (fiesta) rowdy

**estría** [es'tria] nf groove

**estribación** [estriβa'θjon] nf (GEO) spur, foothill

**estribar** [estri'βar] vi: ~ **en** to rest on, be supported by

**estribillo** [estri'βiʎo] nm (LITERATURA) refrain; (MUS) chorus

**estribo** [es'triβo] nm (de jinete) stirrup; (de coche, tren) step; (de puente) support; (GEO) spur; **perder los** ~s to fly off the handle

**estribor** [estri'βor] nm (NAUT) starboard

**estricto, a** [es'trikto, a] adj (riguroso) strict; (severo) severe

**estridente** [estri'ðente] adj (color) loud; (voz) raucous

**estropajo** [estro'paxo] nm scourer

**estropear** [estrope'ar] vt (arruinar) to spoil; (dañar) to damage; ~se vr (objeto) to get damaged; (persona: la piel etc) to be ruined

**estructura** [estruk'tura] nf structure

**estruendo** [es'trwendo] nm (ruido) racket, din; (fig: alboroto) uproar, turmoil

**estrujar** [estru'xar] vt (apretar) to squeeze; (aplastar) to crush; (fig) to drain, bleed

**estuario** [es'twarjo] nm estuary

**estuche** [es'tutʃe] nm box, case

**estudiante** [estu'ðjante] nmf student; **estudiantil** adj student cpd

**estudiar** [estu'ðjar] vt to study

**estudio** [es'tuðjo] nm study; (CINE, ARTE, RADIO) studio; ~s nmpl studies; (erudición) learning sg; ~**so, a** adj studious

**estufa** [es'tufa] nf heater, fire

**estupefaciente** [estupefa'θjente] nm drug, narcotic

**estupefacto, a** [estupe'fakto, a] adj speechless, thunderstruck

**estupendo, a** [estu'pendo, a] adj wonderful, terrific; (fam) great; ¡~! that's great!, fantastic!

**estupidez** [estupi'ðeθ] nf (torpeza) stupidity; (acto) stupid thing (to do)

**estúpido, a** [es'tupiðo, a] adj stupid, silly

**estupor** [estu'por] nm stupor; (fig) astonishment, amazement

**estupro** [es'tupro] nm rape

**estuve** *etc vb ver* **estar**

**esvástica** [ɛs'βastika] *nf* swastika

**ETA** ['eta] (*ESP*) *nf abr* (= Euskadi ta Askatasuna) ETA

**etapa** [e'tapa] *nf* (*de viaje*) stage; (*DEPORTE*) leg; (*parada*) stopping place; (*fig*) stage, phase

**etarra** [e'tarra] *nm/f* member of ETA

*etc. abr* (= etcétera) etc

**etcétera** [et'θetera] *adv* etcetera

**eternidad** [eterni'ðað] *nf* eternity; **eterno, a** *adj* eternal, everlasting

**ética** ['etika] *nf* ethics *pl*

**ético, a** ['etiko, a] *adj* ethical

**etiqueta** [eti'keta] *nf* (*modales*) etiquette; (*rótulo*) label, tag

**Eucaristía** [eukaris'tia] *nf* Eucharist

**eufemismo** [eufe'mismo] *nm* euphemism

**euforia** [eu'forja] *nf* euphoria

**eunuco** [eu'nuko] *nm* eunuch

**eurodiputado, a** [eurodipu'taðo, a] *nm/f* Euro MP

**Europa** [eu'ropa] *nf* Europe; **europeo, a** *adj, nm/f* European

**Euskadi** [eus'kaði] *nm* the Basque Country *o* Provinces *pl*

**euskera** [eus'kera] *nm* (*LING*) Basque

**evacuación** [eβakwa'θjon] *nf* evacuation

**evacuar** [eβa'kwar] *vt* to evacuate

**evadir** [eβa'ðir] *vt* to evade, avoid; ~**se** *vr* to escape

**evaluar** [eβa'lwar] *vt* to evaluate

**evangelio** [eβaŋ'xeljo] *nm* gospel

**evaporar** [eβapo'rar] *vt* to evaporate; ~**se** *vr* to vanish

**evasión** [eβa'sjon] *nf* escape, flight; (*fig*) evasion; ~ **de capitales** flight of capital

**evasiva** [eβa'siβa] *nf* (*pretexto*) excuse

**evasivo, a** [eβa'siβo, a] *adj* evasive, non-committal

**evento** [e'βento] *nm* event

**eventual** [eβen'twal] *adj* possible, conditional (upon circumstances); (*trabajador*) casual, temporary

**evidencia** [eβi'ðenθja] *nf* evidence,

proof; **evidenciar** *vt* (*hacer patente*) to make evident; (*probar*) to prove, show; **evidenciarse** *vr* to be evident

**evidente** [eβi'ðente] *adj* obvious, clear, evident

**evitar** [eβi'tar] *vt* (*evadir*) to avoid; (*impedir*) to prevent

**evocar** [eβo'kar] *vt* to evoke, call forth

**evolución** [eβolu'θjon] *nf* (*desarrollo*) evolution, development; (*cambio*) change; (*MIL*) manoeuvre; **evolucionar** *vi* to evolve; to manoeuvre

**ex** [eks] *adj* ex-: **el ~ ministro** the former minister, the ex-minister

**exacerbar** [eksaθer'βar] *vt* to irritate, annoy

**exactamente** [eksakta'mente] *adv* exactly

**exactitud** [eksakti'tuð] *nf* exactness; (*precisión*) accuracy; (*puntualidad*) punctuality; **exacto, a** *adj* exact; accurate; punctual; **¡exacto!** exactly!

**exageración** [eksaxera'θjon] *nf* exaggeration

**exagerar** [eksaxe'rar] *vt, vi* to exaggerate

**exaltado, a** [eksal'taðo, a] *adj* (*apasionado*) over-excited, worked-up; (*exagerado*) extreme

**exaltar** [eksal'tar] *vt* to exalt, glorify; ~**se** *vr* (*excitarse*) to get excited *o* worked-up

**examen** [ek'samen] *nm* examination

**examinar** [eksami'nar] *vt* to examine; ~**se** *vr* to be examined, take an examination

**exasperar** [eksaspe'rar] *vt* to exasperate; ~**se** *vr* to get exasperated, lose patience

**Exca.** *abr* = Excelencia

**excavadora** [ekskaβa'ðora] *nf* excavator

**excavar** [ekska'βar] *vt* to excavate

**excedencia** [eksθe'ðenθja] *nf*: **estar en ~** to be on leave; **pedir** *o* **solicitar la ~** to ask for leave

**excedente** [eksθe'ðente] *adj, nm* excess, surplus

**exceder** [eksθe'ðer] vt to exceed, surpass; ~**se** vr (extralimitarse) to go too far; (sobrepasarse) to excel o.s.

**excelencia** [eksθe'lenθja] nf excellence; E~ Excellency; **excelente** adj excellent

**excentricidad** [eksθentriθi'ðað] nf eccentricity; **excéntrico, a** adj, nm/f eccentric

**excepción** [eksθep'θjon] nf exception; **excepcional** adj exceptional

**excepto** [eks'θepto] adv excepting, except (for)

**exceptuar** [eksθep'twar] vt to except, exclude

**excesivo, a** [eksθe'siβo, a] adj excessive

**exceso** [eks'θeso] nm (gen) excess; (COM) surplus; ~ **de equipaje/peso** excess luggage/weight

**excitación** [eksθita'θjon] nf (sensación) excitement; (acción) excitation

**excitado, a** [eksθi'taðo, a] adj excited; (emociones) aroused

**excitar** [eksθi'tar] vt to excite; (incitar) to urge; ~**se** vr to get excited

**exclamación** [eksklama'θjon] nf exclamation

**exclamar** [ekskla'mar] vi to exclaim.

**excluir** [eksklu'ir] vt to exclude; (dejar fuera) to shut out; (descartar) to reject; **exclusión** nf exclusion

**exclusiva** [eksklu'siβa] nf (PRENSA) exclusive, scoop; (COM) sole right

**exclusivo, a** [eksklu'siβo, a] adj exclusive; **derecho** ~ sole o exclusive right

**Excmo.** abr = **excelentísimo**

**excomulgar** [ekskomul'yar] vt (REL) to excommunicate

**excomunión** [ekskomu'njon] nf excommunication

**excursión** [ekskur'sjon] nf excursion, outing; **excursionista** nm/f (turista) sightseer

**excusa** [eks'kusa] nf excuse; (disculpa) apology

**excusar** [eksku'sar] vt to excuse; (evitar) to avoid, prevent; ~**se** vr

(disculparse) to apologize

**exento, a** [ek'sento, a] adj exempt

**exequias** [ek'sekjas] nfpl funeral rites

**exhalar** [eksa'lar] vt to exhale, breathe out; (olor etc) to give off; (suspiro) to breathe, heave

**exhaustivo, a** [eksaus'tiβo, a] adj (análisis) thorough; (estudio) exhaustive

**exhausto, a** [ek'sausto, a] adj exhausted

**exhibición** [eksiβi'θjon] nf exhibition, display, show

**exhibir** [eksi'βir] vt to exhibit, display, show

**exhortar** [eksor'tar] vt: ~ **a** to exhort to

**exigencia** [eksi'xenθja] nf demand, requirement; **exigente** adj demanding

**exigir** [eksi'xir] vt (gen) to demand, require; ~ **el pago** to demand payment

**exiliado, a** [eksi'ljaðo, a] adj exiled ♦ nm/f exile

**exilio** [ek'siljo] nm exile

**eximir** [eksi'mir] vt to exempt

**existencia** [eksis'tenθja] nf existence; ~**s** nfpl stock(s) (pl)

**existir** [eksis'tir] vi to exist, be

**éxito** ['eksito] nm (resultado) result, outcome; (triunfo) success; (MUS etc) hit; **tener** ~ to be successful

**exonerar** [eksone'rar] vt to exonerate; ~ **de una obligación** to free from an obligation

**exorbitante** [eksorβi'tante] adj (precio) exorbitant; (cantidad) excessive

**exorcizar** [eksorθi'θar] vt to exorcize

**exótico, a** [ek'sotiko, a] adj exotic

**expandir** [ekspan'dir] vt to expand

**expansión** [ekspan'sjon] nf expansion

**expansivo, a** [ekspan'siβo, a] adj: **onda** ~**a** shock wave

**expatriarse** [ekspa'trjarse] vr to emigrate; (POL) to go into exile

**expectativa** [ekspekta'tiβa] nf (espera) expectation; (perspectiva) prospect

**expedición** [ekspeði'θjon] *nf (excursión)* expedition

**expediente** [ekspe'ðjente] *nm* expedient; *(JUR: procedimento)* action, proceedings *pl; (: papeles)* dossier, file, record

**expedir** [ekspe'ðir] *vt (despachar)* to send, forward; *(pasaporte)* to issue

**expendedor, a** [ekspende'ðor, a] *nm/f (vendedor)* dealer

**expensas** [eks'pensas] *nfpl:* a ~ de at the expense of

**experiencia** [ekspe'rjenθja] *nf* experience

**experimentado, a** [eksperimen'taðo, a] *adj* experienced

**experimentar** [eksperimen'tar] *vt (en laboratorio)* to experiment with; *(probar)* to test, try out; *(notar, observar)* to experience; *(deterioro, pérdida)* to suffer; *experimento nm* experiment

**experto, a** [eks'perto, a] *adj* expert, skilled ♦ *nm/f* expert

**expiar** [ekspi'ar] *vt* to atone for

**expirar** [ekspi'rar] *vi* to expire

**explanada** [ekspla'naða] *nf (llano)* plain

**explayarse** [ekspla'jarse] *vr (en discurso)* to speak at length; ~ con uno to confide in sb

**explicación** [eksplika'θjon] *nf* explanation

**explicar** [ekspli'kar] *vt* to explain; ~se *vr* to explain (o.s.)

**explícito, a** [eks'pliθito, a] *adj* explicit

**explique** *etc vb ver* explicar

**explorador, a** [eksplora'ðor, a] *nm/f (pionero)* explorer; *(MIL)* scout ♦ *nm (MED)* probe; *(TEC) (radar)* scanner

**explorar** [eksplo'rar] *vt* to explore; *(MED)* to probe; *(radar)* to scan

**explosión** [eksplo'sjon] *nf* explosion; **explosivo, a** *adj* explosive

**explotación** [eksplota'θjon] *nf* exploitation; *(de planta etc)* running

**explotar** [eksplo'tar] *vt* to exploit; to

run, operate ♦ *vi* to explode

**exponer** [ekspo'ner] *vt* to expose; *(cuadro)* to display; *(vida)* to risk; *(idea)* to explain; ~se *vr:* ~se a **(hacer)** algo to run the risk of (doing) sth

**exportación** [eksporta'θjon] *nf (acción)* export; *(mercancías)* exports *pl*

**exportar** [ekspor'tar] *vt* to export

**exposición** [eksposi'θjon] *nf (gen)* exposure; *(de arte)* show, exhibition; *(explicación)* explanation; *(narración)* account, statement

**expresamente** [ekspresa'mente] *adv (decir)* clearly; *(a propósito)* expressly

**expresar** [ekspre'sar] *vt* to express; **expresión** *nf* expression

**expresivo, a** [ekspre'sißo, a] *adj (persona, gesto, palabras)* expressive; *(cariñoso)* affectionate

**expreso, a** [eks'preso, a] *pp de* expresar ♦ *adj (explícito)* express; *(claro)* specific, clear; *(tren)* fast ♦ *adv:* **mandar** ~ to send by express (delivery)

**express** [eks'pres] *(AM) adv:* enviar algo ~ to send sth special delivery

**exprimidor** [eksprimi'ðor] *nm* squeezer

**exprimir** [ekspri'mir] *vt (fruta)* to squeeze; *(zumo)* to squeeze out

**expropiar** [ekspro'pjar] *vt* to expropriate

**expuesto, a** [eks'pwesto, a] *pp de* exponer ♦ *adj* exposed; *(cuadro etc)* on show, on display

**expulsar** [ekspul'sar] *vt (echar)* to eject, throw out; *(alumno)* to expel; *(despedir)* to sack, fire; *(DEPORTE)* to send off; **expulsión** *nf* expulsion; sending-off

**exquisito, a** [ekski'sito, a] *adj* exquisite; *(comida)* delicious

**éxtasis** ['ekstasis] *nm* ecstasy

**extender** [eksten'der] *vt* to extend; *(los brazos)* to stretch out, hold out; *(mapa, tela)* to spread (out), open (out); *(mantequilla)* to spread; *(certificado)* to issue; *(cheque, recibo)* to make out; (documento) to draw up; ~se vr (gen) to extend; (persona: en el suelo) to stretch out; (epidemia) to spread; **extendido, a** adj (abierto) spread out, open; (brazos) outstretched; (costumbre) widespread; (pey) rife

**extensión** [eksten'sjon] nf (de terreno, mar) expanse, stretch; (de tiempo) length, duration; (TEL) extension; en toda la ~ de la palabra in every sense of the word

**extenso, a** [eks'tenso, a] adj extensive

**extenuar** [ekste'nwar] vt (debilitar) to weaken

**exterior** [ekste'rjor] adj (de fuera) external; (afuera) outside, exterior; (apariencia) outward; (deuda, relaciones) foreign ♦ nm (gen) exterior, outside; (aspecto) outward appearance; (DEPORTE) wing(er); (países extranjeros) abroad; en el ~ abroad; al ~ outwardly, on the surface

**exterminar** [ekstermi'nar] vt to exterminate; **exterminio** nm extermination

**externo, a** [eks'terno, a] adj (exterior) external, outside; (superficial) outward ♦ nm/f day pupil

**extinguir** [ekstin'gir] vt (fuego) to extinguish, put out; (raza, población) to wipe out; ~se vr (fuego) to go out; (BIO) to die out, become extinct

**extinto, a** [eks'tinto, a] adj extinct

**extintor** [ekstin'tor] nm (fire) extinguisher

**extirpar** [ekstir'par] vt (MED) to remove (surgically)

**extorsión** [ekstor'sjon] nf (FIN, JUR) blackmail; (molestia) inconvenience

**extra** ['ekstra] adj inv (tiempo) extra; (chocolate, vino) good-quality ♦ nm/f extra ♦ nm extra; (bono) bonus

**extracción** [ekstrak'θjon] nf extraction; (en lotería) draw

**extracto** [eks'trakto] nm extract

**extradición** [ekstraði'θjon] nf extradition

**extraer** [ekstra'er] vt to extract, take out

**extraescolar** [ekstraesko'lar] adj: actividad ~ extracurricular activity

**extralimitarse** [ekstralimi'tarse] vr to go too far

**extranjero, a** [ekstran'xero, a] adj foreign ♦ nm/f foreigner ♦ nm foreign countries pl; en el ~ abroad

**extrañar** [ekstra'nar] vt (sorprender) to find strange o odd; (echar de menos) to miss; ~se vr (sorprenderse) to be amazed, be surprised; (distanciarse) to become estranged, grow apart

**extrañeza** [ekstra'neθa] nf (rareza) strangeness, oddness; (asombro) amazement, surprise

**extraño, a** [eks'trano, a] adj (extranjero) foreign; (raro, sorprendente) strange, odd

**extraordinario, a** [ekstraorði'narjo, a] adj extraordinary; (edición, número) special ♦ nm (de periódico) special edition; horas extraordinarias overtime sg

**extrarradio** [ekstra'rraðjo] nm poor suburban area

**extravagancia** [ekstraβa'vanθja] nf oddness; outlandishness; **extravagante** adj (excéntrico) eccentric; (estrafalario) outlandish

**extraviado, a** [ekstra'βjaðo, a] adj lost, missing

**extraviar** [ekstra'βjar] vt (persona: desorientar) to mislead, misdirect; (perder) to lose, misplace; ~se vr to lose one's way, get lost; **extravío** nm loss; (fig) deviation

**extremar** [ekstre'mar] vt to carry to extremes; ~se vr to do one's utmost, make every effort

**extremaunción** [ekstremaun'θjon] nf extreme unction

**extremidad** [ekstremi'ðað] nf (punta) extremity; (fila) edge; ~es nfpl (ANAT) extremities

**extremo, a** [eks'tremo, a] adj extreme; (*último*) last ♦ *nm* end; (*límite, grado sumo*) extreme; **en último** ~ as a last resort

**extrovertido, a** [ekstroßer'tiðo, a] *adj, nm/f* extrovert

**exuberancia** [eksuße'ranθja] *nf* exuberance; **exuberante** *adj* exuberant; (*fig*) luxuriant, lush

**eyacular** [ejaku'lar] *vt, vi* to ejaculate

# F

**f.a.b.** *abr* (= *franco a bordo*) f.o.b.

**fábrica** ['faßrika] *nf* factory; **marca de** ~ trademark; **precio de** ~ factory price

**fabricación** [faßrika'θjon] *nf* (*manufactura*) manufacture; (*producción*) production; **de** ~ **casera** home-made; ~ **en serie** mass production

**fabricante** [faßri'kante] *nm/f* manufacturer

**fabricar** [faßri'kar] *vt* (*manufacturar*) to manufacture, make; (*construir*) to build; (*cuento*) to fabricate, devise

**fábula** ['faßula] *nf* (*cuento*) fable; (*chisme*) rumour; (*mentira*) fib

**fabuloso, a** [faßu'loso, a] *adj* (*oportunidad, tiempo*) fabulous, great

**facción** [fak'θjon] *nf* (*POL*) faction; **facciones** *nfpl* (*del rostro*) features

**faceta** [fa'θeta] *nf* facet

**fácil** ['faθil] *adj* (*simple*) easy; (*probable*) likely

**facilidad** [faθili'ðað] *nf* (*capacidad*) ease; (*sencillez*) simplicity; (*de palabra*) fluency; ~**es** *nfpl* facilities

**facilitar** [faθili'tar] *vt* (*hacer fácil*) to make easy; (*proporcionar*) to provide

**fácilmente** ['faθilmente] *adv* easily

**facsímil** [fak'simil] *nm* facsimile, fax

**factible** [fak'tißle] *adj* feasible

**factor** [fak'tor] *nm* factor

**factura** [fak'tura] *nf* (*cuenta*) bill; (*hechura*) manufacture; **facturar** *vt* (*COM*) to invoice, charge for; (*equipaje*) to register (*BRIT*), check (*US*)

**facultad** [fakul'tað] *nf* (*aptitud, ESCOL etc*) faculty; (*poder*) power

**facha** ['fatʃa] (*fam*) *nf* (*aspecto*) look; (*cara*) face

**fachada** [fa'tʃaða] *nf* (*ARQ*) façade, front

**faena** [fa'ena] *nf* (*trabajo*) work; (*quehacer*) task, job

**faisán** [fai'san] *nm* pheasant

**faja** ['faxa] *nf* (*para la cintura*) sash; (*de mujer*) corset; (*de tierra*) strip

**fajo** ['faxo] *nm* (*de papeles*) bundle; (*de billetes*) wad

**falacia** [fa'laθja] *nf* fallacy

**falda** ['falda] *nf* (*prenda de vestir*) skirt

**falo** ['falo] *nm* phallus

**falsedad** [false'ðað] *nf* falseness; (*hipocresía*) hypocrisy; (*mentira*) falsehood

**falsificar** [falsifi'kar] *vt* (*firma etc*) to forge; (*voto etc*) to rig; (*moneda*) to counterfeit

**falso, a** ['falso, a] *adj* false; (*erróneo*) mistaken; (*documento, moneda etc*) fake; **en** ~ falsely

**falta** ['falta] *nf* (*defecto*) fault, flaw; (*privación*) lack, want; (*ausencia*) absence; (*carencia*) shortage; (*equivocación*) mistake; (*DEPORTE*) foul; **echar en** ~ to miss; **hacer** ~ **hacer algo** to be necessary to do sth; **me hace** ~ **una pluma** I need a pen; ~ **de educación** bad manners *pl*

**faltar** [fal'tar] *vi* (*escasear*) to be lacking, be wanting; (*ausentarse*) to be absent, be missing; **faltan 2 horas para llegar** there are 2 hours to go till arrival; ~ **al respeto a uno** to be disrespectful to sb; **¡no faltaba más!** that's the last straw!

**falto, a** ['falto, a] *adj* (*desposeído*) deficient, lacking; (*necesitado*) poor, wretched

**falla** ['faʎa] *nf* (*defecto*) fault, flaw

**fallar** [fa'ʎar] *vt* (*JUR*) to pronounce sentence on ♦ *vi* (*memoria*) to fail; (*motor*) to miss

**fallecer** [faʎe'θer] *vi* to pass away,

die; **fallecimiento** nm decease, demise

**fallido, a** [fa'ʎiðo, a] adj (gen) frustrated, unsuccessful

**fallo** ['faʎo] nm (JUR) verdict, ruling; (fracaso) failure; ~ **cardíaco** heart failure

**fama** ['fama] nf (renombre) fame; (reputación) reputation

**famélico, a** [fa'meliko, a] adj starving

**familia** [fa'milja] nf family; ~ **política** in-laws pl

**familiar** [fami'ljar] adj (relativo a la familia) family cpd; (conocido, informal) familiar ♦ nm relative, relation; (~idad) nf (gen) familiarity; (informalidad) homeliness; **~izarse** vr: ~izarse con to familiarize o.s. with

**famoso, a** [fa'moso, a] adj (renombrado) famous

**fanático, a** [fa'natiko, a] adj fanatical ♦ nm/f fanatic; (CINE, DEPORTE) fan; **fanatismo** nm fanaticism

**fanfarrón, ona** [fanfa'rron, ona] adj boastful; (pey) showy

**fango** ['fango] nm mud; **~so, a** adj muddy

**fantasía** [fanta'sia] nf fantasy, imagination; **joyas de ~** imitation jewellery sg

**fantasma** [fan'tasma] nm (espectro) ghost, apparition; (presumido) showoff

**fantástico, a** [fan'tastiko, a] adj fantastic

**farmacéutico, a** [farma'θeutiko, a] adj pharmaceutical ♦ nm/f chemist (BRIT), pharmacist

**farmacia** [far'maθja] nf chemist's (shop) (BRIT), pharmacy; ~ **de turno** duty chemist; ~ **de guardia** all-night chemist

**fármaco** ['farmako] nm drug

**faro** ['faro] nm (NAUT: torre) lighthouse; (AUTO) headlamp; (foco) floodlight; **~s antiniebla** fog lamps; **~s delanteros/traseros** headlights/rear lights

**farol** [fa'rol] nm lantern, lamp

**farola** [fa'rola] nf street lamp (BRIT) o light (US)

**farsa** ['farsa] nf (gen) farce

**farsante** [far'sante] nm/f fraud, fake

**fascículo** [fas'θikulo] nm (de revista) part, instalment

**fascinar** [fasθi'nar] vt (gen) to fascinate

**fascismo** [fas'θismo] nm fascism; **fascista** adj, nm/f fascist

**fase** ['fase] nf phase

**fastidiar** [fasti'ðjar] vt (disgustar) to annoy, bother; (estropear) to spoil; **~se** vr (disgustarse) to get annoyed o cross; **¡que se fastidie!** (fam) he'll just have to put up with it!

**fastidio** [fas'tiðjo] nm (disgusto) annoyance; **~so, a** adj (molesto) annoying

**fastuoso, a** [fas'twoso, a] adj (banquete, boda) lavish; (acto) pompous

**fatal** [fa'tal] adj (gen) fatal; (desgraciado) ill-fated; (fam: malo, pésimo) awful; **~idad** nf (destino) fate; (mala suerte) misfortune

**fatiga** [fa'tiɣa] nf (cansancio) fatigue, weariness

**fatigar** [fati'ɣar] vt to tire, weary; **~se** vr to get tired

**fatigoso, a** [fati'ɣoso, a] adj (cansador) tiring

**fatuo, a** ['fatwo, a] adj (vano) fatuous; (presuntuoso) conceited

**fauces** ['fauθes] nfpl jaws, mouth sg

**favor** [fa'βor] nm favour; **estar a ~ de** to be in favour of; **haga el ~ de...** would you be so good as to..., kindly...; **por ~** please; **~able** adj favourable

**favorecer** [faβore'θer] vt to favour; (vestido etc) to become, flatter; **este peinado le favorece** this hairstyle suits him

**favorito, a** [faβo'rito, a] adj, nm/f favourite

**faz** [faθ] nf face; **la ~ de la tierra** the face of the earth

**fe** [fe] nf (REL) faith; (confianza) belief; (documento) certificate; **pres-**

tar ~ a to believe, credit; **actuar con buena/mala** ~ to act in good/bad faith; **dar** ~ **de** to bear witness to

**fealdad** [feal'ðaθ] nf ugliness

**febril** [fe'βril] adj (fig: actividad) hectic; (mente, mirada) feverish

**febrero** [fe'βrero] nm February

**fecundar** [fekun'dar] vt (generar) to fertilize, make fertile; **fecundo, a** adj (fértil) fertile; (fig) prolific; (productivo) productive

**fecha** ['fetʃa] nf date; ~ **de caducidad** (de producto alimenticio) sell-by date; (de contrato etc) expiry date; **con** ~ **adelantada** postdated; **en** ~ **próxima** soon; **hasta la** ~ to date, so far; **poner** ~ to date; **fechar** vt to date

**federación** [feðera'θjon] nf federation

**federal** [feðe'ral] adj federal

**felicidad** [feliθi'ðaθ] nf (satisfacción, contento) happiness; ~**es** nfpl (felicitaciones) best wishes, congratulations

**felicitación** [feliθita'θjon] nf: **¡felicitaciones!** congratulations!

**felicitar** [feliθi'tar] vt to congratulate

**feligrés, esa** [feli'γres, esa] nm/f parishioner

**feliz** [fe'liθ] adj (contento) happy; (afortunado) lucky

**felpudo** [fel'puðo] nm mat

**femenino, a** [feme'nino, a] adj, nm feminine

**feminista** [femi'nista] adj, nm/f feminist

**fenómeno** [fe'nomeno] nm phenomenon; (fig) freak, accident ♦ adj great ♦ excl great!, marvellous!; **fenomenal** adj = **fenómeno**

**feo, a** [fe'o, a] adj (gen) ugly; (desagradable) bad, nasty

**féretro** ['feretro] nm (ataúd) coffin; (sarcófago) bier

**feria** ['ferja] nf (gen) fair; (descanso) holiday, rest day; (AM: mercado) village market; (: cambio) loose o small change

**fermentar** [fermen'tar] vi to ferment

**ferocidad** [feroθi'ðaθ] nf fierceness, ferocity

**feroz** [fe'roθ] adj (cruel) cruel; (salvaje) fierce

**férreo, a** ['ferreo, a] adj iron

**ferretería** [ferrete'ria] nf (tienda) ironmonger's (shop) (BRIT), hardware store

**ferrocarril** [ferroka'rril] nm railway

**ferroviario, a** [ferro'βjarjo, a] adj rail cpd

**fértil** ['fertil] adj (productivo) fertile; (rico) rich; **fertilidad** nf (gen) fertility; (productividad) fruitfulness

**ferviente** [fer'βjente] adj fervent

**fervor** [fer'βor] nm fervour; ~**oso, a** adj fervent

**festejar** [feste'xar] vt (celebrar) to celebrate; **festejo** nm celebration; **festejos** nmpl (fiestas) festivals

**festín** [fes'tin] nm feast, banquet

**festival** [festi'βal] nm festival

**festividad** [festiβi'ðaθ] nf festivity

**festivo, a** [fes'tiβo, a] adj (de fiesta) festive; (fig) witty; (CINE, LITERATURA) humorous; **día** ~ holiday

**fétido, a** ['fetiðo, a] adj (hediondo) foul-smelling

**feto** ['feto] nm foetus

**fiable** ['fjaβle] adj (persona) trustworthy; (máquina) reliable

**fiador, a** [fja'ðor, a] nm/f (JUR) surety, guarantor; (COM) backer; **salir** ~ **por uno** to stand bail for sb

**fiambre** ['fjambre] nm cold meat

**fianza** ['fjanθa] nf surety; (JUR): **libertad bajo** ~ release on bail

**fiar** [fi'ar] vt (salir garante de) to guarantee; (vender a crédito) to sell on credit; (secreto): ~ **a** to confide (to) ♦ vi to trust; ~**se** vr to trust (in), rely on; ~**se de uno** to rely on sb

**fibra** ['fiβra] nf fibre; ~ **óptica** optical fibre

**ficción** [fik'θjon] nf fiction

**ficticio, a** [fik'tiθjo, a] adj (imaginario) fictitious; (falso) fabricated

**ficha** ['fitʃa] nf (TEL) token; (en juegos) counter, marker; (tarjeta) (index) card; **fichar** vt (archivar) to file, index; (DEPORTE) to sign; **estar fichado** to have a record; **fichero** nm box file; (INFORM) file

**fidelidad** [fiðeli'ðað] nf (lealtad) fidelity, loyalty; **alta ~** high fidelity, hi-fi

**fideos** [fi'ðeos] nmpl noodles

**fiebre** [fi'ßeßre] nf (MED) fever; (fig) fever, excitement; **~ amarilla/del heno** yellow/hay fever; **~ palúdica** malaria; **tener ~** to have a temperature

**fiel** [fjel] adj (leal) faithful, loyal; (fiable) reliable; (exacto) accurate, faithful ♦ nm: **los ~es** the faithful

**fieltro** [fi'eltro] nm felt

**fiera** ['fjera] nf (animal feroz) wild animal o beast; (fig) dragon; ver tb **fiero**

**fiero, a** [fi'ero, a] adj (cruel) cruel; (feroz) fierce; (duro) harsh ♦ nm/f (fig) fiend

**fiesta** ['fjesta] nf party; (de pueblo) festival; (vacaciones, tb: ~s) holiday sg; (REL): **~ de guardar** day of obligation

**figura** [fi'yura] nf (gen) figure; (forma, imagen) shape, form; (NAIPES) face card

**figurar** [fixu'rar] vt (representar) to represent; (fingir) to figure ♦ vi to figure; **~se** vr (imaginarse) to imagine; (suponer) to suppose

**fijador** [fixa'ðor] nm (FOTO etc) fixative; (de pelo) gel

**fijar** [fi'xar] vt (gen) to fix; (estampilla) to stick (on), stick (on); (fig) to settle (on), decide; **~se** vr: **~se en** to notice

**fijo, a** [a'fixo, a] adj (gen) fixed; (firme) firm; (permanente) permanent ♦ adv: **mirar ~** to stare

**fila** ['fila] nf row; (MIL) rank; (cadena) line; **ponerse en ~** to line up, get into line

**filántropo, a** [fi'lantropo, a] nm/f philanthropist

**filatelia** [fila'telja] nf philately, stamp collecting

**filete** [fi'lete] nm (carne) fillet steak; (pescado) fillet

**filiación** [filja'θjon] nf (POL) affiliation

**filial** [fi'ljal] adj filial ♦ nf subsidiary

**Filipinas** [fili'pinas] nfpl: **las ~** the Philippines; **filipino, a** adj, nm/f Philippine

**filmar** [fil'mar] vt to film, shoot

**filo** ['filo] nm (gen) edge; **sacar ~ a** to sharpen; **al ~ del mediodía** at about midday; **de doble ~** double-edged

**filón** [fi'lon] nm (MINERÍA) vein, lode; (fig) goldmine

**filosofía** [filoso'fia] nf philosophy; **filósofo, a** nm/f philosopher

**filtrar** [fil'trar] vt, vi to filter, strain; **~se** vr to filter; (fig: dinero) to dwindle; **filtro** nm (TEC, utensilio) filter

**fin** [fin] nm end; (objetivo) aim, purpose; **al ~ y al cabo** when all's said and done; **a ~ de** in order to; **por ~** finally; **en ~** in short; **~ de semana** weekend

**final** [fi'nal] adj final ♦ nm end, conclusion ♦ nf final; **~idad** nf (propósito) purpose, intention; **~ista** nm/f finalist; **~izar** vt to end, finish; (INFORM) to log out o off ♦ vi to end, come to an end

**financiar** [finan'θjar] vt to finance; **financiero, a** adj financial ♦ nm/f financier

**finca** ['finka] nf (bien inmueble) property, land; (casa de campo) country house; (AM) farm

**fingir** [fin'xir] vt (simular) to simulate, feign; (pretextar) to sham, fake ♦ vi (aparentar) to pretend; **~se** vr to pretend to be

**finlandés, esa** [finlan'des, esa] adj Finnish ♦ nm/f Finn ♦ nm (LING) Finnish

**Finlandia** [fin'landja] nf Finland

**fino, a** ['fino, a] adj fine; (delgado) slender; (de buenas maneras) polite, refined; (jerez) fino, dry

**firma** ['firma] nf signature; (COM)

firm, company

**firmamento** [firma'mento] *nm* firmament

**firmar** [fir'mar] *vt* to sign

**firme** ['firme] *adj* firm; (*estable*) stable; (*sólido*) solid; (*constante*) steady; (*decidido*) resolute ♦ *nm* road (surface); **~mente** *adv* firmly; **~za** *nf* firmness; (*constancia*) steadiness; (*solidez*) solidity

**fiscal** [fis'kal] *adj* fiscal ♦ *nm/f* public prosecutor; **año ~** tax o fiscal year

**fisco** ['fisko] *nm* (*hacienda*) treasury, exchequer (*BRIT*)

**fisgar** [fis'ɣar] *vt* to pry into

**fisgonear** [fisɣone'ar] *vt* to poke one's nose into ♦ *vi* to pry, spy

**física** ['fisika] *nf* physics *sg*; *ver tb* **físico**

**físico, a** ['fisiko, a] *adj* physical ♦ *nm* physique ♦ *nm/f* physicist

**fisura** [fi'sura] *nf* crack; (*MED*) (hairline) fracture

**flac(c)ido, a** ['fla(k)θiðo, a] *adj* flabby

**flaco, a** ['flako, a] *adj* (*muy delgado*) skinny, thin; (*débil*) weak, feeble

**flagrante** [fla'ɣrante] *adj* flagrant

**flamante** [fla'mante] (*fam*) *adj* brilliant; (*nuevo*) brand-new

**flamenco, a** [fla'menko, a] *adj* (*de Flandes*) Flemish; (*baile, música*) flamenco ♦ *nm* (*baile, música*) flamenco

**flan** [flan] *nm* creme caramel

**flaqueza** [fla'keθa] *nf* (*delgadez*) thinness, leanness; (*fig*) weakness

**flash** [flaʃ] (*pl* **~s** *o* **~es**) *nm* (*FOTO*) flash

**flauta** ['flauta] *nf* (*MUS*) flute

**fleco** ['fleko] *nm* fringe

**flecha** ['fletʃa] *nf* arrow

**flechazo** [fle'tʃaθo] *nm* love at first sight

**flema** ['flema] *nm* phlegm

**flequillo** [fle'kiʎo] *nm* (*pelo*) fringe

**flete** ['flete] *nm* (*carga*) freight; (*alquiler*) charter; (*precio*) freightage

**flexible** [flek'siβle] *adj* flexible

**flexo** ['flekso] *nm* adjustable table-

lamp

**flojera** [flo'xera] (*AM: fam*) *nf*: me da ~ I can't be bothered

**flojo, a** ['floxo, a] *adj* (*gen*) loose; (*sin fuerzas*) limp; (*débil*) weak

**flor** [flor] *nf* flower; (*piropo*) compliment; **a ~ de** on the surface of; **~ecer** *vi* (*BOT*) to flower, bloom; (*fig*) to flourish; **~eciente** *adj* (*BOT*) in flower, flowering; (*fig*) thriving; **~ero** *nm* vase; **~istería** *nf* florist's (shop)

**flota** ['flota] *nf* fleet

**flotador** [flota'ðor] *nm* (*gen*) float; (*para nadar*) rubber ring

**flotar** [flo'tar] *vi* (*gen*) to float; **flote** *nm*: **a flote** afloat; **salir a flote** (*fig*) to get back on one's feet

**fluctuar** [fluk'twar] *vi* (*oscilar*) to fluctuate

**fluidez** [flui'ðeθ] *nf* fluidity; (*fig*) fluency

**fluido, a** ['fluiðo, a] *adj, nm* fluid

**fluir** [flu'ir] *vi* to flow

**flujo** ['fluxo] *nm* flow; **~ y reflujo** ebb and flow; **~ de sangre** (*MED*) loss of blood

**fluvial** [fluβi'al] *adj* (*navegación, cuenca*) fluvial, river *cpd*

**foca** ['foka] *nf* seal

**foco** ['foko] *nm* focus; (*ELEC*) floodlight; (*AM*) (light) bulb

**fofo, a** ['fofo, a] *adj* soft, spongy; (*carnes*) flabby

**fogata** [fo'ɣata] *nf* bonfire

**fogón** [fo'ɣon] *nm* (*de cocina*) ring, burner

**fogoso, a** [fo'ɣoso, a] *adj* spirited

**folio** ['foljo] *nm* folio, page

**follaje** [fo'ʎaxe] *nm* foliage

**folletín** [foʎe'tin] *nm* newspaper serial

**folleto** [fo'ʎeto] *nm* (*POL*) pamphlet

**follón** [fo'ʎon] (*fam*) *nm* (*lío*) mess; (*conmoción*) fuss; **armar un ~** to kick up a row

**fomentar** [fomen'tar] *vt* (*MED*) to foment; **fomento** *nm* (*promoción*) promotion

**fonda** ['fonda] *nf* inn

**fondear** [fonde'ar] vt to search

**fondo** ['fondo] nm (de mar) bottom; (de coche, sala) back; (ARTE etc) background; (reserva) fund; ~s nmpl (COM) funds, resources; **una investigación a** ~ a thorough investigation; **en el** ~ at bottom, deep down

**fontanería** [fontane'ria] nf plumbing; **fontanero, a** nm/f plumber

**footing** ['futin] nm jogging; **hacer** ~ to jog, go jogging

**foráneo, a** [fo'raneo, a] adj foreign

**forastero, a** [foras'tero, a] nm/f stranger

**forcejear** [forθexe'ar] vi (luchar) to struggle

**forense** [fo'rense] nm/f pathologist

**forjar** [for'xar] vt to forge

**forma** ['forma] nf (figura) form, shape; (molde) mould, pattern; (MED) fitness; (método) way, means; **las** ~ **s** the conventions; **estar en** ~ to be fit

**formación** [forma'θjon] nf (gen) formation; (educación) education; ~ **profesional** vocational training

**formal** [for'mal] adj (gen) formal; (fig: persona) serious; (: de fiar) reliable; ~**idad** nf formality; seriousness; ~**izar** vt (JUR) to formalize; (situación) to put in order, regularize; ~**izarse** vr (situación) to be put in order, be regularized

**formar** [for'mar] vt (componer) to form, shape; (constituir) to make up, constitute; (ESCOL) to train, educate; ~**se** vr (ESCOL) to be trained, educated; (cobrar forma) to form, take form; (desarrollarse) to develop

**formatear** [formate'ar] vt to format

**formativo, a** [forma'tiβo, a] adj (lecturas, años) formative

**formato** [for'mato] nm format

**formidable** [formi'ðaβle] adj (temible) formidable; (asombroso) tremendous

**fórmula** ['formula] nf formula

**formular** [formu'lar] vt (queja) to make, lodge; (petición) to draw up;

(pregunta) to pose

**formulario** [formu'larjo] nm form

**fornido, a** [for'niðo, a] adj well-built

**forrar** [fo'rrar] vt (abrigo) to line; (libro) to cover; **forro** nm (de cuaderno) cover; (COSTURA) lining; (de sillón) upholstery

**fortalecer** [fortale'θer] vt to strengthen

**fortaleza** [forta'leθa] nf (MIL) fortress, stronghold; (fuerza) strength; (determinación) resolution

**fortuito, a** [for'twito, a] adj accidental

**fortuna** [for'tuna] nf (suerte) fortune, (good) luck; (riqueza) fortune, wealth

**forzar** [for'θar] vt (puerta) to force (open); (compeler) to compel

**forzoso, a** [for'θoso, a] adj necessary

**fosa** ['fosa] nf (sepultura) grave; (en tierra) pit; (MED) cavity; ~**s nasales** nostrils

**fósforo** ['fosforo] nm (QUÍMICA) phosphorus; (AM) match

**foso** ['foso] nm ditch; (TEATRO) pit; (AUTO): ~ **de reconocimiento** inspection pit

**foto** ['foto] nf photo, snap(shot); **sacar una** ~ to take a photo o picture

**fotocopia** [foto'kopja] nf photocopy; **fotocopiadora** nf photocopier; **fotocopiar** vt to photocopy

**fotografía** [fotoɣra'fia] nf (ARTE) photography; (una ~) photograph; **fotografiar** vt to photograph

**fotógrafo, a** [fo'toɣrafo, a] nm/f photographer

**fracasar** [fraka'sar] vi (gen) to fail

**fracaso** [fra'kaso] nm (desgracia, revés) failure

**fracción** [frak'θjon] nf fraction; (POL) faction; **fraccionamiento** (AM) nm housing estate

**fractura** [frak'tura] nf fracture, break

**fragancia** [fra'ɣanθja] nf (olor) fragrance, perfume

**frágil** ['fraxil] adj (débil) fragile; (COM) breakable

**fragmento** [fraɣ'mento] nm (pedazo) fragment

**fragua** ['fraɣwa] nf forge; **fraguar** vt to forge; (fig) to concoct ♦ vi to harden

**fraile** ['fraile] nm (REL) friar; (: monje) monk

**frambuesa** [fram'bwesa] nf raspberry

**francés, esa** [fran'θes, esa] adj French ♦ nm/f Frenchman/woman ♦ nm (LING) French

**Francia** ['franθja] nf France

**franco, a** ['franko, a] adj (cándido) frank, open; (COM: exento) free ♦ nm (moneda) franc; **francamente** adv (hablar, decir) frankly; (realmente) really

**francotirador, a** [frankotira'ðor, a] nm/f sniper

**franela** [fra'nela] nf flannel

**franja** ['franxa] nf fringe

**franquear** [franke'ar] vt (camino) to clear; (carta, paquete postal) to frank, stamp; (obstáculo) to overcome

**franqueo** [fran'keo] nm postage

**franqueza** [fran'keθa] nf (candor) frankness

**frasco** ['frasko] nm bottle, flask; ~ al vacío (vacuum) flask

**frase** ['frase] nf sentence; ~ hecha set phrase; (pey) stock phrase

**fraterno, a** [fra'terno, a] adj brotherly, fraternal

**fraude** ['frauðe] nm (cualidad) dishonesty; (acto) fraud; **fraudulento, a** adj fraudulent

**frazada** [fra'saða] (AM) nf blanket

**frecuencia** [fre'kwenθja] nf frequency; **con** ~ frequently, often

**frecuentar** [frekwen'tar] vt to frequent

**fregadero** [freɣa'ðero] nm (kitchen) sink

**fregar** [fre'ɣar] vt (frotar) to scrub; (platos) to wash (up); (AM) to annoy

**fregona** [fre'ɣona] nf (utensilio) mop; (pey: sirvienta) skivvy

**freir** [fre'ir] vt to fry

**frenar** [fre'nar] vt to brake; (fig) to check

**frenazo** [fre'naθo] nm: **dar un** ~ to brake sharply

**frenesí** [frene'si] nm frenzy; **frenético, a** adj frantic

**freno** ['freno] nm (TEC, AUTO) brake; (de cabalgadura) bit; (fig) check

**frente** ['frente] nm (ARQ, POL) front; (de objeto) front part ♦ nf forehead, brow; ~ **a** in front of; (en situación opuesta de) opposite; **al** ~ **de** (fig) at the head of; **chocar de** ~ to crash head-on; **hacer** ~ **a** to face up to

**fresa** ['fresa] (ESP) nf strawberry

**fresco, a** ['fresko, a] adj (nuevo) fresh; (frío) cool; (descarado) cheeky ♦ nm (aire) fresh air; (ARTE) fresco; (AM: jugo) fruit drink ♦ nm/f (fam): **ser un** ~ to have a nerve; **tomar el** ~ to get some fresh air; **frescura** nf freshness; (descaro) cheek, nerve; (calma) calmness

**frialdad** [frial'daθ] nf (gen) coldness; (indiferencia) indifference

**fricción** [frik'θjon] nf (gen) friction; (acto) rub(bing); (MED) massage

**frigidez** [frixi'ðeθ] nf frigidity

**frigorífico** [friɣo'rifiko] nm refrigerator

**frijol** [fri'xol] nm kidney bean

**frío, a** etc ['frio, a] vb ver **freír** ♦ adj cold; (indiferente) indifferent ♦ nm cold; indifference; **hace** ~ it's cold; **tener** ~ to be cold

**frito, a** ['frito, a] adj fried; **me trae** ~ **ese hombre** I'm sick and tired of that man; **fritos** nmpl fried food

**frívolo, a** ['friβolo, a] adj frivolous

**frontal** [fron'tal] adj frontal; **choque** ~ head-on collision

**frontera** [fron'tera] nf frontier; **fronterizo, a** adj frontier cpd; (contiguo) bordering

**frontón** [fron'ton] nm (DEPORTE: cancha) pelota court; (: juego) pelota

**frotar** [fro'tar] vt to rub; ~**se** vr:

~se las manos to rub one's hands

**fructífero, a** [fruk'tifero, a] adj
fruitful

**frugal** [fru'γal] adj frugal

**fruncir** [frun'θir] vt to pucker; (COS-
TURA) to pleat; (fig): ~ **el ceño** to knit
one's brow

**frustrar** [frus'trar] vt to frustrate

**fruta** ['fruta] nf fruit; **frutería** nf fruit
shop; **frutero, a** adj fruit cpd ♦ nm/f
fruiterer ♦ nm fruit bowl

**frutilla** [fru'tiʎa] (AM) nf strawberry

**fruto** ['fruto] nm fruit; (fig: resultado) result; (: utilidad) benefit; ~s
secos nuts; (pasas etc) dried fruit sg

**fue** vb ver **ser**; **ir**

**fuego** ['fweγo] nm (gen) fire; a ~
lento on a low flame o gas; ¿tienes
~? have you (got) a light?; ~s artificiales o de artificio fireworks

**fuente** ['fwente] nf (fountain; (manantial, fig) spring; (origen) source;
(plato) large dish

**fuera** etc ['fwera] vb ver **ser**, **ir** ♦
adv out(side); (en otra parte) away;
(excepto, salvo) except, save ♦ prep:
~ de outside; (fig) besides; ~ de sí
beside o.s.; **por** ~ (on) the outside

**fuerte** ['fwerte] adj strong; (golpe)
hard; (ruido) loud; (comida) rich;
(lluvia) heavy; (dolor) intense ♦ adv
strongly; hard; loud(ly)

**fuerza** etc ['fwerθa] vb ver **forzar** ♦
nf (fortaleza) strength; (TEC,
ELEC) power; (coacción) force;
(MIL: tb: ~s) forces pl; a ~ de by
dint of; **cobrar** ~s to recover one's
strength; **tener** ~ **para** to have the
strength to; **a la** ~ forcibly, by
force; **por** ~ of necessity; ~ **de voluntad** willpower

**fuga** ['fuγa] nf (huida) flight, escape;
(de gas etc) leak

**fugarse** [fu'γarse] vr to flee, escape

**fugaz** [fu'γaθ] adj fleeting

**fugitivo, a** [fuxi'tiβo, a] adj, nm/f fugitive

**fui** vb ver **ser**; **ir**

**fulano, a** [fu'lano, a] nm/f so-and-so,
what's-his-name/what's-her-name

**fulminante** [fulmi'nante] adj (fig:
mirada) fierce; (MED: enfermedad,
ataque) sudden; (fam: éxito, golpe)
sudden

**fumador, a** [fuma'ðor, a] nm/f
smoker

**fumar** [fu'mar] vt, vi to smoke; ~se
vr (disipar) to squander; ~ **en pipa**
to smoke a pipe

**función** [fun'θjon] nf function; (de
puesto) duties pl; (espectáculo)
show; **entrar en funciones** to take
up one's duties

**funcionar** [funθjo'nar] vi (gen) to
function; (máquina) to work; "**no
funciona**" "out of order"

**funcionario, a** [funθjo'narjo, a] nm/
f official; (público) civil servant

**funda** ['funda] nf (gen) cover; (de almohada) pillowcase

**fundación** [funda'θjon] nf foundation

**fundamental** [fundamen'tal] adj
fundamental, basic

**fundamentar** [fundamen'tar] vt (poner base) to lay the foundations of;
(establecer) to found; (fig) to base;
**fundamento** nm (base) foundation

**fundar** [fun'dar] vt to found; ~se vr:
~se en to be founded on

**fundición** [fundi'θjon] nf fusing; (fábrica) foundry

**fundir** [fun'dir] vt (gen) to fuse; (metal) to smelt, melt down; (nieve etc)
to melt; (COM) to merge; (estatua)
to cast; ~se vr (colores etc) to
merge, blend; (unirse) to fuse together; (ELEC: fusible, lámpara etc)
to fuse, blow; (nieve etc) to melt

**fúnebre** ['funeβre] adj funeral cpd,
funeral

**funeral** [fune'ral] nm funeral; **funeraria** nf undertaker's

**funesto, a** [fu'nesto, a] adj (día) ill-
fated; (decisión) fatal

**furgón** [fur'γon] nm wagon; **furgoneta** nf (AUTO, COM) (transit) van
(BRIT), pick-up (truck) (US)

**furia** ['furja] nf (ira) fury; (violencia)
violence; **furibundo, a** adj furious;
**furioso, a** adj (iracundo) furious;

(*violento*) violent; **furor** nm (*cólera*) rage

**furtivo, a** [fur'tiβo, a] adj furtive ♦ nm poacher

**fusible** [fu'siβle] nm fuse

**fusil** [fu'sil] nm rifle; **~ar** vt to shoot

**fusión** [fu'sjon] nf (*gen*) melting; (*unión*) fusion; (*COM*) merger

**fusta** ['fusta] nf (*látigo*) riding crop

**fútbol** ['futβol] nm football; **futbolista** nm footballer

**fútil** ['futil] adj trifling

**futuro, a** [fu'turo, a] adj, nm future

# G

**gabardina** [gaβar'ðina] nf raincoat, gabardine

**gabinete** [gaβi'nete] nm (*POL*) cabinet; (*estudio*) study; (*de abogados etc*) office

**gaceta** [ga'θeta] nf gazette

**gachas** ['gatʃas] nfpl porridge sg

**gafas** ['gafas] nfpl glasses; **~ de sol** sunglasses

**gafe** ['gafe] nm jinx

**gaita** ['gaita] nf bagpipes pl

**gajes** ['gaxes] nmpl: **los ~ del oficio** occupational hazards

**gajo** ['gaxo] nm (*de naranja*) segment

**gala** ['gala] nf (*traje de etiqueta*) full dress; (*fig: lo mejor*) cream, flower; **~s** nfpl (*ropa*) finery sg; **estar de ~** to be in one's best clothes; **hacer ~ de** to display, show off

**galante** [ga'lante] adj gallant; **galantear** vt (*hacer la corte a*) to court, woo; **galantería** nf (*caballerosidad*) gallantry; (*cumplido*) politeness; (*comentario*) compliment

**galápago** [ga'lapaxo] nm (*ZOOL*) turtle

**galaxia** [ga'laksja] nf galaxy

**galera** [ga'lera] nf (*nave*) galley; (*carro*) wagon; (*IMPRENTA*) galley

**galería** [gale'ria] nf (*gen*) gallery; (*balcón*) veranda(h); (*pasillo*) corridor

**Gales** ['gales] nm (tb: País de ~) Wales; **galés, esa** adj Welsh ♦ nm/f Welshman/woman ♦ nm (*LING*) Welsh

**galgo, a** ['galxo, a] nm/f greyhound

**galimatías** [galima'tias] nmpl (*lenguaje*) gibberish sg, nonsense sg

**galón** [ga'lon] nm (*MIL*) stripe; (*COSTURA*) braid; (*medida*) gallon

**galopar** [galo'par] vi to gallop

**gallardía** [gaʎar'ðia] nf (*galantería*) dash; (*valor*) bravery; (*elegancia*) elegance

**gallego, a** [ga'ʎexo, a] adj, nm/f Galician

**galleta** [ga'ʎeta] nf biscuit (*BRIT*), cookie (*US*)

**gallina** [ga'ʎina] nf hen ♦ nm/f (*fam: cobarde*) chicken; **gallinero** nm henhouse; (*TEATRO*) top gallery

**gallo** ['gaʎo] nm cock, rooster

**gama** ['gama] nf (*fig*) range

**gamba** ['gamba] nf (*gen*) prawn (*BRIT*), shrimp (*US*)

**gamberro, a** [gam'berro, a] nm/f hooligan, lout

**gamuza** [ga'muθa] nf chamois

**gana** ['gana] nf (*deseo*) desire, wish; (*apetito*) appetite; (*voluntad*) will; (*añoranza*) longing; **de buena ~** willingly; **de mala ~** reluctantly; **me da ~s de** I feel like, I want to; **no me da la ~** I don't feel like it; **tener ~s de** to feel like

**ganadería** [ganaðe'ria] nf (*ganado*) livestock; (*ganado vacuno*) cattle pl; (*cría, comercio*) cattle raising

**ganado** [ga'naðo] nm livestock; **~ lanar** sheep pl; **~ mayor** cattle pl; **~ porcino** pigs pl

**ganador, a** [gana'ðor, a] adj winning ♦ nm/f winner

**ganancia** [ga'nanθja] nf (*lo ganado*) gain; (*aumento*) increase; (*beneficio*) profit; **~s** nfpl (*ingresos*) earnings; (*beneficios*) profit sg, winnings

**ganar** [ga'nar] vt (*obtener*) to get, obtain; (*sacar ventaja*) to gain; (*salario etc*) to earn; (*DEPORTE, premio*) to win; (*derrotar a*) to beat;

*(alcanzar)* to reach ♦ *vi (DE-PORTE)* to win; **~se** *vr:* **~se la vida** to earn one's living

**ganchillo** [gan'tʃiʎo] *nm* crochet

**gancho** ['gantʃo] *nm (gen)* hook; *(colgador)* hanger

**gandul, a** [gan'dul, a] *adj, nm/f* good-for-nothing, layabout

**ganga** ['ganga] *nf (cosa buena y barata)* bargain; *(buena situación)* cushy job

**gangrena** [gan'grena] *nf* gangrene

**gansada** [gan'saða] *(fam)* nf stupid thing to do

**ganso, a** ['ganso, a] *nm/f (ZOOL)* goose; *(fam)* idiot

**ganzúa** [gan'θua] *nf* skeleton key

**garabatear** [garaβate'ar] *vi, vt (al escribir)* to scribble, scrawl

**garabato** [gara'βato] *nm (escritura)* scrawl, scribble

**garaje** [ga'raxe] *nm* garage

**garante** [ga'rante] *adj* responsible ♦ *nm/f* guarantor

**garantía** [garan'tia] *nf* guarantee

**garantizar** [garanti'θar] *vt (hacerse responsable de)* to vouch for; *(asegurar)* to guarantee

**garbanzo** [gar'βanθo] *nm* chickpea *(BRIT)*, garbanzo *(US)*

**garbo** ['garβo] *nm* grace, elegance

**garfio** ['garfjo] *nm* grappling iron

**garganta** [gar'ganta] *nf (ANAT)* throat; *(de botella)* neck; **gargantilla** *nf* necklace

**gárgaras** ['garγaras] *nfpl:* **hacer ~** to gargle

**garita** [ga'rita] *nf* cabin, hut; *(MIL)* sentry box

**garra** ['garra] *nf (de gato, TEC)* claw; *(de ave)* talon; *(fam)* hand, paw

**garrafa** [ga'rrafa] *nf* carafe, decanter

**garrapata** [garra'pata] *nf* tick

**garrote** [ga'rrote] *nm (palo)* stick; *(porra)* cudgel; *(suplicio)* garrotte

**garza** ['garθa] *nf* heron

**gas** [gas] *nm* gas

**gasa** ['gasa] *nf* gauze

**gaseosa** [gase'osa] *nf* lemonade

**gaseoso, a** [gase'oso, a] *adj* gassy, fizzy

**gasoil** [ga'soil] *nm* diesel (oil)

**gasóleo** [ga'soleo] *nm* = gasoil

**gasolina** [gaso'lina] *nf* petrol, gas(oline) *(US)*; **gasolinera** *nf* petrol *(BRIT)* o gas *(US)* station

**gastado, a** [gas'taðo, a] *adj (rendido)* spent; *(raído)* worn out; *(usado: frase etc)* trite

**gastar** [gas'tar] *vt (dinero, tiempo)* to spend; *(fuerzas)* to use up; *(desperdiciar)* to waste; *(llevar)* to wear; **~se** *vr* to wear out; *(estropearse)* to waste; **~ en** to spend on; **~ bromas** to crack jokes; **¿qué número gastas?** what size (shoe) do you take?

**gastronomía** [gastrono'mia] *nf* gastronomy

**gasto** ['gasto] *nm (desembolso)* expenditure, spending; *(consumo, uso)* use; **~s** *nmpl (desembolsos* expenses; *(cargos)* charges, costs

**gatear** [gate'ar] *vi (andar a gatas)* to go on all fours

**gatillo** [ga'tiʎo] *nm (de arma de fuego)* trigger; *(de dentista)* forceps

**gato, a** ['gato, a] *nm/f* cat ♦ *nm (TEC)* jack; **andar a gatas** to go on all fours

**gaviota** [ga'βjota] *nf* seagull

**gay** [ge] *adj inv, nm* gay, homosexual

**gazpacho** [gaθ'patʃo] *nm* gazpacho

**gel** [xel] *nm (tb:* **~ de baño/ducha**) gel

**gelatina** [xela'tina] *nf* jelly; *(polvos etc)* gelatine

**gema** ['xema] *nf* gem

**gemelo, a** [xe'melo, a] *adj, nm/f* twin; **~s** *nmpl (de camisa)* cufflinks; **~s de campo** field glasses, binoculars

**gemido** [xe'miðo] *nm (quejido)* moan, groan; *(aullido)* howl

**Géminis** ['xeminis] *nm* Gemini

**gemir** [xe'mir] *vi (quejarse)* to moan, groan; *(aullar)* to howl

**generación** [xenera'θjon] *nf* generation

**general** [xene'ral] *adj* general ♦ *nm*

general; **por lo** o **en ~** in general; **G~itat** *nf Catalan parliament;* **~izar** *vt* to generalize; **~izarse** *vr* to become generalized, spread; **~mente** *adv* generally

**generar** [xene'rar] *vt* to generate

**género** ['xenero] *nm (clase)* kind, sort; *(tipo)* type; *(BIO)* genus; *(LING)* gender; *(COM)* material; **~ humano** human race

**generosidad** [xenerosi'ðað] *nf* generosity; **generoso, a** *adj* generous

**genial** [xe'njal] *adj* inspired; *(idea)* brilliant; *(afable)* genial

**genio** ['xenjo] *nm (carácter)* nature, disposition; *(humor)* temper; *(facultad creadora)* genius; **de mal ~** bad-tempered

**genital** [xeni'tal] *adj* genital; **genitales** *nmpl* genitals

**gente** ['xente] *nf (personas)* people *pl; (raza)* race; *(nación)* nation; *(parientes)* relatives *pl*

**gentil** [xen'til] *adj (elegante)* graceful; *(encantador)* charming; **~eza** *nf* grace; charm; *(cortesía)* courtesy

**gentío** [xen'tio] *nm* crowd, throng

**genuino, a** [xe'nwino, a] *adj* genuine

**geografía** [xeoɣra'fia] *nf* geography

**geología** [xeolo'xia] *nf* geology

**geometría** [xeome'tria] *nf* geometry

**gerencia** [xe'renθja] *nf* management; **gerente** *nmf (supervisor)* manager; *(jefe)* director

**geriatría** [xerja'tria] *nf (MED)* geriatrics *sg*

**germen** ['xermen] *nm* germ

**germinar** [xermi'nar] *vi* to germinate

**gesticular** [xestiku'lar] *vi* to gesticulate; *(hacer muecas)* to grimace; **gesticulación** *nf* gesticulation; *(mueca)* grimace

**gestión** [xes'tjon] *nf* management; *(diligencia, acción)* negotiation; **gestionar** *vt (lograr)* to try to arrange; *(llevar)* to manage

**gesto** ['xesto] *nm (mueca)* grimace; *(ademán)* gesture

**Gibraltar** [xiβral'tar] *nm* Gibraltar;

**gibraltareño, a** *adj, nmf* Gibraltarian

**gigante** [xi'ɣante] *adj, nmf* giant; **gigantesco, a** *adj* gigantic

**gilipollas** [xili'poʎas] *(fam) adj inv* daft ♦ *nmf inv* wally

**gimnasia** [xim'nasja] *nf* gymnastics *pl;* **gimnasio** *nm* gymnasium; **gimnasta** *nmf* gymnast

**gimotear** [ximote'ar] *vi* to whine, whimper

**ginebra** [xi'neβra] *nf* gin

**ginecólogo, a** [xine'koloɣo, a] *nmf* gynaecologist

**gira** ['xira] *nf* tour, trip

**girar** [xi'rar] *vt (dar la vuelta)* to turn (around); *(: rápidamente)* to spin; *(COM: giro postal)* to draw; *(comerciar: letra de cambio)* to issue ♦ *vi* to turn (round); *(rápido)* to spin; *(COM)* to draw

**girasol** [xira'sol] *nm* sunflower

**giratorio, a** [xira'torjo, a] *adj (gen)* revolving; *(puente)* swing

**giro** ['xiro] *nm (movimiento)* turn, revolution; *(LING)* expression; *(COM)* draft; **~ bancario/postal** bank giro/postal order

**gis** [xis] *(AM) nm* chalk

**gitano, a** [xi'tano, a] *adj, nmf* gypsy

**glacial** [gla'θjal] *adj* icy, freezing

**glaciar** [gla'θjar] *nm* glacier

**glándula** ['glandula] *nf* gland

**global** [glo'βal] *adj* global

**globo** ['gloβo] *nm (esfera)* globe, sphere; *(aerostato, juguete)* balloon

**glóbulo** ['gloβulo] *nm* globule; *(ANAT)* corpuscle

**gloria** ['glorja] *nf* glory

**glorieta** [glo'rjeta] *nf (de jardín)* bower, arbour; *(plazoleta)* roundabout *(BRIT)*, traffic circle *(US)*

**glorificar** [glorifi'kar] *vt (enaltecer)* to glorify, praise

**glorioso, a** [glo'rjoso, a] *adj* glorious

**glosa** ['glosa] *nf* comment

**glosario** [glo'sarjo] *nm* glossary

**glotón, ona** [glo'ton, ona] *adj* gluttonous, greedy ♦ *nmf* glutton

**glucosa** [glu'kosa] *nf* glucose

**gobernador, a** [goβerna'ðor, a] *adj* governing ♦ *nm/f* governor; **gobernante** *adj* governing

**gobernar** [goβer'nar] *vt* (*dirigir*) to guide, direct; (*POL*) to rule, govern ♦ *vi* to govern; (*NAUT*) to steer

**gobierno** *etc* [go'βjerno] *vb ver* **gobernar** ♦ *nm* (*POL*) government; (*dirección*) guidance, direction; (*NAUT*) steering

**goce** *etc* ['goθe] *vb ver* **gozar** ♦ *nm* enjoyment

**gol** [gol] *nm* goal

**golf** [golf] *nm* golf

**golfa** ['golfa] (*fam*) *nf* (*mujer*) slut, whore

**golfo** ['golfo, a] *nm* (*GEO*) gulf ♦ *nm/f* (*fam: niño*) urchin; (*gamberro*) lout

**golondrina** [golon'drina] *nf* swallow

**golosina** [golo'sina] *nf* titbit; (*dulce*) sweet; **goloso, a** *adj* sweet-toothed

**golpe** ['golpe] *nm* blow; (*de puño*) punch; (*de mano*) smack; (*de remo*) stroke; (*fig: choque*) clash; **no dar** ~ to be bone idle; **de un** ~ with one blow; **de** ~ suddenly; ~ (**de estado**) coup d'état; **golpear** *vt, vi* to strike, knock; (*asestar*) to beat; (*de puño*) to punch; (*golpetear*) to tap

**goma** ['goma] *nf* (*caucho*) rubber; (*elástico*) elastic; (*una* ~) elastic band; ~ **espuma** foam rubber; ~ **de pegar** gum, glue

**gordo, a** ['gorðo, a] *adj* (*gen*) fat; (*persona*) plump; (*enorme*) enormous; **el (premio)** ~ (*en lotería*) first prize; **gordura** *nf* fat; (*corpulencia*) fatness, stoutness

**gorila** [go'rila] *nm* gorilla

**gorjear** [gorxe'ar] *vi* to twitter, chirp

**gorra** ['gorra] *nf* (*gen*) cap; (*de niño*) bonnet; (*militar*) bearskin; **entrar de** ~ (*fam*) to gatecrash; **ir de** ~ to sponge

**gorrión** [go'rrjon] *nm* sparrow

**gorro** ['gorro] *nm* (*gen*) cap; (*de niño, mujer*) bonnet

**gorrón, ona** [go'rron, ona] *nm/f* scrounger; **gorronear** (*fam*) *vi* to

scrounge

**gota** ['gota] *nf* (*gen*) drop; (*de sudor*) bead; (*MED*) gout; **gotear** *vi* to drip; (*lloviznar*) to drizzle; **gotera** *nf* leak

**gozar** [go'θar] *vi* to enjoy o.s.; ~ **de** (*disfrutar*) to enjoy; (*poseer*) to possess

**gozne** ['goθne] *nm* hinge

**gozo** ['goθo] *nm* (*alegría*) joy; (*placer*) pleasure

**gr.** *abr* (= *gramo, gramos*) g

**grabación** [graβa'θjon] *nf* recording

**grabado** [gra'βaðo] *nm* print, engraving

**grabadora** [graβa'ðora] *nf* tape-recorder

**grabar** [gra'βar] *vt* to engrave; (*discos, cintas*) to record

**gracia** ['graθja] *nf* (*encanto*) grace, gracefulness; (*humor*) humour, wit; **¡(muchas) ~s!** thanks (very much)!; ~**s a** thanks to; **tener** ~ (*chiste etc*) to be funny; **no me hace** ~ I am not keen; **gracioso, a** *adj* (*divertido*) funny, amusing; (*cómico*) comical ♦ *nm/f* (*TEATRO*) comic character

**grada** ['graða] *nf* (*de escalera*) step; (*de anfiteatro*) tier, row; ~**s** *nfpl* (*DEPORTE: de estadio*) terraces

**gradación** [graða'θjon] *nf* gradation

**gradería** [graðe'ria] *nf* (*gradas*) (flight of) steps *pl*; (*de anfiteatro*) tiers *pl*, rows *pl*; (*DEPORTE: de estadio*) terraces *pl*; ~ **cubierta** covered stand

**grado** ['graðo] *nm* degree; (*de aceite, vino*) grade; (*grada*) step; (*MIL*) rank; **de buen** ~ willingly

**graduación** [graðwa'θjon] *nf* (*del alcohol*) proof, strength; (*ESCOL*) graduation; (*MIL*) rank

**gradual** [gra'ðwal] *adj* gradual

**graduar** [gra'ðwar] *vt* (*gen*) to graduate; (*MIL*) to commission; ~**se** *vr* to graduate; ~**se la vista** to have one's eyes tested

**gráfica** ['grafika] *nf* graph

**gráfico, a** ['grafiko, a] *adj* graphic

*nm* diagram; ~**s** *nmpl* (*INFORM*) graphics

**grajo** ['graxo] *nm* rook

**Gral** *abr* (= *General*) Gen.

**gramática** [gra'matika] *nf* grammar

**gramo** ['gramo] *nm* gramme (*BRIT*), gram (*US*)

**gran** [gran] *adj ver* **grande**

**grana** ['grana] *nf* (*BOT*) seedling; (*color, tela*) scarlet

**granada** [gra'naða] *nf* pomegranate; (*MIL*) grenade

**granate** [gra'nate] *adj* (*color*) deep red

**Gran Bretaña** [-bre'taŋa] *nf* Great Britain

**grande** ['grande] (*antes de nmsg:* **gran**) *adj* (*de tamaño*) big, large; (*alto*) tall; (*distinguido*) great; (*impresionante*) grand ♦ *nm* grandee; **grandeza** *nf* greatness

**grandioso, a** [gran'djoso, a] *adj* magnificent, grand

**granel** [gra'nel]: **a** ~ *adv* (*COM*) in bulk

**granero** [gra'nero] *nm* granary, barn

**granito** [gra'nito] *nm* (*AGR*) small grain; (*roca*) granite

**granizado** [grani'θaðo] *nm* iced drink

**granizar** [grani'θar] *vi* to hail; **granizo** *nm* hail

**granja** ['granxa] *nf* (*gen*) farm; **granjear** *vt* to win, gain; **granjearse** *vr* to win, gain; **granjero, a** *nm/f* farmer

**grano** ['grano] *nm* grain; (*semilla*) seed; (*baya*) berry; (*MED*) pimple, spot; ~**s** *nmpl* (*cereales*) cereals

**granuja** [gra'nuxa] *nm/f* rogue; (*golfillo*) urchin

**grapa** ['grapa] *nf* staple; (*TEC*) clamp; **grapadora** *nf* stapler

**grasa** ['grasa] *nf* (*gen*) grease; (*de cocina*) fat, lard; (*sebo*) suet; (*mugre*) filth; **grasiento, a** *adj* greasy; (*de aceite*) oily; **graso, a** *adj* (*leche, queso, carne*) fatty; (*pelo, piel*) greasy

**gratificación** [gratifika'θjon] *nf* (*propina*) tip; (*bono*) bonus; (*recompen-*

*sa*) reward

**gratificar** [gratifi'kar] *vt* to tip; to reward

**gratis** ['gratis] *adv* free

**gratitud** [grati'tuð] *nf* gratitude

**grato, a** ['grato, a] *adj* (*agradable*) pleasant, agreeable; (*bienvenido*) welcome

**gratuito, a** [gra'twito, a] *adj* (*gratis*) free; (*sin razón*) gratuitous

**gravamen** [gra'Bamen] *nm* (*carga*) burden; (*impuesto*) tax

**gravar** [gra'Bar] *vt* to burden; (*COM*) to tax

**grave** ['graBe] *adj* heavy; (*serio*) grave, serious; ~**dad** *nf* gravity

**gravilla** [gra'Biʎa] *nf* gravel

**gravitar** [graBi'tar] *vi* to gravitate; ~ **sobre** to rest on

**graznar** [graθ'nar] *vi* (*cuervo*) to squawk; (*pato*) to quack; (*hablar ronco*) to croak

**Grecia** ['greθja] *nf* Greece

**gremio** ['gremjo] *nm* (*asociación*) trade, industry

**greña** ['greŋa] *nf* (*cabellos*) shock of hair; (*maraña*) tangle

**gresca** ['greska] *nf* uproar

**griego, a** ['grjeʝo, a] *adj, nm/f* Greek

**grieta** ['grjeta] *nf* crack

**grifo** ['grifo] *nm* tap; (*AM: AUTO*) petrol (*BRIT*) o gas (*US*) station

**grilletes** [gri'ʎetes] *nmpl* fetters

**grillo** ['griʎo] *nm* (*ZOOL*) cricket; (*BOT*) shoot

**gripe** ['gripe] *nf* flu, influenza

**gris** [gris] *adj* (*color*) grey

**gritar** [gri'tar] *vt, vi* to shout, yell; **grito** *nm* shout, yell; (*de horror*) scream

**grosella** [gro'seʎa] *nf* (*red*)currant; ~ **negra** blackcurrant

**grosería** [grose'ria] *nf* (*actitud*) rudeness; (*comentario*) vulgar comment; **grosero, a** *adj* (*poco cortés*) rude, bad-mannered; (*ordinario*) vulgar, crude

**grosor** [gro'sor] *nm* thickness

**grotesco, a** [gro'tesko, a] *adj* grotesque

**grúa** ['grua] nf (TEC) crane; (de petróleo) derrick

**grueso, a** ['grweso, a] adj thick; (persona) stout ♦ nm bulk; el ~ de the bulk of

**grulla** ['gruʎa] nf crane

**grumo** ['grumo] nm clot, lump

**gruñido** [gru'ɲiðo] nm grunt; (fig) grumble

**gruñir** [gru'ɲir] vi (animal) to growl; (fam) to grumble

**grupa** ['grupa] nf (ZOOL) rump

**grupo** ['grupo] nm group; (TEC) unit, set

**gruta** ['gruta] nf grotto

**guadaña** [gwa'ðaɲa] nf scythe

**guagua** ['gwa'xwa] (AM) nf (niño) baby; (bus) bus

**guante** ['gwante] nm glove

**guapo, a** ['gwapo, a] adj good-looking, attractive; (elegante) smart ♦ nm (fam) tough guy, stud

**guarda** ['gwarða] nm/f (persona) guard, keeper ♦ nm (acto) guarding; (custodia) custody; ~**bosques** nm inv gamekeeper; ~**costas** nm inv coastguard vessel; ~**espaldas** nm/f inv bodyguard; ~**meta** nm/f goalkeeper; **guardar** vt (gen) to keep; (vigilar) to guard, watch over; (dinero: ahorrar) to save; **guardarse** vr (preservarse) to protect o.s.; (evitar) to avoid; **guardar cama** to stay in bed; ~**ropa** nm (armario) wardrobe; (en establecimiento público) cloakroom

**guardería** [gwarðe'ria] nf nursery

**guardia** ['gwarðja] nf (MIL) guard; (cuidado) care, custody ♦ nm/f guard; (policía) policeman/woman; **estar de** ~ to be on guard; **montar** ~ to mount guard; **G~ Civil** Civil Guard; **G~ Nacional** National Guard

**guardián, ana** [gwar'ðjan, ana] nm/ f (gen) guardian, keeper

**guarecer** [gware'θer] vt (proteger) to protect; (abrigar) to shelter; ~**se** vr to take refuge

**guarida** [gwa'riða] nf (de animal) den, lair; (refugio) refuge

**guarnecer** [gwarne'θer] vt (equipar) to provide; (adornar) to adorn; (TEC) to reinforce; **guarnición** nf (de vestimenta) trimming; (de piedra) mount; (CULIN) garnish; (arneses) harness; (MIL) garrison

**guarro, a** ['gwarro, a] nm/f pig

**guasa** ['gwasa] nf joke; **guasón, ona** adj witty; (bromista) joking ♦ nm/f wit; joker

**Guatemala** [gwate'mala] nf Guatemala

**gubernativo, a** [guβerna'tiβo, a] adj governmental

**guerra** ['gerra] nf war; (pelea) struggle; ~ **civil** civil war; ~ **fría** cold war; **dar** ~ to annoy; **guerrear** vi to wage war; **guerrero, a** adj fighting; (carácter) warlike ♦ nm/f warrior

**guerrilla** [ge'rriʎa] nf guerrilla warfare; (tropas) guerrilla band o group

**guía** etc ['gia] vb ver **guiar** ♦ nm/f (persona) guide ♦ nf (libro) guidebook; **G~ Girl Guide; ~ de ferrocarriles** railway timetable; ~ **telefónica** telephone directory

**guiar** [gi'ar] vt to guide, direct; (AUTO) to steer; ~**se** vr: ~**se por** to be guided by

**guijarro** [gi'xarro] nm pebble

**guillotina** [giʎo'tina] nf guillotine

**guinda** ['ginda] nf morello cherry

**guindilla** [gin'diʎa] nf chilli pepper

**guiñapo** [gi'ɲapo] nm (harapo) rag; (persona) reprobate, rogue

**guiñar** [gi'ɲar] vt to wink

**guión** [gi'on] nm (LING) hyphen, dash; (CINE) script; **guionista** nm/f scriptwriter

**guiri** ['giri] (pey) nm/f foreigner

**guirnalda** [gir'nalda] nf garland

**guisado** [gi'saðo] nm stew

**guisante** [gi'sante] nm pea

**guisar** [gi'sar] vt, vi to cook; **guiso** nm cooked dish

**guitarra** [gi'tarra] nf guitar

**gula** ['gula] nf gluttony, greed

**gusano** [gu'sano] nm maggot; (lombriz) earthworm

**gustar** [gus'tar] vt to taste, sample ♦ vi to please, be pleasing; ~ **de algo** to like o enjoy sth; **me gustan las uvas** I like grapes; **le gusta nadar** she likes o enjoys swimming

**gusto** ['gusto] nm (sentido, sabor) taste; (placer) pleasure; **tiene ~ a menta** it tastes of mint; **tener buen ~** to have good taste; **sentirse a ~** to feel at ease; **mucho ~ (en conocerle)** pleased to meet you; **el ~ es mío** the pleasure is mine; **con ~** willingly, gladly; ~**so, a** adj (sabroso) tasty; (agradable) pleasant

# H

**ha** vb ver **haber**

**haba** ['aßa] nf bean

**Habana** [a'Bana] nf: **la ~** Havana

**habano** [a'Bano] nm Havana cigar

**habéis** vb ver **haber**

PALABRA CLAVE

**haber** [a'Ber] vb aux 1 (tiempos compuestos) to have; **había comido** I have/had eaten; **antes/después de ~lo visto** before seeing/after seeing o having seen it
2: **¡~lo dicho antes!** you should have said so before!
3: ~ **de: he de hacerlo** I have to do it; **ha de llegar mañana** it should arrive tomorrow

♦ vb impers 1 (existencia: sg) there is; (: pl) there are; **hay un hermano/dos hermanos** there is one brother/there are two brothers; **¿cuánto hay de aquí a Sucre?** how far is it from here to Sucre?
2 (obligación): **hay que hacer algo** something must be done; **hay que apuntarlo para acordarse** you have to write it down to remember
3: **¡hay que ver!** well I never!
4: **¡no hay de o por (AM) qué!** don't mention it!, not at all!
5: **¿qué hay?** (¿qué pasa?) what's

up?, what's the matter?; (¿qué tal?) how's it going?
♦ ~**se** vr: **habérselas con uno** to have it out with sb
♦ vt: **he aquí unas sugerencias** here are some suggestions; **no hay cintas blancas pero sí las hay rojas** there aren't any white ribbons but there are some red ones
♦ nm (en cuenta) credit side; ~**es** nmpl assets; **¿cuánto tengo en el ~?** how much do I have in my account?; **tiene varias novelas en su ~** he has several novels to his credit

**habichuela** [aßi'tʃwela] nf kidney bean

**hábil** ['aßil] adj (listo) clever, smart; (capaz) fit, capable; (experto) expert; **día ~** working day; **habilidad** nf (gen) skill, ability; (inteligencia) cleverness

**habilitar** [aßili'tar] vt (capacitar) to enable; (dar instrumentos) to equip; (financiar) to finance

**hábilmente** [aßil'mente] adv skilfully, expertly

**habitación** [aßita'θjon] nf (cuarto) room; (casa) dwelling, abode; (BIO: morada) habitat; ~ **sencilla** o individual single room; ~ **doble** o **de matrimonio** double room

**habitante** [aßi'tante] nm/f inhabitant

**habitar** [aßi'tar] vt (residir en) to inhabit; (ocupar) to occupy ♦ vi to live

**hábito** ['aßito] nm habit

**habitual** [aßi'twal] adj usual

**habituar** [aßi'twar] vt to accustom; ~**se** vr: ~**se a** to get used to

**habla** ['aßla] nf (capacidad de hablar) speech; (idioma) language; (dialecto) dialect; **perder el ~** to become speechless; **de ~ francesa** French-speaking; **estar al ~** to be in contact; (TEL) to be on the line; **¡González al ~!** (TEL) González speaking!

**hablador, a** [aßla'ðor, a] adj talkative ♦ nm/f chatterbox

**habladuría** [aßlaðu'ria] nf rumour;

~s *nfpl* gossip *sg*

**hablante** [a'βlante] *adj* speaking ♦ *nm/f* speaker

**hablar** [a'βlar] *vt* to speak, talk ♦ *vi* to speak; ~se *vr* to speak to each other; ~ con to speak to; ~ de to speak of *o* about; "se habla inglés" "English spoken here"; ¡ni ~! it's out of the question!

**habré** *etc vb ver* **haber**

**hacendado** [asen'ðaðo] (*AM*) *nm* large landowner

**hacendoso, a** [aθen'doso, a] *adj* industrious

---

*PALABRA CLAVE*

**hacer** [a'θer] *vt* 1 (*fabricar, producir*) to make; (*construir*) to build; ~ una película/un ruido to make a film/noise; el guisado lo hice yo I made *o* cooked the stew

2 (*ejecutar: trabajo etc*) to do; ~ la colada to do the washing; ~ la comida to do the cooking; ¿qué haces? what are you doing?; ~ el malo *o* el papel del malo (*TEATRO*) to play the villain

3 (*estudios, algunos deportes*) to do; ~ español/económicas to do *o* study Spanish/economics; ~ yoga/gimnasia to do yoga/go to gym

4 (*transformar, incidir en*): esto lo hará más difícil this will make it more difficult; salir te hará sentir mejor going out will make you feel better

5 (*cálculo*): 2 y 2 hacen 4 2 and 2 make 4; éste hace 100 this one makes 100

6 (+ *sub*): esto hará que ganemos this will make us win; harás que no quiera venir you'll stop him wanting to come

7 (*como sustituto de vb*) to do; él bebió y yo hice lo mismo he drank and I did likewise

8: no hace más que criticar all he does is criticize

♦ *vb semi-aux*: ~ + *infin* 1 (*directo*): les hice venir I made *o* had them

come; ~ trabajar a los demás to get others to work

2 (*por intermedio de otros*): ~ reparar algo to get sth repaired

♦ *vi* 1: haz como que no lo sabes act as if you don't know

2 (*ser apropiado*): si os hace if it's alright with you

3: ~ de: ~ de madre para uno to be like a mother to sb; (*TEATRO*): ~ de Otelo to play Othello

♦ *vb impers* 1: hace calor/frío it's hot/cold; *ver tb* bueno; sol; tiempo

2 (*tiempo*): hace 3 años 3 years ago; hace un mes que voy/no voy I've been going/I haven't been for a month

3: ¿cómo has hecho para llegar tan rápido? how did you manage to get here so quickly?

♦ ~se *vr* 1 (*volverse*) to become; se hicieron amigos they became friends

2 (*acostumbrarse*): ~se a to get used to

3: se hace con huevos y leche it's made out of eggs and milk; eso no se hace that's not done

4 (*obtener*): ~se de *o* con algo to get hold of sth

5 (*fingirse*): ~se el sueco to turn a deaf ear

---

**hacia** ['aθja] *prep* (*en dirección de*) towards; (*cerca de*) near; (*actitud*) towards; ~ arriba/abajo up(wards)/down(wards); ~ mediodía about noon

**hacienda** [a'θjenda] *nf* (*propiedad*) property; (*finca*) farm; (*AM*) ranch; ~ pública public finance; (*Ministerio de*) H~ Exchequer (*BRIT*), Treasury Department (*US*)

**hacha** ['atʃa] *nf* axe; (*antorcha*) torch

**hachís** [a'tʃis] *nm* hashish

**hada** ['aða] *nf* fairy

**hago** *etc vb ver* **hacer**

**Haití** [ai'ti] *nm* Haiti

**halagar** [ala'ɣar] *vt* (*lisonjear*) to

flatter

**halago** [a'lavo] *nm* (*adulación*) flattery; **halagüeño, a** *adj* flattering

**halcón** [al'kon] *nm* falcon, hawk

**halterofilia** [altero'filja] *nf* weight-lifting

**hallar** [a'ʎar] *vt* (*gen*) to find; (*descubrir*) to discover; (*toparse con*) to run into; ~*se vr* to be (situated); **hallazgo** *nm* discovery; (*cosa*) find

**hamaca** [a'maka] *nf* hammock

**hambre** ['ambre] *nf* hunger; (*carencia*) famine; (*fig*) longing; **tener** ~ to be hungry; **hambriento, a** *adj* hungry, starving

**hamburguesa** [ambur'vesa] *nf* hamburger

**han** *vb ver* **haber**

**haragán, ana** [ara'van, ana] *adj, nm/f* good-for-nothing

**harapiento, a** [ara'pjento, a] *adj* tattered, in rags

**harapos** [a'rapos] *nmpl* rags

**haré** *etc vb ver* **hacer**

**harina** [a'rina] *nf* flour

**hartar** [ar'tar] *vt* to satiate, glut; (*fig*) to tire, sicken; ~*se vr* (*de comida*) to fill o.s., gorge o.s.; (*cansarse*) to get fed up (de with); **hartazgo** *nm* surfeit, glut; **harto, a** *adj* (*lleno*) full; (*cansado*) fed up ♦ *adv* (*bastante*) enough; (*muy*) very; **estar harto de** to be fed up with

**has** *vb ver* **haber**

**hasta** ['asta] *adv conj* ♦ *prep* (*alcanzando a*) as far as; up to; down to; (*de tiempo: a tal hora*) till, until; (*antes de*) before ♦ *conj*: ~ **que** until; ~ **luego/el sábado** see you soon/ on Saturday

**hastiar** [as'tjar] *vt* (*gen*) to weary; (*aburrir*) to bore; ~*se vr*: ~*se de* to get fed up with; **hastio** *nm* weariness; boredom

**hatillo** [a'tiʎo] *nm* belongings *pl*, kit; (*montón*) bundle, heap

**hay** *vb ver* **haber**

**Haya** ['aja] *nf*: **la** ~ The Hague

**haya** *etc vb ver* **haber** ♦ *nf* beech tree

**haz** [aθ] *vb ver* **hacer** ♦ *nm* bundle, bunch; (*rayo: de luz*) beam

**hazaña** [a'θaɲa] *nf* feat, exploit

**hazmerreír** [aθmerre'ir] *nm inv* laughing stock

**he** *vb ver* **haber**

**hebilla** [e'βiʎa] *nf* buckle, clasp

**hebra** [e'βra] *nf* thread; (*BOT: fibra*) fibre, grain

**hebreo, a** [e'βreo, a] *adj, nm/f* Hebrew ♦ *nm* (*LING*) Hebrew

**hectárea** [ek'tarea] *nf* hectare

**hechizar** [etʃi'θar] *vt* to cast a spell on, bewitch

**hechizo** [e'tʃiθo] *nm* witchcraft, magic; (*acto de magia*) spell, charm

**hecho, a** ['etʃo, a] *pp de* **hacer** ♦ *adj* complete; (*maduro*) mature; (*COSTURA*) ready-to-wear ♦ *nm* deed, act; (*dato*) fact; (*cuestión*) matter; (*suceso*) event ♦ *excl* agreed!, done!; **¡bien** ~! well done!; **de** ~ in fact, as a matter of fact

**hechura** [e'tʃura] *nf* making, creation; (*producto*) product; (*forma*) form, shape; (*de persona*) build; (*TEC*) craftsmanship

**heder** [e'ðer] *vi* to stink, smell; (*fig*) to be unbearable

**hediondo, a** [e'ðjondo, a] *adj* stinking

**hedor** [e'ðor] *nm* stench

**helada** [e'laða] *nf* frost

**heladera** [ela'ðera] (*AM*) *nf* (*refrigerador*) refrigerator

**helado, a** [e'laðo, a] *adj* frozen; (*glacial*) icy; (*fig*) chilly, cold ♦ *nm* ice cream

**helar** [e'lar] *vt* to freeze, ice (up); (*dejar atónito*) to amaze; (*desalentar*) to discourage ♦ *vi* to freeze; ~*se vr* to freeze

**helecho** [e'letʃo] *nm* fern

**hélice** ['eliθe] *nf* spiral; (*TEC*) propeller

**helicóptero** [eli'koptero] *nm* helicopter

**hembra** ['embra] *nf* (*BOT, ZOOL*) female; (*mujer*) woman; (*TEC*) nut

**hemorragia** [emo'rraxja] nf haemorrhage

**hemorroides** [emo'rroiðes] nfpl haemorrhoids, piles

**hemos** vb ver **haber**

**hendidura** [endi'ðura] nf crack, split; (GEO) fissure

**heno** ['eno] nm hay

**herbicida** [erßi'θiða] nm weedkiller

**heredad** [ere'ðað] nf landed property; (granja) farm

**heredar** [ere'ðar] vt to inherit; **heredero, a** nm/f heir(ess)

**hereje** [e'rexe] nm/f heretic

**herencia** [e'renθja] nf inheritance

**herida** [e'riða] nf wound, injury; ver tb **herido**

**herido, a** [e'riðo, a] adj injured, wounded ♦ nm/f casualty

**herir** [e'rir] vt to wound, injure; (fig) to offend

**hermanastro, a** [erma'nastro, a] nm/f stepbrother/sister

**hermandad** [erman'dað] nf brotherhood

**hermano, a** [er'mano, a] nm/f brother/sister; ~ **gemelo** twin brother; ~ **político** brother-in-law; **hermana política** sister-in-law

**hermético, a** [er'metiko, a] adj hermetic; (fig) watertight

**hermoso, a** [er'moso, a] adj beautiful, lovely; (estupendo) splendid; (guapo) handsome; **hermosura** nf beauty

**hernia** ['ernja] nf hernia

**héroe** ['eroe] nm hero

**heroína** [ero'ina] nf (mujer) heroine; (droga) heroin

**heroísmo** [ero'ismo] nm heroism

**herradura** [erra'ðura] nf horseshoe

**herramienta** [erra'mjenta] nf tool

**herrero** [e'rrero] nm blacksmith

**herrumbre** [e'rrumbre] nf rust

**hervidero** [erßi'ðero] nm (fig) swarm; (POL etc) hotbed

**hervir** [er'ßir] vi to boil; (burbujear) to bubble; (fig): ~ **de** to teem with; ~ **a fuego lento** to simmer; **hervor** nm boiling; (fig) ardour, fervour

**heterosexual** [eterosek'swal] adj

**hice** etc vb ver **hacer**

**hidratante** [iðra'tante] adj: **crema** ~ moisturizing cream, moisturizer; **hidratar** vt (piel) to moisturize; **hidrato** nm: **hidratos de carbono** carbohydrates

**hidráulica** [i'ðraulika] nf hydraulics sg

**hidráulico, a** [i'ðrauliko, a] adj hydraulic

**hidro...** [iðro] prefijo hydro..., water...; ~**eléctrico, a** adj hydroelectric; ~**fobia** nf hydrophobia, rabies; **hidrógeno** nm hydrogen

**hiedra** [i'eðra] nf ivy

**hiel** [jel] nf gall, bile; (fig) bitterness

**hiela** etc vb ver **helar**

**hielo** ['jelo] nm (gen) ice; (escarcha) frost; (fig) coldness, reserve

**hiena** ['jena] nf hyena

**hierba** [i'erßa] nf (pasto) grass; (CULIN, MED: planta) herb; **mala** ~ weed; (fig) evil influence; ~**buena** nf mint

**hierro** ['jerro] nm (metal) iron; (objeto) iron object

**hígado** ['iɣaðo] nm liver

**higiene** [i'xjene] nf hygiene; **higiénico, a** adj hygienic

**higo** ['iɣo] nm fig; **higuera** nf fig tree

**hijastro, a** [i'xastro, a] nm/f stepson/daughter

**hijo, a** ['ixo, a] nm/f son/daughter, child; ~s nmpl children, sons and daughters; ~ **de papá/mamá** daddy's/mummy's boy; ~ **de puta** (fam!) bastard (!), son of a bitch (!)

**hilar** [i'lar] vt to spin; ~ **fino** to split hairs

**hilera** [i'lera] nf row, file

**hilo** ['ilo] nm thread; (BOT) fibre; (metal) wire; (de agua) trickle, thin stream; (de luz) beam, ray

**hilvanar** [ilßa'nar] vt (COSTURA) to tack (BRIT), baste (US); (fig) to do hurriedly

**himno** ['imno] nm hymn; ~ **nacional** national anthem

**hincapié** [inka'pje] *nm*: **hacer ~ en** to emphasize

**hincar** [in'kar] *vt* to drive (in), thrust (in); **~se** *vr*: **~se de rodillas** to kneel down

**hincha** ['intʃa] (*fam*) *nm/f* fan

**hinchado, a** [in'tʃaðo, a] *adj* (*gen*) swollen; (*persona*) pompous

**hinchar** [in'tʃar] *vt* (*gen*) to swell; (*inflar*) to blow up, inflate; (*fig*) to exaggerate; **~se** *vr* (*inflarse*) to swell up; (*fam*: *llenarse*) to stuff o.s.; **hinchazón** *nf* (*MED*) swelling; (*altivez*) arrogance

**hinojo** [i'noxo] *nm* fennel

**hipermercado** [ipermer'kaðo] *nm* hypermarket, superstore

**hípico, a** ['ipiko, a] *adj* horse *cpd*

**hipnotismo** [ipno'tismo] *nm* hypnotism; **hipnotizar** *vt* to hypnotize

**hipo** ['ipo] *nm* hiccups *pl*

**hipocresía** [ipokre'sia] *nf* hypocrisy; **hipócrita** *adj* hypocritical ♦ *nm/f* hypocrite

**hipódromo** [i'poðromo] *nm* racetrack

**hipopótamo** [ipo'potamo] *nm* hippopotamus

**hipoteca** [ipo'teka] *nf* mortgage

**hipótesis** [i'potesis] *nf inv* hypothesis

**hiriente** [i'rjente] *adj* offensive, wounding

**hispánico, a** [is'paniko, a] *adj* Hispanic

**hispano, a** [is'pano, a] *adj* Hispanic, Spanish, Hispano- ♦ *nm/f* Spaniard; **H~américa** *nf* Latin America; **~americano, a** *adj*, *nm/f* Latin American

**histeria** [is'terja] *nf* hysteria

**historia** [is'torja] *nf* history; (*cuento*) story, tale; (*chismes*) gossip *sg*; **dejarse de ~s** to come to the point; **pasar a la ~** to go down in history; **~dor, a** *nm/f* historian; **histórial** *nm* (*profesional*) curriculum vitae, C.V.; (*MED*) case history; **histórico, a** *adj* historical; (*fig*) historic

**historieta** [isto'rjeta] *nf* tale, anecdote; (*dibujos*) comic strip

**hito** ['ito] *nm* (*fig*) landmark; (*objetivo*) goal, target

**hizo** *vb ver* **hacer**

**Hnos** *abr* (= *Hermanos*) Bros.

**hocico** [o'θiko] *nm* snout; (*fig*) grimace

**hockey** ['xoki] *nm* hockey; **~ sobre hielo** ice hockey

**hogar** [o'xar] *nm* fireplace, hearth; (*casa*) home; (*vida familiar*) home life; **~eño, a** *adj* home *cpd*; (*persona*) home-loving

**hoguera** [o'xera] *nf* (*gen*) bonfire

**hoja** ['oxa] *nf* (*gen*) leaf; (*de flor*) petal; (*de papel*) sheet; (*página*) page; **~ de afeitar** razor blade

**hojalata** [oxa'lata] *nf* tin(plate)

**hojaldre** [o'xaldre] *nm* (*CULIN*) puff pastry

**hojear** [oxe'ar] *vt* to leaf through, turn the pages of

**hola** ['ola] *excl* hello!

**Holanda** [o'landa] *nf* Holland; **holandés, esa** *adj* Dutch ♦ *nm/f* Dutchman/woman ♦ *nm* (*LING*) Dutch

**holgado, a** [ol'xaðo, a] *adj* loose, baggy; (*rico*) well-to-do

**holgar** [ol'xar] *vi* (*descansar*) to rest; (*sobrar*) to be superfluous; **huelga decir que** it goes without saying that

**holgazán, ana** [olxa'θan, ana] *adj* idle, lazy ♦ *nm/f* loafer

**holgura** [ol'xura] *nf* looseness, bagginess; (*TEC*) play, free movement; (*vida*) comfortable living, luxury

**hollín** [o'ʎin] *nm* soot

**hombre** ['ombre] *nm* (*gen*) man; (*raza humana*): **el ~** man(kind); (*uno*) man ♦ *excl*: **¡sí ~!** (*claro*) of course!; (*para énfasis*) man, old boy; **~ de negocios** businessman; **~ de pro** honest man; **~-rana** frogman

**hombrera** [om'brera] *nf* shoulder strap

**hombro** ['ombro] *nm* shoulder

**hombruno, a** [om'bruno, a] *adj* mannish

**homenaje** [ome'naxe] *nm* (*gen*)

homage; (*tributo*) tribute

**homicida** [omiˈθiða] adj homicidal ♦ *nm/f* murderer; **homicidio** *nm* murder, homicide

**homologar** [omoloˈðar] vt (COM: *productos, tamaños*) to standardize; **homólogo, a** *nm/f*: su *etc* homólogo his *etc* counterpart o opposite number

**homosexual** [omosekˈswal] adj, *nm/f* homosexual

**hondo, a** [ˈondo, a] adj deep; lo ~ the depth(s) (pl), the bottom; ~**nada** *nf* hollow, depression; (*cañón*) ravine; (GEO) lowland

**Honduras** [onˈduras] *nf* Honduras

**hondureño, a** [onduˈreɲo, a] adj, *nm/f* Honduran

**honestidad** [onestiˈðað] *nf* purity, chastity; (*decencia*) decency; **honesto, a** adj chaste; decent, honest; (*justo*) just

**hongo** [ˈongo] *nm* (BOT: *gen*) fungus; (: *comestible*) mushroom; (: *venenoso*) toadstool

**honor** [oˈnor] *nm* (*gen*) honour; (*gloria*) glory; **en ~ a la verdad** to be fair; ~**able** adj honourable

**honorario, a** [onoˈrarjo, a] adj honorary; ~**s** *nmpl* fees

**honra** [ˈonra] *nf* (*gen*) honour; (*renombre*) good name; ~**dez** *nf* honesty; (*de persona*) integrity; ~**do, a** adj honest, upright

**honrar** [onˈrar] vt to honour; ~**se** vr: ~**se con algo/de hacer algo** to be honoured by sth/to do sth

**honroso, a** [onˈroso, a] adj (*honrado*) honourable; (*respetado*) respectable

**hora** [ˈora] *nf* (*una* ~) hour; (*tiempo*) time; ¿**qué ~ es?** what time is it?; ¿**a qué ~?** at what time?; **media ~** half an hour; **a la ~ de recreo** at playtime; **a primera ~** first thing (in the morning); **a última ~** at the last moment; **a altas ~s** in the small hours; ¡**a buena ~!** about time, too!; **dar la ~** to strike the hour; ~**s de oficina/de trabajo** office/working hours; ~**s de visita** visiting times; ~**s extras** o **extraordinarias** overtime *sg*; ~**s punta** rush hours

**horadar** [oraˈðar] vt to drill, bore

**horario, a** [oˈrarjo, a] adj hourly, hour *cpd* ♦ *nm* timetable; ~ **comercial** business hours *pl*

**horca** [ˈorka] *nf* gallows *sg*

**horcajadas** [orkaˈxaðas]: **a ~** adv astride

**horchata** [orˈtʃata] *nf* cold drink made from tiger nuts and water, tiger nut milk

**horizontal** [oriθonˈtal] adj horizontal

**horizonte** [oriˈθonte] *nm* horizon

**horma** [ˈorma] *nf* mould

**hormiga** [orˈmixa] *nf* ant; ~**s** (MED) pins and needles

**hormigón** [ormiˈɣon] *nm* concrete; ~ **armado/pretensado** reinforced/prestressed concrete

**hormigueo** [ormiˈɣeo] *nm* (*comezón*) itch; (*fig*) uneasiness

**hormona** [orˈmona] *nf* hormone

**hornada** [orˈnaða] *nf* batch (*of loaves etc*)

**hornillo** [orˈniʎo] *nm* (*cocina*) portable stove

**horno** [ˈorno] *nm* (CULIN) oven; (TEC) furnace; **alto ~** blast furnace

**horóscopo** [oˈroskopo] *nm* horoscope

**horquilla** [orˈkiʎa] *nf* hairpin; (AGR) pitchfork

**horrendo, a** [oˈrrendo, a] adj horrendous, frightful

**horrible** [oˈrriβle] adj horrible, dreadful

**horripilante** [orripiˈlante] adj hairraising, horrifying

**horror** [oˈrror] *nm* horror, dread; (*atrocidad*) atrocity; ¡**qué ~!** (*fam*) how awful!; ~**izar** vt to horrify, frighten; ~**izarse** vr to be horrified; ~**oso, a** adj horrifying, ghastly

**hortaliza** [ortaˈliθa] *nf* vegetable

**hortelano, a** [orteˈlano, a] *nm/f* (market) gardener

**hortera** [orˈtera] (*fam*) adj tacky

**hosco, a** [ˈosko, a] adj dark; (*perso-*

*na*) sullen, gloomy

**hospedar** [ospe'ðar] *vt* to put up; ~**se** *vr* to stay, lodge

**hospital** [ospi'tal] *nm* hospital

**hospitalario, a** [ospita'larjo, a] *adj* (*acogedor*) hospitable; **hospitalidad** *nf* hospitality

**hostal** [os'tal] *nm* small hotel

**hostelería** [ostele'ria] *nf* hotel business o trade

**hostia** ['ostja] *nf* (*REL*) host, consecrated wafer; (*fam: golpe*) whack, punch ♦ *excl* (*fam!*): ¡~(**s**)! damn!

**hostigar** [osti'xar] *vt* to whip; (*fig*) to harass, pester

**hostil** [os'til] *adj* hostile; ~**idad** *nf* hostility

**hotel** [o'tel] *nm* hotel; ~**ero, a** *adj* hotel *cpd* ♦ *nm/f* hotelier

**hoy** [oi] *adv* (*este día*) today; (*la actualidad*) now(adays) ♦ *nm* present time; ~ (**en**) **día** now(adays)

**hoyo** ['ojo] *nm* hole, pit; **hoyuelo** *nm* dimple

**hoz** [oθ] *nf* sickle

**hube** *etc vb ver* **haber**

**hucha** ['utʃa] *nf* money box

**hueco, a** ['weko, a] *adj* (*vacío*) hollow, empty; (*resonante*) booming ♦ *nm* hollow, cavity

**huelga** *etc* ['welxa] *vb ver* **holgar** ♦ *nf* strike; **declararse en** ~ to go on strike, come out on strike; ~ **de hambre** hunger strike

**huelguista** [wel'xista] *nm/f* striker

**huelo** *etc vb ver* **oler**

**huella** ['weʎa] *nf* (*acto de pisar, pisada*) tread(ing); (*marca del paso*) footprint, footstep; (: *de animal, máquina*) track; ~ **digital** fingerprint

**huérfano, a** ['werfano, a] *adj* orphan(ed) ♦ *nm/f* orphan

**huerta** ['werta] *nf* market garden; (*en Murcia y Valencia*) irrigated region

**huerto** ['werto] *nm* kitchen garden; (*de árboles frutales*) orchard

**hueso** ['weso] *nm* (*ANAT*) bone; (*de fruta*) stone

**huésped, a** ['wespeð, a] *nm/f* (*invi-*

*tado*) guest; (*habitante*) resident; (*anfitrión*) host(ess)

**huesudo, a** [we'suðo, a] *adj* bony, big-boned

**huevera** [we'βera] *nf* eggcup

**huevo** ['weβo] *nm* egg; ~ **duro/escalfado/frito** (*ESP*) o **estrellado** (*AM*)/**pasado por agua** hard-boiled/poached/fried/soft-boiled egg; ~**s revueltos** scrambled eggs

**huida** [u'iða] *nf* escape, flight

**huidizo, a** [ui'ðiθo, a] *adj* (*tímido*) shy; (*pasajero*) fleeting

**huir** [u'ir] *vi* (*escapar*) to flee, escape; (*evadir*) to avoid; ~**se** *vr* (*escaparse*) to escape

**hule** ['ule] *nm* (*encerado*) oilskin

**humanidad** [umani'ðað] *nf* (*género humano*) man(kind); (*cualidad*) humanity

**humanitario, a** [umani'tarjo, a] *adj* humanitarian

**humano, a** [u'mano, a] *adj* (*gen*) human; (*humanitario*) humane ♦ *nm* human; **ser** ~ human being

**humareda** [uma'reða] *nf* cloud of smoke

**humedad** [ume'ðað] *nf* (*del clima*) humidity; (*de pared etc*) dampness; **a prueba de** ~ damp-proof; **humedecer** *vt* to moisten, wet; **humedecerse** *vr* to get wet

**húmedo, a** ['umeðo, a] *adj* (*mojado*) damp, wet; (*tiempo etc*) humid

**humildad** [umil'dað] *nf* humility, humbleness; **humilde** *adj* humble, modest

**humillación** [umiʎa'θjon] *nf* humiliation; **humillante** *adj* humiliating

**humillar** [umi'ʎar] *vt* to humiliate; ~**se** *vr* to humble o.s., grovel

**humo** ['umo] *nm* (*de fuego*) smoke; (*gas nocivo*) fumes *pl*; (*vapor*) steam, vapour; ~**s** *nmpl* (*fig*) conceit *sg*

**humor** [u'mor] *nm* (*disposición*) mood, temper; (*lo que divierte*) humour; **de buen/mal** ~ in a good/bad mood; ~**ista** *nm/f* comic; ~**ístico, a** *adj* funny, humorous

**hundimiento** [undi'mjento] nm (gen) sinking; (colapso) collapse

**hundir** [un'dir] vt to sink; (edificio, plan) to ruin, destroy; ~**se** vr to sink, collapse

**húngaro, a** ['ungaro, a] adj, nm/f Hungarian

**Hungría** [un'gria] nf Hungary

**huracán** [ura'kan] nm hurricane

**huraño, a** [u'raɲo, a] adj shy; (antisocial) unsociable

**hurgar** [ur'var] vt to poke, jab; (remover) to stir (up); ~**se** vr: ~**se (las narices)** to pick one's nose

**hurón, ona** [u'ron, ona] nm (ZOOL) ferret

**hurtadillas** [urta'ðiʎas]: **a ~** adv stealthily, on the sly

**hurtar** [ur'tar] vt to steal; **hurto** nm theft, stealing

**husmear** [usme'ar] vt (oler) to sniff out, scent; (fam) to pry into ♦ vi to smell bad

**huyo** etc vb ver **huir**

## I

**iba** etc vb ver **ir**

**ibérico, a** [i'ßeriko, a] adj Iberian

**iberoamericano, a** [ißeroameri-'kano, a] adj, nm/f Latin American

**Ibiza** [i'ßiθa] nf Ibiza

**iceberg** [iθe'ßer] nm iceberg

**ícono** ['ikono] nm ikon, icon

**iconoclasta** [ikono'klasta] adj iconoclastic ♦ nm/f iconoclast

**ictericia** [ikte'riθja] nf jaundice

**ida** ['iða] nf going, departure; ~ **y vuelta** round trip, return

**idea** [i'ðea] nf idea; **no tengo la menor ~** I haven't a clue

**ideal** [iðe'al] adj, nm ideal; ~**ista** nm/f idealist; ~**izar** vt to idealize

**idear** [iðe'ar] vt to think up; (aparato) to invent; (viaje) to plan

**ídem** ['iðem] pron ditto

**idéntico, a** [i'ðentiko, a] adj identical

**identidad** [iðenti'ðað] nf identity

**identificación** [iðentifika'θjon] nf identification

**identificar** [iðentifi'kar] vt to identify; ~**se** vr: ~**se con** to identify with

**ideología** [iðeolo'xia] nf ideology

**idilio** [i'ðiljo] nm love-affair

**idioma** [i'ðjoma] nm (gen) language

**idiota** [i'ðjota] adj idiotic ♦ nm/f idiot; **idiotez** nf idiocy

**ídolo** ['iðolo] nm (tb: fig) idol

**idóneo, a** [i'ðoneo, a] adj suitable

**iglesia** [i'ɣlesja] nf church

**ignominia** [iɣno'minja] nf ignominy

**ignorancia** [iɣno'ranθja] nf ignorance; **ignorante** adj ignorant, uninformed ♦ nm/f ignoramus

**ignorar** [iɣno'rar] vt not to know, be ignorant of; (no hacer caso a) to ignore

**igual** [i'ɣwal] adj (gen) equal; (similar) like, similar; (mismo) (the) same; (constante) constant; (temperatura) even ♦ nm/f equal; ~ **que** like, the same as; **me da** o **es ~** I don't care; **son ~es** they're the same; **al ~ que** prep, conj like, just like

**igualada** [iɣwa'laða] nf equaliser

**igualar** [iɣwa'lar] vt (gen) to equalize, make equal; (allanar, nivelar) to level (off), even (out); ~**se** vr (platos de balanza) to balance out

**igualdad** [iɣwal'dað] nf equality; (similaridad) sameness; (uniformidad) uniformity

**igualmente** [iɣwal'mente] adv equally; (también) also, likewise ♦ excl the same to you!

**ikurriña** [iku'rriɲa] nf Basque flag

**ilegal** [ile'val] adj illegal

**ilegítimo, a** [ile'xitimo, a] adj illegitimate

**ileso, a** [i'leso, a] adj unhurt

**ilícito, a** [i'liθito] adj illicit

**ilimitado, a** [ilimi'taðo, a] adj unlimited

**ilógico, a** [i'loxiko, a] adj illogical

**iluminación** [ilumina'θjon] nf illumination; (alumbrado) lighting

**iluminar** [ilumi'nar] vt to illuminate,

light (up); (*fig*) to enlighten

**ilusión** [ilu'sjon] *nf* illusion; (*quimera*) delusion; (*esperanza*) hope; **hacerse ilusiones** to build up one's hopes; **ilusionado, a** *adj* excited; **ilusionar** *vi*: **le ilusiona ir de vacaciones** he's looking forward to going on holiday; ~**se** *vr*: ~ (**con**) to get excited (about)

**ilusionista** [ilusjo'nista] *nm/f* conjurer

**iluso, a** [i'luso, a] *adj* easily deceived ♦ *nm/f* dreamer

**ilusorio, a** [ilu'sorjo, a] *adj* (*de ilusión*) illusory, deceptive; (*esperanza*) vain

**ilustración** [ilustra'θjon] *nf* illustration; (*saber*) learning, erudition; **la I~** the Enlightenment; **ilustrado, a** *adj* illustrated; learned

**ilustrar** [ilus'trar] *vt* to illustrate; (*instruir*) to instruct; (*explicar*) to explain, make clear; ~**se** *vr* to acquire knowledge

**ilustre** [i'lustre] *adj* famous, illustrious

**imagen** [i'maxen] *nf* (*gen*) image; (*dibujo*) picture

**imaginación** [imaxina'θjon] *nf* imagination

**imaginar** [imaxi'nar] *vt* (*gen*) to imagine; (*idear*) to think up; (*suponer*) to suppose; ~**se** *vr* to imagine; ~**io, a** *adj* imaginary; **imaginativo, a** *adj* imaginative

**imán** [i'man] *nm* magnet

**imbécil** [im'beθil] *nm/f* imbecile, idiot

**imitación** [imita'θjon] *nf* imitation

**imitar** [imi'tar] *vt* to imitate; (*parodiar*, *remedar*) to mimic, ape

**impaciencia** [impa'θjenθja] *nf* impatience; **impaciente** *adj* impatient; (*nervioso*) anxious

**impacto** [im'pakto] *nm* impact

**impar** [im'par] *adj* odd

**imparcial** [impar'θjal] *adj* impartial, fair

**impartir** [impar'tir] *vt* to impart, give

**impasible** [impa'sißle] *adj* impassive

**impávido, a** [im'paßiðo, a] *adj* fearless, intrepid

**impecable** [impe'kaßle] *adj* impeccable

**impedimento** [impeðí'mento] *nm* impediment, obstacle

**impedir** [impe'ðir] *vt* (*estorbar*) to impede, obstruct; (*estorbar*) to prevent

**impenetrable** [impene'traßle] *adj* impenetrable; (*fig*) incomprehensible

**imperar** [impe'rar] *vi* (*reinar*) to rule, reign; (*fig*) to prevail; reign; (*precio*) to be current

**imperativo, a** [impera'tißo, a] *adj* (*persona*) imperious; (*urgente*, LING) imperative

**imperceptible** [imperθep'tißle] *adj* imperceptible

**imperdible** [imper'ðißle] *nm* safety pin

**imperdonable** [imperðo'naßle] *adj* unforgivable, inexcusable

**imperfección** [imperfek'θjon] *nf* imperfection

**imperfecto, a** [imper'fekto, a] *adj* imperfect

**imperial** [impe'rjal] *adj* imperial; ~**ismo** *nm* imperialism

**imperio** [im'perjo] *nm* empire; (*autoridad*) rule, authority; (*fig*) pride, haughtiness; ~**so, a** *adj* imperious; (*urgente*) urgent; (*imperativo*) imperative

**impermeable** [imperme'aßle] *adj* (*a prueba de agua*) waterproof ♦ *nm* raincoat, mac (BRIT)

**impersonal** [imperso'nal] *adj* impersonal

**impertinencia** [imperti'nenθja] *nf* impertinence; **impertinente** *adj* impertinent

**imperturbable** [impertur'ßaßle] *adj* imperturbable

**ímpetu** [im'petu] *nm* (*impulso*) impetus, impulse; (*impetuosidad*) impetuosity; (*violencia*) violence

**impetuoso, a** [impe'twoso, a] *adj* impetuous; (*río*) rushing; (*acto*) hasty

**impío, a** [im'pio, a] *adj* impious, ungodly

**implacable** [impla'kaβle] *adj* implacable

**implantar** [implan'tar] *vt* to introduce

**implicar** [impli'kar] *vt* to involve; *(entrañar)* to imply

**implícito, a** [im'pliθito, a] *adj (tácito)* implicit; *(sobreentendido)* tacit

**implorar** [implo'rar] *vt* to beg, implore

**imponente** [impo'nente] *adj (impresionante)* impressive, imposing; *(solemne)* grand

**imponer** [impo'ner] *vt (gen)* to impose; *(exigir)* to exact; ~**se** *vr* to assert o.s.; *(prevalecer)* to prevail; **imponible** *adj (COM)* taxable

**impopular** [impopu'lar] *adj* unpopular

**importación** [importa'θjon] *nf (acto)* importing; *(mercancias)* imports *pl*

**importancia** [impor'tanθja] *nf* importance; *(valor)* value, significance; *(extensión)* size, magnitude; **importante** *adj* important; valuable, significant

**importar** [impor'tar] *vt (del extranjero)* to import; *(costar)* to amount to ♦ *vi* to be important, matter; me **importa un rábano** I couldn't care less; **no importa** it doesn't matter; **¿le importa que fume?** do you mind if I smoke?

**importe** [im'porte] *nm (total)* amount; *(valor)* value

**importunar** [importu'nar] *vt* to bother, pester

**imposibilidad** [imposiβili'ðað] *nf* impossibility; **imposibilitar** *vt* to make impossible, prevent

**imposible** [impo'siβle] *adj (gen)* impossible; *(insoportable)* unbearable, intolerable

**imposición** [imposi'θjon] *nf* imposition; *(COM: impuesto)* tax; *(: inversión)* deposit

**impostor, a** [impos'tor, a] *nm/f* impostor

**impotencia** [impo'tenθja] *nf* impotence; **impotente** *adj* impotent

**impracticable** [imprakti'kaβle] *adj (irrealizable)* impracticable; *(intransitable)* impassable

**impreciso, a** [impre'θiso, a] *adj* imprecise, vague

**impregnar** [impreɣ'nar] *vt* to impregnate; ~**se** *vr* to become impregnated

**imprenta** [im'prenta] *nf (acto)* printing; *(aparato)* press; *(casa)* printer's; *(letra)* print

**imprescindible** [impresθin'diβle] *adj* essential, vital

**impresión** [impre'sjon] *nf (gen)* impression; *(IMPRENTA)* printing; *(edición)* edition; *(FOTO)* print; *(marca)* imprint; ~ **digital** fingerprint

**impresionable** [impresjo'naβle] *adj (sensible)* impressionable

**impresionante** [impresjo'nante] *adj* impressive; *(tremendo)* tremendous; *(maravilloso)* great, marvellous

**impresionar** [impresjo'nar] *vt (conmover)* to move; *(afectar)* to impress, strike; *(pelicula fotográfica)* to expose; ~**se** *vr* to be impressed; *(conmoverse)* to be moved

**impreso, a** [im'preso, a] *pp de* **imprimir** ♦ *adj* printed; ~**s** *nmpl* printed matter; **impresora** *nf* printer

**imprevisto, a** [impre'βisto, a] *adj (gen)* unforeseen; *(inesperado)* unexpected

**imprimir** [impri'mir] *vt* to imprint, impress, stamp; *(textos)* to print; *(INFORM)* to output, print out

**improbable** [impro'βaβle] *adj* improbable; *(inverosímil)* unlikely

**improcedente** [improθe'ðente] *adj* inappropriate

**improductivo, a** [improðuk'tiβo, a] *adj* unproductive

**improperio** [impro'perjo] *nm* insult

**impropio, a** [im'propjo, a] *adj* improper

**improvisado, a** [improβi'saðo, a] *adj* improvised

**improvisar** [improβi'sar] *vt* to improvise

**improviso, a** [impro'βiso, a] *adj*: de ~ unexpectedly, suddenly

**imprudencia** [impru'ðenθja] *nf* imprudence; (*indiscreción*) indiscretion; (*descuido*) carelessness; **imprudente** *adj* unwise, imprudent; (*indiscreto*) indiscreet

**impúdico, a** [im'puðiko, a] *adj* shameless; (*lujurioso*) lecherous

**impudor** [impu'ðor] *nm* shamelessness; (*lujuria*) lechery

**impuesto, a** [im'pwesto, a] *adj* imposed ♦ *nm* tax; ~ **sobre el valor añadido** value added tax

**impugnar** [impuɣ'nar] *vt* to oppose, contest; (*refutar*) to refute, impugn

**impulsar** [impul'sar] *vt* = **impeler**

**impulsivo, a** [impul'siβo, a] *adj* impulsive; **impulso** *nm* impulse; (*fuerza, empuje*) thrust, drive; (*fig: sentimiento*) urge, impulse

**impune** [im'pune] *adj* unpunished

**impureza** [impu'reθa] *nf* impurity; (*fig*) lewdness; **impuro, a** *adj* impure; lewd

**imputar** [impu'tar] *vt*: ~ **a** to attribute to

**inacabable** [inaka'βaβle] *adj* (*infinito*) endless; (*interminable*) interminable

**inaccesible** [inakθe'siβle] *adj* inaccessible

**inacción** [inak'θjon] *nf* inactivity

**inaceptable** [inaθep'taβle] *adj* unacceptable

**inactividad** [inaktiβi'ðað] *nf* inactivity; (*COM*) dullness; **inactivo, a** *adj* inactive

**inadecuado, a** [inaðe'kwaðo, a] *adj* (*insuficiente*) inadequate; (*inapto*) unsuitable

**inadmisible** [inaðmi'siβle] *adj* inadmissible

**inadvertido, a** [inaðβer'tiðo, a] *adj* (*no visto*) unnoticed

**inagotable** [inaɣo'taβle] *adj* inexhaustible

**inaguantable** [inaɣwan'taβle] *adj* unbearable

**inalterable** [inalte'raβle] *adj* immutable, unchangeable

**inanición** [inani'θjon] *nf* starvation

**inanimado, a** [inani'maðo, a] *adj* inanimate

**inapreciable** [inapre'θjaβle] *adj* (*cantidad, diferencia*) imperceptible; (*ayuda, servicio*) invaluable

**inaudito, a** [inau'ðito, a] *adj* unheard-of

**inauguración** [inauɣura'θjon] *nf* inauguration; opening

**inaugurar** [inauɣu'rar] *vt* to inaugurate; (*exposición*) to open

**I.N.B.** (*ESP*) *abr* (= *Instituto Nacional de Bachillerato*) ≈ comprehensive school (*BRIT*), ≈ high school (*US*)

**inca** [ˈinka] *nm/f* Inca

**incalculable** [inkalku'laβle] *adj* incalculable

**incandescente** [inkandes'θente] *adj* incandescent

**incansable** [inkan'saβle] *adj* tireless, untiring

**incapacidad** [inkapaθi'ðað] *nf* incapacity; (*incompetencia*) incompetence; ~ **física/mental** physical/mental disability

**incapacitar** [inkapaθi'tar] *vt* (*inhabilitar*) to incapacitate, render unfit; (*descalificar*) to disqualify

**incapaz** [inka'paθ] *adj* incapable

**incautación** [inkauta'θjon] *nf* confiscation

**incautarse** [inkau'tarse] *vr*: ~ **de** to seize, confiscate

**incauto, a** [in'kauto, a] *adj* (*imprudente*) incautious, unwary

**incendiar** [inθen'djar] *vt* to set fire to; (*fig*) to inflame; ~**se** *vr* to catch fire; ~**io, a** *adj* incendiary

**incendio** [in'θendjo] *nm* fire

**incentivo** [inθen'tiβo] *nm* incentive

**incertidumbre** [inθerti'ðumbre] *nf* (*inseguridad*) uncertainty; (*duda*) doubt

**incesante** [inθe'sante] *adj* incessant

**incesto** [in'θesto] *nm* incest

**incidencia** [inθi'ðenθja] *nf* (*MAT*) incidence

**incidente** [inθi'ðente] nm incident

**incidir** [inθi'ðir] vi (influir) to influence; (afectar) to affect; ~ en un error to fall into error

**incienso** [in'θjenso] nm incense

**incierto, a** [in'θjerto, a] adj uncertain

**incineración** [inθinera'θjon] nf incineration; (de cadáveres) cremation

**incinerar** [inθine'rar] vt to burn; (cadáveres) to cremate

**incipiente** [inθi'pjente] adj incipient

**incisión** [inθi'sjon] nf incision

**incisivo, a** [inθi'siβo, a] adj sharp, cutting; (fig) incisive

**incitar** [inθi'tar] vt to incite, rouse

**inclemencia** [inkle'menθja] nf (severidad) harshness, severity; (del tiempo) inclemency

**inclinación** [inklina'θjon] nf (gen) inclination; (de tierras) slope, incline; (de cabeza) nod, bow; (fig) leaning, bent

**inclinar** [inkli'nar] vt to incline; (cabeza) to nod, bow ♦ vi to lean, slope; ~se vr to bow; (encorvarse) to stoop; ~se a (parecerse a) to take after, resemble; ~se ante to bow down to; me inclino a pensar que I'm inclined to think that

**incluir** [inklu'ir] vt to include; (incorporar) to incorporate; (meter) to enclose

**inclusive** [inklu'siβe] adv inclusive ♦ prep including

**incluso, a** [in'kluso, a] adj included ♦ adv inclusively; (hasta) even

**incógnita** [in'koɣnita] nf (MAT) unknown quantity

**incógnito** [in'koɣnito] nm: de ~ incognito

**incoherente** [inkoe'rente] adj incoherent

**incoloro, a** [inko'loro, a] adj colourless

**incólume** [in'kolume] adj (gen) safe; (indemne) intact, unharmed

**incomodar** [inkomo'ðar] vt to inconvenience; (molestar) to bother, trou-

ble; (fastidiar) to annoy; ~se vr to put o.s. out; (fastidiarse) to get annoyed

**incomodidad** [inkomoði'ðað] nf inconvenience; (fastidio, enojo) annoyance; (de vivienda) discomfort

**incómodo, a** [in'komoðo, a] adj (incomfortable) uncomfortable; (molesto) annoying; (inconveniente) inconvenient

**incomparable** [inkompa'raβle] adj incomparable

**incompatible** [inkompa'tiβle] adj incompatible

**incompetencia** [inkompe'tenθja] nf incompetence; **incompetente** adj incompetent

**incompleto, a** [inkom'pleto, a] adj incomplete, unfinished

**incomprensible** [inkompren'siβle] adj incomprehensible

**incomunicado, a** [inkomuni'kaðo, a] adj (aislado) cut off, isolated; (confinado) in solitary confinement

**inconcebible** [inkonθe'βiβle] adj inconceivable

**incondicional** [inkondiθjo'nal] adj unconditional; (apoyo) wholehearted; (partidario) staunch

**inconexo, a** [inko'nekso, a] adj (gen) unconnected; (desunido) disconnected

**inconfundible** [inkonfun'diβle] adj unmistakable

**incongruente** [inkon'grwente] adj incongruous

**inconsciencia** [inkons'θjenθja] nf unconsciousness; (fig) thoughtlessness; **inconsciente** adj unconscious; thoughtless

**inconsecuente** [inkonse'kwente] adj inconsistent

**inconsiderado, a** [inkonsiðe'raðo, a] adj inconsiderate

**inconsistente** [inkonsis'tente] adj weak; (tela) flimsy

**inconstancia** [inkons'tanθja] nf inconstancy; (inestabilidad) unsteadiness; **inconstante** adj inconstant

**incontable** [inkon'taβle] adj countless, innumerable

**incontestable** [inkontes'taβle] *adj* unanswerable; *(innegable)* undeniable

**incontinencia** [inkonti'nenθja] *nf* incontinence

**inconveniencia** [inkombe'njenθja] *nf* unsuitability, inappropriateness; *(descortesía)* impoliteness; **inconveniente** *adj* unsuitable; impolite ♦ *nm* obstacle; *(desventaja)* disadvantage; **el inconveniente es que ...** the trouble is that ...

**incordiar** [inkor'ðjar] *(fam) vt* to bug, annoy

**incorporación** [inkorpora'θjon] *nf* incorporation

**incorporar** [inkorpo'rar] *vt* to incorporate; **~se** *vr* to sit up

**incorrección** [inkorrek'θjon] *nf* *(gen)* incorrectness, inaccuracy; *(descortesía)* bad-mannered behaviour; **incorrecto, a** *adj (gen)* incorrect, wrong; *(comportamiento)* bad-mannered

**incorregible** [inkorre'xiβle] *adj* incorrigible

**incredulidad** [inkreðuli'ðað] *nf* incredulity; *(escepticismo)* scepticism; **incrédulo, a** *adj* incredulous, unbelieving; sceptical

**increíble** [inkre'iβle] *adj* incredible

**incremento** [inkre'mento] *nm* increment; *(aumento)* rise, increase

**increpar** [inkre'par] *vt* to reprimand

**incruento, a** [in'krwento, a] *adj* bloodless

**incrustar** [inkrus'tar] *vt* to incrust; *(piedras: en joya)* to inlay

**incubar** [inku'βar] *vt* to incubate; *(fig)* to hatch

**inculcar** [inkul'kar] *vt* to inculcate

**inculpar** [inkul'par] *vt (acusar)* to accuse; *(achacar, atribuir)* to charge, blame

**inculto, a** [in'kulto, a] *adj (persona)* uneducated; *(grosero)* uncouth ♦ *nm/f* ignoramus

**incumplimiento** [inkumpli'mjento] *nm* non-fulfilment; **~ de contrato**

breach of contract

**incurrir** [inku'rrir] *vi:* **~ en** to incur; *(crimen)* to commit; **~ en un error** to make a mistake

**indagación** [indaɣa'θjon] *nf* investigation; *(búsqueda)* search; *(JUR)* inquest

**indagar** [inda'ɣar] *vt* to investigate; to search; *(averiguar)* to ascertain

**indecente** [inde'θente] *adj* indecent, improper; *(lascivo)* obscene

**indecible** [inde'θiβle] *adj* unspeakable; *(indescriptible)* indescribable

**indeciso, a** [inde'θiso, a] *adj (por decidir)* undecided; *(vacilante)* hesitant

**indefenso, a** [inde'fenso, a] *adj* defenceless

**indefinido, a** [indefi'niðo, a] *adj* indefinite; *(vago)* vague, undefined

**indeleble** [inde'leβle] *adj* indelible

**indemne** [in'demne] *adj (objeto)* undamaged; *(persona)* unharmed, unhurt

**indemnizar** [indemni'θar] *vt* to indemnify; *(compensar)* to compensate

**independencia** [indepen'denθja] *nf* independence

**independiente** [indepen'djente] *adj* *(libre)* independent; *(autónomo)* self-sufficient

**indeterminado, a** [indetermi'naðo, a] *adj* indefinite; *(desconocido)* indeterminate

**India** ['indja] *nf:* **la ~** India

**indicación** [indika'θjon] *nf* indication; *(señal)* sign; *(sugerencia)* suggestion, hint

**indicado, a** [indi'kaðo, a] *adj (momento, método)* right; *(tratamiento)* appropriate; *(solución)* likely

**indicador** [indika'ðor] *nm* indicator; *(TEC)* gauge, meter

**indicar** [indi'kar] *vt (mostrar)* to indicate, show; *(termómetro etc)* to read, register; *(señalar)* to point to

**índice** ['indiθe] *nm* index; *(catálogo)* catalogue; *(ANAT)* index finger, forefinger

**indicio** [in'diθjo] *nm* indication, sign;

*(en pesquisa etc)* clue

**indiferencia** [indife'renθja] *nf* indifference; *(apatia)* apathy; **indiferente** *adj* indifferent

**indígena** [in'dixena] *adj* indigenous, native ♦ *nm/f* native

**indigencia** [indi'xenθja] *nf* poverty, need

**indigestión** [indixes'tjon] *nf* indigestion

**indigesto, a** [indi'xesto, a] *adj* undigested; *(indigestible)* indigestible; *(fig)* turgid

**indignación** [indiγna'θjon] *nf* indignation

**indignar** [indiγ'nar] *vt* to anger, make indignant; ~**se** *vr:* ~**se por** to get indignant about

**indigno, a** [in'diγno, a] *adj (despreciable)* low, contemptible; *(inmerecido)* unworthy

**indio, a** ['indjo, a] *adj, nm/f* Indian

**indirecta** [indi'rekta] *nf* insinuation, innuendo; *(sugerencia)* hint

**indirecto, a** [indi'rekto, a] *adj* indirect

**indiscreción** [indiskre'θjon] *nf (imprudencia)* indiscretion; *(irreflexión)* tactlessness; *(acto)* gaffe, faux pas

**indiscreto, a** [indis'kreto, a] *adj* indiscreet

**indiscriminado, a** [indiskrimi'naðo, a] *adj* indiscriminate

**indiscutible** [indisku'tißle] *adj* indisputable, unquestionable

**indispensable** [indispen'saßle] *adj* indispensable, essential

**indisponer** [indispo'ner] *vt* to spoil, upset; *(salud)* to make ill; ~**se** *vr* to fall ill; ~**se con uno** to fall out with sb

**indisposición** [indisposi'θjon] *nf* indisposition

**indispuesto, a** [indis'pwesto, a] *adj (enfermo)* unwell, indisposed

**indistinto, a** [indis'tinto, a] *adj* indistinct; *(vago)* vague

**individual** [indiβi'ðwal] *adj* individual; *(habitación)* single ♦ *nm (DEPORTE)* singles *sg*

**individuo, a** [indi'ðiβwo, a] *adj, nm* individual

**índole** ['indole] *nf (naturaleza)* nature; *(clase)* sort, kind

**indolencia** [indo'lenθja] *nf* indolence, laziness

**indómito, a** [in'domito, a] *adj* indomitable

**inducir** [indu'θir] *vt* to induce; *(inferir)* to infer; *(persuadir)* to persuade

**indudable** [indu'ðaßle] *adj* undoubted; *(incuestionable)* unquestionable

**indulgencia** [indul'xenθja] *nf* indulgence

**indultar** [indul'tar] *vt (perdonar)* to pardon, reprieve; *(librar de pago)* to exempt; **indulto** *nm* pardon; exemption

**industria** [in'dustrja] *nf* industry; *(habilidad)* skill; **industrial** *adj* industrial ♦ *nm* industrialist

**inédito, a** [in'eðito, a] *adj (texto)* unpublished; *(nuevo)* new

**inefable** [ine'faßle] *adj* ineffable, indescribable

**ineficaz** [inefi'kaθ] *adj (inútil)* ineffective; *(ineficiente)* inefficient

**ineludible** [inelu'ðißle] *adj* inescapable, unavoidable

**ineptitud** [inepti'tuð] *nf* ineptitude, incompetence; **inepto, a** *adj* inept, incompetent

**inequívoco, a** [ine'kiβoko, a] *adj* unequivocal; *(inconfundible)* unmistakable

**inercia** [in'erθja] *nf* inertia; *(pasividad)* passivity

**inerme** [in'erme] *adj (sin armas)* unarmed; *(indefenso)* defenceless

**inerte** [in'erte] *adj* inert; *(inmóvil)* motionless

**inesperado, a** [inespe'raðo, a] *adj* unexpected, unforeseen

**inestable** [ines'taßle] *adj* unstable

**inevitable** [ineβi'taßle] *adj* inevitable

**inexactitud** [ineksakti'tuð] *nf* inaccuracy; **inexacto, a** *adj* inaccurate; *(falso)* untrue

**inexperto, a** [inek'sperto, a] *adj*

(*novato*) inexperienced

**infalible** [infaˈliβle] *adj* infallible; (*plan*) foolproof

**infame** [inˈfame] *adj* infamous; (*horrible*) dreadful; **infamia** *nf* infamy; (*deshonra*) disgrace

**infancia** [inˈfanθja] *nf* infancy, childhood

**infantería** [infanteˈria] *nf* infantry

**infantil** [infanˈtil] *adj* (*pueril*, *aniñado*) infantile; (*cándido*) childlike; (*literatura*, *ropa etc*) children's

**infarto** [inˈfarto] *nm* (tb: ~ de miocardio) heart attack

**infatigable** [infatiˈɣaβle] *adj* tireless, untiring

**infección** [infekˈθjon] *nf* infection; **infeccioso, a** *adj* infectious

**infectar** [infekˈtar] *vt* to infect; ~se *vr* to become infected

**infeliz** [infeˈliθ] *adj* unhappy, wretched ♦ *nm/f* wretch

**inferior** [infeˈrjor] *adj* inferior; (*situación*) lower ♦ *nm/f* inferior, subordinate

**inferir** [infeˈrir] *vt* (*deducir*) to infer, deduce; (*causar*) to cause

**infestar** [infesˈtar] *vt* to infest

**infidelidad** [infiðeliˈðað] *nf* (*gen*) infidelity, unfaithfulness

**infiel** [inˈfjel] *adj* unfaithful, disloyal; (*erróneo*) inaccurate ♦ *nm/f* infidel, unbeliever

**infierno** [inˈfjerno] *nm* hell

**infiltrarse** [infilˈtrarse] *vr*: ~ en to infiltrate in(to); (*persona*) to work one's way in(to)

**ínfimo, a** [ˈinfimo, a] *adj* (*más bajo*) lowest; (*despreciable*) vile, mean

**infinidad** [infiniˈðað] *nf* infinity; (*abundancia*) great quantity

**infinito, a** [infiˈnito, a] *adj*, *nm* infinite

**inflación** [inflaˈθjon] *nf* (*hinchazón*) swelling; (*monetaria*) inflation; (*fig*) conceit; **inflacionario, a** *adj* inflationary

**inflamar** [inflaˈmar] *vt* (MED, fig) to inflame; ~se *vr* to catch fire; to become inflamed

**inflar** [inˈflar] *vt* (*hinchar*) to inflate, blow up; (*fig*) to exaggerate; ~se *vr* to swell (up); (*fig*) to get conceited

**inflexible** [inflekˈsiβle] *adj* inflexible; (*fig*) unbending

**infligir** [infliˈxir] *vt* to inflict

**influencia** [influˈenθja] *nf* influence; **influenciar** *vt* to influence

**influir** [influˈir] *vt* to influence

**influjo** [inˈfluxo] *nm* influence

**influya** *etc vb ver* **influir**

**influyente** [influˈjente] *adj* influential

**información** [informaˈθjon] *nf* information; (*noticias*) news *sg*; (JUR) inquiry; I~ (*oficina*) Information Office; (*mostrador*) Information Desk; (TEL) Directory Enquiries

**informal** [inforˈmal] *adj* (*gen*) informal

**informar** [inforˈmar] *vt* (*gen*) to inform; (*revelar*) to reveal, make known ♦ *vi* (JUR) to plead; (*denunciar*) to inform; (*dar cuenta de*) to report on; ~se *vr* to find out; ~se de to inquire into

**informática** [inforˈmatika] *nf* computer science, information technology

**informe** [inˈforme] *adj* shapeless ♦ *nm* report

**infortunio** [inforˈtunjo] *nm* misfortune

**infracción** [infrakˈθjon] *nf* infraction, infringement

**infranqueable** [infrankeˈaβle] *adj* impassable; (*fig*) insurmountable

**infringir** [infrinˈxir] *vt* to infringe, contravene

**infructuoso, a** [infrukˈtwoso, a] *adj* fruitless, unsuccessful

**infundado, a** [infunˈdaðo, a] *adj* groundless, unfounded

**infundir** [infunˈdir] *vt* to infuse, instil

**infusión** [infuˈsjon] *nf* infusion; ~ de manzanilla camomile tea

**ingeniar** [inxeˈnjar] *vt* to think up, devise; ~se *vr*: ~se para to manage to

**ingeniería** [inxenjeˈria] *nf* engineering; ~ genética genetic engineering; **ingeniero, a** *nm/f* engineer; **ingenie-**

ro de caminos/de sonido civil engineer/sound engineer

**ingenio** [in'xenjo] *nm (talento)* talent; *(agudeza)* wit; *(habilidad)* ingenuity, inventiveness; *(TEC)*: ~ azucarero sugar refinery

**ingenioso, a** [inxe'njoso, a] *adj* ingenious, clever; *(divertido)* witty

**ingenuidad** [inxenwi'ðað] *nf* ingenuousness; *(sencillez)* simplicity; **ingenuo, a** *adj* ingenuous

**ingerir** [inxe'rir] *vt* to ingest; *(tragar)* to swallow; *(consumir)* to consume

**Inglaterra** [ingla'terra] *nf* England

**ingle** ['ingle] *nf* groin

**inglés, esa** [in'gles, esa] *adj* English ♦ *nm/f* Englishman/woman ♦ *nm (LING)* English

**ingratitud** [ingrati'tuð] *nf* ingratitude; **ingrato, a** *adj (agr)* ungrateful

**ingrediente** [ingre'ðjente] *nm* ingredient

**ingresar** [ingre'sar] *vt (dinero)* to deposit ♦ *vi* to come in; ~ **en un club** to join a club; ~ **en el hospital** to go into hospital

**ingreso** [in'greso] *nm (entrada)* entry; (: *en hospital etc)* admission; ~s *nmpl (dinero)* income *sg*; (: *COM)* takings *pl*

**inhabitable** [inaßi'taßle] *adj* uninhabitable

**inhalar** [ina'lar] *vt* to inhale

**inherente** [ine'rente] *adj* inherent

**inhibir** [ini'ßir] *vt* to inhibit; *(REL)* to restrain

**inhóspito, a** [i'nospito, a] *adj (región, paisaje)* inhospitable

**inhumano, a** [inu'mano, a] *adj* inhuman

**INI** ['ini] *(ESP) nm abr (= Instituto Nacional de Industria)* ≈ NEB *(BRIT)*

**inicial** [ini'θjal] *adj, nf* initial

**iniciar** [ini'θjar] *vt (persona)* to initiate; *(empezar)* to begin, commence; *(conversación)* to start up

**iniciativa** [iniθja'tißa] *nf* initiative; **la ~ privada** private enterprise

**ininterrumpido, a** [ininterrum-'piðo, a] *adj* uninterrupted

**injerencia** [inxe'renθja] *nf* interference

**injertar** [inxer'tar] *vt* to graft; **injerto** *nm* graft

**injuria** [in'xurja] *nf (agravio, ofensa)* offence; *(insulto)* insult; **injuriar** *vt* to insult; **injurioso, a** *adj* offensive; insulting

**injusticia** [inxus'tiθja] *nf* injustice

**injusto, a** [in'xusto, a] *adj* unjust, unfair

**inmadurez** [inmaðu'reθ] *nf* immaturity

**inmediaciones** [inmeðja'θjones] *nfpl* neighbourhood *sg*, environs

**inmediato, a** [inme'ðjato, a] *adj* immediate; *(contiguo)* adjoining; *(rápido)* prompt; *(próximo)* neighbouring, next; **de ~** immediately

**inmejorable** [inmexo'raßle] *adj* unsurpassable; *(precio)* unbeatable

**inmenso, a** [in'menso, a] *adj* immense, huge

**inmerecido, a** [inmere'θiðo, a] *adj* undeserved

**inmigración** [inmixra'θjon] *nf* immigration

**inmiscuirse** [inmisku'irse] *vr* to interfere, meddle

**inmobiliaria** [inmoßi'ljarja] *nf* estate agency

**inmobiliario, a** [inmoßi'ljarjo, a] *adj* real-estate *cpd*, property *cpd*

**inmolar** [inmo'lar] *vt* to immolate, sacrifice

**inmoral** [inmo'ral] *adj* immoral

**inmortal** [inmor'tal] *adj* immortal; ~**izar** *vt* to immortalize

**inmóvil** [in'moßil] *adj* immobile

**inmueble** [in'mweßle] *adj*: **bienes** ~**s** real estate, landed property ♦ *nm* property

**inmundicia** [inmun'diθja] *nf* filth; **inmundo, a** *adj* filthy

**inmune** [in'mune] *adj*: ~ **(a)** *(MED)* immune to)

**inmunidad** [inmuni'ðað] *nf* immunity

**inmutarse** [inmu'tarse] *vr* to turn pale; **no se inmutó** he didn't turn a hair

**innato, a** [in'nato, a] *adj* innate

**innecesario, a** [inneθe'sarjo, a] *adj* unnecessary

**innoble** [in'noβle] *adj* ignoble

**innovación** [innoβa'θjon] *nf* innovation

**innovar** [inno'βar] *vt* to introduce

**inocencia** [ino'θenθja] *nf* innocence

**inocentada** [inoθen'taða] *nf* practical joke

**inocente** [ino'θente] *adj* (*ingenuo*) naive, innocent; (*inculpable*) innocent; (*sin malicia*) harmless ♦ *nm/f* simpleton

**inodoro** [ino'ðoro] *nm* toilet, lavatory (BRIT)

**inofensivo, a** [inofen'siβo, a] *adj* inoffensive, harmless

**inolvidable** [inolβi'ðaβle] *adj* unforgettable

**inopinado, a** [inopi'naðo, a] *adj* unexpected

**inoportuno, a** [inopor'tuno, a] *adj* untimely; (*molesto*) inconvenient

**inoxidable** [inoksi'ðaβle] *adj*: **acero ~** stainless steel

**inquebrantable** [inkeβran'taβle] *adj* unbreakable

**inquietar** [inkje'tar] *vt* to worry, trouble; **~se** *vr* to worry, get upset; **inquieto, a** *adj* anxious, worried; **inquietud** *nf* anxiety, worry

**inquilino, a** [inki'lino, a] *nm/f* tenant

**inquirir** [inki'rir] *vt* to enquire into, investigate

**insaciable** [insa'θjaβle] *adj* insatiable

**insalubre** [insa'luβre] *adj* unhealthy

**inscribir** [inskri'βir] *vt* to inscribe; **~ a uno en** (*lista*) to put sb on; (*censo*) to register sb on

**inscripción** [inskrip'θjon] *nf* inscription; (ESCOL *etc*) enrolment; (*censo*) registration

**insecticida** [insekti'θiða] *nm* insecticide

**insecto** [in'sekto] *nm* insect

**inseguridad** [inseɣuri'ðað] *nf* insecurity

**inseguro, a** [inse'ɣuro, a] *adj* insecure; (*inconstante*) unsteady; (*incierto*) uncertain

**insensato, a** [insen'sato, a] *adj* foolish, stupid

**insensibilidad** [insensiβili'ðað] *nf* (*gen*) insensitivity; (*dureza de corazón*) callousness

**insensible** [insen'siβle] *adj* (*gen*) insensitive; (*movimiento*) imperceptible; (*sin sentido*) numb

**insertar** [inser'tar] *vt* to insert

**inservible** [inser'βiβle] *adj* useless

**insidioso, a** [insi'ðjoso, a] *adj* insidious

**insignia** [in'siɣnja] *nf* (*señal distintiva*) badge; (*estandarte*) flag

**insignificante** [insiɣnifi'kante] *adj* insignificant

**insinuar** [insi'nwar] *vt* to insinuate, imply; **~se** *vr*: **~se con uno** to ingratiate o.s. with sb

**insípido, a** [in'sipiðo, a] *adj* insipid

**insistencia** [insis'tenθja] *nf* insistence

**insistir** [insis'tir] *vi* to insist; **~ en algo** to insist on sth; (*enfatizar*) to stress sth

**insolación** [insola'θjon] *nf* (MED) sunstroke

**insolencia** [inso'lenθja] *nf* insolence; **insolente** [inso'lente] *adj* insolent

**insólito, a** [in'solito, a] *adj* unusual

**insoluble** [inso'luβle] *adj* insoluble

**insolvencia** [insol'βenθja] *nf* insolvency

**insomnio** [in'somnjo] *nm* insomnia

**insondable** [inson'daβle] *adj* bottomless; (*fig*) impenetrable

**insonorizado, a** [insonori'θaðo, a] *adj* (*cuarto etc*) soundproof

**insoportable** [insopor'taβle] *adj* unbearable

**insospechado, a** [insospe'tʃaðo, a] *adj* (*inesperado*) unexpected

**inspección** [inspek'θjon] *nf* inspection, check; **inspeccionar** *vt* (*examinar*) to inspect, examine; (*controlar*) to check

**inspector, a** [inspek'tor, a] *nm/f* inspector

**inspiración** [inspira'θjon] *nf* inspiration

**inspirar** [inspi'rar] *vt* to inspire; *(MED)* to inhale; ~**se** *vr*: ~**se en** to be inspired by

**instalación** [instala'θjon] *nf* (*equipo*) fittings *pl*, equipment; ~ **eléctrica** wiring

**instalar** [insta'lar] *vt* (*establecer*) to install; (*erguir*) to set up, erect; ~**se** *vr* to establish o.s.; (*en una vivienda*) to move into

**instancia** [ins'tanθja] *nf* (*JUR*) petition; (*ruego*) request; **en última** ~ as a last resort

**instantánea** [instan'tanea] *nf* snap(shot)

**instantáneo, a** [instan'taneo, a] *adj* instantaneous; **café** ~ instant coffee

**instante** [ins'tante] *nm* instant, moment

**instar** [ins'tar] *vt* to press, urge

**instaurar** [instau'rar] *vt* (*costumbre*) to establish; (*normas, sistema*) to bring in, introduce; (*gobierno*) to instal

**instigar** [insti'ɣar] *vt* to instigate

**instinto** [ins'tinto] *nm* instinct; **por** ~ instinctively

**institución** [institu'θjon] *nf* institution, establishment

**instituir** [institu'ir] *vt* to establish; (*fundar*) to found; **instituto** *nm* (*gen*) institute; **Instituto Nacional de Enseñanza** (*ESP*) ≈ comprehensive (*BRIT*) o high (*US*) school

**institutriz** [institu'triθ] *nf* governess

**instrucción** [instruk'θjon] *nf* instruction

**instructivo, a** [instruk'tiβo, a] *adj* instructive

**instruir** [instru'ir] *vt* (*gen*) to instruct; (*enseñar*) to teach, educate

**instrumento** [instru'mento] *nm* (*gen*) instrument; (*herramienta*) tool, implement

**insubordinarse** [insuβorði'narse] *vr*

to rebel

**insuficiencia** [insufi'θjenθja] *nf* (*carencia*) lack; (*inadecuación*) inadequacy; **insuficiente** *adj* (*gen*) insufficient; (*ESCOL*: *calificación*) unsatisfactory

**insufrible** [insu'friβle] *adj* insufferable

**insular** [insu'lar] *adj* insular

**insultar** [insul'tar] *vt* to insult; **insulto** *nm* insult

**insuperable** [insupe'raβle] *adj* (*excelente*) unsurpassable; (*problema etc*) insurmountable

**insurgente** [insur'xente] *adj, nm/f* insurgent

**insurrección** [insurrek'θjon] *nf* insurrection, rebellion

**intacto, a** [in'takto, a] *adj* intact

**intachable** [inta'tʃaβle] *adj* irreproachable

**integral** [inte'ɣral] *adj* integral; (*completo*) complete; **pan** ~ wholemeal (*BRIT*) o wholewheat (*US*) bread

**integrar** [inte'ɣrar] *vt* to make up, compose; (*MAT, fig*) to integrate

**integridad** [inteɣri'ðað] *nf* wholeness; (*carácter*) integrity; **íntegro, a** *adj* whole, entire; (*honrado*) honest

**intelectual** [intelek'twal] *adj, nm/f* intellectual

**inteligencia** [inteli'xenθja] *nf* intelligence; (*ingenio*) ability; **inteligente** *adj* intelligent

**inteligible** [inteli'xiβle] *adj* intelligible

**intemperie** [intem'perje] *nf*: **a la** ~ out in the open, exposed to the elements

**intempestivo, a** [intempes'tiβo, a] *adj* untimely

**intención** [inten'θjon] *nf* (*gen*) intention, purpose; **con segundas intenciones** maliciously; **con** ~ deliberately

**intencionado, a** [intenθjo'naðo, a] *adj* deliberate; **bien/mal** ~ well-meaning/ill-disposed, hostile

**intensidad** [intensi'ðað] *nf* (*gen*) intensity; (*ELEC, TEC*) strength; **llover con** ~ to rain hard

**intenso, a** [in'tenso, a] *adj* intense; (*sentimiento*) profound, deep

**intentar** [inten'tar] *vt* (*tratar*) to try, attempt; **intento** *nm* (*intención*) intention, purpose; (*tentativa*) attempt

**interactivo, a** [interak'tiβo, a] *adj* (*INFORM*) interactive

**intercalar** [interka'lar] *vt* to insert

**intercambio** [inter'kambjo] *nm* exchange, swap

**interceder** [interθe'ðer] *vi* to intercede

**interceptar** [interθep'tar] *vt* to intercept

**intercesión** [interθe'sjon] *nf* intercession

**interés** [inte'res] *nm* (*gen*) interest; (*parte*) share, part; (*pey*) self-interest; **intereses creados** vested interests

**interesado, a** [intere'saðo, a] *adj* interested; (*prejuiciado*) prejudiced; (*pey*) mercenary, self-seeking

**interesante** [intere'sante] *adj* interesting

**interesar** [intere'sar] *vt, vi* to interest, be of interest to; ~**se** *vr*: ~**se en** *o* **por** to take an interest in

**interface** [inter'faθe] *nm* (*INFORM*) interface

**interfase** [inter'fase] *nm* = **interface**

**interferir** [interfe'rir] *vt* to interfere with; (*TEL*) to jam ♦ *vi* to interfere

**interfono** [inter'fono] *nm* intercom

**interino, a** [inte'rino, a] *adj* temporary ♦ *nm/f* temporary holder of a post; (*MED*) locum; (*ESCOL*) supply teacher

**interior** [inte'rjor] *adj* inner, inside; (*COM*) domestic, internal ♦ *nm* interior, inside; (*fig*) soul, mind; **Ministerio del I**~ ≈ Home Office (*BRIT*), ≈ Department of the Interior (*US*)

**interjección** [interxek'θjon] *nf* interjection

**interlocutor, a** [interloku'tor, a] *nm/f* speaker

**intermediario, a** [interme'ðjarjo, a] *nm/f* intermediary

**intermedio, a** [inter'meðjo, a] *adj* intermediate ♦ *nm* interval

**interminable** [intermi'naβle] *adj* endless

**intermitente** [intermi'tente] *adj* intermittent ♦ *nm* (*AUTO*) indicator

**internacional** [internaθjo'nal] *adj* international

**internado** [inter'naðo] *nm* boarding school

**internar** [inter'nar] *vt* to intern; (*en un manicomio*) to commit; ~**se** *vr* (*penetrar*) to penetrate

**interno, a** [in'terno, a] *adj* internal, interior; (*POL etc*) domestic ♦ *nm/f* (*alumno*) boarder

**interponer** [interpo'ner] *vt* to interpose, put in; ~**se** *vr* to intervene

**interpretación** [interpreta'θjon] *nf* interpretation

**interpretar** [interpre'tar] *vt* to interpret; (*TEATRO, MUS*) to perform, play; **intérprete** *nm/f* (*LING*) interpreter, translator; (*MUS, TEATRO*) performer, artist(e)

**interrogación** [interroɣa'θjon] *nf* interrogation; (*LING*: *tb*: **signo de ~**) question mark

**interrogar** [interro'ɣar] *vt* to interrogate, question

**interrumpir** [interrum'pir] *vt* to interrupt

**interrupción** [interrup'θjon] *nf* interruption

**interruptor** [interrup'tor] *nm* (*ELEC*) switch

**intersección** [intersek'θjon] *nf* intersection

**interurbano, a** [interur'βano, a] *adj*: **llamada interurbana** long-distance call

**intervalo** [inter'βalo] *nm* interval; (*descanso*) break; **a ~s** at intervals, every now and then

**intervenir** [interβe'nir] *vt* (*controlar*) to control, supervise; (*MED*) to operate on ♦ *vi* (*participar*) to take part, participate; (*mediar*) to intervene

**interventor, a** [interβen'tor, a] nm/f inspector; (COM) auditor

**interviú** [inter'βju] nf interview

**intestino** [intes'tino] nm intestine

**intimar** [inti'mar] vi to become friendly

**intimidad** [intimi'ðað] nf intimacy; (familiaridad) familiarity; (vida privada) private life; (JUR) privacy

**íntimo, a** [i'intimo, a] adj intimate

**intolerable** [intole'raβle] adj intolerable, unbearable

**intoxicación** [intoksika'θjon] nf poisoning

**intranquilizarse** [intrankili'θarse] vr to get worried o anxious; **intranquilo, a** adj worried

**intransigente** [intransi'xente] adj intransigent

**intransitable** [intransi'taβle] adj impassable

**intrépido, a** [in'trepiðo, a] adj intrepid

**intriga** [in'triɣa] nf intrigue; (plan) plot; **intrigar** vt, vi to intrigue

**intrincado, a** [intrin'kaðo, a] adj intricate

**intrínseco, a** [in'trinseko, a] adj intrinsic

**introducción** [introðuk'θjon] nf introduction

**introducir** [introðu'θir] vt (gen) to introduce; (moneda etc) to insert; (INFORM) to input, enter

**intromisión** [intromi'sjon] nf interference, meddling

**introvertido, a** [introβer'tiðo, a] adj, nm/f introvert

**intruso, a** [in'truso, a] adj intrusive ♦ nm/f intruder

**intuición** [intwi'θjon] nf intuition

**inundación** [inunda'θjon] nf flood(ing); **inundar** vt to flood; (fig) to swamp, inundate

**inusitado, a** [inusi'taðo, a] adj unusual, rare

**inútil** [in'util] adj useless; (esfuerzo) vain, fruitless; **inutilidad** nf uselessness

**inutilizar** [inutili'θar] vt to make o

render useless; **~se** vr to become useless

**invadir** [imba'ðir] vt to invade

**inválido, a** [im'baliðo, a] adj invalid ♦ nm/f invalid

**invariable** [imba'rjaβle] adj invariable

**invasión** [imba'sjon] nf invasion

**invasor, a** [imba'sor, a] adj invading ♦ nm/f invader

**invención** [imben'θjon] nf invention

**inventar** [imben'tar] vt to invent

**inventario** [imben'tarjo] nm inventory

**inventiva** [imben'tiβa] nf inventiveness

**invento** [im'bento] nm invention

**inventor, a** [imben'tor, a] nm/f inventor

**invernadero** [imberna'ðero] nm greenhouse

**inverosímil** [imbero'simil] adj implausible

**inversión** [imber'sjon] nf (COM) investment

**inverso, a** [im'berso, a] adj inverse, opposite; **en el orden ~** in reverse order; **a la inversa** inversely, the other way round

**inversor, a** [imber'sor, a] nm/f (COM) investor

**invertir** [imber'tir] vt (COM) to invest; (volcar) to turn upside down; (tiempo etc) to spend

**investigación** [imbestiɣa'θjon] nf investigation; (ESCOL) research; **~ de mercado** market research

**investigar** [imbesti'ɣar] vt to investigate; (ESCOL) to do research into

**invierno** [im'bjerno] nm winter

**invisible** [imbi'siβle] adj invisible

**invitado, a** [imbi'taðo, a] nm/f guest

**invitar** [imbi'tar] vt to invite; (incitar) to entice; (pagar) to buy, pay for

**invocar** [imbo'kar] vt to invoke, call on

**involucrar** [imbolu'krar] vt: **~ en** to involve in; **~se** vr (persona): **~ en** to get mixed up in

**involuntario, a** [imbolun'tarjo, a] adj (movimiento, gesto) involuntary; (error) unintentional

**inyección** [injek'θjon] nf injection

**inyectar** [injek'tar] vt to inject

---

*PALABRA CLAVE*

**ir** [ir] vi **1** to go; (a pie) to walk; (viajar) to travel; ~ caminando to walk; fui en tren I went o travelled by train; ¡(ahora) voy! (I'm just) coming!

**2:** ~ (a) por: ~ (a) por el médico to fetch the doctor

**3** (progresar: persona, cosa) to go; el trabajo va muy bien work is going very well; ¿cómo te va? how are things going?; me va muy bien I'm getting on very well; le fue fatal it went awfully badly for him

**4** (funcionar): el coche no va muy bien the car isn't running very well

**5:** te va estupendamente ese color that colour suits you fantastically well

**6** (locuciones): ¿vino? – ¡que va! did he come? – of course not!; vamos, no llores come on, don't cry; ¡vaya coche! what a car!, that's some car!

**7:** no vaya a ser: tienes que correr, no vaya a ser que pierdas el tren you'll have to run so as not to miss the train

**8** (+ pp): iba vestido muy bien he was very well dressed

**9:** no me etc va ni me viene I etc don't care

♦ vb aux **1:** ~ a: voy/iba a hacerlo hoy I am/was going to do it today

**2** (+ gerundio): iba anocheciendo it was getting dark; todo se me iba aclarando everything was gradually becoming clearer to me

**3** (+ pp = pasivo): van vendidos 300 ejemplares 300 copies have been sold so far

♦ ~se vr **1:** ¿por dónde se va al zoológico? which is the way to the zoo?

---

**2** (marcharse) to leave; ya se habrán ido they must already have left o gone

**ira** ['ira] nf anger, rage

**iracundo, a** [ira'kundo, a] adj irascible

**Irak** [i'rak] nm = **Iraq**

**Irán** [i'ran] nm Iran; **iraní** adj, nm/f Iranian

**Iraq** [i'rak] nm Iraq; **iraquí** adj, nm/f Iraqui

**iris** ['iris] nm inv (tb: arco ~) rainbow; (ANAT) iris

**Irlanda** [ir'landa] nf Ireland; **irlandés, esa** adj Irish ♦ nm/f Irishman/woman; los **irlandeses** the Irish

**ironía** [iro'nia] nf irony; **irónico, a** adj ironic(al)

**irreal** [irre'al] adj unreal

**irrecuperable** [irrekupe'raßle] adj irrecoverable, irretrievable

**irreflexión** [irreflek'sjon] nf thoughtlessness

**irregular** [irreɣu'lar] adj (gen) irregular; (situación) abnormal

**irremediable** [irreme'ðjaßle] adj irremediable; (vicio) incurable

**irreparable** [irrepa'raßle] adj (daños) irreparable; (pérdida) irrecoverable

**irresoluto, a** [irreso'luto, a] adj irresolute, hesitant

**irrespetuoso, a** [irrespe'twoso, a] adj disrespectful

**irresponsable** [irrespon'saßle] adj irresponsible

**irreversible** [irreßer'sible] adj irreversible

**irrigar** [irri'ɣar] vt to irrigate

**irrisorio, a** [irri'sorjo, a] adj derisory, ridiculous

**irritar** [irri'tar] vt to irritate, annoy

**irrupción** [irrup'θjon] nf irruption; (invasión) invasion

**isla** ['isla] nf island

**islandés, esa** [islan'des, esa] adj Icelandic ♦ nm/f Icelander

**Islandia** [is'landja] nf Iceland

**isleño, a** [is'leɲo, a] adj island cpd

♦ *nm/f* islander

**Israel** [isra'el] *nm* Israel; **israelí** *adj, nm/f* Israeli

**istmo** ['istmo] *nm* isthmus

**Italia** [i'talja] *nf* Italy; **italiano, a** *adj, nm/f* Italian

**itinerario** [itine'rarjo] *nm* itinerary, route

**IVA** ['iβa] *nm abr* (= *impuesto sobre el valor añadido*) VAT

**izar** [i'θar] *vt* to hoist

**izdo, a** *abr* (= *izquierdo, a*) l.

**izquierda** [iθ'kjerda] *nf* left; (POL) left (wing); **a la ~** (*estar*) on the left; (*torcer etc*) (to the) left

**izquierdista** [iθkjer'δista] *nm/f* left-winger, leftist

**izquierdo, a** [iθ'kjerðo, a] *adj* left

## J

**jabalí** [xaβa'li] *nm* wild boar

**jabalina** [xaβa'lina] *nf* javelin

**jabón** [xa'βon] *nm* soap; **jabonar** *vt* to soap

**jaca** ['xaka] *nf* pony

**jacinto** [xa'θinto] *nm* hyacinth

**jactarse** [xak'tarse] *vr* to boast, brag

**jadear** [xaðe'ar] *vi* to pant, gasp for breath; **jadeo** *nm* panting, gasping

**jaguar** [xa'ɣwar] *nm* jaguar

**jalea** [xa'lea] *nf* jelly

**jaleo** [xa'leo] *nm* racket, uproar; **armar un ~** to kick up a racket

**jalón** [xa'lon] (AM) *nm* tug

**Jamaica** [xa'maika] *nf* Jamaica

**jamás** [xa'mas] *adv* never; (*interrogación*) ever

**jamón** [xa'mon] *nm* ham; **~ dulce**, **~ de York** cooked ham; **~ serrano** cured ham

**Japón** [xa'pon] *nm*: **el ~** Japan; **japonés, esa** *adj, nm/f* Japanese ♦ *nm* (LING) Japanese

**jaque** ['xake] *nm*: **~ mate** checkmate

**jaqueca** [xa'keka] *nf* (very bad) headache, migraine

**jarabe** [xa'raβe] *nm* syrup

**jarcia** ['xarθja] *nf* (NAUT) ropes *pl*, rigging

**jardín** [xar'ðin] *nm* garden; **~ de (la) infancia** (ESP) *o* **de niños** (AM) nursery (school); **jardinería** *nf* gardening; **jardinero, a** *nm/f* gardener

**jarra** ['xarra] *nf* jar; (*jarro*) jug

**jarro** ['xarro] *nm* jug

**jaula** ['xaula] *nf* cage

**jauría** [xau'ria] *nf* pack of hounds

**J. C.** *abr* (= *Jesucristo*) J.C.

**jefa** ['xefa] *nf ver* jefe

**jefatura** [xefa'tura] *nf*: **~ de policía** police headquarters *sg*

**jefe** ['xefe, a] *nm/f* (*gen*) chief, head; (*patrón*) boss; **~ de cocina** chef; **~ de estación** stationmaster; **~ de estado** head of state

**jengibre** [xen'xiβre] *nm* ginger

**jeque** ['xeke] *nm* sheik

**jerarquía** [xerar'kia] *nf* (*orden*) hierarchy; (*rango*) rank; **jerárquico, a** *adj* hierarchic(al)

**jerez** [xe'reθ] *nm* sherry

**jerga** ['xerɣa] *nf* (*tela*) coarse cloth; (*lenguaje*) jargon

**jeringa** [xe'ringa] *nf* syringe; (AM) annoyance, bother; **~ de engrase** grease gun; **jeringar** (AM) *vt* to annoy, bother

**jeroglífico** [xero'xlifiko] *nm* hieroglyphic

**jersey** [xer'sei] (*pl* **~s**) *nm* jersey, pullover, jumper

**Jerusalén** [xerusa'len] *n* Jerusalem

**Jesucristo** [xesu'kristo] *nm* Jesus Christ

**jesuita** [xe'swita] *adj, nm* Jesuit

**Jesús** [xe'sus] *nm* Jesus; **¡~!** good heavens!; (*al estornudar*) bless you!

**jinete, a** [xi'nete, a] *nm/f* horseman/ woman, rider

**jipijapa** [xipi'xapa] (AM) *nm* straw hat

**jirafa** [xi'rafa] *nf* giraffe

**jirón** [xi'ron] *nm* rag, shred

**jocoso, a** [xo'koso, a] *adj* humorous, jocular

**jofaina** [xo'faina] *nf* washbasin

**jornada** [xor'naða] nf (viaje de un día) day's journey; (camino o viaje entero) journey; (día de trabajo) working day

**jornal** [xor'nal] nm (day's) wage; ~**ero** nm (day) labourer

**joroba** [xo'roβa] nf hump, hunched back; ~**do, a** adj hunchbacked ♦ nm/f hunchback

**jota** ['xota] nf (la letra) J; (danza) Aragonese dance; (fam) jot, iota; **no saber ni** ~ to have no idea

**joven** ['xoβen] adj (pl **jóvenes**) young ♦ nm young man, youth ♦ nf young woman, girl

**jovial** [xo'βjal] adj cheerful, jolly

**joya** ['xoja] nf jewel, gem; (fig: persona) gem; **joyería** (joyas) jewellery; (tienda) jeweller's (shop); **joyero** nm (persona) jeweller; (caja) jewel case

**juanete** [xwa'nete] nm (del pie) bunion

**jubilación** [xuβila'θjon] nf (retiro) retirement

**jubilado, a** [xuβi'laðo, a] adj retired ♦ nm/f pensioner (BRIT), senior citizen

**jubilar** [xuβi'lar] vt to pension off, retire; (fam) to discard; ~**se** vr to retire

**júbilo** ['xuβilo] nm joy, rejoicing; **jubiloso, a** adj jubilant

**judía** [xu'ðia] nf (CULIN) bean; ~ **verde** French bean; ver tb **judío**

**judicial** [xuði'θjal] adj judicial

**judío, a** [xu'ðio, a] adj Jewish ♦ nm/f Jew(ess)

**judo** ['juðo] nm judo

**juego** etc ['xwexo] vb ver **jugar** ♦ nm (gen) play; (pasatiempo, partido) game; (en casino) gambling; (conjunto) set; **fuera de** ~ (DEPORTE: persona) offside; (: pelota) out of play; **J**~s **Olímpicos** Olympic Games

**juerga** ['xwerxa] nf binge; (fiesta) party; **ir de** ~ to go out on a binge

**jueves** ['xweβes] nm inv Thursday

**juez** [xweθ] nm/f judge; ~ **de línea** linesman; ~ **de salida** starter

**jugada** [xu'ɣaða] nf play; **buena** ~ good move/shot/stroke etc

**jugador, a** [xuɣa'ðor, a] nm/f player; (en casino) gambler

**jugar** [xu'ɣar] vt, vi to play; (en casino) to gamble; (apostar) to bet; ~ **al fútbol** to play football

**juglar** [xu'ɣlar] nm minstrel

**jugo** ['xuɣo] nm (BOT) juice; (fig) essence, substance; ~ **de fruta** (AM) fruit juice; ~**so, a** adj juicy; (fig) substantial, important

**juguete** [xu'ɣete] nm toy; ~**ar** vi to play; ~**ría** nf toyshop

**juguetón, ona** [xuɣe'ton, ona] adj playful

**juicio** ['xwiθjo] nm judgement; (razón) sanity, reason; (opinión) opinion; **estar fuera de** ~ to be out of one's mind; ~**so, a** adj wise, sensible

**julio** ['xuljo] nm July

**junco** ['xunko] nm rush, reed

**jungla** ['xungla] nf jungle

**junio** ['xunjo] nm June

**junta** ['xunta] nf (asamblea) meeting, assembly; (comité, consejo) board, council, committee; (articulación) joint

**juntar** [xun'tar] vt to join, unite; (maquinaria) to assemble, put together; (dinero) to collect; ~**se** vr to join, meet; (reunirse: personas) to meet, assemble; (arrimarse) to approach, draw closer; ~**se con uno** to join sb

**junto, a** ['xunto, a] adj joined; (unido) united; (anexo) near, close; (contiguo, próximo) next, adjacent ♦ adv: ~ **todo** ~ all at once; ~**s** together; ~ **a** near to, next to

**jurado** [xu'raðo] nm (JUR: individuo) juror; (: grupo) jury; (de concurso: grupo) panel of (judges); (: individuo) member of a panel

**juramento** [xura'mento] nm oath; (maldición) oath, curse; **prestar** ~ to take the oath; **tomar** ~ **a** to swear in, administer the oath to

**jurar** [xu'rar] vt, vi to swear; ~ **en**

falso to commit perjury; **jurárselas a uno** to have it in for sb

**jurídico, a** [xu'riðiko, a] *adj* legal

**jurisdicción** [xurisðik'θjon] *nf* (*poder, autoridad*) jurisdiction; (*territorio*) district

**jurisprudencia** [xurispru'ðenθja] *nf* jurisprudence

**jurista** [xu'rista] *nm/f* jurist

**justamente** [xusta'mente] *adv* justly, fairly; (*precisamente*) just, exactly

**justicia** [xus'tiθja] *nf* justice; (*equidad*) fairness, justice; **justiciero, a** *adj* just, righteous

**justificación** [xustifika'θjon] *nf* justification; **justificar** *vt* to justify

**justo, a** ['xusto, a] *adj* (*equitativo*) just, fair, right; (*preciso*) exact, correct; (*ajustado*) tight ♦ *adv* (*precisamente*) exactly, precisely; (*AM: apenas a tiempo*) just in time

**juvenil** [xuβe'nil] *adj* youthful

**juventud** [xuβen'tuð] *nf* (*adolescencia*) youth; (*jóvenes*) young people *pl*

**juzgado** [xuθ'γaðo] *nm* tribunal, (*JUR*) court

**juzgar** [xuθ'γar] *vt* to judge; **a ~ por ...** to judge by ..., judging by ...

## K

**kg** *abr* (= *kilogramo*) kg

**kilo** ['kilo] *nm* kilo ♦ *pref:* **~gramo** *nm* kilogramme; **~metraje** *nm* distance in kilometres, ≈ mileage; **kilómetro** *nm* kilometre; **~vatio** *nm* kilowatt

**kiosco** ['kjosko] *nm* = **quiosco**

**km** *abr* (= *kilómetro*) km

**kv** *abr* (= *kilovatio*) kw

## L

**l** *abr* (= *litro*) l

**la** [la] *art def* the ♦ *pron* her; (*Ud.*) you; (*cosa*) it ♦ *nm* (*MUS*) la; **~ del sombrero rojo** the girl in the red

hat; *tb ver* **el**

**laberinto** [laβe'rinto] *nm* labyrinth

**labia** ['laβja] *nf* fluency; (*pey*) glib tongue

**labio** ['laβjo] *nm* lip

**labor** [la'βor] *nf* labour; (*AGR*) farm work; (*tarea*) job, task; (*COSTURA*) needlework; **~able** *adj* (*AGR*) workable; **día ~able** working day; **~al** *adj* (*accidente*) at work; (*jornada*) working

**laboratorio** [laβora'torjo] *nm* laboratory

**laborioso, a** [laβo'rjoso, a] *adj* (*persona*) hard-working; (*trabajo*) tough

**laborista** [laβo'rista] *adj:* **Partido L~** Labour Party

**labrado, a** [la'βraðo, a] *adj* worked; (*madera*) carved; (*metal*) wrought ♦ *nm* (*AGR*) cultivated field

**labrador, a** [laβra'ðor, a] *adj* farming *cpd* ♦ *nm/f* farmer

**labranza** [la'βranθa] *nf* (*AGR*) cultivation

**labrar** [la'βrar] *vt* (*gen*) to work; (*madera etc*) to carve; (*fig*) to cause, bring about

**labriego, a** [la'βrjeɣo, a] *nm/f* peasant

**laca** ['laka] *nf* lacquer

**lacayo** [la'kajo] *nm* lackey

**lacio, a** ['laθjo, a] *adj* (*pelo*) lank, straight

**lacónico, a** [la'koniko, a] *adj* laconic

**lacra** ['lakra] *nf* (*fig*) blot; **lacrar** *vt* (*cerrar*) to seal (with sealing wax); **lacre** *nm* sealing wax

**lactancia** [lak'tanθja] *nf* lactation

**lactar** [lak'tar] *vt, vi* to suckle

**lácteo, a** ['lakteo, a] *adj:* **productos ~s** dairy products

**ladear** [laðe'ar] *vt* to tip, tilt ♦ *vi* to tilt; **~se** *vr* to lean

**ladera** [la'ðera] *nf* slope

**lado** ['laðo] *nm* (*gen*) side; (*fig*) protection; (*MIL*) flank; **al ~ de** beside; **poner de ~** to put on its side; **poner a un ~** to put aside; **por todos ~s** on all sides, all round (*BRIT*)

**ladrar** [la'ðrar] *vi* to bark; **ladrido** *nm* bark, barking

**ladrillo** [la'ðriʎo] *nm* (*gen*) brick; (*azulejo*) tile

**ladrón, ona** [la'ðron, ona] *nm/f* thief

**lagartija** [laɣar'tixa] *nf* (*ZOOL*) (small) lizard

**lagarto** [la'ɣarto] *nm* (*ZOOL*) lizard

**lago** ['laɣo] *nm* lake

**lágrima** ['laɣrima] *nf* tear

**laguna** [la'ɣuna] *nf* (*lago*) lagoon; (*hueco*) gap

**laico, a** ['laiko, a] *adj* lay

**lamentable** [lamen'taßle] *adj* lamentable, regrettable; (*miserable*) pitiful

**lamentar** [lamen'tar] *vt* (*sentir*) to regret; (*deplorar*) to lament; **lo lamento mucho** I'm very sorry; **~se** *vr* to lament; **lamento** *nm* lament

**lamer** [la'mer] *vt* to lick

**lámina** ['lamina] *nf* (*plancha delgada*) sheet; (*para estampar, estampa*) plate

**lámpara** ['lampara] *nf* lamp; **~ de alcohol/gas** spirit/gas lamp; **~ de pie** standard lamp

**lamparón** [lampa'ron] *nm* grease spot

**lampiño** [lam'piɲo] *adj* clean-shaven

**lana** ['lana] *nf* wool

**lance** *etc* ['lanθe] *vb ver* **lanzar ♦** *nm* (*golpe*) stroke; (*suceso*) event, incident

**lancha** ['lantʃa] *nf* launch; **~ de pesca** fishing boat; **~ salvavidas/torpedera** lifeboat/torpedo boat

**langosta** [lan'gosta] *nf* (*crustáceo*) lobster; (*: de río*) crayfish; **langostino** *nm* Dublin Bay prawn; (*: de río*) crayfish

**languidecer** [langiðe'θer] *vi* to languish; **languidez** *nf* languor; **languido, a** *adj* (*gen*) languid; (*sin energía*) listless

**lanilla** [la'niʎa] *nf* nap

**lanza** ['lanθa] *nf* (*arma*) lance, spear

**lanzamiento** [lanθa'mjento] *nm* (*gen*) throwing; (*NAUT, COM*) launch, launching; **~ de peso** putting the shot

**lanzar** [lan'θar] *vt* (*gen*) to throw; (*DEPORTE*: *pelota*) to bowl; (*NAUT, COM*) to launch; (*JUR*) to evict; **~se** *vr* to throw o.s.

**lapa** ['lapa] *nf* limpet

**lapicero** [lapi'θero] *nm* propelling (*BRIT*) o mechanical (*US*) pencil; (*AM*: *bolígrafo*) Biro ®

**lápida** ['lapiða] *nf* stone; **~ mortuoria** headstone; **~ conmemorativa** memorial stone; **lapidario, a** *adj, nm* lapidary

**lápiz** ['lapiθ] *nm* pencil; **~ de color** coloured pencil; **~ de labios** lipstick

**lapón, ona** [la'pon, ona] *nm/f* Laplander, Lapp

**lapso** ['lapso] *nm* (*de tiempo*) interval; (*error*) error

**lapsus** ['lapsus] *nm inv* error, mistake

**largar** [lar'ɣar] *vt* (*soltar*) to release; (*aflojar*) to loosen; (*lanzar*) to launch; (*fam*) to let fly; (*velas*) to unfurl; (*AM*) to throw; **~se** *vr* (*fam*) to beat it; **~se a** (*AM*) to start to

**largo, a** ['larɣo, a] *adj* (*longitud*) long; (*tiempo*) lengthy; (*fig*) generous **♦** *nm* length; (*MUS*) largo; **dos años ~s** two long years; **tiene 9 metros de ~** it is 9 metres long; **a lo ~ de** along; (*tiempo*) all through, throughout; **~metraje** *nm* feature film

**laringe** [la'rinxe] *nf* larynx; **laringitis** *nf* laryngitis

**larva** ['larßa] *nf* larva

**las** [las] *art def* the **♦** *pron* them; **~ que cantan** the ones/women/girls who sing; *tb ver* **el**

**lascivo, a** [las'θißo, a] *adj* lewd

**láser** ['laser] *nm* laser

**lástima** ['lastima] *nf* (*pena*) pity; **dar ~** to be pitiful; **es una ~ que** it's a pity that; **¡qué ~!** what a pity!; **ella está hecha una ~** she looks pitiful

**lastimar** [lasti'mar] *vt* (*herir*) to wound; (*ofender*) to offend; **~se** *vr* to hurt o.s.; **lastimero, a** *adj* pitiful, pathetic

**lastre** ['lastre] *nm* (*TEC, NAUT*) ballast; (fig) dead weight

**lata** ['lata] nf (metal) tin; (caja) tin (BRIT), can; (fam) nuisance; **en** ~ tinned (BRIT), canned; **dar (la)** ~ to be a nuisance

**latente** [la'tente] adj latent

**lateral** [late'ral] adj side cpd, lateral ♦ nm (TEATRO) wings

**latido** [la'tiðo] nm (del corazón) beat

**latifundio** [lati'fundjo] nm large estate; **latifundista** nm/f owner of a large estate

**latigazo** [lati'yaθo] nm (golpe) lash; (sonido) crack

**látigo** ['latiyo] nm whip

**latín** [la'tin] nm Latin

**latino, a** [la'tino, a] adj Latin; ~**americano, a** adj, nm/f Latin-American

**latir** [la'tir] vi (corazón, pulso) to beat

**latitud** [lati'tuð] nf (GEO) latitude

**latón** [la'ton] nm brass

**latoso, a** [la'toso, a] adj (molesto) annoying; (aburrido) boring

**laúd** [la'uð] nm lute

**laurel** [lau'rel] nm (BOT) laurel; (CULIN) bay

**lava** ['laβa] nf lava

**lavabo** [la'βaβo] nm (jofaina) wash-basin; (tb: ~s) toilet

**lavado** [la'βaðo] nm washing; (de ropa) laundry; (ARTE) wash; ~ **de cerebro** brainwashing; ~ **en seco** dry-cleaning

**lavadora** [laβa'ðora] nf washing machine

**lavanda** [la'βanda] nf lavender

**lavandería** [laβande'ria] nf laundry; ~ **automática** launderette

**lavaplatos** [laβa'platos] nm inv dish-washer

**lavar** [la'βar] vt to wash; (borrar) to wipe away; ~**se** vr to wash o.s.; ~**se las manos** to wash one's hands; ~**y marcar** (pelo) to shampoo and set; ~ **en seco** to dry-clean

**lavavajillas** [laβaβa'xiʎas] nm inv dishwasher

**laxante** [lak'sante] nm laxative

**lazada** [la'θaða] nf bow

**lazarillo** [laθa'riʎo] nm: **perro** ~ guide dog

**lazo** [la'θo] nm knot; (lazada) bow; (para animales) lasso; (trampa) snare; (vínculo) tie

**le** [le] pron (directo) him (o her); (: usted) you; (indirecto) to him (o her o it); (: usted) to you

**leal** [le'al] adj loyal; ~**tad** nf loyalty

**lección** [lek'θjon] nf lesson

**lector, a** [lek'tor, a] nm/f reader

**lectura** [lek'tura] nf reading

**leche** ['letʃe] nf milk; **tiene mala** ~ (fam!) he's a swine (!); ~ **condensada/en polvo** condensed/powdered milk; ~ **desnatada** skimmed milk; ~**ra** nf (vendedora) milkmaid; (recipiente) (milk) churn; (AM) cow; ~**ro, a** adj dairy

**lecho** ['letʃo] nm (cama, de río) bed; (GEO) layer

**lechón** [le'tʃon] nm sucking (BRIT) o suckling (US) pig

**lechoso, a** [le'tʃoso, a] adj milky

**lechuga** [le'tʃuya] nf lettuce

**lechuza** [le'tʃuθa] nf owl

**leer** [le'er] vt to read

**legado** [le'yaðo] nm (don) bequest; (herencia) legacy; (enviado) legate

**legajo** [le'yaxo] nm file

**legal** [le'yal] adj (gen) legal; (persona) trustworthy; ~**idad** nf legality; ~**izar** vt to legalize; (documento) to authenticate

**legaña** [le'yaɲa] nf sleep (in eyes)

**legar** [le'yar] vt to bequeath, leave

**legendario, a** [lexen'darjo, a] adj legendary

**legión** [le'xjon] nf legion; **legionario, a** adj legionary ♦ nm legionnaire

**legislación** [lexisla'θjon] nf legislation

**legislar** [lexis'lar] vi to legislate

**legislatura** [lexisla'tura] nf (POL) period of office

**legitimar** [lexiti'mar] vt to legitimize; **legítimo, a** adj (genuino) authentic; (legal) legitimate

**lego, a** ['leyo, a] adj (REL) secular;

(*ignorante*) ignorant ♦ *nm* layman

**legua** [le'ɣwa] *nf* league

**legumbres** [le'ɣumbres] *nfpl* pulses

**leído, a** [le'iðo, a] *adj* well-read

**lejanía** [lexa'nia] *nf* distance; **lejano, a** *adj* far-off; (*en el tiempo*) distant; (*fig*) remote

**lejía** [le'xia] *nf* bleach

**lejos** ['lexos] *adv* far, far away; **a lo ~** in the distance; **de o desde ~** from afar; **~ de** far from

**lelo, a** ['lelo, a] *adj* silly ♦ *nm/f* idiot

**lema** ['lema] *nm* motto; (*POL*) slogan

**lencería** [lenθe'ria] *nf* linen, drapery

**lengua** ['lengwa] *nf* tongue; (*LING*) language; **morderse la ~** to hold one's tongue

**lenguado** [len'gwaðo] *nm* sole

**lenguaje** [len'gwaxe] *nm* language

**lengüeta** [len'gweta] *nf* (*ANAT*) epiglottis; (*zapatos, MUS*) tongue

**lente** ['lente] *nf* lens; (*lupa*) magnifying glass; **~s** *nfpl* (*gafas*) glasses; **~s de contacto** contact lenses

**lenteja** [len'texa] *nf* lentil; **lentejuela** *nf* sequin

**lentilla** [len'tiʎa] *nf* contact lens

**lentitud** [lenti'tuð] *nf* slowness; **con ~** slowly

**lento, a** ['lento, a] *adj* slow

**leña** ['lena] *nf* firewood; **~dor, a** *nm/f* woodcutter

**leño** ['leno] *nm* (*trozo de árbol*) log; (*madera*) timber; (*fig*) blockhead

**Leo** ['leo] *nm* Leo

**león** [le'on] *nm* lion; **~ marino** sea lion

**leopardo** [leo'parðo] *nm* leopard

**leotardos** [leo'tarðos] *nmpl* tights

**lepra** ['lepra] *nf* leprosy; **leproso, a** *nm/f* leper

**lerdo, a** ['lerðo, a] *adj* (*lento*) slow; (*patoso*) clumsy

**les** [les] *pron* (*directo*) them; (: *ustedes*) you; (*indirecto*) to them; (: *ustedes*) to you

**lesbiana** [les'βjana] *adj*, *nf* lesbian

**lesión** [le'sjon] *nf* wound, lesion; (*DEPORTE*) injury; **lesionado, a**

*adj* injured ♦ *nm/f* injured person

**letal** [le'tal] *adj* lethal

**letanía** [leta'nia] *nf* litany

**letargo** [le'tarɣo] *nm* lethargy

**letra** ['letra] *nf* letter; (*escritura*) handwriting; (*MUS*) lyrics *pl*; **~ de cambio** bill of exchange; **~ de imprenta** print; **~do, a** *adj* learned; (*fam*) pedantic ♦ *nm* lawyer; **letrero** (*cartel*) sign; (*etiqueta*) label

**letrina** [le'trina] *nf* latrine

**leucemia** [leu'θemja] *nf* leukaemia

**levadizo** [leβa'ðiθo] *adj*: **puente ~** drawbridge

**levadura** [leβa'ðura] *nf* (*para el pan*) yeast; (*de la cerveza*) brewer's yeast

**levantamiento** [leβanta'mjento] *nm* raising, lifting; (*rebelión*) revolt, rising; **~ de pesos** weight-lifting

**levantar** [leβan'tar] *vt* (*gen*) to raise; (*del suelo*) to pick up; (*hacia arriba*) to lift (up); (*plan*) to make, draw up; (*mesa*) to clear; (*campamento*) to strike; (*fig*) to cheer up, hearten; **~se** *vr* to get up; (*enderezarse*) to straighten up; (*rebelarse*) to rebel; **~ el ánimo** to cheer up

**levante** [le'βante] *nm* east coast; **el L~** region of Spain extending from Castellón to Murcia

**levar** [le'βar] *vt* to weigh anchor

**leve** ['leβe] *adj* light; (*fig*) trivial; **~dad** *nf* lightness

**levita** [le'βita] *nf* frock coat

**léxico** ['leksiko] *nm* (*vocabulario*) vocabulary

**ley** [lei] *nf* (*gen*) law; (*metal*) standard

**leyenda** [le'jenda] *nf* legend

**leyó** *etc vb ver* leer

**liar** [li'ar] *vt* to tie (up); (*unir*) to bind; (*envolver*) to wrap (up); (*enredar*) to confuse; (*cigarrillo*) to roll; **~se** *vr* (*fam*) to get involved; **~se a palos** to get involved in a fight

**Líbano** ['liβano] *nm*: **el ~** (the) Lebanon

**libelo** [li'βelo] *nm* satire, lampoon; (*JUR*) petition

**libélula** [li'βelula] *nf* dragonfly

**liberación** [liβera'θjon] nf liberation; *(de la cárcel)* release

**liberal** [liβe'ral] adj, nmf liberal; ~**idad** nf liberality, generosity

**liberar** [liβe'rar] vt to liberate

**libertad** [liβer'taδ] nf liberty, freedom; ~ **de culto/de prensa/de comercio** freedom of worship/of the press/of trade; ~ **condicional** probation; ~ **bajo palabra** parole; ~ **bajo fianza** bail

**libertar** [liβer'tar] vt *(preso)* to set free; *(de una obligación)* to release; *(eximir)* to exempt

**libertino, a** [liβer'tino, a] adj permissive ♦ nm/f permissive person

**libra** ['liβra] nf *(moneda)* pound *(ASTROLOGIA)*: L~ Libra; ~ **esterlina** pound sterling

**libramiento** [liβra'mjento] nm rescue; *(COM)* delivery

**libranza** [li'βranθa] nf *(COM)* draft; *(letra de cambio)* bill of exchange

**librar** [li'βrar] vt *(de peligro)* to save; *(batalla)* to wage, fight; *(de impuestos)* to exempt; *(cheque)* to make out; *(JUR)* to exempt; ~**se** vr: ~**se de** to escape from, free o.s. from

**libre** ['liβre] adj free; *(lugar)* unoccupied; *(asiento)* vacant; *(de deudas)* free of debts; ~ **de impuestos** free of tax; **tiro** ~ **free kick**; **los 100 metros** ~ **the 100 metres free-style** *(race)*; **al aire** ~ **in the open air**

**librería** [liβre'ria] nf *(tienda)* bookshop; **librero, a** nmf bookseller

**libreta** [li'βreta] nf notebook; ~ **de ahorros** savings book

**libro** ['liβro] nm book; ~ **de bolsillo** paperback; ~ **de caja** cashbook; ~ **de cheques** chequebook *(BRIT)*, checkbook *(US)*; ~ **de texto** textbook

**Lic.** abr = **licenciado, a**

**licencia** [li'θenθja] nf *(gen)* licence; *(permiso)* permission; ~ **por enfermedad/con goce de sueldo** sick leave/paid leave; ~ **de caza** game licence; ~**do, a** adj licensed ♦

nm/f graduate; **licenciar** vt *(empleado)* to dismiss; *(permitir)* to permit, allow; *(soldado)* to discharge; *(estudiante)* to confer a degree upon; **licenciarse en letras** to graduate in arts

**licencioso, a** [liθen'θjoso, a] adj licentious

**licitar** [liθi'tar] vt to bid for; *(AM)* to sell by auction

**lícito, a** ['liθito, a] adj *(legal)* lawful; *(justo)* fair, just; *(permisible)* permissible

**licor** [li'kor] nm spirits pl *(BRIT)*, liquor *(US)*; *(de frutas etc)* liqueur

**licuadora** [likwa'δora] nf blender

**licuar** [li'kwar] vt to liquidize

**lid** [liδ] nf combat; *(fig)* controversy

**líder** ['liδer] nm/f leader; **liderato** nm leadership; **liderazgo** nm leadership

**lidia** [li'δja] nf bullfighting; *(una* ~*)* bullfight; **toros de** ~ fighting bulls; **lidiar** vt, vi to fight

**liebre** ['ljeβre] nf hare

**lienzo** ['ljenθo] nm linen; *(ARTE)* canvas; *(ARQ)* wall

**liga** ['liɣa] nf *(de medias)* garter, suspender; *(AM: gomita)* rubber band; *(confederación)* league

**ligadura** [liɣa'δura] nf bond, tie; *(MED, MUS)* ligature

**ligamento** [liɣa'mento] nm *(ANAT)* ligament; *(atadura)* tie; *(unión)* bond

**ligar** [li'ɣar] vt *(atar)* to tie; *(unir)* to join; *(MED)* to bind up; *(MUS)* to slur ♦ vi to mix, blend; *(fam)*: *(él)* **liga mucho** he pulls a lot of women; ~**se** vr to commit o.s.

**ligereza** [lixe'reθa] nf lightness; *(rapidez)* swiftness; *(agilidad)* agility; *(superficialidad)* flippancy

**ligero, a** [li'xero, a] adj *(de peso)* light; *(tela)* thin; *(rápido)* swift, quick; *(ágil)* agile, nimble; *(de importancia)* slight; *(de carácter)* flippant, superficial ♦ adv: **a la ligera** superficially

**liguero** [li'ɣero] nm suspender *(BRIT)* o garter *(US)* belt

**lija** ['lixa] nf *(ZOOL)* dogfish; *(tb: pa-*

pel de ~) sandpaper

**lila** ['lila] *nf* lilac

**lima** ['lima] *nf* file; (*BOT*) lime; ~ **de uñas** nailfile; **limar** *vt* to file

**limitación** [limita'θjon] *nf* limitation, limit; ~ **de velocidad** speed limit

**limitar** [limi'tar] *vt* to limit; (*reducir*) to reduce, cut down ♦ *vi*: ~ **con** to border on; ~**se** *vr*: ~**se a** to limit o.s. to

**límite** ['limite] *nm* (*gen*) limit; (*fin*) end; (*frontera*) border; ~ **de velocidad** speed limit

**limítrofe** [li'mitrofe] *adj* bordering, neighbouring

**limón** [li'mon] *nm* lemon ♦ *adj*: **amarillo** ~ lemon-yellow; **limonada** *nf* lemonade

**limosna** [li'mosna] *nf* alms *pl*; **vivir de** ~ to live on charity

**limpiaparabrisas** [limpjapara'βrisas] *nm inv* windscreen (*BRIT*) o windshield (*US*) wiper

**limpiar** [lim'pjar] *vt* to clean; (*con trapo*) to wipe; (*quitar*) to wipe away; (*zapatos*) to shine, polish; (*fig*) to clean up

**limpieza** [lim'pjeθa] *nf* (*estado*) cleanliness; (*acto*) cleaning; (*: de las calles*) cleansing; (*: de zapatos*) polishing; (*habilidad*) skill; (*: POLICIA*) clean-up; (*pureza*) purity; (*MIL*): **operación de** ~ mopping-up operation; ~ **en seco** dry cleaning

**limpio, a** ['limpjo, a] *adj* clean; (*moralmente*) pure; (*COM*) clear, net; (*fam*) honest ♦ *adv*: **jugar** ~ to play fair; **pasar a** (*ESP*) o **en** (*AM*) ~ to make a clean copy

**linaje** [li'naxe] *nm* lineage, family

**lince** ['linθe] *nm* lynx

**linchar** [lin'tʃar] *vt* to lynch

**lindar** [lin'dar] *vi* to adjoin; ~ **con** to border on; **linde** *nm* o *f* boundary; **lindero, a** *adj* adjoining ♦ *nm* boundary

**lindo, a** ['lindo, a] *adj* pretty, lovely ♦ *adv*: **nos divertimos de lo** ~ we had a marvellous time; **canta muy** ~ (*AM*) he sings beautifully

**línea** ['linea] *nf* (*gen*) line; **en** ~ (*INFORM*) on line; ~ **aérea** airline; ~ **de meta** goal line; (*de carrera*) finishing line; ~ **recta** straight line

**lingote** [lin'gote] *nm* ingot

**lingüista** [lin'gwista] *nm/f* linguist; **lingüística** *nf* linguistics *sg*

**linimento** [lini'mento] *nm* liniment

**lino** ['lino] *nm* linen; (*BOT*) flax

**linóleo** [li'noleo] *nm* lino, linoleum

**linterna** [lin'terna] *nf* lantern, lamp; ~ **eléctrica** o **a pilas** torch (*BRIT*), flashlight (*US*)

**lío** ['lio] *nm* bundle; (*fam*) fuss; (*desorden*) muddle, mess; **armar un** ~ to make a fuss

**liquen** ['liken] *nm* lichen

**liquidación** [likiða'θjon] *nf* liquidation; **venta de** ~ clearance sale

**liquidar** [liki'ðar] *vt* (*mercancías*) to liquidate; (*deudas*) to pay off; (*empresa*) to wind up

**líquido, a** ['likiðo, a] *adj* liquid; (*ganancia*) net ♦ *nm* liquid; ~ **imponible** net taxable income

**lira** ['lira] *nf* (*MUS*) lyre; (*moneda*) lira

**lírico, a** ['liriko, a] *adj* lyrical

**lirio** ['lirjo] *nm* (*BOT*) iris

**lirón** [li'ron] *nm* (*ZOOL*) dormouse; (*fig*) sleepyhead

**Lisboa** [lis'βoa] *n* Lisbon

**lisiado, a** [li'sjaðo, a] *adj* injured ♦ *nm/f* cripple

**lisiar** [li'sjar] *vt* to maim; ~**se** *vr* to injure o.s

**liso, a** ['liso, a] *adj* (*terreno*) flat; (*cabello*) straight; (*superficie*) even; (*tela*) plain

**lisonja** [li'sonxa] *nf* flattery; **lisonjear** *vt* to flatter; (*fig*) to please

**lista** ['lista] *nf* list; (*de alumnos*) school register; (*de libros*) catalogue; (*de platos*) menu; (*de precios*) price list; **pasar** ~ to call the roll; ~ **de correos** poste restante; ~ **de espera** waiting list; **tela a** ~**s** striped material

**listo, a** ['listo, a] *adj* (*perspicaz*) smart, clever; (*preparado*) ready

**listón** [lis'ton] nm (tela) ribbon; (de madera, metal) strip

**litera** [li'tera] nf (en barco, tren) berth; (en dormitorio) bunk, bunk bed

**literal** [lite'ral] adj literal

**literario, a** [lite'rarjo, a] adj literary

**literato, a** [lite'rato, a] adj literary ♦ nm/f writer

**literatura** [litera'tura] nf literature

**litigar** [liti'ɣar] vt to fight ♦ vi (JUR) to go to law; (fig) to dispute, argue

**litigio** [li'tixjo] nm (JUR) lawsuit; (fig): **en ~ con** in dispute with

**litografía** [litoɣra'fia] nf lithography; (una ~) lithograph

**litoral** [lito'ral] adj coastal ♦ nm coast, seaboard

**litro** ['litro] nm litre

**liviano, a** [li'βjano, a] adj (persona) fickle; (cosa, objeto) trivial

**lívido, a** ['liβiðo, a] adj livid

**ll...** see under letter LL, after L

**lo** [lo] art def: ~ **bello** the beautiful, what is beautiful, that which is beautiful ♦ pron (persona) him; (cosa) it; tb ver **el**

**loable** [lo'aβle] adj praiseworthy

**loar** vt to praise

**lobato** [lo'βato] nm (ZOOL) wolf cub; **L~ Cub Scout**

**lobo** ['loβo] nm wolf; ~ **de mar** (fig) sea dog; ~ **marino** seal

**lóbrego, a** ['loβreɣo, a] adj dark; (fig) gloomy

**lóbulo** ['loβulo] nm lobe

**local** [lo'kal] adj local ♦ nm place, site; (oficinas) premises pl; ~**idad** f (barrio) locality; (lugar) location; (TEATRO) seat, ticket; ~**izar** vt (ubicar) to locate, find; (restringir) to localize; (situar) to place

**loción** [lo'θjon] nf lotion

**loco, a** ['loko, a] adj mad ♦ nm/f lunatic, mad person

**locomoción** [lokomo'θjon] nf locomotion

**locomotora** [lokomo'tora] nf engine, locomotive

**locuaz** [lo'kwaθ] adj loquacious

**locución** [loku'θjon] nf expression

**locura** [lo'kura] nf madness; (acto) crazy act

**locutor, a** [loku'tor, a] nm/f (RADIO) announcer; (comentarista) commentator; (TV) newsreader

**locutorio** [loku'torjo] nm (en telefónica) telephone booth

**lodo** ['loðo] nm mud

**lógica** ['loxika] nf logic

**lógico, a** [a 'loxiko, a] adj logical

**logística** [lo'xistika] nf logistics sg

**logotipo** [loɣo'tipo] nm logo

**logrado, a** [lo'ɣraðo, a] adj (interpretación, reproducción) polished, excellent

**lograr** [lo'ɣrar] vt to achieve; (obtener) to get, obtain; ~ **hacer** to manage to do; ~ **que uno venga** to manage to get sb to come

**logro** ['loɣro] nm achievement, success

**loma** ['loma] nf hillock (BRIT), small hill

**lombriz** [lom'briθ] nf worm

**lomo** ['lomo] nm (de animal) back; (CULIN: de cerdo) pork loin; (: de vaca) rib steak; (de libro) spine

**lona** ['lona] nf canvas

**loncha** ['lontʃa] nf = **lonja**

**lonche** ['lontʃe] nm (AM) lunch; ~**ría** (AM) nf snack bar, diner (US)

**Londres** ['londres] n London

**longaniza** [longa'niθa] nf pork sausage

**longitud** [lonxi'tuð] nf length; (GEO) longitude; **tener 3 metros de ~** to be 3 metres long; ~ **de onda** wavelength

**lonja** ['lonxa] nf slice; (de tocino) rasher; ~ **de pescado** fish market

**loro** ['loro] nm parrot

**los** [los] art def the ♦ pron them; (ustedes) you; **mis libros y ~** Ud my books and yours; tb ver **el**

**losa** ['losa] nf stone; ~ **sepulcral** gravestone

**lote** ['lote] nm portion; (COM) lot

**lotería** [lote'ria] nf lottery; (juego) lotto

# loza

**loza** [ˈloθa] *nf* crockery

**lozanía** [loθaˈnia] *nf* (*lujo*) luxuriance; **lozano, a** *adj* luxuriant; (*animado*) lively

**lubricante** [luβriˈkante] *nm* lubricant

**lubricar** [luβriˈkar] *vt* to lubricate

**lucidez** [luθiˈðeθ] *nf* lucidity

**lúcido, a** [ˈluθiðo, a] *adj* (*persona*) lucid; (*mente*) logical; (*idea*) crystal-clear

**luciérnaga** [luˈθjernaɣa] *nf* glowworm

**lucir** [luˈθir] *vt* to illuminate, light (up); (*ostentar*) to show off ♦ *vi* (*brillar*) to shine; ~**se** *vr* (*irónico*) to make a fool of o.s.

**lucro** [ˈlukro] *nm* profit, gain

**lucha** [ˈlutʃa] *nf* fight, struggle; ~ **de clases** class struggle; ~ **libre** wrestling; **luchar** *vi* to fight

**lúdico, a** [ˈluðiko, a] *adj* (*aspecto, actividad*) play *atr*

**luego** [ˈlweɣo] *adv* (*después*) next; (*más tarde*) later, afterwards

**lugar** [luˈɣar] *nm* place; (*sitio*) spot; **en ~ de** instead of; **hacer ~** to make room; **fuera de ~** out of place; **tener ~** to take place; ~ **común** commonplace

**lugareño, a** [luɣaˈreɲo, a] *adj* village *cpd* ♦ *nm/f* villager

**lugarteniente** [luɣarteˈnjente] *nm* deputy

**lúgubre** [ˈluɣuβre] *adj* mournful

**lujo** [ˈluxo] *nm* luxury; (*fig*) profusion, abundance; ~**so, a** *adj* luxurious

**lujuria** [luˈxurja] *nf* lust

**lumbre** [ˈlumbre] *nf* (*gen*) light

**lumbrera** [lumˈbrera] *nf* luminary

**luminoso, a** [lumiˈnoso, a] *adj* luminous, shining

**luna** [ˈluna] *nf* moon; (*de un espejo*) glass; (*de gafas*) lens; (*fig*) crescent; ~ **llena/nueva** full/new moon; **estar en la ~** to have one's head in the clouds; ~ **de miel** honeymoon

**lunar** [luˈnar] *adj* lunar ♦ *nm* (*ANAT*) mole; **tela a ~es** spotted material

**lunes** [ˈlunes] *nm inv* Monday

**lupa** [ˈlupa] *nf* magnifying glass

**lustrar** [lusˈtrar] *vt* (*mueble*) to polish; (*zapatos*) to shine; **lustre** *nm* polish; (*fig*) lustre; **dar lustre a** to polish; **lustroso, a** *adj* shining

**luto** [ˈluto] *nm* mourning; (*congoja*) grief, sorrow; **llevar el** *o* **vestirse de ~** to be in mourning

**Luxemburgo** [luksemˈburɣo] *nm* Luxembourg

**luz** [luθ] (*pl* **luces**) *nf* light; **dar a ~ un niño** to give birth to a child; **sacar a la ~** to bring to light; **dar** *o* **encender** (*ESP*) *o* **prender** (*AM*) **apagar la ~** to switch the light on/off; **a todas luces** by any reckoning; **hacer la ~ sobre** to shed light on; **tener pocas luces** to be dim *o* stupid; ~ **roja/verde** red/green light; ~ **de freno** brake light; **luces de tráfico** traffic lights; **traje de luces** bullfighter's costume

## LL

**llaga** [ˈʎaɣa] *nf* wound

**llama** [ˈʎama] *nf* flame; (*ZOOL*) llama

**llamada** [ʎaˈmaða] *nf* call; ~ **al orden** call to order; ~ **a pie de página** reference note

**llamamiento** [ʎamaˈmjento] *nm* call

**llamar** [ʎaˈmar] *vt* (*atención*) to attract ♦ *vi* (*por teléfono*) to telephone; (*a la puerta*) to knock (*o* ring); (*por señas*) to beckon; (*MIL*) to call up; ~**se** *vr* to be called, be named; **¿cómo se llama usted?** what's your name?

**llamarada** [ʎamaˈraða] *nf* (*llamas*) blaze; (*rubor*) flush; (*fig*) flare-up

**llamativo, a** [ʎamaˈtiβo, a] *adj* showy; (*color*) loud

**llamear** [ʎameˈar] *vi* to blaze

**llano, a** [ˈʎano, a] *adj* (*superficie*) flat; (*persona*) straightforward; (*estilo*) clear ♦ *nm* plain, flat ground

**llanta** ['ʎanta] nf (wheel) rim; (AM): ~ de goma tyre; (: cámara) inner (tube)

**llanto** ['ʎanto] nm weeping

**llanura** [ʎa'nura] nf plain

**llave** ['ʎaβe] nf key; (del agua) tap; (MECANICA) spanner; (de la luz) switch; (MUS) key; ~ inglesa monkey wrench; ~ maestra master key; ~ de contacto (AUTO) ignition key; ~ de paso stopcock; echar ~ a to lock up; ~ro nm keyring

**llegada** [ʎe'ɣaða] nf arrival

**llegar** [ʎe'ɣar] vi to arrive; (alcanzar) to reach; (bastar) to be enough; ~se vr: ~se a to approach; ~ a to manage to, succeed in; ~ a saber to find out; ~ a ser to become; ~ a las manos de to come into the hands of

**llenar** [ʎe'nar] vt to fill; (espacio) to cover; (formulario) to fill in o up; (fig) to heap

**lleno, a** ['ʎeno, a] adj full, filled; (repleto) full up ♦ nm (abundancia) abundance; (TEATRO) full house; dar de ~ contra un muro to hit a wall head-on

**llevadero, a** [ʎeβa'ðero, a] adj bearable, tolerable

**llevar** [ʎe'βar] vt to take; (ropa) to wear; (cargar) to carry; (quitar) to take away; (en coche) to drive; (transportar) to transport; (traer: dinero) to carry; (conducir) to lead; (MAT) to carry ♦ vi (suj: camino etc): ~ a to lead to; ~se vr to carry off, take away; llevamos dos días aquí we have been here for two days; él me lleva 2 años he's 2 years older than me; (COM): ~ los libros to keep the books; ~se bien to get on well (together)

**llorar** [ʎo'rar] vt, vi to cry, weep; ~ de risa to cry with laughter

**lloriquear** [ʎorike'ar] vi to snivel, whimper

**lloro** ['ʎoro] nm crying, weeping; **llorón, ona** adj tearful ♦ nm/f crybaby; ~**so, a** adj (gen) weeping,

tearful; (triste) sad, sorrowful

**llover** [ʎo'βer] vi to rain

**llovizna** [ʎo'βiθna] nf drizzle; **lloviznar** vi to drizzle

**llueve** etc vb ver llover

**lluvia** ['ʎuβja] nf rain; ~ **radioactiva** (radioactive) fallout; **lluvioso, a** adj rainy

# M

**m** abr (= metro) m; (= minuto) m

**macarrones** [maka'rrones] nmpl macaroni sg

**macedonia** [maθe'ðonja] nf: ~ de frutas fruit salad

**macerar** [maθe'rar] vt to macerate

**maceta** [ma'θeta] nf (de flores) pot of flowers; (para plantas) flowerpot

**macizo, a** [ma'θiθo, a] adj (grande) massive; (fuerte, sólido) solid ♦ nm mass, chunk

**machacar** [matʃa'kar] vt to crush, pound ♦ vi (insistir) to go on, keep on

**machete** [ma'tʃete] (AM) nm machete, (large) knife

**machismo** [ma'tʃismo] nm male chauvinism; **machista** adj, nm sexist

**macho** ['matʃo] adj male; (fig) virile ♦ nm male; (fig) he-man

**madeja** [ma'ðexa] nf (de lana) skein, hank; (de pelo) mass, mop

**madera** [ma'ðera] nf wood; (fig) nature, character; **una ~** a piece of wood

**madero** [ma'ðero] nm beam; (fig) ship

**madrastra** [ma'ðrastra] nf stepmother

**madre** ['maðre] adj mother cpd; (AM) tremendous ♦ nf mother; (de vino etc) dregs pl; ~ **política/soltera** mother-in-law/unmarried mother

**Madrid** [ma'ðrið] n Madrid

**madriguera** [maðri'ɣera] nf burrow

**madrileño, a** [maðri'leɲo, a] adj of o from Madrid ♦ nm/f native of Madrid

**madrina** [ma'ðrina] *nf* godmother; (*ARQ*) prop, shore; (*TEC*) brace; ~ **de boda** bridesmaid

**madrugada** [maðru'yaða] *nf* early morning; (*alba*) dawn, daybreak

**madrugador, a** [maðruya'ðor, a] *adj* early-rising

**madrugar** [maðru'yar] *vi* to get up early; (*fig*) to get ahead

**madurar** [maðu'rar] *vt*, *vi* (*fruta*) to ripen; (*fig*) to mature; **madurez** *nf* ripeness; maturity; **maduro, a** *adj* ripe; mature

**maestra** [ma'estra] *nf ver* **maestro**

**maestría** [maes'tria] *nf* mastery; (*habilidad*) skill, expertise

**maestro, a** [ma'estro, a] *adj* masterly; (*perito*) skilled, expert; (*principal*) main; (*educado*) trained ♦ *nm/f* master/mistress; (*profesor*) teacher ♦ *nm* (*autoridad*) authority; (*MUS*) maestro; (*AM*) skilled workman; ~ **albañil** master mason

**magia** ['maxja] *nf* magic; **mágico, a** *adj* magic(al) ♦ *nm/f* magician

**magisterio** [maxis'terjo] *nm* (*enseñanza*) teaching; (*profesión*) teaching profession; (*maestros*) teachers *pl*

**magistrado** [maxis'traðo] *nm* magistrate

**magistral** [maxis'tral] *adj* magisterial; (*fig*) masterly

**magnánimo, a** [may'nanimo, a] *adj* magnanimous

**magnate** [may'nate] *nm* magnate, tycoon

**magnético, a** [may'netiko, a] *adj* magnetic; **magnetizar** *vt* to magnetize

**magnetófon** [mayneto'fon] *nm* tape recorder; **magnetofónico, a** *adj*: **cinta magnetofónica** recording tape

**magnetófono** [mayne'tofono] *nm* = **magnetofón**

**magnífico, a** [may'nifiko, a] *adj* splendid, magnificent

**magnitud** [mayni'tuð] *nf* magnitude

**mago, a** ['mayo, a] *nm/f* magician; **los Reyes M~s** the Magi, the Three Wise Men

**magro, a** ['mayro, a] *adj* (*persona*) thin, lean; (*carne*) lean

**maguey** [ma'yei] *nm* agave

**magullar** [mayu'ʎar] *vt* (*amoratar*) to bruise; (*dañar*) to damage; (*fam*: *golpear*) to bash, beat

**mahometano, a** [maome'tano, a] *adj* Mohammedan

**mahonesa** [mao'nesa] *nf* = **mayonesa**

**maíz** [ma'iθ] *nm* maize (*BRIT*), corn (*US*); sweet corn

**majadero, a** [maxa'ðero, a] *adj* silly, stupid

**majestad** [maxes'tað] *nf* majesty; **majestuoso, a** *adj* majestic

**majo, a** ['maxo, a] *adj* nice; (*guapo*) attractive, good-looking; (*elegante*) smart

**mal** [mal] *adv* badly; (*equivocadamente*) wrongly; (*con dificultad*) with difficulty ♦ *adj* = **malo** ♦ *nm* evil; (*desgracia*) misfortune; (*daño*) harm, damage; (*MED*) illness; ~ **que bien** rightly or wrongly; **ir de** ~ **en peor** to get worse and worse

**mala** ['mala] *nf* spell of bad luck; **estar de** ~**s** to be in a bad mood; *ver tb* **malo**

**malabarismo** [malaβa'rismo] *nm* juggling; **malabarista** *nm/f* juggler

**malaria** [ma'larja] *nf* malaria

**malcriado, a** [mal'krjaðo, a] *adj* (*consentido*) spoiled

**maldad** [mal'dað] *nf* evil, wickedness

**maldecir** [malde'θir] *vt* to curse ♦ *vi*: ~ **de** to speak ill of

**maldición** [maldi'θjon] *nf* curse

**maldito, a** [mal'dito, a] *adj* (*condenado*) damned; (*perverso*) wicked; **¡**~ **sea!** damn it!

**maleante** [male'ante] *adj* wicked ♦ *nm/f* criminal, crook

**maledicencia** [maleði'θenθja] *nf* slander, scandal

**maleducado, a** [maleðu'kaðo, a] *adj* bad-mannered, rude

**malentendido** [malenten'diðo] *nm* misunderstanding

**malestar** [males'tar] nm (gen) discomfort; (fig: inquietud) uneasiness; (POL) unrest

**maleta** [ma'leta] nf case, suitcase; (AUTO) boot (BRIT), trunk (US); **hacer las ~s** to pack; **maletera** (AM) nf = **maletero**; **maletero** nm (AUTO) boot (BRIT), trunk (US); **maletín** nm small case, bag

**malévolo, a** [ma'leβolo, a] adj malicious, spiteful

**maleza** [ma'leθa] nf (hierbas malas) weeds pl; (arbustos) thicket

**malgastar** [malɣas'tar] vt (tiempo, dinero) to waste; (salud) to ruin

**malhechor, a** [male'tʃor, a] nm/f delinquent

**malhumorado, a** [malumo'raðo, a] adj bad-tempered

**malicia** [ma'liθja] nf (maldad) wickedness; (astucia) slyness, guile; (mala intención) malice, spite; (carácter travieso) mischievousness; **malicioso, a** adj wicked, evil; sly, crafty; malicious, spiteful; mischievous

**maligno, a** [ma'liɣno, a] adj evil; (malévolo) malicious; (MED) malignant

**malo, a** ['malo, a] adj bad; (falso) false ♦ nm/f villain; **estar ~** to be ill

**malograr** [malo'ɣrar] vt to spoil; (plan) to upset; (ocasión) to waste; **~se** vr (plan etc) to fail, come to grief; (persona) to die before one's time

**malparado, a** [malpa'raðo, a] adj: **salir ~** to come off badly

**malpensado, a** [malpen'saðo, a] adj (persona) nasty

**malsano, a** [mal'sano, a] adj unhealthy

**Malta** ['malta] nf Malta

**malteada** [malte'aða] (AM) nf milk shake

**maltratar** [maltra'tar] vt to ill-treat, mistreat

**maltrecho, a** [mal'tretʃo, a] adj battered, damaged

**malvado, a** [mal'βaðo, a] adj evil, villainous

**malversar** [malβer'sar] vt to embezzle, misappropriate

**Malvinas** [mal'βinas]: **Islas ~** nfpl Falkland Islands

**malvivir** [malβi'βir] vi to live poorly

**malla** ['maʎa] nf mesh; (de baño) swimsuit; (de ballet, gimnasia) leotard; **~s** nfpl tights; **~ de alambre** wire mesh

**Mallorca** [ma'ʎorka] nf Majorca

**mama** ['mama] nf (de animal) teat; (de mujer) breast

**mamá** [ma'ma] (pl **~s**) (fam) nf mum, mummy

**mamar** [ma'mar] vt (pecho) to suck; (fig) to absorb, assimilate ♦ vi to suck

**mamarracho** [mama'rratʃo] nm sight, mess

**mamífero** [ma'mifero] nm mammal

**mampara** [mam'para] nf (entre habitaciones) partition; (biombo) screen

**mampostería** [mamposte'ria] nf masonry

**manada** [ma'naða] nf (ZOOL) herd; (: de leones) pride; (: de lobos) pack

**Managua** [ma'naɣwa] n Managua

**manantial** [manan'tjal] nm spring; (fuente) fountain; (fig) source

**manar** [ma'nar] vt to run with, flow with ♦ vi to run, flow; (abundar) to abound

**manco, a** ['manko, a] adj (de un brazo) one-armed; (de una mano) one-handed; (fig) defective, faulty

**mancomunar** [mankomu'nar] vt to unite, bring together; (recursos) to pool; (JUR) to make jointly responsible; **mancomunidad** nf union, association; (comunidad) community; (JUR) joint responsibility

**mancha** ['mantʃa] nf stain, mark; (ZOOL) patch; (boceto) sketch, outline; **manchar** vt (gen) to stain, mark; (ensuciar) to soil, dirty

**manchego, a** [man'tʃeɣo, a] adj of o from La Mancha

**mandamiento** [manda'mjento] nm (orden) order, command; (REL) commandment; **~ judicial** warrant

**mandar** [man'dar] vt (ordenar) to order; (dirigir) to lead, command; (enviar) to send; (pedir) to order, ask for ♦ vi to be in charge; (pey) to be bossy; ¿mande? pardon?, excuse me?; ~ **hacer un traje** to have a suit made

**mandarina** [manda'rina] nf (fruta) tangerine, mandarin (orange)

**mandatario, a** [manda'tarjo, a] nm/f (representante) agent; **primer** ~ head of state

**mandato** [man'dato] nm (orden) order; (INFORM) command; (POL: periodo) term of office; (: territorio) mandate; ~ **judicial** (search) warrant

**mandíbula** [man'diβula] nf jaw

**mandil** [man'dil] nm (delantal) apron

**mando** [man'do] nm (MIL) command; (de país) rule; (el primer lugar) lead; (POL) term of office; (TEC) control; ~ **a la izquierda** left-hand drive

**mandón, ona** [man'don, ona] adj bossy, domineering

**manejable** [mane'xaβle] adj manageable

**manejar** [mane'xar] vt to manage; (máquina) to work, operate; (caballo etc) to handle; (casa) to run, manage; (AM: AUTO) to drive; ~**se** vr (comportarse) to act, behave; (arreglárselas) to manage; **manejo** nm management; handling; running; driving; (facilidad de trato) ease, confidence; **manejos** nmpl (intrigas) intrigues

**manera** [ma'nera] nf way, manner, fashion; ~**s** nfpl (modales) manners; **su** ~ **de ser** the way he is; (aire) his manner; **de ninguna** ~ no way, by no means; **de otra** ~ otherwise; **de todas** ~**s** at any rate; **no hay** ~ **de persuadirle** there's no way of convincing him

**manga** ['manga] nf (de camisa) sleeve; (de riego) hose

**mangar** [man'gar] vt (fam) to pinch, nick

**mango** ['mango] nm handle; (BOT) mango

**mangonear** [mangone'ar] vi (meterse) to meddle, interfere; (ser mandón) to boss people about

**manguera** [man'gera] nf (de riego) hose; (tubo) pipe

**manía** [ma'nia] nf (MED) mania; (fig: moda) rage, craze; (disgusto) dislike; (malicia) spite; **maníaco, a** adj maniac(al) ♦ nm/f maniac

**maniatar** [manja'tar] vt to tie the hands of

**maniático, a** [ma'njatiko, a] adj maniac(al) ♦ nm/f maniac

**manicomio** [mani'komjo] nm mental hospital (BRIT), insane asylum (US)

**manifestación** [manifesta'θjon] nf (declaración) statement, declaration; (de emoción) show, display; (POL: desfile) demonstration; (: concentración) mass meeting

**manifestar** [manifes'tar] vt to show, manifest; (declarar) to state, declare; **manifiesto, a** adj clear, manifest ♦ nm manifesto

**manija** [ma'nixa] nf handle

**manillar** [mani'ʎar] nm (de bicicleta) handlebars pl

**maniobra** [ma'njoβra] nf manœuvring; (manejo) handling; (fig) manœuvre; (estratagema) stratagem; ~**s** nfpl (MIL) manœuvres; **maniobrar** vt to manœuvre; (manejar) to handle

**manipulación** [manipula'θjon] nf manipulation

**manipular** [manipu'lar] vt to manipulate; (manejar) to handle

**maniquí** [mani'ki] nm dummy ♦ nm/f model

**manirroto, a** [mani'rroto, a] adj lavish, extravagant ♦ nm/f spendthrift

**manivela** [mani'βela] nf crank

**manjar** [man'xar] nm (tasty) dish

**mano** ['mano] nf hand; (ZOOL) foot, paw; (de pintura) coat; (serie) lot, series; **a** ~ by hand; **a** ~ **derecha/izquierda** on the right(-hand side)/

left(-hand side); **de primera ~** (at) first hand; **de segunda ~** (at) second hand; **robo a ~ armada** armed robbery; **~ de obra** labour, manpower; **estrechar la ~ a uno** to shake sb's hand

**manojo** [ma'noxo] *nm* handful, bunch; **~ de llaves** bunch of keys

**manopla** [ma'nopla] *nf* (*guante*) glove; (*paño*) face cloth

**manoseado, a** [manose'aðo, a] *adj* well-worn

**manosear** [manose'ar] *vt* (*tocar*) to handle, touch; (*desordenar*) to mess up, rumple; (*insistir en*) to overwork; (*AM*) to caress, fondle

**manotazo** [mano'taθo] *nm* slap, smack

**mansalva** [man'salβa]: **a ~** *adv* indiscriminately

**mansedumbre** [manse'ðumbre] *nf* gentleness, meekness

**mansión** [man'sjon] *nf* mansion

**manso, a** ['manso, a] *adj* gentle, mild; (*animal*) tame

**manta** ['manta] *nf* blanket; (*AM*: *poncho*) poncho

**manteca** [man'teka] *nf* fat; (*AM*: butter); **~ de cacahuete/cacao** peanut/cocoa butter; **~ de cerdo** lard

**mantecado** [mante'kaðo] (*AM*) *nm* ice cream

**mantel** [man'tel] *nm* tablecloth

**mantendré** *etc vb ver* **mantener**

**mantener** [mante'ner] *vt* to support, maintain; (*alimentar*) to sustain; (*conservar*) to keep; (*TEC*) to maintain, service; **~se** *vr* (*seguir de pie*) to be still standing; (*no ceder*) to hold one's ground; (*subsistir*) to sustain o.s., keep going; **mantenimiento** *nm* maintenance; sustenance; (*sustento*) support

**mantequilla** [mante'kiʎa] *nf* butter

**mantilla** [man'tiʎa] *nf* mantilla; **~s** *nfpl* (*de bebé*) baby clothes

**manto** ['manto] *nm* (*capa*) cloak; (*de ceremonia*) robe, gown

**mantuve** *etc vb ver* **mantener**

**manual** [ma'nwal] *adj* manual ♦ *nm* manual, handbook

**manufactura** [manufak'tura] *nf* manufacture; (*fábrica*) factory; **manufacturado, a** (*producto*) manufactured

**manuscrito, a** [manus'krito, a] *adj* handwritten ♦ *nm* manuscript

**manutención** [manuten'θjon] *nf* maintenance; (*sustento*) support

**manzana** [man'θana] *nf* apple; (*ARQ*) block (of houses)

**manzanilla** [manθa'niʎa] *nf* (*planta*) camomile; (*infusión*) camomile tea

**manzano** [man'θano] *nm* apple tree

**maña** ['maɲa] *nf* (*gen*) skill, dexterity; (*pey*) guile; (*costumbre*) habit; (*destreza*) trick, knack

**mañana** [ma'ɲana] *adv* tomorrow ♦ *nm* future ♦ *nf* morning; **de o por la ~ in the morning**; **¡hasta ~!** see you tomorrow!; **~ por la ~** tomorrow morning

**mañoso, a** [ma'ɲoso, a] *adj* (*hábil*) skilful; (*astuto*) clever

**mapa** ['mapa] *nm* map

**maqueta** [ma'keta] *nf* (*scale*) model

**maquillaje** [maki'ʎaxe] *nm* make-up; (*acto*) making up

**maquillar** [maki'ʎar] *vt* to make up; **~se** *vr* to put on (some) make-up

**máquina** ['makina] *nf* machine; (*de tren*) locomotive, engine; (*FOTO*) camera; (*AM*: *coche*) car; (*fig*) machinery; (: *proyecto*) plan, project; **escrito a ~** typewritten; **de escribir** typewriter; **~ de coser/lavar** sewing/washing machine

**maquinación** [makina'θjon] *nf* machination, plot

**maquinal** [maki'nal] *adj* (*fig*) mechanical, automatic

**maquinaria** [maki'narja] *nf* (*máquinas*) machinery; (*mecanismo*) mechanism, works *pl*

**maquinilla** [maki'niʎa] *nf*: **~ de afeitar** razor

**maquinista** [maki'nista] *nm/f* (*de tren*) engine driver; (*TEC*) operator; (*NAUT*) engineer

**mar** [mar] *nm o f* sea; ~ **adentro** *o* **afuera** out at sea; **en alta** ~ on the high seas; **la** ~ **de** (*fam*) lots of; **el** M~ **Negro/Báltico** the Black/Baltic Sea

**maraña** [ma'raɲa] *nf* (*maleza*) thicket; (*confusión*) tangle

**maravilla** [mara'βiʎa] *nf* marvel, wonder; (*BOT*) marigold; **maravillar** *vt* to astonish, amaze; **maravillarse** *vr* to be astonished, be amazed; **maravilloso, a** *adj* wonderful, marvellous

**marca** ['marka] *nf* (*gen*) mark; (*sello*) stamp; (*COM*) make, brand; **de** ~ excellent, outstanding; ~ **de fábrica** trademark; ~ **registrada** registered trademark

**marcado, a** [mar'kaðo, a] *adj* marked, strong

**marcador** [marka'ðor] *nm* (*DEPORTE*) scoreboard; (: *persona*) scorer

**marcar** [mar'kar] *vt* (*gen*) to mark; (*número de teléfono*) to dial; (*gol*) to score; (*números*) to record, keep a tally of; (*pelo*) to set ♦ *vi* (*DEPORTE*) to score; (*TEL*) to dial

**marcial** [mar'θjal] *adj* martial, military

**marciano, a** [mar'θjano, a] *adj, nm/f* Martian

**marco** ['marko] *nm* frame; (*DEPORTE*) goal posts *pl*; (*moneda*) mark; (*fig*) framework; ~ **de chimenea** mantelpiece

**marcha** ['martʃa] *nf* march; (*TEC*) running, working; (*AUTO*) gear; (*velocidad*) speed; (*fig*) progress; (*dirección*) course; **poner en** ~ to put into gear; (*fig*) to set in motion, get going; **dar** ~ **atrás** to reverse, put into reverse gear; **estar en** ~ to be under way, be in motion

**marchar** [mar'tʃar] *vi* (*ir*) to go; (*funcionar*) to work, go; ~**se** *vr* to go (away), leave

**marchitar** [martʃi'tar] *vt* to wither, dry up; ~**se** *vr* (*BOT*) to wither; (*fig*) to fade away; **marchito, a** *adj* withered, faded; (*fig*) in decline

**marea** [ma'rea] *nf* tide; (*llovizna*) drizzle

**marear** [mare'ar] *vt* (*fig*) to annoy, upset; (*MED*): ~ **a uno** to make sb feel sick; ~**se** *vr* (*tener náuseas*) to feel sick; (*desvanecerse*) to feel faint; (*aturdirse*) to feel dizzy; (*fam: emborracharse*) to get tipsy

**maremoto** [mare'moto] *nm* tidal wave

**mareo** [ma'reo] *nm* (*náusea*) sick feeling; (*en viaje*) travel sickness; (*aturdimiento*) dizziness; (*fam: lata*) nuisance

**marfil** [mar'fil] *nm* ivory

**margarina** [marɣa'rina] *nf* margarine

**margarita** [marɣa'rita] *nf* (*BOT*) daisy; (*rueda*) ~ daisywheel

**margen** ['marxen] *nm* (*borde*) edge, border; (*fig*) margin, space ♦ *nf* (*de río etc*) bank; **dar** ~ **para** to give an opportunity for; **mantenerse al** ~ to keep out (of things)

**marginar** [marxi'nar] *vt* (*grupo, individuo*) to marginalize, ostracize; *socialmente*: to marginalize, ostracize

**marica** [ma'rika] (*fam*) *nm* sissy

**maricón** [mari'kon] (*fam*) *nm* queer

**marido** [ma'riðo] *nm* husband

**mariguana** [mari'ɣwana] *nf* marijuana, cannabis

**marihuana** [mari'wana] *nf* = **mariguana**

**marina** [ma'rina] *nf* navy; ~ **mercante** merchant navy

**marinero, a** [mari'nero, a] *adj* sea *cpd*; (*barco*) seaworthy ♦ *nm* sailor, seaman

**marino, a** [ma'rino, a] *adj* sea *cpd*, marine ♦ *nm* sailor

**marioneta** [marjo'neta] *nf* puppet

**mariposa** [mari'posa] *nf* butterfly

**mariquita** [mari'kita] *nf* ladybird (*BRIT*), ladybug (*US*)

**mariscos** [ma'riskos] *nmpl* shellfish *inv*, seafood(s)

**marítimo, a** [ma'ritimo, a] *adj* sea *cpd*, maritime

**mármol** ['marmol] *nm* marble

**marqués, esa** [mar'kes, esa] *nm/f* marquis/marchioness

**marrón** [ma'rron] *adj* brown

**marroquí** [marro'ki] *adj*, *nm/f* Moroccan ♦ *nm* Morocco (leather)

**Marruecos** [ma'rrwekos] *nm* Morocco

**martes** ['martes] *nm inv* Tuesday

**martillo** [mar'tiʎo] *nm* hammer; ~ **neumático** pneumatic drill (BRIT), jackhammer

**mártir** ['martir] *nm/f* martyr; **martirio** *nm* martyrdom; (*fig*) torture, torment

**Marxismo** [mark'sismo] *nm* Marxism; **marxista** *adj*, *nm/f* Marxist

**marzo** ['marθo] *nm* March

**mas** [mas] *conj* but

---

PALABRA CLAVE

**más** [mas] *adj*, *adv* 1: ~ (que, de) (*compar*) more (than), ...+ *er* (than); ~ **grande/inteligente** bigger/more intelligent; **trabaja** ~ (**que yo**) he works more (than me); *ver tb* **cada**

2 (*superl*): **el** ~ **the most**, ...+ *est*; **el** ~ **grande/inteligente** (**de**) the biggest/most intelligent (in)

3 (*negativo*): **no tengo** ~ **dinero** I haven't got any more money; **no viene** ~ **por aquí** he doesn't come round here any more

4 (*adicional*): **no le veo** ~ **solución que** ... I see no other solution than to ...; ¿**quién** ~? anybody else?

5 (+ *adj*: *valor superlativo*): ¡**qué perro** ~ **sucio!** what a filthy dog!; ¡**es** ~ **tonto!** he's so stupid!

6 (*locuciones*): ~ **o menos** more or less; **los** ~ **most** people; **es** ~ furthermore; ~ **bien** rather; ¡**qué** ~ **da!** what does it matter!; *ver tb* **no**

7: **por** ~: **por** ~ **que te esfuerces** no matter how hard you try; **por** ~ **que quisiera** ... much as I should like to ...

8: **de** ~: **veo que aquí estoy de** ~ I can see I'm not needed here; **tenemos uno de** ~ we've got one extra

---

♦ *prep*: 2 ~ 2 **son** 4 2 **and** *o* **plus** 2 **are** 4

♦ *nm inv*: **este trabajo tiene sus** ~ **y sus menos** this job's got its good points and its bad points

**masa** ['masa] *nf* (*mezcla*) dough; (*volumen*) volume, mass; (*FÍSICA*) mass; **en** ~ **en masse**; **las** ~**s** (*POL*) the masses

**masacre** [ma'sakre] *nf* massacre

**masaje** [ma'saxe] *nm* massage

**máscara** ['maskara] *nf* (*gen*) mask ♦ *nm/f* masked person; **mascarilla** *nf* (*de belleza*, *MED*) mask

**masculino, a** [masku'lino, a] *adj* masculine; (*BIO*) male

**masificación** [masifika'θjon] *nf* overcrowding

**masivo, a** [ma'siβo, a] *adj* (*en masa*) mass

**masón** [ma'son] *nm* (free)mason

**masoquista** [maso'kista] *nm/f* masochist

**masticar** [masti'kar] *vt* to chew; (*fig*) to ponder

**mástil** ['mastil] *nm* (*de navío*) mast; (*de guitarra*) neck

**mastín** [mas'tin] *nm* mastiff

**masturbación** [masturβa'θjon] *nf* masturbation

**masturbarse** [mastur'βarse] *vr* to masturbate

**mata** ['mata] *nf* (*arbusto*) bush, shrub; (*de hierba*) tuft

**matadero** [mata'ðero] *nm* slaughterhouse, abattoir

**matador, a** [mata'ðor, a] *adj* killing ♦ *nm/f* killer ♦ *nm* (*TAUR*) matador, bullfighter

**matamoscas** [mata'moskas] *nm inv* (*palo*) fly swat

**matanza** [ma'tanθa] *nf* slaughter

**matar** [ma'tar] *vt*, *vi* to kill; ~**se** *vr* (*suicidarse*) to kill o.s., commit suicide; (*morir*) to be get killed; ~ **el hambre** to stave off hunger

**matasellos** [mata'seʎos] *nm inv* postmark

**mate** ['mate] *adj* (*sin brillo*: *color*)

dull, matt ♦ *nm* (*en ajedrez*) (check)mate; (*AM: hierba*) maté; (*: vasija*) gourd

**matemáticas** [mate'matikas] *nfpl* mathematics; **matemático, a** *adj* mathematical ♦ *nm/f* mathematician

**materia** [ma'terja] *nf* (*gen*) matter; (*TEC*) material; (*ESCOL*) subject; **en ~ de** on the subject of; **~ prima** raw material; **material** *adj* material; (*dolor*) physical ♦ *nm* material; (*TEC*) equipment; **materialismo** *nm* materialism; **materialista** *adj* materialist(ic); **materialmente** *adv* materially; (*fig*) absolutely

**maternal** [mater'nal] *adj* motherly, maternal

**maternidad** [materni'ðað] *nf* motherhood, maternity; **materno, a** *adj* maternal; (*lengua*) mother *cpd*

**matinal** [mati'nal] *adj* morning *cpd*

**matiz** [ma'tiθ] *nm* shade; **~ar** *vt* (*variar*) to vary; (*ARTE*) to blend; **~ar de** to tinge with

**matón** [ma'ton] *nm* bully

**matorral** [mato'rral] *nm* thicket

**matraca** [ma'traka] *nf* rattle

**matrícula** [ma'trikula] *nf* (*registro*) register; (*AUTO*) registration number; (*: placa*) number plate; **matricular** *vt* to register, enrol

**matrimonial** [matrimo'njal] *adj* matrimonial

**matrimonio** [matri'monjo] *nm* (*pareja*) (married) couple; (*unión*) marriage

**matriz** [ma'triθ] *nf* (*ANAT*) womb; (*TEC*) mould; **casa ~** (*COM*) head office

**matrona** [ma'trona] *nf* (*persona de edad*) matron

**maullar** [mau'ʎar] *vi* to mew, miaow

**maxilar** [maksi'lar] *nm* jaw(bone)

**máxima** ['maksima] *nf* maxim

**máxime** ['maksime] *adv* especially

**máximo, a** ['maksimo, a] *adj* maximum; (*más alto*) highest; (*más grande*) greatest ♦ *nm* maximum

**mayo** ['majo] *nm* May

**mayonesa** [majo'nesa] *nf* mayon-

naise

**mayor** [ma'jor] *adj* main, chief; (*adulto*) adult; (*de edad avanzada*) elderly; (*MUS*) major; (*compar: de tamaño*) bigger; (*: de edad*) older; (*superl: de tamaño*) biggest; (*: de edad*) oldest ♦ *nm* chief, boss; (*adulto*) adult; **al por ~** wholesale; **~ de edad** adult; **~es** *nmpl* (*antepasados*) ancestors

**mayoral** [majo'ral] *nm* foreman

**mayordomo** [major'ðomo] *nm* butler

**mayoría** [majo'ria] *nf* majority, greater part

**mayorista** [majo'rista] *nm/f* wholesaler

**mayoritario, a** [majori'tarjo, a] *adj* majority *cpd*

**mayúscula** [ma'juskula] *nf* capital letter

**mayúsculo, a** [ma'juskulo, a] *adj* (*fig*) huge, tremendous

**mazapán** [maθa'pan] *nm* marzipan

**mazo** ['maθo] *nm* (*martillo*) mallet; (*de flores*) bunch; (*DEPORTE*) bat

**me** [me] *pron* (*directo*) me; (*indirecto*) (to) me; (*reflexivo*) (to) myself; **¡dámelo!** give it to me!

**mear** [me'ar] (*fam*) *vi* to pee, piss

**mecánica** [me'kanika] *nf* (*ESCOL*) mechanics *sg*; (*mecanismo*) mechanism; *ver tb* **mecánico**

**mecánico, a** [me'kaniko, a] *adj* mechanical ♦ *nm/f* mechanic

**mecanismo** [meka'nismo] *nm* mechanism; (*marcha*) gear

**mecanografía** [mekanovra'fia] *nf* typewriting; **mecanógrafo, a** *nm/f* typist

**mecate** [me'kate] (*AM*) *nm* rope

**mecedora** [meθe'ðora] *nf* rocking chair

**mecer** [me'θer] *vt* (*cuna*) to rock; **~se** *vr* to rock; (*ramo*) to sway

**mecha** ['metʃa] *nf* (*de vela*) wick; (*de bomba*) fuse

**mechero** [me'tʃero] *nm* (cigarette) lighter

**mechón** [me'tʃon] *nm* (*gen*) tuft;

*(manojo)* bundle; *(de pelo)* lock

**medalla** [me'ðaʎa] *nf* medal

**media** ['meðja] *nf (ESP)* stocking; *(AM)* sock; *(promedio)* average

**mediado, a** [me'ðjaðo, a] *adj* half-full; *(trabajo)* half-completed; **a ~s de** in the middle of, halfway through

**mediano, a** [me'ðjano, a] *adj (regular)* medium, average; *(mediocre)* mediocre

**medianoche** [meðja'notʃe] *nf* midnight

**mediante** [me'ðjante] *adv* by (means of), through

**mediar** [me'ðjar] *vi (interceder)* to mediate, intervene

**medicación** [meðika'θjon] *nf* medication, treatment

**medicamento** [meðika'mento] *nm* medicine, drug

**medicina** [meði'θina] *nf* medicine

**medición** [meði'θjon] *nf* measurement

**médico, a** ['meðiko, a] *adj* medical ♦ *nm/f* doctor

**medida** [me'ðiða] *nf* measure; *(medición)* measurement; *(prudencia)* moderation, prudence; **en cierta/gran ~** up to a point/to a great extent; **un traje a la ~** made-to-measure suit; **~ de cuello** collar size; **a ~ de** in proportion to; *(de acuerdo con)* in keeping with; **a ~ que** *(conforme)* as

**medio, a** ['meðjo, a] *adj* half *(a)*; *(punto)* mid, middle; *(promedio)* average ♦ *adv* half ♦ *nm (centro)* middle, centre; *(promedio)* average; *(método)* means, way; *(ambiente)* environment; **~s** *nmpl* means, resources; **~ litro** half a litre; **las tres y media** half past three; **~ Oriente** Middle East; **a ~ terminar** half finished; **pagar a medias** to share the cost; **~ ambiental** *adj (política, efectos)* environmental

**mediocre** [me'ðjokre] *adj* middling, average; *(pey)* mediocre

**mediodía** [meðjo'ðia] *nm* midday, noon

**medir** [me'ðir] *vt, vi (gen)* to measure

**meditar** [meði'tar] *vt* to ponder, think over, meditate on; *(planear)* to think out

**mediterráneo, a** [meðite'rraneo, a] *adj* Mediterranean ♦ *nm:* **el M~** the Mediterranean (Sea)

**médula** ['meðula] *nf (ANAT)* marrow; **~ espinal** spinal cord

**medusa** [me'ðusa] *nf (ESP)* jellyfish

**megafonía** [meðafo'nia] *nf* public address system, PA system; **megáfono** *nm* megaphone

**megalómano, a** [meɣa'lomano, a] *nm/f* megalomaniac

**mejicano, a** [mexi'kano, a] *adj, nm/f* Mexican

**Méjico** ['mexiko] *nm* Mexico

**mejilla** [me'xiʎa] *nf* cheek

**mejillón** [mexi'ʎon] *nm* mussel

**mejor** [me'xor] *adj, adv (compar)* better; *(superl)* best; **a lo ~** probably; *(quizá)* maybe; **~ dicho** rather; **tanto ~** so much the better

**mejora** [me'xora] *nf* improvement; **mejorar** *vt* to improve, make better ♦ *vi* to improve, get better; **mejorarse** *vr* to improve, get better

**melancólico, a** [melan'koliko, a] *adj (triste)* sad, melancholy; *(soñador)* dreamy

**melena** [me'lena] *nf (de persona)* long hair; *(ZOOL)* mane

**melocotón** [meloko'ton] *(ESP) nm* peach

**melodía** [melo'ðia] *nf* melody, tune

**melodrama** [melo'ðrama] *nm* melodrama; **melodramático, a** *adj* melodramatic

**melón** [me'lon] *nm* melon

**mellizo, a** [me'ʎiθo, a] *adj, nm/f* twin; **~s** *nmpl (AM)* cufflinks

**membrete** [mem'brete] *nm* letterhead

**membrillo** [mem'briʎo] *nm* quince; **carne de ~** quince jelly

**memorable** [memo'raßle] *adj* memorable

**memorándum** [memo'randum] *(pl*

**~s)** nm (libro) notebook; (comunicación) memorandum

**memoria** [me'morja] nf (gen) memory; (recuerdo) memory, memoirs; **~ intermedia** (INFORM) buffer; **memorizar** vt to memorize

**menaje** [me'naxe] nm: **~ de cocina** kitchenware

**mencionar** [menθjo'nar] vt to mention

**mendigar** [mendi'γar] vt to beg (for)

**mendigo, a** [men'diγo, a] nm/f beggar

**mendrugo** [men'druγo] nm crust

**menear** [mene'ar] vt to move; (fig) to handle; **~se** vr to shake; (balancearse) to sway; (moverse) to move; (fig) to get a move on

**menester** [menes'ter] nm (necesidad) necessity; **~es** nmpl (deberes) duties; **es ~** it is necessary

**menestra** [me'nestra] nf: **~ de verduras** vegetable stew

**menguante** [men'gwante] adj decreasing, diminishing

**menguar** [men'gwar] vt to lessen, diminish; (fig) to discredit ♦ vi to diminish, decrease; (fig) to decline

**menopausia** [meno'pausja] nf menopause

**menor** [me'nor] adj (más pequeño: compar) smaller; (: superl) smallest; (más joven: compar) younger; (: superl) youngest; (MUS) minor ♦ nm/f (joven) young person, juvenile; **no tengo la ~ idea** I haven't the faintest idea; **al por ~** retail; **~ de edad** person under age

**Menorca** [me'norka] nf Minorca

PALABRA CLAVE

**menos** [menos] adj **1**: **~ (que, de)** (compar: cantidad) less (than); (: número) fewer (than); **con ~ entusiasmo** with less enthusiasm; **~ gente** fewer people; ver tb **cada**
**2** (superl): **es el que ~ culpa tiene** he is the least to blame
♦ adv **1** (compar): **~ (que, de)** less (than); **me gusta ~ que el otro** I

like it less than the other one
**2** (superl): **es el ~ listo** (de su clase) he's the least bright in his class; **de todas ellas es la que ~ me agrada** out of all of them she's the one I like least; **(por) lo ~** at the (very) least
**3** (locuciones): **no quiero verle y ~ visitarle** I don't want to see him let alone visit him; **tenemos 7 de ~** we're seven short

♦ prep except; (cifras) minus; **todos ~ él** everyone except (for) him; **5 ~ 2** 5 minus 2

♦ conj: **a ~ que: a ~ que venga mañana** unless he comes tomorrow

**menospreciar** [menospre'θjar] vt to underrate, undervalue; (despreciar) to scorn, despise

**mensaje** [men'saxe] nm message; **~ro, a** nm/f messenger

**menstruación** [menstrua'θjon] nf menstruation

**menstruar** [mens'trwar] vi to menstruate

**mensual** [men'swal] adj monthly; **1000 ptas ~es** 1000 ptas a month; **~idad** nf (salario) monthly salary; (COM) monthly payment, monthly instalment

**menta** ['menta] nf mint

**mental** [men'tal] adj mental; **~idad** nf mentality; **~izar** vt (opinión pública) to convince; (padres) to convince (mentally); **~izarse** vr: **~izarse (de)** to get used to the idea (of)

**mentar** [men'tar] vt to mention, name

**mente** ['mente] nf mind

**mentir** [men'tir] vi to lie

**mentira** [men'tira] nf (una ~) lie; (acto) lying; (invención) fiction; **parece ~ que ...** it seems incredible that ..., I can't believe that ...

**mentiroso, a** [menti'roso, a] adj lying ♦ nm/f liar

**menú** [me'nu] nm (pl **~s**) nm menu; (AM) set meal

**menudo, a** [me'nuðo, a] adj (peque-

*ño)* small, tiny; *(sin importancia)* petty, insignificant; *;~ negocio!* *(fam)* some deal!; **a ~** often, frequently

**meñique** [me'nike] *nm* little finger

**meollo** [me'noʎo] *nm (fig)* core

**mercaderías** [merkaðe'rias] *nfpl* goods, merchandise *sg*

**mercado** [mer'kaðo] *nm* market; **M~ Común** Common Market

**mercancía** [merkan'θia] *nf* commodity; *~s nfpl* goods, merchandise *sg*

**mercantil** [merkan'til] *adj* mercantile, commercial

**mercenario, a** [merθe'narjo, a] *adj, nm* mercenary

**mercería** [merθe'ria] *nf* haberdashery *(BRIT)*, notions *(US)*; *(tienda)* haberdasher's *(BRIT)*, notions store *(US)*; *(AM)* drapery

**mercurio** [mer'kurjo] *nm* mercury

**merecer** [mere'θer] *vt* to deserve, merit ♦ *vi* to be deserving, be worthy; **merece la pena** it's worthwhile; **merecido, a** *adj* (well) deserved; **llevar su merecido** to get one's deserts

**merendar** [meren'dar] *vt* to have for tea ♦ *vi* to have tea; *(en el campo)* to have a picnic

**merengue** [me'renge] *nm* meringue

**meridiano** [meri'ðjano] *nm (GEO)* meridian

**merienda** [me'rjenda] *nf* (light) tea, afternoon snack; *(de campo)* picnic

**mérito** ['merito] *nm* merit; *(valor)* worth, value

**merluza** [mer'luθa] *nf* hake

**merma** ['merma] *nf* decrease; *(pérdida)* wastage; **mermar** *vt* to reduce, lessen ♦ *vi* to decrease, dwindle

**mermelada** [merme'laða] *nf* jam

**mero, a** ['mero, a] *adj* mere; *(AM: fam)* very

**merodear** [meroðe'ar] *vi:* ~ **por** to prowl about

**mes** [mes] *nm* month; *(salario)* month's pay

**mesa** ['mesa] *nf* table; *(de trabajo)* desk; *(GEO)* plateau; *(ARQ)* land-

ing; **~ directiva** board; **~ redonda** *(reunión)* round table; **poner/quitar la ~** to lay/clear the table; **mesero, a** *(AM) nm/f* waiter/waitress

**meseta** [me'seta] *nf (GEO)* meseta, tableland; *(ARQ)* landing

**mesilla** [me'siʎa] *nf:* ~ **(de noche)** bedside table

**mesón** [me'son] *nm* inn

**mestizo, a** [mes'tiθo, a] *adj* half-caste, of mixed race; *(ZOOL)* crossbred ♦ *nm/f* half-caste

**mesura** [me'sura] *nf (moderación)* moderation, restraint; *(cortesía)* courtesy

**meta** ['meta] *nf* goal; *(de carrera)* finish

**metabolismo** [metaβo'lismo] *nm (BIO)* metabolism

**metáfora** [me'tafora] *nf* metaphor

**metal** [me'tal] *nm (materia)* metal; *(MUS)* brass; **metálico, a** *adj* metallic; *(de metal)* metal ♦ *nm (dinero contante)* cash

**metalurgia** [meta'lurxja] *nf* metallurgy

**meteoro** [mete'oro] *nm* meteor; **~logía** *nf* meteorology

**meter** [me'ter] *vt (colocar)* to put, place; *(introducir)* to put in, insert; *(involucrar)* to involve; *(causar)* to make, cause; **~se** *vr:* **~se en** to go into, enter; *(fig)* to interfere in, meddle in; **~se a** to start; **~se a escritor** to become a writer; **~se con uno** to provoke sb, pick a quarrel with sb

**meticuloso, a** [metiku'loso, a] *adj* meticulous, thorough

**metódico, a** [me'toðiko, a] *adj* methodical

**método** ['metoðo] *nm* method

**metralleta** [metra'ʎeta] *nf* submachine-gun

**métrico, a** [me'triko, a] *adj* metric

**metro** ['metro] *nm* metre; *(tren)* underground *(BRIT)*, subway *(US)*

**México** ['mexiko] *nm* Mexico; **Ciudad de ~** Mexico City

**mezcla** ['meθkla] *nf* mixture; **mez-**

**clar** vt to mix (up); **mezclarse** vr to mix, mingle; **mezclarse en** to get mixed up in, get involved in

**mezquino, a** [meθ'kino, a] adj (cicatero) mean

**mezquita** [meθ'kita] nf mosque

**mg.** abr (= miligramo) mg

**mi** [mi] adj pos my ♦ nm (MUS) E

**mí** [mi] pron me; myself

**mía** ['mia] pron ver **mío**

**miaja** ['mjaxa] nf crumb

**micro** ['mikro] (AM) nm minibus

**microbio** [mi'kroβjo] nm microbe

**micrófono** [mi'krofono] nm microphone

**microondas** [mikro'ondas] nm inv (tb: horno ~) microwave (oven)

**microordenador** [mikro(o)rðena'ðor] nm microcomputer

**microscopio** [mikros'kopjo] nm microscope

**michelín** [mitʃe'lin] fam nm (de grasa) spare tyre

**miedo** ['mjeðo] nm fear; (nerviosismo) apprehension, nervousness; **tener** ~ to be afraid; **de** ~ wonderful, marvellous; **hace un frío de** ~ (fam) it's terribly cold; **~so, a** adj fearful, timid

**miel** [mjel] nf honey

**miembro** ['mjembro] nm limb; (socio) member; ~ **viril** penis

**mientras** ['mjentras] conj while; (duración) as long as ♦ adv meanwhile; ~ **tanto** meanwhile; ~ **más tiene, más quiere** the more he has, the more he wants

**miércoles** ['mjerkoles] nm inv Wednesday

**mierda** ['mjerða] (fam!) nf shit (!)

**miga** ['miɣa] nf crumb; (fig: meollo) essence; **hacer buenas ~s** (fam) to get on well

**migración** [miɣra'θjon] nf migration

**mil** [mil] num thousand; **dos ~ libras** two thousand pounds

**milagro** [mi'laɣro] nm miracle; **~so, a** adj miraculous

**milésima** [mi'lesima] nf (de segundo) thousandth

**mili** ['mili] (fam) nf: **hacer la** ~ to do one's military service

**milicia** [mi'liθja] nf militia; (servicio militar) military service

**milímetro** [mi'limetro] nm millimetre

**militante** [mili'tante] adj militant

**militar** [mili'tar] adj military ♦ nm/f soldier ♦ vi to serve in the army; (fig) to be a member of a party

**milla** ['miʎa] nf mile

**millar** [mi'ʎar] nm thousand

**millón** [mi'ʎon] num million; **millonario, a** nm/f millionaire

**mimar** [mi'mar] vt (gen) to spoil, pamper

**mimbre** ['mimbre] nm wicker

**mímica** ['mimika] nf (para comunicarse) sign language; (imitación) mimicry

**mimo** ['mimo] nm (caricia) caress; (de niño) spoiling; (TEATRO) mime; (: actor) mime artist

**mina** ['mina] nf mine; **minar** vt to mine; (fig) to undermine

**mineral** [mine'ral] adj mineral ♦ nm (GEO) mineral; (mena) ore

**minero, a** [mi'nero, a] adj mining cpd ♦ nm/f miner

**miniatura** [minja'tura] adj inv, nf miniature

**minifalda** [mini'falda] nf miniskirt

**mínimo, a** ['minimo, a] adj, nm minimum

**minino, a** [mi'nino, a] (fam) nm/f puss, pussy

**ministerio** [minis'terjo] nm Ministry; M~ **de Hacienda/del Exterior** Treasury (BRIT), Treasury Department (US)/Foreign Office (BRIT), State Department (US)

**ministro, a** [mi'nistro, a] nm/f minister

**minoría** [mino'ria] nf minority

**minucioso, a** [minu'θjoso, a] adj thorough, meticulous; (prolijo) very detailed

**minúscula** [mi'nuskula] nf small letter

**minúsculo, a** [mi'nuskulo, a] adj

tiny, minute

**minusválido, a** |minus'βaliδo, a|
*adj* (physically) handicapped ♦ *nm/f*
(physically) handicapped person

**minuta** |mi'nuta| *nf (de comida)*
menu

**minutero** |minu'tero| *nm* minute
hand

**minuto** |mi'nuto| *nm* minute

**mío, a** |'mio, a| *pron*: el ~/la mía
mine; **un amigo** ~ a friend of mine;
lo ~ what is mine

**miope** |mi'ope| *adj* short-sighted

**mira** |'mira| *nf (de arma)* sight(s)
*(pl)*; *(fig)* aim, intention

**mirada** |mi'raδa| *nf* look, glance;
*(expresión)* look, expression; **clavar
la** ~ **en** to stare at; **echar una** ~ **a**
to glance at

**mirado, a** |mi'raδo, a| *adj (sensato)*
sensible; *(considerado)* considerate;
**bien/mal** ~ well/not well thought of;
**bien** ~ all things considered

**mirador** |mira'δor| *nm.* viewpoint,
vantage point

**mirar** |mi'rar| *vt* to look at; *(observar)* to watch; *(considerar)* to con-
sider, think over; *(vigilar, cuidar)* to
watch, look after ♦ *vi* to look; *(ARQ)*
to face; ~**se** *vr (dos personas)* to
look at each other; ~ **bien/mal** to
think highly of/have a poor opinion
of; ~**se al espejo** to look at o.s. in
the mirror

**mirilla** |mi'riλa| *nf (agujero)* spyhole,
peephole

**mirlo** |'mirlo| *nm* blackbird

**misa** |'misa| *nf (REL)* mass

**miserable** |mise'raβle| *adj (avaro)*
mean, stingy; *(nimio)* miserable, paltry; *(lugar)* squalid; *(fam)* vile, despicable ♦ *nm/f (malvado)* rogue

**miseria** |mi'serja| *nf* misery; *(pobre-
za)* poverty; *(tacañería)* meanness,
stinginess; *(condiciones)* squalor;
**una** ~ a pittance

**misericordia** |miseri'korδja| *nf
(compasión)* compassion, pity; *(piedad)* mercy

**misil** |mi'sil| *nm* missile

**misión** |mi'sjon| *nf* mission; **misio-
nero, a** *nm/f* missionary

**mismo, a** |'mismo, a| *adj (seme-
jante)* same; *(después de pron)* -self;
*(para énfasis)* very ♦ *adv:* **aquí/hoy**
~ right here/this very day; **ahora** ~
right now ♦ *conj:* **lo** ~ **que** just like,
just as; **el** ~ **traje** the same suit; **en
ese** ~ **momento** at that very moment; **vino el** ~ **Ministro** the minister himself came; **yo** ~ **lo vi** I saw
it myself; **lo** ~ the same (thing); **da
lo** ~ it's all the same; **quedamos en
las mismas** we're no further forward; **por lo** ~ for the same reason

**misterio** |mis'terjo| *nm (gen)* mys-
tery; *(lo secreto)* secrecy; ~**so, a**
*adj* mysterious

**mitad** |mi'taδ| *nf (medio)* half; *(cen-
tro)* middle; **a** ~ **de precio** (at)
half-price; **en** *o* **a** ~ **del camino**
halfway along the road; **cortar por
la** ~ to cut through the middle

**mitigar** |miti'var| *vt* to mitigate; *(do-
lor)* to ease; *(sed)* to quench

**mitin** |'mitin| *(pl* **mitines**) *nm* meet-
ing

**mito** |'mito| *nm* myth

**mixto, a** |'miksto, a| *adj* mixed

**ml.** *abr* (= *mililitro*) ml

**mm.** *abr* (= *milímetro*) mm

**mobiliario** |moβi'ljarjo| *nm* furniture

**moción** |mo'θjon| *nf* motion

**moco** |'moko| *nm* mucus; ~**s** *nmpl*
*(fam)* snot; **quitarse los** ~**s de la
nariz** *(fam)* to wipe one's nose

**mochila** |mo'tʃila| *nf* rucksack
*(BRIT)*, back-pack

**moda** |'moδa| *nf* fashion; *(estilo)*
style; **a la** *o* **de** ~ in fashion, fashionable; **pasado de** ~ out of fashion

**modales** |mo'δales| *nmpl* manners

**modalidad** |moδali'δaδ| *nf* kind,
variety

**modelar** |moδe'lar| *vt* to model

**modelo** |mo'δelo| *adj inv, nm/f* mod-
el

**módem** |'moδem| *nm (INFORM)*
modem

**moderado, a** |moδe'raδo, a| *adj*

moderate

**moderar** [moðe'rar] vt to moderate; (violencia) to restrain, control; (velocidad) to reduce; ~se vr to restrain o.s., control o.s.

**modernizar** [moðerni'θar] vt to modernize

**moderno, a** [mo'ðerno, a] adj modern; (actual) present-day

**modestia** [mo'ðestja] nf modesty; **modesto, a** adj modest

**módico, a** ['moðiko, a] adj moderate, reasonable

**modificar** [moðifi'kar] vt to modify

**modisto, a** [mo'ðisto, a] nm/f dressmaker

**modo** ['moðo] nm (manera, forma) way, manner; (MUS) mode; ~s nmpl manners; de ningún ~ in no way; de todos ~s at any rate; ~ de empleo directions pl (for use)

**modorra** [mo'ðorra] nf drowsiness

**mofa** ['mofa] nf: hacer ~ de to mock; **mofarse** vr: mofarse de to mock, scoff at

**mogollón** [moɣo'ʎon] (fam) adv (gustar, beber) a hell of a lot

**moho** ['moo] nm (BOT) mould, mildew; (en metal) rust; ~so, a adj mouldy; rusty

**mojar** [mo'xar] vt to wet; (humedecer) to damp(en), moisten; (calar) to soak; ~se vr to get wet

**mojón** [mo'xon] nm boundary stone

**molde** ['molde] nm mould; (COSTURA) pattern; (fig) model; ~ar vt to mould

**mole** ['mole] nf mass, bulk; (edificio) pile

**moler** [mo'ler] vt to grind, crush; (cansar) to tire out, exhaust

**molestar** [moles'tar] vt to bother; (fastidiar) to annoy; (incomodar) to inconvenience, put out ♦ vi to be a nuisance; ~se vr to bother; (incomodarse) to go to trouble; (ofenderse) to take offence

**molestia** [mo'lestja] nf bother, trouble; (incomodidad) inconvenience; (MED) discomfort; es una ~ it's a

nuisance; **molesto, a** adj (que fastidia) annoying; (incómodo) inconvenient; (inquieto) uncomfortable, ill at ease; (enfadado) annoyed

**molido, a** [mo'liðo, a] adj: estar ~ (fig) to be exhausted o dead beat

**molinillo** [moli'niʎo] nm: ~ de carne/café mincer/coffee grinder

**molino** [mo'lino] nm (edificio) mill; (máquina) grinder

**momentáneo, a** [momen'taneo, a] adj momentary

**momento** [mo'mento] nm (gen) moment; (TEC) momentum; de ~ at the moment, for the moment

**momia** ['momja] nf mummy

**monarca** [mo'narka] nm/f monarch, ruler; **monarquía** nf monarchy; **monárquico, a** nm/f royalist, monarchist

**monasterio** [monas'terjo] nm monastery

**mondar** [mon'dar] vt (limpiar) to clean; (pelar) to peel; ~se vr: ~se de risa (fam) to split one's sides laughing

**moneda** [mo'neða] nf (tipo de dinero) currency, money; (pieza) coin; una ~ de 5 pesetas a 5 peseta piece; **monedero** nm purse; **monetario, a** adj monetary, financial

**monitor, a** [moni'tor, a] nm/f instructor, coach ♦ nm (TV) set; (INFORM) monitor

**monja** ['monxa] nf nun

**monje** ['monxe] nm monk

**mono, a** ['mono, a] adj (bonito) lovely, pretty; (gracioso) nice, charming ♦ nm/f monkey, ape ♦ nm dungarees pl; (overoles) overalls pl

**monopatín** [monopa'tin] nm skateboard

**monopolio** [mono'poljo] nm monopoly; **monopolizar** vt to monopolize

**monotonía** [monoto'nia] nf (sonido) monotone; (fig) monotony

**monótono, a** [mo'notono, a] adj monotonous

**monstruo** ['monstrwo] nm monster ♦ adj inv fantastic; ~so, a adj monstrous

**montaje** [mon'taxe] nm assembly; (TEATRO) décor; (CINE) montage

**montaña** [mon'taɲa] nf (monte) mountain; (sierra) mountains pl, mountainous area; (AM: selva) forest; ~ **rusa** roller coaster; **montañero, a** nm/f mountaineer ♦ nm/f highlander; **montañismo** nm mountaineering

**montar** [mon'tar] vt (subir a) to mount, get on; (TEC) to assemble, put together; (negocio) to set up; (arma) to cock; (colocar) to lift on to; (CULIN) to beat ♦ vi to mount, get on; (sobresalir) to overlap; ~ **en cólera** to get angry; ~ **a caballo** to ride, go horseriding

**monte** ['monte] nm (montaña) mountain; (bosque) woodland; (área sin cultivar) wild area, wild country; **M~ de Piedad** pawnshop

**monto** ['monto] nm total, amount

**montón** [mon'ton] nm heap, pile; (fig): **un ~ de** heaps of, lots of

**monumento** [monu'mento] nm monument

**monzón** [mon'θon] nm monsoon

**moño** ['moɲo] nm bun

**moqueta** [mo'keta] nf fitted carpet

**mora** ['mora] nf blackberry; ver tb **moro**

**morada** [mo'raða] nf (casa) dwelling, abode

**morado, a** [mo'raðo, a] adj purple, violet ♦ nm bruise

**moral** [mo'ral] adj moral ♦ nf (ética) ethics pl; (moralidad) morals pl, morality; (ánimo) morale

**moraleja** [mora'lexa] nf moral

**moralidad** [morali'ðað] nf morals pl, morality

**morboso, a** [mor'βoso, a] adj morbid

**morcilla** [mor'θiʎa] nf blood sausage, ~ **black** pudding (BRIT)

**mordaz** [mor'ðaθ] adj (crítica) biting, scathing

**mordaza** [mor'ðaθa] nf (para la boca) gag; (TEC) clamp

**morder** [mor'ðer] vt to bite; (mordis-

quear) to nibble; (fig: consumir) to eat away, eat into; **mordisco** nm bite

**moreno, a** [mo'reno, a] adj (color) (dark) brown; (de tez) dark; (de pelo ~) dark-haired; (negro) black

**morfina** [mor'fina] nf morphine

**moribundo, a** [mori'βundo, a] adj dying

**morir** [mo'rir] vi to die; (fuego) to die down; (luz) to go out; ~**se** vr to die; (fig) to be dying; **fue muerto en un accidente** he was killed in an accident; ~**se por algo** to be dying for sth

**moro, a** ['moro, a] adj Moorish ♦ nm/f Moor

**moroso, a** [mo'roso, a] nm/f (COM) bad debtor, defaulter

**morral** [mo'rral] nm haversack

**morro** ['morro] nm (ZOOL) snout, nose; (AUTO, AVIAT) nose

**morsa** ['morsa] nf walrus

**mortaja** [mor'taxa] nf shroud

**mortal** [mor'tal] adj mortal; (golpe) deadly; ~**idad** nf mortality

**mortero** [mor'tero] nm mortar

**mortífero, a** [mor'tifero, a] adj deadly, lethal

**mortificar** [mortifi'kar] vt to mortify

**mosca** ['moska] nf fly

**Moscú** [mos'ku] n Moscow

**mosquearse** [moske'arse] (fam) vr (enojarse) to get cross; (ofenderse) to take offence

**mosquitero** [moski'tero] nm mosquito net

**mosquito** [mos'kito] nm mosquito

**mostaza** [mos'taθa] nf mustard

**mostrador** [mostra'ðor] nm (de tienda) counter; (de café) bar

**mostrar** [mos'trar] vt to show; (exhibir) to display, exhibit; (explicar) to explain; ~**se** vr: ~**se amable** to be kind; to prove to be kind; **no se muestra muy inteligente** he doesn't seem (to be) very intelligent

**mota** ['mota] nf speck, tiny piece; (en diseño) dot

**mote** ['mote] nm (apodo) nickname

**motín** [mo'tin] nm (del pueblo) re-

volt, rising; (*del ejército*) mutiny
**motivar** [moti'βar] vt (*causar*) to cause, motivate; (*explicar*) to explain, justify; **motivo** nm motive, reason
**moto** ['moto] (*fam*) nf = **motocicleta**
**motocicleta** [motoθi'kleta] nf motorbike (*BRIT*), motorcycle
**motor** [mo'tor] nm motor, engine; ~ **a chorro** o **de reacción/de explosión** jet engine/internal combustion engine
**motora** [mo'tora] nf motorboat
**movedizo, a** [moße'ðiθo, a] adj (*inseguro*) unsteady; (*fig*) unsettled, changeable; (*persona*) fickle
**mover** [mo'ßer] vt to move; (*cabeza*) to shake; (*accionar*) to drive; (*fig*) to cause, provoke; **~se** vr to move; (*fig*) to get a move on
**móvil** ['moßil] adj mobile; (*pieza de máquina*) moving; (*mueble*) movable ♦ nm motive; **movilidad** nf mobility; **movilizar** vt to mobilize
**movimiento** [moßi'mjento] nm movement; (*TEC*) motion; (*actividad*) activity
**mozo, a** ['moθo, a] adj (*joven*) young ♦ nm/f (*joven*) youth, young man/girl; (*camarero*) waiter; (*camarera*) waitress
**muchacho, a** [mu'tʃatʃo, a] nm/f (*niño*) boy/girl; (*criado*) servant; (*criada*) maid
**muchedumbre** [mutʃe'ðumbre] nf crowd

PALABRA CLAVE

**mucho, a** ['mutʃo, a] adj **1** (*cantidad*) a lot of, much; (*número*) lots of, a lot of, many; ~ **dinero** a lot of money; **hace** ~ **calor** it's very hot; **muchas amigas** lots o a lot of friends
**2** (*sg: grande*): **ésta es mucha casa para él** this house is much too big for him
♦ pron: **tengo** ~ **que hacer** I've got a lot to do; **~s dicen que** ... a lot of

people say that ...; ver tb **tener**
♦ adv **1: me gusta** ~ I like it a lot; **lo siento** ~ I'm very sorry; **come** ~ he eats a lot; **¿te vas a quedar** ~? are you going to be staying long?
**2** (*respuesta*) very; **¿estás cansado?** – **¡~!** are you tired? - very!
**3** (*locuciones*): **como** ~ at (the) most; **con** ~: **el mejor con** ~ by far the best; **ni** ~ **menos: no es rico ni** ~ **menos** he's far from being rich
**4: por** ~ **que: por** ~ **que le creas** no matter how o however much you believe her

**muda** ['muða] nf change of clothes
**mudanza** [mu'ðanθa] nf (*cambio*) change; (*de casa*) move
**mudar** [mu'ðar] vt to change; (*ZOOL*) to shed ♦ vi to change; **~se** vr (*la ropa*) to change; **~se de casa** to move house
**mudo, a** ['muðo, a] adj dumb; (*callado, CINE*) silent
**mueble** ['mweßle] nm piece of furniture; **~s** nmpl furniture sg
**mueca** ['mweka] nf face, grimace; **hacer ~s a** to make faces at
**muela** ['mwela] nf (*diente*) tooth; (: *de atrás*) molar
**muelle** ['mweʎe] nm spring; (*NAUT*) wharf; (*malecón*) pier
**muero** etc vb ver **morir**
**muerte** ['mwerte] nf death; (*homicidio*) murder; **dar** ~ **a** to kill
**muerto, a** ['mwerto, a] pp de **morir** ♦ adj dead; (*color*) dull ♦ nm/f dead man/woman; (*difunto*) deceased; (*cadáver*) corpse; **estar** ~ **de cansancio** to be dead tired
**muestra** ['mwestra] nf (*señal*) indication, sign; (*demostración*) demonstration; (*prueba*) proof; (*estadística*) sample; (*modelo*) model, pattern; (*testimonio*) token
**muestreo** [mwes'treo] nm sample, sampling
**muestro** etc vb ver **mostrar**
**muevo** etc vb ver **mover**

**mugir** [mu'xir] *vi* (*vaca*) to moo

**mugre** ['muɣre] *nf* dirt, filth; **mugriento, a** *adj* dirty, filthy

**mujer** [mu'xer] *nf* woman; (*esposa*) wife; **~iego** *nm* womanizer

**mula** ['mula] *nf* mule

**mulato, a** [mu'lato, a] *adj, nm/f* mulatto

**muleta** [mu'leta] *nf* (*para andar*) crutch; (*TAUROMAQUIA*) stick with red cape attached

**multa** ['multa] *nf* fine; **poner una ~** a to fine; **multar** *vt* to fine

**multicopista** [multiko'pista] *nm* duplicator

**multinacional** [multinaθjo'nal] *nf* (*COM*) multinational

**múltiple** ['multiple] *adj* multiple; (*pl*) many, numerous

**multiplicar** [multipli'kar] *vt* (*MAT*) to multiply; (*fig*) to increase; **~se** *vr* (*BIO*) to multiply; (*fig*) to be everywhere at once

**multitud** [multi'tuð] *nf* (*muchedumbre*) crowd; **~ de** lots of

**mullido, a** [mu'ʎiðo, a] *adj* (*cama*) soft; (*hierba*) soft, springy

**mundano, a** [mun'dano, a] *adj* worldly; (*de moda*) fashionable

**mundial** [mun'djal] *adj* world-wide, universal; (*guerra, récord*) world (*cpd*)

**mundo** ['mundo] *nm* world; **todo el ~** everybody; **tener ~** to be experienced, know one's way around

**munición** [muni'θjon] *nf* (*MIL: provisiones*) stores *pl*, supplies *pl*; (*: balas*) ammunition

**municipal** [muniθi'pal] *adj* municipal, local

**municipio** [muni'θipjo] *nm* (*ayuntamiento*) town council, corporation; (*territorio administrativo*) town, municipality

**muñeca** [mu'ɲeka] *nf* (*ANAT*) wrist; (*juguete*) doll

**muñeco** [mu'ɲeko] *nm* (*figura*) figure; (*marioneta*) puppet; (*fig*) puppet, pawn

**mural** [mu'ral] *adj* mural, wall *cpd* ♦ *nm* mural

**muralla** [mu'raʎa] *nf* (*city*) wall(s) (*pl*)

**murciélago** [mur'θjelavo] *nm* bat

**murmullo** [mur'muʎo] *nm* murmur(ing); (*cuchicheo*) whispering; (*de arroyo*) murmur, rippling

**murmuración** [murmura'θjon] *nf* gossip; **murmurar** *vi* to murmur, whisper; (*criticar*) to criticize; (*cotillear*) to gossip

**muro** ['muro] *nm* wall

**muscular** [musku'lar] *adj* muscular

**músculo** ['muskulo] *nm* muscle

**museo** [mu'seo] *nm* museum

**musgo** ['musvo] *nm* moss

**música** ['musika] *nf* music; *ver tb* **músico**

**músico, a** ['musiko, a] *adj* musical ♦ *nm/f* musician

**musitar** [musi'tar] *vt, vi* to mutter, mumble

**muslo** ['muslo] *nm* thigh

**mustio, a** ['mustjo, a] *adj* (*persona*) depressed, gloomy; (*planta*) faded, withered

**musulmán, ana** [musul'man, ana] *nm/f* Moslem

**mutación** [muta'θjon] *nf* (*BIO*) mutation; (*: cambio*) (sudden) change

**mutilar** [muti'lar] *vt* to mutilate; (*a una persona*) to maim

**mutismo** [mu'tismo] *nm* (*de persona*) uncommunicativeness; (*de autoridades*) silence

**mutuamente** [mutwa'mente] *adv* mutually

**mutuo, a** ['mutwo, a] *adj* mutual

**muy** [mwi] *adv* very; (*demasiado*) too; **M~ Señor mío** Dear Sir; **~ de noche** very late at night; **eso es ~ de él** that's just like him

# N

**N** *abr* (= *norte*) N

**nabo** ['naβo] *nm* turnip

**nácar** ['nakar] *nm* mother-of-pearl

**nacer** [na'θer] *vi* to be born; (*de huevo*) to hatch; (*vegetal*) to sprout;

(*río*) to rise; **nací en Barcelona** I was born in Barcelona; **nació una sospecha en su mente** a suspicion formed in her mind; **nacido, a** *adj* born; **recién nacido** newborn; **naciente** *adj* new, emerging; (*sol*) rising; **nacimiento** *nm* birth; (*fig*) birth, origin; (*de Navidad*) Nativity; (*linaje*) descent, family; (*de río*) source

**nación** [na'θjon] *nf* nation; **nacional** *adj* national; **nacionalismo** *nm* nationalism; **nacionalista** *nm/f* nationalist; **nacionalizar** *vt* to nationalize; **nacionalizarse** *vr* (*persona*) to become naturalized

**nada** ['naða] *pron* nothing ♦ *adv* not at all, in no way; **no decir** ~ to say nothing, not to say anything; ~ **más** nothing else; **de** ~ don't mention it

**nadador, a** [naða'ðor, a] *nm/f* swimmer

**nadar** [na'ðar] *vi* to swim

**nadie** ['naðje] *pron* nobody, no-one; ~ **habló** nobody spoke; **no había** ~ there was nobody there, there wasn't anybody there

**nado** ['naðo]: **a** ~ *adv*: **pasar a** ~ to swim across

**nafta** ['nafta] (*AM*) *nf* petrol (*BRIT*), gas (*US*)

**naipe** ['naipe] *nm* (playing card); ~**s** *nmpl* cards

**nalgas** ['nalvas] *nfpl* buttocks

**nana** ['nana] *nf* lullaby

**naranja** [na'ranxa] *adj inv, nf* orange; **media** ~ (*fam*) better half; **naranjada** *nf* orangeade; **naranjo** *nm* orange tree

**narciso** [nar'θiso] *nm* narcissus

**narcótico, a** [nar'kotiko, a] *adj, nm* narcotic; **narcotizar** *vt* to drug; **narcotráfico** *nm* drug trafficking *o* running

**nardo** ['narðo] *nm* lily

**narigón, ona** [narɪ'von, ona] *adj* big-nosed

**narigudo, a** [narɪ'xuðo, a] *adj* = **narigón**

**nariz** [na'riθ] *nf* nose; **narices** *nfpl* nostrils; **delante de las narices de**

**uno** under one's (very) nose

**narración** [narra'θjon] *nf* narration; **narrador, a** *nm/f* narrator

**narrar** [na'rrar] *vt* to narrate, recount; **narrativa** *nf* narrative, story

**nata** ['nata] *nf* cream

**natación** [nata'θjon] *nf* swimming

**natal** [na'tal] *adj*: **ciudad** ~ home town; ~**idad** *nf* birth rate

**natillas** [na'tiλas] *nfpl* custard *sg*

**nativo, a** [na'tiβo, a] *adj, nm/f* native

**nato, a** ['nato, a] *adj* born; **un músico** ~ a born musician

**natural** [natu'ral] *adj* natural; (*fruta etc*) fresh ♦ *nm/f* native ♦ *nm* (*disposición*) nature

**naturaleza** [natura'leθa] *nf* nature; (*género*) nature, kind; ~ **muerta** still life

**naturalidad** [naturali'ðað] *nf* naturalness

**naturalmente** [natural'mente] *adv* (*de modo natural*) in a natural way; **¡**~**!** of course!

**naufragar** [naufra'var] *vi* to sink; **naufragio** *nm* shipwreck; **náufrago, a** *nm/f* castaway, shipwrecked person

**nauseabundo, a** [nausea'βundo, a] *adj* nauseating, sickening

**náuseas** ['nauseas] *nfpl* nausea; **me da** ~ it makes me feel sick

**náutico, a** ['nautiko, a] *adj* nautical

**navaja** [na'βaxa] *nf* (*cortaplumas*) clasp knife (*BRIT*), penknife; (*de barbero, peluquero*) razor

**naval** [na'βal] *adj* (*MIL*: *combat, escuela*) naval

**Navarra** [na'βarra] *n* Navarre

**nave** ['naβe] *nf* (*barco*) ship, vessel; (*ARQ*) nave; ~ **espacial** spaceship

**navegación** [naβeva'θjon] *nf* navigation; (*viaje*) sea journey; ~ **aérea** air traffic; ~ **costera** coastal shipping; **navegante** *nm/f* navigator; **navegar** *vi* (*barco*) to sail; (*avión*) to fly ♦ *vt* to sail; to fly; (*dirigir el rumbo*) to navigate

**navidad** [naβi'ðað] *nf* Christmas; ~**es** *nfpl* Christmas time; **navideño,**

a adj Christmas cpd
navío [na'βio] nm ship
nazca etc vb ver nacer
nazi ['naθi] adj, nm/f Nazi
NE abr (= nor(d)este) NE
neblina [ne'βlina] nf mist
nebuloso, a [neβu'loso, a] adj fog-
gy; (calinoso) misty; (indefinido)
nebulous, vague ♦ nf nebula
necedad [neθe'ðað] nf foolishness;
(una ~) foolish act
necesario, a [neθe'sarjo, a] adj necessary
neceser [neθe'ser] nm toilet bag;
(bolsa grande) holdall
necesidad [neθesi'ðað] nf need; (lo
inevitable) necessity; (miseria) poverty, need; en caso de ~ in case of
need o emergency; hacer sus ~es
to relieve o.s
necesitado, a [neθesi'taðo, a] adj
needy, poor; ~ de in need of
necesitar [neθesi'tar] vt to need, require ♦ vi: ~ de to have need of
necio, a ['neθjo, a] adj foolish
necrópolis [ne'kropolis] nf inv cemetery
nectarina [nekta'rina] nf nectarine
nefasto, a [ne'fasto, a] adj ill-fated,
unlucky
negación [neɣa'θjon] nf negation;
(rechazo) refusal, denial
negar [ne'ɣar] vt (renegar, rechazar)
to refuse; (prohibir) to refuse, deny;
(desmentir) to deny; ~se vr: ~se a
to refuse to
negativa [neɣa'tiβa] nf negative;
(rechazo) refusal, denial
negativo, a [neɣa'tiβo, a] adj, nm
negative
negligencia [neɣli'xenθja] nf negligence; negligente adj negligent
negociable [neɣo'θjaβle] adj (COM)
negotiable
negociado [neɣo'θjaðo] nm department, section
negociante [neɣo'θjante] nm/f
businessman/woman
negociar [neɣo'θjar] vt, vi to negotiate; ~ en to deal in, trade in

negocio [ne'ɣoθjo] nm (COM) business; (asunto) affair, business;
(operación comercial) deal, transaction; (AM) firm; (lugar) place of
business; los ~s business sg; hacer
~ to do business
negra ['neɣra] nf (MUS) crotchet;
ver tb negro
negro, a ['neɣro, a] adj black;
(suerte) awful ♦ nm black ♦ nm/f
Negro/Negress, Black
nene, a ['nene, a] nm/f baby, small
child
nenúfar [ne'nufar] nm water lily
neologismo [neolo'xismo] nm neolo-
gism
neón [ne'on] nm: luces/lámpara de
~ neon lights/lamp
neoyorquino, a [neojor'kino, a] adj
(of) New York
nepotismo [nepo'tismo] nm nepo-
tism
nervio ['nerβjo] nm (ANAT) nerve;
(: tendón) tendon; (fig) vigour; nerviosismo nm nervousness, nerves pl;
~so, a adj nervous
neto, a ['neto, a] adj clear; (limpio)
clean; (COM) net
neumático, a [neu'matiko, a] adj
pneumatic ♦ nm (ESP) tyre (BRIT),
tire (US); ~ de recambio spare
tyre
neurasténico, a [neuras'teniko, a]
adj (fig) hysterical
neurólogo, a [neu'roloɣo, a] nm/f
neurologist
neurona [neu'rona] nf (ANAT) nerve
cell
neutral [neu'tral] adj neutral; ~izar
vt to neutralize; (contrarrestar) to
counteract
neutro, a ['neutro, a] adj (BIO,
LING) neuter
neutrón [neu'tron] nm neutron
nevada [ne'βaða] nf snowstorm;
(caída de nieve) snowfall
nevar [ne'βar] vi to snow
nevera [ne'βera] nf refrigerator
(BRIT), icebox (US)
nevería [neβe'ria] (AM) nf ice-cream

parlour

**nexo** ['nekso] nm link, connection

**ni** [ni] conj nor, neither; (tb: ~ siquiera) not ... even; ~ que not even if; ~ blanco ~ negro neither white nor black

**Nicaragua** [nika'rawa] nf Nicaragua; **nicaragüense** adj, nmf Nicaraguan

**nicotina** [niko'tina] nf nicotine

**nicho** ['nitʃo] nm niche

**nido** ['niðo] nm nest; (fig) hiding place

**niebla** ['njeβla] nf fog; (neblina) mist

**niego** etc vb ver **negar**

**nieto, a** ['njeto, a] nm/f grandson/daughter; ~s nmpl grandchildren

**nieve** etc ['njeβe] vb ver **nevar** ♦ nf snow; (AM) icecream

**nimiedad** [nimje'ðað] nf smallmindedness; (trivialidad) triviality

**nimio, a** ['nimjo, a] adj trivial, insignificant

**ninfa** ['ninfa] nf nymph

**ninfómana** [nin'fomana] nf nymphomaniac

**ningún** [nin'gun] adj ver **ninguno**

**ninguno, a** [nin'guno, a] adj (delante de nm: **ningún**) no ♦ pron (nadie) nobody; (ni uno) none, not one; (ni uno ni otro) neither; de ninguna manera by no means, not at all

**niña** ['niɲa] nf (ANAT) pupil; ver tb **niño**

**niñera** [ni'ɲera] nf nursemaid, nanny; **niñería** nf childish act

**niñez** [ni'ɲeθ] nf childhood; (infancia) infancy

**niño, a** ['niɲo, a] adj (joven) young; (inmaduro) immature ♦ nm/f child, boy/girl

**nipón, ona** [ni'pon, ona] adj, nm/f Japanese

**níquel** ['nikel] nm nickel; **niquelar** vt (TEC) to nickel-plate

**níspero** ['nispero] nm medlar

**nitidez** [niti'ðeθ] nf (claridad) clarity; (: de atmósfera) brightness; (: de imagen) sharpness; **nítido, a** adj clear; sharp

**nitrato** [ni'trato] nm nitrate

**nitrógeno** [ni'troxeno] nm nitrogen

**nitroglicerina** [nitroβliθe'rina] nf nitroglycerine

**nivel** [ni'βel] nm (GEO) level; (norma) level, standard; (altura) height; ~ de aceite oil level; ~ de aire spirit level; ~ de vida standard of living; **~ar** vt to level out; (fig) to even up; (COM) to balance

**NN. UU.** nfpl abr (= Naciones Unidas) UN sg

**no** [no] adv no; not; (con verbo) not ♦ excl no!; ~ tengo nada I don't have anything, I have nothing; ~ es el mío it's not mine; **ahora** ~ not now; **¿~ lo sabes?** don't you know?; ~ **mucho** not much; ~ **bien termine**, lo entregaré as soon as I finish I'll hand it over; ~ **más: ayer** ~ **más** just yesterday; **¡pase** ~ **más!** come in!; **¡a que** ~ **lo sabes!** I bet you don't know!; **¡cómo** ~! of course!; **los países** ~ **alineados** the non-aligned countries; **la** ~ **intervención** non-intervention

**noble** ['noβle] adj, nm/f noble; **~za** nf nobility

**noción** [no'θjon] nf notion

**nocivo, a** [no'θiβo, a] adj harmful

**noctámbulo, a** [nok'tambulo, a] nm/f sleepwalker

**nocturno, a** [nok'turno, a] adj (de la noche) nocturnal, night cpd; (de la tarde) evening cpd ♦ nm nocturne

**noche** ['notʃe] nf night, night-time; (la tarde) evening; (fig) darkness; **de** ~, **por la** ~ at night

**nochebuena** [notʃe'βwena] nf Christmas Eve

**nochevieja** [notʃe'βjexa] nf New Year's Eve

**nodriza** [no'ðriθa] nf wet nurse; **buque o nave** ~ supply ship

**nogal** [no'βal] nm walnut tree

**nómada** ['nomaða] adj nomadic ♦ nm/f nomad

**nombramiento** [nombra'mjento] nm naming; (a un empleo) appointment

**nombrar** [nom'brar] vt (*designar*) to name; (*mencionar*) to mention; (*dar puesto a*) to appoint

**nombre** ['nombre] nm name; (*sustantivo*) noun; (*fama*) renown; ~ **y apellidos** name in full; ~ **común/ propio** common/proper noun; ~ **de pila/de soltera** Christian/maiden name; **poner** ~ **a** to call, name

**nomenclatura** [nomenkla'tura] nf nomenclature

**nomeolvides** [nomeol'βiðes] nm inv forget-me-not

**nómina** ['nomina] nf (*lista*) list; (COM) payroll

**nominal** [nomi'nal] adj nominal

**nominar** [nomi'nar] vt to nominate

**nominativo, a** [nomina'tiβo, a] adj (COM): **cheque** ~ **a X** cheque made out to X

**nono, a** ['nono, a] adj ninth

**nordeste** [nor'ðeste] adj north-east, north-eastern, north-easterly ♦ nm north-east

**nórdico, a** ['norðiko, a] adj (*del norte*) northern, northerly; (*escandinavo*) Nordic

**noreste** [no'reste] adj, nm = **nordeste**

**noria** ['norja] nf (AGR) waterwheel; (*de carnaval*) big (BRIT) o Ferris (US) wheel

**norma** ['norma] nf rule (of thumb)

**normal** [nor'mal] adj (*corriente*) normal; (*habitual*) usual, natural; (*gasolina*): ~ **two-star petrol**; ~**idad** nf normality; **restablecer la** ~**idad** to restore order; ~**izar** vt (*reglamentar*) to normalize; (TEC) to standardize; ~**izarse** vr to return to normal

**normando, a** [nor'mando, a] adj, nm/f Norman

**normativa** [norma'tiβa] nf (set of) rules

**noroeste** [noro'este] adj north-west, north-western, north-westerly ♦ nm north-west

**norte** ['norte] adj north, northern, northerly ♦ nm north; (*fig*) guide

**norteamericano, a** [norteameri-'kano, a] adj, nm/f (North) American

**Noruega** [no'rweγa] nf Norway

**noruego, a** [no'rweγo, a] adj, nm/f Norwegian

**nos** [nos] pron (*directo*) us; (*indirecto*) us; to us; from us; (*reflexivo*) (to) ourselves; (*recíproco*) (to) each other; ~ **levantamos a las 7** we get up at 7

**nosotros, as** [no'sotros, as] pron (*sujeto*) we; (*después de prep*) us

**nostalgia** [nos'talxja] nf nostalgia

**nota** ['nota] nf note; (ESCOL) mark

**notable** [no'taβle] adj notable; (ESCOL) outstanding ♦ nm/f notable

**notar** [no'tar] vt to notice, note; ~**se** vr to be obvious; **se nota que ...** one observes that ...

**notarial** [nota'rjal] adj: **acta** ~ affidavit

**notario** [no'tarjo] nm notary

**noticia** [no'tiθja] nf (*información*) piece of news; **las** ~**s** the news sg; **tener** ~**s de alguien** to hear from sb

**noticiero** [noti'θjero] (AM) nm news bulletin

**notificación** [notifika'θjon] nf notification; **notificar** vt to notify, inform

**notoriedad** [notorje'ðað] nf fame, renown; **notorio, a** adj (*público*) well-known; (*evidente*) obvious

**novato, a** [no'βato, a] adj inexperienced ♦ nm/f beginner, novice

**novecientos, as** [noβe'θjentos, as] num nine hundred

**novedad** [noβe'ðað] nf (*calidad de nuevo*) newness; (*noticia*) piece of news; (*cambio*) change, (new) development

**novel** [no'βel] adj new; (*inexperto*) inexperienced ♦ nm/f beginner

**novela** [no'βela] nf novel

**novelero, a** [noβe'lero, a] adj highly imaginative

**noveno, a** [no'βeno, a] adj ninth

**noventa** [no'βenta] num ninety

**novia** ['noβja] nf ver **novio**

**noviazgo** [no'βjaθvo] nm engagement

**novicio, a** [no'βiθjo, a] nm/f novice

**noviembre** [no'βjembre] nm November

**novillada** [noβi'ʎaða] nf (TAUROMAQUIA) bullfight with young bulls; **novillero** nm novice bullfighter; **novillo** nm young bull, bullock; **hacer novillos** (fam) to play truant

**novio, a** ['noβjo, a] nm/f boyfriend/girlfriend; (prometido) fiancé/fiancée; (recién casado) bridegroom/bride; **los ~s** the newly-weds

**nubarrón** [nuβa'rron] nm storm cloud

**nube** ['nuβe] nf cloud

**nublado, a** [nu'βlaðo, a] adj cloudy ♦ nm storm cloud; **nublar** vt (oscurecer) to darken; (confundir) to cloud; **nublarse** vr to grow dark

**nubosidad** [nuβosi'ðað] nf cloudiness; **había mucha ~** it was very cloudy

**nuca** ['nuka] nf nape of the neck

**nuclear** [nukle'ar] adj nuclear

**núcleo** ['nukleo] nm (centro) core; (FISICA) nucleus

**nudillo** [nu'ðiʎo] nm knuckle

**nudista** [nu'ðista] adj (playa) nudist

**nudo** ['nuðo] nm knot; (unión) bond; (de problema) crux; **~so, a** adj knotty

**nuera** ['nwera] nf daughter-in-law

**nuestro, a** ['nwestro, a] adj our ♦ pron ours; **~ padre** our father; **un amigo ~** a friend of ours; **es el ~** it's ours

**nueva** ['nweβa] nf piece of news

**nuevamente** [nweβa'mente] adv (otra vez) again; (de nuevo) anew

**Nueva York** [-'jork] n New York

**Nueva Zelandia** [-θe'landja] nf New Zealand

**nueve** ['nweβe] num nine

**nuevo, a** ['nweβo, a] adj (gen) new; **de ~** again

**nuez** [nweθ] nf (fruto) nut; (del nogal) walnut; **~ de Adán** Adam's apple; **~ moscada** nutmeg

**nulidad** [nuli'ðað] nf (incapacidad) incompetence; (abolición) nullity

**nulo, a** ['nulo, a] adj (inepto, torpe) useless; (inválido) (null and void); (DEPORTE) drawn, tied

**núm.** abr (= número) no

**numeración** [numera'θjon] nf (cifras) numbers pl; (arábiga, romana etc) numerals pl

**numeral** [nume'ral] nm numeral

**numerar** [nume'rar] vt to number

**número** ['numero] nm (gen) number; (tamaño: de zapato) size; (ejemplar: de diario) number, issue; **sin ~** numberless, unnumbered; **~ de matrícula/de teléfono** registration/telephone number; **~ atrasado** back number

**numeroso, a** [nume'roso, a] adj numerous

**nunca** ['nunka] adv (jamás) never; **~ lo pensé** I never thought it; **no viene ~** he never comes; **~ más** never again; **más que ~** more than ever

**nuncio** ['nunθjo] nm (REL) nuncio

**nupcias** ['nupθjas] nfpl wedding sg, nuptials

**nutria** ['nutrja] nf otter

**nutrición** [nutri'θjon] nf nutrition

**nutrido, a** [nu'triðo, a] adj (alimentado) nourished; (fig: grande) large; (abundante) abundant

**nutrir** [nu'trir] vt (alimentar) to nourish; (dar de comer) to feed; (fig) to strengthen; **nutritivo, a** adj nourishing, nutritious

**nylon** [ni'lon] nm nylon

# Ñ

**ñato, a** ['ɲato, a] (AM) adj snub-nosed

**ñoñería** [ɲoɲe'ria] nf insipidness

**ñoño, a** ['ɲoɲo, a] adj (AM: tonto) silly, stupid; (soso) insipid; (persona) spineless

# O

**o** [o] *conj* or

**O** *abr* (= *oeste*) W

**o/** *abr* (= *orden*) o.

**oasis** [o'asis] *nm inv* oasis

**obcecar** [oβθe'kar] *vt* to blind

**obcecarse** [oβθe'karse] *vr* to get/ become stubborn

**obedecer** [oβeðe'θer] *vt* to obey; **obediencia** *nf* obedience; **obediente** *adj* obedient

**obertura** [oβer'tura] *nf* overture

**obesidad** [oβesi'ðað] *nf* obesity; **obeso, a** *adj* obese

**obispo** [o'βispo] *nm* bishop

**objeción** [oβxe'θjon] *nf* objection; **poner objeciones** to raise objections

**objetar** [oβxe'tar] *vt*, *vi* to object

**objetivo, a** [oβxe'tiβo, a] *adj*, *nm* objective

**objeto** [oβ'xeto] *nm* (*cosa*) object; (*fin*) aim

**objetor, a** [oβxe'tor, a] *nm/f* objetor

**oblicuo, a** [o'βlikwo, a] *adj* oblique; (*mirada*) sidelong

**obligación** [oβliγa'θjon] *nf* obligation; (*COM*) bond

**obligar** [oβli'γar] *vt* to force; **~se** *vr* to bind o.s.; **obligatorio, a** *adj* compulsory, obligatory

**oboe** [o'βoe] *nm* oboe

**obra** ['oβra] *nf* work; (*hechura*) piece of work; (*ARQ*) construction, building; (*TEATRO*) play; **~ maestra** masterpiece; **~s públicas** public works; **por ~ de** thanks to (the efforts of); **obrar** *vt* to work; (*tener efecto*) to have an effect on ♦ *vi* to act, behave; (*tener efecto*) to have an effect; **la carta obra en su poder** the letter is in his/her possession

**obrero, a** [o'βrero, a] *adj* (*clase*) working; (*movimiento*) labour *cpd*; **clase obrera** working class ♦ *nm/f* (*gen*) worker; (*sin oficio*) labourer

**obscenidad** [oβsθeni'ðað] *nf* obscen-

ity; **obsceno, a** *adj* obscene

**obscu... = oscu...**

**obsequiar** [oβse'kjar] *vt* (*ofrecer*) to present with; (*agasajar*) to make a fuss of, lavish attention on; **obsequio** *nm* (*regalo*) gift; (*cortesía*) courtesy, attention

**observación** [oβserβa'θjon] *nf* observation; (*reflexión*) remark

**observador, a** [oβserβa'ðor, a] *nm/f* observer

**observar** [oβser'βar] *vt* to observe; (*anotar*) to notice; **~se** *vr* to keep to, observe

**obsesión** [oβse'sjon] *nf* obsession; **obsesionar** *vt* to obsess; **obsesivo, a** *adj* obsessive

**obsoleto, a** [oβso'leto, a] *adj* (*máquina, técnica*) obsolete

**obstaculizar** [oβstakuli'θar] *vt* (*dificultar*) to hinder, hamper

**obstáculo** [oβs'takulo] *nm* (*gen*) obstacle; (*impedimento*) hindrance, drawback

**obstante** [oβs'tante]: **no ~** *adv* nevertheless ♦ *prep* in spite of

**obstinado, a** [oβsti'naðo, a] *adj* (*gen*) obstinate, stubborn

**obstinarse** [oβsti'narse] *vr* to be obstinate; **~ en** to persist in

**obstrucción** [oβstruk'θjon] *nf* obstruction; **obstruir** *vt* to obstruct

**obtener** [oβte'ner] *vt* (*conseguir*) to obtain; (*ganar*) to gain

**obturador** [oβtura'ðor] *nm* (*FOTO*) shutter

**obtuso, a** [oβ'tuso, a] *adj* (*filo*) blunt; (*MAT, fig*) obtuse

**obvio, a** ['oββjo, a] *adj* obvious

**ocasión** [oka'sjon] *nf* (*oportunidad*) opportunity, chance; (*momento*) occasion, time; (*causa*) cause; **de ~** secondhand; **ocasionar** *vt* to cause

**ocaso** [o'kaso] *nm* (*fig*) decline

**occidente** [okθi'ðente] *nm* west

**OCDE** *nf abr* (= *Organización de Cooperación y Desarrollo Económico*) OECD

**océano** [o'θeano] *nm* ocean; **el ~ Índico** the Indian Ocean

**ocio** ['oθjo] nm (tiempo) leisure; (pey) idleness; **~so, a** adj (inactivo) idle; (inútil) useless

**octanaje** [okta'naxe] nm: **de alto ~** high octane; **octano** nm octane

**octavilla** [okta'viʎa] nf leaflet, pamphlet

**octavo, a** [ok'taβo, a] adj eighth

**octogenario, a** [oktoxe'narjo, a] adj octogenarian

**octubre** [ok'tuβre] nm October

**ocular** [oku'lar] adj ocular, eye cpd; **testigo ~** eyewitness

**oculista** [oku'lista] nm/f oculist

**ocultar** [okul'tar] vt (esconder) to hide; (callar) to conceal; **oculto, a** adj hidden; (fig) secret

**ocupación** [okupa'θjon] nf occupation

**ocupado, a** [oku'paðo, a] adj (persona) busy; (plaza) occupied, taken; (teléfono) engaged; **ocupar** vt (gen) to occupy; **ocuparse** vr: **ocuparse de o en** (gen) to concern o.s. with; (cuidar) to look after

**ocurrencia** [oku'rrenθja] nf (suceso) incident, event; (idea) bright idea

**ocurrir** [oku'rrir] vi to happen; **~se** vr: **se me ocurrió que ...** it occurred to me that ...

**ochenta** [o'tʃenta] num eighty

**ocho** ['otʃo] num eight; **~ días** a week

**odiar** [o'ðjar] vt to hate; **odio** nm (gen) hate, hatred; (disgusto) dislike; **odioso, a** adj (gen) hateful; (malo) nasty

**odontólogo, a** [oðon'toloɣo, a] nm/f dentist, dental surgeon

**OEA** nf abr (= Organización de Estados Americanos) OAS

**oeste** [o'este] nm west; **una película del ~** a western

**ofender** [ofen'der] vt (agraviar) to offend; (insultar) to insult; **~se** vr to take offence; **ofensa** nf offence; **ofensiva** nf offensive; **ofensivo, a** adj (insultante) insulting; (MIL) offensive

**oferta** [o'ferta] nf offer; (propuesta) proposal; **la ~ y la demanda** supply and demand; **artículos en ~** goods on offer

**oficial** [ofi'θjal] adj official ♦ nm official; (MIL) officer

**oficina** [ofi'θina] nf office; **~ de correos** post office; **~ de turismo** tourist office; **oficinista** nm/f clerk

**oficio** [o'fiθjo] nm (profesión) profession; (puesto) post; (REL) service; **ser del ~** to be an old hand; **tener mucho ~** to have a lot of experience; **~ de difuntos** funeral service; **de ~** officially

**oficioso, a** [ofi'θjoso, a] adj (pey) officious; (no oficial) unofficial, informal

**ofimática** [ofi'matika] nf office automation

**ofrecer** [ofre'θer] vt (dar) to offer; (proponer) to propose; **~se** vr (persona) to offer o.s., volunteer; (situación) to present itself; **¿qué se le ofrece?, ¿se le ofrece algo?** what can I do for you?, can I get you anything?

**ofrecimiento** [ofreθi'mjento] nm offer, offering

**ofrendar** [ofren'dar] vt to offer, contribute

**oftalmólogo, a** [oftal'moloɣo, a] nm/f ophthalmologist

**ofuscación** [ofuska'θjon] nf (fig) bewilderment

**ofuscar** [ofus'kar] vt (confundir) to bewilder; (enceguecer) to dazzle, blind

**oída** [o'iða] nf: **de ~s** by hearsay

**oído** [o'iðo] nm (ANAT) ear; (sentido) hearing

**oigo** etc vb ver **oír**

**oír** [o'ir] vt (gen) to hear; (atender a) to listen to; **¡oiga!** listen!; **~ misa** to attend mass

**OIT** nf abr (= Organización Internacional del Trabajo) ILO

**ojal** [o'xal] nm buttonhole

**ojalá** [oxa'la] excl if only (it were so)!, some hope! ♦ conj if only ...!, would that ...!; **~ que venga hoy** I hope he comes today

**ojeada** [oxe'aða] *nf* glance

**ojera** [o'xera] *nf*: **tener ~s** to have bags under one's eyes

**ojeriza** [oxe'riθa] *nf* ill-will

**ojeroso, a** [oxe'roso, a] *adj* haggard

**ojo** ['oxo] *nm* eye; (*de puente*) span; (*de cerradura*) keyhole ♦ *excl* careful!; **tener ~ para** to have an eye for; **~ de buey** porthole

**ola** ['ola] *nf* wave

**olé** [o'le] *excl* bravo!, olé!

**oleada** [ole'aða] *nf* big wave, swell; (*fig*) wave

**oleaje** [ole'axe] *nm* swell

**óleo** ['oleo] *nm* oil; **oleoducto** *nm* (oil) pipeline

**oler** [o'ler] *vt* (*gen*) to smell; (*inquirir*) to pry into; (*fig: sospechar*) to sniff out ♦ *vi* to smell; **~ a** to smell of

**olfatear** [olfate'ar] *vt* to smell; (*fig: sospechar*) to sniff out; (*inquirir*) to pry into; **olfato** *nm* sense of smell

**oligarquía** [olivar'kia] *nf* oligarchy

**olimpíada** [olim'piaða] *nf*: **las O~s** the Olympics

**oliva** [o'liβa] *nf* (*aceituna*) olive; **aceite de ~** olive oil; **olivo** *nm* olive tree

**olmo** ['olmo] *nm* elm (tree)

**olor** [o'lor] *nm* smell; **~oso, a** *adj* scented

**olvidadizo, a** [olβiða'ðiθo, a] *adj* (*desmemoriado*) forgetful; (*distraído*) absent-minded

**olvidar** [olβi'ðar] *vt* to forget; (*omitir*) to omit; **~se** *vr* (*fig*) to forget o.s.; **se me olvidó** I forgot

**olvido** [ol'βiðo] *nm* oblivion; (*despiste*) forgetfulness

**olla** ['oʎa] *nf* pan; (*comida*) stew; **~ a presión** o **exprés** pressure cooker; **~ podrida** type of Spanish stew

**ombligo** [om'blixo] *nm* navel

**omisión** [omi'sjon] *nf* (*abstención*) omission; (*descuido*) neglect

**omiso, a** [o'miso, a] *adj*: **hacer caso ~ de** to ignore, pass over

**omitir** [omi'tir] *vt* to omit

**omnipotente** [omnipo'tente] *adj* omnipotent

**omnívoro, a** [om'niβoro, a] *adj* omnivorous

**omóplato** [o'moplato] *nm* shoulder blade

**OMS** *nf abr* (= *Organización Mundial de la Salud*) WHO

**once** ['onθe] *num* eleven; **~s** (*AM*) *nmpl* tea break

**onda** ['onda] *nf* wave; **~ corta/larga/media** short/long/medium wave; **ondear** *vt*, *vi* to wave; (*tener ondas*) to be wavy; (*agua*) to ripple; **ondearse** *vr* to swing, sway

**ondulación** [ondula'θjon] *nf* undulation; **ondulado, a** *adj* wavy ♦ *nm* wave

**ondular** [ondu'lar] *vt* (*el pelo*) to wave ♦ *vi* to undulate; **~se** *vr* to undulate

**ONU** ['onu] *nf abr* (= *Organización de las Naciones Unidas*) UNO

**opaco, a** [o'pako, a] *adj* opaque; (*fig*) dull

**opción** [op'θjon] *nf* (*gen*) option; (*derecho*) right, option

**OPEP** ['opep] *nf abr* (= *Organización de Países Exportadores de Petróleo*) OPEC

**ópera** ['opera] *nf* opera; **~ bufa** o **cómica** comic opera

**operación** [opera'θjon] *nf* (*gen*) operation; (*COM*) transaction, deal

**operador, a** [opera'ðor, a] *nm/f* operator; (*CINE: proyección*) projectionist; (*: rodaje*) cameraman

**operar** [ope'rar] *vt* (*producir*) to produce, bring about; (*MED*) to operate on ♦ *vi* (*COM*) to operate, deal; **~se** *vr* to occur; (*MED*) to have an operation

**opereta** [ope'reta] *nf* operetta

**opinar** [opi'nar] *vt* (*estimar*) to think ♦ *vi* (*enjuiciar*) to give one's opinion; **opinión** *nf* (*creencia*) belief; (*criterio*) opinion

**opio** ['opjo] *nm* opium

**oponente** [opo'nente] *nm/f* opponent

**oponer** [opo'ner] *vt* (*resistencia*) to

put up, offer; (negativa) to raise; ~se vr (objetar) to object; (estar frente a frente) to be opposed; (dos personas) to oppose each other; ~ A a B to set A against B; me opongo a pensar que ... I refuse to believe o think that ...

**oportunidad** [oportuni'ðað] nf (ocasión) opportunity; (posibilidad) chance

**oportunismo** [oportu'nismo] nm opportunism; **oportunista** nm/f opportunist

**oportuno, a** [opor'tuno, a] adj (en su tiempo) opportune, timely; (respuesta) suitable; **en el momento ~** at the right moment

**oposición** [oposi'θjon] nf opposition; **oposiciones** nfpl (ESCOL) public examinations

**opositor, a** [oposi'tor, a] nm/f (adversario) opponent; (candidato): ~ (a) candidate (for)

**opresión** [opre'sjon] nf oppression; **opresivo, a** adj oppressive; **opresor, a** nm/f oppressor

**oprimir** [opri'mir] vt to squeeze; (fig) to oppress

**optar** [op'tar] vi (elegir) to choose; ~ a o por to opt for; **optativo, a** adj optional

**óptico, a** ['optiko, a] adj optic(al) ♦ nm/f optician; **óptica** nf optician's (shop); **desde esta ~** from this point of view

**optimismo** [opti'mismo] nm optimism; **optimista** nm/f optimist

**óptimo, a** ['optimo, a] adj (el mejor) very best

**opuesto, a** [o'pwesto, a] adj (contrario) opposite; (antagónico) opposing

**opulencia** [opu'lenθja] nf opulence; **opulento, a** adj opulent

**oración** [ora'θjon] nf (discurso) speech; (REL) prayer; (LING) sentence

**orador, a** [ora'ðor, a] nm/f (conferenciante) speaker, orator

**oral** [o'ral] adj oral

**orangután** [orangu'tan] nm orangutan

**orar** [o'rar] vi (REL) to pray

**oratoria** [ora'torja] nf oratory

**órbita** ['orβita] nf orbit

**orden** ['orðen] nm (gen) order ♦ nf (gen) order; (INFORM) command; ~ **del día** agenda; **de primer ~** first-rate; **en ~ de prioridad** in order of priority

**ordenado, a** [orðe'naðo, a] adj (metódico) methodical; (arreglado) orderly

**ordenador** [orðena'ðor] nm computer; ~ **central** mainframe computer

**ordenanza** [orðe'nanθa] nf ordinance

**ordenar** [orðe'nar] vt (mandar) to order; (poner orden) to put in order, arrange; ~se vr (REL) to be ordained

**ordeñar** [orðe'nar] vt to milk

**ordinario, a** [orði'narjo, a] adj (común) ordinary, usual; (vulgar) vulgar, common

**orégano** [o'rexano] nm oregano

**oreja** [o'rexa] nf ear; (MECANICA) lug, flange

**orfanato** [orfa'nato] nm orphanage

**orfandad** [orfan'dað] nf orphanhood

**orfebrería** [orfeβre'ria] nf gold/silver work

**orgánico, a** [or'ɣaniko, a] adj organic

**organigrama** [orɣani'ɣrama] nm flow chart

**organismo** [orɣa'nismo] nm (BIO) organism; (POL) organization

**organización** [orɣaniθa'θjon] nf organization; **organizar** vt to organize

**órgano** ['orɣano] nm organ

**orgasmo** [or'ɣasmo] nm orgasm

**orgía** [or'xia] nf orgy

**orgullo** [or'ɣuʎo] nm (altanería) pride; (autorespeto) self-respect; **orgulloso, a** adj (gen) proud; (altanero) haughty

**orientación** [orjenta'θjon] nf (posición) position; (dirección) direction

**orientar** [orjen'tar] vt (situar) to orientate; (señalar) to point; (dirigir) to direct; (guiar) to guide; **~se** vr to get one's bearings; (decidirse) to decide on a course of action

**oriente** [o'rjente] nm east; **Cercano/Medio/Lejano O~** Near/ Middle/Far East

**origen** [o'rixen] nm origin; (nacimiento) lineage, birth

**original** [orixi'nal] adj original; (extraño) odd, strange; **~idad** nf originality

**originar** [orixi'nar] vt to start, cause; **~se** vr to originate; **~io, a** adj (nativo) native; (primordial) original

**orilla** [o'riʎa] nf (borde) border; (de río) bank; (de bosque, tela) edge; (de mar) shore

**orina** [o'rina] nf urine; **orinal** nm (chamber) pot; **orinar** vi to urinate; **orinarse** vr to wet o.s.; **orines** nmpl urine

**oriundo, a** [o'rjundo, a] adj: **~ de** native of

**ornitología** [ornitolo'xia] nf ornithology, bird-watching

**oro** [o'ro] nm gold; **~s** nmpl (NAIPES) hearts

**oropel** [oro'pel] nm tinsel

**orquesta** [or'kesta] nf orchestra; **~ de cámara/sinfónica** chamber/ symphony orchestra

**orquídea** [or'kiðea] nf orchid

**ortiga** [or'tiɣa] nf nettle

**ortodoxo, a** [orto'ðokso, a] adj orthodox

**ortografía** [ortoɣra'fia] nf spelling

**ortopedia** [orto'peðja] nf orthopaedics sg; **ortopédico, a** adj orthopaedic

**oruga** [o'ruɣa] nf caterpillar

**orzuelo** [or'θwelo] nm (MED) stye

**os** [os] pron (gen) you; (a vosotros) to you

**osa** ['osa] nf (she-bear); **O~ Mayor/ Menor** Great/Little Bear

**osadía** [osa'ðia] nf daring

**osar** [o'sar] vi to dare

**oscilación** [osθila'θjon] nf (movimiento) oscillation; (fluctuación) fluc-

tuation; (vacilación) hesitation; (columpio) swinging, movement to and fro

**oscilar** [osθi'lar] vi to oscillate; to fluctuate; to hesitate

**oscurecer** [oskure'θer] vt to darken ♦ vi to grow dark; **~se** vr to grow o get dark

**oscuridad** [oskuri'ðað] nf obscurity; (tinieblas) darkness

**oscuro, a** [os'kuro, a] adj dark; (fig) obscure; **a oscuras** in the dark

**óseo, a** ['oseo, a] adj bony

**oso** ['oso] nm bear; **~ de peluche** teddy bear; **~ hormiguero** anteater

**ostensible** [osten'sißle] adj obvious

**ostentación** [ostenta'θjon] nf (gen) ostentation; (acto) display

**ostentar** [osten'tar] vt (gen) to show; (pey) to flaunt, show off; (poseer) to have, possess

**ostra** ['ostra] nf oyster

**OTAN** ['otan] nf abr (= Organización del Tratado del Atlántico Norte) NATO

**otear** [ote'ar] vt to observe; (fig) to look into

**otitis** [o'titis] nf earache

**otoñal** [oto'nal] adj autumnal

**otoño** [o'tono] nm autumn

**otorgar** [otor'ɣar] vt (conceder) to concede; (dar) to grant

**otorrino, a** [oto'rrino, a] nm/f ear, nose and throat specialist

**otorrinolaringólogo, a** [otorrinolarin'golovo, a] nm/f = **otorrino**

*PALABRA CLAVE*

**otro, a** ['otro, a] adj **1** (distinto: sg) another; (: pl) other; **con ~s amigos** with other o different friends
**2** (adicional): **tráigame ~ café (más), por favor** can I have another coffee please; **~s 10 días más** another ten days
♦ pron **1: el ~** the other one; **(los) ~s** (the) others; **de ~** somebody else's; **que lo haga ~** let somebody else do it

**2** (*recíproco*): se odian (la) una a (la) otra they hate one another *o* each other

**3**: ~ tanto: comer ~ tanto to eat the same *o* as much again; recibió una decena de telegramas y otras tantas llamadas he got about ten telegrams and as many calls

**ovación** [oβa'θjon] *nf* ovation
**oval** [o'βal] *adj* oval; ~**ado, a** *adj* oval; **óvalo** *nm* oval
**ovario** [o'βarjo] *nm* (ANAT) ovary
**oveja** [o'βexa] *nf* sheep
**overol** [oβe'rol] (AM) *nm* overalls *pl*
**ovillo** [o'βiʎo] *nm* (*de lana*) ball of wool; **hacerse un** ~ to curl up
**OVNI** ['oβni] *nm abr* (= *objeto volante no identificado*) UFO
**ovulación** [oβula'θjon] *nf* ovulation; **óvulo** *nm* ovum
**oxidación** [oksiða'θjon] *nf* rusting
**oxidar** [oksi'ðar] *vt* to rust; ~**se** *vr* to go rusty
**óxido** ['oksiðo] *nm* oxide
**oxigenado, a** [oksixe'naðo, a] *adj* (QUIMICA) oxygenated; (*pelo*) bleached
**oxígeno** [ok'sixeno] *nm* oxygen
**oyente** [o'jente] *nm/f* listener, hearer
**oyes** *etc vb ver* **oír**
**ozono** [o'θono] *nm* ozone

# P

**P** *abr* (= *padre*) Fr.
**pabellón** [paβe'ʎon] *nm* bell tent; (ARQ) pavilion; (*de hospital etc*) block, section; (*bandera*) flag
**pacer** [pa'θer] *vi* to graze
**paciencia** [pa'θjenθja] *nf* patience
**paciente** [pa'θjente] *adj*, *nm/f* patient
**pacificación** [paθifika'θjon] *nf* pacification
**pacificar** [paθifi'kar] *vt* to pacify; (*tranquilizar*) to calm
**pacífico, a** [pa'θifiko, a] *adj* (*persona*) peaceable; (*existencia*) peaceful; **el** (*océano*) **P**~ the Pacific (Ocean)

**pacifismo** [paθi'fismo] *nm* pacifism; **pacifista** *nm/f* pacifist
**pacotilla** [pako'tiʎa] *nf*: **de** ~ (*actor, escritor*) third-rate; (*mueble etc*) cheap
**pactar** [pak'tar] *vt* to agree to *o* on ♦ *vi* to come to an agreement
**pacto** ['pakto] *nm* (*tratado*) pact; (*acuerdo*) agreement
**padecer** [paðe'θer] *vt* (*sufrir*) to suffer; (*soportar*) to endure, put up with; (*engaño, error*) to be a victim of; **padecimiento** *nm* suffering
**padrastro** [pa'ðrastro] *nm* stepfather
**padre** ['paðre] *nm* father ♦ *adj* (*fam*): **un éxito** ~ a tremendous success; ~**s** *nmpl* parents
**padrino** [pa'ðrino] *nm* (REL) godfather; (*tb*: ~ **de boda**) best man; (*fig*) sponsor, patron; ~**s** *nmpl* parents
**padrón** [pa'ðron] *nm* (*censo*) census, roll; (*de socios*) register
**paella** [pa'eʎa] *nf* paella, *dish of rice with meat, shellfish etc*
**paga** ['paxa] *nf* (*pago*) payment; (*sueldo*) pay, wages *pl*
**pagadero, a** [paxa'ðero, a] *adj* payable; ~ **a plazos** payable in instalments
**pagano, a** [pa'xano, a] *adj*, *nm/f* pagan, heathen
**pagar** [pa'xar] *vt* to pay; (*las compras, crimen*) to pay for; (*fig*: *favor*) to repay ♦ *vi* to pay; ~ **al contado/a plazos** to pay (in) cash/in instalments
**pagaré** [paxa're] *nm* I.O.U.
**página** ['paxina] *nf* page
**pago** ['paxo] *nm* (*dinero*) payment; (*fig*) return; **estar** ~ to be even *o* quits; ~ **anticipado/a cuenta/contra reembolso/en especie** advance payment/payment on account/cash on delivery/payment in kind
**pág(s).** *abr* (= *página(s)*) p(p).
**pague** *etc vb ver* **pagar**
**país** [pa'is] *nm* (*gen*) country; (*región*) land; **los P**~**es Bajos** the Low Countries; **el P**~ **Vasco** the Basque

Country

**paisaje** [pai'saxe] *nm* countryside, scenery

**paisano, a** [pai'sano, a] *adj* of the same country ♦ *nm/f* (*compatriota*) fellow countryman/woman; **vestir de ~** (*soldado*) to be in civvies; (*guardia*) to be in plain clothes

**paja** ['paxa] *nf* straw; (*fig*) rubbish (*BRIT*), trash (*US*)

**pajarita** [paxa'rita] *nf* (*corbata*) bow tie

**pájaro** ['paxaro] *nm* bird; **~ carpintero** woodpecker

**pajita** [pa'xita] *nf* (drinking) straw

**pala** ['pala] *nf* spade, shovel; (*raqueta etc*) bat; (: *de tenis*) racquet; (*CULIN*) slice; **~ matamoscas** fly swat

**palabra** [pa'laβra] *nf* word; (*facultad*) (power of) speech; (*derecho de hablar*) right to speak; **tomar la ~** (*en mitin*) to take the floor

**palabrota** [pala'brota] *nf* swearword

**palacio** [pa'laθjo] *nm* palace; (*mansión*) mansion, large house; **~ de justicia** courthouse; **~ municipal** town/city hall

**paladar** [pala'ðar] *nm* palate; **paladear** *vt* to taste

**palanca** [pa'lanka] *nf* lever; (*fig*) pull, influence

**palangana** [palan'gana] *nf* washbasin

**palco** ['palko] *nm* box

**Palestina** [pales'tina] *nf* Palestine; **palestino, a** *nm/f* Palestinian

**paleta** [pa'leta] *nf* (*de pintor*) palette; (*de albañil*) trowel; (*de pingpong*) bat; (*AM*) ice lolly

**paleto, a** [pa'leto, a] (*fam, pey*) *nm/f* yokel

**paliar** [pa'ljar] *vt* (*mitigar*) to mitigate, alleviate; **paliativo** *nm* palliative

**palidecer** [paliðe'θer] *vi* to turn pale; **palidez** *nf* paleness; **pálido, a** *adj* pale

**palillo** [pa'liʎo] *nm* small stick; (*mondadientes*) toothpick; (*para comer*) chopstick

**paliza** [pa'liθa] *nf* beating, thrashing

**palma** ['palma] *nf* (*ANAT*) palm; (*árbol*) palm tree; **batir o dar ~s** to clap, applaud; **~da** *nf* slap; **~das** *nfpl* clapping *sg*, applause *sg*

**palmar** [pal'mar] (*fam*) *vi* (*tb: ~la*) to die, kick the bucket

**palmear** [palme'ar] *vi* to clap

**palmera** [pal'mera] *nf* (*BOT*) palm tree

**palmo** ['palmo] *nm* (*medida*) span; (*fig*) small amount; **~ a ~** inch by inch

**palmotear** [palmote'ar] *vi* to clap, applaud

**palo** ['palo] *nm* stick; (*poste*) post; (*de tienda de campaña*) pole; (*mango*) handle, shaft; (*golpe*) blow, hit; (*de golf*) club; (*de béisbol*) bat; (*NAUT*) mast; (*NAIPES*) suit

**paloma** [pa'loma] *nf* dove, pigeon

**palomilla** [palo'miʎa] *nf* moth; (*TEC: tuerca*) wing nut; (: *hierro*) angle iron

**palomitas** [palo'mitas] *nfpl* popcorn *sg*

**palpar** [pal'par] *vt* to touch, feel

**palpitación** [palpita'θjon] *nf* palpitation

**palpitante** [palpi'tante] *adj* palpitating; (*fig*) burning

**palpitar** [palpi'tar] *vi* to palpitate; (*latir*) to beat

**palta** ['palta] (*AM*) *nf* avocado (pear)

**paludismo** [palu'ðismo] *nm* malaria

**pamela** [pa'mela] *nf* picture hat, sun hat

**pampa** ['pampa] (*AM*) *nf* pampas, prairie

**pan** [pan] *nm* bread; (*una barra*) loaf; **~ integral** wholemeal (*BRIT*) *o* wholewheat (*US*) bread; **~ rallado** breadcrumbs *pl*

**pana** ['pana] *nf* corduroy

**panadería** [panaðe'ria] *nf* baker's (shop); **panadero, a** *nm/f* baker

**Panamá** [pana'ma] *nm* Panama; **panameño, a** *adj* Panamanian

**pancarta** [pan'karta] *nf* placard, banner

**panda** ['panda] nm (ZOOL) panda

**pandereta** [pande'reta] nf tambourine

**pandilla** [pan'diʎa] nf set, group; (de criminales) gang; (pey: camarilla) clique

**panecillo** [pane'θiʎo] nm (bread) roll

**panel** [pa'nel] nm panel; ~ **solar** solar panel

**panfleto** [pan'fleto] nm pamphlet

**pánico** ['paniko] nm panic

**panorama** [pano'rama] nm panorama; (vista) view

**pantalón** [panta'lon] nm trousers; **pantalones** nmpl trousers

**pantalla** [pan'taʎa] nf (de cine) screen; (de lámpara) lampshade

**pantano** [pan'tano] nm (ciénaga) marsh, swamp; (depósito de agua) reservoir; (fig) jam, difficulty

**panteón** [pante'on] nm: ~ **familiar** family tomb

**pantera** [pan'tera] nf panther

**pantomima** [panto'mima] nf pantomime

**pantorrilla** [panto'rriʎa] nf calf (of the leg)

**pantufla** [pan'tufla] nf slipper

**panza** ['panθa] nf belly, paunch

**pañal** [pa'ɲal] nm nappy (BRIT), diaper (US); ~es nmpl (fig) early stages, infancy sg

**paño** [pa'ɲo] nm (tela) cloth; (pedazo de tela) (piece of) cloth; (trapo) duster, rag; ~ **higiénico** sanitary towel; ~s **menores** underclothes

**pantis** [pan'tis] nmpl tights

**pañuelo** [pa'ɲwelo] nm handkerchief, hanky (fam); (para la cabeza) (head)scarf

**papa** ['papa] nm: el P~ the Pope ♦ (AM) nf potato

**papá** [pa'pa] (pl ~s) (fam) nm dad(dy), pa (US)

**papada** [pa'paða] nf (ANAT) double chin

**papagayo** [papa'ɣajo] nm parrot

**papanatas** [papa'natas] (fam) nm

inv simpleton

**paparrucha** [papa'rrutʃa] nf piece of nonsense

**papaya** [pa'paja] nf papaya

**papel** [pa'pel] nm paper; (hoja de ~) sheet of paper; (TEATRO, fig) role; ~ **de calco/carbón/de cartas** tracing paper/carbon paper/stationery; ~ **de envolver/pintado** wrapping paper/wallpaper; ~ **de aluminio/ higiénico** aluminium (BRIT) o aluminum (US) foil/toilet paper; ~ **de estaño** o **plata** tinfoil; ~ **de lija** sandpaper; ~ **moneda** paper money; ~ **secante** blotting paper

**papeleo** [pape'leo] nm red tape

**papelera** [pape'lera] nf wastepaper basket; (escritorio) desk

**papelería** [papele'ria] nf stationer's (shop)

**papeleta** [pape'leta] nf (pedazo de papel) slip of paper; (POL) ballot paper; (ESCOL) report

**paperas** [pa'peras] nfpl mumps sg

**papilla** [pa'piʎa] nf (para niños) baby food

**paquete** [pa'kete] nm (de cigarrillos etc) packet; (CORREOS etc) parcel; (AM) package tour; (: fam) nuisance, bore

**par** [par] adj (igual) like, equal; (MAT) even ♦ nm equal; (de guantes) pair; (de veces) couple; (POL) peer; (GOLF, COM) par; **abrir de** ~ **en** ~ to open wide

**para** ['para] prep for; **no es** ~ **comer** it's not for eating; **decir** ~ **sí** to say to o.s.; **¿** ~ **qué lo quieres?** what do you want it for?; **se casaron** ~ **separarse otra vez** they married only to separate again; **lo tendré** ~ **mañana** I'll have it (for) tomorrow; **ir** ~ **casa** to go home, head for home; **profesor es muy estúpido** ~ **ser profesor** he's very stupid for a teacher; **¿quién es usted** ~ **gritar así?** who are you to shout like that?; **tengo bastante** ~ **vivir** I have enough to live on; ver tb **con**

**parabién** [para'βjen] nm congratulations·pl

**parábola** [pa'raßola] nf parable; (MAT) parabola; **parabólica** nf (tb: antena ~) satellite dish

**parabrisas** [para'Brisas] nm inv windscreen (BRIT), windshield (US)

**paracaídas** [paraka'iðas] nm inv parachute; **paracaidista** nm/f parachutist; (MIL) paratrooper

**parachoques** [para'tʃokes] nm inv (AUTO) bumper; (MECANICA etc) shock absorber

**parada** [pa'raða] nf stop; (acto) stopping; (de industria) shutdown, stoppage; (lugar) stopping place; ~ de autobús bus stop

**paradero** [para'ðero] nm stopping-place; (situación) whereabouts

**parado, a** [pa'raðo, a] adj (persona) motionless, standing still; (fábrica) closed, at a standstill; (coche) stopped; (AM) standing (up); (sin empleo) unemployed, idle

**paradoja** [para'ðoxa] nf paradox

**parador** [para'ðor] nm parador, state-run hotel

**paráfrasis** [pa'rafrasis] nf inv paraphrase

**paraguas** [pa'raɣwas] nm inv umbrella

**Paraguay** [para'ɣwai] nm: el ~ Paraguay; **paraguayo, a** adj, nm/f Paraguayan

**paraíso** [para'iso] nm paradise, heaven

**paraje** [pa'raxe] nm place, spot

**paralelo, a** [para'lelo, a] adj parallel

**parálisis** [pa'ralisis] nf inv paralysis; **paralítico, a** adj, nm/f paralytic

**paralizar** [parali'θar] vt to paralyse; ~se vr to become paralysed; (fig) to come to a standstill

**paramilitar** [paramili'tar] adj paramilitary

**páramo** ['paramo] nm bleak plateau

**parangón** [paran'gon] nm: sin ~ incomparable

**paranoico, a** [para'noiko, a] nm/f paranoiac

**parapléjico, a** [para'plexiko, a] adj,

nm/f paraplegic

**parar** [pa'rar] vt to stop; (golpe) to ward off ♦ vi to stop; ~se vr to stop; (AM) to stand up; **ha parado de llover** it has stopped raining; **van a ~ en la comisaría** they're going to end up in the police station; ~se to pay attention to

**pararrayos** [para'rrajos] nm inv lightning conductor

**parásito, a** [pa'rasito, a] nm/f parasite

**parcela** [par'θela] nf plot, piece of ground

**parcial** [par'θjal] adj (pago) part-; (eclipse) partial; (JUR) prejudiced, biased; (POL) partisan; ~idad nf (prejuicio) prejudice, bias

**parco, a** ['parko, a] adj (moderado) moderate

**parche** [partʃe] nm (gen) patch

**pardillo, a** [par'ðiʎo, a] (pey) adj yokel

**parecer** [pare'θer] nm (opinión) opinion, view; (aspecto) looks pl ♦ vi (tener apariencia) to seem, look; (asemejarse) to look o seem like; (aparecer, llegar) to appear; ~se vr to look alike, resemble each other; ~se a to look like, resemble; **según o a lo que parece** evidently, apparently; **me parece que** I think (that), it seems to me that

**parecido, a** [pare'θiðo, a] adj similar ♦ nm similarity, likeness, resemblance; **bien** ~ good-looking, nice-looking

**pared** [pa'reð] nf wall

**pareja** [pa'rexa] nf pair; (dos personas) couple; (otro: de un par) other one (of a pair); (persona) partner

**parentela** [paren'tela] nf relations pl

**parentesco** [paren'tesko] nm relationship

**paréntesis** [pa'rentesis] nm inv parenthesis; (digresión) digression; (en escrito) bracket

**parezco** etc vb ver **parecer**

**pariente, a** [pa'rjente, a] nm/f relative, relation

**parir** [pa'rir] vt to give birth to ♦ vi (mujer) to give birth, have a baby

**París** [pa'ris] n París

**parking** ['parkin] nm car park (BRIT), parking lot (US)

**parlamentar** [parlamen'tar] vi (negociar) to parley

**parlamentario, a** [parlamen'tarjo, a] adj parliamentary ♦ nm/f member of parliament

**parlamento** [parla'mento] nm (POL) parliament

**parlanchín, ina** [parlan'tʃin, ina] adj indiscreet ♦ nm/f chatterbox

**paro** ['paro] nm (huelga) stoppage (of work), strike; (desempleo) unemployment; **subsidio de** ~ unemployment benefit; **hay** ~ **en la industria** work in the industry is at a standstill

**parodia** [pa'roðja] nf parody; **parodiar** vt to parody

**parpadear** [parpaðe'ar] vi (ojos) to blink; (luz) to flicker

**párpado** ['parpaðo] nm eyelid

**parque** ['parke] nm (lugar verde) park; ~ **de atracciones/infantil/ zoológico** fairground/playground/zoo

**parquímetro** [par'kimetro] nm parking meter

**parra** ['parra] nf (grape) vine

**párrafo** ['parrafo] nm paragraph; **echar un** ~ (fam) to have a chat

**parranda** [pa'rranda] nf (fam) spree, binge

**parrilla** [pa'rriʎa] nf (CULIN) grill; (de coche) grille; (carne a la) ~ barbecue; ~**da** nf barbecue

**párroco** ['parroko] nm parish priest

**parroquia** [pa'rrokja] nf parish; (iglesia) parish church; (COM) clientele, customers pl; ~**no, a** nm/f parishioner; client, customer

**parsimonia** [parsi'monja] nf calmness, level-headedness

**parte** ['parte] nm message; (informe) report ♦ nf part; (lado, cara) side; (de reparto) share; (JUR) party; **en alguna** ~ **de Europa** somewhere in Europe; **en/por todas** ~**s** every-

where; **en gran** ~ to a large extent; **la mayor** ~ **de los españoles** most Spaniards; **de un tiempo a esta** ~ for some time past; **de** ~ **de alguien** on sb's behalf; ¿**de** ~ **de quién?** (TEL) who is speaking?; **por** ~ **de** on the part of; **yo por mi** ~ I for my part; **por otra** ~ on the other hand; **dar** ~ to inform; **tomar** ~ to take part

**partición** [parti'θjon] nf division, sharing-out; (POL) partition

**participación** [partiθipa'θjon] nf (acto) participation, taking part; (parte, asunto) share; (de lotería) shared prize; (aviso) notice, notification

**participante** [partiθi'pante] nm/f participant

**participar** [partiθi'par] vt to notify, inform ♦ vi to take part, participate

**partícipe** [par'tiθipe] nm/f participant

**particular** [partiku'lar] adj (especial) particular, special; (individual, personal) private, personal ♦ nm (punto, asunto) particular, point; (individuo) individual; **tiene coche** ~ he has a car of his own; ~**izar** vt to distinguish; (especificar) to specify; (detallar) to give details about

**partida** [par'tiða] nf (salida) departure; (COM) entry, item; (juego) game; (grupo de personas) band, group; **mala** ~ dirty trick; ~ **de nacimiento/matrimonio/defunción** birth/marriage/death certificate

**partidario, a** [parti'ðarjo, a] adj partisan ♦ nm/f supporter, follower

**partido** [par'tiðo] nm (POL) party; (DEPORTE: encuentro) game, match; (: equipo) team; (apoyo) support; **sacar** ~ **de** to profit o benefit from; **tomar** ~ to take sides

**partir** [par'tir] vt (dividir) to split, divide; (compartir, distribuir) to share (out), distribute; (romper) to break open, split open; (rebanada) to cut (off) ♦ vi (ponerse en camino) to set off o out; (comenzar) to start (off o out); **~se** *vr* to crack *o* split *o* break (in two *etc*); **a ~ de** (starting) from

**partitura** [parti'tura] *nf* (MUS) score

**parto** ['parto] *nm* birth; (*fig*) product, creation; **estar de ~** to be in labour

**parvulario** [parβu'larjo] *nm* nursery school, kindergarten

**pasa** ['pasa] *nf* raisin; **~ de Corinto/de Esmirna** currant/sultana

**pasada** [pa'saða] *nf* passing, passage; **de ~** in passing, incidentally; **una mala ~** a dirty trick

**pasadizo** [pasa'ðiθo] *nm* (*pasillo*) passage, corridor; (*callejuela*) alley

**pasado, a** [pa'saðo, a] *adj* past; (*malo: comida, fruta*) bad; (*muy cocido*) overdone; (*anticuado*) out of date ♦ *nm* past; **~ mañana** the day after tomorrow; **el mes ~** last month

**pasador** [pasa'ðor] *nm* (*gen*) bolt; (*de pelo*) hair slide; (*horquilla*) grip

**pasaje** [pa'saxe] *nm* passage; (*pago de viaje*) fare; (*los pasajeros*) passengers *pl*; (*pasillo*) passageway

**pasajero, a** [pasa'xero, a] *adj* passing; (*situación, estado*) temporary; (*amor, enfermedad*) brief ♦ *nm/f* passenger

**pasamanos** [pasa'manos] *nm inv* (hand) rail; (*de escalera*) banisters *pl*

**pasamontañas** [pasamon'taɲas] *nm inv* balaclava helmet

**pasaporte** [pasa'porte] *nm* passport

**pasar** [pa'sar] *vt* to pass; (*tiempo*) to spend; (*desgracias*) to suffer, endure; (*noticia*) to give, pass on; (*río*) to cross; (*barrera*) to pass through; (*falta*) to overlook, tolerate; (*contrincante*) to surpass, do better than; (*coche*) to overtake; (*CINE*) to show; (*enfermedad*) to give, infect with ♦ *vi* (*gen*) to pass; (*terminarse*) to be over; (*ocurrir*) to happen; **~se** *vr* (*flores*) to fade; (*comida*) to go bad *o* off; (*fig*) to overdo it, go too far; **~ de** to go beyond, exceed; **~ por** (AM) to fetch; **~lo bien/mal** to have a good/bad time; **¡pase!** come

in!; **hacer ~** to show in; **~se al enemigo** to go over to the enemy; **se me pasó** I forgot; **no se le pasa nada** he misses nothing; **pase lo que pase** come what may

**pasarela** [pasa'rela] *nf* footbridge; (*en barco*) gangway

**pasatiempo** [pasa'tjempo] *nm* pastime, hobby

**Pascua** ['paskwa] *nf*: **~ (de Resurrección)** Easter; **~ de Navidad** Christmas; **~s** *nfpl* Christmas (time); **¡felices ~s!** Merry Christmas!

**pase** ['pase] *nm* pass; (CINE) performance, showing

**pasear** [pase'ar] *vt* to take for a walk; (*exhibir*) to parade, show off ♦ *vi* to walk, go for a walk; **~se** *vr* to walk, go for a walk; **~ en coche** to go for a drive; **paseo** *nm* (*avenida*) avenue; (*distancia corta*) walk, stroll; **dar un *o* ir de paseo** to go for a walk

**pasillo** [pa'siʎo] *nm* passage, corridor

**pasión** [pa'sjon] *nf* passion

**pasivo, a** [pa'siβo, a] *adj* passive; (*inactivo*) inactive ♦ *nm* (COM) liabilities *pl*, debts *pl*; (LING) passive

**pasmar** [pas'mar] *vt* (*asombrar*) to amaze, astonish; **pasmo** *nm* amazement, astonishment; (*resfriado*) chill; (*fig*) wonder, marvel; **pasmoso, a** *adj* amazing, astonishing

**paso, a** ['paso, a] *adj* dried ♦ *nm* step; (*modo de andar*) walk; (*huella*) footprint; (*rapidez*) speed, pace, rate; (*camino accesible*) way through, passage; (*cruce*) crossing; (*pasaje*) passing, passage; (GEO) pass; (*estrecho*) strait; **~ a nivel** (FERRO) level-crossing; **~ de peatones** pedestrian crossing; **a ese ~** (*fig*) at that rate; **salir al ~ de *o* a** to waylay; **estar de ~** to be passing through; **~ elevado** flyover; **prohibido el ~** no entry; **ceda el ~** give way

**pasota** [pa'sota] (*fam*) *adj, nm/f*

dropout; **ser un (tipo)** ~ to be a bit of a dropout; (*ser indiferente*) not to care about anything

**pasta** ['pasta] *nf* paste; (CULIN: *masa*) dough; (: *de bizcochos etc*) pastry; (*fam*) dough; ~s *nfpl* (*bizcochos*) pastries, small cakes; (*fideos, espaguetis etc*) pasta; ~ de dientes *o* dentífrica toothpaste

**pastar** [pas'tar] *vt, vi* to graze

**pastel** [pas'tel] *nm* (*dulce*) cake; ~ de carne meat pie; (ARTE) pastel; ~ería *nf* cake shop

**pasteurizado, a** [pasteuri'θaðo, a] *adj* pasteurised

**pastilla** [pas'tiʎa] *nf* (*de jabón, chocolate*) bar; (*píldora*) tablet, pill

**pasto** ['pasto] *nm* (*hierba*) grass; (*lugar*) pasture, field

**pastor, a** [pas'tor, a] *nm/f* shepherd/ess ♦ *nm* (REL) clergyman, pastor; ~ alemán Alsatian

**pata** ['pata] *nf* (*pierna*) leg; (*pie*) foot; (*de muebles*) leg; ~s arriba upside down; **meter la** ~ (*fam*) to put one's foot in it; (TEC): ~ de cabra crowbar; **tener buena/mala** ~ to be lucky/unlucky; ~da *nf* kick; (*en el suelo*) stamp

**patalear** [patale'ar] *vi* (*en el suelo*) to stamp one's feet

**patata** [pa'tata] *nf* potato; ~s fritas *o* a la española chips, French fries o ~s fritas (*de bolsa*) crisps

**paté** [pa'te] *nm* paté

**patear** [pate'ar] *vt* (*pisar*) to stamp on, trample (on); (*pegar con el pie*) to kick ♦ *vi* to stamp (with rage), stamp one's feet

**patentar** [paten'tar] *vt* to patent

**patente** [pa'tente] *adj* obvious, evident; (COM) patent ♦ *nf* patent

**paternal** [pater'nal] *adj* fatherly, paternal; **paterno, a** *adj* paternal

**patético, a** [pa'tetiko, a] *adj* pathetic, moving

**patilla** [pa'tiʎa] *nf* (*de gafas*) side(piece)

**patillas** [pa'tiʎas] *nfpl* sideburns

**patín** [pa'tin] *nm* skate; (*de trineo*) runner; **patinaje** *nm* skating; **patinar** *vi* to skate; (*resbalarse*) to skid, slip; (*fam*) to slip up, blunder

**patio** ['patjo] *nm* (*de casa*) patio, courtyard; ~ de recreo playground

**pato** ['pato] *nm* duck; **pagar el** ~ (*fam*) to take the blame, carry the can

**patológico, a** [pato'loxiko, a] *adj* pathological

**patoso, a** [pa'toso, a] *adj* (*fam*) clumsy

**patraña** [pa'traɲa] *nf* story, fib

**patria** ['patrja] *nf* native land, mother country

**patrimonio** [patri'monjo] *nm* inheritance; (*fig*) heritage

**patriota** [pa'trjota] *nm/f* patriot; **patriotismo** *nm* patriotism

**patrocinar** [patroθi'nar] *vt* to sponsor; (*apoyar*) to back, support; **patrocinio** *nm* sponsorship; backing, support

**patrón, ona** [pa'tron, ona] *nm/f* (*jefe*) boss, chief, master/mistress; (*propietario*) landlord/lady; (REL) patron saint ♦ *nm* (TEC, COSTURA) pattern

**patronal** [patro'nal] *adj*: **la clase** ~ management

**patronato** [patro'nato] *nm* sponsorship; (*acto*) patronage; (*fundación benéfica*) trust, foundation

**patrulla** [pa'truʎa] *nf* patrol

**pausa** ['pausa] *nf* pause, break

**pausado, a** [pau'saðo, a] *adj* slow, deliberate

**pauta** ['pauta] *nf* line, guide line

**pavimento** [paßi'mento] *nm* (*con losas*) pavement, paving

**pavo** ['paßo] *nm* turkey; ~ real peacock

**pavor** [pa'ßor] *nm* dread, terror

**payaso, a** [pa'jaso, a] *nm/f* clown

**payo, a** ['pajo] *nm/f* (*para gitanos*) non-gipsy

**paz** [paθ] *nf* peace; (*tranquilidad*) peacefulness, tranquillity; **hacer las paces** to make peace; (*fig*) to make up

**P.D.** abr (= posdata) P.S., p.s.

**peaje** [pe'axe] nm toll

**peatón** [pea'ton] nm pedestrian

**peca** ['peka] nf freckle

**pecado** [pe'kaðo] nm sin; **pecador, a** adj sinful ♦ nm/f sinner

**pecaminoso, a** [pekami'noso, a] adj sinful

**pecar** [pe'kar] vi (REL) to sin; (fig): **peca de generoso** he is generous to a fault

**peculiar** [peku'ljar] adj special, peculiar; (característico) typical, characteristic; ~**idad** nf peculiarity; special feature, characteristic

**pecho** ['petʃo] nm (ANAT) chest; (de mujer) breast(s) (pl), bosom; (fig: corazón) heart, breast; (: valor) courage, spirit; **dar el ~ a** breast-feed; **tomar algo a ~** to take sth to heart

**pechuga** [pe'tʃuɣa] nf breast

**pedal** [pe'ðal] nm pedal; ~**ear** vi to pedal

**pedante** [pe'ðante] adj pedantic ♦ nm/f pedant; ~**ría** nf pedantry

**pedazo** [pe'ðaθo] nm piece, bit; **hacerse ~s** (romperse) to smash, shatter

**pedernal** [peðer'nal] nm flint

**pediatra** [pe'ðjatra] nm/f paediatrician

**pedido** [pe'ðiðo] nm (COM: mandado) order; (petición) request

**pedir** [pe'ðir] vt to ask for, request; (comida, cuenta) to order; (exigir: precio) to ask; (necesitar) to need, demand, require ♦ vi to ask; **me pidió que cerrara la puerta** he asked me to shut the door; **¿cuánto piden por el coche?** how much are they asking for the car?

**pedo** [pe'ðo] nm (fam!) nm fart

**pega** ['peɣa] nf snag; **poner ~s (a)** to complain (about)

**pegadizo, a** [peɣa'ðiθo, a] adj (MUS) catchy

**pegajoso, a** [peɣa'xoso, a] adj sticky, adhesive

**pegamento** [peɣa'mento] nm gum, glue

**pegar** [pe'ɣar] vt (papel, sellos) to stick (on); (cartel) to stick up; (coser) to sew (on); (unir: partes) to join, fix together; (MED) to give, infect with; (dar: golpe) to give, deal ♦ vi (adherirse) to stick, adhere; (ir juntos: colores) to match, go together; (golpear) to hit; (quemar: el sol) to strike hot, burn (fig); ~**se** vr (gen) to stick; (dos personas) to hit each other, fight; ~ **un grito** to let out a yell; ~ **un salto** to jump (with fright); ~ **en** to touch; ~**se un tiro** to shoot o.s.

**pegatina** [peɣa'tina] nf sticker

**pegote** [pe'ɣote] nm (fig) mess; (fam, pey) eyesore, sight

**peinado** [pei'naðo] nm (en peluquería) hairdo; (estilo) hair style

**peinar** [pei'nar] vt to comb; (hacer estilo) to style; ~**se** vr to comb one's hair

**peine** ['peine] nm comb; ~**ta** nf ornamental comb

**p.ej.** abr (= por ejemplo) e.g.

**Pekín** [pe'kin] n Peking(n)

**pelado, a** [pe'laðo, a] adj (fruta, patata etc) peeled; (cabeza) shorn; (campo, fig) bare; (fam: sin dinero) broke

**pelaje** [pe'laxe] nm (ZOOL) fur, coat; (fig) appearance

**pelar** [pe'lar] vt (fruta, patatas etc) to peel; (cortar el pelo a) to cut the hair of; (quitar la piel: animal) to skin; ~**se** vr (la piel) to peel off; **voy a ~me** I'm going to get my hair cut

**peldaño** [pel'daño] nm step

**pelea** [pe'lea] nf (lucha) fight; (discusión) quarrel, row

**peleado, a** [pele'aðo, a] adj: **estar** ~ (con uno) to have fallen out (with sb)

**pelear** [pele'ar] vi to fight; ~**se** vr to fight; (reñirse) to fall out, quarrel

**peletería** [pelete'ria] nf furrier's, fur shop

**pelícano** [pe'likano] *nm* pelican

**película** [pe'likula] *nf* film; (*cobertura ligera*) thin covering; (*FOTO: rollo*) roll o reel of film

**peligro** [pe'liɣro] *nm* danger; (*riesgo*) risk; **correr un ~** to run the risk of; **~so, a** *adj* dangerous; risky

**pelirrojo, a** [peli'rroxo, a] *adj* red-haired, red-headed ♦ *nm/f* redhead

**pelma** ['pelma] (*fam*) *nm/f* pain (in the neck)

**pelmazo** [pel'maθo] (*fam*) *nm* = **pelma**

**pelo** ['pelo] *nm* (*cabellos*) hair; (*de barba, bigote*) whisker; (*de animal: pellejo*) hair, fur, coat; **al ~** just right; **venir al ~** to be exactly what one needs; **un hombre de ~ en pecho** a brave man; **por los ~s** by the skin of one's teeth; **no tener ~s en la lengua** to be outspoken, not mince words; **tomar el ~ a uno** to pull sb's leg

**pelota** [pe'lota] *nf* ball; (*fam: cabeza*) nut; **en ~** stark naked; **hacer la ~ (a uno)** (*fam*) to creep (to sb); **~ vasca** pelota

**pelotari** [pelo'tari] *nm* pelota player

**pelotón** [pelo'ton] *nm* (*MIL*) squad, detachment

**peluca** [pe'luka] *nf* wig

**peluche** [pe'lutʃe] *nm*: **oso/muñeco de ~** teddy bear/soft toy

**peludo, a** [pe'luðo, a] *adj* hairy, shaggy

**peluquería** [peluke'ria] *nf* hairdresser's; (*para hombres*) barber's (shop); **peluquero, a** *nm/f* hairdresser; barber

**pelusa** [pe'lusa] *nf* (*BOT*) down; (*COSTURA*) fluff

**pellejo** [pe'ʎexo] *nm* (*de animal*) skin, hide

**pellizcar** [peʎiθ'kar] *vt* to pinch, nip

**pena** ['pena] *nf* (*congoja*) grief, sadness; (*remordimiento*) regret; (*dificultad*) trouble, pain; (*dolor*) pain; (*JUR*) sentence; **merecer o valer la ~** to be worthwhile; **a duras ~s** with great difficulty; **~ de muerte** death

penalty; **~ pecuniaria** fine; **¡qué ~!** what a shame!

**penal** [pe'nal] *adj* penal ♦ *nm* (*cárcel*) prison

**penalidad** [penali'ðað] *nf* (*problema, dificultad*) trouble, hardship; (*castigo*) penalty, punishment; **~es** *nfpl* trouble, hardship

**penalti** [pe'nalti] (*pl* **~s** *o* **~es**) *nm* penalty (kick)

**penalty** [pe'nalti] (*pl* **~s** *o* **~es**) *nm* = **penalti**

**penar** [pe'nar] *vt* to penalize; (*castigar*) to punish ♦ *vi* to suffer

**pendiente** [pen'djente] *adj* pending, unsettled ♦ *nm* earring ♦ *nf* hill, slope

**pene** ['pene] *nm* penis

**penetración** [penetra'θjon] *nf* (*acto*) penetration; (*agudeza*) sharpness, insight

**penetrante** [pene'trante] *adj* (*herida*) deep; (*persona, arma*) sharp; (*sonido*) penetrating, piercing; (*mirada*) searching; (*viento, ironía*) biting

**penetrar** [pene'trar] *vt* to penetrate, pierce; (*entender*) to grasp ♦ *vi* to penetrate, go in; (*entrar*) to enter, go in; (*líquido*) to soak in; (*fig*) to pierce

**penicilina** [peniθi'lina] *nf* penicillin

**península** [pe'ninsula] *nf* peninsula; **peninsular** *adj* peninsular

**penique** [pe'nike] *nm* penny

**penitencia** [peni'tenθja] *nf* (*remordimiento*) penitence; (*castigo*) penance

**penoso, a** [pe'noso, a] *adj* (*difícil*) arduous, difficult

**pensador, a** [pensa'ðor, a] *nm/f* thinker

**pensamiento** [pensa'mjento] *nm* thought; (*mente*) mind; (*idea*) idea

**pensar** [pen'sar] *vt* to think; (*considerar*) to think over, think out; (*proponerse*) to intend, plan; (*imaginarse*) to think up, invent ♦ *vi* to think; **~ en** to aim at, aspire to; **pensativo, a** *adj* thoughtful, pensive

**pensión** [pen'sjon] *nf* (*casa*) boarding o guest house; (*dinero*) pension;

(*cama y comida*) board and lodging; ~ **completa** full board; **pensionista** *nmf* (*jubilado*) (old-age) pensioner; (*huésped*) lodger

**penúltimo, a** [pe'nultimo, a] *adj* penultimate, last but one

**penumbra** [pe'numbra] *nf* half-light

**penuria** [pe'nurja] *nf* shortage, want

**peña** ['peɲa] *nf* (*roca*) rock; (*cuesta*) cliff, crag; (*grupo*) group, circle; (*AM*: *club*) folk club

**peñasco** [pe'ɲasko] *nm* large rock, boulder

**peñón** [pe'ɲon] *nm* wall of rock; **el P**~ the Rock (of Gibraltar)

**peón** [pe'on] *nm* labourer; (*AM*) farm labourer, farmhand; (*AJEDREZ*) pawn

**peonza** [pe'onθa] *nf* spinning top

**peor** [pe'or] *adj* (*comparativo*) worse; (*superlativo*) worst ♦ *adv* worse; worst; **de mal en** ~ from bad to worse

**pepinillo** [pepi'niλo] *nm* gherkin

**pepino** [pe'pino] *nm* cucumber; (**no**) **me importa un** ~ I don't care one bit

**pepita** [pe'pita] *nf* (*BOT*) pip; (*MINERIA*) nugget

**pequeñez** [peke'neθ] *nf* smallness, littleness; (*trivialidad*) trifle, triviality

**pequeño, a** [pe'keɲo, a] *adj* small, little

**pera** ['pera] *nf* pear; **peral** *nm* pear tree

**percance** [per'kanθe] *nm* setback, misfortune

**percatarse** [perka'tarse] *vr*: ~ **de** to notice, take note of

**percepción** [perθep'θjon] *nf* (*vista*) perception; (*idea*) notion, idea

**perceptible** [perθep'tiβle] *adj* perceptible, noticeable; (*COM*) payable, receivable

**percibir** [perθi'βir] *vt* to perceive, notice; (*COM*) to earn, get

**percusión** [perku'sjon] *nf* percussion

**percha** ['pertʃa] *nf* (*ganchos*) coat hooks *pl*; (*colgador*) coat hanger; (*de*

*ave*) perch

**perdedor, a** [perðe'ðor, a] *adj* losing ♦ *nm/f* loser

**perder** [per'ðer] *vt* to lose; (*tiempo, palabras*) to waste; (*oportunidad*) to lose, miss; (*tren*) to miss ♦ *vi* to lose; ~**se** *vr* (*extraviarse*) to get lost; (*desaparecer*) to disappear, be lost to view; (*arruinarse*) to be ruined; **echar a** ~ (*comida*) to spoil, ruin; (*oportunidad*) to waste

**perdición** [perði'θjon] *nf* perdition, ruin

**pérdida** ['perðiða] *nf* loss; (*de tiempo*) waste; ~**s** *nfpl* (*COM*) losses

**perdido, a** [per'ðiðo, a] *adj* lost

**perdiz** [per'ðiθ] *nf* partridge

**perdón** [per'ðon] *nm* (*disculpa*) pardon, forgiveness; (*clemencia*) mercy; **¡~!** sorry!, I beg your pardon!; **perdonar** *vt* to pardon, forgive; (*la vida*) to spare; (*excusar*) to exempt, excuse; **¡perdone (usted)!** sorry!, I beg your pardon!

**perdurable** [perðu'raβle] *adj* lasting; (*eterno*) everlasting

**perdurar** [perðu'rar] *vi* (*resistir*) to last, endure; (*seguir existiendo*) to stand, still exist

**perecedero, a** [pereθe'ðero, a] *adj* (*COM etc*) perishable

**perecer** [pere'θer] *vi* (*morir*) to perish, die; (*objeto*) to shatter

**peregrinación** [pereɣrina'θjon] *nf* (*REL*) pilgrimage

**peregrino, a** [pere'ðrino, a] *adj* (*idea*) strange, absurd ♦ *nm/f* pilgrim

**perejil** [pere'xil] *nm* parsley

**perenne** [pe'renne] *adj* everlasting, perennial

**perentorio, a** [peren'torjo, a] *adj* (*urgente*) urgent, peremptory; (*fijo*) set, fixed

**pereza** [pe'reθa] *nf* laziness, idleness; **perezoso, a** *adj* lazy, idle

**perfección** [perfek'θjon] *nf* perfection; **perfeccionar** *vt* to perfect; (*mejorar*) to improve; (*acabar*) to complete, finish

**perfectamente** [perfekta'mente] adv perfectly

**perfecto, a** [per'fekto, a] adj perfect; (terminado) complete, finished

**perfidia** [per'fiðja] nf perfidy, treachery

**perfil** [per'fil] nm profile; (contorno) silhouette, outline; (ARQ) (cross) section; ~es nmpl features; (fig) social graces; ~ar vt (trazar) to outline; (fig) to shape, give character to

**perforación** [perfora'θjon] nf perforation; (con taladro) drilling; **perforadora** nf punch

**perforar** [perfo'rar] vt to perforate; (agujero) to drill, bore; (papel) to punch a hole in ♦ vi to drill, bore

**perfume** [per'fume] nm perfume, scent

**pericia** [pe'riθja] nf skill, expertise

**periferia** [peri'ferja] nf periphery; (de ciudad) outskirts pl

**periférico** [peri'feriko] (AM) nm ring road (BRIT), beltway (US)

**perímetro** [pe'rimetro] nm perimeter

**periódico, a** [pe'rjoðiko, a] adj periodic(al) ♦ nm newspaper

**periodismo** [perjo'ðismo] nm journalism; **periodista** nm/f journalist

**periodo** [pe'rjoðo] nm = periodo

**período** [pe'rjoðo] nm = periodo

**periquito** [peri'kito] nm budgerigar, budgie

**perito, a** [pe'rito, a] adj (experto) expert; (diestro) skilled, skilful ♦ nm/f expert; skilled worker; (técnico) technician

**perjudicar** [perxuði'kar] vt (gen) to damage, harm; **perjudicial** adj damaging, harmful; (en detrimento) detrimental; **perjuicio** nm damage, harm

**perjurar** [perxu'rar] vi to commit perjury

**perla** ['perla] nf pearl; **me viene de** ~ it suits me fine

**permanecer** [permane'θer] vi (quedarse) to stay, remain; (seguir) to continue to be

**permanencia** [perma'nenθja] nf permanence; (estancia) stay

**permanente** [perma'nente] adj permanent, constant ♦ nf perm

**permisible** [permi'sible] adj permissible, allowable

**permisivo, a** [permi'siβo, a] adj permissive

**permiso** [per'miso] nm permission; (licencia) permit, licence; **con** ~ excuse me; **estar de** ~ (MIL) to be on leave; ~ **de conducir** driving licence (BRIT), driver's license (US)

**permitir** [permi'tir] vt to permit, allow

**pernera** [per'nera] nf trouser leg

**pernicioso, a** [perni'θjoso, a] adj (maligno, MED) pernicious; (persona) wicked

**pero** ['pero] conj but; (aún) yet ♦ nm (defecto) flaw, defect; (reparo) objection

**perpendicular** [perpendiku'lar] adj perpendicular

**perpetrar** [perpe'trar] vt to perpetrate

**perpetuar** [perpe'twar] vt to perpetuate; **perpetuo, a** adj perpetual

**perplejo, a** [per'plexo, a] adj perplexed, bewildered

**perra** ['perra] nf (ZOOL) bitch; (fam: dinero) money; **estar sin una** ~ to be flat broke

**perrera** [pe'rrera] nf kennel

**perro** ['perro] nm dog

**persa** ['persa] adj, nm/f Persian

**persecución** [perseku'θjon] nf pursuit, chase; (REL, POL) persecution

**perseguir** [perse'xir] vt to pursue, hunt; (cortejar) to chase after; (molestar) to pester, annoy; (REL, POL) to persecute

**perseverante** [perseβe'rante] adj persevering, persistent

**perseverar** [perseβe'rar] vi to persevere, persistent; ~ **en** to persevere in, persist with

**persiana** [per'sjana] nf (Venetian) blind

**persignarse** [persix'narse] vr to

cross o.s.

**persistente** [persis'tente] adj persistent

**persistir** [persis'tir] vi to persist

**persona** [per'sona] nf person; ~ mayor elderly person; 10 ~s 10 people

**personaje** [perso'naxe] nm important person, celebrity; (TEATRO etc) character

**personal** [perso'nal] adj (particular) personal; (para una persona) single, for one person ♦ nm personnel, staff; ~idad nf personality

**personarse** [perso'narse] vr to appear in person

**personificar** [personifi'kar] vt to personify

**perspectiva** [perspek'tißa] nf perspective; (vista, panorama) view, panorama; (posibilidad futura) outlook, prospect

**perspicacia** [perspi'kaθja] nf (fig) discernment, perspicacity

**perspicaz** [perspi'kaθ] adj shrewd

**persuadir** [perswa'ðir] vt (gen) to persuade; (convencer) to convince; ~se vr to become convinced; **persuasión** nf persuasion; **persuasivo, a** adj persuasive; convincing

**pertenecer** [pertene'θer] vi to belong; (fig) to concern; **perteneciente** adj: **perteneciente a** belonging to; **pertenencia** nf ownership; **pertenencias** nfpl (bienes) possessions, property sg

**pertenezca** etc vb ver **pertenecer**

**pértiga** ['pertixa] nf: **salto de** ~ pole vault

**pertinaz** [perti'naθ] adj (persistente) persistent; (terco) obstinate

**pertinente** [perti'nente] adj relevant, pertinent; (apropiado) appropriate; ~ a concerning, relevant to

**perturbación** [perturßa'θjon] nf (POL) disturbance; (MED) upset, disturbance

**perturbado, a** [pertur'ßaðo, a] adj mentally unbalanced

**perturbador, a** [perturßa'ðor, a]

adj perturbing, disturbing; (subversivo) subversive

**perturbar** [pertur'ßar] vt (el orden) to disturb; (MED) to upset, disturb; (mentalmente) to perturb

**Perú** [pe'ru] nm: el ~ Peru; **peruano, a**, adj, nm/f Peruvian

**perversión** [perßer'sjon] nf perversion; **perverso, a** adj perverse; (depravado) depraved

**pervertido, a** [perßer'tiðo, a] adj perverted ♦ nm/f pervert

**pervertir** [perßer'tir] vt to pervert, corrupt

**pesa** ['pesa] nf weight; (DEPORTE) shot

**pesadez** [pesa'ðeθ] nf (peso) heaviness; (lentitud) slowness; (aburrimiento) tediousness

**pesadilla** [pesa'ðiʎa] nf nightmare, bad dream

**pesado, a** [pe'saðo, a] adj heavy; (lento) slow; (difícil, duro) tough, hard; (aburrido) boring, tedious; (tiempo) sultry

**pesadumbre** [pesa'ðumbre] nf grief, sorrow

**pésame** ['pesame] nm expression of condolence, message of sympathy; **dar el** ~ to express one's condolences

**pesar** [pe'sar] vt to weigh ♦ vi to weigh; (ser pesado) to weigh a lot, be heavy; (fig: opinión) to carry weight; **no pesa mucho** it doesn't weigh much ♦ nm (arrepentimiento) regret; (pena) grief, sorrow; **a** ~ **de** o **pese a** (que) in spite of, despite

**pesca** ['peska] nf (acto) fishing; (lo pescado) catch; **ir de** ~ to go fishing

**pescadería** [peskaðe'ria] nf fish shop, fishmonger's (BRIT)

**pescadilla** [peska'ðiʎa] nf (pez) whiting

**pescado** [pes'kaðo] nm fish

**pescador, a** [peska'ðor, a] nm/f fisherman/woman

**pescar** [pes'kar] vt (tomar) to catch; (intentar tomar) to fish for; (conseguir: trabajo) to manage to get ♦ vi to fish, go fishing

**pescuezo** [pes'kweθo] *nm* (ZOOL) neck

**pesebre** [pe'seβre] *nm* manger

**peseta** [pe'seta] *nf* peseta

**pesimista** [pesi'mista] *adj* pessimistic ♦ *nm/f* pessimist

**pésimo, a** ['pesimo, a] *adj* awful, dreadful

**peso** ['peso] *nm* weight; (*moneda*) scales *pl*; (*moneda*) peso; ~ **bruto/neto** gross/net weight; **vender a** ~ to sell by weight

**pesquero, a** [pes'kero, a] *adj* fishing *cpd*

**pesquisa** [pes'kisa] *nf* inquiry, investigation

**pestaña** [pes'taɲa] *nf* (ANAT) eyelash; (*borde*) rim; **pestañear** *vi* to blink

**peste** ['peste] *nf* plague; (*mal olor*) stink, stench

**pesticida** [pesti'θiða] *nm* pesticide

**pestilencia** [pesti'lenθja] *nf* (*mal olor*) stink, stench

**pestillo** [pes'tiʎo] *nm* (*cerrojo*) bolt; (*picaporte*) doorhandle

**petaca** [pe'taka] *nf* (*de cigarros*) cigarette case; (*de pipa*) tobacco pouch; (AM: *maleta*) suitcase

**pétalo** ['petalo] *nm* petal

**petardo** [pe'tarðo] *nm* firework, firecracker

**petición** [peti'θjon] *nf* (*pedido*) request, plea; (*memorial*) petition; (JUR) plea

**petrificar** [petrifi'kar] *vt* to petrify

**petróleo** [pe'troleo] *nm* oil, petroleum; **petrolero, a** *adj* petroleum *cpd* ♦ *nm* (COM: *persona*) oil man; (*buque*) oil) tanker

**peyorativo, a** [pejora'tiβo, a] *adj* pejorative

**pez** [peθ] *nm* fish

**pezón** [pe'θon] *nm* teat, nipple

**pezuña** [pe'θuɲa] *nf* hoof

**piadoso, a** [pja'ðoso, a] *adj* (*devoto*) pious, devout; (*misericordioso*) kind, merciful

**pianista** [pja'nista] *nm/f* pianist

**piano** ['pjano] *nm* piano

**piar** [pjar] *vi* to cheep

**pibe, a** ['piβe, a] (AM) *nm/f* boy/girl

**picadero** [pika'ðero] *nm* riding school

**picadillo** [pika'ðiʎo] *nm* mince, minced meat

**picado, a** [pi'kaðo, a] *adj* pricked, punctured; (CULIN) minced, chopped; (*mar*) choppy; (*diente*) bad; (*tabaco*) cut; (*enfadado*) cross

**picador** [pika'ðor] *nm* (TAUR) picador; (*minero*) faceworker

**picadura** [pika'ðura] *nf* (*pinchazo*) puncture; (*de abeja*) sting; (*de mosquito*) bite; (*tabaco picado*) cut tobacco

**picante** [pi'kante] *adj* hot; (*comentario*) racy, spicy

**picaporte** [pika'porte] *nm* (*manija*) doorhandle; (*pestillo*) latch

**picar** [pi'kar] *vt* (*agujerear, perforar*) to prick, puncture; (*abeja*) to sting; (*mosquito, serpiente*) to bite; (CULIN) to mince, chop; (*incitar*) to incite, goad; (*dañar, irritar*) to annoy, bother; (*quemar: lengua*) to burn, sting ♦ *vi* (*pez*) to bite, take the bait; (*sol*) to burn, scorch; (*abeja, MED*) to sting; (*mosquito*) to bite; ~**se** *vr* (*agriarse*) to turn sour, go off; (*ofenderse*) to take offence

**picardía** [pikar'ðia] *nf* villainy; (*astucia*) slyness, craftiness; (*una* ~) dirty trick; (*palabra*) rude/bad word o expression

**pícaro, a** ['pikaro, a] *adj* (*malicioso*) villainous; (*travieso*) mischievous ♦ *nm* (*astuto*) crafty sort; (*sinvergüenza*) rascal, scoundrel

**pico** ['piko] *nm* (*de ave*) beak; (*punta*) sharp point; (TEC) pick, pickaxe; (GEO) peak, summit; **y** ~ **and a bit**

**picotear** [pikote'ar] *vt* to peck ♦ *vi* to nibble, pick

**picudo, a** [pi'kuðo, a] *adj* pointed, with a point

**pichón** [pi'tʃon] *nm* young pigeon

**pidió** *etc vb ver* **pedir**

**pido** etc vb ver **pedir**

**pie** [pje] (pl ~s) nm foot; (fig: motivo) motive, basis; (: fundamento) foothold; **ir a** ~ to go on foot, walk; **estar de** ~ to be standing (up); **ponerse de** ~ to stand up; **de** ~s **a cabeza** from top to bottom; **al** ~ **de la letra** (citar) literally, verbatim; (copiar) exactly, word for word; **en** ~ **de guerra** on a war footing; **dar** ~ **a** to give cause for; **hacer** ~ (en el agua) to touch (the) bottom

**piedad** [pje'ðað] nf (lástima) pity, compassion; (clemencia) mercy; (devoción) piety, devotion

**piedra** ['pjeðra] nf stone; (roca) rock; (de mechero) flint; (METEOROLOGIA) hailstone

**piel** [pjel] nf (ANAT) skin; (ZOOL) skin, hide, fur; (cuero) leather; (BOT) skin, peel

**pienso** etc vb ver **pensar**

**pierdo** etc vb ver **perder**

**pierna** ['pjerna] nf leg

**pieza** ['pjeθa] nf piece; (habitación) room; ~ **de recambio** o **repuesto** spare (part)

**pigmeo, a** [pi'γmeo, a] adj, nm/f pigmy

**pijama** [pi'xama] nm pyjamas pl

**pila** ['pila] nf (ELEC) battery; (montón) heap, pile; (lavabo) sink

**píldora** ['pildora] nf pill; **la** ~ **(anti-conceptiva)** the (contraceptive) pill

**pileta** [pi'leta] nf basin, bowl; (AM) swimming pool

**piloto** [pi'loto] nm pilot; (de aparato) (pilot) light; (AUTO: luz) tail o rear light; (: conductor) driver

**pillaje** [pi'ʎaxe] nm pillage, plunder

**pillar** [pi'ʎar] vt (saquear) to pillage, plunder; (fam: coger) to catch; (: agarrar) to grasp, seize; (: entender) to grasp, catch on to; ~**se** vr: ~**se un dedo con la puerta** to catch one's finger in the door

**pillo, a** ['piʎo, a] adj villainous; (astuto) sly, crafty ♦ nm/f rascal, rogue, scoundrel

**pimentón** [pimen'ton] nm paprika

**pimienta** [pi'mjenta] nf pepper

**pimiento** [pi'mjento] nm pepper, pimiento

**pinacoteca** [pinako'teka] nf art gallery

**pinar** [pi'nar] nm pine forest (BRIT), pine grove (US)

**pincel** [pin'θel] nm paintbrush

**pinchadiscos** [pintʃa'ðiskos] nm/f inv disc-jockey, DJ

**pinchar** [pin'tʃar] vt (perforar) to prick, pierce; (neumático) to puncture; (fig) to prod

**pinchazo** [pin'tʃaθo] nm (perforación) prick; (de neumático) puncture; (fig) prod

**pincho** ['pintʃo] nm savoury (snack); ~ **moruno** shish kebab; ~ **de tortilla** small slice of omelette

**ping-pong** ['pin'pon] nm table tennis

**pingüino** [pin'gwino] nm penguin

**pino** ['pino] nm pine (tree)

**pinta** ['pinta] nf spot; (de líquidos) spot, drop; (aspecto) appearance, look(s) (pl); ~**do, a** adj spotted; (de muchos colores) colourful; ~**das** nfpl graffiti sg

**pintar** [pin'tar] vt to paint ♦ vi to paint; (fam) to count, be important; ~**se** vr to put on make-up

**pintor, a** [pin'tor, a] nm/f painter

**pintoresco, a** [pinto'resko, a] adj picturesque

**pintura** [pin'tura] nf painting; ~ **a la acuarela** watercolour; ~ **al óleo** oil painting

**pinza** ['pinθa] nf (ZOOL) claw; (para colgar ropa) clothes peg; (TEC) pincers pl; ~**s** nfpl (para depilar etc) tweezers pl

**piña** ['piɲa] nf (fruto del pino) pine cone; (fruta) pineapple; (fig) group

**piñón** [pi'ɲon] nm (fruto) pine nut; (TEC) pinion

**pío, a** ['pio, a] adj (devoto) pious, devout; (misericordioso) merciful

**piojo** ['pjoxo] nm louse

**pionero, a** [pjo'nero, a] adj pioneering ♦ nm/f pioneer

**pipa** ['pipa] nf pipe; **~s** nfpl (BOT) (edible) sunflower seeds

**pipí** [pi'pi] (fam) nm: **hacer ~** to have a wee(-wee) (BRIT), have to go (wee-wee) (US)

**pique** ['pike] nm (resentimiento) pique, resentment; (rivalidad) rivalry, competition; **irse a ~** to sink; (es- peranza, familia) to be ruined

**piqueta** [pi'keta] nf pick(axe)

**piquete** [pi'kete] nm (agujerito) small hole; (MIL) squad, party; (de obreros) picket

**piragua** [pi'raɣwa] nf canoe; **pira- güismo** nm canoeing

**pirámide** [pi'ramiðe] nf pyramid

**pirata** [pi'rata] adj, nm pirate ♦ nm/ f: **~ informático/a** hacker

**Pirineo(s)** [piri'neo(s)] nm(pl) Pyr- enees pl

**pirómano, a** [pi'romano, a] nm/f (MED, JUR) arsonist

**piropo** [pi'ropo] nm compliment, (piece of) flattery

**pirueta** [pi'rweta] nf pirouette

**pis** [pis] (fam) nm pee, piss; **hacer ~** to have a pee; (para niños) to wee-wee

**pisada** [pi'saða] nf (paso) footstep; (huella) footprint

**pisar** [pi'sar] vt (caminar sobre) to walk on, tread on; (apretar con el pie) to press; (fig) to trample on, walk all over ♦ vi to tread, step, walk

**piscina** [pis'θina] nf swimming pool

**Piscis** ['pisθis] nm Pisces

**piso** ['piso] nm (suelo, planta) floor; (apartamento) flat (BRIT), apartment; **primer ~** (ESP) first floor; (AM) ground floor

**pisotear** [pisote'ar] vt to trample (on o underfoot)

**pista** ['pista] nf track, trail; (indicio) clue; **~ de aterrizaje** runway; **~ de baile** dance floor; **~ de hielo** ice rink; **~ de tenis** tennis court

**pistola** [pis'tola] nf pistol; (TEC) spray-gun; **pistolero, a** nm/f gunman/woman, gangster

**pistón** [pis'ton] nm (TEC) piston; (MUS) key

**pitar** [pi'tar] vt (silbato) to blow; (re- chiflar) to whistle at, boo ♦ vi to whistle; (AUTO) to sound o toot one's horn; (AM) to smoke

**pitillo** [pi'tiʎo] nm cigarette

**pito** ['pito] nm whistle; (de coche) horn

**pitón** [pi'ton] nm (ZOOL) python

**pitonisa** [pito'nisa] nf fortune-teller

**pitorreo** [pito'rreo] nm joke; **estar de ~** to be joking

**pizarra** [pi'θarra] nf (piedra) slate; (encerado) blackboard

**pizca** ['piθka] nf pinch, spot; (fig) spot, speck; **ni ~** not a bit

**placa** ['plaka] nf plate; (distintivo) badge, insignia; **~ de matrícula** number plate

**placentero, a** [plaθen'tero, a] adj pleasant, agreeable

**placer** [pla'θer] nm pleasure ♦ vt to please

**plácido, a** ['plaθiðo, a] adj placid

**plaga** ['plaɣa] nf pest; (MED) plague; (abundancia) abundance;

**plagar** vt to infest, plague; (llenar) to fill

**plagio** ['plaxjo] nm plagiarism

**plan** [plan] nm (esquema, proyecto) plan; (idea, intento) idea, intention; **tener ~** (fam) to have a date; **tener un ~** (fam) to have an affair; **en ~ económico** (fam) on the cheap; **va- mos en ~ de turismo** we're going as tourists; **si te pones en ese ~ ...** if that's your attitude ...

**plana** ['plana] nf sheet (of paper), page; (TEC) trowel; **en primera ~** on the front page; **~ mayor** staff

**plancha** ['plantʃa] nf (para planchar) iron; (rótulo) plate, sheet; (NAUT) gangway; **a la ~** (CULIN) grilled; **~do** nm ironing; **planchar** vt to iron ♦ vi to do the ironing

**planeador** [planea'ðor] nm glider

**planear** [plane'ar] vt to plan ♦ vi to glide

**planeta** [pla'neta] nm planet

**planicie** [pla'niθje] nf plain

**planificación** [planifika'θjon] nf planning; ~ **familiar** family planning

**plano, a** ['plano, a] adj flat, level, even ♦ nm (MAT, TEC, AVIAT) plane; (FOTO) shot; (ARQ) plan; (GEO) map; (de ciudad) map, street plan; **primer** ~ close-up; **caer de** ~ to fall flat

**planta** ['planta] nf (BOT, TEC) plant; (ANAT) sole of the foot, foot; (piso) floor; (AM: personal) staff; ~ **baja** ground floor

**plantación** [planta'θjon] nf (AGR) plantation; (acto) planting

**plantar** [plan'tar] vt (BOT) to plant; (levantar) to erect, set up; ~**se** vr to stand firm; ~ **a uno en la calle** to throw sb out; **dejar plantado a uno** (fam) to stand sb up

**plantear** [plante'ar] vt (problema) to pose; (dificultad) to raise

**plantilla** [plan'tiΛa] nf (de zapato) insole; (personal) personnel; **ser de** ~ to be on the staff

**plantón** [plan'ton] nm (MIL) guard, sentry; (fam) long wait; **dar (un)** ~ **a uno** to stand sb up

**plasmar** [plas'mar] vt (dar forma) to mould, shape; (representar) to represent ♦ vi: ~ **en** to take the form of

**plasta** ['plasta] nf (fam) adj inv boring ♦ nm/f bore

**Plasticina** [plasti'θina] ® nf Plasticine ®

**plástico, a** ['plastiko, a] adj plastic ♦ nm plastic

**Plastilina** [plasti'lina] ® nf Plasticine ®

**plata** ['plata] nf (metal) silver; (cosas hechas de ~) silverware; (AM) cash, dough; **hablar en** ~ to speak bluntly o frankly

**plataforma** [plata'forma] nf platform; ~ **de lanzamiento/perforación** launch(ing) pad/drilling rig

**plátano** ['platano] nm (fruta) banana; (árbol) banana tree

**platea** [pla'tea] nf (TEATRO) pit

**plateado, a** [plate'aðo, a] adj silver; (TEC) silver-plated

**plática** ['platika] nf talk, chat; **platicar** vi to talk, chat

**platillo** [pla'tiΛo] nm saucer; ~**s** nmpl (MUS) cymbals; ~ **volador** o **volante** flying saucer

**platino** [pla'tino] nm platinum; ~**s** nmpl (AUTO) contact points

**plato** ['plato] nm plate, dish; (parte de comida) course; (comida) dish; ~ **combinado** set main course (served on one plate); ~ **fuerte** main course; **primer** ~ first course

**playa** ['plaja] nf beach; (costa) seaside; ~ **de estacionamiento** (AM) car park

**playera** [pla'jera] nf (AM: camiseta) T-shirt; ~**s** nfpl (zapatos) (slip-on) canvas shoes

**plaza** ['plaθa] nf square; (mercado) market(place); (sitio) room, space; (en vehículo) seat, place; (colocación) post, job; ~ **de toros** bullring

**plazo** ['plaθo] nm (lapso de tiempo) time, period; (fecha de vencimiento) expiry date; (pago parcial) instalment; **a corto/largo** ~ short-/long-term; **comprar algo a** ~**s** to buy sth on hire purchase (Brit) o on time (US)

**plazoleta** [plaθo'leta] nf small square

**pleamar** [plea'mar] nf high tide

**plebe** ['pleβe] nf: **la** ~ the common people pl, the masses pl; (pey) the plebs pl; ~**yo, a** adj plebeian; (pey) coarse, common

**plebiscito** [pleβis'θito] nm plebiscite

**plegable** [ple'γaβle] adj pliable; (silla) folding

**plegar** [ple'γar] vt (doblar) to fold, bend; (COSTURA) to pleat; ~**se** vr to yield, submit

**pleito** ['pleito] nm (JUR) lawsuit, case; (fig) dispute, feud

**plenilunio** [pleni'lunjo] nm full moon

**plenitud** [pleni'tuð] nf plenitude, fullness; (abundancia) abundance

**pleno, a** ['pleno, a] adj full; (com-

_pleto)_ complete ♦ _nm_ plenum; **en ~ día** in broad daylight; **en ~ verano** at the height of summer; **en plena cara** full in the face

**pleuresía** [pleure'sia] _nf_ pleurisy

**pliego** _etc_ ['pljeɣo] _vb ver_ **plegar** ♦ _nm (hoja)_ sheet (of paper); _(carta)_ sealed letter/document; **~ de condiciones** details _pl_, specifications _pl_

**pliegue** _etc_ ['pljeɣe] _vb ver_ **plegar** ♦ _nm_ fold, crease; _(de vestido)_ pleat

**plomero** [plo'mero] _nm (AM)_ plumber

**plomo** ['plomo] _nm (metal)_ lead; _(ELEC)_ fuse; **sin ~** unleaded

**pluma** ['pluma] _nf_ feather; _(para escribir)_: _(estilográfica)_ ink pen; **~ fuente** _(AM)_ fountain pen

**plumero** [plu'mero] _nm (quitapolvos)_ feather duster

**plumón** [plu'mon] _nm (AM: fino)_ felt-tip pen; _(: ancho)_ marker

**plural** [plu'ral] _adj_ plural; **~idad** _nf_ plurality; **una ~idad de votos** a majority of votes

**pluriempleo** [pluriem'pleo] _nm_ having more than one job

**plus** [plus] _nm_ bonus; **~valía** _nf (COM)_ appreciation

**población** [poβla'θjon] _nf_ population; _(pueblo, ciudad)_ town, city

**poblado, a** [po'βlaðo, a] _adj_ inhabited ♦ _nm (aldea)_ village; _(pueblo) (small)_ town; **densamente ~** densely populated

**poblador, a** [poβla'ðor, a] _nm/f_ settler, colonist

**poblar** [po'βlar] _vt (colonizar)_ to colonize; _(fundar)_ to found; _(habitar)_ to inhabit

**pobre** ['poβre] _adj_ poor ♦ _nm/f_ poor person; **~za** _nf_ poverty

**pocilga** [po'θilɣa] _nf_ pigsty

**pócima** ['poθima] _nf =_ **poción**

---

PALABRA CLAVE

**poco, a** ['poko, a] _adj_ **1** _(sg)_ little, not much; **~ tiempo** little o not much time; **de ~ interés** of little interest, not very interesting; **poca**

**cosa** not much

**2** _(pl)_ few, not many; **unos ~s** a few, some; **~s niños comen lo que les conviene** few children eat what they should

♦ _adv_ **1** little, not much; **cuesta ~** it doesn't cost much

**2** _(+ adj: = negativo, antónimo)_: **~ amable/inteligente** not very nice/intelligent

**3: por ~ me caigo** I almost fell

**4: a ~: a ~ de haberse casado** shortly after getting married

**5: ~ a ~** little by little

♦ _nm_ a little, a bit; **un ~ triste/de dinero** a little sad/money

---

**podar** [po'ðar] _vt_ to prune

---

PALABRA CLAVE

**poder** [po'ðer] _vi_ **1** _(capacidad)_ can, be able to; **no puedo hacerlo** I can't do it, I'm unable to do it

**2** _(permiso)_ can, may, be allowed to; **¿se puede?** may I (o we)?; **puedes irte ahora** you may go now; **no se puede fumar en este hospital** smoking is not allowed in this hospital

**3** _(posibilidad)_ may, might, could; **puede llegar mañana** he may o might arrive tomorrow; **pudiste haberte hecho daño** you might o could have hurt yourself; **¡podías habérmelo dicho antes!** you might have told me before!

**4: puede ser:** **puede ser** perhaps; **puede ser que lo sepa Tomás** Tomás may o might know

**5: ¡no puedo más!** I've had enough!; **no pude menos que dejarlo** I couldn't help but leave it; **es tonto a más no ~** he's as stupid as they come

**6: ~ con: no puedo con este crío** this kid's too much for me

♦ _nm_ power; **~ adquisitivo** purchasing power; **detentar** o **ocupar** o **estar en el ~** to be in power

**poderoso, a** [poðe'roso, a] adj (político, pais) powerful

**podio** ['poðjo] nm (DEPORTE) podium

**podium** ['poðjum] = podio

**podrido, a** [po'ðriðo, a] adj rotten, bad; (fig) rotten, corrupt

**podrir** [po'ðrir] = pudrir

**poema** [po'ema] nm poem

**poesía** [poe'sia] nf poetry

**poeta** [po'eta] nm/f poet; **poético, a** adj poetic(al)

**poetisa** [poe'tisa] nf (woman) poet

**póker** ['poker] nm poker

**polaco, a** [po'lako, a] adj Polish ♦ nm/f Pole

**polar** [po'lar] adj polar; **~idad** nf polarity; **~izarse** vr to polarize

**polea** [po'lea] nf pulley

**polémica** [po'lemika] nf polemics sg; (una ~) controversy, polemic

**polen** ['polen] nm pollen

**policía** [poli'θia] nm/f policeman/woman ♦ nf police; **~co, a** adj police cpd; **novela policíaca** detective story; **policial** adj police cpd

**polideportivo** [poliðepor'tiβo] nm sports centre o complex

**polietileno** [polieti'leno] nm polythene (BRIT), polyethylene (US)

**poligamia** [poli'xamja] nf polygamy

**polilla** [po'liʎa] nf moth

**polio** ['poljo] nf polio

**política** [po'litika] nf politics sg; (económica, agraria etc) policy; ver tb **político**

**político, a** [po'litiko, a] adj (discreto) tactful; (de familia) -in-law ♦ nm/f politician; **padre ~** father-in-law

**póliza** ['poliθa] nf certificate, voucher; (impuesto) tax stamp; **~ de seguros** insurance policy

**polizón** [poli'θon] nm (en barco etc) stowaway

**polo** ['polo] nm (GEO, ELEC) pole; (helado) ice lolly; (DEPORTE) polo; (suéter) polo-neck; **~ Norte/Sur** North/South Pole

**Polonia** [po'lonja] nf Poland

**poltrona** [pol'trona] nf easy chair

**polución** [polu'θjon] nf pollution

**polvera** [pol'βera] nf powder compact

**polvo** ['polβo] nm dust; (QUÍMICA, CULIN, MED) powder; **~s** nmpl (maquillaje) powder sg; **~ de talco** talcum powder; **estar hecho ~** (fam) to be worn out o exhausted

**pólvora** ['polβora] nf gunpowder; (fuegos artificiales) fireworks pl

**polvoriento, a** [polβo'rjento, a] adj (superficie) dusty; (sustancia) powdery

**pollera** [po'ʎera] (AM) nf skirt

**pollería** [poʎe'ria] nf poulterer's (shop)

**pollo** ['poʎo] nm chicken

**pomada** [po'maða] nf (MED) cream, ointment

**pomelo** [po'melo] nm grapefruit

**pómez** ['pomeθ] nf: **piedra ~** pumicestone

**pomo** ['pomo] nm doorknob

**pompa** ['pompa] nf (burbuja) bubble; (bomba) pump; (esplendor) pomp, splendour; **pomposo, a** adj splendid, magnificent; (pey) pompous

**pómulo** ['pomulo] nm cheekbone

**pon** [pon] vb ver **poner**

**ponche** ['pontʃe] nm punch

**poncho** ['pontʃo] (AM) nm poncho

**ponderar** [ponde'rar] vt (considerar) to weigh up, consider; (elogiar) to praise highly, speak in praise of

**pondré** etc vb ver **poner**

PALABRA CLAVE

**poner** [po'ner] vt **1** (colocar) to put; (telegrama) to send; (obra de teatro) to put on; (película) to show; **ponlo más fuerte** turn it up; **¿qué ponen en el Excelsior?** what's on at the Excelsior?

**2** (tienda) to open; (instalar: gas etc) to put in; (radio, TV) to switch o turn on

**3** (suponer): **pongamos que ...** let's suppose that ...

**4** (*contribuir*): **el gobierno ha puesto otro millón** the government has contributed another million

**5** (*TELEC*): **póngame con el Sr. López** can you put me through to Mr. López?

**6**: **~ de: le han puesto de director general** they've appointed him general manager

**7** (+ *adj*) to make; **me estás poniendo nerviosa** you're making me nervous

**8** (*dar nombre*): **al hijo le pusieron Diego** they called their son Diego

♦ *vi* (*gallina*) to lay

♦ **~se** *vr* **1** (*colocarse*): **se puso a mi lado** he came and stood beside me; **tú pónte en esa silla** you go and sit on that chair

**2** (*vestido, cosméticos*) to put on; **¿por qué no te pones el vestido nuevo?** why don't you put on *o* wear your new dress?

**3** (+ *adj*) to turn; to get; become; **se puso muy serio** he got very serious; **después de lavarla la tela se puso azul** after washing it the material turned blue

**4**: **~se a: se puso a llorar** he started to cry; **tienes que ~te a estudiar** you must get down to studying

**5**: **~se a bien con uno** to make it up with sb; **~se a mal con uno** to get on the wrong side of sb

**pongo** *etc vb ver* **poner**

**poniente** [po'njente] *nm* (*occidente*) west; (*viento*) west wind

**pontífice** [pon'tifiθe] *nm* pope, pontiff

**popa** ['popa] *nf* stern

**popular** [popu'lar] *adj* popular; (*cultura*) of the people, folk *cpd*; **~idad** *nf* popularity; **~izarse** *vr* to become popular

**por** [por] *prep* **1** (*objetivo*) for; **luchar ~ la patria** to fight for one's country

**2** (+ *infin*): **~ no llegar tarde** so as not to arrive late; **~ citar unos ejemplos** to give a few examples

**3** (*causa*) out of, because of; **~ escasez de fondos** through *o* for lack of funds

**4** (*tiempo*): **~ la mañana/noche** in the morning/at night; **se queda ~ una semana** she's staying (for) a week

**5** (*lugar*): **pasar ~ Madrid** to pass through Madrid; **ir a Guayaquil ~ Quito** to go to Guayaquil via Quito; **caminar ~ la calle** to walk down the street; *ver tb* **todo**

**6** (*cambio, precio*): **te doy uno nuevo ~ el que tienes** I'll give you a new one (in return) for the one you've got

**7** (*valor distributivo*): **550 pesetas ~ hora/cabeza** 550 pesetas an *o* per hour/a *o* per head

**8** (*modo, medio*) by; **~ correo/avión** by post/air; **día ~ día** day by day; **entrar ~ la entrada principal** to go in through the main entrance

**9**: **10 ~ 10 son 100** 10 by 10 is 100

**10** (*en lugar de*): **vino él ~ su jefe** he came instead of his boss

**11**: **~ mí que revienten** as far as I'm concerned they can drop dead

**porcelana** [porθe'lana] *nf* porcelain; (*china*) china

**porcentaje** [porθen'taxe] *nm* percentage

**porción** [por'θjon] *nf* (*parte*) portion, share; (*cantidad*) quantity, amount

**pordiosero, a** [porðjo'sero, a] *nm/f* beggar

**porfiar** [por'fjar] *vi* to persist, insist; (*disputar*) to argue stubbornly

**pormenor** [porme'nor] *nm* detail, particular

**pornografía** [pornoɣra'fia] *nf* pornography

**poro** ['poro] *nm* pore; **~so, a** *adj* porous

**porque** ['porke] *conj* (*a causa de*)

**because;** (*ya que*) since; (*con el fin de*) so that, in order that

**porqué** [por'ke] *nm* reason, cause

**porquería** [porke'ria] *nf* (*suciedad*) filth, dirt; (*acción*) dirty trick; (*objeto*) small thing, trifle; (*fig*) rubbish

**porra** ['porra] *nf* (*arma*) stick, club

**porrazo** [po'rraθo] *nm* blow, bump

**porro** ['porro] *nm* (*droga*) joint (*fam*)

**porrón** [po'rron] *nm* glass wine jar with a long spout

**portaaviones** [porta(a)βjones] *nm inv* aircraft carrier

**portada** [por'taða] *nf* (*de revista*) cover

**portador, a** [porta'ðor, a] *nm/f* carrier, bearer; (*COM*) bearer, payee

**portaequipajes** [portaeki'paxes] *nm inv* (*AUTO: maletero*) boot; (: *baca*) luggage rack

**portal** [por'tal] *nm* (*entrada*) vestibule, hall; (*portada*) porch, doorway; (*puerta de entrada*) main door; (*DEPORTE*) goal

**portamaletas** [portama'letas] *nm inv* (*AUTO: maletero*) boot; (: *baca*) roof rack

**portarse** [por'tarse] *vr* to behave, conduct o.s.

**portátil** [por'tatil] *adj* portable

**portavoz** [porta'βoθ] *nm/f* (*persona*) spokesman/woman

**portazo** [por'taθo] *nm*: **dar un ~** to slam the door

**porte** ['porte] *nm* (*COM*) transport; (*precio*) transport charges *pl*

**portento** [por'tento] *nm* marvel, wonder; **~so, a** *adj* marvellous, extraordinary

**porteño, a** [por'teɲo, a] *adj* of o from Buenos Aires

**portería** [porte'ria] *nf* (*oficina*) porter's office; (*gol*) goal

**portero, a** [por'tero, a] *nm/f* porter; (*conserje*) caretaker; (*ujier*) doorman; (*DEPORTE*) goalkeeper; ~ **automático** intercom

**pórtico** ['portiko] *nm* (*patio*) portico, porch; (*fig*) gateway; (*arcada*) arcade

**portorriqueño, a** [portorri'keɲo, a] *adj* Puerto Rican

**Portugal** [portu'val] *nm* Portugal; **portugués, esa** *adj, nm/f* Portuguese ♦ *nm* (*LING*) Portuguese

**porvenir** [porβe'nir] *nm* future

**pos** [pos] *prep*: **en ~ de** after, in pursuit of

**posada** [po'saða] *nf* (*refugio*) shelter, lodging; (*mesón*) guest house; **dar ~ a** to give shelter to, take in

**posaderas** [posa'ðeras] *nfpl* backside *sg*, buttocks

**posar** [po'sar] *vt* (*en el suelo*) to lay down, put down; (*la mano*) to place, put gently ♦ *vi* to sit, pose; **~se** *vr* to settle; (*pájaro*) to perch; (*avión*) to land, come down

**posdata** [pos'ðata] *nf* postscript

**pose** [po'se] *nf* pose

**poseedor, a** [posee'ðor, a] *nm/f* owner, possessor; (*de récord, puesto*) holder

**poseer** [pose'er] *vt* to possess, own; (*ventaja*) to enjoy; (*récord, puesto*) to hold

**posesión** [pose'sjon] *nf* possession; **posesionarse** *vr*: **posesionarse de** to take possession of, take over

**posesivo, a** [pose'siβo, a] *adj* possessive

**posibilidad** [posiβili'ðað] *nf* possibility; (*oportunidad*) chance; **posibilitar** *vt* to make possible; (*hacer realizable*) to make feasible

**posible** [po'siβle] *adj* possible; (*realizable*) feasible; **de ser ~** if possible; **en lo ~** as far as possible

**posición** [posi'θjon] *nf* position; (*rango social*) status

**positivo, a** [posi'tiβo, a] *adj* positive

**poso** ['poso] *nm* sediment; (*heces*) dregs *pl*

**posponer** [pospo'ner] *vt* to put behind/below; (*aplazar*) to postpone

**posta** ['posta] *nf*: **a ~** deliberately, on purpose

**postal** [pos'tal] *adj* postal ♦ *nf* postcard

**poste** ['poste] *nm* (*de telégrafos etc*) post, pole; (*columna*) pillar

**póster** ['poster] (*pl* **pósteres, pósters**) *nm* poster

**postergar** [poster'xar] *vt* to postpone, delay

**posteridad** [posteri'ðað] *nf* posterity

**posterior** [poste'rjor] *adj* back, rear; (*siguiente*) following, subsequent; (*más tarde*) later; ~**idad** *nf*: **con** ~**idad** later, subsequently

**postizo, a** [pos'tiθo, a] *adj* false, artificial ♦ *nm* hairpiece

**postor, a** [pos'tor, a] *nm/f* bidder

**postre** ['postre] *nm* sweet, dessert

**postrero, a** [pos'trero, a] (*delante de nmsg*: **postrer**) *adj* (*último*) last; (*que viene detrás*) rear

**postulado** [postu'laðo] *nm* postulate

**póstumo, a** ['postumo, a] *adj* posthumous

**postura** [pos'tura] *nf* (*del cuerpo*) posture, position; (*fig*) attitude, position

**potable** [po'taβle] *adj* drinkable; **agua** ~ drinking water

**potaje** [po'taxe] *nm* thick vegetable soup

**pote** ['pote] *nm* pot, jar

**potencia** [po'tenθja] *nf* power

**potencial** [poten'θjal] *adj, nm* potential

**potenciar** [poten'θjar] *vt* to boost

**potente** [po'tente] *adj* powerful

**potro, a** ['potro, a] *nm/f* (*ZOOL*) colt/filly ♦ *nm* (*de gimnasia*) vaulting horse

**pozo** ['poθo] *nm* well; (*de río*) deep pool; (*de mina*) shaft

**P.P.** *abr* (= *porte pagado*) CP

**práctica** ['praktika] *nf* practice; (*método*) method; (*arte, capacidad*) skill; **en la** ~ in practice

**practicable** [prakti'kaβle] *adj* practicable; (*camino*) passable

**practicante** [prakti'kante] *nm/f* (*MED*: *ayudante de doctor*) medical assistant; (*enfermero*) nurse; (*quien practica algo*) practitioner ♦ *adj* practising

**practicar** [prakti'kar] *vt* to practise; (*DEPORTE*) to go in for (*BRIT*) o out for (*US*), play; (*realizar*) to carry out, perform

**práctico, a** ['praktiko, a] *adj* practical; (*instruido*: *persona*) skilled, expert

**practique** *etc vb ver* **practicar**

**pradera** [pra'ðera] *nf* meadow; (*US etc*) prairie

**prado** ['praðo] *nm* (*campo*) meadow, field; (*pastizal*) pasture

**Praga** ['praxa] *n* Prague

**pragmático, a** [praɣ'matiko, a] *adj* pragmatic

**preámbulo** [pre'ambulo] *nm* preamble, introduction

**precario, a** [pre'karjo, a] *adj* precarious

**precaución** [prekau'θjon] *nf* (*medida preventiva*) preventive measure, precaution; (*prudencia*) caution, wariness

**precaver** [preka'βer] *vt* to guard against; (*impedir*) to forestall; ~*vr*: ~**se de** o **contra algo** to (be on one's) guard against sth; **precavido, a** *adj* cautious, wary

**precedente** [preθe'ðente] *adj* preceding; (*anterior*) former ♦ *nm* precedent

**preceder** [preθe'ðer] *vt, vi* to precede, go before, come before

**precepto** [pre'θepto] *nm* precept

**preciado, a** [pre'θjaðo, a] *adj* (*estimado*) esteemed, valuable

**preciarse** [pre'θjarse] *vr* to pride o.s. on, boast of; ~**se de** to pride o.s. on, boast of being

**precinto** [pre'θinto] *nm* (*tb*: ~ **de garantía**) seal

**precio** ['preθjo] *nm* price; (*costo*) cost; (*valor*) value, worth; (*de viaje*) fare; ~ **al contado** o **de coste** o **de oportunidad** cash/cost/bargain price; ~ **al detalle** o **al por menor** retail price; ~ **tope** top price

**preciosidad** [preθjosi'ðað] *nf* (*valor*) (high) value, (great) worth; (*encanto*) charm; (*cosa bonita*) beautiful thing; **es una** ~ it's lovely, it's really beautiful

**precioso, a** [pre'θjoso, a] *adj* precious; *(de mucho valor)* valuable; *(fam)* lovely, beautiful

**precipicio** [preθi'piθjo] *nm* cliff, precipice; *(fig)* abyss

**precipitación** [preθipita'θjon] *nf* haste; *(lluvia)* rainfall

**precipitado, a** [preθipi'taðo, a] *adj (conducta)* hasty, rash; *(salida)* hasty, sudden

**precipitar** [preθipi'tar] *vt (arrojar)* to hurl down, throw; *(apresurar)* to hasten; *(acelerar)* to speed up, accelerate; ~**se** *vr* to throw o.s.; *(apresurarse)* to rush; *(actuar sin pensar)* to act rashly

**precisamente** [preθisa'mente] *adv* precisely; *(exactamente)* precisely, exactly

**precisar** [preθi'sar] *vt (necesitar)* to need, require; *(fijar)* to determine exactly, fix; *(especificar)* to specify

**precisión** [preθi'sjon] *nf (exactitud)* precision

**preciso, a** [pre'θiso, a] *adj (exacto)* precise; *(necesario)* necessary, essential

**preconcebido, a** [prekonθe'βiðo, a] *adj* preconceived

**precoz** [pre'koθ] *adj (persona)* precocious; *(calvicie etc)* premature

**precursor, a** [prekur'sor, a] *nm/f* predecessor, forerunner

**predecir** [preðe'θir] *vt* to predict, forecast

**predestinado, a** [preðesti'naðo, a] *adj* predestined

**predicar** [preði'kar] *vt, vi* to preach

**predicción** [preðik'θjon] *nf* prediction

**predilecto, a** [preði'lekto, a] *adj* favourite

**predisponer** [preðispo'ner] *vt* to predispose; *(pey)* to prejudice; **predisposición** [preðisposi'θjon] *nf* inclination; prejudice, bias

**predominante** [preðomi'nante] *adj* predominant

**predominar** [preðomi'nar] *vt* to dominate ♦ *vi* to predominate; *(prevalecer)* to prevail; **predominio** *nm* predominance; prevalence

**preescolar** [pre(e)sko'lar] *adj* preschool

**prefabricado, a** [prefaβri'kaðo, a] *adj* prefabricated

**prefacio** [pre'faθjo] *nm* preface

**preferencia** [prefe'renθja] *nf* preference; **de** ~ preferably, for preference

**preferible** [prefe'riβle] *adj* preferable

**preferir** [prefe'rir] *vt* to prefer

**prefiero** *etc vb ver* **preferir**

**pregonar** [prevo'nar] *vt* to proclaim, announce

**pregunta** [pre'vunta] *nf* question; **hacer una** ~ to ask o put (forth (US)) a question

**preguntar** [prevun'tar] *vt* to ask; *(cuestionar)* to question ♦ *vi* to ask; ~**se** *vr* to wonder; ~ **por alguien** to ask for sb

**preguntón, ona** [prevun'ton, ona] *adj* inquisitive

**prehistórico, a** [preis'toriko, a] *adj* prehistoric

**prejuicio** [pre'xwiθjo] *nm (acto)* prejudgement; *(idea preconcebida)* preconception; *(parcialidad)* prejudice, bias

**preliminar** [prelimi'nar] *adj* preliminary

**preludio** [pre'luðjo] *nm* prelude

**prematuro, a** [prema'turo, a] *adj* premature

**premeditación** [premeðita'θjon] *nf* premeditation

**premeditar** [premeði'tar] *vt* to premeditate

**premiar** [pre'mjar] *vt* to reward; *(en un concurso)* to give a prize to

**premio** [pre'mjo] *nm* reward; prize; *(COM)* premium

**premonición** [premoni'θjon] *nf* premonition

**prenatal** [prena'tal] *adj* antenatal, prenatal

**prenda** ['prenda] *nf (ropa)* garment;

article of clothing; (*garantía*) pledge; ~**s** *nfpl* (*talentos*) talents, gifts

**prendedor** [prende'ðor] *nm* brooch

**prender** [pren'der] *vt* (*captar*) to catch, capture; (*detener*) to arrest; (*COSTURA*) to pin, attach; (*sujetar*) to fasten ♦ *vi* to catch; (*arraigar*) to take root; ~**se** *vr* (*encenderse*) to catch fire

**prendido, a** [pren'diðo, a] (*AM*) *adj* (*luz etc*) on

**prensa** ['prensa] *nf* press; **la P~** the press; **prensar** *vt* to press

**preñado, a** [pre'naðo, a] *adj* (*ZOOL*) pregnant; ~ **de** pregnant with, full of

**preocupación** [preokupa'θjon] *nf* worry, concern; (*ansiedad*) anxiety

**preocupado, a** [preoku'paðo, a] *adj* worried, concerned; (*ansioso*) anxious

**preocupar** [preoku'par] *vt* to worry; ~**se** *vr* to worry; ~**se de algo** (*hacerse cargo*) to take care of sth

**preparación** [prepara'θjon] *nf* (*acto*) preparation; (*estado*) readiness; (*entrenamiento*) training

**preparado, a** [prepa'raðo, a] *adj* (*dispuesto*) prepared; (*CULIN*) ready (to serve) ♦ *nm* preparation

**preparar** [prepa'rar] *vt* (*disponer*) to prepare, get ready; (*TEC*: *tratar*) to prepare, process; (*entrenar*) to teach, train; ~**se** *vr*: ~**se a** o **para** to prepare to o for, get ready to o for; **preparativo, a** *adj* preparatory, preliminary; **preparativos** *nmpl* preparations; **preparatoria** (*AM*) *nf* sixth-form college (*BRIT*), senior high school (*US*)

**prerrogativa** [prerroɣa'tiβa] *nf* prerogative, privilege

**presa** ['presa] *nf* (*cosa apresada*) catch; (*víctima*) victim; (*de animal*) prey; (*de agua*) dam

**presagiar** [presa'xjar] *vt* to presage, forebode; **presagio** *nm* omen

**prescindir** [presθin'dir] *vi*: ~ **de** (*privarse de*) to do without, go without; (*descartar*) to dispense with

**prescribir** [preskri'βir] *vt* to prescribe; **prescripción** *nf* prescription

**presencia** [pre'senθja] *nf* presence; **presencial** *adj*: **testigo presencial** eyewitness; **presenciar** *vt* to be present at; (*asistir a*) to attend; (*ver*) to see, witness

**presentación** [presenta'θjon] *nf* presentation; (*introducción*) introduction

**presentador, a** [presenta'ðor, a] *nm/f* presenter, compère

**presentar** [presen'tar] *vt* to present; (*ofrecer*) to offer; (*mostrar*) to show, display; (*a una persona*) to introduce; ~**se** *vr* (*llegar inesperadamente*) to appear, turn up; (*ofrecerse como candidato*) to run, stand; (*aparecer*) to show, appear; (*solicitar empleo*) to apply

**presente** [pre'sente] *adj* present ♦ *nm* present; **hacer** ~ to state, declare; **tener** ~ to remember, bear in mind

**presentimiento** [presenti'mjento] *nm* premonition, presentiment

**presentir** [presen'tir] *vt* to have a premonition of

**preservación** [preserβa'θjon] *nf* protection, preservation

**preservar** [preser'βar] *vt* to protect, preserve; **preservativo** *nm* sheath, condom

**presidencia** [presi'ðenθja] *nf* presidency; (*de comité*) chairmanship

**presidente** [presi'ðente] *nm/f* president; (*de comité*) chairman/woman

**presidiario** [presi'ðjarjo] *nm* convict

**presidio** [pre'sidjo] *nm* prison, penitentiary

**presidir** [presi'ðir] *vt* (*dirigir*) to preside at, preside over; (: *comité*) to take the chair at; (*dominar*) to dominate, rule ♦ *vi* to preside; to take the chair

**presión** [pre'sjon] *nf* pressure; **presionar** *vt* to press; (*fig*) to press, put pressure on ♦ *vi*: **presionar para** to press for

**preso, a** ['preso, a] *nm/f* prisoner;

**tomar** o **llevar ~ a uno** to arrest sb, take sb prisoner

**prestaciones** [presta'θjones] *nfpl* (*TEC, AUT*) features

**prestado, a** [pres'taðo, a] *adj* on loan; **pedir ~** to borrow

**prestamista** [presta'mista] *nm/f* moneylender

**préstamo** ['prestamo] *nm* loan; **~ hipotecario** mortgage

**prestar** [pres'tar] *vt* to lend, loan; (*atención*) to pay; (*ayuda*) to give

**presteza** [pres'teθa] *nf* speed, promptness

**prestigio** [pres'tixjo] *nm* prestige; **~so, a** *adj* (*honorable*) prestigious; (*famoso, renombrado*) renowned, famous

**presumido, a** [presu'miðo, a] *adj* (*persona*) vain

**presumir** [presu'mir] *vt* to presume ♦ *vi* (*tener aires*) to be conceited; **según cabe ~** as may be presumed, presumably; **presunción** *nf* presumption; (*sospecha*) suspicion; **presunto, a** *adj* (*supuesto*) supposed, presumed; (*así llamado*) so-called; **presuntuoso, a** *adj* conceited, presumptuous

**presuponer** [presupo'ner] *vt* to presuppose

**presupuesto** [presu'pwesto] *pp de* **presuponer** ♦ *nm* (*FINANZAS*) budget; (*estimación: de costo*) estimate

**pretencioso, a** [preten'θjoso, a] *adj* pretentious

**pretender** [preten'der] *vt* (*intentar*) to try to, seek to; (*reivindicar*) to claim; (*buscar*) to seek, try for; (*cortejar*) to woo, court; **~ que** to expect that; **pretendiente** *nm/f* (*candidato*) candidate, applicant; (*amante*) suitor; **pretensión** *nf* (*aspiración*) aspiration; (*reivindicación*) claim; (*orgullo*) pretension

**pretexto** [pre'teksto] *nm* pretext; (*excusa*) excuse

**prevalecer** [preβale'θer] *vi* to prevail

**prevención** [preβen'θjon] *nf* (*preparación*) preparation; (*estado*) preparedness, readiness; (*el evitar*) prevention; (*previsión*) foresight, forethought; (*precaución*) precaution

**prevenido, a** [preβe'niðo, a] *adj* prepared, ready; (*cauteloso*) cautious

**prevenir** [preβe'nir] *vt* (*impedir*) to prevent; (*prever*) to foresee, anticipate; (*predisponer*) to prejudice, bias; (*avisar*) to warn; (*preparar*) to prepare, get ready; **~se** *vr* to get ready, prepare; **~se contra** to take precautions against; **preventivo, a** *adj* preventive, precautionary

**prever** [pre'βer] *vt* to foresee

**previo, a** ['preβjo, a] *adj* (*anterior*) previous; (*preliminar*) preliminary ♦ *prep*: **~ acuerdo de los otros** subject to the agreement of the others

**previsión** [preβi'sjon] *nf* (*perspicacia*) foresight; (*predicción*) forecast; **previsto, a** *adj* anticipated, forecast

**prima** ['prima] *nf* (*COM*) bonus; **~ de seguro** insurance premium; *ver tb* **primo**

**primacía** [prima'θia] *nf* primacy

**primario, a** [pri'marjo, a] *adj* primary

**primavera** [prima'βera] *nf* spring(-time)

**primera** [pri'mera] *nf* (*AUTO*) first gear; (*FERRO*: *tb*: **~ clase**) first class; **de ~** (*fam*) first-class, first-rate

**primero, a** [pri'mero, a] (*delante de nmsg*: **primer**) *adj* first; (*principal*) prime ♦ *adv* first; (*más bien*) sooner, rather; **primera plana** front page

**primicia** [pri'miθja] *nf* (*PRENSA*) (*tb*: **~ informativa**) scoop

**primitivo, a** [primi'tiβo, a] *adj* primitive; (*original*) original

**primo, a** ['primo, a] *adj* prime ♦ *nm/f* cousin; (*fam*) fool, idiot; **~ hermano** first cousin; **materias primas** raw materials

**primogénito, a** [primo'xenito, a] *adj* first-born

**primordial** [primor'ðjal] *adj* basic, fundamental

**primoroso, a** [primo'roso, a] *adj*

exquisite, delicate
**princesa** [prin'θesa] *nf* princess
**principal** [prinθi'pal] *adj* principal, main ♦ *nm* (*jefe*) chief, principal
**príncipe** ['prinθipe] *nm* prince
**principiante** [prinθi'pjante] *nm/f* beginner
**principio** [prin'θipjo] *nm* (*comienzo*) beginning, start; (*origen*) origin; (*primera etapa*) rudiment, basic idea; (*moral*) principle; a ~s de at the beginning of
**pringoso, a** [prin'ɣoso, a] *adj* (*grasiento*) greasy; (*pegajoso*) sticky
**pringue** ['pringe] *nm* (*grasa*) grease, fat, dripping
**prioridad** [prjori'ðað] *nf* priority
**prisa** ['prisa] *nf* (*apresuramiento*) hurry, haste; (*rapidez*) speed; (*urgencia*) (sense of) urgency; a o de ~ quickly; (*correr*) ~ to be urgent; darse ~ to hurry up; estar de o tener ~ to be in a hurry
**prisión** [pri'sjon] *nf* (*cárcel*) prison; (*período de cárcel*) imprisonment; **prisionero, a** [prisjo'nero, a] *nm/f* prisoner
**prismáticos** [pris'matikos] *nmpl* binoculars
**privación** [priβa'θjon] *nf* deprivation; (*falta*) want, privation
**privado, a** [pri'βaðo, a] *adj* private
**privar** [pri'βar] *vt* to deprive; **privativo, a** *adj* exclusive
**privilegiado, a** [priβile'xjaðo, a] *adj* privileged; (*memoria*) very good
**privilegiar** [priβile'xjar] *vt* to grant a privilege to; (*favorecer*) to favour
**privilegio** [priβi'lexjo] *nm* privilege; (*concesión*) concession
**pro** [pro] *nm* o *f* profit, advantage ♦ *prep*: **asociación ~ ciegos** association for the blind ♦ *prefijo*: ~ **soviético/americano** pro-Soviet/ American; **en ~ de** on behalf of, for; **los ~s y los contras** the pros and cons
**proa** ['proa] *nf* bow, prow; **de ~** bow *cpd*, fore
**probabilidad** [proβaβili'ðað] *nf* probability, likelihood; (*oportunidad,*

*posibilidad*) chance, prospect; **probable** *adj* probable, likely
**probador** [proβa'ðor] *nm* (*en tienda*) fitting room
**probar** [pro'βar] *vt* (*demostrar*) to prove; (*someter a prueba*) to test, try out; (*ropa*) to try on; (*comida*) to taste ♦ *vi* to try; ~**se un traje** to try on a suit
**probeta** [pro'βeta] *nf* test tube
**problema** [pro'βlema] *nm* problem
**procedente** [proθe'ðente] *adj* (*razonable*) reasonable; (*conforme a derecho*) proper, fitting; ~ **de** coming from, originating in
**proceder** [proθe'ðer] *vi* (*avanzar*) to proceed; (*actuar*) to act; (*ser correcto*) to be right (and proper), be fitting ♦ *nm* (*comportamiento*) behaviour, conduct; ~ **de** to come from, originate in; **procedimiento** *nm* procedure; (*proceso*) process; (*método*) means *pl*, method
**procesado, a** [proθe'saðo, a] *nm/f* accused
**procesador** [proθesa'ðor] *nm*: ~ **de textos** word processor
**procesar** [proθe'sar] *vt* to try, put on trial
**procesión** [proθe'sjon] *nf* procession
**proceso** [pro'θeso] *nm* process; (*JUR*) trial; (*lapso*) course (of time)
**proclamar** [prokla'mar] *vt* to proclaim
**procreación** [prokrea'θjon] *nf* procreation
**procrear** [prokre'ar] *vt, vi* to procreate
**procurador, a** [prokura'ðor, a] *nm/f* attorney
**procurar** [proku'rar] *vt* (*intentar*) to try, endeavour; (*conseguir*) to get, obtain; (*asegurar*) to secure; (*producir*) to produce
**prodigio** [pro'ðixjo] *nm* prodigy; (*milagro*) wonder, marvel; ~**so, a** *adj* prodigious, marvellous
**pródigo, a** ['proðiɣo, a] *adj*: **hijo ~** prodigal son
**producción** [proðuk'θjon] *nf* (*gen*)

production; (*producto*) product; ~ **en serie** mass production

**producir** [produ'θir] *vt* to produce; (*causar*) to cause, bring about; ~**se** *vr* (*cambio*) to come about; (*accidente*) to take place; (*problema etc*) to arise; (*hacerse*) to be produced, be made; (*estallar*) to break out

**productividad** [produktiβi'ðað] *nf* productivity; **productivo, a** *adj* productive; (*provechoso*) profitable

**producto** [pro'ðukto] *nm* product; (*producción*) production

**productor, a** [pro'ðuk'tor, a] *adj* productive, producing ♦ *nm/f* producer

**proeza** [pro'eθa] *nf* exploit, feat

**profanar** [profa'nar] *vt* to desecrate, profane; **profano, a** *adj* profane ♦ *nm/f* layman/woman

**profecía** [profe'θia] *nf* prophecy

**proferir** [profe'rir] *vt* (*palabra, sonido*) to utter; (*injuria*) to hurl, let fly

**profesar** [profe'sar] *vt* (*practicar*) to practise

**profesión** [profe'sjon] *nf* profession; **profesional** *adj* professional

**profesor, a** [profe'sor, a] *nm/f* teacher; ~**ado** *nm* teaching profession

**profeta** [pro'feta] *nm/f* prophet; **profetizar** *vt, vi* to prophesy

**prófugo, a** [pro'fuɣo, a] *nm/f* fugitive; (*MIL: desertor*) deserter

**profundidad** [profundi'ðað] *nf* depth; **profundizar** *vt* (*fig*) to profundizar en to go deeply into; **profundo, a** *adj* deep; (*misterio, pensador*) profound

**profusión** [profu'sjon] *nf* (*abundancia*) profusion; (*prodigalidad*) extravagance

**progenitor** [proxeni'tor] *nm* ancestor; ~**es** *nmpl* (*padres*) parents

**programa** [pro'ɣrama] *nm* programme (*BRIT*), program (*US*); ~**ción** *nf* programming; ~**dor, a** *nm/f* programmer; **programar** *vt* to program

**progresar** [proɣre'sar] *vi* to pro-

gress, make progress; **progresista** *adj, nm/f* progressive; **progresivo, a** *adj* progressive; (*gradual*) gradual; (*continuo*) continuous; **progreso** *nm* progress

**prohibición** [proiβi'θjon] *nf* prohibition, ban

**prohibir** [proi'βir] *vt* to prohibit, ban, forbid; **se prohíbe fumar, prohibido fumar** no smoking

**prójimo, a** ['proximo, a] *nm/f* fellow man; (*vecino*) neighbour

**proletariado** [proleta'rjaðo] *nm* proletariat

**proletario, a** [prole'tarjo, a] *adj, nm/f* proletarian

**proliferación** [prolifera'θjon] *nf* proliferation

**proliferar** [prolife'rar] *vi* to proliferate; **prolífico, a** *adj* prolific

**prólogo** [pro'loɣo] *nm* prologue

**prolongación** [prolonɡa'θjon] *nf* extension; **prolongado, a** *adj* (*largo*) long; (*alargado*) lengthy

**prolongar** [prolon'ɡar] *vt* to extend; (*reunión etc*) to prolong; (*calle, tubo*) to extend

**promedio** [pro'meðjo] *nm* average; (*de distancia*) middle, mid-point

**promesa** [pro'mesa] *nf* promise

**prometer** [prome'ter] *vt* to promise ♦ *vi* to show promise; ~**se** *vr* (*novios*) to get engaged; **prometido, a** *adj* promised; engaged ♦ *nm/f* fiancé/fiancée

**prominente** [promi'nente] *adj* prominent

**promiscuo, a** [pro'miskwo, a] *adj* promiscuous

**promoción** [promo'θjon] *nf* promotion

**promotor** [promo'tor] *nm* promoter; (*instigador*) instigator

**promover** [promo'βer] *vt* to promote; (*causar*) to cause; (*instigar*) to instigate, stir up

**promulgar** [promul'ɣar] *vt* to promulgate; (*fig*) to proclaim

**pronombre** [pro'nombre] *nm* pronoun

**pronosticar** [pronosti'kar] vt to predict, foretell, forecast; **pronóstico** nm prediction, forecast; **pronóstico del tiempo** weather forecast

**pronto, a** ['pronto, a] adj (rápido) prompt, quick; (preparado) ready ♦ adv quickly, promptly; (en seguida) at once, right away; (dentro de poco) soon; (temprano) early ♦ nm: **tener ~s de enojo** to be quick-tempered; **al ~** at first; **de ~** suddenly; **por lo ~** meanwhile, for the present

**pronunciación** [pronunθja'θjon] nf pronunciation

**pronunciar** [pronun'θjar] vt to pronounce; (discurso) to make, deliver; **~se** vr to revolt, rebel; (declararse) to declare o.s.

**propagación** [propaɣa'θjon] nf propagation

**propaganda** [propa'ɣanda] nf (política) propaganda; (comercial) advertising

**propagar** [propa'ɣar] vt to propagate

**propensión** [propen'sjon] nf inclination, propensity; **propenso, a** adj inclined to: **ser propenso a** to be inclined to, have a tendency to

**propicio, a** [pro'piθjo, a] adj favourable, propitious

**propiedad** [propje'ðað] nf property; (posesión) possession, ownership; **~ particular** private property

**propietario, a** [propje'tarjo, a] nm/f owner, proprietor

**propina** [pro'pina] nf tip

**propio, a** ['propjo, a] adj own, of one's own; (característico) characteristic, typical; (debido) proper; (mismo) selfsame, very; **el ~ ministro** the minister himself; **¿tienes casa propia?** have you a house of your own?

**proponer** [propo'ner] vt to propose, put forward; (problema) to pose; **~se** vr to propose, intend

**proporción** [propor'θjon] nf proportion; (MAT) ratio; **proporciones** nfpl (dimensiones) dimensions; (fig) size sg; **proporcionado, a** adj

proportionate; (regular) medium, middling; (justo) just right; **proporcionar** vt (dar) to give, supply, provide

**proposición** [proposi'θjon] nf proposition; (propuesta) proposal

**propósito** [pro'posito] nm purpose; (intento) aim, intention ♦ adv: **a ~** by the way, incidentally; (a posta) on purpose, deliberately; **a ~ de** about, with regard to

**propuesta** [pro'pwesta] vb ver **proponer** ♦ nf proposal

**propulsar** [propul'sar] vt to drive, propel; (fig) to promote, encourage; **propulsión** nf propulsion; **propulsión a chorro** o **por reacción** jet propulsion

**prórroga** ['prorroɣa] nf extension; (JUR) stay; (COM) deferment; (DEPORTE) extra time; **prorrogar** vt (período) to extend; (decisión) to defer, postpone

**prorrumpir** [prorrum'pir] vi to burst forth, break out

**prosa** ['prosa] nf prose

**proscrito, a** [pro'skrito, a] adj (prohibido, desterrado) banned

**proseguir** [prose'xir] vt to continue, carry on ♦ vi to continue, go on

**prospección** [prospek'θjon] nf exploration; (del oro) prospecting

**prospecto** [pros'pekto] nm prospectus

**prosperar** [prospe'rar] vi to prosper, thrive, flourish; **prosperidad** nf prosperity; (éxito) success; **próspero, a** adj prosperous, flourishing; (que tiene éxito) successful

**prostíbulo** [pros'tißulo] nm brothel (BRIT), house of prostitution (US)

**prostitución** [prostitu'θjon] nf prostitution

**prostituir** [prosti'twir] vt to prostitute; **~se** vr to prostitute o.s., become a prostitute

**prostituta** [prosti'tuta] nf prostitute

**protagonista** [protaɣo'nista] nm/f protagonist

**protagonizar** [protaɣoni'θar] vt to

take the chief rôle in

**protección** [protek'θjon] *nf* protection

**protector, a** [protek'tor, a] *adj* protective, protecting ♦ *nm/f* protector

**proteger** [prote'xer] *vt* to protect; **protegido, a** *nm/f* protégé/protégée

**proteína** [prote'ina] *nf* protein

**protesta** [pro'testa] *nf* protest; (*declaración*) protestation

**protestante** [protes'tante] *adj* Protestant

**protestar** [protes'tar] *vt* to protest, declare; (*fe*) to protest ♦ *vi* to protest

**protocolo** [proto'kolo] *nm* protocol

**prototipo** [proto'tipo] *nm* prototype

**prov.** *abr* (= *provincia*) prov

**provecho** [pro'βetʃo] *nm* advantage, benefit; (*FINANZAS*) profit; ¡**buen ~!** bon appétit!; **en ~ de** to the benefit of; **sacar ~ de** to benefit from, profit by

**proveer** [proβe'er] *vt* to provide, supply ♦ *vi*: **~ a** to provide for

**provenir** [proβe'nir] *vi*: **~ de** to come from, stem from

**proverbio** [pro'βerβjo] *nm* proverb

**providencia** [proβi'ðenθja] *nf* providence; (*previsión*) foresight

**provincia** [pro'βinθja] *nf* province; **~no, a** *adj* provincial; (*del campo*) country *cpd*

**provisión** [proβi'sjon] *nf* provision; (*abastecimiento*) provision, supply; (*medida*) measure, step

**provisional** [proβisjo'nal] *adj* provisional

**provocación** [proβoka'θjon] *nf* provocation

**provocar** [proβo'kar] *vt* to provoke; (*alentar*) to tempt, invite; (*causar*) to bring about, lead to; (*promover*) to promote; (*estimular*) to rouse, stimulate; ¿**te provoca un café?** (*AM*) would you like a coffee?; **provocativo, a** *adj* provocative

**próximamente** [proksima'mente] *adv* shortly, soon

**proximidad** [proksimi'ðað] *nf* close-

ness, proximity; **próximo, a** *adj* near, close; (*vecino*) neighbouring; (*siguiente*) next

**proyectar** [projek'tar] *vt* (*objeto*) to hurl, throw; (*luz*) to cast, shed; (*CINE*) to screen, show; (*planear*) to plan

**proyectil** [projek'til] *nm* projectile, missile

**proyecto** [pro'jekto] *nm* plan; (*estimación de costo*) detailed estimate

**proyector** [projek'tor] *nm* (*CINE*) projector

**prudencia** [pru'ðenθja] *nf* (*sabiduría*) wisdom; (*cuidado*) care; **prudente** *adj* sensible, wise; (*conductor*) careful

**prueba** *etc* ['prweßa] *vb ver* **probar** ♦ *nf* proof; (*ensayo*) test, trial; (*degustación*) tasting, sampling; (*de ropa*) fitting; **a ~** on trial; **a ~ de** proof against; **a ~ de agua/fuego** waterproof/fireproof; **someter a ~** to put to the test

**prurito** [pru'rito] *nm* itch; (*de bebé*) nappy (*BRIT*) o diaper (*US*) rash

**psico...** [siko] *prefijo* psycho...; **~análisis** *nm inv* psychoanalysis; **~logía** *nf* psychology; **~lógico, a** *adj* psychological; **psicólogo, a** *nm/f* psychologist; **psicópata** *nm/f* psychopath; **~sis** *nf inv* psychosis

**psiquiatra** [si'kjatra] *nm/f* psychiatrist; **psiquiátrico, a** *adj* psychiatric; **psíquico, a** ['sikiko, a] *adj* psychic(al)

**PSOE** [pe'soe] *nm abr* = Partido Socialista Obrero Español

**pta(s)** *abr* = peseta(s)

**pts** *abr* = pesetas

**púa** ['pua] *nf* sharp point; (*BOT, ZOOL*) prickle, spine; (*para guitarra*) plectrum (*BRIT*), pick (*US*); **alambre de ~** barbed wire

**pubertad** [puβer'tað] *nf* puberty

**publicación** [puβlika'θjon] *nf* publication

**publicar** [puβli'kar] *vt* (*editar*) to publish; (*hacer público*) to publicize; (*divulgar*) to make public, divulge

**publicidad** [puβliθi'ðað] *nf* publicity; (COM: propaganda) advertising; **publicitario, a** *adj* publicity *cpd*; advertising *cpd*

**público, a** ['puβliko, a] *adj* public ♦ *nm* public; (TEATRO etc) audience

**puchero** [pu'tʃero] *nm* (CULIN: guiso) stew; (: olla) cooking pot; **hacer ~s** to pout

**pude** *etc vb ver* **poder**

**púdico, a** ['puðiko, a] *adj* modest

**pudiente** [pu'ðjente] *adj* (rico) wealthy, well-to-do

**pudiera** *etc vb ver* **poder**

**pudor** [pu'ðor] *nm* modesty

**pudrir** [pu'ðrir] *vt* to rot; (fam) to upset, annoy; ~**se** *vr* to rot, decay

**pueblo** ['pweβlo] *nm* people; (nación) nation; (aldea) village

**puedo** *etc vb ver* **poder**

**puente** ['pwente] *nm* bridge; **hacer ~** (inf) to take an extra day off work between 2 public holidays; to take a long weekend; ~ **aéreo** shuttle service; ~ **colgante** suspension bridge

**puerco, a** ['pwerko, a] *nm/f* pig/sow ♦ *adj* (sucio) dirty, filthy; (obsceno) disgusting; ~ **de mar** porpoise; ~ **marino** dolphin

**pueril** [pwe'ril] *adj* childish

**puerro** ['pwerro] *nm* leek

**puerta** ['pwerta] *nf* door; (de jardín) gate; (portería) doorway; (fig) gateway; (portería) goal; **a la ~** at the door; **a ~ cerrada** behind closed doors; ~ **giratoria** revolving door

**puerto** ['pwerto] *nm* port; (paso) pass; (fig) haven, refuge

**Puerto Rico** [pwerto'riko] *nm* Puerto Rico; **puertorriqueño, a** *adj, nm/f* Puerto Rican

**pues** [pwes] *adv* (entonces) then; (bueno) well, well then; (así que) so ♦ *conj* (ya que) since; ~**!** (sí) yes!, certainly!

**puesta** ['pwesta] *nf* (apuesta) bet, stake; ~ **en marcha** starting; ~ **del sol** sunset

**puesto, a** ['pwesto, a] *pp de* **poner** ♦ *adj*: **tener algo ~** to have sth on,

be wearing sth ♦ *nm* (lugar, posición) place; (trabajo) post, job; (COM) stall ♦ *conj*: ~ **que** since, as

**púgil** ['puxil] *nm* boxer

**pugna** ['puɣna] *nf* battle, conflict; ~ (**luchar**) to struggle, fight; (pelear) to fight

**pujar** [pu'xar] *vi* (en subasta) to bid; (esforzarse) to struggle, strain

**pulcro, a** ['pulkro, a] *adj* neat, tidy; (bello) exquisite

**pulga** ['pulɣa] *nf* flea

**pulgada** [pul'ɣaða] *nf* inch

**pulgar** [pul'ɣar] *nm* thumb

**pulir** [pu'lir] *vt* to polish; (alisar) to smooth; (fig) to polish up, touch up

**pulmón** [pul'mon] *nm* lung; **pulmonía** *nf* pneumonia

**pulpa** ['pulpa] *nf* pulp; (de fruta) flesh, soft part

**pulpería** [pulpe'ria] *nf* (AM) (tienda) small grocery store

**púlpito** ['pulpito] *nm* pulpit

**pulpo** ['pulpo] *nm* octopus

**pulsación** [pulsa'θjon] *nf* beat, pulsation; (ANAT) throb(bing)

**pulsar** [pul'sar] *vt* (tecla) to touch, tap; (MUS) to play; (botón) to press, push ♦ *vi* to pulsate; (latir) to beat, throb; (MED): ~ **a uno** to take sb's pulse

**pulsera** [pul'sera] *nf* bracelet

**pulso** ['pulso] *nm* (ANAT) pulse; (: muñeca) wrist; (fuerza) strength; (firmeza) steadiness, steady hand; (tacto) tact, good sense

**pulverizador** [pulβeriθa'ðor] *nm* spray, spray gun

**pulverizar** [pulβeri'θar] *vt* to pulverize; (líquido) to spray

**pulla** ['puʎa] *nf* cutting remark; (expresión grosera) obscene remark

**puna** ['puna] *nf* (AM) mountain sickness

**punitivo, a** [puni'tiβo, a] *adj* punitive

**punta** ['punta] *nf* point, tip; (extremidad) end; (fig) touch, trace; **horas ~s** peak hours, rush hours; **sacar ~ a** to sharpen; **estar de ~** to be edgy

**puntada** [pun'taða] nf (COSTURA) stitch

**puntal** [pun'tal] nm prop, support

**puntapié** [punta'pje] nm kick

**puntear** [punte'ar] vt to tick, mark

**puntería** [punte'ria] nf (de arma) aim, aiming; (destreza) marksmanship

**puntero, a** [pun'tero, a] adj leading ♦ nm (palo) pointer

**puntiagudo, a** [puntja'ɣuðo, a] adj sharp, pointed

**puntilla** [pun'tiʎa] nf (encaje) lace edging o trim; (andar) de ~s (to walk) on tiptoe

**punto** ['punto] nm (gen) point; (señal diminuta) spot, dot; (COSTURA, MED) stitch; (lugar) spot, place; (momento) point, moment; a ~ ready; estar a ~ de to be on the point of o about to; en ~ on the dot; ~ muerto dead centre; (AUTO) neutral (gear); ~ final full stop (BRIT), period (US); ~ y coma semicolon; ~ de interrogación question mark; ~ de vista point of view, viewpoint; hacer ~ (tejer) to knit

**puntuación** [puntwa'θjon] nf (puntos: en examen) mark(s) (pl); (: DEPORTE) score

**puntual** [pun'twal] adj (a tiempo) punctual; (exacto) exact, accurate; (seguro) reliable; ~idad nf punctuality; exactness, accuracy; reliability; ~izar vt to fix, specify

**puntuar** [pun'twar] vi (DEPORTE) to score, count

**punzada** [pun'θaða] nf (de dolor) twinge

**punzante** [pun'θante] adj (dolor) shooting, sharp; (herramienta) sharp; **punzar** vt to prick, pierce ♦ vi to shoot, stab

**puñado** [pu'ɲaðo] nm handful

**puñal** [pu'ɲal] nm dagger; ~**ada** nf stab

**puñetazo** [puɲe'taθo] nm punch

**puño** ['puɲo] nm (ANAT) fist; (cantidad) fistful, handful; (COSTURA)

cuff; (de herramienta) handle

**pupila** [pu'pila] nf pupil

**pupitre** [pu'pitre] nm desk

**puré** [pu're] nm puree; (sopa) (thick) soup; ~ de patatas mashed potatoes

**pureza** [pu'reθa] nf purity

**purga** ['purɣa] nf purge; **purgante** adj, nm purgative; **purgar** vt to purge

**purgatorio** [purɣa'torjo] nm purgatory

**purificar** [purifi'kar] vt to purify; (refinar) to refine

**puritano, a** [puri'tano, a] adj (actitud) puritanical; (iglesia, tradición) puritan ♦ nm/f puritan

**puro, a** ['puro, a] adj pure; (cielo) clear; (verdad) simple, plain ♦ adv: de ~ cansado out of sheer tiredness ♦ nm cigar

**púrpura** ['purpura] nf purple; **purpúreo, a** adj purple

**pus** [pus] nm pus

**puse** etc vb ver **poner**

**pusiera** etc vb ver **poner**

**pústula** ['pustula] nf pimple, sore

**puta** ['puta] nf whore, prostitute

**putrefacción** [putrefak'θjon] nf rotting, putrefaction

**pútrido, a** ['putriðo, a] adj rotten

**PVP** abr (ESP: = precio venta al público) RRP

# Q

_PALABRA CLAVE_

**que** [ke] conj **1** (con oración subordinada: muchas veces no se traduce) that; **dijo ~ vendría** he said (that) he would come; **espero ~ lo encuentres** I hope (that) you find it; **ver tb** el

**2** (en oración independiente): **¡~ entre!** send him in; **¡que se mejore tu padre!** I hope your father gets better!

**3** (enfático): **¿me quieres? – ¡~ sí!** do you love me? – of course!

**4** (*consecutivo*: *muchas veces no se traduce*) that; **es tan grande ~ no lo puedo levantar** it's so big (that) I can't lift it

**5** (*comparaciones*) than; **yo ~ tú/él** if I were you/him; *ver tb* **más; menos; mismo**

**6** (*valor disyuntivo*): **~ le guste o no** whether he likes it or not; **~ venga o ~ no venga** whether he comes or not

**7** (*porque*): **no puedo, ~ tengo ~ quedarme en casa** I can't, I've got to stay in

♦ *pron* **1** (*cosa*) that, which; (+ *prep*) which; **el sombrero ~ te compraste** the hat (that o which) you bought; **la cama en ~ dormí** the bed (that o which) I slept in

**2** (*persona*: *suj*) that, who; (: *objeto*) that, whom; **el amigo ~ me acompañó al museo** the friend that o who went to the museum with me; **la chica ~ invité** the girl (that o whom) I invited

**qué** [ke] *adj* what?, which? ♦ *pron* what?; **¡~ divertido!** how funny!; **¿~ edad tienes?** how old are you?; **¿de ~ me hablas?** what are you saying to me?; **¿~ tal?** how are you?, how are things?; **¿~ hay (de nuevo)?** what's new?

**quebrada** [ke'βraða] *nf* ravine; *ver tb* **quebrado**

**quebradizo, a** [keβra'ðiθo, a] *adj* fragile; (*persona*) frail

**quebrado, a** [ke'βraðo, a] *adj* (*roto*) broken ♦ *nm/f* bankrupt ♦ *nm* (MAT) fraction

**quebrantar** [keβran'tar] *vt* (*infringir*) to violate, transgress; **~se** *vr* (*persona*) to fail in health

**quebranto** [ke'βranto] *nm* damage, harm; (*decaimiento*) exhaustion; (*dolor*) grief, pain

**quebrar** [ke'βrar] *vt* to break, smash ♦ *vi* to go bankrupt; **~se** *vr* to break, get broken; (MED) to be ruptured

**quedar** [ke'ðar] *vi* to stay, remain; (*encontrarse*: *sitio*) to be; (*restar*) to remain, be left; **~se** *vr* to remain, stay (behind); **~se (con) algo** to keep sth; **~ en** (*acordar*) to agree on/to; **~ en nada** to come to nothing; **~ por hacer** to be still to be done; **~ ciego/mudo** to be left blind/dumb; **no te queda bien ese vestido** that dress doesn't suit you; **eso queda muy lejos** that's a long way (away); **quedamos a las seis** we agreed to meet at six

**quedo, a** ['keðo, a] *adj* still ♦ *adv* softly, gently

**quehacer** [kea'θer] *nm* task, job; **~es (domésticos)** *nmpl* household chores

**queja** ['kexa] *nf* complaint; **quejarse** *vr* (*enfermo*) to moan, groan; (*protestar*) to complain; **quejarse de que** to complain (about the fact) that; **quejido** *nm* moan

**quemado, a** [ke'maðo, a] *adj* burnt

**quemadura** [kema'ðura] *nf* burn, scald

**quemar** [ke'mar] *vt* to burn; (*fig*: *malgastar*) to burn up, squander ♦ *vi* to be burning hot; **~se** *vr* (*consumirse*) to burn (up); (*del sol*) to get sunburnt

**quemarropa** [kema'rropa]: **a ~** *adv* point-blank

**quemazón** [kema'θon] *nf* burn; (*calor*) intense heat; (*sensación*) itch

**quepo** *etc vb ver* **caber**

**querella** [ke'reʎa] *nf* (JUR) charge; (*disputa*) dispute; **~se** *vr* (JUR) to file a complaint

---

PALABRA CLAVE

**querer** [ke'rer] *vt* **1** (*desear*) to want; **quiero más dinero** I want more money; **quisiera o querría un té** I'd like a tea; **sin ~** unintentionally; **quiero ayudar/que vayas** I want to help/you to go

**2** (*preguntas*: *para pedir algo*): **¿quiere abrir la ventana?** could you open the window?; **¿quieres**

echarme una mano? can you give me a hand?

**3** (*amar*) to love; (*tener cariño a*) to be fond of; **quiere mucho a sus hijos** he's very fond of his children

**4** (*requerir*): **esta planta quiere más luz** this plant needs more light

**5**: **le pedí que me dejara ir pero no quiso** I asked him to let me go but he refused

**querido, a** [ke'riðo, a] *adj* dear ♦ *nm/f* darling; (*amante*) lover

**queso** ['keso] *nm* cheese; ~ **crema** cream cheese

**quicio** ['kiθjo] *nm* hinge; **sacar a uno de** ~ to get on sb's nerves

**quiebra** ['kjeβra] *nf* break, split; (*COM*) bankruptcy; (*ECON*) slump

**quiebro** ['kjeβro] *nm* (*del cuerpo*) swerve

**quien** [kjen] *pron* who; **hay** ~ **piensa que** there are those who think that; **no hay** ~ **lo haga** no-one will do it

**quién** [kjen] *pron* who, whom; ¿~ **es?** who's there?

**quienquiera** [kjen'kjera] (*pl* **quienesquiera**) *pron* whoever

**quiero** *etc vb ver* **querer**

**quieto, a** ['kjeto, a] *adj* still; (*carácter*) placid; **quietud** *nf* stillness

**quilate** [ki'late] *nm* carat

**quilla** ['kiʎa] *nf* keel

**quimera** [ki'mera] *nf* chimera; **quimérico, a** *adj* fantastic

**químico, a** ['kimiko, a] *adj* chemical ♦ *nm/f* chemist ♦ *nf* chemistry

**quincalla** [kin'kaʎa] *nf* hardware, ironmongery (*BRIT*)

**quince** ['kinθe] *num* fifteen; ~ **días** a fortnight; **~añero, a** *nm/f* teenager; **~na** *nf* fortnight; (*pago*) fortnightly pay; **~nal** *adj* fortnightly

**quiniela** [ki'njela] *nf* football pools *pl*; **~s** *nfpl* (*impreso*) pools coupon *sg*

**quinientos, as** [ki'njentos, as] *adj, num* five hundred

**quinina** [ki'nina] *nf* quinine

**quinqui** ['kinki] *nm* delinquent

**quinto, a** ['kinto, a] *adj* fifth ♦ *nf* country house; (*MIL*) call-up, draft

**quiosco** ['kjosko] *nm* (*de música*) bandstand; (*de periódicos*) news stand

**quirófano** [ki'rofano] *nm* operating theatre

**quirúrgico, a** [ki'rurxiko, a] *adj* surgical

**quise** *etc vb ver* **querer**

**quisiera** *etc vb ver* **querer**

**quisquilloso, a** [kiski'ʎoso, a] *adj* (*susceptible*) touchy; (*meticuloso*) pernickety

**quiste** ['kiste] *nm* cyst

**quitaesmalte** [kitaes'malte] *nm* nail-polish remover

**quitamanchas** [kita'mantʃas] *nm inv* stain remover

**quitanieves** [kita'njeβes] *nm inv* snowplough (*BRIT*), snowplow (*US*)

**quitar** [ki'tar] *vt* to remove, take away; (*ropa*) to take off; (*dolor*) to relieve; **¡quita de ahí!** get away!; **~se** *vr* to withdraw; (*ropa*) to take off; **se quitó el sombrero** he took off his hat

**quitasol** [kita'sol] *nm* sunshade (*BRIT*), parasol

**quite** ['kite] *nm* (*esgrima*) parry; (*evasión*) dodge

**Quito** ['kito] *n* Quito

**quizá(s)** [ki'θa(s)] *adv* perhaps, maybe

# R

**rábano** ['raβano] *nm* radish; **me importa un** ~ I don't give a damn

**rabia** ['raβja] *nf* (*MED*) rabies *sg*; (*fig: ira*) fury, rage; **rabiar** *vi* to have rabies; to rage with fury; **rabiar por algo** to long for sth

**rabieta** [ra'βjeta] *nf* tantrum, fit of temper

**rabino** [ra'βino] *nm* rabbi

**rabioso, a** [ra'βjoso, a] *adj* rabid; (*fig*) furious

**rabo** ['raβo] nm tail

**racial** [ra'θjal] adj racial, race cpd

**racimo** [ra'θimo] nm bunch

**raciocinio** [raθjo'θinjo] nm reason

**ración** [ra'θjon] nf portion; **raciones** nfpl rations

**racional** [raθjo'nal] adj (razonable) reasonable; (lógico) rational; **~izar** vt to rationalize

**racionar** [raθjo'nar] vt to ration (out)

**racismo** [ra'θismo] nm racialism, racism; **racista** adj, nmf racist

**racha** ['ratʃa] nf gust of wind: **buena/mala ~** (fig) spell of good/bad luck

**radar** [ra'ðar] nm radar

**radiactivo, a** [raðiak'tiβo, a] adj = **radioactivo**

**radiador** [raðia'ðor] nm radiator

**radiante** [ra'ðjante] adj radiant

**radical** [raði'kal] adj, nmf radical

**radicar** [raði'kar] vi to take root; **~ en** to lie o consist in; **~se** vr to establish o.s., put down (one's) roots

**radio** ['raðjo] nf radio; (aparato) radio (set) ♦ nm (MAT) radius; (QUIMICA) radium; **~actividad** nf radioactivity; **~activo, a** adj radioactive; **~difusión** nf broadcasting; **~emisora** nf transmitter, radio station; **~escucha** nmf listener; **~grafía** nf X-ray; **~grafiar** vt to X-ray; **~terapia** nf radiotherapy; **~yente** nmf listener

**ráfaga** ['rafaɣa] nf gust; (de luz) flash; (de tiros) burst

**raido, a** [ra'iðo, a] adj (ropa) threadbare

**raigambre** [rai'ɣambre] nf (BOT) roots pl; (fig) tradition

**raíz** [ra'iθ] nf root; **~ cuadrada** square root; **a ~ de** as a result of

**raja** ['raxa] nf (de melón etc) slice; (grieta) crack; **rajar** vt to slash; (fam) to slash; **rajarse** vr to split, crack; **rajarse de** to back out of

**rajatabla** [raxa'taβla]: **a ~** adv (estrictamente) strictly, to the letter

**rallador** [raʎa'ðor] nm grater

**rallar** [ra'ʎar] vt to grate

**RAM** [ram] nf abr (= memoria de acceso aleatorio) RAM

**rama** ['rama] nf branch; **~je** nm branches pl, foliage; **ramal** nm (de cuerda) strand; (FERRO) branch line (BRIT); (AUTO) branch (road) (BRIT)

**rambla** ['rambla] nf (avenida) avenue

**ramera** [ra'mera] nf whore

**ramificación** [ramifika'θjon] nf ramification

**ramificarse** [ramifi'karse] vr to branch out

**ramillete** [rami'ʎete] nm bouquet

**ramo** ['ramo] nm branch; (sección) department, section

**rampa** ['rampa] nf ramp

**ramplón, ona** [ram'plon, ona] adj uncouth, coarse

**rana** ['rana] nf frog; **salto de ~** leapfrog

**rancio, a** ['ranθjo, a] adj (comestibles) rancid; (vino) aged, mellow; (fig) ancient

**ranchero** [ran'tʃero] nm (AM) rancher; smallholder

**rancho** ['rantʃo] nm grub (fam); (AM: grande) ranch; (: pequeño) small farm

**rango** ['rango] nm rank, standing

**ranura** [ra'nura] nf groove; (de teléfono etc) slot

**rapar** [ra'par] vt to shave; (los cabellos) to crop

**rapaz** [ra'paθ] (nf: **rapaza**) nmf young boy/girl ♦ adj (ZOOL) predatory

**rape** ['rape] nm quick shave; (pez) angler fish; **al ~** cropped

**rapé** [ra'pe] nm snuff

**rapidez** [rapi'ðeθ] nf speed, rapidity; **rápido, a** adj fast, quick ♦ adv quickly ♦ nm (FERRO) express; **rápidos** nmpl rapids

**rapiña** [ra'piɲa] nf robbery; **ave de ~** bird of prey

**raptar** [rap'tar] vt to kidnap; **rapto** nm kidnapping; (impulso) sudden impulse; (éxtasis) ecstasy, rapture

**raqueta** [ra'keta] nf racquet

**raquítico, a** [ra'kitiko, a] adj stunted; (fig) poor, inadequate; **raquitismo** nm rickets sg

**rareza** [ra'reθa] nf rarity; (fig) eccentricity

**raro, a** ['raro, a] adj (poco común) rare; (extraño) odd, strange; (excepcional) remarkable

**ras** [ras] nm: a ~ de level with; a ~ de tierra at ground level

**rasar** [ra'sar] vt (igualar) to level

**rascacielos** [raska'θjelos] nm inv skyscraper

**rascar** [ras'kar] vt (con las uñas etc) to scratch; (raspar) to scrape; ~se vr to scratch (o.s.)

**rasgar** [ras'var] vt to tear, rip (up)

**rasgo** ['rasvo] nm (con pluma) stroke; ~s nmpl (facciones) features, characteristics; a grandes ~s in outline, broadly

**rasguñar** [rasxu'nar] vt to scratch; **rasguño** nm scratch

**raso, a** ['raso, a] adj (liso) flat, level; (a baja altura) very low ♦ nm satin; cielo ~ clear sky

**raspadura** [raspa'ðura] nf (acto) scrape, scraping; (marca) scratch; ~s nfpl (de papel etc) scrapings

**raspar** [ras'par] vt to scrape; (arañar) to scratch; (limar) to file

**rastra** ['rastra] nf (AGR) rake; a ~s by dragging; (fig) unwillingly

**rastreador** [rastrea'ðor] nm tracker; ~ de minas minesweeper

**rastrear** [rastre'ar] vt (seguir) to track

**rastrero, a** [ras'trero, a] adj (BOT, ZOOL) creeping; (fig) despicable, mean

**rastrillo** [ras'triʎo] nm rake

**rastro** ['rastro] nm (AGR) rake; (pista) track, trail; (vestigio) trace; el R~ the Madrid fleamarket

**rastrojo** [ras'troxo] nm stubble

**rasurador** [rasura'ðor] nm (AM) electric shaver

**rasuradora** [rasura'ðora] (AM) nf = rasurador

**rasurarse** [rasu'rarse] vr to shave

**rata** ['rata] nf rat

**ratear** [rate'ar] vt (robar) to steal

**ratero, a** [ra'tero, a] adj light-fingered ♦ nm/f (carterista) pickpocket; (AM: de casas) burglar

**ratificar** [ratifi'kar] vt to ratify

**rato** ['rato] nm while, short time; a ~s from time to time; **hay para** ~ there's still a long way to go; **al poco** ~ soon afterwards; **pasar el** ~ to kill time; **pasar un buen/mal** ~ to have a good/rough time

**ratón** [ra'ton] nm mouse; **ratonera** nf mousetrap

**raudal** [rau'ðal] nm torrent; a ~es in abundance

**raya** ['raja] nf line; (marca) scratch; (en tela) stripe; (de pelo) parting; (límite) boundary; (pez) ray; (puntuación) dash; a ~s striped; **pasarse de la** ~ to go too far; **tener a** ~ to keep in check; **rayar** vt to line; to scratch; (subrayar) to underline ♦ vi: **rayar en** o **con** to border on

**rayo** ['rajo] nm (del sol) ray, beam; (de luz) shaft; (en una tormenta) (flash of) lightning; ~s X X-rays

**raza** ['raθa] nf race; ~ **humana** human race

**razón** [ra'θon] nf reason; (justicia) right, justice; (razonamiento) reasoning; (motivo) reason, motive; (MAT) ratio; **a** ~ **de 10 cada día** at the rate of 10 a day; **"~: ..."** "inquiries to ..."; **en** ~ **de** with regard to; **dar** ~ **a uno** to agree that sb is right; **tener** ~ to be right; ~ **directa/inversa** direct/inverse proportion; **de ser** raison d'être; **razonable** adj reasonable; (justo, moderado) fair; **razonamiento** nm (juicio) judgement; (argumento) reasoning; **razonar** vt, vi to reason, argue

**reacción** [reak'θjon] nf reaction; **avión a** ~ jet plane; ~ **en cadena** chain reaction; **reaccionar** vi to react; **reaccionario, a** adj reactionary

**reacio, a** [re'aθjo, a] adj stubborn

**reactivar** [reakti'βar] vt to revitalize

**reactor** [reak'tor] nm reactor

**readaptación** [readapta'θjon] nf: ~ profesional industrial retraining

**reajuste** [rea'xuste] nm readjustment

**real** [re'al] adj real; (del rey, fig) royal

**realce** [re'alθe] nm (TEC) embossing; (lustre, fig) splendour; (ARTE) highlight; **poner de ~** to emphasize

**realidad** [reali'ðað] nf reality, fact; (verdad) truth

**realista** [rea'lista] nm/f realist

**realización** [realiθa'θjon] nf fulfilment; (COM) selling up (BRIT), conversion into money (US)

**realizador, a** [realiθa'ðor, a] nm/f (TV etc) producer

**realizar** [reali'θar] vt (objetivo) to achieve; (plan) to carry out; (viaje) to make, undertake; (COM) to sell up (BRIT), convert into money (US); ~se vr to come about, come true

**realmente** [real'mente] adv really, actually

**realquilar** [realki'lar] vt (subarrendar) to sublet

**realzar** [real'θar] vt (TEC) to raise; (embellecer) to enhance; (acentuar) to highlight

**reanimar** [reani'mar] vt to revive; (alentar) to encourage; ~se vr to revive

**reanudar** [reanu'ðar] vt (renovar) to renew; (historia, viaje) to resume

**reaparición** [reapari'θjon] nf reappearance

**rearme** [re'arme] nm rearmament

**rebaja** [re'βaxa] nf (COM) reduction; (: descuento) discount; ~s nfpl (COM) sale; **rebajar** vt (bajar) to lower; (reducir) to reduce; (disminuir) to lessen; (humillar) to humble

**rebanada** [reβa'naða] nf slice

**rebañar** [reβa'ɲar] vt (comida) to scrape up; (plato) to scrape clean

**rebaño** [re'βaɲo] nm herd; (de ovejas) flock

**rebasar** [reβa'sar] vt (tb: ~ de) to exceed

**rebatir** [reβa'tir] vt to refute

**rebeca** [re'βeka] nf cardigan

**rebelarse** [reβe'larse] vr to rebel, revolt

**rebelde** [re'βelde] adj rebellious; (niño) unruly ♦ nm/f rebel; **rebeldía** nf rebelliousness; (desobediencia) disobedience

**rebelión** [reβe'ljon] nf rebellion

**reblandecer** [reβlande'θer] vt to soften

**rebobinar** [reβoβi'nar] vt (cinta, película de video) to rewind

**rebosante** [reβo'sante] adj overflowing

**rebosar** [reβo'sar] vi (líquido, recipiente) to overflow; (abundar) to abound, be plentiful

**rebotar** [reβo'tar] vt to bounce; (rechazar) to repel ♦ vi (pelota) to bounce; (bala) to ricochet; **rebote** nm rebound; **de rebote** on the rebound

**rebozado, a** [reβo'θaðo, a] adj fried in batter o breadcrumbs

**rebozar** [reβo'θar] vt to wrap up; (CULIN) to fry in batter o breadcrumbs

**rebuscado, a** [reβus'kaðo, a] adj (amanerado) affected; (palabra) recherché; (idea) far-fetched

**rebuscar** [reβus'kar] vi: ~ (en/por) to search carefully (in/for)

**rebuznar** [reβuθ'nar] vi to bray

**recabar** [reka'βar] vt (obtener) to manage to get

**recado** [re'kaðo] nm message; **tomar un ~** (TEL) to take a message

**recaer** [reka'er] vi to relapse; ~ **en** to fall to o on; (criminal etc) to fall back into, relapse into; **recaída** nf relapse

**recalcar** [rekal'kar] vt (fig) to stress, emphasize

**recalcitrante** [rekalθi'trante] adj recalcitrant

**recalentar** [rekalen'tar] vt (volver a calentar) to reheat; (calentar demasiado) to overheat

**recámara** [re'kamara] (AM) nf bedroom

**recambio** [re'kambjo] *nm* spare; (*de pluma*) refill

**recapacitar** [rekapaθi'tar] *vi* to reflect

**recargado, a** [rekar'xaðo, a] *adj* overloaded

**recargar** [rekar'xar] *vt* to overload; (*batería*) to recharge; **recargo** *nm* surcharge; (*aumento*) increase

**recatado, a** [reka'taðo, a] *adj* (*modesto*) modest, demure; (*prudente*) cautious

**recato** [re'kato] *nm* (*modestia*) modesty, demureness; (*cautela*) caution

**recaudación** [rekauða'θjon] *nf* (*acción*) collection; (*cantidad*) takings *pl*; (*en deporte*) gate; **recaudador, a** *nm/f* tax collector

**recelar** [reθe'lar] *vt*: ~ **que** (*sospechar*) to suspect that; (*temer*) to fear that ♦ *vi*: ~ **de** to distrust; **recelo** *nm* distrust, suspicion; **receloso, a** *adj* distrustful, suspicious

**recepción** [reθep'θjon] *nf* reception; **recepcionista** *nm/f* receptionist

**receptáculo** [reθep'takulo] *nm* receptacle

**receptivo, a** [reθep'tiβo, a] *adj* receptive

**receptor, a** [reθep'tor, a] *nm/f* recipient ♦ *nm* (*TEL*) receiver

**recesión** [reθe'sjon] *nf* (*COM*) recession

**receta** [re'θeta] *nf* (*CULIN*) recipe; (*MED*) prescription

**recibidor, a** [reθiβi'ðor, a] *nm* entrance hall

**recibimiento** [reθiβi'mjento] *nm* reception, welcome

**recibir** [reθi'βir] *vt* to receive; (*dar la bienvenida*) to welcome ♦ *vi* to entertain; ~**se** *vr*: ~**se de** to qualify as; **recibo** *nm* receipt

**reciclar** [reθi'klar] *vt* to recycle

**recién** [re'θjen] *adv* recently, newly; **los** ~ **casados** the newly-weds; **el** ~ **llegado** the newcomer; **el** ~ **nacido** the newborn child

**reciente** [re'θjente] *adj* recent; (*fresco*) fresh; ~**mente** *adv* recently

**recinto** [re'θinto] *nm* enclosure; (*área*) area, place

**recio, a** [re'θjo, a] *adj* strong, tough; (*voz*) loud ♦ *adv* hard; loud(ly)

**recipiente** [reθi'pjente] *nm* receptacle

**reciprocidad** [reθiproθi'ðað] *nf* reciprocity; **recíproco, a** *adj* reciprocal

**recital** [reθi'tal] *nm* (*MUS*) recital; (*LITERATURA*) reading

**recitar** [reθi'tar] *vt* to recite

**reclamación** [reklama'θjon] *nf* claim, demand; (*queja*) complaint

**reclamar** [rekla'mar] *vt* to claim, demand ♦ *vi*: ~ **contra** to complain about; ~ **a uno en justicia** to take sb to court; **reclamo** *nm* (*anuncio*) advertisement; (*tentación*) attraction

**reclinar** [rekli'nar] *vt* to recline, lean; ~**se** *vr* to lean back

**recluir** [reklu'ir] *vt* to intern, confine

**reclusión** [reklu'sjon] *nf* (*prisión*) prison; (*refugio*) seclusion; ~ **perpetua** life imprisonment

**recluta** [re'kluta] *nm/f* recruit ♦ *nf* recruitment; **reclutar** (*datos*) to collect; (*dinero*) to collect up

**reclutamiento** [rekluta'mjento] *nm* recruitment

**recobrar** [reko'βrar] *vt* (*salud*) to recover; (*rescatar*) to get back; ~**se** *vr* to recover

**recodo** [re'koðo] *nm* (*de río, camino*) bend

**recoger** [reko'xer] *vt* to collect; (*AGR*) to harvest; (*levantar*) to pick up; (*juntar*) to gather; (*pasar a buscar*) to come for; get; (*dar asilo*) to give shelter to; (*faldas*) to gather up; (*pelo*) to put up; ~**se** *vr* (*retirarse*) to retire; **recogido, a** *adj* (*lugar*) quiet, secluded; (*pequeño*) small ♦ *nf* (*CORREOS*) collection; (*AGR*) harvest

**recolección** [rekolek'θjon] *nf* (*AGR*) harvesting; (*colecta*) collection

**recomendación** [rekomenda'θjon] *nf* (*sugerencia*) suggestion, recommendation; (*referencia*) reference

**recomendar** [rekomen'dar] *vt* to

suggest, recommend; (*confiar*) to entrust

**recompensa** [rekom'pensa] *nf* reward, recompense; **recompensar** *vt* to reward, recompense

**recomponer** [rekompo'ner] *vt* to mend

**reconciliación** [rekonθilja'θjon] *nf* reconciliation

**reconciliar** [rekonθi'ljar] *vt* to reconcile; ~**se** *vr* to become reconciled

**recóndito, a** [re'kondito, a] *adj* (*lugar*) hidden, secret

**reconfortar** [rekonfor'tar] *vt* to comfort

**reconocer** [rekono'θer] *vt* to recognize; (*registrar*) to search; (*MED*) to examine; **reconocido, a** *adj* recognized; (*agradecido*) grateful; **reconocimiento** *nm* recognition; search; examination; gratitude; (*confesión*) admission

**reconquista** [rekon'kista] *nf* reconquest; **la R~** the Reconquest (of Spain)

**reconstituyente** [rekonstitu'jente] *nm* tonic

**reconstruir** [rekonstru'ir] *vt* to reconstruct

**reconversión** [rekonßer'sjon] *nf*: ~ **industrial** industrial rationalization

**recopilación** [rekopila'θjon] *nf* (*resumen*) summary; (*compilación*) compilation; **recopilar** *vt* to compile

**récord** ['rekorð] (*pl* ~**s**) *adj inv*, *nm* record

**recordar** [rekor'ðar] *vt* (*acordarse de*) to remember; (*acordar a otro*) to remind ♦ *vi* to remember

**recorrer** [reko'rrer] *vt* (*país*) to cross, travel through; (*distancia*) to cover; (*registrar*) to search; (*repasar*) to look over; **recorrido** *nm* run, journey; **tren de largo recorrido** main-line train

**recortado, a** [rekor'taðo, a] *adj* uneven, irregular

**recortar** [rekor'tar] *vt* to cut out; **recorte** *nm* (*acción, de prensa*) cutting; (*de telas, chapas*) trimming

**recostado, a** [rekos'taðo, a] *adj* leaning; **estar** ~ to be lying down

**recostar** [rekos'tar] *vt* to lean; ~**se** *vr* to lie down

**recoveco** [reko'Beko] *nm* (*de camino, río etc*) bend; (*en casa*) cubby hole

**recreación** [rekrea'θjon] *nf* recreation

**recrear** [rekre'ar] *vt* (*entretener*) to entertain; (*volver a crear*) to recreate; **recreativo, a** *adj* recreational; **recreo** *nm* recreation; (*ESCOL*) break, playtime

**recriminar** [rekrimi'nar] *vt* to reproach ♦ *vi* to recriminate; ~**se** *vr* to reproach each other

**recrudecer** [rekruðe'θer] *vt, vi* to worsen; ~**se** *vr* to worsen again; **recrudecimiento** [rekruðeθi'mjento] *nm* upsurge

**recta** ['rekta] *nf* straight line

**rectángulo, a** [rek'tangulo, a] *adj* rectangular ♦ *nm* rectangle

**rectificar** [rektifi'kar] *vt* to rectify; (*volverse recto*) to straighten ♦ *vi* to correct o.s.

**rectitud** [rekti'tuð] *nf* straightness; (*fig*) rectitude

**recto, a** ['rekto, a] *adj* straight; (*persona*) honest, upright ♦ *nm* rectum

**rector, a** [rek'tor, a] *adj* governing

**recuadro** [re'kwaðro] *nm* box; (*TIPOGRAFÍA*) inset

**recubrir** [reku'ßrir] *vt*: ~ (**con**) (*pintura, crema*) to cover (with)

**recuento** [re'kwento] *nm* inventory; **hacer el** ~ **de** to count o reckon up

**recuerdo** [re'kwerðo] *nm* souvenir; ~**s** *nmpl* (*memorias*) memories; ¡~**s a tu madre!** give my regards to your mother!

**recular** [reku'lar] *vi* to back down

**recuperable** [rekupe'raßle] *adj* recoverable

**recuperación** [rekupera'θjon] *nf* recovery

**recuperar** [rekupe'rar] *vt* to recover; (*tiempo*) to make up; ~**se** *vr* to recuperate

**recurrir** [reku'rrir] vi (JUR) to appeal; ~ a to resort to; (persona) to turn to; recurso nm resort; (medios) means pl, resources pl; (JUR) appeal

**recusar** [reku'sar] vt to reject, refuse

**rechazar** [retʃa'θar] vt to repel, drive back; (idea) to reject; (oferta) to turn down

**rechazo** [re'tʃaθo] nm (de fusil) recoil; (rebote) rebound; (negación) rebuff

**rechifla** [re'tʃifla] nf hissing, booing; (fig) derision

**rechinar** [retʃi'nar] vi to creak; (dientes) to grind

**rechistar** [retʃis'tar] vi: sin ~ without a murmur

**rechoncho, a** [re'tʃontʃo, a] (fam) adj thickset (BRIT), heavy-set (US)

**rechupete** [retʃu'pete] (LAM): de ~ (comida) delicious, scrumptious

**red** [reð] nf net, mesh; (FERRO etc) network; (trampa) trap

**redacción** [reðak'θjon] nf (acción) editing; (personal) editorial staff; (ESCOL) essay, composition

**redactar** [reðak'tar] vt to draw up, draft; (periódico) to edit

**redactor, a** [reðak'tor, a] nm/f editor

**redada** [re'ðaða] nf: ~ policial police raid, round-up

**rededor** [reðe'ðor] nm: al o en ~ around, round about

**redención** [reðen'θjon] nf redemption

**redicho, a** [re'ðitʃo, a] adj affected

**redil** [re'ðil] nm sheepfold

**redimir** [reði'mir] vt to redeem

**rédito** ['reðito] nm interest, yield

**redoblar** [reðo'βlar] vt to redouble ♦ vi (tambor) to play a roll on the drums

**redomado, a** [reðo'maðo, a] adj (astuto) sly, crafty; (perfecto) utter

**redonda** [re'ðonda] nf: a la ~ around, round about

**redondear** [reðonde'ar] vt to round,

round off

**redondel** [reðon'del] nm (círculo) circle; (TAUR) bullring, arena; (AUTO) roundabout

**redondo, a** [re'ðondo, a] adj (circular) round; (completo) complete

**reducción** [reðuk'θjon] nf reduction

**reducido, a** [reðu'θiðo, a] adj reduced; (limitado) limited; (pequeño) small

**reducir** [reðu'θir] vt to reduce; to limit; ~se vr to diminish

**redundancia** [reðun'danθja] nf redundancy

**reembolsar** [re(e)mbol'sar] vt (persona) to reimburse; (dinero) to repay, pay back; (depósito) to refund; **reembolso** nm reimbursement; refund

**reemplazar** [re(e)mpla'θar] vt to replace; **reemplazo** nm replacement; de reemplazo (MIL) reserve

**reencuentro** [re(e)n'kwentro] nm reunion

**referencia** [refe'renθja] nf reference; con ~ a with reference to

**referéndum** [refe'rendum] (pl ~s) nm referendum

**referente** [refe'rente] adj: ~ a concerning, relating to

**referir** [refe'rir] vt (contar) to tell, recount; (relacionar) to refer, relate; ~se vr: ~se a to refer to

**refilón** [refi'lon]: de ~ adv obliquely

**refinado, a** [refi'naðo, a] adj refined

**refinamiento** [refina'mjento] nm refinement

**refinar** [refi'nar] vt to refine; **refinería** nf refinery

**reflejar** [refle'xar] vt to reflect; **reflejo, a** adj reflected; (movimiento) reflex ♦ nm reflection; (ANAT) reflex

**reflexión** [reflek'sjon] nf reflection; **reflexionar** vt to reflect on ♦ vi to reflect; (detenerse) to pause (to think)

**reflexivo, a** [reflek'siβo, a] adj thoughtful; (LING) reflexive

**reflujo** [re'fluxo] nm ebb

**reforma** [re'forma] nf reform; (ARQ etc) repair; ~ agraria agrarian reform

**reformar** [refor'mar] *vt* to reform; *(modificar)* to change, alter; *(ARQ)* to repair; ~**se** *vr* to mend one's ways

**reformatorio** [reforma'torjo] *nm* reformatory

**reforzar** [refor'θar] *vt* to strengthen; *(ARQ)* to reinforce; *(fig)* to encourage

**refractario, a** [refrak'tarjo, a] *adj* *(TEC)* heat-resistant

**refrán** [re'fran] *nm* proverb, saying

**refregar** [refre'γar] *vt* to scrub

**refrenar** [refre'nar] *vt* to check, restrain

**refrendar** [refren'dar] *vt* (*firma*) to endorse, countersign; *(ley)* to approve

**refrescante** [refres'kante] *adj* refreshing, cooling

**refrescar** [refres'kar] *vt* to refresh ♦ *vi* to cool down; ~**se** *vr* to get cooler; *(tomar aire fresco)* to go out for a breath of fresh air; *(beber)* to have a drink

**refresco** [re'fresko] *nm* soft drink, cool drink; "~**s**" "refreshments"

**refriega** [re'frjeγa] *nf* scuffle, brawl

**refrigeración** [refrixera'θjon] *nf* refrigeration; *(de sala)* air-conditioning

**refrigerador** [refrixera'ðor] *nm* refrigerator *(BRIT)*, icebox *(US)*

**refrigeradora** [refrixera'ðora] *nf* = refrigerador

**refrigerar** [refrixe'rar] *vt* to refrigerate; *(sala)* to air-condition

**refuerzo** [re'fwerθo] *nm* reinforcement; *(TEC)* support

**refugiado, a** [refu'xjaðo, a] *nm/f* refugee

**refugiarse** [refu'xjarse] *vr* to take refuge, shelter

**refugio** [re'fuxjo] *nm* refuge; *(protección)* shelter

**refulgir** [reful'xir] *vi* to shine, be dazzling

**refunfuñar** [refunfu'ɲar] *vi* to grunt, growl; *(quejarse)* to grumble

**refutar** [refu'tar] *vt* to refute

**regadera** [reγa'ðera] *nf* watering can

**regadío** [reγa'ðio] *nm* irrigated land

**regalado, a** [reγa'laðo, a] *adj* comfortable, luxurious; *(gratis)* free, for nothing

**regalar** [reγa'lar] *vt* (*dar*) to give (as a present); *(entregar)* to give away; *(mimar)* to pamper, make a fuss of

**regalía** [reγa'lia] *nf* privilege, prerogative; *(COM)* bonus; *(de autor)* royalty

**regaliz** [reγa'liθ] *nm* liquorice

**regalo** [re'γalo] *nm* *(obsequio)* gift, present; *(gusto)* pleasure; *(comodidad)* comfort

**regañadientes** [reγaɲa'ðjentes]: **a ~** *adv* reluctantly

**regañar** [reγa'ɲar] *vt* to scold ♦ *vi* to grumble; **regañón, ona** *adj* nagging

**regar** [re'γar] *vt* to water, irrigate; *(fig)* to scatter, sprinkle

**regatear** [reγate'ar] *vt* (*COM*) to bargain over; *(escatimar)* to be mean with ♦ *vi* to bargain, haggle; *(DEPORTE)* to dribble; **regateo** *nm* bargaining; dribbling; *(del cuerpo)* swerve, dodge

**regazo** [re'γaθo] *nm* lap

**regeneración** [rexenera'θjon] *nf* regeneration

**regenerar** [rexene'rar] *vt* to regenerate

**regentar** [rexen'tar] *vt* to direct, manage; **regente** *nm* *(COM)* manager; *(POL)* regent

**régimen** ['reximen] *(pl* **regímenes***) nm* regime; *(MED)* diet

**regimiento** [rexi'mjento] *nm* regiment

**regio, a** ['rexjo, a] *adj* royal, regal; *(fig: suntuoso)* splendid; *(AM: fam)* great, terrific

**región** [re'xjon] *nf* region; **regionalista** *nm/f* regionalist

**regir** [re'xir] *vt* to govern, rule; *(dirigir)* to manage, run ♦ *vi* to apply, be in force

**registrador** [rexistra'ðor] *nm* registrar, recorder

**registrar** [rexis'trar] *vt* *(buscar)* to

search; (: *en cajón*) to look through; (*inspeccionar*) to inspect; (*anotar*) to register, record; (*INFORM*) to log; ~**se** *vr* to register; (: *ocurrir*) to happen

**registro** [re'xistro] *nm* (*acto*) registration; (*MUS, libro*) register; (*inspección*) inspection, search; ~ **civil** registryoffice

**regla** ['rexla] *nf* (*ley*) rule, regulation; (*de medir*) ruler, rule; (*MED: período*) period

**reglamentación** [rexlamenta'θjon] *nf* (*acto*) regulation; (*lista*) rules *pl*

**reglamentar** [rexlamen'tar] *vt* to regulate; **reglamentario, a** *adj* statutory; **reglamento** *nm* rules *pl*, regulations *pl*

**regocijarse** [rexoθi'xarse] *vr*: ~ **de** to rejoice at, be happy about; **regocijo** *nm* joy, happiness

**regodearse** [rexoðe'arse] *vr* to be glad, be delighted; **regodeo** *nm* delight

**regresar** [rexre'sar] *vi* to come back, go back, return; **regresivo, a** *adj* backward; (*fig*) regressive; **regreso** *nm* return

**reguero** [re'xero] *nm* (*de sangre etc*) trickle; (*de humo*) trail

**regulador** [rexula'ðor] *nm* regulator; (*de radio etc*) knob, control

**regular** [rexu'lar] *adj* regular; (*normal*) normal, usual; (*común*) ordinary; (*organizado*) regular, orderly; (*mediano*) average; (*fam*) not bad, so-so ♦ *adv* so-so, alright ♦ *vt* (*controlar*) to control, regulate; (*TEC*) to adjust; **por lo** ~ as a rule; **~idad** *nf* regularity; **~izar** *vt* to regularize

**regusto** [re'xusto] *nm* aftertaste

**rehabilitación** [reaβilita'θjon] *nf* rehabilitation; (*ARQ*) restoration

**rehabilitar** [reaβili'tar] *vt* to rehabilitate; (*ARQ*) to restore; (*reintegrar*) to reinstate

**rehacer** [rea'θer] *vt* (*reparar*) to mend, repair; (*volver a hacer*) to redo, repeat; ~**se** *vr* (*MED*) to recover

**rehén** [re'en] *nm* hostage

**rehuir** [reu'ir] *vt* to avoid, shun

**rehusar** [reu'sar] *vt, vi* to refuse

**reina** ['reina] *nf* queen; ~**do** *nm* reign

**reinante** [rei'nante] *adj* (*fig*) prevailing

**reinar** [rei'nar] *vi* to reign

**reincidir** [reinθi'ðir] *vi* to relapse

**reincorporarse** [reinkorpo'rarse] *vr*: ~ **a** to rejoin

**reino** ['reino] *nm* kingdom; **el R~ Unido** the United Kingdom

**reintegrar** [reinte'xrar] *vt* (*reconstituir*) to reconstruct; (*persona*) to reinstate; (*dinero*) to refund, pay back; ~**se** *vr*: ~**se a** to return to

**reír** [re'ir] *vi* to laugh; ~**se** *vr* to laugh; ~**se de** to laugh at

**reiterar** [reite'rar] *vt* to reiterate

**reivindicación** [reiβindika'θjon] *nf* (*demanda*) claim, demand; (*justificación*) vindication

**reivindicar** [reiβindi'kar] *vt* to claim

**reja** ['rexa] *nf* (*de ventana*) grille, bars *pl*; (*en la calle*) grating

**rejilla** [re'xiʎa] *nf* grating, grille; (*muebles*) wickerwork; (*de ventilación*) vent; (*de coche etc*) luggage rack

**rejoneador** [rexonea'ðor] *nm* mounted bullfighter

**rejuvenecer** [rexuβene'θer] *vt, vi* to rejuvenate

**relación** [rela'θjon] *nf* relation, relationship; (*MAT*) ratio; (*narración*) report; **relaciones públicas** public relations; **con ~ a, en ~ con** in relation to; **relacionar** *vt* to relate, connect; **relacionarse** *vr* to be connected, be linked

**relajación** [relaxa'θjon] *nf* relaxation

**relajado, a** [rela'xaðo, a] *adj* (*disoluto*) loose; (*cómodo*) relaxed; (*MED*) ruptured

**relajar** [rela'xar] *vt* to relax; ~**se** *vr* to relax

**relamerse** [rela'merse] *vr* to lick one's lips

**relamido, a** [rela'miðo, a] *adj* (*pul-*

cro) overdressed; (*afectado*) affected

**relámpago** [re'lampayo] *nm* flash of lightning; **visita/huelga** ~ lightning visit/strike; **relampaguear** *vi* to flash

**relatar** [rela'tar] *vt* to tell, relate

**relativo, a** [rela'tiβo, a] *adj* relative; **en lo** ~ **a** concerning

**relato** [re'lato] *nm* (*narración*) story, tale

**relegar** [rele'xar] *vt* to relegate

**relevante** [rele'βante] *adj* eminent, outstanding

**relevar** [rele'βar] *vt* (*sustituir*) to relieve; ~**se** *vr* to relay; ~ **a uno de un cargo** to relieve sb of his post

**relevo** [re'leβo] *nm* relief; **carrera de** ~**s** relay race

**relieve** [re'ljeβe] *nm* (*ARTE, TEC*) relief; (*fig*) prominence, importance; **bajo** ~ bas-relief

**religión** [reli'xjon] *nf* religion; **religioso, a** *adj* religious ♦ *nm/f* monk/nun

**relinchar** [relin'tʃar] *vi* to neigh; **relincho** *nm* neigh; (*acto*) neighing

**reliquia** [re'likja] *nf* relic; ~ **de familia** heirloom

**reloj** [re'lo(x)] *nm* clock; ~ (**de pulsera**) wristwatch; ~ **despertador** alarm (clock); **poner el** ~ to set one's watch (o the clock); ~**ero, a** *nm/f* clockmaker; watchmaker

**reluciente** [relu'θjente] *adj* brilliant, shining

**relucir** [relu'θir] *vi* to shine; (*fig*) to excel

**relumbrar** [relum'brar] *vi* to dazzle, shine brilliantly

**rellano** [re'ʎano] *nm* (*ARQ*) landing

**rellenar** [reʎe'nar] *vt* (*llenar*) to fill up; (*CULIN*) to stuff; (*COSTURA*) to pad; **relleno, a** *adj* full up; stuffed ♦ *nm* stuffing; (*de tapicería*) padding

**remachar** [rema'tʃar] *vt* to rivet; (*fig*) to hammer home, drive home; **remache** *nm* rivet

**remanente** [rema'nente] *nm* remainder; (*COM*) balance; (*de producto*) surplus

**remangar** [reman'gar] *vt* to roll up

**remanso** [re'manso] *nm* pool

**remar** [re'mar] *vi* to row

**rematado, a** [rema'taðo, a] *adj* complete, utter

**rematar** [rema'tar] *vt* to finish off; (*COM*) to sell off cheap ♦ *vi* to end, finish off; (*DEPORTE*) to shoot

**remate** [re'mate] *nm* end, finish; (*punta*) tip; (*DEPORTE*) shot; (*ARQ*) top; (*COM*) auction sale; **de o para** ~ to crown it all (*BRIT*), to top it off

**remedar** [reme'ðar] *vt* to imitate

**remediar** [reme'ðjar] *vt* to remedy; (*subsanar*) to make good, repair; (*evitar*) to avoid

**remedio** [re'meðjo] *nm* remedy; (*alivio*) relief, help; (*JUR*) recourse, remedy; **poner** ~ **a** to correct, stop; **no tener más** ~ to have no alternative; **¡qué** ~! there's no choice!; **sin** ~ hopeless

**remedo** [re'meðo] *nm* imitation; (*pey*) parody

**remendar** [remen'dar] *vt* to repair; (*con parche*) to patch

**remesa** [re'mesa] *nf* remittance; (*COM*) shipment

**remiendo** [re'mjendo] *nm* mend; (*con parche*) patch; (*cosido*) darn

**remilgado, a** [remil'gaðo, a] *adj* prim; (*afectado*) affected

**remilgo** [re'milɣo] *nm* primness; (*afectación*) affectation

**reminiscencia** [reminis'θenθja] *nf* reminiscence

**remiso, a** [re'miso, a] *adj* slack, slow

**remite** [re'mite] *nm* (*en sobre*) name and address of sender

**remitir** [remi'tir] *vt* to remit, send ♦ *vi* to slacken; (*en carta*): **remite: X** sender: X; **remitente** *nm/f* sender

**remo** [re'mo] *nm* (*de barco*) oar; (*DEPORTE*) rowing

**remojar** [remo'xar] *vt* to steep, soak; (*galleta etc*) to dip, dunk

**remojo** [re'moxo] *nm*: **dejar la ropa en** ~ to leave clothes to soak

**remolacha** [remo'latʃa] *nf* beet, beetroot

beetroot

**remolcador** [remolka'ðor] *nm* (*NAUT*) tug; (*AUTO*) breakdown lorry

**remolcar** [remol'kar] *vt* to tow

**remolino** [remo'lino] *nm* eddy; (*de agua*) whirlpool; (*de viento*) whirlwind; (*de gente*) crowd

**remolque** [re'molke] *nm* tow, towing; (*cuerda*) towrope; **llevar a** ~ to tow

**remontar** [remon'tar] *vt* to mend; ~**se** *vr* to soar; ~**se a** (*COM*) to amount to; ~ **el vuelo** to soar

**remorder** [remor'ðer] *vt* to distress, disturb; ~**le la conciencia a uno** to have a guilty conscience; **remordimiento** *nm* remorse

**remoto, a** [re'moto, a] *adj* remote

**remover** [remo'ßer] *vt* to stir; (*tierra*) to turn over; (*objetos*) to move round

**remozar** [remo'θar] *vt* (*ARQ*) to refurbish

**remuneración** [remunera'θjon] *nf* remuneration

**remunerar** [remune'rar] *vt* to remunerate; (*premiar*) to reward

**renacer** [rena'θer] *vi* to be reborn; (*fig*) to revive; **renacimiento** *nm* rebirth; **el Renacimiento** the Renaissance

**renacuajo** [rena'kwaxo] *nm* (*ZOOL*) tadpole

**renal** [re'nal] *adj* renal, kidney *cpd*

**rencilla** [ren'θiʎa] *nf* quarrel

**rencor** [ren'kor] *nm* rancour, bitterness; ~**oso, a** *adj* spiteful

**rendición** [rendi'θjon] *nf* surrender

**rendido, a** [ren'diðo, a] *adj* (*sumiso*) submissive; (*cansado*) worn-out, exhausted

**rendija** [ren'dixa] *nf* (*hendedura*) crack, cleft

**rendimiento** [rendi'mjento] *nm* (*producción*) output; (*TEC, COM*) efficiency

**rendir** [ren'dir] *vt* (*vencer*) to defeat; (*producir*) to produce; (*dar beneficio*) to yield; (*agotar*) to exhaust ♦

*vi* to pay; ~**se** *vr* (*someterse*) to surrender; (*cansarse*) to wear o.s. out; ~ **homenaje** *o* **culto a** to pay homage to

**renegar** [rene'xar] *vi* (*renunciar*) to renounce; (*blasfemar*) to blaspheme; (*quejarse*) to complain

**RENFE** ['renfe] *nf abr* (= *Red Nacional de los Ferrocarriles Españoles*) ≈ BR (*BRIT*)

**renglón** [ren'glon] *nm* (*línea*) line; (*COM*) item, article; **a** ~ **seguido** immediately after

**renombrado, a** [renom'braðo, a] *adj* renowned

**renombre** [re'nombre] *nm* renown

**renovación** [renoßa'θjon] *nf* (*de contrato*) renewal; (*ARQ*) renovation

**renovar** [reno'ßar] *vt* to renew; (*ARQ*) to renovate

**renta** ['renta] *nf* (*ingresos*) income; (*beneficio*) profit; (*alquiler*) rent; ~ **vitalicia** annuity; **rentable** *adj* profitable; **rentar** *vt* to produce, yield

**renuncia** [re'nunθja] *nf* resignation

**renunciar** [renun'θjar] *vt* to renounce; (*tabaco, alcohol etc*) ~ **a** to give up; (*oferta, oportunidad*) to turn down; (*puesto*) to resign ♦ *vi* to resign

**reñido, a** [re'ɲiðo, a] *adj* (*batalla*) bitter, hard-fought; **estar** ~ **con uno** to be on bad terms with sb

**reñir** [re'ɲir] *vt* (*regañar*) to scold ♦ *vi* (*estar peleado*) to quarrel, fall out; (*combatir*) to fight

**reo** [re'o] *nm/f* culprit, offender; ~ **de muerte** prisoner condemned to death

**reojo** [re'oxo] : **de** ~ *adv* out of the corner of one's eye

**reparación** [repara'θjon] *nf* (*acto*) mending, repairing; (*TEC*) repair; (*fig*) amends, reparation

**reparar** [repa'rar] *vt* to repair; (*fig*) to make amends for; (*observar*) to observe ♦ *vi*: ~ **en** (*darse cuenta de*) to notice; (*prestar atención a*) to pay attention to

**reparo** [re'paro] *nm* (*advertencia*)

observation; (*duda*) doubt; (*dificultad*) difficulty; **poner** ~**s (a)** to raise objections (to)

**repartición** [reparti'θjon] *nf* distribution; (*división*) division; **repartidor, a** *nm/f* distributor

**repartir** [repar'tir] *vt* to distribute, share out; (*CORREOS*) to deliver; **reparto** *nm* distribution; delivery; (*TEATRO, CINE*) cast; (*AM: urbanización*) housing estate (*BRIT*), real estate development (*US*)

**repasar** [repa'sar] *vt* (*ESCOL*) to revise; (*MECÁNICA*) to check, overhaul; (*COSTURA*) to mend; **repaso** *nm* revision; overhaul, checkup; mending

**repatriar** [repa'trjar] *vt* to repatriate

**repecho** [re'petʃo] *nm* steep incline

**repelente** [repe'lente] *adj* repellent, repulsive

**repeler** [repe'ler] *vt* to repel

**repensar** [repen'sar] *vt* to reconsider

**repente** [re'pente] *nm*: **de** ~ suddenly; ~ **de ira** fit of anger

**repentino, a** [repen'tino, a] *adj* sudden

**repercusión** [reperku'sjon] *nf* repercussion

**repercutir** [reperku'tir] *vi* (*objeto*) to rebound; (*sonido*) to echo; ~ **en** (*fig*) to have repercussions on

**repertorio** [reper'torjo] *nm* list; (*TEATRO*) repertoire

**repetición** [repeti'θjon] *nf* repetition

**repetir** [repe'tir] *vt* to repeat; (*plato*) to have a second helping of ♦ *vi* to repeat; (*sabor*) to come back; ~**se** *vr* (*volver sobre un tema*) to repeat o.s.

**repetitivo, a** [repeti'tiβo, a] *adj* repetitive, repetitious

**repicar** [repi'kar] *vt* (*campanas*) to ring

**repique** [re'pike] *nm* pealing, ringing; ~**teo** *nm* pealing; (*de tambor*) drumming

**repisa** [re'pisa] *nf* ledge, shelf; (*de ventana*) windowsill; ~ **de chimenea** mantelpiece

**repito** *etc vb ver* **repetir**

**replantearse** [replante'arse] *vr*: ~ **un problema** to reconsider a problem

**replegarse** [reple'ɣarse] *vr* to fall back, retreat

**repleto, a** [re'pleto, a] *adj* replete, full up

**réplica** ['replika] *nf* answer; (*ARTE*) replica

**replicar** [repli'kar] *vi* to answer; (*objetar*) to argue, answer back

**repliegue** [re'pljeɣe] *nm* (*MIL*) withdrawal

**repoblación** [repoβla'θjon] *nf* repopulation; (*de río*) restocking; ~ **forestal** reafforestation

**repoblar** [repo'βlar] *vt* to repopulate; (*con árboles*) to reafforest

**repollo** [re'poʎo] *nm* cabbage

**reponer** [repo'ner] *vt* to replace, put back; (*TEATRO*) to revive; ~**se** *vr* to recover; ~ **que** to reply that

**reportaje** [repor'taxe] *nm* report, article

**reportero, a** [repor'tero, a] *nm/f* reporter

**reposacabezas** [reposaka'βeθas] *nm inv* headrest

**reposado, a** [repo'saðo, a] *adj* (*descansado*) restful; (*tranquilo*) calm

**reposar** [repo'sar] *vi* to rest, repose

**reposición** [reposi'θjon] *nf* replacement; (*CINE*) remake

**reposo** [re'poso] *nm* rest

**repostar** [repos'tar] *vt* to replenish; (*AUTO*) to fill up (with petrol (*BRIT*) o gasoline (*US*))

**repostería** [reposte'ria] *nf* confectioner's (shop); **repostero, a** *nm/f* confectioner

**reprender** [repren'der] *vt* to reprimand

**represa** [re'presa] *nf* dam; (*lago artificial*) lake, pool

**represalia** [repre'salja] *nf* reprisal

**representación** [representa'θjon] *nf* representation; (*TEATRO*) performance; **representante** *nm/f* representative; performer

**representar** [represen'tar] *vt* to represent; (*TEATRO*) to perform; (*edad*) to look; **~se** *vr* to imagine; **representativo, a** *adj* representative

**represión** [repre'sjon] *nf* repression

**reprimenda** [repri'menda] *nf* reprimand, rebuke

**reprimir** [repri'mir] *vt* to repress

**reprobar** [repro'ßar] *vt* to censure, reprove

**reprochar** [repro't∫ar] *vt* to reproach; **reproche** *nm* reproach

**reproducción** [reproðuk'θjon] *nf* reproduction

**reproducir** [reproðu'θir] *vt* to reproduce; **~se** *vr* to breed; (*situación*) to recur

**reproductor, a** [reproðuk'tor, a] *adj* reproductive

**reptil** [rep'til] *nm* reptile

**república** [re'pußlika] *nf* republic; **republicano, a** *adj, nm/f* republican

**repudiar** [repu'ðjar] *vt* to repudiate; (*fe*) to renounce

**repuesto** [re'pwesto] *nm* (*pieza de recambio*) spare (part); (*abastecimiento*) supply; **rueda de ~** spare wheel

**repugnancia** [repuɣ'nanθja] *nf* repugnance; **repugnante** *adj* repugnant, repulsive

**repugnar** [repuɣ'nar] *vt* to disgust

**repulsa** [re'pulsa] *nf* rebuff

**repulsión** [repul'sjon] *nf* repulsion, aversion; **repulsivo, a** *adj* repulsive

**reputación** [reputa'θjon] *nf* reputation

**reputar** [repu'tar] *vt* to consider, deem

**requemado, a** [reke'maðo, a] *adj* (*quemado*) scorched; (*bronceado*) tanned

**requerimiento** [rekeri'mjento] *nm* request; (*JUR*) summons

**requerir** [reke'rir] *vt* (*pedir*) to ask, request; (*exigir*) to require; (*llamar*) to send for, summon

**requesón** [reke'son] *nm* cottage cheese

**requete...** [re'kete] *prefijo* extremely

**réquiem** ['rekjem] (*pl* **~s**) *nm* requiem

**requisito** [reki'sito] *nm* requirement, requisite

**res** [res] *nf* beast, animal

**resaca** [re'saka] *nf* (*en el mar*) undertow, undercurrent; (*fig*) backlash; (*fam*) hangover

**resaltar** [resal'tar] *vi* to project, stick out; (*fig*) to stand out

**resarcir** [resar'θir] *vt* to compensate; **~se** *vr* to make up for

**resbaladizo, a** [resßala'ðiθo, a] *adj* slippery

**resbalar** [resßa'lar] *vi* to slip, slide; (*fig*) to slip (up); **~se** *vr* to slip, slide; to slip (up); **resbalón** *nm* (*acción*) slip

**rescatar** [reska'tar] *vt* (*salvar*) to save, rescue; (*objeto*) to get back, recover; (*cautivos*) to ransom

**rescate** [res'kate] *nm* rescue; (*de objeto*) recovery; **pagar un ~** to pay a ransom

**rescindir** [resθin'dir] *vt* to rescind

**rescisión** [resθi'sjon] *nf* cancellation

**rescoldo** [res'koldo] *nm* embers *pl*

**resecar** [rese'kar] *vt* to dry thoroughly; (*MED*) to cut out, remove; **~se** *vr* to dry up

**reseco, a** [re'seko, a] *adj* very dry; (*fig*) skinny

**resentido, a** [resen'tiðo, a] *adj* resentful

**resentimiento** [resenti'mjento] *nm* resentment, bitterness

**resentirse** [resen'tirse] *vr* (*debilitarse: persona*) to suffer; **~ de** (*consecuencias*) to feel the effects of; **~ de** (*o por*) **algo** to resent sth, be bitter about sth

**reseña** [re'seɲa] *nf* (*cuenta*) account; (*informe*) report; (*LITERATURA*) review

**reseñar** [rese'ɲar] *vt* to describe; (*LITERATURA*) to review

**reserva** [re'serßa] *nf* reserve; (*reservación*) reservation; **a ~ de que ...** unless ...; **con toda ~** in strictest confidence

**reservado, a** [reser'βaðo, a] *adj* reserved; (*retraído*) cold, distant ♦ *nm* private room

**reservar** [reser'βar] *vt* (*guardar*) to keep; (*habitación, entrada*) to reserve; **~se** *vr* to save o.s.; (*callar*) to keep to o.s.

**resfriado** [resfri'aðo] *nm* cold; **resfriarse** *vr* to cool; (*MED*) to catch (a) cold

**resguardar** [reswar'ðar] *vt* to protect, shield; **~se** *vr*: **~se de** to guard against; **resguardo** *nm* defence; (*vale*) voucher; (*recibo*) receipt, slip

**residencia** [resi'ðenθja] *nf* residence; **~l** *nf* (*urbanización*) housing estate

**residente** [resi'ðente] *adj, nmf* resident

**residir** [resi'ðir] *vi* to reside, live; **~ en** to reside in, lie in

**residuo** [re'siðwo] *nm* residue

**resignación** [resiɣna'θjon] *nf* resignation; **resignarse** *vr*: **resignarse a** *o* **con** to resign o.s. to, be resigned to

**resina** [re'sina] *nf* resin

**resistencia** [resis'tenθja] *nf* (*dureza*) endurance, strength; (*oposición, ELEC*) resistance; **resistente** *adj* strong, hardy; resistant

**resistir** [resis'tir] *vt* (*soportar*) to bear; (*oponerse a*) to resist, oppose; (*aguantar*) to put up with ♦ *vi* to resist; (*aguantar*) to last, endure; **~se** *vr*: **~se a** to refuse to, resist

**resolución** [resolu'θjon] *nf* resolution; (*decisión*) decision; **resoluto, a** *adj* resolute

**resolver** [resol'βer] *vt* to resolve; (*solucionar*) to solve, resolve; (*decidir*) to decide, settle; **~se** *vr* to make up one's mind

**resollar** [reso'ʎar] *vi* to breathe noisily, wheeze

**resonancia** [reso'nanθja] *nf* (*del sonido*) resonance; (*repercusión*) repercussion

**resonar** [reso'nar] *vi* to ring, echo

**resoplar** [reso'plar] *vi* to snort; **resoplido** *nm* heavy breathing

**resorte** [re'sorte] *nm* spring; (*fig*) lever

**respaldar** [respal'dar] *vt* to back (up), support; **~se** *vr* to lean back; **~se con** *o* **en** (*fig*) to take one's stand on; **respaldo** *nm* (*de sillón*) back; (*fig*) support, backing

**respectivo, a** [respek'tiβo, a] *adj* respective; **en lo ~ a** with regard to

**respecto** [res'pekto] *nm*: **al ~** on this matter; **con ~ a, ~ de** with regard to, in relation to

**respetable** [respe'taβle] *adj* respectable

**respetar** [respe'tar] *vt* to respect; **respeto** *nm* respect; (*acatamiento*) deference; **respetos** *nmpl* respects; **respetuoso, a** *adj* respectful

**respingo** [res'pingo] *nm* start, jump

**respiración** [respira'θjon] *nf* breathing; (*MED*) respiration; (*ventilación*) ventilation

**respirar** [respi'rar] *vi* to breathe; **respiratorio, a** *adj* respiratory; **respiro** *nm* breathing; (*fig: descanso*) respite

**resplandecer** [resplande'θer] *vi* to shine; **resplandeciente** *adj* resplendent, shining; **resplandor** *nm* brilliance, brightness; (*de luz, fuego*) blaze

**responder** [respon'der] *vt* to answer ♦ *vi* to answer; (*fig*) to respond; (*pey*) to answer back; **~ de** *o* **por** to answer for; **respondón, ona** *adj* cheeky

**responsabilidad** [responsaβili'ðað] *nf* responsibility

**responsabilizarse** [responsaβili-'θarse] *vr* to make o.s. responsible, take charge

**responsable** [respon'saβle] *adj* responsible

**respuesta** [res'pwesta] *nf* answer, reply

**resquebrajar** [reskeβra'xar] *vt* to crack, split; **~se** *vr* to crack, split

**resquemor** [reske'mor] *nm* resentment

**resquicio** [res'kiθjo] *nm* chink; (*hen-*

*dedura)* crack

**resta** ['resta] *nf (MAT)* remainder

**restablecer** [restaßle'θer] *vt* to re-establish, restore; **~se** *vr* to recover

**restallar** [resta'ʎar] *vi* to crack

**restante** [res'tante] *adj* remaining; **lo ~** the remainder

**restar** [res'tar] *vt (MAT)* to subtract; *(fig)* to take away ♦ *vi* to remain, be left

**restauración** [restaura'θjon] *nf* restoration

**restaurante** [restau'rante] *nm* restaurant

**restaurar** [restau'rar] *vt* to restore

**restitución** [restitu'θjon] *nf* return, restitution

**restituir** [restitu'ir] *vt (devolver)* to return, give back; *(rehabilitar)* to restore

**resto** ['resto] *nm (residuo)* rest, remainder; *(apuesta)* stake; **~s** *nmpl* remains

**restregar** [restre'ɣar] *vt* to scrub, rub

**restricción** [restrik'θjon] *nf* restriction

**restrictivo, a** [restrik'tißo, a] *adj* restrictive

**restringir** [restrin'xir] *vt* to restrict, limit

**resucitar** [resuθi'tar] *vt, vi* to resuscitate, revive

**resuelto, a** [re'swelto, a] *pp de* resolver ♦ *adj* resolute, determined

**resuello** [re'sweʎo] *nm (aliento)* breath; **estar sin ~** to be breathless

**resultado** [resul'taðo] *nm* result; *(conclusión)* outcome; **resultante** *adj* resulting, resultant

**resultar** [resul'tar] *vi (ser)* to be; *(llegar a ser)* to turn out to be; *(salir bien)* to turn out well; *(COM)* to amount to; **~ de** to stem from; **me resulta difícil hacerlo** it's difficult for me to do it

**resumen** [re'sumen] *(pl* **resúmenes)** *nm* summary, résumé; **en ~** in short

**resumir** [resu'mir] *vt* to sum up; *(cortar)* to abridge, cut down; *(con-*

*densar)* to summarize

**resurgir** [resur'xir] *vi (reaparecer)* to reappear

**resurrección** [resurre(k)'θjon] *nf* resurrection

**retablo** [re'taßlo] *nm* altarpiece

**retaguardia** [reta'ɣwarðja] *nf* rearguard

**retahíla** [reta'ila] *nf* series, string

**retal** [re'tal] *nm* remnant

**retar** [re'tar] *vt* to challenge; *(desafiar)* to defy, dare

**retardar** [retar'ðar] *vt (demorar)* to delay; *(hacer más lento)* to slow down; *(retener)* to hold back

**retazo** [re'taθo] *nm* snippet *(BRIT)*, fragment

**retener** [rete'ner] *vt (intereses)* to withhold

**reticente** [reti'θente] *adj (tono)* insinuating; *(postura)* reluctant; **ser ~ a hacer algo** to be reluctant o unwilling to do sth

**retina** [re'tina] *nf* retina

**retintín** [retin'tin] *nm* jangle, jingle

**retirada** [reti'raða] *nf (MIL, refugio)* retreat; *(de dinero)* withdrawal; *(de embajador)* recall; **retirado, a** *adj (lugar)* remote; *(vida)* quiet; *(jubilado)* retired

**retirar** [reti'rar] *vt* to withdraw; *(quitar)* to remove; *(jubilar)* to retire, pension off; **~se** *vr* to retreat, withdraw; *(acostarse)* to retire, go to bed; **retiro** *nm* retreat; retirement; *(pago)* pension

**reto** ['reto] *nm* dare, challenge

**retocar** [reto'kar] *vt (fotografía)* to touch up, retouch

**retoño** [re'toɲo] *nm* sprout, shoot; *(fig)* offspring, child

**retoque** [re'toke] *nm* retouching

**retorcer** [retor'θer] *vt* to twist; *(manos, lavado)* to wring; **~se** *vr* to become twisted; *(mover el cuerpo)* to writhe

**retorcido, a** [retor'θiðo, a] *adj (persona)* devious

**retórica** [re'torika] *nf* rhetoric; *(pey)* affectedness; **retórico, a** *adj* rhetorical

**retornar** [retor'nar] vt to return, give back ♦ vi to return, go/come back; **retorno** nm return

**retortijón** [retorti'xon] nm twist, twisting

**retozar** [reto'θar] vi (juguetear) to frolic, romp; (saltar) to gambol; **retozón, ona** adj playful

**retracción** [retrak'θjon] nf retraction

**retractarse** [retrak'tarse] vr to retract; **me retracto** I take that back

**retraerse** [retra'erse] vr to retreat, withdraw; **retraído, a** adj shy, retiring; **retraimiento** nm retirement; (timidez) shyness

**retransmisión** [retransmi'sjon] nf repeat (broadcast)

**retransmitir** [retransmi'tir] vt (mensaje) to relay; (TV etc) to repeat, transmit; (: en vivo) to broadcast live

**retrasado, a** [retra'saðo, a] adj late; (MED) mentally retarded; (país etc) backward, underdeveloped

**retrasar** [retra'sar] vt (demorar) to postpone, put off; (retardar) to slow down ♦ vi (atrasarse) to be late; (reloj) to be slow; (producción) to fall (away); (quedarse atrás) to lag behind; ~se vr to be late; to be slow; to fall away; to lag behind

**retraso** [re'traso] nm (demora) delay; (lentitud) slowness; (tardanza) lateness; (atraso) backwardness; ~s (FINANZAS) nmpl arrears; **llegar con** ~ to arrive late; ~ **mental** mental deficiency

**retratar** [retra'tar] vt (ARTE) to paint the portrait of; (fotografiar) to photograph; (fig) to depict, describe; ~**se** vr to have one's portrait painted; to have one's photograph taken; **retrato** nm portrait; (fig) likeness; **retrato-robot** nm identikit picture

**retreta** [re'treta] nf retreat

**retrete** [re'trete] nm toilet

**retribución** [retriβu'θjon] nf (recompensa) reward; (pago) pay, payment

**retribuir** [retri'βwir] vt (recompensar) to reward; (pagar) to pay

**retro...** ['retro] prefijo retro...

**retroactivo, a** [retroak'tiβo, a] adj retroactive, retrospective

**retroceder** [retroθe'ðer] vi (echarse atrás) to move back(wards); (fig) to back down

**retroceso** [retro'θeso] nm backward movement; (MED) relapse; (fig) backing down

**retrógrado, a** [re'troɣraðo, a] adj retrograde, retrogressive; (POL) reactionary

**retropropulsión** [retropropul'sjon] nf jet propulsion

**retrospectivo, a** [retrospek'tiβo, a] adj retrospective

**retrovisor** [retroβi'sor] nm (tb: espejo ~) rear-view mirror

**retumbar** [retum'bar] vi to echo, resound

**reuma** ['reuma] nm rheumatism

**reumatismo** [reuma'tismo] nm = reuma

**reunificar** [reunifi'kar] vt to reunify

**reunión** [reu'njon] nf (asamblea) meeting; (fiesta) party

**reunir** [reu'nir] vt (juntar) to reunite, join (together); (recoger) to gather (together); (personas) to get together; (cualidades) to combine; ~**se** vr (personas: en asamblea) to meet, gather

**revalidar** [reβali'ðar] vt (ratificar) to confirm, ratify

**revalorizar** [reβalori'θar] vt to revalue, reassess

**revancha** [re'βantʃa] nf revenge

**revelación** [reβela'θjon] nf revelation

**revelado** [reβe'laðo] nm developing

**revelar** [reβe'lar] vt to reveal; (FOTO) to develop

**reventa** [re'βenta] nf (de entradas: para concierto) touting

**reventar** [reβen'tar] vt to burst, explode

**reventón** [reβen'ton] nm (AUTO) blow-out (BRIT), flat (US)

**reverberación** [reßerßera'θjon] nf reverberation

**reverberar** [reßerße'rar] vi to reverberate

**reverencia** [reße'renθja] nf reverence; **reverenciar** vt to revere

**reverendo, a** [reße'rendo, a] adj reverend

**reverente** [reße'rente] adj reverent

**reversible** [reßer'sißle] adj (prenda) reversible

**reverso** [re'ßerso] nm back, other side; (de moneda) reverse

**revertir** [reßer'tir] vi to revert

**revés** [re'ßes] nm back, wrong side; (fig) reverse, setback; (DEPORTE) backhand; **al ~** the wrong way round; (de arriba abajo) upside down; (ropa) inside out; **volver algo al ~** to turn sth round; (ropa) to turn sth inside out

**revestir** [reßes'tir] vt (poner) to put on; (cubrir) to cover, coat; **~ con o de** to invest with

**revisar** [reßi'sar] vt (examinar) to check; (texto etc) to revise; **revisión** nf revision

**revisor, a** [reßi'sor, a] nm/f inspector; (FERRO) ticket collector

**revista** [re'ßista] nf magazine, review; (TEATRO) revue; (inspección) inspection; **pasar ~ a** to review, inspect

**revivir** [reßi'ßir] vi to revive

**revocación** [reßoka'θjon] nf repeal

**revocar** [reßo'kar] vt to revoke

**revolcarse** [reßol'karse] vr to roll about

**revolotear** [reßolote'ar] vi to flutter

**revoltijo** [reßol'tixo] nm mess, jumble

**revoltoso, a** [reßol'toso, a] adj (travieso) naughty, unruly

**revolución** [reßolu'θjon] nf revolution; **revolucionar** vt to revolutionize; **revolucionario, a** adj, nm/f revolutionary

**revolver** [reßol'ßer] vt (desordenar) to disturb, mess up; (mover) to move about; (POL) to stir up ♦ vi: **~ en** to go through, rummage (about) in; **~se** (volver contra) to turn on o against

**revólver** [re'ßolßer] nm revolver

**revuelo** [re'ßwelo] nm fluttering; (fig) commotion

**revuelta** [re'ßwelta] nf (motín) revolt; (agitación) commotion

**revuelto, a** [re'ßwelto, a] pp de **revolver** ♦ adj (mezclado) mixed-up, in disorder

**revulsivo** [reßul'sißo] nm enema

**rey** [rei] nm king; **Día de R~es** Twelfth Night

**reyerta** [re'jerta] nf quarrel, brawl

**rezagado, a** [reθa'ɣaðo, a] nm/f straggler

**rezagar** [reθa'ɣar] vt (dejar atrás) to leave behind; (retrasar) to delay, postpone

**rezar** [re'θar] vi to pray; **~ con** (fam) to concern, have to do with; **rezo** nm prayer

**rezongar** [reθoŋ'gar] vi to grumble

**rezumar** [reθu'mar] vt to ooze

**ría** ['ria] nf estuary

**riada** [ri'aða] nf flood

**ribera** [ri'ßera] nf (de río) bank; (: área) riverside

**ribete** [ri'ßete] nm (de vestido) border; (fig) addition; **~ar** vt to edge, border

**ricino** [ri'θino] nm: **aceite de ~** castor oil

**rico, a** ['riko, a] adj rich; (adinerado) wealthy, rich; (lujoso) luxurious; (comida) delicious; (niño) lovely, cute ♦ nm/f rich person

**rictus** ['riktus] nm (mueca) sneer, grin

**ridiculez** [riðiku'leθ] nf absurdity

**ridiculizar** [riðikuli'θar] vt to ridicule

**ridículo, a** [ri'ðikulo, a] adj ridiculous; **hacer el ~** to make a fool of o.s.; **poner a uno en ~** to make a fool of sb

**riego** ['rjeɣo] nm (aspersión) watering; (irrigación) irrigation

**riel** [rjel] nm rail

**rienda** ['rjenda] nf rein; **dar ~ suel-**

ta a to give free rein to

**riesgo** ['rjesɣo] *nm* risk; **correr el ~ de** to run the risk of

**rifa** ['rifa] *nf* (*lotería*) raffle; **rifar** *vt* to raffle

**rifle** ['rifle] *nm* rifle

**rigidez** [rixi'ðeθ] *nf* rigidity, stiffness; (*fig*) strictness; **rígido, a** *adj* rigid, stiff; strict, inflexible

**rigor** [ri'vor] *nm* strictness, rigour; (*inclemencia*) harshness; **de ~ de** rigueur, essential; **riguroso, a** *adj* rigorous; harsh; (*severo*) severe

**rimar** [ri'mar] *vi* to rhyme

**rimbombante** [rimbom'bante] *adj* (*fig*) pompous

**rímel** ['rimel] *nm* mascara

**rímmel** ['rimel] *nm* = **rímel**

**rincón** [rin'kon] *nm* corner (*inside*)

**rinoceronte** [rinoθe'ronte] *nm* rhinoceros

**riña** ['riɲa] *nf* (*disputa*) argument; (*pelea*) brawl

**riñón** [ri'ɲon] *nm* kidney; **tener riñones** to have guts

**río** *etc* ['rio] *vb ver* **reír** ♦ *nm* river; (*fig*) torrent, stream; **~ abajo/arriba** downstream/upstream; **~ de la Plata** River Plate

**rioja** [ri'oxa] *nm* (*vino*) rioja (wine)

**rioplatense** [riopla'tense] *adj* **de o** from the River Plate region

**riqueza** [ri'keθa] *nf* wealth, riches *pl*; (*cualidad*) richness

**risa** ['risa] *nf* laughter; (*una ~*) laugh; **¡qué ~!** what a laugh!

**risco** ['risko] *nm* crag, cliff

**risible** [ri'sißle] *adj* ludicrous, laughable

**risotada** [riso'taða] *nf* guffaw, loud laugh

**ristra** ['ristra] *nf* string

**risueño, a** [ri'sweɲo, a] *adj* (*sonriente*) smiling; (*contento*) cheerful

**ritmo** ['ritmo] *nm* rhythm; **a ~ lento** slowly; **trabajar a ~ lento** to go slow

**rito** ['rito] *nm* rite

**ritual** [ri'twal] *adj, nm* ritual

**rival** [ri'ßal] *adj, nm/f* rival; **~idad** *nf*

rivalry; **~izar** *vi*: **~izar con** to rival, vie with

**rizado, a** [ri'θaðo, a] *adj* curly ♦ *nm* curls *pl*

**rizar** [ri'θar] *vt* to curl; **~se** *vr* (*pelo*) to curl; (*agua*) to ripple; **rizo** *nm* curl; ripple

**RNE** *nf abr* = **Radio Nacional de España**

**robar** [ro'ßar] *vt* to rob; (*objeto*) to steal; (*casa etc*) to break into; (*NAIPES*) to draw

**roble** ['roßle] *nm* oak; **~dal** *nm* = **robledo**; **~do** *nm* oakwood

**robo** ['roßo] *nm* robbery, theft

**robot** [ro'ßot] *nm* robot; **~ (de cocina)** food processor

**robustecer** [roßuste'θer] *vt* to strengthen

**robusto, a** [ro'ßusto, a] *adj* robust, strong

**roca** ['roka] *nf* rock

**roce** ['roθe] *nm* (*caricia*) brush; (*TEC*) friction; (*en la piel*) graze; **tener ~ con** to be in close contact with

**rociar** [ro'θjar] *vt* to spray

**rocín** [ro'θin] *nm* nag, hack

**rocío** [ro'θio] *nm* dew

**rocoso, a** [ro'koso, a] *adj* rocky

**rodado, a** [ro'ðaðo, a] *adj* (*con ruedas*) wheeled

**rodaja** [ro'ðaxa] *nf* (*raja*) slice

**rodaje** [ro'ðaxe] *nm* (*CINE*) shooting, filming; (*AUTO*): **en ~** running in

**rodar** [ro'ðar] *vt* (*vehículo*) to wheel (along); (*escalera*) to roll down; (*viajar por*) to travel (over) ♦ *vi* to roll; (*coche*) to go, run; (*CINE*) to shoot, film

**rodear** [roðe'ar] *vt* to surround ♦ *vi* to go round; **~se** *vr*: **se de amigos** to surround o.s. with friends

**rodeo** [ro'ðeo] *nm* (*ruta indirecta*) detour; (*evasión*) evasion; (*AM*) rodeo; **hablar sin ~s** to come to the point, speak plainly

**rodilla** [ro'ðiʎa] *nf* knee; **de ~s** kneeling; **ponerse de ~s** to kneel (down)

**rodillo** [ro'ðiʎo] nm roller; (CULIN) rolling-pin

**roedor, a** [roe'ðor, a] adj gnawing ♦ nm rodent

**roer** [ro'er] vt (masticar) to gnaw; (corroer, fig) to corrode

**rogar** [ro'var] vt, vi (pedir) to ask for; (suplicar) to beg, plead; se ruega no fumar please do not smoke

**rojizo, a** [ro'xiθo, a] adj reddish

**rojo, a** ['roxo, a] adj, nm red; al ~ vivo red-hot

**rol** [rol] nm list, roll; (AM: papel) role

**rollizo, a** [ro'ʎiθo, a] adj (objeto) cylindrical; (persona) plump

**rollo** ['roʎo] nm roll; (de cuerda) coil; (madera) log; (fam) bore; ¡qué ~! what a carry-on!

**ROM** [rom] nf abr (= memoria de sólo lectura) ROM

**Roma** ['roma] n Rome

**romance** [ro'manθe] nm (idioma castellano) Romance language; (LITERATURA) ballad; hablar en ~ to speak plainly

**romanticismo** [romanti'θismo] nm romanticism

**romántico, a** [ro'mantiko, a] adj romantic

**rombo** ['rombo] nm (GEOM) rhombus

**romería** [rome'ria] nf (REL) pilgrimage; (excursión) trip, outing

**romero, a** [ro'mero, a] nm/f pilgrim ♦ nm rosemary

**romo, a** ['romo, a] adj blunt; (fig) dull

**rompecabezas** [rompeka'βeθas] nm inv riddle, puzzle; (juego) jigsaw (puzzle)

**rompeolas** [rompe'olas] nm inv breakwater

**romper** [rom'per] vt to break; (hacer pedazos) to smash; (papel, tela etc) to tear, rip ♦ vi (olas) to break; (sol, diente) to break through; ~ un contrato to break a contract; ~ a (empezar a) to start (suddenly) to; ~ a llorar to burst into tears; ~

con uno to fall out with sb

**rompimiento** [rompi'mjento] nm (acto) breaking; (fig) break; (quiebra) crack

**ron** [ron] nm rum

**roncar** [ron'kar] vi to snore

**ronco, a** ['ronko, a] adj (afónico) hoarse; (áspero) raucous

**ronda** ['ronda] nf (gen) round; (patrulla) patrol; **rondar** vt to patrol ♦ vi to patrol; (fig) to prowl round

**ronquido** [ron'kiðo] nm snore, snoring

**ronronear** [ronrone'ar] vi to purr; **ronroneo** nm purr

**roña** ['roɲa] nf (VETERINARIA) mange; (mugre) dirt, grime; (óxido) rust

**roñoso, a** [ro'ɲoso, a] adj (mugriento) filthy; (tacaño) mean

**ropa** ['ropa] nf clothes pl, clothing; ~ blanca linen; ~ de cama bed linen; ~ interior underwear; ~ para lavar washing; ~je nm gown, robes pl

**ropero** [ro'pero] nm linen cupboard; (guardarropa) wardrobe

**rosa** ['rosa] adj pink ♦ nf rose; (ANAT) red birthmark; ~ de los vientos the compass

**rosado, a** [ro'saðo, a] adj pink ♦ nm rosé

**rosal** [ro'sal] nm rosebush

**rosario** [ro'sarjo] nm (REL) rosary; rezar el ~ to say the rosary

**rosca** ['roska] nf (de tornillo) thread; (de humo) coil, spiral; (pan, postre) ring-shaped roll/pastry

**rosetón** [rose'ton] nm rosette; (ARQ) rose window

**rosquilla** [ros'kiʎa] nf doughnut-shaped fritter

**rostro** ['rostro] nm (cara) face

**rotación** [rota'θjon] nf rotation; ~ de cultivos crop rotation

**rotativo, a** [rota'tiβo, a] adj rotary

**roto, a** ['roto, a] pp de **romper** ♦ adj broken

**rótula** ['rotula] nf kneecap; (TEC) ball-and-socket joint

**rotulador** [rotula'ðor] nm felt-tip pen

**rotular** [rotu'lar] vt (carta, documento) to head, entitle; (objeto) to label; **rótulo** nm heading, title; label; (letrero) sign

**rotundamente** [rotunda'mente] adv (negar) flatly; (responder, afirmar) emphatically; **rotundo, a** adj round; (enfático) emphatic

**rotura** [ro'tura] nf (rompimiento) breaking; (MED) fracture

**roturar** [rotu'rar] vt to plough

**rozadura** [roθa'ðura] nf abrasion, graze

**rozar** [ro'θar] vt (frotar) to rub; (arañar) to scratch; (tocar ligeramente) to shave, touch lightly; **~se** vr to rub (together); **~se con** (fam) to rub shoulders with

**rte.** abr (= remite, remitente) sender

**RTVE** nf abr = Radiotelevisión Española

**rubí** [ru'βi] nm ruby; (de reloj) jewel

**rubio, a** ['ruβjo, a] adj fair-haired, blond(e) ♦ nm/f blond/blonde; **tabaco ~** Virginia tobacco

**rubor** [ru'βor] nm (sonrojo) blush; (timidez) bashfulness; **~izarse** vr to blush

**rúbrica** ['ruβrika] nf (título) title, heading; (de la firma) flourish; **rubricar** vt (firmar) to sign with a flourish; (concluir) to sign and seal

**rudeza** [ru'ðeθa] nf (tosquedad) coarseness; (sencillez) simplicity

**rudimentario, a** [ruðimen'tarjo, a] adj (conocimientos, noción) rudimentary; **rudimento** nm rudiment

**rudo, a** ['ruðo, a] adj (sin pulir) unpolished; (grosero) coarse; (violento) violent; (sencillo) simple

**rueda** ['rweða] nf wheel; (círculo) ring, circle; (rodaja) slice, round; **~ delantera/trasera/de repuesto** front/back/spare wheel; **~ de prensa** press conference

**ruedo** ['rweðo] nm (contorno) edge, border; (de vestido) hem; (círculo) circle; (TAUR) arena, bullring

**ruego** etc ['rweɣo] vb ver **rogar** ♦

nm request

**rufián** [ru'fjan] nm scoundrel

**rugby** ['ruɣβi] nm rugby

**rugido** [ru'xiðo] nm roar

**rugir** [ru'xir] vi to roar

**rugoso, a** [ru'ɣoso, a] adj (arrugado) wrinkled; (áspero) rough; (desigual) ridged

**ruido** ['rwiðo] nm noise; (sonido) sound; (alboroto) racket, row; (escándalo) commotion, rumpus; **~so, a** adj noisy, loud; (fig) sensational

**ruin** [rwin] adj contemptible, mean

**ruina** ['rwina] nf ruin; (colapso) collapse; (de persona) ruin, downfall

**ruindad** [rwin'dað] nf lowness, meanness; (acto) low o mean act

**ruinoso, a** [rwi'noso, a] adj ruinous; (destartalado) dilapidated, tumbledown; (COM) disastrous

**ruiseñor** [rwise'ɲor] nm nightingale

**ruleta** [ru'leta] nf roulette

**rulo** ['rulo] nm (para el pelo) curler

**Rumania** [ru'manja] nf Rumania

**rumba** ['rumba] nf rumba

**rumbo** ['rumbo] nm (ruta) route, direction; (ángulo de dirección) bearing; (fig) course of events: **ir con ~ a** to be heading for

**rumboso, a** [rum'boso, a] adj (generoso) generous

**rumiante** [ru'mjante] nm ruminant

**rumiar** [ru'mjar] vt to chew; (fig) to chew over ♦ vi to chew the cud

**rumor** [ru'mor] nm (ruido sordo) low sound; (murmuración) murmur, buzz

**rumorearse** vr: **se rumorea que** it is rumoured that

**runrún** [run'run] nm (voces) murmur, sound of voices; (fig) rumour

**rupestre** [ru'pestre] adj rock cpd

**ruptura** [rup'tura] nf rupture

**rural** [ru'ral] adj rural

**Rusia** ['rusja] nf Russia; **ruso, a** adj, nm/f Russian

**rústica** ['rustika] nf: **libro en ~** paperback (book); ver tb **rústico**

**rústico, a** ['rustiko, a] adj rustic; (ordinario) coarse, uncouth ♦ nm/f yokel

**ruta** ['ruta] nf route
**rutina** [ru'tina] nf routine; **~rio, a** adj routine

# S

**S** abr (= santo, a) St; (= sur) S
**s.** abr (= siglo) C.; (= siguiente) foll
**S.A.** abr (= Sociedad Anónima) Ltd. (BRIT), Inc. (US)
**sábado** ['saβaðo] nm Saturday
**sábana** ['saβana] nf sheet
**sabandija** [saβan'dixa] nf bug, insect
**sabañón** [saβa'ɲon] nm chilblain
**saber** [sa'βer] vt to know; (llegar a conocer) to find out, learn; (tener capacidad de) to know how to ♦ vi: ~ **a** to taste of, taste like ♦ nm knowledge, learning; **a ~** namely; ¿**sabes conducir/nadar?** can you drive/ swim?; ¿**sabes francés?** do you speak French?; **~ de memoria** to know by heart; **hacer ~ algo a uno** to inform sb of sth, let sb know sth
**sabiduría** [saβiðu'ria] nf (conocimientos) wisdom; (instrucción) learning
**sabiendas** [sa'βjendas]: **a ~** adv knowingly
**sabio, a** [sa'βjo,a] adj (docto) learned; (prudente) wise, sensible
**sabor** [sa'βor] nm taste, flavour; **~ear** vt to taste, savour; (fig) to relish
**sabotaje** [saβo'taxe] nm sabotage
**saboteador, a** [saβotea'ðor, a] nm/f saboteur
**sabotear** [saβote'ar] vt to sabotage
**sabré** etc vb ver **saber**
**sabroso, a** [sa'βroso, a] adj tasty; (fig: fam) racy, salty
**sacacorchos** [saka'kortʃos] nm inv corkscrew
**sacapuntas** [saka'puntas] nm inv pencil sharpener
**sacar** [sa'kar] vt to take out; (fig: extraer) to get (out); (quitar) to remove, get out; (hacer salir) to bring out; (conclusión) to draw; (novela

etc) to publish, bring out; (ropa) to take off; (obra) to make; (premio) to receive; (entradas) to get; (TENIS) to serve; **~ adelante** (niño) to bring up; (negocio) to carry on, go on with; **~ a uno a bailar** to get sb up to dance; **~ una foto** to take a photo; **~ la lengua** to stick out one's tongue; **~ buenas/malas notas** to get good/bad marks
**sacarina** [saka'rina] nf saccharin(e)
**sacerdote** [saθer'ðote] nm priest
**saciar** [sa'θjar] vt (hambre, sed) to satisfy; **~se** vr (de comida) to get full up; **comer hasta ~se** to eat one's fill
**saco** ['sako] nm bag; (grande) sack; (su contenido) bagful; (AM) jacket; **~ de dormir** sleeping bag
**sacramento** [sakra'mento] nm sacrament
**sacrificar** [sakrifi'kar] vt to sacrifice; **sacrificio** nm sacrifice
**sacrilegio** [sakri'lexjo] nm sacrilege; **sacrílego, a** adj sacrilegious
**sacristía** [sakris'tia] nf sacristy
**sacro, a** ['sakro, a] adj sacred
**sacudida** [saku'ðiða] nf (agitación) shake, shaking; (sacudimiento) jolt, bump; **~ eléctrica** electric shock
**sacudir** [saku'ðir] vt to shake; (golpear) to hit
**sádico, a** ['saðiko, a] adj sadistic ♦ nm/f sadist; **sadismo** nm sadism
**saeta** [sa'eta] nf (flecha) arrow
**sagacidad** [saɣaθi'ðað] nf shrewdness, cleverness; **sagaz** adj shrewd, clever
**sagitario** [saxi'tarjo] nm Sagittarius
**sagrado, a** [sa'ɣraðo, a] adj sacred, holy
**Sáhara** ['saara] nm: **el ~** the Sahara (desert)
**sal** [sal] vb ver **salir** ♦ nf salt
**sala** ['sala] nf (cuarto grande) large room; (~ de estar) living room; (TEATRO) house, auditorium; (de hospital) ward; **~ de apelación** court; **~ de espera** waiting room; **~ de estar** living room; **~ de fiestas**

dance hall

**salado, a** [sa'laðo, a] adj salty; (fig)
witty, amusing; **agua salada** salt
water

**salar** [sa'lar] vt to salt, add salt to

**salarial** [sala'rjal] adj (aumento, revisión) wage cpd, salary cpd

**salario** [sa'larjo] nm wage, pay

**salchicha** [sal'tʃitʃa] nf (pork) sausage; **salchichón** nm (salami-type)
sausage

**saldar** [sal'dar] vt to pay; (vender) to
sell off; (fig) to settle, resolve; **saldo**
nm (pago) settlement; (de una cuenta) balance; (lo restante) remnant(s)
(pl), remainder; **~s** nmpl (en tienda) sale

**saldré** etc vb ver **salir**

**salero** [sa'lero] nm salt cellar

**salgo** etc vb ver **salir**

**salida** [sa'liða] nf (puerta etc) exit,
way out; (acto) leaving, going out;
(de tren, AVIAT) departure; (TEC)
output, production; (fig) way out;
(COM) opening; (GEO, válvula) outlet; (de gas) leak; **calle sin ~** cul-
de-sac; **~ de incendios** fire escape

**saliente** [sa'ljente] adj (ARQ) projecting; (sol) rising; (fig) outstanding

---

*PALABRA CLAVE*

**salir** [sa'lir] vi **1** (partir: tb: **~ de**) to
leave; **Juan ha salido** Juan is out;
**salió de la cocina** he came out of
the kitchen

**2** (aparecer) to appear; (disco, libro)
to come out; **anoche salió en la
tele** she appeared o was on TV last
night; **salió en todos los periódicos**
it was in all the papers

**3** (resultar): **la muchacha nos salió muy trabajadora** the girl turned
out to be a very hard worker; **la
comida te ha salido deliciosa** the
food was delicious; **sale muy caro**
it's very expensive

**4**: **~le a uno algo**: **la entrevista
que hice me salió bien/mal** the interview I did went o turned out well/
badly

**5**: **~ adelante**: **no sé como haré
para ~ adelante** I don't know how
I'll get by

♦ **~se** vr (líquido) to spill; (animal)
to escape

**saliva** [sa'liβa] nf saliva

**salmo** ['salmo] nm psalm

**salmón** [sal'mon] nm salmon

**salmuera** [sal'mwera] nf pickle,
brine

**salón** [sa'lon] nm (de casa) living
room, lounge; (muebles) lounge
suite; (de baile) beauty parlour; **~
de baile** dance hall

**salpicadero** [salpika'ðero] nm
(AUTO) dashboard

**salpicar** [salpi'kar] vt (rociar) to
sprinkle, spatter; (esparcir) to scatter

**salsa** ['salsa] nf sauce; (con carne
asada) gravy; (fig) spice

**saltamontes** [salta'montes] nm inv
grasshopper

**saltar** [sal'tar] vt to jump (over), leap
(over); (dejar de lado) to skip, miss
♦ vi to jump, leap; (pelota) to
bounce; (al aire) to fly up; (quebrarse) to break; (al agua) to dive;
(fig) to explode, blow up

**salto** ['salto] nm jump, leap; (al
agua) dive; **~ de agua** waterfall; **~
de altura** high jump

**saltón, ona** [sal'ton, ona] adj (ojos)
bulging, popping; (dientes) protrud-
ing

**salud** [sa'luð] nf health; **¡(a su) ~!**
cheers!, good health!; **~able** adj (de
buena ~) healthy; (provechoso)
good, beneficial

**saludar** [salu'ðar] vt to greet; (MIL)
to salute; **saludo** nm greeting; **saludos** (en carta) "best wishes", "regards"

**salva** ['salβa] nf: **~ de aplausos** ovation

**salvación** [salβa'θjon] nf salvation;
(rescate) rescue

**salvado** [sal'βaðo] nm bran

**salvaguardar** [salβaɣwar'ðar] vt to

safeguard

**salvajada** [salβa'xaða] nf (una ~) atrocity

**salvaje** [sal'βaxe] adj wild; (tribu) savage; **salvajismo** nm savagery

**salvamento** [salβa'mento] nm rescue

**salvar** [sal'βar] vt (rescatar) to save, rescue; (resolver) to overcome, resolve; (cubrir distancias) to cover, travel; (hacer excepción) to except, exclude; (un barco) to salvage

**salvavidas** [salβa'βiðas] adj inv: **bote/chaleco/cinturón ~** lifeboat/life jacket/life belt

**salvo, a** [salβo, a] adj safe ♦ adv except (for), save; **a ~** out of danger; **~ que** unless; **~conducto** nm safe-conduct

**san** [san] adj saint; **S~ Juan** St. John

**sanar** [sa'nar] vt (herida) to heal; (persona) to cure ♦ vi (persona) to get well, recover; (herida) to heal

**sanatorio** [sana'torjo] nm sanatorium

**sanción** [san'θjon] nf sanction; **sancionar** vt to sanction

**sandalia** [san'dalja] nf sandal

**sandez** [san'deθ] nf foolishness

**sandía** [san'dia] nf watermelon

**sandwich** [sandwitʃ] (pl ~s, ~es) nm sandwich

**saneamiento** [sanea'mjento] nm sanitation

**sanear** [sane'ar] vt (terreno) to drain

**sangrar** [san'grar] vt, vi to bleed; **sangre** nf blood

**sangría** [san'gria] nf sangria, sweetened drink of red wine with fruit

**sangriento, a** [san'grjento, a] adj bloody

**sanguijuela** [sangi'xwela] nf (ZOOL, fig) leech

**sanguinario, a** [sangi'narjo, a] adj bloodthirsty

**sanguíneo, a** [san'gineo, a] adj blood cpd

**sanidad** [sani'ðað] nf sanitation; (calidad de sano) health, healthiness; ~

**pública** public health

**sanitario, a** [sani'tarjo, a] adj sanitary; (de la salud) health; **~s** nmpl toilets (BRIT), washroom (US)

**sano, a** ['sano, a] adj healthy; (sin daños) sound; (comida) wholesome; (entero) whole, intact; **~ y salvo** safe and sound

**Santiago** [san'tjaɣo] nm: **~ (de Chile)** Santiago

**santiamén** [santja'men] nm: **en un ~** in no time at all

**santidad** [santi'ðað] nf holiness, sanctity

**santiguarse** [santi'ɣwarse] vr to make the sign of the cross

**santo, a** ['santo, a] adj holy; (fig) wonderful, miraculous ♦ nm/f saint ♦ nm saint's day; **~ y seña** password

**santuario** [san'twarjo] nm sanctuary, shrine

**saña** ['saɲa] nf rage, fury

**sapo** ['sapo] nm toad

**saque** ['sake] nm (TENIS) service, serve; (FUTBOL) throw-in; **~ de esquina** corner (kick)

**saquear** [sake'ar] vt (MIL) to sack; (robar) to loot, plunder; (fig) to ransack; **saqueo** nm sacking; looting, plundering; ransacking

**sarampión** [saram'pjon] nm measles sg

**sarcasmo** [sar'kasmo] nm sarcasm; **sarcástico, a** adj sarcastic

**sardina** [sar'ðina] nf sardine

**sargento** [sar'xento] nm sergeant

**sarmiento** [sar'mjento] nm (BOT) vine shoot

**sarna** ['sarna] nf itch; (MED) scabies

**sarpullido** [sarpu'ʎiðo] nm (MED) rash

**sarro** ['sarro] nm (en dientes) tartar, plaque

**sartén** [sar'ten] nf frying pan

**sastre** ['sastre] nm tailor; **~ría** (f) (arte) tailoring; (tienda) tailor's (shop)

**Satanás** [sata'nas] nm Satan

**satélite** [sa'telite] nm satellite

**sátira** ['satira] nf satire

**satisfacción** [satisfak'θjon] *nf* satisfaction

**satisfacer** [satisfa'θer] *vt* to satisfy; (*gastos*) to meet; (*pérdida*) to make good; **~se** *vr* to satisfy o.s., to be satisfied; (*vengarse*) to take revenge; **satisfecho, a** *adj* satisfied; (*contento*) content(ed), happy; (*tb: satisfecho de sí mismo*) self-satisfied, smug

**saturar** [satu'rar] *vt* to saturate

**sauce** ['sauθe] *nm* willow; **~ llorón** weeping willow

**sauna** ['sauna] *nf* sauna

**savia** ['saβja] *nf* sap

**saxofón** [sakso'fon] *nm* saxophone

**sazonar** [saθo'nar] *vt* to ripen; (*CULIN*) to flavour, season

---

*PALABRA CLAVE*

**se** [se] *pron* **1** (*reflexivo: sg: m*) himself; (: *f*) herself; (: *pl*) themselves; (: *cosa*) itself; (: *de Vd*) yourself; (: *de Vds*) yourselves; **~ está preparando** she's preparing herself; *para usos léxicos del pron ver el vb en cuestión, p.ej.* **arrepentirse**

**2** (*con complemento indirecto*) to him; to her; to them; to it; to you; a usted **~ lo dije ayer** I told you yesterday; **~ compró un sombrero** he bought himself a hat; **~ rompió la pierna** he broke his leg

**3** (*uso recíproco*) each other, one another; **~ miraron (el uno al otro)** they looked at each other *o* one another

**4** (*en oraciones pasivas*): **se han vendido muchos libros** a lot of books have been sold

**5** (*impers*): **~ dice que** people say that, it is said that; **allí ~ come muy bien** the food there is very good, you can eat very well there

---

**SE** *abr* (= *sudeste*) SE

**sé** *vb ver* **saber**; **ser**

**sea** *etc vb ver* **ser**

**sebo** ['seβo] *nm* fat, grease

**secador** [seka'ðor] *nm*: **~ de pelo** hair-dryer

**secadora** [seka'ðora] *nf* (*ELEC*) tumble dryer

**secar** [se'kar] *vt* to dry; **~se** *vr* to dry (off); (*río, planta*) to dry up

**sección** [sek'θjon] *nf* section

**seco, a** ['seko, a] *adj* dry; (*carácter*) cold; (*respuesta*) sharp, curt; **habrá pan a secas** there will be just bread; **decir algo a secas** to say sth curtly; **parar en ~** to stop dead

**secretaría** [sekreta'ria] *nf* secretariat

**secretario, a** [sekre'tarjo, a] *nm/f* secretary

**secreto, a** [se'kreto, a] *adj* secret; (*persona*) secretive ♦ *nm* secret; (*calidad*) secrecy

**secta** ['sekta] *nf* sect; **~rio, a** *adj* sectarian

**sector** [sek'tor] *nm* sector

**secuela** [se'kwela] *nf* consequence

**secuencia** [se'kwenθja] *nf* sequence

**secuestrar** [sekwes'trar] *vt* to kidnap; (*bienes*) to seize, confiscate; **secuestro** *nm* kidnapping; seizure, confiscation

**secular** [seku'lar] *adj* secular

**secundar** [sekun'dar] *vt* to second, support

**secundario, a** [sekun'darjo, a] *adj* secondary

**sed** [seð] *nf* thirst; **tener ~** to be thirsty

**seda** ['seða] *nf* silk

**sedal** [se'ðal] *nm* fishing line

**sedante** [se'ðante] *nm* sedative

**sede** ['seðe] *nf* (*de gobierno*) seat; (*de compañía*) headquarters *pl*; **Santa S~** Holy See

**sedentario, a** [seðen'tarjo, a] *adj* sedentary

**sediento, a** [se'ðjento, a] *adj* thirsty

**sedimento** [seði'mento] *nm* sediment

**sedoso, a** [se'ðoso, a] *adj* silky, silken

**seducción** [seðuk'θjon] *nf* seduction

**seducir** [seðu'θir] *vt* to seduce; (*sobornar*) to bribe; (*cautivar*) to charm, fascinate; (*atraer*) to attract;

**seductor, a** adj seductive; charming, fascinating; attractive; (engañoso) deceptive, misleading ♦ nm/f seducer

**segar** [se'ɣar] vt (mies) to reap, cut; (hierba) to mow, cut

**seglar** [se'ɣlar] adj secular, lay

**segregación** [seɣreɣa'θjon] nf segregation. ~ **racial** racial segregation

**segregar** [seɣre'ɣar] vt to segregate, separate

**seguida, a** [se'ɣiða] nf: **en** ~ at once, right away

**seguido, a** [se'ɣiðo, a] adj (continuo) continuous, unbroken; (recto) straight ♦ adv (directo) straight (on); (después) after; (AM: a menudo) often; ~**s** consecutive, successive; **5 días** ~**s** 5 days running, 5 days in a row

**seguimiento** [seɣi'mjento] nm chase, pursuit; (continuación) continuation

**seguir** [se'ɣir] vt to follow; (venir después) to follow on, come after; (proseguir) to continue; (perseguir) to chase, pursue ♦ vi (gen) to follow; (continuar) to continue, carry o go on; ~**se** vr to follow; **sigo sin comprender** I still don't understand; **sigue lloviendo** it's still raining

**según** [se'ɣun] prep according to ♦ adv: ¿**irás?** - ~ are you going? - it all depends ♦ conj as; ~ **caminamos** while we walk

**segunda** [se'ɣunda] nf double meaning; (tb: ~ **clase**) second class; (tb: ~ **marcha**) second (gear)

**segundo, a** [se'ɣundo, a] adj second ♦ nm second; **de segunda mano** second hand; **segunda enseñanza** secondary education

**seguramente** [seɣura'mente] adv surely; (con certeza) for sure, with certainty

**seguridad** [seɣuri'ðað] nf safety; (del orden, de casa etc) security; (certidumbre) certainty; (confianza) confidence; (estabilidad) stability; ~ **social** social security

**seguro, a** [se'ɣuro, a] adj (cierto)

sure, certain; (fiel) trustworthy; (libre del peligro) safe; (bien defendido, firme) secure ♦ adv for sure, certainly ♦ nm (COM) insurance; ~ **contra terceros/a todo riesgo** third party/comprehensive insurance; ~**s sociales** social security

**seis** [seis] num six

**seísmo** [se'ismo] nm tremor, earthquake

**selección** [selek'θjon] nf selection; **seleccionar** vt to pick, choose, select

**selectividad** [selektiβi'ðað] (ESP) nf university entrance examination

**selecto, a** [se'lekto, a] adj select, choice; (escogido) selected

**selva** [ˈselβa] nf (bosque) forest, woods pl; (jungla) jungle

**sellar** [se'ʎar] vt (documento oficial) to seal; (pasaporte, visado) to stamp

**sello** [ˈseʎo] nm stamp; (precinto) seal

**semáforo** [se'maforo] nm (AUTO) traffic lights pl; (FERRO) signal

**semana** [se'mana] nf week; **entre** ~ during the week; **S~ Santa** Holy Week; **semanal** adj weekly

**semblante** [sem'blante] nm face; (fig) look

**sembrar** [sem'brar] vt to sow; (objetos) to sprinkle, scatter about; (noticias etc) to spread

**semejante** [seme'xante] adj (parecido) similar ♦ nm fellow man, fellow creature; ~**s** alike, similar; **nunca hizo cosa** ~ he never did any such thing; **semejanza** nf similarity, resemblance

**semejar** [seme'xar] vi to seem like, resemble; ~**se** vr to look alike, be similar

**semen** [ˈsemen] nm semen; ~**tal** nm stud

**semestral** [semes'tral] adj halfyearly, bi-annual

**semicírculo** [semi'θirkulo] nm semicircle

**semifinal** [semifi'nal] nf semifinal

**semilla** [se'miʎa] nf seed

**seminario** [semi'narjo] nm (REL)

seminary; (ESCOL) seminar

**sémola** ['semola] nf semolina

**sempiterno, a** [sempi'terno, a] adj everlasting

**Sena** ['sena] nm: el ~ the (river) Seine

**senado** [se'naðo] nm senate; **senador, a** nm/f senator

**sencillez** [senθi'ceθ] nf simplicity; (de persona) naturalness; **sencillo, a** adj simple; natural, unaffected

**senda** ['senda] nf path, track

**sendero** [sen'dero] nm path, track

**sendos, as** ['sendos, as] adj pl: les dio ~ golpes he hit both of them

**senil** [se'nil] adj senile

**seno** ['seno] nm (ANAT) bosom, bust; (fig) bosom; ~s breasts

**sensación** [sensa'θjon] nf sensation; (sentido) sense; (sentimiento) feeling; **sensacional** adj sensational

**sensato, a** [sen'sato, a] adj sensible

**sensible** [sen'sible] adj sensitive; (apreciable) perceptible, appreciable; (pérdida) considerable; ~**ro, a** adj sentimental

**sensitivo, a** [sensi'tiβo, a] adj sense cpd

**sensorial** [senso'rjal] adj sensory

**sensual** [sen'swal] adj sensual

**sentada** [sen'taða] nf sitting; (protesta) sit-in

**sentado, a** [sen'taðo, a] adj (establecido) settled; (carácter) sensible; **estar** ~ to sit, be sitting (down); **dar por** ~ to take for granted, assume

**sentar** [sen'tar] vt to sit, seat; (fig) to establish ♦ vi (vestido) to suit; (alimento): **bien/mal a** to agree/disagree with; ~**se** vr (persona) to sit, sit down; (el tiempo) to settle (down); (los depósitos) to settle

**sentencia** [sen'tenθja] nf (máxima) maxim, saying; (JUR) sentence; **sentenciar** vt to sentence

**sentido, a** [sen'tiðo, a] adj (pérdida) regrettable; (carácter) sensitive ♦ nm sense; (sentimiento) feeling; (significado) sense, meaning; (dirección) direction; **mi más** ~ **pésame** my deepest sympathy; ~ **del humor** sense of humour; ~ **único** one-way (street); **tener** ~ to make sense

**sentimental** [sentimen'tal] adj sentimental; **vida** ~ love life

**sentimiento** [senti'mjento] nm (emoción) feeling, emotion; (sentido) sense; (pesar) regret, sorrow

**sentir** [sen'tir] vt to feel; (percibir) to perceive, sense; (lamentar) to regret, be sorry for ♦ vi (tener la sensación) to feel; (lamentarse) to feel sorry ♦ nm opinion, judgement; ~**se bien/mal** to feel well/ill; **lo siento** I'm sorry

**seña** ['sena] nf sign; (MIL) password; ~**s** nfpl (dirección) address sg; ~**s personales** personal description sg

**señal** [se'nal] nf sign; (síntoma) symptom; (FERRO, TELEC) signal; (marca) mark; (COM) deposit; **en** ~ **de** as a token of, as a sign of; ~**ar** vt to mark; (indicar) to point out, indicate; (fijar) to fix, settle

**señor** [se'nor] nm (hombre) man; (caballero) gentleman; (dueño) owner, master; (trato: antes de nombre propio) Mr; (: hablando directamente) sir; **muy** ~ **mío** Dear Sir; **el** ~ **alcalde/presidente** the mayor/president

**señora** [se'nora] nf (dama) lady; (trato: antes de nombre propio) Mrs; (: hablando directamente) madam; (esposa) wife; **Nuestra S~** Our Lady

**señorita** [seno'rita] nf (con nombre y/o apellido) Miss; (mujer joven) young lady

**señorito** [seno'rito] nm young gentleman; (pey) rich kid

**señuelo** [se'nwelo] nm decoy

**sepa** etc vb ver **saber**

**separación** [separa'θjon] nf separation; (división) division; (distancia) gap

**separar** [sepa'rar] vt to separate; (dividir) to divide; ~**se** vr (parte) to come away; (*partes*) to come apart; (*persona*) to leave, go away; (*matrimonio*) to separate; **separatismo** *nm* separatism

**sepia** ['sepja] *nf* cuttlefish

**septiembre** [sep'tjembre] *nm* September

**séptimo, a** ['septimo, a] *adj, nm* seventh

**sepulcral** [sepul'kral] *adj* (*fig: silencio, atmósfera*) gloomy; **sepulcro** *nm* tomb, grave

**sepultar** [sepul'tar] *vt* to bury; **sepultura** *nf* (*acto*) burial; (*tumba*) grave, tomb

**sequedad** [seke'ðað] *nf* dryness; (*fig*) brusqueness, curtness

**sequía** [se'kia] *nf* drought

**séquito** ['sekito] *nm* (*de rey etc*) retinue; (*POL*) followers *pl*

---

PALABRA CLAVE

**ser** [ser] *vi* **1** (*descripción*) to be; es médica/muy alta she's a doctor/very tall; **la familia es de Cuzco** his (o her *etc*) family is from Cuzco; **soy Ana** (*TELEC*) Ana speaking o here

**2** (*propiedad*): **es de Joaquín** it's Joaquín's, it belongs to Joaquín

**3** (*horas, fechas, números*): **es la una** it's one o'clock; **son las seis y media** it's half-past six; **es el 1 de junio** it's the first of June; **somos/son seis** there are six of us/them

**4** (*en oraciones pasivas*): **ha sido descubierto ya** it's already been discovered

**5**: **es de esperar que ...** it is to be hoped o I *etc* hope that ...

**6** (*locuciones con sub*): **o sea** that is to say; **sea él sea su hermana** either him or his sister

**7**: **a no ~ por él** ... but for him ...

**8**: **a no ~ que**: **a no ~ que tenga uno ya** unless he's got one already

♦ *nm* being; **~ humano** human being

**serenarse** [sere'narse] *vr* to calm

down

**sereno, a** [se'reno, a] *adj* (*persona*) calm, unruffled; (*el tiempo*) fine, settled; (*ambiente*) calm, peaceful ♦ *nm* night watchman

**serial** [ser'jal] *nm* serial

**serie** ['serje] *nf* series; (*cadena*) sequence, succession; **fuera de ~** out of order; (*fig*) special, out of the ordinary; **fabricación en ~** mass production

**seriedad** [serje'ðað] *nf* seriousness; (*formalidad*) reliability; (*de crisis*) gravity, seriousness; **serio, a** *adj* serious; reliable, dependable; grave, serious; **en serio** *adv* seriously

**sermón** [ser'mon] *nm* (*REL*) sermon

**serpentear** [serpente'ar] *vi* to wriggle; (*camino, río*) to wind, snake

**serpentina** [serpen'tina] *nf* streamer

**serpiente** [ser'pjente] *nf* snake; **~ boa** boa constrictor; **~ de cascabel** rattlesnake

**serranía** [serra'nia] *nf* mountainous area

**serrar** [se'rrar] *vt* = **aserrar**

**serrín** [se'rrin] *nm* = **aserrín**

**serrucho** [se'rrutʃo] *nm* saw

**servicio** [ser'βiθjo] *nm* service; **~s** *nmpl* toilet(s); **~ incluido** service charge included; **~ militar** military service

**servidumbre** [serβi'ðumbre] *nf* (*sujeción*) servitude; (*criados*) servants *pl*, staff

**servil** [ser'βil] *adj* servile

**servilleta** [serβi'ʎeta] *nf* serviette, napkin

**servir** [ser'βir] *vt* to serve ♦ *vi* to serve; (*tener utilidad*) to be of use, be useful; **~se** *vr* to serve o help o.s.; **~se de algo** to make use of sth, use sth; **sírvase pasar** please come in

**sesenta** [se'senta] *num* sixty

**sesgo** ['sesɣo] *nm* slant; (*fig*) slant, twist

**sesión** [se'sjon] *nf* (*POL*) session, sitting; (*CINE*) showing

**seso** ['seso] *nm* brain; **sesudo, a** *adj*

sensible, wise

**seta** ['seta] *nf* mushroom; ~ venenosa toadstool

**setecientos, as** [sete'θjentos, as] *adj, num* seven hundred

**setenta** [se'tenta] *num* seventy

**seudónimo** [seu'ðonimo] *nm* pseudonym

**severidad** [seβeri'ðað] *nf* severity; **severo, a** *adj* severe

**Sevilla** [se'βiʎa] *n* Seville; **sevillano, a** *adj* of o from Seville ♦ *nm/f* native o inhabitant of Seville

**sexo** ['sekso] *nm* sex

**sexto, a** ['seksto, a] *adj, nm* sixth

**sexual** [sek'swal] *adj* sexual; **vida** ~ sex life

**si** [si] *conj* if; **me pregunto** ~ ... I wonder if o whether ...

**sí** [si] *adv* yes ♦ *nm* consent ♦ *pron* (*uso impersonal*) oneself; (*sg: m*) himself; (: *f*) herself; (: *de cosa*) itself; (*de usted*) yourself; (*pl*) themselves; (*de ustedes*) yourselves; (*recíproco*) each other; **él no quiere pero yo** ~ he doesn't want to but I do; **ella** ~ **vendrá** she will certainly come, she is sure to come; **claro que** ~ of course; **creo que** ~ I think so

**siamés, esa** [sja'mes, esa] *adj, nm/f* Siamese

**SIDA** ['siða] *nm abr* (= *Síndrome de Inmuno-deficiencia Adquirida*) AIDS

**siderúrgico, a** [siðe'rurxiko, a] *adj* iron and steel *cpd*

**sidra** ['siðra] *nf* cider

**siembra** ['sjembra] *nf* sowing

**siempre** ['sjempre] *adv* always; (*todo el tiempo*) all the time; ~ **que** (*cada vez*) whenever; (*dado que*) provided that; **como** ~ as usual; **para** ~ for ever

**sien** [sjen] *nf* temple

**siento** *etc vb ver* sentar; sentir

**sierra** ['sjerra] *nf* (*TEC*) saw; (*cadena de montañas*) mountain range

**siervo, a** ['sjerβo, a] *nm/f* slave

**siesta** ['sjesta] *nf* siesta, nap; **echar la** ~ to have an afternoon nap o a

siesta

**siete** ['sjete] *num* seven

**sífilis** ['sifilis] *nf* syphilis

**sifón** [si'fon] *nm* syphon; **whisky con** ~ whisky and soda

**sigilo** [si'xilo] *nm* secrecy, discretion; (*al moverse*) stealth

**sigla** ['sixla] *nf* abbreviation; acronym

**siglo** ['sixlo] *nm* century; (*fig*) age

**significación** [sixnifika'θjon] *nf* significance

**significado** [sixnifi'kaðo] *nm* significance; (*de palabra etc*) meaning

**significar** [sixnifi'kar] *vt* to mean, signify; (*notificar*) to make known, express; **significativo, a** *adj* significant

**signo** ['sixno] *nm* sign; ~ **de admiración** o **exclamación** exclamation mark; ~ **de interrogación** question mark

**sigo** *etc vb ver* seguir

**siguiente** [si'xjente] *adj* next, following

**siguió** *etc vb ver* seguir

**sílaba** ['silaβa] *nf* syllable

**silbar** [sil'βar] *vt, vi* to whistle; **silbato** *nm* whistle; **silbido** *nm* whistle, whistling

**silenciador** [silenθja'ðor] *nm* silencer

**silenciar** [silen'θjar] *vt* (*persona*) to silence; (*escándalo*) to hush up; **silencio** *nm* silence, quiet; **silencioso, a** *adj* silent, quiet

**silicio** [si'liθjo] *nm* silicon

**silueta** [si'lweta] *nf* silhouette; (*de edificio*) outline; (*figura*) figure

**silvestre** [sil'βestre] *adj* (*BOT*) wild; (*fig*) rustic, rural

**silla** ['siʎa] *nf* (*asiento*) chair; (*tb*: ~ **de montar**) saddle; ~ **de ruedas** wheelchair

**sillón** [si'ʎon] *nm* armchair, easy chair

**simbólico, a** [sim'boliko, a] *adj* symbolic(al)

**simbolizar** [simboli'θar] *vt* to symbolize

**símbolo** ['simbolo] *nm* symbol

**simetría** [sime'tria] *nf* symmetry

**simiente** [si'mjente] *nf* seed

**similar** [simi'lar] *adj* similar

**simio** ['simjo] *nm* ape

**simpatía** [simpa'tia] *nf* liking; (*afecto*) affection; (*amabilidad*) kindness; (*solidaridad*) mutual support, solidarity; **simpático, a** *adj* nice, pleasant; kind

**simpatizante** [simpati'θante] *nm/f* sympathizer

**simpatizar** [simpati'θar] *vi*: ~ **con** to get on well with

**simple** ['simple] *adj* simple; (*elemental*) simple, easy; (*mero*) mere; (*puro*) pure, sheer ♦ *nm/f* simpleton; **~za** *nf* simpleness; (*necedad*) silly thing; **simplificar** *vt* to simplify

**simposio** [sim'posjo] *nm* symposium

**simular** [simu'lar] *vt* to simulate

**simultáneo, a** [simul'taneo, a] *adj* simultaneous

**sin** [sin] *prep* without; **la ropa está ~ lavar** the clothes are unwashed; **~ que** without; **~ embargo** however, still

**sinagoga** [sina'ɣoɣa] *nf* synagogue

**sinceridad** [sinθeri'ðað] *nf* sincerity; **sincero, a** *adj* sincere

**sincronizar** [sinkroni'θar] *vt* to synchronize

**sindical** [sindi'kal] *adj* union *cpd*, trade-union *cpd*; **~ista** *adj, nm/f* trade-unionist

**sindicato** [sindi'kato] *nm* (*de trabajadores*) trade(s) union; (*de negociantes*) syndicate

**síndrome** ['sindrome] *nm* (*MED*) syndrome; ~ **de abstinencia** (*MED*) withdrawal symptoms *cpd*

**sinfín** [sin'fin] *nm*: **un ~ de** a great many, no end of

**sinfonía** [sinfo'nia] *nf* symphony

**singular** [singu'lar] *adj* singular; (*fig*) outstanding, exceptional; (*pey*) peculiar, odd; **~idad** *nf* singularity, peculiarity; **~izarse** *vr* to distinguish o.s., stand out

**siniestro, a** [si'njestro, a] *adj* left;

(*fig*) sinister ♦ *nm* (*accidente*) accident

**sinnúmero** [sin'numero] *nm* = **sinfín**

**sino** ['sino] *nm* fate, destiny ♦ *conj* (*pero*) but; (*salvo*) except, save

**sinónimo, a** [si'nonimo, a] *adj* synonymous ♦ *nm* synonym

**síntesis** ['sintesis] *nf* synthesis; **sintético, a** *adj* synthetic

**sintetizar** [sinteti'θar] *vt* to synthesize

**sintió** *vb ver* **sentir**

**síntoma** ['sintoma] *nm* symptom

**sintonía** [sinto'nia] *nf* (*RADIO, MUS: de programa*) tuning; **sintonizar** *vt* (*RADIO: emisora*) to tune (in)

**sinvergüenza** [simber'ɣwenθa] *nm/f* rogue, scoundrel; **¡es un ~!** he's got a nerve!

**sionismo** [sjo'nismo] *nm* Zionism

**siquiera** [si'kjera] *conj* even if, even though ♦ *adv* at least; **ni ~** not even

**sirena** [si'rena] *nf* siren

**Siria** ['sirja] *nf* Syria

**sirviente, a** [sir'βjente, a] *nm/f* servant

**sirvo** *etc vb ver* **servir**

**sisear** [sise'ar] *vt, vi* to hiss

**sistema** [sis'tema] *nm* system; (*método*) method; **sistemático, a** *adj* systematic

**sitiar** [si'tjar] *vt* to besiege, lay siege to

**sitio** ['sitjo] *nm* (*lugar*) place; (*espacio*) room, space; (*MIL*) siege

**situación** [sitwa'θjon] *nf* situation, position; (*estatus*) position, standing

**situado, a** [situ'aðo] *adj* situated, placed

**situar** [si'twar] *vt* to place, put; (*edificio*) to locate, situate

**slip** [slip] *nm* pants *pl*, briefs *pl*

**smoking** ['smokin, es'mokin] (*pl* ~s) *nm* dinner jacket (*BRIT*), tuxedo (*US*)

**snob** [es'nob] = **esnob**

**SO** *abr* (= *suroeste*) SW

**sobaco** [so'βako] *nm* armpit

**sobar** [so'βar] *vt* (*ropa*) to rumple,

*(libro)* to dirty (with one's fingers); *(comida)* to play around with

**soberanía** [soβeraˈnia] *nf* sovereignty; **soberano, a** *adj* sovereign; *(fig)* supreme ♦ *nm/f* sovereign

**soberbia** [soˈβerβja] *nf* pride; haughtiness, arrogance; magnificence

**soberbio, a** [soˈβerβjo, a] *adj (orgulloso)* proud; *(altivo)* haughty, arrogant; *(fig)* magnificent, superb

**sobornar** [soβorˈnar] *vt* to bribe; **soborno** *nm* bribe

**sobra** [ˈsoβra] *nf* excess, surplus; ~s *nfpl* left-overs, scraps; **de ~** surplus, extra; **tengo de ~** I've more than enough; **~do, a** *adj (más que suficiente)* more than enough; *(superfluo)* excessive ♦ *adv* too, exceedingly; **sobrante** *adj* remaining, extra ♦ *nm* surplus, remainder

**sobrar** [soˈβrar] *vt* to exceed, surpass ♦ *vi (tener de más)* to be more than enough; *(quedar)* to remain, be left (over)

**sobrasada** [soβraˈsaða] *nf* pork sausage spread

**sobre** [ˈsoβre] *prep (gen)* on; *(encima)* on (top of); *(por encima de, arriba de)* over, above; *(más que)* more than; *(además)* in addition to, besides; *(alrededor de)* about ♦ *nm* envelope; **~ todo** above all

**sobrecama** [soβreˈkama] *nf* bedspread

**sobrecargar** [soβrekarˈxar] *vt (camión)* to overload; *(COM)* to surcharge

**sobredosis** [soβreˈðosis] *nf inv* overdose

**sobreentender** [soβre(e)ntenˈder] *vt (adivinar)* to deduce, infer; **~se** *vr:* **se sobreentiende que ...** it is implied that ...

**sobrehumano, a** [soβreuˈmano, a] *adj* superhuman

**sobrellevar** [soβreʎeˈβar] *vt (fig)* to bear, endure

**sobremesa** [soβreˈmesa] *nf:* **durante la ~** after dinner; **ordenador de ~** desktop computer

**sobrenatural** [soβrenatuˈral] *adj* supernatural

**sobrenombre** [soβreˈnombre] *nm* nickname

**sobrepasar** [soβrepaˈsar] *vt* to exceed, surpass

**sobreponer** [soβrepoˈner] *vt (poner encima)* to put on top; *(añadir)* to add; **~se** *vr:* **~se a** to overcome

**sobresaliente** [soβresaˈljente] *adj* projecting; *(fig)* outstanding, excellent

**sobresalir** [soβresaˈlir] *vi* to project, jut out; *(fig)* to stand out, excel

**sobresaltar** [soβresalˈtar] *vt (asustar)* to scare, frighten; *(sobrecoger)* to startle; **sobresalto** *nm (movimiento)* start; *(susto)* scare; *(turbación)* sudden shock

**sobretodo** [soβreˈtoðo] *nm* overcoat

**sobrevenir** [soβreβeˈnir] *vi (ocurrir)* to happen (unexpectedly); *(resultar)* to follow, ensue

**sobreviviente** [soβreβiˈβjente] *adj* surviving ♦ *nm/f* survivor

**sobrevivir** [soβreβiˈβir] *vi* to survive

**sobrevolar** [soβreβoˈlar] *vt* to fly over

**sobriedad** [soβrjeˈðað] *nf* sobriety, soberness; *(moderación)* moderation, restraint

**sobrino, a** [soˈβrino, a] *nm/f* nephew/niece

**sobrio, a** [ˈsoβrjo, a] *adj (moderado)* moderate, restrained

**socarrón, ona** [sokaˈrron, ona] *adj (sarcástico)* sarcastic, ironic(al)

**socavar** [sokaˈβar] *vt (tb fig)* to undermine

**socavón** [sokaˈβon] *nm (hoyo)* hole

**sociable** [soˈθjaβle] *adj (persona)* sociable, friendly; *(animal)* social

**social** [soˈθjal] *adj* social; *(COM)* company *cpd*

**socialdemócrata** [soθjaldeˈmokrata] *nm/f* social democrat

**socialista** [soθjaˈlista] *adj, nm/f* socialist

**socializar** [soθjaliˈθar] *vt* to socialize

**sociedad** [soθjeˈðað] *nf* society;

(COM) company; ~ **anónima** limited company; ~ **de consumo** consumer society

**socio, a** ['soθjo, a] nm/f (miembro) member; (COM) partner

**sociología** [soθjolo'xia] nf sociology; **sociólogo, a** nm/f sociologist

**socorrer** [soko'rrer] vt to help; **socorrista** nm/f first aider; (en piscina, playa) lifeguard; **socorro** nm (ayuda) help, aid; (MIL) relief; **¡socorro!** help!

**soda** ['soða] nf (sosa) soda; (bebida) soda (water)

**sofá** [so'fa] (pl ~s) nm sofa, settee; ~**-cama** nm studio couch; sofa bed

**sofisticación** [sofistika'θjon] nf sophistication

**sofocar** [sofo'kar] vt to suffocate; (apagar) to smother, put out; ~**se** vr to suffocate; (fig) to blush, feel embarrassed; **sofoco** nm suffocation; embarrassment

**sofreír** [sofre'ir] vt (CULIN) to fry lightly

**soga** ['soɣa] nf rope

**sois** vb ver **ser**

**soja** ['soxa] nf soya

**sojuzgar** [soxuθ'ɣar] vt to subdue, rule despotically

**sol** [sol] nm sun; (luz) sunshine, sunlight; **hace** ~ it is sunny

**solamente** [sola'mente] adv only, just

**solapa** [so'lapa] nf (de chaqueta) lapel; (de libro) jacket

**solapado, a** [sola'paðo, a] adj (intenciones) underhand; (gestos, movimiento) sly

**solar** [so'lar] adj solar, sun cpd

**solaz** [so'laθ] nm recreation, relaxation; ~**ar** vt (divertir) to amuse

**soldada** [sol'daða] nf pay

**soldado** [sol'daðo] nm soldier; ~ **raso** private

**soldador** [solda'ðor] nm soldering iron; (persona) welder

**soldar** [sol'dar] vt to solder, weld; (unir) to join, unite

**soleado, a** [sole'aðo, a] adj sunny

**soledad** [sole'ðað] nf solitude; (estado infeliz) loneliness

**solemne** [so'lemne] adj solemn; **solemnidad** nf solemnity

**soler** [so'ler] vi to be in the habit of, be accustomed to; **suele salir a las ocho** she usually goes out at 8 o'clock

**solfeo** [sol'feo] nm solfa

**solicitar** [soliθi'tar] vt (permiso) to ask for, seek; (puesto) to apply for; (votos) to canvass for; (atención) to attract; (persona) to pursue, chase after

**solícito, a** [so'liθito, a] adj (diligente) diligent; (cuidadoso) careful; **solicitud** nf (calidad) great care; (petición) request; (a un puesto) application

**solidaridad** [soliðari'ðað] nf solidarity; **solidario, a** adj (participación) joint, common; (compromiso) mutually binding

**solidez** [soli'ðeθ] nf solidity; **sólido, a** adj solid

**soliloquio** [soli'lokjo] nm soliloquy

**solista** [so'lista] nm/f soloist

**solitario, a** [soli'tarjo, a] adj (persona) lonely, solitary; (lugar) lonely, desolate ♦ nm/f (recluso) recluse; (en la sociedad) loner ♦ nm solitaire

**solo, a** ['solo, a] adj (único) single, sole; (sin compañía) alone; (solitario) lonely; **hay una sola dificultad** there is just one difficulty; **a solas** alone, by oneself

**sólo** ['solo] adv only, just

**solomillo** [solo'miλo] nm sirloin

**soltar** [sol'tar] vt (dejar ir) to let go; (desprender) to unfasten, loosen; (librar) to release, set free; (risa etc) to let out

**soltero, a** [sol'tero, a] adj single, unmarried ♦ nm/f bachelor/single woman; **solterón, ona** nm/f old bachelor/spinster

**soltura** [sol'tura] nf looseness, slackness; (de los miembros) agility, ease of movement; (en el hablar) fluency, ease

**soluble** [so'luβle] *adj* (*QUÍMICA*) soluble; (*problema*) solvable; ~ **en agua** soluble in water

**solución** [solu'θjon] *nf* solution; **solucionar** *vt* (*problema*) to solve; (*asunto*) to settle, resolve

**solventar** [solβen'tar] *vt* (*pagar*) to settle, pay; (*resolver*) to resolve; **solvente** (*ECON: empresa, persona*) solvent

**sollozar** [soλo'θar] *vi* to sob; **sollozo** *nm* sob

**sombra** ['sombra] *nf* shadow; (*como protección*) shade; ~**s** *nfpl* (*oscuridad*) darkness *sg*, shadows; **tener buena/mala** ~ to be lucky/unlucky

**sombrero** [som'brero] *nm* hat

**sombrilla** [som'briλa] *nf* parasol, sunshade

**sombrío, a** [som'brio, a] *adj* (*oscuro*) dark; (*fig*) sombre, sad; (*persona*) gloomy

**somero, a** [so'mero, a] *adj* superficial

**someter** [some'ter] *vt* (*país*) to conquer; (*persona*) to subject to one's will; (*informe*) to present, submit; ~**se** *vr* to give in, yield, submit; ~ **a** to subject to

**somier** [so'mjer] (*pl* **somiers**) *n* spring mattress

**somnífero** [som'nifero] *nm* sleeping pill

**somnolencia** [somno'lenθja] *nf* sleepiness, drowsiness

**somos** *vb ver* **ser**

**son** [son] *vb ver* **ser** ♦ *nm* sound; **en** ~ **de broma** as a joke

**sonajero** [sona'xero] *nm* (baby's) rattle

**sonambulismo** [sonambu'lismo] *nm* sleepwalking; **sonámbulo, a** *nm/f* sleepwalker

**sonar** [so'nar] *vt* to ring ♦ *vi* to sound; (*hacer ruido*) to make a noise; (*pronunciarse*) to be sounded, be pronounced; (*ser conocido*) to sound familiar; (*campana*) to ring; (*reloj*) to strike, chime; ~**se** *vr*: ~**se (las narices)** to blow one's nose;

**me suena ese nombre** that name rings a bell

**sonda** ['sonda] *nf* (*NAUT*) sounding; (*TEC*) bore, drill; (*MED*) probe

**sondear** [sonde'ar] *vt* to sound; to bore (into), drill; to probe, sound; (*fig*) to sound out; **sondeo** *nm* sounding; boring, drilling; (*fig*) poll, enquiry

**sónico, a** ['soniko, a] *adj* sonic, sound *cpd*

**sonido** [so'niðo] *nm* sound

**sonoro, a** [so'noro, a] *adj* sonorous; (*resonante*) loud, resonant

**sonreír** [sonre'ir] *vi* to smile; ~**se** *vr* to smile; **sonriente** *adj* smiling; **sonrisa** *nf* smile

**sonrojarse** [sonro'xarse] *vr* to blush, go red; **sonrojo** *nm* blush

**sonsacar** [sonsa'kar] *vt* to coax

**soñador, a** [soɲa'ðor, a] *nm/f* dreamer

**soñar** [so'ɲar] *vt*, *vi* to dream; ~ **con** to dream about *o* of

**soñoliento, a** [soɲo'ljento, a] *adj* sleepy, drowsy

**sopa** ['sopa] *nf* soup

**sopesar** [sope'sar] *vt* to consider, weigh up

**soplar** [so'plar] *vt* (*polvo*) to blow away, blow off; (*inflar*) to blow up; (*vela*) to blow out ♦ *vi* to blow; **soplo** *nm* blow, puff; (*de viento*) puff, gust

**soplón, ona** [so'plon, ona] (*fam*), *nm/f* (*niño*) telltale; (*de policía*) grass (*fam*)

**sopor** [so'por] *nm* drowsiness

**soporífero** [sopo'rifero] *nm* sleeping pill

**soportable** [sopor'taβle] *adj* bearable

**soportar** [sopor'tar] *vt* to bear, carry; (*fig*) to bear, put up with; **soporte** *nm* support; (*fig*) pillar, support

**soprano** [so'prano] *nf* soprano

**sorber** [sor'βer] *vt* (*chupar*) to sip; (*inhalar*) to inhale; (*tragar*) to swallow (up); (*absorber*) to soak up, absorb

**sorbete** [sor'βete] *nm* iced fruit drink

**sorbo** ['sorβo] *nm* (*trago: grande*) gulp, swallow; (: *pequeño*) sip

**sordera** [sor'δera] *nf* deafness

**sórdido, a** ['sorδiδo, a] *adj* dirty, squalid

**sordo, a** ['sorδo, a] *adj* (*persona*) deaf ♦ *nm/f* deaf person; **~mudo, a** *adj* deaf and dumb

**sorna** ['sorna] *nf* sarcastic tone

**soroche** [so'rotʃe] (*AM*) *nm* mountain sickness

**sorprendente** [sorpren'dente] *adj* surprising

**sorprender** [sorpren'der] *vt* to surprise; **sorpresa** *nf* surprise

**sortear** [sorte'ar] *vt* to draw lots for; (*rifar*) to raffle; (*dificultad*) to avoid; **sorteo** *nm* (*en lotería*) draw; (*rifa*) raffle

**sortija** [sor'tixa] *nf* ring; (*rizo*) ringlet, curl

**sosegado, a** [sose'xaδo, a] *adj* quiet, calm

**sosegar** [sose'xar] *vt* to quieten, calm; (*el ánimo*) to reassure ♦ *vi* to rest; **sosiego** *nm* quiet(ness), calm(ness)

**soslayo** [sos'lajo]: **de ~** *adv* obliquely, sideways

**soso, a** ['soso, a] *adj* (*CULIN*) tasteless; (*fig*) dull, uninteresting

**sospecha** [sos'petʃa] *nf* suspicion; **sospechar** *vt* to suspect; **sospechoso, a** *adj* suspicious; (*testimonio, opinión*) suspect ♦ *nm/f* suspect

**sostén** [sos'ten] *nm* (*apoyo*) support; (*sujetador*) bra; (*alimentación*) sustenance, food

**sostener** [soste'ner] *vt* to support; (*mantener*) to keep up, maintain; (*alimentar*) to sustain, keep going; **~se** *vr* to support o.s.; (*seguir*) to continue, remain; **sostenido, a** *adj* continuous, sustained; (*prolongado*) prolonged

**sotana** [so'tana] *nf* (*REL*) cassock

**sótano** ['sotano] *nm* basement

**soviético, a** [so'βjetiko, a] *adj* So-

viet; **los ~s** the Soviets

**soy** *vb ver* **ser**

**Sr.** *abr* (= *Señor*) Mr

**Sra.** *abr* (= *Señora*) Mrs

**S.R.C.** *abr* (= *se ruega contestación*) R.S.V.P.

**Sres.** *abr* (= *Señores*) Messrs

**Srta.** *abr* (= *Señorita*) Miss

**Sta.** *abr* (= *Santa*) St

**status** ['status, e'status] *nm inv* status

**Sto.** *abr* (= *Santo*) St

**su** [su] *pron* (*de él*) his; (*de ella*) her; (*de una cosa*) its; (*de ellos, ellas*) their; (*de usted, ustedes*) your

**suave** ['swaβe] *adj* gentle; (*superficie*) smooth; (*trabajo*) easy; (*música, voz*) soft, sweet; **suavidad** *nf* gentleness; smoothness; softness, sweetness; **suavizar** *vt* to soften; (*quitar la aspereza*) to smooth (out)

**subalimentado, a** [suβalimen'taδo, a] *adj* undernourished

**subasta** [su'βasta] *nf* auction; **subastar** *vt* to auction (off)

**subcampeón, ona** [suβkampe'on, ona] *nm/f* runner-up

**subconsciente** [suβkon'sθjente] *adj, nm* subconscious

**subdesarrollado, a** [suβδesarro-'ʎaδo, a] *adj* underdeveloped

**subdesarrollo** [suβδesa'rroʎo] *nm* underdevelopment

**subdirector, a** [suβδirek'tor, a] *nm/f* assistant director

**súbdito, a** ['suβδito, a] *nm/f* subject

**subestimar** [suβesti'mar] *vt* to underestimate, underrate

**subida** [su'βiδa] *nf* (*de montaña etc*) ascent, climb; (*de precio*) rise, increase; (*pendiente*) slope, hill

**subir** [su'βir] *vt* (*objeto*) to raise, lift up; (*cuesta, calle*) to go up; (*colina, montaña*) to climb; (*precio*) to raise, put up ♦ *vi* to go up, come up; (*a un coche*) to get in; (*a un autobús, tren o avión*) to get on, board; (*precio*) to rise, go up; (*río, marea*) to rise; **~se** *vr* to get up, climb

**súbito, a** ['suβito, a] *adj* (*repentino*)

sudden; (*imprevisto*) unexpected
**subjetivo, a** [suβxe'tiβo, a] *adj* subjective
**sublevación** [suβleβa'θjon] *nf* revolt, rising
**sublevar** [suβle'βar] *vt* to rouse to revolt; **~se** *vr* to revolt, rise
**sublime** [su'βlime] *adj* sublime
**submarino, a** [suβma'rino, a] *adj* underwater ♦ *nm* submarine
**subnormal** [suβnor'mal] *adj* subnormal ♦ *nm/f* subnormal person
**subordinado, a** [suβorði'naðo, a] *adj, nm/f* subordinate
**subrayar** [suβra'jar] *vt* to underline
**subsanar** [suβsa'nar] *vt* (*reparar*) to make good; (*perdonar*) to excuse; (*sobreponerse a*) to overcome
**subscribir** [suβskri'βir] *vt* = **suscribir**
**subsidio** [suβ'siðjo] *nm* (*ayuda*) aid, financial help; (*subvención*) subsidy, grant; (*de enfermedad, paro etc*) benefit, allowance
**subsistencia** [suβsis'tenθja] *nf* subsistence
**subsistir** [suβsis'tir] *vi* to subsist; (*vivir*) to live; (*sobrevivir*) to survive, endure
**subterráneo, a** [suβte'rraneo, a] *adj* underground, subterranean ♦ *nm* underpass, underground passage
**subtítulo** [suβ'titulo] *nm* (*CINE*) subtitle
**suburbano, a** [suβur'βano, a] *adj* suburban
**suburbio** [su'βurβjo] *nm* (*barrio*) slum quarter; (*afueras*) suburbs *pl*
**subvención** [suββen'θjon] *nf* (*ECON*) subsidy, grant; **subvencionar** *vt* to subsidize
**subversión** [suββer'sjon] *nf* subversion; **subversivo, a** *adj* subversive
**subyugar** [suβju'ɣar] *vt* (*país*) to subjugate, subdue; (*enemigo*) to overpower; (*voluntad*) to dominate
**succión** [suk'θjon] *nf* suction
**sucedáneo, a** [suθe'ðaneo, a] *adj* substitute ♦ *nm* substitute (food)
**suceder** [suθe'ðer] *vt, vi* to happen;

(*seguir*) to succeed, follow; **lo que sucede es que ...** the fact is that ...;
**sucesión** *nf* succession; (*serie*) sequence, series
**sucesivamente** [suθesiβa'mente] *adv*: **y así ~** and so on
**sucesivo, a** [suθe'siβo, a] *adj* successive, following; **en lo ~** in future, from now on
**suceso** [su'θeso] *nm* (*hecho*) event, happening; (*incidente*) incident
**suciedad** [suθje'ðað] *nf* (*estado*) dirtiness; (*mugre*) dirt, filth
**sucinto, a** [su'θinto, a] *adj* (*conciso*) succinct, concise
**sucio, a** ['suθjo, a] *adj* dirty
**suculento, a** [suku'lento, a] *adj* succulent
**sucumbir** [sukum'bir] *vi* to succumb
**sucursal** [sukur'sal] *nf* branch (office)
**Sudáfrica** [suð'afrika] *nf* South Africa
**Sudamérica** [suða'merika] *nf* South America; **sudamericano, a** *adj, nm/f* South American
**sudar** [su'ðar] *vt, vi* to sweat
**sudeste** [su'ðeste] *nm* south-east
**sudoeste** [suðo'este] *nm* south-west
**sudor** [su'ðor] *nm* sweat; **~oso, a** *adj* sweaty, sweating
**Suecia** ['sweθja] *nf* Sweden; **sueco, a** *adj* Swedish ♦ *nm/f* Swede
**suegro, a** ['sweɣro, a] *nm/f* father-/mother-in-law
**suela** ['swela] *nf* sole
**sueldo** ['sweldo] *nm* pay, wage(s) (*pl*)
**suele** *etc vb ver* **soler**
**suelo** ['swelo] *nm* (*tierra*) ground; (*de casa*) floor
**suelto, a** ['swelto, a] *adj* loose; (*libre*) free; (*separado*) detached; (*ágil*) quick, agile; (*corriente*) fluent, flowing ♦ *nm* (*loose*) change, small change
**sueño** *etc* ['sweɲo] *vb ver* **soñar** ♦ *nm* sleep; (*somnolencia*) sleepiness, drowsiness; (*lo soñado, fig*) dream; **tener ~** to be sleepy

**suero** ['swero] *nm* (MED) serum; (de leche) whey

**suerte** ['swerte] *nf* (fortuna) luck; (azar) chance; (destino) fate, destiny; (condición) lot; (género) sort, kind; **tener ~** to be lucky; **de otra ~** otherwise, if not; **de ~ que** so that, in such a way that

**suéter** ['sweter] *nm* sweater

**suficiente** [sufi'θjente] *adj* enough, sufficient ♦ *nm* (ESCOL) pass

**sufragio** [su'fraxjo] *nm* (voto) vote; (derecho de voto) suffrage

**sufrido, a** [su'friðo, a] *adj* (persona) tough; (paciente) long-suffering, patient

**sufrimiento** [sufri'mjento] *nm* (dolor) suffering

**sufrir** [su'frir] *vt* (padecer) to suffer; (soportar) to bear, put up with; (apoyar) to hold up, support ♦ *vi* to suffer

**sugerencia** [suxe'renθja] *nf* suggestion

**sugerir** [suxe'rir] *vt* to suggest; (sutilmente) to hint

**sugestión** [suxes'tjon] *nf* suggestion; (sutil) hint; **sugestionar** *vt* to influence

**sugestivo, a** [suxes'tiβo, a] *adj* stimulating; (fascinante) fascinating

**suicida** [sui'θiða] *adj* suicidal ♦ *nm/f* suicidal person; (muerto) suicide, person who has committed suicide; **suicidarse** *vr* to commit suicide, kill o.s.; **suicidio** *nm* suicide

**Suiza** ['swiθa] *nf* Switzerland; **suizo, a** *adj, nm/f* Swiss

**sujeción** [suxe'θjon] *nf* subjection

**sujetador** [suxeta'ðor] *nm* fastener, clip; (sostén) bra

**sujetar** [suxe'tar] *vt* (fijar) to fasten; (detener) to hold down; (fig) to subject, subjugate; **~se** *vr* to subject o.s.; **sujeto, a** *adj* fastened, secure ♦ *nm* subject; (individuo) individual; **sujeto a** a subject to

**suma** ['suma] *nf* (cantidad) total, sum; (de dinero) sum; (acto) adding (up), addition; **en ~** in short

**sumamente** [suma'mente] *adv* extremely, exceedingly

**sumar** [su'mar] *vt* to add (up); (reunir) to collect, gather ♦ *vi* to add up

**sumario, a** [su'marjo, a] *adj* brief, concise ♦ *nm* summary

**sumergir** [sumer'xir] *vt* to submerge; (hundir) to sink; (bañar) to immerse, dip

**suministrar** [sumini'strar] *vt* to supply, provide; **suministro** *nm* supply; (acto) supplying, providing

**sumir** [su'mir] *vt* to sink, submerge; (fig) to plunge

**sumisión** [sumi'sjon] *nf* (acto) submission; (calidad) submissiveness, docility; **sumiso, a** *adj* submissive, docile

**sumo, a** ['sumo, a] *adj* great, extreme; (mayor) highest, supreme

**suntuoso, a** [sun'twoso, a] *adj* sumptuous, magnificent

**supe** *etc vb ver* **saber**

**supeditar** [supeði'tar] *vt*: **~ algo a** algo to subordinate sth to sth

**super...** [super] *prefijo* super..., over...; **~bueno** *adj* great, fantastic

**súper** ['super] *nf* (gasolina) three-star (petrol)

**superar** [supe'rar] *vt* (sobreponerse a) to overcome; (rebasar) to surpass, do better than; (pasar) to go beyond; **~se** *vr* to excel o.s.

**superávit** [supe'raβit] *nm inv* surplus

**superficial** [superfi'θjal] *adj* superficial; (medida) surface *cpd*, of the surface

**superficie** [super'fiθje] *nf* surface; (área) area

**superfluo, a** [su'perflwo, a] *adj* superfluous

**superior** [supe'rjor] *adj* (piso, clase) upper; (temperatura, número, nivel) higher; (mejor: calidad, producto) superior, better ♦ *nm/f* superior; **~idad** *nf* superiority

**supermercado** [supermer'kaðo] *nm* supermarket

**superponer** [superpo'ner] *vt* to superimpose

**supersónico, a** [super'soniko, a] *adj* supersonic

**superstición** [supersti'θjon] *nf* superstition; **supersticioso, a** *adj* superstitious

**supervisar** [superβi'sar] *vt* to supervise

**supervivencia** [superβiβen'θja] *nf* survival

**superviviente** [superβi'βjente] *adj* surviving

**supiera** *etc vb ver* **saber**

**suplantar** [suplan'tar] *vt (persona)* to supplant; *(documento etc)* to falsify

**suplemento** [suple'mento] *nm* supplement

**suplente** [su'plente] *adj, nm/f* substitute

**supletorio, a** [suple'torjo, a] *adj* supplementary ♦ *nm* supplement; **mesa supletoria** spare table

**súplica** ['suplika] *nf* request; *(JUR)* petition

**suplicar** [supli'kar] *vt (cosa)* to beg (for), plead for; *(persona)* to beg, plead with

**suplicio** [su'pliθjo] *nm* torture

**suplir** [su'plir] *vt (compensar)* to make good, make up for; *(reemplazar)* to replace, substitute ♦ *vi:* ~ **a** to take the place of, substitute for

**supo** *etc vb ver* **saber**

**suponer** [supo'ner] *vt* to suppose ♦ *vi* to have authority; **suposición** *nf* supposition

**supremacía** [suprema'θia] *nf* supremacy

**supremo, a** [su'premo, a] *adj* supreme

**supresión** [supre'sjon] *nf* suppression; *(de derecho)* abolition; *(de dificultad)* removal; *(de palabra etc)* deletion; *(de restricción)* cancellation, lifting

**suprimir** [supri'mir] *vt* to suppress; *(derecho, costumbre)* to abolish; *(dificultad)* to remove; *(palabra etc)* to delete; *(restricción)* to cancel, lift

**supuesto, a** [su'pwesto, a] *pp de* su-

poner ♦ *adj (hipotético)* supposed; *(falso)* false ♦ *nm* assumption, hypothesis; ~ **que** since; **por** ~ of course

**sur** [sur] *nm* south

**surcar** [sur'kar] *vt* to plough; *(superficie)* to cut, score; **surco** *nm (en metal, disco)* groove; *(AGR)* furrow

**surgir** [sur'xir] *vi* to arise, emerge; *(dificultad)* to come up, crop up

**surtido, a** [sur'tiðo, a] *adj* mixed, assorted ♦ *nm (selección)* selection, assortment; *(abastecimiento)* supply, stock

**surtir** [sur'tir] *vt* to supply, provide ♦ *vi* to spout, spurt

**susceptible** [susθep'tiβle] *adj* susceptible; *(sensible)* sensitive; ~ **de** capable of

**suscitar** [susθi'tar] *vt* to cause, provoke; *(interés, sospechas)* to arouse

**suscribir** [suskri'βir] *vt (firmar)* to sign; *(respaldar)* to subscribe to, endorse; ~**se** *vr* to subscribe; **suscripción** *nf* subscription

**susodicho, a** [suso'ðitʃo, a] *adj* above-mentioned

**suspender** [suspen'der] *vt (objeto)* to hang (up), suspend; *(trabajo)* to stop, suspend; *(ESCOL)* to fail; **suspensión** *nf* suspension; *(fig)* stoppage, suspension

**suspenso, a** [sus'penso, a] *adj* hanging, suspended; *(ESCOL)* failed ♦ *nm:* **quedar** *o* **estar en** ~ to be pending

**suspicacia** [suspi'kaθja] *nf* suspicion, mistrust; **suspicaz** *adj* suspicious, distrustful

**suspirar** [suspi'rar] *vi* to sigh; **suspiro** *nm* sigh

**sustancia** [sus'tanθja] *nf* substance

**sustentar** [susten'tar] *vt (alimentar)* to sustain, nourish; *(objeto)* to hold up, support; *(idea, teoría)* to maintain, uphold; *(fig)* to sustain, keep going; **sustento** *nm* support; *(alimento)* sustenance, food

**sustituir** [sustitu'ir] *vt* to substitute, replace; **sustituto, a** *nm/f* substitute, replacement

**susto** ['susto] *nm* fright, scare

**sustraer** [sustra'er] *vt* to remove, take away; (*MAT*) to subtract

**susurrar** [susu'rrar] *vi* to whisper; **susurro** *nm* whisper

**sutil** [su'til] *adj* (*aroma, diferencia*) subtle; (*tenue*) thin; (*inteligencia, persona*) sharp; **~eza** *nf* subtlety; thinness

**suyo, a** ['sujo, a] (*con artículo o después del verbo ser*) *adj* (*de él*) his; (*de ella*) hers; (*de ellos, ellas*) theirs; (*de Ud, Uds*) yours; **un amigo ~** a friend of his (*o hers o theirs o yours*)

## T

**tabacalera** [taβaka'lera] *nf*: **T~** Spanish state tobacco monopoly

**tabaco** [ta'βako] *nm* tobacco; (*fam*) cigarettes *pl*

**taberna** [ta'βerna] *nf* bar, pub (*BRIT*); **tabernero, a** *nm/f* (*encargado*) publican; (*camarero*) barman/maid

**tabique** [ta'βike] *nm* partition (wall)

**tabla** ['taβla] *nf* (*de madera*) plank; (*estante*) shelf; (*de vestido*) pleat; (*ARTE*) panel; **~s** *nfpl*: **estar o quedar en ~s** to draw; **~do** *nm* (*plataforma*) platform; (*TEATRO*) stage

**tablao** [ta'βlao] *nm* (*tb*: **~ flamenco**) flamenco show

**tablero** [ta'βlero] *nm* (*de madera*) plank, board; (*de ajedrez, damas*) board; (*AUTO*) dashboard; **~ de anuncios** notice (*BRIT*) *o* bulletin (*US*) board

**tableta** [ta'βleta] *nf* (*MED*) tablet; (*de chocolate*) bar

**tablón** [ta'βlon] *nm* (*de suelo*) plank; (*de techo*) beam; **~ de anuncios** notice board (*BRIT*), bulletin board (*US*)

**tabú** [ta'βu] *nm* taboo

**tabular** [taβu'lar] *vt* to tabulate

**taburete** [taβu'rete] *nm* stool

**tacaño, a** [ta'kaɲo, a] *adj* (*avaro*) mean

**tácito, a** ['taθito, a] *adj* tacit

**taciturno, a** [taθi'turno, a] *adj* (*callado*) silent; (*malhumorado*) sullen

**taco** ['tako] *nm* (*BILLAR*) cue; (*libro de billetes*) book; (*AM*: *de zapato*) heel; (*tarugo*) peg; (*palabrota*) swear word

**tacón** [ta'kon] *nm* heel; **de ~ alto** high-heeled; **taconeo** *nm* (heel) stamping

**táctica** ['taktika] *nf* tactics *pl*

**táctico, a** ['taktiko, a] *adj* tactical

**tacto** ['takto] *nm* touch; (*fig*) tact

**tacha** ['tatʃa] *nf* flaw; (*TEC*) stud; **tachar** *vt* (*borrar*) to cross out; **tachar de** to accuse of

**tafetán** [tafe'tan] *nm* taffeta

**tafilete** [tafi'lete] *nm* morocco leather

**tahona** [ta'ona] *nf* (*panadería*) bakery

**taimado, a** [tai'maðo, a] *adj* (*astuto*) sly

**taita** ['taita] (*fam*) *nm* dad, daddy

**tajada** [ta'xaða] *nf* slice

**tajante** [ta'xante] *adj* sharp

**tajo** ['taxo] *nm* (*corte*) cut; (*GEO*) cleft

**tal** [tal] *adj* such; **~ vez** perhaps ♦ *pron* (*persona*) someone, such a one; (*cosa*) something, such a thing; **~ como** such as; **~ para cual** tit for tat; (*dos iguales*) two of a kind ♦ *adv*: **~ como** (*igual*) just as; **~ cual** (*como es*) just as it is; **¿qué ~?** how are things?; **¿qué ~ te gusta?** how do you like it? ♦ *conj*: **con ~ de que** provided that

**taladrar** [tala'ðrar] *vt* to drill; **taladro** *nm* drill; (*hoyo*) drill hole

**talante** [ta'lante] *nm* (*humor*) mood; (*voluntad*) will, willingness

**talar** [ta'lar] *vt* to fell, cut down; (*devastar*) to devastate

**talco** ['talko] *nm* (*polvos*) talcum powder

**talego** [ta'lexo] *nm* sack

**talento** [ta'lento] *nm* talent; (*capaci-*

*dad)* ability

**TALGO** [tal'ɣo] *(ESP) nm abr* (= *tren articulado ligero Goicoechea-Oriol)* ≈ HST *(BRIT)*

**talismán** [talis'man] *nm* talisman

**talón** [ta'lon] *nm (ANAT)* heel; *(COM)* counterfoil; *(cheque)* cheque *(BRIT)*, check *(US)*

**talonario** [talo'narjo] *nm (de cheques)* chequebook *(BRIT)*, checkbook *(US)*; *(de billetes)* book of tickets; *(de recibos)* receipt book

**talla** ['taʎa] *nf (estatura, fig, MED)* height, stature; *(palo)* measuring rod; *(ARTE)* carving; *(medida)* size

**tallado, a** [ta'ʎaðo, a] *adj* carved ♦ *nm* carving

**tallar** [ta'ʎar] *vt (madera)* to carve; *(metal etc)* to engrave; *(medir)* to measure

**tallarines** [taʎa'rines] *nmpl* noodles

**talle** ['taʎe] *nm (ANAT)* waist; *(fig)* appearance

**taller** [ta'ʎer] *nm (TEC)* workshop; *(de artista)* studio

**tallo** ['taʎo] *nm (de planta)* stem; *(de hierba)* blade; *(brote)* shoot

**tamaño, a** [ta'maɲo, a] *adj (tan grande)* such a big; *(tan pequeño)* such a small ♦ *nm* size; **de ∼** natural full-size

**tamarindo** [tama'rindo] *nm* tamarind

**tambalearse** [tambale'arse] *vr (persona)* to stagger; *(vehículo)* to sway

**también** [tam'bjen] *adv (igualmente)* also, too, as well; *(además)* besides

**tambor** [tam'bor] *nm (ANAT)* drum; *(ANAT)* eardrum; **∼ del freno** brake drum

**tamiz** [ta'miθ] *nm* sieve; **∼ar** *vt* to sieve

**tampoco** [tam'poko] *adv* ∼nor, neither; **yo ∼ lo compré** I didn't buy it either

**tampón** [tam'pon] *nm* tampon

**tan** [tan] *adv* so; **∼ es así que ...** so much so that ....

**tanda** ['tanda] *nf (gen)* series; *(turno)* shift

**tangente** [tan'xente] *nf* tangent

**Tánger** ['tanxer] *n* Tangier(s)

**tangible** [tan'xiβle] *adj* tangible

**tanque** ['tanke] *nm (cisterna, MIL)* tank; *(AUTO)* tanker

**tantear** [tante'ar] *vt (calcular)* to reckon (up); *(medir)* to take the measure of; *(probar)* to test, try out; *(tomar la medida: persona)* to take the measurements of; *(situación)* to weigh up; *(persona: opinión)* to sound out ♦ *vi (DEPORTE)* to score; **tanteo** *nm (cálculo)* (rough) calculation; *(prueba)* test, trial; *(DEPORTE)* scoring

**tanto, a** ['tanto, a] *adj (cantidad)* so much, as much; **∼s** so many, as many; **20 y ∼s** 20-odd ♦ *adv (cantidad)* so much, as much; *(tiempo)* so long, as long ♦ *conj*: **en ∼ que** while; **hasta ∼ (que)** until such time as ♦ *nm (suma)* certain amount; *(proporción)* so much; *(punto)* point; *(gol)* goal; **un ∼ perezoso** somewhat lazy ♦ *pron*: **cado uno paga ∼** each one pays so much; **∼ tú como yo** both you and I; **∼ como eso** it's not as bad as that; **∼ más ... cuanto que** it's all the more ... because; **∼ mejor/peor** so much the better/the worse; **∼ si viene como si va** whether he comes or whether he goes; **∼ es así que** so much so that; **por o por lo ∼** therefore; **me he vuelto ronco de o con ∼ hablar** I have become hoarse with so much talking; **a ∼s de agosto** on such and such a day in August

**tapa** ['tapa] *nf (de caja, olla)* lid; *(de botella)* top; *(de libro)* cover; *(comida)* snack

**tapadera** [tapa'ðera] *nf* lid, cover

**tapar** [ta'par] *vt (cubrir)* to cover; *(envolver)* to wrap o cover up; *(la vista)* to obstruct; *(persona, falta)* to conceal; *(AM)* to fill; **∼se** *vr* to wrap o.s. up

**taparrabo** [tapa'rraβo] *nm* loincloth

**tapete** [ta'pete] *nm* table cover

**tapia** ['tapja] *nf (garden) wall*; **tapiar** *vt* to wall in

**tapicería** [tapiθe'ria] nf tapestry; (para muebles) upholstery; (tienda) upholsterer's (shop)

**tapiz** [ta'piθ] nm (alfombra) carpet; (tela tejida) tapestry; **~ar** vt (muebles) to upholster

**tapón** [ta'pon] nm (corcho) stopper; (TEC) plug; **~ de rosca** screw-top

**taquigrafía** [takiɣra'fia] nf shorthand; **taquígrafo, a** nm/f shorthand writer, stenographer

**taquilla** [ta'kiʎa] nf (donde se compra) booking office; (suma recogida) takings pl; **taquillero, a** adj: **función taquillera** box office success ♦ nm/f ticket clerk

**tara** ['tara] nf (defecto) defect; (COM) tare

**tarántula** [ta'rantula] nf tarantula

**tararear** [tarare'ar] vi to hum

**tardanza** [tar'ðanθa] nf (demora) delay

**tardar** [tar'ðar] vi (tomar tiempo) to take a long time; (llegar tarde) to be late; (demorar) to delay; **¿tarda mucho el tren?** does the train take (very) long?; **a más ~** at the latest; **no tardes en venir** come soon

**tarde** ['tarðe] adv late ♦ nf (de día) afternoon; (al anochecer) evening; **de ~ en ~** from time to time; **¡buenas ~s!** good afternoon!; **a o por la ~** in the afternoon; in the evening

**tardío, a** [tar'ðio, a] adj (retrasado) late; (lento) slow (to arrive)

**tarea** [ta'rea] nf task; (faena) chore; (ESCOL) homework

**tarifa** [ta'rifa] nf (lista de precios) price list; (precio) tariff

**tarima** [ta'rima] nf (plataforma) platform

**tarjeta** [tar'xeta] nf card; **~ postal/ de crédito/de Navidad** postcard/ credit card/Christmas card

**tarro** ['tarro] nm jar, pot

**tarta** ['tarta] nf (pastel) cake; (torta) tart

**tartamudear** [tartamuðe'ar] vi to stammer; **tartamudo, a** adj stammering ♦ nm/f stammerer

**tártaro, a** ['tartaro, a] adj: **salsa tártara** tartare sauce

**tasa** ['tasa] nf (precio) (fixed) price, rate; (valoración) valuation; (medida, norma) measure, standard; **~ de cambio/interés** exchange/interest rate; **~ción** nf valuation; **~dor, a** nm/f valuer

**tasar** [ta'sar] vt (arreglar el precio) to fix a price for; (valorar) to value, assess

**tasca** ['taska] (fam) nf pub

**tatarabuelo, a** [tatara'βwelo, a] nm/f great-great-grandfather/mother

**tatuaje** [ta'twaxe] nm (dibujo) tattoo; (acto) tattooing

**tatuar** [ta'twar] vt to tattoo

**taurino, a** [tau'rino, a] adj bullfighting cpd

**Tauro** ['tauro] nm Taurus

**tauromaquia** [tauro'makja] nf tauromachy, (art of) bullfighting

**taxi** ['taksi] nm taxi

**taxista** [tak'sista] nm/f taxi driver

**taza** ['taθa] nf cup; (de retrete) bowl; **~ para café** coffee cup; **tazón** nm (taza grande) mug, large cup; (de fuente) basin

**te** [te] pron (complemento de objeto) you; (complemento indirecto) (to) you; (reflexivo) (to) yourself; **¿~ duele mucho el brazo?** does your arm hurt a lot?; **~ equivocas** you're wrong; **¡cálma~!** calm down!

**té** [te] nm tea

**tea** ['tea] nf torch

**teatral** [tea'tral] adj theatre cpd; (fig) theatrical

**teatro** [te'atro] nm theatre; (LITERATURA) plays pl, drama

**tebeo** [te'βeo] nm comic

**tecla** ['tekla] nf key; **~do** nm keyboard; **teclear** vi (MUS) to strum; (con los dedos) to tap ♦ vt (INFORM) to key in

**técnica** ['teknika] nf technique; (arte, oficio) craft, ver tb **técnico**

**técnico, a** ['tekniko, a] adj technical ♦ nm/f technician; (experto) expert

**tecnócrata** [tek'nokrata] nm/f technocrat

**tecnología** [teknolo'xia] *nf* technology; **tecnológico, a** *adj* technological

**techo** ['tetʃo] *nm* (*externo*) roof; (*interno*) ceiling; ~ **corredizo** sunroof

**tedio** ['teðjo] *nm* boredom, tedium; ~**so, a** *adj* boring, tedious

**teja** ['texa] *nf* (*azulejo*) tile; (*BOT*) lime (tree); ~**do** *nm* (tiled) roof

**tejemaneje** [texema'nexe] *nm* (*lío*) fuss; (*intriga*) intrigue

**tejer** [te'xer] *vt* to weave; (*hacer punto*) to knit; (*fig*) to fabricate; **tejido** *nm* (*tela*) material, fabric; (*telaraña*) web; (*ANAT*) tissue

**tel** *abr* (= *teléfono*) tel

**tela** ['tela] *nf* (*tejido*) material; (*telaraña*) web; (*en líquido*) skin; **telar** *nm* (*máquina*) loom; **telares** *nmpl* (*fábrica*) textile mill *sg*

**telaraña** [tela'raɲa] *nf* cobweb

**tele** ['tele] (*fam*) *nf* telly (*BRIT*), tube (*US*)

**tele...** ['tele] *pref* tele...; ~**comunicación** *nf* telecommunication; ~**control** *nm* remote control; ~**diario** *nm* television news; ~**difusión** *nf* (*television*) broadcast; ~**dirigido, a** *adj* remote-controlled

**teleférico** [tele'feriko] *nm* (*tren*) cable-railway; (*de esquí*) ski-lift

**telefonear** [telefone'ar] *vi* to telephone

**telefónico, a** [tele'foniko, a] *adj* telephone *cpd*

**telefonillo** [telefo'niʎo] *nm* (*de puerta*) intercom

**telefonista** [telefo'nista] *nm/f* telephonist

**teléfono** [te'lefono] *nm* (tele)phone; **estar hablando al** ~ to be on the phone; **llamar a uno por** ~ to ring sb (up) *o* phone sb (up); ~ **móvil** car phone; ~ **portátil** mobile phone

**telegrafía** [teleɣra'fia] *nf* telegraphy

**telégrafo** [te'leɣrafo] *nm* telegraph

**telegrama** [tele'ɣrama] *nm* telegram

**tele:** ~**impresor** *nm* teleprinter

(*BRIT*), teletype (*US*); ~**objetivo** *nm* telephoto lens; ~**patía** *nf* telepathy; ~**pático, a** *adj* telepathic; ~**scópico, a** *adj* telescopic; ~**scopio** *nm* telescope; ~**silla** *nm* chairlift; ~**spectador, a** *nm/f* viewer; ~**squí** *nm* ski-lift; ~**tarjeta** *nf* phonecard; ~**tipo** *nm* teletype

**televidente** [teleβi'ðente] *nm/f* viewer

**televisar** [teleβi'sar] *vt* to televise

**televisión** [teleβi'sjon] *nf* television; ~ **en colores** colour television

**televisor** [teleβi'sor] *nm* television set

**télex** ['teleks] *nm inv* telex

**telón** [te'lon] *nm* curtain; ~ **de acero** (*POL*) iron curtain; ~ **de fondo** backcloth, background

**tema** ['tema] *nm* (*asunto*) subject, topic; (*MUS*) theme ♦ *nf* (*obsesión*) obsession; **temática** *nf* (*social, histórica, artística*) range of topics; **temático, a** *adj* thematic

**temblar** [tem'blar] *vi* to shake, tremble; (*de frío*) to shiver; **temblón, ona** *adj* shaking; **temblor** *nm* trembling; (*de tierra*) earthquake; **tembloroso, a** *adj* trembling

**temer** [te'mer] *vt* to fear ♦ *vi* to be afraid; **temo que llegue tarde** I am afraid he may be late

**temerario, a** [teme'rarjo, a] *adj* (*descuidado*) reckless; (*irreflexivo*) hasty; **temeridad** *nf* (*imprudencia*) rashness; (*audacia*) boldness

**temeroso, a** [teme'roso, a] *adj* (*miedoso*) fearful; (*que inspira temor*) frightful

**temible** [te'miβle] *adj* fearsome

**temor** [te'mor] *nm* (*miedo*) fear; (*duda*) suspicion

**témpano** ['tempano] *nm:* ~ **de hielo** ice-floe

**temperamento** [tempera'mento] *nm* temperament

**temperatura** [tempera'tura] *nf* temperature

**tempestad** [tempes'tað] *nf* storm; **tempestuoso, a** *adj* stormy

**templado, a** [tem'plaðo, a] *adj*
(*moderado*) moderate; (: *en el comer*) frugal; (: *en el beber*) abs-
temious; (*agua*) lukewarm; (*clima*)
mild; (*MUS*) well-tuned; **templanza**
*nf* moderation; abstemiousness; mildness

**templar** [tem'plar] *vt* (*moderar*) to
moderate; (*furia*) to restrain; (*calor*)
to reduce; (*afinar*) to tune (up);
(*acero*) to temper; (*tuerca*) to tight-
en up; **temple** *nm* (*ajuste*) temper-
ing; (*afinación*) tuning; (*clima*) temperature; (*pintura*) tempera

**templo** ['templo] *nm* (*iglesia*)
church; (*pagano etc*) temple

**temporada** [tempo'raða] *nf* time,
period; (*estación*) season

**temporal** [tempo'ral] *adj* (*no permanente*) temporary; (*REL*) temporal
♦ *nm* storm

**tempranero, a** [tempra'nero, a] *adj*
(*BOT*) early; (*persona*) early-rising

**temprano, a** [tem'prano, a] *adj* early; (*demasiado pronto*) too soon, too
early

**ten** *vb ver* **tener**

**tenaces** [te'naθes] *adj pl ver* **tenaz**

**tenacidad** [tenaθi'ðað] *nf* tenacity;
(*dureza*) toughness; (*terquedad*)
stubbornness

**tenacillas** [tena'θiʎas] *nfpl* tongs;
(*para el pelo*) curling tongs (*BRIT*) o
iron *sg* (*US*); (*MED*) forceps

**tenaz** [te'naθ] *adj* (*material*) tough;
(*persona*) tenacious; (*creencia, resistencia*) stubborn

**tenaza(s)** [te'naθa(s)] *nf(pl)* (*MED*)
forceps; (*TEC*) pliers; (*ZOOL*) pincers

**tendedero** [tende'ðero] *nm* (*para
ropa*) drying place; (*cuerda*) clothes
line

**tendencia** [ten'denθja] *nf* tendency;
(*proceso*) trend; **tener** ~ **a** to tend
to, have a tendency to; **tendencioso,
a** *adj* tendentious

**tender** [ten'der] *vt* (*extender*) to
spread out; (*colgar*) to hang out;
(*vía férrea, cable*) to lay; (*estirar*)

stretch ♦ *vi*: ~ **a** to tend to, have a
tendency towards; **~se** *vr* to lie
down; ~ **la cama/la mesa** (*AM*) to
make the bed/lay (*BRIT*) o set (*US*)
the table

**tenderete** [tende'rete] *nm* (*puesto*)
stall; (*exposición*) display of goods

**tendero, a** [ten'dero, a] *nm/f* shopkeeper

**tendido, a** [ten'diðo, a] *adj* (*acostado*) lying down, flat; (*colgado*) hanging ♦ *nm* (*TAUR*) front rows of
seats; **a galope** ~ flat out

**tendón** [ten'don] *nm* tendon

**tendré** *etc vb ver* **tener**

**tenebroso, a** [tene'Broso, a] *adj*
(*oscuro*) dark; (*fig*) gloomy; (*complot*) sinister

**tenedor** [tene'ðor] *nm* (*CULIN*)
fork; (*poseedor*) holder; ~ **de libros**
book-keeper

**teneduría** [teneðu'ria] *nf* keeping; ~
**de libros** book-keeping

**tenencia** [te'nenθja] *nf* (*de casa*)
tenancy; (*de oficio*) tenure; (*de propiedad*) possession

---

*PALABRA CLAVE*

**tener** [te'ner] *vt* **1** (*poseer, gen*) to
have; (*en la mano*) to hold; ¿tienes
un boli? have you got a pen?; va a
~ **un niño** she's going to have a
baby; ¡ten (o tenga)!, ¡aquí tienes
(o tiene)! here you are!

**2** (*edad, medidas*) to be; **tiene 7
años** she's 7 years old; **tiene 15
cm de largo** it's 15 cm long; *ver* **calor, hambre** *etc*

**3** (*considerar*): **lo tengo por brillante** I consider him to be brilliant
; ~ **en mucho a uno** to think very
highly of sb

**4** (+ *pp*: = *pretérito*): **tengo termi-
nada ya la mitad del trabajo** I've
done half the work already

**5**: ~ **que hacer algo** to have to do
sth; **tengo que acabar este trabajo
hoy** I have to finish this job today

**6**: ¿**qué tienes, estás enfermo?**
what's the matter with you, are you

ill?
♦ ~se vr 1: ~se en pie to stand up
2: ~se por to think o.s.; se tiene
por muy listo he thinks himself
very clever

tengo etc vb ver tener

tenia ['tenja] nf tapeworm

teniente [te'njente] nm (rango) lieutenant; (ayudante) deputy

tenis ['tenis] nm tennis; ~ de mesa
table tennis; ~ta nm/f tennis player

tenor [te'nor] nm (sentido) meaning;
(MUS) tenor; a ~ de on the lines of

tensar [ten'sar] vt to tauten; (arco)
to draw

tensión [ten'sjon] nf tension; (TEC)
stress; (MED): ~ arterial blood
pressure; tener la ~ alta to have
high blood pressure

tenso, a ['tenso, a] adj tense

tentación [tenta'θjon] nf temptation

tentáculo [ten'takulo] nm tentacle

tentador, a [tenta'ðor, a] adj tempting ♦ nm/f tempter/temptress

tentar [ten'tar] vt (tocar) to touch,
feel; (seducir) to tempt; (atraer) to
attract; tentativa de asesinato attempted murder

tentativa [tenta'tiβa] nf attempt; tentativa de asesinato attempted murder

tentempié [tentem'pje] (fam) nm
snack

tenue ['tenwe] adj (delgado) thin,
slender; (neblina) light; (lazo, vínculo) slight

teñir [te'nir] vt to dye; (fig) to tinge;
~se vr to dye; ~se el pelo to dye
one's hair

teología [teolo'xia] nf theology

teorema [teo'rema] nm theorem

teoría [teo'ria] nf theory; en ~ in
theory; teóricamente adv theoreti-
cally; teórico, a [te'oriko, a] adj
teoretic(al) ♦ nm/f theoretician, theorist; teorizar
vi to theorize

terapéutico, a [tera'peutiko, a] adj
therapeutic

terapia [te'rapja] nf therapy

tercer [ter'θer] adj ver tercero

tercermundista [terθermun'dista]
adj Third World cpd

tercero, a [ter'θero, a] adj (delante
de nmsg: tercer) third ♦ nm (JUR)
third party

terceto [ter'θeto] nm trio

terciado, a [ter'θjaðo, a] adj slant-
ing

terciar [ter'θjar] vt (llevar) to wear
(across the shoulder) ♦ vi (participar) to take part; (hacer de árbitro)
to mediate; ~se vr to come up; ~io,
a adj tertiary

tercio ['terθjo] nm third

terciopelo [terθjo'pelo] nm velvet

terco, a ['terko, a] adj obstinate

tergal [ter'val] ® nm type of polyester

tergiversar [terxiβer'sar] vt to distort

termal [ter'mal] adj thermal

termas ['termas] nfpl hot springs

térmico, a ['termiko, a] adj thermal

terminación [termina'θjon] nf (final)
end; (conclusión) conclusion, ending

terminal [termi'nal] adj, nm, nf terminal

terminante [termi'nante] adj (final)
final, definitive; (tajante) categorical; ~mente adv: ~mente prohibido strictly forbidden

terminar [termi'nar] vt (completar)
to complete, finish; (concluir) to end
♦ vi (llegar a su fin) to end; (parar)
to stop; (acabar) to finish; ~se vr to
come to an end; ~ por hacer algo
to end up (by) doing sth

término ['termino] nm end, conclusion; (parada) terminus; (límite)
boundary; ~ medio average; (fig)
middle way; en último ~ (a fin de
cuentas) in the last analysis; (como
último recurso) as a last resort; en
~s de in terms of

terminología [terminolo'xia] nf ter-
minology

termodinámico, a [termoði'namiko, a] adj thermodynamic

termómetro [ter'mometro] nm thermometer

termonuclear [termonukle'ar] adj
thermonuclear

**termo(s)** ['termo(s)] ® *nm* Thermos
(flask) ®

**termostato** [termo'stato] *nm* thermostat

**ternero, a** [ter'nero, a] *nm/f* (animal) calf ♦ *nf* (carne) veal

**ternura** [ter'nura] *nf* (trato) tenderness; (palabra) endearment; (cariño) fondness

**terquedad** [terke'ðað] *nf* obstinacy;
(dureza) harshness

**terrado** [te'rraðo] *nm* terrace

**terraplén** [terra'plen] *nm* (AGR) terrace; (cuesta) slope

**terrateniente** [terrate'njente] *nm/f*
landowner

**terraza** [te'rraθa] *nf* (balcón) balcony; (techo) (flat) roof; (AGR) terrace

**terremoto** [terre'moto] *nm* earthquake

**terrenal** [terre'nal] *adj* earthly

**terreno** [te'rreno] *nm* (tierra) land;
(parcela) plot; (suelo) soil; (fig)
field; **un ~** a piece of land

**terrestre** [te'rrestre] *adj* terrestrial;
(ruta) land *cpd*

**terrible** [te'rriβle] *adj* terrible, awful

**territorio** [terri'torjo] *nm* territory

**terrón** [te'rron] *nm* (de azúcar)
lump; (de tierra) clod, lump

**terror** [te'rror] *nm* terror; **~ífico, a**
*adj* terrifying; **~ista** *adj, nm/f* terror-
ist

**terruño** [te'rruɲo] *nm* (parcela) plot;
(fig) native soil

**terso, a** ['terso, a] *adj* (liso) smooth;
(pulido) polished; **tersura** *nf* smoothness

**tertulia** [ter'tulja] *nf* (reunión informal) social gathering; (grupo) group,
circle

**tesis** ['tesis] *nf inv* thesis

**tesón** [te'son] *nm* (firmeza)
firmness; (tenacidad) tenacity

**tesorero, a** [teso'rero, a] *nm/f* treasurer

**tesoro** [te'soro] *nm* treasure; (COM,
POL) treasury

**testaferro** [testa'ferro] *nm* figure-
head

**testamentaría** [testamenta'ria] *nf*
execution of a will

**testamentario, a** [testamen'tarjo,
a] *adj* testamentary ♦ *nm/f* executor/
executrix

**testamento** [testa'mento] *nm* will

**testar** [tes'tar] *vi* to make a will

**testarudo, a** [testa'ruðo, a] *adj*
stubborn

**testículo** [tes'tikulo] *nm* testicle

**testificar** [testifi'kar] *vt* to testify;
(fig) to attest ♦ *vi* to give evidence

**testigo** [tes'tiɣo] *nm/f* witness; **~ de
cargo/descargo** witness for the
prosecution/defence; **~ ocular** eye
witness

**testimoniar** [testimo'njar] *vt* to testify to; (fig) to show; **testimonio** *nm*
testimony

**teta** ['teta] *nf* (de biberón) teat;
(ANAT: pezón) nipple; (: fam)
breast

**tétanos** ['tetanos] *nm* tetanus

**tetera** [te'tera] *nf* teapot

**tétrico, a** ['tetriko, a] *adj* gloomy,
dismal

**textil** [teks'til] *adj* textile

**texto** ['teksto] *nm* text; **textual** *adj*
textual

**textura** [teks'tura] *nf* (de tejido) texture

**tez** [teθ] *nf* (cutis) complexion;
(color) colouring

**ti** [ti] *pron* you; (reflexivo) yourself

**tía** ['tia] *nf* (pariente) aunt; (fam)
chick, bird

**tibieza** [ti'βjeθa] *nf* (temperatura)
tepidness; (fig) coolness; **tibio, a** *adj*
lukewarm

**tiburón** [tiβu'ron] *nm* shark

**tic** [tik] *nm* (ruido) click; (de reloj)
tick; (MED): **~ nervioso** nervous
tic

**tictac** [tik'tak] *nm* (de reloj) tick tock

**tiempo** ['tjempo] *nm* time; (época,
período) age, period; (METEORO-
LOGIA) weather; (LING) tense;
(DEPORTE) half; **a ~** in time; **a un
o al mismo ~** at the same time; **al**

**poco** ~ very soon (after); **se quedó poco** ~ he didn't stay very long; **hace poco** ~ not long ago; **mucho** ~ a long time; **de** ~ **en** ~ from time to time; **hace buen/mal** ~ the weather is fine/bad; **estar a** ~ to be in time; **hace** ~ some time ago; **hacer** ~ to while away the time; **motor de 2** ~**s** two-stroke engine; **primer** ~ first half

**tienda** ['tjenda] *nf* shop, store; ~ **(de campaña)** tent

**tienes** *etc vb ver* **tener**

**tienta** *etc* ['tjenta] *vb ver* **tentar** ♦ *nf*: **andar a** ~**s** to grope one's way along

**tiento** ['tjento] *vb ver* **tentar** ♦ *nm* (*tacto*) touch; (*precaución*) wariness

**tierno, a** ['tjerno, a] *adj* (*blando*) tender; (*fresco*) fresh; (*amable*) sweet

**tierra** ['tjerra] *nf* earth; (*suelo*) soil; (*mundo*) earth, world; (*país*) country, land; ~ **adentro** inland

**tieso, a** ['tjeso, a] *adj* (*rígido*) rigid; (*duro*) stiff; (*fam*: *orgulloso*) conceited

**tiesto** ['tjesto] *nm* flowerpot

**tifoidea** [tifoi'ðea] *nf* typhoid

**tifón** [ti'fon] *nm* typhoon

**tifus** ['tifus] *nm* typhus

**tigre** ['tiɣre] *nm* tiger

**tijera** [ti'xera] *nf* scissors *pl*; (*ZOOL*) claw; ~**s** *nfpl* scissors; (*para plantas*) shears

**tijereta** [tixe'reta] *nf* earwig

**tijeretear** [tixerete'ar] *vt* to snip

**tildar** [til'dar] *vt*: ~ **de** to brand as

**tilde** ['tilde] *nf* (*TIP*) tilde

**tilín** [ti'lin] *nm* tinkle

**tilo** ['tilo] *nm* lime tree

**timar** [ti'mar] *vt* (*robar*) to steal; (*estafar*) to swindle

**timbal** [tim'bal] *nm* small drum

**timbrar** [tim'brar] *vt* to stamp

**timbre** ['timbre] *nm* (*sello*) stamp; (*campanilla*) bell; (*tono*) timbre; (*COM*) stamp duty

**timidez** [timi'ðeθ] *nf* shyness; **tímido, a** *adj* shy

**timo** ['timo] *nm* swindle

**timón** [ti'mon] *nm* helm, rudder; **timonel** *nm* helmsman

**tímpano** ['timpano] *nm* (*ANAT*) eardrum; (*MUS*) small drum

**tina** ['tina] *nf* tub; (*baño*) bath(tub); **tinaja** *nf* large jar

**tinglado** [tin'glaðo] *nm* (*cobertizo*) shed; (*fig*: *truco*) trick; (*intriga*) intrigue

**tinieblas** [ti'njeβlas] *nfpl* darkness *sg*; (*sombras*) shadows

**tino** ['tino] *nm* (*habilidad*) skill; (*juicio*) insight

**tinta** ['tinta] *nf* ink; (*TEC*) dye; (*ARTE*) colour

**tinte** ['tinte] *nm* (*acto*) dyeing

**tintero** [tin'tero] *nm* inkwell

**tintinear** [tintine'ar] *vt* to tinkle

**tinto** ['tinto, a] *adj* (*teñido*) dyed ♦ *nm* red wine

**tintorería** [tintore'ria] *nf* dry cleaner's

**tintura** [tin'tura] *nf* (*acto*) dyeing; (*QUIMICA*) dye; (*farmacéutico*) tincture

**tío** ['tio] *nm* (*pariente*) uncle; (*fam*: *individuo*) bloke (*BRIT*), guy

**tiovivo** [tio'βiβo] *nm* merry-go-round

**típico, a** ['tipiko, a] *adj* typical

**tipo** ['tipo] *nm* (*clase*) type, kind; (*norma*) norm; (*patrón*) pattern; (*hombre*) fellow; (*ANAT*: *de hombre*) build; (: *de mujer*) figure; (*IMPRENTA*) type; ~ **bancario/de descuento/de interés/de cambio** bank/discount/interest/exchange rate

**tipografía** [tipoɣra'fia] *nf* (*tipo*) printing cpd; (*lugar*) printing press; **tipográfico, a** *adj* printing cpd

**tíquet** ['tiket] (*pl* ~**s**) *nm* ticket; (*en tienda*) cash slip

**tiquismiquis** [tikis'mikis] *nm inv* fussy person ♦ *nmpl* (*querellas*) squabbling *sg*; (*escrúpulos*) silly scruples

**tira** ['tira] *nf* strip; (*fig*) abundance; ~ **y afloja** give and take

**tirabuzón** [tiraβu'θon] *nm* (*rizo*) curl

**tirachinas** [tira'tʃinas] *nm inv* catapult

**tirada** [ti'raða] nf (acto) cast, throw; (distancia) distance; (serie) series; (TIP) printing, edition; **de una ~ at** one go

**tiradero** [tira'ðero] nm rubbish dump

**tirado, a** [ti'raðo, a] adj (barato) dirt-cheap; (fam: fácil) very easy

**tirador** [tira'ðor] nm (mango) handle

**tiranía** [tira'nia] nf tyranny; **tirano, a** adj tyrannical ♦ nm/f tyrant

**tirante** [ti'rante] adj (cuerda etc) tight, taut; (relaciones) strained ♦ nm (ARQ) brace; (TEC) stay; (correa) shoulder strap; **~s** nmpl (de pantalón) braces (BRIT), suspenders (US); **tirantez** nf tightness; (fig) tension

**tirar** [ti'rar] vt to throw; (dejar caer) to drop; (volcar) to upset; (derribar) to knock down o over; (jalar) to pull; (desechar) to throw out o away; (disipar) to squander; (imprimir) to print; (dar: golpe) to deal ♦ vi (disparar) to shoot; (jalar) to pull; (fig) to draw; (fam: andar) to go; (tender a, buscar realizar) to tend to; (DEPORTE) to shoot; **~se** vr to throw o.s.; (fig) to cheapen o.s.; **~ abajo** to bring down, destroy; **tira más a su padre** he takes more after his father; **ir tirando** to manage; **a todo ~** at the most

**tirita** [ti'rita] nf (sticking) plaster (BRIT), bandaid (US)

**tiritar** [tiri'tar] vi to shiver

**tiro** ['tiro] nm (lanzamiento) throw; (disparo) shot; (disparar) shooting; (DEPORTE) shot; (GOLF, TENIS) drive; (alcance) range; (golpe) blow; (engaño) hoax; **~ al blanco** target practice; **caballo de ~** cart-horse; **andar de ~s largos** to be all dressed up; **al ~ (AM)** at once

**tirón** [ti'ron] nm (sacudida) pull, tug; **de un ~** in one go, all at once

**tiroteo** [tiro'teo] nm exchange of shots, shooting

**tísico, a** ['tisiko, a] adj consumptive

**tisis** ['tisis] nf inv consumption,

tuberculosis

**títere** ['titere] nm puppet

**titiritero, a** [titiri'tero, a] nm/f puppeteer

**titubeante** [tituβe'ante] adj (inestable) shaky, tottering; (farfullante) stammering; (dudoso) hesitant

**titubear** [tituβe'ar] vi to stagger; to stammer; (fig) to hesitate; **titubeo** nm staggering; stammering; hesitation

**titulado, a** [titu'laðo, a] adj (libro) entitled; (persona) titled

**titular** [titu'lar] adj titular ♦ nm/f occupant ♦ nm headline ♦ vt to title; **~se** vr to be entitled; **título** nm title; (de diario) headline; (certificado) professional qualification; (universitario) (university) degree; (fig) right; **a título de** in the capacity of

**tiza** ['tiθa] nf chalk

**tiznar** [tiθ'nar] vt to blacken; (fig) to tarnish

**tizón** [ti'θon] nm brand; (fig) stain

**toalla** [to'aʎa] nf towel

**tobillo** [to'βiʎo] nm ankle

**tobogán** [toβo'ɣan] nm toboggan; (montaña rusa) roller-coaster; (resbaladilla) chute, slide

**toca** ['toka] nf headdress

**tocadiscos** [toka'ðiskos] nm inv record-player

**tocado, a** [to'kaðo, a] adj (fam) touched ♦ nm headdress

**tocador** [toka'ðor] nm (mueble) dressing table; (cuarto) boudoir; (fam) ladies' toilet (BRIT) o room (US)

**tocante** [to'kante]: **~ a** prep with regard to

**tocar** [to'kar] vt to touch; (MUS) to play; (topar con) to run into, strike; (referirse a) to allude to; (padecer) to suffer ♦ vi (a la puerta) to knock (on o at the door); (ser de turno) to fall to, be the turn of; (ser hora) to be due; (barco, avión) to call at; (atañer) to concern; **~se** vr (cu-

brisse la cabeza) to cover one's
head; (*tener contacto*) to touch (each
other); **por lo que a mí me toca** as
far as I am concerned

**tocayo, a** [to'kajo, a] *nm/f* name-
sake

**tocino** [to'θino] *nm* bacon

**todavía** [toða'βia] *adv* (*aun*) even;
(*aún*) still, yet; ~ **más** yet more; ~
**no** not yet

---

*PALABRA CLAVE*

**todo, a** [toðo, a] *adj* **1** (*con artículo
sg*) all; **toda la carne** all the meat;
**toda la noche** all night, the whole
night; ~ **el libro** the whole book;
**toda una botella** a whole bottle; ~
**lo contrario** quite the opposite; **está
toda sucia** she's all dirty; **por** ~ **el
país** throughout the whole country
**2** (*con artículo pl*) all; every; **los
libros** all the books; **todas las noches** every night; ~**s los que quieran salir** all those who want to leave
♦ *pron* **1** everything, all; ~**s** everyone, everybody; **lo sabemos** ~ we
know everything; ~**s querían más
tiempo** everybody *o* everyone
wanted more time; **nos marchamos**
~**s** all of us left
**2**: **con** ~: **con** ~ **él me sigue gus-
tando** even so I still like him
♦ *adv* all; **vaya** ~ **seguido** keep
straight on *o* ahead
♦ *nm*: **como un** ~ as a whole; **del**
~: **no me agrada del** ~ I don't entirely like it

---

**todopoderoso, a** [toðopoðe'roso,
a] *adj* all powerful; (*REL*) almighty

**toga** ['toxa] *nf* toga; (*ESCOL*) gown

**Tokio** ['tokjo] *n* Tokyo

**toldo** ['toldo] *nm* (*para el sol*) sunshade (*BRIT*), parasol; (*tienda*) marquee

**tolerancia** [tole'ranθja] *nf* tolerance;
**tolerante** *adj* (*sociedad*) liberal;
(*persona*) open-minded

**tolerar** [tole'rar] *vt* to tolerate; (*resistir*) to endure

**toma** ['toma] *nf* (*acto*) taking;
(*MED*) dose; ~ **(de corriente)**
socket

**tomar** [to'mar] *vt* to take; (*aspecto*)
to take on; (*beber*) to drink; ~ **vi** to
take; (*AM*) to drink; ~**se** *vr* to take;
~**se por** to consider o.s. to be; ~ **a
bien/a mal** to take well/badly; ~ **en
serio** to take seriously; ~ **el pelo a
alguien** to pull sb's leg; ~**la con
uno** to pick a quarrel with sb

**tomate** [to'mate] *nm* tomato

**tomavistas** [toma'βistas] *nm inv* movie camera

**tomillo** [to'miʎo] *nm* thyme

**tomo** ['tomo] *nm* (*libro*) volume

**ton** [ton] *abr* = **tonada** ♦ *nm*: **sin
~ ni son** without rhyme *o* reason

**tonada** [to'naða] *nf* tune

**tonalidad** [tonali'ðað] *nf* tone

**tonel** [to'nel] *nm* barrel

**tonelada** [tone'laða] *nf* ton; **tonelaje**
*nm* tonnage

**tónica** ['tonika] *nf* (*MUS*) tonic; (*fig*)
keynote

**tónico, a** ['toniko, a] *adj* tonic ♦ *nm*
(*MED*) tonic

**tonificar** [tonifi'kar] *vt* to tone up

**tono** ['tono] *nm* tone; **fuera de** ~ inappropriate; **darse** ~ to put on airs

**tontería** [tonte'ria] *nf* (*estupidez*)
foolishness; (*cosa*) stupid thing;
(*acto*) foolish act; ~**s** *nfpl* (*disparates*) rubbish *sg*, nonsense *sg*

**tonto, a** ['tonto, a] *adj* stupid, silly
♦ *nm/f* fool; (*payaso*) clown

**topar** [to'par] *vt* (*tropezar*) to bump
into; (*encontrar*) to find, come
across; (*ZOOL*) to butt ♦ *vi*: ~ **contra** *o* **en** to run into; ~ **con** to run
up against

**tope** ['tope] *adj* maximum ♦ *nm* (*fin*)
end; (*límite*) limit; (*FERRO*) buffer;
(*AUTO*) bumper; **al** ~ end to end

**tópico, a** ['topiko, a] *adj* topical ♦
*nm* platitude

**topo** ['topo] *nm* (*ZOOL*) mole; (*fig*)
blunderer

**topografía** [topoxra'fia] *nf* topog-
raphy; **topógrafo, a** *nm/f* topog-

rapher

**toque** etc ['toke] vb ver tocar ♦ nm touch; (MUS) beat; (de campana) peal; (fig) crux; **dar un ~ a** to test; **~ de queda** curfew; **~tear** vt to handle

**toqué** vb ver tocar

**toquilla** [to'kiʎa] nf (pañuelo) head-scarf; (chal) shawl

**tórax** ['toraks] nm thorax

**torbellino** [torbe'ʎino] nm whirl-wind; (fig) whirl

**torcedura** [torθe'ðura] nf twist; (MED) sprain

**torcer** [tor'θer] vt to twist; (la esquina) to turn; (MED) to sprain ♦ vi (desviar) to turn off; **~se** vr (la-dearse) to bend; (desviarse) to go astray; (fracasar) to go wrong; **torci-do, a** adj twisted; (fig) crooked ♦ nm curl

**tordo, a** ['torðo, a] adj dappled ♦ nm thrush

**torear** [tore'ar] vt (fig: evadir) to avoid; (jugar con) to tease ♦ vi to fight bulls; **toreo** nm bullfighting; **to-rero, a** nm/f bullfighter

**tormenta** [tor'menta] nf storm; (fig: confusión) turmoil

**tormento** [tor'mento] nm torture; (fig) anguish

**tornar** [tor'nar] vt (devolver) to re-turn, give back; (transformar) to transform ♦ vi to go back; **~se** vr (ponerse) to become

**tornasolado, a** [tornaso'laðo, a] adj (brillante) iridescent; (reluciente) shimmering

**torneo** [tor'neo] nm tournament

**tornillo** [tor'niʎo] nm screw

**torniquete** [torni'kete] nm (puerta) turnstile; (MED) tourniquet

**torno** ['torno] nm (TEC) winch; (tambor) drum; **en ~** (a) round, about

**toro** ['toro] nm bull; (fam) he-man; **los ~s** bullfighting

**toronja** [to'ronxa] nf grapefruit

**torpe** ['torpe] adj (poco hábil) clum-sy, awkward; (necio) dim; (lento) slow

**torpedo** [tor'peðo] nm torpedo

**torpeza** [tor'peθa] nf (falta de agili-dad) clumsiness; (lentitud) slowness; (error) mistake

**torre** ['torre] nf tower; (de petróleo) derrick

**torrefacto, a** [torre'fakto, a] adj roasted

**torrente** [to'rrente] nm torrent

**tórrido, a** [to'rriðo, a] adj torrid

**torrija** [to'rrixa] nf French toast

**torsión** [tor'sjon] nf twisting

**torso** ['torso] nm torso

**torta** ['torta] nf cake; (fam) slap

**tortícolis** [tor'tikolis] nm inv stiff neck

**tortilla** [tor'tiʎa] nf omelette; (AM) maize pancake; **~ francesa/ española** plain/potato omelette

**tórtola** ['tortola] nf turtledove

**tortuga** [tor'tuxa] nf tortoise

**tortuoso, a** [tor'twoso, a] adj wind-ing

**tortura** [tor'tura] nf torture; **torturar** vt to torture

**tos** [tos] nf cough; **~ ferina** whoop-ing cough

**tosco, a** ['tosko, a] adj coarse

**toser** [to'ser] vi to cough

**tostada** [tos'taða] nf piece of toast; **tostado, a** adj toasted; (por el sol) dark brown; (piel) tanned

**tostador** [tosta'ðor] nm toaster

**tostar** [tos'tar] vt to toast; (café) to roast; (persona) to tan; **~se** vr to get brown

**total** [to'tal] adj total ♦ adv in short; (al fin y al cabo) when all is said and done ♦ nm total; **~ que** to cut (BRIT) o make (US) a long story short

**totalidad** [totali'ðað] nf whole

**totalitario, a** [totali'tarjo, a] adj to-talitarian

**tóxico, a** ['toksiko, a] adj toxic ♦ nm poison; **toxicómano, a** nm/f drug addict

**toxina** [tok'sina] nf toxin

**tozudo, a** [to'θuðo, a] adj obstinate

**traba** ['traβa] nf bond, tie; (cadena) shackle

**trabajador, a** [traβaxa'ðor, a] adj hard-working ♦ nm/f worker

**trabajar** [traβa'xar] vt to work; (AGR) to till; (empeñarse en) to work at; (empujar: persona) to push; (convencer) to persuade ♦ vi to work; (esforzarse) to strive; **trabajo** nm work; (tarea) task; (POL) labour; (fig) effort; **tomarse el trabajo de** to take the trouble to; **trabajo por turno/a destajo** shift work/piecework; **trabajoso, a** adj hard

**trabalenguas** [traβa'lenɡwas] nm inv tongue twister

**trabar** [tra'βar] vt (juntar) to join, unite; (atar) to tie down, fetter; (agarrar) to seize; (amistad) to strike up; **~se** vr to become entangled; **trabársele a uno la lengua** to be tongue-tied

**tracción** [trak'θjon] nf traction; **~ delantera/trasera** front-wheel/rear-wheel drive

**tractor** [trak'tor] nm tractor

**tradición** [traði'θjon] nf tradition; **tradicional** adj traditional

**traducción** [traðuk'θjon] nf translation

**traducir** [traðu'θir] vt to translate; **traductor, a** nm/f translator

**traer** [tra'er] vt to bring; (llevar) to carry; (ropa) to wear; (incluir) to carry; (fig) to cause; **~se** vr: **~se algo** to be up to sth

**traficar** [trafi'kar] vi to trade

**tráfico** ['trafiko] nm (COM) trade; (AUTO) traffic

**tragaluz** [traɣa'luθ] nm skylight

**tragaperras** [traɣa'perras] nm o f inv slot machine

**tragar** [tra'ɣar] vt to swallow; (devorar) to devour, bolt down; **~se** vr to swallow

**tragedia** [tra'xeðja] nf tragedy; **trágico, a** adj tragic

**trago** ['traɣo] nm (líquido) drink; (bocado) gulp; (fam: de bebida)

swig; (desgracia) blow

**traición** [trai'θjon] nf treachery; (JUR) treason; (una ~) act of treachery; **traicionar** vt to betray

**traicionero, a** [traiθjo'nero, a] adj treacherous

**traidor, a** [trai'ðor, a] adj treacherous ♦ nm/f traitor

**traigo** etc vb ver **traer**

**traje** ['traxe] vb ver **traer** ♦ nm (de hombre) suit; (de mujer) dress; (vestido típico) costume; **~ de baño** swimsuit; **~ de luces** bullfighter's costume

**trajera** etc vb ver **traer**

**trajín** [tra'xin] nm haulage; (fam: movimiento) bustle; **trajinar** vt (llevar) to carry, transport ♦ vi (moverse) to bustle about; (viajar) to travel around

**trama** ['trama] nf (intriga) plot; (de tejido) weft (BRIT), woof (US); **tramar** vt to plot; (TEC) to weave

**tramitar** [trami'tar] vt (asunto) to transact; (negociar) to negotiate; (manejar) to handle

**trámite** ['tramite] nm (paso) step; (JUR) transaction; **~s** nmpl (burocracia) procedure sg; (JUR) proceedings

**tramo** ['tramo] nm (de tierra) plot; (de escalera) flight; (de via) section

**tramoya** [tra'moja] nf (TEATRO) piece of stage machinery; (fig) scheme; **tramoyista** nm/f scene shifter; (fig) trickster

**trampa** ['trampa] nf trap; (en el suelo) trapdoor; (engaño) trick; (fam) fiddle; **trampear** vt, vi to cheat

**trampolín** [trampo'lin] nm trampoline; (de piscina etc) diving board

**tramposo, a** [tram'poso, a] adj crooked, cheating ♦ nm/f crook, cheat

**tranca** ['tranka] nf (palo) stick; (de puerta, ventana) bar; **trancar** vt to bar

**trance** ['tranθe] nm (momento difícil) difficult moment o juncture; (estado hipnotizado) trance

**tranco** ['tranko] nm stride

**tranquilidad** [traŋkili'ðað] nf (calma) calmness, stillness; (paz) peacefulness

**tranquilizar** [traŋkili'θar] vt (calmar) to calm (down); (asegurar) to reassure; ~**se** vr to calm down; **tranquilo, a** adj (calmado) calm; (apacible) peaceful; (mar) calm; (mente) untroubled

**transacción** [transak'θjon] nf transaction

**transbordador** [transβorða'ðor] nm ferry

**transbordar** [transβor'ðar] vt to transfer; **transbordo** nm transfer; **hacer transbordo** to change (trains)

**transcurrir** [transku'rrir] vi (tiempo) to pass; (hecho) to turn out

**transcurso** [trans'kurso] nm: ~ **del tiempo** lapse (of time)

**transeúnte** [transe'unte] adj transient ♦ nm/f passer-by

**transferencia** [transfe'renθja] nf transference; (COM) transfer

**transferir** [transfe'rir] vt to transfer

**transformador** [transforma'ðor] nm (ELEC) transformer

**transformar** [transfor'mar] vt to transform; (convertir) to convert

**tránsfuga** ['transfuya] nm/f (MIL) deserter; (POL) turncoat

**transfusión** [transfu'sjon] nf transfusion

**transición** [transi'θjon] nf transition

**transigir** [transi'xir] vi to compromise, make concessions

**transistor** [transis'tor] nm transistor

**transitar** [transi'tar] vi to go (from place to place); **tránsito** nm transit; (AUTO) traffic; **transitorio, a** adj transitory

**transmisión** [transmi'sjon] nf (TEC) transmission; (transferencia) transfer; ~ **en directo/exterior** live/outside broadcast

**transmitir** [transmi'tir] vt to transmit; (RADIO, TV) to broadcast

**transparencia** [transpa'renθja] nf transparency; (claridad) clearness,

clarity; (foto) slide

**transparentar** [transparen'tar] vt to reveal ♦ vi to be transparent; **transparente** adj transparent; (claro) clear; (ligero) diaphanous

**transpirar** [transpi'rar] vi to perspire; (fig) to transpire

**transportar** [transpor'tar] vt to transport; (llevar) to carry; **transporte** nm transport; (COM) haulage

**transversal** [transβer'sal] adj transverse, cross

**tranvía** [tram'bia] nm tram

**trapecio** [tra'peθjo] nm trapeze; **trapecista** nm/f trapeze artist

**trapero, a** [tra'pero, a] nm/f ragman

**trapiche** [tra'pitʃe] nm (fam) nm scheme, fiddle

**trapo** ['trapo] nm (tela) rag; (de cocina) cloth; **poner un** ~ **a** (o por) to dust

**tráquea** ['trakea] nf windpipe

**traqueteo** [trake'teo] nm (golpeteo) rattling

**tras** [tras] prep (detrás) behind; (después) after

**trasatlántico** [trasat'lantiko] nm (barco) (cabin) cruiser

**trascendencia** [trasθen'denθja] nf (importancia) importance; (FILOSOFIA) transcendence

**trascendental** [trasθenden'tal] adj important; (FILOSOFIA) transcendental

**trascender** [trasθen'der] vi (noticias) to come out; (suceso) to have a wide effect

**trasero, a** [tra'sero, a] adj back, rear ♦ nm (ANAT) bottom

**trasfondo** [tras'fondo] nm background

**trasgredir** [trasxre'ðir] vt to contravene

**trashumante** [trasu'mante] adj (animales) migrating

**trasladar** [trasla'ðar] vt to move; (persona) to transfer; (postergar) to postpone; (copiar) to copy; ~**se** vr (mudarse) to move; **traslado** nm move; (mudanza) move, removal

**traslucir** [traslu'θir] vt to show; ~se vr to be translucent; (fig) to be revealed

**trasluz** [tras'luθ] nm reflected light; al ~ against o up to the light

**trasnochador, a** [trasnotʃa'ðor, a] nm/f night owl

**trasnochar** [trasno'tʃar] vi (acostarse tarde) to stay up late; (no dormir) to have a sleepless night

**traspapelar** [traspape'lar] vt (documento, carta) to mislay, misplace

**traspasar** [traspa'sar] vt (suj: bala etc) to pierce, go through; (propiedad) to sell, transfer; (calle) to cross over; (límites) to go beyond; (ley) to break; **traspaso** nm (venta) transfer, sale

**traspié** [tras'pje] nm (tropezón) trip; (fig) blunder

**trasplantar** [trasplan'tar] vt to transplant

**traste** ['traste] nm (MUS) fret; dar al ~ con algo to ruin sth

**trastero** [tras'tero] nm storage room

**trastienda** [tras'tjenda] nf back of shop

**trasto** ['trasto] (pey) nm (cosa) piece of junk; (persona) dead loss

**trastornado, a** [trastor'naðo, a] adj (loco) mad, crazy

**trastornar** [trastor'nar] vt to overturn, upset; (fig: ideas) to confuse; (: nervios) to shatter; (: persona) to drive crazy; ~se vr (volverse loco) to go mad o crazy; **trastorno** nm (acto) overturning; (confusión) confusion

**tratable** [tra'taβle] adj friendly

**tratado** [tra'taðo] nm (POL) treaty; (COM) agreement

**tratamiento** [trata'mjento] nm treatment; ~ de textos (INFORM) word processing cpd

**tratar** [tra'tar] vt (ocuparse de) to treat; (manejar, TEC) to handle; (MED) to treat; (dirigirse a: persona) to address ♦ vi: ~ de (hablar sobre) to deal with, be about; (intentar) to try to; ~se vr to treat each

other; ~ con (COM) to trade in; (negociar) to negotiate with; (tener contactos) to have dealings with; ¿de qué se trata? what's it about?; **trato** nm dealings pl; (relaciones) relationship; (comportamiento) manner; (COM) agreement; (título) (form of) address

**trauma** ['trauma] nm trauma

**través** [tra'βes] nm (fig) reverse; al ~ across, crossways; a ~ de across; (sobre) over; (por) through

**travesaño** [traβe'saɲo] nm (ARQ) crossbeam; (DEPORTE) crossbar

**travesía** [traβe'sia] nf (calle) cross-street; (NAUT) crossing

**travesura** [traβe'sura] nf (broma) prank; (ingenio) wit

**traviesa** [tra'βjesa] nf (ARQ) crossbeam

**travieso, a** [tra'βjeso, a] adj (niño) naughty

**trayecto** [tra'jekto] nm (ruta) road, way; (viaje) journey; (tramo) stretch; (curso) course; ~ria nf trajectory; (fig) path

**traza** ['traθa] nf (aspecto) looks pl; (señal) sign; ~do, a adj: bien ~do shapely, well-formed ♦ nm (ARQ) plan, design; (fig) outline

**trazar** [tra'θar] vt (ARQ) to plan; (ARTE) to sketch; (fig) to trace; (plan) to follow; **trazo** nm (línea) line; (bosquejo) sketch

**trébol** ['treβol] nm (BOT) clover

**trece** ['treθe] num thirteen

**trecho** ['tretʃo] nm (distancia) distance; (de tiempo) while; (fam) piece; de ~ en ~ at intervals

**tregua** ['trexwa] nf (MIL) truce; (fig) lull

**treinta** ['treinta] num thirty

**tremendo, a** [tre'mendo, a] adj (terrible) terrible; (imponente: cosa) imposing; (fam: fabuloso) tremendous

**trémulo, a** ['tremulo, a] adj quivering

**tren** [tren] nm train; ~ de aterrizaje undercarriage

**trenza** ['trenθa] nf (de pelo) plait (BRIT), braid (US); **trenzar** vt (pelo) to plait, braid; **trenzarse** vr (AM) to become involved

**trepadora** [trepa'ðora] nf (BOT) climber

**trepar** [tre'par] vt, vi to climb

**trepidante** [trepi'ðante] adj (acción) fast; (ritmo) hectic

**trepidar** [trepi'ðar] vi to shake, vibrate

**tres** [tres] num three

**tresillo** [tre'siʎo] nm three-piece suite; (MUS) triplet

**treta** ['treta] nf (COM etc) gimmick; (fig) trick

**triángulo** ['trjaŋgulo] nm triangle

**tribu** ['triβu] nf tribe

**tribuna** [tri'βuna] nf (plataforma) platform; (DEPORTE) (grand)stand; (fig) public speaking

**tribunal** [triβu'nal] nm (JUR) court; (comisión, fig) tribunal

**tributar** [triβu'tar] vt (gen) to pay; tributo (COM) tax

**tributo** [tri'βuto] nm (COM) tax

**tricotar** [triko'tar] vi to knit

**trigal** [tri'val] nm wheat field

**trigo** ['trivo] nm wheat

**trigueño, a** [tri'veɲo, a] adj (pelo) corn-coloured; (piel) olive-skinned

**trillado, a** [tri'ʎaðo, a] adj (camino) beaten; (fig) trite, hackneyed; **trilladora** nf threshing machine

**trillar** [tri'ʎar] vt (AGR) to thresh

**trimestral** [trimes'tral] adj quarterly; (ESCOL) termly

**trimestre** [tri'mestre] nm (ESCOL) term

**trinar** [tri'nar] vi (pájaros) to sing; (rabiar) to fume, be angry

**trincar** [trin'kar] vt (atar) to tie up; (inmovilizar) to pinion

**trinchar** [trin'tʃar] vt to carve

**trinchera** [trin'tʃera] nf (fosa) trench

**trineo** [tri'neo] nm sledge

**trinidad** [trini'ðað] nf trio; (REL): la T~ the Trinity

**trino** ['trino] nm trill

**tripa** ['tripa] nf (ANAT) intestine; (fam: tb: ~s) insides pl

**triple** ['triple] adj triple

**triplicado, a** [tripli'kaðo, a] adj: por ~ in triplicate

**tripulación** [tripula'θjon] nf crew

**tripulante** [tripu'lante] nm/f crewman/woman

**tripular** [tripu'lar] vt (barco) to man; (AUTO) to drive

**triquiñuela** [triki'pwela] nf trick

**tris** [tris] nm inv crack; en un ~ in an instant

**triste** ['triste] adj (afligido) sad; (sombrío) melancholy, gloomy; (lamentable) sorry, miserable; ~za nf (aflicción) sadness; (melancolía) melancholy

**triturar** [tritu'rar] vt (moler) to grind; (mascar) to chew

**triunfar** [trjun'far] vi (tener éxito) to triumph; (ganar) to win; **triunfo** nm triumph

**trivial** [tri'βjal] adj trivial; ~izar vt to minimize, play down

**triza** ['triθa] nf: hacer ~s to smash to bits; (papel) to tear to shreds

**trocar** [tro'kar] vt to exchange

**trocear** [troθe'ar] vt (carne, manzana) to cut up, cut into pieces

**trocha** ['trotʃa] nf short cut

**troche** ['trotʃe]: a ~ y moche adv helter-skelter, pell-mell

**trofeo** [tro'feo] nm (premio) trophy; (éxito) success

**tromba** ['tromba] nf whirlwind

**trombón** [trom'bon] nm trombone

**trombosis** [trom'bosis] nf inv thrombosis

**trompa** ['trompa] nf horn; (trompo) humming top; (hocico) snout; (fam): cogerse una ~ to get tight

**trompazo** [trom'paθo] nm bump, bang

**trompeta** [trom'peta] nf trumpet; (clarín) bugle

**trompicón** [trompi'kon]: a ~es adv in fits and starts

**trompo** ['trompo] nm spinning top

**trompón** [trom'pon] nm bump, bang

**tronar** [tro'nar] vt (AM) to shoot ♦ vi to thunder; (fig) to rage

**tronco** ['tronko] nm (de árbol, ANAT) trunk

**tronchar** [tron'tʃar] vt (árbol) to chop down; (fig: vida) to cut short; (: esperanza) to shatter; (persona) to tire out; **~se** vr to fall down

**tronera** [tro'nera] nf (MIL) loophole; (ARQ) small window

**trono** ['trono] nm throne

**tropa** ['tropa] nf (MIL) troop; (soldados) soldiers pl

**tropel** [tro'pel] nm (muchedumbre) crowd

**tropezar** [trope'θar] vi to trip, stumble; (fig) to slip up; **~ con** to run into; (topar con) to bump into; **tropezón** nm trip; (fig) blunder

**tropical** [tropi'kal] adj tropical

**trópico** ['tropiko] nm tropic

**tropiezo** [tro'pjeθo] vb ver **tropezar ♦** nm (error) slip, blunder; (desgracia) misfortune; (obstáculo) snag

**trotamundos** [trota'mundos] nm inv globetrotter

**trotar** [tro'tar] vi to trot; **trote** nm trot; (fam) travelling; **de mucho trote** hard-wearing

**trozo** ['troθo] nm bit, piece

**truco** ['truko] nm (habilidad) knack; (engaño) trick

**trucha** ['trutʃa] nf trout

**trueno** ['trweno] nm thunder; (estampido) bang

**trueque** etc ['trweke] vb ver **trocar ♦** nm exchange; (COM) barter

**trufa** ['trufa] nf (BOT) truffle

**truhán, ana** [tru'an, ana] nm/f rogue

**truncar** [trun'kar] vt (cortar) to truncate; (fig: la vida etc) to cut short; (: el desarrollo) to stunt

**tu** [tu] adj your

**tú** [tu] pron you

**tubérculo** [tu'βerkulo] nm (BOT) tuber

**tuberculosis** [tuβerku'losis] nf inv tuberculosis

**tubería** [tuβe'ria] nf pipes pl; (conducto) pipeline

**tubo** ['tuβo] nm tube, pipe; **~ de ensayo** test tube; **~ de escape** ex-

haust (pipe)

**tuerca** ['twerka] nf nut

**tuerto, a** ['twerto, a] adj blind in one eye ♦ nm/f one-eyed person

**tuerza** etc vb ver **torcer**

**tuétano** ['twetano] nm marrow; (BOT) pith

**tufo** ['tufo] nm vapour; (fig: pey) stench

**tugurio** [tu'ɣurio] nm slum

**tul** [tul] nm tulle

**tulipán** [tuli'pan] nm tulip

**tullido, a** [tu'ʎiðo, a] adj crippled

**tumba** ['tumba] nf (sepultura) tomb

**tumbar** [tum'bar] vt to knock down; **~se** vr (echarse) to lie down; (extenderse) to stretch out

**tumbo** ['tumbo] nm (caída) fall; (de vehículo) jolt

**tumbona** [tum'bona] nf (butaca) easy chair; (de playa) deckchair (BRIT), beach chair (US)

**tumor** [tu'mor] nm tumour

**tumulto** [tu'multo] nm turmoil

**tuna** ['tuna] nf (BOT) prickly pear; (MUS) student music group; ver tb **tuno**

**tunante** [tu'nante] nm/f rascal

**tunda** ['tunda] nf (golpeo) beating

**túnel** ['tunel] nm tunnel

**Túnez** ['tuneθ] nm Tunisia; (ciudad) Tunis

**tuno, a** ['tuno, a] nm/f (fam) rogue ♦ nm member of student music group

**tuntún** [tun'tun]: **al ~** adv thoughtlessly

**tupido, a** [tu'piðo, a] adj (denso) dense; (tela) close-woven; (fig) dim

**turba** ['turβa] nf crowd

**turbación** [turβa'θjon] nf (molestia) disturbance; (preocupación) worry

**turbado, a** adj (molesto) disturbed; (preocupado) worried

**turbante** [tur'βante] nm turban

**turbar** [tur'βar] vt (molestar) to disturb; (incomodar) to upset; **~se** vr to be disturbed

**turbina** [tur'βina] nf turbine

**turbio, a** ['turβjo, a] adj cloudy;

*(tema etc)* confused ♦ *adv* indistinctly

**turbulencia** [turβu'lenθja] *nf* turbulence; *(fig)* restlessness; **turbulento, a** *adj* turbulent; *(fig: intranquilo)* restless; *(: ruidoso)* noisy

**turco, a** ['turko, a] *adj* Turkish ♦ *nm/f* Turk

**turismo** [tu'rismo] *nm* tourism; *(coche)* saloon car; **turista** *nmf* tourist; **turístico, a** *adj* tourist *cpd*

**turnar** [tur'nar] *vi* to take (it in) turns; **~se** *vr* to take (it in) turns; **turno** *nm (INDUSTRIA)* shift; *(oportunidad, orden de prioridad)* opportunity; *(juegos etc)* turn

**turquesa** [tur'kesa] *nf* turquoise

**Turquía** [tur'kia] *nf* Turkey

**turrón** [tu'rron] *nm (dulce)* nougat

**tutear** [tute'ar] *vt* to address as familiar "tú"; **~se** *vr* to be on familiar terms

**tutela** [tu'tela] *nf (legal)* guardianship; *(instrucción)* guidance; **tutelar** *adj* tutelary ♦ *vt* to protect

**tutor, a** [tu'tor, a] *nm/f (legal)* guardian; *(ESCOL)* tutor

**tuve** *etc vb ver* **tener**

**tuviera** *etc vb ver* **tener**

**tuyo, a** ['tujo, a] *adj* yours, of yours ♦ *pron* yours; **un amigo ~** a friend of yours; **los ~s** *(fam)* your relations, your family

**TV** ['te'βe] *nf abr (= televisión)* TV

**TVE** *nf abr* = **Televisión Española**

---

# U

**u** [u] *conj* or

**ubicar** [uβi'kar] *vt* to place, situate; *(: fig)* to install in a post; *(AM: encontrar)* to find; **~se** *vr* to lie, to be located

**ubre** ['uβre] *nf* udder

**Ud(s)** *abr* = **usted(es)**

**ufanarse** [ufa'narse] *vr* to boast; **~ de** to pride o.s. on; **ufano, a** *adj (arrogante)* arrogant; *(presumido)* conceited

**UGT** *nf abr* = **Unión General de Trabajadores**

**ujier** [u'xjer] *nm* usher; *(portero)* doorkeeper

**úlcera** ['ulθera] *nf* ulcer

**ulcerar** [ulθe'rar] *vt* to make sore; **~se** *vr* to ulcerate

**ulterior** [ulte'rjor] *adj (más allá)* farther, further; *(subsecuente, siguiente)* subsequent

**últimamente** [ultima'mente] *adv (recientemente)* lately, recently

**ultimar** [ulti'mar] *vt* to finish; *(finalizar)* to finalize; *(AM: rematar)* to finish off

**ultimátum** [ulti'matum] *(pl* **~s)** ultimatum

**último, a** ['ultimo, a] *adj* last; *(más reciente)* latest, most recent; *(más bajo)* bottom; *(más alto)* top; *(fig)* final, extreme; **en las últimas** on one's last legs; **por ~** finally

**ultra** ['ultra] *adj* ultra ♦ *nm/f* extreme right-winger

**ultrajar** [ultra'xar] *vt (escandalizar)* to outrage; *(insultar)* to insult, abuse; **ultraje** *nm* outrage; insult

**ultramar** [ultra'mar] *nm*: **de o en ~** abroad, overseas

**ultramarinos** [ultrama'rinos] *nmpl* groceries; **tienda de ~** grocer's (shop)

**ultranza** [ul'tranθa]: **a ~** *adv (a todo trance)* at all costs; *(completo)* outright

**ultrasónico, a** [ultra'soniko, a] *adj* ultrasonic

**ultratumba** [ultra'tumba] *nf*: **la vida de ~** the next life

**ulular** [ulu'lar] *vi* to howl; *(búho)* to hoot

**umbral** [um'bral] *nm (gen)* threshold

**umbrío, a** [um'brio, a] *adj* shady

---

PALABRA CLAVE

**un, una** [un, 'una] *art indef* a; *(antes de vocal)* an; **una mujer/ naranja** a woman/an orange ♦ *adj*: **unos** (o **unas**): **hay unos regalos para ti** there are some presents for you; **hay unas cervezas en la nevera** there are some beers in the fridge

**unánime** [u'nanime] *adj* unanimous; **unanimidad** *nf* unanimity

**undécimo, a** [un'deθimo, a] *adj* eleventh

**ungir** [un'xir] *vt* to rub with ointment; (*REL*) to anoint

**ungüento** [un'gwento] *nm* ointment; (*fig*) salve, balm

**únicamente** ['unikamente] *adv* solely, only

**único, a** ['uniko, a] *adj* only, sole; (*sin par*) unique

**unidad** [uni'ðað] *nf* unity; (*COM, TEC etc*) unit

**unido, a** [u'niðo, a] *adj* joined, linked; (*fig*) united

**unificar** [unifi'kar] *vt* to unite, unify

**uniformar** [unifor'mar] *vt* to make uniform, level up; (*persona*) to put into uniform

**uniforme** [uni'forme] *adj* uniform, equal; (*superficie*) even ♦ *nm* uniform; **uniformidad** *nf* uniformity; (*llaneza*) levelness, evenness

**unilateral** [unilate'ral] *adj* unilateral

**unión** [u'njon] *nf* union; (*acto*) uniting, joining; (*calidad*) unity; (*TEC*) joint; (*fig*) closeness, togetherness; **la U~ Soviética** the Soviet Union

**unir** [u'nir] *vt* (*juntar*) to join, unite; (*atar*) to tie, fasten; (*combinar*) to combine; ~**se** *vr* to join together, unite; (*empresas*) to merge

**unísono** [u'nisono] *nm*: **al ~ in unison**

**universal** [unißer'sal] *adj* universal; (*mundial*) world *cpd*

**universidad** [unißersi'ðað] *nf* university

**universitario, a** [unißersi'tarjo, a] *adj* university *cpd* ♦ *nm/f* (*profesor*) lecturer; (*estudiante*) (university) student; (*graduado*) graduate

**universo** [uni'ßerso] *nm* universe

---

**uno, a** ['uno, a] *adj* one; **es todo ~** it's all one and the same; ~**s pocos** a few; ~**s cien** about a hundred
♦ *pron* **1** one; **quiero ~ solo** I only want one; ~ **de ellos** one of them
**2** (*alguien*) somebody, someone; **conozco a ~ que se le parece** I know somebody *o* someone who looks like you; ~ **mismo** oneself; ~**s querían quedarse** some (people) wanted to stay
**3**: (**los**) ~**s ...** (**los**) **otros ...** some ... others; each other, one another; **una y otra son muy agradables** they're both very nice
♦ *nf* one; **es la una** it's one o'clock
♦ *nm* (number) one

**untar** [un'tar] *vt* to rub; (*engrasar*) to grease, oil; (*fig*) to bribe

**uña** ['uɲa] *nf* (*ANAT*) nail; (*garra*) claw; (*casco*) hoof; (*arrancaclavos*) claw

**uranio** [u'ranjo] *nm* uranium

**urbanidad** [urßani'ðað] *nf* courtesy, politeness

**urbanismo** [urßa'nismo] *nm* town planning

**urbanización** [urßaniθa'θjon] *nf* (*barrio, colonia*) housing estate

**urbanizar** [urßani'θar] *vt* (*zona*) to develop, urbanize

**urbano, a** [ur'ßano, a] *adj* (*de ciudad*) urban; (*cortés*) courteous, polite

**urbe** [ur'ße] *nf* large city

**urdimbre** [ur'ðimbre] *nf* (*de tejido*) warp; (*intriga*) intrigue

**urdir** [ur'ðir] *vt* to warp; (*fig*) to plot, contrive

**urgencia** [ur'xenθja] *nf* urgency; (*prisa*) haste, rush; (*emergencia*) emergency; **servicios de ~** emergency services; **urgente** *adj* urgent

**urgir** [ur'xir] *vi* to be urgent; **me urge** I'm in a hurry for it

**urinario, a** [uri'narjo, a] *adj* urinary ♦ *nm* urinal

**urna** ['urna] *nf* urn; (*POL*) ballot box

**urraca** [u'rraka] *nf* magpie

**URSS** *nf*: la ~ the USSR

**Uruguay** [uru'ɣwai] *nm*: el ~ Uruguay; **uruguayo, a** *adj, nm/f* Uruguayan

**usado, a** [u'saðo, a] *adj* used; *(ropa etc)* worn

**usanza** [u'sanθa] *nf* custom, usage

**usar** [u'sar] *vt* to use; *(ropa)* to wear; *(tener costumbre)* to be in the habit of; ~se *vr* to be used; **uso** *nm* use; wear; *(costumbre)* usage, custom; *(moda)* fashion; **al uso** in keeping with custom; **al uso de** in the style of

**usted** [us'teð] *pron* (*sg*) you *sg*; (*pl*): ~es you *pl*

**usual** [u'swal] *adj* usual

**usuario, a** [u'swarjo, a] *nm/f* user

**usufructo** [usu'frukto] *nm* use

**usura** [u'sura] *nf* usury; **usurero, a** *nm/f* usurer

**usurpar** [usur'par] *vt* to usurp

**utensilio** [uten'siljo] *nm* tool; *(CULIN)* utensil

**útero** ['utero] *nm* uterus, womb

**útil** ['util] *adj* useful ♦ *nm* tool; **utilidad** *nf* usefulness; *(COM)* profit; **utilizar** *vt* to use, utilize

**utopía** [uto'pia] *nf* Utopia; **utópico, a** *adj* Utopian

**uva** ['uβa] *nf* grape

# V

**v** *abr* (= *voltio*) V

**va** *vb ver* **ir**

**vaca** ['baka] *nf* (*animal*) cow; **carne de ~** beef

**vacaciones** [baka'θjones] *nfpl* holidays

**vacante** [ba'kante] *adj* vacant, empty ♦ *nf* vacancy

**vaciar** [ba'θjar] *vt* to empty out; *(ahuecar)* to hollow out; *(moldear)* to cast ♦ *vi* (*río*): ~ **(en)** to flow (into); ~se *vr* to empty out

**vacilación** [baθila'θjon] *nf* hesitation

**vacilante** [baθi'lante] *adj* unsteady;

*(habla)* faltering; *(fig)* hesitant

**vacilar** [baθi'lar] *vi* to be unsteady; *(al hablar)* to falter; *(fig)* to hesitate, waver; *(memoria)* to fail

**vacío, a** [ba'θio, a] *adj* empty; *(puesto)* vacant; *(desocupado)* idle; *(vano)* vain ♦ *nm* emptiness; *(FISICA)* vacuum; *(un ~)* (empty) space

**vacuna** [ba'kuna] *nf* vaccine; **vacunar** *vt* to vaccinate

**vacuno, a** [ba'kuno, a] *adj* cow *cpd*; **ganado ~** cattle

**vacuo, a** ['bakwo, a] *adj* empty

**vadear** [baðe'ar] *vt* (*río*) to ford; **vado** *nm* ford

**vagabundo, a** [baɣa'βundo, a] *adj* wandering; *(pey)* vagrant ♦ *nm* tramp

**vagamente** [baɣa'mente] *adv* vaguely

**vagancia** [ba'ɣanθja] *nf* *(pereza)* idleness, laziness

**vagar** [ba'ɣar] *vi* to wander; *(no hacer nada)* to idle

**vagina** [ba'xina] *nf* vagina

**vago, a** ['baɣo, a] *adj* vague; *(perezoso)* lazy; *(ambulante)* wandering ♦ *nm/f* *(vagabundo)* tramp; *(flojo)* lazybones *sg*, idler

**vagón** [ba'ɣon] *nm* *(FERRO: de pasajeros)* carriage; *(: de mercancías)* wagon

**vaguedad** [baɣe'ðað] *nf* vagueness

**vaho** ['bao] *nm* *(vapor)* vapour, steam; *(respiración)* breath

**vaina** ['baina] *nf* sheath

**vainilla** [bai'niʎa] *nf* vanilla

**vainita** [bai'nita] *nf* (*AM*) green o French bean

**vais** *vb ver* **ir**

**vaivén** [bai'βen] *nm* to-and-fro movement; *(de tránsito)* coming and going; **vaivenes** *nmpl* (*fig*) ups and downs

**vajilla** [ba'xiʎa] *nf* crockery, dishes *pl*; **lavar la ~** to do the washing-up (*BRIT*), wash the dishes (*US*)

**valdré** *etc vb ver* **valer**

**vale** ['bale] *nm* voucher; *(recibo)* receipt; (*pagaré*) IOU

**valedero, a** [bale'ðero, a] *adj* valid

**valenciano, a** [balen'θjano, a] *adj* Valencian

**valentía** [balen'tia] *nf* courage, bravery; (*acción*) heroic deed

**valer** [ba'ler] *vt* to be worth; (*MAT*) to equal; (*costar*) to cost ♦ *vi* (*ser útil*) to be useful; (*ser válido*) to be valid; ~**se** *vr* to defend o.s.; ~**se de** to make use of, take advantage of; ~ **la pena** to be worthwhile; **¿vale?** (*ESP*) OK?

**valeroso, a** [bale'roso, a] *adj* brave, valiant

**valgo** *etc vb ver* **valer**

**valía** [ba'lia] *nf* worth, value

**validar** [bali'ðar] *vt* to validate; **validez** *nf* validity; **válido, a** *adj* valid

**valiente** [ba'ljente] *adj* brave, valiant ♦ *nm* hero

**valioso, a** [ba'ljoso, a] *adj* valuable; (*rico*) wealthy

**valor** [ba'lor] *nm* value, worth; (*precio*) price; (*valentía*) valour, courage; (*importancia*) importance; ~**es** *nmpl* (*COM*) securities; ~**ar** *vt* to value

**vals** [bals] *nm inv* waltz

**válvula** ['balβula] *nf* valve

**valla** ['baʎa] *nf* fence; (*DEPORTE*) hurdle; (*fig*) barrier; ~ **publicitaria** hoarding; **vallar** *vt* to fence in

**valle** ['baʎe] *nm* valley

**vamos** *vb ver* **ir**

**vampiro, resa** [bam'piro, 'resa] *nm/f* vampire

**van** *vb ver* **ir**

**vanagloriarse** [banaɣlo'rjarse] *vr* to boast

**vandalismo** [banda'lismo] *nm* vandalism; **vándalo, a** *nm/f* vandal

**vanguardia** [ban'gwarðja] *nf* vanguard; (*ARTE etc*) avant-garde

**vanidad** [bani'ðað] *nf* vanity; **vanidoso, a** *adj* vain, conceited

**vano, a** ['bano, a] *adj* (*irreal*) unreal, vain; (*inútil*) useless; (*persona*) vain, conceited; (*frívolo*) frivolous

**vapor** [ba'por] *nm* vapour; (*vaho*)

steam; **al** ~ (*CULIN*) steamed; ~**izador** *nm* atomizer; ~**izar** *vt* to vaporize; ~**oso, a** *adj* vaporous

**vapulear** [bapule'ar] *vt* to beat, thrash

**vaquero, a** [ba'kero, a] *adj* cattle *cpd* ♦ *nm* cowboy; ~**s** *nmpl* (*pantalones*) jeans

**vaquilla** [ba'kiʎa] *nf* (*ZOOL*) heifer

**vara** ['bara] *nf* stick; (*TEC*) rod; ~ **mágica** magic wand

**variable** [ba'rjaβle] *adj, nf* variable

**variación** [barja'θjon] *nf* variation

**variar** [bar'jar] *vt* to vary; (*modificar*) to modify; (*cambiar de posición*) to switch around ♦ *vi* to vary

**varices** [ba'riθes] *nfpl* varicose veins

**variedad** [barje'ðað] *nf* variety

**varilla** [ba'riʎa] *nf* stick; (*BOT*) twig; (*TEC*) rod; (*de rueda*) spoke

**vario, a** ['barjo, a] *adj* varied; ~**s** various, several

**varita** [ba'rita] *nf*: ~ **mágica** magic wand

**varón** [ba'ron] *nm* male, man; **varonil** *adj* manly, virile

**Varsovia** [bar'soβja] *n* Warsaw

**vas** *vb ver* **ir**

**vasco, a** ['basko, a] *adj, nm/f* Basque

**vascongado, a** [baskon'gaðo, a] *adj* Basque; **las Vascongadas** the Basque Country

**vascuence** [bas'kwenθe] *adj* = **vascongado**

**vaselina** [base'lina] *nf* Vaseline ®

**vasija** [ba'sixa] *nf* container, vessel

**vaso** ['baso] *nm* glass, tumbler; (*ANAT*) vessel

**vástago** [bastaɣo] *nm* (*BOT*) shoot; (*TEC*) rod; (*fig*) offspring

**vasto, a** ['basto, a] *adj* vast, huge

**Vaticano** [bati'kano] *nm*: **el** ~ **the** Vatican

**vaticinio** [bati'θinjo] *nm* prophecy

**vatio** ['batjo] *nm* (*ELEC*) watt

**vaya** *etc vb ver* **ir**

**Vd(s)** *abr* = **usted(es)**

**ve** *vb ver* **ir**; **ver**

**vecindad** [beθin'dað] *nf* neighbourhood; (*habitantes*) residents pl

**vecindario** [beθin'darjo] nm neighbourhood; residents pl

**vecino, a** [be'θino, a] adj neighbouring ♦ nm/f neighbour; (*residente*) resident

**veda** ['beða] nf prohibition

**vedado** [be'ðaðo] nm preserve

**vedar** [be'ðar] vt (*prohibir*) to ban, prohibit; (*impedir*) to stop, prevent

**vegetación** [bexeta'θjon] nf vegetation

**vegetariano, a** [bexeta'rjano, a] adj, nm/f vegetarian

**vegetal** [bexe'tal] adj, nm vegetable

**vehemencia** [be(e)'menθja] nf (*insistencia*) vehemence; (*pasión*) passion; (*fervor*) fervour; (*violencia*) violence; **vehemente** adj vehement; passionate; fervent

**vehículo** [be'ikulo] nm vehicle; (*MED*) carrier

**veía** etc vb ver **ver**

**veinte** ['beinte] num twenty

**vejación** [bexa'θjon] nf vexation; (*humillación*) humiliation

**vejar** [be'xar] vt (*irritar*) to annoy, vex; (*humillar*) to humiliate

**vejez** [be'xeθ] nf old age

**vejiga** [be'xixa] nf (*ANAT*) bladder

**vela** ['bela] nf (*de cera*) candle; (*NAUT*) sail; (*insomnio*) sleeplessness; (*vigilia*) vigil; (*MIL*) sentry duty; **estar a dos ~s** (*fam*) to be skint

**velado, a** [be'laðo, a] adj veiled; (*sonido*) muffled; (*FOTO*) blurred ♦ nf soirée

**velar** [be'lar] vt (*vigilar*) to keep watch over ♦ vi to stay awake; **~ por** to watch over, look after

**velatorio** [bela'torjo] nm (*funeral*) wake

**veleidad** [belei'ðað] nf (*ligereza*) fickleness; (*capricho*) whim

**velero** [be'lero] nm (*NAUT*) sailing ship; (*AVIAT*) glider

**veleta** [be'leta] nf weather vane

**veliz** [be'lis] (*AM*) nm suitcase

**velo** ['belo] nm veil

**velocidad** [beloθi'ðað] nf speed; (*TEC, AUTO*) gear

**velocímetro** [belo'θimetro] nm speedometer

**veloz** [be'loθ] adj fast

**vello** ['beλo] nm down, fuzz

**ven** vb ver **venir**

**vena** ['bena] nf vein

**venado** [be'naðo] nm deer

**vencedor, a** [benθe'ðor, a] adj victorious ♦ nm/f victor, winner

**vencer** [ben'θer] vt (*dominar*) to defeat, beat; (*derrotar*) to vanquish; (*superar, controlar*) to overcome, master ♦ vi (*triunfar*) to win (through), triumph; (*plazo*) to expire; **vencido, a** (*derrotado*) defeated, beaten; (*COM*) due ♦ adv: **pagar vencido** to pay in arrears; **vencimiento** nm (*COM*) maturity

**venda** ['benda] nf bandage; **~je** nm bandage, dressing; **vendar** vt to bandage; **vendar los ojos** to blindfold

**vendaval** [benda'ßal] nm (*viento*) gale

**vendedor, a** [bende'ðor, a] nm/f seller

**vender** [ben'der] vt to sell; **~ al contado/al por mayor/al por menor** to sell for cash/wholesale/retail

**vendimia** [ben'dimja] nf grape harvest

**vendré** etc vb ver **venir**

**veneno** [be'neno] nm poison; (*de serpiente*) venom; **~so, a** adj poisonous; venomous

**venerable** [bene'raßle] adj venerable; **venerar** vt (*respetar*) to revere; (*adorar*) to worship

**venéreo, a** [be'nereo, a] adj: **enfermedad venérea** venereal disease

**venezolano, a** [beneθo'lano, a] adj Venezuelan

**Venezuela** [bene'θwela] nf Venezuela

**venganza** [ben'ganθa] nf vengeance, revenge; **vengar** vt to avenge; **vengarse** vr to take revenge; **vengativo, a** adj (*persona*) vindictive

**vengo** *etc vb ver* **venir**

**venia** ['benja] *nf (perdón)* pardon; *(permiso)* consent

**venial** [be'njal] *adj* venial

**venida** [be'niða] *nf (llegada)* arrival; *(regreso)* return

**venidero, a** [beni'ðero, a] *adj* coming, future

**venir** [be'nir] *vi* to come; *(llegar)* to arrive; *(ocurrir)* to happen; *(fig.):* ~ **de** to stem from; ~ **bien/mal** to be suitable/unsuitable; **el año que viene** next year; ~**se abajo** to collapse

**venta** ['benta] *nf (COM)* sale; ~ **a plazos** hire purchase; ~ **al contado/al por mayor/al por menor** *o* **al detalle** cash sale/wholesale/retail; ~ **con derecho a retorno** sale or return; **"en** ~**"** "for sale"

**ventaja** *nf* advantage; **ventajoso, a** *adj* advantageous

**ventana** [ben'tana] *nf* window; **ventanilla** *nf (de taquilla)* window *(of booking office etc)*

**ventilación** [bentila'θjon] *nf* ventilation; *(corriente)* draught; **ventilar** *vt* to ventilate; *(para secar)* to put out to dry; *(fig)* to air, discuss

**ventisca** [ben'tiska] *nf* blizzard; *(nieve amontonada)* snowdrift

**ventrílocuo, a** [ben'trilokwo, a] *nm/f* ventriloquist

**ventura** [ben'tura] *nf (felicidad)* happiness; *(buena suerte)* luck; *(destino)* fortune; **a la (buena)** ~ at random; **venturoso, a** *adj* happy; *(afortunado)* lucky, fortunate

**veo** *etc vb ver* **ver**

**ver** [ber] *vt* to see; *(mirar)* to look at, watch; *(entender)* to understand; *(investigar)* to look into; ♦ *vi* to see; to understand; ~**se** *vr (encontrarse)* to meet; *(dejarse* ~) to be seen; *(hallarse: en un apuro)* to find o.s.; ♦ *nm* looks *pl*, appearance; **a** ~ let's see; **dejarse** ~ to become apparent; **no tener nada que** ~ **con** to have nothing to do with; **a mi modo de** ~ as I see it

**vera** ['bera] *nf* edge, verge; *(de río)* bank

**veracidad** [beraθi'ðað] *nf* truthfulness

**veranear** [berane'ar] *vi* to spend the summer; **veraneo** *nm* summer holiday; **veraniego, a** *adj* summer *cpd*

**verano** [be'rano] *nm* summer

**veras** ['beras] *nfpl* truth *sg*; **de** ~ really, truly

**veraz** [be'raθ] *adj* truthful

**verbal** [ber'βal] *adj* verbal

**verbena** [ber'βena] *nf (fiesta)* fair; *(baile)* open-air dance

**verbo** ['berβo] *nm* verb; **verboso, a** *adj* verbose

**verdad** [ber'ðað] *nf* truth; *(fiabilidad)* reliability; **de** ~ real, proper; **a decir** ~ to tell the truth; ~**ero, a** *adj (veraz)* true, truthful; *(fiable)* reliable; *(fig)* real

**verde** ['berðe] *adj* green; *(chiste)* blue, dirty ♦ *nm* green; **viejo** ~ dirty old man; ~**ar** *vi* to turn green; **verdor** *nm (lo* ~) greenness; *(BOT)* verdure

**verdugo** [ber'ðuɣo] *nm* executioner

**verdulero, a** [ber'ðulero, a] *nm/f* greengrocer

**verduras** [ber'ðuras] *nfpl (CULIN)* greens

**vereda** [be'reða] *nf* path; *(AM)* pavement *(BRIT)*, sidewalk *(US)*

**veredicto** [bere'ðikto] *nm* verdict

**vergonzoso, a** [berɣon'θoso, a] *adj* shameful; *(tímido)* timid, bashful

**vergüenza** [ber'ɣwenθa] *nf* shame, sense of shame; *(timidez)* bashfulness; *(pudor)* modesty; **me da** ~ I'm ashamed

**verídico, a** [be'riðiko, a] *adj* true, truthful

**verificar** [berifi'kar] *vt* to check; *(corroborar)* to verify; *(llevar a cabo)* to carry out; ~**se** *vr* to occur, happen

**verja** ['berxa] *nf (cancela)* iron gate; *(valla)* iron railings *pl*; *(de ventana)* grille

**vermut** [ber'mut] *(pl* ~**s**) *nm* vermouth

**verosímil** [bero'simil] *adj* likely, probable; (*relato*) credible

**verruga** [be'rruɣa] *nf* wart

**versado, a** [ber'saðo, a] *adj*: ~ **en** versed in

**versátil** [ber'satil] *adj* versatile

**versión** [ber'sjon] *nf* version

**verso** ['berso] *nm* verse; **un** ~ **a** line of poetry

**vértebra** ['berteβra] *nf* vertebra

**verter** [ber'ter] *vt* (*líquido: adrede*) to empty, pour (out); (*: sin querer*) to spill; (*basura*) to dump ♦ *vi* to flow

**vertical** [berti'kal] *adj* vertical

**vértice** ['bertiθe] *nm* vertex, apex

**vertiente** [ber'tjente] *nf* slope; (*fig*) aspect

**vertiginoso, a** [bertixi'noso, a] *adj* giddy, dizzy

**vértigo** ['bertiɣo] *nm* vertigo; (*mareo*) dizziness

**vesícula** [be'sikula] *nf* blister

**vespertino, a** [besper'tino, a] *adj* evening *cpd*

**vestíbulo** [bes'tiβulo] *nm* hall; (*de teatro*) foyer

**vestido** [bes'tiðo] *pp de* **vestir**; ~ **de azul/marinero** dressed in blue/as a sailor ♦ *nm* (*ropa*) clothes *pl*, clothing; (*de mujer*) dress, frock

**vestigio** [bes'tixjo] *nm* (*huella*) trace; ~**s** *nmpl* (*restos*) remains

**vestimenta** [besti'menta] *nf* clothing

**vestir** [bes'tir] *vt* (*poner: ropa*) to put on; (*llevar: ropa*) to wear; (*proveer de ropa a*) to clothe; (*suj: sastre*) to make clothes for ♦ *vi* to dress; (*verse bien*) to look good; ~**se** *vr* to get dressed, dress o.s.

**vestuario** [bes'twarjo] *nm* clothes *pl*, wardrobe; (*TEATRO: cuarto*) dressing room; (*DEPORTE*) changing room

**veta** ['beta] *nf* (*vena*) vein, seam; (*en carne*) streak; (*de madera*) grain

**vetar** [be'tar] *vt* to veto

**veterano, a** [bete'rano, a] *adj, nm* veteran

**veterinaria** [beteri'narja] *nf* veterinary science; *ver tb* **veterinario**

**veterinario, a** [beteri'narjo, a] *nm/f* vet(erinary surgeon)

**veto** ['beto] *nm* veto

**vetusto, a** [be'tusto, a] *adj* ancient

**vez** [beθ] *nf* time; (*turno*) turn; **a la** ~ **que** at the same time as; **a su** ~ in its turn; **otra** ~ again; **una** ~ once; **de una** ~ in one go; **de una** ~ **para siempre** once and for all; **en** ~ **de** instead of; **a o algunas veces** sometimes; **una y otra** ~ repeatedly; **de** ~ **en cuando** from time to time; **7 veces 9** 7 times 9; **hacer las veces de** to stand in for; **tal** ~ perhaps

**vía** ['bia] *nf* track, route; (*FERRO*) line; (*fig*) way; (*ANAT*) passage, tube ♦ *prep* via, by way of; **por** ~ **judicial** by legal means; **por** ~ **oficial** through official channels; **en** ~**s de** in the process of; ~ **aérea** airway; **V~ Láctea** Milky Way; ~ **pública** public road *o* thoroughfare

**viable** ['bjaβle] *adj* (*solución, plan, alternativa*) feasible

**viaducto** [bja'ðukto] *nm* viaduct

**viajante** [bja'xante] *nm* commercial traveller

**viajar** [bja'xar] *vi* to travel; **viaje** *nm* journey; (*gira*) tour; (*NAUT*) voyage; **estar de viaje** to be on a journey; **viaje de ida y vuelta** round trip; **viaje de novios** honeymoon; **viajero, a** *adj* travelling; (*ZOOL*) migratory ♦ *nm/f* (*quien viaja*) traveller; (*pasajero*) passenger

**vial** [bjal] *adj* road *cpd*, traffic *cpd*

**víbora** ['biβora] *nf* viper; (*AM*) poisonous snake

**vibración** [biβra'θjon] *nf* vibration

**vibrar** [bi'βrar] *vt, vi* to vibrate

**vicario** [bi'karjo] *nm* curate

**vicepresidente** [biθepresi'ðente] *nm/f* vice-president

**viceversa** [biθe'βersa] *adv* vice versa

**viciado, a** [bi'θjaðo, a] *adj* (*corrompido*) corrupt; (*contaminado*) foul, contaminated; **viciar** *vt* (*pervertir*) to pervert; (*JUR*) to nullify; (*estropear*) to spoil; **viciarse** *vr* to become corrupted

**vicio** ['biθjo] *nm* vice; (*mala costumbre*) bad habit; **~so, a** *adj* (*muy malo*) vicious; (*corrompido*) depraved ♦ *nm/f* depraved person

**vicisitud** [biθisi'tuð] *nf* vicissitude

**víctima** ['biktima] *nf* victim

**victoria** [bik'torja] *nf* victory; **victorioso, a** *adj* victorious

**vicuña** [bi'kuɲa] *nf* vicuna

**vid** [bið] *nf* vine

**vida** ['biða] *nf* (*gen*) life; (*duración*) lifetime; **de por ~** for life; **en la/mi ~** never; **estar con ~** to be still alive; **ganarse la ~** to earn one's living

**vídeo** ['bideo] *nm* video ♦ *adj inv*: **película ~** video film; **~cámara** *nf* camcorder; **~club** *nm* video club

**vidriero, a** [bi'ðrjero, a] *nm/f* glazier ♦ *nf* (*ventana*) stained-glass window; (*AM*: *de tienda*) shop window; (*puerta*) glass door

**vidrio** ['biðrjo] *nm* glass

**vieira** ['bjeira] *nf* scallop

**viejo, a** ['bjexo, a] *adj* old ♦ *nm/f* old man/woman; **hacerse ~** to get old

**Viena** ['bjena] *n* Vienna

**vienes** *etc vb ver* **venir**

**vienés, esa** [bje'nes, esa] *adj* Viennese

**viento** ['bjento] *nm* wind; **hacer ~** to be windy

**vientre** ['bjentre] *nm* belly; (*matriz*) womb

**viernes** ['bjernes] *nm inv* Friday; **V~ Santo** Good Friday

**Vietnam** [bjet'nam] *nm*: **el ~** Vietnam; **vietnamita** *adj* Vietnamese

**viga** ['biva] *nf* beam, rafter; (*de metal*) girder

**vigencia** [bi'xenθja] *nf* validity; **estar en ~** to be in force; **vigente** *adj* valid, in force; (*imperante*) prevailing

**vigésimo, a** [bi'xesimo, a] *adj* twentieth

**vigía** [bi'xia] *nm* look-out ♦ *nf* (*ata-*

*laya*) watchtower; (*acción*) watching

**vigilancia** [bixi'lanθja] *nf*: **tener a uno bajo ~** to keep watch on sb

**vigilar** [bixi'lar] *vt* to watch over ♦ *vi* (*gen*) to be vigilant; (*hacer guardia*) to keep watch; **~ por** to take care of

**vigilia** [vi'xilja] *nf* wakefulness, being awake; (*REL*) fast

**vigor** [bi'yor] *nm* vigour, vitality; **en ~** in force; **entrar/poner en ~** to come/put into effect; **~oso, a** *adj* vigorous

**VIH** *nm abr de* **virus de la inmunodeficiencia humana** HIV; **~ positivo/negativo** HIV-positive/-negative

**vil** [bil] *adj* vile, low; **~eza** *nf* vileness; (*acto*) base deed

**vilipendiar** [bilipen'djar] *vt* to vilify, revile

**vilo** ['bilo]: **en ~** *adv* in the air, suspended; (*fig*) on tenterhooks, in suspense

**villa** ['biʎa] *nf* (*casa*) villa; (*pueblo*) small town; (*municipalidad*) municipality; **~ miseria** (*AM*) shantytown

**villancico** [biʎan'θiko] *nm* (Christmas) carol

**villorrio** [bi'ʎorrjo] (*AM*) *nm* shantytown

**vinagre** [bi'naɣre] *nm* vinegar

**vinagreta** [bina'ɣreta] *nf* vinaigrette, French dressing

**vinatero, a** [bina'tero, a] *adj* wine *cpd* ♦ *nm* wine merchant

**vinculación** [binkula'θjon] *nf* (*lazo*) link, bond; (*acción*) linking

**vincular** [binku'lar] *vt* to link, bind; **vínculo** *nm* link, bond

**vine** *etc vb ver* **venir**

**vinicultura** [binikul'tura] *nf* wine growing

**viniera** *etc vb ver* **venir**

**vino** ['bino] *vb ver* **venir** ♦ *nm* wine; **~ blanco/tinto** white/red wine

**viña** ['biɲa] *nf* vineyard; **viñedo** *nm* vineyard

**viola** ['bjola] *nf* viola

**violación** [bjola'θjon] *nf* violation; (*estupro*): **~ (sexual)** rape

**violar** [bjo'lar] *vt* to violate; (*cometer estupro*) to rape

**violencia** [bjo'lenθja] *nf* (*fuerza*) violence, force; (*embarazo*) embarrassment; (*acto injusto*) unjust act; **violentar** *vt* to force; (*casa*) to break into; (*agredir*) to assault; (*violar*) to violate; **violento, a** *adj* violent; (*furioso*) furious; (*situación*) embarrassing; (*acto*) forced, unnatural

**violeta** [bjo'leta] *nf* violet

**violín** [bjo'lin] *nm* violin

**violón** [bjo'lon] *nm* double bass

**viraje** [bi'raxe] *nm* turn; (*de vehículo*) swerve; (*de carretera*) bend; (*fig*) change of direction; **virar** *vi* to change direction

**virgen** ['birxen] *adj, nf* virgin

**Virgo** ['birγo] *nm* Virgo

**viril** [bi'ril] *adj* virile; **~idad** *nf* virility

**virtud** [bir'tuð] *nf* virtue; **en ~ de** by virtue of; **virtuoso, a** *adj* virtuous ♦ *nm/f* virtuoso

**viruela** [bi'rwela] *nf* smallpox; **~s** *nfpl* (*granos*) pockmarks

**virulento, a** [biru'lento, a] *adj* virulent

**virus** ['birus] *nm inv* virus

**visa** ['bisa] (*AM*) *nf* = **visado**

**visado** [bi'saðo] *nm* visa

**víscera** ['bisθera] *nf* (*ANAT, ZOOL*) gut, bowel; **~s** *nfpl* entrails

**visceral** [bisθe'ral] *adj* (*odio*) intense; **reacción ~** gut reaction

**viscoso, a** [bis'koso, a] *adj* viscous

**visera** [bi'sera] *nf* visor

**visibilidad** [bisiβili'ðað] *nf* visibility; **visible** *adj* visible; (*fig*) obvious

**visillos** [bi'siʎos] *nmpl* lace curtains

**visión** [bi'sjon] *nf* (*ANAT*) vision, (*eye*)sight; (*fantasía*) vision, fantasy

**visita** [bi'sita] *nf* call, visit; (*persona*) visitor; **hacer una ~** to pay a visit

**visitar** [bisi'tar] *vt* to visit, call on

**vislumbrar** [bislum'brar] *vt* to glimpse, catch a glimpse of; **vislumbre** *nf* glimpse; (*centelleo*) gleam; (*idea vaga*) glimmer

**viso** ['biso] *nm* (*del metal*) glint,

gleam; (*de tela*) sheen; (*aspecto*) appearance

**visón** [bi'son] *nm* mink

**visor** [bi'sor] *nm* (*FOTO*) viewfinder

**víspera** ['bispera] *nf*: **la ~ de ...** the day before ...

**vista** ['bista] *nf* sight, vision; (*capacidad de ver*) (eye)sight; (*mirada*) look(s) (*pl*) ♦ *nm* customs officer; **a primera ~** at first glance; **hacer la ~ gorda** to turn a blind eye; **volver la ~** to look back; **está a la ~ que** it's obvious that; **en ~ de** in view of; **en ~ de que** in view of the fact that; **¡hasta la ~!** so long!, see you!; **con ~s a** with a view to; **~zo** *nm* glance; **dar** o **echar un ~zo a** to glance at

**visto, a** [a [bisto, a] *pp* de *ver* ♦ *vb ver tb* **vestir** ♦ *adj* seen; (*considerado*) obvious; **~ bueno** approval; **"~ bueno"** "approved"; **por lo ~** apparently; **está ~ que** it's clear that; **está bien/mal ~** it's acceptable/unacceptable; **~ que** conj since, considering that

**vistoso, a** [bis'toso, a] *adj* colourful

**visual** [bi'swal] *adj* visual

**vital** [bi'tal] *adj* life *cpd*, living *cpd*; (*fig*) vital; (*persona*) lively, vivacious; **~icio, a** *adj* for life; **~idad** *nf* (*de persona, negocio*) energy; (*de ciudad*) liveliness

**vitamina** [bita'mina] *nf* vitamin

**viticultor, a** [bitikul'tor, a] *nm/f* wine grower; **viticultura** *nf* wine growing

**vitorear** [bitore'ar] *vt* to cheer, acclaim

**vítores** ['bitores] *nmpl* cheers

**vitrina** [bi'trina] *nf* show case; (*AM*) shop window

**vituperio** [bitu'perjo] *nm* (*condena*) condemnation; (*censura*) censure; (*insulto*) insult

**viudez** *nf* widowhood

**viudo, a** ['bjuðo, a] *nm/f* widower/widow

**viva** ['biβa] *excl* hurrah!: **¡~ el rey!** long live the king!

**vivacidad** [biβaθi'ðað] *nf* (*vigor*) vigour; (*vida*) liveliness

**vivaracho, a** [biβa'ratʃo, a] *adj* jaunty, lively; (*ojos*) bright, twinkling

**vivaz** [bi'βaθ] *adj* lively

**víveres** ['biβeres] *nmpl* provisions

**vivero** [bi'βero] *nm* (*para plantas*) nursery; (*para peces*) fish farm; (*fig*) hotbed

**viveza** [bi'βeθa] *nf* liveliness; (*agudeza: mental*) sharpness

**vivienda** [bi'βjenda] *nf* housing; (*una ~*) house; (*piso*) flat (*BRIT*), apartment (*US*)

**viviente** [bi'βjente] *adj* living

**vivir** [bi'βir] *vt, vi* to live ♦ *nm* life, living

**vivo, a** ['biβo, a] *adj* living, alive; (*fig: descripción*) vivid; (*persona: astuto*) smart, clever; **en ~** (*transmisión etc*) live

**vocablo** [bo'kaβlo] *nm* (*palabra*) word; (*término*) term

**vocabulario** [bokaβu'larjo] *nm* vocabulary

**vocación** [boka'θjon] *nf* vocation; **vocacional** (*AM*) *nf* ≈ technical college

**vocal** [bo'kal] *adj* vocal ♦ *nf* vowel; **~izar** *vt* to vocalize

**vocear** [boθe'ar] *vt* (*para vender*) to cry; (*aclamar*) to acclaim; (*fig*) to proclaim ♦ *vi* to yell; **vocerío** *nm* shouting

**vocero** [bo'θero] *nm/f* spokesman/woman

**voces** ['boθes] *pl de* **voz**

**vociferar** [boθife'rar] *vt* to shout ♦ *vi* to yell

**vodka** ['boðka] *nm o f* vodka

**vol** *abr* = **volumen**

**volador, a** [bola'ðor, a] *adj* flying

**volandas** [bo'landas]: **en ~** *adv* in the air; (*fig*) swiftly

**volante** [bo'lante] *adj* flying ♦ *nm* (*de coche*) steering wheel; (*de reloj*) balance

**volar** [bo'lar] *vt* (*edificio*) to blow up ♦ *vi* to fly

**volátil** [bo'latil] *adj* volatile

**volcán** [bol'kan] *nm* volcano; **~ico, a** *adj* volcanic

**volcar** [bol'kar] *vt* to upset, overturn; (*tumbar, derribar*) to knock over; (*vaciar*) to empty out ♦ *vi* to overturn; **~se** *vr* to tip over

**voleibol** [bolei'βol] *nm* volleyball

**volqué** *etc vb ver* **volcar**

**voltaje** [bol'taxe] *nm* voltage

**voltear** [bolte'ar] *vt* to turn over; (*volcar*) to turn upside down

**voltereta** [bolte'reta] *nf* somersault

**voltio** ['boltjo] *nm* volt

**voluble** [bo'luβle] *adj* fickle

**volumen** [bo'lumen] (*pl* **volúmenes**) *nm* volume; **voluminoso, a** *adj* voluminous; (*enorme*) massive

**voluntad** [bolun'tað] *nf* will; (*resolución*) willpower; (*deseo*) desire, wish

**voluntario, a** [bolun'tarjo, a] *adj* voluntary ♦ *nm/f* volunteer

**voluntarioso, a** [bolunta'rjoso, a] *adj* headstrong

**voluptuoso, a** [boluptwoso, a] *adj* voluptuous

**volver** [bol'βer] *vt* (*gen*) to turn; (*dar vuelta a*) to turn (over); (*voltear*) to turn round, turn upside down; (*poner al revés*) to turn inside out; (*devolver*) to return ♦ *vi* to return, go back, come back; **~se** *vr* to turn round; **~ la espalda** to turn one's back; **~ triste** *etc* a uno to make sb sad *etc*; **~ a hacer** to do again; **~ en sí** to come to; **~se insoportable/muy caro** to get o become unbearable/very expensive; **~se loco** to go mad

**vomitar** [bomi'tar] *vt, vi* to vomit

**vómito** ['bomito] *nm* (*acto*) vomiting; (*resultado*) vomit

**voraz** [bo'raθ] *adj* voracious

**vos** [bos] (*AM*) *pron* you

**vosotros, as** [bo'sotros, as] *pron* you; (*reflexivo*): **entre/para ~** among/for yourselves

**votación** [bota'θjon] *nf* (*acto*) voting; (*voto*) vote

**votar** [bo'tar] *vi* to vote; **voto** *nm*

vote; (*promesa*) vow; **votos** (good) wishes

**voy** *vb ver* **ir**

**voz** [boθ] *nf* voice; (*grito*) shout; (*chisme*) rumour; (*LING*) word; **dar voces** to shout, yell; **a media** ~ in a low voice; **a** ~ **en cuello** *o* **en grito** at the top of one's voice; **de viva** ~ verbally; **en** ~ **alta** aloud; ~ **de mando** command

**vuelco** ['bwelko] *vb ver* **volcar** ♦ *nm* spill, overturning

**vuelo** ['bwelo] *vb ver* **volar** ♦ *nm* flight; (*encaje*) lace, frill; **coger al** ~ to catch in flight; ~ **charter/ regular** charter/scheduled flight; ~ **libre** (*DEPORTE*) hang-gliding

**vuelque** *etc vb ver* **volcar**

**vuelta** ['bwelta] *nf* (*gen*) turn; (*curva*) bend, curve; (*regreso*) return; (*revolución*) revolution; (*circuito*) lap; (*de papel, tela*) reverse; (*cambio*) change; **a la** ~ on one's return; **a** ~ **de correo** by return of post; **dar** ~**s** (*suj: cabeza*) to spin; **dar** ~**s a una idea** to turn over an idea (in one's head); **estar de** ~ to be back; **dar una** ~ to go for a walk; (*en coche*) to go for a drive; ~ **ciclista** (*DEPORTE*) (cycle) tour

**vuelto** *pp de* **volver**

**vuelvo** *etc vb ver* **volver**

**vuestro, a** ['bwestro, a] *adj* your; **un amigo** ~ a friend of yours ♦ *pron:* **el** ~/**la vuestra**, **los** ~**s/las vuestras** yours

**vulgar** [bul'ɣar] *adj* (*ordinario*) vulgar; (*común*) common; ~**idad** *nf* commonness; (*acto*) vulgarity; (*expresión*) coarse expression; ~**idades** *nfpl* (*banalidades*) banalities; ~**izar** *vt* to popularize

**vulgo** ['bulɣo] *nm* common people

**vulnerable** [bulne'raßle] *adj* vulnerable

**vulnerar** [bulne'rar] *vt* (*ley, acuerdo*) to violate, breach; (*derechos, intimidad*) to violate; (*reputación*) to damage

# W

**Walkman** [wak'man] ® (*MUS*) Walkman ®

**wáter** ['bater] *nm* toilet

**whisky** ['wiski] *nm* whisky, whiskey

# X

**xenofobia** [kseno'foßja] *nf* xenophobia

**xilófono** [ksi'lofono] *nm* xylophone

# Y

**y** [i] *conj* and

**ya** [ja] *adv* (*gen*) already; (*ahora*) now; (*en seguida*) at once; (*pronto*) soon ♦ *excl* all right! ♦ *conj* (*ahora que*) now that; ~ **lo sé** I know; ~ **que** since

**yacer** [ja'θer] *vi* to lie

**yacimiento** [jaθi'mjento] *nm* deposit

**yanqui** ['janki] *adj, nm/f* Yankee

**yate** ['jate] *nm* yacht

**yazco** *etc vb ver* **yacer**

**yedra** ['jeðra] *nf* ivy

**yegua** ['jexwa] *nf* mare

**yema** ['jema] *nf* (*del huevo*) yoke; (*BOT*) leaf bud; (*fig*) best part; ~ **del dedo** fingertip

**yergo** *etc vb ver* **erguir**

**yermo, a** ['jermo, a] *adj* (*despoblado*) uninhabited; (*estéril, fig*) barren ♦ *nm* wasteland

**yerno** ['jerno] *nm* son-in-law

**yerro** *etc vb ver* **errar**

**yerto, a** ['jerto, a] *adj* stiff

**yeso** ['jeso] *nm* (*GEO*) gypsum; (*ARQ*) plaster

**yo** ['jo] *pron* I; **soy** ~ it's me, it is I

**yodo** ['joðo] *nm* iodine

**yoga** ['joxa] *nm* yoga

**yogur(t)** [jo'xur(t)] *nm* yoghurt

**yugo** ['juxo] *nm* yoke

**Yugoslavia** [juɣos'laßja] *nf* Yugoslavia

**yugular** [juɣu'lar] adj jugular

**yunque** ['junke] nm anvil

**yunta** ['junta] nf yoke; **yuntero** nm ploughman

**yute** ['jute] nm jute

**yuxtaponer** [jukstapo'ner] vt to juxtapose; **yuxtaposición** nf juxtaposition

# Z

**zafar** [θa'far] vt (soltar) to untie; (superficie) to clear; **~se** vr (escaparse) to escape; (TEC) to slip off

**zafio, a** ['θafjo, a] adj coarse

**zafiro** [θa'firo] nm sapphire

**zaga** ['θaɣa] nf: a la ~ behind, in the rear

**zaguán** [θa'ɣwan] nm hallway

**zaherir** [θae'rir] vt (criticar) to criticize

**zaino, a** ['θaino, a] adj (color de caballo) chestnut

**zalamería** [θalame'ria] nf flattery; **zalamero, a** adj flattering; (relamido) suave

**zamarra** [θa'marra] nf (piel) sheepskin; (chaqueta) sheepskin jacket

**zambullirse** [θambu'ʎirse] vr to dive; (ocultarse) to hide o.s.

**zampar** [θam'par] vt to gobble down ♦ vi gobble (up)

**zanahoria** [θana'orja] nf carrot

**zancada** [θan'kaða] nf stride

**zancadilla** [θanka'ðiʎa] nf trip; (fig) stratagem

**zanco** [θanko] nm stilt

**zancudo, a** [θan'kuðo, a] adj longlegged ♦ nm (AM) mosquito

**zángano** ['θangano] nm drone

**zanja** ['θanxa] nf (ditch); **zanjar** vt (superar) to surmount; (resolver) to resolve

**zapata** [θa'pata] nf half-boot; (MECANICA) shoe

**zapatear** [θapate'ar] vi to tap with one's foot

**zapatería** [θapate'ria] nf (oficio) shoemaking; (tienda) shoe shop; (fa-

brica) shoe factory; **zapatero, a** nm/f shoemaker

**zapatilla** [θapa'tiʎa] nf slipper; ~ de deporte training shoe

**zapato** [θa'pato] nm shoe

**zar** [θar] nm tsar, czar

**zarandear** [θarande'ar] (fam) vt to shake vigorously

**zarpa** ['θarpa] nf (garra) claw

**zarpar** [θar'par] vi to weigh anchor

**zarza** ['θarθa] nf (BOT) bramble; **zarzal** nm (matorral) bramble patch

**zarzamora** [θarθa'mora] nf blackberry

**zarzuela** [θar'θwela] nf Spanish light opera

**zigzag** [θiɣ'θaɣ] nm zigzag; **zigzaguear** vi to zigzag

**zinc** [θink] nm zinc

**zócalo** ['θokalo] nm (ARQ) plinth, base

**zodíaco** [θo'ðiako] nm (ASTRO) zodiac

**zona** ['θona] nf zone; ~ fronteriza border area

**zoo** ['θoo] nm zoo

**zoología** [θoolo'xia] nf zoology; **zoológico, a** adj zoological ♦ nm (tb: parque ~) zoo; **zoólogo, a** nm/f zoologist

**zoom** [θum] nm zoom lens

**zopilote** [θopi'lote] nm (AM) buzzard

**zoquete** [θo'kete] nm (madera) block; (fam) blockhead

**zorro, a** ['θorro, a] adj crafty ♦ nm/f fox/vixen

**zozobra** [θo'θobra] nf (fig) anxiety; **zozobrar** vi (hundirse) to capsize; (fig) to fail

**zueco** ['θweko] nm clog

**zumbar** [θum'bar] vt (golpear) to hit ♦ vi to buzz; **zumbido** nm buzzing

**zumo** ['θumo] nm juice

**zurcir** [θur'θir] vt (coser) to darn

**zurdo, a** ['θurðo, a] adj (mano) left; (persona) left-handed

**zurrar** [θu'rrar] (fam) vt to wallop

**zurrón** [θu'rron] nm pouch

# ENGLISH-SPANISH
# INGLÉS-ESPAÑOL

## A

**A** [eɪ] n (MUS) la m

---
KEYWORD
---

**a** [ə] indef art (before vowel or silent h: an) **1** un(a); ~ **book** un libro; **an apple** una manzana; **she's** ~ **doctor** (ella) es médica
**2** (instead of the number "one") un(a); ~ **year ago** hace un año; ~ **hundred/thousand** etc **pounds** cien/mil etc libras
**3** (in expressing ratios, prices etc): **3** ~ **day/week** 3 al día/a la semana; **10 km an hour** 10 km por hora; **£5** ~ **person** £5 por persona; **30p** ~ **kilo** 30p el kilo

**A.A.** n abbr (= Automobile Association: BRIT) ≈ RACE m (SP); (= Alcoholics Anonymous) Alcohólicos Anónimos
**A.A.A.** (US) n abbr (= American Automobile Association) ≈ RACE m (SP)
**aback** [əˈbæk] adv: **to be taken** ~ quedar desconcertado
**abandon** [əˈbændən] vt abandonar; (give up) renunciar a ♦ n abandono; (wild behaviour): **with** ~ sin reparos
**abate** [əˈbeɪt] vi (storm) amainar; (anger) aplacarse; (terror) disminuir
**abattoir** [ˈæbətwɑː*] (BRIT) n matadero
**abbey** [ˈæbɪ] n abadía
**abbot** [ˈæbət] n abad m
**abbreviation** [əˌbriːvɪˈeɪʃən] n (short form) abreviatura
**abdicate** [ˈæbdɪkeɪt] vt renunciar a ♦ vi abdicar; **abdication** [-ˈkeɪʃən] n renuncia; (of monarch) abdicación f
**abdomen** [ˈæbdəmən] n abdomen m
**abduct** [æbˈdʌkt] vt raptar, secuestrar
**abet** [əˈbet] vt see **aid**

**abeyance** [əˈbeɪəns] n: **in** ~ (law) en desuso; (matter) en suspenso
**abhor** [əbˈhɔː*] vt aborrecer, abominar (de)
**abide** [əˈbaɪd] vt: **I can't** ~ **it/him** no lo/le puedo ver; ~ **by** vt fus atenerse a
**ability** [əˈbɪlɪtɪ] n habilidad f, capacidad f; (talent) talento
**abject** [ˈæbdʒekt] adj (poverty) miserable; (apology) rastrero
**ablaze** [əˈbleɪz] adj en llamas, ardiendo
**able** [ˈeɪbl] adj capaz; (skilled) hábil; **to be** ~ **to do sth** poder hacer algo; ~-**bodied** adj sano; **ably** adv hábilmente
**abnormal** [æbˈnɔːməl] adj anormal
**aboard** [əˈbɔːd] adv a bordo ♦ prep a bordo de
**abode** [əˈbəʊd] n: **of no fixed** ~ sin domicilio fijo
**abolish** [əˈbɒlɪʃ] vt suprimir, abolir; **abolition** [æbəˈlɪʃən] n supresión f, abolición f
**aborigine** [æbəˈrɪdʒɪnɪ] n aborigen m/f
**abort** [əˈbɔːt] vt, vi abortar; ~**ion** [əˈbɔːʃən] n aborto; **to have an** ~**ion** abortar, hacerse abortar; ~**ive** adj malogrado
**abound** [əˈbaʊnd] vi: **to** ~ (**in** or **with**) abundar (de o en)

---
KEYWORD
---

**about** [əˈbaʊt] adv **1** (approximately) más o menos, aproximadamente; ~ **a hundred/thousand** etc unos(unas) cien/mil etc; **it takes** ~ **10 hours** se tarda unas o más o menos 10 horas; **at** ~ **2 o'clock** sobre las dos; **I've just** ~ **finished** casi he terminado
**2** (referring to place) por todas partes; **to leave things lying** ~ dejar

las cosas (tiradas) por ahí; **to run** ~ correr por todas partes; **to walk** ~ pasearse, ir y venir

**3**: **to be** ~ **to do** sth estar a punto de hacer algo

♦ *prep* **1** (*relating to*) de, sobre, acerca de; **a book** ~ **London** un libro sobre *or* acerca de Londres; **what is it** ~? ¿de qué se trata?, ¿qué pasa?; **we talked** ~ **it** hablamos de eso *or* ello; **what** *or* **how** ~ **doing this?** ¿qué tal si hacemos esto?

**2** (*referring to place*) por; **to walk** ~ **the town** caminar por la ciudad

**above** [ə'bʌv] *adv* encima, por encima, arriba ♦ *prep* encima de; (*greater than*: in number) más de; (: in rank) superior a; **mentioned** ~ susodicho; ~ **all** sobre todo; ~ **board** *adj* legítimo

**abrasive** [ə'breɪzɪv] *adj* abrasivo; (*manner*) brusco

**abreast** [ə'brest] *adv* de frente; **to keep** ~ **of** (*fig*) mantenerse al corriente de

**abridge** [ə'brɪdʒ] *vt* abreviar

**abroad** [ə'brɔːd] *adv* (*to be*) en el extranjero; (*to go*) al extranjero

**abrupt** [ə'brʌpt] *adj* (*sudden*) brusco; (*curt*) áspero

**abruptly** [ə'brʌptlɪ] *adv* (*leave*) repentinamente; (*speak*) bruscamente

**abscess** ['æbsɪs] *n* absceso

**abscond** [əb'skɒnd] *vi* (*thief*): **to** ~ **with** fugarse con; (*prisoner*): **to** ~ (**from**) escaparse (de)

**absence** ['æbsəns] *n* ausencia

**absent** ['æbsənt] *adj* ausente; ~**ee** [-'tiː] *n* ausente *m/f*; ~**-minded** *adj* distraído

**absolute** ['æbsəluːt] *adj* absoluto; ~**ly** [-'luːtlɪ] *adv* (*totally*) totalmente; (*certainly*!) ¡por supuesto (que sí)!

**absolve** [əb'zɒlv] *vt*: **to** ~ **sb** (**from**) absolver a alguien (de)

**absorb** [əb'zɔːb] *vt* absorber; **to be** ~**ed in a book** estar absorto en un libro; ~**ent cotton** (*US*) *n* algodón *m*

hidrófilo; ~**ing** *adj* absorbente

**absorption** [əb'zɔːpʃən] *n* absorción *f*

**abstain** [əb'steɪn] *vi*: **to** ~ (**from**) abstenerse (de)

**abstinence** ['æbstɪnəns] *n* abstinencia

**abstract** ['æbstrækt] *adj* abstracto

**absurd** [əb'sɜːd] *adj* absurdo

**abundance** [ə'bʌndəns] *n* abundancia

**abuse** [*n* ə'bjuːs, *vb* ə'bjuːz] *n* (*insults*) insultos *mpl*, injurias *fpl*; (*ill-treatment*) malos tratos *mpl*; (*misuse*) abuso ♦ *vt* insultar; maltratar; abusar de; **abusive** *adj* ofensivo

**abysmal** [ə'bɪzməl] *adj* pésimo; (*failure*) garrafal; (*ignorance*) supino

**abyss** [ə'bɪs] *n* abismo

**AC** *abbr* (= *alternating current*) corriente *f* alterna

**academic** [ækə'demɪk] *adj* académico, universitario; (*pej*: *issue*) puramente teórico ♦ *n* estudioso/a; profesor(a) *m/f* universitario/a

**academy** [ə'kædəmɪ] *n* (*learned body*) academia; (*school*) instituto, colegio; ~ **of music** conservatorio

**accelerate** [æk'seləreɪt] *vt, vi* acelerar; **accelerator** (*BRIT*) *n* acelerador *m*

**accent** ['æksənt] *n* acento; (*fig*) énfasis *m*

**accept** [ək'sept] *vt* aceptar; (*responsibility, blame*) admitir; ~**able** *adj* aceptable; ~**ance** *n* aceptación *f*

**access** ['ækses] *n* acceso; **to have** ~ **to** tener libre acceso a; ~**ible** [-'sesəbl] *adj* (*place, person*) accesible; (*knowledge etc*) asequible

**accessory** [æk'sesərɪ] *n* accesorio; (*LAW*): ~ **to** cómplice de

**accident** ['æksɪdənt] *n* accidente *m*; (*chance event*) casualidad *f*; **by** ~ (*unintentionally*) sin querer; (*by chance*) por casualidad; ~**al** [-'dentl] *adj* accidental, fortuito; ~**ally** [-'dentlɪ] *adv* sin querer; por casualidad; ~**-prone** *adj* propenso a los accidentes

**acclaim** [əˈkleɪm] vt aclamar, aplaudir ♦ n aclamación f, aplausos mpl

**acclimate** [əˈklaɪmət] (US) vt = acclimatize

**acclimatize** [əˈklaɪmətaɪz] (BRIT) vt: **to become ~d** aclimatarse

**accolade** [ˈækəleɪd] n premio

**accommodate** [əˈkɒmədeɪt] vt (subj: person) alojar, hospedar; (: car, hotel etc) tener cabida para; (oblige, help) complacer; **accommodating** adj servicial, complaciente

**accommodation** [əkɒməˈdeɪʃən] n (US **accommodations** npl) alojamiento

**accompaniment** [əˈkʌmpənɪmənt] n (MUS) acompañamiento

**accompany** [əˈkʌmpənɪ] vt acompañar

**accomplice** [əˈkʌmplɪs] n cómplice m/f

**accomplish** [əˈkʌmplɪʃ] vt (finish) concluir; (achieve) lograr; **~ed** adj experto, hábil; **~ment** n (skill: gen pl) talento; (completion) realización f

**accord** [əˈkɔːd] n acuerdo ♦ vt conceder; **of his own ~** espontáneamente; **~ance** n: **in ~ance with** de acuerdo con; **~ing: ~ing to** prep según; (in accordance with) conforme a; **~ingly** adv (appropriately) de acuerdo con esto; (as a result) en consecuencia

**accordion** [əˈkɔːdɪən] n acordeón m

**accost** [əˈkɒst] vt abordar, dirigirse a

**account** [əˈkaʊnt] n (COMM) cuenta; (report) informe m; **~s** npl (COMM) cuentas fpl; **of no ~** de ninguna importancia; **on ~** a cuenta; **on no ~** bajo ningún concepto; **on ~ of** a causa de, por motivo de; **to take into ~, take ~ of** tener en cuenta; **~ for** vt fus (explain) explicar; (represent) representar; **~able** adj: **~able to** responsable (ante)

**accountancy** [əˈkaʊntənsɪ] n contabilidad f

**accountant** [əˈkaʊntənt] n contable m/f, contador(a) m/f

**account number** n (at bank etc) número de cuenta

**accredited** [əˈkredɪtɪd] adj (agent etc) autorizado

**accrued interest** [əˈkruːd-] n interés m acumulado

**accumulate** [əˈkjuːmjuleɪt] vt acumular ♦ vi acumularse

**accuracy** [ˈækjurəsɪ] n (of total) exactitud f; (of description etc) precisión f

**accurate** [ˈækjurɪt] adj (total) exacto; (description) preciso; (person) cuidadoso; (device) de precisión; **~ly** adv con precisión

**accusation** [ækjuˈzeɪʃən] n acusación f

**accuse** [əˈkjuːz] vt: **to ~ sb (of sth)** acusar a uno (de algo); **~d** n (LAW) acusado/a

**accustom** [əˈkʌstəm] vt acostumbrar; **~ed** adj: **~ed to** acostumbrado a

**ace** [eɪs] n as m

**ache** [eɪk] n dolor m ♦ vi doler; **my head ~s** me duele la cabeza

**achieve** [əˈtʃiːv] vt (aim, result) alcanzar; (success) lograr, conseguir; **~ment** n (completion) realización f; (success) éxito

**acid** [ˈæsɪd] adj (CHEM, inf: LSD) ácido; (taste) agrio ♦ n (CHEM, inf: LSD) ácido; **~ rain** n lluvia ácida

**acknowledge** [əkˈnɒlɪdʒ] vt (letter: also: **~ receipt of**) acusar recibo de; (fact, situation, person) reconocer; **~ment** n acuse m de recibo

**acne** [ˈæknɪ] n acné m

**acorn** [ˈeɪkɔːn] n bellota

**acoustic** [əˈkuːstɪk] adj acústico; **~s** n, npl acústica sg

**acquaint** [əˈkweɪnt] vt: **to ~ sb with sth** (inform) poner a uno al corriente de algo; **to be ~ed with** (person) conocer; **~ance** n (person) conocido/a; (with person, subject) conocimiento

**acquiesce** [ækwɪˈes] vi: **to ~ (to)** consentir (en)

**acquire** [əˈkwaɪə*] vt adquirir; **acquisition** [ækwɪˈzɪʃən] n adquisición f

**acquit** [ə'kwɪt] vt absolver, exculpar; to ~ o.s. well salir con éxito

**acre** ['eɪkə*] n acre m

**acrid** ['ækrɪd] adj acre

**acrimonious** [ækrɪ'məʊnɪəs] adj (remark) mordaz; (argument) reñido

**acrobat** ['ækrəbæt] n acróbata m/f

**acronym** ['ækrənɪm] n siglas fpl

**across** [ə'krɒs] prep (on the other side of) al otro lado de, del otro lado de; (crosswise) a través de ♦ adv de un lado a otro, de una parte a otra; a través, al través; (measurement): the road is 10m ~ la carretera tiene 10m de ancho; to run/swim ~ atravesar corriendo/nadando; ~ from enfrente de

**acrylic** [ə'krɪlɪk] adj acrílico ♦ n acrílica

**act** [ækt] n acto, acción f; (of play) acto; (in music hall etc) número; (LAW) decreto, ley f ♦ vi (behave) comportarse; (have effect: drug, chemical) hacer efecto; (THEATRE) actuar; (pretend) fingir; (take action) obrar ♦ vt (part) hacer el papel de; in the ~ of: to catch sb in the ~ of ... pillar a uno en el momento en que ...; to ~ as actuar or hacer de; ~ing adj suplente ♦ n (activity) actuación f; (profession) profesión f de actor

**action** ['ækʃən] n acción f, acto; (MIL) acción f, batalla; (LAW) proceso, demanda; out of ~ (person) fuera de combate; (thing) estropeado; to take ~ tomar medidas; ~ replay n (TV) repetición f

**activate** ['æktɪveɪt] vt activar

**active** ['æktɪv] adj activo, enérgico; (volcano) en actividad; ~ly adv (participate) activamente; (discourage, dislike) enérgicamente; **activist** n activista m/f; **activity** [-'tɪvɪtɪ] n actividad f

**actor** ['æktə*] n actor m

**actress** ['æktrɪs] n actriz f

**actual** ['æktjʊəl] adj verdadero, real; (emphatic use) propiamente dicho; ~ly adv realmente, en realidad;

(even) incluso

**acumen** ['ækjʊmən] n perspicacia

**acute** [ə'kjuːt] adj agudo

**ad** [æd] n abbr = advertisement

**A.D.** adv abbr (= anno Domini) A.C

**adamant** ['ædəmənt] adj firme, inflexible

**adapt** [ə'dæpt] vt adaptar ♦ vi: to ~ (to) adaptarse a, ajustarse (a); ~able adj adaptable; ~er or ~or n (ELEC) adaptador m

**add** [æd] vt añadir, agregar; (figures: also: ~ up) sumar ♦ vi: to ~ to (increase) aumentar, acrecentar; it doesn't ~ up (fig) no tiene sentido

**adder** ['ædə*] n víbora

**addict** ['ædɪkt] n adicto/a; (enthusiast) entusiasta m/f; ~ed [ə'dɪktɪd] adj: to be ~ed to ser adicto a; (football etc) ser fanático de; ~ion [ə'dɪkʃən] n (to drugs etc) adicción f; ~ive [ə'dɪktɪv] adj que causa adicción

**addition** [ə'dɪʃən] n (adding up) adición f; (thing added) añadidura, añadido; in ~ además, por añadidura; in ~ to además de; ~al adj adicional

**additive** ['ædɪtɪv] n aditivo

**address** [ə'drɛs] n dirección f, señas fpl; (speech) discurso ♦ vt (letter) dirigir; (speak to) dirigirse a, dirigir la palabra a; (problem) tratar

**adept** ['ædɛpt] adj: ~ at experto or hábil en

**adequate** ['ædɪkwɪt] adj (satisfactory) adecuado; (enough) suficiente

**adhere** [əd'hɪə*] vi: to ~ to (stick to) pegarse a; (fig: abide by) observar; (: belief etc) ser partidario de

**adhesive** [əd'hiːzɪv] n adhesivo; ~ tape n (BRIT) cinta adhesiva; (US: MED) esparadrapo

**ad hoc** [æd'hɒk] adj ad hoc

**adjacent** [ə'dʒeɪsənt] adj: ~ to contiguo a, inmediato a

**adjective** ['ædʒɛktɪv] n adjetivo

**adjoining** [ə'dʒɔɪnɪŋ] adj contiguo, vecino

**adjourn** [ə'dʒɜːn] vt aplazar ♦ vi

suspenderse

**adjudicate** [ə'dʒu:dɪkeɪt] *vi* sentenciar

**adjust** [ə'dʒʌst] *vt* (*change*) modificar; (*clothing*) arreglar; (*machine*) ajustar ♦ *vi*: to ~ (to) adaptarse (a); ~**able** *adj* ajustable; ~**ment** *n* adaptación *f*; (*to machine*, *prices*) ajuste *m*

**ad-lib** [æd'lɪb] *vt*, *vi* improvisar; **ad lib** *adv* de forma improvisada

**administer** [əd'mɪnɪstə*] *vt* administrar; **administration** [-'treɪʃən] *n* (*management*) administración *f*; (*government*) gobierno; **administrative** [-trətɪv] *adj* administrativo

**admiral** ['ædmərəl] *n* almirante *m*; **A~ty** (*BRIT*) *n* Ministerio de Marina, Almirantazgo

**admiration** [ædmə'reɪʃən] *n* admiración *f*

**admire** [əd'maɪə*] *vt* admirar; ~**r** *n* (*fan*) admirador(a) *m/f*

**admission** [əd'mɪʃən] *n* (*to university*, *club*) ingreso; (*entry fee*) entrada; (*confession*) confesión *f*

**admit** [əd'mɪt] *vt* (*confess*) confesar; (*permit to enter*) dejar entrar, dar entrada a; (*to club*, *organization*) admitir; (*accept: defeat*) reconocer; **to be ~ted to hospital** ingresar en el hospital; ~ **to** *vt fus* confesarse culpable de; ~**tance** *n* entrada; ~**tedly** *adv* es cierto or verdad que

**admonish** [əd'mɒnɪʃ] *vt* amonestar

**ad nauseam** [æd'nɔ:sɪæm] *adv* hasta el cansancio

**ado** [ə'du:] *n*: **without (any) more** ~ sin más (ni más)

**adolescent** [ædəu'lɛsnt] *adj*, *n* adolescente *m/f*

**adopt** [ə'dɒpt] *vt* adoptar; ~**ed** *adj* adoptivo; ~**ive** *adj* adoptivo; ~**ion** [ə'dɒpʃən] *n* adopción *f*

**adore** [ə'dɔ:*] *vt* adorar

**Adriatic** [eɪdrɪ'ætɪk] *n*: **the ~ (Sea)** el (Mar) Adriático

**adrift** [ə'drɪft] *adv* a la deriva

**adult** ['ædʌlt] *n* adulto/a ♦ *adj* (*grown-up*) adulto; (*for adults*) para

adultos

**adultery** [ə'dʌltərɪ] *n* adulterio

**advance** [əd'vɑ:ns] *n* (*progress*) adelanto, progreso; (*money*) anticipo, préstamo; (*MIL*) avance *m* ♦ *adj*: ~ **booking** venta anticipada; ~ **notice**, ~ **warning** previo aviso ♦ *vt* (*money*) anticipar; (*theory*, *idea*) proponer (para la discusión) ♦ *vi* avanzar, adelantarse; **to make ~s (to sb)** hacer proposiciones a alguien; **in** ~ por adelantado; ~**d** *adj* avanzado; (*SCOL: studies*) adelantado; ~**ment** *n* progreso; (*in job*) ascenso

**advantage** [əd'vɑ:ntɪdʒ] *n* (*also TENNIS*) ventaja; **to take ~ of** (*person*) aprovecharse de; (*opportunity*) aprovechar; ~**ous** [ædvən-'teɪdʒəs] *adj*: ~**ous (to)** ventajoso (para)

**Advent** ['ædvənt] *n* (*REL*) Adviento

**adventure** [əd'ventʃə*] *n* aventura; **adventurous** [-tʃərəs] *adj* atrevido; aventurero

**adverb** ['ædvə:b] *n* adverbio

**adverse** ['ædvə:s] *adj* adverso, contrario

**adversity** [əd'və:sɪtɪ] *n* infortunio

**advert** ['ædvə:t] (*BRIT*) *n abbr* = **advertisement**

**advertise** ['ædvətaɪz] *vi* (*in newspaper etc*) anunciar, hacer publicidad; **to ~ for** (*staff*, *accommodation etc*) buscar por medio de anuncios ♦ *vt* anunciar; ~**ment** [əd'və:tɪsmənt] *n* (*COMM*) anuncio; ~**r** *n* anunciante *m/f*; **advertising** *n* publicidad *f*, anuncios *mpl*; (*industry*) industria publicitaria

**advice** [əd'vaɪs] *n* consejo, consejos *mpl*; (*notification*) aviso; **a piece of** ~ un consejo; **to take legal** ~ consultar con un abogado

**advisable** [əd'vaɪzəbl] *adj* aconsejable, conveniente

**advise** [əd'vaɪz] *vt* aconsejar; (*inform*): **to ~ sb of sth** informar a uno de algo; **to ~ sb against sth/doing sth** desaconsejar algo a uno/aconsejar a uno que no haga algo;

**~dly** [əd'vaɪzɪdlɪ] adv (deliberately) deliberadamente; **~r** n = **advisor**; **advisor** n consejero/a (consultant) asesor(a) m/f; **advisory** adj consultivo

**advocate** ['ædvəkeɪt] vt abogar por ♦ n [-kɪt] (lawyer) abogado/a; (supporter): ~ **of** defensor(a) m/f de

**Aegean** [i:'dʒi:ən] n: the ~ (Sea) el (Mar) Egeo

**aerial** ['ɛərɪəl] n antena ♦ adj aéreo

**aerobics** [ɛə'rəubɪks] n aerobic m

**aeroplane** ['ɛərəpleɪn] (BRIT) n avión m

**aerosol** ['ɛərəsɒl] n aerosol m

**aesthetic** [i:s'θɛtɪk] adj estético

**afar** [ə'fɑ:*] adv: **from ~** desde lejos

**affair** [ə'fɛə*] n asunto; (also: love ~) aventura (amorosa)

**affect** [ə'fɛkt] vt (influence) afectar, influir en; (afflict, concern) afectar; (move) conmover; **~ed** adj afectado

**affection** [ə'fɛkʃən] n afecto, cariño; **~ate** adj afectuoso, cariñoso

**affiliated** [əfɪlɪ'eɪtɪd] adj afiliado

**affinity** [ə'fɪnɪtɪ] n (bond, rapport): **to feel an ~ with** sentirse identificado con; (resemblance) afinidad f

**afflict** [ə'flɪkt] vt afligir

**affluence** ['æfluəns] n opulencia, riqueza

**affluent** ['æfluənt] adj (wealthy) acomodado, rico; **the ~ society** la sociedad opulenta

**afford** [ə'fɔ:d] vt (provide) proporcionar; **can we ~ (to buy) it?** ¿tenemos bastante dinero para comprarlo?

**Afghanistan** [æf'gænɪstæn] n Afganistán m

**afield** [ə'fi:ld] adv: **far ~** muy lejos

**afloat** [ə'fləut] adv (floating) a flote

**afoot** [ə'fut] adv: **there is something ~** algo se está tramando

**afraid** [ə'freɪd] adj: **to be ~ of** (person) tener miedo a; (thing) tener miedo de; **to be ~ to** tener miedo de, temer; **I am ~ that** me temo que; **I am ~ not/so** lo siento, pero no/es así

**afresh** [ə'frɛʃ] adv de nuevo, otra vez

**Africa** ['æfrɪkə] n África; **~n** adj, n africano/a m/f

**aft** [ɑ:ft] adv (to be) en popa; (to go) a popa

**after** ['ɑ:ftə*] prep (time) después de; (place, order) detrás de, tras ♦ adv después ♦ conj después (de) que; **what/who are you ~?** ¿qué/a quién busca usted?; ~ **having done/he left** después de que marchó; **to name sb ~ sb** llamar a uno por uno; **it's twenty ~ eight** (US) son las ocho y veinte; **to ask ~ sb** preguntar por alguien; ~ **all** después de todo, al fin y al cabo; ~ **you!** ¡pase usted!; **~-effects** npl consecuencias fpl, efectos mpl; **~math** n consecuencias fpl, resultados mpl; **~noon** n tarde f; **~s** (inf) n (dessert) postre m; **~-sales service** (BRIT) n servicio de asistencia pos-venta; **~-shave (lotion)** n aftershave m; **~thought** n ocurrencia (tardía); **~wards** (US **~ward**) adv después, más tarde

**again** [ə'gɛn] adv otra vez, de nuevo; **to do sth ~** volver a hacer algo; **~ and ~** una y otra vez

**against** [ə'gɛnst] prep (in opposition to) en contra de; (leaning on, touching) junto, junto a

**age** [eɪdʒ] n edad f; (period) época f ♦ vi envejecer(se) ♦ vt envejecer; **is 20 years of ~** tiene 20 años; **to come of ~** llegar a la mayoría de edad; **it's been ~s since I saw you** hace siglos que no te veo; **~d 10** de 10 años de edad; **the ~d** ['eɪdʒɪd] npl los ancianos; **~ group** n: **to be in the same ~ group** tener la misma edad; **~ limit** n edad f mínima (or máxima)

**agency** ['eɪdʒənsɪ] n agencia

**agenda** [ə'dʒɛndə] n orden m del día

**agent** ['eɪdʒənt] n agente m/f; (COMM: holding concession) representante m/f, delegado/a; (CHEM, fig) agente m

**aggravate** ['ægrəveɪt] vt (situation) agravar; (person) irritar

**aggregate** [ˈægrɪgeɪt] n conjunto

**aggressive** [əˈgresɪv] adj (belligerent) agresivo; (assertive) enérgico

**aggrieved** [əˈgriːvd] adj ofendido, agraviado

**aghast** [əˈgɑːst] adj horrorizado

**agile** [ˈædʒaɪl] adj ágil

**agitate** [ˈædʒɪteɪt] vt (trouble) inquietar ♦ vi: to ~ for/against hacer campaña pro or en favor de/en contra de; **agitator** n agitador(a) m/f

**AGM** n abbr (= annual general meeting) asamblea anual

**ago** [əˈgəʊ] adv: 2 days ~ hace 2 días; **not long** ~ hace poco; **how long** ~? ¿hace cuánto tiempo?

**agog** [əˈgɒg] adj (eager) ansioso; (excited) emocionado

**agonizing** [ˈægənaɪzɪŋ] adj (pain) atroz; (decision, wait) angustioso

**agony** [ˈægənɪ] n (pain) dolor m agudo; (distress) angustia; **to be in** ~ retorcerse de dolor

**agree** [əˈgriː] vt (price, date) acordar, quedar en ♦ vi (have same opinion): **to** ~ (**with/that**) estar de acuerdo (con/que); (consent) acceder; **to** ~ **with** (subj: person) estar de acuerdo con, ponerse de acuerdo con; (: food) sentar bien a; (LING) concordar con; **to** ~ **to sth/to do sth** consentir en algo/aceptar hacer algo; **to** ~ **that** (admit) estar de acuerdo en que; ~**able** adj (sensation) agradable; (person) simpático; (willing) de acuerdo, conforme; ~**d** adj (time, place) convenido; (contract) contrato; **in** ~**ment** de acuerdo, conforme

**agricultural** [ægrɪˈkʌltʃərəl] adj agrícola

**agriculture** [ˈægrɪkʌltʃəˈ] n agricultura

**aground** [əˈgraʊnd] adv: **to run** ~ (NAUT) encallar, embarrancar

**ahead** [əˈhed] adv (in front) delante; (into the future): **she had no time to think** ~ no tenía tiempo de hacer planes para el futuro; ~ **of** delante

de; (in advance of) antes de; ~ **of time** antes de la hora; **go right** or **straight** ~ (direction) siga adelante; (permission) hazlo (or hágalo)

**aid** [eɪd] n ayuda, auxilio; (device) aparato ♦ vt ayudar, auxiliar; **in** ~ **of** a beneficio de; **to** ~ **and abet** (LAW) ser cómplice de

**aide** [eɪd] n (person, also: MIL) ayudante m/f

**AIDS** [eɪdz] n abbr (= acquired immune deficiency syndrome) SIDA m

**ailing** [ˈeɪlɪŋ] adj (person) enfermizo; (economy) debilitado

**ailment** [ˈeɪlmənt] n enfermedad f, achaque m

**aim** [eɪm] vt (gun, camera) apuntar; (missile, remark) dirigir; (blow) asestar ♦ vi (also: take ~) apuntar ♦ n (in shooting: skill) puntería; (objective) propósito, meta; **to** ~ **at** (with weapon) apuntar a; (objective) aspirar a, pretender; **to** ~ **to do** tener la intención de hacer; ~**less** adj sin propósito, sin objeto

**ain't** [eɪnt] (inf) = **am not**; **aren't**; **isn't**

**air** [eə*] n aire m; (appearance) aspecto ♦ vt (room) ventilar; (clothes, ideas) airear ♦ cpd aéreo; **to throw sth into the** ~ (ball etc) lanzar algo al aire; **by** ~ (travel) en avión; **to be on the** ~ (RADIO, TV) estar en antena; ~**bed** n (BRIT) n colchón m neumático; ~**borne** adj (in the air) en el aire; ~-**conditioned** adj climatizado; ~ **conditioning** n aire acondicionado; ~**craft** n inv avión m; ~**craft carrier** n porta(a)viones m inv; ~**field** n campo de aviación; ~ **force** n fuerzas fpl aéreas, aviación f; ~ **freshener** n ambientador m; ~**gun** n escopeta de aire comprimido; ~ **hostess** (BRIT) n azafata; ~**letter** (BRIT) n carta aérea; ~**line** n línea aérea; ~**liner** n avión m de pasajeros; ~**mail** n: **by** ~**mail** por avión; ~**plane** (US) n avión m; ~**port** n aeropuerto; ~ **raid** n ataque m

aéreo; **~sick** *adj*: to be ~sick
marearse (en avión); **~space** *n*
espacio aéreo; ~ **terminal** *n* terminal *f*; **~tight** *adj* hermético; **~**-**traffic controller** *n* controlador(a)
*m/f* aéreo/a; **~y** *adj (room)* bien ventilado; *(fig: manner)* desenfadado

**aisle** [aɪl] *n (of church)* nave *f; (of theatre, supermarket)* pasillo

**ajar** [ə'dʒɑː*] *adj* entreabierto

**akin** [ə'kɪn] *adj*: **~ to** parecido a

**alacrity** [ə'lækrɪtɪ] *n* presteza

**alarm** [ə'lɑːm] *n (in shop, bank)* alarma; *(anxiety)* inquietud *f* ♦ *vt* asustar, inquietar; ~ **call** *n (in hotel etc)*
alarma; ~ **clock** *n* despertador *m*

**alas** [ə'læs] *adv* desgraciadamente

**albeit** [ɔːl'biːɪt] *conj* aunque

**album** ['ælbəm] *n* álbum *m*; *(L.P.)*
elepé *m*

**alcohol** ['ælkəhɒl] *n* alcohol *m*; **~ic**
[-'hɒlɪk] *adj, n* alcohólico/a *m/f*

**alcove** ['ælkəʊv] *n* nicho, hueco

**ale** [eɪl] *n* cerveza

**alert** [ə'lɜːt] *adj (attentive)* atento;
*(to danger, opportunity)* alerta ♦ *n*
alerta *m*, alarma ♦ *vt* poner sobre
aviso; **to be on the ~** *(also MIL)* estar alerta *or* sobre aviso

**algebra** ['ældʒɪbrə] *n* álgebra

**Algeria** [æl'dʒɪərɪə] *n* Argelia

**alias** ['eɪlɪəs] *adv* alias, conocido por
♦ *n (of criminal)* apodo; *(of writer)*
seudónimo

**alibi** ['ælɪbaɪ] *n* coartada

**alien** ['eɪlɪən] *n (foreigner)* extranjero/a; *(extraterrestrial)* extraterrestre *m/f* ♦ *adj*: **~ to** ajeno a;
**~ate** *vt* enajenar, alejar

**alight** [ə'laɪt] *adj* ardiendo; *(eyes)*
brillante ♦ *vi (person)* apearse, bajar; *(bird)* posarse

**align** [ə'laɪn] *vt* alinear

**alike** [ə'laɪk] *adj* semejantes, iguales
♦ *adv* igualmente, del mismo modo;
**to look ~** parecerse

**alimony** ['ælɪmənɪ] *n* manutención *f*

**alive** [ə'laɪv] *adj* vivo; *(lively)* alegre

---

┌─────────────┐
│ KEYWORD │
└─────────────┘

**all** [ɔːl] *adj (sg)* todo/a; *(pl)* todos/as;
~ **day** todo el día; ~ **night** toda la
noche; ~ **men** todos los hombres; ~
**five** came vinieron los cinco; ~ **the
books** todos los libros; ~ **his** life
toda su vida
♦ *pron* **1** todo; I ate it ~, I ate ~
of it me lo comí todo; ~ **of us** went
fuimos todos; ~ **the boys** went fueron todos los chicos; is that ~? ¿eso
es todo?, ¿algo más?; *(in shop)* ¿algo
más?, ¿alguna cosa más?
**2** *(in phrases)*: **above** ~ sobre todo;
por encima de todo; **after** ~ después
de todo; **at** ~: **not at** ~ *(in answer
to question)* ¡en absoluto!; *(in answer
to thanks)* ¡de nada!, ¡no hay de
qué!; **I'm not at** ~ **tired** no estoy
nada cansado/a; **anything at** ~ will
do cualquier cosa viene bien; **in** ~ a
fin de cuentas
♦ *adv*: ~ **alone** completamente
solo/a; **it's not as hard as** ~ **that**
no es tan difícil como lo pintas; ~
**the more/the better** tanto más/
mejor; ~ **but** casi; **the score is** 2 ~
están empatados a 2

**allay** [ə'leɪ] *vt (fears)* aquietar

**all clear** *n (after attack etc)* fin *m* de
la alerta; *(fig)* luz *f* verde

**allegation** [ælɪ'ɡeɪʃən] *n* alegato

**allege** [ə'ledʒ] *vt* pretender; **~dly**
[ə'ledʒɪdlɪ] *adv* supuestamente, según se
afirma

**allegiance** [ə'liːdʒəns] *n* lealtad *f*

**allergy** ['ælədʒɪ] *n* alergia

**alleviate** [ə'liːvɪeɪt] *vt* aliviar

**alley** ['ælɪ] *n* callejuela

**alliance** [ə'laɪəns] *n* alianza

**allied** ['ælaɪd] *adj* aliado

**alligator** ['ælɪɡeɪtə*] *n (ZOOL)* caimán *m*

**all-in** *(BRIT) adj, adv (charge)* todo
incluido; ~ **wrestling** *n* lucha libre

**all-night** *adj (cafe, shop)* abierto
toda la noche; *(party)* que dura toda
la noche

**allocate** ['æləkeɪt] vt (money etc) asignar

**allot** [ə'lɒt] vt asignar; **~ment** n ración f; (garden) parcela

**all-out** adj (effort etc) supremo; **all out** adv con todas las fuerzas

**allow** [ə'lau] vt permitir, dejar; -(a claim) admitir; (sum, time etc) dar, conceder; (concede): **to ~ that** reconocer que; **to ~ sb to do** permitir a alguien hacer; **he is ~ed to ...** se le permite ...; **~ for** vt fus tener en cuenta; **~ance** n subvención f; (welfare payment) subsidio, pensión f; (pocket money) dinero de bolsillo; (tax ~) desgravación f; **to make ~ances for** (person) disculpar a; (thing) tener en cuenta

**alloy** ['ælɔɪ] n mezcla

**all:** **~ right** adv bien; (as answer) ¡conforme!, ¡está bien!; **~rounder** n: **he's a good ~rounder** se le da bien todo; **~-time** adj (record) de todos los tiempos

**allude** [ə'lu:d] vi: **to ~ to** aludir a

**alluring** [ə'ljuərɪŋ] adj atractivo, tentador(a)

**allusion** [ə'lu:ʒən] n referencia, alusión f

**ally** ['ælaɪ] n aliado/a ♦ vt: **to ~ o.s. with** aliarse con

**almighty** [ɔːl'maɪtɪ] adj todopoderoso; (row etc) imponente

**almond** ['ɑːmənd] n almendra

**almost** ['ɔːlməust] adv casi

**alms** [ɑːmz] npl limosna

**aloft** [ə'lɒft] adv arriba

**alone** [ə'ləun] adj, adv solo; **to leave sb ~** dejar a uno en paz; **to leave sth ~** no tocar algo, dejar algo sin tocar; **let ~ ...** y mucho menos ...

**along** [ə'lɒŋ] prep a lo largo de, por ♦ adv: **is he coming ~ with us?** ¿viene con nosotros?; **he was limping ~** iba cojeando; **~ with** junto con; **all ~** (all the time) desde el principio; **~side** prep al lado de ♦ adv al lado

**aloof** [ə'lu:f] adj reservado ♦ adv: **to stand ~** mantenerse apartado

**aloud** [ə'laud] adv en voz alta

**alphabet** ['ælfəbet] n alfabeto

**Alps** [ælps] npl: **the ~** los Alpes

**already** [ɔːl'redɪ] adv ya

**alright** [ɔːl'raɪt] (BRIT) adv = **all right**

**Alsatian** [æl'seɪʃən] n (dog) pastor m alemán

**also** ['ɔːlsəu] adv también, además

**altar** ['ɔltə*] n altar m

**alter** ['ɔltə*] vt cambiar, modificar ♦ vi cambiar

**alteration** [ɔltə'reɪʃən] n cambio; (to clothes) arreglo; (to building) arreglos mpl

**alternate** [adj ɔl'tɜːnɪt, vb 'ɔltɜːneɪt] adj (actions etc) alternativo; (events) alterno; (US) = **alternative** ♦ vi: **to ~ (with)** alternar (con); **on ~ days** un día sí y otro no; **alternating current** [-neɪtɪŋ] n corriente f alterna

**alternative** [ɔl'tɜːnətɪv] adj alternativo ♦ n alternativa; **~ly** adv: **~ly one could ...** por otra parte se podría ...

**although** [ɔːl'ðəu] conj aunque

**altitude** ['æltɪtjuːd] n altura

**alto** ['æltəu] n (female) contralto f; (male) alto

**altogether** [ɔːltə'geðə*] adv completamente, del todo; (on the whole) en total, en conjunto

**aluminium** [ælju'mɪnɪəm] (BRIT) n aluminio

**aluminum** [ə'luːmɪnəm] (US) n = **aluminium**

**always** ['ɔːlweɪz] adv siempre

**Alzheimer's (disease)** ['ælts-haɪməz-] n enfermedad f de Alzheimer

**am** [æm] vb see **be**

**a.m.** adv abbr (= ante meridiem) de la mañana

**amalgamate** [ə'mælgəmeɪt] vi amalgamarse ♦ vt amalgamar, unir

**amass** [ə'mæs] vt amontonar, acumular

**amateur** ['æmətə*] n aficionado/a, amateur m/f; **~ish** adj inexperto, superficial

**amaze** [ə'meɪz] vt asombrar, pasmar; **to be ~d (at)** quedar pasmado (de); **~ment** n asombro, sorpresa; **amazing** adj extraordinario; (fantastic) increíble

**Amazon** ['æməzən] n (GEO) Amazonas m

**ambassador** [æm'bæsədə*] n embajador(a) m/f

**amber** ['æmbə*] n ámbar m; **at ~** (BRIT: AUT) en el amarillo

**ambiguity** [æmbɪ'gjuɪtɪ] n ambigüedad f

**ambiguous** [æm'bɪgjuəs] adj ambiguo

**ambition** [æm'bɪʃən] n ambición f; **ambitious** [-ʃəs] adj ambicioso

**amble** ['æmbl] vi (gen: ~ along) deambular, andar sin prisa

**ambulance** ['æmbjuləns] n ambulancia

**ambush** ['æmbuʃ] n emboscada ♦ vt tender una emboscada a

**amenable** [ə'mi:nəbl] adj: **to be ~ to** dejarse influir por

**amend** [ə'mend] vt enmendar; **to make ~s** dar cumplida satisfacción; **~ment** n enmienda

**amenities** [ə'mi:nɪtɪz] npl comodidades fpl

**America** [ə'merɪkə] n (USA) Estados mpl Unidos; **~n** adj, n norteamericano/a m/f; estadounidense m/f

**amiable** ['eɪmɪəbl] adj amable, simpático

**amicable** ['æmɪkəbl] adj amistoso, amigable

**amid(st)** [ə'mɪd(st)] prep entre, en medio de

**amiss** [ə'mɪs] adv: **to take sth ~** tomar algo a mal; **there's something ~** pasa algo

**ammonia** [ə'məunɪə] n amoníaco

**ammunition** [æmju'nɪʃən] n municiones fpl

**amnesty** ['æmnɪstɪ] n amnistía

**amok** [ə'mɔk] adv: **to run ~** enloquecerse, desbocarse

**among(st)** [ə'mʌŋ(st)] prep entre, en medio de

**amorous** ['æmərəs] adj amoroso

**amount** [ə'maunt] n (gen) cantidad f; (of bill etc) suma, importe m ♦ vi: **to ~ to** sumar; (be same as) equivaler a, significar

**amp(ère)** ['æmp(ɛə*)] n amperio

**amphibious** [æm'fɪbɪəs] adj anfibio

**amphitheatre** ['æmfɪθɪətə*] (US **amphitheater**) n anfiteatro

**ample** ['æmpl] adj (large) grande; (abundant) abundante; (enough) bastante, suficiente

**amplifier** ['æmplɪfaɪə*] n amplificador m

**amputate** ['æmpjuteɪt] vt amputar

**amuse** [ə'mju:z] vt divertir; (distract) distraer, entretener; **~ment** n diversión f; (pastime) pasatiempo; (laughter) risa; **~ment arcade** n salón m de juegos

**an** [æn] indef art see **a**

**anaemia** [ə'ni:mɪə] n (US **anemia**) anemia; **anaemic** [-mɪk] (US **anemic**) adj anémico; (fig) soso, insípido

**anaesthetic** [ænɪs'θetɪk] n (US **anesthetic**) anestesia; **anaesthetist** [æ'ni:sθɪtɪst] (US **anesthetist**) n anestesista m/f

**analog(ue)** ['ænəlɔg] adj (computer, watch) analógico

**analogy** [ə'nælədʒɪ] n analogía

**analyse** ['ænəlaɪz] (US **analyze**) vt analizar; **analyses** [ə'næləsi:z] npl of analysis; **analysis** [ə'næləsɪs] (pl **analyses**) n análisis m inv; **analyst** [-lɪst] n (political ~, psycho~) analista m/f; **analytic(al)** [ænə'lɪtɪk(əl)] adj analítico

**analyze** ['ænəlaɪz] (US) vt = analyse

**anarchist** ['ænəkɪst] n anarquista m/f

**anarchy** ['ænəkɪ] n anarquía

**anatomy** [ə'nætəmɪ] n anatomía

**ancestor** ['ænsɪstə*] n antepasado

**anchor** ['æŋkə*] n ancla, áncora f ♦ vi (also: **to drop ~**) anclar ♦ vt anclar; **to weigh ~** levar anclas

**anchovy** ['æntʃəvɪ] n anchoa
**ancient** ['eɪnʃənt] adj antiguo
**ancillary** [æn'sɪlərɪ] adj auxiliar
**and** [ænd] conj y; (before i-, hi- + consonant) e; men ~ women hombres y mujeres; **father** ~ son padre e hijo; **trees** ~ **grass** árboles y hierba; ~ so on etcétera, y así sucesivamente; **try** ~ **come** procura venir; **he talked** ~ **talked** habló sin parar; **better** ~ **better** cada vez mejor
**Andes** ['ændiːz] npl: **the** ~ los Andes
**anemia** etc [ə'niːmɪə] (US) = **anaemia** etc
**anesthetic** etc [ænɪs'θetɪk] (US) = **anaesthetic** etc
**anew** [ə'njuː] adv de nuevo, otra vez
**angel** ['eɪndʒəl] n ángel m
**anger** ['æŋgə*] n cólera
**angina** [æn'dʒaɪnə] n angina (del pecho)
**angle** ['æŋgl] n ángulo; **from their** ~ desde su punto de vista
**angler** ['æŋglə*] n pescador(a) m/f (de caña)
**Anglican** ['æŋglɪkən] adj, n anglicano/a m/f
**angling** ['æŋglɪŋ] n pesca con caña
**Anglo...** ['æŋgləu] prefix anglo...
**angrily** ['æŋgrɪlɪ] adv coléricamente, airadamente
**angry** ['æŋgrɪ] adj enfadado, airado; (wound) inflamado; **to be** ~ **with sb/at sth** estar enfadado con alguien/por algo; **to get** ~ enfadarse, enojarse
**anguish** ['æŋgwɪʃ] n (physical) tormentos mpl; (mental) angustia
**angular** ['æŋgjulə*] adj (shape) angular; (features) anguloso
**animal** ['ænɪml] n animal m; (pej: person) bestia ♦ adj animal
**animate** ['ænɪmeɪt] adj vivo; ~d [-meɪtɪd] adj animado
**animosity** [ænɪ'mɒsɪtɪ] n animosidad f, rencor m
**aniseed** ['ænɪsiːd] n anís m
**ankle** ['æŋkl] n tobillo m; ~ **sock** n calcetín m corto

**annex** [n 'æneks, vb æ'neks] n (also: BRIT: **annexe**) (building) edificio anexo ♦ vt (territory) anexionar
**annihilate** [ə'naɪəleɪt] vt aniquilar
**anniversary** [ænɪ'vɜːsərɪ] n aniversario
**announce** [ə'nauns] vt anunciar; ~**ment** n anuncio; (official) declaración f; ~ **r** n (RADIO) locutor(a) m/f; (TV) presentador(a) m/f
**annoy** [ə'nɔɪ] vt molestar, fastidiar; **don't get** ~**ed!** ¡no se enfade!; ~**ance** n enojo; ~**ing** adj molesto, fastidioso; (person) pesado
**annual** ['ænjuəl] adj anual ♦ n (BOT) anual m; (book) anuario; ~**ly** adv anualmente, cada año
**annul** [ə'nʌl] vt anular
**annum** ['ænəm] n see **per**
**anomaly** [ə'nɒməlɪ] n anomalía
**anonymous** [ə'nɒnɪməs] adj anónimo
**anorak** ['ænəræk] n anorak m
**another** [ə'nʌðə*] adj (one more, a different one) otro, otra; see **one**
**answer** ['ɑːnsə*] n contestación f, respuesta; (to problem) solución f ♦ vi contestar, responder ♦ vt (reply to) contestar a, responder a; (problem) resolver; (prayer) escuchar; **in** ~ **to your letter** contestando or en contestación a su carta; **to** ~ **the phone** contestar or coger el teléfono; **to** ~ **the bell** or **the door** acudir a la puerta; ~ **back** vi replicar, ser respondón/ona; ~ **for** vt fus responder de or por; ~ **to** vt fus (description) corresponder a; ~**able** adj: ~**able to sb for sth** responsable ante uno de algo; ~**ing machine** n contestador m automático
**ant** [ænt] n hormiga
**antagonism** [æn'tægənɪzm] n antagonismo, hostilidad f
**antagonize** [æn'tægənaɪz] vt provocar la enemistad de
**Antarctic** [ænt'ɑːktɪk] n: **the** ~ el Antártico
**antelope** ['æntɪləup] n antílope m

**antenatal** ['æntɪ'neɪtl] adj antenatal, prenatal; ~ **clinic** n clínica prenatal

**antenna** [æn'tɛnə] (pl ~e) n antena

**anthem** ['ænθəm] n: **national** ~ himno nacional

**anthology** [æn'θɒlədʒɪ] n antología

**anthropology** [ænθrə'pɒlədʒɪ] n antropología

**anti...** [æntɪ] prefix anti...; ~**aircraft** [-'ɛəkrɑːft] adj antiaéreo; ~**biotic** [-baɪ'ɒtɪk] n antibiótico; ~**body** ['æntɪbɒdɪ] n anticuerpo

**anticipate** [æn'tɪsɪpeɪt] vt prever; (expect) esperar, contar con; (look forward to) esperar con ilusión; (do first) anticiparse a, adelantarse a; **anticipation** [-'peɪʃən] n (expectation) previsión f; (eagerness) ilusión f, expectación f

**anticlimax** [æntɪ'klaɪmæks] n decepción f

**anticlockwise** [æntɪ'klɒkwaɪz] (BRIT) adv en dirección contraria a la de las agujas del reloj

**antics** ['æntɪks] npl gracias fpl

**anticyclone** [æntɪ'saɪkləʊn] n anticiclón m

**antidote** ['æntɪdəʊt] n antídoto

**antifreeze** ['æntɪfriːz] n anticongelante m

**antihistamine** [æntɪ'hɪstəmiːn] n antihistamínico

**antipathy** [æn'tɪpəθɪ] n (between people) antipatía; (to person, thing) aversión f

**antiquated** ['æntɪkweɪtɪd] adj anticuado

**antique** [æn'tiːk] n antigüedad f ♦ adj antiguo; ~ **dealer** n anticuario/a; ~ **shop** n tienda de antigüedades

**antiquity** [æn'tɪkwɪtɪ] n antigüedad f

**anti-Semitism** [æntɪ'semɪtɪzm] n antisemitismo

**antiseptic** [æntɪ'septɪk] adj, n antiséptico

**antlers** ['æntləz] npl cuernas fpl, cornamenta sg

**anus** ['eɪnəs] n ano

**anvil** ['ænvɪl] n yunque m

**anxiety** [æŋ'zaɪətɪ] n inquietud f;

(MED) ansiedad f; ~ **to do** do deseo de hacer

**anxious** ['æŋkʃəs] adj inquieto, preocupado; (worrying) preocupante; (keen): **to be** ~ **to do** tener muchas ganas de hacer

KEYWORD

**any** ['enɪ] adj **1** (in questions etc) algún/alguna; **have you** ~ **butter/children?** ¿tienes mantequilla/hijos?; **if there are** ~ **tickets left** si quedan billetes, si queda algún billete

**2** (with negative): **I haven't** ~ **money/books** no tengo dinero/libros

**3** (no matter which) cualquier; ~ **excuse will do** valdrá or servirá cualquier excusa; **choose** ~ **book you like** escoge el libro que quieras; ~ **teacher you ask will tell you** cualquier profesor al que preguntes te lo dirá

**4** (in phrases): **in** ~ **case** de todas formas, en cualquier caso; ~ **day now** cualquier día (de estos); **at** ~ **moment** en cualquier momento, de un momento a otro; **at** ~ **rate** en todo caso; ~ **time**: **come** (at) ~ **time** venga cuando quieras; **he might come** (at) ~ **time** podría llegar de un momento a otro

♦ pron **1** (in questions etc): **have you got** ~? ¿tienes alguno(s)/a(s)?; **can** ~ **of you sing?** ¿sabéis/saben cantar alguno de vosotros/ustedes?

**2** (with negative): **I haven't** ~ (of them) no tengo ninguno

**3** (no matter which one(s)): **take** ~ **of those books** (you like) toma cualquier libro que quieras de ésos

♦ adv **1** (in questions etc): **do you want** ~ **more soup/sandwiches?** ¿quieres más sopa/bocadillos?; **are you feeling** ~ **better?** ¿te sientes algo mejor?

**2** (with negative): **I can't hear him** ~ **more** ya no le oigo; **don't wait** ~ **longer** no esperes más

**anybody** ['ɛnibɔdi] *pron* cualquiera; (*in interrogative sentences*) alguien; (*in negative sentences*): **I don't see ~** no veo a nadie; **if ~ should phone ...** si llama alguien ...

**anyhow** ['ɛnihau] *adv* (*at any rate*) de todos modos, de todas formas; (*haphazard*): **do it ~ you like** hazlo como quieras; **she leaves things just ~** deja las cosas como quiera o de cualquier modo; **I shall go ~** de todos modos iré

**anyone** ['ɛniwʌn] *pron* = **anybody**

**anything** ['ɛniθiŋ] *pron* (*in questions etc*) algo, alguna cosa; (*with negative*) nada; **can you see ~?** ¿ves algo?; **if ~ happens to me ...** si algo me ocurre ...; (*no matter what*): **you can ~ = you like** puedes decir lo que quieras; **~ will do** vale todo o cualquier cosa; **he'll eat ~** come de todo o lo que sea

**anyway** ['ɛniwei] *adv* (*at any rate*) de todos modos, de todas formas; **I shall go ~** iré de todos modos; (*besides*): **~, I couldn't come even if I wanted to** además, no podría venir aunque quisiera; **why are you phoning ~?** ¿entonces, por qué llamas?; **¿por qué llamas, pues?**

**anywhere** ['ɛniwɛə*] *adv* (*in questions etc*): **can you see him ~?** ¿le ves por algún lado?; **are you going ~?** ¿vas a algún sitio?; (*with negative*): **I can't see him ~** no le veo por ninguna parte; **~ in the world** (*no matter where*) en cualquier parte (del mundo); **put the books down ~** deja los libros donde quieras

**apart** [ə'pɑːt] *adv* (*aside*) aparte; (*situation*): **~ (from)** separado (de); (*movement*): **to pull ~** separar; **10 miles ~** separados por 10 millas; **to take ~** desmontar; **~ from** *prep* aparte de

**apartheid** [ə'pɑːteit] *n* apartheid *m*

**apartment** [ə'pɑːtmənt] *n* (*US*) piso (*SP*), departamento (*AM*), apartamento; (*room*) cuarto; **~ building**

(*US*) *n* edificio de apartamentos

**apathetic** [æpə'θɛtik] *adj* apático, indiferente

**apathy** ['æpəθi] *n* apatía, indiferencia

**ape** [eip] *n* mono ♦ *vt* imitar, remedar

**aperitif** [ə'pɛritif] *n* aperitivo

**aperture** ['æpətjuə*] *n* rendija, resquicio; (*PHOT*) abertura

**apex** ['eipɛks] *n* ápice *m*; (*fig*) cumbre *f*

**apiece** [ə'piːs] *adv* cada uno

**aplomb** [ə'plɔm] *n* aplomo

**apologetic** [əpɔlə'dʒɛtik] *adj* de disculpa; (*person*) arrepentido

**apologize** [ə'pɔlədʒaiz] *vi*: **to ~ (for sth to sb)** disculparse (con alguien de algo)

**apology** [ə'pɔlədʒi] *n* disculpa, excusa

**apostrophe** [ə'pɔstrəfi] *n* apóstrofo *m*

**appal** [ə'pɔːl] *vt* horrorizar, espantar; **~ling** *adj* espantoso; (*awful*) pésimo

**apparatus** [æpə'reitəs] *n* (*equipment*) equipo; (*organization*) aparato; (*in gymnasium*) aparatos *mpl*

**apparel** [ə'pærl] (*US*) *n* ropa

**apparent** [ə'pærənt] *adj* aparente; (*obvious*) evidente; **~ly** *adv* por lo visto, al parecer

**appeal** [ə'piːl] *vi* (*LAW*) apelar ♦ *n* (*LAW*) apelación *f*; (*request*) llamamiento; (*plea*) petición *f*; (*charm*) atractivo; **to ~** for reclamar; **to ~ to** (*be attractive to*) atraer; **it doesn't ~ to me** no me atrae, no me llama la atención; **~ing** *adj* (*attractive*) atractivo

**appear** [ə'piə*] *vi* aparecer, presentarse; (*LAW*) comparecer; (*publication*) salir (a luz); (*seem*) parecer; **to ~ on TV/in "Hamlet"** salir por la tele/hacer un papel en "Hamlet"; **it would ~ that** parecería que; **~ance** *n* aparición *f*; (*look*) apariencia, aspecto

**appease** [ə'piːz] *vt* (*pacify*) apaciguar; (*satisfy*) satisfacer

**appendices** [əˈpendɪsiːz] npl of appendix

**appendicitis** [əpendɪˈsaɪtɪs] n appendicitis f

**appendix** [əˈpendɪks] (pl appendices) n apéndice m

**appetite** [ˈæpɪtaɪt] n apetito; (fig) deseo, anhelo

**appetizer** [ˈæpɪtaɪzə*] n (drink) aperitivo; (food) tapas fpl (SP)

**appetizing** [ˈæpɪtaɪzɪŋ] adj apetitoso

**applaud** [əˈplɔːd] vt, vi aplaudir

**applause** [əˈplɔːz] n aplausos mpl

**apple** [ˈæpl] n manzana; ~ **tree** n manzano

**appliance** [əˈplaɪəns] n aparato

**applicable** [əˈplɪkəbl] adj (relevant): to be ~ (to) ser aplicable a

**applicant** [ˈæplɪkənt] n candidato/a; solicitante m/f

**application** [æplɪˈkeɪʃən] n aplicación f; (for a job etc) solicitud f, petición f; ~ **form** n solicitud f

**applied** [əˈplaɪd] adj aplicado

**apply** [əˈplaɪ] vt (paint etc) poner; (law etc: put into practice) poner en vigor ♦ vi: to ~ to (ask) dirigirse a; (be applicable) ser aplicable a; to ~ for (permit, grant, job) solicitar; to ~ o.s. to aplicarse a, dedicarse a

**appoint** [əˈpɔɪnt] vt (to post) nombrar; ~**ed** adj: at the ~**ed** time a la hora señalada; ~**ment** n (with client) cita; (act) nombramiento; (post) puesto; (at hairdresser etc): **to have an ~ment** tener hora; **to make an ~ment** (with sb) citarse (con uno)

**appraisal** [əˈpreɪzl] n valoración f

**appreciable** [əˈpriːʃəbl] adj sensible

**appreciate** [əˈpriːʃɪeɪt] vt apreciar, tener en mucho; (be grateful for) agradecer; (be aware of) comprender ♦ vi (COMM) aumentar(se) en valor; **appreciation** [-ˈeɪʃən] n apreciación f; (gratitude) reconocimiento, agradecimiento; (COMM) aumento en valor

**appreciative** [əˈpriːʃɪətɪv] adj apreciativo; (comment) agradecido

**apprehend** [æprɪˈhend] vt detener

**apprehension** [æprɪˈhenʃən] n (fear) aprensión f; **apprehensive** [-ˈhensɪv] adj aprensivo

**apprentice** [əˈprentɪs] n aprendiz/a m/f; ~**ship** n aprendizaje

**approach** [əˈprəʊtʃ] vi acercarse ♦ vt acercarse a; (ask, apply to) dirigirse a; (situation, problem) abordar ♦ n acercamiento; (access) acceso; (to problem, situation): ~ (to) actitud f (ante); ~**able** adj (person) abordable; (place) accesible

**appropriate** [adj əˈprəʊprɪət, vb əˈprəʊprɪeɪt] adj apropiado, conveniente ♦ vt (take) apropiarse de

**approval** [əˈpruːvl] n aprobación f, visto bueno; (permission) consentimiento; **on ~** (COMM) a prueba

**approve** [əˈpruːv] vt aprobar; ~ **of** vt fus (thing) aprobar; (person): **they don't ~ of her** (ella) no les parece bien

**approximate** [əˈprɒksɪmɪt] adj aproximado; ~**ly** adv aproximadamente, más o menos

**apricot** [ˈeɪprɪkɒt] n albaricoque m (SP), damasco (AM)

**April** [ˈeɪprəl] n abril m; ~ **Fools' Day** n el primero de abril; ≈ día m de los Inocentes (28 December)

**apron** [ˈeɪprən] n delantal m

**apt** [æpt] adj acertado, apropiado; (likely): ~ **to do** propenso a hacer

**aquarium** [əˈkweərɪəm] n acuario

**Aquarius** [əˈkweərɪəs] n Acuario

**aqueduct** [ˈækwɪdʌkt] n acueducto

**Arab** [ˈærəb] adj, n árabe m/f

**Arabian** [əˈreɪbɪən] adj árabe

**Arabic** [ˈærəbɪk] adj árabe; (numerals) arábigo ♦ n árabe m

**arable** [ˈærəbl] adj cultivable

**Aragon** [ˈærəgən] n Aragón m

**arbitrary** [ˈɑːbɪtrərɪ] adj arbitrario

**arbitration** [ɑːbɪˈtreɪʃən] n arbitraje m

**arcade** [ɑːˈkeɪd] n (round a square) soportales mpl; (shopping mall) galería comercial

**arch** [ɑːtʃ] n arco; (of foot) arco del

pie ♦ *vt* arquear

**archaeologist** [ɑːkɪˈɒlədʒɪst] (*US* **archeologist**) *n* arqueólogo/a

**archaeology** [ɑːkɪˈɒlədʒɪ] (*US* **archeology**) *n* arqueología

**archaic** [ɑːˈkeɪɪk] *adj* arcaico

**archbishop** [ɑːtʃˈbɪʃəp] *n* arzobispo

**arch-enemy** *n* enemigo jurado

**archeology** *etc* [ɑːkɪˈɒlədʒɪ] (*US*) = **archaeology** *etc*

**archery** [ˈɑːtʃərɪ] *n* tiro al arco

**archipelago** [ɑːkɪˈpeləgəʊ] *n* archipiélago

**architect** [ˈɑːkɪtɛkt] *n* arquitecto/a; ~**ural** [-ˈtɛktʃərəl] *adj* arquitectónico; ~**ure** *n* arquitectura

**archives** [ˈɑːkaɪvz] *npl* archivo

**Arctic** [ˈɑːktɪk] *adj* ártico ♦ *n*: **the** ~ el Artico

**ardent** [ˈɑːdənt] *adj* ardiente, apasionado

**arduous** [ˈɑːdjʊəs] *adj* (*task*) arduo; (*journey*) agotador(a)

**are** [ɑː*] *vb see* **be**

**area** [ˈɛərɪə] *n* área, región *f*; (*part of place*) zona; (*MATH etc*) área, superficie *f*; (*in room: e.g. dining* ~) parte *f*; (*of knowledge, experience*) campo

**arena** [əˈriːnə] *n* estadio; (*of circus*) pista

**aren't** [ɑːnt] = **are not**

**Argentina** [ɑːdʒənˈtiːnə] *n* Argentina; **Argentinian** [-ˈtɪnɪən] *adj, n* argentino/a *m/f*

**arguably** [ˈɑːgjʊəblɪ] *adv* posiblemente

**argue** [ˈɑːgjuː] *vi* (*quarrel*) discutir, pelearse; (*reason*) razonar, argumentar; **to** ~ **that** sostener que

**argument** [ˈɑːgjʊmənt] *n* discusión *f*, pelea; (*reasons*) argumento; ~**ative** [-ˈmɛntətɪv] *adj* discutidor(a)

**Aries** [ˈɛəriːz] *n* Aries *m*

**arise** [əˈraɪz] (*pt* **arose**, *pp* **arisen**) *vi* surgir, presentarse

**arisen** [əˈrɪzn] *pp of* **arise**

**aristocrat** [ˈærɪstəkræt] *n* aristócrata *m/f*

**arithmetic** [əˈrɪθmətɪk] *n* aritmética

**ark** [ɑːk] *n*: Noah's A~ el Arca *f* de Noé

**arm** [ɑːm] *n* brazo ♦ *vt* armar; ~**s** *npl* armas *fpl*; ~ **in** ~ cogidos del brazo

**armaments** [ˈɑːməmənts] *npl* armamento

**armchair** [ˈɑːmtʃɛə*] *n* sillón *m*, butaca

**armed** [ɑːmd] *adj* armado; ~ **robbery** *n* robo a mano armada

**armour** [ˈɑːmə*] (*US* **armor**) *n* armadura; (*MIL: tanks*) blindaje *m*; ~**ed car** *n* coche (*SP*) *m* or carro (*AM*) blindado

**armpit** [ˈɑːmpɪt] *n* sobaco, axila

**armrest** [ˈɑːmrɛst] *n* apoyabrazos *m inv*

**army** [ˈɑːmɪ] *n* ejército; (*fig*) multitud *f*

**aroma** [əˈrəʊmə] *n* aroma *m*, fragancia

**arose** [əˈrəʊz] *pt of* **arise**

**around** [əˈraʊnd] *adv* alrededor; (*in the area*): **there is no one else** ~ no hay nadie más por aquí ♦ *prep* alrededor de

**arouse** [əˈraʊz] *vt* despertar; (*anger*) provocar

**arrange** [əˈreɪndʒ] *vt* arreglar, ordenar; (*organize*) organizar; **to** ~ **to do sth** quedar en hacer algo; ~**ment** *n* arreglo; (*agreement*) acuerdo; ~**ments** *npl* (*preparations*) preparativos *mpl*

**array** [əˈreɪ] *n*: ~ **of** (*things*) serie *f* de; (*people*) conjunto de

**arrears** [əˈrɪəz] *npl* atrasos *mpl*; **to be in** ~ **with one's rent** estar retrasado en el pago del alquiler

**arrest** [əˈrɛst] *vt* detener; (*sb's attention*) llamar ♦ *n* detención *f*; **under** ~ detenido

**arrival** [əˈraɪvl] *n* llegada; **new** ~ recién llegado/a; (*baby*) recién nacido

**arrive** [əˈraɪv] *vi* llegar; (*baby*) nacer

**arrogant** [ˈærəgənt] *adj* arrogante

**arrow** [ˈærəʊ] *n* flecha

**arse** [ɑːs] (*BRIT: inf!*) *n* culo, trasero

**arsenal** ['ɑːsɪnl] n arsenal m

**arson** ['ɑːsn] n incendio premeditado

**art** [ɑːt] n arte m; (skill) destreza; A~s npl (SCOL) Letras fpl

**artery** ['ɑːtərɪ] n arteria

**artful** ['ɑːtful] adj astuto

**art gallery** n pinacoteca; (saleroom) galería de arte

**arthritis** [ɑː'θraɪtɪs] n artritis f

**artichoke** ['ɑːtɪtʃəuk] n alcachofa; Jerusalem ~ aguaturma

**article** ['ɑːtɪkl] n artículo; (BRIT: LAW: training) ~s npl contrato de aprendizaje; ~ of clothing prenda de vestir

**articulate** [adj ɑː'tɪkjulɪt, vb ɑː'tɪkjuleɪt] adj claro, bien expresado ♦ vt expresar; ~d lorry (BRIT) n trailer m

**artificial** [ɑːtɪ'fɪʃəl] adj artificial; (affected) afectado

**artillery** [ɑː'tɪlərɪ] n artillería

**artisan** ['ɑːtɪzæn] n artesano

**artist** ['ɑːtɪst] n artista m/f; (MUS) intérprete m/f; ~ic [ɑː'tɪstɪk] adj artístico; ~ry n arte m, habilidad f (artística)

**art school** n escuela de bellas artes

---

KEYWORD

**as** [æz] conj 1 (referring to time) cuando, mientras; a medida que; ~ the years went by al paso de los años; he came in ~ I was leaving entró cuando me marchaba; ~ from tomorrow desde or a partir de mañana

2 (in comparisons): ~ big ~ tan grande como; twice ~ big ~ el doble de grande que; ~ much money/ many books ~ tanto dinero/tantos libros como; ~ soon ~ en cuanto

3 (since, because) como, ya que; he left early ~ he had to be home by 10 se fue temprano como tenía que estar en casa a las 10

4 (referring to manner, way): do ~ you wish haz lo que quieras; ~ she said como dijo; he gave it to me ~ a present me lo dio de regalo

5 (in the capacity of): he works ~ a barman trabaja de barman; ~ chairman of the company, he ... como presidente de la compañía, ...

6 (concerning): ~ for or to that por or en lo que respecta a eso

7: ~ if or though como si; he looked ~ if he was ill parecía como si estuviera enfermo, tenía aspecto de enfermo

see also long; such; well

---

**a.s.a.p.** abbr (= as soon as possible) cuanto antes

**asbestos** [æz'bɛstəs] n asbesto, amianto

**ascend** [ə'sɛnd] vt subir; (throne) ascender or subir a; ~ancy n ascendiente m, dominio

**ascent** [ə'sɛnt] n subida; (slope) cuesta, pendiente f

**ascertain** [æsə'teɪn] vt averiguar

**ascribe** [ə'skraɪb] vt: to ~ sth to atribuir algo a

**ash** [æʃ] n ceniza; (tree) fresno

**ashamed** [ə'ʃeɪmd] adj avergonzado, apenado (AM); to be ~ of avergonzarse de

**ashen** ['æʃn] adj pálido

**ashore** [ə'ʃɔː*] adv en tierra; (swim etc) a tierra

**ashtray** ['æʃtreɪ] n cenicero

**Ash Wednesday** n miércoles m de Ceniza

**Asia** ['eɪʃə] n Asia; ~n adj, n asiático/a m/f

**aside** [ə'saɪd] adv a un lado ♦ n aparte m

**ask** [ɑːsk] vt (question) preguntar; (invite) invitar; to ~ sb sth/to do sth preguntar algo a uno/pedir a alguien que haga algo; to ~ sb about sth preguntar algo a alguien; to ~ (sb) a question hacer una pregunta (a alguien); to ~ sb out to dinner invitar a cenar a uno; ~ after vt fus preguntar por; ~ for vt fus pedir; (trouble) buscar

**askance** [ə'skɑːns] adv: to look ~ at sb/sth mirar con recelo a uno/

mirar algo con recelo

**askew** [ə'skju:] *adv* torcido, ladeado

**asking price** *n* precio inicial

**asleep** [ə'sli:p] *adj* dormido; **to fall ~** dormirse, quedarse dormido

**asparagus** [əs'pærəgəs] *n (plant)* espárrago; *(food)* espárragos *mpl*

**aspect** [ˈæspekt] *n* aspecto, apariencia; *(direction in which a building etc faces)* orientación *f*

**aspersions** [əs'pə:ʃənz] *npl:* **to cast ~ on** difamar a, calumniar a

**asphyxiation** [æsfɪksɪ'eɪʃən] *n* asfixia

**aspirations** [æspə'reɪʃənz] *npl* ambición *f*

**aspire** [əs'paɪə*] *vi:* **to ~ to** aspirar a, ambicionar

**aspirin** [ˈæsprɪn] *n* aspirina

**ass** [æs] *n* asno, burro; *(inf: idiot)* imbécil *mf*; *(US: inf!)* culo, trasero

**assailant** [ə'seɪlənt] *n* asaltador(a) *m/f*, agresor(a) *m/f*

**assassin** [ə'sæsɪn] *n* asesino/a; **~ate** *vt* asesinar; **~ation** [-'neɪʃən] *n* asesinato

**assault** [ə'sɔ:lt] *n* asalto; *(LAW)* agresión *f* ♦ *vt* asaltar, atacar; *(sexually)* violar

**assemble** [ə'sɛmbl] *vt* reunir, juntar; *(TECH)* montar ♦ *vi* reunirse, juntarse

**assembly** [ə'sɛmblɪ] *n* reunión *f*, asamblea; *(parliament)* parlamento *m*; *(construction)* montaje *m*; **~ line** *n* cadena de montaje

**assent** [ə'sɛnt] *n* asentimiento, aprobación *f*

**assert** [ə'sə:t] *vt* afirmar; *(authority)* hacer valer; **~ion** [-ʃən] *n* afirmación *f*

**assess** [ə'sɛs] *vt* valorar, calcular; *(tax, damages)* fijar; *(for tax)* gravar; **~ment** *n* valoración *f*; *(for tax)* gravamen *m*; **~or** *n* asesor(a) *m/f*

**asset** [ˈæsɛt] *n* ventaja; **~s** *npl* *(COMM)* activo; *(property, funds)* fondos *mpl*

**assign** [ə'saɪn] *vt:* **to ~ (to)** *(date)* fijar (para); *(task)* asignar (a); *(re-*

*sources)* destinar (a); **~ment** *n* tarea

**assist** [ə'sɪst] *vt* ayudar; **~ance** *n* ayuda, auxilio; **~ant** *n* ayudante *m/f*; *(BRIT: also:* **shop ~ant)** dependiente/a *m/f*

**associate** [*adj, n* ə'səuʃɪɪt, *vb* ə'səuʃɪeɪt] *adj* asociado ♦ *n (at work)* colega *m/f* ♦ *vt* asociar; *(ideas)* relacionar ♦ *vi:* **to ~ with sb** tratar con alguien

**association** [əsəusɪ'eɪʃən] *n* asociación *f*

**assorted** [ə'sɔ:tɪd] *adj* surtido, variado

**assortment** [ə'sɔ:tmənt] *n (of shapes, colours)* surtido; *(of books)* colección *f*; *(of people)* mezcla

**assume** [ə'sju:m] *vt* suponer; *(responsibilities)* asumir; *(attitude)* adoptar, tomar; **~d name** *n* nombre *m* falso

**assumption** [ə'sʌmpʃən] *n* suposición *f*, presunción *f*; *(of power etc)* toma

**assurance** [ə'ʃuərəns] *n* garantía, promesa; *(confidence)* confianza, aplomo; *(insurance)* seguro

**assure** [ə'ʃuə*] *vt* asegurar

**asthma** [ˈæsmə] *n* asma

**astonish** [ə'stɒnɪʃ] *vt* asombrar, pasmar; **~ment** *n* asombro, sorpresa

**astound** [ə'staund] *vt* asombrar, pasmar

**astray** [ə'streɪ] *adv:* **to go ~** extraviarse; **to lead ~** *(morally)* llevar por mal camino

**astride** [ə'straɪd] *prep* a caballo or horcajadas sobre

**astrology** [æs'trɒlədʒɪ] *n* astrología

**astronaut** [ˈæstrənɔ:t] *n* astronauta *m/f*

**astronomy** [əs'trɒnəmɪ] *n* astronomía

**astute** [əs'tju:t] *adj* astuto

**asylum** [ə'saɪləm] *n (refuge)* asilo; *(mental hospital)* manicomio

---
**KEYWORD**
---

**at** [æt] *prep* **1** *(referring to position)*

**ate** en; (*direction*) a; ~ **the top** en lo alto; ~ **home/school** en casa/la escuela; **to look** ~ **sth/sb** mirar algo/a uno
**2** (*referring to time*): ~ **4 o'clock** a las 4; ~ **night** por la noche; ~ **Christmas** en Navidad; ~ **times** a veces
**3** (*referring to rates, speed etc*): ~ **£1 a kilo** a una libra el kilo; **two ~ a time** de dos en dos; ~ **50 km/h** a 50 km/h
**4** (*referring to manner*): ~ **a stroke** de un golpe; ~ **peace** en paz
**5** (*referring to activity*): **to be** ~ **work** estar trabajando; (*in the office etc*) estar en el trabajo; **to play** ~ **cowboys** jugar a los vaqueros; **to be good** ~ **sth** ser bueno en algo
**6** (*referring to cause*): **shocked/surprised/annoyed** ~ **sth** asombrado/sorprendido/fastidiado por algo; **I went** ~ **his suggestion** fui a instancias suyas

**ate** [eɪt] *pt of* eat
**atheist** ['eɪθɪɪst] *n* ateo/a
**Athens** ['æθɪnz] *n* Atenas
**athlete** ['æθliːt] *n* atleta *m/f*
**athletic** [æθ'lɛtɪk] *adj* atlético; ~**s** *n* atletismo
**Atlantic** [ət'læntɪk] *adj* atlántico ♦ *n*: **the** ~ (**Ocean**) el (Océano) Atlántico
**atlas** ['ætləs] *n* atlas *m*
**atmosphere** ['ætmɔsfɪə*] *n* atmósfera; (*of place*) ambiente *m*
**atom** ['ætəm] *n* átomo; ~**ic** [ə'tɔmɪk] *adj* atómico; ~(**ic**) **bomb** *n* bomba atómica; ~**izer** ['ætəmaɪzə*] *n* atomizador *m*
**atone** [ə'təun] *vi*: **to** ~ **for** expiar
**atrocious** [ə'trəuʃəs] *adj* atroz
**attach** [ə'tætʃ] *vt* (*fasten*) atar; (*join*) unir, sujetar; (*document, letter*) adjuntar; (*importance etc*) dar, conceder; **to be** ~**ed to sb/sth** (*to like*) tener cariño a alguien/algo
**attaché** [ə'tæʃeɪ] *n* agregado/a; ~ **case** *n* maletín *m*

**attachment** [ə'tætʃmənt] *n* (*tool*) accesorio; (*love*): ~ (**to**) apego (a)
**attack** [ə'tæk] *vt* (*MIL*) atacar; (*subj: criminal*) agredir, asaltar; (*criticize*) criticar; (*task*) emprender ♦ *n* ataque *m*, asalto; (*on sb's life*) atentado; (*fig: criticism*) crítica; (*of illness*) ataque *m*; **heart** ~ infarto (de miocardio); ~**er** *n* agresor/a *m/f*, asaltante *m/f*
**attain** [ə'teɪn] *vt* (*also*: ~ **to**) alcanzar; (*achieve*) lograr, conseguir; ~**ments** *npl* logros *mpl*
**attempt** [ə'tɛmpt] *n* tentativa, intento; (*attack*) atentado ♦ *vt* intentar; ~**ed** *adj*: ~**ed burglary/murder/suicide** tentativa *or* intento de robo/asesinato/suicidio
**attend** [ə'tɛnd] *vt* asistir a; (*patient*) atender; ~ **to** *vt fus* ocuparse de; (*customer, patient*) atender a; ~**ance** *n* asistencia, presencia; (*people present*) concurrencia; ~**ant** *n* ayudante *m/f*; (*in garage etc*) encargado/a ♦ *adj* (*dangers*) concomitante
**attention** [ə'tɛnʃən] *n* atención *f*; (*care*) atenciones *fpl* ♦ *excl* (*MIL*) ¡firme(s)!; **for the** ~ **of** ... (*ADMIN*) atención ....
**attentive** [ə'tɛntɪv] *adj* atento
**attest** [ə'tɛst] *vi*: **to** ~ **to** demostrar; (*LAW: confirm*) dar fe de
**attic** ['ætɪk] *n* desván *m*
**attitude** ['ætɪtjuːd] *n* actitud *f*; (*disposition*) disposición *f*
**attorney** [ə'tɜːnɪ] *n* (*lawyer*) abogado/a; **A~ General** (*BRIT*) ≈ Presidente *m* del Consejo del Poder Judicial (*SP*); (*US*) ≈ ministro de justicia
**attract** [ə'trækt] *vt* atraer; (*sb's attention*) llamar; ~**ion** [ə'trækʃən] *n* encanto; (*gen pl: amusements*) diversiones *fpl*; (*PHYSICS*) atracción *f*; (*fig: towards sb, sth*) atractivo; ~**ive** *adj* guapo; (*interesting*) atrayente
**attribute** [*n* 'ætrɪbjuːt, *vb* ə'trɪbjuːt] *n* atributo ♦ *vt*: **to** ~ **sth to** atribuir

algo a

**attrition** [ə'trɪʃən] *n*: war of ~ guerra de agotamiento

**aubergine** ['əubəʒi:n] (*BRIT*) *n* berenjena; (*colour*) morado

**auburn** ['ɔ:bən] *adj* color castaño rojizo

**auction** ['ɔ:kʃən] *n* (*also: sale by ~*) subasta ♦ *vt* subastar; **~eer** [-'nɪə*] *n* subastador(a) *m/f*

**audacity** [ɔ:'dæsɪtɪ] *n* audacia, atrevimiento; (*pej*) descaro

**audible** ['ɔ:dɪbl] *adj* audible, que se puede oír

**audience** ['ɔ:dɪəns] *n* público; (*RADIO*) radioescuchas *mpl*; (*TV*) telespectadores *mpl*; (*interview*) audiencia

**audio-typist** ['ɔ:dɪəu'taɪpɪst] *n* mecanógrafo/a de dictáfono

**audio-visual** ['ɔ:dɪəu'vɪzjuəl] *adj* audiovisual; **~ aid** *n* ayuda audiovisual

**audit** ['ɔ:dɪt] *vt* revisar, intervenir

**audition** [ɔ:'dɪʃən] *n* audición *f*

**auditor** ['ɔ:dɪtə*] *n* interventor(a) *m/f*, censor(a) *m/f* de cuentas

**augment** [ɔ:g'ment] *vt* aumentar

**augur** ['ɔ:gə*] *vi*: it ~s well es un buen augurio

**August** ['ɔ:gəst] *n* agosto

**aunt** [ɑ:nt] *n* tía; **~ie**, **~y** *n diminutive of* **aunt**

**au pair** ['əu'pɛə*] *n* (*also: ~ girl*) au pair *f*

**auspices** ['ɔ:spɪsɪz] *npl*: under the ~ of bajo los auspicios de

**auspicious** [ɔ:s'pɪʃəs] *adj* propicio, de buen augurio

**austerity** [ɔ'stɛrɪtɪ] *n* austeridad *f*

**Australia** [ɔs'treɪlɪə] *n* Australia; **~n** *adj*, *n* australiano/a *m/f*

**Austria** ['ɔstrɪə] *n* Austria; **~n** *adj*, *n* austríaco/a *m/f*

**authentic** [ɔ:'θentɪk] *adj* auténtico

**author** ['ɔ:θə*] *n* autor(a) *m/f*

**authoritarian** [ɔ:θɔrɪ'tɛərɪən] *adj* autoritario

**authoritative** [ɔ:'θɔrɪtətɪv] *adj* autorizado; (*manner*) autoritario

**authority** [ɔ:'θɔrɪtɪ] *n* autoridad *f*;

(*official permission*) autorización *f*; **the authorities** *npl* las autoridades

**authorize** ['ɔ:θəraɪz] *vt* autorizar

**auto** ['ɔ:təu] (*US*) *n* coche *m* (*SP*), carro (*AM*), automóvil *m*

**autobiography** [ɔ:təbaɪ'ɔgrəfɪ] *n* autobiografía

**autograph** ['ɔ:təgrɑ:f] *n* autógrafo ♦ *vt* (*photo etc*) dedicar; (*programme*) firmar

**automated** ['ɔ:təmeɪtɪd] *adj* automatizado

**automatic** [ɔ:tə'mætɪk] *adj* automático ♦ *n* (*gun*) pistola automática; (*car*) coche *m* automático; **~ally** *adv* automáticamente

**automation** [ɔ:tə'meɪʃən] *n* reconversión *f*

**automaton** [ɔ:'tɔmətən] (*pl* **automata**) *n* autómata *m*

**automobile** ['ɔ:təməbi:l] (*US*) *n* coche *m* (*SP*), carro (*AM*), automóvil *m*

**autonomy** [ɔ:'tɔnəmɪ] *n* autonomía

**autopsy** ['ɔ:tɔpsɪ] *n* autopsia

**autumn** ['ɔ:təm] *n* otoño

**auxiliary** [ɔ:g'zɪlɪərɪ] *adj*, *n* auxiliar *m/f*

**avail** [ə'veɪl] *vt*: to ~ o.s. of aprovechar(se) de ♦ *n*: to no ~ en vano, sin resultado

**available** [ə'veɪləbl] *adj* disponible; (*unoccupied*) libre; (*person: unattached*) soltero y sin compromiso

**avalanche** ['ævəlɑ:nʃ] *n* alud *m*, avalancha

**avant-garde** ['ævɑŋ'gɑ:d] *adj* de vanguardia

**Ave.** *abbr* = **avenue**

**avenge** [ə'vendʒ] *vt* vengar

**avenue** ['ævənju:] *n* avenida; (*fig*) camino

**average** ['ævərɪdʒ] *n* promedio, término medio ♦ *adj* medio, de término medio; (*ordinary*) regular, corriente ♦ *vt* sacar un promedio de; **on** ~ por regla general; **~ out** *vi*: to ~ out at salir en un promedio de

**averse** [ə'vɜ:s] *adj*: to be ~ to sth/doing sentir aversión o antipatía por algo/por hacer

**avert** [ə'vɜːt] vt prevenir; (blow) desviar; (one's eyes) apartar

**aviary** ['eɪvɪərɪ] n pajarera, avería

**avid** ['ævɪd] adj ávido, ansioso

**avocado** [ævə'kɑːdəʊ] n (also: BRIT: ~ pear) aguacate m (SP), palta (AM)

**avoid** [ə'vɔɪd] vt evitar, eludir

**await** [ə'weɪt] vt esperar, aguardar

**awake** [ə'weɪk] (pt awoke, pp awoken or awaked) adj despierto ♦ vt despertar ♦ vi despertarse; to be ~ estar despierto; **~ning** n el despertar

**award** [ə'wɔːd] n premio; (LAW: damages) indemnización f ♦ vt otorgar, conceder; (LAW: damages) adjudicar

**aware** [ə'weə*] adj: ~ (of) consciente (de); to become ~ of/that (realize) darse cuenta de/de que; (learn) enterarse de/de que; **~ness** n conciencia; (knowledge) conocimiento

**awash** [ə'wɒʃ] adj: ~ with (also fig) inundado de

**away** [ə'weɪ] adv fuera; (movement): she went ~ se marchó; (far ~) lejos; two kilometres ~ a dos kilómetros de distancia; two hours ~ by car a dos horas en coche; the holiday was two weeks ~ faltaban dos semanas para las vacaciones; he's ~ for a week estará ausente una semana; to take ~ (from) quitar a; (subtract) substraer de; to work/pedal ~ seguir trabajando/pedaleando; to fade ~ (colour) desvanecerse; (sound) apagarse; **~ game** n (SPORT) partido de fuera

**awe** [ɔː] n admiración f respetuosa; **~-inspiring** adj imponente; **~some** adj imponente

**awful** ['ɔːfəl] adj horroroso; (quantity): an ~ lot (of) cantidad (of); **~ly** adv (very) terriblemente

**awhile** [ə'waɪl] adv (durante) un rato, algún tiempo

**awkward** ['ɔːkwəd] adj desmañado, torpe; (shape) incómodo; (embarrassing) delicado, difícil

**awning** ['ɔːnɪŋ] n (of tent, caravan, shop) toldo

**awoke** [ə'wəʊk] pt of awake

**awoken** [ə'wəʊkən] pp of awake

**awry** [ə'raɪ] adv: to be ~ estar descolocado or mal puesto; to go ~ salir mal, fracasar

**axe** [æks] (US ax) n hacha f (project) cortar; (jobs) reducir

**axes** ['æksiːz] npl of axis

**axis** ['æksɪs] (pl axes) n eje m

**axle** ['æksl] n eje m, árbol m

**ay(e)** [aɪ] excl sí

# B

**B** [biː] n (MUS) si m

**B.A.** abbr = Bachelor of Arts

**babble** ['bæbl] vi barbotear; (brook) murmurar

**baby** ['beɪbɪ] n bebé m/f; (US: inf: darling) mi amor; ~ carriage n (US) cochecito; **~-sit** vi hacer de canguro; **~-sitter** n canguro/a

**bachelor** ['bætʃələ*] n soltero; B~ of Arts/Science licenciado/a en Filosofía y Letras/Ciencias

**back** [bæk] n (of person) espalda; (of animal) lomo; (of hand) dorso; (as opposed to front) parte f de atrás; (of chair) respaldo; (of page) reverso; (of book) final m; (of crowd): the ones at the ~ los del fondo; (FOOTBALL) defensa m ♦ vt (candidate: also: ~ up) respaldar, apoyar; (horse: at races) apostar a; (car) dar marcha atrás a or con ♦ vi (car etc) ir or dar marcha atrás ♦ adv atrás ♦ adj (payment, rent) atrasado; (seats, wheels) de atrás ♦ adv (not forward) (hacia) atrás; (returned): he's ~ está de vuelta, ha vuelto; he ran ~ volvió corriendo; (restitution): throw the ball ~ devuelve la pelota; can I have it ~? ¿me lo devuelve?; (again): he called ~ llamó de nuevo; ~ down vi echarse atrás; ~ out vi (of promise) volverse atrás; ~ up vt (person) apoyar, respaldar; (: *theory*) defender; (*COMPUT*) hacer una copia preventiva *or* de reserva; ~**bencher** (*BRIT*) *n* miembro del parlamento sin cargo relevante; ~**cloth** *n* telón *m* de fondo; ~**date** *vt* (*pay rise*) dar efecto retroactivo a; (*letter*) poner fecha atrasada a; ~**drop** *n* ~**cloth**; ~**fire** *vi* (*AUT*) petardear; (*plans*) fallar, salir mal; ~**ground** *n* fondo; (*of events*) antecedentes *mpl*; (*basic knowledge*) bases *fpl*; (*experience*) conocimientos *mpl*, educación *f*; ~**ground** *n* origen *m*, antecedentes *mpl*; ~**hand** *n* (*TENNIS*: *also*: ~*hand stroke*) revés *m*; ~**hander** (*BRIT*) *n* (*bribe*) soborno; ~**ing** *n* (*fig*) apoyo, respaldo; ~**lash** *n* reacción *f*; ~**log** *n*: ~**log of work** trabajo atrasado; ~**number** *n* (*of magazine etc*) número atrasado; ~**pack** *n* mochila; ~ **pay** *n* pago atrasado; ~**side** (*inf*) *n* trasero, culo; ~**stage** *adv* entre bastidores; ~**stroke** *n* espalda; ~**up** *adj* suplementario; (*COMPUT*) de reserva ♦ *n* (*support*) apoyo; (*also*: ~*up file*) copia preventiva *or* de reserva; ~**ward** *adj* (*person*, *country*) atrasado; ~**wards** *adv* hacia atrás; (*read a list*) al revés; (*fall*) de espaldas; ~**water** *n* (*fig*) lugar *m* atrasado *or* apartado; ~**yard** *n* traspatio

**bacon** ['beɪkən] *n* tocino, beicon *m*

**bad** [bæd] *adj* malo; (*mistake*, *accident*) grave; (*food*) podrido, pasado; **his ~ leg** su pierna lisiada; **to go ~** (*food*) caducar

**bade** [bæd, beɪd] *pt of* **bid**

**badge** [bædʒ] *n* insignia; (*policeman's*) chapa, placa

**badger** ['bædʒə*] *n* tejón *m*

**badly** ['bædlɪ] *adv* mal; **to reflect ~ on sb** influir negativamente en la reputación de uno; ~ **wounded** gravemente herido; **he needs it ~** le hace gran falta; **to be ~ off (for money)** andar mal de dinero

**badminton** ['bædmɪntən] *n* bádmin-

ton *m*

**bad-tempered** *adj* de mal genio *or* carácter; (*temporarily*) de mal humor

**baffle** ['bæfl] *vt* desconcertar, confundir

**bag** [bæg] *n* bolsa; (*handbag*) bolso; (*satchel*) mochila; (*case*) maleta; ~**s of** (*inf*) un montón de; ~**gage** *n* equipaje *m*; ~**gy** *adj* amplio; ~**pipes** *npl* gaita

**Bahamas** [bə'hɑːməz] *npl*: **the ~ las** Islas Bahamas

**bail** [beɪl] *n* fianza ♦ *vt* (*prisoner*: *gen*: *grant* ~ *to*) poner en libertad bajo fianza; (*boat*: *also*: ~ *out*) achicar; **on ~** (*prisoner*) bajo fianza; **to ~ sb out** obtener la libertad de uno bajo fianza; *see also* **bale**

**bailiff** ['beɪlɪf] *n* alguacil *m*

**bait** [beɪt] *n* cebo ♦ *vt* poner cebo en; (*tease*) tomar el pelo a

**bake** [beɪk] *vt* cocer (al horno) ♦ *vi* cocerse; ~**d beans** *npl* judías *fpl* en salsa de tomate; ~**r** *n* panadero; ~**ry** *n* panadería; (*for cakes*) pastelería; **baking** *n* (*act*) amasar *m*; (*batch*) hornada; **baking powder** *n* levadura (en polvo)

**balance** ['bæləns] *n* equilibrio; (*COMM*: *sum*) balance *m*; (*remainder*) resto; (*scales*) balanza ♦ *vt* equilibrar; (*budget*) nivelar; (*account*) saldar; (*make equal*) equilibrar; ~ **of trade/payments** balanza de comercio/pagos; ~**d** *adj* (*personality*, *diet*) equilibrado; (*report*) objetivo; ~ **sheet** *n* balance *m*

**balcony** ['bælkənɪ] *n* (*open*) balcón *m*; (*closed*) galería; (*in theatre*) anfiteatro

**bald** [bɔːld] *adj* calvo; (*tyre*) liso

**bale** [beɪl] *n* (*AGR*) paca, fardo; (*of papers etc*) fajo; ~ **out** *vi* lanzarse en paracaídas

**Balearics** [bælɪ'ærɪks] *npl*: **the ~ las** Baleares

**ball** [bɔːl] *n* pelota; (*football*) balón *m*; (*of wool*, *string*) ovillo; (*dance*) baile *m*; **to play ~** (*fig*) cooperar

**ballast** ['bæləst] n lastre m
**ball bearings** npl cojinetes mpl de
bolas
**ballerina** [bælə'ri:nə] n bailarina
**ballet** ['bæleɪ] n ballet m; ~ **dancer**
n bailarín/ina m/f
**ballistics** [bə'lıstıks] n balística
**balloon** [bə'lu:n] n globo
**ballot** ['bælət] n votación f; ~ **paper**
n papeleta (para votar)
**ball-point (pen)** ['bɔːlpɔɪnt-] n bolígrafo
**ballroom** ['bɔːlrum] n salón m de
baile
**balm** [baːm] n bálsamo
**Baltic** ['bɔːltɪk] n: the ~ (Sea) el
(Mar) Báltico
**balustrade** ['bæləstreɪd] n barandilla
**ban** [bæn] n prohibición f, proscrip-
ción f ♦ vt prohibir, proscribir
**banal** [bə'nɑːl] adj banal, vulgar
**banana** [bə'nɑːnə] n plátano (SP),
banana (AM)
**band** [bænd] n grupo; (strip) faja,
tira; (stripe) lista; (MUS: jazz) orquesta; (: rock) grupo; (: MIL) banda; ~ **together** vi juntarse, asociar-
se
**bandage** ['bændɪdʒ] n venda, vendaje m ♦ vt vendar
**Bandaid** ['bændeɪd] ® (US) n tirita
**bandit** ['bændɪt] n bandido
**bandwagon** ['bændwægən] n: to
jump on the ~ subirse al carro
**bandy** ['bændɪ] vt (jokes, insults)
cambiar
**bandy-legged** ['bændɪ'lɛgd] adj estevado
**bang** [bæŋ] n (of gun, exhaust): (trees)
llido, detonación f; (of door) portazo;
(blow) golpe m ♦ vt (door) cerrar de
golpe; (one's head) golpear ♦ vi (estallar; (door) cerrar de golpe
**Bangladesh** [bæŋglə'dɛʃ] n Bangladesh m
**bangs** [bæŋz] (US) npl flequillo
**banish** ['bænɪʃ] vt desterrar
**banister(s)** ['bænɪstə(z)] n(pl) barandilla, pasamanos m inv
**bank** [bæŋk] n (COMM) banco; (of

river, lake) ribera, orilla; (of earth)
terraplén m ♦ vi (AVIAT) ladearse;
~ **on** vt fus contar con; ~ **account** n
cuenta de banco; ~ **card** n tarjeta
bancaria; ~**er** n banquero; ~**er's
card** (BRIT) n ~ = card; B~ **holiday** (BRIT) n día m festivo; ~**ing** n
banca; ~**note** n billete m de banco;
~ **rate** n tipo de interés bancario
**bankrupt** ['bæŋkrʌpt] adj quebrado,
insolvente; to go ~ hacer bancarrota; to be ~ estar en quiebra; ~**cy** n
quiebra
**bank statement** n balance m or
detalle m de cuenta
**banner** ['bænə*] n pancarta
**banns** [bænz] npl amonestaciones fpl
**banquet** ['bæŋkwɪt] n banquete m
**baptism** ['bæptɪzəm] n bautismo;
(act) bautizo
**baptize** [bæp'taɪz] vt bautizar
**bar** [bɑː*] n (pub) bar m; (counter)
mostrador m; (rod) barra; (of window, cage) reja; (of soap) pastilla;
(of chocolate) tableta; (fig: hindrance) obstáculo; (prohibition) pros-
cripción f; (MUS) barra ♦ vt (road)
obstruir; (person) excluir; (activity)
prohibir; **behind** ~**s** entre rejas; the
B~ (LAW) la abogacía; ~ **none** sin
excepción
**barbaric** [bɑː'bærɪk] adj bárbaro
**barbecue** ['bɑːbɪkjuː] n barbacoa
**barbed wire** ['bɑːbd-] n alambre m
de púas
**barber** ['bɑːbə*] n peluquero, barbero
**bar code** n código de barras
**bare** [bɛə*] adj desnudo; (trees) sin
hojas; (necessities etc) básico ♦ vt
desnudar; (teeth) enseñar; ~**back**
adv a pelo, sin silla; ~**faced** adj descarado; ~**foot** adj, adv descalzo; ~
**ly** adv apenas
**bargain** ['bɑːgɪn] n pacto, negocio;
(good buy) ganga ♦ vi negociar;
(haggle) regatear; **into the** ~
además, por añadidura; ~ **for** vt fus:
he got more than he ~ed for le resultó peor de lo que esperaba

**barge** [bɑːdʒ] n barcaza; ~ **in** vi irrumpir; (interrupt: conversation) interrumpir

**bark** [bɑːk] n (of tree) corteza; (of dog) ladrido ♦ vi ladrar; ~ **sugar** n azúcar m cande

**barley** [ˈbɑːlɪ] n cebada; ~**ess** n baronesa

**barmaid** [ˈbɑːmeɪd] n camarera

**barman** [ˈbɑːmən] n camarero, barman m

**barn** [bɑːn] n granero

**barometer** [bəˈrɒmɪtə*] n barómetro

**baron** [ˈbærən] n barón m; (press etc) magnate m; ~**ess** n baronesa

**barracks** [ˈbærəks] npl cuartel m

**barrage** [ˈbærɑːʒ] n (MIL) descarga, bombardeo; (dam) presa; (of criticism) lluvia, aluvión n

**barrel** [ˈbærəl] n barril m; (of gun) cañón m

**barren** [ˈbærən] adj estéril

**barricade** [bærɪˈkeɪd] n barricada ♦ vt cerrar con barricadas; **to** ~ **o.s. (in)** hacerse fuerte (en)

**barrier** [ˈbærɪə*] n barrera

**barring** [ˈbɑːrɪŋ] prep excepto, salvo

**barrister** [ˈbærɪstə*] (BRIT) n abogado/a

**barrow** [ˈbærəu] n (cart) carretilla (de mano)

**bartender** [ˈbɑːtɛndə*] (US) n camarero, barman m

**barter** [ˈbɑːtə*] vi: **to** ~ **sth for sth** trocar algo por algo

**base** [beɪs] n base f ♦ vt: **to** ~ **sth on** basar or fundar algo en ♦ adj bajo, infame

**baseball** [ˈbeɪsbɔːl] n béisbol m

**basement** [ˈbeɪsmənt] n sótano

**bases**[1] [ˈbeɪsiːz] npl of **basis**

**bases**[2] [ˈbeɪsiːz] npl of **base**

**bash** [bæʃ] (inf) vt golpear

**bashful** [ˈbæʃful] adj tímido, vergonzoso

**basic** [ˈbeɪsɪk] adj básico; ~**ally** adv fundamentalmente, en el fondo; (simply) sencillamente; **the** ~**s** npl los fundamentos

**basil** [ˈbæzl] n albahaca

**basin** [ˈbeɪsn] n cuenco, tazón m; (GEO) cuenca; (also: wash~) lavabo

**basis** [ˈbeɪsɪs] (pl **bases**) n base f; **on a part-time/trial** ~ a tiempo parcial/a prueba

**bask** [bɑːsk] vi: **to** ~ **in the sun** tomar el sol

**basket** [ˈbɑːskɪt] n cesta, cesto; canasta; ~**ball** n baloncesto

**Basque** [bæsk] adj, n vasco/a m/f; ~ **Country** n Euskadi m, País m Vasco

**bass** [beɪs] n (MUS: instrument) bajo; (double ~) contrabajo; (singer) bajo

**bassoon** [bəˈsuːn] n fagot m

**bastard** [ˈbɑːstəd] n bastardo; (inf!) hijo de puta (!)

**bastion** [ˈbæstɪən] n baluarte m

**bat** [bæt] n (ZOOL) murciélago; (for ball games) palo; (BRIT: for table tennis) pala ♦ vt: **he didn't** ~ **an eyelid** ni pestañeó

**batch** [bætʃ] n (of bread) hornada; (of letters etc) lote m

**bated** [ˈbeɪtɪd] adj: **with** ~ **breath** sin respirar

**bath** [bɑːθ, pl bɑːðz] n (action) baño; (~tub) baño (SP), bañera (SP), tina (AM) ♦ vt bañar; **to have a** ~ bañarse, tomar un baño; see also **baths**

**bathe** [beɪð] vi bañarse ♦ vt (wound) lavar; ~**r** n bañista m/f

**bathing** [ˈbeɪðɪŋ] n el bañarse; ~ **cap** n gorro de baño; ~ **costume** (US = **suit**) n traje m de baño

**bath**: ~**robe** n (man's) batín m; (woman's) bata; ~**room** n (cuarto de) baño; ~**s** [bɑːðz] npl (also: swimming ~) piscina; ~ **towel** n toalla de baño

**baton** [ˈbætən] n (MUS) batuta; (ATHLETICS) testigo; (weapon) porra

**batter** [ˈbætə*] vt maltratar; (subj: rain etc) azotar ♦ n masa (para rebozar); ~**ed** adj (hat, pan) estropeado

**battery** [ˈbætərɪ] n (AUT) batería; (of torch) pila

**battle** [ˈbætl] n batalla; (fig) lucha ♦ vi luchar; ~**ship** n acorazado

**bawdy** ['bɔːdɪ] *adj* (*joke*) verde

**bawl** [bɔːl] *vi* chillar, gritar; (*child*) berrear

**bay** [beɪ] *n* (GEO) bahía; B~ of Biscay ≈ mar Cantábrico; to hold sb at ~ mantener a alguien a raya; ~ leaf *n* hoja de laurel

**bay window** *n* ventana salediza

**bazaar** [bə'zɑː*] *n* bazar *m*; (*fete*) venta con fines benéficos

**B. & B.** *n abbr* (= bed and breakfast) cama y desayuno

**BBC** *n abbr* (= British Broadcasting Corporation) cadena de radio y televisión estatal británica

**B.C.** *adv abbr* (= before Christ) a. de C

---

KEYWORD

**be** [biː] (*pt* was, were, *pp* been) *aux vb* **1** (*with present participle: forming continuous tenses*): what are you doing? ¿qué estás haciendo?, ¿qué haces?; they're coming tomorrow vienen mañana; I've been waiting for you for hours llevo horas esperándote

**2** (*with pp: forming passives*): ser (*but often replaced by active or reflective constructions*); to ~ murdered ser asesinado; the box had been opened habían abierto la caja; the thief was nowhere to ~ seen no se veía al ladrón por ninguna parte

**3** (*in tag questions*): it was fun, wasn't it? fue divertido, ¿no? or ¿verdad?; he's good-looking, isn't he? es guapo, ¿no te parece?; she's back again, is she? entonces, ¿ha vuelto?

**4** (+ *to* + *infin*): the house is to ~ sold (*necessity*) hay que vender la casa; (*future*) van a vender la casa; he's not to open it no tiene que abrirlo

♦ *vb* + *complement* **1** (*with n or num complement, but see also* **3, 4, 5** *and impers vb*): he's a doctor es médico; 2 and 2 are 4 2 y 2 son 4

**2** (*with adj complement: expressing permanent or inherent quality*) ser; (:

*expressing state seen as temporary or reversible*) estar; I'm English soy inglés/esa; she's tall/pretty es alta/bonita; he's young es joven; I'm careful/good/quiet ten cuidado/pórtate bien/cállate; I'm tired estoy cansado/a; it's dirty está sucio/a

**3** (*of health*) estar; how are you? ¿cómo estás?; he's very ill está muy enfermo; I'm better now ya estoy mejor

**4** (*of age*) tener; how old are you? ¿cuántos años tienes?; I'm sixteen (years old) tengo dieciséis años

**5** (*cost*) costar; ser; how much was the meal? ¿cuánto fue or costó la comida?; that'll ~ £5.75, please son £5.75, por favor; this shirt is £17 esta camisa cuesta £17

♦ *vi* **1** (*exist, occur etc*) existir, haber; the best singer that ever was el mejor cantante que existió jamás; is there a God? ¿hay un Dios?, ¿existe Dios?; that as it may sea como sea; so ~ it así sea

**2** (*referring to place*) estar; I won't ~ here tomorrow no estaré aquí mañana

**3** (*referring to movement*): where have you been? ¿dónde has estado?

♦ *impers vb* **1** (*referring to time*): it's 5 o'clock son las 5; it's the 28th of April estamos a 28 de abril

**2** (*referring to distance*): it's 10 km to the village el pueblo está a 10 km

**3** (*referring to the weather*): it's too hot/cold hace demasiado calor/frío; it's windy today hace viento hoy

**4** (*emphatic*): it's me soy yo; it was Maria who paid the bill fue María la que pagó la cuenta

---

**beach** [biːtʃ] *n* playa ♦ *vt* varar

**beacon** ['biːkən] *n* (*lighthouse*) faro; (*marker*) guía

**bead** [biːd] *n* cuenta; (*of sweat etc*) gota

**beak** [biːk] *n* pico

**beaker** ['biːkə*] *n* vaso de plástico

**beam** [biːm] *n* (ARCH) viga, travesaño; (*of light*) rayo, haz *m* de luz ♦ *vi* brillar; (*smile*) sonreír

**bean** [biːn] *n* judía; (*runner/broad* ~) habichuela/haba; **coffee** ~ grano de café; **~sprouts** *npl* brotes *mpl* de soja

**bear** [bɛə*] (*pt* **bore**, *pp* **borne**) *n* oso ♦ *vt* (*weight etc*) llevar; (*cost*) pagar; (*responsibility*) tener; (*endure*) soportar, aguantar; (*children*) parir, tener; (*fruit*) dar ♦ *vi*: **to ~ right/left** torcer a la derecha/izquierda ♦ *vt* (*suspicions*) corroborar, confirmar; (*person*) dar la razón a; **~ out** *vt* (*suspicions*) corroborar, confirmar; (*person*) dar la razón a; **~ up** *vi* (*remain cheerful*) mantenerse animado

**beard** [biəd] *n* barba; **~ed** *adj* con barba, barbudo

**bearer** ['bɛərə*] *n* portador(a) *m/f*

**bearing** ['bɛəriŋ] *n* porte *m*, comportamiento; (*connection*) relación *f*; **~s** *npl* (*also*: **ball** ~**s**) cojinetes *mpl* a bolas; **to take a ~** tomar marcaciones; **to find one's ~s** orientarse

**beast** [biːst] *n* bestia; (*inf*) bruto, salvaje *m*; **~ly** (*inf*) *adj* horrible

**beat** [biːt] (*pt* **beat**, *pp* **beaten**) *n* (*of heart*) latido; (*MUS*) ritmo, compás *m*; (*of policeman*) ronda ♦ *vt* pegar, golpear; (*eggs*) batir; (*defeat: opponent*) vencer, derrotar; (: *record*) sobrepasar ♦ *vi* (*heart*) latir; (*drum*) redoblar; (*rain, wind*) azotar; **off the ~en track** aislado; **to ~ it** largarse; **~ off** *vt* rechazar; **~ up** *vt* (*attack*) dar una paliza a; **~ing** *n* paliza

**beautiful** ['bjuːtiful] *adj* precioso, hermoso, bello; **~ly** *adv* maravillosamente

**beauty** ['bjuːti] *n* belleza; ~ **salon** *n* salón *m* de belleza; ~ **spot** *n* (*TOURISM*) lugar *m* pintoresco

**beaver** ['biːvə*] *n* castor *m*

**became** [bɪ'keɪm] *pt of* **become**

**because** [bɪ'kɔz] *conj* porque; ~ **of** debido a, a causa de

**beck** [bɛk] *n*: **to be at the ~ and call of** estar a disposición de

**beckon** ['bɛkən] *vt* (*also*: ~ **to**) llamar con señas

**become** [bɪ'kʌm] (*irreg: like* **come**) *vt* (*suit*) favorecer, sentar bien a ♦ *vi* (+*n*) hacerse, llegar a ser; (+*adj*) ponerse, volverse; **to ~ fat** engordar

**becoming** [bɪ'kʌmiŋ] *adj* (*behaviour*) decoroso; (*clothes*) favorecedor(a)

**bed** [bɛd] *n* cama; (*of flowers*) macizo; (*of coal, clay*) capa; (*of river*) lecho; (*of sea*) fondo; **to go to ~** acostarse; ~ **and breakfast** *n* (*place*) pensión *f*; (*terms*) cama y desayuno; **~clothes** *npl* ropa de cama; **~ding** *n* ropa de cama

**bedlam** ['bɛdləm] *n* desbarajuste *m*

**bedraggled** [bɪ'dræɡld] *adj* (*untidy: person*) desastrado; (*clothes, hair*) desordenado

**bed**: **~ridden** *adj* postrado en cama; **~room** *n* dormitorio; **~side** *n*: **at the ~side of** a la cabecera de; **~sit(ter)** (*BRIT*) *n* estudio (*SP*), suite *m* (*AM*); **~spread** *n* cubrecama *m*, colcha; **~time** *n* hora de acostarse

**bee** [biː] *n* abeja

**beech** [biːtʃ] *n* haya

**beef** [biːf] *n* carne *f* de vaca; **roast** ~ rosbif *m*; **~burger** *n* hamburguesa; **B~eater** *n* alabardero de la Torre de Londres

**beehive** ['biːhaɪv] *n* colmena

**beeline** ['biːlaɪn] *n*: **to make a ~ for** ir derecho a

**been** [biːn] *pp of* **be**

**beer** [bɪə*] *n* cerveza

**beet** [biːt] (*US*) *n* (*also*: **red** ~) remolacha

**beetle** ['biːtl] *n* escarabajo

**beetroot** ['biːtruːt] (*BRIT*) *n* remolacha

**before** [bɪ'fɔː*] *prep* (*of time*) antes de; (*of space*) delante de ♦ *conj* antes (de) que ♦ *adv* antes, anteriormente; delante, adelante; ~ **going** antes de marcharse; ~ **she goes** antes de que se vaya; **the week** ~ la semana anterior; **I've never seen it** ~ no lo he visto nunca; **~hand** *adv* de antemano, con anticipación

**beg** [beg] *vi* pedir limosna ♦ *vt* pedir, rogar; (*entreat*) suplicar; **to ~ sb to do sth** rogar a uno que haga algo; *see also* **pardon**

**began** [bɪ'gæn] *pt of* **begin**

**beggar** ['begə*] *n* mendigo/a

**begin** [bɪ'gɪn] (*pt* **began**, *pp* **begun**) *vt, vi* empezar, comenzar; **to ~ doing** *or* **to do sth** empezar a hacer algo; **~ner** *n* principiante *m/f*; **~ning** *n* principio, comienzo

**begun** [bɪ'gʌn] *pp of* **begin**

**behalf** [bɪ'hɑːf] *n*: **on ~ of** en nombre de, por; (*for benefit of*) en beneficio de; **on my/his ~** por mí/él

**behave** [bɪ'heɪv] *vi* (*person*) portarse, comportarse; (*well: also*: **~ o.s.**) portarse bien; **behaviour** (*US* **behavior**) *n* comportamiento, conducta

**behead** [bɪ'hed] *vt* decapitar

**beheld** [bɪ'held] *pt, pp of* **behold**

**behind** [bɪ'haɪnd] *prep* detrás de; (*supporting*): **to be ~ sb** apoyar a alguien; (*lower in rank etc*) estar por detrás de ♦ *adv* detrás, por detrás, atrás ♦ *n* trasero; **to be ~** (*schedule*) ir retrasado; **~ the scenes** (*fig*) entre bastidores

**behold** [bɪ'hould] (*irreg: like* **hold**) *vt* contemplar

**beige** [beɪʒ] *adj* color beige

**being** ['biːɪŋ] *n* ser *m*; (*existence*): **in ~** existente; **to come into ~** aparecer

**belated** [bɪ'leɪtɪd] *adj* atrasado, tardío

**belch** [beltʃ] *vi* eructar ♦ *vt* (*gen*: **~ out: smoke etc**) arrojar

**belfry** ['belfrɪ] *n* campanario

**Belgian** ['beldʒən] *adj, n* belga *m/f*

**Belgium** ['beldʒəm] *n* Bélgica

**belie** [bɪ'laɪ] *vt* desmentir, contradecir

**belief** [bɪ'liːf] *n* opinión *f*; (*faith*) fe *f*

**believe** [bɪ'liːv] *vt, vi* creer; **to ~ in** creer en; **~r** *n* partidario/a; (*REL*) creyente *m/f*, fiel *m/f*

**belittle** [bɪ'lɪtl] *vt* quitar importancia a

**bell** [bel] *n* campana; (*small*) campanilla; (*on door*) timbre *m*

**belligerent** [bɪ'lɪdʒərənt] *adj* agresivo

**bellow** ['beləu] *vi* bramar; (*person*) rugir; **~s** *npl* fuelle *m*

**belly** ['belɪ] *n* barriga, panza

**belong** [bɪ'lɒŋ] *vi*: **to ~** to pertenecer a; (*club etc*) ser socio de; **this book ~s here** este libro va aquí; **~ings** *npl* pertenencias *fpl*

**beloved** [bɪ'lʌvɪd] *adj* querido/a

**below** [bɪ'ləu] *prep* bajo, debajo de; (*less than*) inferior a ♦ *adv* abajo, (por) debajo; **see ~** véase más abajo

**belt** [belt] *n* cinturón *m*; (*TECH*) correa, cinta ♦ *vt* (*thrash*) pegar con correa; **~way** (*US*) *n* (*AUT*) carretera de circunvalación

**bemused** [bɪ'mjuːzd] *adj* aturdido

**bench** [bentʃ] *n* banco; (*BRIT: POL*): **the Government/Opposition ~es** (los asientos de) los miembros del Gobierno/de la Oposición; **the B~** (*LAW: judges*) magistratura

**bend** [bend] (*pt, pp* **bent**) *vt* doblar ♦ *vi* inclinarse ♦ *n* (*BRIT: in road, river*) curva; (*in pipe*) codo; **~ down** *vi* inclinarse, doblarse; **~ over** *vi* inclinarse

**beneath** [bɪ'niːθ] *prep* bajo, debajo de; (*unworthy of*) indigno de ♦ *adv* abajo, (por) debajo

**benefactor** ['benɪfæktə*] *n* bienhechor *m*

**beneficial** [benɪ'fɪʃəl] *adj* beneficioso

**benefit** ['benɪfɪt] *n* beneficio; (*allowance of money*) subsidio ♦ *vt* beneficiar ♦ *vi*: **he'll ~ from it** se sacará provecho

**benevolent** [bɪ'nevələnt] *adj* (*person*) benévolo

**benign** [bɪ'naɪn] *adj* benigno; (*smile*) afable

**bent** [bent] *pt, pp of* **bend** ♦ *n* inclinación *f* ♦ *adj*: **to be ~ on** estar empeñado en

**bequest** [bɪ'kwest] *n* legado

**bereaved** [bɪ'riːvd] *npl*: **the ~** los

*íntimos de una persona afligidos por su muerte*

**beret** ['berei] *n* boina

**Berlin** [bəː'lɪn] *n* Berlín

**berm** [bəːm] (US) *n* (AUT) arcén *m*

**Bermuda** [bəː'mjuːdə] *n* las Bermudas

**berry** ['beri] *n* baya

**berserk** [bə'səːk] *adj*: to go ~ perder los estribos

**berth** [bəːθ] *n* (bed) litera; (cabin) camarote *m*; (for ship) amarradero ♦ *vi* atracar, amarrar

**beseech** [bɪ'siːtʃ] (pt, pp **besought**) *vt* suplicar

**beset** [bɪ'sɛt] (pt, pp **beset**) *vt* (person) acosar

**beside** [bɪ'saɪd] *prep* junto a, al lado de; to be ~ o.s. with anger estar fuera de sí; that's ~ the point eso no tiene nada que ver

**besides** [bɪ'saɪdz] *adv* además ♦ *prep* además de

**besiege** [bɪ'siːdʒ] *vt* sitiar; (fig) asediar

**besought** [bɪ'sɔːt] *pt, pp* of **beseech**

**best** [bɛst] *adj* (el/la) mejor ♦ *adv* (lo) mejor; the ~ part of (quantity) la mayor parte de; at ~ en el mejor de los casos; to make the ~ of sth sacar el mejor partido de algo; to do one's ~ hacer todo lo posible; to the ~ of my knowledge que yo sepa; to the ~ of my ability como mejor puedo; ~ man *n* padrino de boda

**bestow** [bɪ'stəu] *vt* (title) otorgar

**bestseller** ['bɛst'sɛlə*] *n* éxito de librería, bestseller *m*

**bet** [bɛt] (pt, pp **bet** or **betted**) *n* apuesta ♦ *vt*: to ~ money on apostar dinero por; to ~ sb sth apostar algo a uno ♦ *vi* apostar

**betray** [bɪ'treɪ] *vt* traicionar; (trust) faltar a; ~al *n* traición ♦ *f*

**better** ['bɛtə*] *adj, adv* mejor ♦ *vt* superar ♦ *n*: to get the ~ of sb quedar por encima de alguien; you had ~ do it más vale que lo hagas; he thought ~ of it cambió de parecer; to get ~ (MED) mejorar(se)

~ **off** *adj* mejor; (wealthier) más acomodado

**betting** ['bɛtɪŋ] *n* juego, el apostar; ~ **shop** (BRIT) *n* agencia de apuestas

**between** [bɪ'twiːn] *prep* entre ♦ *adv* (time) mientras tanto; (place) en medio

**beverage** ['bɛvərɪdʒ] *n* bebida

**beware** [bɪ'wɛə*] *vi*: to ~ (of) tener cuidado (con); "~ of the dog" "perro peligroso"

**bewildered** [bɪ'wɪldəd] *adj* aturdido, perplejo

**bewitching** [bɪ'wɪtʃɪŋ] *adj* hechicero, encantador(a)

**beyond** [bɪ'jɔnd] *prep* más allá de; (past: understanding) fuera de; (after: date) después de, más allá de; (above) superior a ♦ *adv* (in space) más allá; (in time) posteriormente; ~ **doubt** fuera de toda duda; ~ **repair** irreparable

**bias** ['baɪəs] *n* (prejudice) prejuicio, (preference) predisposición *f*; ~(**s**)**ed** *adj* parcial

**bib** [bɪb] *n* babero

**Bible** ['baɪbl] *n* Biblia

**bicarbonate of soda** [baɪ'kɑːbə-nɪt-] *n* bicarbonato sódico

**bicker** ['bɪkə*] *vi* pelearse

**bicycle** ['baɪsɪkl] *n* bicicleta

**bid** [bɪd] (pt **bade** or **bid**, pp **bidden** or **bid**) *n* oferta, postura; (in tender) licitación *f*; (attempt) tentativa, conato ♦ *vi* hacer una oferta ♦ *vt* (offer) ofrecer; to ~ sb good day dar a uno los buenos días; ~**der** *n*: the highest ~**der** el mejor postor; ~**ding** *n* (at auction) ofertas *fpl*

**bide** [baɪd] *vt*: to ~ one's time esperar el momento adecuado

**bifocals** [baɪ'fəuklz] *npl* gafas *fpl* (SP) or anteojos *mpl* (AM) bifocales

**big** [bɪg] *adj* grande; (brother, sister) mayor

**bigheaded** ['bɪg'hɛdɪd] *adj* engreído

**bigot** ['bɪgət] *n* fanático/a, intolerante *m/f*; ~**ed** *adj* fanático, intolerante; ~**ry** *n* fanatismo, intolerancia

**big top** n (at circus) carpa

**bike** [baik] n bici f

**bikini** [bɪ'ki:nɪ] n bikini m

**bile** [baɪl] n bilis f

**bilingual** [baɪ'lɪŋgwəl] adj bilingüe

**bill** [bɪl] n cuenta; (invoice) factura; (POL) proyecto de ley; (US: banknote) billete m; (of bird) pico; (of show) programa m; "post no ~s" "prohibido fijar carteles"; to fit or fill the ~ (fig) cumplir con los requisitos; ~**board** (US) n cartelera

**billet** ['bɪlɪt] n alojamiento

**billfold** ['bɪlfəʊld] (US) n cartera

**billiards** ['bɪljədz] n billar m

**billion** ['bɪljən] n (BRIT) billón m (millón de millones); (US) mil millones

**bin** [bɪn] n (for rubbish) cubo (SP) or bote m (AM) de la basura; (container) recipiente m

**bind** [baɪnd] (pt, pp bound) vt atar; (book) encuadernar; (oblige) obligar ♦ n (inf: nuisance) lata; ~**ing** adj (contract) obligatorio

**binge** [bɪndʒ] (inf) n: to go on a ~ ir de juerga

**bingo** ['bɪŋgəʊ] n bingo m

**binoculars** [bɪ'nɒkjʊləz] npl prismáticos mpl

**bio...** [baɪə] prefix: ~**chemistry** n bioquímica; ~**graphy** [baɪ'ɒgrəfɪ] n biografía; ~**logical** adj biológico; ~**logy** [baɪ'ɒlədʒɪ] n biología

**birch** [bɜːtʃ] n (tree) abedul m

**bird** [bɜːd] n ave f, pájaro; (BRIT: inf: girl) chica; ~**'s eye view** n (aerial view) vista de pájaro; (overview) visión f de conjunto; ~ **watcher** n ornitólogo/a

**Biro** ['baɪrəʊ] ® n bolígrafo

**birth** [bɜːθ] n nacimiento; to give ~ to parir, dar a luz; (fig) ~ **certificate** n partida de nacimiento; ~ **control** n (policy) control m de natalidad; (methods) métodos mpl anticonceptivos; ~**day** n cumpleaños m inv ♦ cpd (cake, card etc) de cumpleaños; ~**place** n lugar m de nacimiento; ~ **rate** n (tasa de) natalidad f

**biscuit** ['bɪskɪt] (BRIT) n galleta, bizcocho (AM)

**bisect** [baɪ'sɛkt] vt bisecar

**bishop** ['bɪʃəp] n obispo; (CHESS) alfil m

**bit** [bɪt] pt of bite ♦ n trozo, pedazo, pedacito; (COMPUT) bit m, bitio; (for horse) freno, bocado; a ~ of un poco de; a ~ **mad** un poco loco; ~ **by** ~ poco a poco

**bitch** [bɪtʃ] n perra; (inf!: woman) zorra (!)

**bite** [baɪt] (pt bit, pp bitten) vt, vi morder; (insect etc) picar ♦ n (insect ~) picadura; (mouthful) bocado; to ~ one's nails comerse las uñas; let's have a ~ (to eat) (inf) vamos a comer algo

**bitter** ['bɪtə*] adj amargo; (wind) cortante, penetrante; (battle) encarnizado ♦ n (BRIT: beer) cerveza típica británica a base de lúpulos; ~**ness** n lo amargo, amargura; (anger) rencor m

**bizarre** [bɪ'zɑː*] adj raro, extraño

**blab** [blæb] (inf) vi soplar

**black** [blæk] adj negro; (tea, coffee) solo ♦ n color m negro; (person): B~ negro/a ♦ vt (BRIT: INDUSTRY) boicotear; to give sb a ~ eye ponerle a uno el ojo morado; ~ **and blue** (bruised) amoratado; to be in the ~ (bank account) estar en números negros; ~**berry** n zarzamora; ~**bird** n mirlo; ~**board** n pizarra; ~ **coffee** n café m solo; ~**currant** n grosella negra; ~**en** vt (fig) desacreditar; ~ **ice** n hielo invisible en la carretera; ~**leg** (BRIT) n esquirol m, rompehuelgas m inv; ~**list** n lista negra; ~**mail** n chantaje m ♦ vt chantajear; ~ **market** n mercado negro; ~**out** n (MIL) oscurecimiento; (power cut) apagón m; (TV, RADIO) interrupción f de programas; (fainting) desmayo; **B~ Sea** n: the B~ Sea el Mar Negro; ~**sheep** n (fig) oveja negra; ~**smith** n herrero; ~ **spot** n (AUT) lugar m peligroso; (for unemployment etc) punto negro

**bladder** ['blædə*] n vejiga

**blade** [bleɪd] n hoja; (of propeller) paleta; **a ~ of grass** una brizna de hierba

**blame** [bleɪm] n culpa ♦ vt: **to ~ sb for sth** echar a uno la culpa de algo; **to be to ~** tener la culpa de; **~less** adj inocente

**bland** [blænd] adj (music, taste) soso

**blank** [blæŋk] adj en blanco; (look) sin expresión ♦ n (of memory): **my mind is a ~** no puedo recordar nada; (on form) blanco, espacio en blanco; (cartridge) cartucho sin bala or de fogueo; **~ cheque** n cheque m en blanco

**blanket** ['blæŋkɪt] n manta (SP), cobija (AM); (of snow) capa; (of fog) manto

**blare** [blɛə*] vi sonar estrepitosamente

**blasé** ['blɑːzeɪ] adj hastiado

**blasphemy** ['blæsfɪmɪ] n blasfemia

**blast** [blɑːst] n (of wind) ráfaga, soplo; (of explosive) explosión f ♦ vt (blow up) volar; **~-off** n (SPACE) lanzamiento

**blatant** ['bleɪtənt] adj descarado

**blaze** [bleɪz] n (fire) fuego; (fig: of colour) despliegue m; (: of glory) esplendor m ♦ vi arder en llamas; (fig) brillar ♦ vt: **to ~ a trail** (fig) abrir (un) camino; **in a ~ of publicity** con gran publicidad

**blazer** ['bleɪzə*] n chaqueta de uniforme de colegial o de socio de club

**bleach** [bliːtʃ] n (also: household ~) lejía ♦ vt blanquear; **~ed** adj (hair) teñido (de rubio); **~ers** (US) npl (SPORT) gradas fpl al sol

**bleak** [bliːk] adj (countryside) desierto; (prospect) poco prometedor(a); (weather) crudo; (smile) triste

**bleary-eyed** ['blɪərɪ'aɪd] adj: **to be ~** tener ojos de cansado

**bleat** [bliːt] vi balar

**bleed** [bliːd] (pt, pp bled) vt, vi sangrar; **my nose is ~ing** me está sangrando la nariz

**bleeper** ['bliːpə*] n busca m

**blemish** ['blemɪʃ] n marca, mancha; (on reputation) tacha

**blend** [blend] n mezcla ♦ vt mezclar; (colours etc) combinar, mezclar ♦ vi (colours etc: also: ~ in) combinarse, mezclarse

**bless** [bles] (pt, pp blessed or blest) vt bendecir; **~ you!** (after sneeze) ¡Jesús!; **~ing** n (approval) aprobación f; (godsend) don m del cielo, bendición f; (advantage) beneficio, ventaja

**blew** [bluː] pt of blow

**blight** [blaɪt] vt (hopes etc) frustrar, arruinar

**blimey** ['blaɪmɪ] (BRIT: inf) excl ¡caray!

**blind** [blaɪnd] adj ciego; (fig): **~ (to)** ciego (a) ♦ n (for window) persiana ♦ vt cegar; (dazzle) deslumbrar; (deceive): **to ~ sb to ...** cegar a uno a ...; **the ~** npl los ciegos; **~ alley** n callejón m sin salida; **~ corner** (BRIT) n esquina escondida; **~fold** n venda ♦ adv con los ojos vendados ♦ vt vendar los ojos a; **~ly** adv a ciegas, ciegamente; **~ness** n ceguera; **~ spot** n (AUT) ángulo ciego

**blink** [blɪŋk] vi parpadear, pestañear; (light) oscilar; **~ers** npl anteojeras fpl

**bliss** [blɪs] n felicidad f

**blister** ['blɪstə*] n ampolla ♦ vi (paint) ampollarse

**blithely** ['blaɪðlɪ] adv alegremente

**blitz** [blɪts] n (MIL) bombardeo aéreo

**blizzard** ['blɪzəd] n ventisca

**bloated** ['bləutɪd] adj hinchado; (person: full) ahíto

**blob** [blɔb] n (drop) gota; (indistinct object) bulto

**bloc** [blɔk] n (POL) bloque m

**block** [blɔk] n bloque m; (in pipes) obstáculo; (of buildings) manzana (SP), cuadra (AM) ♦ vt obstruir, cerrar; (progress) estorbar; **~ of flats** (BRIT) bloque m de pisos; **mental ~** bloqueo mental; **~ade** [-'keɪd] n bloqueo ♦ *vt* bloquear; **~age** *n* estorbo, obstrucción *f*; **~buster** *n* (book) bestseller *m*; (film) éxito de público; **~ letters** *npl* letras *fpl* de molde

**bloke** [bləuk] (BRIT: inf) *n* tipo, tío

**blond(e)** [blɔnd] *adj, n* rubio/a *m/f*

**blood** [blʌd] *n* sangre *f*; **~ donor** *n* donante *m/f* de sangre; **~ group** *n* grupo sanguíneo; **~hound** *n* sabueso; **~ poisoning** *n* envenenamiento de la sangre; **~ pressure** *n* presión *f* sanguínea; **~shed** *n* derramamiento de sangre; **~shot** *adj* inyectado en sangre; **~stream** *n* corriente *f* sanguínea; **~ test** *n* análisis *m inv* de sangre; **~thirsty** *adj* sanguinario; **~ vessel** *n* vaso sanguíneo; **~y** *adj* sangriento; (nose etc) lleno de sangre; (BRIT: inf!): **this ~** ... ! este condenado *o* puñetero ... (!) ♦ *adv*: **~y strong/good** (BRIT: inf!) terriblemente fuerte/bueno; **~y-minded** (BRIT: inf) *adj* malicioso

**bloom** [bluːm] *n* flor *f* ♦ *vi* florecer

**blossom** [ˈblɔsəm] *n* flor *f* ♦ *vi* (also fig) florecer

**blot** [blɔt] *n* borrón *m*; (fig) mancha ♦ *vt* (stain) manchar; **~ out** *vt* (view) tapar

**blotchy** [ˈblɔtʃɪ] *adj* (complexion) lleno de manchas

**blotting paper** [ˈblɔtɪŋ-] *n* papel *m* secante

**blouse** [blauz] *n* blusa

**blow** [bləu] (pt blew, pp blown) *n* golpe *m*; (with sword) espadazo ♦ *vi* soplar; (dust, sand etc) volar; (fuse) fundirse ♦ *vt* (subj: wind) llevarse; (fuse) quemar; (instrument) tocar; **to ~ one's nose** sonarse; **~ away** *vt* llevarse, arrancar; **~ down** *vt* derribar; **~ off** *vt* arrebatar; **~ out** *vi* apagarse; **~ over** *vi* amainar; **~ up** *vi* estallar ♦ *vt* volar; (tyre) inflar; (PHOT) ampliar; **~-dry** *n* moldeado (con secador); **~lamp** (BRIT) *n* soplete *m*, lámpara de soldar; **~out** *n* (of tyre) pinchazo; **~torch** *n* = **blowlamp**

**blue** [bluː] *adj* azul; (depressed) deprimido; **~ film/joke** película/chiste verde; **out of the ~** (fig) de repente; **~bell** *n* campanilla, campánula azul; **~bottle** *n* moscarda, mosca azul; **~print** *n* (fig) anteproyecto

**bluff** [blʌf] *vi* tirarse un farol, farolear ♦ *n* farol *m*; **to call sb's ~** cogera uno la palabra

**blunder** [ˈblʌndə*] *n* patinazo, metedura de pata ♦ *vi* cometer un error, meter la pata

**blunt** [blʌnt] *adj* (pencil) despuntado; (knife) desafilado, romo; (person) franco, directo

**blur** [bləː*] *n* (shape): **to become a ~** hacerse borroso ♦ *vt* (vision) enturbiar; (distinction) borrar

**blurb** [bləːb] *n* comentario de sobrecubierta

**blurt out** [bləːt-] *vt* descolgarse con, dejar escapar

**blush** [blʌʃ] *vi* ruborizarse, ponerse colorado ♦ *n* rubor *m*

**blustering** [ˈblʌstərɪŋ] *adj* (person) fanfarrón/ona

**blustery** [ˈblʌstərɪ] *adj* (weather) tempestuoso, tormentoso

**boar** [bɔː*] *n* verraco, cerdo

**board** [bɔːd] *n* (card~) cartón *m*; (wooden) tabla, tablero; (on wall) tablón *m*; (for chess etc) tablero; (committee) junta, consejo; (in firm) mesa *o* junta directiva; (NAUT, AVIAT): **on ~** a bordo ♦ *vt* (ship) embarcarse en; (train) subir a; **full ~** (BRIT) pensión completa; **half ~** (BRIT) media pensión; **to go by the ~** (fig) ser abandonado *o* olvidado; **~ up** *vt* (door) tapiar; **~ and lodging** *n* casa y comida; **~er** *n* (SCOL) interno/a; **~ing card** (BRIT) *n* tarjeta de embarque; **~ing house** *n* casa de huéspedes; **~ing pass** (US) *n* = **~ing card**; **~ing school** *n* internado; **~room** *n* sala de juntas

**boast** [bəust] *vi*: **to ~** (about *or* of) alardear (de)

**boat** [bəut] *n* barco, buque *m*; (small) barca, bote *m*; **~er** *n* (hat) canotié *m*

**bob** [bɔb] *vi* (*also*: ~ *up and down*) menearse, balancearse; ~ **up** *vi* (re)aparecer de repente

**bobby** ['bɔbɪ] *n* (*BRIT*: *inf*) *n* poli *m*

**bobsleigh** ['bɔbsleɪ] *n* bob *m*

**bode** [bəud] *vi*: **to** ~ **well/ill (for)** ser prometedor/poco prometedor (para)

**bodily** ['bɔdɪlɪ] *adj* corporal ♦ *adv* (*move*: *person*) en peso

**body** ['bɔdɪ] *n* cuerpo; (*corpse*) cadáver *m*; (*of car*) caja, carrocería; (*fig*: *group*) grupo; (: *organization*) organismo; ~**building** *n* culturismo; ~**guard** *n* guardaespaldas *m inv*; ~**work** *n* carrocería

**bog** [bɔg] *n* pantano, ciénaga ♦ *vt*: **to get** ~**ged down** (*fig*) empantanarse, atascarse

**boggle** ['bɔgl] *vi*: **the mind** ~**s**! ¡no puedo creerlo!

**bogus** ['bəugəs] *adj* falso, fraudulento

**boil** [bɔɪl] *vt* (*water*) hervir; (*eggs*) pasar por agua, cocer ♦ *vi* hervir; (*fig*: *with anger*) estar furioso; (: *with heat*) asfixiarse ♦ *n* (*MED*) furúnculo, divieso; **to come to the** ~, **to come to a** ~ (*US*) comenzar a hervir; **to** ~ **down to** (*fig*) reducirse a; ~ **over** *vi* salirse, rebosar (*anger etc*) llegar al colmo; ~**ed egg** *n* huevo cocido (*SP*) or pasado (*AM*); ~**ed potatoes** *npl* patatas *fpl* (*SP*) or papas *fpl* (*AM*) hervidas; ~**er** *n* caldera; ~**er suit** *n* (*BRIT*) *n* mono; ~**ing point** *n* punto de ebullición

**boisterous** ['bɔɪstərəs] *adj* (*noisy*) bullicioso; (*excitable*) exuberante; (*crowd*) tumultuoso

**bold** [bəuld] *adj* valiente, audaz; (*pej*) descarado; (*colour*) llamativo

**Bolivia** [bə'lɪvɪə] *n* Bolivia; ~**n** *adj*, *n* boliviano/a *m/f*

**bollard** ['bɔləd] *n* (*AUT*) poste *m*

**bolster** ['bəulstə*] *vt*: ~ **up** *vt* reforzar

**bolt** [bəult] *n* (*lock*) cerrojo; (*with nut*) perno, tornillo ♦ *adv*: ~ **up-right** rígido, erguido ♦ *vt* (*door*)

echar el cerrojo a; (*also*: ~ *together*) sujetar con tornillos; (*food*) engullir ♦ *vi* fugarse; (*horse*) desbocarse

**bomb** [bɔm] *n* bomba ♦ *vt* bombardear; ~**ard** [-'bɑːd] *vt* bombardear; (*fig*): **to** ~ **with questions** acribillar a preguntas; ~**ardment** [-'bɑːdmənt] *n* bombardeo

**bombastic** [bɔm'bæstɪk] *adj* rimbombante; (*person*) farolero

**bomb**: ~ **disposal** *n* desmontaje *m* de explosivos; ~**er** *n* (*AVIAT*) bombardero; ~**shell** *n* (*fig*) bomba

**bona fide** ['bəunə'faɪdɪ] *adj* genuino, auténtico

**bond** [bɔnd] *n* (*promise*) fianza; (*FINANCE*) bono; (*link*) vínculo, lazo; (*COMM*): **in** ~ en depósito bajo fianza

**bondage** ['bɔndɪdʒ] *n* esclavitud *f*

**bone** [bəun] *n* hueso; (*of fish*) espina ♦ *vt* deshuesar; quitar las espinas a; ~ **idle** *adj* gandul

**bonfire** ['bɔnfaɪə*] *n* hoguera, fogata

**bonnet** ['bɔnɪt] *n* gorra; (*BRIT*: *of car*) capó *m*

**bonus** ['bəunəs] *n* (*payment*) paga extraordinaria, plus *m*; (*fig*) bendición *f*

**bony** ['bəunɪ] *adj* (*arm*, *face*) huesudo; (*MED*: *tissue*) óseo; (*meat*) lleno de huesos; (*fish*) lleno de espinas

**boo** [buː] *excl* ¡uh! ♦ *vt* abuchear, rechiflar

**booby trap** ['buːbɪ-] *n* trampa explosiva

**book** [buk] *n* libro; (*of tickets*) taco; (*of stamps etc*) librito ♦ *vt* (*ticket*) sacar; (*seat*, *room*) reservar; ~**s** *npl* (*COMM*) cuentas *fpl*, contabilidad *f*; ~**case** *n* librería, estante *m* para libros; ~**ing office** *n* (*BRIT*: *RAIL*) despacho de billetes (*SP*) or boletos (*AM*); (*THEATRE*) taquilla (*SP*), boletería (*AM*); ~**keeping** *n* contabilidad *f*; ~**let** *n* folleto; ~**maker** *n* corredor *m* de apuestas; ~**seller** *n* librero; ~**shop**, ~ **store** *n* librería

**boom** [buːm] *n* (*noise*) trueno, estampido; (*in prices etc*) alza rápida;

(*ECON, in population*) boom *m* ♦ *vi*
(*cannon*) hacer gran estruendo, retumbar; (*ECON*) estar en alza

**boon** [bu:n] *n* favor *m*, beneficio

**boost** [bu:st] *n* estímulo, empuje *m*
♦ *vt* estimular, empujar; *n*
(*MED*) reinyección *f*

**boot** [bu:t] *n* bota; (*BRIT: of car*)
maleta, maletero ♦ *vt* (*COMPUT*)
arrancar; to ~ (*in addition*) además,
por añadidura

**booth** [bu:ð] *n* (*at fair*) barraca;
(*telephone* ~, *voting* ~) cabina

**booty** ['bu:tɪ] *n* botín *m*

**booze** [bu:z] (*inf*) *n* bebida

**border** ['bɔ:də*] *n* borde *m*, margen
*m*; (*of a country*) frontera; (*for flowers*) arriate *m* ♦ *vt* (*road*) bordear;
(*another country: also:* ~ *on*) lindar
con; **B~s** *n*: **the B~s** *región fronteriza entre Escocia y Inglaterra*; **~
on** *vt fus* (*insanity etc*) rayar en;
~**line** *n*: **on the** ~**line** en el límite;
~**line case** *n* caso dudoso

**bore** [bɔ:*] *pt of* **bear** ♦ *vt* (*hole*) hacer un agujero en; (*well*) perforar;
(*person*) aburrir ♦ *n* (*person*) pelmazo, pesado; (*of gun*) calibre *m*; **to be
~d** estar aburrido; ~**dom** *n* aburrimiento

**boring** ['bɔ:rɪŋ] *adj* aburrido

**born** [bɔ:n] *adj*: **to be** ~ nacer; **I
was** ~ **in 1960** nací en 1960

**borne** [bɔ:n] *pp of* **bear**

**borough** ['bʌrə] *n* municipio

**borrow** ['bɔrəʊ] *vt*: **to** ~ **sth** (*from
sb*) tomar algo prestado (a alguien)

**bosom** ['buzəm] *n* pecho; ~ **friend**
*n* amigo íntimo

**boss** [bɔs] *n* jefe *m* ♦ *vt* (*also:
~ about or around*) mangonear; ~**y** *adj*
mandón/ona

**bosun** ['bəusn] *n* contramaestre *m*

**botany** ['bɔtənɪ] *n* botánica

**botch** [bɔtʃ] *vt* (*also:* ~ *up*) arruinar, estropear

**both** [bəuθ] *adj, pron* ambos/as, los/
las dos; ~ **of us went, we** ~ **went**
fuimos los dos, ambos fuimos ♦ *adv*:
~ **A and B** tanto A como B

**bother** ['bɔðə*] *vt* (*worry*) preocupar; (*disturb*) molestar, fastidiar
♦ *vi* (*also:* ~ *o.s.*) molestarse ♦ *n*
(*trouble*) dificultad *f*; (*nuisance*) molestia, lata; **to** ~ **doing** tomarse la
molestia de hacer

**bottle** ['bɔtl] *n* botella; (*small*) frasco; (*baby's*) biberón *m* ♦ *vt* embotellar; ~ **up** *vt* suprimir; ~ **bank** *n*
contenedor de vidrio; ~**neck** *n*
(*AUT*) embotellamiento; (*in supply*)
obstáculo; ~**opener** *n* abrebotellas
*m inv*

**bottom** ['bɔtəm] *n* (*of box, sea*) fondo; (*buttocks*) trasero, culo; (*of
page*) pie *m*; (*of list*) final *m*; (*of
class*) último/a ♦ *adj* (*lowest*) más
bajo; (*last*) último; ~**less** *adj* sin
fondo, inacabable

**bough** [bau] *n* rama

**bought** [bɔ:t] *pt, pp of* **buy**

**boulder** ['bəuldə*] *n* canto rodado

**bounce** [bauns] *vi* (*ball*) (re)botar;
(*cheque*) ser rechazado ♦ *vt* hacer
(re)botar ♦ *n* (*rebound*) (re)bote *m*;
~**r** (*inf*) *n* gorila *m* (*que echa a los
alborotadores de un bar, club etc*)

**bound** [baund] *pt, pp of* **bind** ♦ *n*
(*leap*) salto; (*gen pl: limit*) límite *m*
♦ *vi* (*leap*) saltar ♦ *vt* (*border*) rodear ♦ *adj*: ~ **by** rodeado de; **to be
~ to do sth** (*obliged*) tener el deber
de hacer algo; **he's** ~ **to come** es
seguro que vendrá; **out of** ~**s** prohibido el paso; ~ **for** con destino a

**boundary** ['baundrɪ] *n* límite *m*

**boundless** ['baundlɪs] *adj* ilimitado

**bouquet** ['bukeɪ] *n* (*of flowers*) ramo

**bourgeois** ['buəʒwa:] *adj* burgués/
esa *m/f*

**bout** [baut] *n* (*of malaria etc*) ataque
*m*; (*of activity*) período; (*BOXING
etc*) combate *m*, encuentro

**bow**[1] [bau] *n* (*knot*) lazo; (*weapon,
MUS*) arco

**bow**[2] [bau] *n* (*of the head*) reverencia; (*NAUT: also:* ~*s*) proa ♦ *vi* inclinarse, hacer una reverencia;
(*yield*): **to** ~ **to or before** ceder
ante, someterse a

**bowels** [bauəlz] *npl* intestinos *mpl*, vientre *m*; (*fig*) entrañas *fpl*

**bowl** [bəul] *n* tazón *m*, cuenco; (*ball*) bola ♦ *vi* (*CRICKET*) arrojar la pelota

**bow-legged** ['bəu'legid] *adj* estevado

**bowler** ['bəulə*] *n* (*CRICKET*) lanzador *m* (de la pelota); (*BRIT*: *also*: ~ *hat*) hongo, bombín *m*

**bowling** ['bəuliŋ] *n* (*game*) bochas *fpl*, bolos *mpl*; ~ **alley** *n* bolera; ~ **green** *n* pista para bochas

**bowls** [bəulz] *n* juego de las bochas, bolos *mpl*

**bow tie** ['bəu-] *n* corbata de lazo, pajarita

**box** [bɔks] *n* (*also*: *cardboard* ~) caja, cajón *m*; (*THEATRE*) palco ♦ *vt* encajonar ♦ *vi* (*SPORT*) boxear; ~**er** *n* (*person*) boxeador *m*; ~**ing** *n* (*SPORT*) boxeo; **B~ing Day** *n* (*BRIT*) *n* día en que se dan los aguinaldos, 26 de diciembre; ~**ing gloves** *npl* guantes *mpl* de boxeo; ~**ing ring** *n* ring *m*, cuadrilátero; ~ **office** *n* taquilla (*SP*), boletería (*AM*); ~**room** *n* trastero

**boy** [bɔi] *n* (*young*) niño, muchacho, chico; (*son*) hijo

**boycott** ['bɔikɔt] *n* boicot *m* ♦ *vt* boicotear

**boyfriend** ['bɔifrend] *n* novio

**boyish** ['bɔiiʃ] *adj* juvenil; (*girl*) con aspecto de muchacho

**B.R.** *n* *abbr* (= *British Rail*) ≈ RENFE *f* (*SP*)

**bra** [brɑ:] *n* sostén *m*, sujetador *m*

**brace** [breis] *n* (*BRIT*: *also*: ~**s**: *on teeth*) corrector *m*, aparato; (*tool*) berbiquí *m*; (*of knees*, *shoulders*) tensionar; ~**s** *npl* (*BRIT*) tirantes *mpl*, to ~ **o.s.** (*fig*) prepararse

**bracelet** ['breislit] *n* pulsera, brazalete *m*

**bracing** ['breisiŋ] *adj* vigorizante, tónico

**bracket** ['brækit] *n* (*TECH*) soporte *m*, puntal *m*; (*group*) clase *f*, categoría; (*also*: *brace* ~) soporte *m*, abra-

zadera; (*also*: *round* ~) paréntesis *inv*; (*also*: *square* ~) corchete *m* ♦ *vt* (*word etc*) poner entre paréntesis

**brag** [bræg] *vi* jactarse

**braid** [breid] *n* (*trimming*) galón *m*; (*of hair*) trenza

**brain** [brein] *n* cerebro; ~**s** *npl* sesos *mpl*; **she's got** ~**s** es muy lista; ~**child** *n* invento; ~**wash** *vt* lavar el cerebro; ~**wave** *n* idea luminosa; ~**y** *adj* muy inteligente

**braise** [breiz] *vt* cocer a fuego lento

**brake** [breik] *n* (*on vehicle*) freno ♦ *vi* frenar; ~ **fluid** *n* líquido de frenos; ~ **light** *n* luz *f* de frenado

**bran** [bræn] *n* salvado

**branch** [brɑ:ntʃ] *n* rama; (*COMM*) sucursal *f*; ~ **out** *vi* (*fig*) extenderse

**brand** [brænd] *n* marca; (*fig*: *type*) tipo ♦ *vt* (*cattle*) marcar con hierro candente

**brandish** ['brændiʃ] *vt* blandir

**brand-new** ['brænd'nju:] *adj* flamante, completamente nuevo

**brandy** ['brændi] *n* coñac *m*

**brash** [bræʃ] *adj* (*forward*) descarado

**brass** [brɑ:s] *n* latón *m*; **the** ~ (*MUS*) los cobres; ~ **band** *n* banda de metal

**brassière** ['bræsiə*] *n* sostén *m*, sujetador *m*

**brat** [bræt] (*pej*) *n* mocoso/a

**bravado** [brə'vɑ:dəu] *n* fanfarronería

**brave** [breiv] *adj* valiente, valeroso ♦ *vt* (*face up to*) desafiar; ~**ry** *n* valor *m*, valentía

**brawl** [brɔ:l] *n* pelea, reyerta

**brawny** ['brɔ:ni] *adj* fornido, musculoso

**bray** [brei] *vi* rebuznar

**brazen** ['breizn] *adj* descarado, cínico ♦ *vt*: to ~ **it out** echarle cara

**brazier** ['breiziə*] *n* brasero

**Brazil** [brə'zil] *n* (el) Brasil; ~**ian** *adj*, *n* brasileño/a *m/f*

**breach** [bri:tʃ] *vt* abrir brecha en ♦ *n* (*gap*) brecha; (*breaking*): ~ **of contract** infracción *f* de contrato; ~ **of the peace** perturbación *f* del órden público

**bread** [bred] n pan m; ~ **and butter** n pan con mantequilla; (fig) pan (de cada día); ~**bin** (US =**box**) n panera; ~**crumbs** npl migajas fpl; (CULIN) pan rallado; ~**line** n: **on the** ~**line** en la miseria

**breadth** [brεtθ] n anchura; (fig) amplitud f

**breadwinner** ['brεdwɪnə*] n sustento m de la familia

**break** [breɪk] (pt **broke**, pp **broken**) vt romper; (promise) faltar a; (law) violar, infringir; (record) batir ♦ vi romperse, quebrarse; (storm) estallar; (weather) cambiar; (dawn) despuntar; (news etc) darse a conocer ♦ n (gap) abertura; (fracture) fractura; (time) intervalo; (: at school) (período de) recreo; (chance) oportunidad f; **to** ~ **the news to sb** comunicar la noticia a uno; ~ **down** vt (figures, data) analizar, descomponer ♦ vi (machine) estropearse; (AUT) averiarse; (person) romper a llorar; (talks) fracasar; ~ **even** vi cubrir los gastos; ~ **free** or **loose** vi escaparse; ~ **in** vt (horse etc) domar ♦ vi (burglar) forzar una entrada; (interrupt) interrumpir; ~ **into** vt fus (house) forzar; ~ **off** vi (speaker) pararse, detenerse; (branch) partir; ~ **open** vt (door etc) abrir por la fuerza, forzar; ~ **out** vi estallar; (prisoner) escaparse; **to** ~ **out in spots** salirle a uno granos; ~ **up** vi (ship) hacerse pedazos; (crowd, meeting) disolverse; (marriage) deshacerse; (SCOL) terminar (el curso) ♦ vt (rocks etc) partir; (journey) partir; (fight etc) acabar con; ~**age** n rotura; ~**down** n (AUT) avería; (in communications) interrupción f; (MED: also: **nervous** ~**down**) colapso, crisis f nerviosa; (of marriage, talks) análisis m inv; ~**down van** (BRIT) n (camión m) grúa; ~**er** n (ola) rompiente f

**breakfast** ['brεkfəst] n desayuno

**break-:** ~**in** n robo con allanamiento

de morada; ~**ing and entering** n (LAW) violación f de domicilio, allanamiento de morada; ~**through** n (also fig) avance m; ~**water** n rompeolas m inv

**breast** [brεst] n (of woman) pecho, seno; (chest) pecho; (of bird) pechuga; ~**feed** (irreg: like **feed**) vt, vi amamantar, criar a los pechos; ~**stroke** n braza (de pecho)

**breath** [breθ] n aliento, respiración f; **to take a deep** ~ respirar hondo; **out of** ~ sin aliento, sofocado

**Breathalyser** ['brεθəlaɪzə*] ® (BRIT) n alcoholímetro m

**breathe** [briːð] vt, vi respirar; ~ **in** vt, vi aspirar; ~ **out** vt, vi espirar; ~**r** n respiro; **breathing** n respiración f

**breath-:** ~**less** adj sin aliento, jadeante; ~**taking** adj imponente, pasmoso

**breed** [briːd] (pt, pp **bred**) vt criar ♦ vi reproducirse, procrear ♦ n (ZOOL) raza, casta; (type) tipo; ~**ing** n (of person) educación f

**breeze** [briːz] n brisa

**breezy** ['briːzi] adj de mucho viento, ventoso; (person) despreocupado

**brevity** ['brεvɪti] n brevedad f

**brew** [bruː] vt (tea) hacer; (beer) elaborar ♦ vi (fig: trouble) prepararse; (storm) amenazar; ~**ery** n fábrica de cerveza, cervecería

**bribe** [braɪb] n soborno ♦ vt sobornar, cohechar; ~**ry** n soborno, cohecho

**bric-a-brac** ['brɪkəbræk] n inv baratijas fpl

**brick** [brɪk] n ladrillo; ~**layer** n albañil m

**bridal** ['braɪdl] adj nupcial

**bride** [braɪd] n novia; ~**groom** n novio; ~**smaid** n dama de honor

**bridge** [brɪdʒ] n puente m; (NAUT) puente m de mando; (of nose) caballete m; (CARDS) bridge m ♦ vt (fig): **to** ~ **a gap** llenar un vacío

**bridle** ['braɪdl] n brida, freno; ~**path** n camino de herradura

**brief** [bri:f] adj breve, corto ♦ n (LAW) escrito; (task) cometido, encargo ♦ vt informar; ~s npl (for men) calzoncillos mpl; (for women) bragas fpl; ~**case** n cartera (SP), portafolio (AM); ~**ing** n (PRESS) informe m; ~**ly** adv (glance) fugazmente; (say) en pocas palabras

**brigadier** [brɪɡə'dɪə*] n general m de brigada

**bright** [braɪt] adj brillante; (room) luminoso; (day) de sol; (person: clever) listo, inteligente; (: lively) alegre; (colour) vivo; (future) prometedor(a); ~**en** (also: ~**en up**) vt (room) hacer más alegre; (event) alegrar ♦ vi (weather) despejarse; (person) animarse, alegrarse; (prospects) mejorar

**brilliance** ['brɪljəns] n brillo, brillantez f; (of talent etc) brillantez

**brilliant** ['brɪljənt] adj brillante; (inf) fenomenal

**brim** [brɪm] n borde m; (of hat) ala

**brine** [braɪn] n (CULIN) salmuera

**bring** [brɪŋ] (pt, pp **brought**) vt (thing, person: with you) traer; (: to sb) llevar, conducir; (trouble, satisfaction) causar; ~ **about** vt ocasionar, producir; ~ **back** vt volver a traer; (return) devolver; ~ **down** vt (government, plane) derribar; (price) rebajar; ~ **forward** vt adelantar; ~ **off** vt (task, plan) lograr, conseguir; ~ **out** vt sacar; (book etc) publicar; (meaning) subrayar; ~ **round** vt (unconscious person) hacer volver en sí; ~ **up** vt subir; (person) educar, criar; (question) sacar a colación; (food: vomit) devolver, vomitar

**brink** [brɪŋk] n borde m

**brisk** [brɪsk] adj (abrupt: tone) brusco; (person) enérgico, vigoroso; (pace) rápido; (trade) activo

**bristle** ['brɪsl] n cerda ♦ vi: to ~ in anger temblar de rabia

**Britain** ['brɪtən] n (also: Great ~) Gran Bretaña

**British** ['brɪtɪʃ] adj británico ♦ npl:

the ~ los británicos; ~ **Isles** npl: the ~ las Islas Británicas; ~ **Rail** n = RENFE f (SP)

**Briton** ['brɪtən] n británico/a

**brittle** ['brɪtl] adj quebradizo, frágil

**broach** [brəʊtʃ] vt (subject) abordar

**broad** [brɔːd] adj ancho; (range) amplio; (smile) abierto; (general: outlines etc) general; (accent) cerrado; **in ~ daylight** en pleno día; ~**cast** (irreg: like **cast**) n emisión f ♦ vt (RADIO) emitir; (TV) transmitir ♦ vi emitir; transmitir; ~**en** vt ampliar ♦ vi ensancharse; to ~ one's mind hacer más tolerante a uno; ~**ly** adv en general; ~-**minded** adj tolerante, liberal

**broccoli** ['brɒkəlɪ] n brécol m

**brochure** ['brəʊʃjuə*] n folleto

**broil** [brɔɪl] vt (CULIN) asar a la parrilla

**broke** [brəʊk] pt of **break** ♦ adj (inf) pelado, sin blanca

**broken** ['brəʊkən] pp of **break**; ~ roto; (machine: also: ~ **down**) averiado; ~ **leg** pierna rota; **in ~ English** en un inglés imperfecto; ~-**hearted** adj con el corazón partido

**broker** ['brəʊkə*] n agente m/f, bolsista m/f; (insurance ~) agente de seguros

**brolly** ['brɒlɪ] (BRIT: inf) n paraguas m inv

**bronchitis** [brɒŋ'kaɪtɪs] n bronquitis f

**bronze** [brɒnz] n bronce m

**brooch** [brəʊtʃ] n prendedor m, broche m

**brood** [bru:d] n camada, cría ♦ vi (person) dejarse obsesionar

**broom** [bru:m] n escoba; (BOT) retama; ~**stick** n palo de escoba

**Bros.** abbr (= **Brothers**) Hnos

**broth** [brɒθ] n caldo

**brothel** ['brɒθl] n burdel m

**brother** ['brʌðə*] n hermano; ~-**in-law** n cuñado

**brought** [brɔːt] pt, pp of **bring**

**brow** [braʊ] n (forehead) frente m; (eye~) ceja; (of hill) cumbre f

**brown** [braun] *adj* (*colour*) marrón; (*hair*) castaño; (*tanned*) bronceado, moreno ♦ *n* (*colour*) color *m* marrón or pardo ♦ *vt* (*CULIN*) dorar; ~ **bread** *n* pan integral

**brownie** ['brauni] *n* niña exploradora; (*US: cake*) pastel de chocolate con nueces

**brown paper** *n* papel *m* de estraza

**brown sugar** *n* azúcar *m* terciado

**browse** [brauz] *vi* (*through book*) hojear; (*in shop*) mirar

**bruise** [bru:z] *n* cardenal *m* (*SP*), moretón *n* (*AM*) ♦ *vt* magullar

**brunch** [brʌntʃ] *n* desayuno-almuerzo

**brunette** [bru:'nɛt] *n* morena

**brunt** [brʌnt] *n*: **to bear the ~ of** llevar el peso de

**brush** [brʌʃ] *n* cepillo; (*for painting, shaving etc*) brocha; (*artist's*) pincel *m*; (*with police etc*) roce *m* ♦ *vt* (*sweep*) barrer; (*groom*) cepillar; (*also*: ~ *against*) rozar al pasar; ~ **aside** *vt* rechazar, no hacer caso a; ~ **up** *vt* (*knowledge*) repasar, refrescar; ~**wood** *n* (*sticks*) leña

**brusque** [bru:sk] *adj* brusco, áspero

**Brussels** ['brʌslz] *n* Bruselas; ~ **sprout** *n* col *f* de Bruselas

**brute** [bru:t] *n* bruto; (*person*) bestia ♦ *adj*: **by ~ force** a fuerza bruta

**B.Sc.** *abbr* (= *Bachelor of Science*) licenciado en Ciencias

**bubble** ['bʌbl] *n* burbuja ♦ *vi* burbujear, borbotar; ~ **bath** *n* espuma para el baño; ~ **gum** *n* chicle *m* de globo

**buck** [bʌk] *n* (*rabbit*) conejo macho; (*deer*) gamo; (*US: inf*) dólar *m* ♦ *vi* corcovear; **to pass the ~ (to sb)** echar (a uno) el muerto; ~ **up** *vi* (*cheer up*) animarse, cobrar ánimo

**bucket** ['bʌkɪt] *n* cubo, balde *m*

**buckle** ['bʌkl] *n* hebilla ♦ *vt* abrochar con hebilla ♦ *vi* combarse

**bud** [bʌd] *n* (*of plant*) brote *m*, yema; (*of flower*) capullo ♦ *vi* brotar, echar brotes

**Buddhism** ['budɪzm] *n* Budismo

**budding** ['bʌdɪŋ] *adj* en ciernes, en

embrión

**buddy** ['bʌdɪ] (*US*) *n* compañero, compinche *m*

**budge** [bʌdʒ] *vt* mover; (*fig*) hacer ceder ♦ *vi* moverse, ceder

**budgerigar** ['bʌdʒərɪgɑ:*] *n* periquito

**budget** ['bʌdʒɪt] *n* presupuesto ♦ *vi*: **to ~ for sth** presupuestar algo

**budgie** ['bʌdʒɪ] *n* = **budgerigar**

**buff** [bʌf] *adj* (*colour*) color de ante *m*; (*inf: enthusiast*) entusiasta *m/f*

**buffalo** ['bʌfələu] (*pl* ~ *or* ~**es**) *n* (*BRIT*) búfalo; (*US: bison*) bisonte *m*

**buffer** ['bʌfə*] *n* (*COMPUT*) memoria intermedia; (*RAIL*) tope *m*

**buffet¹** ['bufeɪ] *n* (*BRIT: in station*) bar *m*, cafetería; (*food*) buffet *m*; ~ **car** (*BRIT*) *n* (*RAIL*) coche-comedor *m*

**buffet²** ['bʌfɪt] *vt* golpear

**bug** [bʌg] *n* (*esp US: insect*) bicho, sabandija; (*COMPUT*) error *m*; (*germ*) microbio, bacilo; (*spy device*) micrófono oculto ♦ *vt* (*inf: annoy*) fastidiar; (*room*) poner micrófono oculto en

**buggy** [bʌgɪ] *n* cochecito de niño

**bugle** ['bju:gl] *n* corneta, clarín *m*

**build** [bɪld] (*pt, pp* **built**) *n* (*of person*) tipo ♦ *vt* construir, edificar; ~ **up** *vt* (*morale, forces, production*) acrecentar; (*stocks*) acumular; ~**er** *n* (*contractor*) contratista *m/f*; ~**ing** *n* construcción *f*; (*structure*) edificio; ~**ing society** (*BRIT*) *n* sociedad *f* inmobiliaria, cooperativa de construcciones

**built** [bɪlt] *pt, pp of* **build** ♦ *adj*: ~-**in** (*wardrobe etc*) empotrado; ~-**up area** *n* zona urbanizada

**bulb** [bʌlb] *n* (*BOT*) bulbo; (*ELEC*) bombilla (*SP*), foco (*AM*)

**Bulgaria** [bʌl'geərɪə] *n* Bulgaria; ~**n** *adj, n* búlgaro/a *m/f*

**bulge** [bʌldʒ] *n* bulto, protuberancia ♦ *vi* bombearse, pandearse; (*pocket etc*): **to ~ (with)** rebosar (de)

**bulk** [bʌlk] *n* masa, mole *f*; **in ~**

(*COMM*) a granel; **the ~ of** la mayor parte de; **~y** *adj* voluminoso, abultado

**bull** [bul] *n* toro; (*male elephant, whale*) macho; **~dog** *n* dogo

**bulldozer** ['buldəuzə*] *n* bulldozer *m*

**bullet** ['bulit] *n* bala

**bulletin** ['bulitin] *n* anuncio, parte *m*; (*journal*) boletín *m*

**bulletproof** ['bulitpru:f] *adj* a prueba de balas

**bullfight** ['bulfait] *n* corrida de toros; **~er** *n* torero; **~ing** *n* los toros, el toreo

**bullion** ['buljən] *n* oro (*or* plata) en barras

**bullock** ['buldk] *n* novillo

**bullring** ['bulrin] *n* plaza de toros

**bull's-eye** *n* centro del blanco

**bully** ['buli] *n* valentón *m*, matón *m* ♦ *vt* intimidar, tiranizar

**bum** [bʌm] *n* (*inf*: *backside*) culo; (*esp US*: *tramp*) vagabundo

**bumblebee** ['bʌmblbi:] *n* abejorro

**bump** [bʌmp] *n* (*blow*) tope *m*, choque *m*; (*jolt*) sacudida; (*on road etc*) bache *m*; (*on head etc*) chichón *m* ♦ *vt* (*strike*) chocar contra; **~ into** *vt fus* chocar contra, tropezar con; (*person*) topar con; **~er** *n* (*AUT*) parachoques *m inv* ♦ *adj*: **~er crop/ harvest** cosecha abundante; **~er cars** *npl* coches *mpl* de choque

**bumptious** ['bʌmpʃəs] *adj* engreído, presuntuoso

**bumpy** ['bʌmpi] *adj* (*road*) lleno de baches

**bun** [bʌn] *n* (*BRIT*: *cake*) pastel *m*; (*US*: *bread*) bollo; (*of hair*) moño

**bunch** [bʌntʃ] *n* (*of flowers*) ramo; (*of keys*) manojo; (*of bananas*) piña; (*of people*) grupo; (*pej*) pandilla; **~es** *npl* (*in hair*) coletas *fpl*

**bundle** ['bʌndl] *n* bulto, fardo; (*of sticks*) haz *m*; (*of papers*) legajo ♦ *vt* (*also*: **~ up**) atar, envolver; (*to put sth/sb into*) meter algo/a alguien precipitadamente en

**bungalow** ['bʌngələu] *n* bungalow *m*, chalé *m*

**bungle** ['bʌngl] *vt* hacer mal

**bunion** ['bʌnjən] *n* juanete *m*

**bunk** [bʌnk] *n* litera; **~ beds** *npl* literas *fpl*

**bunker** ['bʌnkə*] *n* (*coal store*) carbonera; (*MIL*) refugio; (*GOLF*) bunker *m*

**bunny** ['bʌni] *n* (*also*: **~ rabbit**) conejito

**bunting** ['bʌntin] *n* banderitas *fpl*

**buoy** [bɔi] *n* boya; **~ up** *vt* (*fig*) animar; **~ant** *adj* (*ship*) capaz de flotar; (*economy*) boyante; (*person*) optimista

**burden** ['bə:dn] *n* carga ♦ *vt* cargar

**bureau** [bjuə'rəu] *n* (*pl* **bureaux**) (*BRIT*: *writing desk*) escritorio, buró *m*; (*US*: *chest of drawers*) cómoda; (*office*) oficina, agencia

**bureaucracy** [bjuə'rɔkrəsi] *n* burocracia

**bureaux** [bjuə'rəu] *npl of* **bureau**

**burglar** ['bə:glə*] *n* ladrón/ona *m/f*; **~ alarm** *n* alarma *f* antirrobo; **~y** *n* robo con allanamiento, robo de una casa

**burial** ['beriəl] *n* entierro

**burly** ['bə:li] *adj* fornido, membrudo

**Burma** ['bə:mə] *n* Birmania

**burn** [bə:n] *n* (*pt, pp* **burned** *or* **burnt**) *vt* quemar; (*house*) incendiar ♦ *vi* quemarse, arder; incendiarse; (*sting*) escocer ♦ *n* quemadura; **~ down** *vt* incendiar; **~er** *n* (*on cooker etc*) quemador *m*; **~ing** (*building etc*) en llamas; (*hot*: *sand etc*) abrasador; (*ambition*) ardiente; **burnt** [bə:nt] *pt, pp of* **burn**

**burrow** ['bʌrəu] *n* madriguera ♦ *vi* hacer una madriguera; (*rummage*) hurgar

**bursary** ['bə:səri] *n* (*BRIT*) beca

**burst** [bə:st] (*pt, pp* **burst**) *vt* reventar; (*subj*: *river*: *banks etc*) romper ♦ *vi* reventarse; (*tyre*) pincharse ♦ *n* (*of gunfire*) ráfaga; (*also*: **~ pipe**) reventón *m*; **a ~ of energy/speed/ enthusiasm** una explosión de energía/un ímpetu de velocidad/un arranque de entusiasmo; **to ~ into**

flames estallar en llamas; **to ~ into
tears** deshacerse en lágrimas; **to ~
out laughing** soltar la carcajada; **to
~ open** abrirse de golpe; **to be
~ing with** (*subj: container*) estar
lleno a rebosar de; (*person*) reventar
por o de; **~ into** *vt fus* (*room etc*)
irrumpir en

**bury** ['bɛrɪ] *vt* enterrar; (*body*) enterrar, sepultar

**bus** [bʌs] *n* autobús *m*

**bush** [buʃ] *n* arbusto; (*scrub land*)
monte *m*; **to beat about the ~** an-
dar(se) con rodeos; **~y** *adj* (*thick*)
espeso, poblado

**busily** ['bɪzɪlɪ] *adv* afanosamente

**business** ['bɪznɪs] *n* (*matter*) asunto;
(*trading*) comercio, negocios *mpl*;
(*firm*) empresa, casa; (*occupation*)
oficio; **to be away on ~** estar en
viaje de negocios; **it's my ~ to ...**
me toca o corresponde ...; **it's none
of my ~** yo no tengo nada que ver;
**he means ~** habla en serio; **~like**
*adj* eficiente; **~man** *n* hombre *m* de
negocios; **~ trip** *n* viaje *m* de negocios; **~woman** *n* mujer *f* de negocios

**busker** ['bʌskə*] *n* (*BRIT*) músico/a
ambulante

**bus-stop** ['bʌsstɔp] *n* parada de
autobús

**bust** [bʌst] *n* (*ANAT*) pecho; (*sculpture*) busto ♦ *adj* (*inf: broken*) roto,
estropeado; **to go ~** quebrar

**bustle** ['bʌsl] *n* bullicio, movimiento
♦ *vi* menearse, apresurarse; **bust-
ling** *adj* (*town*) animado, bullicioso

**busy** ['bɪzɪ] *adj* ocupado, atareado;
(*shop, street*) concurrido, animado;
(*TEL: line*) comunicando ♦ *vt*: **to ~
o.s. with** ocuparse en; **~body** *n*
entrometido/a; **~ signal** (*US*) *n*
(*TEL*) señal *f* de comunicando

---

KEYWORD

**but** [bʌt] *conj* 1 pero; **he's not very
bright, ~ he's hard-working** no es
muy inteligente, pero es trabajador
2 (*in direct contradiction*) sino; **he's
not English ~ French** no es inglés

sino francés; **he didn't sing ~ he
shouted** no cantó sino que gritó
3 (*showing disagreement, surprise
etc*): **~ that's far too expensive!**
¡pero eso es carísimo!; **~ it does
work!** ¡(pero) sí que funciona!

♦ *prep* (*apart from, except*) menos,
salvo; **we've had nothing ~ trouble** no hemos tenido más que problemas; **no-one ~ him can do it** nadie
más que él puede hacerlo; **who ~ a
lunatic would do such a thing?**
¡sólo un loco haría una cosa así!; **~
for you/your help** si no fuera por ti/
tu ayuda; **anything ~ that** cualquier cosa menos eso

♦ *adv* (*just, only*): **she's ~ a child**
no es más que una niña; **had I ~
known** si lo hubiera sabido; **I can ~
try** al menos lo puedo intentar; **it's
all ~ finished** está casi acabado

**butcher** ['butʃə*] *n* carnicero ♦ *vt*
hacer una carnicería con; (*cattle etc*)
matar; **~'s (shop)** *n* carnicería

**butler** ['bʌtlə*] *n* mayordomo

**butt** [bʌt] *n* (*barrel*) tonel *m*; (*of
gun*) culata; (*of cigarette*) colilla;
(*BRIT: fig: target*) blanco ♦ *vt* dar
cabezadas contra, top(et)ar; **~ in** *vi*
(*interrupt*) interrumpir

**butter** ['bʌtə*] *n* mantequilla ♦ *vt*
untar con mantequilla; **~cup** *n* botón
*m* de oro

**butterfly** ['bʌtəflaɪ] *n* mariposa;
(*SWIMMING: also: ~ stroke*) braza
de mariposa

**buttocks** ['bʌtəks] *npl* nalgas *fpl*

**button** ['bʌtn] *n* botón *m*; (*US*) placa, chapa ♦ *vt* (*also: ~ up*) abotonar, abrochar ♦ *vi* abrocharse

**buttress** ['bʌtrɪs] *n* contrafuerte *m*

**buxom** ['bʌksəm] *adj* exuberante

**buy** [baɪ] (*pt, pp* **bought**) *vt* comprar
♦ *n* compra; **to ~ sb sth/sth from
sb** comprarle algo a alguien; **to ~
sb a drink** invitar a alguien a tomar
algo; **~er** *n* comprador(a) *m/f*

**buzz** [bʌz] *n* zumbido; (*inf: phone
call*) llamada (por teléfono) ♦ *vi*

zumbar; **~er** n timbre m; **~word** n palabra que está de moda

KEYWORD

**by** [baɪ] prep **1** (referring to cause, agent) por; de; **killed ~ lightning** muerto por un relámpago; **a painting ~ Picasso** un cuadro de Picasso **2** (referring to method, manner, means): **~ bus/car/train** en autobús/coche/tren; **to pay ~ cheque** pagar con un cheque; **~ moonlight/candlelight** a la luz de la luna/una vela; **~ saving hard, he ... ahorrando, ...**
**3** (via, through) por; **we came ~ Dover** vinimos por Dover
**4** (close to, past): **the house ~ the river** la casa junto al río; **she rushed ~ me** pasó a mi lado como una exhalación; **I go ~ the post office every day** paso por delante de Correos todos los días
**5** (time: not later than) para; (: during): **~ daylight** de día; **~ 4 o'clock** para las cuatro; **~ this time tomorrow** mañana a estas horas; **~ the time I got here it was too late** cuando llegué ya era demasiado tarde
**6** (amount): **~ the metre/kilo** por metro/kilo; **paid ~ the hour** pagado por hora
**7** (MATH, measure): **to divide/multiply ~ 3** dividir/multiplicar por 3; **a room 3 metres ~ 4** una habitación de 3 metros por 4; **it's broader ~ a metre** es un metro más ancho
**8** (according to) según, de acuerdo con; **it's 3 o'clock ~ my watch** según mi reloj, son las tres; **it's all right ~ me** por mí, está bien
**9**: (all) **~ oneself** etc todo solo; **he did it (all) ~ himself** lo hizo él solo; **he was standing (all) ~ himself** estaba de pie solo en un rincón
**10**: **~ the way** a propósito, por cierto; **this wasn't my idea, ~ the way** pues, no fue idea mía

♦ adv **1** see **go**; **pass** etc
**2**: **~ and ~** finalmente; **they'll come back ~ and ~** acabarán volviendo; **~ and large** en líneas generales, en general

**bye(-bye)** ['baɪ('baɪ)] excl adiós, hasta luego
**by(e)-law** n ordenanza municipal
**by-election** (BRIT) n elección f parcial
**bygone** ['baɪgɒn] adj pasado, del pasado ♦ n: **let ~s be ~s** lo pasado, pasado está
**bypass** ['baɪpɑːs] n carretera de circunvalación; (operación f de) by-pass m ♦ vt evitar
**by-product** n subproducto, derivado; (of situation) consecuencia
**bystander** ['baɪstændə*] n espectador(a) m/f
**byte** [baɪt] n (COMPUT) byte m, octeto
**byword** ['baɪwəːd] n: **to be a ~ for** ser conocidísimo por
**by-your-leave** n: **without so much as a ~** sin decir nada, sin dar ningún tipo de explicación

# C

**C** [siː] n (MUS) do m; abbr = **centigrade**
**C.A.** abbr = **chartered accountant**
**cab** [kæb] n taxi m; (of truck) cabina
**cabbage** ['kæbɪdʒ] n col f, berza
**cabin** ['kæbɪn] n cabaña; (on ship) camarote m; (on plane) cabina; **~ cruiser** n yate m de motor
**cabinet** ['kæbɪnɪt] n (POL) consejo de ministros; (furniture) armario; (also: display ~) vitrina
**cable** ['keɪbl] n cable m ♦ vt cablegrafiar; **~-car** n teleférico; **~ television** n televisión f por cable
**cache** [kæʃ] n (of weapons, drugs etc) alijo
**cackle** ['kækl] vi lanzar risotadas; (hen) cacarear

**cacti** ['kæktaɪ] npl of **cactus**

**cactus** ['kæktəs] (pl **cacti**) cacto

**cadge** [kædʒ] (inf) vt gorronear

**Caesarean** [siːˈzɛərɪən] adj: ~ (section) cesárea

**café** ['kæfeɪ] n café m

**cafeteria** [kæfɪˈtɪərɪə] n cafetería

**cage** [keɪdʒ] n jaula

**cagey** ['keɪdʒɪ] (inf) adj cauteloso, reservado

**cagoule** [kəˈguːl] n chubasquero

**cajole** [kəˈdʒəʊl] vt engatusar

**cake** [keɪk] n (CULIN: large) tarta, (: small) pastel m; (of soap) pastilla; ~d adj: ~d with cubierto de

**calculate** ['kælkjuleɪt] vt calcular; **calculating** adj (scheming) calculador(a); **calculation** [-'leɪʃən] n cálculo, cómputo; **calculator** n calculadora

**calendar** ['kæləndə*] n calendario; ~ **month/year** n mes m/año civil

**calf** [kɑːf] (pl **calves**) n (of cow) ternero, becerro; (of other animals) cría; (also: ~skin) piel f de becerro; (ANAT) pantorrilla

**calibre** ['kælɪbə*] (US **caliber**) n calibre m

**call** [kɔːl] vt llamar; (meeting) convocar ♦ vi (shout) llamar; (TEL) llamar (por teléfono), telefonear (esp AM); (visit: also: ~ in, ~ round) hacer una visita ♦ n llamada; (of bird) canto; **to be** ~**ed** llamarse; **on** ~ (nurse, doctor etc) de guardia; ~ **back** vi (return) volver; (TEL) volver a llamar; ~ **for** vt fus (demand) pedir, exigir; (fetch) venir por (SP), pasar por (AM); ~ **off** vt (cancel: meeting, race) cancelar; (: deal) anular; ~ **on** vt fus (visit) visitar; (turn to) acudir a; ~ **out** vi gritar, dar voces; ~ **up** vt (MIL) llamar al servicio militar; ~**box** (BRIT) n cabina telefónica; ~**er** n visita; (TEL) usuario/a; ~ **girl** n prostituta; ~-**in** (US) n (programa m) coloquio (por teléfono); ~**ing** n vocación f; (occupation) profesión f; ~**ing card** (US) n tarjeta comercial or de visita

**callous** ['kæləs] adj insensible, cruel

**calm** [kɑːm] adj tranquilo; (sea) liso, en calma ♦ n calma, tranquilidad f ♦ vt calmar, tranquilizar; ~ **down** vi calmarse, tranquilizarse ♦ vt calmar, tranquilizar

**Calor gas** ['kælə*-] ® n butano

**calorie** ['kælərɪ] n caloría

**calves** [kɑːvz] npl of **calf**

**camber** ['kæmbə*] n (of road) combadura, comba

**Cambodia** [kæmˈbəʊdʒə] n Camboya

**camcorder** ['kæmkɔːdə*] n cámara de vídeo portátil

**came** [keɪm] pt of **come**

**camel** ['kæməl] n camello

**cameo** ['kæmɪəʊ] n camafeo

**camera** ['kæmərə] n máquina fotográfica; (CINEMA, TV) cámara; **in** ~ (LAW) a puerta cerrada; ~**man** n cámara m

**camouflage** ['kæməflɑːʒ] n camuflaje m ♦ vt camuflar

**camp** [kæmp] n campamento, camping m; (MIL) campamento; (for prisoners) campo; (fig: faction) bando ♦ vi acampar ♦ adj afectado, afeminado

**campaign** [kæmˈpeɪn] n (MIL, POL etc) campaña ♦ vi hacer campaña

**camp**: ~**bed** (BRIT) n cama de campaña; ~**er** n campista m/f; (vehicle) caravana; ~**ing** n camping m; **to go** ~**ing** hacer camping; ~**site** n camping m

**campus** ['kæmpəs] n ciudad f universitaria

**can¹** [kæn] n (of oil, water) bidón m; (tin) lata, bote m ♦ vt enlatar

───────────
KEYWORD
───────────

**can²** (negative **cannot**, **can't**; conditional and pt **could**) aux vb **1** (be able to) poder; **you** ~ **do it if you try** puedes hacerlo si lo intentas; **I** ~**'t see you** no te veo

**2** (know how to) saber; **I** ~ **swim/play tennis/drive** sé nadar/jugar al tenis/conducir; ~ **you speak French?** ¿hablas or sabes hablar francés?

**3** (may) poder; ~ **I use your phone?** ¿me dejas or puedo usar tu teléfono?

**4** (expressing disbelief, puzzlement etc): **it ~'t be true!** ¡no puede ser (verdad)!; **what CAN we want?** ¿qué querrá?

**5** (expressing possibility, suggestion etc): **he could be in the library** podría estar en la biblioteca; **she could have been delayed** pudo haberse retrasado

---

**Canada** ['kænədə] n (el) Canadá; **Canadian** [kə'neɪdɪən] adj, n canadiense m/f

**canal** [kə'næl] n canal m

**canary** [kə'nɛərɪ] n canario; **C~ Islands** npl las (Islas) Canarias

**cancel** ['kænsəl] vt cancelar; (train) suprimir; (cross out) tachar, borrar; **~lation** [-'leɪʃən] n cancelación f; supresión f

**cancer** ['kænsə*] n cáncer m; **C~** (ASTROLOGY) Cáncer m

**candid** ['kændɪd] adj franco, abierto

**candidate** ['kændɪdeɪt] n candidato/a

**candle** ['kændl] n vela; (in church) cirio; **~light** n: **by ~light** a la luz de una vela; **~stick** n (single) candelero; (low) palmatoria; (bigger, ornate) candelabro

**candour** ['kændə*] (US **candor**) n franqueza

**candy** ['kændɪ] n azúcar m cande; (US) caramelo; **~-floss** (BRIT) n algodón m (azucarado)

**cane** [keɪn] n (BOT) caña; (stick) vara, palmeta; (for furniture) mimbre f ♦ (BRIT) vt (SCOL) castigar (con vara)

**canister** ['kænɪstə*] n bote m, lata; (of gas) bombona

**cannabis** ['kænəbɪs] n marijuana

**canned** [kænd] adj en lata, de lata

**cannibal** ['kænɪbəl] n caníbal m/f

**cannon** ['kænən] (pl ~ or ~s) n cañón m

**cannot** ['kænɔt] = can not

**canoe** [kə'nuː] n canoa; (SPORT) piragua

**canon** ['kænən] n (clergyman) canónigo; (standard) canon m

**can opener** n abrelatas m inv

**canopy** ['kænəpɪ] n dosel m; toldo

**can't** [kænt] = can not

**cantankerous** [kæn'tæŋkərəs] adj quisquilloso

**canteen** [kæn'tiːn] n (eating place) cantina; (BRIT: of cutlery) juego

**canter** ['kæntə*] vi ir a medio galope

**canvas** ['kænvəs] n (material) lona; (painting) lienzo; (NAUT) velas fpl

**canvass** ['kænvəs] vi (POL): **to ~ for** solicitar votos por ♦ vt (COMM) sondear

**canyon** ['kænjən] n cañón m

**cap** [kæp] n (hat) gorra; (of pen) capuchón m; (of bottle) tapa, tapón m; (contraceptive) diafragma m; (for toy gun) cápsula ♦ vt (outdo) superar; (limit) recortar

**capability** [keɪpə'bɪlɪtɪ] n capacidad f

**capable** ['keɪpəbl] adj capaz

**capacity** [kə'pæsɪtɪ] n capacidad f; (position) calidad f

**cape** [keɪp] n capa; (GEO) cabo

**caper** ['keɪpə*] n (CULIN: gen: ~s) alcaparra; (prank) broma

**capital** ['kæpɪtl] n (also: ~ **city**) capital f; (money) capital m; (also: ~ **letter**) mayúscula; **~ gains tax** n impuesto sobre las ganancias de capital; **~ism** n capitalismo; **~ist** adj, n capitalista m/f; **~ize** on vt fus aprovechar; **~ punishment** n pena de muerte

**capitulate** [kə'pɪtjuleɪt] vi capitular, rendirse

**Capricorn** ['kæprɪkɔːn] n (ASTROLOGY) Capricornio

**capsize** [kæp'saɪz] vt volcar, hacer zozobrar ♦ vi volcarse, zozobrar

**capsule** ['kæpsjuːl] n cápsula

**captain** ['kæptɪn] n capitán m

**caption** ['kæpʃən] n (heading) título; (to picture) leyenda

**captive** ['kæptɪv] adj, n cautivo/a m/f

**capture** ['kæptʃə*] vt prender, apresar; (animal, COMPUT) capturar; (place) tomar; (attention) captar, llamar ♦ n apresamiento; captura; toma; (data ~) formulación f de datos

**car** [ka:*] n coche m, carro (AM), automóvil m; (US: RAIL) vagón m

**carafe** [kə'ræf] n jarra

**carat** ['kærət] n quilate m

**caravan** ['kærəvæn] n (BRIT) caravana, ruló f; (in desert) caravana; ~ **site** (BRIT) n camping m para caravanas

**carbohydrate** [ka:bəu'haidreit] n hidrato de carbono; (food) fécula

**carbon** ['ka:bən] n carbono; ~ **paper** n papel m de carbón

**carburettor** [ka:bju'retə*] (US **carburetor**) n carburador m

**carcass** ['ka:kəs] n cadáver m (de animal)

**card** [ka:d] n (material) cartulina; (index ~ etc) ficha; (playing ~) carta, naipe m; (visiting ~, greetings ~ etc) tarjeta; ~**board** n cartón m

**cardigan** ['ka:dɪgən] n rebeca

**cardinal** ['ka:dɪnl] adj cardinal; (importance, principal) esencial ♦ n cardenal m

**card index** n fichero

**care** [keə*] n cuidado; (worry) inquietud f; (charge) cargo, custodia ♦ vi: **to ~ about** (person, animal) tener cariño a; (thing, idea) preocuparse por; ~ **of** en casa de, al cuidado de; **in sb's** ~ a cargo de uno; **to take** ~ **to** cuidarse de, tener cuidado de; **to take** ~ **of** cuidar; (problem etc) ocuparse de; **I don't** ~ no me importa; **I couldn't** ~ **less** no me trae sin cuidado; ~ **for** vt fus cuidar a; (like) querer

**career** [kə'rɪə*] n profesión f; (in work, school) carrera ♦ vi (also: ~ **along**) correr a toda velocidad; ~ **woman** n mujer f dedicada a su profesión

**carefree** ['keəfri:] adj despreocupado

**careful** ['keəful] adj cuidadoso; (cautious) cauteloso; (be) ~! ¡tenga cuidado!; ~**ly** adv con cuidado, cuidadosamente; con cautela

**careless** ['keəlis] adj descuidado; (heedless) poco atento; ~**ness** n descuido; falta de atención

**carer** ['keərə*] n enfermero/a m/f (official); (unpaid) persona que cuida a un pariente o vecino

**caress** [kə'res] n caricia ♦ vt acariciar

**caretaker** ['keəteikə*] n portero/a, conserje m/f

**car-ferry** n transbordador m para coches

**cargo** ['ka:gəu] (pl ~**es**) n cargamento, carga

**car hire** n alquiler m de automóviles

**Caribbean** [kærɪ'bi:ən] n: **the** ~ **(Sea)** el (Mar) Caribe

**caring** ['keərɪŋ] adj humanitario; (behaviour) afectuoso

**carnation** [ka:'neiʃən] n clavel m

**carnival** ['ka:nɪvəl] n carnaval m; (US: funfair) parque m de atracciones

**carol** ['kærəl] n (Christmas) ~ villancico

**car park** (BRIT) n aparcamiento, parking m

**carpenter** ['ka:pintə*] n carpintero/a.

**carpet** ['ka:pit] n alfombra; (fitted) moqueta ♦ vt alfombrar; ~ **slippers** npl zapatillas fpl; ~ **sweeper** n aparato para barrer alfombras

**car phone** n teléfono movil

**carriage** ['kærɪdʒ] n (BRIT: RAIL) vagón m; (horse-drawn) coche m; (of goods) transporte m; (: cost) porte m, flete m; ~**way** (BRIT) n (part of road) calzada

**carrier** ['kærɪə*] n (transport company) transportista, empresa de transportes; (MED) portador m; ~ **bag** (BRIT) n bolsa de papel or plástico

**carrot** ['kærət] n zanahoria

**carry** ['kærɪ] vt (subj: person) llevar; (transport) transportar; (involve: responsibilities etc) entrañar, implicar; (MED) ser portador de ♦ vi (sound) oírse; **to get carried away** (fig) entusiasmarse; ~ **on** vi (continue) seguir (adelante), continuar ♦ vt proseguir, continuar; ~ **out** vt (orders) cumplir; (investigation) llevar a cabo, realizar; ~ **cot** (BRIT) n cuna portátil; ~**on** (inf) n (fuss) lío

**cart** [kɑ:t] n carro, carreta ♦ vt (inf: transport) acarrear

**carton** ['kɑ:tən] n (box) caja (de cartón); (of milk etc) bote m; (of yogurt) tarrina

**cartoon** [kɑ:'tu:n] n (PRESS) caricatura; (comic strip) tira cómica; (film) dibujos mpl animados

**cartridge** ['kɑ:trɪdʒ] n cartucho; (of pen) recambio; (of record player) cápsula

**carve** [kɑ:v] vt (meat) trinchar; (wood, stone) cincelar, esculpir; (initials etc) grabar; ~ **up** vt dividir, repartir; **carving** n (object) escultura; (design) talla; (art) tallado; **carving knife** n trinchante m

**car wash** n lavado de coches

**case** [keɪs] n (container) caja; (MED) caso; (for jewels etc) estuche m; (LAW) causa, proceso; (BRIT: also: suit~) maleta; **in** ~ **of** en caso de; **in any** ~ en todo caso; **just in** ~ por si acaso

**cash** [kæʃ] n dinero en efectivo, dinero contante ♦ vt cobrar, hacer efectivo; **to pay (in)** ~ pagar al contado; ~ **on delivery** cóbrese al entregar; ~**book** n libro de caja; ~ **card** n tarjeta f dinero; ~**desk** (BRIT) n caja; ~ **dispenser** n cajero automático

**cashew** [kæ'ʃu:] n (also: ~ **nut**) anacardo

**cash flow** n flujo de fondos, cash flow m

**cashier** [kæ'ʃɪə*] n cajero/a

**cashmere** ['kæʃmɪə*] n cachemira

**cash register** n caja

**casing** ['keɪsɪŋ] n revestimiento

**casino** [kə'si:nəu] n casino

**casket** ['kɑ:skɪt] n cofre m, estuche m; (US: coffin) ataúd m

**casserole** ['kæsərəul] n (food, pot) cazuela

**cassette** [kæ'set] n cassette f; ~ **player/recorder** n tocacassettes m inv, cassette m

**cast** [kɑ:st] (pt, pp cast) vt (throw) echar, arrojar, lanzar; (glance, eyes) dirigir; (THEATRE): **to** ~ **sb as Othello** dar a uno el papel de Otelo ♦ vi (FISHING) lanzar ♦ n (THEATRE) reparto; (also: plaster ~) vaciado; **to** ~ **one's vote** votar; **to** ~ **doubt** on suscitar dudas acerca de; ~ **off** vi (NAUT) desamarrar; (KNITTING) cerrar (los puntos); ~ **on** vi (KNITTING) poner los puntos

**castanets** [kæstə'nets] npl castañuelas fpl

**castaway** ['kɑ:stəweɪ] n náufrago/a

**caste** [kɑ:st] n casta

**caster sugar** ['kɑ:stə*-] (BRIT) n azúcar m extrafino

**Castile** [kæs'ti:l] n Castilla; **Castilian** adj, n castellano/a m/f

**casting vote** ['kɑ:stɪŋ-] (BRIT) n voto decisivo

**cast iron** n hierro fundido

**castle** ['kɑ:sl] n castillo; (CHESS) torre f

**castor** ['kɑ:stə*] n (wheel) ruedecilla; ~ **oil** n aceite m de ricino

**casual** ['kæʒjul] adj fortuito; (irregular: work etc) eventual, temporero; (unconcerned) despreocupado; (clothes) de sport; ~**ly** adv de manera despreocupada; (dress) de sport

**casualty** ['kæʒjultɪ] n víctima, herido; (dead) muerto; (MED: department) urgencias fpl

**cat** [kæt] n gato; (big ~) felino

**Catalan** ['kætələn] adj, n catalán/ana m/f

**catalogue** ['kætəlɔg] (US **catalog**) n catálogo ♦ vt catalogar

**Catalonia** [kætə'ləunɪə] n Cataluña

**catalyst** ['kætəlɪst] n catalizador m

**catalytic convertor** [kætə'lɪtɪk

kən'vɜ:tə*] n catalizador m

**catapult** ['kætəpʌlt] n tirachinas m inv

**catarrh** [kə'tɑ:*] n catarro m

**catastrophe** [kə'tæstrəfɪ] n catástrofe f

**catch** [kætʃ] (pt, pp **caught**) vt coger (SP), agarrar (AM); (arrest) detener; (grasp) asir; (breath) contener; (surprise: person) sorprender; (attract: attention) captar; (hear) oír; (MED) contagiarse de, coger; (also: ~ up) alcanzar ♦ vi (fire) encenderse; (in branches etc) engancharse ♦ n (fish etc) pesca; (act of catching) cogida; (hidden problem) dificultad f; (game) pilla-pilla; (of lock) pestillo, cerradura; to ~ **fire** encenderse; to ~ **sight of** divisar; to ~ **on** vi (understand) caer en la cuenta; (grow popular) hacerse popular; to ~ **up** vi (fig) ponerse al día

**catching** ['kætʃɪŋ] adj (MED) contagioso

**catchment area** ['kætʃmənt-] (BRIT) n zona de captación

**catchphrase** ['kætʃfreɪz] n lema m, eslogan m

**catchy** ['kætʃɪ] adj (tune) pegadizo

**category** ['kætɪgərɪ] n categoría, clase f

**cater** ['keɪtə*] vi: to ~ **for** (BRIT) abastecer a; (needs) atender a; (COMM: parties etc) proveer comida a; ~**er** n abastecedor(a) m/f, proveedor(a) m/f; ~**ing** n (trade) hostelería

**caterpillar** ['kætəpɪlə*] n oruga, gusano; ~ **track** n rodado de oruga

**cathedral** [kə'θi:drəl] n catedral f

**catholic** ['kæθəlɪk] adj (tastes etc) amplio; **C~** adj, n (REL) católico/a m/f

**cat's-eye** (BRIT) n (AUT) catafoto m

**cattle** ['kætl] npl ganado

**catty** ['kætɪ] adj malicioso, rencoroso

**caucus** ['kɔ:kəs] n (POL) camarilla política; (: US: to elect candidates) comité m electoral

**caught** [kɔ:t] pt, pp of **catch**

**cauliflower** ['kɔlɪflauə*] n coliflor f

**cause** [kɔ:z] n causa, motivo, razón f; (principle: also: POL) causa ♦ vt causar

**caustic** ['kɔ:stɪk] adj cáustico; (fig) mordaz

**caution** ['kɔ:ʃən] n cautela, prudencia; (warning) advertencia, amonestación f ♦ vt amonestar

**cautious** ['kɔ:ʃəs] adj cauteloso, prudente, precavido; ~**ly** adv con cautela

**cavalier** [kævə'lɪə*] adj arrogante, desdeñoso

**cavalry** ['kævəlrɪ] n caballería

**cave** [keɪv] n cueva, caverna; ~ **in** vi (roof etc) derrumbarse, hundirse; ~**man** n cavernícola m, troglodita m

**cavity** ['kævɪtɪ] n hueco, cavidad f; (in tooth) caries f inv

**cavort** [kə'vɔ:t] vi dar brincos

**CB** n abbr (= Citizens' Band (Radio)) banda ciudadana

**CBI** n abbr (= Confederation of British Industry) ≈ C.E.O.E. f (SP)

**cc** abbr = **cubic centimetres**; **carbon copy**

**CD** n abbr (= compact disc) DC m; (player) (reproductor m de) disco compacto; ~**-ROM** [si:di:'rɔm] n abbr CD-ROM m

**cease** [si:s] vt, vi cesar; ~**fire** n alto m el fuego; ~**less** adj incesante

**cedar** ['si:də*] n cedro

**ceiling** ['si:lɪŋ] n techo; (fig) límite m

**celebrate** ['selɪbreɪt] vt celebrar ♦ vi divertirse; ~**d** adj célebre; **celebration** [-'breɪʃən] n fiesta, celebración f

**celery** ['selərɪ] n apio

**celibacy** ['selɪbəsɪ] n celibato

**cell** [sel] n celda; (BIOL) célula; (ELEC) elemento

**cellar** ['selə*] n sótano; (for wine) bodega

**'cello** ['tʃeləu] n violoncelo

**cellophane** ['seləfeɪn] n celofán m

**cellphone** ['selfəun] n teléfono celular

**Celt** [kelt, selt] adj, n celta m/f; ~**ic** adj celta

**cement** [sə'ment] n cemento; ~ **mix-**

er n hormigonera

**cemetery** ['sɛmɪtrɪ] n cementerio

**censor** ['sɛnsə*] n censor m ♦ vt (cut) censurar; ~ship n censura

**censure** ['sɛnʃə*] vt censurar

**census** ['sɛnsəs] n censo

**cent** [sɛnt] n (US: coin) centavo, céntimo; see also **per**

**centenary** [sɛn'tiːnərɪ] n centenario

**center** ['sɛntə*] (US) = **centre**

**centi...** [sɛntɪ] prefix: ~**grade** adj centígrado, ~**litre** (US ~**liter**) n centilitro; ~**metre** (US ~**meter**) n centímetro

**centipede** ['sɛntɪpiːd] n ciempiés m inv

**central** ['sɛntrəl] adj central; (of house etc) central; **C~ America** n Centroamérica; ~ **heating** n calefacción f central; ~**ize** vt centralizar

**centre** ['sɛntə*] (US **center**) n centro; (fig) núcleo ♦ vt centrar; ~-**forward** n (SPORT) delantero centro; ~-**half** n (SPORT) medio centro

**century** ['sɛntjʊrɪ] n siglo; 20th ~ siglo veinte

**ceramic** [sɪ'ræmɪk] adj cerámico; ~**s** n cerámica

**cereal** ['siːrɪəl] n cereal m

**cerebral** ['sɛrɪbrəl] adj cerebral; intelectual

**ceremony** ['sɛrɪmənɪ] n ceremonia; **to stand on** ~ hacer ceremonias, estar de cumplido

**certain** ['sɜːtən] adj seguro; (person): **a** ~ **Mr Smith** un tal Sr Smith; (particular, some) cierto; **for** ~ a ciencia cierta; ~**ly** adv (undoubtedly) ciertamente; (of course) desde luego, por supuesto; ~**ty** n certeza, certidumbre f, seguridad f; (inevitability) certeza

**certificate** [sə'tɪfɪkɪt] n certificado

**certified** ['sɜːtɪfaɪd]: ~ **mail** (US) n correo certificado; ~ **public accountant** (US) n contable m/f diplomado/a

**certify** ['sɜːtɪfaɪ] vt certificar; (award diploma to) conceder un diploma a; (declare insane) declarar loco

**cervical** ['sɜːvɪkl] adj cervical

**cervix** ['sɜːvɪks] n cuello del útero

**cf.** abbr (= compare) cfr

**CFC** n abbr clorofluorocarbono

**ch.** abbr (= chapter) cap

**chafe** [tʃeɪf] vt (rub) rozar

**chagrin** [ʃ'grɪn] n (annoyance) disgusto; (disappointment) decepción f

**chain** [tʃeɪn] n cadena; (of mountains) cordillera; (of events) sucesión f ♦ vt (also: ~ **up**) encadenar; ~ re-**action** n reacción f en cadena; ~-**smoke** vi fumar un cigarrillo tras otro; ~ **store** n tienda de una cadena, gran almacén

**chair** [tʃɛə*] n silla; (armchair) sillón m, butaca; (of university) cátedra; (of meeting etc) presidencia ♦ vt (meeting) presidir; ~**lift** n telesilla; ~**man** n presidente m

**chalet** ['ʃæleɪ] n chalet m

**chalk** [tʃɔːk] n (GEO) creta; (for writing) tiza (SP), gis m (AM)

**challenge** ['tʃælɪndʒ] n desafío, reto ♦ vt desafiar, retar; (statement, right) poner en duda; **to** ~ **sb to do sth** retar a uno a que haga algo; ~**ing** adj exigente; (tone) desafío

**chamber** ['tʃeɪmbə*] n cámara, sala; (POL) cámara; (BRIT: LAW: gen pl) despacho; ~ **of commerce** n cámara de comercio; ~**maid** n camarera; ~ **music** n música de cámara

**chamois** ['ʃæmwɑː] n gamuza

**champagne** [ʃæm'peɪn] n champaña m, champán m

**champion** ['tʃæmpɪən] n campeón/ona m/f; (of cause) defensor(a) m/f; ~**ship** n campeonato

**chance** [tʃɑːns] n (opportunity) ocasión f, oportunidad f; (likelihood) posibilidad f; (risk) riesgo ♦ vt arriesgar, probar ♦ adj fortuito, casual; **to** ~ **it** arriesgarse, intentarlo; **to take a** ~ arriesgarse; **by** ~ por casualidad

**chancellor** ['tʃɑːnsələ*] n canciller m; **C~ of the Exchequer** (BRIT) n Ministro de Hacienda

**chandelier** [ʃændə'lɪə*] n araña (de
luces)

**change** [tʃeɪndʒ] vt cambiar; (replace) cambiar, reemplazar; (gear,
clothes, job) cambiar de; (transform) transformar ♦ vi cambiar(se);
(trains) hacer transbordo; (traffic
lights) cambiar de color; (be transformed): to ~ into transformarse en
♦ n cambio; (alteration) modificación f, transformación f; (of clothes)
muda; (coins) suelto, sencillo; (money returned) vuelta; to ~ gear
(AUT) cambiar de marcha; to ~
one's mind cambiar de opinión or
idea; for a ~ para variar; ~able
adj (weather) cambiable; ~
machine n máquina de cambio;
~over n (to new system) cambio

**changing** [tʃeɪndʒɪŋ] adj cambiante; ~ room n (BRIT) vestuario

**channel** [tʃænl] n (TV) canal m; (of
river) cauce m; (groove) conducto;
(fig: medium) medio ♦ vt (river etc)
encauzar; the (English) C~ el Canal de la Mancha; the C~ Islands
las Islas Normandas

**chant** [tʃɑːnt] n (of crowd) gritos
mpl; (REL) canto ♦ vt (slogan,
word) repetir a gritos

**chaos** [keɪɔs] n caos m

**chap** [tʃæp] (BRIT: inf) n (man) tío,
tipo

**chapel** [tʃæpəl] n capilla

**chaperone** [ʃæpərəun] n carabina

**chaplain** [tʃæplɪn] n capellán m

**chapped** [tʃæpt] adj agrietado

**chapter** [tʃæptə*] n capítulo

**char** [tʃɑː*] vt (burn) carbonizar,
chamuscar ♦ n (BRIT) = charlady

**character** [kærɪktə*] n carácter m,
naturaleza, índole f; (moral strength,
personality) carácter; (in novel, film)
personaje m; ~istic [-'rɪstɪk] adj característico ♦ n característica; ~ize
vt caracterizar

**charcoal** [tʃɑːkəul] n carbón m vegetal; (ART) carboncillo

**charge** [tʃɑːdʒ] n (LAW) cargo, acusación f; (cost) precio, coste m; (re-

sponsibility) cargo ♦ vt (LAW): to ~
(with) acusar (de); (battery) cargar; (price) pedir; (customer) cobrar ♦ vi precipitarse; (MIL) cargar, atacar; ~s npl: to reverse the
~s (BRIT: TEL) revertir el cobro;
to take ~ of hacerse cargo de, encargarse de; to be in ~ of estar encargado de; (business) mandar; how
much do you ~? ¿cuánto cobra usted?; to ~ an expense (up) to sb's
account cargar algo a cuenta de alguien; ~ card n tarjeta de cuenta

**charitable** [tʃærɪtəbl] adj benéfico

**charity** [tʃærɪtɪ] n caridad f; (organization) sociedad f benéfica; (money,
gifts) limosnas fpl

**charlady** [tʃɑːleɪdɪ] (BRIT) n mujer
f de la limpieza

**charlatan** [tʃɑːlətən] n farsante m/f

**charm** [tʃɑːm] n encanto, atractivo;
(talisman) hechizo; (on bracelet) dije
m ♦ vt encantar; ~ing adj encanta-
dor(a)

**chart** [tʃɑːt] n (diagram) cuadro;
(graph) gráfica; (map) carta de navegación ♦ vt (course) trazar; (progress) seguir; ~s npl (Top 40): the
~s = los 40 principales (SP)

**charter** [tʃɑːtə*] vt (plane) alquilar;
(ship) fletar ♦ n (document) carta;
(of university, company) estatutos
mpl; ~ed accountant (BRIT) n contable m/f diplomado/a; ~ flight n
vuelo chárter

**charwoman** [tʃɑːwumən] n = charlady

**chase** [tʃeɪs] vt (pursue) perseguir;
(also: ~ away) ahuyentar ♦ n persecución f

**chasm** [kæzəm] n sima

**chassis** [ʃæsɪ] n chasis m

**chat** [tʃæt] vi (also: have a ~) charlar ♦ n charla; ~ show (BRIT) n
programa m de entrevistas

**chatter** [tʃætə*] vi (person) charlar;
(teeth) castañetear ♦ n (of birds)
parloteo; (of people) charla, cháchar-
ra; ~box (inf) n parlanchín/ina m/f

**chatty** [tʃætɪ] adj (style) informal;

(*person*) hablador(a)

**chauffeur** ['ʃəufə*] n chófer m

**chauvinist** ['ʃəuvɪnɪst] n (*male ~*) machista m; (*nationalist*) chovinista m/f

**cheap** [tʃiːp] adj barato; (*joke*) de mal gusto; (*poor quality*) de mala calidad ♦ adv barato; **~er** adj más barato; **~ly** adv barato, a bajo precio

**cheat** [tʃiːt] vi hacer trampa ♦ vt: to ~ sb (out of sth) estafar (algo) a uno ♦ n (*person*) tramposo/a

**check** [tʃek] vt (*examine*) controlar; (*facts*) comprobar; (*halt*) parar, detener; (*restrain*) refrenar, restringir ♦ n (*inspection*) control m, inspección f; (*curb*) freno; (*US: bill*) nota, cuenta; (*US*) = **cheque**; (*pattern: gen pl*) cuadro ♦ adj (*also*: **~ed**: *pattern, cloth*) a cuadros; **~ in** vi (*at hotel*) firmar el registro; (*at airport*) facturar el equipaje ♦ vt (*luggage*) facturar; **~ out** vi (*of hotel*) marcharse; **~ up** vi: to ~ up on sth comprobar algo; to ~ up on sb investigar a alguien; (*check etc*) **~ered** (*US*) adj = **chequered**; **~ers** (*US*) n juego de damas; **~-in (desk)** n mostrador m de facturación; **~ing account** (*US*) n cuenta corriente; **~mate** n jaque m mate; **~out** n caja; **~point** n (*punto de*) control m; **~room** (*US*) n consigna; **~up** n (*MED*) reconocimiento general

**cheek** [tʃiːk] n mejilla; (*impudence*) descaro; **what a ~!** ¡qué cara!; **~bone** n pómulo; **~y** adj fresco, descarado

**cheep** [tʃiːp] vi piar

**cheer** [tʃɪə*] vt vitorear, aplaudir; (*gladden*) alegrar, animar ♦ vi dar vivas ♦ n viva m; **~s** npl aplausos mpl; **~s!** ¡salud!; **~ up** vi animarse ♦ vt alegrar, animar; **~ful** adj alegre

**cheerio** [tʃɪərɪ'əu] (*BRIT*) excl ¡hasta luego!

**cheese** [tʃiːz] n queso; **~board** n tabla de quesos

**cheetah** ['tʃiːtə] n leopardo cazador

**chef** [ʃef] n jefe/a m/f de cocina

**chemical** ['kemɪkəl] adj químico ♦ n producto químico

**chemist** ['kemɪst] n (*BRIT: pharmacist*) farmacéutico/a; (*scientist*) químico/a; **~ry** n química; **~'s (shop)** (*BRIT*) n farmacia

**cheque** [tʃek] (*US* **check**) n cheque m; **~book** n talonario de cheques (*SP*), chequera (*AM*); **~ card** n tarjeta de cheque

**chequered** ['tʃekəd] (*US* **checkered**) adj (*fig*) accidentado

**cherish** ['tʃerɪʃ] vt (*love*) querer, apreciar; (*protect*) cuidar; (*hope etc*) abrigar

**cherry** ['tʃerɪ] n cereza; (*also*: ~ **tree**) cerezo

**chess** [tʃes] n ajedrez m; **~board** n tablero de ajedrez

**chest** [tʃest] n (*ANAT*) pecho; (*box*) cofre m, cajón m; **~ of drawers** n cómoda

**chestnut** ['tʃesnʌt] n castaña; (*also*: **~ tree**) n castaño

**chew** [tʃuː] vt mascar, masticar; **~ing gum** n chicle m

**chic** [ʃik] adj elegante

**chick** [tʃik] n pollito, polluelo; (*inf: girl*) chica

**chicken** ['tʃikɪn] n gallina, pollo; (*food*) pollo; (*inf: coward*) gallina m/f; **~ out** (*inf*) vi rajarse; **~pox** n varicela

**chicory** ['tʃɪkərɪ] n (*for coffee*) achicoria; (*salad*) escarola

**chief** [tʃiːf] n jefe/a m/f ♦ adj principal; **~ executive** n director/a m/f general; **~ly** adv principalmente

**chiffon** ['ʃifɔn] n gasa

**chilblain** ['tʃilblein] n sabañón m

**child** [tʃaild] (*pl* **children**) n niño/a; (*offspring*) hijo/a; **~birth** n parto; **~hood** n niñez f, infancia; **~ish** adj pueril, aniñado; **~like** adj de niño/a; **~ minder** (*BRIT*) n niñera; **~ren** ['tʃildrən] npl of **child**

**Chile** ['tʃili] n Chile m; **~an** adj, n chileno/a m/f

**chill** [tʃɪl] n frío; (MED) resfriado ♦ vt enfriar; (CULIN) congelar

**chilli** [ˈtʃɪlɪ] (BRIT) n chile m (SP), ají m (AM)

**chilly** [ˈtʃɪlɪ] adj frío

**chime** [tʃaɪm] n repique m; (of clock) campanada ♦ vi repicar; sonar

**chimney** [ˈtʃɪmnɪ] n chimenea; ~ **sweep** n deshollinador m

**chimpanzee** [tʃɪmpænˈziː] n chimpancé m

**chin** [tʃɪn] n mentón m, barbilla

**china** [ˈtʃaɪnə] n porcelana; (crockery) loza

**China** [ˈtʃaɪnə] n China; **Chinese** [tʃaɪˈniːz] adj chino, n inv chino/a; (LING) chino

**chink** [tʃɪŋk] n (opening) grieta, hendedura; (noise) tintineo

**chip** [tʃɪp] n (gen pl: CULIN: BRIT) patata (SP) o papa (AM) frita; (: US: also: potato ~) patata or papa frita; (of wood) astilla; (of glass, stone) lasca; (at poker) ficha; (COMPUT) chip m ♦ vt (cup, plate) desconchar; ~ **in** (inf) vi interrumpir; (contribute) compartir los gastos

**chiropodist** [kɪˈrɔpədɪst] (BRIT) n pedicuro/a, callista m/f

**chirp** [tʃəːp] vi (bird) gorjear, piar

**chisel** [ˈtʃɪzl] n (for wood) escoplo; (for stone) cincel m

**chit** [tʃɪt] n nota

**chitchat** [ˈtʃɪttʃæt] n chismes mpl, habladurías fpl

**chivalry** [ˈʃɪvəlrɪ] n caballerosidad f

**chives** [tʃaɪvz] npl cebollinos mpl

**chlorine** [ˈklɔːriːn] n cloro

**chock-a-block** [ˈtʃɔkəˈblɔk] adj, **chockfull** [tʃɔkˈful] adj atestado

**chocolate** [ˈtʃɔklɪt] n chocolate m; (sweet) bombón m

**choice** [tʃɔɪs] n elección f, selección f; (option) opción f; (preference) preferencia ♦ adj escogido

**choir** [ˈkwaɪə*] n coro; ~**boy** n niño de coro

**choke** [tʃəuk] vi ahogarse; (on food) atragantarse ♦ vt estrangular, aho-

gar; (block): **to be** ~**d with** estar atascado de ♦ n (AUT) estárter m

**cholesterol** [kəˈlestərɔl] n colesterol m

**choose** [tʃuːz] (pt chose, pp chosen) vt escoger, elegir; (team) seleccionar; **to** ~ **to do sth** optar por hacer algo

**choosy** [ˈtʃuːzɪ] adj delicado

**chop** [tʃɔp] vt (wood) cortar, tajar; (CULIN: also: ~ **up**) picar ♦ n (CULIN) chuleta; ~**s** npl (jaws) boca, labios mpl

**chopper** [ˈtʃɔpə*] n (helicopter) helicóptero

**choppy** [ˈtʃɔpɪ] adj (sea) picado, agitado

**chopsticks** [ˈtʃɔpstɪks] npl palillos mpl

**chord** [kɔːd] n (MUS) acorde m

**chore** [tʃɔː*] n faena, tarea; (routine task) trabajo rutinario

**chortle** [ˈtʃɔːtl] vi reír entre dientes

**chorus** [ˈkɔːrəs] n coro; (repeated part of song) estribillo

**chose** [tʃəuz] pt of choose

**chosen** [ˈtʃəuzn] pp of choose

**Christ** [kraɪst] n Cristo

**christen** [ˈkrɪsn] vt bautizar

**Christian** [ˈkrɪstɪən] adj, n cristiano/a m/f; ~**ity** [-ˈænɪtɪ] n cristianismo; ~ **name** n nombre m de pila

**Christmas** [ˈkrɪsməs] n Navidad f; **Merry** ~! ¡Felices Pascuas!; ~ **card** n crismas m inv, tarjeta de Navidad; ~ **Day** n día m de Navidad; ~ **Eve** n Nochebuena; ~ **tree** n árbol m de Navidad

**chrome** [krəum] n cromo

**chronic** [ˈkrɔnɪk] adj crónico

**chronological** [krɔnəˈlɔdʒɪkəl] adj cronológico

**chubby** [ˈtʃʌbɪ] adj regordete

**chuck** [tʃʌk] (inf) vt lanzar, arrojar; (BRIT: also: ~ **up**) abandonar; ~ **out** vt (person) echar (fuera); (rubbish etc) tirar

**chuckle** [ˈtʃʌkl] vi reírse entre dientes

**chug** [tʃʌg] vi resoplar; (car, boat)

*also:* ~ *along*) avanzar traqueteando

**chum** [tʃʌm] *n* compañero/a

**chunk** [tʃʌŋk] *n* pedazo, trozo

**church** [tʃɜːtʃ] *n* iglesia; **~yard** *n* cementerio

**churlish** [tʃɜːlɪʃ] *adj* grosero

**churn** [tʃɜːn] *n* (*for butter*) mantequera; (*for milk*) lechera; ~ **out** *vt* producir en serie

**chute** [ʃuːt] *n* (*also: rubbish* ~) vertedero; (*for coal etc*) rampa de caída

**chutney** [tʃʌtnɪ] *n* condimento a base de frutas de la India

**CIA** (*US*) *n abbr* = *Central Intelligence Agency*) CIA *f*

**CID** (*BRIT*) *n abbr* (= *Criminal Investigation Department*) ≈ B.I.C. *f* (*SP*)

**cider** [saɪdə*] *n* sidra

**cigar** [sɪɡɑː*] *n* puro

**cigarette** [sɪɡəˈret] *n* cigarrillo (*SP*), cigarro (*AM*); pitillo; ~ **case** *n* pitillera; ~ **end** *n* colilla

**Cinderella** [sɪndəˈrelə] *n* Cenicienta

**cinders** [sɪndəz] *npl* cenizas *fpl*

**cine-camera** [sɪnɪ-] (*BRIT*) *n* cámara cinematográfica

**cinema** [sɪnəmə] *n* cine *m*

**cinnamon** [sɪnəmən] *n* canela

**circle** [sɜːkl] *n* círculo *m*; (*in theatre*) anfiteatro ♦ *vi* dar vueltas ♦ *vt* (*surround*) rodear, cercar; (*move round*) dar la vuelta a

**circuit** [sɜːkɪt] *n* circuito *m*; (*tour*) gira; (*track*) pista; (*lap*) vuelta; **~ous** [sɜːˈkjuːtəs] *adj* indirecto

**circular** [sɜːkjulə*] *adj* circular ♦ *n* circular *f*

**circulate** [sɜːkjuleɪt] *vi* circular; (*person: at party etc*) hablar con los invitados ♦ *vt* poner en circulación; **circulation** [-ˈleɪʃən] *n* circulación *f*; (*of newspaper*) tirada

**circumcise** [sɜːkəmsaɪz] *vt* circuncidar

**circumspect** [sɜːkəmspekt] *adj* prudente

**circumstances** [sɜːkəmstənsɪz] *npl* circunstancias *fpl*; (*financial condition*) situación *f* económica

**circumvent** [sɜːkəmvent] *vt* burlar

**circus** [sɜːkəs] *n* circo

**CIS** *n abbr* (= *Commonwealth of Independent States*) CEI *f*

**cistern** [sɪstən] *n* tanque *m*, depósito; (*in toilet*) cisterna

**citizen** [sɪtɪzn] *n* (*POL*) ciudadano/a; (*of city*) vecino/a, habitante *m*/*f*; **~ship** *n* ciudadanía

**citrus fruits** [sɪtrəs-] *npl* agrios *mpl*

**city** [sɪtɪ] *n* ciudad *f*; **the C~** centro financiero de Londres

**civic** [sɪvɪk] *adj* cívico; (*authorities*) municipal; ~ **centre** (*BRIT*) *n* centro público

**civil** [sɪvɪl] *adj* civil; (*polite*) atento, cortés; ~ **engineer** *n* ingeniero de caminos (, canales y puertos); **~ian** [sɪˈvɪlɪən] *adj* civil (*no militar*) ♦ *n* civil *m*/*f*, paisano/a

**civilization** [sɪvɪlaɪˈzeɪʃən] *n* civilización *f*

**civilized** [sɪvɪlaɪzd] *adj* civilizado

**civil:** ~ **law** *n* derecho civil; ~ **servant** *n* funcionario/a del Estado; **C~ Service** *n* administración *f* pública; ~ **war** *n* guerra civil

**clad** [klæd] *adj:* ~ (**in**) vestido (de)

**claim** [kleɪm] *vt* exigir, reclamar; (*rights etc*) reivindicar; (*assert*) pretender ♦ *vi* (*for insurance*) reclamar ♦ *n* reclamación *f*; pretensión *f*; **~ant** *n* demandante *m*/*f*

**clairvoyant** [kleəˈvɔɪənt] *n* clarividente *m*/*f*

**clam** [klæm] *n* almeja

**clamber** [klæmbə*] *vi* trepar

**clammy** [klæmɪ] *adj* frío y húmedo

**clamour** [klæmə*] (*US* **clamor**) *vi:* to ~ **for** clamar por, pedir a voces

**clamp** [klæmp] *n* abrazadera, grapa ♦ *vt* (*2 things together*) cerrar fuertemente; (*one thing on another*) afianzar (con abrazadera); ~ **down on** *vt fus* (*subj: government, police*) reforzar la lucha contra

**clang** [klæŋ] *vi* sonar, hacer estruendo

**clap** [klæp] *vi* aplaudir; **~ping** *n* aplausos *mpl*

**claret** ['klærət] n clarete m

**clarify** ['klærɪfaɪ] vt aclarar

**clarinet** [klærɪ'net] n clarinete m

**clash** [klæʃ] n enfrentamiento; choque m; desacuerdo; estruendo ♦ vi (fight) enfrentarse; (beliefs) chocar; (disagree) estar en desacuerdo; (colours) desentonar; (two events) coincidir

**clasp** [klɑːsp] n (hold) apretón m; (of necklace, bag) cierre m ♦ vt apretar; abrazar

**class** [klɑːs] n clase f ♦ vt clasificar

**classic** ['klæsɪk] adj, n clásico; ~al adj clásico

**classified** ['klæsɪfaɪd] adj (information) reservado; ~ **advertisement** n anuncio por palabras

**classify** ['klæsɪfaɪ] vt clasificar

**classmate** ['klɑːsmeɪt] n compañero/a de clase

**classroom** ['klɑːsrum] n aula

**clatter** ['klætə*] n estrépito ♦ vi hacer ruido or estrépito

**clause** [klɔːz] n cláusula; (LING) oración f

**claw** [klɔː] n (of cat) uña; (of bird of prey) garra; (of lobster) pinza; ~ **at** vt fus arañar

**clay** [kleɪ] n arcilla

**clean** [kliːn] adj limpio; (record, reputation) bueno, intachable; (joke) decente ♦ vt limpiar; (hands etc) lavar; ~ **out** vt limpiar; ~ **up** vt limpiar, asear; ~**cut** adj (person) bien parecido; ~**er** n (person) asistenta; (substance) producto para la limpieza; ~**er's** n tintorería; ~**ing** n limpieza; ~**liness** ['klenlɪnɪs] n limpieza

**cleanse** [klenz] vt limpiar; ~**r** n (for face) crema limpiadora

**clean-shaven** adj sin barba, afeitado

**cleansing department** (BRIT) n departamento de limpieza

**clear** [klɪə*] adj claro; (road, way) libre; (conscience) limpio, tranquilo; (skin) terso; (sky) despejado ♦ v saltar por encima de; (cheque) aceptar ♦ vi (fog etc) despejarse ♦ adv: ~ **of** a distancia de; **to** ~ **the table** recoger or levantar la mesa; ~ **up** vt limpiar; (mystery) aclarar, resolver; ~**ance** n (removal) despeje m; (permission) acreditada f; ~**cut** adj bien definido, nítido; ~**ing** n (in wood) claro; ~**ing bank** (BRIT) n cámara de compensación; ~**ly** adv claramente; (evidently) sin duda; ~**way** (BRIT) n carretera donde no se puede parar

**cleaver** ['kliːvə] n cuchilla (de carnicero)

**clef** [klef] n (MUS) clave f

**cleft** [kleft] n (in rock) grieta, hendedura

**clench** [klentʃ] vt apretar, cerrar

**clergy** ['klɜːdʒɪ] n clero; ~**man** n clérigo

**clerical** ['klerɪkəl] adj de oficina; (REL) clerical

**clerk** [klɑːk, (US) klɜːrk] (BRIT) n oficinista m/f; (US) dependiente/a m/f, vendedor(a) m/f

**clever** ['klevə*] adj (intelligent) inteligente, listo; (skilful) hábil; (device, arrangement) ingenioso

**click** [klɪk] vt (tongue) chasquear; (heels) taconear

**client** ['klaɪənt] n cliente m/f

**cliff** [klɪf] n acantilado

**climate** ['klaɪmɪt] n clima m

**climax** ['klaɪmæks] n (of battle, career) apogeo; (of film, book) punto culminante; (sexual) orgasmo

**climb** [klaɪm] vi subir; (plant) trepar; (move with effort): **to** ~ **over a wall/into a car** trepar a una tapia/subir a un coche ♦ vt (stairs) subir; (tree) trepar a; (mountain) escalar ♦ n subida; ~**down** n vuelta atrás; ~**er** n alpinista m/f (SP), andinista m/f (AM); ~**ing** n alpinismo (SP), andinismo (AM)

**clinch** [klɪntʃ] vt (deal) cerrar; (argument) ingeniar

**cling** [klɪŋ] (pt, pp **clung**) vi: **to** ~ **to** agarrarse a; (clothes) pegarse a

51

**clinic** ['klɪnɪk] n clínica; ~**al** adj clínico; (fig) frío

**clink** [klɪŋk] vi tintinar

**clip** [klɪp] n (for hair) horquilla; (also: paper ~) sujetapapeles m inv, clip m; (TV, CINEMA) fragmento ♦ vt (cut) cortar; (also: ~ together) unir; ~**pers** npl (for gardening) tijeras fpl; ~**ping** n (newspaper) recorte m

**clique** [kliːk] n camarilla

**cloak** [kləʊk] n capa, manto ♦ vt (fig) encubrir, disimular; ~**room** n guardarropa; (BRIT: WC) lavabo (SP), aseos mpl (SP), baño (AM)

**clock** [klɒk] n reloj m; ~ **in** or **on** vi fichar, picar; ~ **off** or **out** vi fichar or picar la salida; ~**wise** adv en el sentido de las agujas del reloj; ~**work** n aparato de relojería ♦ adj (toy) de cuerda

**clog** [klɒg] n zueco, chanclo ♦ vt atascar ♦ vi (also: ~ **up**) atascarse

**cloister** ['klɔɪstə*] n claustro

**close**[1] [kləʊs] adj (near): ~ (to) cerca (de); (friend) íntimo; (connection) estrecho; (examination) detallado, minucioso; (weather) bochornoso; **to have a** ~ **shave** (fig) escaparse por un pelo ♦ adv cerca; ~ **by**, ~ **at hand** muy cerca; ~ **to** prep cerca de

**close**[2] [kləʊz] vt (shut) cerrar; (end) concluir, terminar ♦ vi (shop etc) cerrarse; (end) concluirse, terminarse ♦ n (end) fin m, final m, conclusión f; ~ **down** vi cerrarse definitivamente; ~**d** adj (shop etc) cerrado; ~**d shop** n taller m gremial

**close-knit** [kləʊs'nɪt] adj (fig) muy unido

**closely** ['kləʊslɪ] adv (study) con detalle; (watch) de cerca; (resemble) estrechamente

**closet** ['klɒzɪt] n armario

**close-up** ['kləʊsʌp] n primer plano

**closure** ['kləʊʒə*] n cierre m

**clot** [klɒt] n (gen: blood ~) coágulo; (inf: idiot) imbécil m/f ♦ vi (blood) coagularse

**cloth** [klɒθ] n (material) tela, paño; (rag) trapo

**clothe** [kləʊð] vt vestir; ~**s** npl ropa; ~**s brush** n cepillo (para la ropa); ~**s line** n cuerda (para tender la ropa); ~**s peg** (US ~**s pin**) n pinza

**clothing** ['kləʊðɪŋ] n = **clothes**

**cloud** [klaʊd] n nube f; ~**burst** n aguacero; ~**y** adj nublado, nuboso; (liquid) turbio

**clout** [klaʊt] vt dar un tortazo a

**clove** [kləʊv] n clavo; ~ **of garlic** diente m de ajo

**clover** ['kləʊvə*] n trébol m

**clown** [klaʊn] n payaso ♦ vi (also: ~ **about**, ~ **around**) hacer el payaso

**cloying** ['klɔɪɪŋ] adj empalagoso

**club** [klʌb] n (society) club m; (weapon) porra, cachiporra; (golf ~) palo ♦ vt aporrear ♦ vi: **to** ~ **together** (for gift) comprar entre todos; ~**s** npl (CARDS) tréboles mpl; ~ **car** (US) n (RAIL) coche m salón; ~**house** n local social, sobre todo en clubs deportivos

**cluck** [klʌk] vi cloquear

**clue** [kluː] n pista; (in crosswords) indicación f; **I haven't a** ~ no tengo ni idea

**clump** [klʌmp] n (of trees) grupo

**clumsy** ['klʌmzɪ] adj (person) torpe, desmañado; (tool) difícil de manejar; (movement) desgarbado

**clung** [klʌŋ] pt, pp of **cling**

**cluster** ['klʌstə*] n grupo ♦ vi agruparse, apiñarse

**clutch** [klʌtʃ] n (AUT) embrague m; (grasp): **in one's ~es** se garras fpl ♦ vt asir; agarrar

**clutter** ['klʌtə*] vt atestar

**cm** abbr (= centimetre) cm

**CND** n abbr (= Campaign for Nuclear Disarmament) plataforma por desarme nuclear

**Co.** abbr = **county; company**

**c/o** abbr (= care of) c/a, a/c

**coach** [kəʊtʃ] n autocar m (SP), coche m de línea; (horse-drawn) coche m; (of train) vagón m, coche m;

*(SPORT)* entrenador(a) m/f, instructor(a) m/f; *(tutor)* profesor(a) m/f particular ♦ vt *(SPORT)* entrenar; *(student)* preparar, enseñar; ~ **trip** n excursión f en autocar

**coal** [kəul] n carbón m; ~ **face** n frente m de carbón; ~**field** n yacimiento de carbón

**coalition** [kəuəˈlɪʃən] n coalición f

**coal:** ~**man** [ˈkəulmən] n carbonero; ~ **merchant** n = **coalman**; ~**mine** [ˈkəulmaɪn] n mina de carbón

**coarse** [kɔːs] adj basto, burdo; *(vulgar)* grosero, ordinario

**coast** [kəust] n costa, litoral m ♦ vi *(AUT)* ir en punto muerto; ~**al** adj costero, costanero; ~**guard** n guardacostas m inv; ~**line** n litoral m

**coat** [kəut] n abrigo; *(of animal)* pelaje m, lana; *(of paint)* mano f, capa ♦ vt cubrir, revestir; ~ **of arms** n escudo de armas; ~ **hanger** n percha *(SP)*, gancho *(AM)*; ~**ing** n capa, baño

**coax** [kəuks] vt engatusar

**cob** [kɔb] n see **corn**

**cobbler** [ˈkɔblə] n zapatero (remendón)

**cobbles** [ˈkɔblz] npl, **cobblestones** [ˈkɔblstəunz] npl adoquines mpl

**cobweb** [ˈkɔbweb] n telaraña

**cock** [kɔk] n *(rooster)* gallo; *(male bird)* macho ♦ vt *(gun)* amartillar; ~**erel** n gallito; ~**eyed** adj *(idea)* disparatado

**cockle** [ˈkɔkl] n berberecho

**cockney** [ˈkɔknɪ] n habitante de ciertos barrios de Londres

**cockpit** [ˈkɔkpɪt] n cabina

**cockroach** [ˈkɔkrəutʃ] n cucaracha

**cocktail** [ˈkɔkteɪl] n cóctel m; ~ **cabinet** n mueble-bar m; ~ **party** n coctel m, cóctel m

**cocoa** [ˈkəukəu] n cacao; *(drink)* chocolate m

**coconut** [ˈkəukənʌt] n coco

**cocoon** [kəˈkuːn] n *(ZOOL)* capullo

**cod** [kɔd] n bacalao

**C.O.D.** abbr (= cash on delivery) C.A.E

**code** [kəud] n código; *(cipher)* clave f; *(dialling ~)* prefijo; *(post ~)* código postal

**cod-liver oil** [ˈkɔdlɪvə*-] n aceite m de hígado de bacalao

**coercion** [kəuˈɜːʃən] n coacción f

**coffee** [ˈkɔfɪ] n café m; ~ **bar** *(BRIT)* n cafetería; ~ **bean** n grano de café; ~ **break** n descanso (para tomar café); ~**pot** n cafetera; ~ **table** n mesita (para servir el café)

**coffin** [ˈkɔfɪn] n ataúd m

**cog** [kɔg] n *(wheel)* rueda dentada; *(tooth)* diente m

**cogent** [ˈkəudʒənt] adj convincente

**cognac** [ˈkɔnjæk] n coñac m

**coil** [kɔɪl] n rollo; *(ELEC)* bobina, carrete m; *(contraceptive)* espiral f ♦ vt enrollar

**coin** [kɔɪn] n moneda ♦ vt *(word)* inventar, idear; ~**age** n moneda; ~**box** *(BRIT)* n cabina telefónica

**coincide** [kəunˈsaɪd] vi coincidir; *(agree)* estar de acuerdo; **coincidence** [kəuˈɪnsɪdəns] n casualidad f

**coke** [kəuk] n *(coal)* coque m

**Coke** [kəuk] ® n Coca Cola ®

**colander** [ˈkɔləndə*] n colador m, escurridor m

**cold** [kəuld] adj frío ♦ n frío; *(MED)* resfriado; **it's** ~ hace frío; **to be** ~ *(person)* tener frío; **to catch** ~ resfriarse; **to catch a** ~ resfriarse, acatarrarse; **in** ~ **blood** a sangre fría; ~**-shoulder** vt dar o volver la espalda a; ~ **sore** n herpes mpl o fpl

**coleslaw** [ˈkəulslɔː] n especie de ensalada de col

**colic** [ˈkɔlɪk] n cólico

**collapse** [kəˈlæps] vi hundirse, derrumbarse; *(MED)* sufrir un colapso ♦ n hundimiento, derrumbamiento; *(MED)* colapso; **collapsible** adj plegable

**collar** [ˈkɔlə*] n *(of coat, shirt)* cuello; *(of dog etc)* collar; ~**bone** n clavícula

**collateral** [kɔˈlætərəl] n garantía colateral

**colleague** ['kɒliːg] n colega m/f

**collect** [kə'lekt] vt (litter, mail etc)
recoger; (as a hobby) coleccionar;
(BRIT: call and pick up) recoger;
(debts, subscriptions etc) recaudar ♦
vi reunirse; (dust) acumularse; **to
call ~** (US: TEL) llamar a cobro revertido; **~ion** [kə'lekʃən] n colección
f; (of mail, for charity) recogida

**collector** [kə'lektə*] n coleccionista
m/f

**college** ['kɒlɪdʒ] n colegio mayor; (of
agriculture, technology) escuela universitaria

**collide** [kə'laɪd] vi chocar

**collie** ['kɒlɪ] n perro pastor escocés,
collie m

**colliery** ['kɒlɪərɪ] (BRIT) n mina de
carbón

**collision** [kə'lɪʒən] n choque m

**colloquial** [kə'ləukwɪəl] adj familiar,
coloquial

**collusion** [kə'luːʒən] n confabulación
f, connivencia

**Colombia** [kə'lɒmbɪə] n Colombia;
**~n** adj, n colombiano/a

**colon** ['kəulən] n (sign) dos puntos;
(MED) colon m

**colonel** ['kɔːnl] n coronel m

**colonial** [kə'ləunɪəl] adj colonial

**colony** ['kɒlənɪ] n colonia

**colour** ['kʌlə*] (US color) n color m
♦ vt color(e)ar; (dye) teñir; (fig: account) adornar ♦ vi (blush) sonrojarse; ~s
npl (of party, club) colores mpl; in
~ en color; **~ in** vt colorear; **~ bar**
n segregación f racial; **~-blind** adj
daltónico; **~ed** adj de color; (photo)
en color; **~ film** n película en color;
**~ful** adj lleno de color; (story) fantástico; (person) excéntrico; **~ing** n
(complexion) tez f; (in food) colorante
m; **~ scheme** n combinación f de
colores; **~ television** n televisión f
en color

**colt** [kəult] n potro

**column** ['kɒləm] n columna; **~ist**
['kɒləmnɪst] n columnista m/f

**coma** ['kəumə] n coma m

**comb** [kəum] n peine m; (ornamental) peineta ♦ vt (hair) peinar;
(area) registrar a fondo

**combat** ['kɒmbæt] n combate m ♦ vt
combatir

**combination** [kɒmbɪ'neɪʃən] n combinación f

**combine** [vb kəm'baɪn, n 'kɒmbaɪn]
vt combinar; (qualities) reunir ♦ vi
combinarse ♦ n (ECON) cartel m; **~
(harvester)** n cosechadora

────── KEYWORD ──────

**come** [kʌm] (pt **came**, pp **come**) vi
**1** (movement towards) venir; **to ~
running** venir corriendo
**2** (arrive) llegar; **he's ~ here to
work** ha venido aquí para trabajar;
**to ~ home** volver a casa
**3** (reach): **to ~ to** llegar a; **the bill
came to £40** la cuenta ascendía a
cuarenta libras
**4** (occur): **an idea came to me** se
me ocurrió una idea
**5** (be, become): **to ~ loose/undone**
etc aflojarse/desabrocharse, desatarse
etc; **I've ~ to like him** por fin ha
llegado a gustarme

**come about** vi suceder, ocurrir
**come across** vt fus (person) topar
con; (thing) dar con
**come away** vi (leave) marcharse;
(become detached) desprenderse
**come back** vi (return) volver
**come by** vt fus (acquire) conseguir
**come down** vi (price) bajar; (tree,
building) ser derribado
**come forward** vi presentarse
**come from** vt fus (place, source) ser
de
**come in** vi (visitor) entrar; (train,
report) llegar; (fashion) ponerse de
moda; (on deal etc) entrar
**come in for** vt fus (criticism etc) recibir
**come into** vt fus (money) heredar;
(be involved) tener que ver con; **~
into fashion** ponerse de moda
**come off** vi (button) soltarse, des-

prenderse; (*attempt*) salir bien
**come on** *vi* (*pupil*) progresar; (*work, project*) desarrollarse; (*lights*) encenderse; (*electricity*) volver; ~ **on!** ¡vamos!
**come out** *vi* (*fact*) salir a la luz; (*book, sun*) salir; (*stain*) quitarse
**come round** *vi* (*after faint, operation*) volver en sí
**come to** *vi* (*wake*) volver en sí
**come up** *vi* (*sun*) salir; (*problem*) surgir; (*event*) aproximarse; (*in conversation*) mencionarse
**come up against** *vt fus* (*resistance etc*) tropezar con
**come up with** *vt fus* (*idea*) sugerir; (*money*) conseguir
**come upon** *vt fus* (*find*) dar con

**comeback** [ˈkʌmbæk] *n*: to make a ~ (*THEATRE*) volver a las tablas
**comedian** [kəˈmiːdɪən] *n* cómico; **comedienne** [-ˈɛn] *n* cómica
**comedy** [ˈkɒmɪdɪ] *n* comedia; (*humour*) comicidad *f*
**comet** [ˈkɒmɪt] *n* cometa *m*
**comeuppance** [kʌmˈʌpəns] *n*: to get one's ~ llevar su merecido
**comfort** [ˈkʌmfət] *n* bienestar *m*; (*relief*) alivio ♦ *vt* consolar; ~s *npl* (*of home etc*) comodidades *fpl*; ~**able** *adj* cómodo; (*financially*) acomodado; (*easy*) fácil; ~**ably** *adv* (*sit*) cómodamente; (*live*) holgadamente; ~ **station** (*US*) *n* servicios *mpl*

**comic** [ˈkɒmɪk] *adj* (*also*: ~al) cómico ♦ *n* (*comedian*) cómico; (*BRIT: for children*) tebeo; (*BRIT: for adults*) comic*m*; ~ **strip** *n* tira cómica
**coming** [ˈkʌmɪŋ] *n* venida, llegada ♦ *adj* que viene; ~(s) **and going(s)** *n(pl)* ir y venir *m*, ajetreo
**comma** [ˈkɒmə] *n* coma
**command** [kəˈmɑːnd] *n* orden *f*, mandato; (*MIL: authority*) mando; (*mastery*) dominio ♦ *vt* (*troops*) mandar; (*give orders to*): to ~ **sb** to do mandar *or* ordenar a uno hacer; ~**eer** [kɒmənˈdɪə*] *vt* requisar;

~**er** *n* (*MIL*) comandante *m/f*, jefe/a *m/f*; ~**ment** *n* (*REL*) mandamiento
**commemorate** [kəˈmɛməreɪt] *vt* conmemorar
**commence** [kəˈmɛns] *vt, vi* comenzar, empezar
**commend** [kəˈmɛnd] *vt* elogiar, alabar; (*recommend*) recomendar
**commensurate** [kəˈmɛnʃərɪt] *adj*: ~ **with** en proporción a, que corresponde a
**comment** [ˈkɒmɛnt] *n* comentario ♦ *vi*: to ~ **on** hacer comentarios sobre; "no ~" (*written*) "sin comentarios"; (*spoken*) "no tengo nada que decir"; ~**ary** [ˈkɒməntərɪ] *n* comentario; ~**ator** [ˈkɒməntəɪtə*] *n* comentarista *m/f*
**commerce** [ˈkɒməːs] *n* comercio
**commercial** [kəˈməːʃəl] *adj* comercial ♦ *n* (*TV, RADIO*) anuncio
**commiserate** [kəˈmɪzəreɪt] *vi*: to ~ **with** compadecerse de, condolerse de
**commission** [kəˈmɪʃən] *n* (*committee, fee*) comisión *f* ♦ *vt* (*work of art*) encargar; **out of** ~ fuera de servicio; ~**aire** [kəmɪʃəˈnɛə*] (*BRIT*) *n* portero; ~**er** *n* (*POLICE*) comisario de policía
**commit** [kəˈmɪt] *vt* (*act*) cometer; (*resources*) dedicar; (to sb's care) entregar; to ~ **o.s.** (**to do**) comprometerse a (hacer); to ~ **suicide** suicidarse; ~**ment** *n* compromiso; (*ideology etc*) entrega
**committee** [kəˈmɪtɪ] *n* comité *m*
**commodity** [kəˈmɒdɪtɪ] *n* mercancía
**common** [ˈkɒmən] *adj* común; (*pej*) ordinario ♦ *n* campo común; **the C~s** *npl* (*BRIT*) (la Cámara de) los Comunes *mpl*; **in** ~ en común; ~**er** *n* plebeyo; ~ **law** *n* ley *f* consuetudinaria; ~**ly** *adv* comúnmente; **C~ Market** *n* Mercado Común; ~**place** *adj* de lo más común; ~**room** *n* sala común; ~ **sense** *n* sentido común; **the C~wealth** *n* la Commonwealth
**commotion** [kəˈməʊʃən] *n* tumulto, confusión *f*
**commune** [*n* ˈkɒmjuːn, *vb* kəˈmjuːn]

*n* (*group*) comuna ♦ *vi*: **to ~ with** comulgar *or* conversar con

**communicate** [kə'mju:nɪkeɪt] *vt* comunicar ♦ *vi*: **to ~ (with)** comunicarse (con); (*in writing*) estar en contacto (con)

**communication** [kəmju:nɪ'keɪʃən] *n* comunicación *f*; **~ cord** (*BRIT*) *n* timbre *m* de alarma

**communion** [kə'mju:nɪən] *n* (*also: Holy C~*) comunión *f*

**communiqué** [kə'mju:nɪkeɪ] *n* comunicado, parte *f*

**communism** [kɔmjunɪzəm] *n* comunismo; **communist** *adj*, *n* comunista *m/f*

**community** [kə'mju:nɪtɪ] *n* comunidad *f*; (*large group*) colectividad *f*; **~ centre** *n* centro social; **~ chest** (*US*) *n* arca comunitaria, fondo común; **~ home** (*BRIT*) *n* correccional *m*

**commutation ticket** [kɔmju-'teɪʃən-] (*US*) *n* billete *m* de abono

**commute** [kə'mju:t] *vi* viajar a diario de la casa al trabajo ♦ *vt* conmutar; **~r** *n* persona (que ... *see vi*)

**compact** [*adj* kəm'pækt, *n* 'kɔmpækt] *adj* compacto ♦ *n* (*also: powder ~*) polvera; **~ disc** *n* compact disc *m*; **~ disc player** *n* reproductor *m* de disco compacto, compact disc *m*

**companion** [kəm'pænɪən] *n* compañero/a; **~ship** *n* compañerismo

**company** ['kʌmpənɪ] *n* compañía; (*COMM*) sociedad *f*, compañía; **to keep sb ~** acompañar a uno; **~ secretary** (*BRIT*) *n* secretario/a de compañía

**comparative** [kəm'pærətɪv] *adj* relativo; (*study*) comparativo; **~ly** *adv* (*relatively*) relativamente

**compare** [kəm'peə*] *vt*: **to ~ sth/sb with/to** comparar algo a uno con ♦ *vi*: **to ~ (with)** compararse (con); **comparison** [-'pærɪsn] *n* comparación *f*

**compartment** [kəm'pɔ:tmənt] *n* (*also: RAIL*) compartim(i)ento

**compass** ['kʌmpəs] *n* brújula; **~es** *npl* (*MATH*) compás *m*

**compassion** [kəm'pæʃən] *n* compasión *f*; **~ate** *adj* compasivo

**compatible** [kəm'pætɪbl] *adj* compatible

**compel** [kəm'pel] *vt* obligar; **~ling** *adj* (*fig*: *argument*) convincente

**compensate** ['kɔmpənseɪt] *vt* compensar ♦ *vi*: **to ~ for** compensar; **compensation** [-'seɪʃən] *n* (*for loss*) indemnización *f*

**compère** ['kɔmpeə*] *n* presentador *m*

**compete** [kəm'pi:t] *vi* (*take part*) tomar parte, concurrir; (*vie with*): **to ~ with** competir con, hacer competencia a

**competence** ['kɔmpɪtəns] *n* capacidad *f*, aptitud *f*

**competent** ['kɔmpɪtənt] *adj* competente, capaz

**competition** [kɔmpɪ'tɪʃən] *n* (*contest*) concurso; (*rivalry*) competencia

**competitive** [kəm'petɪtɪv] *adj* (*ECON*, *SPORT*) competitivo

**competitor** [kəm'petɪtə*] *n* (*rival*) competidor(a) *m/f*; (*participant*) concursante *m/f*

**compile** [kəm'paɪl] *vt* compilar

**complacency** [kəm'pleɪsnsɪ] *n* autosatisfacción *f*

**complacent** [kəm'pleɪsnt] *adj* autocomplaciente

**complain** [kəm'pleɪn] *vi* quejarse; (*COMM*) reclamar; **~t** *n* queja; reclamación *f*; (*MED*) enfermedad *f*

**complement** [*n* 'kɔmplɪmənt, *vb* 'kɔmplɪment] *n* complemento; (*esp of ship's crew*) dotación *f* ♦ *vt* (*enhance*) complementar; **~ary** [kɔmplɪ'mentərɪ] *adj* complementario

**complete** [kəm'pli:t] *adj* (*full*) completo; (*finished*) acabado ♦ *vt* (*fulfil*) completar; (*finish*) acabar; (*a form*) llenar; **~ly** *adv* completamente; **completion** [-'pli:ʃən] *n* terminación *f*; (*of contract*) realización *f*

**complex** ['kɔmpleks] *adj*, *n* complejo

**complexion** [kəm'plekʃən] *n* (*of face*) tez *f*, cutis *m*

**compliance** [kəm'plaɪəns] n (submission) sumisión f; (agreement) conformidad f; in ~ with de acuerdo con

**complicate** ['kɒmplɪkeɪt] vt complicar; ~**d** adj complicado; **complication** [-'keɪʃən] n complicación f

**complicity** [kəm'plɪsɪtɪ] n complicidad f

**compliment** ['kɒmplɪmənt] n (formal) cumplido ♦ vt felicitar; ~**s** npl (regards) saludos mpl; **to pay sb a ~** hacer cumplidos a uno; ~**ary** [-'mentərɪ] adj lisonjero; (free) de favor

**comply** [kəm'plaɪ] vi: **to ~ with** cumplir con

**component** [kəm'pəʊnənt] adj componente ♦ n (TECH) pieza

**compose** [kəm'pəʊz] vt: **to be ~d of** componerse de; (music etc) componer; **to ~ o.s.** tranquilizarse; ~**d** adj sosegado; ~**r** n (MUS) compositor(a) m/f; **composition** [kɒmpə'zɪʃən] n composición f

**compost** ['kɒmpɒst] n abono (vegetal)

**composure** [kəm'pəʊʒə*] n serenidad f, calma

**compound** ['kɒmpaʊnd] n (CHEM) compuesto, f; (LING) palabra compuesta; (enclosure) recinto ♦ adj compuesto; (fracture) complicado

**comprehend** [kɒmprɪ'hend] vt comprender; **comprehension** [-'henʃən] n comprensión f

**comprehensive** [kɒmprɪ'hensɪv] adj exhaustivo; (INSURANCE) contra todo riesgo; ~ (**school**) n centro estatal de enseñanza secundaria; ≈ Instituto Nacional de Bachillerato (SP)

**compress** [vb kəm'pres, n 'kɒmpres] vt comprimir; (information) condensar ♦ n (MED) compresa

**comprise** [kəm'praɪz] vt (also: **be ~d of**) comprender, constar de; (constitute) constituir

**compromise** ['kɒmprəmaɪz] n (agreement) arreglo ♦ vt comprometer ♦ vi transigir

**compulsion** [kəm'pʌlʃən] n compulsión f; (force) obligación f

**compulsive** [kəm'pʌlsɪv] adj compulsivo; (viewing, reading) obligado

**compulsory** [kəm'pʌlsərɪ] adj obligatorio

**computer** [kəm'pju:tə*] n ordenador m, computador m, computadora; ~**game** n juego para ordenador; ~**ize** vt (data) computerizar; (system) informatizar; ~ **programmer** n programador(a) m/f; ~ **programming** n programación f; ~ **science** n informática; **computing** [kəm'pju:tɪŋ] n (activity, science) informática

**comrade** ['kɒmrɪd] n (POL, MIL) camarada; (friend) compañero/a; ~**ship** n camaradería, compañerismo

**con** [kɒn] vt (deceive) engañar; (cheat) estafar ♦ n estafa

**conceal** [kən'si:l] vt ocultar

**conceit** [kən'si:t] n presunción f; ~**ed** adj presumido

**conceivable** [kən'si:vəbl] adj concebible

**conceive** [kən'si:v] vt, vi concebir

**concentrate** ['kɒnsəntreɪt] vi concentrarse ♦ vt concentrar

**concentration** [kɒnsən'treɪʃən] n concentración f

**concept** ['kɒnsept] n concepto

**conception** [kən'sepʃən] n (idea) concepto, idea; (BIOL) concepción f

**concern** [kən'sɜːn] n (matter) asunto; (COMM) empresa; (anxiety) preocupación f ♦ vt (worry) preocupar; (involve) afectar; (relate to) tener que ver con; **to be ~ed** (**about**) interesarse (por), preocuparse (por); ~**ing** prep sobre, acerca de

**concert** ['kɒnsət] n concierto; ~**ed** [kən'sɜːtɪd] adj (efforts etc) concertado; ~ **hall** n sala de conciertos

**concertina** [kɒnsə'ti:nə] n concertina

**concerto** [kən'tʃɜːtəʊ] n concierto

**concession** [kən'seʃən] n concesión f; **tax ~** privilegio fiscal

**concise** [kən'saɪs] adj conciso

**conclude** [kən'klu:d] vt concluir; (treaty etc) firmar; (agreement) llegar a; (decide) llegar a la conclusión de; **conclusion** [-'klu:ʒən] n conclusión f; firma; **conclusive** [-'klu:sɪv] adj decisivo, concluyente

**concoct** [kən'kɒkt] vt confeccionar; (plot) tramar; **~ion** n [-'kɒkʃən] n mezcla

**concourse** ['kɒŋkɔːs] n vestíbulo

**concrete** ['kɒŋkriːt] n hormigón m ♦ adj de hormigón; (fig) concreto

**concur** [kən'kɔː*] vi estar de acuerdo, asentir

**concurrently** [kən'kʌrntlɪ] adv al mismo tiempo

**concussion** [kən'kʌʃən] n conmoción f cerebral

**condemn** [kən'dɛm] vt condenar; (building) declarar en ruina; **~ation** [kɒndɛm'neɪʃən] n condena

**condense** [kən'dɛns] vi condensarse ♦ vt condensar, abreviar; **~d milk** n leche f condensada

**condescending** [kɒndɪ'sɛndɪŋ] adj condescendiente

**condition** [kən'dɪʃən] n condición f, estado; (requirement) condición f ♦ vt condicionar; **on ~ that** a condición (de) que; **~al** adj condicional; **~er** n suavizante

**condolences** [kən'dəʊlənsɪz] npl pésame m

**condom** ['kɒndəm] n condón m

**condone** [kən'dəʊn] vt condonar

**conducive** [kən'djuːsɪv] adj: **~ to** conducente a

**conduct** [n 'kɒndʌkt, vb kən'dʌkt] n conducta, comportamiento ♦ vt (lead) conducir; (manage) llevar a cabo, dirigir; (MUS) dirigir; **to ~ o.s.** comportarse; **~ed tour** (BRIT) n visita acompañada; **~or** n (of orchestra) director m; (US: on train) revisor(a) m/f; (on bus) cobrador m; (ELEC) conductor m; **~ress** n (on bus) cobradora

**cone** [kəʊn] n cono; (pine ~) piña; (on road) pivote m; (for ice-cream) cucurucho

**confectioner** [kən'fɛkʃənə*] n repostero/a; **~'s (shop)** n confitería;

**~y** n dulces mpl

**confer** [kən'fɜː*] vt: **to ~ sth on** otorgar algo a ♦ vi conferenciar

**conference** ['kɒnfərns] n (meeting) reunión f; (convention) congreso

**confess** [kən'fɛs] vt confesar ♦ vi admitir; **~ion** [-'fɛʃən] n confesión f

**confetti** [kən'fɛtɪ] n confeti m

**confide** [kən'faɪd] vi: **to ~ in** confiar en

**confidence** ['kɒnfɪdns] n (also: self ~) confianza; (secret) confidencia; **in ~** (speak, write) en confianza; **~ trick** n timo; **confident** adj seguro de sí mismo; (certain) seguro; **confidential** [kɒnfɪ'dɛnʃəl] adj confidencial

**confine** [kən'faɪn] vt (limit) limitar; (shut up) encerrar; **~d** adj (space) reducido; **~ment** n (prison) prisión f; **~s** ['kɒnfaɪnz] mpl confines mpl

**confirm** [kən'fɜːm] vt confirmar; **~ation** [kɒnfə'meɪʃən] n confirmación f; **~ed** adj empedernido

**confiscate** ['kɒnfɪskeɪt] vt confiscar

**conflict** [n 'kɒnflɪkt, vb kən'flɪkt] n conflicto ♦ vi (opinions) chocar; **~ing** adj contradictorio

**conform** [kən'fɔːm] vi conformarse; **to ~ to** ajustarse a

**confound** [kən'faʊnd] vt confundir

**confront** [kən'frʌnt] vt (problems) hacer frente a; (enemy, danger) enfrentarse con; **~ation** [kɒnfrən-'teɪʃən] n enfrentamiento

**confuse** [kən'fjuːz] vt (perplex) aturdir, desconcertar; (mix up) confundir; (complicate) complicar; **~d** adj confuso; (person) perplejo; **confusing** adj confuso; **confusion** [-'fjuːʒən] n confusión f

**congeal** [kən'dʒiːl] vi (blood) coagularse; (sauce etc) cuajarse

**congenial** [kən'dʒiːnɪəl] adj agradable

**congenital** [kən'dʒenɪtl] adj congénito

**congested** [kən'dʒestɪd] adj congestionado

**congestion** [kən'dʒestʃən] n congestión f

**conglomerate** [kən'glomərət] n (COMM, GEO) conglomerado

**congratulate** [kən'grætjuleɪt] vt: to ~ sb (on) felicitar a uno (por); **congratulations** [-'leɪʃənz] npl felicitaciones fpl; ~! ¡enhorabuena!

**congregate** ['kɒŋgrɪgeɪt] vi congregarse; **congregation** [-'geɪʃən] n (of a church) feligreses mpl

**congress** ['kɒŋgres] n congreso; (US): C~ Congreso; ~**man** (US) n miembro del Congreso

**conifer** ['kɒnɪfə*] n conífera

**conjecture** [kən'dʒektʃə*] n conjetura

**conjugal** ['kɒndʒugl] adj conyugal

**conjugate** ['kɒndʒugeɪt] vt conjugar

**conjunctivitis** [kəndʒʌŋktɪ'vaɪtɪs] n conjuntivitis f

**conjure** [kʌndʒə*] vi hacer juegos de manos; ~ **up** vt (ghost, spirit) hacer aparecer; (memories) evocar; ~**r** n ilusionista m/f

**conk out** [kɒŋk-] (inf) vi averiarse

**con man** ['kɒn-] n estafador m

**connect** [kə'nekt] vt juntar, unir; (ELEC) conectar; (TEL: subscriber) poner; (TEL: caller) poner al habla; (fig) relacionar, asociar ♦ vi: to ~ **with** (train) enlazar con; to be ~**ed with** (associated) estar relacionado con; ~**ion** [-ʃən] n juntura, unión f; (ELEC) conexión f; (RAIL) enlace m; (TEL) comunicación f; (fig) relación f

**connive** [kə'naɪv] vi: to ~ **at** hacer la vista gorda a

**connoisseur** [kɒnɪ'sə*] n experto/a, entendido/a

**conquer** ['kɒŋkə*] vt (territory) conquistar; (enemy, feelings) vencer; ~**or** n conquistador m

**conquest** ['kɒŋkwest] n conquista

**cons** [kɒnz] npl see **convenience**; **pro**

**conscience** ['kɒnʃəns] n conciencia

**conscientious** [kɒnʃɪ'enʃəs] adj concienzudo; (objection) de conciencia

**conscious** ['kɒnʃəs] adj (deliberate) deliberado; (awake, aware) consciente; ~**ness** n conciencia; (MED) conocimiento

**conscript** ['kɒnskrɪpt] n recluta m; ~**ion** [kən'skrɪpʃən] n servicio militar (obligatorio)

**consecrate** ['kɒnsɪkreɪt] vt consagrar

**consensus** [kən'sensəs] n consenso

**consent** [kən'sent] n consentimiento ♦ vi: to ~ (to) consentir (en)

**consequence** ['kɒnsɪkwəns] n consecuencia; (significance) importancia

**consequently** ['kɒnsɪkwəntlɪ] adv por consiguiente

**conservation** [kɒnsə'veɪʃən] n conservación f

**conservative** [kən'sə:vətɪv] adj conservador(a); (estimate etc) cauteloso; C~ (BRIT) adj, n (POL) conservador(a) m/f

**conservatory** [kən'sə:vətrɪ] n invernadero; (MUS) conservatorio

**conserve** [kən'sə:v] vt conservar ♦ n conserva

**consider** [kən'sɪdə*] vt considerar; (take into account) tener en cuenta; (study) estudiar, examinar; to ~ **doing sth** pensar en (la posibilidad de) hacer algo; ~**able** adj considerable; ~**ably** adv notablemente

**considerate** [kən'sɪdərɪt] adj considerado; **consideration** [-'reɪʃən] n consideración f; (factor) factor m; to **give sth further consideration** estudiar algo más a fondo

**considering** [kən'sɪdərɪŋ] prep teniendo en cuenta

**consign** [kən'saɪn] vt: to ~ **to** (sth unwanted) relegar a; (person) destinar a; ~**ment** n envío

**consist** [kən'sɪst] vi: to ~ **of** consistir en

**consistency** [kən'sɪstənsɪ] n (of argument etc) coherencia; consecuencia; (thickness) consistencia

**consistent** [kən'sɪstənt] adj (person) consecuente; (argument etc) coherente

**consolation** [kɔnsə'leiʃən] *n* consuelo

**console¹** [kən'səul] *vt* consolar

**console²** ['kɔnsəul] *n* consola

**consonant** ['kɔnsənənt] *n* consonante *f*

**consortium** [kən'sɔ:tiəm] *n* consorcio

**conspicuous** [kən'spikjuəs] *adj* (*visible*) visible

**conspiracy** [kən'spirəsi] *n* conjura, complot *m*

**conspire** [kən'spaiə*] *vi* conspirar; (*events etc*) unirse

**constable** ['kʌnstəbl] (*BRIT*) *n* policía *m/f*; **chief** ~ = jefe *m* de policía

**constabulary** [kən'stæbjuləri] *n* = policía

**constant** ['kɔnstənt] *adj* constante; ~**ly** *adv* constantemente

**constipated** ['kɔnstipeitid] *adj* estreñido; **constipation** [kɔnsti'peiʃən] *n* estreñimiento

**constituency** [kən'stitjuənsi] *n* (*POL: area*) distrito electoral; (: *electors*) electorado; **constituent** [-ənt] *n* (*POL*) elector(a) *m/f*; (*part*) componente *m*

**constitute** ['kɔnstitju:t] *vt* constituir; (*make up: whole*) componer

**constitution** [kɔnsti'tju:ʃən] *n* constitución *f*; ~**al** *adj* constitucional

**constraint** [kən'streint] *n* obligación *f*; (*limit*) restricción *f*

**construct** [kən'strʌkt] *vt* construir; ~**ion** [-ʃən] *n* construcción *f*; ~**ive** *adj* constructivo

**construe** [kən'stru:] *vt* interpretar

**consul** ['kɔnsl] *n* cónsul *m/f*; ~**ate** ['kɔnsjulit] *n* consulado

**consult** [kən'sʌlt] *vt* consultar; ~**ant** *n* (*BRIT: MED*) especialista *m/f*; (*other specialist*) asesor(a) *m/f*; ~**ation** [kɔnsəl'teiʃən] *n* consulta; ~**ing room** (*BRIT*) *n* consultorio

**consume** [kən'sju:m] *vt* (*eat*) comerse; (*drink*) beberse; (*fire etc, COMM*) consumir; ~**r** *n* consumidor(a) *m/f*; ~**r goods** *npl* bienes *mpl* de consumo; ~**rism** *n* consumismo

**consummate** ['kɔnsʌmeit] *vt* consumar

**consumption** [kən'sʌmpʃən] *n* consumo

**cont.** *abbr* (= *continued*) sigue

**contact** ['kɔntækt] *n* contacto; (*person*) contacto; (: *pej*) enchufe *m* ♦ *vt* ponerse en contacto con; ~ **lenses** *npl* lentes *fpl* de contacto

**contagious** [kən'teidʒəs] *adj* contagioso

**contain** [kən'tein] *vt* contener; **to** ~ **o.s.** contenerse; ~**er** *n* recipiente *m*; (*for shipping etc*) contenedor *m*

**contaminate** [kən'tæmineit] *vt* contaminar

**cont'd** *abbr* (= *continued*) sigue

**contemplate** ['kɔntəmpleit] *vt* contemplar; (*reflect upon*) considerar

**contemporary** [kən'tempərəri] *adj*, *n* contemporáneo/a *m/f*

**contempt** [kən'tempt] *n* desprecio; ~ **of court** (*LAW*) desacato a (los tribunales); ~**ible** *adj* despreciable; ~**uous** *adj* desdeñoso

**contend** [kən'tend] *vt* (*argue*) afirmar ♦ *vi*: **to** ~ **with/for** luchar contra/por; ~**er** *n* (*SPORT*) contendiente *m/f*

**content** [*adj, vb* kən'tent, *n* 'kɔntent] *adj* (*happy*) contento; (*satisfied*) satisfecho ♦ *vt* contentar; satisfacer ♦ *n* contenido; ~**s** *npl* contenido; (*table of*) ~**s** índice *m* de materias; ~**ed** *adj* contento; satisfecho

**contention** [kən'tenʃən] *n* (*assertion*) aseveración *f*; (*disagreement*) discusión *f*

**contentment** [kən'tentmənt] *n* contento

**contest** [*n* 'kɔntest, *vb* kən'test] *n* lucha; (*competition*) concurso ♦ *vt* (*dispute*) impugnar; (*POL*) presentarse como candidato/a en; ~**ant** [kən'testənt] *n* concursante *m/f*; (*in fight*) contendiente *m/f*

**context** ['kɔntekst] *n* contexto

**continent** ['kɔntinənt] *n* continente *m*; **the C~** (*BRIT*) el continente europeo; ~**al** [-'nentl] *adj* continen-

tal; ~**al quilt** (BRIT) n edredón m
**contingency** [kən'tɪndʒənsɪ] n contingencia
**continual** [kən'tɪnjuəl] adj continuo; ~**ly** adv constantemente
**continuation** [kəntɪnju'eɪʃən] n prolongación f; (after interruption) reanudación f
**continue** [kən'tɪnjuː] vi, vt seguir, continuar
**continuous** [kən'tɪnjuəs] adj continuo; ~ **stationery** n papel m continuo
**contort** [kən'tɔːt] vt retorcer; ~**ion** [-'tɔːʃən] n (movement) contorsión f
**contour** ['kɒntuə*] n contorno; (also: ~ **line**) curva de nivel
**contraband** ['kɒntrəbænd] n contrabando
**contraception** [kɒntrə'sepʃən] n contracepción f
**contraceptive** [kɒntrə'septɪv] adj, n anticonceptivo
**contract** [n 'kɒntrækt, vb kən'trækt] n contrato ♦ vi (COMM): **to** ~ **to do sth** comprometerse por contrato a hacer algo; (become smaller) contraerse, encogerse ♦ vt contraer; ~**ion** [kən'trækʃən] n contracción f; ~**or** n contratista m/f
**contradict** [kɒntrə'dɪkt] vt contradecir; ~**ion** [-ʃən] n contradicción f; ~**ory** adj contradictorio
**contraption** [kən'træpʃən] (pej) n artilugio m
**contrary**[1] ['kɒntrərɪ] adj contrario
♦ n lo contrario; **on the** ~ al contrario; **unless you hear to the** ~ a no ser que le digan lo contrario
**contrary**[2] [kən'treərɪ] adj (perverse) terco
**contrast** [n 'kɒntrɑːst, vt kən'trɑːst] n contraste m ♦ vt comparar; **in** ~ **to** en contraste con; ~**ing** adj (opinions) opuesto; (colours) que hace contraste
**contravene** [kɒntrə'viːn] vt infringir
**contribute** [kən'trɪbjuːt] vi contribuir ♦ vt: **to** ~ **£10/an article to** contribuir con 10 libras/un artículo a;

**to** ~ **to** (charity) donar a; (newspaper) escribir para; (discussion) intervenir en; **contribution** [kɒntrɪ'bjuːʃən] n (donation) donativo; (BRIT: for social security) cotización f; (to debate) intervención f; (to journal) colaboración f; **contributor** n contribuyente m/f; (to newspaper) colaborador(a) m/f
**contrive** [kən'traɪv] vt (invent) idear ♦ vi: **to** ~ **to do** lograr hacer
**control** [kən'trəul] vt controlar; (process etc) dirigir; (machinery) manejar; (temper) dominar; (disease) contener ♦ n control m; ~**s** npl (of vehicle) instrumentos mpl de mando; (of radio) controles mpl; (governmental) medidas fpl de control; **under** ~ bajo control; **to be in** ~ **of** tener el mando de; **the car went out of** ~ se perdió el control del coche; ~ **panel** n tablero de instrumentos; ~ **room** n sala de mando; ~ **tower** n (AVIAT) torre f de control
**controversial** [kɒntrə'vɜːʃl] adj polémico
**controversy** ['kɒntrəvɜːsɪ] n polémica
**conurbation** [kɒnɜː'beɪʃən] n urbanización f
**convalesce** [kɒnvə'les] vi convalecer
**convector** [kən'vektə*] n calentador m de aire
**convene** [kən'viːn] vt convocar ♦ vi reunirse
**convenience** [kən'viːnɪəns] n (easiness) comodidad f; (suitability) idoneidad f; (advantage) ventaja; **at your** ~ cuando le sea conveniente; **all modern** ~**s, all mod cons** (BRIT) todo confort
**convenient** [kən'viːnɪənt] adj (useful) útil; (place, time) conveniente
**convent** ['kɒnvənt] n convento
**convention** [kən'venʃən] n convención f; (meeting) asamblea; (agreement) convenio; ~**al** adj convencional
**converge** [kən'vɜːdʒ] vi convergir; (people): **to** ~ **on** dirigirse todos a

**conversant** [kən'vɜːsnt] *adj:* to be ~ with estar al tanto de

**conversation** [kɒnvə'seɪʃən] *n* conversación *f;* ~al *adj* familiar; ~al skill facilidad *f* de palabra

**converse** [kən'vɜːs, *vb* kən'vɜːs] *n* inversa ♦ *vi* conversar; ~ly [-'vɜːslɪ] *adv* a la inversa

**conversion** [kən'vɜːʃən] *n* conversión *f*

**convert** [*vb* kən'vɜːt, *n* 'kɒnvɜːt] *vt* (*REL, COMM*) convertir; (*alter):* to ~ sth into/to transformar algo en/ convertir algo a ♦ *n* converso/a; ~ible *adj* convertible ♦ *n* descapotable *m*

**convey** [kən'veɪ] *vt* llevar; (*thanks*) comunicar; (*idea*) expresar; ~or belt *n* cinta transportadora

**convict** [*vb* kən'vɪkt, *n* 'kɒnvɪkt] *vt* (*find guilty*) declarar culpable a ♦ *n* presidiario/a; ~ion *n* condena; (*belief, certainty*) convicción *f*

**convince** [kən'vɪns] *vt* convencer; ~d *adj:* ~d of/that convencido de/de que; **convincing** *adj* convincente

**convoluted** ['kɒnvəluːtɪd] *adj* (*argument etc*) enrevesado

**convoy** ['kɒnvɔɪ] *n* convoy *m*

**convulse** [kən'vʌls] *vt:* to be ~d with laughter desternillarse de risa; **convulsion** [-'vʌlʃən] *n* convulsión *f*

**coo** [kuː] *vi* arrullar

**cook** [kuk] *vt* (*stew etc*) guisar; (*meal*) preparar ♦ *vi* cocer; (*person*) cocinar ♦ *n* cocinero/a; ~ book *n* libro de cocina; ~er *n* cocina; ~ery *n* cocina; ~ery book (*BRIT*) *n* = ~ book; ~ie (*US*) *n* galleta; ~ing *n* cocina

**cool** [kuːl] *adj* fresco; (*not afraid*) tranquilo; (*unfriendly*) frío ♦ *vt* enfriar ♦ *vi* enfriarse; ~ness *n* frescura; tranquilidad *f;* (*indifference*) falta de entusiasmo

**coop** [kuːp] *n* gallinero ♦ *vt:* to ~ up (*fig*) encerrar

**cooperate** [kəu'ɒpəreɪt] *vi* cooperar, colaborar; **cooperation** [-'reɪʃən] *n* cooperación *f*, colaboración *f;* co-

**operative** [-rətɪv] *adj* (*business*) cooperativo; (*person*) servicial ♦ *n* cooperativa

**coordinate** [*vb* kəu'ɔːdɪneɪt, *n* kəu'ɔːdɪnət] *vt* coordinar ♦ *n* (*MATH*) coordenada; ~s *npl* (*clothes*) coordinados *mpl;* **coordination** [-'neɪʃən] *n* coordinación *f*

**co-ownership** [kəu'əunəʃɪp] *n* copropiedad *f*

**cop** [kɒp] (*inf*) *n* poli *m* (*SP*), tira *m* (*AM*)

**cope** [kəup] *vi:* to ~ with (*problem*) hacer frente a

**copious** ['kəupɪəs] *adj* copioso, abundante

**copper** ['kɒpə*] *n* (*metal*) cobre *m;* (*BRIT: inf*) poli *m;* ~s *npl* (*money*) calderilla (*SP*), centavos *mpl* (*AM*)

**coppice** ['kɒpɪs] *n* bosquecillo

**copulate** ['kɒpjuleɪt] *vi* copularse

**copy** ['kɒpɪ] *n* copia; (*of book etc*) ejemplar *m* ♦ *vt* copiar; ~right *n* derechos *mpl* de autor

**coral** ['kɒrəl] *n* coral *m;* ~ reef *n* arrecife *m* (de coral)

**cord** [kɔːd] *n* cuerda; (*ELEC*) cable *m;* (*fabric*) pana

**cordial** ['kɔːdɪəl] *adj* cordial ♦ *n* cordial *m*

**cordon** ['kɔːdn] *n* cordón *m;* ~ off *vt* acordonar

**corduroy** ['kɔːdərɔɪ] *n* pana

**core** [kɔː*] *n* centro, núcleo; (*of fruit*) corazón *m;* (*of problem*) meollo ♦ *vt* quitar el corazón a

**coriander** [kɒrɪ'ændə*] *n* culantro

**cork** [kɔːk] *n* corcho; (*tree*) alcornoque *m;* ~screw *n* sacacorchos *m inv*

**corn** [kɔːn] *n* (*BRIT: cereal crop*) trigo; (*US: maize*) maíz *m;* (*on foot*) callo; ~ on the cob (*CULIN*) maíz en la mazorca (*SP*), choclo (*AM*)

**corned beef** ['kɔːnd-] *n* carne *f* acecinada (en lata)

**corner** ['kɔːnə*] *n* (*outside*) esquina; (*inside*) rincón *m;* (*in road*) curva; (*FOOTBALL*) córner *m;* (*BOXING*) esquina ♦ *vt* (*trap*) arrinconar; (*COMM*) acaparar ♦ *vi* (*in car*) tomar las curvas; ~**stone** n (also fig) piedra angular

**cornet** ['kɔːnɪt] n (MUS) corneta; (BRIT: of ice-cream) cucurucho

**cornflakes** ['kɔːnfleɪks] npl copos mpl de maíz, cornflakes mpl

**cornflour** ['kɔːnflauə*] (BRIT), **cornstarch** ['kɔːnstɑːtʃ] (US) n harina de maíz

**Cornwall** ['kɔːnwəl] n Cornualles m

**corny** ['kɔːnɪ] (inf) adj gastado

**coronary** ['kɔrənərɪ] n (also: ~ thrombosis) infarto

**coronation** [kɔrə'neɪʃən] n coronación f

**coroner** ['kɔrənə*] n juez m (de instrucción)

**corporal** ['kɔːpərl] n cabo ♦ adj: ~ punishment castigo corporal

**corporate** ['kɔːpərɪt] adj (action, ownership) colectivo; (finance, image) corporativo

**corporation** [kɔːpə'reɪʃən] n (of town) ayuntamiento; (COMM) corporación f

**corps** [kɔː*, pl kɔːz] n inv cuerpo; diplomatic ~ cuerpo diplomático; press ~ gabinete m de prensa

**corpse** [kɔːps] n cadáver m

**corral** [kə'rɑːl] n corral m

**correct** [kə'rɛkt] adj justo, exacto; (proper) correcto ♦ vt corregir; (exam) corregir, calificar; ~**ion** [-ʃən] n (act) corrección f; (instance) rectificación f

**correspond** [kɔrɪs'pɔnd] vi (write): to ~ (with) escribirse (con); (be equivalent to): to ~ (to) corresponder (a); (be in accordance): to ~ (with) corresponder (con); ~**ence** n correspondencia; ~**ence course** n curso por correspondencia; ~**ent** n corresponsal m/f

**corridor** ['kɔrɪdɔː*] n pasillo

**corroborate** [kə'rɔbəreɪt] vt corroborar

**corrode** [kə'rəud] vt corroer ♦ vi corroerse; **corrosion** [-'rəuʒən] n corrosión f

**corrugated** ['kɔrəgeɪtɪd] adj ondula-

do; ~ **iron** n chapa ondulada

**corrupt** [kə'rʌpt] adj (person) corrupto; (COMPUT) corrompido ♦ vt corromper; (COMPUT) degradar; ~**ion** [-ʃən] n corrupción f

**corset** ['kɔːsɪt] n faja

**Corsica** ['kɔːsɪkə] n Córcega

**cosmetic** [kɔz'mɛtɪk] adj, n cosmético

**cosmonaut** ['kɔzmənɔːt] n cosmonauta m/f

**cosmopolitan** [kɔzmə'pɔlɪtn] adj cosmopolita

**cosset** ['kɔsɪt] vt mimar

**cost** [kɔst] (pt, pp cost) n (price) precio; ~**s** npl (COMM) costes mpl; (LAW) costas fpl ♦ vi costar, valer ♦ vt preparar el presupuesto de; **how much does it** ~? ¿cuánto cuesta?; **to** ~ **sb time/effort** costarle a uno tiempo/esfuerzo; **it** ~ **him his life** le costó la vida; **at all** ~**s** cueste lo que cueste

**co-star** ['kəustɑː*] n coprotagonista m/f

**Costa Rica** ['kɔstə'riːkə] n Costa Rica; ~**n** adj, n costarriqueño/a m/f

**cost-effective** [kɔstɪ'fɛktɪv] adj rentable

**costly** ['kɔstlɪ] adj costoso

**cost-of-living** [kɔstəv'lɪvɪŋ] adj: ~ **allowance** plus m de carestía de vida; ~ **index** índice m del costo de vida

**cost price** (BRIT) n precio de coste

**costume** ['kɔstjuːm] n traje m; (BRIT: also: swimming ~) traje de baño; ~ **jewellery** n bisutería

**cosy** ['kəuzɪ] (US **cozy**) adj (person) cómodo; (room) acogedor/a

**cot** [kɔt] n (BRIT: child's) cuna; (US: campbed) cama de campaña

**cottage** ['kɔtɪdʒ] n casita de campo; (rustic) barraca; ~ **cheese** n requesón m

**cotton** ['kɔtn] n algodón m; (thread) hilo; ~ **on to** (inf) vt fus caer en la cuenta de; ~ **candy** (US) n algodón m (azucarado); ~ **wool** (BRIT) n algodón m (hidrófilo)

**couch** [kautʃ] n sofá m; (doctor's etc) diván m

**couchette** [ku:'ʃet] n litera

**cough** [kɔf] vi toser ♦ n tos f; **~ drop** n pastilla para la tos

**could** [kud] pt of **can²**; **~n't** = could not

**council** ['kaunsl] n consejo; **city** or **town ~** consejo municipal; **~ estate** (BRIT) n urbanización f de viviendas municipales de alquiler; **~ house** (BRIT) n vivienda municipal de alquiler; **~lor** n concejal(a) m/f

**counsel** ['kaunsl] n (advice) consejo; (lawyer) abogado/a ♦ vt aconsejar; **~lor** n consejero/a; **~or** (US) n abogado/a

**count** [kaunt] vt contar; (include) incluir ♦ vi contar ♦ n cuenta; (of votes) escrutinio; (level) nivel m; (nobleman) conde m; **~ on** vt fus contar con; **~down** n cuenta atrás

**countenance** ['kauntinəns] n semblante m, rostro ♦ vt (tolerate) aprobar, tolerar

**counter** ['kauntə*] n (in shop) mostrador m; (in games) ficha ♦ vt contrarrestar ♦ adv: **to run ~ to** ser contrario a, ir en contra de; **~act** vt contrarrestar

**counterfeit** ['kauntəfit] n falsificación f, simulación f ♦ vt falsificar ♦ adj falso, falsificado

**counterfoil** ['kauntəfɔil] n talón m

**countermand** ['kauntəmɑ:nd] vt revocar, cancelar

**counterpart** ['kauntəpɑ:t] n homólogo/a

**counter-productive** [kauntəprə-'dʌktɪv] adj contraproducente

**countersign** ['kauntəsain] vt refrendar

**countess** ['kauntis] n condesa

**countless** ['kauntlis] adj innumerable

**country** ['kʌntri] n país m; (native land) patria; (as opposed to town) campo; (region) región f, tierra; **~ dancing** (BRIT) n baile m regional; **~ house** n casa de campo; **~man** n

(compatriot) compatriota m; (rural) campesino, paisano; **~side** n campo

**county** ['kaunti] n condado

**coup** [ku:] (pl ~s) n (also: ~ d'état) golpe m (de estado); (achievement) éxito

**coupé** ['ku:pei] n cupé m

**couple** ['kʌpl] n (of things) par m; (of people) pareja; (married ~) matrimonio; **a ~ of** un par de

**coupon** ['ku:pɔn] n cupón m; (voucher) valé m

**courage** ['kʌridʒ] n valor m, valentía; **~ous** [kə'reidʒəs] adj valiente

**courgette** [kuə'ʒet] (BRIT) n calabacín m (SP), calabacita (AM)

**courier** ['kuriə*] n mensajero/a; (for tourists) guía m/f (de turismo)

**course** [kɔ:s] n (direction) dirección f; (of river, SCOL) curso; (process) transcurso; (MED): **~ of treatment** tratamiento; (of ship) rumbo; (part of meal) plato; (GOLF) campo; **of ~** desde luego, naturalmente; **of ~!** ¡claro!

**court** [kɔ:t] n (royal) corte f; (LAW) tribunal m, juzgado; (TENNIS etc) pista, cancha ♦ vt (woman) cortejar a; **to take to ~** demandar

**courteous** ['kə:tiəs] adj cortés

**courtesan** [kɔ:tiˈzæn] n cortesana

**courtesy** ['kə:təsi] n cortesía; **(by) ~ of** por cortesía de

**court-house** ['kɔ:thaus] (US) n palacio de justicia

**courtier** ['kɔ:tiə*] n cortesano

**court-martial** (pl **courts-martial**) n consejo de guerra

**courtroom** ['kɔ:trum] n sala de justicia

**courtyard** ['kɔ:tjɑ:d] n patio

**cousin** ['kʌzn] n primo/a; **first ~** primo/a carnal, primo/a hermano/a

**cove** [kəuv] n cala, ensenada

**covenant** ['kʌvənənt] n pacto

**cover** ['kʌvə*] vt cubrir; (feelings, mistake) ocultar; (with lid) tapar; (book etc) forrar; (distance) recorrer; (include) abarcar; (protect: also: INSURANCE) cubrir; (PRESS) investigar; (*discuss*) tratar ♦ *n* cubierta; (*lid*) tapa; (*for chair etc*) funda; (*envelope*) sobre *m*; (*for book*) forro; (*of magazine*) portada; (*shelter*) abrigo; (INSURANCE) cobertura; (*of spy*) cobertura; ~s *npl* (*on bed*) sábanas; mantas; **to take** ~ (*shelter*) protegerse, resguardarse; **under** ~ (*indoors*) bajo techo; **under** ~ **of darkness** al amparo de la oscuridad; **under separate** ~ (COMM) por separado; **to up** *vi*: **to** ~ **up for sb** encubrir a uno; ~**age** *n* (TV, PRESS) cobertura; ~**alls** (US) *npl* mono; ~**charge** *n* precio del cubierto; ~**ing** *n* capa; ~**ing letter** (US ~ **letter**) *n* carta de explicación; ~**note** *n* (INSURANCE) póliza provisional

**covert** ['kʌvət] *adj* secreto, encubierto

**cover-up** *n* encubrimiento

**covet** ['kʌvɪt] *vt* codiciar

**cow** [kau] *n* vaca; (*inf!*: *woman*) bruja ♦ *vt* intimidar

**coward** ['kauəd] *n* cobarde *m/f*; ~**ice** [-ɪs] *n* cobardía; ~**ly** *adj* cobarde

**cowboy** ['kaubɔɪ] *n* vaquero

**cower** ['kauə*] *vi* encogerse (de miedo)

**coy** [kɔɪ] *adj* tímido

**cozy** ['kəuzɪ] (US) *adj* = **cosy**

**CPA** (US) *n abbr* = **certified public accountant**

**crab** [kræb] *n* cangrejo; ~ **apple** *n* manzana silvestre

**crack** [kræk] *n* grieta; (*noise*) crujido; (*drug*) crack ♦ *vt* agrietar, romper; (*nut*) cascar; (*solve: problem*) resolver; (: *code*) descifrar; (*whip etc*) chasquear; (*knuckles*) crujir; (*joke*) contar ♦ *adj* (*expert*) de primera; ~ **down on** *vt fus* adoptar fuertes medidas contra; ~ **up** *vi* (MED) sufrir una crisis nerviosa; ~**er** *n* (*biscuit*) crácker *m*; (*Christmas* ~**er**) petardo sorpresa

**crackle** ['krækl] *vi* crepitar

**cradle** ['kreɪdl] *n* cuna

**craft** [krɑːft] *n* (*skill*) arte *m*; (*trade*)

oficio; (*cunning*) astucia; (*boat*: *pl inv*) barco; (*plane*: *pl inv*) avión *m*

**craftsman** ['krɑːftsmən] *n* artesano; ~**ship** *n* (*quality*) destreza

**crafty** ['krɑːftɪ] *adj* astuto

**crag** [kræg] *n* peñasco

**cram** [kræm] *vt* (*fill*): **to** ~ **sth with** llenar algo (a reventar) de; (*put*): **to** ~ **sth into** meter algo a la fuerza en ♦ *vi* (*for exams*) empollar

**cramp** [kræmp] *n* (MED) calambre *m*; ~**ed** *adj* apretado, estrecho

**cranberry** ['krænbərɪ] *n* arándano agrio

**crane** [kreɪn] *n* (TECH) grúa; (*bird*) grulla

**crank** [kræŋk] *n* manivela; (*person*) chiflado; ~**shaft** *n* cigüeñal *m*

**cranny** ['krænɪ] *n see* **nook**

**crash** [kræʃ] *n* (*noise*) estrépito; (*of cars etc*) choque *m*; (*of plane*) accidente *m* de aviación; (COMM) quiebra ♦ *vt* (*car, plane*) estrellar ♦ *vi* (*car, plane*) estrellarse; (*two cars*) chocar; (COMM) quebrar; ~ **course** *n* curso acelerado; ~ **helmet** *n* casco (protector); ~ **landing** *n* aterrizaje *m* forzado

**crass** [kræs] *adj* grosero, maleducado

**crate** [kreɪt] *n* cajón *m* de embalaje; (*for bottles*) caja

**crater** ['kreɪtə*] *n* cráter *m*

**cravat(e)** [krə'væt] *n* pañuelo

**crave** [kreɪv] *vt*, *vi*: **to** ~ **(for)** ansiar, anhelar

**crawl** [krɔːl] *vi* (*drag o.s.*) arrastrarse; (*child*) andar a gatas, gatear; (*vehicle*) avanzar (lentamente) ♦ *n* (SWIMMING) crol *m*

**crayfish** ['kreɪfɪʃ] *n inv* (*freshwater*) cangrejo de río; (*saltwater*) cigala

**crayon** ['kreɪən] *n* lápiz *m* de color

**craze** [kreɪz] *n* (*fashion*) moda

**crazy** ['kreɪzɪ] *adj* (*person*) loco; (*idea*) disparatado; (*inf*: *keen*): ~ **about sb/sth** loco por uno/algo; ~ **paving** (BRIT) *n* pavimento de baldosas irregulares

**creak** [kriːk] *vi* (*floorboard*) crujir; (*hinge etc*) chirriar, rechinar

**cream** [kri:m] n (of milk) nata, crema; (lotion) crema f; (fig) flor f y nata ♦ adj (colour) color crema; ~ **cake** n pastel m de nata; ~ **cheese** n queso blanco; ~**y** adj cremoso; (colour) color crema

**crease** [kri:s] n (fold) pliegue m; (in trousers) raya; (wrinkle: gen) arruga f ♦ vt (wrinkle) arrugar ♦ vi (wrinkle up) arrugarse

**create** [kri:'eɪt] vt crear; **creation** [-ʃən] n creación f; **creative** adj creativo; **creator** n creador(a) m/f

**creature** ['kri:tʃə*] n (animal) animal m, bicho; (person) criatura

**crèche** [krɛʃ] n guardería (infantil)

**credence** ['kri:dəns] n: **to lend** or **give** ~ **to** creer en, dar crédito a

**credentials** [krɪ'denʃlz] npl (references) referencias fpl; (identity papers) documentos mpl de identidad

**credible** ['kredɪbl] adj creíble; (trustworthy) digno de confianza

**credit** ['kredɪt] n crédito m; (merit) honor m, mérito f vt (COMM) abonar; (believe: also: **give** ~ **to**) creer, prestar fe a ♦ adj crediticio; ~**s** npl (CINEMA) fichas fpl técnicas; **to be in** ~ (person) tener saldo a favor; **to** ~ **sb with** (fig) reconocer a uno el mérito de; ~ **card** n tarjeta de crédito; ~**or** n acreedor(a) m/f

**creed** [kri:d] n credo

**creek** [kri:k] n cala, ensenada; (US) riachuelo

**creep** [kri:p] (pt, pp **crept**) vi arrastrarse; ~**er** n enredadera; ~**y** adj (frightening) horripilante

**cremate** [krɪ'meɪt] vt incinerar

**crematorium** [kremə'tɔ:rɪəm] (pl **crematoria**) n crematorio

**crêpe** [kreɪp] n (fabric) crespón m; (also: ~ **rubber**) crepé m; ~ **bandage** (BRIT) n venda de crepé

**crept** [krept] pt, pp of **creep**

**crescent** ['kresnt] n media luna; (street) calle f (en forma de semicírculo)

**cress** [kres] n berro

**crest** [krest] n (of bird) cresta; (of

hill) cima, cumbre f; (of coat of arms) blasón m; ~-**fallen** adj alicaído

**crevice** ['krevɪs] n grieta, hendedura

**crew** [kru:] n (of ship etc) tripulación f; (TV, CINEMA) equipo; ~-**cut** n corte m al rape; ~-**neck** n cuello a la caja

**crib** [krɪb] n cuna ♦ vt (inf) plagiar

**crick** [krɪk] n (in neck) tortícolis f

**cricket** ['krɪkɪt] n (insect) grillo; (game) críquet m

**crime** [kraɪm] n (no pl: illegal activities) crimen m; (illegal action) delito; **criminal** ['krɪmɪnl] n criminal m/f, delincuente m/f ♦ adj criminal; (illegal) delictivo; (law) penal

**crimson** ['krɪmzn] adj carmesí

**cringe** [krɪndʒ] vi agacharse, encogerse

**crinkle** ['krɪŋkl] vt arrugar

**cripple** ['krɪpl] n lisiado/a, cojo/a ♦ vt lisiar, mutilar

**crises** ['kraɪsi:z] npl of **crisis**

**crisis** ['kraɪsɪs] (pl **crises**) n crisis f inv

**crisp** [krɪsp] adj fresco; (vegetables etc) crujiente; (manner) seco; ~**s** (BRIT) npl patatas fpl (SP) or papas fpl (AM) fritas

**criss-cross** ['krɪskrɔs] adj entrelazado

**criterion** [kraɪ'tɪərɪən] (pl **criteria**) n criterio

**critic** ['krɪtɪk] n crítico/a, m/f; ~**al** adj crítico; (illness) grave; ~**ally** adv (speak etc) en tono crítico; (ill) gravemente; ~**ism** ['krɪtɪsɪzm] n crítica; ~**ize** ['krɪtɪsaɪz] vt criticar

**croak** [krəuk] vi (frog) croar; (raven) graznar; (person) gruñir

**Croatia** [krəu'eɪʃə] n Croacia

**crochet** ['krəuʃeɪ] n ganchillo

**crockery** ['krɔkərɪ] n loza, vajilla

**crocodile** ['krɔkədaɪl] n cocodrilo

**crocus** ['krəukəs] n croco, crocus m

**croft** [krɔft] n granja pequeña

**crony** ['krəunɪ] (inf: pej) n compinche m/f

**crook** [kruk] n ladrón/ona m/f; (of shepherd) cayado; ~**ed** ['krukɪd] adj torcido; (*dishonest*) nada honrado

**crop** [krɔp] *n* (*produce*) cultivo; (*amount produced*) cosecha; (*riding* ~) látigo de montar ♦ *vt* cortar, recortar; ~ **up** *vi* surgir, presentarse

**croquette** [krə'kɛt] *n* croqueta

**cross** [krɔs] *n* cruz *f*; (*hybrid*) cruce *m* ♦ *vt* (*street etc*) cruzar, atravesar ♦ *adj* de mal humor, enojado; ~ **out** *vt* tachar; ~ **over** *vi* cruzar; ~**bar** *n* travesaño; ~**country (race)** *n* carrera a campo traviesa, cross *m*; ~-**examine** *vt* interrogar; ~-**eyed** *adj* bizco; ~**fire** *n* fuego cruzado; ~**ing** *n* (*sea passage*) travesía; (*also*: *pedestrian* ~*ing*) paso para peatones; ~**ing guard** (*US*) *n* persona encargada de ayudar a los niños a cruzar la calle; ~ **purposes** *npl*: **to be at** ~ **purposes** no comprenderse uno a otro; ~-**reference** *n* referencia, llamada; ~**roads** *n* cruce *m*, encrucijada; ~ **section** *n* corte *m* transversal; (*of population*) muestra (representativa); ~**walk** (*US*) *n* paso de peatones; ~**wind** *n* viento de costado; ~**word** *n* crucigrama *m*

**crotch** [krɔtʃ] *n* (*ANAT, of garment*) entrepierna

**crotchet** ['krɔtʃɪt] *n* (*MUS*) negra

**crotchety** ['krɔtʃɪtɪ] *adj* antipático

**crouch** [krautʃ] *vi* agacharse, acurrucarse

**crow** [krəu] *n* (*bird*) cuervo; (*of cock*) canto, cacareo ♦ *vi* (*cock*) cantar

**crowbar** ['krəuba:*] *n* palanca

**crowd** [kraud] *n* muchedumbre *f*, multitud *f* ♦ *vt* (*fill*) llenar ♦ *vi* (*gather*): **to** ~ **round** reunirse en torno a; (*cram*): **to** ~ **in** entrar en tropel; ~**ed** *adj* (*full*) atestado; (*densely populated*) superpoblado

**crown** [kraun] *n* corona; (*of head*) coronilla; (*for tooth*) funda; (*of hill*) cumbre *f* ♦ *vt* coronar; (*fig*) completar, rematar; ~ **jewels** *npl* joyas *fpl* reales; ~ **prince** *n* príncipe *m* heredero

**crow's feet** *npl* patas *fpl* de gallo

**crucial** ['kru:ʃl] *adj* decisivo

**crucifix** ['kru:sɪfɪks] *n* crucifijo; ~**ion** [-'fɪkʃən] *n* crucifixión *f*

**crude** [kru:d] *adj* (*materials*) bruto; (*fig: basic*) tosco; (: *vulgar*) ordinario; ~ (**oil**) *n* (petróleo) crudo

**cruel** ['kruəl] *adj* cruel; ~**ty** *n* crueldad *f*

**cruise** [kru:z] *n* crucero ♦ *vi* (*ship*) hacer un crucero; (*car*) ir a velocidad de crucero; ~**r** *n* (*motorboat*) yate *m* de motor; (*warship*) crucero

**crumb** [krʌm] *n* miga, migaja

**crumble** ['krʌmbl] *vt* desmenuzar ♦ *vi* desmenuzarse; (*building, fig also*) desmoronarse; **crumbly** *adj* que se desmigaja fácilmente

**crumpet** ['krʌmpɪt] *n* ≈ bollo para tostar

**crumple** ['krʌmpl] *vt* (*paper*) estrujar; (*material*) arrugar

**crunch** [krʌntʃ] *vt* (*with teeth*) mascar; (*underfoot*) hacer crujir ♦ *n* (*fig*) hora o momento de la verdad; ~**y** *adj* crujiente

**crusade** [kru:'seɪd] *n* cruzada

**crush** [krʌʃ] *n* (*crowd*) aglomeración *f*; (*infatuation*): **to have a** ~ **on sb** estar loco por uno; (*drink*): **lemon** ~ limonada ♦ *vt* aplastar; (*paper*) estrujar; (*cloth*) arrugar; (*fruit*) exprimir; (*opposition*) aplastar; (*hopes*) destruir

**crust** [krʌst] *n* corteza; (*of snow, ice*) costra

**crutch** [krʌtʃ] *n* muleta

**crux** [krʌks] *n*: **the** ~ **of** lo esencial de, el quid de

**cry** [kraɪ] *vi* llorar; (*shout: also*: ~ **out**) gritar ♦ *n* (*shriek*) chillido; (*shout*) grito; ~ **off** *vi* echarse atrás

**cryptic** ['krɪptɪk] *adj* enigmático, secreto

**crystal** ['krɪstl] *n* cristal *m*; ~-**clear** *adj* claro como el agua

**cub** [kʌb] *n* cachorro; (*also*: ~ **scout**) niño explorador

**Cuba** ['kju:bə] *n* Cuba; ~**n** *adj, n* cubano/a *m/f*

**cubbyhole** ['kʌbɪhəul] *n* cuchitril *m*

**cube** [kju:b] n cubo ♦ vt (MATH) cubicar; **cubic** adj cúbico

**cubicle** ['kju:bɪkl] n (at pool) caseta; (for bed) cubículo

**cuckoo** ['kuku:] n cuco; ~ **clock** n reloj m de cucú

**cucumber** ['kju:kʌmbə*] n pepino

**cuddle** ['kʌdl] vt abrazar ♦ vi abrazarse

**cue** [kju:] n (snooker ~) taco; (THEATRE etc) señal f

**cuff** [kʌf] n (of sleeve) puño; (US: of trousers) vuelta; (blow) bofetada; **off the ~** adv de improviso; ~**links** npl gemelos mpl

**cuisine** [kwɪ'zi:n] n cocina

**cul-de-sac** ['kʌldəsæk] n callejón m sin salida

**cull** [kʌl] vt (idea) sacar ♦ n (of animals) matanza selectiva

**culminate** ['kʌlmɪneɪt] vi: **to ~ in** terminar en; **culmination** [-'neɪʃən] n culminación f, colmo

**culottes** [ku:'lɔts] npl falda pantalón f

**culprit** ['kʌlprɪt] n culpable m/f

**cult** [kʌlt] n culto

**cultivate** ['kʌltɪveɪt] vt (also fig) cultivar; ~**d** adj culto; **cultivation** [-'veɪʃən] n cultivo

**cultural** ['kʌltʃərəl] adj cultural

**culture** ['kʌltʃə*] n (also fig) cultura; (BIO) cultivo; ~**d** adj culto

**cumbersome** ['kʌmbəsəm] adj de mucho bulto, voluminoso; (process) enrevesado

**cunning** ['kʌnɪŋ] n astucia ♦ adj astuto

**cup** [kʌp] n taza; (as prize) copa

**cupboard** ['kʌbəd] n armario; (kitchen) alacena

**cup-tie** ['kʌptaɪ] (BRIT) n partido de copa

**curate** ['kjuərɪt] n cura m

**curator** [kjuə'reɪtə*] n director(a) m/f

ción f; (fig: solution) remedio

**curfew** ['kə:fju:] n toque m de queda

**curio** ['kjuərɪəu] n curiosidad f

**curiosity** [kjuərɪ'ɔsɪtɪ] n curiosidad f

**curious** ['kjuərɪəs] adj curioso; (person: interested): **to be ~** sentir curiosidad

**curl** [kə:l] n rizo ♦ vt (hair) rizar ♦ vi rizarse; ~ **up** vi (person) hacerse un ovillo; ~**er** n rulo; ~**y** adj rizado

**currant** ['kʌrnt] n pasa (de Corinto); (black~, red~) grosella

**currency** ['kʌrənsɪ] n moneda; **to gain ~** (fig) difundirse

**current** ['kʌrnt] n corriente f ♦ adj (accepted) corriente; (present) actual; ~ **account** (BRIT) n cuenta corriente; ~ **affairs** npl noticias fpl de actualidad; ~**ly** adv actualmente

**curriculum** [kə'rɪkjuləm] (pl ~**s** or **curricula**) n plan m de estudios; ~ **vitae** n currículum m

**curry** ['kʌrɪ] n curry m ♦ vt: **to ~ favour with** buscar favores con; ~ **powder** n curry m en polvo

**curse** [kə:s] vi soltar tacos ♦ vt maldecir ♦ n maldición f; (swearword) palabrota, taco

**cursor** ['kə:sə*] n (COMPUT) cursor m

**cursory** ['kə:sərɪ] adj rápido, superficial

**curt** [kə:t] adj corto, seco

**curtail** [kə:'teɪl] vt (visit etc) acortar; (freedom) restringir; (expenses etc) reducir

**curtain** ['kə:tn] n cortina; (THEATRE) telón m

**curts(e)y** ['kə:tsɪ] vi hacer una reverencia

**curve** [kə:v] n curva ♦ vi (road) hacer una curva; (line etc) curvarse

**cushion** ['kuʃən] n cojín m; (of air) colchón m ♦ vt (shock) amortiguar

**custard** ['kʌstəd] n natillas fpl

**custody** ['kʌstədɪ] n custodia; **to take into ~** detener

**custom** ['kʌstəm] n costumbre f; (COMM) clientela; ~**ary** adj acostumbrado

**customer** [ˈkʌstəmə*] n cliente m/f
**customized** [ˈkʌstəmaɪzd] adj (car etc) hecho a encargo
**custom-made** adj hecho a la medida
**customs** [ˈkʌstəmz] npl aduana; ~ **duty** n derechos mpl de aduana; ~ **officer** n aduanero/a
**cut** [kʌt] (pt, pp cut) vt cortar; (price) rebajar; (text, programme) acortar; (reduce) reducir ♦ vi cortar ♦ n (of garment) corte m; (in skin) cortadura; (in salary etc) rebaja; (in spending) reducción f, recorte m; (slice of meat) tajada; **to ~ a tooth** echar un diente; ~ **down** vt (tree) derribar; (reduce) reducir; ~ **off** vt cortar; (person, place) aislar; (TEL) desconectar; ~ **out** vt (shape) recortar; (stop: activity etc) dejar; (remove) quitar; ~ **up** vt cortar (en pedazos); ~**back** n reducción f
**cute** [kjuːt] adj mono
**cuticle** [ˈkjuːtɪkl] n cutícula
**cutlery** [ˈkʌtlərɪ] n cubiertos mpl
**cutlet** [ˈkʌtlɪt] n chuleta; (nut etc cutlet) plato vegetariano hecho con nueces y verdura en forma de chuleta
**cut:** ~**out** n (switch) dispositivo de seguridad, disyuntor m; (cardboard ~) recortable m; ~**price** (US ~**rate**) adj a precio reducido; ~**throat** n asesino/a ♦ adj feroz
**cutting** [ˈkʌtɪŋ] adj (remark) mordaz ♦ n (BRIT: from newspaper) recorte m; (from plant) esqueje m
**CV** n abbr = curriculum vitae
**cwt** abbr = hundredweight(s)
**cyanide** [ˈsaɪənaɪd] n cianuro
**cycle** [ˈsaɪkl] n ciclo; (bicycle) bicicleta ♦ vi ir en bicicleta; **cycling** n ciclismo; **cyclist** n ciclista m/f
**cyclone** [ˈsaɪkləun] n ciclón m
**cygnet** [ˈsɪgnɪt] n pollo de cisne
**cylinder** [ˈsɪlɪndə*] n cilindro; (of gas) bombona; ~**head gasket** n junta de culata
**cymbals** [ˈsɪmblz] npl platillos mpl
**cynic** [ˈsɪnɪk] n cínico/a; ~**al** adj cíni-

co; ~**ism** [ˈsɪnɪsɪzəm] n cinismo
**cypress** [ˈsaɪprɪs] n ciprés m
**Cyprus** [ˈsaɪprəs] n Chipre f
**cyst** [sɪst] n quiste m; ~**itis** [-ˈtaɪtɪs] n cistitis f
**czar** [zɑː*] n zar m
**Czech** [tʃɛk] adj, n checo/a m/f
**Czechoslovakia** [tʃɛkəsləˈvækɪə] n Checoslovaquia; ~**n** adj, n checo/a m/f

# D

**D** [diː] n (MUS) re m
**dab** [dæb] vt (eyes, wound) tocar (ligeramente); (paint, cream) poner un poco de
**dabble** [ˈdæbl] vi: **to ~ in** ser algo aficionado a
**dad** [dæd] n = **daddy**
**daddy** [ˈdædɪ] n papá m
**daffodil** [ˈdæfədɪl] n narciso
**daft** [dɑːft] adj tonto
**dagger** [ˈdægə*] n puñal m, daga
**daily** [ˈdeɪlɪ] adj diario, cotidiano ♦ adv todos los días, cada día
**dainty** [ˈdeɪntɪ] adj delicado
**dairy** [ˈdɛərɪ] n (shop) lechería; (on farm) vaquería; ~ **farm** n granja; ~ **products** npl productos mpl lácteos; ~ **store** (US) n lechería
**dais** [ˈdeɪɪs] n estrado
**daisy** [ˈdeɪzɪ] n margarita; ~ **wheel** n margarita
**dale** [deɪl] n valle m
**dam** [dæm] n presa ♦ vt construir una presa sobre, represar
**damage** [ˈdæmɪdʒ] n lesión f; daño; (dents etc) desperfectos mpl; (fig) perjuicio ♦ vt dañar, perjudicar; (spoil, break) estropear; ~**s** npl (LAW) daños mpl y perjuicios
**damn** [dæm] vt condenar; (curse) maldecir ♦ n (inf): **I don't give a ~** me importa un pito ♦ adj (inf: also: ~**ed**) maldito; ~ **(it)!** ¡maldito sea!; ~**ing** adj (evidence) irrecusable
**damp** [dæmp] adj húmedo, mojado ♦ n humedad f ♦ vt (also: ~**en:** cloth,

*rag*) mojar; (: *enthusiasm*) enfriar

**damson** ['dæmzən] *n* ciruela damascena

**dance** [dɑːns] *n* baile *m* ♦ *vi* bailar; ~ **hall** *n* salón *m* de baile; ~**r** *n* bailador(a) *m/f*; (*professional*) bailarín/ina *m/f*; **dancing** *n* baile *m*

**dandelion** ['dændɪlaɪən] *n* diente *m* de león

**dandruff** ['dændrəf] *n* caspa

**Dane** [deɪn] *n* danés/esa *m/f*

**danger** ['deɪndʒə*] *n* peligro; (*risk*) riesgo; ~! (*on sign*) ¡peligro de muerte!; **to be in ~ of** correr riesgo de; ~**ous** *adj* peligroso; ~**ously** *adv* peligrosamente

**dangle** ['dæŋgl] *vt* colgar ♦ *vi* pender, colgar

**Danish** ['deɪnɪʃ] *adj* danés/esa ♦ *n* (*LING*) danés *m*

**dapper** ['dæpə*] *adj* pulcro, apuesto

**dare** [dɛə*] *vt*: **to ~ sb to do** desafiar a uno a hacer ♦ *vi*: **to ~ (to) do sth** atreverse a hacer algo; **I ~ say** (*I suppose*) puede ser (que); ~**devil** *n* temerario/a, atrevido/a; **daring** *adj* atrevido, osado ♦ *n* atrevimiento, osadía

**dark** [dɑːk] *adj* oscuro; (*hair, complexion*) moreno ♦ *n*: **in the ~ about** a oscuras; **to be in the ~ about** (*fig*) no saber nada de; **after ~** después del anochecer; ~**en** *vt* (*colour*) hacer más oscuro ♦ *vi* oscurecerse; ~**glasses** *npl* gafas *fpl* negras (*SP*), anteojos *mpl* negros (*AM*); ~**ness** *n* oscuridad *f*; ~**room** *n* cuarto oscuro

**darling** ['dɑːlɪŋ] *adj, n* querido/a *m/f*

**darn** [dɑːn] *vt* zurcir

**dart** [dɑːt] *n* dardo; (*in sewing*) sisa ♦ *vi* precipitarse; ~ **away/along** *vi* salir/marchar disparado; ~**board** *n* diana; ~**s** *n* dardos *mpl*

**dash** [dæʃ] *n* (*small quantity: of liquid*) gota, chorrito; (: *of solid*) pizca; (*sign*) raya ♦ *vt* (*throw*) tirar; (*hopes*) defraudar ♦ *vi* precipitarse, ir de prisa; ~ **away** *or* **off** *vi* marcharse apresuradamente

**dashboard** ['dæʃbɔːd] *n* (*AUT*) sal-

picadero

**dashing** ['dæʃɪŋ] *adj* gallardo

**data** ['deɪtə] *npl* datos *mpl*; ~**base** *n* base *f* de datos; ~ **processing** *n* proceso de datos

**date** [deɪt] *n* (*day*) fecha; (*with friend*) cita; (*fruit*) dátil *m* ♦ *vt* fechar; (*person*) salir con; ~ **of birth** fecha de nacimiento; **to ~** *adv* hasta la fecha; ~**d** *adj* anticuado

**daub** [dɔːb] *vt* embadurnar

**daughter** ['dɔːtə*] *n* hija; ~**-in-law** *n* nuera, hija política

**daunting** ['dɔːntɪŋ] *adj* desalentador(a)

**dawdle** ['dɔːdl] *vi* (*go slowly*) andar muy despacio

**dawn** [dɔːn] *n* alba, amanecer *m*; (*fig*) nacimiento ♦ *vi* (*day*) amanecer; (*fig*): **it ~ed on him that ...** cayó en la cuenta de que ....

**day** [deɪ] *n* día *m*; (*working ~*) jornada; (*hey~*) tiempos *mpl*, días *mpl*; **the ~ before/after** el día anterior/siguiente; **the ~ after tomorrow** pasado mañana; **the ~ before yesterday** anteayer; **the following ~** el día siguiente; **by ~** de día; ~**break** *n* amanecer *m*; ~**dream** *vi* soñar despierto; ~**light** *n* luz *f* (del día); ~ **return** (*BRIT*) *n* billete *m* de ida y vuelta (en un día); ~**time** *n* día *m*; ~**-to-** *adj* cotidiano

**daze** [deɪz] *vt* (*stun*) aturdir ♦ *n*: **in a ~** aturdido

**dazzle** ['dæzl] *vt* deslumbrar

**DC** *abbr* (= *direct current*) corriente *f* continua

**dead** [dɛd] *adj* muerto; (*limb*) dormido; (*telephone*) cortado; (*battery*) agotado ♦ *adv* (*completely*) totalmente; (*exactly*) exactamente; **to shoot sb ~** matar a uno a tiros; ~ **tired** muerto de cansancio; **to stop ~** parar en seco; **the ~** *npl* los muertos; **to be a ~ loss** (*inf: person*) ser un inútil; ~**en** *vt* (*blow, sound*) amortiguar; (*pain etc*) aliviar; ~ **end** *n* callejón *m* sin salida; ~ **heat** *n* (*SPORT*) empate *m*; ~**line**

*n* fecha (*or* hora) tope; **~lock** *n*: **to reach ~lock** llegar a un punto muerto; **~ly** *adj* mortal, fatal; **~pan** *adj* sin expresión; **the D~ Sea** *n* el Mar Muerto

**deaf** [dɛf] *adj* sordo; **~en** *vt* ensordecer; **~ness** *n* sordera

**deal** [diːl] (*pt, pp* **dealt**) *n* (*agreement*) pacto, convenio; (*business ~*) trato ♦ *vt* dar; (*card*) repartir; **a great ~ (of)** bastante, mucho; **~ in** *vt fus* tratar en, comerciar en; **~ with** *vt fus* (*people*) tratar con; (*problem*) ocuparse de; (*subject*) tratar de; **~ings** *npl* (COMM) transacciones *fpl*; (*relations*) relaciones *fpl*

**dealt** [dɛlt] *pt, pp* of **deal**

**dean** [diːn] *n* (REL) deán *m*; (SCOL: BRIT; (: US) decano; *(: US)* decano *m*

**dear** [dɪə*] *adj* querido; (*expensive*) caro ♦ *n*: **my ~** mi querido/a ♦ *excl*: **~ me!** ¡Dios mío!; **D~ Sir/Madam** (*in letter*) Muy Señor Mío, Estimado Señor/Estimada Señora; **D~ Mr/Mrs X** Estimado/a Señor(a) X; **~ly** *adv* (*love*) mucho; (*pay*) caro

**death** [dɛθ] *n* muerte *f*; **~ certificate** *n* partida de defunción; **~ly** *adj* (*white*) como un muerto; (*silence*) sepulcral; **~ penalty** *n* pena de muerte; **~ rate** *n* mortalidad *f*; **~ toll** *n* número de víctimas

**debacle** [deɪ'bɑːkl] *n* desastre *m*

**debar** [dɪ'bɑː*] *vt*: **to ~ sb from doing** prohibir a uno hacer

**debase** [dɪ'beɪs] *vt* degradar

**debatable** [dɪ'beɪtəbl] *adj* discutible

**debate** [dɪ'beɪt] *n* debate *m* ♦ *vt* discutir

**debauchery** [dɪ'bɔːtʃərɪ] *n* libertinaje *m*

**debilitating** [dɪ'bɪlɪteɪtɪŋ] *adj* (*illness etc*) debilitante

**debit** ['dɛbɪt] *n* debe *m* ♦ *vt*: **to ~ a sum to sb** *or* **to sb's account** cargar una suma en cuenta a alguien

**debris** ['dɛbriː] *n* escombros *mpl*

**debt** [dɛt] *n* deuda; **to be in ~** tener

deudas; **~or** *n* deudor(a) *m/f*

**debunk** [diː'bʌŋk] *vt* desprestigiar, desacreditar

**début** ['deɪbjuː] *n* presentación *f*

**decade** ['dɛkeɪd] *n* decenio, década

**decadence** ['dɛkədəns] *n* decadencia

**decaffeinated** [dɪ'kæfɪneɪtɪd] *adj* descafeinado

**decanter** [dɪ'kæntə*] *n* garrafa

**decay** [dɪ'keɪ] *n* (*of building*) desmoronamiento; (*of tooth*) caries *f inv* ♦ *vi* (*rot*) pudrirse

**deceased** [dɪ'siːst] *n*: **the ~** el/la difunto/a

**deceit** [dɪ'siːt] *n* engaño; **~ful** *adj* engañoso; **deceive** [dɪ'siːv] *vt* engañar

**December** [dɪ'sɛmbə*] *n* diciembre *m*

**decent** ['diːsənt] *adj* (*proper*) decente; (*person: kind*) amable, bueno

**deception** [dɪ'sɛpʃən] *n* engaño

**deceptive** [dɪ'sɛptɪv] *adj* engañoso

**decibel** ['dɛsɪbɛl] *n* decibel(io) *m*

**decide** [dɪ'saɪd] *vt* (*person*) decidir; (*question, argument*) resolver ♦ *vi* decidir; **to ~ to do/that** decidir hacer/que; **to ~ on sth** decidirse por algo; **~d** *adj* (*resolute*) decidido; (*clear, definite*) indudable; **~dly** [-dɪdlɪ] *adv* decididamente; (*emphatically*) con energía

**deciduous** [dɪ'sɪdjʊəs] *adj* de hoja caduca

**decimal** ['dɛsɪməl] *adj* decimal ♦ *n* decimal *m*; **~ point** *n* coma decimal

**decimate** ['dɛsɪmeɪt] *vt* diezmar

**decipher** [dɪ'saɪfə*] *vt* descifrar

**decision** [dɪ'sɪʒən] *n* decisión *f*

**decisive** [dɪ'saɪsɪv] *adj* decisivo; (*person*) decidido

**deck** [dɛk] *n* (NAUT) cubierta; (*of bus*) piso; (*record ~*) platina; (*of cards*) baraja; **~chair** *n* tumbona

**declaration** [dɛklə'reɪʃən] *n* declaración *f*

**declare** [dɪ'klɛə*] *vt* declarar

**decline** [dɪ'klaɪn] *n* disminución *f*, descenso ♦ *vt* rehusar ♦ *vi* (*person, business*) decaer; (*strength*) disminuir

**decode** [diː'kəʊd] vt descifrar

**decoder** [diː'kəʊdə*] n (TV) decodificador m

**decompose** [diːkəm'pəʊz] vi descomponerse

**décor** ['deɪkɔː*] n decoración f; (THEATRE) decorado

**decorate** ['dekəreɪt] vt (adorn): to ~ (with) adornar (de), decorar (de); (paint) pintar; (paper) empapelar; **decoration** [-'reɪʃən] n adorno; (act) decoración f; (medal) condecoración f; **decorative** ['dekərətɪv] adj decorativo; **decorator** n (workman) pintor m (decorador)

**decorum** [dɪ'kɔːrəm] n decoro

**decoy** ['diːkɔɪ] n señuelo

**decrease** [n 'diːkriːs, vb diːkriːs] n: ~ (in) disminución f ♦ vt disminuir, reducir ♦ vi reducirse

**decree** [dɪ'kriː] n decreto; ~ **nisi** n sentencia provisional de divorcio

**dedicate** ['dedɪkeɪt] vt dedicar; **dedication** [-'keɪʃən] n (devotion) dedicación f; (in book) dedicatoria

**deduce** [dɪ'djuːs] vt deducir

**deduct** [dɪ'dʌkt] vt restar; descontar; ~**ion** [dɪ'dʌkʃən] n (amount deducted) descuento; (conclusion) deducción f, conclusión f

**deed** [diːd] n hecho, acto; (feat) hazaña; (LAW) escritura

**deem** [diːm] vt juzgar

**deep** [diːp] adj profundo; (expressing measurements) ~ de profundidad; (voice) bajo; (breath) profundo; (colour) intenso ♦ adv: the spectators stood 20 ~ los espectadores se formaron de 20 en fondo; to be 4 metres ~ tener 4 metros de profundidad; ~**en** vt ahondar, profundizar ♦ vi aumentar, crecer; ~**freeze** n congelador m; ~**fry** vt freír en aceite abundante; ~**ly** adv (breathe) a pleno pulmón; (interested, moved, grateful) profundamente, hondamente; ~**sea diving** n buceo de altura; ~**seated** adj (beliefs) (profundamente) arraigado

**deer** [dɪə*] n inv ciervo

**deface** [dɪ'feɪs] vt (wall, surface) estropear, pintarrajear

**default** [dɪ'fɔːlt] n: by ~ (win) por incomparecencia ♦ adj (COMPUT) por defecto

**defeat** [dɪ'fiːt] n derrota ♦ vt derrotar, vencer; ~**ist** adj, n derrotista m/f

**defect** [n 'diːfekt, vb dɪ'fekt] n defecto ♦ vi: to ~ to the enemy pasarse al enemigo; ~**ive** [dɪ'fektɪv] adj defectuoso

**defence** [dɪ'fens] (US **defense**) n defensa; ~**less** adj indefenso

**defend** [dɪ'fend] vt defender; ~**ant** n acusado/a; (in civil case) demandado/a; ~**er** n defensor(a) m/f; (SPORT) defensa m/f

**defense** [dɪ'fens] (US) n = **defence**

**defensive** [dɪ'fensɪv] adj defensivo ♦ n: on the ~ a la defensiva

**defer** [dɪ'fɜː*] vt aplazar; ~**ence** ['defərəns] n deferencia, respeto

**defiance** [dɪ'faɪəns] n desafío; **in** ~ **of** en contra de; **defiant** [dɪ'faɪənt] adj (challenging) desafiante, retador(a)

**deficiency** [dɪ'fɪʃənsɪ] n (lack) falta; (defect) defecto; **deficient** [dɪ'fɪʃənt] adj deficiente

**deficit** ['defɪsɪt] n déficit m

**defile** [dɪ'faɪl] vt manchar

**define** [dɪ'faɪn] vt (word etc) definir; (limits etc) determinar

**definite** ['defɪnɪt] adj (fixed) determinado; (obvious) claro; (certain) indudable; he was ~ **about** it no dejó lugar a dudas (sobre ello); ~**ly** adv desde luego, por supuesto

**definition** [defɪ'nɪʃən] n definición f; (clearness) nitidez f

**deflate** [diː'fleɪt] vt desinflar

**deflect** [dɪ'flekt] vt desviar

**defraud** [dɪ'frɔːd] vt: to ~ **sb** of **sth** estafar algo a uno

**defrost** [diː'frɒst] vt descongelar; ~**er** (US) n (demister) eliminador m de vaho

**deft** [deft] adj diestro, hábil

**defunct** [dɪ'fʌŋkt] adj difunto; (organization etc) ya que no existe

**defuse** [diːˈfjuːz] vt desactivar; (situation) calmar

**defy** [dɪˈfaɪ] vt (resist) oponerse a; (challenge) desafiar; (fig): **it defies description** resulta imposible describirlo

**degenerate** [vb dɪˈdʒenəreɪt, adj dɪˈdʒenərɪt] vi degenerar ♦ adj degenerado

**degree** [dɪˈgriː] n grado; (SCOL) título; **to have a ~ in maths** tener una licenciatura en matemáticas; **by ~s** (gradually) poco a poco, por etapas; **to some ~** hasta cierto punto

**dehydrated** [diːhaɪˈdreɪtd] adj deshidratado; (milk) en polvo

**de-ice** [diːˈaɪs] vt deshelar

**deign** [deɪn] vi: **to ~ to do** dignarse hacer

**deity** [ˈdiːɪtɪ] n deidad f, divinidad f

**dejected** [dɪˈdʒektɪd] adj abatido, desanimado

**delay** [dɪˈleɪ] vt demorar, aplazar; (person) entretener; (train) retrasar ♦ vi tardar ♦ n demora, retraso; **to be ~ed** retrasarse; **without ~** en seguida, sin tardar

**delectable** [dɪˈlektəbl] adj (person) encantador(a); (food) delicioso

**delegate** [n ˈdelɪgɪt, vb ˈdelɪgeɪt] n delegado/a ♦ vt (person) delegar en; (task) delegar

**delete** [dɪˈliːt] vt suprimir, tachar

**deliberate** [adj dɪˈlɪbərɪt, vb dɪˈlɪbəreɪt] adj (intentional) intencionado; (slow) pausado, lento ♦ vi deliberar; **~ly** adv (on purpose) a propósito

**delicacy** [ˈdelɪkəsɪ] n delicadeza; (choice food) manjar m

**delicate** [ˈdelɪkɪt] adj delicado; (fragile) frágil

**delicatessen** [delɪkəˈtesn] n ultramarinos mpl finos

**delicious** [dɪˈlɪʃəs] adj delicioso

**delight** [dɪˈlaɪt] n (feeling) placer m, deleite m; (person, experience etc) encanto, delicia ♦ vt encantar, deleitar; **to take ~ in** deleitarse en; **~ed** adj: **~ed** (at or with/to do) encan-

tado (con/de hacer); **~ful** adj encantador(a), delicioso

**delinquent** [dɪˈlɪŋkwənt] adj, n delincuente m/f

**delirious** [dɪˈlɪrɪəs] adj: **to be ~** delirar, desvariar; **to be ~ with** estar loco de

**deliver** [dɪˈlɪvə*] vt (distribute) repartir; (hand over) entregar; (message) comunicar; (speech) pronunciar; (MED) asistir al parto de; **~y** n reparto; entrega; (of speaker) modo de expresarse; (MED) parto, alumbramiento; **to take ~y of** recibir

**delude** [dɪˈluːd] vt engañar

**deluge** [ˈdeljuːdʒ] n diluvio

**delusion** [dɪˈluːʒən] n ilusión f, engaño

**de luxe** [dəˈlʌks] adj de lujo

**delve** [delv] vi: **to ~ into** (subject) ahondar en; (cupboard etc) hurgar en

**demand** [dɪˈmɑːnd] vt (gen) exigir; (rights) reclamar ♦ n exigencia; (claim) reclamación f; (ECON) demanda; **to be in ~** ser muy solicitado; **on ~** a solicitud; **~ing** adj (boss) exigente; (work) absorbente

**demean** [dɪˈmiːn] vt: **to ~ o.s.** rebajarse

**demeanour** [dɪˈmiːnə*] (US demeanor) n porte m, conducta

**demented** [dɪˈmentɪd] adj demente

**demise** [dɪˈmaɪz] n (death) fallecimiento

**demister** [diːˈmɪstə*] n (AUT) eliminador m de vaho

**demo** [ˈdeməu] (inf) n abbr (= demonstration) manifestación f

**democracy** [dɪˈmɔkrəsɪ] n democracia; democrat [ˈdeməkræt] n demócrata m/f; **democratic** [deməˈkrætɪk] adj democrático; (US) demócrata

**demolish** [dɪˈmɔlɪʃ] vt derribar, demoler; (fig: argument) destruir

**demolition** [deməˈlɪʃən] n derribo, demolición f; destrucción f

**demon** [ˈdiːmən] n (evil spirit) demonio

**demonstrate** ['demənstreɪt] vt demostrar; (skill, appliance) mostrar ♦ vi manifestarse; **demonstration** [-'streɪʃən] n (POL) manifestación f; (proof, exhibition) demostración f; **demonstrator** n (POL) manifestante m/f; (COMM) demostrador(a) m/f; vendedor(a) m/f

**demoralize** [dɪ'mɔrəlaɪz] vt desmoralizar

**demote** [dɪ'məʊt] vt degradar

**demure** [dɪ'mjʊə*] adj recatado

**den** [dɛn] n (of animal) guarida; (room) habitación f

**denatured alcohol** [diː'neɪtʃəd-] (US) n alcohol m desnaturalizado

**denial** [dɪ'naɪəl] n (refusal) negativa; (of report etc) negación f

**denim** ['dɛnɪm] n tela vaquera; ~s npl vaqueros mpl

**Denmark** ['dɛnmɑːk] n Dinamarca

**denomination** [dɪnɔmɪ'neɪʃən] n valor m; (REL) confesión f

**denote** [dɪ'nəʊt] vt indicar, significar

**denounce** [dɪ'naʊns] vt denunciar

**dense** [dɛns] adj (crowd) denso; (thick) espeso; (: foliage etc) tupido; (inf: stupid) torpe; ~ly adv: ~ly populated con una alta densidad de población

**density** ['dɛnsɪtɪ] n densidad f; **single/double-~ disk** n (COMPUT) disco de densidad sencilla/doble densidad

**dent** [dɛnt] n abolladura ♦ vt (also: make a ~ in) abollar

**dental** ['dɛntl] adj dental; ~ **surgeon** n odontólogo/a

**dentist** ['dɛntɪst] n dentista m/f; ~**ry** n odontología f

**dentures** ['dɛntʃəz] npl dentadura (postiza)

**denunciation** [dɪnʌnsɪ'eɪʃən] n denuncia, denunciación f

**deny** [dɪ'naɪ] vt negar; (charge) rechazar

**deodorant** [diː'əʊdərənt] n desodorante m

**depart** [dɪ'pɑːt] vi irse, marcharse; (train) salir; **to ~ from** (fig: differ

*from) apartarse de

**department** [dɪ'pɑːtmənt] n (COMM) sección f; (SCOL) departamento; (POL) ministerio; ~ **store** n gran almacén m

**departure** [dɪ'pɑːtʃə*] n partida, ida; (of train) salida; (of employee) marcha; **a new** ~ un nuevo rumbo; ~ **lounge** n (at airport) sala de embarque

**depend** [dɪ'pɛnd] vi: **to** ~ **on** depender de; (rely on) contar con; **it** ~**s** depende, según; ~**ing on the result** según el resultado; ~**able** adj (person) formal, serio; (watch) exacto; (car) seguro; ~**ant** n dependiente m/f; ~**ence** n dependencia; ~**ent** adj: **to be** ~**ent on** depender de ♦ n = **dependant**

**depict** [dɪ'pɪkt] vt (in picture) pintar; (describe) representar

**depleted** [dɪ'pliːtɪd] adj reducido

**deplorable** [dɪ'plɔːrəbl] adj deplorable

**deploy** [dɪ'plɔɪ] vt desplegar

**depopulation** [diːpɔpjʊ'leɪʃən] n despoblación f

**deport** [dɪ'pɔːt] vt deportar; ~**ment** n comportamiento; (way of walking) porte m

**depose** [dɪ'pəʊz] vt deponer

**deposit** [dɪ'pɔzɪt] n depósito; (CHEM) sedimento; (of ore, oil) yacimiento ♦ vt (gen) depositar; ~ **account** (BRIT) n cuenta de ahorros

**depot** ['dɛpəʊ] n (storehouse) depósito; (for vehicles) parque m; (US) estación f

**depreciate** [dɪ'priːʃɪeɪt] vi depreciarse, perder valor; **depreciation** [-'eɪʃən] n depreciación f

**depress** [dɪ'prɛs] vt deprimir; (wages etc) hacer bajar; (press down) apretar; ~**ed** adj deprimido; ~**ing** adj deprimente; ~**ion** [dɪ'prɛʃən] n depresión f

**deprivation** [dɛprɪ'veɪʃən] n privación f

**deprive** [dɪ'praɪv] vt: **to** ~ **sb of** privar a uno de; ~**d** adj necesitado

**depth** [depθ] n profundidad f; (of cupboard) fondo; **to be in the ~s of despair** sentir la mayor desesperación; **to be out of one's ~** (in water) no hacer pie; (fig) sentirse totalmente perdido

**deputation** [depju'teɪʃən] n delegación f

**deputize** ['depjutaɪz] vi: **to ~ for sb** suplir a uno

**deputy** ['depjutɪ] adj: **~ head** subdirector(a) m/f ♦ n sustituto/a, suplente m/f; (US: POL) adjunto/a; (US: also: **~ sheriff**) agente m (del sheriff)

**derail** [dɪ'reɪl] vt: **to be ~ed** descarrilarse; **~ment** n descarrilamiento

**deranged** [dɪ'reɪndʒd] adj trastornado

**derby** ['dɜːbɪ] (US) n (hat) hongo

**derelict** ['derɪlɪkt] adj abandonado

**derisory** [dɪ'raɪzərɪ] adj (sum) irrisorio

**derivative** [dɪ'rɪvətɪv] n derivado

**derive** [dɪ'raɪv] vt (benefit etc) obtener ♦ vi: **to ~ from** derivarse de

**derogatory** [dɪ'rɔgətərɪ] adj despectivo

**descend** [dɪ'sɛnd] vt, vi descender, bajar; **to ~ from** descender de; **to ~ to** rebajarse a; **~ant** n descendiente m/f

**descent** [dɪ'sɛnt] n descenso; (origin) descendencia

**describe** [dɪs'kraɪb] vt describir; **description** [-'krɪpʃən] n descripción f; (sort) clase f, género

**desecrate** ['desɪkreɪt] vt profanar

**desert** [n 'dezət, vb dɪ'zɜːt] n desierto ♦ vt abandonar ♦ vi (MIL) desertar; **~er** [dɪ'zɜːtə*] n desertor(a) m/f; **~ion** [dɪ'zɜːʃən] n deserción f; (LAW) abandono; **~ island** n isla desierta; **~s** [dɪ'zɜːts] npl: **to get one's just ~s** llevar su merecido

**deserve** [dɪ'zɜːv] vt merecer, ser digno de; **deserving** adj (person) digno de; (action, cause) meritorio

**design** [dɪ'zaɪn] n (sketch) bosquejo; (layout, shape) diseño; (pattern) dibujo; (intention) intención f ♦ vt diseñar

**designate** [vb 'dezɪgneɪt, adj 'dezɪgnɪt] vt (appoint) nombrar; (destine) designar ♦ adj designado

**designer** [dɪ'zaɪnə*] n diseñador/a m/f; (fashion ~) modisto/a, diseñador(a) m/f de moda

**desirable** [dɪ'zaɪərəbl] adj (proper) deseable; (attractive) atractivo

**desire** [dɪ'zaɪə*] n deseo ♦ vt desear

**desk** [desk] n (in office) escritorio; (for pupil) pupitre m; (in hotel, at airport) recepción f; (BRIT: in shop, restaurant) caja

**desolate** ['desəlɪt] adj (place) desierto; (person) afligido; **desolation** [-'leɪʃən] n (of place) desolación f; (of person) aflicción f

**despair** [dɪs'pɛə*] n desesperación f ♦ vi: **to ~ of** perder la esperanza de

**despatch** [dɪs'pætʃ] n, vt = **dispatch**

**desperate** ['despərɪt] adj desesperado; (fugitive) peligroso; **to be ~ for sth/to do** necesitar urgentemente algo/hacer; **~ly** adv desesperadamente; (very) terriblemente, gravemente

**desperation** [despə'reɪʃən] n desesperación f; **in (sheer) ~** (absolutamente) desesperado

**despicable** [dɪs'pɪkəbl] adj vil, despreciable

**despise** [dɪs'paɪz] vt despreciar

**despite** [dɪs'paɪt] prep a pesar de, pese a

**despondent** [dɪs'pɒndənt] adj deprimido, abatido

**dessert** [dɪ'zɜːt] n postre m; **~spoon** n cuchara (de postre)

**destination** [destɪ'neɪʃən] n destino

**destiny** ['destɪnɪ] n destino

**destitute** ['destɪtjuːt] adj desamparado, indigente

**destroy** [dɪs'trɔɪ] vt destruir; (animal) sacrificar; **~er** n (NAUT) destructor m

**destruction** [dɪs'trʌkʃən] n destrucción f; **destructive** [dɪs'trʌktɪv] adj destructivo, destructor(a)

**detach** [dɪ'tætʃ] vt separar; (unstick)

despegar; ~**able** adj de quita y pon; ~**ed** adj (attitude) objetivo, imparcial; ~**ed house** n ≈ chalé m, ≈ chalet m; ~**ment** n (aloofness) frialdad f; (MIL) destacamento

**detail** ['di:teɪl] n detalle m; (no pl: in picture etc) detalles mpl; (trifle) pequeñez f ♦ vt detallar; (MIL) destacar; **in** ~ detalladamente; ~**ed** adj detallado

**detain** [dɪ'teɪn] vt retener; (in captivity) detener

**detect** [dɪ'tekt] vt descubrir; (MED, POLICE) identificar; (MIL, RADAR, TECH) detectar; ~**ion** [dɪ'tekʃən] n descubrimiento; identificación f; ~**ive** n detective m/f; ~**ive story** n novela policíaca; ~**or** n detector m

**détente** [deɪ'tɑ:nt] n distensión f

**detention** [dɪ'tenʃən] n detención f, arresto; (SCOL) castigo

**deter** [dɪ'tə:*] vt (dissuade) disuadir

**detergent** [dɪ'tə:dʒənt] n detergente m

**deteriorate** [dɪ'tɪərɪəreɪt] vi deteriorarse; **deterioration** [-'reɪʃən] n deterioro

**determination** [dɪtə:mɪ'neɪʃən] n resolución f; (establishment) establecimiento

**determine** [dɪ'tə:mɪn] vt determinar; ~**d** adj (person) resuelto, decidido; ~**d to** do resuelto a hacer

**deterrent** [dɪ'terənt] n (MIL) fuerza de disuasión

**detest** [dɪ'test] vt aborrecer

**detonate** ['detəneɪt] vi estallar ♦ vt hacer detonar

**detour** ['di:tuə*] n (gen, US: AUT) desviación f

**detract** [dɪ'trækt] vt: **to** ~ **from** quitar mérito a, desvirtuar

**detriment** ['detrɪmənt] n: **to the** ~ **of** en perjuicio de; ~**al** [detrɪ'mentl] adj: ~**al (to)** perjudicial (a)

**devaluation** [di:vælju:'eɪʃən] n devaluación f

**devalue** [di:'vælju:] vt (currency) devaluar; (fig) quitar mérito a

**devastate** ['devəsteɪt] vt devastar;

(fig): **to be** ~**d by** quedar destrozado por; **devastating** adj devastador(a); (fig) arrollador(a)

**develop** [dɪ'veləp] vt desarrollar; (PHOT) revelar; (disease) coger; (habit) adquirir; (fault) empezar a tener ♦ vi desarrollarse; (advance) progresar; (facts, symptoms) aparecer; ~**ing country** n país m en (vías de) desarrollo; ~**er** n promotor m; ~**ment** n desarrollo; (advance) progreso; (of affair, case) desenvolvimiento; (of land) urbanización f

**deviate** ['di:vɪeɪt] vi: **to** ~ (**from**) desviarse (de); **deviation** [-'eɪʃən] n desviación f

**device** [dɪ'vaɪs] n (apparatus) aparato, mecanismo

**devil** ['devl] n diablo, demonio; ~**ish** adj diabólico

**devious** ['di:vɪəs] adj taimado

**devise** [dɪ'vaɪz] vt idear, inventar

**devoid** [dɪ'vɔɪd] adj: ~ **of** desprovisto de

**devolution** [di:və'lu:ʃən] n (POL) descentralización f

**devote** [dɪ'vəut] vt: **to** ~ **sth to** dedicar algo a; ~**d** adj (loyal) leal, fiel; **to be** ~**d to** sb querer con devoción a alguien; **the book is** ~**d to politics** el libro trata de la política; ~**e** [devəu'ti:] n entusiasta m/f; (REL) devoto/a

**devotion** [dɪ'vəuʃən] n dedicación f; (REL) devoción f

**devour** [dɪ'vauə*] vt devorar

**devout** [dɪ'vaut] adj devoto

**dew** [dju:] n rocío

**dexterity** [deks'terɪtɪ] n destreza

**diabetes** [daɪə'bi:ti:z] n diabetes f; **diabetic** [-'betɪk] adj, n diabético/a m/f

**diabolical** [daɪə'bɒlɪkəl] (inf) adj (weather, behaviour) pésimo

**diagnose** [daɪəg'nəuz] vt diagnosticar; **diagnoses** [-'nəusi:z] npl of diagnosis; **diagnosis** [-'nəusɪs] (pl -ses) n diagnóstico

**diagonal** [daɪ'ægənl] adj, n diagonal f

**diagram** 76 **diminish**

**diagram** ['daɪəgræm] n diagrama m, esquema m

**dial** ['daɪəl] n esfera, cuadrante m, cara (AM); (on radio etc) selector m; (of phone) disco ♦ vt (number) marcar

**dialling** ['daɪəlɪŋ]: ~ **code** (US dial code) n prefijo; ~ **tone** (US dial tone) n (BRIT) señal f or tono de marcar

**dialogue** ['daɪəlɔg] (US dialog) n diálogo

**diameter** [daɪ'æmɪtə*] n diámetro

**diamond** ['daɪəmənd] n diamante m; (shape) rombo; ~s npl (CARDS) diamantes mpl

**diaper** ['daɪəpə*] (US) n pañal m

**diaphragm** ['daɪəfræm] n diafragma m

**diarrhoea** [daɪə'riːə] (US diarrhea) n diarrea

**diary** ['daɪərɪ] n (daily account) diario; (book) agenda

**dice** [daɪs] n inv dados mpl ♦ vt (CULIN) cortar en cuadritos

**dichotomy** [daɪ'kɔtəmɪ] n dicotomía

**Dictaphone** ['dɪktəfəun] ® n dictáfono ®

**dictate** [dɪk'teɪt] vt dictar; (conditions) imponer; **dictation** [-'teɪʃən] n dictado; (giving of orders) órdenes fpl

**dictator** [dɪk'teɪtə*] n dictador m; ~**ship** n dictadura

**dictionary** ['dɪkʃənrɪ] n diccionario

**did** [dɪd] pt of do

**didn't** ['dɪdnt] = did not

**die** [daɪ] vi morir; (fig: fade) desvanecerse, desaparecer; **to be dying for sth/to do sth** morirse por ganas de hacer algo; ~ **away** vi (sound, light) perderse; ~ **down** vi apagarse; (wind) amainar; ~ **out** vi desaparecer

**diehard** ['daɪhɑːd] n reaccionario/a

**diesel** ['diːzəl] n vehículo con motor Diesel; ~ **engine** n motor m Diesel; ~ (**oil**) n gasoil m

**diet** ['daɪət] n dieta; (restricted food) régimen m ♦ vi (also: be on a ~) estar a dieta, hacer régimen

**differ** ['dɪfə*] vi: **to ~ (from)** (be different) ser distinto a, diferenciarse de; (disagree) discrepar (de); ~**ence** n diferencia; (disagreement) desacuerdo; ~**ent** adj diferente, distinto; ~**entiate** [-'renʃɪeɪt] vi: **to ~entiate (between)** distinguir (entre); ~**ently** adv de otro modo, en forma distinta

**difficult** ['dɪfɪkəlt] adj difícil; ~**y** n dificultad f

**diffident** ['dɪfɪdənt] adj tímido

**diffuse** [adj dɪ'fjuːs, vb dɪ'fjuːz] adj difuso ♦ vt difundir

**dig** [dɪg] (pt, pp dug) vt (hole, ground) cavar ♦ n (prod) empujón m; (archaeological) excavación f; (remark) indirecta; **to ~ one's nails into** clavar las uñas en; ~ **into** vt fus (savings) consumir; ~ **out** vt (hole) excavar; (fig) sacar; ~ **up** vt (information) desenterrar; (plant) desarraigar

**digest** [vb daɪ'dʒɛst, n 'daɪdʒɛst] vt (food) digerir; (facts) asimilar ♦ n resumen m; ~**ion** [dɪ'dʒɛstʃən] n digestión f

**digit** ['dɪdʒɪt] n (number) dígito; (finger) dedo; ~**al** adj digital

**dignified** ['dɪgnɪfaɪd] adj grave, solemne

**dignity** ['dɪgnɪtɪ] n dignidad f

**digress** [daɪ'grɛs] vi: **to ~ from** apartarse de

**digs** [dɪgz] (BRIT: inf) npl pensión f, alojamiento

**dilapidated** [dɪ'læpɪdeɪtɪd] adj desmoronado, ruinoso

**dilemma** [daɪ'lɛmə] n dilema m

**diligent** ['dɪlɪdʒənt] adj diligente

**dilute** [daɪ'luːt] vt diluir

**dim** [dɪm] adj (light) débil; (outline) indistinto; (room) oscuro; (inf: stupid) lerdo ♦ vt (light) bajar

**dime** [daɪm] (US) n moneda de diez centavos

**dimension** [dɪ'mɛnʃən] n dimensión f

**diminish** [dɪ'mɪnɪʃ] vt, vi disminuir

**diminutive** [dɪ'mɪnjutɪv] adj diminuto ♦ n (LING) diminutivo

**dimmers** ['dɪməz] (US) npl (AUT: dipped headlights) luces fpl cortas; (: parking lights) luces fpl de posición

**dimple** ['dɪmpl] n hoyuelo

**din** [dɪn] n estruendo, estrépito

**dine** [daɪn] vi cenar; **~r** n (person) comensal m/f; (US) restaurante m económico

**dinghy** ['dɪŋgɪ] n bote m; (also: rubber ~) lancha (neumática)

**dingy** ['dɪndʒɪ] adj (room) sombrío; (colour) sucio

**dining car** n (BRIT) (RAIL) coche-comedor m

**dining room** n comedor m

**dinner** ['dɪnə*] n (evening meal) cena; (lunch) comida; (public) cena, banquete m; ~ **jacket** n smoking m; ~ **party** n cena; ~ **time** n (evening) hora de cenar; (midday) hora de comer

**dinosaur** ['daɪnəsɔ:*] n dinosaurio

**dint** [dɪnt] n: by ~ of a fuerza de

**diocese** ['daɪəsɪs] n diócesis f inv

**dip** [dɪp] n (slope) pendiente m; (in sea) baño; (CULIN) salsa ♦ vt (in water) mojar; (ladle etc) meter; (BRIT: AUT): to ~ one's lights poner luces de cruce ♦ vi (road etc) descender, bajar

**diphthong** ['dɪfθɔŋ] n diptongo

**diploma** [dɪ'pləumə] n diploma m

**diplomacy** [dɪ'pləuməsɪ] n diplomacia

**diplomat** ['dɪpləmæt] n diplomático/a; **~ic** [dɪplə'mætɪk] adj diplomático

**diprod** ['dɪprɒd] (US) n = dipstick

**dipstick** ['dɪpstɪk] (BRIT) n (AUT) varilla de nivel (del aceite)

**dipswitch** ['dɪpswɪtʃ] (BRIT) n (AUT) interruptor m

**dire** [daɪə*] adj calamitoso

**direct** [daɪ'rɛkt] adj directo; (challenge) claro; (person) franco ♦ vt dirigir; (order): to ~ sb to do sth mandar a uno hacer algo ♦ adv derecho; **can you ~ me to...?** ¿puede

indicarme dónde está...?; ~ **debit** (BRIT) n domiciliación f bancaria de recibos

**direction** [dɪ'rɛkʃən] n dirección f; **sense of** ~ sentido de la dirección; **~s** npl (instructions) instrucciones fpl; ~ **for use** modo de empleo

**directly** [dɪ'rɛktlɪ] adv (in straight line) directamente; (at once) en seguida

**director** [dɪ'rɛktə*] n director(a) m/f

**directory** [dɪ'rɛktərɪ] n (TEL) guía (telefónica); (COMPUT) directorio

**dirt** [də:t] n suciedad f; (earth) tierra; **~-cheap** adj baratísimo; **~y** adj sucio; (joke) verde (SP), colorado (AM) ♦ vt ensuciar; (stain) manchar; **~y trick** n juego sucio

**disability** [dɪsə'bɪlɪtɪ] n incapacidad f

**disabled** [dɪs'eɪbld] adj: **to be physically** ~ ser minusválido/a; **to be mentally** ~ ser deficiente mental

**disadvantage** [dɪsəd'vɑːntɪdʒ] n desventaja, inconveniente m

**disaffection** [dɪsə'fɛkʃən] n descontento

**disagree** [dɪsə'gri:] vi (differ) discrepar; **to** ~ (with) no estar de acuerdo (con); **~able** adj desagradable; (person) antipático; **~ment** n desacuerdo

**disallow** [dɪsə'lau] vt (goal) anular; (claim) rechazar

**disappear** [dɪsə'pɪə*] vi desaparecer; **~ance** n desaparición f

**disappoint** [dɪsə'pɔɪnt] vt decepcionar, defraudar; **~ed** adj decepcionado; **~ing** adj decepcionante; **~ment** n decepción f

**disapproval** [dɪsə'pru:vəl] n desaprobación f

**disapprove** [dɪsə'pru:v] vi: **to** ~ **of** ver mal

**disarm** [dɪs'ɑːm] vt desarmar; **~ament** n desarme m; **~ing** adj (smile etc) que desarma

**disarray** [dɪsə'reɪ] n: **in** ~ (army, organization) desorganizado; (hair, clothes) desarreglado

**disaster** [dɪ'zɑːstə*] n desastre m

**disband** [dɪs'bænd] vt disolver ♦ vi
desbandarse

**disbelief** [dɪsbə'liːf] n incredulidad f

**disc** [dɪsk] n disco; (COMPUT) =
disk

**discard** [dɪs'kɑːd] vt (old things) tirar; (fig) descartar

**discern** [dɪ'səːn] vt percibir, discernir; (understand) comprender; ~ing
adj perspicaz

**discharge** [vb dɪs'tʃɑːdʒ, n
'dɪstʃɑːdʒ] vt (task, duty) cumplir;
(waste) verter; (patient) dar de alta;
(employee) despedir; (soldier) licenciar; (defendant) poner en libertad ♦
n (ELEC) descarga; (MED) supura-
ción f; (dismissal) despedida; (of
duty) desempeño; (of debt) pago,
descargo

**disciple** [dɪ'saɪpl] n discípulo

**discipline** ['dɪsɪplɪn] n disciplina ♦
vt disciplinar; (punish) castigar

**disc jockey** n pinchadiscos m/f inv

**disclaim** [dɪs'kleɪm] vt negar

**disclose** [dɪs'kləʊz] vt revelar; **dis-
closure** [-'kləʊʒə*] n revelación f

**disco** ['dɪskəʊ] n abbr = discothèque

**discoloured** [dɪs'kʌləd] (US discol-
ored) adj descolorido

**discomfort** [dɪs'kʌmfət] n incomodidad f; (unease) inquietud f; (physical) malestar m

**disconcert** [dɪskən'səːt] vt desconcertar

**disconnect** [dɪskə'nekt] vt separar;
(ELEC etc) desconectar

**discontent** [dɪskən'tent] n descontento; **~ed** adj descontento

**discontinue** [dɪskən'tɪnjuː] vt interrumpir; (payments) suspender;
**"~d"** (COMM) "ya no se fabrica"

**discord** ['dɪskɔːd] n discordia;
(MUS) disonancia; **~ant** [dɪs'kɔːdənt]
adj discorde

**discothèque** ['dɪskəʊtek] n discoteca

**discount** [n 'dɪskaʊnt, vb dɪs'kaʊnt]
n descuento ♦ vt descontar

**discourage** [dɪs'kʌrɪdʒ] vt desalentar; (advise against): **to ~ sb from**

doing disuadir a uno de hacer;
**discouraging** adj desalentador(a)

**discover** [dɪs'kʌvə*] vt descubrir;
(error) darse cuenta de; **~y** n descubrimiento

**discredit** [dɪs'kredɪt] vt desacreditar

**discreet** [dɪs'kriːt] adj (tactful) discreto; (careful) circunspecto, prudente

**discrepancy** [dɪs'krepənsɪ] n diferencia

**discretion** [dɪs'kreʃən] n (tact) discreción f; **at the ~ of** a criterio de

**discriminate** [dɪs'krɪmɪneɪt] vi: **to
~ between** distinguir entre; **to ~
against** discriminar contra; **dis-
criminating** adj entendido; **discrimination** [-'neɪʃən] n (discernment)
perspicacia; (bias) discriminación f

**discuss** [dɪs'kʌs] vt discutir; (a
theme) tratar; **~ion** [dɪs'kʌʃən] n
discusión f

**disdain** [dɪs'deɪn] n desdén m

**disease** [dɪ'ziːz] n enfermedad f

**disembark** [dɪsɪm'bɑːk] vt, vi desembarcar

**disenchanted** [dɪsɪn'tʃɑːntɪd] adj:
**~ (with)** desilusionado (con)

**disengage** [dɪsɪn'geɪdʒ] vt: **to ~ the
clutch** (AUT) desembragar

**disentangle** [dɪsɪn'tæŋgl] vt soltar;
(wire, thread) desenredar

**disfigure** [dɪs'fɪgə*] vt (person) desfigurar; (object) afear

**disgrace** [dɪs'greɪs] n ignominia;
(shame) vergüenza, escándalo ♦ vt
deshonrar; **~ful** adj vergonzoso

**disgruntled** [dɪs'grʌntld] adj disgustado, descontento

**disguise** [dɪs'gaɪz] n disfraz m ♦ vt
disfrazar; **in ~** disfrazado

**disgust** [dɪs'gʌst] n repugnancia ♦ vt
repugnar, dar asco a; **~ing** adj repugnante, asqueroso; (behaviour etc)
vergonzoso

**dish** [dɪʃ] n (gen) plato; **to do or
wash the ~es** fregar los platos; **~
up** vt servir; **~ out** vt repartir;
**~cloth** n estropajo

**dishearten** [dɪs'hɑːtn] vt desalentar

**dishevelled** [dɪˈʃevəld] *adj* (*hair*) despeinado; (*appearance*) desarreglado

**dishonest** [dɪsˈɔnɪst] *adj* (*person*) poco honrado, tramposo; (*means*) fraudulento; **~y** *n* falta de honradez

**dishonour** [dɪsˈɔnə*] (*US* **dishonor**) *n* deshonra; **~able** *adj* deshonroso

**dishtowel** [ˈdɪʃtauəl] (*US*) *n* estropajo

**dishwasher** [ˈdɪʃwɔʃə*] *n* lavaplatos *m inv*

**disillusion** [dɪsɪˈluːʒən] *vt* desilusionar

**disincentive** [dɪsɪnˈsentɪv] *n* desincentivo

**disinfect** [dɪsɪnˈfekt] *vt* desinfectar; **~ant** *n* desinfectante *m*

**disintegrate** [dɪsˈɪntɪgreɪt] *vi* disgregarse, desintegrarse

**disinterested** [dɪsˈɪntrəstɪd] *adj* interesado

**disjointed** [dɪsˈdʒɔɪntɪd] *adj* inconexo

**disk** [dɪsk] *n* (*esp US*) = **disc**; (*COMPUT*) disco, disquete *m*; **single-/double-sided** ~ disco de una cara/dos caras; ~ **drive** *n* disc drive *m*; **~ette** *n* = **disk**

**dislike** [dɪsˈlaɪk] *n* antipatía, aversión *f* ♦ *vt* tener antipatía a

**dislocate** [ˈdɪsləkeɪt] *vt* dislocar

**dislodge** [dɪsˈlɔdʒ] *vt* sacar

**disloyal** [dɪsˈlɔɪəl] *adj* desleal

**dismal** [ˈdɪzml] *adj* (*gloomy*) deprimente, triste; (*very bad*) malísimo, fatal

**dismantle** [dɪsˈmæntl] *vt* desmontar, desarmar

**dismay** [dɪsˈmeɪ] *n* consternación *f* ♦ *vt* consternar

**dismiss** [dɪsˈmɪs] *vt* (*worker*) despedir; (*pupils*) dejar marchar; (*soldiers*) dar permiso para irse; (*idea, LAW*) rechazar; (*possibility*) descartar; **~al** *n* despido

**dismount** [dɪsˈmaunt] *vi* apearse

**disobedience** [dɪsəˈbiːdɪəns] *n* desobediencia

**disobedient** [dɪsəˈbiːdɪənt] *adj* desobediente

**disobey** [dɪsəˈbeɪ] *vt* desobedecer

**disorder** [dɪsˈɔːdə*] *n* desorden *m*; (*rioting*) disturbios *mpl*; (*MED*) trastorno; **~ly** *adj* desordenado; (*meeting*) alborotado; (*conduct*) escandaloso

**disorientated** [dɪsˈɔːrɪənteɪtəd] *adj* desorientado

**disown** [dɪsˈaun] *vt* (*action*) renegar de; (*person*) negar cualquier tipo de relación con

**disparaging** [dɪsˈpærɪdʒɪŋ] *adj* despreciativo

**disparate** [ˈdɪspərɪt] *adj* dispar

**disparity** [dɪsˈpærɪtɪ] *n* disparidad *f*

**dispassionate** [dɪsˈpæʃənɪt] *adj* (*unbiased*) imparcial

**dispatch** [dɪsˈpætʃ] *vt* enviar ♦ *n* (*sending*) envío; (*PRESS*) informe *m*; (*MIL*) parte *m*

**dispel** [dɪsˈpel] *vt* disipar

**dispense** [dɪsˈpens] *vt* (*medicines*) preparar; ~ **with** *vt fus* prescindir de; **~r** *n* (*container*) distribuidor *m* automático; **dispensing chemist** (*BRIT*) *n* farmacia

**disperse** [dɪsˈpəːs] *vt* dispersar ♦ *vi* dispersarse

**dispirited** [dɪsˈpɪrɪtɪd] *adj* desanimado, desalentado

**displace** [dɪsˈpleɪs] *vt* desplazar, reemplazar; **~d person** *n* (*POL*) desplazado/a

**display** [dɪsˈpleɪ] *n* (*in shop window*) escaparate *m*; (*exhibition*) exposición *f*; (*COMPUT*) visualización *f*; (*of feeling*) manifestación *f* ♦ *vt* exponer; manifestar; (*ostentatiously*) lucir

**displease** [dɪsˈpliːz] *vt* (*offend*) ofender; (*annoy*) fastidiar; **~d** *adj*: **~d with** disgustado con; **displeasure** [-ˈpleʒə*] *n* disgusto

**disposable** [dɪsˈpauzəbl] *adj* desechable; (*income*) disponible; **~ nappy** *n* pañal *m* desechable

**disposal** [dɪsˈpauzl] *n* (*of rubbish*) destrucción *f*; **at one's ~** a su disposición

**dispose** [dɪsˈpauz] *vi*: **to ~ of** (*un-*)

*wanted goods)* deshacerse de; *(problem etc)* resolver; **~d** *adj:* **~d to do** dispuesto a hacer; **to be well-~ towards** estar bien dispuesto hacia uno; **disposition** [-'zɪʃən] *n (nature)* temperamento; *(inclination)* propensión *f*

**disproportionate** [dɪsprə'pɔːʃənət] *adj* desproporcionado

**disprove** [dɪs'pruːv] *vt* refutar

**dispute** [dɪs'pjuːt] *n* disputa; *(also: industrial ~)* conflicto *(laboral)* ♦ *vt (argue)* disputar, discutir; *(question)* cuestionar

**disqualify** [dɪs'kwɔlɪfaɪ] *vt (SPORT)* desclasificar; **to ~ sb for sth/from doing sth** incapacitar a algn para algo/hacer algo

**disquiet** [dɪs'kwaɪət] *n* preocupación *f*, inquietud *f*

**disregard** [dɪsrɪ'gɑːd] *vt (ignore)* no hacer caso de

**disrepair** [dɪsrɪ'peə*] *n:* **to fall into ~** *(building)* desmoronarse

**disreputable** [dɪs'repjutəbl] *adj (person)* de mala fama; *(behaviour)* vergonzoso

**disrespectful** [dɪsrɪ'spektful] *adj* irrespetuoso

**disrupt** [dɪs'rʌpt] *vt (plans)* desbaratar, trastornar; *(conversation)* interrumpir; **~ion** [-'rʌpʃən] *n (disturbance)* trastorno; *(interruption)* interrupción *f*

**dissatisfaction** [dɪssætɪs'fækʃən] *n* disgusto, descontento

**dissect** [dɪ'sekt] *vt* disecar

**dissent** [dɪ'sent] *n* disensión *f*

**dissertation** [dɪsə'teɪʃən] *n* tesina

**disservice** [dɪs'sɜːvɪs] *n:* **to do sb a ~** perjudicar a alguien

**dissident** ['dɪsɪdnt] *adj, n* disidente *m/f*

**dissimilar** [dɪ'sɪmɪlə*] *adj* distinto

**dissipate** ['dɪsɪpeɪt] *vt* disipar; *(waste)* desperdiciar

**dissociate** [dɪ'səuʃɪeɪt] *vt* disociar

**dissolute** ['dɪsəluːt] *adj* disoluto

**dissolution** [dɪsə'luːʃən] *n* disolución *f*

**dissolve** [dɪ'zɔlv] *vt* disolver ♦ *vi* disolverse; **to ~ in(to) tears** deshacerse en lágrimas

**dissuade** [dɪ'sweɪd] *vt:* **to ~ sb (from)** disuadir a uno (de)

**distance** ['dɪstns] *n* distancia; **in the ~** a lo lejos

**distant** ['dɪstnt] *adj* lejano; *(manner)* reservado, frío

**distaste** [dɪs'teɪst] *n* repugnancia; **~ful** *adj* repugnante, desagradable

**distended** [dɪ'stendɪd] *adj (stomach)* hinchado

**distil** [dɪs'tɪl] *(US **distill**)* *vt* destilar; **~lery** *n* destilería

**distinct** [dɪs'tɪŋkt] *adj (different)* distinto; *(clear)* claro; *(unmistakeable)* inequívoco; **as ~ from** a diferencia de; **~ion** [dɪs'tɪŋkʃən] *n (distinction f; (honour)* honor *m; (in exam)* sobresaliente *m;* **~ive** *adj* distintivo

**distinguish** [dɪs'tɪŋgwɪʃ] *vt* distinguir; **to ~ o.s.** destacarse; **~ed** *adj (eminent)* distinguido; **~ing** *adj (feature)* distintivo

**distort** [dɪs'tɔːt] *vt* distorsionar; *(shape, image)* deformar; **~ion** [dɪs'tɔːʃən] *n* distorsión *f;* deformación *f*

**distract** [dɪs'trækt] *vt* distraer; **~ed** *adj* distraído; **~ion** [dɪs'trækʃən] *n* distracción *f; (confusion)* aturdimiento

**distraught** [dɪs'trɔːt] *adj* loco de inquietud

**distress** [dɪs'tres] *n (anguish)* angustia, aflicción *f* ♦ *vt* afligir; **~ing** *adj* angustioso; doloroso; **~ signal** *n* señal *f* de socorro

**distribute** [dɪs'trɪbjuːt] *vt* distribuir; *(share out)* repartir; **distribution** [-'bjuːʃən] *n* distribución *f,* reparto; **distributor** *n (AUT)* distribuidor *m; (COMM)* distribuidora

**district** ['dɪstrɪkt] *n (of country)* zona, región *f; (of town)* barrio; *(ADMIN)* distrito; **~ attorney** *(US) n* fiscal *m/f;* **~ nurse** *(BRIT)* n enfermera que atiende a pacientes a domicilio

**distrust** [dɪs'trʌst] n desconfianza ♦ vt desconfiar de

**disturb** [dɪs'təːb] vt (person: bother, interrupt) molestar; (: upset) perturbar, inquietar; (disorganize) alterar; **~ance** n (upheaval) perturbación f; (political etc: gen pl) disturbio; (of mind) trastorno; **~ed** adj (worried, upset) preocupado, angustiado; **emotionally ~ed** trastornado; (childhood) inseguro; **~ing** adj inquietante, perturbador(a)

**disuse** [dɪs'juːs] n: **to fall into ~** caer en desuso

**disused** [dɪs'juːzd] adj abandonado

**ditch** [dɪtʃ] n zanja; (irrigation ~) acequia ♦ vt (inf: partner) deshacerse de; (: plan, car etc) abandonar

**dither** ['dɪðə*] (pej) vi vacilar

**ditto** ['dɪtəu] adv ídem, lo mismo

**divan** [dɪ'væn] n (also: ~ bed) cama turca

**dive** [daɪv] n (from board) salto; (underwater) buceo; (of submarine) sumersión f ♦ vi (swimmer: into water) saltar; (: under water) zambullirse, bucear; (fish, submarine) sumergirse; (bird) lanzarse en picado; **to ~ into** (bag etc) meter la mano en; (place) meterse de prisa en; **~r** n (underwater) buzo

**diverge** [daɪ'vəːdʒ] vi divergir

**diverse** [daɪ'vəːs] adj diversos/as, varios/as

**diversion** [daɪ'vəːʃən] n (BRIT: AUT) desviación f; (distraction, MIL) diversión f; (of funds) distracción f

**divert** [daɪ'vəːt] vt (turn aside) desviar

**divide** [dɪ'vaɪd] vt dividir; (separate) separar ♦ vi dividirse; (road) bifurcarse; **~d highway** (US) n carretera de doble calzada

**dividend** ['dɪvɪdend] n dividendo; (fig): **to pay ~s** proporcionar beneficios

**divine** [dɪ'vaɪn] adj (also fig) divino

**diving** ['daɪvɪŋ] n (SPORT) salto; (underwater) buceo; **~ board** n

trampolín m

**divinity** [dɪ'vɪnɪtɪ] n divinidad f; (SCOL) teología

**division** [dɪ'vɪʒən] n división f; (sharing out) reparto; (disagreement) diferencias fpl; (COMM) sección f

**divorce** [dɪ'vɔːs] n divorcio ♦ vt divorciarse de; **~d** adj divorciado; **~e** [-'siː] n divorciado/a

**divulge** [daɪ'vʌldʒ] vt divulgar, revelar

**D.I.Y.** (BRIT) adj, n abbr = **do-it-yourself**

**dizzy** ['dɪzɪ] adj (spell) de mareo; **to feel ~** marearse

**DJ** n abbr = **disc jockey**

---
KEYWORD
---

**do** [duː] (pt did, pp done) n (inf: party etc): **we're having a little ~ on Saturday** damos una fiestecita el sábado; **it was rather a grand ~** fue un acontecimiento a lo grande

♦ aux vb **1** (in negative constructions: not translated) **I don't understand** no entiendo

**2** (to form questions: not translated) **didn't you know?** ¿no lo sabías?; **what ~ you think?** ¿qué opinas?

**3** (for emphasis, in polite expressions): **people ~ make mistakes sometimes** sí que se cometen errores a veces; **she does seem rather late** a mí también me parece que se ha retrasado; **~ sit down/help yourself** siéntate/sírvete por favor; **~ take care!** ¡ten cuidado!, ¡te pido!

**4** (used to avoid repeating vb): **she sings better than I ~** canta mejor que yo; **~ you agree? — yes, I ~/no, I don't** ¿estás de acuerdo? — sí (lo estoy)/no (lo estoy); **she lives in Glasgow — so ~ I** vive en Glasgow — yo también; **he didn't like it and neither did we** no le gustó y a nosotros tampoco; **who made this mess? — I did** ¿quién hizo esta chapuza? — yo; **he asked me to help**

him and I did me pidió que le ayudara y lo hice

**5** (*in question tags*): **you like him, don't you?** te gusta, ¿verdad? or ¿no?; **I don't know him, ~ I?** creo que no le conozco

♦ vt **1** (*gen, carry out, perform etc*): **what are you ~ing tonight?** ¿qué haces esta noche?; **what can I ~ for you?** ¿en qué puedo servirle?; **to ~ the washing-up/cooking** fregar los platos/cocinar; **to ~ one's teeth/hair/nails** lavarse los dientes/arreglarse el pelo/arreglarse las uñas

**2** (*AUT etc*): **the car was ~ing 100** el coche iba a 100; **we've done 200 km already** ya hemos hecho 200 km; **he can ~ 100 in that car** puede dar los 100 en ese coche

♦ vi **1** (*act, behave*) hacer; **~ as I ~** haz como yo

**2** (*get on, fare*): **he's ~ing well/badly at school** va bien/mal en la escuela; **the firm is ~ing well** la empresa anda or va bien; **how ~ you ~?** mucho gusto; (*less formal*) ¿qué tal?

**3** (*suit*): **will it ~?** ¿sirve?, ¿está or va bien?

**4** (*be sufficient*) bastar; **will £10 ~?** ¿será bastante con £10?; **that'll ~** así está bien; **that'll ~!** (*in annoyance*) ¡ya está bien!, ¡basta ya!; **to make ~ (with)** arreglárselas (con)

**do away with** vt fus (*kill, disease*) eliminar; (*abolish: law etc*) abolir; (*withdraw*) retirar

**do up** vt (*laces*) atar; (*zip, dress, shirt*) abrochar; (*renovate: room, house*) renovar

**do with** vt fus (*need*): **I could ~ with a drink/some help** no me vendría mal un trago/un poco de ayuda; (*be connected*) tener que ver con; **what has it got to ~ with you?** ¿qué tiene que ver contigo?

**do without** vi pasar sin; **if you're late for tea then you'll ~ without** si llegas tarde para la merienda te pasarás sin él ♦ vt fus pasar sin; **I can**

**~ without a car** puedo pasar sin coche

**dock** [dɔk] n (*NAUT*) muelle m; (*LAW*) banquillo (de los acusados); **~s** npl (*NAUT*) muelles mpl, puerto sg ♦ vi (*enter*) atracar (la) muelle; (*SPACE*) acoplarse; **~er** n trabajador m portuario, estibador m; **~yard** n astillero

**doctor** ['dɔktə*] n médico/a; (*PhD etc*) doctor(a) m/f ♦ vt (*drink etc*) adulterar; **D~ of Philosophy** n Doctor en Filosofía y Letras

**doctrine** ['dɔktrɪn] n doctrina

**document** ['dɔkjumənt] n documento; **~ary** [-'mentərɪ] adj documental ♦ n documental m

**dodge** [dɔdʒ] n (*fig*) truco ♦ vt evadir; (*blow*) esquivar

**dodgems** ['dɔdʒəmz] (*BRIT*) npl coches mpl de choque

**doe** [dəu] n (*deer*) cierva, gama; (*rabbit*) coneja

**does** [dʌz] vb see **do**; **~n't** = **does not**

**dog** [dɔg] n perro ♦ vt seguir los pasos de; (*subj: bad luck*) perseguir; **~ collar** n collar m de perro; (*of clergyman*) alzacuellos m inv; **~-eared** adj sobado

**dogged** ['dɔgɪd] adj tenaz, obstinado

**dogsbody** ['dɔgzbɔdɪ] (*BRIT*: *inf*) n burro de carga

**doings** ['duːɪŋz] npl (*activities*) actividades fpl

**do-it-yourself** n bricolaje m

**doldrums** ['dɔldrəmz] npl: **to be in the ~** (*person*) estar abatido; (*business*) estar estancado

**dole** [dəul] (*BRIT*) n (*payment*) subsidio de paro; **on the ~** parado; **~ out** vt repartir

**doleful** ['dəulful] adj triste, lúgubre

**doll** [dɔl] n muñeca; (*US*: *inf*: *woman*) muñeca, gachí f; **~ed-up** (*inf*) adj arreglada

**dollar** ['dɔlə*] n dólar m

**dolphin** ['dɔlfɪn] n delfín m

**domain** [də'meɪn] n (*fig*) campo, competencia; (*land*) dominios mpl

**dome** [dəʊm] n (ARCH) cúpula

**domestic** [dəˈmestɪk] adj (animal, duty) doméstico; (flight, policy) nacional; ~**ated** adj domesticado; (home-loving) casero, hogareño

**dominant** [ˈdɒmɪnənt] adj dominante

**dominate** [ˈdɒmɪneɪt] vt dominar

**domineering** [dɒmɪˈnɪərɪŋ] adj dominante

**dominion** [dəˈmɪnɪən] n dominio

**domino** [ˈdɒmɪnəʊ] (pl ~es) n ficha de dominó; ~**es** n (game) dominó

**don** [dɒn] (BRIT) n profesor(a) m/f universitario/a

**donate** [dəˈneɪt] vt donar; **donation** [dəˈneɪʃən] n donativo

**done** [dʌn] pp of **do**

**donkey** [ˈdɒŋkɪ] n burro

**donor** [ˈdəʊnə*] n donante m/f

**don't** [dəʊnt] = **do not**

**doodle** [ˈduːdl] vi hacer dibujitos or garabatos

**doom** [duːm] n (fate) suerte f ♦ vt: **to be ~ed to failure** estar condenado al fracaso; ~**sday** n día m del juicio final

**door** [dɔː*] n puerta; ~**bell** n timbre m; ~ **handle** n tirador m; (of car) manija; ~**man** n (in hotel) portero; ~**mat** n felpudo, estera; ~**step** n peldaño; ~**to-** adj de puerta en puerta; ~**way** n entrada, puerta

**dope** [dəʊp] n (inf: illegal drug) droga; (: person) imbécil m/f ♦ vt (horse etc) drogar

**dopey** [ˈdəʊpɪ] (inf) adj (groggy) atontado; (stupid) imbécil

**dormant** [ˈdɔːmənt] adj inactivo

**dormice** [ˈdɔːmaɪs] npl of **dormouse**

**dormitory** [ˈdɔːmɪtrɪ] n (BRIT) dormitorio; (US) colegio mayor

**dormouse** [ˈdɔːmaʊs] (pl ~mice) n lirón m

**DOS** n abbr (= disk operating system) DOS m

**dosage** [ˈdəʊsɪdʒ] n dosis f inv

**dose** [dəʊs] n dósis f inv

**doss house** [ˈdɒs-] (BRIT) n pensión f de mala muerte

**dossier** [ˈdɒsɪeɪ] n expediente m, dosier m

**dot** [dɒt] n punto ♦ vi: ~**ted with** salpicado de; **on the ~** en punto

**dote** [dəʊt]: **to ~ on** vt fus adorar, idolatrar

**dot-matrix printer** n impresora matricial (or de matriz) de puntos

**double** [ˈdʌbl] adj doble ♦ adv (twice): **to cost** ~ costar el doble ♦ n doble m ♦ vt doblar ♦ vi doblarse; **on the ~, at the ~** (BRIT) corriendo; ~ **bass** n contrabajo; ~ **bed** n cama de matrimonio; ~ **bend** (BRIT) n doble curva; ~**breasted** adj cruzado; ~**cross** vt (trick) engañar; (betray) traicionar; ~**decker** n autobús m de dos pisos; ~ **glazing** (BRIT) n doble acristalamiento; ~ **room** n habitación f doble; ~**s** n (TENNIS) juego de dobles; **doubly** adv doblemente

**doubt** [daʊt] n duda ♦ vt dudar; (suspect) dudar de; **to ~ that** dudar que; ~**ful** adj dudoso; (person): **to be ~ful about sth** tener dudas sobre algo; ~**less** adv sin duda

**dough** [dəʊ] n masa, pasta; ~**nut** n ≈ rosquilla

**douse** [daʊs] vt (drench) mojar; (extinguish) apagar

**dove** [dʌv] n paloma

**dovetail** [ˈdʌvteɪl] vi (fig) encajar

**dowdy** [ˈdaʊdɪ] adj (person) mal vestido; (clothes) pasado de moda

**down** [daʊn] n (feathers) plumón m, flojel m ♦ adv (~wards) abajo, hacia abajo; (on the ground) por or en tierra ♦ prep abajo ♦ vt (inf: drink) beberse; ~ **with X!** ¡abajo X!; ~**and-out** n vagabundo/a; ~**at-heel** adj venido a menos; (appearance) desaliñado; ~**cast** adj (eyes) abatido; ~**fall** n caída, ruina; ~**hearted** adj desanimado; ~**hill** adv: **to go** ~**hill** (also fig) ir cuesta abajo; ~ **payment** n entrada, pago al contado; ~**pour** n aguacero; ~**right** adj (nonsense, lie) manifiesto; (refusal) terminante

**Down's syndrome** [daʊnz-] n síndrome m de Down

**down**: ~stairs adv (below) (en la casa de) abajo; (~wards) escaleras abajo; ~stream adv aguas or río abajo; ~-to-earth adj práctico; ~town adv en el centro de la ciudad; ~ under adv en Australia or Nueva Zelanda); ~ward [-wəd] adj, adv hacia abajo; ~wards [-wədz] adv hacia abajo

**dowry** ['dauri] n dote f

**doz.** abbr = dozen

**doze** [dəuz] vi dormitar; ~ off vi quedarse medio dormido

**dozen** ['dʌzn] n docena; a ~ books una docena de libros; ~s of cantidad de

**Dr.** abbr = doctor; drive

**drab** [dræb] adj gris, monótono

**draft** [drɑːft] n (first copy) borrador m; (POL: of bill) anteproyecto; (US: call-up) quinta ♦ vt (plan) preparar; (write roughly) hacer un borrador de; see also draught

**draftsman** ['drɑːftsmən] (US) n = draughtsman

**drag** [dræg] vt arrastrar; (river) dragar, rastrear ♦ vi (time) pasar despacio; (play, film etc) hacerse pesado ♦ n (inf) lata; (women's clothing): in ~ vestido de travesti; ~ on vi ser interminable

**dragon** ['drægən] n dragón m

**dragonfly** ['drægənflai] n libélula

**drain** [drein] n desaguadero; (in street) sumidero; (source of loss): to be a ~ on consumir, agotar ♦ vt (land, marshes) desecar; (reservoir) desecar; (vegetables) escurrir ♦ vi escurrirse; ~age n (act) desagüe m; (MED, AGR) drenaje m; (sewage) alcantarillado; ~board (US) n = ~ing board; ['dreinbɔːd] (US) n = ~ing board; ~ing board n escurridera, escurridor m; ~pipe n tubo de desagüe

**drama** ['drɑːmə] n (art) teatro; (play) drama m; (excitement) emoción f; ~tic [drə'mætik] adj dramático; (sudden, marked) espectacular; ~tist ['dræmətist] n dramaturgo/a; ~tize ['dræmətaiz] vt (events) dra-

matizar; (adapt: for TV, cinema) adaptar a la televisión/al cine

**drank** [dræŋk] pt of drink

**drape** [dreip] vt (cloth) colocar; (flag) colgar; ~s (US) npl cortinas fpl

**drastic** ['dræstik] adj (measure) severo; (change) radical, drástico

**draught** [drɑːft] (US **draft**) n (of air) corriente f de aire; (NAUT) calado; on ~ (beer) de barril; ~board (BRIT) n tablero de damas; ~s (BRIT) n (game) juego de damas

**draughtsman** ['drɑːftsmən] (US **draftsman**) n delineante m

**draw** [drɔː] (pt **drew**, pp **drawn**) vt (picture) dibujar; (cart) tirar de; (curtain) correr; (take out) sacar; (attract) atraer; (money) retirar; (wages) cobrar ♦ vi (SPORT) empatar ♦ n (SPORT) empate m; (lottery) sorteo; ~ near vi acercarse; ~ out vi (lengthen) alargarse ♦ vt sacar; ~ up vi (stop) pararse ♦ vt (chair) acercar; (document) redactar; ~back n inconveniente m, desventaja; ~bridge n puente m levadizo

**drawer** [drɔː*] n cajón m

**drawing** ['drɔːiŋ] n dibujo; ~ board n tablero de (dibujante); ~ pin (BRIT) n chincheta; ~ room n salón m

**drawl** [drɔːl] n habla lenta y cansina

**drawn** [drɔːn] pp of draw

**dread** [dred] n pavor m, terror m ♦ vt temer, tener miedo or pavor a; ~ful adj horroroso

**dream** [driːm] (pt, pp **dreamed** or **dreamt**) n sueño ♦ vt, vi soñar; ~er n soñador(a) m/f; **dreamt** [dremt] pt, pp of dream; ~y adj (distracted) soñador(a), distraído; (music) suave

**dreary** ['driəri] adj monótono

**dredge** [dredʒ] vt dragar

**dregs** [dregz] npl posos mpl; (of humanity) hez f

**drench** [drentʃ] vt empapar

**dress** [dres] n vestido; (clothing) ropa ♦ vt vestir; (wound) vendar ♦

*vi* vestirse; **to get ~ed** vestirse; **~ up** *vi* vestirse de etiqueta; (*in fancy dress*) disfrazarse; **~ circle** (BRIT) *n* principal *m*; **~er** *n* (*furniture*) aparador *m*; (*: US*) cómoda (con espejo); **~ing** *n* (MED) vendaje *m*; (CULIN) aliño; **~ing gown** (BRIT) *n* bata; **~ing room** *n* (THEATRE) camarín *m*, (SPORT) vestuario; **~ing table** *n* tocador *m*; **~maker** *n* modista, costurera; **~ rehearsal** *n* ensayo general

**drew** |dru:| *pt of* **draw**

**dribble** ['drɪbl] *vi* (*baby*) babear ♦ *vt* (*ball*) regatear

**dried** |draɪd| *adj* (*fruit*) seco; (*milk*) en polvo

**drier** ['draɪə*] *n* = **dryer**

**drift** |drɪft| *n* (*of current etc*) flujo; (*of snow*) ventisquero; (*meaning*) significado ♦ *vi* (*boat*) ir a la deriva; (*sand, snow*) amontonarse; **~wood** *n* madera de deriva

**drill** |drɪl| *n* (**~ bit**) broca; (*tool for DIY etc*) taladro; (*of dentist*) fresa; (*for mining etc*) perforadora, barrena; (MIL) instrucción ♦ *vt* perforar, taladrar; (*troops*) enseñar la instrucción a ♦ *vi* (*for oil*) perforar

**drink** |drɪŋk| (*pt* **drank**, *pp* **drunk**) *n* bebida; (*sip*) trago ♦ *vt, vi* beber; **to have a ~** tomar algo; tomar una copa *or* un trago; **a ~ of water** un trago de agua; **~er** *n* bebedor(a) *m/f*; **~ing water** *n* agua potable

**drip** |drɪp| *n* (*act*) goteo; (*one ~*) gota; (MED) gota a gota *m* ♦ *vi* gotear; **~-dry** *adj* (*shirt*) inarrugable; **~ping** *n* (*animal fat*) pringue *m*

**drive** |draɪv| (*pt* **drove**, *pp* **driven**) *n* (*journey*) viaje *m* en coche; (*also: ~way*) entrada; (*energy*) energía, vigor *m*; (COMPUT: *also: disk ~*) drive *m* ♦ *vt* (*car*) conducir (SP), manejar (AM); (*nail*) clavar; (*push*) empujar; (TECH: *motor*) impulsar ♦ *vi* (AUT: *at controls*) conducir; (*: travel*) pasearse en coche; **left-/right-hand ~** conducción *f* a la izquierda/derecha; **to ~ sb mad** vol-

verle loco a uno

**drivel** ['drɪvl] (*inf*) *n* tonterías *fpl*

**driven** ['drɪvn] *pp of* **drive**

**driver** ['draɪvə*] *n* conductor(a) *m/f* (SP), chofer *m* (AM); (*of taxi, bus*) chofer; **~'s license** (US) *n* carnet *m* de conducir

**driveway** ['draɪvweɪ] *n* entrada

**driving** ['draɪvɪŋ] *n* el conducir (SP), el manejar (AM); **~ instructor** *n* instructor(a) *m/f* de conducción *or* manejo; **~ lesson** *n* clase *f* de conducción *or* manejo; **~ licence** (BRIT) *n* permiso de conducir; **~ school** *n* autoescuela; **~ test** *n* examen *m* de conducción *or* manejo

**drizzle** ['drɪzl] *n* llovizna

**drone** |drəun| *n* (*noise*) zumbido; (*bee*) zángano

**drool** |dru:l| *vi* babear

**droop** |dru:p| *vi* (*flower*) marchitarse; (*shoulders*) encorvarse; (*head*) inclinarse

**drop** |drɒp| *n* (*of water*) gota; (*lessening*) baja; (*fall*) caída ♦ *vt* dejar caer; (*voice, eyes, price*) bajar; (*passenger*) dejar; (*omit*) omitir ♦ *vi* (*object*) caer; (*wind*) amainar; **~s** *npl* (MED) gotas *fpl*; **~ off** *vi* (*sleep*) dormirse ♦ *vt* (*passenger*) dejar; **~ out** *vi* (*withdraw*) retirarse; (*university*) marginado/a; (SCOL) estudiante *que abandona los estudios*; **~per** *n* cuentagotas *m inv*; **~pings** *npl* excremento

**drought** |draut| *n* sequía

**drove** |drəuv| *pt of* **drive**

**drown** |draun| *vt* ahogar ♦ *vi* ahogarse

**drowsy** ['drauzɪ] *adj* soñoliento; **to be ~** tener sueño

**drudgery** ['drʌdʒərɪ] *n* trabajo monótono

**drug** |drʌg| *n* medicamento; (*narcotic*) droga ♦ *vt* drogar; **to be on ~s** drogarse; (*passenger*) **~ addict** *n* drogadicto/a; **~gist** (US) *n* farmacéutico; **~store** (US) *n* farmacia

**drum** |drʌm| *n* tambor *m*; (*for oil, petrol*) bidón *m*; **~s** *npl* batería;

**~mer** n tambor m

**drunk** [drʌŋk] pp of **drink** ♦ adj borracho ♦ n (also: **~ard**) borracho/a; **~en** adj borracho; (laughter, party) de borrachos

**dry** [draɪ] adj seco; (day) sin lluvia; (climate) árido, seco ♦ vt secar; (tears) enjugarse ♦ vi secarse; **~** vi (river) secarse; **~-cleaner's** n tintorería; **~-cleaning** n lavado en seco; **~er** n (for hair) secador m; (US: for clothes) secadora; **~ness** n sequedad f; **~ rot** n putrefacción f fungoide

**DSS** n abbr = Department of Social Security

**dual** ['djuəl] adj doble; **~ carriageway** (BRIT) n carretera de doble calzada; **~ nationality** n doble nacionalidad f; **~-purpose** adj de doble uso

**dubbed** [dʌbd] adj (CINEMA) doblado

**dubious** ['djuːbɪəs] adj indeciso; (reputation, company) sospechoso

**duchess** ['dʌtʃɪs] n duquesa

**duck** [dʌk] n pato ♦ vi agacharse; **~ling** n patito

**duct** [dʌkt] n conducto, canal m

**dud** [dʌd] n (object, tool) engaño, engañifa ♦ adj: **~ cheque** (BRIT) cheque m sin fondos

**due** [djuː] adj (owed) n: he is **~** £10 se le deben 10 libras; (expected: event): the meeting is **~** on Wednesday la reunión tendrá lugar el miércoles; (: arrival) the train is **~** at 8am el tren tiene su llegada para las 8; (proper) debido ♦ n: to give sb his (or her) **~** ser justo con alguien ♦ adv: **~** north derecho al norte; **~s** npl (for club, union) cuota; (in harbour) derechos mpl; in **~** course a su debido tiempo; **~** to debido a; to be **~** to deberse a

**duet** [djuːˈɛt] n dúo

**duffel** ['dʌfl] adj: **~ bag** n bolsa de lona; **~ coat** n trenca, abrigo de tres cuartos

**dug** [dʌg] pt, pp of **dig**

**duke** [djuːk] n duque m

**dull** [dʌl] adj (light) débil; (stupid) torpe; (boring) pesado; (sound, pain) sordo; (weather, day) gris ♦ vt (pain, grief) aliviar; (mind, senses) entorpecer

**duly** ['djuːlɪ] adv debidamente; (on time) a su debido tiempo

**dumb** [dʌm] n mudo; (pej: stupid) estúpido; **~founded** [dʌmˈfaundɪd] adj pasmado

**dummy** ['dʌmɪ] n (tailor's ~) maniquí m; (mock-up) maqueta; (BRIT: for baby) chupete m ♦ adj falso, postizo

**dump** [dʌmp] n (also: rubbish ~) basurero, vertedero; (inf: place) cuchitril m ♦ vt (put down) dejar; (get rid of) deshacerse de; (COMPUT: data) transferir

**dumpling** ['dʌmplɪŋ] n bola de masa hervida

**dumpy** ['dʌmpɪ] adj regordete/a

**dunce** [dʌns] n zopenco

**dung** [dʌŋ] n estiércol m

**dungarees** [dʌŋgəˈriːz] npl mono

**dungeon** ['dʌndʒən] n calabozo

**duo** ['djuːəu] n (gen, MUS) dúo

**dupe** [djuːp] n (victim) víctima f ♦ vt engañar

**duplex** ['djuːplɛks] n dúplex m

**duplicate** [n 'djuːplɪkət, vb 'djuːplɪkeɪt] n duplicado ♦ vt duplicar; (photocopy) fotocopiar; (repeat) repetir; in **~** por duplicado

**durable** ['djuərəbl] adj duradero

**duration** [djuəˈreɪʃən] n duración f

**duress** [djuəˈrɛs] n: under **~** por compulsión

**during** ['djuərɪŋ] prep durante

**dusk** [dʌsk] n crepúsculo, anochecer m

**dust** [dʌst] n polvo ♦ vt quitar el polvo a, desempolvar; (cake etc): to **~** with espolvorear de; **~bin** (BRIT) n cubo de la basura (SP), balde m (AM); **~er** n paño, trapo; **~man** (BRIT) n basurero; **~y** adj polvoriento

**Dutch** [dʌtʃ] adj holandés/esa ♦ n

(*LING*) holandés *m*; **the ~** *npl* los holandeses; **to go ~** (*inf*) pagar cada uno lo suyo; **~man/woman** *n* holandés/esa *m/f*

**dutiful** ['dju:tɪfʊl] *adj* obediente, sumiso

**duty** ['dju:tɪ] *n* deber *m*; (*tax*) derechos *mpl* de aduana; **on ~** de servicio; (*at night etc*) de guardia; **off ~** libre (de servicio); **~-free** *adj* libre de impuestos

**duvet** ['du:veɪ] (*BRIT*) *n* edredón *m*

**dwarf** [dwɔ:f] (*pl* **dwarves**) *n* enano/a ♦ *vt* empequeñecer; **dwarves** [dwɔːvz] *npl of* **dwarf**

**dwell** [dwɛl] (*pt, pp* **dwelt**) *vi* morar; **~ on** *vt fus* explayarse en; **~ing** *n* vivienda

**dwindle** ['dwɪndl] *vi* menguar, disminuir

**dye** [daɪ] *n* tinte *m* ♦ *vt* teñir

**dying** ['daɪɪŋ] *adj* moribundo, agonizante

**dyke** [daɪk] (*BRIT*) *n* dique *m*

**dynamic** [daɪ'næmɪk] *adj* dinámico

**dynamite** ['daɪnəmaɪt] *n* dinamita

**dynamo** ['daɪnəməʊ] *n* dínamo *f*

**dynasty** ['dɪnəstɪ] *n* dinastía

# E

**E** [i:] *n* (*MUS*) mi *m*

**each** [i:tʃ] *adj* cada *inv* ♦ *pron* cada uno; **~ other** el uno al otro; **they hate ~ other** se odian (entre ellos *or* mutuamente); **they have 2 books ~** tienen 2 libros por persona

**eager** ['i:gə*] *adj* (*keen*) entusiasmado; **to be ~ to do sth** tener muchas ganas de hacer algo, impacientarse por hacer algo; **to be ~ for** tener muchas ganas de

**eagle** ['i:gl] *n* águila

**ear** [ɪə*] *n* oreja; oído; (*of corn*) espiga; **~ache** *n* dolor *m* de oídos; **~drum** *n* tímpano

**earl** [ə:l] *n* conde *m*

**earlier** ['ə:lɪə*] *adj* anterior ♦ *adv* antes

**early** ['ə:lɪ] *adv* temprano; (*before time*) con tiempo, con anticipación ♦ *adj* temprano; (*settlers etc*) primitivo; (*death, departure*) prematuro; (*reply*) pronto; **to have an ~ night** acostarse temprano; **in the ~ or ~ in the spring/19th century** a principios de primavera/del siglo diecinueve; **~ retirement** *n* jubilación *f* anticipada

**earmark** ['ɪəmɑːk] *vt*: **to ~ (for)** reservar (para), destinar (a)

**earn** [ə:n] *vt* (*salary*) percibir; (*interest*) devengar; (*praise*) merecerse

**earnest** ['ə:nɪst] *adj* (*wish*) fervoroso; (*person*) serio, formal; **in ~** *n* en serio

**earnings** ['ə:nɪŋz] *npl* (*personal*) sueldo, ingresos *mpl*; (*company*) ganancias *fpl*

**ear**: **~phones** *npl* auriculares *mpl*; **~ring** *n* pendiente *m*, arete *m*; **~shot** *n*: **within ~shot** al alcance del oído

**earth** [ə:θ] *n* tierra; (*BRIT*: *ELEC*) cable *m* de toma de tierra ♦ *vt* (*BRIT*: *ELEC*) conectar a tierra; **~enware** *n* loza (de barro); **~quake** *n* terremoto; **~y** *adj* (*fig*: *vulgar*) grosero

**ease** [i:z] *n* facilidad *f*; (*comfort*) comodidad *f* ♦ *vt* (*lessen*: *problem*) mitigar; (*: pain*) aliviar; (*: tension*) reducir; **to ~ sth in/out** meter/sacar algo con cuidado; **at ~!** (*MIL*) ¡descansen!; **~ off** *or* **up** *vi* (*wind, rain*) amainar; (*slow down*) aflojar la marcha

**easel** ['i:zl] *n* caballete *m*

**easily** ['i:zɪlɪ] *adv* fácilmente

**east** [i:st] *n* este *m* ♦ *adj* del este, oriental; (*wind*) este ♦ *adv* al este, hacia el este; **the E~** el Oriente; (*POL*) los países del Este

**Easter** ['i:stə*] *n* Pascua (de Resurrección); **~ egg** *n* huevo de Pascua

**easterly** ['i:stəlɪ] *adj* (*to the east*) al este; (*from the east*) del este

**eastern** ['i:stən] *adj* del este, oriental; (*oriental*) oriental; (*communist*) del este

**East Germany** n Alemania Oriental
**eastward(s)** ['i:stwəd(z)] *adv* hacia el este
**easy** ['i:zɪ] *adj* fácil; (*simple*) sencillo; (*comfortable*) holgado, cómodo; (*relaxed*) tranquilo ♦ *adv*: to take it or things ~ (*not worry*) tomarlo con calma; (*rest*) descansar; ~ **chair** n sillón m; ~**-going** *adj* acomodadizo
**eat** [i:t] (*pt* ate, *pp* eaten) *vt* comer; ~ **into** *vt fus* corroer; (*savings*) mermar; ~ **away at** *vt fus* corroer; mermar
**eau de Cologne** [əʊdəkə'ləʊn] n (agua de) Colonia
**eaves** [i:vz] *npl* alero
**eavesdrop** ['i:vzdrɒp] *vi*: to ~ (on) escuchar a escondidas
**ebb** [eb] n reflujo ♦ *vi* bajar; (*fig*: *also*: ~ **away**) decaer
**ebony** ['ebənɪ] n ébano
**EC** n *abbr* (= *European Community*) CE f
**eccentric** [ɪk'sentrɪk] *adj*, n excéntrico/a m/f
**echo** ['ekəʊ] (*pl* ~**es**) n eco m ♦ *vt* (*sound*) repetir ♦ *vi* resonar, hacer eco
**éclair** [ɪ'kleə*] n pastelillo relleno de crema y con chocolate por encima
**eclipse** [ɪ'klɪps] n eclipse m
**ecology** [ɪ'kɒlədʒɪ] n ecología
**economic** [i:kə'nɒmɪk] *adj* económico; (*business etc*) rentable; ~**al** *adj* económico; ~s n (*SCOL*) economía ♦ *npl* (*of project etc*) rentabilidad f
**economize** [ɪ'kɒnəmaɪz] *vi* economizar, ahorrar
**economy** [ɪ'kɒnəmɪ] n economía; ~ **class** n (*AVIAT*) clase f económica; ~ **size** n tamaño económico
**ecstasy** ['ekstəsɪ] n éxtasis m *inv*; **ecstatic** [-'tætɪk] *adj* extático
**ECU** ['eɪkju:] n (= *European Currency Unit*) ECU m
**Ecuador** ['ekwədɔ:*] n Ecuador m; **E~ian** *adj*, n ecuatoriano/a m/f
**eczema** ['eksɪmə] n eczema m

**edge** [edʒ] n (*of knife etc*) filo; (*of object*) borde m; (*of lake etc*) orilla ♦ *vt* (*SEWING*) ribetear; **on** ~ (*fig*) = edgy; **to** ~ **away from** alejarse poco a poco de; ~**ways** *adv*: he couldn't get a word in ~**ways** no pudo meter ni baza
**edgy** ['edʒɪ] *adj* nervioso, inquieto
**edible** ['edɪbl] *adj* comestible
**Edinburgh** ['edɪnbərə] n Edimburgo
**edit** ['edɪt] *vt* (*be the editor of*) dirigir; (*text, report*) corregir, preparar; ~**ion** [ɪ'dɪʃən] n edición f; ~**or** n (*of newspaper*) director(a) m/f; (*of column*): **foreign/political** ~**or** encargado de la sección de extranjero/política; (*of book*) redactor(a) m/f; ~**orial** [-'tɔ:rɪəl] *adj* editorial ♦ n editorial m
**educate** ['edjukeɪt] *vt* (*gen*) educar; (*instruct*) instruir
**education** [edju'keɪʃən] n educación f; (*schooling*) enseñanza; (*SCOL*) pedagogía; ~**al** *adj* (*policy etc*) educacional; (*experience*) docente; (*toy*) educativo
**EEC** n *abbr* (= *European Economic Community*) CEE f
**eel** [i:l] n anguila
**eerie** ['ɪərɪ] *adj* misterioso
**effect** [ɪ'fekt] n efecto ♦ *vt* efectuar, llevar a cabo; **to take** ~ (*law*) entrar en vigor o vigencia; (*drug*) surtir efecto; **in** ~ en realidad; ~**ive** *adj* eficaz; (*actual*) verdadero; ~**ively** *adv* eficazmente; (*in reality*) efectivamente; ~**iveness** n eficacia
**effeminate** [ɪ'femɪnɪt] *adj* afeminado
**efficiency** [ɪ'fɪʃənsɪ] n eficiencia; rendimiento
**efficient** [ɪ'fɪʃənt] *adj* eficiente; (*machine*) de buen rendimiento
**effort** ['efət] n esfuerzo; ~**less** *adj* sin ningún esfuerzo; (*style*) natural
**effrontery** [ɪ'frʌntərɪ] n descaro
**effusive** [ɪ'fju:sɪv] *adj* efusivo
**e.g.** *adv abbr* (= *exempli gratia*) p. ej.
**egg** [eg] n huevo; **hard-boiled/soft-boiled** ~ huevo duro/pasado por

agua; ~ **on** *vt* incitar; ~**cup** *n* huevera; ~ **plant** (*esp US*) *n* berenjena; ~**shell** *n* cáscara de huevo

**ego** ['i:gəu] *n* ego; ~**tism** *n* egoísmo; ~**tist** *n* egoísta *m/f*

**Egypt** ['i:dʒɪpt] *n* Egipto; ~**ian** [ɪ'dʒɪpʃən] *adj*, *n* egipcio/a *m/f*

**eiderdown** ['aɪdədaun] *n* edredón *m*

**eight** [eɪt] *num* ocho; ~**een** *num* diez y ocho, dieciocho; ~**h** [eɪtθ] *num* octavo; ~**y** *num* ochenta

**Eire** ['ɛərə] *n* Eire *m*

**either** ['aɪðə\*] *adj* cualquiera de los dos; (*both*, *each*) cada ♦ *pron:* ~ (**of them**) cualquiera (de los dos) ♦ *adv* tampoco; **on** ~ **side** en ambos lados; **I don't like** ~ no me gusta ninguno/a de los/las dos; **no, I don't** ~ no, yo tampoco ♦ *conj:* ~ **yes or no** o sí o no

**eject** [ɪ'dʒɛkt] *vt* echar, expulsar; (*tenant*) desahuciar; ~**or seat** *n* asiento proyectable

**eke** [i:k]: **to** ~ **out** *vt* hacer que alcance

**elaborate** [*adj* ɪ'læbərɪt, *vb* ɪ'læbəreɪt] *adj* (*complex*) complejo ♦ *vt* (*expand*) ampliar; (*refine*) refinar ♦ *vi* explicar con más detalles

**elapse** [ɪ'læps] *vi* transcurrir

**elastic** [ɪ'læstɪk] *n* elástico ♦ *adj* elástico; (*fig*) flexible; ~ **band** (*BRIT*) *n* gomita

**elated** [ɪ'leɪtɪd] *adj:* **to be** ~ regocijarse

**elbow** ['ɛlbəu] *n* codo

**elder** ['ɛldə\*] *adj* mayor ♦ *n* (*tree*) saúco; (*person*) mayor; ~**ly** *adj* de edad, mayor ♦ *npl:* **the** ~**ly** los mayores

**eldest** ['ɛldɪst] *adj*, *n* el/la mayor

**elect** [ɪ'lɛkt] *vt* elegir ♦ *adj:* **the president** ~ el presidente electo; **to** ~ **to do** optar por hacer; ~**ion** [ɪ'lɛkʃən] *n* elección *f*; ~**ioneering** [ɪlɛkʃə'nɪərɪŋ] *n* campaña electoral; ~**or** *n* elector/a; ~**oral** *adj* electoral; ~**orate** *n* electorado

**electric** [ɪ'lɛktrɪk] *adj* eléctrico; ~**al** *adj* eléctrico; ~ **blanket** *n* manta

eléctrica; ~ **fire** *n* estufa eléctrica

**electrician** [ɪlɛk'trɪʃən] *n* electricista *m/f*

**electricity** [ɪlɛk'trɪsɪtɪ] *n* electricidad *f*

**electrify** [ɪ'lɛktrɪfaɪ] *vt* (*RAIL*) electrificar; (*fig: audience*) electrizar

**electron** [ɪ'lɛktrɔn] *n* electrón *m*

**electronic** [ɪlɛk'trɔnɪk] *adj* electrónico; ~ **mail** *n* correo electrónico; ~**s** *n* electrónica

**elegant** ['ɛlɪgənt] *adj* elegante

**element** ['ɛlɪmənt] *n* elemento; (*of kettle etc*) resistencia; ~**ary** [ɛlɪ'mɛntərɪ] *adj* elemental; (*primitive*) rudimentario; (*school*) primario

**elephant** ['ɛlɪfənt] *n* elefante *m*

**elevation** [ɛlɪ'veɪʃən] *n* elevación *f*; (*height*) altura

**elevator** ['ɛlɪveɪtə\*] *n* (*US*) ascensor *m*; (*in warehouse etc*) montacargas *m inv*

**eleven** [ɪ'lɛvn] *num* once; ~**ses** (*BRIT*) *npl* café *m* de las once; ~**th** *num* undécimo

**elf** [ɛlf] (*pl* **elves**) *n* duende *m*

**elicit** [ɪ'lɪsɪt] *vt:* **to** ~ (**from**) sacar (de)

**eligible** ['ɛlɪdʒəbl] *adj:* **an** ~ **young man/woman** un buen partido; **to be** ~ **for sth** llenar los requisitos para algo

**eliminate** [ɪ'lɪmɪneɪt] *vt* (*eradicate*) suprimir; (*opponent*) eliminar

**elm** [ɛlm] *n* olmo

**elongated** ['i:lɔŋgeɪtɪd] *adj* alargado

**elope** [ɪ'ləup] *vi* fugarse (para casarse); ~**ment** *n* fuga

**eloquent** ['ɛləkwənt] *adj* elocuente

**else** [ɛls] *adv:* **something** ~ otra cosa; **somewhere** ~ en otra parte; **everywhere** ~ en todas partes menos aquí; **where** ~? ¿dónde más?, ¿en qué otra parte?; **there was little** ~ **to do** apenas quedaba otra cosa que hacer; **nobody** ~ **spoke** no habló nadie más; ~**where** *adv* (*be*) en otra parte; (*go*) a otra parte

**elucidate** [ɪ'lu:sɪdeɪt] *vt* aclarar

**elude** [ɪ'lu:d] *vt* (*subj: idea etc*) escaparse a; (capture) esquivar

**elusive** [ɪ'luːsɪv] adj esquivo; (quality) difícil de encontrar

**emaciated** [ɪ'meɪsɪeɪtɪd] adj demacrado

**emanate** ['eməneɪt] vi: to ~ from (idea) surgir de; (light, sound) proceder de

**emancipate** [ɪ'mænsɪpeɪt] vt emancipar

**embankment** [ɪm'bæŋkmənt] n terraplén m

**embargo** [ɪm'bɑːgəu] (pl ~es) n prohibición f, embargo m

**embark** [ɪm'bɑːk] vi embarcarse ♦ vt embarcar; to ~ on (journey) emprender; (course of action) lanzarse a; ~ation [embɑː'keɪʃən] n (people) embarco; (goods) embarque m

**embarrass** [ɪm'bærəs] vt avergonzar; (government etc) dejar en mal lugar; ~ed adj (laugh, silence) embarazoso; ~ing adj (situation) violento; (question) embarazoso; ~ment n (shame) vergüenza; (problem): to be an ~ment for sb poner en un aprieto a uno

**embassy** ['embəsɪ] n embajada

**embedded** [ɪm'bedɪd] adj (object) empotrado; (thorn etc) clavado

**embellish** [ɪm'belɪʃ] vt embellecer; (story) adornar

**embers** ['embəz] npl rescoldo, ascua

**embezzle** [ɪm'bezl] vt desfalcar, malversar

**embitter** [ɪm'bɪtə*] vt (fig: sour) amargar

**embody** [ɪm'bɒdɪ] vt (spirit) encarnar; (include) incorporar

**embossed** [ɪm'bɒst] adj realzado

**embrace** [ɪm'breɪs] vt abrazar, dar un abrazo a; (include) abarcar ♦ vi abrazarse ♦ n abrazo

**embroider** [ɪm'brɔɪdə*] vt bordar; ~y n bordado

**embryo** ['embrɪəu] n embrión m

**emerald** ['emərəld] n esmeralda

**emerge** [ɪ'mɜːdʒ] vi salir, (arise) surgir

**emergency** [ɪ'mɜːdʒənsɪ] n crisis f

inv; in an ~ en caso de urgencia; state of ~ estado de emergencia; ~ cord (US) n timbre m de alarma; ~ exit n salida de emergencia; ~ landing n aterrizaje m forzoso; ~ services npl (fire, police, ambulance) servicios mpl de urgencia or emergencia

**emergent** [ɪ'mɜːdʒənt] adj (nation) recién independizado; (group) recién aparecido

**emery board** ['emərɪ-] n lima de uñas

**emigrate** ['emɪgreɪt] vi emigrar

**emissions** [ɪ'mɪʃənz] npl emisión f

**emit** [ɪ'mɪt] vt emitir; (smoke) arrojar; (smell) despedir; (sound) producir

**emotion** [ɪ'məuʃən] n emoción f; ~al adj (needs) emocional; (person) sentimental; (scene) conmovedor(a), emocionante; (speech) emocionado

**emperor** ['empərə*] n emperador m

**emphases** ['emfəsiːz] npl of emphasis

**emphasis** ['emfəsɪs] (pl ~ses) n énfasis m inv

**emphasize** ['emfəsaɪz] vt (word, point) subrayar, recalcar; (feature) hacer resaltar

**emphatic** [em'fætɪk] adj (reply) categórico; (person) insistente; ~ally adv con énfasis; (certainly) sin ningún género de dudas

**empire** ['empaɪə*] n (also fig) imperio

**employ** [ɪm'plɔɪ] vt emplear; ~ee [-'iː] n empleado/a; ~er n patrón/ona m/f; empresario; ~ment n (work) trabajo; ~ment agency n agencia de colocaciones

**empower** [ɪm'pauə*] vt: to ~ sb to do sth autorizar a uno para hacer algo

**empress** ['empris] n emperatriz f

**emptiness** ['emptɪnɪs] n vacío; (of life etc) vaciedad f

**empty** ['emptɪ] adj vacío; (place) desierto; (house) desocupado; (threat) vano ♦ vt vaciar; (place) dejar vacío

♦ vi vaciarse; (house etc) quedar desocupado; **~-handed** adj con las manos vacías

**emulate** ['emjuleit] vt emular

**emulsion** [ɪ'mʌlʃən] n emulsión f; (also: ~ paint) pintura emulsión

**enable** [ɪ'neɪbl] vt: to ~ sb to do sth permitir a algn hacer algo

**enact** [ɪn'ækt] vt (law) promulgar; (play) representar; (role) hacer

**enamel** [ɪ'næml] n esmalte m; (also: ~ paint) pintura esmaltada

**enamoured** [ɪ'næməd] adj: to be ~ of (person) estar enamorado de; (activity etc) tener gran afición a; (idea) aferrarse a

**encased** [ɪn'keɪst] adj: ~ in (covered) revestido de

**enchant** [ɪn'tʃɑːnt] vt encantar; **~ing** adj encantador(a)

**encircle** [ɪn'sɜːkl] vt rodear

**encl.** abbr (= enclosed) adj

**enclose** [ɪn'kləʊz] vt (land) cercar; (letter etc) adjuntar; **please find ~d** le mandamos adjunto

**enclosure** [ɪn'kləʊʒə*] n cercado, recinto

**encompass** [ɪn'kʌmpəs] vt abarcar

**encore** [ɔŋ'kɔː*] excl ¡otra!, ¡bis! ♦ n bis m

**encounter** [ɪn'kaʊntə*] n encuentro ♦ vt encontrar, encontrarse con; (difficulty) tropezar con

**encourage** [ɪn'kʌrɪdʒ] vt alentar, animar; (activity) fomentar; (growth) estimular; **~ment** n estímulo; (of industry) fomento

**encroach** [ɪn'krəʊtʃ] vi: to ~ (up)on invadir; (rights) usurpar; (time) adueñarse de

**encumber** [ɪn'kʌmbə*] vt: to be ~d with (baggage etc, debts) estar cargado de

**encyclop(a)edia** [ensaɪkləʊ'piːdɪə] n enciclopedia

**end** [end] n (gen, also aim) fin m; (of table) extremo; (of street) final m; (SPORT) lado ♦ vt terminar, acabar; (also: bring to an ~, put an ~ to) acabar con ♦ vi terminar, aca-

bar; **in the** ~ al fin; **on** ~ (object) de punta, de cabeza; to stand on ~ (hair) erizarse; **for hours on** ~ hora tras hora; **~ up** vi: to ~ up in terminar en; (place) ir a parar en

**endanger** [ɪn'deɪndʒə*] vt poner en peligro

**endearing** [ɪn'dɪərɪŋ] adj simpático, atractivo

**endeavour** [ɪn'devə*] (US endeavor) n esfuerzo; (attempt) tentativa ♦ vi: to ~ to do esforzarse por hacer; (try) procurar hacer

**ending** ['endɪŋ] n (of book) desenlace m; (LING) terminación f

**endive** ['endaɪv] n (chicory) endibia; (curly) escarola

**endless** ['endlɪs] adj interminable, inacabable

**endorse** [ɪn'dɔːs] vt (cheque) endosar; (approve) aprobar; **~ment** n (on driving licence) nota de inhabilitación

**endow** [ɪn'dau] vt (provide with money): to ~ (with) dotar (de); to be ~ed with (fig) estar dotado de

**endurance** [ɪn'djuərəns] n resistencia

**endure** [ɪn'djuə*] vt (bear) aguantar, soportar ♦ vi (last) durar

**enemy** ['enəmɪ] adj, n enemigo/a m/f

**energetic** [enə'dʒetɪk] adj enérgico

**energy** ['enədʒɪ] n energía

**enforce** [ɪn'fɔːs] vt (LAW) hacer cumplir

**engage** [ɪn'geɪdʒ] vt (attention) llamar; (interest) ocupar; (in conversation) abordar; (worker) contratar; (AUT): to ~ the clutch embragar ♦ vi (TECH) engranar; to ~ in dedicarse a, ocuparse en; **~d** adj (BRIT: busy, in use) ocupado; (betrothed) prometido; to get **~d** prometerse; **~d tone** (BRIT) n (TEL) señal f de comunicando; **~ment** n (appointment) compromiso, cita; (booking) contratación f; (to marry) compromiso; (period) noviazgo; **~ment ring** n anillo de prometida

**engaging** [ɪn'geɪdʒɪŋ] adj atractivo

**engender** [ɪn'dʒɛndə*] vt engendrar

**engine** ['ɛndʒɪn] n (AUT) motor m; (RAIL) locomotora; **~ driver** n maquinista m/f

**engineer** [ɛndʒɪ'nɪə*] n ingeniero m; (BRIT: for repairs) mecánico m; (on ship, US: RAIL) maquinista m; **~ing** n ingeniería f

**England** ['ɪŋglənd] n Inglaterra f

**English** ['ɪŋglɪʃ] adj inglés/esa ♦ n (LING) inglés m; **the ~** npl los ingleses mpl; **the ~ Channel** n (el Canal de) la Mancha; **~man/woman** n inglés/esa m/f

**engraving** [ɪn'greɪvɪŋ] n grabado m

**engrossed** [ɪn'grəust] adj: **~** in absorto en

**engulf** [ɪn'gʌlf] vt (subj: water) sumergir, hundir; (: fire) prender; (: fear) apoderarse de

**enhance** [ɪn'hɑːns] vt (gen) aumentar; (beauty) realzar

**enjoy** [ɪn'dʒɔɪ] vt (health, fortune) disfrutar de, gozar de; (like) gustarle a uno; **to ~ o.s.** divertirse; **~able** adj agradable; (amusing) divertido; **~ment** n (joy) placer m; (activity) diversión f

**enlarge** [ɪn'lɑːdʒ] vt aumentar; (broaden) extender; (PHOT) ampliar ♦ vi: **to ~ on** (subject) tratar con más detalles; **~ment** n (PHOT) ampliación f

**enlighten** [ɪn'laɪtn] vt (inform) informar; **~ed** adj comprensivo; **the E~ment** n (HISTORY) ≈ la Ilustración, ≈ el Siglo de las Luces

**enlist** [ɪn'lɪst] vt alistar; (support) conseguir ♦ vi alistarse

**enmity** ['ɛnmɪtɪ] n enemistad f

**enormous** [ɪ'nɔːməs] adj enorme

**enough** [ɪ'nʌf] adj: **~ time/books** bastante tiempo/bastantes libros ♦ pron bastante(s) ♦ adv: **big ~** bastante grande; **he has not worked ~** no ha trabajado bastante; **have you got ~?** ¿tiene usted bastante(s)?; **~ to eat** lo suficiente para comer; **~!** ¡basta ya!; **that's ~, thanks** con eso basta, gracias

I've had **~ of him** estoy harto de él; **... which, funnily or oddly ~** ... lo que, por extraño que parezca...

**enquire** [ɪn'kwaɪə*] vt, vi = **inquire**

**enrage** [ɪn'reɪdʒ] vt enfurecer

**enrich** [ɪn'rɪtʃ] vt enriquecer

**enrol** [ɪn'rəul] vt (members) inscribir; (SCOL) matricular ♦ vi inscribirse; (SCOL) matricularse; **~ment** n inscripción f; matriculación f

**en route** [ɒn'ruːt] adv durante el viaje

**ensue** [ɪn'sjuː] vi seguirse; (result) resultar

**ensure** [ɪn'ʃuə*] vt asegurar

**entail** [ɪn'teɪl] vt suponer

**entangled** [ɪn'tæŋgld] adj: **to become ~** (in) quedarse enredado (en) or enmarañado (en)

**enter** ['ɛntə*] vt (room) entrar en; (club) hacerse socio de; (army) alistarse en; (sb for a competition) inscribir; (write down) anotar, apuntar; (COMPUT) meter ♦ vi entrar; **~ for** vt fus presentarse para; **~ into** vt fus (discussion etc) entablar; (agreement) llegar a, firmar

**enterprise** ['ɛntəpraɪz] n empresa; (spirit) iniciativa; **free ~** la libre empresa; **private ~** la iniciativa privada; **enterprising** adj emprendedor(a)

**entertain** [ɛntə'teɪn] vt (amuse) divertir; (invite: guest) invitar (a casa); (idea) abrigar; **~er** n artista m/f; **~ing** adj divertido, entretenido; **~ment** n (amusement) diversión f; (show) espectáculo

**enthralled** [ɪn'θrɔːld] adj encantado

**enthusiasm** [ɪn'θuːzɪæzm] n entusiasmo

**enthusiast** [ɪn'θuːzɪæst] n entusiasta m/f; **~ic** [-'æstɪk] adj entusiasta; **to be ~ic about** entusiasmarse por

**entice** [ɪn'taɪs] vt tentar

**entire** [ɪn'taɪə*] adj entero; **~ly** adv totalmente, enteramente; **~ty** [ɪn'taɪərətɪ] n: **in its ~ty** en su totalidad

**entitle** [ɪn'taɪtl] vt: **to ~ sb to sth** dar a uno derecho a algo; **~d** adj (*book*) titulado; **to be ~d** to do tener derecho a hacer

**entourage** [ɒntu'rɑːʒ] *n* séquito

**entrails** ['entreɪlz] *npl* entrañas *fpl*

**entrance** [*n* 'entrəns, *vb* ɪn'trɑːns] *n* entrada ♦ *vt* encantar, hechizar; **to gain ~ to** (*university etc*) ingresar en; **~ examination** *n* examen *m* de ingreso; **~ fee** *n* cuota; **~ ramp** (*US n*) (*AUT*) rampa de acceso

**entrant** ['entrənt] *n* (*in race, competition*) participante *m/f*; (*in examination*) candidato/a

**entreat** [en'triːt] *vt* rogar, suplicar

**entrenched** [en'trentʃd] *adj* inamovible

**entrepreneur** [ɒntrəprə'nɜː] *n* empresario

**entrust** [ɪn'trʌst] *vt*: **to ~ sth to sb** confiar algo a uno

**entry** ['entrɪ] *n* entrada; (*in competition*) participación *f*; (*in register*) apunte *m*; (*in account*) partida; (*in reference book*) artículo; **"no ~"** "prohibido el paso"; (*AUT*) "dirección prohibida"; **~ form** *n* hoja de inscripción; **~ phone** *n* portero automático

**enunciate** [ɪ'nʌnsɪeɪt] *vt* pronunciar; (*principle etc*) enunciar

**envelop** [ɪn'veləp] *vt* envolver

**envelope** ['envələup] *n* sobre *m*

**envious** ['envɪəs] *adj* envidioso; (*look*) de envidia

**environment** [ɪn'vaɪərənmənt] *n* (*surroundings*) entorno; (*natural world*): **the ~** el medio ambiente; **~al** [-'mentl] *adj* ambiental; medioambiental; **~-friendly** *adj* no perjudicial para el medio ambiente

**envisage** [ɪn'vɪzɪdʒ] *vt* prever

**envoy** ['envɔɪ] *n* enviado

**envy** ['envɪ] *n* envidia ♦ *vt* tener envidia a; **to ~ sb sth** envidiar algo a uno

**epic** ['epɪk] *n* épica ♦ *adj* épico

**epidemic** [epɪ'demɪk] *n* epidemia

**epilepsy** ['epɪlepsɪ] *n* epilepsia

**episode** ['epɪsəud] *n* episodio

**epitomize** [ɪ'pɪtəmaɪz] *vt* epitomar,

resumir

**equable** ['ekwəbl] *adj* (*climate*) templado; (*character*) tranquilo, afable

**equal** ['iːkwl] *adj* igual; (*treatment*) equitativo ♦ *n* igual *m/f* ♦ *vt* ser igual a; (*fig*) igualar; **to be ~ to** (*task*) estar a la altura de; **~ity** [iː'kwɒlɪtɪ] *n* igualdad *f*; **~ize** *vi* (*SPORT*) empatar; **~ly** *adv* igualmente; (*share etc*) a partes iguales

**equate** [ɪ'kweɪt] *vt*: **to ~ sth with** equiparar algo con; **equation** [ɪ'kweɪʒən] *n* (*MATH*) ecuación *f*

**equator** [ɪ'kweɪtə*] *n* ecuador *m*

**equilibrium** [iːkwɪ'lɪbrɪəm] *n* equilibrio

**equip** [ɪ'kwɪp] *vt* equipar; (*person*) proveer; **to be well ~ped** estar bien equipado; **~ment** *n* equipo, (*tools*) avíos *mpl*

**equitable** ['ekwɪtəbl] *adj* equitativo

**equities** ['ekwɪtɪz] (*BRIT*) *npl* (*COMM*) derechos *mpl* sobre or en el activo

**equivalent** [ɪ'kwɪvələnt] *adj*: **~ (to)** equivalente (a) ♦ *n* equivalente *m*

**equivocal** [ɪ'kwɪvəkl] *adj* (*ambiguous*) ambiguo; (*open to suspicion*) equívoco

**era** ['ɪərə] *n* era, época

**eradicate** [ɪ'rædɪkeɪt] *vt* erradicar

**erase** [ɪ'reɪz] *vt* borrar; **~r** *n* goma de borrar

**erect** [ɪ'rekt] *adj* erguido ♦ *vt* erigir, levantar; (*assemble*) montar; **~ion** [-ʃən] *n* construcción *f*; (*assembly*) montaje *m*; (*PHYSIOL*) erección *f*

**ERM** *n abbr* (= *Exchange Rate Mechanism*) tipo de cambio europeo

**ermine** ['ɜːmɪn] *n* armiño

**erode** [ɪ'rəud] *vt* (*GEO*) erosionar; (*metal*) corroer, desgastar; (*fig*) desgastar

**erotic** [ɪ'rɒtɪk] *adj* erótico

**err** [ɜː*] *vi* (*formal*) equivocarse

**errand** ['ernd] *n* recado (*SP*), mandado (*AM*)

**erratic** [ɪ'rætɪk] *adj* desigual, poco uniforme

**erroneous** [ɪ'rəunɪəs] *adj* erróneo

**error** ['ɛrə\*] n error m, equivocación f

**erupt** [ɪ'rʌpt] vi entrar en erupción; (fig) estallar; **~ion** [ɪ'rʌpʃən] n erupción f; (of war) estallido

**escalate** ['ɛskəleɪt] vi extenderse, intensificarse

**escalator** ['ɛskəleɪtə\*] n escalera móvil

**escapade** [ɛskə'peɪd] n travesura

**escape** [ɪ'skeɪp] n fuga ♦ vi escaparse; (flee) huir, evadirse; (leak) fugarse ♦ vt (responsibility etc) evitar, eludir; (consequences) escapar a; (elude): **his name ~s me** no me sale su nombre; **to ~ from** (place) escaparse de; (person) escaparse a

**escort** [n 'ɛskɔːt, vb ɪ'skɔːt] n acompañante m/f; (MIL) escolta f ♦ vt acompañar

**Eskimo** ['ɛskɪməu] n esquimal m/f

**especially** [ɪ'spɛʃlɪ] adv (above all) sobre todo; (particularly) en particular, especialmente

**espionage** ['ɛspɪənɑːʒ] n espionaje m

**esplanade** [ɛsplə'neɪd] n (by sea) paseo marítimo

**espouse** [ɪ'spauz] vt adherirse a

**Esquire** [ɪ'skwaɪə] n (abbr Esq.) n: J. Brown, ~ Sr. D. J. Brown

**essay** ['ɛseɪ] n (LITERATURE) ensayo; (SCOL: short) redacción f; (: long) trabajo

**essence** ['ɛsns] n esencia

**essential** [ɪ'sɛnʃl] adj (necessary) imprescindible; (basic) esencial; **~s** npl lo imprescindible, lo esencial; **~ly** adv esencialmente

**establish** [ɪ'stæblɪʃ] vt establecer; (prove) demostrar; (relations) entablar; (reputation) ganarse; **~ed** adj (business) conocido; (practice) arraigado; **~ment** n establecimiento; the E~ment la clase dirigente

**estate** [ɪ'steɪt] n (land) finca, hacienda; (inheritance) herencia; (BRIT: also: housing ~) urbanización f; **~ agent** (BRIT) n agente m/f inmobiliario/a; **~ car** (BRIT) n fur-

goneta

**esteem** [ɪ'stiːm] n: **to hold sb in high ~** estimar en mucho a uno

**esthetic** [ɪs'θɛtɪk] (US) adj = **aesthetic**

**estimate** [n 'ɛstɪmət, vb 'ɛstɪmeɪt] n estimación f, apreciación f; (assessment) tasa, cálculo; (COMM) presupuesto ♦ vt estimar, tasar; calcular; **estimation** [-'meɪʃən] n opinión f, juicio; cálculo

**estranged** [ɪ'streɪndʒd] adj separado

**estuary** ['ɛstjuərɪ] n estuario, ría

**etc** abbr (= et cetera) etc

**etching** ['ɛtʃɪŋ] n aguafuerte m or f

**eternal** [ɪ'tɜːnl] adj eterno

**eternity** [ɪ'tɜːnɪtɪ] n eternidad f

**ethical** ['ɛθɪkl] adj ético; **ethics** ['ɛθɪks] n ética ♦ npl moralidad f

**Ethiopia** [iːθɪ'əupɪə] n Etiopía f

**ethnic** ['ɛθnɪk] adj étnico

**ethos** ['iːθɔs] n genio, carácter m

**etiquette** ['ɛtɪkɛt] n etiqueta f

**Eurocheque** ['juərəutʃɛk] n Eurocheque m

**Europe** ['juərəp] n Europa f; **~an** [-'piːən] adj, n europeo/a m/f

**evacuate** [ɪ'vækjueɪt] vt (people) evacuar; (place) desocupar; **evacuation** [-'eɪʃən] n evacuación f

**evade** [ɪ'veɪd] vt evadir, eludir

**evaluate** [ɪ'væljueɪt] vt evaluar

**evaporate** [ɪ'væpəreɪt] vi evaporarse; (fig) desvanecerse; **~d milk** n leche f evaporada

**evasion** [ɪ'veɪʒən] n evasión f

**eve** [iːv] n: **on the ~ of** en vísperas de

**even** ['iːvn] adj (level) llano; (smooth) liso; (speed, temperature) uniforme; (number) par ♦ adv hasta, incluso; (introducing a comparison) aún, todavía; **~ if, ~ though** aunque + sub; **~ more** aun más; **~ so** aun así; **not ~** ni siquiera; **~ he was there** hasta él estuvo allí; **~ on Sundays** incluso los domingos; **to get ~ with sb** ajustar cuentas con uno; **~ out** vi nivelarse

**evening** ['iːvnɪŋ] n tarde f; (late) no-

che f; **in the ~** por la tarde; **~ class**
n clase f nocturna; **~ dress** n (no pl:
formal clothes) traje m de etiqueta;
(woman's) traje m de noche

**event** [ɪ'vɛnt] n suceso, acontecimiento; (SPORT) prueba; **in the ~ of** en
caso de; **~ful** adj (life) activo; (day)
ajetreado

**eventual** [ɪ'vɛntʃuəl] adj final; **~ity**
[-'ælɪtɪ] n eventualidad f; **~ly** adv
(finally) finalmente; (in time) con el
tiempo

**ever** ['ɛvə*] adv (at any time) nunca,
jamás; (at all times) siempre; (in
question) why **~ not?** ¿por qué
no?; **the best ~** lo nunca visto;
**have you ~ seen it?** ¿lo ha visto
usted alguna vez?; **better than ~**
mejor que nunca; **~ since** adv desde
entonces ♦ conj después de que;
**~green** n árbol m de hoja perenne;
**~lasting** adj eterno, perpetuo

---
**KEYWORD**
---

**every** ['ɛvrɪ] adj 1 (each) cada; **~
one of them** (persons) todos ellos/
as; (objects) cada uno de ellos/as; **~
shop in the town was closed** todas
las tiendas de la ciudad estaban ce-
rradas

2 (all possible) todo; **I gave you ~
assistance** te di toda la ayuda posible; **I have ~ confidence in him**
tiene toda mi confianza; **we wish
you ~ success** te deseamos toda
suerte de éxitos

3 (showing recurrence) todo/a; **~
day/week** todos los días/todas las semanas; **~ other car had been broken into** habían forzado un de cada
dos coches; **she visits me ~ other/
third day** me visita cada dos/tres
días; **~ now and then** de vez en
cuando

**everybody** ['ɛvrɪbɒdɪ] pron =
everyone

**everyday** ['ɛvrɪdeɪ] adj (daily) cotidiano, de todos los días; (usual) acostumbrado

**everyone** ['ɛvrɪwʌn] pron todos/as,
todo el mundo

**everything** ['ɛvrɪθɪŋ] pron todo; **this
shop sells ~** esta tienda vende de
todo

**everywhere** ['ɛvrɪwɛə*] adv: **I've
been looking for you ~** te he estado buscando por todas partes; **~ you
go you meet ...** en todas partes en-
cuentras ...

**evict** [ɪ'vɪkt] vt desahuciar; **~ion**
[ɪ'vɪkʃən] n desahucio

**evidence** ['ɛvɪdəns] n (proof) prueba; (of witness) testimonio; (sign)
indicios mpl; **to give ~** prestar declaración, dar testimonio

**evident** ['ɛvɪdənt] adj evidente, manifiesto; **~ly** adv por lo visto

**evil** ['iːvl] adj malo; (influence) funesto ♦ n mal m

**evocative** [ɪ'vɒkətɪv] adj sugestivo,
evocador(a)

**evoke** [ɪ'vəuk] vt evocar

**evolution** [iːvə'luːʃən] n evolución f

**evolve** [ɪ'vɒlv] vt desarrollar ♦ vi
evolucionar, desarrollarse

**ewe** [juː] n oveja

**ex-** [ɛks] prefix ex

**exact** [ɪg'zækt] adj exacto; (person)
meticuloso ♦ vt: **to ~ sth (from)**
exigir algo (de); **~ing** adj exigente;
(conditions) arduo; **~ly** adv exactamente; (indicating agreement) exacto

**exaggerate** [ɪg'zædʒəreɪt] vt, vi exagerar; **exaggeration** [-'reɪʃən] n exageración f

**exalted** [ɪg'zɔːltɪd] adj eminente

**exam** [ɪg'zæm] n abbr (SCOL) = examination

**examination** [ɪgzæmɪ'neɪʃən] n examen m; (MED) reconocimiento

**examine** [ɪg'zæmɪn] vt examinar;
(inspect) inspeccionar, escudriñar;
(MED) reconocer; **~r** n examina-
dor(a) m/f

**example** [ɪg'zɑːmpl] n ejemplo; **for
~** por ejemplo

**exasperate** [ɪg'zɑːspəreɪt] vt exasperar, irritar; **exasperation** [-ʃən] n

exasperación f, irritación f
**excavate** ['ɛkskəveɪt] vt excavar
**exceed** [ɪk'siːd] vt (amount) exceder; (number) pasar de; (speed limit) sobrepasar; (powers) excederse en; (hopes) superar; ~**ingly** adv sumamente, sobremanera
**excel** [ɪk'sɛl] vi: ~ (at/in) sobresalir (en)
**excellent** ['ɛksələnt] adj excelente
**except** [ɪk'sɛpt] prep (also: ~ for, ~ing) excepto, salvo ♦ vt exceptuar, excluir; ~ **if/when** excepto si/cuando; ~ **that** salvo que; ~**ion** [ɪk'sɛpʃən] n excepción f; **to take** ~**ion to** ofenderse por; ~**ional** [ɪk'sɛpʃənl] adj excepcional
**excerpt** ['ɛksəːpt] n extracto
**excess** [ɪk'sɛs] n exceso; ~**es** npl (of cruelty etc) atrocidades fpl; ~ **baggage** n exceso de equipaje; ~ **fare** n suplemento; ~**ive** adj excesivo
**exchange** [ɪks'tʃeɪndʒ] n intercambio; (conversation) diálogo; (also: telephone ~) central f (telefónica) ♦ vt: **to** ~ (**for**) cambiar (por); ~ **rate** n tipo de cambio
**exchequer** [ɪks'tʃɛkə*] (BRIT) n: **the** ~ la Hacienda del Fisco
**excise** ['ɛksaɪz] n impuestos mpl sobre el alcohol y el tabaco
**excite** [ɪk'saɪt] vt (stimulate) estimular; (arouse) excitar; **to get** ~**d** emocionarse; ~**ment** n (agitation) excitación f; (exhilaration) emoción f; **exciting** adj emocionante
**exclaim** [ɪk'skleɪm] vi exclamar; **exclamation** [ɛksklə'meɪʃən] n exclamación f; **exclamation mark** n punto de admiración
**exclude** [ɪk'skluːd] vt excluir; exceptuar
**exclusive** [ɪk'skluːsɪv] adj exclusivo; (club, district) selecto; ~ **of tax** excluyendo impuestos; ~**ly** adv únicamente
**excommunicate** [ɛkskə'mjuːnɪkeɪt] vt excomulgar
**excruciating** [ɪk'skruːʃɪeɪtɪŋ] adj (pain) agudísimo, atroz; (noise, em-

barrassment) horrible
**excursion** [ɪk'skəːʃən] n (tourist ~) excursión f
**excuse** [n ɪk'skjuːs, vb ɪk'skjuːz] n disculpa, excusa; (pretext) pretexto ♦ vt (justify) justificar; (forgive) disculpar, perdonar; **to** ~ **sb from doing sth** dispensar a uno de hacer algo; ~ **me!** (attracting attention) ¡por favor!; (apologizing) ¡perdón!; **if you will** ~ **me** con su permiso
**ex-directory** ['ɛksdɪ'rɛktərɪ] (BRIT) adj que no consta en la guía
**execute** ['ɛksɪkjuːt] vt (plan) realizar; (order) cumplir; (person) ajusticiar, ejecutar; **execution** [-'kjuːʃən] n realización f; cumplimiento; ejecución f; **executioner** [-'kjuːʃənə*] n verdugo
**executive** [ɪg'zɛkjutɪv] n (person, committee) ejecutivo; (POL: committee) poder m ejecutivo ♦ adj ejecutivo
**executor** [ɪg'zɛkjutə*] n albacea m, testamentario
**exemplify** [ɪg'zɛmplɪfaɪ] vt ejemplificar; (illustrate) ilustrar
**exempt** [ɪg'zɛmpt] adj: ~ **from** exento de ♦ vt: **to** ~ **sb from** eximir a uno de; ~**ion** [-ʃən] n exención f
**exercise** ['ɛksəsaɪz] n ejercicio ♦ vt (patience) usar de; (right) valerse de; (dog) llevar de paseo; (mind) preocupar ♦ vi (also: **to take** ~) hacer ejercicio(s); ~ **bike** n ciclostátic ® m, bicicleta estática; ~ **book** n cuaderno
**exert** [ɪg'zəːt] vt ejercer; **to** ~ **o.s.** esforzarse; ~**ion** [-ʃən] n esfuerzo
**exhale** [ɛks'heɪl] vt despedir ♦ vi exhalar
**exhaust** [ɪg'zɔːst] n (AUT: also: ~ **pipe**) escape m; (: fumes) gases mpl de escape ♦ vt agotar; ~**ed** adj agotado; ~**ion** [-tʃən] n agotamiento; **nervous** ~**ion** postración f nerviosa; ~**ive** adj exhaustivo
**exhibit** [ɪg'zɪbɪt] n (ART) obra expuesta; (LAW) objeto expuesto ♦ vt

(*show: emotions*) manifestar; (: *courage, skill*) demostrar; (*paintings*) exponer; ~**ion** [ɛksɪ'bɪʃən] n exposición f; (*of talent etc*) demostración f

**exhilarating** [ɪg'zɪləreɪtɪŋ] adj estimulante, tónico

**exile** ['ɛksaɪl] n exilio; (*person*) exiliado/a ♦ vt desterrar, exiliar

**exist** [ɪg'zɪst] vi existir; (*live*) vivir; ~**ence** n existencia; ~**ing** adj existente, actual

**exit** ['ɛksɪt] n salida ♦ vi (THEATRE) hacer mutis; (COMPUT) salir (al sistema); ~ **ramp** (US) n (AUT) vía de acceso

**exodus** ['ɛksədəs] n éxodo

**exonerate** [ɪg'zɒnəreɪt] vt: to ~ **from** exculpar de

**exotic** [ɪg'zɒtɪk] adj exótico

**expand** [ɪk'spænd] vt ampliar; (*number*) aumentar ♦ vi (*population*) aumentar; (*trade etc*) expandirse; (*gas, metal*) dilatarse

**expanse** [ɪk'spæns] n extensión f

**expansion** [ɪk'spænʃən] n (*of population*) aumento; (*of trade*) expansión f

**expect** [ɪk'spɛkt] vt esperar; (*require*) contar con; (*suppose*) suponer ♦ vi: to be ~**ing** (*pregnant woman*) estar embarazada; ~**ancy** n (*anticipation*) esperanza; **life** ~**ancy** esperanza de vida; ~**ant mother** n futura madre f; ~**ation** [ɛkspɛk'teɪʃən] n (*hope*) esperanza; (*belief*) expectativa

**expedient** [ɪk'spiːdɪənt] adj conveniente, oportuno ♦ n recurso, expediente m

**expedition** [ɛkspə'dɪʃən] n expedición f

**expel** [ɪk'spɛl] vt arrojar; (*from place*) expulsar

**expend** [ɪk'spɛnd] vt (*money*) gastar; (*time, energy*) consumir; ~**able** adj prescindible; ~**iture** n gastos mpl, desembolso; consumo

**expense** [ɪk'spɛns] n gasto, gastos mpl; (*high cost*) costa; ~**s** npl (COMM) gastos mpl; **at the** ~ **of** a costa de; ~ **account** n cuenta de gastos

**expensive** [ɪk'spɛnsɪv] adj caro, costoso

**experience** [ɪk'spɪərɪəns] n experiencia ♦ vt experimentar; (*suffer*) sufrir; ~**d** adj experimentado

**experiment** [ɪk'spɛrɪmənt] n experimento ♦ vi hacer experimentos; ~**al** [-'mɛntl] adj experimental

**expert** ['ɛkspɜːt] adj experto, perito ♦ n experto/a, perito/a; (*specialist*) especialista m/f; ~**ise** [-'tiːz] n pericia

**expire** [ɪk'spaɪə*] vi caducar, vencer; **expiry** n vencimiento

**explain** [ɪk'spleɪn] vt explicar; **explanation** [ɛksplə'neɪʃən] n explicación f; **explanatory** [ɪk'splænətrɪ] adj explicativo; aclaratorio

**explicit** [ɪk'splɪsɪt] adj explícito

**explode** [ɪk'spləud] vi estallar, explotar; (*population*) crecer rápidamente; (*with anger*) reventar

**exploit** [*n* 'ɛksplɔɪt, *vb* ɪk'splɔɪt] n hazaña ♦ vt explotar; ~**ation** [-'teɪʃən] n explotación f

**exploratory** [ɪk'splɒrətrɪ] adj de exploración; (*fig: talks*) exploratorio, preliminar

**explore** [ɪk'splɔː*] vt explorar; (*fig*) examinar, investigar; ~**r** n explorador(a) m/f

**explosion** [ɪk'spləuʒən] n (*also fig*) explosión f; **explosive** [ɪk'spləusɪv] adj, n explosivo

**exponent** [ɪk'spəunənt] n (*of theory etc*) partidario/a; (*of skill etc*) exponente m/f

**export** [*vb* ɛk'spɔːt, *n* 'ɛkspɔːt] vt exportar ♦ n (*process*) exportación f; (*product*) producto de exportación ♦ cpd de exportación; ~**er** n exportador m

**expose** [ɪk'spəuz] vt exponer; (*unmask*) desenmascarar; ~**d** adj expuesto

**exposure** [ɪk'spəuʒə*] n exposición f; (*publicity*) publicidad f; (PHOT: *speed*) velocidad f de obturación; (: *shot*) fotografía; **to die from ~**

(MED) morir de frío; ~ **meter** n fotómetro

**expound** [ɪkˈspaund] vt exponer

**express** [ɪkˈsprɛs] adj (definite) expreso, explícito; (BRIT: letter etc) urgente ♦ n (train) rápido ♦ vt expresar; ~**ion** [ɪkˈsprɛʃən] n expresión f; (of actor etc) sentimiento; ~**ly** adv expresamente; ~**way** (US) n (urban motorway) autopista

**exquisite** [ɛkˈskwɪzɪt] adj exquisito

**extend** [ɪkˈstɛnd] vt (visit, street) prolongar; (building) ampliar; (invitation) ofrecer ♦ vi (land) extenderse; (period of time) prolongarse

**extension** [ɪkˈstɛnʃən] n extensión f; (building) ampliación f; (of time) prolongación f; (TEL: in private house) línea derivada; (: in office) extensión f

**extensive** [ɪkˈstɛnsɪv] adj extenso; (damage) importante; (knowledge) amplio; ~**ly** adv: he's travelled ~**ly** ha viajado por muchos países

**extent** [ɪkˈstɛnt] n (breadth) extensión f; (scope) alcance m; to some ~ hasta cierto punto; to the ~ of... hasta el punto de...; to such an ~ that... hasta tal punto que...; to what ~? ¿hasta qué punto?

**extenuating** [ɪkˈstɛnjueɪtɪŋ] adj: ~ **circumstances** circunstancias fpl atenuantes

**exterior** [ɛkˈstɪərɪə*] adj exterior, externo ♦ n exterior m

**exterminate** [ɪkˈstəːmɪneɪt] vt exterminar

**external** [ɛkˈstəːnl] adj externo

**extinct** [ɪkˈstɪŋkt] adj (volcano) extinguido; (race) extinto

**extinguish** [ɪkˈstɪŋgwɪʃ] vt extinguir, apagar; ~**er** n extintor m

**extort** [ɪkˈstɔːt] vt obtener por fuerza; ~**ion** [ɪkˈstɔːʃən] n extorsión f; ~**ionate** [ɪkˈstɔːʃnət] adj excesivo, exorbitante

**extra** [ˈɛkstrə] adj adicional ♦ adv (in addition) de más ♦ n (luxury, addition) extra m; (CINEMA, THEATRE) extra m/f, comparsa m/f

**extra...** [ˈɛkstrə] prefix extra....

**extract** [vb ɪkˈstrækt, n ˈɛkstrækt] vt sacar; (tooth) extraer; (money, promise) obtener ♦ n extracto

**extracurricular** [ɛkstrəkəˈrɪkjulə*] adj extraescolar, extra-académico

**extradite** [ˈɛkstrədaɪt] vt extraditar

**extramarital** [ɛkstrəˈmærɪtl] adj extramatrimonial

**extramural** [ɛkstrəˈmjuərl] adj extraescolar

**extraordinary** [ɪkˈstrɔːdnrɪ] adj extraordinario; (odd) raro

**extravagance** [ɪkˈstrævəgəns] n derroche m, despilfarro; (thing bought) extravagancia

**extravagant** [ɪkˈstrævəgənt] adj (lavish: person) pródigo; (: gift) (demasiado) caro; (wasteful) despilfarrador(a)

**extreme** [ɪkˈstriːm] adj extremo, extremado ♦ n extremo; ~**ly** adv sumamente, extremadamente

**extremity** [ɪkˈstrɛmətɪ] n extremidad f, punta; (of situation) extremo

**extricate** [ˈɛkstrɪkeɪt] vt: to ~ **sth/ sb** from librar algo/a uno de

**extrovert** [ˈɛkstrəvəːt] n extrovertido/a

**exuberant** [ɪgˈzjuːbərnt] adj (person) eufórico; (imagination) exuberante

**exude** [ɪgˈzjuːd] vt (confidence) rebosar; (liquid, smell) rezumar

**eye** [aɪ] n ojo ♦ vt mirar de soslayo, ojear; to keep an ~ **on** vigilar; ~**ball** n globo del ojo; ~**bath** n ojera; ~**brow** n ceja; ~**brow pencil** n lápiz m de cejas; ~**drops** npl gotas fpl para los ojos, colino; ~**lash** n pestaña; ~**lid** n párpado; ~**liner** n lápiz m de ojos; ~**opener** n revelación f, gran sorpresa; ~**shadow** n sombreador m de ojos; ~**sight** n vista; ~**sore** n monstruosidad f; ~ **witness** n testigo m/f presencial

# F

**F** [ef] n (MUS) fa m

**F.** abbr = **Fahrenheit**

**fable** ['feibl] n fábula

**fabric** ['fæbrik] n tejido, tela

**fabrication** [fæbri'keiʃən] n (lie) invención f; (making) fabricación f

**fabulous** ['fæbjuləs] adj fabuloso

**façade** [fə'sɑːd] n fachada

**face** [feis] n (ANAT) cara, rostro; (of clock) esfera (SP), cara (AM); (of mountain) cara, ladera; (of building) fachada ♦ vt (direction) estar de cara a; (situation) hacer frente a; (facts) aceptar; **~ down** (person, card) boca abajo; **to lose ~** desprestigiarse; **to make** or **pull a ~** hacer muecas; **in the ~ of** (difficulties etc) ante; **on the ~ of it** a primera vista; **~ to ~** cara a cara; **~ up to** vt fus hacer frente a, arrostrar; **~ cloth** (BRIT) n manopla; **~ cream** n crema (de belleza); **~ lift** n estirado facial; (of building) renovación f; **~ powder** n polvos mpl; **~-saving** adj que salva las apariencias

**facetious** [fə'siːʃəs] adj gracioso

**face value** n (of stamp) valor m nominal; **to take sth at ~** (fig) tomar algo en sentido literal

**facile** ['fæsail] adj superficial

**facilities** [fə'silitiz] npl (buildings) instalaciones fpl; (equipment) servicios mpl; **credit ~** facilidades fpl de crédito

**facing** ['feisiŋ] prep frente a

**facsimile** [fæk'simili] n (replica) facsímil(e) m; (machine) telefax m; (fax) fax m

**fact** [fækt] n hecho; **in ~** en realidad

**factor** ['fæktə*] n factor m

**factory** ['fæktəri] n fábrica

**factual** ['fæktjuəl] adj basado en los hechos

**faculty** ['fækəlti] n facultad f; (US: teaching staff) personal m docente

**fad** [fæd] n novedad f, moda

**fade** [feid] vi desteñirse; (sound, smile) desvanecerse; (light) apagarse; (flower) marchitarse; (hope, memory) perderse

**fag** [fæg] (BRIT: inf) n (cigarette) pitillo (SP), cigarro

**fail** [feil] vt (candidate) suspender; (exam) no aprobar (SP), reprobar (AM); (subj: memory etc) fallar a ♦ vi suspender; (be unsuccessful) fracasar; (strength, brakes) fallar; (light) acabarse; **to ~ to do sth** (neglect) dejar de hacer algo; (be unable) no poder hacer algo; **without ~** sin falta; **~ing** n falta, defecto ♦ prep a falta de; **~ure** ['feiljə*] n fracaso; (person) fracasado/a; (mechanical etc) fallo

**faint** [feint] adj débil; (recollection) vago; (mark) apenas visible ♦ n desmayo ♦ vi desmayarse; **to feel ~** estar mareado, marearse

**fair** [feə*] adj justo; (hair, person) rubio; (weather) bueno; (good enough) regular; (considerable) considerable ♦ adv (play) limpio ♦ n feria; (BRIT: funfair) parque m de atracciones; **~ly** adv (justly) con justicia; (quite) bastante; **~ness** n justicia, imparcialidad f; **~ play** n juego limpio

**fairy** ['feəri] n hada; **~ tale** n cuento de hadas

**faith** [feiθ] n fe f; (trust) confianza f; (sect) religión f; **~ful** adj (loyal: troops etc) leal; (spouse) fiel; (account) exacto; **~fully** adv fielmente; **yours ~fully** (BRIT: in letters) le saluda atentamente

**fake** [feik] n (painting etc) falsificación f; (person) impostor(a) m/f ♦ adj falso ♦ vt fingir; (painting etc) falsificar

**falcon** ['fɔːlkən] n halcón m

**fall** [fɔːl] (pt fell, pp fallen) n caída; (in price etc) descenso; (US) otoño ♦ vi caer(se); (price) bajar, descender; **~s** npl (water~) cascada, salto de agua; **to ~ flat** (on one's face) caerse (boca abajo); (plan) fracasar; (*joke, story*) no hacer gracia; ~ **back** *vi* retroceder; ~ **back on** *vt fus* (*remedy etc*) recurrir a; ~ **behind** *vi* quedarse atrás; ~ **down** *vi* (*person*) caerse; (*building, hopes*) derrumbarse; ~ **for** *vt fus* (*trick*) dejarse engañar por; (*person*) enamorarse de; ~ **in** *vi* (*roof*) hundirse; (*MIL*) alinearse; ~ **off** *vi* caerse; (*diminish*) disminuir; ~ **out** *vi* (*friends etc*) reñir; (*hair, teeth*) caerse; ~ **through** *vi* (*plan, project*) fracasar

**fallacy** ['fæləsɪ] *n* error *m*

**fallen** ['fɔːlən] *pp* of **fall**

**fallout** ['fɔːlaʊt] *n* lluvia radioactiva; ~ **shelter** *n* refugio antiatómico

**fallow** ['fæləʊ] *adj* en barbecho

**false** [fɔːls] *adj* falso; under ~ pretences con engaños; ~ **alarm** *n* falsa alarma; ~ **teeth** (*BRIT*) *npl* dentadura postiza

**falter** ['fɔːltə*] *vi* vacilar; (*engine*) fallar

**fame** [feɪm] *n* fama

**familiar** [fə'mɪlɪə*] *adj* conocido, familiar; (*tone*) de confianza; to be ~ **with** (*subject*) conocer (bien)

**family** ['fæmɪlɪ] *n* familia; ~ **business** *n* negocio familiar; ~ **doctor** *n* médico/a de cabecera

**famine** ['fæmɪn] *n* hambre *f*, hambruna

**famished** ['fæmɪʃt] *adj* hambriento

**famous** ['feɪməs] *adj* famoso, célebre; ~**ly** *adv* (*get on*) estupendamente

**fan** [fæn] *n* abanico *m*; (*ELEC*) ventilador *m*; (*of pop star*) fan *m/f*; (*SPORT*) hincha *m/f* ♦ *vt* abanicar; (*fire, quarrel*) atizar; ~ **out** *vi* desparramarse

**fanatic** [fə'nætɪk] *n* fanático/a

**fan belt** *n* correa del ventilador

**fanciful** ['fænsɪfʊl] *adj* (*design, name*) fantástico

**fancy** ['fænsɪ] *n* (*whim*) capricho, antojo; (*imagination*) imaginación *f* ♦ *adj* (*luxury*) lujoso, de lujo ♦ *vt* (*feel like, want*) tener ganas de; (*imagine*)

imaginarse; (*think*) creer; to take a ~ to sb tomar cariño a uno; he **fancies her** (*inf*) le gusta (ella) mucho; ~ **dress** *n* disfraz *m*; ~**dress ball** *n* baile *m* de disfraces

**fanfare** ['fænfɛə*] *n* fanfarria (de trompeta)

**fang** [fæŋ] *n* colmillo

**fantastic** [fæn'tæstɪk] *adj* (*enormous*) enorme; (*strange, wonderful*) fantástico

**fantasy** ['fæntəzɪ] *n* (*dream*) sueño; (*unreality*) fantasía

**far** [fɑː*] *adj* (*distant*) lejano ♦ *adv* lejos; (*much, greatly*) mucho; ~ **away, ~ off** (a lo lejos); ~ **better** mucho mejor; ~ **from** lejos de; by ~ con mucho; go as ~ as the farm vaya hasta la granja; as ~ as I know que yo sepa; how ~? ¿hasta dónde?; (*fig*) ¿hasta qué punto?; ~**away** *adj* remoto; (*look*) distraído

**farce** [fɑːs] *n* farsa; **farcical** *adj* absurdo

**fare** [fɛə*] *n* (*on trains, buses*) precio (del billete); (*in taxi: cost*) tarifa; (*food*) comida; **half** ~ medio pasaje *m*; **full** ~ pasaje completo

**Far East** *n*: the ~ el Extremo Oriente

**farewell** [fɛə'wɛl] *excl, n* adiós *m*

**farm** [fɑːm] *n* granja (*SP*), finca (*AM*), estancia (*AM*) ♦ *vt* cultivar; ~**er** *n* granjero (*SP*), estanciero (*AM*); ~**hand** *n* peón *m*; ~**house** *n* granja, casa de hacienda (*AM*); ~**ing** *n* agricultura; (*of crops*) cultivo; (*of animals*) cría; ~**land** *n* tierra de cultivo; ~ **worker** *n* = ~**hand**; ~**yard** *n* corral *m*

**far-reaching** [fɑː'riːtʃɪŋ] *adj* (*reform, effect*) de gran alcance

**fart** [fɑːt] (*inf!*) *vi* tirarse un pedo

**farther** ['fɑːðə*] *adv* más lejos, más allá ♦ *adj* más lejano

**farthest** ['fɑːðɪst] *superlative* of **far**

**fascinate** ['fæsɪneɪt] *vt* fascinar; **fascination** [-'neɪʃən] *n* fascinación *f*

**fascism** ['fæʃɪzəm] *n* fascismo

**fashion** ['fæʃən] *n* moda; (~ *in-*

dustry) industria de la moda; (*manner*) manera ♦ *vt* formar; **in** ~ **a** la moda; **out of** ~ pasado de moda; ~**able** *adj* de moda; ~ **show** *n* desfile *m* de modelos

**fast** [fɑːst] *adj* rápido; (*dye, colour*) resistente; (*clock*): **to be** ~ estar adelantado ♦ *adv* rápidamente, de prisa; (*stuck, held*) firmemente ♦ *n* ayuno ♦ *vi* ayunar; ~ **asleep** profundamente dormido

**fasten** [ˈfɑːsn] *vt* atar, sujetar; (*coat, belt*) abrochar ♦ *vi* atarse; abrocharse; ~**er** *n* cierre *m*; (*of door etc*) cerrojo; ~**ing** *n* = ~**er**

**fast food** *n* comida rápida, platos *mpl* preparados

**fastidious** [fæsˈtɪdɪəs] *adj* (*fussy*) quisquilloso

**fat** [fæt] *adj* gordo; (*book*) grueso; (*profit*) grande, pingüe ♦ *n* grasa; (*on person*) carnes *fpl*; (*lard*) manteca

**fatal** [ˈfeɪtl] *adj* (*mistake*) fatal; (*injury*) mortal; ~**istic** [-ˈlɪstɪk] *adj* fatalista; ~**ity** [fəˈtælɪtɪ] *n* (*road death etc*) víctima; ~**ly** *adv* fatalmente; mortalmente

**fate** [feɪt] *n* destino; (*of person*) suerte *f*; ~**ful** *adj* fatídico

**father** [ˈfɑːðəʳ] *n* padre *m*; ~-**in-law** *n* suegro; ~**ly** *adj* paternal

**fathom** [ˈfæðəm] *n* braza ♦ *vt* (*mystery*) desentrañar; (*understand*) lograr comprender

**fatigue** [fəˈtiːg] *n* fatiga, cansancio

**fatten** [ˈfætn] *vt, vi* engordar

**fatty** [ˈfætɪ] *adj* (*food*) graso ♦ *n* (*inf*) gordito/a, gordinflón/ona *m/f*

**fatuous** [ˈfætjʊəs] *adj* fatuo, necio

**faucet** [ˈfɔːsɪt] (*US*) *n* grifo (*SP*), llave *f* (*AM*)

**fault** [fɔːlt] *n* (*blame*) culpa; (*defect: in person, machine*) defecto; (*GEO*) falla ♦ *vt* criticar; **it's my** ~ es culpa mía; **to find** ~ **with** criticar, poner peros a; **at** ~ culpable; ~**y** *adj* defectuoso

**fauna** [ˈfɔːnə] *n* fauna

**faux pas** [ˈfəʊˈpɑː] *n* plancha

**favour** [ˈfeɪvəʳ] (*US* **favor**) *n* favor *m*; (*approval*) aprobación *f* ♦ *vt* (*proposition*) estar a favor de, aprobar; (*assist*) ser propicio a; **to do sb a** ~ hacer un favor a uno; **to find** ~ **with sb** caer en gracia a uno; **in** ~ **of** a favor de; ~**able** *adj* favorable; ~**ite** [-rɪt] *adj, n* favorito, favorita

**fawn** [fɔːn] *n* cervato ♦ *adj* (*also*: ~ **coloured**) color de cervato, leonado ♦ *vi*: **to** ~ (**up**)**on** adular

**fax** [fæks] *n* (*document*) fax *m*; (*machine*) telefax *m* ♦ *vt* mandar por telefax

**FBI** (*US*) *n abbr* (= *Federal Bureau of Investigation*) = BIC *f* (*SP*)

**fear** [fɪəʳ] *n* miedo, temor *m* ♦ *vt* tener miedo de, temer; **for** ~ **of** por si; ~**ful** *adj* temeroso, miedoso; (*awful*) terrible; ~**less** *adj* audaz

**feasible** [ˈfiːzəbl] *adj* factible

**feast** [fiːst] *n* banquete *m*; (*REL: also*: ~ **day**) fiesta ♦ *vi* festejar

**feat** [fiːt] *n* hazaña

**feather** [ˈfeðəʳ] *n* pluma

**feature** [ˈfiːtʃəʳ] *n* característica; (*article*) artículo de fondo ♦ *vt* (*subj: film*) presentar ♦ *vi*: **to** ~ **in** tener un papel destacado en; ~**s** *npl* (*of face*) facciones *fpl*; ~ **film** *n* largometraje *m*

**February** [ˈfebruərɪ] *n* febrero

**fed** [fed] *pt, pp* de **feed**

**federal** [ˈfedərəl] *adj* federal

**fed-up** [ˈfedˈʌp] *adj*: **to be** ~ (**with**) estar harto de

**fee** [fiː] *n* pago; (*professional*) derechos *mpl*, honorarios *mpl*; (*of club*) cuota; **school** ~**s** matrícula

**feeble** [ˈfiːbl] *adj* débil; (*joke*) flojo

**feed** [fiːd] (*pt, pp* **fed**) *n* comida; (*of animal*) pienso; (*on printer*) dispositivo de alimentación ♦ *vt* alimentar; (*BRIT: baby: breast*~) dar el pecho a; (*animal*) dar de comer a; (*data, information*) ~ **into** meter en; ~ **on** *vt fus* alimentarse de; ~**back** *n* reacción *f*, feedback *m*; ~**ing bottle** (*BRIT*) *n* biberón *m*

**feel** [fiːl] (*pt, pp* **felt**) *n* (*sensation*)

sensación f; (sense of touch) tacto; (impression): to have the ~ of parecerse a ♦ vt tocar; (pain etc) sentir; (think, believe) creer; to ~ hungry/cold tener hambre/frío; to ~ lonely/better sentirse solo/mejor; I don't ~ well no me siento bien; it ~s soft es suave al tacto; to ~ like (want) tener ganas de; ~ about or around vi tantear; ~er n (of insect) antena; to put out a ~er or ~ers (fig) sondear; ~ing n (physical) sensación f; (foreboding) presentimiento; (emotion) sentimiento

**feet** [fiːt] npl of **foot**

**feign** [feɪn] vt fingir

**fell** [fel] pt of **fall** ♦ vt (tree) talar

**fellow** ['feləʊ] n tipo, tio (SP); (comrade) compañero; (of learned society) socio/a ♦ cpd: ~ **citizen** n conciudadano/a; ~ **countryman** n compatriota m; ~ **men** npl semejantes mpl; ~**ship** n compañerismo; (grant) beca

**felony** ['feləni] n crimen m

**felt** [felt] pt, pp of **feel** ♦ n fieltro; ~-**tip pen** n rotulador m

**female** ['fiːmeɪl] n (pej: woman) mujer f, tía; (ZOOL) hembra ♦ adj femenino; hembra

**feminine** ['femɪnɪn] adj femenino

**feminist** ['femɪnɪst] n feminista

**fence** [fens] n valla, cerca ♦ vt (also: ~ **in**) cercar ♦ vi (SPORT) hacer esgrima; **fencing** n esgrima

**fend** [fend] vi: to ~ **for o.s.** valerse por sí mismo; ~ **off** vt (attack) rechazar; (questions) evadir

**fender** ['fendə*] n guardafuego; (US: AUT) parachoques m inv

**ferment** [vb fə'ment, n 'fɜːment] vi fermentar ♦ n (fig) agitación f

**fern** [fɜːn] n helecho

**ferocious** [fə'rəʊʃəs] adj feroz; **ferocity** [-'rɒsɪtɪ] n ferocidad f

**ferret** ['ferɪt] n hurón m; ~ **out** vt desentrañar

**ferry** ['ferɪ] n (small) barca (de pasaje), balsa; (large: also: ~**boat**) transbordador m (SP), embarcadero

(AM) ♦ vt transportar

**fertile** ['fɜːtaɪl] adj fértil; (BIOL) fecundo; **fertility** [fə'tɪlɪtɪ] n fertilidad f; fecundidad f; **fertilize** ['fɜːtɪlaɪz] vt (BIOL) fecundar; (AGR) abonar; **fertilizer** n abono

**fervent** ['fɜːvənt] adj ferviente, entusiasta

**fervour** ['fɜːvə*] n fervor m, ardor m

**fester** ['festə*] vi ulcerarse

**festival** ['festɪvəl] n (REL) fiesta; (ART, MUS) festival m

**festive** ['festɪv] adj festivo; **the ~ season** (BRIT: Christmas) las Navidades

**festivities** [fes'tɪvɪtɪz] npl fiestas fpl

**festoon** [fes'tuːn] vt: to ~ **with** engalanar de

**fetch** [fetʃ] vt ir a buscar; (sell for) venderse por

**fetching** ['fetʃɪŋ] adj atractivo

**fête** [feɪt] n fiesta

**fetish** ['fetɪʃ] n obsesión f

**fetus** ['fiːtəs] (US) n = **foetus**

**feud** [fjuːd] n (hostility) enemistad f; (quarrel) disputa

**fever** ['fiːvə*] n fiebre f; ~**ish** adj febril

**few** [fjuː] adj (not many) pocos; **a ~** adj unos pocos, algunos ♦ pron pocos; algunos; ~**er** adj menos; ~**est** adj los/las menos

**fiancé** [fɪ'ɒnseɪ] n novio, prometido; ~**e** n novia, prometida

**fiasco** [fɪ'æskəʊ] n desastre m

**fib** [fɪb] n mentirilla

**fibre** ['faɪbə*] (US **fiber**) n fibra; ~-**glass** n fibra de vidrio

**fickle** ['fɪkl] adj inconstante

**fiction** ['fɪkʃən] n ficción f; ~**al** adj novelesco; **fictitious** [fɪk'tɪʃəs] adj ficticio

**fiddle** ['fɪdl] n (MUS) violín m; (cheating) trampa ♦ vt (BRIT: accounts) falsificar; ~ **with** vt fus juguetear con

**fidget** ['fɪdʒɪt] vi enredar; **stop ~ing!** ¡estáte quieto!

**field** [fiːld] n campo; (fig) campo, esfera; (SPORT) campo, cancha (AM);

~ **marshal** n mariscal m; **~work** n trabajo de campo

**fiend** [fiːnd] n demonio; **~ish** adj diabólico

**fierce** [fɪəs] adj feroz; (*wind, heat*) fuerte; (*fighting, enemy*) encarnizado

**fiery** ['faɪərɪ] adj (*burning*) ardiente; (*temperament*) apasionado

**fifteen** [fɪf'tiːn] num quince

**fifth** [fɪfθ] num quinto

**fifty** ['fɪftɪ] num cincuenta; **~-~** adj (*deal, split*) a medias ♦ adv a medias, mitad por mitad

**fig** [fɪg] n higo

**fight** [faɪt] (*pt, pp* **fought**) n (*gen*) pelea; (*MIL*) combate m; (*struggle*) lucha ♦ vt luchar contra; (*cancer, alcoholism*) combatir; (*election*) intentar ganar; (*emotion*) resistir ♦ vi pelear, luchar; **~er** n combatiente m/f; (*plane*) caza m; (*pej: leader*) figura decorativa; **~ing** n combate m, pelea

**figment** ['fɪgmənt] n: a ~ of the imagination una quimera

**figurative** ['fɪgjʊrətɪv] adj (*meaning*) figurado; (*style*) figurativo

**figure** ['fɪgə*] n (*DRAWING, GEOM*) figura, dibujo; (*number, cipher*) cifra; (*body, outline*) tipo; (*personality*) figura ♦ vt (*esp US*) imaginar ♦ vi (*appear*) figurar; ~ **out** vt (*work out*) resolver; **~head** n (*NAUT*) mascarón m de proa; (*pej: leader*) figura decorativa; ~ **of speech** n figura retórica

**filch** [fɪltʃ] (*inf*) vt hurtar, robar

**file** [faɪl] n (*tool*) lima; (*dossier*) expediente m; (*folder*) carpeta; (*COMPUT*) fichero; (*row*) fila ♦ vt limar; (*LAW: claim*) presentar; (*store*) archivar; ~ **in/out** vi entrar/salir en fila; **filing cabinet** n fichero, archivador m

**fill** [fɪl] vt (*space*) to ~ (**with**) llenar (de); (*vacancy, need*) cubrir ♦ n: to eat one's ~ llenarse; ~ **in** vt rellenar; ~ **up** vt llenar (hasta el borde) ♦ vi (*AUT*) poner gasolina

**fillet** ['fɪlɪt] n filete m; ~ **steak** n filete m de ternera

**filling** ['fɪlɪŋ] n (*CULIN*) relleno; (*for tooth*) empaste m; ~ **station** n estación f de servicio

**film** [fɪlm] n película ♦ vt (*scene*) filmar ♦ vi rodar (una película); ~ **star** n astro, estrella de cine; **~strip** n tira de película

**filter** ['fɪltə*] n filtro ♦ vt filtrar; **~ lane** (*BRIT*) n carril m de selección; **~-tipped** adj con filtro

**filth** [fɪlθ] n suciedad f; **~y** adj sucio; (*language*) obsceno

**fin** [fɪn] n (*gen*) aleta

**final** ['faɪnl] adj (*last*) final, último; (*definitive*) definitivo, terminante ♦ n (*BRIT: SPORT*) final f; **~s** npl (*SCOL*) examen m final; (*US: SPORT*) final f

**finale** [fɪ'nɑːlɪ] n final m

**final:** **~ist** n (*SPORT*) finalista m/f; **~ize** vt concluir, completar; **~ly** adv (*lastly*) por último, finalmente; (*eventually*) por fin

**finance** [faɪ'næns] n (*money*) fondos mpl; **~s** npl finanzas fpl; (*personal ~s*) situación f económica ♦ vt financiar; **financial** [-'nænʃəl] adj financiero; **financier** n financiero/a

**find** [faɪnd] (*pt, pp* **found**) vt encontrar, hallar; (*come upon*) descubrir ♦ n hallazgo; descubrimiento; to ~ **sb guilty** (*LAW*) declarar culpable a uno; ~ **out** vt averiguar; (*truth, secret*) descubrir; to ~ **out about** (*subject*) informarse sobre; (*by chance*) enterarse de; **~ings** npl (*LAW*) veredicto, fallo; (*of report*) recomendaciones fpl

**fine** [faɪn] adj excelente; (*thin*) fino ♦ adv (*well*) bien ♦ n (*LAW*) multa ♦ vt (*LAW*) multar; to be ~ (*person*) estar bien; (*weather*) hacer buen tiempo; ~ **arts** npl bellas artes fpl

**finery** ['faɪnərɪ] n adornos mpl

**finesse** [fɪ'nes] n sutileza

**finger** ['fɪŋgə*] n dedo ♦ vt (*touch*) manosear; **little/index** ~ (dedo) meñique m/índice m; **~nail** n uña; **~print** n huella dactilar; **~tip** n yema del dedo

**finicky** ['fɪnɪkɪ] adj delicado

**finish** ['fɪnɪʃ] n (end) fin m; (SPORT) meta; (polish etc) acabado ♦ vt, vi terminar; **to ~ doing sth** acabar de hacer algo; **to ~ third** llegar el tercero; **~ off** vt acabar, terminar; (kill) acabar con; **~ up** vt acabar, terminar ♦ vi ir a parar, terminar; **~ing line** n línea de llegada or meta; **~ing school** n academia para señoritas

**finite** ['faɪnaɪt] adj finito; (verb) conjugado

**Finland** ['fɪnlənd] n Finlandia

**Finn** [fɪn] n finlandés/esa m/f; **~ish** adj finlandés/esa ♦ n (LING) finlandés m abeto

**fir** [fə:*] n abeto

**fire** ['faɪə*] n fuego; (in hearth) lumbre f; (accidental) incendio; (heater) estufa ♦ vt (gun) disparar; (interest) despertar; (inf: dismiss) despedir ♦ vi (shoot) disparar; **on ~** ardiendo, en llamas; **~ alarm** n alarma de incendios; **~arm** n arma de fuego; **~ brigade** (US **~ department**) n (cuerpo de bomberos mpl; **~ engine** n coche m de bomberos; **~ escape** n escalera de incendios; **~ extinguisher** n extintor m (de incendios); **~guard** n rejilla de protección; **~man** n bombero; **~place** n chimenea; **~side** n: **by the ~side** al lado de la chimenea; **~ station** n parque m de bomberos; **~wood** n leña; **~works** npl fuegos mpl artificiales

**firing squad** ['faɪrɪŋ-] n pelotón m de ejecución

**firm** [fə:m] adj firme; (look, voice) resuelto ♦ n firma, empresa; **~ly** adv firmemente; resueltamente

**first** [fə:st] adj primero ♦ adv (before others) primero; (when listing reasons etc) en primer lugar, primeramente ♦ n (person: in race) primero/a; (AUT) primera; (BRIT: SCOL) título de licenciado con calificación de sobresaliente; **at ~** al principio; **~ of all** ante todo; **~ aid** n

primera ayuda, primeros auxilios mpl; **~-aid kit** n botiquín m; **~-class** adj (excellent) de primera (categoría); (ticket etc) de primera clase; **~-hand** adj de primera mano; **F~ Lady** (esp US) n primera dama; **~ly** adv en primer lugar; **~ name** n nombre m de (pila); **~-rate** adj estupendo

**fish** [fɪʃ] n inv pez m; (food) pescado ♦ vt, vi pescar; **to go ~ing** ir de pesca; **~erman** n pescador m; **~ farm** n criadero de peces; **~ fingers** (BRIT) npl croquetas fpl de pescado; **~ing boat** n barca de pesca; **~ing line** n sedal m; **~ing rod** n caña (de pescar); **~monger's (shop)** (BRIT) n pescadería; **~ sticks** (US) npl = **~ fingers**; **~y** (inf) adj sospechoso

**fist** [fɪst] n puño

**fit** [fɪt] adj (healthy) en (buena) forma; (proper) adecuado, apropiado ♦ vt (subj: clothes) estar or sentar bien a; (instal) poner; (equip) proveer, dotar; (facts) cuadrar or corresponder con ♦ vi (clothes) sentar bien; (in space, gap) caber; (facts) coincidir ♦ n (MED) ataque m; **to ~ to** (ready) a punto de; **~ for** apropiado para; **a ~ of anger/pride** un arranque de cólera/orgullo; **this dress is a good ~** este vestido me sienta bien; **by ~s and starts** a rachas; **~ in** vi (fig: person) llevarse bien (con todos); **~ful** adj espasmódico, intermitente; **~ment** n módulo adosable; **~ness** n (MED) salud f; **~ted carpet** n moqueta; **~ted kitchen** n cocina amueblada; **~ter** n ajustador m; **~ting** adj apropiado ♦ n (of dress) prueba; (of piece of equipment) instalación f; **~ting room** n probador m; **~tings** npl instalaciones fpl

**five** [faɪv] num cinco; **~r** (inf: BRIT) n billete m de cinco libras; (: US) billete m de cinco dólares

**fix** [fɪks] vt (secure) fijar, asegurar; (mend) arreglar; (prepare) preparar ♦ n: **to be in a ~** estar en un aprieto; **~ up** vt (meeting) arreglar; **to**

~ **sb up with sth** proveer a uno de algo; ~**ation** n obsesión f; ~**ed** [fɪkst] adj (prices etc) fijo

**fizzle** ['fɪzl] vi apagarse

**fizzy** ['fɪzɪ] adj (drink) gaseoso

**fjord** [fjɔ:d] n fiordo

**flabbergasted** ['flæbəgɑ:stɪd] adj pasmado, alucinado

**flabby** ['flæbɪ] adj gordo

**flag** [flæg] n bandera; (stone) losa f ♦ vi decaer; **to ~ sb down** hacer señas a uno para que se pare; ~**pole** n asta de bandera; ~**ship** n buque m insignia; (fig) bandera

**flair** [fleə*] n aptitud f especial

**flak** [flæk] n (MIL) fuego antiaéreo; (inf: criticism) lluvia de críticas

**flake** [fleɪk] n (of rust, paint) escama; (of snow, soap powder) copo ♦ vi (also: ~ off) desconcharse

**flamboyant** [flæm'bɔɪənt] adj (dress) vistoso; (person) extravagante

**flame** [fleɪm] n llama

**flamingo** [flə'mɪŋgəu] n flamenco

**flammable** ['flæməbl] adj inflamable

**flan** [flæn] n (BRIT) tarta

**flank** [flæŋk] n (of person) ijar m; (of army) flanco ♦ vt flanquear

**flannel** ['flænl] n (BRIT: also: face ~) manopla; (fabric) franela; ~**s** npl (trousers) pantalones mpl de franela

**flap** [flæp] n (of pocket, envelope) solapa ♦ vt (wings, arms) agitar ♦ vi (sail, flag) ondear

**flare** [fleə*] n llamarada; (MIL) bengala; (in skirt etc) vuelo; ~ **up** vi encenderse; (fig: person) encolerizarse; (: revolt) estallar

**flash** [flæʃ] n relámpago; (also: news ~) noticias fpl de última hora; (PHOT) flash m ♦ vt (light, headlights) lanzar un destello con; (news, message) transmitir; (smile) lanzar ♦ vi brillar; (hazard light etc) lanzar destellos; **in a ~** en un instante; **he ~ed by** or **past** pasó como un rayo;

~**back** n (CINEMA) flashback m; ~**bulb** n bombilla fusible; ~**cube** n cubo de flash; ~**light** n linterna

**flashy** ['flæʃɪ] (pej) adj ostentoso

**flask** [flɑ:sk] n frasco; (also: vacuum ~) termo

**flat** [flæt] adj llano; (smooth) liso; (tyre) desinflado; (battery) descargado; (beer) muerto; (refusal etc) rotundo; (MUS) desafinado; (rate) fijo ♦ n (BRIT: apartment) piso (SP), departamento (AM), apartamento; (AUT) pinchazo; (MUS) bemol m; **to work ~ out** trabajar a toda mecha; ~**ly** adv terminantemente, de plano; ~**ten** vt (also: ~**ten out**) allanar; (smooth out) alisar; (building, plants) arrasar

**flatter** [flætə*] vt adular, halagar; ~**ing** adj halagüeño; (dress) que favorece; ~**y** n adulación f

**flaunt** [flɔ:nt] vt ostentar, lucir

**flavour** ['fleɪvə*] (US **flavor**) n sabor m, gusto ♦ vt sazonar, condimentar; **strawberry ~ed** con sabor a fresa; ~**ing** n (in product) aromatizante m

**flaw** [flɔ:] n defecto; ~**less** adj impecable

**flax** [flæks] n lino; ~**en** adj rubio

**flea** [fli:] n pulga

**fleck** [flek] n (mark) mota

**flee** [fli:] (pt, pp **fled**) vt huir de ♦ vi huir, fugarse

**fleece** [fli:s] n vellón m; (wool) lana ♦ vt (inf) desplumar

**fleet** [fli:t] n flota; (of lorries etc) escuadra

**fleeting** ['fli:tɪŋ] adj fugaz

**Flemish** ['flemɪʃ] adj flamenco

**flesh** [fleʃ] n carne f; (skin) piel f; (of fruit) pulpa; ~ **wound** n herida superficial

**flew** [flu:] pt of **fly**

**flex** [fleks] n cordón m ♦ vt (muscles) tensar; ~**ibility** [-'bɪlɪtɪ] n flexibilidad f; ~**ible** adj flexible

**flick** [flɪk] n capirotazo; chasquido ♦ vt (with hand) dar un capirotazo a; (whip etc) chasquear; (switch) accionar; ~ **through** vt fus hojear

**flicker** ['flıkə*] vi (light) parpadear; (flame) vacilar

**flier** ['flaıə*] n aviador(a) m/f

**flight** [flaıt] n vuelo; (escape) huida, fuga; (also: ~ of steps) tramo (de escaleras); ~ **attendant** (US) n camarero/azafata; (AVIAT) cabina de mandos; (NAUT) cubierta de aterrizaje

**flimsy** ['flımzı] adj (thin) muy ligero; (building) endeble; (excuse) flojo

**flinch** [flıntʃ] vi encogerse; to ~ **from** retroceder ante

**fling** [flıŋ] (pt, pp **flung**) vt arrojar

**flint** [flınt] n pedernal m; (in lighter) piedra

**flip** [flıp] vt dar la vuelta a; (switch: turn on) encender; (: turn off) apagar; (coin) echar a cara o cruz

**flippant** ['flıpənt] adj poco serio

**flipper** ['flıpə*] n aleta

**flirt** [flə:t] vi coquetear, flirtear ♦ n coqueta

**flit** [flıt] vi revolotear

**float** [fləut] n flotador m; (in procession) carroza; (money) reserva ♦ vi flotar; (swimmer) hacer la plancha

**flock** [flɔk] n (of sheep) rebaño; (of birds) bandada ♦ vi: **to ~ to** acudir en tropel a

**flog** [flɔg] vt azotar

**flood** [flʌd] n inundación f; (of letters, imports etc) avalancha ♦ vt inundar ♦ vi (place) inundarse; (people): **to ~ into** inundar; ~**ing** n inundaciones fpl; ~**light** n foco

**floor** [flɔ:*] n suelo; (storey) piso; (of sea) fondo ♦ vt (subj: question) dejar sin respuesta; (: blow) derribar; **ground ~, first ~** (US) planta baja; **first ~, second ~** (US) primer piso; ~**board** n tabla; ~ **show** n cabaret m

**flop** [flɔp] n fracaso ♦ vi (fail) fracasar; (fall) derrumbarse

**floppy** ['flɔpı] adj flojo ♦ n (COMPUT: also: ~ **disk**) floppy m

**flora** ['flɔ:rə] n flora

**floral** ['flɔ:rl] adj (pattern) floreado

**florid** ['flɔrıd] adj florido; (complexion) rubicundo

**florist** ['flɔrıst] n florista m/f; ~'**s** (shop) n florería

**flounce** [flauns] n volante m; ~ **out** vi salir enfadado

**flounder** ['flaundə*] vi (swimmer) patalear; (fig: economy) estar en dificultades ♦ n (ZOOL) platija

**flour** ['flauə*] n harina

**flourish** ['flʌrıʃ] vi florecer ♦ n ademán m, movimiento (ostentoso); ~**ing** adj floreciente

**flout** [flaut] vt burlarse de

**flow** [fləu] n (movement) flujo; (of traffic) circulación f; (tide) corriente f ♦ vi (river, blood) fluir; (traffic) circular; ~ **chart** n organigrama m

**flower** ['flauə*] n flor f ♦ vi florecer; ~ **bed** n macizo; ~**pot** n tiesto; ~**y** adj (fragrance) floral; (pattern) floreado; (speech) florido

**flown** [fləun] pp of **fly**

**flu** [flu:] n: **to have** ~ tener la gripe

**fluctuate** ['flʌktjueıt] vi fluctuar

**fluent** ['flu:ənt] adj (linguist) que habla perfectamente; (speech) elocuente; **he speaks** ~ **French, he's** ~ **in French** domina el francés; ~**ly** adv con fluidez

**fluff** [flʌf] n pelusa; ~**y** adj de pelo suave

**fluid** ['flu:ıd] adj (movement) fluido, líquido; (situation) inestable ♦ n fluido, líquido

**fluke** [flu:k] (inf) n chiripa

**flung** [flʌŋ] pt, pp of **fling**

**fluoride** ['fluəraıd] n fluoruro

**flurry** ['flʌrı] n (of snow) temporal m; ~ **of activity** frenesí m de actividad

**flush** [flʌʃ] n rubor m; (fig: of youth etc) resplandor m ♦ vt limpiar con agua ♦ vi ruborizarse ♦ adj: ~ **with** a ras de; **to** ~ **the toilet** hacer funcionar la cisterna; ~ **out** vt (game, birds) levantar; ~**ed** adj ruborizado

**flustered** ['flʌstəd] adj aturdido

**flute** [flu:t] n flauta

**flutter** ['flʌtə*] n (of wings) revoloteo, aleteo; **a** ~ **of panic/**

**excitement** una oleada de pánico/
excitación ♦ vi revolotear

**flux** [flʌks] n: **to be in a state of ~**
estar continuamente cambiando

**fly** [flaɪ] (pt **flew**, pp **flown**) n mosca;
(on trousers: also: **flies**) bragueta ♦
vt (plane) pilot(e)ar; (cargo) transportar (en avión); (distances) recorrer (en avión) ♦ vi volar; (passengers) ir en avión; (escape) evadirse;
(flag) ondear; **~ away** or **off** vi emprender el vuelo; **~ing** n (activity)
(el) volar; (action) vuelo ♦ adj:
**~ing visit** visita relámpago; **with
~ing colours** con lucimiento; **~ing
saucer** n platillo volante; **~ing
start** n: **to get off to a ~ing start** empezar con buen pie; **~over** (BRIT) n
paso a desnivel or superior; **~sheet**
n (for tent) doble techo

**foal** [fəul] n potro

**foam** [fəum] n espuma ♦ vi hacer espuma; **~ rubber** n goma-espuma

**fob** [fɔb] vt: **to ~ sb off with sth**
despachar a uno con algo

**focal point** [ˈfəukl-] n (fig) centro de
atención

**focus** [ˈfəukəs] (pl **~es**) n foco; (centre) centro ♦ vt (field glasses etc)
enfocar ♦ vi: **to ~ (on)** enfocar (a);
(issue etc) centrarse en; **in/out of ~**
enfocado/desenfocado

**fodder** [ˈfɔdə*] n pienso

**foetus** [ˈfiːtəs] (US **fetus**) n feto

**fog** [fɔg] n niebla; **~gy** adj: **it's ~gy**
hay niebla, está brumoso; **~ lamp**
(US ~ **light**) n (AUT) faro de niebla

**foil** [fɔɪl] vt frustrar ♦ n hoja; (kitch-
en ~) papel m (de) aluminio;
(complement) complemento; (FENC-
ING) florete m

**fold** [fəuld] n (bend, crease) pliegue
m; (AGR) redil m ♦ vt doblar;
(arms) cruzar; **~ up** vi plegarse, doblarse; (business) quebrar ♦ vt
(map etc) plegar; **~er** n (for papers)
carpeta; **~ing** adj (chair, bed) plegable

**foliage** [ˈfəulɪɪdʒ] n follaje m

**folk** [fəuk] npl gente f ♦ adj popular,

folklórico; **~s** npl (family) familia
sg, parientes mpl; **~lore** [ˈfəuklɔː*] n
folklore m; **~ song** n canción f popular or folklórica

**follow** [ˈfɔləu] vt seguir ♦ vi seguir;
(result) resultar; **to ~ suit** hacer lo
mismo; **~ up** vt (letter, offer) responder a; (case) investigar; **~er** n
(of person, belief) partidario/a; **~ing**
adj siguiente ♦ n afición f, partida-
rios mpl

**folly** [ˈfɔlɪ] n locura

**fond** [fɔnd] adj (memory, smile etc)
cariñoso; (hopes) ilusorio; **to be ~
of** tener cariño a; (pastime, food) ser
aficionado a

**fondle** [ˈfɔndl] vt acariciar

**font** [fɔnt] n pila bautismal; (TYP)
fundición f

**food** [fuːd] n comida; **~ mixer** n batidora; **~ poisoning** n intoxicación f
alimenticia; **~ processor** n robot m
de cocina; **~stuffs** npl comestibles
mpl

**fool** [fuːl] n tonto/a; (CULIN) puré m
de frutas con nata ♦ vt engañar ♦ vi
(gen: ~ around) bromear; **~hardy**
adj temerario; **~ish** adj tonto; (careless) imprudente; **~proof** adj (plan
etc) infalible

**foot** [fut] (pl **feet**) n pie m; (measure) pie m (= 304 mm); (of animal)
pata ♦ vt (bill) pagar; **on ~** a pie;
**~age** n (CINEMA) imágenes fpl;
**~ball** n balón m; (game: BRIT) fútbol m; (: US) fútbol m americano;
**~ball player** (BRIT: also: **~baller**)
futbolista m; (US) jugador m de fútbol americano; **~brake** n freno de
pie; **~bridge** n puente m para peatones; **~hills** npl estribaciones fpl;
**~hold** n pie m firme; **~ing** n (fig)
posición f; **to lose one's ~ing** perder el pie; **~lights** npl candilejas fpl;
**~man** n lacayo; **~note** n nota (al
pie de la página); **~path** n sendero;
**~print** n huella, pisada; **~step** n
paso; **~wear** n calzado

KEYWORD

**for** [fɔː] prep 1 (indicating destination, intention) para; the train ~ London el tren con destino a or de Londres; he left ~ Rome marchó para Roma; he went ~ the paper fue por el periódico; is this ~ me? ¿es esto para mí?; it's time ~ lunch es la hora de comer

2 (indicating purpose) para; what('s it) ~? ¿para qué (es)?; to pray ~ peace rezar por la paz

3 (on behalf of, representing): the MP ~ Hove el diputado por Hove; he works ~ the government/a local firm trabaja para el gobierno/en una empresa local; I'll ask him ~ you se lo pediré por ti; G ~ George G de Gerona

4 (because of) por esta razón; ~ fear of being criticized por temor a ser criticado

5 (with regard to) para; it's cold ~ July hace frío para julio; he has a gift ~ languages tiene don de lenguas

6 (in exchange for) por; I sold it ~ £5 lo vendí por £5; to pay 50 pence ~ a ticket pagar 50 peniques por un billete

7 (in favour of): are you ~ or against us? ¿estás con nosotros o contra nosotros?; I'm all ~ it estoy totalmente a favor; vote ~ X vote (a) X

8 (referring to distance): there are roadworks ~ 5 km hay obras en 5 km; we walked ~ miles caminamos kilómetros y kilómetros

9 (referring to time): he was away ~ 2 years estuvo fuera (durante) dos años; it hasn't rained ~ 3 weeks no ha llovido durante or en 3 semanas; I have known her ~ years la conozco desde hace años; can you do it ~ tomorrow? ¿lo podrás hacer para mañana?

10 (with infinitive clauses): it is not ~ me to decide la decisión no es cosa mía; it would be best ~ you to leave sería mejor que te fueras; there is still time ~ you to do it todavía te queda tiempo para hacerlo; ~ this to be possible ... para que esto sea posible ...

11 (in spite of) a pesar de; ~ all his complaints a pesar de sus quejas
♦ conj (since, as: rather formal) puesto que

**forage** ['fɔrɪdʒ] vi (animal) forrajear; (person): to ~ for hurgar en busca de

**foray** ['fɔreɪ] n incursión f

**forbad(e)** [fə'bæd] pt of forbid

**forbid** [fə'bɪd] (pt forbad(e), pp forbidden) vt prohibir; to ~ sb to do sth prohibir a uno hacer algo; ~ding adj amenazador(a)

**force** [fɔːs] n fuerza ♦ vt forzar; (push) meter a la fuerza; to ~ o.s. to do hacer un esfuerzo por hacer; the F~s npl (BRIT) las Fuerzas Armadas; in ~ en vigor; ~d [fɔːst] adj forzado; ~-feed vt alimentar a la fuerza; ~ful adj enérgico

**forcibly** ['fɔːsəblɪ] adv a la fuerza; (speak) enérgicamente

**ford** [fɔːd] n vado

**fore** [fɔː*] n: to come to the ~ empezar a destacar

**forearm** ['fɔːrɑːm] n antebrazo

**foreboding** [fɔː'bəudɪŋ] n presentimiento

**forecast** ['fɔːkɑːst] n pronóstico ♦ vt (irreg: like cast) pronosticar

**forecourt** ['fɔːkɔːt] n patio

**forefathers** ['fɔːfɑːðəz] npl antepasados mpl

**forefinger** ['fɔːfɪŋgə*] n (dedo) índice m

**forefront** ['fɔːfrʌnt] n: in the ~ of en la vanguardia de

**forego** vt = forgo

**foregone** ['fɔːgɒn] pp of forego ♦ adj: it's a ~ conclusion es una conclusión evidente

**foreground** ['fɔːgraund] n primer plano

**forehead** ['fɔrɪd] n frente f

**foreign** ['fɔrɪn] adj extranjero; (trade) exterior; (object) extraño; **~er** n extranjero/a; **~ exchange** n divisas fpl; **F~ Office** (BRIT) n Ministerio de Asuntos Exteriores; **F~ Secretary** (BRIT) n Ministro de Asuntos Exteriores

**foreleg** ['fɔːleg] n pata delantera

**foreman** ['fɔːmən] n capataz m; (in construction) maestro de obras

**foremost** ['fɔːməust] adj principal ♦ adv: **first and ~** ante todo

**forensic** [fə'rensɪk] adj forense

**forerunner** ['fɔːrʌnə*] n precursor(a) m/f

**foresaw** [fɔː'sɔː] pt of foresee

**foresee** [fɔː'siː] (pt foresaw, pp foreseen) vt prever; **~able** adj previsible

**foreshadow** [fɔː'ʃædəu] vt prefigurar, anunciar

**foresight** ['fɔːsaɪt] n previsión f

**forest** ['fɔrɪst] n bosque m

**forestall** [fɔː'stɔːl] vt prevenir

**forestry** ['fɔrɪstrɪ] n silvicultura

**foretaste** ['fɔːteɪst] n muestra

**foretell** [fɔː'tel] (pt, pp foretold) vt predecir, pronosticar

**foretold** [fɔː'təuld] pt, pp of foretell

**forever** [fə'revə*] adv para siempre; (endlessly) constantemente

**forewent** [fɔː'went] pt of forego

**foreword** ['fɔːwəːd] n prefacio

**forfeit** ['fɔːfɪt] vt perder

**forgave** [fə'geɪv] pt of forgive

**forge** [fɔːdʒ] n herrería ♦ vt (signature, money) falsificar; (metal) forjar; **~ ahead** vi avanzar mucho; **~ry** n falsificación f

**forget** [fə'get] (pt forgot, pp forgotten) vt olvidar ♦ vi olvidarse; **~ful** adj despistado; **~-me-not** n nomeolvides f inv

**forgive** [fə'gɪv] (pt forgave, pp forgiven) vt perdonar; to ~ sb for sth perdonar algo a uno; **~ness** n perdón m

**forgo** [fɔː'gəu] (pt forwent, pp forgone) vt (give up) renunciar a; (go

(without) privarse de

**forgot** [fə'gɔt] pt of forget

**forgotten** [fə'gɔtn] pp of forget

**fork** [fɔːk] n (for eating) tenedor m; (for gardening) horca; (of roads) bifurcación f ♦ vi bifurcarse; **~ out** (inf) vt (pay) desembolsar; **~-lift truck** n máquina elevadora

**forlorn** [fə'lɔːn] adj (person) triste, melancólico; (place) abandonado; (attempt, hope) desesperado

**form** [fɔːm] n forma; (BRIT: SCOL) clase f; (document) formulario ♦ vt formar; (idea) concebir; (habit) adquirir; **in top** ~ en plena forma; **to ~ a queue** hacer cola

**formal** ['fɔːml] adj (offer, receipt) por escrito; (person etc) correcto; (occasion, dinner) de etiqueta; (dress) correcto; (garden) (de estilo) clásico; (MATH) de etiqueta; **~ity** [-'mælɪtɪ] n (procedure) trámite m; corrección f; etiqueta; **~ly** adv oficialmente

**format** ['fɔːmæt] n formato ♦ vt (COMPUT) formatear

**formative** ['fɔːmətɪv] adj (years) de formación; (influence) formativo

**former** ['fɔːmə*] adj anterior; (earlier) antiguo; (ex) ex; the ~ ... the latter ... aquél ... éste ...; **~ly** adv antes

**formula** ['fɔːmjulə] n fórmula

**forsake** [fə'seɪk] (pt forsook, pp forsaken) vt (gen) abandonar; (plan) renunciar a

**forsaken** [fə'seɪkən] pp of forsake

**fort** [fɔːt] n fuerte m

**forte** ['fɔːtɪ] n fuerte m

**forth** [fɔːθ] adv: **back and** ~ de acá para allá; **and so** ~ y así sucesivamente; **~coming** adj próximo, venidero; (help, information) disponible; (character) comunicativo; **~right** adj franco; **~with** adv en el acto

**fortify** ['fɔːtɪfaɪ] vt (city) fortificar; (person) fortalecer

**fortitude** ['fɔːtɪtjuːd] n fortaleza

**fortnight** ['fɔːtnaɪt] (BRIT) n quince días mpl; quincena; **~ly** adj de cada quince días, quincenal ♦ adv cada quince días, quincenalmente

**fortress** ['fɔːtrɪs] n fortaleza

**fortunate** ['fɔːtʃənɪt] adj afortunado;
**it is ~ that ...** (es una) suerte que
...; **~ly** adv afortunadamente

**fortune** ['fɔːtʃən] n suerte f;
(wealth) fortuna; **~-teller** n adivino/a

**forty** ['fɔːtɪ] num cuarenta

**forum** ['fɔːrəm] n foro

**forward** ['fɔːwəd] adj (movement,
position) avanzado; (front) delantero; (in time) adelantado; (not shy)
atrevido ♦ n (SPORT) delantero ♦ vt
(letter) remitir; (career) promocio-
nar; **to move ~** avanzar; **~(s)** adv
(hacia) adelante

**fossil** ['fɔsl] n fósil m

**foster** ['fɔstə*] vt (child) acoger en
una familia; fomentar; **~ child** n
hijo/a adoptivo/a

**fought** [fɔːt] pt, pp of **fight**

**foul** [faul] adj sucio, puerco; (weather, smell etc) asqueroso; (language)
grosero; (temper) malísimo ♦ n
(SPORT) falta ♦ vt (dirty) ensuciar;
**~ play** n (LAW) muerte f violenta

**found** [faund] pt, pp of **find** ♦ vt fundar; **~ation** [-'deɪʃən] n (act) fundación f; (basis) base f; (also: **~ation
cream**) crema base; **~ations** npl (of
building) cimientos mpl

**founder** ['faundə*] n fundador(a) m/f
♦ vi hundirse

**foundry** ['faundrɪ] n fundición f

**fountain** ['fauntɪn] n fuente f; **~ pen**
n pluma (estilográfica) (SP), pluma-
fuente f (AM)

**four** [fɔː*] num cuatro; **on all ~s** a
gatas; **~-poster (bed)** n cama de dosel; **~some** ['fɔːsəm] n grupo de cuatro personas; **~teen** num catorce;
**~th** num cuarto

**fowl** [faul] n ave f (de corral)

**fox** [fɔks] n zorro ♦ vt confundir

**foyer** ['fɔɪeɪ] n vestíbulo

**fraction** ['frækʃən] n fracción f

**fracture** ['fræktʃə*] n fractura

**fragile** ['frædʒaɪl] adj frágil

**fragment** ['frægmənt] n fragmento

**fragrant** ['freɪgrənt] adj fragante,

oloroso

**frail** [freɪl] adj frágil; (person) débil

**frame** [freɪm] n (TECH) armazón m;
(of person) cuerpo; (of picture, door
etc) marco; (of spectacles: also: **~s**)
montura ♦ vt enmarcar; **~ of mind**
n estado de ánimo; **~work** n marco

**France** [frɑːns] n Francia

**franchise** ['fræntʃaɪz] n (POL) derecho de voz, sufragio; (COMM) licencia, concesión f

**frank** [fræŋk] adj franco ♦ vt (letter)
franquear; **~ly** adv francamente;
**~ness** n franqueza

**frantic** ['fræntɪk] adj (distraught)
desesperado; (hectic) frenético

**fraternity** [frə'tɜːnɪtɪ] n (feeling) fra-
ternidad f; (group of people) círculos
mpl

**fraud** [frɔːd] n fraude m; (person)
impostor/a m/f

**fraught** [frɔːt] adj: **~ with** lleno de

**fray** [freɪ] n combate m, lucha ♦ vi
deshilacharse; **tempers were ~ed**
el ambiente se ponía tenso

**freak** [friːk] n (person) fenómeno;
(event) suceso anormal

**freckle** ['frekl] n peca

**free** [friː] adj libre; (gratis) gratuito
♦ vt (prisoner etc) poner en libertad;
(jammed object) soltar; **~** (of
charge), **for ~** gratis; **~dom**
['friːdəm] n libertad f; **~-for-all** n riña general; **~ gift** n prima; **~hold** n
propiedad f vitalicia; **~ kick** n tiro libre; **~lance** adj independiente ♦ adv
por cuenta propia; **~ly** adv libremente; (liberally) generosamente;
**F~mason** n francmasón m; **F~post**
n porte m pagado; **~-range** adj (hen,
eggs) de granja; **~ trade** n libre
comercio; **~way** (US) n autopista;
**~ will** n libre albedrío; **of one's
own ~ will** por su propia voluntad

**freeze** [friːz] (pt **froze**, pp **frozen**) vi
(weather) helar; (pipe, person) hel-
arse ♦ vt helar; (food, prices, salaries)
congelar ♦ n helada; (on arms, wages)
congela-
ción f; **~-dried** adj liofilizado; **~r** n

congelador *m* (SP), congeladora (AM)

**freezing** ['fri:zɪŋ] *adj* helado; **3 degrees below** ~ tres grados bajo cero; ~ **point** *n* punto de congelación

**freight** [freɪt] *n* (*goods*) carga; (*money charged*) flete *m*; ~ **train** (US) *n* tren *m* de mercancías

**French** [frentʃ] *adj* francés/esa ♦ *n* (LING) francés *m*; **the** ~ *npl* los franceses; ~ **bean** *n* judía verde; ~ **fried potatoes** *npl* patatas *fpl* (SP) or papas *fpl* (AM) fritas; ~ **fries** (US) *npl* = ~ **fried potatoes**; ~**man/woman** *n* francés/esa *m/f*; ~ **window** *n* puerta de cristal

**frenzy** ['frenzɪ] *n* frenesí *m*

**frequent** [*adj* 'fri:kwənt, *vb* fri'kwɛnt] *adj* frecuente ♦ *vt* frecuentar; ~**ly** [-əntlɪ] *adv* frecuentemente, a menudo

**fresh** [freʃ] *adj* fresco; (*bread*) tierno; (*new*) nuevo; ~**en** *vi* (*wind, air*) soplar más recio; ~**en up** *vi* (*person*) arreglarse, lavarse; ~**er** (BRIT: *inf*) *n* (SCOL) estudiante *m/f* de primer año; ~**ly** *adv* (*made, painted etc*) recién; ~**man** (US) *n* = ~**er**; ~**ness** *n* frescura; ~**water** *adj* (*fish*) de agua dulce

**fret** [fret] *vi* inquietarse

**friar** ['fraɪə*] *n* fraile *m*; (*before name*) fray

**friction** ['frɪkʃən] *n* fricción *f*

**Friday** ['fraɪdɪ] *n* viernes *m* *inv*

**fridge** [frɪdʒ] (BRIT) *n* nevera (SP), refrigeradora (AM)

**fried** [fraɪd] *adj* frito

**friend** [frend] *n* amigo/a; ~**ly** *adj* simpático; (*government*) amigo; (*place*) acogedor(a); (*match*) amistoso; ~**ship** *n* amistad *f*

**frieze** [fri:z] *n* friso

**frigate** ['frɪɡɪt] *n* fragata

**fright** [fraɪt] *n* (*terror*) terror *m*; (*scare*) susto; **to take** ~ asustarse; ~**en** *vt* asustar; ~**ened** *adj* asustado; ~**ening** *adj* espantoso; ~**ful** *adj* espantoso, horrible

**frigid** ['frɪdʒɪd] *adj* (MED) frígido,

frío

**frill** [frɪl] *n* volante *m*

**fringe** [frɪndʒ] *n* (BRIT: *of hair*) flequillo; (*on lampshade etc*) flecos *mpl*; (*of forest etc*) borde *m*, margen *m*; ~ **benefits** *npl* beneficios *mpl* marginales

**frisk** [frɪsk] *vt* cachear, registrar

**frisky** ['frɪskɪ] *adj* juguetón/ona

**fritter** ['frɪtə*] *n* buñuelo; ~ **away** *vt* desperdiciar

**frivolous** ['frɪvələs] *adj* frívolo

**frizzy** ['frɪzɪ] *adj* rizado

**fro** [frəu] *see* **to**

**frock** [frɔk] *n* vestido

**frog** [frɔɡ] *n* rana; ~**man** *n* hombrerana *m*

**frolic** ['frɔlɪk] *vi* juguetear

┌─────────────────┐
│ **KEYWORD** │
└─────────────────┘

**from** [frɔm] *prep* **1** (*indicating starting place*) de, desde; **where do you come** ~? ¿de dónde eres?; **London to Glasgow** de Londres a Glasgow; **to escape** ~ **sth/sb** escaparse de algo/alguien

**2** (*indicating origin etc*) de; **a letter/telephone call** ~ **my sister** una carta/llamada de mi hermana; **tell him** ~ **me that ...** dígale de mi parte que ...

**3** (*indicating time*): ~ **one o'clock to or until or till two** de (la or desde) la una a or hasta las dos; ~ **January (on)** a partir de enero

**4** (*indicating distance*) de; **the hotel is 1 km from the beach** el hotel está a 1 km de la playa

**5** (*indicating price, number etc*) de; **prices range** ~ **£10 to £50** los precios van desde £10 a or hasta £50; **the interest rate was increased** ~ **9% to 10%** el tipo de interés fue incrementado de un 9% a un 10%

**6** (*indicating difference*) de; **he can't tell red** ~ **green** no sabe distinguir el rojo del verde; **to be different** ~ **sb/sth** ser diferente a algo/alguien

**7** (*because of, on the basis of*): ~

what he says por lo que dice; **weak ~ hunger** debilitado por el hambre

**front** [frʌnt] n (foremost part) parte f delantera; (of house) fachada; (of dress) delantero; (of promenade: also: sea ~) paseo marítimo; (MIL, POL, METEOROLOGY) frente m; (fig: appearances) apariencias fpl ♦ adj (wheel, leg) delantero; (row, line) primero; **in ~ (of)** delante (de); **~age** ['frʌntɪdʒ] n (of building) fachada; **~ door** n puerta principal; **~ier** ['frʌntɪə*] n frontera; **~ page** n primera plana; **~ room** n (BRIT) salón m, sala; **~-wheel drive** n tracción f delantera

**frost** [frɔst] n helada; (also: hoar~) escarcha; **~bite** n congelación f; **~ed** adj (glass) deslustrado; **~y** adj (weather) de helada; (welcome etc) glacial

**froth** [frɔθ] n espuma

**frown** [fraun] vi fruncir el ceño

**froze** [frəuz] pt of **freeze**

**frozen** ['frəuzn] pp of **freeze**

**fruit** [fru:t] n inv (fresh) fruto; (fig) fruto; resultados mpl; **~erer** n frutero/a; **~erer's (shop)** n frutería; **~ful** adj provechoso; **~ion** [fru:'ɪʃən] n: **to come to ~ion** realizarse; **~ juice** n zumo (SP) or jugo (AM) de fruta; **~ machine** (BRIT) n máquina f tragaperras; **~ salad** n macedonia (SP) or ensalada (AM) de frutas

**frustrate** [frʌs'treɪt] vt frustrar; **~d** adj frustrado

**fry** [fraɪ] (pt, pp **fried**) vt freír; **small ~** gente f menuda; **~ing pan** n sartén f

**ft.** abbr = **foot**; **feet**

**fuddy-duddy** ['fʌdɪdʌdɪ] (pej) n carroza m/f

**fudge** [fʌdʒ] n (CULIN) caramelo blando

**fuel** [fjuəl] n (for heating) combustible m; (coal) carbón m; (wood) leña; (for engine) carburante m; **~ oil** n fuel oil m; **~ tank** n depósito (de combustible)

**fugitive** ['fju:dʒɪtɪv] n fugitivo/a

**fulfil** [ful'fɪl] vt (function) cumplir con; (condition) satisfacer; (wish, desire) realizar; **~ment** n satisfacción f; (of promise, desire) realización f

**full** [ful] adj lleno; (fig) pleno; (complete) completo; (maximum) máximo; (information) detallado; (price) íntegro; (skirt) amplio ♦ adv: **to know ~ well** that saber perfectamente que; **I'm ~ (up)** no puedo más; **~ employment** pleno empleo; **a ~ two hours** dos horas completas; **at ~ speed** a máxima velocidad; **in ~** (reproduce, quote) íntegramente; **~-length** adj (novel etc) entero; (coat) largo; (portrait) de cuerpo entero; **~ moon** n luna llena; **~-scale** adj (attack, war) en gran escala; (model) de tamaño natural; **~ stop** n punto; **~-time** adj (work) de tiempo completo ♦ adv: **to work ~-time** trabajar a tiempo completo; **~y** adv completamente; (at least) por lo menos; **~y-fledged** adj (teacher, barrister) diplomado

**fulsome** ['fulsəm] (pej) adj (praise, gratitude) excesivo, exagerado

**fumble** ['fʌmbl] vi: **to ~ with** manejar torpemente

**fume** [fju:m] vi (rage) estar furioso; **~s** npl humo, gases mpl

**fun** [fʌn] n (amusement) diversión f; **to have ~** divertirse; **for ~** en broma; **make ~ of** vt fus burlarse de

**function** ['fʌŋkʃən] n función f ♦ vi funcionar; **~al** (operational) en buen estado; (practical) funcional

**fund** [fʌnd] n fondo; (reserve) reserva; **~s** npl (money) fondos mpl

**fundamental** [fʌndə'mentl] adj fundamental

**funeral** ['fju:nərəl] n (burial) entierro; (ceremony) funerales mpl; **~ parlour** (BRIT) n funeraria; **~ service** n misa de difuntos, funeral m

**funfair** ['fʌnfeə*] (BRIT) n parque m de atracciones

**fungi** ['fʌŋgaɪ] npl of **fungus**

**fungus** ['fʌŋgəs] (pl **fungi**) n hongo; (mould) moho

**funnel** ['fʌnl] n embudo; (of ship) chimenea

**funny** ['fʌnɪ] adj gracioso, divertido; (strange) curioso, raro

**fur** [fəː*] n piel f; (BRIT: in kettle etc) sarro; ~ **coat** n abrigo de pieles

**furious** ['fjuərɪəs] adj furioso; (effort) violento

**furlong** ['fəːlɔŋ] n octava parte de una milla, = 201.17 m

**furlough** ['fəːləu] n (MIL) permiso

**furnace** ['fəːnɪs] n horno

**furnish** ['fəːnɪʃ] vt amueblar; (supply) suministrar; (information) facilitar; ~**ings** npl muebles mpl

**furniture** ['fəːnɪtʃə*] n muebles mpl; piece of ~ mueble m

**furrow** ['fʌrəu] n surco

**furry** ['fəːrɪ] adj peludo

**further** ['fəːðə*] adj (new) nuevo, adicional ♦ adv más lejos; (more) más; (moreover) además ♦ vt promover, adelantar; ~ **education** n educación f superior; ~**more** [fəːðə'mɔː*] adv además

**furthest** ['fəːðɪst] superlative of **far**

**fury** ['fjuərɪ] n furia

**fuse** [fjuːz] (US **fuze**) n fusible m; (for bomb etc) mecha ♦ vt (metal) fundir; (fig) fusionar ♦ vi fundirse; fusionarse; (BRIT: ELEC): to ~ **the lights** fundir los plomos; ~ **box** n caja de fusibles

**fuss** [fʌs] n (excitement) conmoción f; (trouble) alboroto; **to make a** ~ armar un jaleo o lío; **to make a** ~ **of sb** mimar a uno; ~**y** adj (person) exigente; (too ornate) recargado

**futile** ['fjuːtaɪl] adj vano

**future** ['fjuːtʃə*] adj futuro; (coming) venidero ♦ n futuro; (prospects) porvenir; **the** ~ de ahora en adelante

**fuze** [fjuːz] (US) = **fuse**

**fuzzy** ['fʌzɪ] adj (PHOT) borroso; (hair) muy rizado

# G

**G** [dʒiː] n (MUS) sol m

**g.** abbr (= **gram(s)**) gr

**G7** abbr (= Group of Seven) el grupo de los 7

**gabble** ['gæbl] vi hablar atropelladamente

**gable** ['geɪbl] n aguilón m

**gadget** ['gædʒɪt] n aparato

**Gaelic** ['geɪlɪk] adj, n (LING) gaélico

**gaffe** [gæf] n plancha

**gag** [gæg] n (on mouth) mordaza; (joke) chiste m ♦ vt amordazar

**gaiety** ['geɪtɪ] n alegría

**gaily** ['geɪlɪ] adv alegremente

**gain** [geɪn] n: ~ (**in**) aumento (de); (profit) ganancia ♦ vt ganar ♦ vi (watch) adelantarse; **to** ~ **from/by sth** sacar provecho de algo; **to** ~ **on sb** ganar terreno a uno; **to** ~ **3 lbs** (**in weight**) engordar 3 libras

**gait** [geɪt] n (mode of) andar m

**gal.** abbr = **gallon**

**gala** ['gɑːlə] n fiesta

**gale** [geɪl] n (wind) vendaval m

**gallant** ['gælənt] adj valiente; (towards ladies) atento; ~**ry** n valentía; galantería

**gall bladder** ['gɔːl-] n vesícula biliar

**gallery** ['gælərɪ] n (also: **art** ~: public) pinacoteca; (: private) galería de arte; (for spectators) tribuna

**galley** ['gælɪ] n (ship's kitchen) cocina

**gallon** ['gælən] n galón m (BRIT = 4,546 litros, US = 3,785 litros)

**gallop** ['gæləp] n galope m ♦ vi galopar

**gallows** ['gæləuz] n horca

**gallstone** ['gɔːlstəun] n cálculo biliario

**galore** [gə'lɔː*] adv en cantidad, en abundancia

**galvanize** ['gælvənaɪz] vt: **to** ~ **sb into action** animar a uno para que haga algo

**gambit** ['gæmbɪt] n (fig): (opening)

~ estrategia (inicial)

**gamble** ['gæmbl] n (risk) riesgo ♦ vt jugar, apostar ♦ vi (take a risk) jugárselas; (bet) apostar; to ~ on apostar a; (success etc) contar con; ~r n jugador(a) m/f; **gambling** n juego

**game** [geɪm] n juego; (match) partido; (of cards) partida; (HUNTING) caza ♦ adj (willing): to be ~ for anything atreverse a todo; **big** ~ caza mayor; ~**keeper** n guardabosques m inv

**gammon** ['gæmən] n (bacon) tocino ahumado; (ham) jamón m ahumado

**gamut** ['gæmət] n gama

**gang** [gæŋ] n (of criminals) pandilla; (of friends etc) grupo; (of workmen) brigada; ~ **up** vi: to ~ up on sb aliarse contra uno

**gangster** ['gæŋstə*] n gángster m

**gangway** ['gæŋweɪ] n (on ship) pasarela; (BRIT: in theatre, bus etc) pasillo

**gaol** [dʒeɪl] (BRIT) n, vt = **jail**

**gap** [gæp] n vacío, hueco (AM); (in trees, traffic) claro; (in time) intervalo; (difference): ~ (between) diferencia (entre)

**gape** [geɪp] vi mirar boquiabierto; (shirt etc) abrirse (completamente); **gaping** adj (completamente) abierto

**garage** ['gærɑːʒ] n garaje m; (for repairs) taller m

**garbage** ['gɑːbɪdʒ] (US) n basura; (inf: nonsense) tonterías fpl; ~ **can** n cubo (SP) or bote m (AM) de la basura

**garbled** ['gɑːbld] adj (distorted) falsificado, amañado

**garden** ['gɑːdn] n jardín m; ~**s** npl (park) parque m; ~**er** n jardinero/a; ~**ing** n jardinería

**gargle** ['gɑːgl] vi hacer gárgaras, gargarear (AM)

**garish** ['gɛərɪʃ] adj chillón/ona

**garland** ['gɑːlənd] n guirnalda

**garlic** ['gɑːlɪk] n ajo

**garment** ['gɑːmənt] n prenda (de vestir)

**garnish** ['gɑːnɪʃ] vt (CULIN) aderezar

**garrison** ['gærɪsn] n guarnición f

**garrulous** ['gærʊləs] adj charlatán/ana

**garter** ['gɑːtə*] n (for sock) liga; (US) liguero

**gas** [gæs] n gas m; (fuel) combustible m; (US: gasoline) gasolina ♦ vt asfixiar con gas; ~ **cooker** (BRIT) n cocina de gas; ~ **cylinder** n bombona de gas; ~ **fire** n estufa de gas

**gash** [gæʃ] n raja; (wound) cuchillada ♦ vt rajar; acuchillar

**gasket** ['gæskɪt] n (AUT) junta de culata

**gas mask** n careta antigás

**gas meter** n contador m de gas

**gasoline** ['gæsəliːn] (US) n gasolina

**gasp** [gɑːsp] n boqueada; (of shock etc) grito sofocado ♦ vi (pant) jadear; ~ **out** vt (say) decir con voz entrecortada

**gas station** (US) n gasolinera

**gastric** ['gæstrɪk] adj gástrico

**gate** [geɪt] n puerta; (iron ~) verja; ~**crash** (BRIT) vt colarse en; ~**way** n (also fig) puerta

**gather** ['gæðə*] vt (flowers, fruit) coger (SP), recoger; (assemble) reunir; (pick up) recoger; (SEWING) fruncir; (understand) entender ♦ vi (assemble) reunirse; to ~ **speed** ganar velocidad; ~**ing** n reunión f, asamblea

**gauche** [ɡəʊʃ] adj torpe

**gaudy** ['ɡɔːdɪ] adj chillón/ona

**gauge** [ɡeɪdʒ] n (instrument) indicador m ♦ vt medir; (fig) juzgar

**gaunt** [ɡɔːnt] adj (haggard) demacrado; (stark) desolado

**gauntlet** ['ɡɔːntlɪt] n guante m; (fig): to run the ~ of exponerse a; to throw down the ~ arrojar el guante

**gauze** [ɡɔːz] n gasa

**gave** [ɡeɪv] pt of **give**

**gay** [ɡeɪ] adj (homosexual) gay; (joyful) alegre; (colour) vivo

**gaze** [ɡeɪz] n mirada fija ♦ vi: to ~

at sth mirar algo fijamente

**gazelle** [gə'zɛl] n gacela

**gazetteer** [gæzə'tɪə*] n diccionario geográfico

**gazumping** [gə'zʌmpɪŋ] (BRIT) n la subida del precio de una casa una vez que ya ha sido apalabrado

**GB** abbr = **Great Britain**

**GCE** n abbr (BRIT) = General Certificate of Education

**GCSE** (BRIT) n abbr (= General Certificate of Secondary Education) examen de reválida que se hace a los 16 años

**gear** [gɪə*] n equipo, herramientas fpl; (TECH) engranaje m; (AUT) velocidad f, marcha ♦ vt (fig: adapt): to ~ sth to adaptar or ajustar algo a; **top** or **high** (US)/**low** ~ cuarta/ primera velocidad f; **in** ~ en marcha; ~ **box** n caja de cambios; ~ **lever** n palanca de cambio; ~ **shift** (US) n = ~ **lever**

**geese** [giːs] npl of **goose**

**gel** [dʒɛl] n gel m

**gem** [dʒɛm] n piedra preciosa

**Gemini** ['dʒɛmɪnaɪ] n Géminis m, Gemelos mpl

**gender** ['dʒɛndə*] n género

**gene** [dʒiːn] n gen(e) m

**general** ['dʒɛnərl] n general m ♦ adj general; **in** ~ en general; ~ **delivery** (US) n lista de correos; ~ **election** n elecciones fpl generales; ~**ization** [-aɪ'zeɪʃən] n generalización f; ~**ly** adv generalmente, en general; ~ **practitioner** n médico general

**generate** ['dʒɛnəreɪt] vt (ELEC) generar; (jobs, profits) producir

**generation** [dʒɛnə'reɪʃən] n generación f

**generator** ['dʒɛnəreɪtə*] n generador m

**generosity** [dʒɛnə'rɒsɪtɪ] n generosidad f

**generous** ['dʒɛnərəs] adj generoso

**genetic engineering** [dʒɪ'nɛtɪkˌɛndʒɪ'nɪərɪŋ] n ingeniería genética

**Geneva** [dʒɪ'niːvə] n Ginebra

**genial** ['dʒiːnɪəl] adj afable, simpático

**genitals** ['dʒɛnɪtlz] npl (órganos mpl) genitales mpl

**genius** ['dʒiːnɪəs] n genio

**genteel** [dʒɛn'tiːl] adj fino, elegante

**gentle** ['dʒɛntl] adj apacible, dulce; (animal) manso; (breeze, curve etc) suave

**gentleman** ['dʒɛntlmən] n señor m; (well-bred man) caballero

**gentleness** ['dʒɛntlnɪs] n apacibilidad f, dulzura; mansedumbre f; suavidad f

**gently** ['dʒɛntlɪ] adv dulcemente; suavemente

**gentry** ['dʒɛntrɪ] n alta burguesía

**gents** [dʒɛnts] n aseos mpl (de caballeros)

**genuine** ['dʒɛnjuɪn] adj auténtico; (person) sincero

**geography** [dʒɪ'ɒgrəfɪ] n geografía

**geology** [dʒɪ'ɒlədʒɪ] n geología

**geometric(al)** [dʒɪə'mɛtrɪk(l)] adj geométrico

**geranium** [dʒɪ'reɪnjəm] n geranio

**geriatric** [dʒɛrɪ'ætrɪk] adj, n geriátrico/a m/f

**germ** [dʒəːm] n (microbe) microbio, bacteria; (seed, also fig) germen m

**German** ['dʒəːmən] adj alemán/ana ♦ n alemán/ana m/f; (LING) alemán m; ~ **measles** n rubéola

**Germany** ['dʒəːmənɪ] n Alemania

**gesture** ['dʒɛstjə*] n gesto; (symbol) muestra

┌─────────────────────┐
│ KEYWORD │
└─────────────────────┘

**get** [gɛt] (pt, pp got, pp **gotten** (US)) vi 1 (become, be) ponerse, volverse; **to** ~ **old/tired** envejecer/cansarse; **to** ~ **drunk** emborracharse; **to** ~ **dirty** ensuciarse; **to** ~ **married** casarse; **when do I** ~ **paid?** ¿cuándo me pagan or se me paga?; **it's** ~**ting late** se está haciendo tarde

**2** (go): **to** ~ **to/from** llegar a/de; **to** ~ **home** llegar a casa

**3** (begin) empezar a; **to** ~ **to know sb** (llegar a) conocer a uno; **I'm**

~ting to like him me está empezando a gustar; let's ~ going or started ¡vamos a empezar)!

**4** *(modal aux vb)*: **you've got to do it** tienes que hacerlo

♦ *vt* **1**: to ~ **sth done** *(finish)* terminar algo; *(have done)* mandar hacer algo; to ~ **one's hair cut** cortarse el pelo; to ~ **the car going** or to go arrancar el coche; to ~ **sth to do sth** conseguir or hacer que alguien haga algo; to ~ **sth/sb ready** preparar algo/a alguien

**2** *(obtain: money, permission, results)* conseguir; *(find: job, flat)* encontrar; *(fetch: person, doctor)* buscar; *(object)* ir a buscar, traer; to ~ **sth for sb** conseguir algo para alguien; ~ **me Mr Jones, please** *(TEL)* póngame or comuníqueme *(AM)* con el Sr. Jones, por favor; **can I ~ you a drink?** ¿quieres algo de beber?

**3** *(receive: present, letter)* recibir; *(acquire: reputation)* alcanzar; *(: prize)* ganar; **what did you ~ for your birthday?** ¿qué te regalaron por tu cumpleaños?; **how much did you ~ for the painting?** ¿cuánto sacaste por el cuadro?

**4** *(catch)* coger, agarrar *(AM)*; *(hit: target etc)* dar en; to ~ **sb by the arm/throat** coger or agarrar a uno por el brazo/cuello; ~ **him!** ¡cógelo! *(SP)*, ¡atrápalo! *(AM)*; **the bullet got him in the leg** la bala le dio en la pierna

**5** *(take, move)* llevar; to ~ **sth to sb** hacer llegar algo a alguien; **do you think we'll ~ it through the door?** ¿crees que lo podremos meter por la puerta?

**6** *(catch, take: plane, bus etc)* coger *(SP)*, tomar *(AM)*; **where do I ~ the train for Birmingham?** ¿dónde se coge or se toma el tren para Birmingham?

**7** *(understand)* entender; *(hear)* oír; **I've got it!** ¡ya lo tengo!, ¡eureka!; **I don't ~ your meaning** no te en-

tiendo; **I'm sorry, I didn't ~ your name** lo siento, no cogí tu nombre

**8** *(have, possess)*: **to have got** tener

**get about** *vi* salir mucho; *(news)* divulgarse

**get along** *vi* *(agree)* llevarse bien; *(depart)* marcharse; *(manage)* = **get by**

**get at** *vt fus* *(attack)* atacar; *(reach)* alcanzar

**get away** *vi* marcharse; *(escape)* escaparse

**get away with** *vt fus* hacer impunemente

**get back** *vi* *(return)* volver ♦ *vt* recobrar

**get by** *vi* *(pass)* lograr pasar; *(manage)* arreglárselas

**get down** *vi* ♦ *vt fus* bajar ♦ *vt* bajar; *(depress)* deprimir

**get down to** *vt fus* *(work)* ponerse a

**get in** *vi* entrar; *(train)* llegar; *(arrive home)* volver a casa, regresar

**get into** *vt fus* entrar en; *(vehicle)* subir a; to ~ **into a rage** enfadarse

**get off** *vi* *(from train etc)* bajar; *(depart: person, car)* marcharse ♦ *vt* *(remove)* quitar ♦ *vt fus* *(train, bus)* bajar de

**get on** *vi* *(at exam etc)*: **how are you ~ting on?** ¿cómo te va?; *(agree)*: to ~ **on (with)** llevarse bien (con) ♦ *vt fus* subir a

**get out** *vi* salir; *(of vehicle)* bajar ♦ *vt* sacar

**get out of** *vt fus* salir de; *(duty etc)* escaparse de

**get over** *vt fus* *(illness)* recobrarse de

**get round** *vt fus* rodear; *(fig: person)* engatusar a

**get through** *vi* *(TEL)* lograr comunicarse

**get through to** *vt fus* *(TEL)* comunicar con

**get together** *vi* reunirse ♦ *vt* reunir, juntar

**get up** *vi* *(rise)* levantarse ♦ *vt fus* subir

**get up to** vt fus (reach) llegar a; (prank) hacer

**geyser** ['gi:zə*] n (water heater) calentador m de agua; (GEO) géiser m
**ghastly** ['gɑːstlɪ] adj horrible
**gherkin** ['gɜːkɪn] n pepinillo
**ghetto blaster** ['gɛtəʊblɑːstə*] n cassette m portátil de gran tamaño
**ghost** [gəʊst] n fantasma m
**giant** ['dʒaɪənt] n gigante m/f ♦ adj gigantesco, gigante
**gibberish** ['dʒɪbərɪʃ] n galimatías m
**gibe** [dʒaɪb] n = **jibe**
**giblets** ['dʒɪblɪts] npl menudillos mpl
**Gibraltar** [dʒɪ'brɔːltə*] n Gibraltar m
**giddy** ['gɪdɪ] adj mareado
**gift** [gɪft] n regalo; (ability) talento; ~**ed** adj dotado; ~ **token** or **voucher** n vale m canjeable por un regalo
**gigantic** [dʒaɪ'gæntɪk] adj gigantesco
**giggle** ['gɪgl] vi reírse tontamente
**gill** [dʒɪl] n (measure) = 0.25 pints (BRIT = 0.148l, US = 0.118l)
**gills** [gɪlz] npl (of fish) branquias fpl, agallas fpl
**gilt** [gɪlt] adj, n dorado; ~**-edged** (COMM) de máxima garantía
**gimmick** ['gɪmɪk] n truco
**gin** [dʒɪn] n ginebra
**ginger** ['dʒɪndʒə*] n jengibre m; ~ **ale**, ~ **beer** n (BRIT) gaseosa de jengibre; ~**bread** n pan m (or galleta) de jengibre
**gingerly** ['dʒɪndʒəlɪ] adv con cautela
**gipsy** ['dʒɪpsɪ] n = **gypsy**
**giraffe** [dʒɪ'rɑːf] n jirafa
**girder** ['gɜːdə*] n viga
**girdle** ['gɜːdl] n (corset) faja
**girl** [gɜːl] n (small) niña; (young woman) chica, joven f, muchacha; (daughter) hija; **an English** ~ una (chica) inglesa; ~**friend** n (of girl) amiga; (of boy) novia; ~**ish** adj de niña
**giro** ['dʒaɪərəʊ] n (BRIT: bank) giro bancario; (post office ~) giro postal; (state benefit) cheque quincenal del subsidio de desempleo

**girth** [gɜːθ] n circunferencia; (of saddle) cincha
**gist** [dʒɪst] n lo esencial
**give** [gɪv] (pt gave, pp given) vt dar; (deliver) entregar; (as gift) regalar ♦ vi (break) romperse; (stretch: fabric) dar de sí; **to** ~ **sb sth**, ~ **sth to sb** dar algo a uno; ~ **away** vt (give free) regalar; (betray) traicionar; (disclose) revelar; ~ **back** vt devolver; ~ **in** vi ceder ♦ vt entregar; ~ **off** vt despedir; ~ **out** vt distribuir; ~ **up** vi rendirse, darse por vencido ♦ vt renunciar a; **to** ~ **up smoking** dejar de fumar; **to** ~ **o.s. up** entregarse; ~ **way** vi ceder; (BRIT: AUT) ceder el paso
**glacier** ['glæsɪə*] n glaciar m
**glad** [glæd] adj contento
**gladly** ['glædlɪ] adv con mucho gusto
**glamorous** ['glæmərəs] adj encantador/a, atractivo; **glamour** ['glæmə*] n encanto, atractivo
**glance** [glɑːns] n ojeada, mirada ♦ vi: **to** ~ **at** echar una ojeada a; ~ **off** vt rebotar en; **glancing** adj (blow) oblicuo
**gland** [glænd] n glándula
**glare** [glɛə*] n (of anger) mirada feroz; (of light) deslumbramiento, brillo; **to be in the** ~ **of publicity** ser el foco de la atención pública ♦ vi deslumbrar; **to** ~ **at** mirar con odio a; **glaring** adj (mistake) manifiesto
**glass** [glɑːs] n vidrio, cristal m; (for drinking) vaso; (: with stem) copa; ~**es** npl (spectacles) gafas fpl; ~**house** n invernadero; ~**ware** n cristalería; ~**y** adj (eyes) vidrioso
**glaze** [gleɪz] vt (window) poner cristales a; (pottery) vidriar ♦ n vidriado; **glazier** ['gleɪzɪə*] n vidriero/a
**gleam** [gliːm] vi brillar
**glean** [gliːn] vt (information) recoger
**glee** [gliː] n alegría, regocijo
**glen** [glɛn] n cañada
**glib** [glɪb] adj de mucha labia; (promise, response) poco sincero
**glide** [glaɪd] vi deslizarse; (AVIAT, birds) planear; ~**r** n (AVIAT) pla-

neador *m*; **gliding** *n* (*AVIAT*) vuelo sin motor

**glimmer** ['glɪmə*] *n* luz *f* tenue; (*of interest*) muestra; (*of hope*) rayo

**glimpse** [glɪmps] *n* vislumbre *m* ♦ *vt* vislumbrar, entrever

**glint** [glɪnt] *vi* centellear

**glisten** ['glɪsn] *vi* relucir, brillar

**glitter** ['glɪtə*] *vi* relucir, brillar

**gloat** [gləut] *vi*: **to ~ over** recrearse en

**global** ['gləubl] *adj* mundial

**globe** [gləub] *n* globo; (*model*) globo terráqueo

**gloom** [glu:m] *n* tinieblas *fpl*, oscuridad *f*; (*sadness*) tristeza, melancolía; **~y** *adj* (*dark*) oscuro; (*sad*) triste; (*pessimistic*) pesimista

**glorious** ['glɔ:rɪəs] *adj* glorioso; (*weather etc*) magnífico

**glory** ['glɔ:rɪ] *n* gloria

**gloss** [glɔs] *n* (*shine*) brillo; (*paint*) pintura de aceite; **~ over** *vt fus* disimular

**glossary** ['glɔsərɪ] *n* glosario

**glossy** ['glɔsɪ] *adj* lustroso; (*magazine*) de lujo

**glove** [glʌv] *n* guante *m*; **~ compartment** *n* (*AUT*) guantera

**glow** [gləu] *vi* brillar

**glower** ['glauə*] *vi*: **to ~ at** mirar con ceño

**glue** [glu:] *n* goma (de pegar), cemento ♦ *vt* pegar

**glum** [glʌm] *adj* (*person, tone*) melancólico

**glut** [glʌt] *n* superabundancia

**glutton** ['glʌtn] *n* glotón/ona *m/f*; **a ~ for work** un(a) trabajador(a) incansable

**gnarled** [nɑ:ld] *adj* nudoso

**gnat** [næt] *n* mosquito

**gnaw** [nɔ:] *vt* roer

**gnome** [nəum] *n* gnomo

**go** [gəu] (*pt* went, *pp* gone; *pl* ~es) *vi* ir; (*travel*) viajar; (*depart*) irse, marcharse; (*work*) funcionar, marchar; (*be sold*) venderse; (*fit, suit*): **to ~ with** hacer juego con; (*become*) ponerse; (*break*

*etc*) estropearse, romperse ♦ *n*: **to have a ~** (**at**) probar suerte (con); **to be on the ~** no parar; **whose ~ is it?** ¿a quién le toca?; **he's going to do it** va a hacerlo; **to ~ for a walk** ir de paseo; **to ~ dancing** ir a bailar; **how did it ~?** ¿qué tal salió *or* resultó?, ¿cómo ha ido?; **to ~ round the back** pasar por detrás; **~ about** *vt* (*rumour*) propagarse ♦ *vt fus*: **how do I ~ about this?** ¿cómo me las arreglo para hacer esto?; **~ ahead** *vi* seguir adelante; **~ along** *vi* ir ♦ *vt fus* bordear; **to ~ along with** (*agree*) estar de acuerdo con; **~ away** *vi* irse, marcharse; **~ back** *vi* volver; **~ back on** *vt fus* (*promise*) faltar a; **~ by** *vi* (*time*) pasar ♦ *vt fus* guiarse por; **~ down** *vi* bajar; (*ship*) hundirse; (*sun*) ponerse ♦ *vt fus* bajar; **~ for** *vt fus* (*fetch*) ir por; (*like*) gustar; (*attack*) atacar; **~ in** *vi* entrar; **~ in for** *vt fus* (*competition*) presentarse a; **~ into** *vt fus* entrar en; (*investigate*) investigar; (*embark on*) dedicarse a; **~ off** *vi* irse, marcharse; (*food*) pasarse; (*explode*) estallar; (*event*) realizarse ♦ *vt fus* dejar de gustar; **I'm going off him/the idea** ya no me gusta tanto él/la idea; **~ on** *vi* (*continue*) seguir, continuar; (*happen*) pasar, ocurrir; **to ~ on doing sth** seguir haciendo algo; **~ out** *vi* salir; (*fire, light*) apagarse; **~ over** *vi* (*ship*) zozobrar ♦ *vt fus* (*check*) revisar; **~ through** *vt fus* (*town etc*) atravesar; **~ up** *vi*, *vt fus* subir; **~ without** *vt fus* pasarse sin

**goad** [gəud] *vt* aguijonear

**go-ahead** *adj* (*person*) dinámico; (*firm*) innovador/a ♦ *n* luz *f* verde

**goal** [gəul] *n* meta; (*score*) gol *m*; **~keeper** *n* portero; **~-post** *n* poste *m* (de la portería)

**goat** [gəut] *n* cabra

**gobble** ['gɔbl] *vt* (*also*: **~ down, ~ up**) tragarse, engullir

**go-between** *n* intermediario/a

**god** [gɔd] *n* dios *m*; **G~** *n* Dios *m*;

~**child** n ahijado/a; ~**daughter** n ahijada; ~**dess** n diosa; ~**father** n padrino; ~**forsaken** adj dejado de la mano de Dios; ~**mother** n madrina; ~**send** n don ♦ adj del cielo; ~**son** n ahijado

**goggles** ['gɔglz] npl gafas fpl

**going** ['gəʊɪŋ] n (conditions) estado del terreno ♦ adj: **the** ~ **rate** la tarifa corriente or en vigor

**gold** [gəʊld] n oro ♦ adj de oro; ~**en** adj (made of ~) de oro; (~ in colour) dorado; ~**fish** n pez m de colores; ~**mine** n (also fig) mina de oro; ~**plated** adj chapado en oro; ~**smith** n orfebre m/f

**golf** [gɔlf] n golf m; ~ **ball** n ~ (for game) pelota de golf; (on typewriter) esfera; ~ **club** n club m de golf; (stick) palo (de golf); ~ **course** n campo de golf; ~**er** n golfista m/f

**gone** [gɔn] pp of **go**

**good** [gʊd] adj bueno; (pleasant) agradable; (kind) bueno, amable; (well-behaved) educado ♦ n bien m, provecho; ~**s** npl (COMM) mercancías fpl; ~! ¡qué bien!; **to be** ~ **at** tener aptitud para; **to be** ~ **for** servir para; **it's** ~ **for you** te hace bien; **would you be** ~ **enough to** ...? ¿podría hacerme el favor de ...?; ¿sería tan amable de ...?; **a** ~ **deal** (of) mucho; **a** ~ **many** muchos; **to make** ~ repairar; **it's no** ~ **complaining** no vale la pena (de) quejarse; **for** ~ para siempre, definitivamente; ~ **morning/afternoon** ¡buenos días/buenas tardes!; ~ **evening!** ¡buenas noches!; ~ **night!** ¡buenas noches!; ~**bye!** ¡adiós!; **to say** ~**bye** despedirse; G~ **Friday** n Viernes m Santo; ~**looking** adj guapo; ~**natured** adj amable, simpático; ~**ness** n (of person) bondad f; **for** ~**ness sake!** ¡por Dios!; ~**ness gracious!** ¡Dios mío!; ~**s train** (BRIT) n tren m de mercancías; ~**will** n buena voluntad f

**goose** [guːs] (pl **geese**) n ganso, oca

**gooseberry** ['gʊzbərɪ] n grosella espinosa; **to play** ~ hacer de carabina

**gooseflesh** ['guːsfleʃ] n = **goose pimples**

**goose pimples** npl carne f de gallina

**gore** [gɔː] vt cornear ♦ n sangre f

**gorge** [gɔːdʒ] n barranco ♦ vr: **to** ~ **o.s. (on)** atracarse (de)

**gorgeous** ['gɔːdʒəs] adj (thing) precioso; (weather) espléndido; (person) guapísimo

**gorilla** [gə'rɪlə] n gorila m

**gorse** [gɔːs] n tojo

**gory** ['gɔːrɪ] adj sangriento

**go-slow** (BRIT) n huelga de manos caídas

**gospel** ['gɔspl] n evangelio

**gossip** ['gɔsɪp] n (scandal) cotilleo, chismes mpl; (chat) charla; (scandalmonger) cotilla m/f, chismoso/a ♦ vi cotillear

**got** [gɔt] pt, pp of **get**; ~**ten** (US) pp of **get**

**gout** [gaʊt] n gota

**govern** ['gʌvən] vt gobernar; (influence) dominar

**governess** ['gʌvənɪs] n institutriz f

**government** ['gʌvnmənt] n gobierno

**governor** ['gʌvənə] n gobernador(a) m/f; (of school etc) miembro del consejo; (of jail) director(a) m/f

**gown** [gaʊn] n traje m; (of teacher, BRIT: of judge) toga

**G.P.** n abbr = **general practitioner**

**grab** [græb] vt coger (SP) or agarrar (AM), arrebatar ♦ vi: **to** ~ **at** intentar agarrar

**grace** [greɪs] n gracia ♦ vt honrar; (adorn) adornar; **5 days'** ~ un plazo de 5 días; ~**ful** adj grácil, ágil; (style, shape) elegante, gracioso; **gracious** ['greɪʃəs] adj amable

**grade** [greɪd] n (quality) clase f, calidad f; (in hierarchy) grado; (SCOL: mark) nota; (US: school class) curso ♦ vt clasificar; ~ **crossing** (US) n paso a nivel; ~ **school** (US) n escuela primaria

**gradient** ['greɪdɪənt] n pendiente f

**gradual** ['grædjʊəl] adj paulatino;

~ly adv paulatinamente

**graduate** [n 'grædjuət, vb 'grædjuert] n (US: of high school) graduado/a; (of university) licenciado/a ♦ vi graduarse; licenciarse; **graduation** [-'eɪʃən] n (ceremony) entrega del título

**graffiti** [grə'fiːtɪ] n pintadas fpl

**graft** [grɑːft] n (AGR, MED) injerto; (BRIT: inf) trabajo duro; (bribery) corrupción f ♦ vt injertar

**grain** [greɪn] n (single particle) grano; (corn) granos mpl, cereales mpl; (of wood) fibra

**gram** [græm] n (US) gramo

**grammar** ['græmə*] n gramática; ~ **school** (BRIT) n = instituto de segunda enseñanza, liceo (SP)

**grammatical** [grə'mætɪkl] adj gramatical

**gramme** [græm] n = **gram**

**gramophone** ['græməfəʊn] (BRIT) n tocadiscos m inv

**grand** [grænd] adj magnífico, imponente; (wonderful) estupendo; (gesture etc) grandioso; ~**children** npl nietos mpl; ~**dad** (inf) n yayo, abuelito; ~**daughter** n nieta; ~**eur** ['grændʒə*] n magnificencia, lo grandioso; ~**father** n abuelo; ~**ma** (inf) n yaya, abuelita; ~**mother** n abuela; ~**pa** (inf) n = **dad**; ~**parents** npl abuelos mpl; ~ **piano** n piano de cola; ~**son** n nieto; ~**stand** n (SPORT) tribuna

**granite** ['grænɪt] n granito

**granny** ['grænɪ] (inf) n abuelita, yaya

**grant** [grɑːnt] vt (concede) conceder; (admit) reconocer ♦ n (SCOL) beca; (ADMIN) subvención f; **to take sth/sb for ~ed** dar algo por sentado/no hacer ningún caso a uno

**granulated sugar** ['grænjuːleɪtɪd-] (BRIT) n azúcar m blanquilla

**granule** ['grænjuːl] n grano, gránulo

**grape** [greɪp] n uva

**grapefruit** ['greɪpfruːt] n pomelo (SP), toronja (AM)

**graph** [grɑːf] n gráfica; ~**ic** adj gráfico; ~**ics** n artes fpl gráficas ♦ npl (drawings) dibujos mpl

**grapple** ['græpl] vi: **to ~ with** sth/sb agarrar a algo/uno

**grasp** [grɑːsp] vt agarrar, asir; (understand) comprender ♦ n (grip) asimiento; (understanding) comprensión f; ~**ing** adj (mean) avaro

**grass** [grɑːs] n hierba; (lawn) césped m; ~**hopper** n saltamontes m inv; ~-**roots** npl (fig) popular

**grate** [greɪt] n parrilla de chimenea ♦ vi: **to ~ (on)** chirriar (sobre) ♦ vt (CULIN) rallar

**grateful** ['greɪtful] adj agradecido

**grater** ['greɪtə*] n rallador m

**gratifying** ['grætɪfaɪɪŋ] adj grato

**grating** ['greɪtɪŋ] n (iron bars) reja ♦ adj (noise) áspero

**gratitude** ['grætɪtjuːd] n agradecimiento

**gratuity** [grə'tjuːɪtɪ] n gratificación f

**grave** [greɪv] n tumba ♦ adj serio, grave

**gravel** ['grævl] n grava

**gravestone** ['greɪvstəʊn] n lápida

**graveyard** ['greɪvjɑːd] n cementerio

**gravity** ['grævɪtɪ] n gravedad f

**gravy** ['greɪvɪ] n salsa de carne

**gray** [greɪ] adj = **grey**

**graze** [greɪz] vi pacer ♦ vt (touch lightly) rozar; (scrape) raspar ♦ n (MED) abrasión f

**grease** [griːs] n (fat) grasa; (lubricant) lubricante m ♦ vt engrasar; ~**proof paper** (BRIT) n papel m apergaminado; **greasy** adj grasiento

**great** [greɪt] adj grande; (inf) magnífico, estupendo; **G~ Britain** n Gran Bretaña; ~**grandfather** n bisabuelo; ~**grandmother** n bisabuela; ~**ly** adv muy; (with verb) mucho; ~**ness** n grandeza

**Greece** [griːs] n Grecia

**greed** [griːd] n (also: ~iness) codicia, avaricia; (for food) gula; (for power etc) avidez f; ~**y** adj avaro; (for food) glotón/ona

**Greek** [griːk] adj griego ♦ n griego/a

a; (LING) griego

**green** [griːn] adj (also POL) verde; (inexperienced) novato ♦ n verde m; (stretch of grass) césped m; (GOLF) green m; ~s npl (vegetables) verduras fpl; ~ **belt** n zona verde; ~ **card** n (AUT) carta verde; (US: work permit) permiso de trabajo para los extranjeros en EE. UU; ~**ery** n verdura; ~**grocer** (BRIT) n verdulero/a; ~**house** n invernadero; ~**house effect** n efecto invernado; ~**house gas** n gases mpl de invernado; ~**ish** adj verdoso

**Greenland** ['griːnlənd] n Groenlandia

**greet** [griːt] vt (welcome) dar la bienvenida a; (receive: news) recibir; ~**ing** n (welcome) bienvenida; ~**ing(s) card** n tarjeta de felicitación

**grenade** [grɪ'neɪd] n granada

**grew** [gruː] pt of **grow**

**grey** [greɪ] adj gris; (weather) sombrío; ~**haired** adj canoso; ~**hound** n galgo

**grid** [grɪd] n reja; (ELEC) red f

**grief** [griːf] n dolor m, pena

**grievance** ['griːvəns] n motivo de queja, agravio

**grieve** [griːv] vi afligirse, acongojarse ♦ vt dar pena a; **to** ~ **for** llorar por

**grievous** ['griːvəs] adj: ~ **bodily harm** (LAW) daños mpl corporales graves

**grill** [grɪl] n (on cooker) parrilla; (also: mixed ~) parrillada ♦ vt (BRIT) asar a la parrilla; (inf: question) interrogar

**grille** [grɪl] n reja; (AUT) rejilla

**grim** [grɪm] adj (place) sombrío; (situation) triste; (person) ceñudo

**grimace** [grɪ'meɪs] n mueca ♦ vi hacer muecas

**grime** [graɪm] n mugre f, suciedad f

**grin** [grɪn] n sonrisa abierta ♦ vi sonreír abiertamente

**grind** [graɪnd] (pt, pp **ground**) vt (coffee, pepper etc) moler; (US: meat) picar; (make sharp) afilar ♦ n (work) rutina

**grip** [grɪp] n (hold) asimiento; (control) control m, dominio; (of tyre etc): **to have a good/bad** ~ agarrarse bien/mal; (handle) asidero; (holdall) maletín m ♦ vt (viewer, reader) fascinar; **to get to** ~**s with** enfrentarse con; ~**ping** adj absorbente

**grisly** ['grɪzlɪ] adj horripilante, horrible

**gristle** ['grɪsl] n ternilla

**grit** [grɪt] n gravilla; (courage) valor m ♦ vt (road) poner gravilla en; **to** ~ **one's teeth** apretar los dientes

**groan** [grəun] n gemido; quejido ♦ vi gemir; quejarse

**grocer** ['grəusə*] n tendero de ultramarinos (SP); ~**ies** npl comestibles mpl; ~**'s (shop)** n tienda de ultramarinos or de abarrotes (AM)

**groggy** ['grɒgɪ] adj atontado

**groin** [grɔɪn] n ingle f

**groom** [gruːm] n mozo/a de cuadra; (also: bride~) novio ♦ vt (horse) almohazar; (fig): **to** ~ **sb for** preparar a uno para; **well~ed** de buena presencia

**groove** [gruːv] n ranura, surco

**grope** [grəup] **to** ~ **for** vt fus buscar a tientas

**gross** [grəus] adj (neglect, injustice) grave; (vulgar: behaviour) grosero; (: appearance) de mal gusto; (COMM) bruto; ~**ly** adv (greatly) enormemente

**grotesque** [grə'tesk] adj grotesco

**grotto** ['grɒtəu] n gruta

**grotty** ['grɒtɪ] (inf) adj horrible

**ground** [graund] pt, pp of **grind** ♦ n suelo, tierra; (SPORT) campo, terreno; (reason: gen pl) causa, razón f; (US: also: ~ wire) tierra ♦ vt (plane) mantener en tierra; (US: ELEC) conectar con tierra; ~**s** npl (of coffee etc) poso; (gardens etc) jardines mpl, parque m; **on the** ~ en el suelo; **to the** ~ al suelo; **to gain/lose** ~ ganar/perder terreno; ~**cloth** (US) n = ~**sheet**; ~**ing** n (in education) conocimientos mpl bási-

cos; ~**less** adj infundado; ~**sheet**
(BRIT) n tela impermeable; suelo;
~ **staff** n personal m de tierra;
~**swell** n (of opinion) marejada;
~**work** n preparación f

**group** [gruːp] n grupo; (musical)
conjunto ♦ vt (also: ~ together)
agrupar ♦ vi (also: ~ together) agruparse

**grouse** [graus] n inv (bird) urogallo
♦ vi (complain) quejarse

**grove** [grəuv] n arboleda

**grovel** ['grɔvl] vi (fig): to ~ before
humillarse ante

**grow** [grəu] (pt grew, pp grown) vi
crecer; (increase) aumentar; (expand) desarrollarse; (become) volverse; to ~ **rich/weak** enriquecer-
se/debilitarse ♦ vt cultivar; (hair,
beard) dejar crecer; ~ **up** vi crecer,
hacerse hombre/mujer; ~**er** n culti-
vador(a) m/f, productor(a) m/f; ~**ing**
adj creciente

**growl** [graul] vi gruñir

**grown** [grəun] pp of **grow**; ~**up** n
adulto, mayor m/f

**growth** [grəuθ] n crecimiento, desarrollo; (what has grown) brote m;
(MED) tumor m

**grub** [grʌb] n larva, gusano; (inf:
food) comida

**grubby** ['grʌbɪ] adj sucio, mugriento

**grudge** [grʌdʒ] n (motivo de) rencor
m ♦ vt: to ~ **sb sth** dar algo a uno
de mala gana; to bear **sb a** ~ guardar rencor a uno

**gruelling** ['gruəlɪŋ] adj penoso, duro

**gruesome** ['gruːsəm] adj horrible

**gruff** [grʌf] adj (voice) ronco; (manner) brusco

**grumble** ['grʌmbl] vi refunfuñar,
quejarse

**grumpy** ['grʌmpɪ] adj gruñón/ona

**grunt** [grʌnt] vi gruñir

**G-string** ['dʒiːstrɪŋ] n taparrabo

**guarantee** [gærən'tiː] n garantía f ♦
vt garantizar

**guard** [gɑːd] n (squad) guardia; (one
man) guardia m; (BRIT: RAIL) jefe
m de tren; (on machine) dispositivo

de seguridad; (also: fire~) rejilla de
protección ♦ vt guardar; (prisoner)
vigilar; to be on one's ~ estar alerta; ~ **against** vt fus (prevent) protegerse de; ~**ed** adj (fig) cauteloso;
~**ian** n guardián/ana m/f; (of minor)
tutor(a) m/f; ~'s **van** n (BRIT:
RAIL) furgón m

**Guatemala** [gwætɪ'mɑːlə] n Guatemala; ~**n** adj, n guatemalteco/a m/f

**guerrilla** [gə'rɪlə] n guerrillero/a

**guess** [gɛs] vi adivinar; (US) suponer ♦ vt adivinar; suponer ♦ n suposición f, conjetura f; to take or have
a ~ tratar de adivinar; ~**work** n
conjeturas fpl

**guest** [gɛst] n invitado/a; (in hotel)
huésped/a m/f; ~**house** n casa de
huéspedes, pensión f; ~ **room** n
cuarto de huéspedes

**guffaw** [gʌ'fɔː] vi reírse a carcajadas

**guidance** ['gaɪdəns] n (advice) consejos mpl

**guide** [gaɪd] n (person) guía m/f;
(book, fig) guía ♦ vt (round museum
etc) guiar; (lead) conducir; (direct)
orientar; (girl) ~ n exploradora;
~**book** n guía; ~ **dog** n perro m
guía; ~**lines** npl (advice) directrices
fpl

**guild** [gɪld] n gremio

**guile** [gaɪl] n astucia

**guillotine** ['gɪlətiːn] n guillotina

**guilt** [gɪlt] n culpabilidad f; ~**y** adj
culpable

**guinea** ['gɪnɪ] n (BRIT) (old) guinea
(= 21 chelines)

**guinea pig** n cobaya; (fig) conejillo
de Indias

**guise** [gaɪz] n: in or under the ~ of
bajo apariencia de

**guitar** [gɪ'tɑː] n guitarra

**gulf** [gʌlf] n golfo; (abyss) abismo

**gull** [gʌl] n gaviota

**gullet** ['gʌlɪt] n esófago

**gullible** ['gʌlɪbl] adj crédulo

**gully** ['gʌlɪ] n barranco

**gulp** [gʌlp] vi tragar saliva ♦ vt
(also: ~ down) tragarse

**gum** [gʌm] n (ANAT) encía; (glue) goma, cemento; (sweet) caramelo de goma; (also: chewing-~) chicle m ♦ vt pegar con goma; ~boots (BRIT) npl botas fpl de goma

**gumption** ['gʌmpʃən] n sentido común

**gun** [gʌn] n (small) pistola, revólver m; (shotgun) escopeta; (rifle) fusil m; (cannon) cañón m; ~boat n cañonero; ~fire n disparos mpl; ~man n pistolero; ~point n: at ~point a mano armada; ~powder n pólvora; ~shot n escopetazo

**gurgle** ['gɜːgl] vi gorgotear; (water) borbotear

**gush** [gʌʃ] n vi salir a raudales; (person) deshacerse en efusiones

**gust** [gʌst] n (of wind) ráfaga

**gusto** ['gʌstəu] n entusiasmo

**gut** [gʌt] n intestino; ~s npl (ANAT) tripas fpl; (courage) valor m

**gutter** ['gʌtə*] n (of roof) canalón m; (in street) cuneta

**guy** [gai] n (also: ~rope) cuerda; (inf: man) tío (SP), tipo; (also: G~ Fawkes) monigote m

**guzzle** ['gʌzl] vi tragar ♦ vt engullir

**gym** [dʒim] n (also: gymnasium) gimnasio; (also: gymnastics) gimnasia; ~nast n gimnasta m/f; ~ shoes npl zapatillas fpl (de deporte); ~ slip (BRIT) n túnica de colegiala

**gynaecologist** [gaini'kɔlədʒist] (US gynecologist) n ginecólogo/a

**gypsy** ['dʒipsi] n gitano/a

**gyrate** [dʒai'reit] vi girar

# H

**haberdashery** [hæbə'dæʃəri] (BRIT) n mercería

**habit** ['hæbit] n hábito, costumbre f; (drug ~) adicción f; (costume) hábito

**habitual** [hə'bitjuəl] adj acostumbrado, habitual; (drinker, liar) empedernido

**hack** [hæk] vt (cut) cortar; (slice) ta-

jar ♦ n (pej: writer) escritor(a) m/f a sueldo; ~er n (COMPUT) pirata m/f informático

**hackneyed** ['hæknid] adj trillado

**had** [hæd] pt, pp of have

**haddock** ['hædək] (pl ~ or ~s) n especie de merluza

**hadn't** ['hædnt] = had not

**haemorrhage** ['heməridʒ] (US hemorrhage) n hemorragia

**haemorrhoids** ['heməroidz] (US hemorrhoids) npl hemorroides fpl

**haggard** ['hægəd] adj ojeroso

**haggle** ['hægl] vi regatear

**Hague** [heig] n: The ~ La Haya

**hail** [heil] n granizo; (fig) lluvia ♦ vt saludar; (taxi) llamar a; (acclaim) aclamar ♦ vi granizar; ~stone n (piedra de) granizo

**hair** [heə*] n pelo, cabellos mpl; (one ~) pelo, cabello; (on legs etc) vello; to do one's ~ arreglarse el pelo; to have grey ~ tener canas fpl; ~brush n cepillo (para el pelo); ~cut n corte m (de pelo); ~do n peinado; ~dresser n peluquero/a; ~dresser's n peluquería; ~dryer n secador m de pelo; ~grip n horquilla; ~net n redecilla; ~piece n postizo; ~pin n horquilla; ~pin bend (US ~pin curve) n curva de horquilla; ~raising adj espeluznante; ~removing cream n crema depilatoria; ~ spray n laca; ~style n peinado; ~y adj peludo; velludo; (inf: frightening) espeluznante

**hake** [heik] (pl inv or ~s) n merluza

**half** [hɑːf] (pl halves) n mitad f; (of beer) ~ caña (SP), media pinta; (RAIL, BUS) billete m de niño ♦ adj medio ♦ adv medio, a medias; two and a ~ dos y media; ~ a dozen media docena; ~ a pound media libra; to cut sth in ~ cortar algo por la mitad; ~caste n mestizo/a; ~hearted adj indiferente, poco entusiasta; ~hour n media hora; ~mast n: at ~mast (flag) a media asta; ~price adj, adv a mitad de precio; ~ term (BRIT) n (SCOL) va-

*caciones de mediados del trimestre;* ~**-time** *n* descanso; ~**way** *adv* a medio camino; *(in period of time)* a mitad de

**hall** [hɔːl] *n (for concerts)* sala; *(entrance way)* hall *m*; vestíbulo; ~ **of residence** *(BRIT) n* residencia

**hallmark** ['hɔːlmɑːk] *n* sello

**hallo** [hə'ləʊ] *excl* = **hello**

**Hallowe'en** [hæləʊ'iːn] *n* víspera de Todos los Santos

**hallucination** [həluːsɪ'neɪʃən] *n* alucinación *f*

**hallway** ['hɔːlweɪ] *n* vestíbulo

**halo** ['heɪləʊ] *n (of saint)* halo, aureola

**halt** [hɔːlt] *n (stop)* alto, parada ♦ *vt* parar; interrumpir ♦ *vi* pararse

**halve** [hɑːv] *vt* partir por la mitad

**halves** [hɑːvz] *npl of* **half**

**ham** [hæm] *n* jamón *m (cocido)*

**hamburger** ['hæmbɜːgə*] *n* hamburguesa

**hamlet** ['hæmlɪt] *n* aldea

**hammer** ['hæmə*] *n* martillo ♦ *vt (nail)* clavar; *(force):* **to ~ an idea into sb/a message across** meter una idea en la cabeza a uno/ machacar una idea ♦ *vi* dar golpes

**hammock** ['hæmək] *n* hamaca

**hamper** ['hæmpə*] *vt* estorbar ♦ *n* cesto

**hand** [hænd] *n* mano *f*; *(of clock)* aguja; *(writing)* letra; *(worker)* obrero ♦ *vt* dar, pasar; **to give** *or* **lend sb a ~** echar una mano a uno, ayudar a uno; **at ~** a mano; **in ~** *(time)* libre; *(job etc)* entre manos; **on ~** *(person, services)* a mano, al alcance; **to ~** *(information etc)* a mano; **on the one ~ ..., on the other ~ ...** por una parte ... por otra (parte) ...; ~ **in** *vt* entregar; ~ **out** *vt* distribuir; ~ **over** *vt (deliver)* entregar; ~**bag** *n* bolso *(SP)*, cartera *(AM)*; ~**book** *n* manual *m*; ~**brake** *n* freno de mano; ~**cuffs** *npl* esposas *fpl*; ~**ful** *n* puñado

**handicap** ['hændɪkæp] *n* minusvalía; *(disadvantage)* desventaja; *(SPORT)* handicap *m* ♦ *vt* estorbar; **mentally/physically** ~**ped** deficiente *m/f (mental)/*minusválido/a *(físico/a)*

**handicraft** ['hændɪkrɑːft] *n* artesanía

**handiwork** ['hændɪwɜːk] *n* artesanía; *(object)* objeto de artesanía

**handkerchief** ['hæŋkətʃɪf] *n* pañuelo

**handle** ['hændl] *n (of door etc)* tirador *m*; *(of cup etc)* asa; *(of knife etc)* mango; *(for winding)* manivela ♦ *vt (touch)* tocar; *(deal with etc)* manejar; "~ **with care**" "(manéjese) con cuidado"; **to fly off the** ~ perder los estribos; ~**bar(s)** *n(pl)* manillar *m*

**hand:** ~**-luggage** *n* equipaje *m* de mano; ~**made** ['hændmeɪd] *adj* hecho a mano; ~**out** ['hændaʊt] *n (money etc)* limosna; *(leaflet)* folleto; ~**rail** ['hændreɪl] *n* pasamanos *m inv*; ~**shake** [hændʃeɪk] *n* apretón *m* de manos

**handsome** ['hænsəm] *adj* guapo; *(building)* bello; *(fig: profit)* considerable

**handwriting** ['hændraɪtɪŋ] *n* letra

**handy** ['hændɪ] *adj (close at hand)* a la mano; *(tool etc)* práctico; *(skilful)* hábil, diestro; ~**man** *n* manitas *m inv*

**hang** [hæŋ] *(pt, pp* **hung)** *vt* colgar; *(criminal: pt, pp* **hanged)** ahorcar ♦ *vi (painting, coat etc)* colgar; *(hair, drapery)* caer; **to get the ~ of sth** *(inf)* lograr dominar algo; ~ **about** *or* **around** *vi* haraganear; ~ **on** *vi (wait)* esperar; ~ **up** *vi (TEL)* colgar ♦ *vt* colgar

**hanger** ['hæŋə*] *n* percha; ~**-on** *n* parásito

**hang-gliding** ['-glaɪdɪŋ] *n* vuelo libre

**hangover** ['hæŋəʊvə*] *n (after drinking)* resaca

**hang-up** *n* complejo

**hanker** ['hæŋkə*] *vi:* **to ~ after** añorar

**hankie, hanky** ['hæŋkɪ] *n abbr* = **handkerchief**

**haphazard** [hæp'hæzəd] adj fortuito

**happen** ['hæpən] vi suceder, ocurrir; (chance): **he ~ed to hear/see** dió la casualidad de que oyó/vió; **as it ~s** da la casualidad de que; **~ing** n suceso, acontecimiento

**happily** ['hæpɪlɪ] adv (luckily) afortunadamente; (cheerfully) alegremente

**happiness** ['hæpɪns] n felicidad f; (cheerfulness) alegría

**happy** ['hæpɪ] adj feliz; (cheerful) alegre; **to be ~ (with)** estar contento (con); **to be ~ to do** estar encantado de hacer; **~ birthday!** ¡feliz cumpleaños!; **~-go-lucky** adj despreocupado

**harass** ['hærəs] vt acosar, hostigar; **~ment** n persecución f

**harbour** ['hɑːbə*] (US harbor) n puerto ♦ vt (fugitive) dar abrigo a; (hope etc) abrigar

**hard** [hɑːd] adj duro; (difficult) difícil; (work) arduo; (person) severo; (fact) innegable ♦ adv (work) mucho, duro; (think) profundamente; **to look ~ at** clavar los ojos en; **to try ~** esforzarse; **no ~ feelings!** ¡sin rencor(es)!; **to be ~ of hearing** ser duro de oído; **to be ~ done by** ser tratado injustamente; **~back** n libro en cartoné; **~ cash** n dinero contante; **~ disk** n (COMPUT) disco duro or rígido; **~en** vt endurecer; (fig) curtir ♦ vi endurecerse; curtirse; **~-headed** adj realista; **~ labour** n trabajos mpl forzados

**hardly** ['hɑːdlɪ] adv apenas; **~ ever** casi nunca

**hardship** ['hɑːdʃɪp] n privación f

**hard-up** (inf) adj sin un duro (SP), sin plata (AM)

**hardware** ['hɑːdwɛə*] n ferretería f; (COMPUT) hardware m; (MIL) armamento; **~ shop** n ferretería

**hard-wearing** adj resistente, duradero

**hard-working** adj trabajador(a)

**hardy** ['hɑːdɪ] adj fuerte; (plant) resistente

**hare** [hɛə*] n liebre f; **~-brained** adj

descabellado

**harem** [hɑː'riːm] n harén m

**harm** [hɑːm] n daño, mal m ♦ vt (person) hacer daño a; (health, interests) perjudicar; (thing) dañar; **out of ~'s way** a salvo; **~ful** adj dañino; **~less** adj (person) inofensivo; (joke etc) inocente

**harmony** ['hɑːmənɪ] n armonía

**harness** ['hɑːnɪs] n arreos mpl; (for child) arnés m; (safety ~) arneses mpl ♦ vt (horse) enjaezar; (resources) aprovechar

**harp** [hɑːp] n arpa ♦ vi: **to ~ on (about)** machacar (con)

**harpoon** [hɑː'puːn] n arpón m

**harrowing** ['hærəʊɪŋ] adj angustioso

**harsh** [hɑːʃ] adj (cruel) duro, cruel; (severe) severo; (sound) áspero; (light) deslumbrador(a)

**harvest** ['hɑːvɪst] n (~ time) siega; (of cereals etc) cosecha; (of grapes) vendimia ♦ vt cosechar

**has** [hæz] vb see **have**

**hash** [hæʃ] n (CULIN) picadillo; (fig: mess) lío

**hashish** ['hæʃɪʃ] n hachís m

**hasn't** ['hæznt] = **has not**

**hassle** ['hæsl] (inf) n lata

**haste** [heɪst] n prisa; **~n** ['heɪsn] vt acelerar ♦ vi darse prisa; **hastily** adv de prisa; precipitadamente; **hasty** adj apresurado; (rash) precipitado

**hat** [hæt] n sombrero

**hatch** [hætʃ] n (NAUT: also: **~way**) escotilla; (also: service **~**) ventanilla ♦ vi (bird) salir del cascarón ♦ vt incubar; (plot) tramar; **5 eggs have ~ed** han salido 5 pollos

**hatchback** ['hætʃbæk] n (AUT) tres or cinco puertas m

**hatchet** ['hætʃɪt] n hacha

**hate** [heɪt] vt odiar, aborrecer ♦ n odio; **~ful** adj odioso; **hatred** ['heɪtrɪd] n odio

**haughty** ['hɔːtɪ] adj altanero

**haul** [hɔːl] vt tirar ♦ n (of fish) redada; (of stolen goods etc) botín m; **~age** (BRIT) n transporte m;

(costs) gastos mpl de transporte; ~ier (US ~er) n transportista m/f

**haunch** [hɔːntʃ] n anca; (of meat) pierna

**haunt** [hɔːnt] vt (subj: ghost) aparecerse en; (obsess) obsesionar ♦ n guarida

---

KEYWORD

---

**have** [hæv] (pt, pp had) aux vb **1** (gen) haber; to ~ arrived/eaten haber llegado/comido; having finished or when he had finished, he left cuando hubo acabado, se fue

**2** (in tag questions): you've done it, ~n't you? lo has hecho, ¿verdad? or ¿no?

**3** (in short answers and questions): I ~n't no; so I ~ pues, es verdad; we ~n't paid — yes we ~! no hemos pagado — ¡sí que hemos pagado! I've been there before, ~ you? he estado allí antes, ¿y tú?

♦ modal aux vb (be obliged): to ~ (got) to do sth tener que hacer algo; you ~n't to tell her no hay que or no debes decírselo

♦ vt **1** (possess): he has (got) blue eyes/dark hair tiene los ojos azules/ el pelo negro

**2** (referring to meals etc): to ~ breakfast/lunch/dinner desayunar/ comer/cenar; to ~ a drink/a cigarette tomar algo/fumar un cigarrillo

**3** (receive) recibir; (obtain) obtener; may I ~ your address? ¿puedes darme tu dirección?; you can ~ it for £5 te lo puedes quedar por £5; I must ~ it by tomorrow lo necesito para mañana; to ~ a baby tener un niño or bebé

**4** (maintain, allow): I won't ~ it/ this nonsense! ¡no lo permitiré!/¡no permitiré estas tonterías!; we can't ~ that no podemos permitir eso

**5**: to ~ sth done hacer or mandar hacer algo; to ~ one's hair cut cortarse el pelo; to ~ sb do sth hacer que alguien haga algo

**6** (experience, suffer): to ~ a cold/ flu tener un resfriado/la gripe; she had her bag stolen/her arm broken le robaron el bolso/se rompió el brazo; to ~ an operation operarse

**7** (+ noun): to ~ a swim/walk/ bath/rest nadar/dar un paseo/darse un baño/descansar; let's ~ a look vamos a ver; to ~ a meeting/party celebrar una reunión/una fiesta; let me ~ a try déjame intentarlo

**have out** vt: to ~ it out with sb (settle a problem etc) dejar las cosas en claro con alguien

**haven** ['heɪvn] n puerto; (fig) refugio

**haven't** ['hævnt] = have not

**haversack** ['hævəsæk] n mochila

**havoc** ['hævək] n estragos mpl

**hawk** [hɔːk] n halcón m

**hay** [heɪ] n heno; ~ fever n fiebre f del heno; ~stack n almiar m

**haywire** ['heɪwaɪə*] (inf) adj: to go ~ (plan) embrollarse

**hazard** ['hæzəd] n peligro ♦ vt aventurar; ~ous adj peligroso; ~ warning lights npl (AUT) señales fpl de emergencia

**haze** [heɪz] n neblina

**hazelnut** ['heɪzlnʌt] n avellana

**hazy** ['heɪzɪ] adj brumoso; (idea) vago

**he** [hiː] pron él; ~ who ... él que ..., quien ...

**head** [hed] n cabeza; (leader) jefe/a m/f; (of school) director(a) m/f ♦ vt (list) encabezar; (group) capitanear; (company) dirigir; ~s (or tails) cara (o cruz); ~ first de cabeza; ~ over heels (in love) perdidamente; to ~ the ball cabecear (la pelota); ~ for vt fus dirigirse a; (disaster) ir camino de; ~ache n dolor m de cabeza; ~dress n tocado; ~ing n título; ~lamp (BRIT) n = ~light; ~land n promontorio; ~light n faro; ~line n titular m; (rush) precipitadamente; ~master/mistress n director(a) m/f (de escuela); ~ office n oficina central, central f; ~-on adj (collision) de frente; **~phones** npl auriculares mpl; **~quarters** npl sede f central; (MIL) cuartel m general; **~rest** n reposa-cabezas m inv; **~room** n (in car) altura interior; (under bridge) (límite m de) altura; **~scarf** n pañuelo; **~strong** adj testarudo; **~waiter** n maitre m; **~way** n: to make **~way** (fig) hacer progresos; **~wind** n viento contrario; **~y** adj (experience, period) apasionante; (wine) cabezón; (atmosphere) embriagador(a)

**heal** [hi:l] vt curar ♦ vi cicatrizarse

**health** [hɛlθ] n salud f; **~ food** n alimentos mpl orgánicos; **the H~ Service** (BRIT) n el servicio de salud pública; ≈ el Insalud (SP); **~y** adj sano, saludable

**heap** [hi:p] n montón m ♦ vt: to **~ (up)** amontonar; to **~ sth with** llenar algo hasta arriba de; **~s of** un montón de

**hear** [hɪə*] (pt, pp **heard**) vt (also LAW) oír; (news) saber ♦ vi oír; to **~ about** oír hablar de; to **~ from** sb tener noticias de uno; **heard** [hɜːd] pt, pp of **hear**; **~ing** n (sense) oído; (LAW) vista; **~ing aid** n audífono; **~say** n rumores mpl, habillias fpl

**hearse** [hɜːs] n coche m fúnebre

**heart** [hɑːt] n corazón m; (fig) valor m; (of lettuce) cogollo; **~s** npl (CARDS) corazones mpl; to lose/take **~** descorazonarse/cobrar ánimo; at **~** en el fondo; by **~** (learn, know) de memoria; **~ attack** n infarto (de miocardio); **~beat** n latido (del corazón); **~breaking** adj desgarrador(a); **~broken** adj: she was **~broken about** it esto le partió el corazón; **~burn** n acedía; **~ failure** n fallo cardíaco; **~felt** adj (deeply felt) más sentido

**hearth** [hɑːθ] n fireplace chimenea

**heartless** [hɑːtlɪs] adj cruel

**hearty** [hɑːtɪ] adj (person) campechano; (laugh) sano; (dislike, support) absoluto

**heat** [hiːt] n calor m; (SPORT: also: qualifying **~**) prueba eliminatoria ♦ vt calentar; **~ up** vi calentarse ♦ vt calentar; **~ed** adj caliente; (fig) acalorado; **~er** n estufa; (in car) calefacción f

**heath** [hiːθ] (BRIT) n brezal m

**heather** [ˈhɛðə*] n brezo

**heating** [ˈhiːtɪŋ] n calefacción f

**heatstroke** [ˈhiːtstrəuk] n insolación f

**heatwave** [ˈhiːtweɪv] n ola de calor

**heave** [hiːv] vt (pull) tirar; (push) empujar con esfuerzo; (lift) levantar (con esfuerzo) ♦ vi (chest) palpitar; (retch) tener náuseas ♦ n tirón m; empujón m; to **~ a sigh** suspirar

**heaven** [ˈhɛvn] n cielo; (fig) una maravilla; **~ly** adj celestial; (fig) maravilloso

**heavily** [ˈhɛvɪlɪ] adv pesadamente; (drink, smoke) con exceso; (sleep, sigh) profundamente; (depend) mucho

**heavy** [ˈhɛvɪ] adj pesado; (work, blow) duro; (sea, rain, meal) fuerte; (drinker, smoker) grande; (responsibility) gravedad; (schedule) ocupado; (weather) bochornoso; **~ goods vehicle** n vehículo pesado; **~weight** n (SPORT) peso pesado

**Hebrew** [ˈhiːbruː] adj, n (LING) hebreo

**heckle** [ˈhɛkl] vt interrumpir

**hectic** [ˈhɛktɪk] adj agitado

**he'd** [hiːd] = he would; he had

**hedge** [hɛdʒ] n seto ♦ vi contestar con evasivas; to **~ one's bets** (fig) cubrirse

**hedgehog** [ˈhɛdʒhɔg] n erizo

**heed** [hiːd] vt (also: **take ~ of**) (pay attention to) hacer caso de; **~less** adj: to be **~less (of)** no hacer caso (de)

**heel** [hiːl] n talón m; (of shoe) tacón m ♦ vt (shoe) poner tacón a

**hefty** [ˈhɛftɪ] adj (person) fornido; (parcel, profit) gordo

**heifer** [ˈhɛfə*] n novilla, ternera

**height** [haɪt] n (of person) estatura;

(of building) altura; (high ground) cerro; (altitude) altitud f; (fig: of season): at the ~ of winter en pleno invierno; (: of power etc) cúspide f; (: of stupidity etc) colmo; ~en vt elevar; (fig) aumentar

**heir** [ɛəˠ] n heredero; ~ess n heredera; ~loom n reliquia de familia

**held** [hɛld] pt, pp of **hold**

**helicopter** ['hɛlɪkɔptəˠ] n helicóptero

**helium** ['hiːlɪəm] n helio

**hell** [hɛl] n infierno; ~! (inf) ¡demonios!

**he'll** [hiːl] = he will; he shall

**hello** [hə'ləu] excl ¡hola!; (to attract attention) ¡oiga!; (surprise) ¡caramba!

**helm** [hɛlm] n (NAUT) timón m

**helmet** ['hɛlmɪt] n casco

**help** [hɛlp] n ayuda; (cleaner etc) criada, asistenta ♦ vt ayudar; ~! ¡socorro!; ~ yourself sírvete; he can't ~ it no es culpa suya; ~er n ayudante m/f; ~ful adj útil; (person) servicial; (advice) útil; ~ing n ración f; ~less adj (incapable) incapaz; (defenceless) indefenso

**hem** [hɛm] n dobladillo ♦ vt poner o coser el dobladillo; ~ in vt cercar

**hemorrhage** ['hɛmərɪdʒ] (US) n = **haemorrhage**

**hemorrhoids** ['hɛmərɔɪdz] (US) npl = **haemorrhoids**

**hen** [hɛn] n gallina; (female bird) hembra

**hence** [hɛns] adv (therefore) por lo tanto; 2 years ~ de aquí a 2 años; ~forth adv de hoy en adelante

**henchman** ['hɛntʃmən] (pej) n escuaz m

**hepatitis** [hɛpə'taɪtɪs] n hepatitis f

**her** [həːˠ] pron (direct) la; (indirect) le; (stressed, after prep) ella ♦ adj su; see also **me**, **my**

**herald** ['hɛrəld] n heraldo ♦ vt anunciar; ~ry n heráldica

**herb** [həːb] n hierba

**herd** [həːd] n rebaño

**here** [hɪəˠ] adv aquí; (at this point) en este punto; ~! (present) ¡presen-

te!; ~ is/are aquí está/están; ~ she is aquí está; ~after adv en el futuro; ~by adv (in letter) por la presente

**heredity** [hɪ'rɛdɪtɪ] n herencia

**heritage** ['hɛrɪtɪdʒ] n patrimonio

**hermit** ['həːmɪt] n ermitaño/a

**hernia** ['həːnɪə] n hernia

**hero** ['hɪərəu] (pl ~es) n héroe m; (in book, film) protagonista m; ~ic [hɪ'rəuɪk] adj heroico

**heroin** ['hɛrəuɪn] n heroína

**heroine** ['hɛrəuɪn] n heroína; (in book, film) protagonista

**heron** ['hɛrən] n garza

**herring** ['hɛrɪŋ] n arenque m

**hers** [həːz] pron (el) suyo/(la) suya etc; see also **mine**

**herself** [həːˈsɛlf] pron (reflexive) se; (emphatic) ella misma; (after prep) sí (misma); see also **oneself**

**he's** [hiːz] = he is; he has

**hesitant** ['hɛzɪtənt] adj vacilante

**hesitate** ['hɛzɪteɪt] vi vacilar; (in speech) titubear; (be unwilling) resistirse a; **hesitation** [-'teɪʃən] n indecisión f; titubeo; dudas fpl

**heterosexual** [hɛtərəu'sɛksjuəl] adj heterosexual

**hew** [hjuː] vt (stone, wood) labrar

**heyday** ['heɪdeɪ] n: the ~ of en el apogeo de

**HGV** n abbr = heavy goods vehicle

**hi** [haɪ] excl ¡hola!; (to attract attention) ¡oiga!

**hiatus** [haɪ'eɪtəs] n vacío

**hibernate** ['haɪbəneɪt] vi invernar

**hiccough** ['hɪkʌp] = **hiccup**

**hiccup** ['hɪkʌp] vi hipar; ~s npl hipo

**hide** [haɪd] (pt hid, pp hidden) n (skin) piel f ♦ vt esconder, ocultar ♦ vi: to ~ (from sb) esconderse or ocultarse (de uno); ~-and-seek n escondite m; ~away n escondrijo

**hideous** ['hɪdɪəs] adj horrible

**hiding** ['haɪdɪŋ] n (beating) paliza; to be in ~ (concealed) estar escondido

**hierarchy** ['haɪərɑːkɪ] n jerarquía

**hi-fi** ['haɪfaɪ] n estéreo, hifi m ♦ adj de alta fidelidad

**high** [haɪ] adj alto; (speed, number) grande; (price) elevado; (wind) fuerte; (voice) agudo ♦ adv alto, a gran altura; **it is 20 m** ~ tiene 20 m de altura; ~ **in the air** en las alturas; ~**brow** adj intelectual; ~**chair** n silla alta; ~**er education** n educación f or enseñanza superior; ~**handed** adj despótico; ~**heeled** de tacón alto; ~ **jump** n (SPORT) salto de altura; **the H**~**lands** npl las tierras altas de Escocia; ~**light** n (fig: of event) punto culminante; (in hair) reflejo ♦ vt subrayar; ~**ly** adv (paid) muy bien; (critical, confidential) sumamente; (a lot): **to speak/think** ~**ly of** hablar muy bien de/tener en mucho a; ~**ly strung** adj hipertenso; ~**ness** n altura; **Her** or **His H**~**ness** Su Alteza; ~**pitched** adj agudo; ~**rise block** n torre f de pisos; ~**school** n ~ Instituto Nacional de Bachillerato (SP); ~ **season** (BRIT) n temporada alta; ~ **street** (BRIT) n calle f mayor; ~**way** n carretera; (US) carretera nacional; autopista; **H**~**way Code** (BRIT) n código de la circulación

**hijack** ['haɪdʒæk] vt secuestrar; ~**er** n secuestrador(a) m/f

**hike** [haɪk] vi (go walking) ir de excursión (a pie) ♦ n caminata; ~**r** n excursionista m/f

**hilarious** [hɪ'lɛərɪəs] adj divertidísimo

**hill** [hɪl] n colina; (high) montaña; (slope) cuesta; ~**side** n ladera; ~**y** adj montañoso

**hilt** [hɪlt] n (of sword) empuñadura; **to the** ~ (fig: support) incondicionalmente

**him** [hɪm] pron (direct) le, lo; (indirect) le; (stressed, after prep) él; see also **me**; ~**self** pron (reflexive) se; (emphatic) él mismo; (after prep) sí (mismo); see also **oneself**

**hind** [haɪnd] adj posterior

**hinder** ['hɪndə*] vt estorbar, impedir; **hindrance** ['hɪndrəns] n estorbo

**hindsight** ['haɪndsaɪt] n: **with** ~ en

retrospectiva

**Hindu** ['hɪnduː] n hindú m/f

**hinge** [hɪndʒ] n bisagra, gozne m ♦ vi (fig): **to** ~ **on** depender de

**hint** [hɪnt] n indirecta; (advice) consejo; (sign) dejo ♦ vt: **to** ~ **that** insinuar que ♦ vi: **to** ~ **at** hacer alusión a

**hip** [hɪp] n cadera

**hippopotamus** [hɪpə'pɒtəməs] (pl ~es or -mi) n hipopótamo

**hire** ['haɪə*] vt (BRIT: car, equipment) alquilar; (worker) contratar ♦ n alquiler m; **for** ~ se alquila; (taxi) libre; ~ **purchase** (BRIT) n compra a plazos

**his** [hɪz] pron (el) suyo/(la) suya etc ♦ adj su; see also **my, mine**

**Hispanic** [hɪs'pænɪk] adj hispánico

**hiss** [hɪs] vi silbar

**historian** [hɪ'stɔːrɪən] n historiador(a) m/f

**historic(al)** [hɪ'stɒrɪk(l)] adj histórico

**history** ['hɪstərɪ] n historia

**hit** [hɪt] (pt, pp hit) vt (strike) golpear, pegar; (reach: target) alcanzar; (collide with: car) chocar contra; (fig: affect) afectar ♦ n golpe m; (success) éxito; **to** ~ **it off with** sb llevarse bien con uno; ~**and-run driver** n conductor(a) que atropella y huye

**hitch** [hɪtʃ] vt (fasten) atar, amarrar; (also: ~ **up**) remangar ♦ n (difficulty) dificultad f; **to** ~ **a lift** hacer autostop

**hitch-hike** vi hacer autostop; ~**r** n autostopista m/f

**hi-tech** [haɪ'tek] adj de alta tecnología

**hitherto** ['hɪðə'tuː] adv hasta ahora

**HIV** n abbr (= human immunodeficiency virus) VIH m; **HIV-negative/positive** adj VIH negativo/positivo

**hive** [haɪv] n colmena; ~ **off** (inf) vt (privatize) privatizar

**HMS** abbr = **His (Her) Majesty's Ship**

**hoard** [hɔːd] n (treasure) tesoro; (stockpile) provisión f ♦ vt acumular; (*goods in short supply*) acaparar; **~ing** *n* (*for posters*) cartelera

**hoarse** [hɔːs] *adj* ronco

**hoax** [həuks] *n* trampa

**hob** [hɔb] *n* quemador *m*

**hobble** [ˈhɔbl] *vi* cojear

**hobby** [ˈhɔbɪ] *n* pasatiempo, afición *f*; **~horse** *n* (*fig*) caballo de batalla

**hobo** [ˈhəubəu] (*US*) *n* vagabundo

**hockey** [ˈhɔkɪ] *n* hockey *m*

**hog** [hɔg] *n* cerdo, puerco ♦ *vt* (*fig*) acaparar; **to go the whole ~** poner toda la carne en el asador

**hoist** [hɔɪst] *n* (*crane*) grúa ♦ *vt* levantar, alzar; (*flag, sail*) izar

**hold** [həuld] (*pt, pp* **held**) *vt* sostener; (*contain*) contener; (*have: power, qualification*) tener; (*keep back*) retener; (*believe*) sostener; (*consider*) considerar; (*keep in position*): **to ~ one's head up** mantener la cabeza alta; (*meeting*) celebrar ♦ *vi* (*withstand pressure*) resistir; (*be valid*) valer ♦ *n* (*grasp*) asimiento; (*fig*) dominio; **~ the line!** (*TEL*) ¡no cuelgue!; **to ~ one's own** defenderse; **to catch** *or* **get (a) ~** of agarrarse *or* asirse de; **~ back** *vt* retener; (*secret*) ocultar; **~ down** *vt* (*person*) sujetar; (*job*) mantener; **~ off** *vt* (*enemy*) rechazar; **~ on** *vi* agarrarse bien; (*wait*) esperar; **~ on!** (*TEL*) ¡(espere) un momento!; **~ on to** *vt fus* agarrarse a; (*keep*) guardar; **~ out** *vt* ofrecer ♦ *vi* (*resist*) resistir; **~ up** *vt* (*raise*) levantar; (*support*) apoyar; (*delay*) retrasar; (*rob*) asaltar; **~all** (*BRIT*) *n* bolsa; **~er** *n* (*container*) receptáculo; (*of ticket, record*) poseedor/a *m/f*; (*of office, title etc*) titular *m/f*; **~ing** *n* (*share*) interés *m*; (*farmland*) parcela; **~up** *n* (*robbery*) atraco; (*delay*) retraso; (*BRIT*: *in traffic*) embotellamiento

**hole** [həul] *n* agujero ♦ *vt* agujerear

**holiday** [ˈhɔlədɪ] *n* vacaciones *fpl*; (*public*) (día *m* de) fiesta, día *m* feriado; **on ~** de vacaciones; **~ camp** *n* (*BRIT*: *also*: **~ centre**) cen-

tro de vacaciones; **~maker** (*BRIT*) *n* turista *m/f*; **~ resort** *n* centro turístico

**Holland** [ˈhɔlənd] *n* Holanda

**hollow** [ˈhɔləu] *adj* hueco; (*claim*) vacío; (*eyes*) hundido; (*sound*) sordo ♦ *n* hueco; (*in ground*) hoyo ♦ *vt*: **to ~ out** excavar

**holly** [ˈhɔlɪ] *n* acebo

**holocaust** [ˈhɔləkɔːst] *n* holocausto

**holy** [ˈhəulɪ] *adj* santo, sagrado; (*water*) bendito

**homage** [ˈhɔmɪdʒ] *n* homenaje *m*

**home** [həum] *n* casa; (*country*) patria; (*institution*) asilo ♦ *cpd* (*domestic*) casero, de casa; (*ECON, POL*) nacional ♦ *adv* (*direction*) a casa; (*right in: nail etc*) a fondo; **at ~** en casa; (*in country*) en el país; **to go/come ~** ir/volver a casa; **make yourself at ~** ¡estás en tu casa!; **~ address** *n* domicilio; **~land** *n* tierra natal; **~less** *adj* sin hogar, sin casa; **~ly** *adj* (*simple*) sencillo; **~made** *adj* casero; **H~ Office** (*BRIT*) *n* Ministerio del Interior; **~ rule** *n* autonomía; **H~ Secretary** (*BRIT*) *n* Ministro del Interior; **~sick** *adj*: **to be ~sick** tener morriña, sentir nostalgia; **~ town** *n* ciudad *f* natal; **~ward** [ˈhəumwəd] *adj* (*journey*) hacia casa; **~work** *n* deberes *mpl*

**homicide** [ˈhɔmɪsaɪd] (*US*) *n* homicidio

**homosexual** [hɔməuˈsɛksjuəl] *adj, n* homosexual *m/f*

**Honduran** [hɔnˈdjuərən] *adj, n* hondureño/a *m/f*

**Honduras** [hɔnˈdjuərəs] *n* Honduras

**honest** [ˈɔnɪst] *adj* honrado; (*sincere*) franco, sincero; **~ly** *adv* honradamente; francamente; **~y** *n* honradez *f*

**honey** [ˈhʌnɪ] *n* miel *f*; **~comb** *n* panal *m*; **~moon** *n* luna de miel; **~suckle** *n* madreselva

**honk** [hɔŋk] *vi* (*AUT*) tocar el pito, pitar

**honorary** ['ɔnərəri] adj (member, president) de honor; (title) honorífico; ~ **degree** doctorado honoris causa

**honour** ['ɔnə*] (US **honor**) vt honrar; (commitment, promise) cumplir con ♦ n honor m, honra; ~**able** adj honorable; ~**s degree** n (SCOL) título de licenciado con calificación alta

**hood** [hud] n capucha; (BRIT: AUT) capota; (US: AUT) capó m; (of cooker) campana de humos

**hoodwink** ['hudwıŋk] (BRIT) vt timar

**hoof** [hu:f] (pl **hooves**) n pezuña

**hook** [huk] n gancho; (on dress) corchete m, broche m; (for fishing) anzuelo ♦ vt enganchar; (fish) pescar

**hooligan** ['hu:lıgən] n gamberro

**hoop** [hu:p] n aro

**hooray** [hu:'reı] excl = **hurray**

**hoot** [hu:t] (BRIT) vi (AUT) tocar el pito, pitar; (siren) sonar la sirena; (owl) ulular; ~**er** (BRIT) n (AUT) pito, claxon m; (NAUT) sirena

**Hoover** ['hu:və*] ® (BRIT) n aspiradora ♦ vt **h~** pasar la aspiradora por

**hooves** [hu:vz] npl of **hoof**

**hop** [hɔp] vi saltar, brincar; (on one foot) saltar con un pie

**hope** [həup] vt, vi esperar ♦ n esperanza; **I ~ so**/**not** espero que sí/no; ~**ful** adj (person) sonar la alarma; (situation) prometedor(a); ~**fully** adv con esperanza; (one hopes): ~**fully he will recover** esperamos que se recupere; ~**less** adj desesperado; (person): **to be** ~**less** ser un desastre

**hops** [hɔps] npl lúpulo

**horde** [hɔːd] n (fig) multitud f

**horizon** [hə'raızn] n horizonte m; ~**tal** [hɔrı'zɔntl] adj horizontal

**hormone** ['hɔːməun] n hormona

**horn** [hɔːn] n cuerno; (MUS: also: French ~) trompa; (AUT) pito, claxon m

**hornet** ['hɔːnıt] n avispón m

**horny** ['hɔːnı] (inf) adj cachondo

**horoscope** ['hɔrəskəup] n horóscopo

**horrible** ['hɔrıbl] adj horrible

**horrid** ['hɔrıd] adj horrible, horroroso

**horrify** ['hɔrıfaı] vt horrorizar

**horror** ['hɔrə*] n horror m; ~ **film** n película de horror

**hors d'œuvre** [ɔː'dəːvrə] n entremeses mpl

**horse** [hɔːs] n caballo; **on** ~**back** a caballo; ~**chestnut** n (tree) castaño de Indias; (nut) castaña de Indias; ~**man/woman** n jinete/a m/f; ~**power** n caballo de (fuerza); ~**racing** n carreras fpl de caballos; ~**radish** n rábano picante; ~**shoe** n herradura

**hose** [həuz] n (also: ~**pipe**) manguera

**hosiery** ['həuzıərı] n (in shop) (sección f de) medias fpl

**hospitable** [hɔs'pıtəbl] adj hospitalario

**hospital** ['hɔspıtl] n hospital m

**hospitality** [hɔspı'tælıtı] n hospitalidad f

**host** [həust] n anfitrión m; (TV, RADIO) presentador m; (REL) hostia; (large number): **a ~ of** multitud de

**hostage** ['hɔstıdʒ] n rehén m

**hostel** ['hɔstl] n hostal m; (youth) ~ n albergue m juvenil

**hostess** ['həustıs] n anfitriona; (BRIT: air ~) azafata; (TV, RADIO) presentadora

**hostile** ['hɔstaıl] adj hostil

**hot** [hɔt] adj caliente; (weather) caluroso, de calor; (as opposed to warm) muy caliente; (spicy) picante; (fig) ardiente, acalorado; **to be ~** (person) tener calor; (object) estar caliente; (weather) hacer calor; ~**bed** n (fig) semillero; ~ **dog** n perro caliente

**hotel** [həu'tɛl] n hotel m; ~**ier** n hotelero; (manager) director m

**hot: ~headed** adj exaltado; ~**house** n invernadero; ~ **line** n (POL) teléfono rojo; ~**ly** adv con pasión, apasionadamente; ~**plate** n (on cooker) placa calentadora; ~**-water bottle** n bolsa de agua caliente

**hound** [haund] vt acosar ♦ n perro (de caza)

**hour** ['auə*] n hora; ~**ly** adj (de) cada hora

**house** [n haus, pl 'hauzɪz, vb hauz] n (gen, firm) casa; (POL) cámara; (THEATRE) sala ♦ vt (person) alojar; (collection) albergar; **on the** ~ (fig) la casa invita; ~ **arrest** n arresto m domiciliario; ~**boat** n casa flotante; ~**bound** adj confinado en casa; ~**breaking** n allanamiento de morada; ~**coat** n bata; ~**hold** n familia; (home) casa; ~**keeper** n ama de llaves; ~**keeping** n (work) trabajos mpl domésticos; ~**keeping** (**money**) n dinero para gastos domésticos; ~**warming party** n fiesta de estreno de una casa; ~**wife** n ama de casa; ~**work** n faenas fpl (de la casa)

**housing** ['hauzɪŋ] n (act) alojamiento; (houses) viviendas fpl; ~ **development** n urbanización f; ~ **estate** (BRIT) n = **development**

**hovel** ['hɔvl] n casucha

**hover** ['hɔvə*] vi flotar (en el aire); ~**craft** n aerodeslizador m

**how** [hau] adv (in what way) cómo; ~ **are you?** ¿cómo estás?; ~ **much milk/many people?** ¿cuánta leche/gente?; ~ **much does it cost?** ¿cuánto cuesta?; ~ **long have you been here?** ¿cuánto hace que estás aquí?; ~ **old are you?** ¿cuántos años tienes?; ~ **tall is he?** ¿cómo es de alto?; ~ **is school?** ¿cómo (te) va (en) la escuela?; ~ **was the film?** ¿qué tal la película?; ~ **lovely/awful!** ¡qué bonito/horror!

**howl** [haul] n aullido ♦ vi aullar; (person) dar alaridos; (wind) ulular

**H.P.** n abbr (in premonition) presentimiento; ~**back** n joroba m/f; ~**ed** adj jorobado

**h.p.** n abbr = **horse power**

**HQ** n abbr = **headquarters**

**hub** [hʌb] n (of wheel) cubo; (fig) centro

**hubbub** ['hʌbʌb] n barahúnda

**hubcap** ['hʌbkæp] n tapacubos m inv

**huddle** ['hʌdl] vi: ~ **together** acurrucarse

**hue** [hju:] n color m, matiz m; ~ **and cry** n clamor m

**huff** [hʌf] n: **in a** ~ enojado

**hug** [hʌg] vt abrazar; (thing) apretar con los brazos

**huge** [hju:dʒ] adj enorme

**hulk** [hʌlk] n (of ship) barco viejo; (person, building etc) mole f

**hull** [hʌl] n (of ship) casco

**hullo** [hə'ləu] excl = **hello**

**hum** [hʌm] vt tararear, canturrear ♦ vi tararear, canturrear; (insect) zumbar

**human** ['hju:mən] adj, n humano

**humane** [hju:'meɪn] adj humano, humanitario

**humanitarian** [hju:mænɪ'tɛərɪən] adj humanitario

**humanity** [hju:'mænɪtɪ] n humanidad f

**humble** ['hʌmbl] adj humilde ♦ vt humillar

**humbug** ['hʌmbʌg] n tonterías fpl; (BRIT: sweet) caramelo de menta

**humdrum** ['hʌmdrʌm] adj (boring) monótono, aburrido

**humid** ['hju:mɪd] adj húmedo

**humiliate** [hju:'mɪlɪeɪt] vt humillar

**humorous** ['hju:mərəs] adj gracioso, divertido

**humour** ['hju:mə*] (US **humor**) n humorismo, sentido del humor; (mood) humor m ♦ vt (person) complacer

**hump** [hʌmp] n (in ground) montículo; (camel's) giba; ~**backed** adj: ~**backed bridge** puente m (de fuerte pendiente)

**hunch** [hʌntʃ] n (premonition) presentimiento; ~**back** n joroba m/f; ~**ed** adj jorobado

**hundred** ['hʌndrəd] num ciento; (before n) cien; ~**s of** centenares de; ~**weight** n (BRIT) = 50.8 kg; 112 lb; (US) = 45.3 kg; 100 lb

**hung** [hʌŋ] pt, pp of **hang**

**Hungarian** [hʌŋ'gɛərɪən] adj, n húngaro/a m/f

**Hungary** ['hʌŋgərɪ] n Hungría

**hunger** ['hʌŋgəʳ] n hambre f ♦ vi: to ~ for (fig) tener hambre de, anhelar; ~ **strike** n huelga de hambre

**hungry** ['hʌŋgrɪ] adj: ~ (for) hambriento (de); **to be** ~ tener hambre

**hunk** [hʌŋk] n (of bread etc) trozo, pedazo

**hunt** [hʌnt] vt (seek) buscar; (SPORT) cazar ♦ vi (search): **to** ~ (for) buscar; (SPORT) cazar ♦ n búsqueda; caza, cacería; ~**er** n cazador(a) m/f; ~**ing** n caza

**hurdle** ['hɜːdl] n (SPORT) valla; (fig) obstáculo

**hurl** [hɜːl] vt lanzar, arrojar

**hurrah** [hu'rɑː] excl = **hurray**

**hurray** [hu'reɪ] excl ¡viva!

**hurricane** ['hʌrɪkən] n huracán m

**hurried** ['hʌrɪd] adj (rushed) hecho de prisa; ~**ly** adv con prisa, apresuradamente

**hurry** ['hʌrɪ] n prisa ♦ vi (also: ~ up) apresurarse, darse prisa ♦ vt (also: ~ up: person) dar prisa a; (: work) apresurar, hacer de prisa; **to be in a** ~ tener prisa

**hurt** [hɜːt] (pt, pp **hurt**) vt hacer daño a ♦ vi doler ♦ adj lastimado; ~**ful** adj (remark etc) hiriente

**hurtle** ['hɜːtl] vi: **to** ~ **past** pasar como un rayo; **to** ~ **down** ir a toda velocidad

**husband** ['hʌzbənd] n marido

**hush** [hʌʃ] n silencio ♦ vt hacer callar; ~! ¡chitón!, ¡cállate!; ~ **up** vt encubrir

**husk** [hʌsk] n (of wheat) cáscara

**husky** ['hʌskɪ] adj ronco ♦ n perro esquimal

**hustle** ['hʌsl] vt (hurry) dar prisa a ♦ n: ~ **and bustle** ajetreo

**hut** [hʌt] n cabaña; (shed) cobertizo

**hutch** [hʌtʃ] n conejera

**hyacinth** ['haɪəsɪnθ] n jacinto

**hydrant** ['haɪdrənt] n (also: fire ~) boca de incendios

**hydraulic** [haɪ'drɔːlɪk] adj hidráulico

**hydroelectric** [haɪdrəʊ'lɛktrɪk] adj hidroeléctrico

**hydrofoil** ['haɪdrəfɔɪl] n aerodeslizador m

**hydrogen** ['haɪdrədʒən] n hidrógeno

**hygiene** ['haɪdʒiːn] n higiene f; **hygienic** [-'dʒiːnɪk] adj higiénico

**hymn** [hɪm] n himno

**hype** [haɪp] (inf) n bombardeo publicitario

**hypermarket** ['haɪpəmɑːkɪt] n hipermercado

**hyphen** ['haɪfn] n guión m

**hypnotize** ['hɪpnətaɪz] vt hipnotizar

**hypochondriac** [haɪpəʊ'kɒndrɪæk] n hipocondríaco/a

**hypocrisy** [hɪ'pɒkrɪsɪ] n hipocresía

**hypocrite** ['hɪpəkrɪt] n hipócrita m/f; **hypocritical** [hɪpə'krɪtɪkl] adj hipócrita

**hypothesis** [haɪ'pɒθɪsɪs] (pl **hypotheses**) n hipótesis f inv

**hysteria** [hɪ'stɪərɪə] n histeria; **hysterical** [-'stɛrɪkl] adj histérico; (funny) para morirse de risa; **hysterics** [-'stɛrɪks] npl histeria; **to be in hysterics** (fig) morirse de risa

# I

**I** [aɪ] pron yo

**ice** [aɪs] n hielo; (~ cream) helado ♦ vt (cake) alcorzar ♦ vi (also: ~ over, ~ up) helarse; ~**berg** n iceberg m; ~**box** n (BRIT) congelador m; (US) nevera (SP), refrigeradora (AM); ~ **cream** n helado; ~ **cube** n cubito de hielo; ~**d** adj (cake) escarchado; (drink) helado; ~ **hockey** n hockey m sobre hielo

**Iceland** ['aɪslənd] n Islandia

**ice:** ~ **lolly** (BRIT) n polo; ~ **rink** n pista de hielo; ~ **skating** n patinaje m sobre hielo

**icicle** ['aɪsɪkl] n carámbano

**icing** ['aɪsɪŋ] n (CULIN) alcorza; ~ **sugar** (BRIT) n azúcar m glas(eado)

**icy** ['aɪsɪ] adj helado

**I'd** [aɪd] = I would; I had

**idea** [aɪ'dɪə] n idea

**ideal** [aɪ'dɪəl] n ideal m ♦ adj ideal;

~**ist** n idealista m/f
**identical** [aɪ'dɛntɪkl] adj idéntico
**identification** [aɪdɛntɪfɪ'keɪʃən] n identificación f; (**means of**) ~ documentos mpl personales
**identify** [aɪ'dɛntɪfaɪ] vt identificar
**Identikit** [aɪ'dɛntɪkɪt] ® n ~ (**picture**) retrato-robot m
**identity** [aɪ'dɛntɪtɪ] n identidad f; ~ **card** n carnet m de identidad
**ideology** [aɪdɪ'ɔlədʒɪ] n ideología f
**idiom** ['ɪdɪəm] n modismo; (style of speaking) lenguaje m; ~**atic** [-'mætɪk] adj idiomático
**idiosyncrasy** [ɪdɪəʊ'sɪŋkrəsɪ] n idiosincrasia
**idiot** ['ɪdɪət] n idiota m/f; ~**ic** [-'ɔtɪk] adj tonto
**idle** ['aɪdl] adj (inactive) ocioso; (lazy) holgazán/ana; (unemployed) parado, desocupado; (machinery etc) parado; (talk etc) frívolo ♦ vi (machine) marchar en vacío; ~ **away** vt: **to** ~ **away the time** malgastar el tiempo
**idol** ['aɪdl] n ídolo; ~**ize** vt idolatrar
**idyllic** [ɪ'dɪlɪk] adj idílico
**i.e.** abbr (= that is) esto es
**if** [ɪf] conj si; ~ **necessary** si fuera necesario, si hiciese falta; ~ **I were you** yo en tu lugar; ~ **so/not** de ser así/si no; ~ **only I could**! ¡ojalá pudiera!; see also **as; even**
**igloo** ['ɪɡluː] n iglú m
**ignite** [ɪɡ'naɪt] vt (set fire to) encender ♦ vi encenderse
**ignition** [ɪɡ'nɪʃən] n (AUT: process) ignición f; (AUT: mechanism) encendido; **to switch on/off the** ~ arrancar/apagar el motor; ~ **key** n (AUT) llave f de contacto
**ignorance** ['ɪɡnərəns] n ignorancia
**ignorant** ['ɪɡnərənt] adj ignorante; **to be** ~ **of** ignorar
**ignore** [ɪɡ'nɔː*] vt (person, advice) no hacer caso de; (fact) pasar por alto
**ill** [ɪl] adj enfermo, malo ♦ n mal m ♦ adv mal; **to be taken** ~ ponerse enfermo; ~**-advised** adj (decision) im-

prudente; ~**-at-ease** adj incómodo
**I'll** [aɪl] = **I will; I shall**
**illegal** [ɪ'liːɡl] adj ilegal
**illegible** [ɪ'lɛdʒɪbl] adj ilegible
**illegitimate** [ɪlɪ'dʒɪtɪmət] adj ilegítimo
**ill-fated** adj malogrado
**ill feeling** n rencor m
**illicit** [ɪ'lɪsɪt] adj ilícito
**illiterate** [ɪ'lɪtərət] adj analfabeto
**ill-mannered** adj mal educado
**illness** ['ɪlnɪs] n enfermedad f
**ill-treat** vt maltratar
**illuminate** [ɪ'luːmɪneɪt] vt (room, street) iluminar, alumbrar; **illumination** [-'neɪʃən] n alumbrado; **illuminations** npl (decorative lights) iluminaciones fpl, luces fpl
**illusion** [ɪ'luːʒən] n ilusión f; (trick) truco
**illustrate** [ɪ'lʌstreɪt] vt ilustrar
**illustration** [ɪlə'streɪʃən] n (act of illustrating) ilustración f; (example) ejemplo, ilustración f; (in book) lámina
**illustrious** [ɪ'lʌstrɪəs] adj ilustre
**ill will** n rencor m
**I'm** [aɪm] = **I am**
**image** ['ɪmɪdʒ] n imagen f; ~**ry** [-ərɪ] n imágenes fpl
**imaginary** [ɪ'mædʒɪnərɪ] adj imaginario
**imagination** [ɪmædʒɪ'neɪʃən] n imaginación f; (inventiveness) inventiva
**imaginative** [ɪ'mædʒɪnətɪv] adj imaginativo
**imagine** [ɪ'mædʒɪn] vt imaginarse
**imbalance** [ɪm'bæləns] n desequilibrio
**imbecile** ['ɪmbəsiːl] n imbécil m/f
**imitate** ['ɪmɪteɪt] vt imitar; **imitation** [-'teɪʃən] n imitación f; (copy) copia
**immaculate** [ɪ'mækjulət] adj inmaculado
**immaterial** [ɪmə'tɪərɪəl] adj (unimportant) sin importancia
**immature** [ɪmə'tjuə*] adj (person) inmaduro
**immediate** [ɪ'miːdɪət] adj inmedia-

to; (pressing) urgente, apremiante; (nearest: family) próximo; (: neighbourhood) inmediato; **~ly** adv (at once) en seguida; (directly) inmediatamente; **~ly next** to muy junto a

**immense** [ɪ'mɛns] adj inmenso, enorme; (importance) enorme

**immerse** [ɪ'məːs] vt (submerge) sumergir; **to be ~d in** (fig) estar absorto en

**immersion heater** [ɪ'məːʃən] n (BRIT) n calentador m de inmersión

**immigrant** ['ɪmɪgrənt] n inmigrante m/f; **immigration** [ɪmɪ'greɪʃən] n inmigración f

**imminent** ['ɪmɪnənt] adj inminente

**immobile** [ɪ'məubaɪl] adj inmóvil

**immoral** [ɪ'mɔrl] adj inmoral

**immortal** [ɪ'mɔːtl] adj inmortal

**immune** [ɪ'mjuːn] adj: **~ (to)** inmune (a); **immunity** n (MED, of diplomat) inmunidad f

**immunize** ['ɪmjunaɪz] vt inmunizar

**imp** [ɪmp] n diablillo; (child) pícaro

**impact** ['ɪmpækt] n impacto

**impair** [ɪm'pɛə*] vt perjudicar

**impale** [ɪm'peɪl] vt empalar

**impart** [ɪm'pɑːt] vt comunicar; (flavour) proporcionar

**impartial** [ɪm'pɑːʃl] adj imparcial

**impassable** [ɪm'pɑːsəbl] adj (barrier) infranqueable; (river, road) intransitable

**impasse** [æm'pɑːs] n punto muerto

**impassive** [ɪm'pæsɪv] adj impasible

**impatience** [ɪm'peɪʃəns] n impaciencia

**impatient** [ɪm'peɪʃənt] adj impaciente; **to get** or **grow ~** impacientarse

**impeccable** [ɪm'pɛkəbl] adj impecable

**impede** [ɪm'piːd] vt estorbar

**impediment** [ɪm'pɛdɪmənt] n obstáculo, estorbo; (also: speech ~) defecto (del habla)

**impending** [ɪm'pɛndɪŋ] adj inminente

**impenetrable** [ɪm'pɛnɪtrəbl] adj impenetrable; (fig) insondable

**imperative** [ɪm'pɛrətɪv] adj (tone)

imperioso; (need) imprescindible ♦ n (LING) imperativo

**imperfect** [ɪm'pəːfɪkt] adj (goods etc) defectuoso ♦ n (LING: also: ~ tense) imperfecto; **~ion** [-'fɛkʃən] n (blemish) desperfecto; (fault) defecto

**imperial** [ɪm'pɪərɪəl] adj imperial; **~ism** n imperialismo

**impersonal** [ɪm'pəːsənl] adj impersonal

**impersonate** [ɪm'pəːsəneɪt] vt hacerse pasar por; (THEATRE) imitar

**impertinent** [ɪm'pəːtɪnənt] adj impertinente, insolente

**impervious** [ɪm'pəːvɪəs] adj impermeable; (fig): **~ to** insensible a

**impetuous** [ɪm'pɛtjuəs] adj impetuoso

**impetus** ['ɪmpətəs] n ímpetu m; (fig) impulso

**impinge** [ɪm'pɪndʒ]: **to ~ on** vt fus (affect) afectar a

**implacable** [ɪm'plækəbl] adj implacable

**implement** [n 'ɪmplɪmənt, vb 'ɪmplɪmɛnt] n herramienta; (for cooking) utensilio ♦ vt (regulation) hacer efectivo; (plan) realizar

**implicate** ['ɪmplɪkeɪt] vt (in crime etc) involucrar; **implication** [-'keɪʃən] n consecuencia; (involvement) implicación f

**implicit** [ɪm'plɪsɪt] adj implícito; (belief, trust) absoluto

**implore** [ɪm'plɔː*] vt (person) suplicar

**imply** [ɪm'plaɪ] vt (involve) suponer; (hint) dar a entender que

**impolite** [ɪmpə'laɪt] adj mal educado

**import** [vb ɪm'pɔːt, n 'ɪmpɔːt] vt importar ♦ n (COMM) importación f; (: article) producto importado; (meaning) significado, sentido

**importance** [ɪm'pɔːtəns] n importancia

**important** [ɪm'pɔːtənt] adj importante; **it's not ~** no importa, no tiene importancia

**importer** [ɪm'pɔːtə*] n importador(a) m/f

**impose** [ɪm'pəuz] *vt* imponer ♦ *vi*:
to ~ on sb abusar de uno; **imposing**
*adj* imponente, impresionante

**imposition** [ɪmpə'zɪʃn] *n* (*of tax
etc*) imposición *f*; **to be an ~ on**
(*person*) molestar a

**impossible** [ɪm'pɒsɪbl] *adj* imposible; (*person*) insoportable

**impostor** [ɪm'pɒstə*] *n* impostor/a
*m/f*

**impotent** ['ɪmpətənt] *adj* impotente

**impound** [ɪm'paund] *vt* embargar

**impoverished** [ɪm'pɒvərɪʃt] *adj* necesitado

**impracticable** [ɪm'præktɪkəbl] *adj*
no factible, irrealizable

**impractical** [ɪm'præktɪkl] *adj* (*person, plan*) poco práctico

**imprecise** [ɪmprɪ'saɪs] *adj* impreciso

**impregnable** [ɪm'prɛgnəbl] *adj*
(*castle*) inexpugnable

**impregnate** ['ɪmprɛgneɪt] *vt* (*saturate*) impregnar

**impress** [ɪm'prɛs] *vt* impresionar;
(*mark*) estampar; **to ~ sth on sb**
hacer entender algo a uno

**impression** [ɪm'prɛʃən] *n* impresión
*f*; (*imitation*) imitación *f*; **to be
under the ~ that** tener la
impresión de que; **~able** *adj*
impresionable; **~ist** *n* impresionista
*m/f*

**impressive** [ɪm'prɛsɪv] *adj* impresionante

**imprint** ['ɪmprɪnt] *n* (*outline*) huella;
(*PUBLISHING*) pie *m* de impren-
ta

**imprison** [ɪm'prɪzn] *vt* encarcelar;
**~ment** *n* encarcelamiento; (*term of
~ment*) cárcel *f*

**improbable** [ɪm'prɒbəbl] *adj* improbable, inverosímil

**impromptu** [ɪm'prɒmptju:] *adj* improvisado

**improper** [ɪm'prɒpə*] *adj* (*unsuitable: conduct etc*) incorrecto; (: *activities*) deshonesto

**improve** [ɪm'pru:v] *vt* mejorar; (*foreign language*) perfeccionar ♦ *vi* mejorarse; **~ment** *n* mejoramiento;

perfección *f*; progreso

**improvise** ['ɪmprəvaɪz] *vt, vi* improvisar

**impudent** ['ɪmpjudnt] *adj* descarado,
insolente

**impulse** ['ɪmpʌls] *n* impulso; **to act
on ~** obrar sin reflexión; **impulsive**
[-'pʌlsɪv] *adj* irreflexivo

**impunity** [ɪm'pju:nɪtɪ] *n*: **with ~** impunemente

**impure** [ɪm'pjuə*] *adj* (*adulterated*)
adulterado; (*morally*) impuro; **impurity** *n* impureza

─── KEYWORD ───

**in** [ɪn] *prep* **1** (*indicating place, position, with place names*) en; **~ the
house/garden** en (la) casa/el jardín;
**~ here/there** aquí/ahí *or* allí dentro;
**~ London/England** en Londres/
Inglaterra

**2** (*indicating time*) en; **~ spring** en
(la) primavera; **~ the afternoon**
por la tarde; **at 4 o'clock ~ the
afternoon** a las 4 de la tarde; **I did
it ~ 3 hours/days** lo hice en 3
horas/días; **I'll see you ~ 2 weeks
or ~ 2 weeks' time** te veré dentro
de 2 semanas

**3** (*indicating manner etc*) en; **~ a
loud/soft voice** en voz alta/baja; **~
pencil/ink** a lápiz/bolígrafo; **the boy
~ the blue shirt** el chico de la camisa azul

**4** (*indicating circumstances*): **~ the
sun/shade/rain** al sol/a la sombra/
bajo la lluvia; **a change ~ policy**
un cambio de política

**5** (*indicating mood, state*): **~ tears**
en lágrimas, llorando; **~ anger/
despair** enfadado/desesperado; **to
live ~ luxury** vivir lujosamente

**6** (*with ratios, numbers*): **1 ~ 10
households, 1 household ~ 10** una
de cada 10 familias; **20 pence ~ the
pound** 20 peniques por libra; **they
lined up ~ twos** se alinearon de dos
en dos

**7** (*referring to people, works*) en; entre; **the disease is common ~**

**children** la enfermedad es común entre los niños; ~ **(the works of) Dickens** en (las obras de) Dickens
**8** (indicating profession etc): to be ~ **teaching** estar en la enseñanza
**9** (after superlative) de; **the best pupil ~ the class** el/la mejor alumno/a de la clase
**10** (with present participle): ~ **saying this** al decir esto
♦ adv: to be ~ (person: at home) estar en casa; (work) estar; (train, ship, plane) haber llegado; (in fashion) estar de moda; **she'll be ~ later today** llegará más tarde hoy; **to ask sb ~** hacer pasar a uno; **to run/limp** etc ~ entrar corriendo/cojeando etc
♦ npl: **the ~s and outs** (of proposal, situation etc) los detalles

**in.** abbr = **inch**
**inability** [ɪnəˈbɪlɪtɪ] n: ~ (to do) incapacidad f (de hacer)
**inaccessible** [ɪnəkˈsesɪbl] adj (also fig) inaccesible
**inaccurate** [ɪnˈækjʊrɪt] adj inexacto, incorrecto
**inactivity** [ɪnækˈtɪvɪtɪ] n inactividad f
**inadequate** [ɪnˈædɪkwət] adj (income, reply etc) insuficiente; (person) incapaz
**inadvertently** [ɪnədˈvəːtntlɪ] adv por descuido
**inadvisable** [ɪnədˈvaɪzəbl] adj poco aconsejable
**inane** [ɪˈneɪn] adj necio, fatuo
**inanimate** [ɪnˈænɪmət] adj inanimado
**inappropriate** [ɪnəˈprəʊprɪət] adj inadecuado; (improper) poco oportuno
**inarticulate** [ɪnɑːˈtɪkjʊlət] adj (person) incapaz de expresarse; (speech) mal pronunciado
**inasmuch as** [ɪnəzˈmʌtʃ-] conj puesto que, ya que
**inaudible** [ɪnˈɔːdɪbl] adj inaudible
**inaugurate** [ɪˈnɔːgjʊreɪt] vt inaugurar; **inauguration** [-ˈreɪʃən] n cere-

monia de apertura
**inborn** [ɪnˈbɔːn] adj (quality) innato
**inbred** [ɪnˈbred] adj innato; (family) engendrado por endogamia
**Inc.** abbr (US: = incorporated) S.A.
**incapable** [ɪnˈkeɪpəbl] adj incapaz
**incapacitate** [ɪnkəˈpæsɪteɪt] vt: to ~ **sb** incapacitar a uno
**incarcerate** [ɪnˈkɑːsəreɪt] vt encarcelar
**incarnation** [ɪnkɑːˈneɪʃən] n encarnación f
**incendiary** [ɪnˈsendɪərɪ] adj incendiario
**incense** [n ˈɪnsens, vb ɪnˈsens] n incienso ♦ vt (anger) indignar, encolerizar
**incentive** [ɪnˈsentɪv] n incentivo, estímulo
**incessant** [ɪnˈsesnt] adj incesante, continuo; **~ly** adv constantemente
**incest** [ˈɪnsest] n incesto
**inch** [ɪntʃ] n pulgada; **to be within an ~ of** estar a dos dedos de; **he didn't give an ~** no dio concesión alguna; **~ forward** vi avanzar palmo a palmo
**incidence** [ˈɪnsɪdns] n (of crime, disease) incidencia
**incident** [ˈɪnsɪdnt] n incidente m
**incidental** [ɪnsɪˈdentl] adj accesorio; **~ to** relacionado con; **~ly** [-ˈdentlɪ] adv (by the way) a propósito
**incinerator** [ɪnˈsɪnəreɪtə*] n incinerador m
**incisive** [ɪnˈsaɪsɪv] adj (remark etc) incisivo
**incite** [ɪnˈsaɪt] vt provocar
**inclination** [ɪnklɪˈneɪʃən] n (tendency) tendencia, inclinación f; (desire) deseo; (disposition) propensión f
**incline** [n ˈɪnklaɪn, vb ɪnˈklaɪn] n pendiente m, cuesta ♦ vt (head) poner de lado ♦ vi inclinarse; **to be ~d to** (tend) ser propenso a
**include** [ɪnˈkluːd] vt (incorporate) incluir; (in letter) adjuntar; **including** prep incluso, incluído
**inclusion** [ɪnˈkluːʒən] n inclusión f
**inclusive** [ɪnˈkluːsɪv] adj inclusivo; ~

of tax incluidos los impuestos

**incognito** [ɪnkɒgˈniːtəu] *adv* de incógnito

**incoherent** [ɪnkəuˈhɪərənt] *adj* incoherente

**income** [ˈɪŋkʌm] *n* (*earned*) ingresos *mpl*; (*from property etc*) renta; (*from investment etc*) rédito; ~ **tax** *n* impuesto sobre la renta

**incoming** [ˈɪnkʌmɪŋ] *adj* (*flight, government etc*) entrante

**incomparable** [ɪnˈkɒmpərəbl] *adj* incomparable, sin par

**incompatible** [ɪnkəmˈpætɪbl] *adj* incompatible

**incompetent** [ɪnˈkɒmpɪtənt] *adj* incompetente

**incomplete** [ɪnkəmˈpliːt] *adj* (*partial: achievement etc*) incompleto; (*unfinished: painting etc*) inacabado

**incomprehensible** [ɪnkɒmprɪˈhensɪbl] *adj* incomprensible

**inconceivable** [ɪnkənˈsiːvəbl] *adj* inconcebible

**incongruous** [ɪnˈkɒŋgruəs] *adj* (*strange*) discordante; (*inappropriate*) incongruente

**inconsiderate** [ɪnkənˈsɪdərət] *adj* desconsiderado

**inconsistent** [ɪnkənˈsɪstnt] *adj* inconsecuente; (*contradictory*) incongruente; ~ **with** (que) no concuerda con

**inconspicuous** [ɪnkənˈspɪkjuəs] *adj* (*colour, building etc*) discreto; (*person*) que llama poco la atención

**inconvenience** [ɪnkənˈviːnjəns] *n* inconvenientes *mpl*; (*trouble*) molestia, incomodidad ♦ *vt* incomodar

**inconvenient** [ɪnkənˈviːnjənt] *adj* incómodo, poco práctico; (*time, place, visitor*) inoportuno

**incorporate** [ɪnˈkɔːpəreɪt] *vt* incorporar; (*contain*) comprender; (*add*) agregar; ~**d** *adj*: ~**d company** (*US*) ≈ sociedad *f* anónima

**incorrect** [ɪnkəˈrekt] *adj* incorrecto

**incorrigible** [ɪnˈkɒrɪdʒəbl] *adj* incorregible

**incorruptible** [ɪnkəˈrʌptɪbl] *adj* inso-

---

bornable

**increase** [*n* ˈɪnkriːs, *vb* ɪnˈkriːs] *n* aumento ♦ *vi* aumentar; (*grow*) crecer; (*price*) subir ♦ *vt* aumentar; (*price*) subir; **increasing** *adj* creciente; **increasingly** *adv* cada vez más, más y más

**incredible** [ɪnˈkredɪbl] *adj* increíble

**incredulous** [ɪnˈkredjuləs] *adj* incrédulo

**incriminate** [ɪnˈkrɪmɪneɪt] *vt* incriminar

**incubator** [ˈɪnkjubeɪtə*] *n* incubadora

**incumbent** [ɪnˈkʌmbənt] *n* titular *m/f* ♦ *adj*: **it is ~ on him to...** le incumbe...

**incur** [ɪnˈkə:*] *vt* (*expenditure*) incurrir; (*loss*) sufrir; (*anger, disapproval*) provocar

**incurable** [ɪnˈkjuərəbl] *adj* incurable

**indebted** [ɪnˈdetɪd] *adj*: **to be ~ to sb** estar agradecido a uno

**indecent** [ɪnˈdiːsnt] *adj* indecente; ~ **assault** (*BRIT*) *n* atentado contra el pudor; ~ **exposure** *n* exhibicionismo

**indecisive** [ɪndɪˈsaɪsɪv] *adj* indeciso

**indeed** [ɪnˈdiːd] *adv* efectivamente, en realidad; (*in fact*) en efecto; (*furthermore*) es más; **yes ~!** ¡claro que sí!

**indefinitely** [ɪnˈdefɪnɪtlɪ] *adv* (*wait*) indefinidamente

**indelible** [ɪnˈdelɪbl] *adj* imborrable

**indemnity** [ɪnˈdemnɪtɪ] *n* (*insurance*) indemnidad *f*; (*compensation*) indemnización *f*

**independence** [ɪndɪˈpendns] *n* independencia

**independent** [ɪndɪˈpendənt] *adj* independiente

**indestructible** [ɪndɪsˈtrʌktəbl] *adj* indestructible

**index** [ˈɪndeks] (*pl* ~**es**) *n* (*in book*) índice *m*; (: *in library etc*) catálogo; (*pl* **indices**: *ratio, sign*) exponente *m*; ~ **card** *n* ficha; ~**ed** (*US*) *adj* = ~-**linked**; ~ **finger** *n* índice *m*; ~-**linked** (*BRIT*) *adj* vinculado al índice del coste de la vida

**India** ['ɪndɪə] n la India; ~n adj, n indio/a m/f; **Red** ~n piel roja m/f; ~n **Ocean** n: the ~n **Ocean** el Océano Índico

**indicate** ['ɪndɪkeɪt] vt indicar; **indication** [-'keɪʃən] n indicio, señal f; **indicative** [ɪn'dɪkətɪv] adj: to be indicative of indicar ♦ n (LING) indicativo; **indicator** n indicador m; (AUT) intermitente m

**indices** ['ɪndɪsiːz] npl of **index**

**indictment** [ɪn'daɪtmənt] n acusación f

**indifference** [ɪn'dɪfrəns] n indiferencia

**indifferent** [ɪn'dɪfrənt] adj indiferente; (mediocre) regular

**indigenous** [ɪn'dɪdʒɪnəs] adj indígena

**indigestion** [ɪndɪ'dʒestʃən] n indigestión f

**indignant** [ɪn'dɪgnənt] adj: to be ~ at sth/with sb indignarse por algo/con uno

**indigo** ['ɪndɪgəu] adj de color añil ♦ n añil m

**indirect** [ɪndɪ'rekt] adj indirecto; ~ly adv indirectamente

**indiscreet** [ɪndɪ'skriːt] adj indiscreto, imprudente

**indiscriminate** [ɪndɪ'skrɪmɪnət] adj indiscriminado

**indispensable** [ɪndɪ'spensəbl] adj indispensable, imprescindible

**indisposed** [ɪndɪ'spəuzd] adj (unwell) indispuesto

**indisputable** [ɪndɪ'spjuːtəbl] adj incontestable

**indistinct** [ɪndɪ'stɪŋkt] adj (noise, memory etc) confuso

**individual** [ɪndɪ'vɪdjuəl] n individuo ♦ adj individual; (personal) personal; (particular) particular; ~ist n individualista m/f; ~ly adv (singly) individualmente

**indoctrinate** [ɪn'dɔktrɪneɪt] vt adoctrinar

**indolent** ['ɪndələnt] adj indolente, perezoso

**indoor** ['ɪndɔː*] adj (swimming pool)

cubierto; (plant) de interior; (sport) bajo cubierta; ~s [ɪn'dɔːz] adv dentro

**induce** [ɪn'djuːs] vt inducir, persuadir; (bring about) producir; (birth) provocar; ~ment n (incentive) incentivo; (pej: bribe) soborno

**indulge** [ɪn'dʌldʒ] vt (whim) satisfacer; (person) complacer; (child) mimar ♦ vi: to ~ in darse el gusto de; ~nce n vicio; (leniency) indulgencia; ~nt adj indulgente

**industrial** [ɪn'dʌstrɪəl] adj industrial; ~ **action** n huelga; ~ **estate** (BRIT) n polígono (SP) o zona (AM) industrial; ~**ist** n industrial m/f; ~**ize** vt industrializar; ~ **park** (US) n = ~ **estate**

**industrious** [ɪn'dʌstrɪəs] adj trabajador(a); (student) aplicado

**industry** ['ɪndəstrɪ] n industria; (diligence) aplicación f

**inebriated** [ɪn'iːbrɪeɪtɪd] adj borracho

**inedible** [ɪn'edɪbl] adj incomible; (poisonous) no comestible

**ineffective** [ɪnɪ'fektɪv] adj ineficaz, inútil

**ineffectual** [ɪnɪ'fektjuəl] adj = ineffective

**inefficiency** [ɪnɪ'fɪʃənsɪ] n ineficacia

**inefficient** [ɪnɪ'fɪʃənt] adj ineficaz, ineficiente

**inept** [ɪ'nept] adj incompetente

**inequality** [ɪnɪ'kwɔlɪtɪ] n desigualdad f

**inert** [ɪ'nɜːt] adj inerte, inactivo; (immobile) inmóvil; ~**ia** [ɪ'nɜːʃə] n inercia; (laziness) pereza

**inescapable** [ɪnɪ'skeɪpəbl] adj ineludible

**inevitable** [ɪn'evɪtəbl] adj inevitable; **inevitably** adv inevitablemente

**inexcusable** [ɪnɪks'kjuːzəbl] adj imperdonable

**inexhaustible** [ɪnɪg'zɔːstɪbl] adj inagotable

**inexpensive** [ɪnɪk'spensɪv] adj económico

**inexperience** [ɪnɪk'spɪərɪəns] n falta

de experiencia; **~d** adj inexperto
**inextricably** [ɪnɪksˈtrɪkəblɪ] adv indisolublemente
**infallible** [ɪnˈfælɪbl] adj infalible
**infamous** [ˈɪnfəməs] adj infame
**infancy** [ˈɪnfənsɪ] n infancia
**infant** [ˈɪnfənt] n niño/a; (baby) niño pequeño, bebé m; **~ile** adj infantil; (pej) aniñado; **~ school** (BRIT) n parvulario
**infantry** [ˈɪnfəntrɪ] n infantería
**infatuated** [ɪnˈfætjueɪtɪd] adj: **~ with** (in love) loco por
**infatuation** [ɪnfætjuˈeɪʃən] n enamoramiento, pasión f
**infect** [ɪnˈfɛkt] vt (wound) infectar; (food) contaminar; (person, animal) contagiar; **~ion** [ɪnˈfɛkʃən] n infección f; (fig) contagio; **~ious** [ɪnˈfɛkʃəs] adj (also fig) contagioso
**infer** [ɪnˈfɜː*] vt deducir, inferir; **~ence** [ˈɪnfərəns] n deducción f, inferencia
**inferior** [ɪnˈfɪərɪə*] adj, n inferior m/f; **~ity** [-rɪˈɒrətɪ] n inferioridad f; **~ity complex** n complejo de inferioridad
**inferno** [ɪnˈfɜːnəu] n (fire) hoguera
**infertile** [ɪnˈfɜːtaɪl] adj estéril; (person) infecundo; **infertility** [-ˈtɪlɪtɪ] n esterilidad f, infecundidad f
**infested** [ɪnˈfɛstɪd] adj: **~ with** plagado de
**in-fighting** n (fig) lucha(s) f(pl) interna(s)
**infiltrate** [ˈɪnfɪltreɪt] vt infiltrar en
**infinite** [ˈɪnfɪnɪt] adj infinito
**infinitive** [ɪnˈfɪnɪtɪv] n infinitivo
**infinity** [ɪnˈfɪnɪtɪ] n infinito; (an ~) infinidad f
**infirm** [ɪnˈfɜːm] adj enfermo, débil; **~ary** n hospital m; **~ity** n debilidad f; (illness) enfermedad f, achaque m
**inflamed** [ɪnˈfleɪmd] adj: **to become ~** inflamarse
**inflammable** [ɪnˈflæməbl] adj inflamable
**inflammation** [ɪnfləˈmeɪʃən] n inflamación f
**inflatable** [ɪnˈfleɪtəbl] adj (ball,

boat) inflable
**inflate** [ɪnˈfleɪt] vt (tyre, price etc) inflar; (fig) hinchar; **inflation** [ɪnˈfleɪʃən] n (ECON) inflación f
**inflexible** [ɪnˈflɛksəbl] adj (rule) rígido; (person) inflexible
**inflict** [ɪnˈflɪkt] vt: **to ~ sth on sb** infligir algo en uno
**influence** [ˈɪnfluəns] n influencia ♦ vt influir en, influenciar; **under the ~ of alcohol** en estado de embriaguez; **influential** [-ˈɛnʃl] adj influyente
**influenza** [ɪnfluˈɛnzə] n gripe f
**influx** [ˈɪnflʌks] n afluencia
**inform** [ɪnˈfɔːm] vt: **to ~ sb of sth** informar a uno sobre or de algo ♦ vi: **to ~ on sb** delatar a uno
**informal** [ɪnˈfɔːml] adj (manner, tone) familiar; (dress, interview, occasion) informal; (visit, meeting) extraoficial; **~ity** [-ˈmælɪtɪ] n informalidad f; sencillez f
**informant** [ɪnˈfɔːmənt] n informante m/f
**information** [ɪnfəˈmeɪʃən] n información f; (knowledge) conocimientos mpl; **a piece of ~** un dato; **~ office** n información f
**informative** [ɪnˈfɔːmətɪv] adj informativo
**informer** [ɪnˈfɔːmə*] n (also: police **~**) soplón/ona m/f
**infra-red** [ɪnfrəˈrɛd] adj infrarrojo
**infrastructure** [ˈɪnfrəstrʌktʃə*] n (of system etc) infraestructura
**infringe** [ɪnˈfrɪndʒ] vt infringir, violar ♦ vi: **to ~ on** abusar de; **~ment** n infracción f; (of rights) usurpación f
**infuriating** [ɪnˈfjuərɪeɪtɪŋ] adj (habit, noise) enloquecedor/a
**ingenious** [ɪnˈdʒiːnjəs] adj ingenioso; **ingenuity** [-dʒɪˈnjuːɪtɪ] n ingeniosidad f
**ingenuous** [ɪnˈdʒɛnjuəs] adj ingenuo
**ingot** [ˈɪŋɡət] n lingote m, barra
**ingrained** [ɪnˈɡreɪnd] adj arraigado
**ingratiate** [ɪnˈɡreɪʃɪeɪt] vt: **to ~ o.s. with** congraciarse con

**ingredient** [ɪn'griːdɪənt] n ingrediente m

**inhabit** [ɪn'hæbɪt] vt vivir en; ~**ant** n habitante m/f

**inhale** [ɪn'heɪl] vt inhalar ♦ vi (breathe in) aspirar; (in smoking) tragar

**inherent** [ɪn'hɪərənt] adj: ~ **in** or **to** inherente a

**inherit** [ɪn'herɪt] vt heredar; ~**ance** n herencia; (fig) patrimonio

**inhibit** [ɪn'hɪbɪt] vt inhibir, impedir; ~**ed** adj (PSYCH) cohibido; ~**ion** [-'bɪʃən] n cohibición f

**inhospitable** [ɪnhɒs'pɪtəbl] adj (person) inhospitalario; (place) inhóspito

**inhuman** [ɪn'hjuːmən] adj inhumano

**iniquity** [ɪ'nɪkwɪtɪ] n iniquidad f; (injustice) injusticia

**initial** [ɪ'nɪʃl] adj primero ♦ n inicial f ♦ vt firmar con las iniciales; ~**s** npl (as signature) iniciales fpl; (abbreviation) siglas fpl; ~**ly** adv al principio

**initiate** [ɪ'nɪʃɪeɪt] vt iniciar; **to ~ proceedings against sb** (LAW) entablar proceso contra uno; **initiation** [-'eɪʃən] n (into secret etc) iniciación f; (beginning) comienzo

**initiative** [ɪ'nɪʃɪətɪv] n iniciativa

**inject** [ɪn'dʒekt] vt inyectar; **to ~ sb with sth** inyectar algo a uno; ~**ion** [ɪn'dʒekʃən] n inyección f

**injunction** [ɪn'dʒʌŋkʃən] n interdicto

**injure** ['ɪndʒə*] vt (hurt) herir, lastimar; (fig: reputation etc) perjudicar; ~**d** adj (person, arm) herido, lastimado; **injury** n herida, lesión f; (wrong) perjuicio, daño; **injury time** n (SPORT) (tiempo de) descuento

**injustice** [ɪn'dʒʌstɪs] n injusticia

**ink** [ɪŋk] n tinta

**inkling** ['ɪŋklɪŋ] n sospecha; (idea) idea

**inlaid** ['ɪnleɪd] adj (with wood, gems etc) incrustado

**inland** [adj 'ɪnlænd, adv ɪn'lænd] adj (waterway, port etc) interior ♦ adv tierra adentro; **I~ Revenue** (BRIT) n departamento de impuestos; ≈ Ha-

cienda (SP)

**in-laws** npl suegros mpl

**inlet** ['ɪnlet] n (GEO) ensenada, cala; (TECH) admisión f, entrada

**inmate** ['ɪnmeɪt] n (in prison) preso/a; presidiario/a; (in asylum) internado/a

**inn** [ɪn] n posada, mesón m

**innate** [ɪ'neɪt] adj innato

**inner** ['ɪnə*] adj (courtyard, calm) interior; (feelings) íntimo; ~ **city** n barrios deprimidos del centro de una ciudad; ~ **tube** n (of tyre) cámara (SP) or llanta (AM)

**innings** ['ɪnɪŋz] n (CRICKET) entrada, turno

**innocence** ['ɪnəsns] n inocencia

**innocent** ['ɪnəsnt] adj inocente

**innocuous** [ɪ'nɒkjuəs] adj inocuo

**innovation** [ɪnəu'veɪʃən] n novedad f

**innuendo** [ɪnju'endəu] (pl ~es) n indirecta

**inoculation** [ɪnɒkju'leɪʃən] n inoculación f

**inopportune** [ɪn'ɒpətjuːn] adj inoportuno

**inordinately** [ɪ'nɔːdɪnɪtlɪ] adv desmesuradamente

**in-patient** n paciente m/f interno/a

**input** ['ɪnput] n entrada; (of resources) inversión f; (COMPUT) entrada de datos

**inquest** ['ɪnkwest] n (coroner's) encuesta judicial

**inquire** [ɪn'kwaɪə*] vi preguntar ♦ vt: **to ~ whether** preguntar si; **to ~ about** (person) preguntar por; (fact) informarse de; ~ **into** vt fus investigar, indagar; **inquiry** n pregunta; (investigation) investigación f, pesquisa; **inquiry office** (BRIT) n oficina de información

**inquisitive** [ɪn'kwɪzɪtɪv] adj (curious) curioso

**inroads** ['ɪnrəudz] npl: **to make ~ into** mermar

**ins** abbr = **inches**

**insane** [ɪn'seɪn] adj loco; (MED) demente

**insanity** [ɪn'sænɪtɪ] n demencia, locu-

ra
**insatiable** [ɪn'seɪʃəbl] *adj* insaciable
**inscription** [ɪn'skrɪpʃən] *n* inscripción *f*; (*in book*) dedicatoria
**inscrutable** [ɪn'skru:təbl] *adj* inescrutable, insondable
**insect** ['ɪnsɛkt] *n* insecto; ~**icide** [ɪn'sɛktɪsaɪd] *n* insecticida *m*
**insecure** [ɪnsɪ'kjuə*] *adj* inseguro
**insemination** [ɪnsɛmɪ'neɪʃn] *n*: **artificial ~** inseminación *f* artificial
**insensitive** [ɪn'sɛnsɪtɪv] *adj* insensible
**inseparable** [ɪn'sɛprəbl] *adj* inseparable
**insert** [*vb* ɪn'sɜːt, *n* 'ɪnsɜːt] *vt* (*into sth*) introducir ♦ *n* encarte *m*; ~**ion** [ɪn'sɜːʃən] *n* inserción *f*
**in-service** *adj* (*training, course*) a cargo de la empresa
**inshore** [ɪn'fɔː*] *adj* de bajura ♦ *adv* (*be*) cerca de la orilla; (*move*) hacia la orilla
**inside** ['ɪn'saɪd] *n* interior *m* ♦ *adj* interior, interno ♦ *adv* (*be*) (por) dentro; (*with haste*) hacia dentro ♦ *prep* dentro de; (*of time*): **~ 10 minutes** en menos de 10 minutos; ~**s** *npl* (*inf: stomach*) tripas *fpl*; ~ **information** *n* información *f* confidencial; ~ **lane** *n* (AUT: *in Britain*) carril *m* izquierdo; (AUT: *in US, Europe etc*) carril *m* derecho; ~ **out** (*turn*) al revés; (*know*) a fondo
**insider dealing, insider trading** *n* (STOCK EXCHANGE) abuso de información privilegiada
**insidious** [ɪn'sɪdɪəs] *adj* insidioso
**insight** ['ɪnsaɪt] *n* perspicacia
**insignia** [ɪn'sɪgnɪə] *npl* insignias *fpl*
**insignificant** [ɪnsɪg'nɪfɪkənt] *adj* insignificante
**insincere** [ɪnsɪn'sɪə*] *adj* poco sincero
**insinuate** [ɪn'sɪnjʊeɪt] *vt* insinuar
**insipid** [ɪn'sɪpɪd] *adj* soso, insulso
**insist** [ɪn'sɪst] *vi* insistir; **to ~ on** insistir en; **to ~ that** insistir en que; (*claim*) exigir que; ~**ence** *n* (*determination*) empeño; ~**ent** *adj* insis-

tente; (*noise, action*) persistente
**insole** ['ɪnsəʊl] *n* plantilla
**insolent** ['ɪnsələnt] *adj* insolente, descarado
**insoluble** [ɪn'sɒljʊbl] *adj* insoluble
**insomnia** [ɪn'sɒmnɪə] *n* insomnio
**inspect** [ɪn'spɛkt] *vt* inspeccionar, examinar; (*troops*) pasar revista a; ~**ion** [ɪn'spɛkʃən] *n* inspección *f*, examen *m*; (*of troops*) revista; ~**or** *n* inspector(a) *m/f*; (BRIT: *on buses, trains*) revisor(a) *m/f*
**inspiration** [ɪnspə'reɪʃən] *n* inspiración *f*; **inspire** [ɪn'spaɪə*] *vt* inspirar
**instability** [ɪnstə'bɪlɪtɪ] *n* inestabilidad *f*
**install** [ɪn'stɔːl] *vt* instalar; (*official*) nombrar; ~**ation** [ɪnstə'leɪʃən] *n* instalación *f*
**instalment** [ɪn'stɔːlmənt] (US **installment**) *n* plazo; (*of story*) entrega; (*of TV serial etc*) capítulo; **in ~s** (*pay, receive*) a plazos
**instance** ['ɪnstəns] *n* ejemplo, caso; **for ~** por ejemplo; **in the first ~** en primer lugar
**instant** ['ɪnstənt] *n* instante *m*, momento ♦ *adj* inmediato; (*coffee etc*) instantáneo; ~**ly** *adv* en seguida
**instead** [ɪn'stɛd] *adv* en cambio; ~ **of** en lugar de, en vez de
**instep** ['ɪnstɛp] *n* empeine *m*
**instil** [ɪn'stɪl] *vt*: **to ~ sth into** inculcar algo a
**instinct** ['ɪnstɪŋkt] *n* instinto; ~**ive** ['-stɪŋktɪv] *adj* instintivo
**institute** ['ɪnstɪtjuːt] *n* instituto; (*professional body*) colegio ♦ *vt* (*begin*) iniciar, empezar; (*proceedings*) entablar; (*system, rule*) establecer
**institution** [ɪnstɪ'tjuːʃən] *n* institución *f*; (MED: *home*) asilo; ~ (*asylum*) manicomio; (*of system etc*) establecimiento; (*of custom*) iniciación *f*

**instruct** [ɪn'strʌkt] *vt*: **to ~ sb in sth** instruir a uno en *or* sobre algo; **to ~ sb to do sth** dar instrucciones a uno de hacer algo; ~**ion**

[ɪn'strʌkʃən] n (teaching) instrucción f; ~**ions** npl (orders) órdenes fpl; ~**ions** (for use) modo de empleo; ~**ive** adj instructivo; ~**or**n instructor(a) m/f

**instrument** ['ɪnstrəmənt] n instrumento; ~**al** [-'mentl] adj (MUS) instrumental; **to be ~al in** ser (el) artífice de; ~ **panel** n tablero de (instrumentos)

**insubordination** [ɪnsəbɔːdɪ'neɪʃən] n insubordinación f

**insufferable** [ɪn'sʌfrəbl] adj insoportable

**insufficient** [ɪnsə'fɪʃənt] adj insuficiente

**insular** ['ɪnsjulə*] adj insular; (person) estrecho de miras

**insulate** ['ɪnsjuleɪt] vt aislar; **insulating tape** n cinta aislante; **insulation** [-'leɪʃən] n aislamiento f

**insulin** ['ɪnsjulɪn] n insulina

**insult** [n 'ɪnsʌlt, vb ɪn'sʌlt] n insulto ♦ vt insultar; ~**ing** adj insultante

**insurance** [ɪn'ʃuərəns] n seguro; **fire/life** ~ seguro contra incendios/sobre la vida; ~ **agent** n agente m/f de seguros; ~ **policy** n póliza de (seguros)

**insure** [ɪn'ʃuə*] vt asegurar

**intact** [ɪn'tækt] adj íntegro, (unharmed) intacto

**intake** ['ɪnteɪk] n (of food) ingestión f; (of air) consumo; (BRIT: SCOL): **an** ~ **of 200 a year** 200 matriculados al año

**integral** ['ɪntɪgrəl] adj (whole) íntegro; (part) integrante

**integrate** ['ɪntɪgreɪt] vt integrar ♦ vi integrarse

**integrity** [ɪn'tegrɪtɪ] n honradez f, rectitud f

**intellect** ['ɪntəlekt] n intelecto; ~**ual** [-'lektjuəl] adj, n intelectual m/f

**intelligence** [ɪn'telɪdʒəns] n inteligencia

**intelligent** [ɪn'telɪdʒənt] adj inteligente; **intelligentsia** [ɪntelɪ'dʒentsɪə] n intelectualidad f

**intelligible** [ɪn'telɪdʒɪbl] adj inteligi-ble, comprensible

**intend** [ɪn'tend] vt (gift etc): **to** ~ **sth for** destinar algo a; **to** ~ **to do sth** tener intención de or pensar hacer algo; ~**ed** adj intencionado

**intense** [ɪn'tens] adj intenso; ~**ly** adv (extremely) sumamente

**intensify** [ɪn'tensɪfaɪ] vt intensificar; (increase) aumentar

**intensive** [ɪn'tensɪv] adj intensivo; ~ **care unit** n unidad f de vigilancia intensiva

**intent** [ɪn'tent] n propósito; (LAW) premeditación f ♦ adj (absorbed) absorto; (attentive) atento; **to all** ~**s and purposes** prácticamente; **to be** ~ **on doing sth** estar resuelto a hacer algo

**intention** [ɪn'tenʃən] n intención f, propósito; ~**al** adj deliberado; ~**ally** adv a propósito

**intently** [ɪn'tentlɪ] adv atentamente, fijamente

**interact** [ɪntər'ækt] vi influirse mutuamente; ~**ion** [-'ækʃən] n interacción f; ~**ive** adj (COMPUT) interactivo

**intercede** [ɪntə'siːd] vi: **to** ~ (**with**) interceder (con)

**intercept** [ɪntə'sept] vt interceptar

**interchange** [n 'ɪntətʃeɪndʒ] n intercambio; (on motorway) intersección f; ~**able** adj intercambiable

**intercom** ['ɪntəkɔm] n interfono

**intercourse** ['ɪntəkɔːs] n (sexual) relaciones fpl sexuales

**interest** ['ɪntrɪst] n (also COMM) interés m ♦ vt interesar; **to be** ~**ed in** interesarse por; ~**ing** adj interesante; ~ **rate** n tipo or tasa de interés

**interface** ['ɪntəfeɪs] n (COMPUT) junción f

**interfere** [ɪntə'fɪə*] vi: **to** ~ **in** (quarrel, other people's business) entrometerse en; **to** ~ **with** (hinder) estorbar; (damage) estropear

**interference** [ɪntə'fɪərəns] n intromisión f; (RADIO, TV) interferencia

**interim** ['ɪntərɪm] n: **in the** ~ en el ínterin ♦ adj provisional

**interior** [ɪn'tɪərɪə*] n interior m ♦
adj interior; ~ **designer** n interiorista m/f

**interjection** [ɪntə'dʒɛkʃən] n interposición f; (LING) interjección f

**interlock** [ɪntə'lɔk] vi entrelazarse

**interlude** ['ɪntəluːd] n intervalo; (THEATRE) intermedio

**intermarry** [ɪntə'mærɪ] vi casarse personas de distintas razas (or religiones etc)

**intermediary** [ɪntə'miːdɪərɪ] n intermediario/a

**intermediate** [ɪntə'miːdɪət] adj intermedio

**interminable** [ɪn'təːmɪnəbl] adj inacabable

**intermission** [ɪntə'mɪʃən] n intermisión f; (THEATRE) descanso

**intermittent** [ɪntə'mɪtnt] adj intermitente

**intern** [vb ɪn'təːn, n 'ɪntəːn] vt internar ♦ n (US) interno/a

**internal** [ɪn'təːnl] adj (layout, pipes, security) interior; (injury, structure, memo) internal; ~**ly** adv: "**not to be taken** ~**ly**" "uso externo"; I~ **Revenue Service** (US) n departamento de impuestos; ≈ Hacienda (SP)

**international** [ɪntə'næʃənl] adj internacional ♦ n (BRIT: match) partido internacional

**interplay** ['ɪntəpleɪ] n interacción f

**interpret** [ɪn'təːprɪt] vt interpretar; (translate) traducir; (understand) entender ♦ vi hacer de intérprete; ~**ation** [-'teɪʃən] n interpretación f; traducción f; entendimiento f; ~**er** n intérprete m/f

**interrelated** [ɪntərɪ'leɪtɪd] adj interrelacionado

**interrogate** [ɪn'tɛrəugeɪt] vt interrogar; **interrogation** [-'geɪʃən] n interrogatorio; **interrogative** [ɪntə'rɔgətɪv] adj (LING) interrogativo

**interrupt** [ɪntə'rʌpt] vt, vi interrumpir; ~**ion** [-'rʌpʃən] n interrupción f

**intersect** [ɪntə'sɛkt] vi (roads) cruzarse; ~**ion** [-'sɛkʃən] n (of roads)

cruce m

**intersperse** [ɪntə'spəːs] vt: to ~ **with** salpicar de

**intertwine** [ɪntə'twaɪn] vt entrelazarse

**interval** ['ɪntəvl] n intervalo; (BRIT: THEATRE, SPORT) descanso; (: SCOL) recreo; **at** ~s a ratos, de vez en cuando

**intervene** [ɪntə'viːn] vi intervenir; (event) interponerse; (time) transcurrir; **intervention** [-'vɛnʃən] n intervención f

**interview** ['ɪntəvjuː] n entrevista ♦ vt entrevistarse con; ~**er** n entrevistador(a) m/f

**intestine** [ɪn'tɛstɪn] n intestino

**intimacy** ['ɪntɪməsɪ] n intimidad f

**intimate** [adj 'ɪntɪmət, vb 'ɪntɪmeɪt] adj íntimo; (friendship) estrecho; (knowledge) profundo ♦ vt dar a entender

**intimidate** [ɪn'tɪmɪdeɪt] vt intimidar, amedrentar

**into** ['ɪntu] prep en; (towards) a; (inside) hacia el interior de; ~ **3 pieces/French** en 3 pedazos/al francés

**intolerable** [ɪn'tɔlərəbl] adj intolerable, insoportable

**intolerant** [ɪn'tɔlərənt] adj: ~ (**of**) intolerante (con or para)

**intonation** [ɪntəu'neɪʃən] n entonación f

**intoxicated** [ɪn'tɔksɪkeɪtɪd] adj embriagado; **intoxication** [ɪntɔksɪ'keɪʃən] n embriaguez f

**intractable** [ɪn'træktəbl] adj (person) intratable; (problem) espinoso

**intransitive** [ɪn'trænsɪtɪv] adj intransitivo

**intravenous** [ɪntrə'viːnəs] adj intravenoso

**in-tray** n bandeja de entrada

**intricate** ['ɪntrɪkət] adj (design, pattern) intrincado

**intrigue** [ɪn'triːg] n intriga ♦ vt fascinar; **intriguing** adj fascinante

**intrinsic** [ɪn'trɪnsɪk] adj intrínseco

**introduce** [ɪntrə'djuːs] vt introducir,

meter; (*speaker, TV show etc*) presentar; **to ~ sb** (**to** sb) presentar uno (a otro); **to ~ sb to** (*pastime, technique*) introducir a uno a; **introduction** [-'dʌkʃən] *n* introducción *f*; (*of person*) presentación *f*; **introductory** [-'dʌktərɪ] *adj* introductorio; (*lesson, offer*) de introducción

**introvert** ['ɪntrəvɜːt] *n* introvertido/a ♦ *adj* (*also*: **~ed**) introvertido

**intrude** [ɪn'truːd] *vi* (*person*) entrometerse; **to ~ on** estorbar; **~r** *n* intruso/a *m/f*; **intrusion** [-ʒən] *n* invasión *f*

**intuition** [ɪntjuː'ɪʃən] *n* intuición *f*

**inundate** ['ɪnʌndeɪt] *vt*: **to ~ with** inundar de

**invade** [ɪn'veɪd] *vt* invadir

**invalid** [*n* 'ɪnvəlɪd, *adj* ɪn'vælɪd] *n* (*MED*) minusválido/a ♦ *adj* (*not valid*) inválido,nulo

**invaluable** [ɪn'væljuəbl] *adj* inestimable

**invariable** [ɪn'veərɪəbl] *adj* invariable

**invasion** [ɪn'veɪʒən] *n* invasión *f*

**invent** [ɪn'vent] *vt* inventar; **~ion** [ɪn'venʃən] *n* invento; (*lie*) ficción *f*, mentira; **~ive** *adj* inventivo; **~or** *n* inventor(a) *m/f*

**inventory** ['ɪnvəntrɪ] *n* inventario

**invert** [ɪn'vɜːt] *vt* invertir

**invertebrate** [ɪn'vɜːtɪbrət] *n* invertebrado

**inverted commas** [ɪn'vɜːtɪd] (*BRIT*) *npl* comillas *fpl*

**invest** [ɪn'vest] *vt* invertir ♦ *vi*: **to ~ in** (*company etc*) invertir dinero en; (*fig*: *sth useful*) comprar

**investigate** [ɪn'vestɪgeɪt] *vt* investigar; **investigation** [-'geɪʃən] *n* investigación *f*, pesquisa; **investigator** *n* investigador(a) *m/f*

**investment** [ɪn'vestmənt] *n* inversión *f*

**investor** [ɪn'vestə*] *n* inversionista *m/f*

**inveterate** [ɪn'vetərət] *adj* empedernido

**invidious** [ɪn'vɪdɪəs] *adj* odioso

**invigilator** [ɪn'vɪdʒɪleɪtə*] *n* persona que vigila en un examen

**invigorating** [ɪn'vɪgəreɪtɪŋ] *adj* vigorizante

**invincible** [ɪn'vɪnsɪbl] *adj* invencible

**invisible** [ɪn'vɪzɪbl] *adj* invisible

**invitation** [ɪnvɪ'teɪʃən] *n* invitación *f*

**invite** [ɪn'vaɪt] *vt* invitar; (*opinions etc*) solicitar, pedir; **inviting** *adj* atractivo; (*food*) apetitoso

**invoice** ['ɪnvɔɪs] *n* factura ♦ *vt* facturar

**invoke** [ɪn'vəʊk] *vt* (*law, principle*) recurrir a

**involuntary** [ɪn'vɒləntrɪ] *adj* involuntario

**involve** [ɪn'vɒlv] *vt* suponer, implicar; tener que ver con; (*concern, affect*) corresponder; **to ~ sb** (**in sth**) comprometer a uno (con algo); **~d** *adj* complicado; **to be ~d in** (*take part*) tomar parte en; (*be engrossed*) estar muy metido en; **~ment** *n* participación *f*; dedicación *f*

**inward** ['ɪnwəd] *adj* (*movement*) interior, interno; (*thought, feeling*) íntimo; **~(s)** *adv* hacia dentro

**I/O** *abbr* (*COMPUT* = *input/output*) entrada/salida

**iodine** ['aɪədiːn] *n* yodo

**ion** ['aɪən] *n* ion *m*

**iota** [aɪ'əʊtə] *n* jota, ápice *m*

**IOU** *n abbr* (= *I owe you*) pagaré *m*

**IQ** *n abbr* (= *intelligence quotient*) coeficiente *m* intelectual

**IRA** *n abbr* (= *Irish Republican Army*) IRA *m*

**Iran** [ɪ'rɑːn] *n* Irán *m*; **~ian** [ɪ'reɪnɪən] *adj, n* iraní *m/f*

**Iraq** [ɪ'rɑːk] *n* Iraq; **~i** *adj, n* iraquí *m/f*

**irascible** [ɪ'ræsɪbl] *adj* irascible

**irate** [aɪ'reɪt] *adj* enojado, airado

**Ireland** ['aɪələnd] *n* Irlanda

**iris** ['aɪrɪs] (*pl* **~es**) *n* (*ANAT*) iris *m*; (*BOT*) lirio

**Irish** ['aɪrɪʃ] *adj* irlandés/esa ♦ *npl*: **the ~** los irlandeses; **~man/woman** *n* irlandés/esa *m/f*; **~ Sea** *n*: **the ~ Sea** el mar de Irlanda

**irksome** ['əːksʌm] *adj* fastidioso

**iron** ['aɪən] *n* hierro; (*for clothes*) plancha ♦ *cpd* de hierro ♦ *vt* (*clothes*) planchar; ~ **out** *vt* (*fig*) allanar; I~ **Curtain** *n*: **the** I~ **Curtain** el Telón de Acero

**ironic(al)** [aɪ'rɒnɪk(l)] *adj* irónico

**ironing** ['aɪənɪŋ] *n* (*activity*) planchado; (*clothes: ironed*) ropa planchada; (: *to be ironed*) ropa por planchar; ~ **board** *n* tabla de planchar

**ironmonger's (shop)** ['aɪənmʌŋgə*z*] (*BRIT*) *n* ferretería, quincallería

**irony** ['aɪrənɪ] *n* ironía

**irrational** [ɪ'ræʃənl] *adj* irracional

**irreconcilable** [ɪrəkən'saɪləbl] *adj* (*ideas*) incompatible; (*enemies*) irreconciliable

**irregular** [ɪ'regjʊlə*] *adj* irregular; (*surface*) desigual; (*action, event*) anómalo; (*behaviour*) poco ortodoxo

**irrelevant** [ɪ'reləvənt] *adj* fuera de lugar, inoportuno

**irreplaceable** [ɪrɪ'pleɪsəbl] *adj* irremplazable

**irrepressible** [ɪrɪ'presəbl] *adj* incontenible

**irresistible** [ɪrɪ'zɪstɪbl] *adj* irresistible

**irresolute** [ɪ'rezəluːt] *adj* indeciso

**irrespective** [ɪrɪ'spektɪv]: ~ **of** *prep* sin tener en cuenta, no importa

**irresponsible** [ɪrɪ'spɒnsɪbl] *adj* (*act*) irresponsable; (*person*) poco serio

**irrigate** ['ɪrɪgeɪt] *vt* regar; **irrigation** [-'geɪʃən] *n* riego

**irritable** ['ɪrɪtəbl] *adj* (*person*) de mal humor

**irritate** ['ɪrɪteɪt] *vt* fastidiar; (*MED*) picar; **irritating** *adj* fastidioso; **irritation** [-'teɪʃən] *n* fastidio; irritación; picazón *f*, picor *m*

**IRS** (*US*) *n abbr* = **Internal Revenue Service**

**is** [ɪz] *vb see* **be**

**Islam** ['ɪzlɑːm] *n* Islam *m*; ~**ic** [ɪz'læmɪk] *adj* islámico

**island** ['aɪlənd] *n* isla; ~**er** *n* isleño/a

**isle** [aɪl] *n* isla

**isn't** ['ɪznt] = **is not**

**isolate** ['aɪsəleɪt] *vt* aislar; ~**d** *adj* aislado; **isolation** [-'leɪʃən] *n* aislamiento

**Israel** ['ɪzreɪl] *n* Israel *m*; ~**i** [ɪz'reɪlɪ] *adj*, *n* israelí *m/f*

**issue** ['ɪsjuː] *n* (*problem, subject, most important part*) cuestión *f*; (*outcome*) resultado; (*of banknotes etc*) emisión *f*; (*of newspaper etc*) edición *f*; (*offspring*) sucesión *f*, descendencia ♦ *vt* (*rations, equipment*) distribuir, repartir; (*orders*) dar; (*certificate, passport*) expedir; (*decree*) promulgar; (*magazine*) publicar; (*cheques*) extender; (*banknotes, stamps*) emitir; **at** ~ en cuestión; **to take** ~ **with sb** (**over**) estar en desacuerdo con uno (sobre); **to make an** ~ **of sth** hacer una cuestión de algo

**Istanbul** [ɪstæn'buːl] *n* Estambul *m*

**isthmus** ['ɪsməs] *n* istmo

┌─────────────────────────────┐
│ KEYWORD │
└─────────────────────────────┘

**it** [ɪt] *pron* **1** (*specific: subject: not generally translated*) él/ella; (: *direct object*) lo, la; (: *indirect object* le); (*after prep*) él/ella; (*abstract concept*) ello; ~**'s on the table** está en la mesa; **I can't find** ~ no lo (*or* la) encuentro; **give** ~ **to me** dámelo (*or* dámela); **I spoke to him about** ~ le hablé del asunto; **what did you learn from** ~? ¿qué aprendiste de él (*or* ella)?; **did you go to** ~? (*party, concert etc*) ¿fuiste?

**2** (*impersonal*): ~**'s raining** llueve, está lloviendo; ~**'s 6 o'clock/the 10th of August** son las 6/es el 10 de agosto; **how far is** ~? — ~**'s 10 miles/2 hours on the train** ¿a qué distancia está? — a 10 millas/2 horas en tren; **who is** ~? — ~**'s me** ¿quién es? — soy yo

**Italian** [ɪ'tæljən] *adj* italiano ♦ *n* italiano/a; (*LING*) italiano

**italics** [ɪ'tælɪks] *npl* cursiva

**Italy** ['ɪtəlɪ] n Italia

**itch** [ɪtʃ] n picazón f ♦ vi (part of body) picar; **to ~ to do sth** rabiar por hacer algo; **~y** adj: **my hand is ~y** me pica la mano

**it'd** ['ɪtd] = **it would; it had**

**item** ['aɪtəm] n artículo; (on agenda) asunto (a tratar); (also: news ~) noticia; **~ize** vt detallar

**itinerant** [ɪ'tɪnərənt] adj ambulante

**itinerary** [aɪ'tɪnərərɪ] n itinerario

**it'll** ['ɪtl] = **it will; it shall**

**its** [ɪts] adj su; sus pl

**it's** [ɪts] = **it is; it has**

**itself** [ɪt'self] pron (reflexive) sí mismo/a; (emphatic) él mismo/ella misma

**ITV** n abbr (BRIT: = Independent Television) cadena de televisión comercial independiente del Estado

**I.U.D.** n abbr (= intra-uterine device) DIU m

**I've** [aɪv] = **I have**

**ivory** ['aɪvərɪ] n marfil m; (colour) (color) de marfil; **~ tower** n torre f de marfil

**ivy** ['aɪvɪ] n (BOT) hiedra

# J

**jab** [dʒæb] vt: **to ~ sth into sth** clavar algo en algo ♦ n (inf) (injection) pinchazo

**jack** [dʒæk] n (AUT) gato; (CARDS) sota; **~ up** vt (AUT) levantar con gato

**jackal** ['dʒækɔːl] n (ZOOL) chacal m

**jacket** ['dʒækɪt] n chaqueta, americana, saco (AM); (of book) sobrecubierta

**jack-knife** vi colear

**jack plug** n (ELEC) enchufe m de clavija

**jackpot** ['dʒækpɒt] n premio gordo

**jaded** ['dʒeɪdɪd] adj (tired) cansado; (fed-up) hastiado

**jagged** ['dʒægɪd] adj dentado

**jail** [dʒeɪl] n cárcel f ♦ vt encarcelar

**jam** [dʒæm] n mermelada; (also:

**traffic ~)** embotellamiento; (inf: difficulty) apuro ♦ vt (passage etc) obstruir; (mechanism, drawer etc) atascar; (RADIO) interferir ♦ vi atascarse, trabarse; **to ~ sth into** sth meter algo a la fuerza en algo

**Jamaica** [dʒə'meɪkə] n Jamaica

**jangle** ['dʒæŋgl] vi entrechocar (ruidosamente)

**janitor** ['dʒænɪtə*] n (caretaker) portero, conserje m

**January** ['dʒænjuərɪ] n enero

**Japan** [dʒə'pæn] n (el) Japón; **~ese** [dʒæpə'niːz] adj japonés/esa ♦ n inv japonés/esa m/f; (LING) japonés m

**jar** [dʒɑː*] n tarro, bote m ♦ vi (sound) chirriar; (colours) desentonar

**jargon** ['dʒɑːgən] n jerga

**jasmine** ['dʒæzmɪn] n jazmín m

**jaundice** ['dʒɔːndɪs] n icteria; **~d** adj desilusionado, poco entusiasta

**jaunt** [dʒɔːnt] n excursión f; **~y** adj alegre

**javelin** ['dʒævlɪn] n jabalina

**jaw** [dʒɔː] n mandíbula

**jay** [dʒeɪ*] n (ZOOL) arrendajo

**jaywalker** ['dʒeɪwɔːkə*] n peatón/ona m/f imprudente

**jazz** [dʒæz] n jazz m; **~ up** vt (liven up) animar, avivar

**jealous** ['dʒeləs] adj celoso; (envious) envidioso; **~y** n celos mpl; envidia

**jeans** [dʒiːnz] npl vaqueros mpl, tejanos mpl

**jeep** [dʒiːp] n jeep m

**jeer** [dʒɪə*] vi: **to ~ (at)** (mock) mofarse (de)

**jelly** ['dʒelɪ] n (jam) jalea; (dessert etc) gelatina; **~fish** ~ inv medusa (SP), aguaviva (AM)

**jeopardy** ['dʒepədɪ] n: **to be in ~** estar en peligro

**jerk** [dʒɜːk] n (jolt) sacudida; (wrench) tirón m; (inf) imbécil m/f ♦ vt tirar bruscamente de ♦ vi (vehicle) traquetear

**jerkin** ['dʒɜːkɪn] n chaleco

**jersey** ['dʒɜːzɪ] n jersey m; (fabric)

(tejido de) punto

**jest** [dʒɛst] n broma

**Jesus** ['dʒiːzəs] n Jesús m

**jet** [dʒɛt] n (of gas, liquid) chorro; (AVIAT) avión m a reacción; ~-**black** adj negro de azabache; ~ **engine** n motor m a reacción; ~ **lag** n desorientación f después de un largo vuelo

**jettison** ['dʒɛtɪsn] vt desechar

**jetty** ['dʒɛtɪ] n muelle m, embarcadero

**Jew** [dʒuː] n judío

**jewel** ['dʒuːəl] n joya; (in watch) rubí m; ~**ler** n joyero/a; ~**ler's (shop)** (US ~**ry store**) n joyería; ~**lery** (US ~**ry**) n joyas fpl, alhajas fpl

**Jewess** ['dʒuːɪs] n judía

**Jewish** ['dʒuːɪʃ] adj judío

**jibe** [dʒaɪb] n mofa

**jiffy** ['dʒɪfɪ] (inf) n: **in a ~** en un santiamén

**jig** [dʒɪg] n giga

**jigsaw** ['dʒɪgsɔː] n (also: ~ **puzzle**) rompecabezas m inv, puzle m

**jilt** [dʒɪlt] vt dejar plantado a

**jingle** ['dʒɪŋgl] n musiquilla ♦ vi tintinear

**jinx** [dʒɪŋks] n: **there's a ~ on it** está gafado

**jitters** ['dʒɪtəz] (inf) npl: **to get the ~** ponerse nervioso

**job** [dʒɔb] n (task) tarea; (post) empleo; **it's not my ~** no me incumbe a mí; **it's a good ~ that ...** menos mal que ...; **just the ~!** ¡estupendo!; ~ **centre** (BRIT) n oficina estatal de colocaciones; ~**less** adj sin trabajo

**jockey** ['dʒɔkɪ] n jockey m/f ♦ vi: **to ~ for position** maniobrar para conseguir una posición

**jocular** ['dʒɔkjulə*] adj gracioso

**jog** [dʒɔg] vt empujar (ligeramente) ♦ vi (run) hacer footing; **to ~ sb's memory** refrescar la memoria a uno; ~ **along** vi (fig) ir tirando; ~**ging** n footing m

**join** [dʒɔɪn] vt (things) juntar, unir; (club) hacerse socio de; (POL:

**party**) afiliarse a; (queue) ponerse en; (meet: people) reunirse con ♦ vi (roads) juntarse; (rivers) confluir ♦ n juntura; ~ **in** vi tomar parte, participar ♦ vt fus tomar parte or participar en; ~ **up** vi reunirse; (MIL) alistarse

**joiner** ['dʒɔɪnə*] (BRIT) n carpintero/a; ~**y** n carpintería

**joint** [dʒɔɪnt] n (TECH) junta, unión f; (ANAT) articulación f; (BRIT: CULIN) pieza de carne (para asar); (inf: place) tugurio; (: of cannabis) porro ♦ adj (common) común; (combined) combinado; ~ **account** (with bank etc) cuenta común

**joke** [dʒəuk] n chiste m; (also: practical ~) broma ♦ vi bromear; **to play a ~ on** gastar una broma a; ~**r** n (CARDS) comodín m

**jolly** ['dʒɔlɪ] adj (merry) alegre; (enjoyable) divertido ♦ adv (BRIT: inf) muy, terriblemente

**jolt** [dʒəult] n (jerk) sacudida; (shock) susto ♦ vt (physically) sacudir; (emotionally) asustar

**jostle** ['dʒɔsl] vt dar empellones a, codear

**jot** [dʒɔt] n: **not one** ~ ni jota, ni pizca; ~ **down** vt apuntar; ~**ter** (BRIT) n bloc m

**journal** ['dʒəːnl] n (magazine) revista; (diary) periódico, diario; ~**ism** n periodismo; ~**ist** n periodista m/f, reportero/a

**journey** ['dʒəːnɪ] n viaje m; (distance covered) trayecto

**jovial** ['dʒəuvɪəl] adj risueño, jovial

**joy** [dʒɔɪ] n alegría; ~**ful** adj alegre; ~**ous** adj alegre; ~ **ride** n (illegal) paseo en coche robado; ~**rider** n gamberro que roba un coche para dar una vuelta y luego abandonarlo; ~ **stick** n (AVIAT) palanca de mando; (COMPUT) palanca de control

**J.P.** n abbr = **Justice of the Peace**

**Jr** abbr = **junior**

**jubilant** ['dʒuːbɪlnt] adj jubiloso

**jubilee** ['dʒuːbɪliː] n aniversario

**judge** [dʒʌdʒ] n juez m/f; (fig: expert) perito ♦ vt juzgar; (consider) considerar; **judg(e)ment** n juicio

**judiciary** [dʒuːˈdɪʃɪərɪ] n poder m judicial

**judicious** [dʒuːˈdɪʃəs] adj juicioso

**judo** [ˈdʒuːdəu] n judo

**jug** [dʒʌg] n jarra

**juggernaut** [ˈdʒʌgənɔːt] n (BRIT) (huge truck) trailer m

**juggle** [ˈdʒʌgl] vi hacer juegos malabares; ~r n malabarista m/f

**Jugoslav** [ˈjuːgəuslɑːv] etc = **Yugoslav** etc

**juice** [dʒuːs] n zumo, jugo (esp AM); **juicy** adj jugoso

**jukebox** [ˈdʒuːkbɒks] n tocadiscos m inv tragaperras

**July** [dʒuːˈlaɪ] n julio

**jumble** [ˈdʒʌmbl] n revoltijo ♦ vt (also: ~ up) revolver; ~ **sale** (BRIT) n venta de objetos usados con fines benéficos

**jumbo (jet)** [ˈdʒʌmbəu-] n jumbo

**jump** [dʒʌmp] vi saltar, dar saltos; (with fear, surprise) pegar un bote; (increase) aumentar ♦ vt saltar ♦ n salto; aumento; to ~ **the queue** (BRIT) colarse; ~ **cables** (US) npl = **jump leads**

**jumper** [ˈdʒʌmpə*] n (BRIT: pullover) suéter m, jersey m; (US: dress) mandil m

**jump leads** (BRIT) npl cables mpl puente de batería

**jumpy** [ˈdʒʌmpɪ] (inf) adj nervioso

**Jun.** abbr = **junior**

**junction** [ˈdʒʌŋkʃən] n (BRIT: of roads) cruce m; (RAIL) empalme m

**juncture** [ˈdʒʌŋktʃə*] n: **at this** ~ en este momento, en esta coyuntura

**June** [dʒuːn] n junio

**jungle** [ˈdʒʌŋgl] n selva, jungla

**junior** [ˈdʒuːnɪə*] adj (in age) menor, más joven; (brother/sister etc): 7 **years her** ~ siete años menor que ella; (position) subalterno ♦ n menor m/f, joven m/f; ~ **school** (BRIT) n escuela primaria

**junk** [dʒʌŋk] n (cheap goods) baratijas fpl; (rubbish) basura; ~ **food** n

alimentos preparados y envasados de escaso valor nutritivo

**junkie** [ˈdʒʌŋkɪ] (inf) n drogadicto/a, yonqui m/f

**junk mail** n propaganda de buzón

**junk shop** n tienda de objetos usados

**Junr** abbr = **junior**

**jurisdiction** [dʒuərɪsˈdɪkʃən] n jurisdicción f

**juror** [ˈdʒuərə*] n jurado

**jury** [ˈdʒuərɪ] n jurado

**just** [dʒʌst] adj justo ♦ adv (exactly) exactamente; (only) solo, solamente; **he's** ~ **done it/left** acaba de hacerlo/irse; ~ **right** perfecto; ~ **two o'clock** las dos en punto; **she's** ~ **as clever as you** es tan lista como tú; ~ **as well that** ... menos mal que ...; ~ **as he was leaving** en el momento en que se marchaba; ~ **before/enough** justo antes/lo suficiente; ~ **here** aquí mismo; **he** ~ **missed** ha fallado por poco; ~ **listen to this** escucha esto un momento

**justice** [ˈdʒʌstɪs] n justicia; (US: judge) juez m; **to do** ~ **to** (fig) hacer justicia a; **J**~ **of the Peace** n juez m de paz

**justify** [ˈdʒʌstɪfaɪ] vt justificar; (text) alinear

**jut** [dʒʌt] vi (also: ~ **out**) sobresalir

**juvenile** [ˈdʒuːvənaɪl] adj (court) de menores; (humour, mentality) infantil ♦ n menor m de edad

**juxtapose** [ˈdʒʌkstəpəuz] vt yuxtaponer

# K

**K** abbr (= one thousand) mil; (= kilobyte) kilobyte m, kilooocteto

**kaleidoscope** [kəˈlaɪdəskəup] n calidoscopio

**kangaroo** [kæŋgəˈruː] n canguro

**karate** [kəˈrɑːtɪ] n karate m

**kebab** [kəˈbæb] n pincho moruno

**keel** [kiːl] n quilla; **on an even** ~

*(fig)* en equilibrio

**keen** [ki:n] *adj (interest, desire)* grande, vivo; *(eye, intelligence)* agudo; *(competition)* reñido; *(edge)* afilado; *(eager)* entusiasta; **to be ~ to do** *or* **on doing sth** tener muchas ganas de hacer algo; **to be ~ on sth/sb** interesarse por algo/uno

**keep** [ki:p] *(pt, pp* **kept***) vt (preserve, store)* guardar; *(hold back)* quedarse con; *(maintain)* mantener; *(detain)* detener; *(shop)* ser propietario de; *(feed: family etc)* mantener; *(promise)* cumplir; *(chickens, bees etc)* criar; *(accounts)* llevar; *(diary)* escribir; *(prevent): to ~ sb from doing sth* impedir a uno hacer algo ♦ *vi (food)* conservarse; *(remain)* seguir, continuar ♦ *n (of castle)* torreón *m; (food etc)* comida, subsistencia; *(inf):* **for ~s** para siempre; **to ~ doing sth** seguir haciendo algo; **to ~ sb happy** tener a uno contento; **to ~ a place tidy** mantener un lugar limpio; **to ~ sth to o.s.** guardar algo para sí mismo; **to ~ sth (back) from sb** ocultar algo a uno; **to ~ time** *(clock)* mantener la hora exacta; **~ on** *vi:* **to ~ on doing** seguir *or* continuar haciendo; **to ~ on (about sth)** no parar de hablar (de algo); **~ out** *vi (stay out)* permanecer fuera; "**~ out**" "prohibida la entrada"; **~ up** *vt* mantener, conservar ♦ *vi* no retrasarse; **to ~ up with** *(pace)* ir al paso de; *(level)* mantenerse a la altura de; **~er** *n* guardián/ana *m/f;* **~-fit** *n* gimnasia (para mantenerse en forma); **~ing** *n (care)* cuidado; **in ~ing with** de acuerdo con; **~sake** *n* recuerdo

**kennel** ['kɛnl] *n* perrera; **~s** *npl* residencia canina

**Kenya** ['kɛnjə] *n* Kenia

**kept** [kɛpt] *pt, pp of* **keep**

**kerb** [kə:b] *(BRIT) n* bordillo

**kernel** ['kə:nl] *n (nut)* almendra; *(fig)* meollo

**ketchup** ['kɛtʃəp] *n* salsa de tomate, catsup *m*

**kettle** ['kɛtl] *n* hervidor *m* de agua; **~ drum** *n (MUS)* timbal *m*

**key** [ki:] *n* llave *f; (MUS)* tono; *(of piano, typewriter)* tecla ♦ *adj (issue etc)* clave *inv* ♦ *vt (also: ~ in)* teclear; **~board** *n* teclado; **~ed up** *adj (person)* nervioso; **~hole** *n* ojo (de la cerradura); **~note** *n (MUS)* tónica; *(of speech)* punto principal *or* clave; **~ring** *n* llavero

**khaki** ['ka:ki] *n* caqui

**kick** [kik] *vt* dar una patada *or* un puntapié a; *(inf: habit)* quitarse de ♦ *vi (horse)* dar coces ♦ *n* patada; puntapié *m; (of animal)* coz *f; (thrill):* **he does it for ~s** lo hace por pura diversión; **~ off** *vi (SPORT)* hacer el saque inicial

**kid** [kid] *n (inf: child)* chiquillo/a; *(animal)* cabrito; *(leather)* cabritilla ♦ *vi (inf)* bromear

**kidnap** ['kidnæp] *vt* secuestrar; **~per** *n* secuestrador(a) *m/f;* **~ping** *n* secuestro

**kidney** ['kidni] *n* riñón *m*

**kill** [kil] *vt* matar; *(murder)* asesinar ♦ *n* matanza; **to ~ time** matar el tiempo; **~er** *n* asesino/a; **~ing** *n (one)* asesinato; *(several)* matanza; **to make a ~ing** *(fig)* hacer su agosto; **~joy** *(BRIT) n* aguafiestas *m/f inv*

**kiln** [kiln] *n* horno

**kilo** ['ki:ləu] *n* kilo; **~byte** *n (COMPUT)* kilobyte *m,* kilococteto; **~gram(me)** ['kiləugræm] *n* kilo, kilogramo; **~metre** ['kiləmi:tə] *(US* **~meter)** *n* kilómetro; **~watt** ['kiləuwɔt] *n* kilovatio

**kilt** [kilt] *n* falda escocesa

**kin** [kin] *n see* **kith; next**

**kind** [kaind] *adj* amable, atento ♦ *n* clase *f,* especie *f; (species)* género; **in ~** *(COMM)* en especie; **a ~ of** una especie de; **to be two of a ~** ser tal para cual

**kindergarten** ['kindəgɑ:tn] *n* jardín *m* de la infancia

**kind-hearted** *adj* bondadoso, de buen corazón

**kindle** ['kɪndl] vt encender; (arouse) despertar

**kindly** ['kaɪndlɪ] adj bondadoso; cariñoso ♦ adv bondadosamente, amablemente; **will you ~ ...** sea usted tan amable de ...

**kindness** ['kaɪndnɪs] n (quality) bondad f, amabilidad f; (act) favor m

**kindred** ['kɪndrɪd] n familia ♦ adj: **~ spirits** almas fpl gemelas

**kinetic** [kɪ'nɛtɪk] adj cinético

**king** [kɪŋ] n rey m; ~**dom** n reino; ~**fisher** n martín m pescador; ~**size** adj de tamaño extra

**kinky** ['kɪŋkɪ] adj (pej: person, behaviour) extraño; (: sexually) perverso

**kiosk** ['ki:ɔsk] n quiosco m; (BRIT: TEL) cabina

**kipper** ['kɪpə*] n arenque m ahumado

**kiss** [kɪs] n beso ♦ vt besar; to ~ (each other) besarse; ~ **of life** n respiración f boca a boca

**kit** [kɪt] n (equipment) equipo; (tools etc) (caja de herramientas fpl; (assembly ~) juego de armar

**kitchen** ['kɪtʃɪn] n cocina; ~ **sink** n fregadero

**kite** [kaɪt] n (toy) cometa

**kith** [kɪθ] n: ~ **and kin** parientes mpl y allegados

**kitten** ['kɪtn] n gatito/a

**kitty** ['kɪtɪ] n (pool of money) fondo común

**kleptomaniac** [klɛptəʊ'meɪnɪæk] n cleptómano/a

**km** abbr (= kilometre) km

**knack** [næk] n: **to have the ~** of doing sth tener el don de hacer algo

**knapsack** ['næpsæk] n mochila

**knead** [ni:d] vt amasar

**knee** [ni:] n rodilla; ~**cap** n rótula

**kneel** [ni:l] (pt, pp knelt) vi (also: ~ down) arrodillarse

**knell** [nɛl] n toque m de difuntos

**knelt** [nɛlt] pt, pp of kneel

**knew** [nju:] pt of know

**knickers** ['nɪkəz] (BRIT) npl bragas fpl

**knife** [naɪf] (pl knives) n cuchillo ♦ vt acuchillar

**knight** [naɪt] n caballero; (CHESS) caballo; ~**hood** (BRIT) n (title): **to receive a ~hood** recibir el título de Sir

**knit** [nɪt] vt tejer, tricotar ♦ vi hacer punto, tricotar; (bones) soldarse; **to ~ one's brows** fruncir el ceño; ~**ting** n labor f de punto; ~**ting machine** n máquina de tricotar; ~**ting needle** n aguja de tejer punto; ~**wear** n prendas fpl de punto

**knives** [naɪvz] npl of knife

**knob** [nɔb] n (of door) tirador m; (of stick) puño; (on radio, TV) botón m

**knock** [nɔk] vt (strike) golpear; (bump into) chocar contra; (inf) criticar ♦ vi (at door etc): **to ~ at/on** llamar a ♦ n golpe m; (on door) llamada; ~ **down** vt atropellar; ~ **off** (inf) vi (finish) salir del trabajo ♦ vt (from price) descontar; (inf: steal) birlar; ~ **out** vt dejar sin sentido; (BOXING) poner fuera de combate, dejar K.O.; (in competition) eliminar; ~ **over** vt (object) tirar; (person) atropellar; ~**er** n (on door) aldabón m; ~**out** n (BOXING) K.O. m, knockout m ♦ cpd (competition etc) eliminatorio

**knot** [nɔt] n nudo ♦ vt anudar; ~**ty** adj (fig) complicado

**know** [nəʊ] (pt knew, pp known) vt (facts) saber; (be acquainted with) conocer; (recognize) reconocer, conocer; **to ~ how to swim** saber nadar; **to ~ about o of sb/sth** saber de uno/algo; ~**all** n sabelotodo m/f; ~**how** n conocimientos mpl; ~**ing** adj (look) de complicidad; ~**ingly** adv (purposely) adrede; (smile, look) con complicidad

**knowledge** ['nɔlɪdʒ] n conocimiento; (learning) saber m, conocimientos mpl; ~**able** adj entendido

**known** [nəʊn] pp of know

**knuckle** ['nʌkl] n nudillo

**K.O.** n abbr = knockout

**Koran** [kɔ'rɑ:n] n Corán m

**Korea** [kə'rɪə] n Corea

**kosher** ['kəʊʃə*] adj autorizado por la ley judía

# L

**L** (BRIT) abbr = learner driver

**l.** abbr (= litre) l

**lab** [læb] n abbr = laboratory

**label** ['leɪbl] n etiqueta ♦ vt poner etiqueta a

**labor** etc ['leɪbə*] (US) = labour

**laboratory** [lə'bɒrətərɪ] n laboratorio

**laborious** [lə'bɔːrɪəs] adj penoso

**labour** ['leɪbə*] (US **labor**) n (hard work) trabajo; (~ force) mano f de obra; (MED): to be in ~ estar de parto ♦ vi: to ~ (at sth) trabajar (en algo) ♦ vt: to ~ a point insistir en un punto; L~, the L~ party (BRIT) el partido laborista, los laboristas mpl; ~ed adj (breathing) fatigoso; ~er n peón m; farm ~er peón m; (day ~er) jornalero

**labyrinth** ['læbərɪnθ] n laberinto

**lace** [leɪs] n encaje m; (of shoe etc) cordón m ♦ vt (shoes: also: ~ up) atarse (los zapatos)

**lack** [læk] n (absence) falta ♦ vt faltarle a uno, carecer de; **through** o **for** ~ of por falta de; **to be ~ing** faltar, no haber; **to be ~ing in sth** faltarle a uno algo

**lacquer** ['lækə*] n laca

**lad** [læd] n muchacho, chico

**ladder** ['lædə*] n escalera (de mano); (BRIT: in tights) carrera

**laden** ['leɪdn] adj: ~ (with) cargado (de)

**ladle** ['leɪdl] n cucharón m

**lady** ['leɪdɪ] n señora; (dignified, graceful) dama; "**ladies and gentlemen ...**" "señoras y caballeros ..."; **young** ~ señorita; **the ladies' (room)** los servicios de señoras; **~bird** (US **~bug**) n mariquita; **~like** adj fino; **L~ship** n: **your L~ship** su Señoría

**lag** [læg] n retraso ♦ vi (also: ~ be-

hind) retrasarse, quedarse atrás ♦ vt (pipes) revestir

**lager** ['lɑːgə*] n cerveza (rubia)

**lagoon** [lə'guːn] n laguna

**laid** [leɪd] pt, pp of **lay**; **~ back** (inf) adj relajado; **~ up** adj: **to be ~ up (with)** tener que guardar cama (a causa de)

**lain** [leɪn] pp of **lie**

**lair** [lɛə*] n guarida

**lake** [leɪk] n lago

**lamb** [læm] n cordero; (meat) (carne f de) cordero; ~ **chop** n chuleta de cordero; **~swool** n lana de cordero

**lame** [leɪm] adj cojo; (excuse) poco convincente

**lament** [lə'ment] n quejo ♦ vt lamentarse de

**laminated** ['læmɪneɪtɪd] adj (metal) laminado; (wood) contrachapado; (surface) plastificado

**lamp** [læmp] n lámpara

**lampoon** [læm'puːn] vt satirizar

**lamp:** **~post** (BRIT) n (poste m del farol m; **~shade** n pantalla

**lance** [lɑːns] n lanza ♦ vt (MED) abrir con lanceta

**land** [lænd] n tierra; (country) país m; (piece of ~) terreno; (estate) tierras fpl, finca ♦ vi (from ship) desembarcar; (AVIAT) aterrizar; (fig: fall) caer, terminar ♦ vt (passengers, goods) desembarcar; **to ~ sb with sth** (inf) hacer cargar a uno con algo; ~ **up** vi: **to ~ up in/at** ir a parar a/en; **~ing** n aterrizaje m; (of staircase) rellano; **~ing gear** n (AVIAT) tren m de aterrizaje; **~ing strip** n pista de aterrizaje; **~lady** n (of rented house, pub etc) dueña; **~lord** n propietario; (of pub etc) patrón m; **~mark** n lugar m conocido; **to be a ~mark** (fig) marcar un hito histórico; **~owner** n terrateniente m/f

**landscape** ['lænskeɪp] n paisaje m; ~ **gardener** n arquitecto de jardines

**landslide** ['lændslaɪd] n (GEO) corrimiento de tierras; (fig: POL) victoria arrolladora

**lane** [leɪn] n (in country) camino; (AUT) carril m; (in race) calle f

**language** [ˈlæŋgwɪdʒ] n lenguaje m; (national tongue) idioma m, lengua; **bad ~** palabrotas fpl; **~ laboratory** n laboratorio de idiomas

**languish** [ˈlæŋgwɪʃ] vi languidecer

**lank** [læŋk] adj (hair) lacio

**lanky** [ˈlæŋkɪ] adj larguirucho

**lantern** [ˈlæntn] n linterna, farol m

**lap** [læp] n (of track) vuelta; (of body) regazo; **to sit on sb's ~** sentarse en las rodillas de alguien ♦ vt (also: **~ up**) beber a lengüetadas ♦ vi (waves) chapotear; **~ up** vt (fig) tragarse

**lapel** [ləˈpel] n solapa

**Lapland** [ˈlæplænd] n Laponia

**lapse** [læps] n fallo; (moral) desliz m; (of time) intervalo ♦ vi caducar; (time) pasar, transcurrir; **to ~ into bad habits** caer en malos hábitos

**laptop (computer)** [ˈlæptɔp-] n ordenador m portátil

**larceny** [ˈlɑːsənɪ] n latrocinio

**larch** [lɑːtʃ] n alerce m

**lard** [lɑːd] n manteca (de cerdo)

**larder** [ˈlɑːdə*] n despensa

**large** [lɑːdʒ] adj grande; **at ~** (free) en libertad; (generally) en general; **~ly** adv (mostly) en su mayor parte; (introducing reason) en gran parte; **~-scale** adj (map) en gran escala; (fig) importante

**largesse** [lɑːˈʒes] n generosidad f

**lark** [lɑːk] n (bird) alondra; (joke) broma; **~ about** vi bromear, hacer el tonto

**laryngitis** [lærɪnˈdʒaɪtɪs] n laringitis f

**larynx** [ˈlærɪŋks] n laringe f

**laser** [ˈleɪzə*] n láser m; **~ printer** n impresora (por) láser

**lash** [læʃ] n latigazo; (also: eye~) pestaña ♦ vt azotar; (tie): **to ~ to/together** atar a/atar; **~ out** vi: **to ~ out (at sb)** (hit) arremeter (contra uno); **to ~ out against sb** lanzar invectivas contra uno

**lass** [læs] n (BRIT) chica

**lasso** [læˈsuː] n lazo

**last** [lɑːst] adj último; (end: of series etc) final ♦ adv (most recently) la última vez; (finally) por último ♦ vi durar; (continue) continuar, seguir; **~ night** anoche; **~ week** la semana pasada; **at ~** por fin; **but one** penúltimo; **~-ditch** adj (attempt) último, desesperado; **~-ing** adj duradero; **~ly** adv por último, finalmente; **~-minute** adj de última hora

**latch** [lætʃ] n pestillo

**late** [leɪt] adj (far on: in time, process etc) avanzado; (dead) fallecido ♦ adv tarde; (behind time, schedule) con retraso; **of ~** últimamente; **at night** a última hora de la noche; **in ~ May** hacia fines de mayo; **the Mr X** el difunto Sr X; **~comer** n recién llegado/a; **~ly** adv últimamente

**later** [ˈleɪtə*] adj (date etc) posterior; (version etc) más reciente ♦ adv más tarde, después

**lateral** [ˈlætərl] adj lateral

**latest** [ˈleɪtɪst] adj último; **at the ~** a más tardar

**lathe** [leɪð] n torno

**lather** [ˈlɑːðə*] n espuma (de jabón) ♦ vt enjabonar

**Latin** [ˈlætɪn] n latín m ♦ adj latino; **~ America** n América latina; **~ American** adj, n latinoamericano/a

**latitude** [ˈlætɪtjuːd] n latitud f; (fig) libertad f

**latrine** [ləˈtriːn] n letrina

**latter** [ˈlætə*] adj (líter, of two) segundo ♦ n: **the ~** el último, éste; **~ly** adv últimamente

**lattice** [ˈlætɪs] n enrejado

**laudable** [ˈlɔːdəbl] adj loable

**laugh** [lɑːf] n risa ♦ vi reír(se); (to do sth) **for a ~** (hacer algo) en broma; **~ at** vt fus reírse de; **~ off** vt tomar algo a risa; **~able** adj ridículo; **~ing stock** n: **the ~ing stock of** el hazmerreír de; **~ter** n risa

**launch** [lɔːntʃ] n lanzamiento; (boat) lancha ♦ vt (ship) botar; (rocket etc) lanzar; (fig) comenzar; **~(ing)**

**launder** ['lɔːndə*] vt lavar
**launderette** [lɔːn'drɛt] (BRIT) n lavandería (automática)
**laundromat** ['lɔːndrəmæt] (US) n = launderette
**laundry** ['lɔːndrɪ] n (dirty) ropa sucia; (clean) colada; (room) lavadero m
**laureate** ['lɔːrɪət] adj see poet
**lavatory** ['lævətərɪ] n wáter m
**lavender** ['lævəndə*] n lavanda
**lavish** ['lævɪʃ] adj (amount) abundante; (person): ~ with pródigo en ♦ vt: to ~ sth on sb colmar a uno de algo
**law** [lɔː] n ley f; (SCOL) derecho m; (a rule) regla; (professions connected with ~) jurisprudencia; ~-abiding adj respetuoso de la ley; ~ and order n orden m público; ~ court n tribunal m (de justicia); ~-ful adj legítimo, lícito; ~-less adj (action) criminal
**lawn** [lɔːn] n césped m; ~mower n cortacésped m; ~ tennis n tenis m sobre hierba
**law school** (US) n (SCOL) facultad f de derecho
**lawsuit** ['lɔːsuːt] n pleito
**lawyer** ['lɔːjə*] n abogado/a; (for sales, wills etc) notario/a
**lax** [læks] adj laxo
**laxative** ['læksətɪv] n laxante m
**lay** [leɪ] (pt, pp laid) pt of lie ♦ adj laico; (not expert) lego ♦ vt (place) colocar; (eggs, table) poner; (cable) tender; (carpet) extender; ~ aside or by vt dejar a un lado; ~ down vt (pen etc) dejar; (rules etc) establecer; to ~ down the law (pej) imponer las normas; ~ off vt (workers) despedir; ~ on vt (meal, facilities) proveer; ~ out vt (spread out) disponer, exponer; ~about (inf) n vago/a; ~-by n (BRIT: AUT) área de aparcamiento
**layer** ['leɪə*] n capa
**layman** ['leɪmən] n lego
**layout** ['leɪaut] n (design) plan m,

trazado; (PRESS) composición f
**laze** [leɪz] vi (also: ~ about): holgazanear
**lazy** ['leɪzɪ] adj perezoso, vago; (movement) lento
**lb.** abbr = pound (weight)
**lead**[1] [liːd] (pt, pp led) n (front position) delantera; (clue) pista; (ELEC) cable m; (for dog) correa; (THEATRE) papel m principal ♦ vt (walk etc in front of) ir a la cabeza de; (guide): to ~ sb somewhere conducir a uno a algún sitio; (be leader of) dirigir; (start, guide: activity) protagonizar ♦ vi (road, pipe etc) conducir a; (SPORT) ir primero; to be in the ~ (SPORT) llevar la delantera; (fig) ir a la cabeza; to ~ the way (also fig) llevar la delantera; ~ away vt llevar; ~ back vt (person, route) llevar de vuelta; ~ on vt (tease) engañar; ~ to vt fus producir, provocar; ~ up to vt fus (events) conducir a; (in conversation) preparar el terreno para
**lead**[2] [lɛd] n (metal) plomo; (in pencil) mina
**leader** ['liːdə*] n jefe/a m/f, líder m; (SPORT) líder m; ~ship n dirección f; (position) mando; (quality) iniciativa
**leading** ['liːdɪŋ] adj (main) principal; (first) primero; (front) delantero; ~ lady n (THEATRE) primera actriz f; ~ light n (person) figura principal; ~ man n (THEATRE) primer galán m
**lead singer** n cantante m/f
**leaf** [liːf] (pl leaves) n hoja ♦ vi: to ~ through hojear; to turn over a new ~ reformarse
**leaflet** ['liːflɪt] n folleto
**league** [liːg] n sociedad f; (FOOTBALL) liga; to be in ~ with haberse confabulado con
**leak** [liːk] n (of liquid, gas) escape m, fuga; (in pipe) agujero; (in roof) gotera; (in security) filtración f ♦ vi (shoes, ship) hacer agua; (pipe) tener (un) escape; (roof) gotear; (liq-

_uid, gas_) escaparse, fugarse; _(fig)_ divulgarse♦ _vt (fig)_ difundir

**lean** [liːn] _(pt, pp_ **leaned** _or_ **leant**) _adj (thin)_ flaco; _(meat)_ magro♦ _vt:_ **to ~ sth on sth** apoyar algo en algo ♦ _vi (slope)_ inclinarse; **to ~ against** apoyarse contra; **to ~ on** apoyarse en; **~ back/forward** _vi_ inclinarse hacia atrás/adelante; **~ out** _vi_ asomarse; **~ over** _vi_ inclinarse; **~ing** _n:_ **~ing (towards)** inclinación _f_ (hacia); **leant** [lɛnt] _pt, pp of_ **lean**

**leap** [liːp] _(pt, pp_ **leaped** _or_ **leapt**) _n_ salto♦ _vi_ saltar; **~frog** _n_ pídola; **leapt** [lɛpt] _pt, pp of_ **leap**; **~ year** _n_ año bisiesto

**learn** [ləːn] _(pt, pp_ **learned** _or_ **learnt**) _vt_ aprender♦ _vi_ aprender; **to ~ about sth** enterarse de algo; **to ~ to do sth** aprender a hacer algo; **~ed** [ˈləːnɪd] _adj_ erudito; **~er** _n (BRIT: also:_ **~er driver)** principiante _m/f_; **~ing** _n_ el saber _m_, conocimientos _mpl_; **learnt** [ləːnt] _pt, pp of_ **learn**

**lease** [liːs] _n_ arriendo♦ _vt_ arrendar

**leash** [liːʃ] _n_ correa

**least** [liːst] _adj:_ **the ~** _(slightest)_ el menor, el más pequeño; _(smallest amount of)_ mínimo♦ _adv (+ vb)_ menos; _(+ adj):_ **the ~ expensive** el/la menos costoso/a; **the ~ possible effort** el menor esfuerzo posible; **at ~** por lo menos, al menos; **you could at ~ have written** por lo menos podías haber escrito; **not in the ~** en absoluto

**leather** [ˈlɛðə*] _n_ cuero

**leave** [liːv] _(pt, pp_ **left**) _vt_ dejar; _(go away from)_ abandonar; _(place etc: permanently)_ salir de ♦ _vi_ irse; _(train etc)_ salir♦ _n_ permiso; **to ~ sth to sb** _(money etc)_ legar algo a uno; _(responsibility etc)_ encargar algo a uno de algo; **to be left** quedar, sobrar; **there's some milk left over** sobra _or_ queda algo de leche; **on ~** de permiso; **~ behind** _vt (on purpose)_ dejar; _(accidentally)_ dejarse; **~ out** _vt_ omitir; **~ of absence** _n_

permiso de ausentarse

**leaves** [liːvz] _npl of_ **leaf**

**Lebanon** [ˈlɛbənən] _n:_ **the ~** el Líbano

**lecherous** [ˈlɛtʃərəs] _(pej) adj_ lascivo

**lecture** [ˈlɛktʃə*] _n_ conferencia; _(SCOL)_ clase _f_ ♦ _vi_ dar una clase♦ _vt (scold):_ **to ~ sb on** _or_ **about sth** echar una reprimenda a uno por algo; **to give a ~ on** dar una conferencia sobre; **~r** _n_ conferenciante _m/f_; _(BRIT: at university)_ profesor _m/f_

**led** [lɛd] _pt, pp of_ **lead**

**ledge** [lɛdʒ] _n_ repisa; _(of window)_ alféizar _m_; _(of mountain)_ saliente _m_

**ledger** [ˈlɛdʒə*] _n_ libro mayor

**leech** [liːtʃ] _n_ sanguijuela

**leek** [liːk] _n_ puerro

**leer** [lɪə*] _vi:_ **to ~ at sb** mirar de manera lasciva a uno

**leeway** [ˈliːweɪ] _n (fig):_ **to have some ~** tener cierta libertad de acción

**left** [lɛft] _pt, pp of_ **leave** ♦ _adj_ izquierdo; _(remaining):_ **there are 2 ~** quedan dos _n_ izquierda♦ _adv_ a la izquierda; **on** _or_ **to the ~** a la izquierda; **the L-~** _(POL)_ la izquierda; **~-handed** _adj_ zurdo; **the ~ hand side** la izquierda; **~-luggage (office)** _(BRIT)_ _n_ consigna; **~-overs** _npl_ sobras _fpl_; **~-wing** _adj (POL)_ de izquierda, izquierdista

**leg** [lɛg] _n_ pierna; _(of animal, chair)_ pata; _(trouser ~)_ pernera; _(CULIN: of lamb)_ pierna; _(of chicken)_ pata; _(of journey)_ etapa

**legacy** [ˈlɛgəsɪ] _n_ herencia

**legal** [ˈliːgl] _adj (permitted by law)_ lícito; _(of law)_ legal; **~ holiday** _(US)_ _n_ fiesta oficial; **~ize** _vt_ legalizar; **~ly** _adv_ legalmente; **~ tender** _n_ moneda de curso legal

**legend** [ˈlɛdʒənd] _n (also fig: person)_ leyenda

**legislation** [lɛdʒɪsˈleɪʃən] _n_ legislación _f_

**legislature** [ˈlɛdʒɪslətʃə*] _n_ cuerpo

legislativo

**legitimate** [lɪˈdʒɪtɪmət] adj legítimo

**leg-room** n espacio para las piernas

**leisure** [ˈlɛʒə*] n ocio, tiempo libre; at ~ con tranquilidad; ~ **centre** n centro de recreo; **~ly** adj sin prisa, lento

**lemon** [ˈlɛmən] n limón m; **~ade** [-ˈneɪd] n (fizzy) gaseosa; ~ **tea** n té m con limón

**lend** [lɛnd] (pt, pp lent) vt: to ~ sth to sb prestar algo a alguien; **~ing library** n biblioteca de préstamo

**length** [lɛŋθ] n (size) largo, longitud f; (distance): the ~ of todo lo largo de; (of swimming pool, cloth) largo; (of wood, string) trozo; (amount of time) duración f; at ~ (at last) por fin, finalmente; (lengthily) largamente; **~en** vt alargar ♦ vi alargarse; **~ways** adv a lo largo; **~y** adj largo, extenso

**lenient** [ˈliːnɪənt] adj indulgente

**lens** [lɛnz] n (of spectacles) lente f; (of camera) objetivo

**lent** [lɛnt] pt, pp of **lend**

**Lent** [lɛnt] n Cuaresma

**lentil** [ˈlɛntl] n lenteja

**Leo** [ˈliːəu] n Leo

**leotard** [ˈliːətɑːd] n mallas fpl

**leprosy** [ˈlɛprəsɪ] n lepra

**lesbian** [ˈlɛzbɪən] n lesbiana

**less** [lɛs] adj (in size, degree etc) menor; (in quality) menos ♦ pron, adv menos ♦ prep: ~ **tax/10% discount** menos impuestos/el 10 por ciento de descuento; ~ **than half** menos de la mitad; ~ **than ever** menos que nunca; ~ **and** ~ cada vez menos; **the** ~ **he works...** cuanto menos trabaja....

**lessen** [ˈlɛsn] vi disminuir, reducirse ♦ vt disminuir, reducir

**lesser** [ˈlɛsə*] adj menor; to a ~ extent en menor grado

**lesson** [ˈlɛsn] n clase f; (warning) lección f

**lest** [lɛst] conj para que

**let** [lɛt] (pt, pp let) vt (allow) dejar, permitir; (BRIT: lease) alquilar; to ~ sb do sth dejar que uno haga

algo; to ~ sb know sth comunicar algo a uno; **~'s go** ¡vamos!; ~ **him come** que venga; "**to** ~" "se alquila"; ~ **down** vt (tyre) desinflar; (disappoint) defraudar; ~ **go** vi, vt soltar; ~ **in** vt dejar entrar; (visitor etc) hacer pasar; ~ **off** vt (culprit) dejar escapar; (gun) disparar; (bomb) accionar; (firework) hacer estallar; ~ **on** (inf) vi divulgar; ~ **out** vt dejar salir; (sound) soltar; ~ **up** vi disminuir

**lethal** [ˈliːθl] adj (weapon) mortífero; (poison, wound) mortal

**lethargic** [lɛˈθɑːdʒɪk] adj letárgico

**letter** [ˈlɛtə*] n (of alphabet) letra; (correspondence) carta; ~ **bomb** n carta-bomba; **~box** (BRIT) n buzón m; **~ing** n letras fpl

**lettuce** [ˈlɛtɪs] n lechuga

**let-up** [ˈlɛtʌp] n disminución f

**leukaemia** [luːˈkiːmɪə] (US **leukemia**) n leucemia

**level** [ˈlɛvl] adj (flat) llano ♦ adv: to **draw** ~ **with** llegar a la altura de ♦ n nivel m; (height) altura ♦ vt nivelar; allanar; (destroy: building) derribar; (: forest) arrasar; **to be** ~ **with** estar a nivel de; "**A**" ~**s** (BRIT) npl ≈ exámenes mpl de bachillerato superior, B.U.P.; "**O**" ~**s** (BRIT) npl ≈ exámenes mpl de octavo de básica; **on the** ~ (fig: honest) serio; ~ **off** or **out** vi (prices etc) estabilizarse; ~ **crossing** (BRIT) n paso a nivel; **~headed** adj sensato

**lever** [ˈliːvə*] n (also fig) palanca ♦ vt: to ~ **up** levantar con palanca; **~age** n (using bar etc) apalancamiento; (fig: influence) influencia

**levity** [ˈlɛvɪtɪ] n frivolidad f

**levy** [ˈlɛvɪ] n impuesto ♦ vt exigir, recaudar

**lewd** [luːd] adj lascivo; (joke) obsceno, colorado (AM)

**liability** [laɪəˈbɪlɪtɪ] n (pej: person, thing) estorbo, lastre m; (JUR: responsibility) responsabilidad f; **liabilities** npl (COMM) pasivo

**liable** [ˈlaɪəbl] adj (subject): ~ **to** su-

**jeto** a; *(responsible)*: ~ **for** responsable de; *(likely)*: ~ **to do** propenso a hacer

**liaise** [lɪ'eɪz] *vi*: **to** ~ **with** enlazar con; **liaison** [lɪ'eɪzɔn] *n* *(coordination)* enlace *m*; *(affair)* relaciones *fpl* amorosas

**liar** ['laɪə*] *n* mentiroso/a

**libel** ['laɪbl] *n* calumnia ♦ *vt* calumniar

**liberal** ['lɪbərl] *adj* liberal; *(offer, amount etc)* generoso

**liberate** ['lɪbəreɪt] *vt* *(people: from poverty etc)* librar; *(prisoner)* libertar; *(country)* librar

**liberty** ['lɪbətɪ] *n* libertad *f*; *(criminal)*: **to be at** ~ estar en libertad; **to be at** ~ **to do** estar libre para hacer; **to take the** ~ **of doing sth** tomarse la libertad de hacer algo

**Libra** ['liːbrə] *n* Libra

**librarian** [laɪ'breərɪən] *n* bibliotecario/a

**library** ['laɪbrərɪ] *n* biblioteca

**libretto** [lɪ'bretəu] *n* libreto

**Libya** ['lɪbɪə] *n* Libia; ~**n** *adj*, *n* libio/a *m/f*

**lice** [laɪs] *npl* de **louse**

**licence** ['laɪsns] *(US* **license**) *n* licencia; *(permit)* permiso; *(also: driving* ~, *US: driver's* ~) carnet *m* de conducir *(SP)*, permiso *(AM)*

**license** ['laɪsns] *n (US)* = **licence** ♦ *vt* autorizar, dar permiso a; ~**d** *adj (for alcohol)* autorizado para vender bebidas alcohólicas; *(car)* matriculado; ~ **plate** *n (US)* n placa de matrícula)

**lichen** ['laɪkən] *n* líquen *m*

**lick** [lɪk] *vt* lamer; *(inf: defeat)* dar una paliza a; **to** ~ **one's lips** relamerse

**licorice** ['lɪkərɪs] *(US)* n = **liquorice**

**lid** [lɪd] *n (of box, case)* tapa; *(of pan)* tapadera

**lido** ['laɪdəu] *n (BRIT)* piscina

**lie** [laɪ] *(pt* **lay**, *pp* **lain**) *vi (rest)* estar echado, estar acostado; *(of object: be situated)* estar, encontrarse; *(tell lies: pt, pp* **lied**) mentir ♦ *n*

mentira; **to** ~ **low** *(fig)* mantenerse a escondidas; ~ **about** *or* **around** *vi (things)* estar tirado; *(BRIT: people)* estar tumbado; ~**down** *(BRIT)* n: **to have a** ~**down** echarse (una siesta); ~**in** *(BRIT)* n: **to have a** ~**in** quedarse en la cama

**lieu** [luː]: **in** ~ **of** *prep* en lugar de

**lieutenant** [lef'tenənt, *(US)* luː'tenənt] *n (MIL)* teniente *m*

**life** [laɪf] *(pl* **lives**) *n* vida; **to come to** ~ animarse; ~ **assurance** *(BRIT)* n seguro de vida; ~**belt** *(BRIT)* n cinturón *m* salvavidas; ~**boat** *n* lancha de socorro; ~**guard** *n* vigilante *m/f*, socorrista *m/f*; ~ **imprisonment** *n* cadena perpetua; ~ **insurance** *n* = ~ **assurance**; ~ **jacket** *n* chaleco salvavidas; ~**less** *adj* sin vida; *(dull)* soso; ~**like** *adj (model etc)* que parece vivo; *(realistic)* realista; ~**line** *n (fig)* cordón *m* umbilical; ~**long** *adj* de toda la vida; ~ **preserver** *(US)* n = ~**belt**; ~ **sentence** *n* cadena perpetua; ~ **size** *adj* de tamaño natural; ~ **span** *n* vida; ~**style** *n* estilo de vida; ~ **support system** *n (MED)* sistema *m* de respiración asistida; ~**time** *n (of person)* vida; *(of thing)* periodo de vida

**lift** [lɪft] *vt* levantar; *(end: ban, rule)* levantar, suprimir ♦ *vi (fog)* disparcarse ♦ *n (BRIT: machine)* ascensor *m*; **to give sb a** ~ *(BRIT)* llevar a uno en el coche; ~**off** *n* despegue *m*

**light** [laɪt] *(pt, pp* **lighted** *or* **lit**) *n* luz *f*; *(lamp)* luz *f*, lámpara; *(AUT)* faro; *(for cigarette etc)*: **have you got a** ~? ¿tienes fuego? ♦ *vt (candle, cigarette, fire)* encender *(SP)*, prender *(AM)*; *(room)* alumbrar ♦ *adj (colour)* claro; *(not heavy, also fig)* ligero; *(room)* con mucha luz; *(gentle, graceful)* ágil; ~**s** *npl (traffic* ~**s)** semáforos *mpl*; **to come to** ~ salir a luz; **in the** ~ **of** *(new evidence etc)* a la luz de; ~ **up** *vi (smoke)* encender un cigarrillo; *(face)* iluminarse ♦ *vt (illuminate)* iluminar, alumbrar; (set fire to) encender; ~ **bulb** n bombilla (SP), foco (AM); ~**en** vt (make less heavy) aligerar; ~**er** n also: cigarette ~er) encendedor m, mechero; ~**headed** adj (dizzy) mareado; (excited) exaltado; ~**hearted** adj (person) alegre; (remark etc) divertido; ~**house** n faro; ~**ing** n (system) alumbrado; ~**ly** adv ligeramente; (not seriously) con poca seriedad; to get off ~**ly** est castigado con poca severidad; ~**ness** n (in weight) ligereza

**lightning** ['laɪtnɪŋ] n relámpago, rayo; ~ **conductor** (US ~ **rod**) n pararrayos m inv

**light:** ~ **pen** n lápiz m óptico; ~**weight** adj (suit) ligero ♦ n (BOXING) peso ligero; ~ **year** n año luz

**like** [laɪk] vt gustarle a uno ♦ prep como ♦ adj parecido, semejante ♦ n: and the ~ y otros por el estilo; his ~s and dislikes sus gustos y aversiones; I would ~, I'd ~ me gustaría; (for purchase) quisiera; would you ~ a coffee? ¿te apetece un café?; I ~ swimming me gusta nadar; she ~s apples le gustan las manzanas; to be or look ~ sb/sth parecerse a alguien/algo that looks, does it look/taste/sound ~? ¿cómo es/a qué sabe/cómo suena?; that's just ~ him es muy de él, es característico de él; do it ~ this hazlo así; it is nothing ~ ... no tiene parecido alguno con ...; ~**able** adj simpático, agradable

**likelihood** ['laɪklɪhʊd] n probabilidad f

**likely** ['laɪklɪ] adj probable; he's ~ to leave es probable que se vaya; not ~! ¡ni hablar!

**likeness** ['laɪknɪs] n semejanza, parecido; that's a good ~ se parece mucho

**likewise** ['laɪkwaɪz] adv igualmente; to do ~ hacer lo mismo

**liking** ['laɪkɪŋ] n: ~ (for) (person) cariño (a); (thing) afición (a); to be

to sb's ~ ser del gusto de uno

**lilac** ['laɪlək] n (tree) lilo; (flower) lila

**lily** ['lɪlɪ] n lirio, azucena; ~ of the valley n lirio de los valles

**limb** [lɪm] n miembro

**limber** ['lɪmbə*]: to ~ up vi (SPORT) hacer ejercicios de calentamiento

**limbo** ['lɪmbəʊ] n: to be in ~ (fig) quedar a la expectativa

**lime** [laɪm] n (tree) limero; (fruit) lima; (GEO) cal f

**limelight** ['laɪmlaɪt] n: to be in the ~ (fig) ser el centro de atención

**limerick** ['lɪmərɪk] n especie de poema humorístico

**limestone** ['laɪmstəʊn] n piedra caliza

**limit** ['lɪmɪt] n límite m ♦ vt limitar; ~**ation** n limitación f; (weak point) punto flaco; (restriction) restricción f; ~**ed** adj limitado; to be ~ed to limitarse a; ~**ed** (**liability**) **company** (BRIT) n sociedad f anónima

**limousine** ['lɪməziːn] n limusina

**limp** [lɪmp] n: to have a ~ tener cojera ♦ vi cojear ♦ adj flojo; (material) fláccido

**limpet** ['lɪmpɪt] n lapa

**line** [laɪn] n línea; (rope) cuerda; (for fishing) sedal m; (wire) hilo; (row, series) fila, hilera; (of writing) renglón m, línea; (of song) verso; (on face) arruga; (RAIL) vía ♦ vt (road etc) llenar; (SEWING) forrar; to ~ the streets llenar las aceras; in ~ with alineado con; (according to) de acuerdo con; ~ **up** vi hacer cola ♦ vt alinear; (prepare) preparar; organizar

**lined** ['laɪnd] adj (face) arrugado; (paper) rayado

**linen** ['lɪnɪn] n ropa blanca; (cloth) lino

**liner** ['laɪnə*] n vapor m de línea, transatlántico; (for bin) bolsa (de basura)

**linesman** ['laɪnzmən] n (SPORT) juez m de línea

**line-up** n (US: queue) cola; (SPORT) alineación f

**linger** ['lɪŋgə*] vi retrasarse, tardar en marcharse; (smell, tradition) persistir

**lingerie** ['lænʒəriː] n lencería

**lingo** ['lɪŋgəu] (pl ~es) (inf) n jerga

**linguist** ['lɪŋgwɪst] n lingüista m/f; **~ic** adj lingüístico; **~ics** n lingüística

**lining** ['laɪnɪŋ] n forro; (ANAT) (membrana) mucosa

**link** [lɪŋk] n (of a chain) eslabón m; (relationship) relación f, vínculo ♦ vt vincular, unir; (associate): to ~ with or to relacionar con; **~s** npl (GOLF) campo de golf; **~ up** vt acoplar ♦ vi unirse

**lino** ['laɪnəu] n = **linoleum**

**linoleum** [lɪ'nəulɪəm] n linóleo

**lion** ['laɪən] n león m; **~ess** n leona

**lip** [lɪp] n labio; **~read** vi leer los labios; **~ salve** n crema protectora para labios; **~ service** n: to pay ~ service to sth (pej) prometer algo de boquilla; **~stick** n lápiz m de labios, carmín m

**liqueur** [lɪ'kjuə*] n licor m

**liquid** ['lɪkwɪd] adj, n líquido; **~ize** [-aɪz] vt (CULIN) licuar; **~izer** [-aɪzə*] n licuadora

**liquor** ['lɪkə*] n licor m, bebidas fpl alcohólicas

**liquorice** ['lɪkərɪs] (BRIT) n regaliz m

**liquor store** (US) n bodega, tienda de vinos y bebidas alcohólicas

**Lisbon** ['lɪzbən] n Lisboa

**lisp** [lɪsp] n ceceo ♦ vi cecear

**list** [lɪst] n lista ♦ vt (mention) enumerar; (put on a list) poner en una lista; **~ed building** (BRIT) n monumento declarado de interés histórico-artístico

**listen** ['lɪsn] vi escuchar, oír; to ~ to sb/sth escuchar a uno/algo; **~er** n oyente m/f; (RADIO) radioyente m/f

**listless** ['lɪstlɪs] adj apático, indiferente

**lit** [lɪt] pt, pp of **light**

**litany** ['lɪtənɪ] n letanía

**liter** ['liːtə*] (US) n = **litre**

**literacy** ['lɪtərəsɪ] n capacidad f de leer y escribir

**literal** ['lɪtərl] adj literal

**literary** ['lɪtərərɪ] adj literario

**literate** ['lɪtərət] adj que sabe leer y escribir; (educated) culto

**literature** ['lɪtrɪtʃə*] n literatura; (brochures etc) folletos mpl

**lithe** [laɪð] adj ágil

**litigation** [lɪtɪ'geɪʃən] n litigio

**litre** ['liːtə*] (US **liter**) n litro

**litter** ['lɪtə*] n (rubbish) basura; (young animals) camada, cría; **~ bin** (BRIT) n papelera; **~ed** adj: **~ed with** (scattered) lleno de

**little** ['lɪtl] adj (small) pequeño; (not much) poco ♦ adv poco; a ~ poco (de); **~ house/bird** casita/pajarito; a ~ bit un poquito; **~ by ~** poco a poco; **~ finger** n dedo meñique

**live** [vi, vb: lɪv adj laɪv] vi vivir ♦ adj (animal) vivo; (wire) conectado; (broadcast) en directo; (shell) cargado; **~ down** vt hacer olvidar; **~ on** vt fus (food, salary) vivir de; **~ together** vi vivir juntos; **~ up to** vt fus (fulfil) cumplir con

**livelihood** ['laɪvlɪhud] n sustento

**lively** ['laɪvlɪ] adj vivo; (interesting: place, book) animado

**liven up** ['laɪvn-] vt animar ♦ vi animarse

**liver** ['lɪvə*] n hígado

**lives** [laɪvz] npl of **life**

**livestock** ['laɪvstɔk] n ganado

**livid** ['lɪvɪd] adj lívido; (furious) furioso

**living** ['lɪvɪŋ] adj (alive) vivo ♦ n: to earn or make a ~ ganarse la vida; **~ conditions** npl condiciones fpl de vida; **~ room** n sala (de estar); **~ standards** npl nivel m de vida; **~ wage** n jornal m suficiente para vivir

**lizard** ['lɪzəd] n lagarto; (small) lagartija

**load** [ləud] n carga; (weight) peso ♦

**loaf** vt (COMPUT) cargar; (also: ~ up):
to ~ (with) cargar (con or de); a ~
of rubbish (inf) tonterías fpl; a ~
of, ~s of (fig) (gran) cantidad de,
montones de; ~ed adj (vehicle): to
be ~ed with estar cargado de;
(question) intencionado; (inf: rich)
forrado (de dinero)

**loaf** [ləuf] (pl **loaves**) n (barra de)
pan m

**loan** [ləun] n préstamo ♦ vt prestar;
on ~ prestado

**loath** [ləuθ] adj: to be ~ to do sth
estar poco dispuesto a hacer algo

**loathe** [ləuð] vt aborrecer; (person)
odiar; **loathing** n aversión f; odio

**loaves** [ləuvz] npl of **loaf**

**lobby** ['lɒbɪ] n vestíbulo, sala de espera; (POL: pressure group) grupo
de presión ♦ vt presionar

**lobe** [ləub] n lóbulo

**lobster** ['lɒbstə*] n langosta

**local** ['ləukl] adj local ♦ n (pub) bar
m; the ~s los vecinos, los del lugar;
~ anaesthetic n (MED) anestesia local; ~ authority n municipio, ayuntamiento (SP); ~ call n (TEL) llamada local; ~ government n gobierno municipal; ~ity [-'kælɪtɪ] n localidad f; ~ly [-kəlɪ] adv en la vecindad;
por aquí

**locate** [ləu'keɪt] vt (find) localizar;
(situate): to be ~d in estar situado
en

**location** [ləu'keɪʃən] n situación f;
on ~ (CINEMA) en exteriores

**loch** [lɒx] n lago

**lock** [lɒk] n (of door, box) cerradura;
(of canal) esclusa; (of hair) mechón
m ♦ vt (with key) cerrar (con llave)
♦ vi (door etc) cerrarse (con llave);
(wheels) trabarse; ~ in vt encerrar;
~ out vt (person) cerrar la puerta
a; ~ up vt (criminal) meter en la
cárcel; (mental patient) encerrar;
(house) cerrar (con llave) ♦ vi echar
la llave

**locker** ['lɒkə*] n casillero

**locket** ['lɒkɪt] n medallón m

**locksmith** ['lɒksmɪθ] n cerrajero/a

**lockup** ['lɒkʌp] n (jail, cell) cárcel f

**locomotive** [ləukə'məutɪv] n locomotora

**locum** ['ləukəm] n (MED) (médico/a)
interino/a

**locust** ['ləukəst] n langosta

**lodge** [lɒdʒ] n casita (del guarda) ♦
vi (person): to ~ (with) alojarse
(en casa de); (bullet, bone) incrus-
tarse ♦ vt (complaint) presentar; ~r
n huésped, m/f

**lodgings** ['lɒdʒɪŋz] npl alojamiento

**loft** [lɒft] n desván m

**lofty** ['lɒftɪ] adj (noble) sublime;
(haughty) altanero

**log** [lɒg] n (of wood) leño, tronco;
(written account) diario ♦ vt anotar

**logbook** ['lɒgbuk] n (NAUT) diario
de a bordo; (AVIAT) libro de vuelo;
(of car) documentación f (del coche
(SP) or carro (AM))

**loggerheads** ['lɒgəhedz] npl: to be
at ~ (with) estar en desacuerdo
(con)

**logic** ['lɒdʒɪk] n lógica; ~al adj lógico

**logo** ['ləugəu] n logotipo

**loin** [lɔɪn] n (CULIN) lomo, solomillo

**loiter** ['lɔɪtə*] vi (linger) entretenerse

**loll** [lɒl] vi (also: ~ about) repantigar-
se

**lollipop** ['lɒlɪpɒp] n chupa-chup m ®,
piruli m; ~ lady/man (BRIT) n persona encargada de ayudar a los niños
a cruzar la calle

**London** ['lʌndən] n Londres; ~er n
londinense m/f

**lone** [ləun] adj solitario

**loneliness** ['ləunlɪnɪs] n soledad f;
aislamiento

**lonely** ['ləunlɪ] adj (situation) solitario; (person) solo; (place) aislado

**long** [lɒŋ] adj largo ♦ adv mucho
tiempo, largamente ♦ vi: to ~ for
sth anhelar algo; so or as ~ as
mientras, con tal que; don't be ~!
¡no tardes!; ¡vuelve pronto!; how ~
is the street? ¿cuánto tiene la calle
de largo?; how ~ is the lesson?
¿cuánto dura la clase?; 6 metres ~

que mide 6 metros, de 6 metros de largo; **6 months** ~ que dura 6 meses, de 6 meses de duración; **all night** ~ toda la noche; **he no** ~er **comes** ya no viene; ~ **before** mucho antes; **before** ~ (+*future*) dentro de poco; (+*past*) poco tiempo después; **at** ~ last al fin, por fin; ~ **distance** adj (*race*) de larga distancia; (*call*) interurbano; ~all adj de pelo largo; ~**hand** n escritura sin abreviaturas; ~**ing** n anhelo, ansia; (*nostalgia*) nostalgia ♦ adj anhelante

**longitude** ['lɒŋgɪtjuːd] n longitud f

**long:** ~ **jump** n salto de longitud; ~**life** adj (*batteries*) de larga duración; (*milk*) uperizado; ~**lost** adj desaparecido hace mucho tiempo; ~**playing record** n elepé m, disco de larga duración; **L~ Range** adj (*plan*) de gran alcance; (*missile*) de largo alcance; ~**sighted** (*BRIT*) adj presbita; ~**standing** adj de mucho tiempo; ~**suffering** adj sufrido; ~ **term** adj a largo plazo; ~ **wave** n onda larga; ~**winded** adj prolijo

**loo** [luː] (*BRIT: inf*) n water m

**look** [luk] vi mirar; (*seem*) parecer; (*building etc*): to ~ **south/on to the sea** dar al sur/al mar ♦ n (*gen*): to **have a** ~ mirar; (*glance*) mirada; (*appearance*) aire m, aspecto; ~s npl (*good* ~s) belleza; ~ **(here)!** (*expressing annoyance etc*) ¡oye!; ~! (*expressing surprise*) ¡mira!; ~ **after** vt fus (*care for*) cuidar a; (*deal with*) encargarse de; ~ **at** vt fus mirar; (*read quickly*) echar un vistazo a; ~ **back** vi mirar hacia atrás; ~ **down on** vt fus (*fig*) despreciar, mirar con desprecio; ~ **for** vt fus buscar; ~ **forward to** vt fus esperar con ilusión; (*in letters*): **we** ~ **forward to hearing from you** quedamos a la espera de sus gratas noticias; ~ **into** vt investigar; ~ **on** vi mirar (*como espectador*); ~ **out** vi (*beware*): to ~ **out (for)** tener cuidado (de); ~ **out for** vt fus (*seek*) buscar; (*await*) esperar; ~ **round** vi

volver la cabeza; ~ **through** vt fus (*examine*) examinar; ~ **to** vt fus (*rely on*) contar con; ~ **up** vi mirar hacia arriba; (*improve*) mejorar ♦ vt (*word*) buscar; ~ **up to** vt fus admirar; ~**out** n (*tower etc*) puesto de observación; (*person*) vigía m/f; **to be on the** ~**out for sth** estar al acecho de algo

**loom** [luːm] vi: ~ **(up)** (*threaten*) surgir, amenazar; (*event: approach*) aproximarse

**loony** ['luːnɪ] (*inf*) n, adj loco/a m/f

**loop** [luːp] n lazo ♦ vt: **to** ~ **sth round sth** pasar algo alrededor de algo; ~**hole** n escapatoria

**loose** [luːs] adj suelto; (*clothes*) ancho; (*morals, discipline*) relajado; **to be on the** ~ estar en libertad; **to be at a** ~ **end or at** ~ **ends** (*US*) no saber qué hacer; ~ **change** n cambio; ~ **chippings** (*on road*) grava villa suelta; ~**ly** adv libremente, aproximadamente; ~**n** vt aflojar

**loot** [luːt] n botín m ♦ vt saquear

**lop off** [lɒp-] vt (*branches*) podar

**lop-sided** adj torcido

**lord** [lɔːd] n señor m; **L~ Smith** Lord Smith; **the L~** el Señor; **my** ~ (*to bishop*) Ilustrísima; (*to noble etc*) Señor; **good L~!** ¡Dios mío!; **the (House of) L~s** (*BRIT*) la Cámara de los Lores; ~**ship** n: **your L~ship** su Señoría

**lore** [lɔː] n tradiciones fpl

**lorry** ['lɒrɪ] (*BRIT*) n camión m; ~ **driver** n camionero/a m/f

**lose** [luːz] (*pt, pp* **lost**) vt perder ♦ vi perder, ser vencido; to ~ (*time*) (*clock*) atrasarse; ~**r** n perdedor/a m/f

**loss** [lɒs] n pérdida; **heavy** ~**es** (*MIL*) grandes pérdidas; **to be at a** ~ no saber qué hacer; **to make a** ~ sufrir pérdidas

**lost** [lɒst] pt, pp de **lose** ♦ adj perdido; ~ **property** (*US* ~ **and found**) n objetos mpl perdidos

**lot** [lɒt] n (*group: of things*) grupo; (*at auctions*) lote m; **the** ~ el todo, todos; **a ~** (large number: of books etc) muchos; (a great deal) mucho, bastante; **a ~ of, ~s of** mucho(s) (pl); **I read a ~** leo bastante; **to draw ~s (for sth)** echar suertes (para decidir algo)

**lotion** ['ləʊʃən] n loción f

**lottery** ['lɒtərɪ] n lotería f

**loud** [laʊd] adj (voice, sound) fuerte; (laugh, shout) estrepitoso; (condemnation etc) enérgico; (gaudy) chillón/ona ♦ adv (speak etc) fuerte; **out ~** en voz alta; **~hailer** (BRIT) n megáfono; **~ly** adv (noisily) fuerte; (aloud) en voz alta; **~speaker** n altavoz m

**lounge** [laʊndʒ] n salón m, sala (de estar); (at airport etc) sala; (BRIT: also: **~bar**) salón-bar m ♦ vi (also: **~ about** or **around**) reposar, holgazanear; **~ suit** (BRIT) n traje m de calle

**louse** [laʊs] (pl lice) n piojo

**lousy** ['laʊzɪ] (inf) adj (bad quality) malísimo, asqueroso; (ill) fatal

**lout** [laʊt] n gamberro m

**lovable** ['lʌvəbl] adj amable, simpático

**love** [lʌv] n (romantic, sexual) amor m; (kind, caring) cariño ♦ vt amar, querer; (thing, activity) encantar a uno; "**~ from Anne**" (on letter) "un abrazo (de) Anne"; **to ~ to do** encantarle a uno hacer; **to be/fall in ~ with** estar enamorado/enamorarse de; **to make ~** hacer el amor; **for the ~ of** por amor de; "**15 ~**" (TENNIS) "15 a cero"; **I ~ paella** me encanta la paella; **~ affair** n aventura sentimental; **~ letter** n carta de amor; **~ life** n vida sentimental

**lovely** ['lʌvlɪ] adj (delightful) encantador(a); (beautiful) precioso

**lover** ['lʌvə*] n amante m/f; (person in love) enamorado m; (amateur): **a ~ of** un(a) aficionado/a or un(a) amante de

**loving** ['lʌvɪŋ] adj amoroso, cariñoso; (action) tierno

**low** [ləʊ] adj, adv bajo ♦ n (METEOROLOGY) área de baja presión; **to be ~ on** (supplies etc) andar mal de; **to feel ~** sentirse deprimido; **to turn (down) ~** bajar; **~-alcohol** adj bajo en contenido en alcohol; **~-cut** (dress) escotado

**lower** ['ləʊə*] adj más bajo; (less important) menos importante ♦ vt bajar; (reduce) reducir ♦ vr: **to ~ o.s. to** (fig) rebajarse a

**low: ~-fat** adj (milk, yoghurt) desnatado; (diet) bajo en calorías; **~lands** npl (GEO) tierras fpl bajas; **~ly** adj humilde, inferior

**loyal** ['lɔɪəl] adj leal; **~ty** n lealtad f

**lozenge** ['lɒzɪndʒ] n (MED) pastilla

**L.P.** n abbr (= long-playing record) elepé m

**L-plates** ['el-] (BRIT) npl placas fpl de aprendiz de conductor

**Ltd** abbr (= limited company) S.A

**lubricate** ['lu:brɪkeɪt] vt lubricar, engrasar

**lucid** ['lu:sɪd] adj lúcido

**luck** [lʌk] n suerte f; **bad ~** mala suerte; **good ~!** ¡que tengas suerte!, ¡suerte!; **bad** or **hard** or **tough ~!** ¡qué pena!; **~ily** adv afortunadamente; **~y** adj afortunado; (at cards etc) con suerte; (object) que trae suerte

**ludicrous** ['lu:dɪkrəs] adj absurdo

**lug** [lʌg] vt (drag) arrastrar

**luggage** ['lʌgɪdʒ] n equipaje m; **~ rack** n (on car) baca, portaequipajes m inv

**lukewarm** ['lu:kwɔ:m] adj tibio

**lull** [lʌl] n tregua ♦ vt: **to ~ sb to sleep** arrullar a uno; **to ~ sb into a false sense of security** dar a alguien una falsa sensación de seguridad

**lullaby** ['lʌləbaɪ] n nana

**lumbago** [lʌm'beɪgəʊ] n lumbago

**lumber** ['lʌmbə*] n (junk) trastos mpl viejos; (wood) maderas mpl; **~ with**: **to be ~ed with** tener que cargar con algo; **~jack** n maderero

**luminous** ['lu:mɪnəs] adj luminoso

**lump** [lʌmp] n terrón m; (fragment)

trozo; (swelling) bulto ♦ vt (also: ~ together) juntar; ~ **sum** n suma global; **~y** adj (sauce) lleno de grumos; (mattress) lleno de bultos

**lunar** ['lu:nə*] adj lunar

**lunatic** ['lu:nətɪk] adj loco

**lunch** [lʌntʃ] n almuerzo, comida ♦ vi almorzar

**luncheon** ['lʌntʃən] n almuerzo; ~ **meat** n tipo de fiambre; ~ **voucher** (BRIT) n vale m de comida

**lunch time** n hora de comer

**lung** [lʌŋ] n pulmón m

**lunge** [lʌndʒ] vi (also: ~ forward) abalanzarse; **to** ~ **at** arremeter contra

**lurch** [lə:tʃ] vi dar sacudidas ♦ n sacudida; **to leave sb in the** ~ dejar a uno plantado

**lure** [luə*] n (attraction) atracción f ♦ vt tentar

**lurid** ['luərɪd] adj (colour) chillón/ona; (account) espeluznante

**lurk** [lə:k] vi (person, animal) estar al acecho; (fig) acechar

**luscious** ['lʌʃəs] adj (attractive: person, thing) precioso; (food) delicioso

**lush** [lʌʃ] adj exuberante

**lust** [lʌst] n lujuria; (greed) codicia; ~ **after** or **for** vt fus codiciar

**lustre** ['lʌstə*] (US **luster**) n lustre m, brillo

**lusty** ['lʌstɪ] adj robusto, fuerte

**Luxembourg** ['lʌksəmbə:g] n Luxemburgo

**luxuriant** [lʌg'zjuərɪənt] adj exuberante

**luxurious** [lʌg'zjuərɪəs] adj lujoso

**luxury** ['lʌkʃərɪ] n lujo ♦ cpd de lujo

**lying** ['laɪɪŋ] n mentiras fpl ♦ adj mentiroso

**lyrical** ['lɪrɪkl] adj lírico

**lyrics** ['lɪrɪks] npl (of song) letra

# M

**m.** abbr = metre; mile; million

**M.A.** abbr = Master of Arts

**mac** [mæk] (BRIT) n impermeable m

**macaroni** [mækə'rəunɪ] n macarrones mpl

**machine** [mə'ʃi:n] n máquina ♦ vt (dress etc) coser a máquina; (TECH) hacer a máquina; ~ **gun** n ametralladora; ~ **language** n (COMPUT) lenguaje m máquina; **~ry** n maquinaria; (fig) mecanismo

**macho** ['mætʃəu] adj machista

**mackerel** ['mækrl] n inv caballa

**mackintosh** ['mækɪntɔʃ] (BRIT) n impermeable m

**mad** [mæd] adj loco; (idea) disparatado; (angry) furioso; (keen): **to be** ~ **about sth** volverse loco a uno algo

**madam** ['mædəm] n señora

**madden** ['mædn] vt volver loco

**made** [meɪd] pt, pp of **make**

**Madeira** [mə'dɪərə] n (GEO) Madera; (wine) vino de Madera

**made-to-measure** (BRIT) adj hecho a la medida

**madly** ['mædlɪ] adv locamente

**madman** ['mædmən] n loco

**madness** ['mædnɪs] n locura

**Madrid** [mə'drɪd] n Madrid

**Mafia** ['mæfɪə] n Mafia

**magazine** [mægə'zi:n] n revista; (RADIO, TV) programa m magazina

**maggot** ['mægət] n gusano

**magic** ['mædʒɪk] n magia ♦ adj mágico; **~ian** [mə'dʒɪʃən] n mago/a; (conjurer) prestidigitador(a) m/f

**magistrate** ['mædʒɪstreɪt] n juez m/f (municipal)

**magnet** ['mægnɪt] n imán m; **~ic** [-'netɪk] adj magnético; (personality) atrayente; **~ic tape** n cinta magnética

**magnificent** [mæg'nɪfɪsnt] adj magnífico

**magnify** ['mægnɪfaɪ] vt (object) ampliar; (sound) aumentar; **~ing glass** n lupa

**magpie** ['mægpaɪ] n urraca

**mahogany** [mə'hɔgənɪ] n caoba

**maid** [meɪd] n criada; **old** ~ (pej) solterona

**maiden** ['meɪdn] n doncella ♦ adj (aunt etc) solterona; (speech, voy-

*age*) inaugural; **~ name** *n* nombre *m* de soltera

**mail** [meɪl] *n* correo; (*letters*) cartas *fpl* ♦ *vt* echar al correo; **~box** (*US*) *n* buzón *m*; **~ing list** *n* lista de direcciones; **~order** *n* pedido postal

**maim** [meɪm] *vt* mutilar, lisiar

**main** [meɪn] *adj* principal, mayor ♦ *n* (*pipe*) cañería maestra; (*US*) red *f* eléctrica; **the ~s** *npl* (*BRIT: ELEC*) la red eléctrica; **in the ~** en general; **~frame** *n* (*COMPUT*) ordenador *m* central; **~land** *n* tierra firme; **~ly** *adv* principalmente; **~ road** *n* carretera; **~stay** *n* (*fig*) pilar *m*; **~stream** *n* corriente *f* principal

**maintain** [meɪnˈteɪn] *vt* mantener; **maintenance** [ˈmeɪntənəns] *n* mantenimiento; (*LAW*) manutención *f*

**maize** [meɪz] (*BRIT*) *n* maíz *m* (*SP*), choclo (*AM*)

**majestic** [məˈdʒestɪk] *adj* majestuoso

**majesty** [ˈmædʒɪstɪ] *n* majestad *f*; (*title*): **Your M~** Su Majestad

**major** [ˈmeɪdʒə*] *n* (*MIL*) comandante *m* ♦ *adj* (*important*) principal; (*MUS*) mayor

**Majorca** [məˈjɔːkə] *n* Mallorca

**majority** [məˈdʒɒrɪtɪ] *n* mayoría

**make** [meɪk] (*pt, pp* **made**) *vt* hacer; (*manufacture*) fabricar; (*mistake*) cometer; (*speech*) pronunciar; (*cause to be*): **to ~ sb sad** poner triste a alguien; (*force*): **to ~ sb do sth** obligar a alguien a hacer algo; (*earn*) ganar; (*equal*): **2 and 2 ~ 4** 2 y 2 son 4 ♦ *n* marca; **to ~ the bed** hacer la cama; **to ~ a fool of sb** poner a alguien en ridículo; **to ~ a profit/loss** obtener ganancias/sufrir pérdidas; **to ~ it** (*arrive*) llegar; (*achieve sth*) tener éxito; **what time do you ~ it?** ¿qué hora tienes?; **to ~ do with** contentarse con; **~ out** *vt* (*decipher*) descifrar; (*understand*) entender; (*see*) distinguir; (*cheque*) extender; **~ up** *vt* (*invent*) inventar; (*prepare*) hacer; (*constitute*) constituir ♦ *vi* reconciliarse; (*with cosmetics*) maquillarse; **~ up for** *vt fus*

compensar; **~believe** *n* ficción *f*, invención *f*; **~r** *n* fabricante *m/f*; (*of film, programme*) autor(a) *m/f*; **~shift** *adj* improvisado; **~up** *n* maquillaje *m*; **~up remover** *n* desmaquillador *m*

**making** [ˈmeɪkɪŋ] *n* (*fig*): **in the ~** en vías de formación; **to have the ~s of** (*person*) tener madera de

**malaise** [mæˈleɪz] *n* malestar *m*

**Malaysia** [məˈleɪzɪə] *n* Malasia, Malaysia

**male** [meɪl] *n* (*BIOL*) macho ♦ *adj* (*sex, attitude*) masculino; (*child etc*) varón

**malfunction** [mælˈfʌŋkʃən] *n* mal funcionamiento

**malice** [ˈmælɪs] *n* malicia; **malicious** [məˈlɪʃəs] *adj* malicioso; rencoroso

**malign** [məˈlaɪn] *vt* difamar, calumniar

**malignant** [məˈlɪɡnənt] *adj* (*MED*) maligno

**mall** [mɔːl] (*US*) *n* (*also: shopping ~*) centro comercial

**mallet** [ˈmælɪt] *n* mazo

**malnutrition** [mælnjuːˈtrɪʃən] *n* desnutrición *f*

**malpractice** [mælˈpræktɪs] *n* negligencia profesional

**malt** [mɔːlt] *n* malta; (*whisky*) whisky *m* de malta

**Malta** [ˈmɔːltə] *n* Malta; **Maltese** *adj, n inv* maltés/esa *m/f*

**mammal** [ˈmæml] *n* mamífero

**mammoth** [ˈmæməθ] *n* mamut *m* ♦ *adj* gigantesco

**man** [mæn] (*pl* **men**) *n* hombre *m*; (*~kind*) el hombre ♦ *vt* (*NAUT*) tripular; (*MIL*) guarnecer; (*operate: machine*) manejar; **an old ~** un viejo; **~ and wife** marido y mujer

**manage** [ˈmænɪdʒ] *vi* arreglárselas, ir tirando ♦ *vt* (*be in charge of*) dirigir; (*control: person*) manejar; (*ship*) gobernar; **~able** *adj* manejable; **~ment** *n* dirección *f*; **~r** *n* director(a) *m/f*; (*of pop star*) mánager *m/f*; (*SPORT*) entrenador(a) *m/f*; **~ress** *n* directora; entrenadora,

~**rial** [-ɔ'dʒɪərɪəl] adj directivo; **managing director** n director(a) m/f general

**mandarin** ['mændərɪn] n (also: ~ orange) mandarina; (person) mandarín m

**mandate** ['mændeɪt] n mandato

**mandatory** ['mændətərɪ] adj obligatorio

**mane** [meɪn] n (of horse) crin f; (of lion) melena

**maneuver** [mə'nuːvə*] n (US) = maneuvre

**manfully** ['mænfəlɪ] adv valientemente

**mangle** ['mæŋgl] vt mutilar, destrozar

**mangy** ['meɪndʒɪ] adj (animal) sarnoso

**manhandle** ['mænhændl] vt maltratar

**manhole** ['mænhəul] n agujero de acceso

**manhood** ['mænhud] n edad f viril; (state) virilidad f

**man-hour** n hora-hombre f

**manhunt** ['mænhʌnt] n (POLICE) búsqueda y captura

**mania** ['meɪnɪə] n manía; ~**c** ['meɪnɪæk] n maníaco/a; (fig) maniático

**manic** ['mænɪk] adj frenético; ~**depressive** n maníaco/a depresivo/a

**manicure** ['mænɪkjuə*] n manicura

**manifest** ['mænɪfest] vt manifestar, mostrar ♦ adj manifiesto

**manifesto** [mænɪ'festəu] n manifiesto

**manipulate** [mə'nɪpjuleɪt] vt manipular

**mankind** [mæn'kaɪnd] n humanidad f, género humano

**manly** ['mænlɪ] adj varonil

**man-made** adj artificial

**manner** ['mænə*] n manera, modo; (behaviour) conducta, manera de ser; (type): all ~ of things toda clase de cosas; ~**s** npl (behaviour) modales mpl; bad ~**s** mala educación; ~**ism** n peculiaridad f de len-

guaje (or de comportamiento)

**manoeuvre** [mə'nuːvə*] (US maneuver) vt, vi maniobrar ♦ n maniobra

**manor** ['mænə*] n (also: ~ house) casa solariega

**manpower** ['mænpauə*] n mano f de obra

**mansion** ['mænʃən] n palacio, casa grande

**manslaughter** ['mænslɔːtə*] n homicidio no premeditado

**mantelpiece** ['mæntlpiːs] n repisa, chimenea

**manual** ['mænjuəl] adj manual ♦ n manual m

**manufacture** [mænju'fæktʃə*] vt fabricar ♦ n fabricación f; ~**r** n fabricante m/f

**manure** [mə'njuə*] n estiércol m

**manuscript** ['mænjuskrɪpt] n manuscrito

**many** ['menɪ] adj, pron muchos/as; a great ~ muchísimos, un buen número de; ~ a time muchas veces

**map** [mæp] n mapa m; **to ~ out** vt proyectar

**maple** ['meɪpl] n arce m (SP), maple m (AM)

**mar** [mɑː*] vt estropear

**marathon** ['mærəθən] n maratón m

**marauder** [mə'rɔːdə*] n merodeador(a) m/f

**marble** ['mɑːbl] n mármol m; (toy) canica

**March** [mɑːtʃ] n marzo

**march** [mɑːtʃ] vi (MIL) marchar; (demonstrators) manifestarse ♦ n marcha; (demonstration) manifestación f

**mare** [meə*] n yegua

**margarine** [mɑːdʒə'riːn] n margarina

**margin** ['mɑːdʒɪn] n margen m; (COMM: profit ~) margen m de beneficios; ~**al** adj marginal; ~**al seat** n (POL) escaño electoral difícil de asegurar

**marigold** ['mærɪgəuld] n caléndula

**marijuana** [mærɪ'wɑːnə] n marijuana

**marina** [mə'riːnə] n puerto deportivo

**marinate** ['mærɪneɪt] vt marinar

**marine** [mə'riːn] adj marino ♦ n soldado de marina

**marital** ['mærɪtl] adj matrimonial; ~ **status** estado civil

**marjoram** ['mɑːdʒərəm] n mejorana

**mark** [mɑːk] n marca, señal f; (in snow, mud etc) huella; (stain) mancha; (BRIT: SCOL) nota; (currency) marco ♦ vt marcar; manchar; (damage: furniture) rayar; (indicate: place etc) señalar; (BRIT: SCOL) calificar, corregir; **to ~ time** marcar el paso; (fig) marcar(se) un ritmo; ~**ed** adj (obvious) marcado, acusado; ~**er** n (sign) marcador m; (bookmark) señal f (de libro)

**market** ['mɑːkɪt] n mercado ♦ vt (COMM) comercializar; ~ **garden** (BRIT) n huerto; ~**ing** n márketing m; ~**place** n mercado; ~ **research** n análisis m inv de mercados

**marksman** ['mɑːksmən] n tirador m

**marmalade** ['mɑːməleɪd] n mermelada de naranja

**maroon** [mə'ruːn] vt: **to be** ~**ed** quedar aislado; (fig) quedar abandonado

**marquee** [mɑː'kiː] n entoldado

**marquess** ['mɑːkwɪs] n marqués m

**marquis** ['mɑːkwɪs] n = **marquess**

**marriage** ['mærɪdʒ] n (relationship, institution) matrimonio; (wedding) boda; (act) casamiento; ~ **bureau** n agencia matrimonial; ~ **certificate** n partida de casamiento

**married** ['mærɪd] adj casado; (life, love) conyugal

**marrow** ['mærəʊ] n médula; (vegetable) calabacín m

**marry** ['mærɪ] vt casarse con; (subj: father, priest etc) casar ♦ vi (also: **get married**) casarse

**Mars** [mɑːz] n Marte m

**marsh** [mɑːʃ] n pantano; (salt ~) marisma

**marshal** ['mɑːʃl] n (MIL) mariscal m; (at sports meeting etc) oficial m;

(US: of police, fire department) jefe/a m/f ♦ vt (thoughts etc) ordenar; (soldiers) formar

**marshy** ['mɑːʃɪ] adj pantanoso

**martial** ['mɑːʃl] adj marcial; ~ **law** n ley f marcial

**martyr** ['mɑːtə*] n mártir m/f; ~**dom** n martirio

**marvel** ['mɑːvl] n maravilla, prodigio ♦ vi: **to ~ (at)** maravillarse (de); ~**lous** (US ~**ous**) adj maravilloso

**Marxist** ['mɑːksɪst] adj, n marxista m/f

**marzipan** ['mɑːzɪpæn] n mazapán m

**mascara** [mæs'kɑːrə] n rímel m

**masculine** ['mæskjulɪn] adj masculino

**mash** [mæʃ] vt machacar; ~**ed potatoes** npl puré m de patatas (SP) or papas (AM)

**mask** [mɑːsk] n máscara ♦ vt (cover): **to ~ one's face** ocultarse la cara; (hide: feelings) esconder

**masochist** ['mæsəkɪst] n masoquista m/f

**mason** ['meɪsn] n (also: **stone~**) albañil m; (also: **free~**) masón m; ~**ry** n (in building) mampostería

**masquerade** [mæskə'reɪd] vi: **to ~ as** disfrazarse de, hacerse pasar por

**mass** [mæs] n (people) muchedumbre f; (of air, liquid etc) masa; (of detail, hair etc) gran cantidad f; (REL) misa ♦ cpd masivo ♦ vi reunirse; concentrarse; **the ~es** npl las masas; ~**es of** (inf) montones de

**massacre** ['mæskə*] n masacre f

**massage** ['mæsɑːʒ] n masaje m ♦ vt dar masaje en

**masseur** [mæ'sɜː*] n masajista m

**masseuse** [mæ'sɜːz] n masajista f

**massive** ['mæsɪv] adj enorme; (support, changes) masivo

**mass media** npl medios mpl de comunicación

**mass-production** n fabricación f en serie

**mast** [mɑːst] n (NAUT) mástil m; (RADIO etc) torre f

**master** ['mɑːstə*] n (of servant)

**masturbate** 167 **me**

amo; (of situation) dueño, maestro; (in primary school) maestro; (in secondary school) profesor m; (title for boys): **M~ X** Señorito **X** ♦ vt dominar; **M~ of Arts/Science** n licenciatura superior en Letras/Ciencias; **~ly** adj magistral; **~mind** n inteligencia superior ♦ vt dirigir, planear; **~piece** n obra maestra; **~y** n maestría

**masturbate** ['mæstəbeɪt] vi masturbarse

**mat** [mæt] n estera; (also: door~) felpudo; (also: table ~) salvamanteles m inv, posavasos m inv ♦ adj = **matt**

**match** [mætʃ] n cerilla, fósforo; (game) partido; (equal) igual m/f ♦ vt (go well with) hacer juego con; (equal) igualar; (correspond to) corresponderse con; (pair: also: ~ up) casar con ♦ vi hacer juego; **to be a good ~** hacer juego; **~box** n caja de cerillas; **~ing** adj que hace juego

**mate** [meɪt] n (work~) colega m/f; (inf: friend) amigo/a; (animal) macho m/hembra f; (in merchant navy) segundo de a bordo ♦ vi acoplarse, aparearse ♦ vt aparear

**material** [mə'tɪərɪəl] n (substance) materia; (information) material m; (cloth) tela, tejido ♦ adj material; (important) esencial; **~s** npl materiales mpl; **~istic** [-'lɪstɪk] adj materialista; **~ize** vi materializarse

**maternal** [mə'tɜ:nl] adj maternal

**maternity** [mə'tɜ:nɪtɪ] n maternidad f; **~ dress** n vestido premamá

**math** [mæθ] (US) n = **mathematics**

**mathematical** [mæθə'mætɪkl] adj matemático

**mathematician** [mæθəmə'tɪʃən] n matemático/a

**mathematics** [mæθə'mætɪks] n matemáticas fpl

**maths** [mæθs] (BRIT) n = **mathematics**

**matinée** ['mætɪneɪ] n sesión f de tarde

**matrices** ['meɪtrɪsi:z] npl of **matrix**

**matriculation** [mətrɪkju'leɪʃən] n (formalización f de) matrícula

**matrimony** ['mætrɪmənɪ] n matrimonio

**matrix** ['meɪtrɪks] (pl **matrices**) n matriz f

**matron** ['meɪtrən] n enfermera f jefe; (in school) ama de llaves

**matt(t)** [mæt] adj mate

**matted** ['mætɪd] adj enmarañado

**matter** ['mætə*] n cuestión f, asunto; (PHYSICS) sustancia, materia; (reading ~) material m; (MED: pus) pus m ♦ vi importar; **~s** npl (affairs) asuntos mpl, temas mpl; **it doesn't ~** no importa; **what's the ~?** ¿qué pasa?; **no ~ what** pase lo que pase; **as a ~ of course** por rutina; **as a ~ of fact** de hecho; **~-of-fact** adj prosaico, práctico

**mattress** ['mætrɪs] n colchón m

**mature** [mə'tjuə*] adj maduro ♦ vi madurar; **maturity** n madurez f

**maul** [mɔ:l] vt magullar

**mauve** [məuv] adj de color malva (SP) or guinda (AM)

**maverick** ['mævərɪk] n hombre/mujer m/f poco ortodoxo/a

**maxim** ['mæksɪm] n máxima

**maximum** ['mæksɪməm] (pl maxima) adj máximo ♦ n máximo

**May** [meɪ] n mayo

**may** [meɪ] (conditional: **might**) vi (indicating possibility): **he ~ come** puede que venga; (be allowed to): **~ I smoke?** ¿puedo fumar?; (wishes): **~ God bless you!** ¡que Dios le bendiga!; **you ~ as well go** bien puedes irte

**maybe** ['meɪbi:] adv quizá(s)

**May Day** n el primero de Mayo

**mayhem** ['meɪhem] n caos m total

**mayonnaise** [meɪə'neɪz] n mayonesa

**mayor** [meə*] n alcalde m; **~ess** n alcaldesa

**maze** [meɪz] n laberinto

**M.D.** abbr = **Doctor of Medicine**

**me** [mi:] pron (direct) me; (stressed, after pron) mí; **can you hear ~?**

¿me oyes?; **he heard ME!** me oyó a mí; **it's ~** soy yo; **give them to ~** dámelos/las; **with/without ~** conmigo/sin mí

**meadow** ['mɛdəu] n prado, pradera

**meagre** ['miːgə*] (US **meager**) adj escaso, pobre

**meal** [miːl] n comida; (flour) harina; **~time** n hora de comer

**mean** [miːn] (pt, pp **meant**) adj (with money) tacaño; (unkind) mezquino, malo; (shabby) humilde; (average) medio ♦ vt (signify) querer decir, significar; (refer to) referirse a; (intend): **to ~ to do sth** pensar or pretender hacer algo ♦ n medio, término medio; **~s** npl (way) medio, manera; (money) recursos mpl, medios mpl; **by ~s of** mediante, por medio de; **by all ~s!** ¡naturalmente!, ¡claro que sí!; **do you ~ it?** ¿lo dices en serio?; **what do you ~?** ¿qué quiere decir?; **to be meant for sb/sth** ser para uno/algo

**meander** [mɪ'ændə*] vi (river) serpentear

**meaning** ['miːnɪŋ] n significado, sentido; (purpose) sentido, propósito; **~ful** adj significativo; **~less** adj sin sentido

**meanness** ['miːnnɪs] n (with money) tacañería; (unkindness) maldad f, mezquindad f; (shabbiness) humildad f

**meant** [mɛnt] pt, pp of **mean**

**meantime** ['miːntaɪm] adv (also: **in the ~**) mientras tanto

**meanwhile** ['miːnwaɪl] adv = **meantime**

**measles** ['miːzlz] n sarampión m

**measly** ['miːzlɪ] (inf) adj miserable

**measure** ['mɛʒə*] vt, vi medir ♦ n medida; (ruler) regla; **~d** adj (tone, step) comedido; **~ments** npl medidas fpl

**meat** [miːt] n carne f; **cold ~** fiambre m; **~ball** n albóndiga; **~ pie** n pastel m de carne

**Mecca** ['mɛkə] n La Meca

**mechanic** [mɪ'kænɪk] n mecánico/a;

**~s** n mecánica ♦ npl mecanismo; **~al** adj mecánico

**mechanism** ['mɛkənɪzəm] n mecanismo

**medal** ['mɛdl] n medalla; **~lion** [mɪ'dælɪən] n medallón m; **~list** (US **~ist**) n (SPORT) medallista m/f

**meddle** ['mɛdl] vi: **to ~ in** entrometerse en; **to ~ with sth** manosear algo

**media** ['miːdɪə] npl medios mpl de comunicación ♦ npl of **medium**

**mediaeval** [mɛdɪ'iːvl] adj = **medieval**

**mediate** ['miːdɪeɪt] vi mediar; **mediator** n intermediario/a, mediador(a) m/f

**Medicaid** ['mɛdɪkeɪd] (US) n programa de ayuda médica para los pobres

**medical** ['mɛdɪkl] adj médico ♦ n reconocimiento médico

**Medicare** ['mɛdɪkeə*] (US) n programa de ayuda médica para los ancianos

**medication** [mɛdɪ'keɪʃən] n medicación f

**medicine** ['mɛdsɪn] n medicina; (drug) medicamento

**medieval** [mɛdɪ'iːvl] adj medieval

**mediocre** [miːdɪ'əukə*] adj mediocre

**meditate** ['mɛdɪteɪt] vi meditar

**Mediterranean** [mɛdɪtə'reɪnɪən] adj mediterráneo; **the ~ (Sea)** el (Mar) Mediterráneo

**medium** ['miːdɪəm] (pl **media**) adj mediano, regular ♦ n (means) medio; (pl **mediums**: person) médium m/f; **~ wave** n onda media

**medley** ['mɛdlɪ] n mezcla; (MUS) popurrí m

**meek** [miːk] adj manso, sumiso

**meet** [miːt] (pt, pp **met**) vt encontrar; (accidentally) encontrarse con, tropezar con; (by arrangement) reunirse con; (for the first time) conocer; (go and fetch) ir a buscar; (opponent) enfrentarse con; (obligations) cumplir; (encounter: problem) hacer frente a; (need) satisfacer ♦

*vi* encontrarse; (*in session*) reunirse; (*join: objects*) unirse; (*for the first time*) conocerse; ~ **with** *vt fus* (*difficulty*) tropezar con; **to** ~ **with success** tener éxito; ~**ing** *n* encuentro; (*arranged*) cita, compromiso; (*business* ~) reunión *f*; (*POL*) mitin *m*

**megabyte** ['megəbaɪt] *n* (*COMPUT*) megabyte *m*, megaocteto

**megaphone** ['megəfəun] *n* megáfono

**melancholy** ['melənkəlɪ] *n* melancolía ♦ *adj* melancólico

**mellow** ['meləu] *adj* (*wine*) añejo; (*sound, colour*) suave ♦ *vi* (*person*) ablandar

**melody** ['melədɪ] *n* melodía

**melon** ['melən] *n* melón *m*

**melt** [melt] *vi* (*metal*) fundirse; (*snow*) derretirse ♦ *vt* fundir; ~**down** *n* (*in nuclear reactor*) fusión *f* de un reactor (nuclear); ~**ing pot** *n* (*fig*) crisol *m*

**member** ['membə*] *n* (*gen, ANAT*) miembro; (*of club*) socio/a; **M**~ **of Parliament** (*BRIT*) diputado/a; **M**~ **of the European Parliament** (*BRIT*) eurodiputado/a; ~**ship** *n* (*members*) número de miembros; (*state*) filiación *f*; ~**ship card** *n* carnet *m* de socio

**memento** [mə'mentəu] *n* recuerdo

**memo** ['meməu] *n* apunte *m*, nota

**memoirs** ['memwɑːz] *npl* memorias *fpl*

**memorandum** [memə'rændəm] (*pl* **memoranda**) *n* apunte *m*, nota; (*official note*) acta

**memorial** [mɪ'mɔːrɪəl] *n* monumento conmemorativo ♦ *adj* conmemorativo

**memorize** ['meməraɪz] *vt* aprender de memoria

**memory** ['memərɪ] *n* (*also: COMPUT*) memoria; (*instance*) recuerdo; (*of dead person*): **in** ~ **of** a la memoria de

**men** [men] *npl of* **man**

**menace** ['menəs] *n* amenaza ♦ *vt* amenazar; **menacing** *adj* amenazador(a)

**mend** [mend] *vt* reparar, arreglar; (*darn*) zurcir ♦ *vi* reponerse ♦ *n* arreglo, reparación *f*; zurcido ♦ *n*: **to be on the** ~ ir mejorando; **to one's ways** enmendarse; ~**ing** *n* reparación *f*; (*clothes*) ropa por remendar

**menial** ['miːnɪəl] (*often pej*) *adj* bajo

**meningitis** [menɪn'dʒaɪtɪs] *n* meningitis *f*

**menopause** ['menəupɔːz] *n* menopausia

**menstruation** [menstru'eɪʃən] *n* menstruación *f*

**mental** ['mentl] *adj* mental; ~**ity** [-'tælɪtɪ] *n* mentalidad *f*

**mention** ['menʃən] *n* mención *f* ♦ *vt* mencionar; (*speak of*) hablar de; **don't** ~ **it!** ¡de nada!

**menu** ['menjuː] *n* (*set* ~) menú *m*; (*printed*) carta; (*COMPUT*) menú *m*

**MEP** *n abbr* = **Member of the European Parliament**

**mercenary** ['məːsɪnərɪ] *adj, n* mercenario/a

**merchandise** ['məːtʃəndaɪz] *n* mercancías *fpl*

**merchant** ['məːtʃənt] *n* comerciante *m/f*; ~ **bank** (*BRIT*) banco comercial; ~ **navy** (*US* ~ **marine**) *n* marina mercante

**merciful** ['məːsɪful] *adj* compasivo; (*fortunate*) afortunado

**merciless** ['məːsɪlɪs] *adj* despiadado

**mercury** ['məːkjurɪ] *n* mercurio

**mercy** ['məːsɪ] *n* compasión *f*; (*REL*) misericordia; **at the** ~ **of** a la merced de

**mere** [mɪə*] *adj* simple, mero; ~**ly** *adv* simplemente, sólo

**merge** [məːdʒ] *vt* (*join*) unir ♦ *vi* unirse; (*COMM*) fusionarse; (*colours etc*) fundirse; ~**r** *n* (*COMM*) fusión *f*

**meringue** [mə'ræŋ] *n* merengue *m*

**merit** ['merɪt] *n* mérito ♦ *vt* merecer

**mermaid** ['məːmeɪd] *n* sirena

**merry** ['merɪ] *adj* alegre; **M**~ **Christmas!** ¡Felices Pascuas!; ~-**go-round** *n* tiovivo

**mesh** [meʃ] *n* malla

**mesmerize** ['mɛzməraɪz] vt hipnoti-zar

**mess** [mɛs] n (muddle: of situation) confusión f; (: of room) revoltijo; (dirt) porquería; (MIL) comedor m; ~ **about** or **around** (inf) vi perder el tiempo; (pass the time) entretenerse; ~ **about** or **around with** (inf) vt fus divertirse con; ~ **up** vt (spoil) estropear; (dirty) ensuciar

**message** ['mɛsɪdʒ] n recado, mensa-je m

**messenger** ['mɛsɪndʒə*] n men-sajero/a

**Messrs** abbr (on letters: = Mes-sieurs) Sres

**messy** ['mɛsɪ] adj (dirty) sucio; (un-tidy) desordenado

**met** [mɛt] pt, pp of **meet**

**metabolism** [mɛ'tæbəlɪzəm] n meta-bolismo

**metal** ['mɛtl] n metal m; ~**lic** [-'tælɪk] adj metálico

**metaphor** ['mɛtəfə*] n metáfora

**mete** [miːt]: to ~ **out** vt (punish-ment) imponer

**meteor** ['miːtɪə*] n meteoro; ~**ite** [-aɪt] n meteorito

**meteorology** [miːtɪə'rɔlədʒɪ] n me-teorología

**meter** ['miːtə*] n (instrument) conta-dor m; (US: unit) = **metre** ♦ vt (US: POST) franquear

**method** ['mɛθəd] n método

**Methodist** ['mɛθədɪst] adj, n meto-dista m/f

**meths** [mɛθs] (BRIT) n = **meth-ylated spirit**

**methylated spirit** ['mɛθɪleɪtɪd-] (BRIT) n alcohol m metilado or des-naturalizado

**metre** ['miːtə*] (US **meter**) n metro

**metric** ['mɛtrɪk] adj métrico

**metropolis** [mɪ'trɔpəlɪs] n metrópoli f

**metropolitan** [mɛtrə'pɔlɪtən] adj metropolitano; **the M~ Police** (BRIT) n la policía londinense

**mettle** ['mɛtl] n: to be on one's ~ estar dispuesto a mostrar todo lo que

uno vale

**mew** [mjuː] vi (cat) maullar

**mews** [mjuːz] n: ~ **flat** (BRIT) piso acondicionado en antiguos establos o cocheras

**Mexican** ['mɛksɪkən] adj, n mejicano/a m/f, mexicano/a m/f

**Mexico** ['mɛksɪkəu] n Méjico (SP), México (AM); ~ **City** n Ciudad f de Méjico or México

**miaow** [miː'au] vi maullar

**mice** [maɪs] npl of **mouse**

**micro...** [maɪkrəu] prefix micro...; ~**chip** n microplaqueta; ~**(com-puter)** n microordenador m; ~**phone** n micrófono; ~**processor** n micro-procesador m; ~**scope** n micros-copio; ~**wave** n (also: ~**wave oven**) horno microondas

**mid** [mɪd] adj: in ~ **May** a mediados de mayo; in ~ **afternoon** a media tarde; in ~ **air** en el aire; ~**day** n mediodía m

**middle** ['mɪdl] n centro; (half-way point) medio; (waist) cintura ♦ adj de en medio; (course, way) interme-dio; in the ~ of the night en plena noche; ~**aged** adj de mediana edad; the **M~ Ages** npl la Edad Media; ~**class** adj de clase media; the ~**class(es)** n(pl) la clase media; **M~ East** n Oriente m Medio; ~**man** n (pl) intermediario; ~ **name** n segundo nombre; ~**of-the-road** adj modera-do; ~**weight** n (BOXING) peso me-dio; ~**middling** adj mediano

**midge** [mɪdʒ] n mosquito

**midget** ['mɪdʒɪt] n enano/a

**Midlands** ['mɪdləndz] npl: the ~ la región central de Inglaterra

**midnight** ['mɪdnaɪt] n medianoche f

**midriff** ['mɪdrɪf] n diafragma m

**midst** [mɪdst] n: in the ~ of (crowd) en medio de; (situation, ac-tion) en mitad de

**midsummer** [mɪd'sʌmə*] n: in ~ en pleno verano

**midway** [mɪd'weɪ] adj, adv: ~ (be-tween) a medio camino (entre); ~ **through** a la mitad (de)

**midweek** [mɪd'wiːk] *adv* entre semana

**midwife** ['mɪdwaɪf] (*pl* **midwives**) *n* comadrona, partera

**midwinter** [mɪd'wɪntə*] *n*: **in ~** en pleno invierno

**might** [maɪt] *vb see* **may ♦** *n* fuerza, poder *m*; **~y** *adj* fuerte, poderoso

**migraine** ['miːɡreɪn] *n* jaqueca

**migrant** ['maɪɡrənt] *n adj* (*bird*) migratorio; (*worker*) emigrante

**migrate** [maɪ'ɡreɪt] *vi* emigrar

**mike** [maɪk] *n abbr* (= *microphone*) micro

**mild** [maɪld] *adj* (*person*) apacible; (*climate*) templado; (*slight*) ligero; (*taste*) suave; (*illness*) leve

**mildew** ['mɪldjuː] *n* moho

**mildly** ['maɪldlɪ] *adv* ligeramente, suavemente; **to put it ~** para no decir más

**mile** [maɪl] *n* milla; **~age** *n* número de millas, ~ kilometraje *m*; **~ometer** *n* ~ cuentakilómetros *m inv*; **~stone** *n* mojón *m*

**milieu** ['miːljə:] *n* (medio) ambiente *m*

**militant** ['mɪlɪtnt] *adj*, *n* militante *m/f*

**military** ['mɪlɪtərɪ] *adj* militar

**militate** ['mɪlɪteɪt] *vi*: **to ~ against** ir en contra de, perjudicar

**militia** [mɪ'lɪʃə] *n* milicia

**milk** [mɪlk] *n* leche *f* ♦ *vt* (*cow*) ordeñar; (*fig*) chupar; **~ chocolate** *n* chocolate *m* con leche; **~man** *n* lechero; **~ shake** *n* batido, malteada (*AM*); **~y** *adj* lechoso; **M~y Way** *n* Vía Láctea

**mill** [mɪl] *n* (*windmill etc*) molino; (*coffee ~*) molinillo; (*factory*) fábrica ♦ *vt* moler ♦ *vi* (*also*: **~ about**) arremolinarse

**millennium** [mɪ'lɛnɪəm] (*pl* **~s** *or* **millennia**) *n* milenio, milenario

**miller** ['mɪlə*] *n* molinero

**milli...** ['mɪlɪ] *prefix*: **~gram(me)** *n* miligramo; **~metre** (*US* **~meter**) *n* milímetro

**millinery** ['mɪlɪnrɪ] *n* sombrerería

**million** ['mɪljən] *n* millón *m*; **a ~ times** un millón de veces; **~aire** *n* millonario/a

**milometer** [maɪ'lɔmɪtə*] (*BRIT*) *n* = **mileometer**

**mime** [maɪm] *n* mímica; (*actor*) mimo/a ♦ *vt* remedar ♦ *vi* actuar de mimo

**mimic** ['mɪmɪk] *n* imitador(a) *m/f* ♦ *adj* mímico ♦ *vt* remedar, imitar

**min.** *abbr* = **minute(s)**; **minimum**

**minaret** [mɪnə'rɛt] *n* alminar *m*

**mince** [mɪns] *vt* picar ♦ *vi* (*in walking*) andar con pasos menudos ♦ *n* (*BRIT*: *CULIN*) carne *f* picada; **~meat** *n* conserva de fruta picada; (*US*: *meat*) carne *f* picada; **~ pie** *n* empanadilla rellena de fruta picada; **~r** *n* picadora de carne

**mind** [maɪnd] *n* mente *f*; (*intellect*) intelecto; (*contrasted with matter*) espíritu ♦ *vt* (*attend to, look after*) ocuparse de, cuidar; (*be careful of*) tener cuidado con; (*object to*): **I don't ~ the noise** no me molesta el ruido; **it is on my ~** me preocupa; **to bear sth in ~** tomar *or* tener algo en cuenta; **to make up one's ~** decidirse; **I don't ~** me es igual; **~ you, ...** te advierto que ...; **never ~!** ¡es igual!, ¡no importa!; (*don't worry*) ¡no te preocupes!; **"~ the step"** "cuidado con el escalón"; **~er** *n* guardaespaldas *m inv*; (*child ~er*) ≈ niñera; **~ful** *adj*: **~ful of** consciente de; **~less** *adj* (*crime*) sin motivo; (*work*) de autómata

**mine[1]** [maɪn] *pron* el mío/la mía *etc*; **a friend of ~** un(a) amigo/a mío/mía ♦ *adj*: **this book is ~** este libro es mío

**mine[2]** [maɪn] *n* mina ♦ *vt* (*coal*) extraer; (*bomb*: *beach etc*) minar; **~field** *n* campo de minas; **miner** *n* minero/a

**mineral** ['mɪnərəl] *adj* mineral ♦ *n* mineral *m*; **~s** *npl* (*BRIT*: *soft drinks*) refrescos *mpl*; **~ water** *n* agua mineral

**mingle** ['mɪŋɡl] *vi*: **to ~ with** mezclarse con

**miniature** ['mɪnətʃə*] adj (en) miniatura ♦ n miniatura

**minibus** ['mɪnɪbʌs] n microbús m

**minim** ['mɪnɪm] n (MUS) blanca

**minimal** ['mɪnɪml] adj mínimo

**minimize** ['mɪnɪmaɪz] vt minimizar; (play down) empequeñecer

**minimum** ['mɪnɪməm] (pl minima) n, adj mínimo

**mining** ['maɪnɪŋ] n explotación f minera

**miniskirt** ['mɪnɪskə:t] n minifalda

**minister** ['mɪnɪstə*] n (BRIT: POL) ministro/a (SP), secretario/a (AM); (REL) pastor m ♦ vi: to ~ to atender a

**ministry** ['mɪnɪstrɪ] n (BRIT: POL) ministerio (SP), secretaría (AM); (REL) sacerdocio

**mink** [mɪŋk] n visón m

**minnow** ['mɪnəʊ] n pececillo (de agua dulce)

**minor** ['maɪnə*] adj (repairs, injuries) leve; (poet, planet) menor; (MUS) menor ♦ n (LAW) menor m de edad

**Minorca** [mɪ'nɔ:kə] n Menorca

**minority** [maɪ'nɒrɪtɪ] n minoría

**mint** [mɪnt] n (plant) menta, hierbabuena; (sweet) caramelo de menta ♦ vt (coins) acuñar; **the (Royal) M~, the (US) M~** la Casa de la Moneda; **in ~ condition** en perfecto estado

**minus** ['maɪnəs] n (also: ~ sign) signo de menos ♦ prep menos; **12 ~ 6 equals 6** 12 menos 6 son 6; **~ 24°C** menos 24 grados

**minute** [n 'mɪnɪt, adj maɪ'nju:t] n minuto; (fig) momento; **~s** npl (of meeting) actas fpl ♦ adj diminuto; (search) minucioso; **at the last ~** a última hora

**miracle** ['mɪrəkl] n milagro

**mirage** ['mɪrɑ:ʒ] n espejismo

**mirror** ['mɪrə*] n espejo; (in car) retrovisor m

**mirth** [mə:θ] n alegría

**misadventure** [mɪsəd'ventʃə*] n desgracia

**misapprehension** [mɪsæprɪ'henʃən] n equivocación f

**misappropriate** [mɪsə'prəʊprɪeɪt] vt malversar

**misbehave** [mɪsbɪ'heɪv] vi portarse mal

**miscalculate** [mɪs'kælkjʊleɪt] vt calcular mal

**miscarriage** ['mɪskærɪdʒ] n (MED) aborto; ~ **of justice** error m judicial

**miscellaneous** [mɪsɪ'leɪnɪəs] adj varios/as, diversos/as

**mischief** ['mɪstʃɪf] n travesuras fpl, diabluras fpl; (maliciousness) malicia; **mischievous** [-ʃɪvəs] adj travieso

**misconception** [mɪskən'sepʃən] n idea equivocada; equivocación f

**misconduct** [mɪs'kɒndʌkt] n mala conducta; **professional ~** falta profesional

**misdemeanour** [mɪsdɪ'mi:nə*] (US **misdemeanor**) n delito, ofensa

**miser** ['maɪzə*] n avaro/a

**miserable** ['mɪzərəbl] adj (unhappy) triste, desgraciado; (unpleasant, contemptible) miserable

**miserly** ['maɪzəlɪ] adj avariento, tacaño

**misery** ['mɪzərɪ] n tristeza; (wretchedness) miseria, desdicha

**misfire** [mɪs'faɪə*] vi fallar

**misfit** ['mɪsfɪt] n inadaptado/a

**misfortune** [mɪs'fɔ:tʃən] n desgracia

**misgiving** [mɪs'gɪvɪŋ] n (apprehension) presentimiento; **to have ~s about sth** tener dudas acerca de algo

**misguided** [mɪs'gaɪdɪd] adj equivocado

**mishandle** [mɪs'hændl] vt (mismanage) manejar mal

**mishap** ['mɪshæp] n desgracia, contratiempo

**misinform** [mɪsɪn'fɔ:m] vt informar mal

**misinterpret** [mɪsɪn'tə:prɪt] vt interpretar mal

**misjudge** [mɪs'dʒʌdʒ] vt juzgar mal

**mislay** [mɪs'leɪ] (irreg) vt extraviar,

perder

**mislead** [mɪsˈliːd] (irreg) vt llevar a conclusiones erróneas; ~ing adj engañoso

**mismanage** [mɪsˈmænɪdʒ] vt administrar mal

**misnomer** [mɪsˈnəumə*] n término inapropiado or equivocado

**misogynist** [mɪˈsɔdʒɪnɪst] n misógino

**misplace** [mɪsˈpleɪs] vt extraviar

**misprint** [ˈmɪsprɪnt] n errata, error m de imprenta

**Miss** [mɪs] n Señorita

**miss** [mɪs] vt (train etc) perder; (fail to hit: target) errar; (regret the absence of): I ~ him (yo) he echo de menos or a faltar; (fail to see): you can't ~ it no tiene pérdida ♦ vi fallar ♦ n (shot) tiro fallido or perdido; ~ out (BRIT) vt omitir

**misshapen** [mɪsˈʃeɪpən] adj deforme

**missile** [ˈmɪsaɪl] n (AVIAT) mísil m; (object thrown) proyectil m

**missing** [ˈmɪsɪŋ] adj (pupil) ausente; (thing) perdido; (MIL): ~ in action desaparecido en combate

**mission** [ˈmɪʃən] n misión f; (official representation) delegación f; ~ary n misionero/a

**misspent** [ˈmɪsˈspent] adj: his ~ youth su juventud disipada

**mist** [mɪst] n (light) neblina; (heavy) niebla; (at sea) bruma ♦ vi (eyes: also: ~ over, ~ up) llenarse de lágrimas; (BRIT: windows: also: ~ over, ~ up) empañarse

**mistake** [mɪsˈteɪk] (vt: irreg) n error m ♦ vt entender mal; by ~ por equivocación; to make a ~ equivocarse; to ~ A for B confundir A con B; **mistaken** pp of mistake ♦ adj equivocado; to be mistaken equivocarse, engañarse

**mister** [ˈmɪstə*] (inf) n señor m; see Mr

**mistletoe** [ˈmɪsltəu] n muérdago

**mistook** [mɪsˈtuk] pt of mistake

**mistress** [ˈmɪstrɪs] n (lover) amante f; (of house) señora (de la casa);

(BRIT: in primary school) maestra; (in secondary school) profesora; (of situation) dueña

**mistrust** [mɪsˈtrʌst] vt desconfiar de

**misty** [ˈmɪstɪ] adj (day) de niebla; (glasses etc) empañado

**misunderstand** [mɪsʌndəˈstænd] (irreg) vt, vi entender mal; ~ing n malentendido

**misuse** [n mɪsˈjuːs, vb mɪsˈjuːz] n mal uso; (of power) abuso; (of funds) malversación f ♦ vt abusar de; malversar

**mitt(en)** [ˈmɪt(n)] n manopla

**mix** [mɪks] vt mezclar; (combine) unir ♦ vi mezclarse; (people) llevarse bien ♦ n mezcla; ~ up vt mezclar; (confuse) confundir; ~ed adj mixto; (feelings etc) encontrado; ~ed-up adj (confused) confuso, revuelto; ~er n (for food) licuadora; (for drinks) coctelera; (person): he's a good ~ tiene don de gentes; ~ture n mezcla; (also: cough ~) jarabe m; ~-up n confusión f

**mm** abbr (= millimetre) mm

**moan** [məun] n gemido ♦ vi gemir; (inf: complain): to ~ (about) quejarse (de)

**moat** [məut] n foso

**mob** [mɔb] n multitud f ♦ vt acosar

**mobile** [ˈməubaɪl] adj móvil ♦ n móvil m; ~ home n caravana; ~ phone n teléfono portátil

**mock** [mɔk] vt (ridicule) ridiculizar; (laugh at) burlarse de ♦ adj fingido; ~ exam examen preparatorio antes de los exámenes oficiales; ~ery n burla; ~-up adj n maqueta

**mod** [mɔd] adj see convenience

**mode** [məud] n modo

**model** [ˈmɔdl] n modelo; (fashion ~, artist's ~) modelo m/f ♦ adj modelo ♦ vt (with clay etc) modelar (copy): to ~ o.s. on tomar como modelo a ♦ vi ser modelo; ~ railway n ferrocarril m de juguete; to ~ clothes pasar modelos, ser modelo

**modem** [ˈməudəm] n modem m

**moderate** [adj ˈmɔdərət, vb

['mɔdəreit] adj moderado/a ♦ vi moderarse, calmarse ♦ vt moderar

**modern** ['mɔdən] adj moderno; ~ize vt modernizar

**modest** ['mɔdɪst] adj modesto; (small) módico; ~y n modestia

**modicum** ['mɔdɪkəm] n: a ~ of un mínimo de

**modify** ['mɔdɪfaɪ] vt modificar

**mogul** ['məugəl] n (fig) magnate m

**mohair** ['məuhɛə*] n mohair m

**moist** [mɔist] adj húmedo; ~en ['mɔisn] vt humedecer; ~ure ['mɔistʃə*] n humedad f; ~urizer ['mɔistʃəraizə*] n crema hidratante

**molar** ['məulə*] n muela

**mold** [məuld] (US) n, vt = mould

**mole** [məul] n (animal, spy) topo; (spot) lunar m

**molecule** ['mɔlikju:l] n molécula

**molest** [məu'lest] vt importunar; (assault sexually) abusar sexualmente de

**mollycoddle** ['mɔlikɔdl] vt mimar

**molt** [məult] (US) vi = moult

**molten** ['məultən] adj fundido; (lava) líquido

**mom** [mɔm] (US) n = mum

**moment** ['məumənt] n momento; at the ~ de momento, por ahora; ~ary adj momentáneo; ~ous [-'mentəs] adj trascendental, importante

**momentum** [məu'mentəm] n momento; (fig) ímpetu m; to gather ~ cobrar velocidad; (fig) ganar fuerza

**mommy** ['mɔmi] (US) n = mummy

**Monaco** ['mɔnəkəu] n Mónaco

**monarch** ['mɔnək] n monarca m/f; ~y n monarquía

**monastery** ['mɔnəstəri] n monasterio

**Monday** ['mʌndi] n lunes m inv

**monetary** ['mʌnitəri] adj monetario

**money** ['mʌni] n dinero; (currency) moneda; to make ~ ganar dinero; ~ order n giro; ~-spinner (inf) n: to be a ~-spinner dar mucho dinero

**mongrel** ['mʌngrəl] n (dog) perro mestizo

**monitor** ['mɔnitə*] n (SCOL) moni-

tor m; (also: television ~) receptor m de control; (of computer) monitor m ♦ vt controlar

**monk** [mʌŋk] n monje m

**monkey** ['mʌŋki] n mono; ~ nut (BRIT) n cacahuete m (SP), maní (AM); ~ wrench n llave f inglesa

**mono** ['mɔnəu] adj (recording) mono

**monopoly** [mə'nɔpəli] n monopolio

**monotone** ['mɔnətəun] n voz f (or tono) monocorde

**monotonous** [mə'nɔtənəs] adj monótono

**monsoon** [mɔn'su:n] n monzón m

**monster** ['mɔnstə*] n monstruo

**monstrosity** [mɔns'trɔsiti] n monstruosidad f

**monstrous** ['mɔnstrəs] adj (huge) enorme; (atrocious, ugly) monstruoso

**month** [mʌnθ] n mes m; ~ly adj mensual ♦ adv mensualmente

**monument** ['mɔnjumənt] n monumento; ~al [-'mentl] adj monumental

**moo** [mu:] vi mugir

**mood** [mu:d] n humor m; (of crowd, group) clima m; to be in a good/bad ~ estar de buen/mal humor; ~y adj (changeable) de humor variable; (sullen) malhumorado

**moon** [mu:n] n luna; ~light n luz f de la luna; ~lighting n pluriempleo; ~lit adj: a ~lit night una noche de luna

**Moor** [muə*] n moro/a

**moor** [muə*] n páramo ♦ vt (ship) amarrar ♦ vi echar las amarras

**Moorish** ['muəriʃ] adj moro; (architecture) árabe, morisco

**moorland** ['muələnd] n páramo, brezal m

**moose** [mu:s] n inv alce m

**mop** [mɔp] n fregona; (of hair) greña, melena ♦ vt fregar; ~ up vt limpiar

**mope** [məup] vi estar o andar deprimido

**moped** ['məuped] n ciclomotor m

**moral** ['mɔrl] adj moral ♦ n moraleja; ~s npl moralidad f, moral f

**morale** [mɔ'rɑ:l] n moral f

**morality** [mə'rælɪtɪ] n moralidad f

**morass** [mə'ræs] n pantano

**morbid** ['mɔːbɪd] adj (interest) morboso

KEYWORD

**more** [mɔː*] adj 1 (greater in number etc) más; ~ people/work than before más gente/trabajo que antes 2 (additional) más; do you want (some) ~ tea? ¿quieres más té?; is there any ~ wine? ¿queda vino?; it'll take a few ~ weeks tardará unas semanas más; it's 2 kms ~ to the house faltan 2 kms para la casa; ~ time/letters than we expected más tiempo del que/ más cartas de las que esperábamos
♦ pron (greater amount, additional amount) más; ~ than 10 más de 10; it cost ~ than the other one/than we expected costó más que el otro/ más de lo que esperábamos; is there any ~? ¿hay más?; many/much ~ muchos(as)/mucho(a) más
♦ adv más; ~ dangerous/easily (than) más peligroso/fácilmente (que); ~ and ~ expensive cada vez más caro; ~ or less más o menos; ~ than ever más que nunca

**moreover** [mɔː'rəuvə*] adv además, por otra parte

**morgue** [mɔːg] n depósito de cadáveres

**Mormon** ['mɔːmən] n mormón/ona m/f

**morning** ['mɔːnɪŋ] n mañana; (early ~) madrugada ♦ cpd matutino, de la mañana; in the ~ por la mañana; 7 o'clock in the ~ las 7 de la mañana; ~ sickness n náuseas fpl matutinas

**Morocco** [mə'rɔkəu] n Marruecos m

**moron** ['mɔːrɔn] (inf) n imbécil m/f

**morose** [mə'rəus] adj hosco, malhumorado

**morphine** ['mɔːfiːn] n morfina

**Morse** [mɔːs] n (also: ~ code) (código) Morse

**morsel** ['mɔːsl] n (of food) bocado

**mortar** ['mɔːtə*] n argamasa; (implement) mortero

**mortgage** ['mɔːgɪdʒ] n hipoteca ♦ vt hipotecar; ~ company (US) n ≈ banco hipotecario

**mortify** ['mɔːtɪfaɪ] vt mortificar, humillar

**mortuary** ['mɔːtjuərɪ] n depósito de cadáveres

**Moscow** ['mɔskəu] n Moscú

**Moslem** ['mɔzləm] adj, n = **Muslim**

**mosque** [mɔsk] n mezquita

**mosquito** [mɔs'kiːtəu] (pl ~es) n mosquito (SP), zancudo (AM)

**moss** [mɔs] n musgo

**most** [məust] adj la mayor parte de, la mayoría de ♦ pron la mayor parte, la mayoría ♦ adv el más; (very) muy; the ~ (also: + adj) el más; of them la mayor parte de ellos; I saw the ~ yo vi el que más; at the (very) ~ a lo sumo, todo lo más; to make the ~ of aprovechar (al máximo); a ~ interesting book un libro interesantísimo

**mostly** ['məustlɪ] adv en su mayor parte, principalmente

**MOT** (BRIT) n abbr (= Ministry of Transport): the ~ (test) inspección (anual) obligatoria de coches y camiones

**motel** [məu'tel] n motel m

**moth** [mɔθ] n mariposa nocturna; (clothes) polilla; ~ball n bola de naftalina

**mother** ['mʌðə*] n madre f ♦ adj materno ♦ vt (care for) cuidar (como una madre); ~hood n maternidad f; ~-in-law n suegra; ~ly adj maternal; ~-of-pearl n nácar m; ~-to-be n futura madre f; ~ tongue n lengua materna

**motif** [məu'tiːf] n motivo

**motion** ['məuʃən] n movimiento; (gesture) ademán m, señal f; (at meeting) moción f ♦ vt, vi: to ~ (to) sb to do sth hacer señas a uno para que haga algo; ~less adj inmóvil; ~ picture n película

**motivated** ['məutiveitid] adj motivado

**motive** ['məutiv] n motivo

**motley** ['mɔtli] adj variado

**motor** ['məutə*] n motor m; (BRIT: inf: vehicle) coche m (SP), carro (AM), automóvil m ♦ adj motor (f: motora or motriz); ~**bike** n moto f; ~**boat** n lancha motora; ~**car** (BRIT) n coche m, carro, automóvil m; ~**cycle** n motocicleta; ~**cycle racing** n motociclismo; ~**cyclist** n motociclista m/f; ~**ing** (BRIT) n automovilismo; ~**ist** n conductor(a) m/f, automovilista m/f; ~ **racing** (BRIT) n carreras fpl de coches, automovilismo; ~ **vehicle** n automóvil m; ~**way** (BRIT) n autopista

**mottled** ['mɔtld] adj abigarrado, multicolor

**motto** ['mɔtəu] (pl ~es) n lema m; (watchword) consigna

**mould** [məuld] (US **mold**) n molde m; (mildew) moho ♦ vt moldear; (fig) formar; ~**y** adj enmohecido

**moult** [məult] (US **molt**) vi mudar la piel (or las plumas)

**mound** [maund] n montón m, montículo

**mount** [maunt] n monte m ♦ vt montar, subir a; (jewel) engarzar; (picture) enmarcar; (exhibition etc) organizar ♦ vi (increase) aumentar; ~ **up** vi aumentar

**mountain** ['mauntin] n montaña ♦ cpd de montaña; ~ **bike** n bicicleta de montaña; ~**eer** [-'niə*] n montañero/a (SP), andinista m/f (AM); ~**eering** [-'niəriŋ] n montañismo, andinismo; ~**ous** adj montañoso; ~ **rescue team** n equipo de rescate de montaña; ~**side** n ladera de la montaña

**mourn** [mɔːn] vt llorar, lamentar ♦ vi: to ~ **for** llorar la muerte de; ~**er** n doliente m/f; dolorido/a ♦ ~**ful** adj triste, lúgubre; ~**ing** n luto; **in** ~**ing** de luto

**mouse** [maus] (pl **mice**) n (ZOOL, COMPUT) ratón m; ~**trap** n ratone-

ra

**mousse** [muːs] n (CULIN) crema batida; (for hair) espuma (moldeadora)

**moustache** [məs'tɑːʃ] (US **mustache**) n bigote m

**mousy** ['mausi] adj (hair) pardusco

**mouth** [mauθ] (pl mauðz) n boca; (of river) desembocadura; ~**ful** n bocado; ~ **organ** n armónica; ~**piece** n (of musical instrument) boquilla; (spokesman) portavoz m/f; ~**wash** n enjuague m; ~**watering** adj apetitoso

**movable** ['muːvəbl] adj movible

**move** [muːv] n (movement) movimiento; (in game) jugada; (: turn to play) turno; (change: of house) mudanza; (: of job) cambio de trabajo ♦ vt mover; (emotionally) conmover; (POL: resolution etc) proponer ♦ vi moverse; (traffic) circular; (also: ~ house) trasladarse, mudarse; to ~ **sb to do sth** mover a uno a hacer algo; to **get a** ~ **on** darse prisa; ~ **about or around** vi moverse; (travel) viajar; ~ **along** vi avanzar; ~ **away** vi alejarse; ~ **back** vi retroceder; ~ **forward** vi avanzar; ~ **in** vi (to a house) instalarse; (police, soldiers) intervenir; ~ **on** vi ponerse en camino; ~ **out** vi (of house) mudarse; ~ **over** vi apartarse, hacer sitio; ~ **up** vi (employee) ser ascendido

**moveable** ['muːvəbl] adj = movable

**movement** ['muːvmənt] n movimiento

**movie** ['muːvi] n película; **to go to the** ~**s** ir al cine; ~ **camera** n cámara cinematográfica

**moving** ['muːviŋ] adj (emotional) conmovedor(a); (that moves) móvil

**mow** [məu] (pt **mowed**, pp **mowed** or **mown**) vt (grass, corn) cortar, segar; ~ **down** vt (shoot) acribillar; ~**er** n (also: lawn~er) cortacéspedes m inv, segadora

**MP** n abbr = Member of Parliament

**m.p.h.** abbr = miles per hour (60 m.p.h. = 96 k.p.h.)

**Mr** ['mɪstə*] (US **Mr.**) n: ~ Smith (el) Sr. Smith

**Mrs** ['mɪsɪz] (US **Mrs.**) n: ~ Smith (la) Sra. Smith

**Ms** [mɪz] (US **Ms.**) n (= Miss or Mrs): ~ Smith (la) Sr(t)a. Smith

**M.Sc.** abbr = Master of Science

**much** [mʌtʃ] adj mucho ♦ adv mucho; (before pp) muy ♦ pron mucho; **how** ~ **is it?** ¿cuánto es?, ¿cuánto cuesta?; **too** ~ demasiado; **it's not** ~ no es mucho; **as** ~ **as** tanto como; **however** ~ **he tries** por mucho que se esfuerce

**muck** [mʌk] n suciedad f; (dirt) porquería f; **~ about** or **around** (inf) vi perder el tiempo; (enjoy o.s.) entretenerse; ~ **up** (inf) vt arruinar, estropear

**mud** [mʌd] n barro, lodo

**muddle** ['mʌdl] n desorden m, confusión f; (mix-up) embrollo, lío ♦ vt (also: ~ **up**) embrollar, confundir; ~ **through** vi salir del paso

**muddy** ['mʌdɪ] adj fangoso, cubierto de lodo

**mudguard** ['mʌdgɑːd] n guardabarros m inv

**muffin** ['mʌfɪn] n panecillo dulce

**muffle** ['mʌfl] vt (sound) amortiguar; (against cold) embozar; **~d** adj (noise etc) amortiguado, apagado; **~r** (US) n (AUT) silenciador m

**mug** [mʌg] n taza grande (sin platillo); (for beer) jarra; (inf: face) jeta; (: fool) bobo ♦ vt (assault) asaltar; **~ging** n asalto

**muggy** ['mʌgɪ] adj bochornoso

**mule** [mjuːl] n mula

**mull over** [mʌl-] vt meditar sobre

**multi...** ['mʌltɪ] prefix multi...

**multi-level** [mʌltɪ'levl] (US) adj = multistorey

**multiple** ['mʌltɪpl] adj múltiple ♦ n múltiplo; ~ **sclerosis** n esclerosis f múltiple

**multiplication** [mʌltɪplɪ'keɪʃən] n multiplicación f

**multiply** ['mʌltɪplaɪ] vt multiplicar ♦ vi multiplicarse

**multistorey** [mʌltɪ'stɔːrɪ] (BRIT) adj de muchos pisos

**multitude** ['mʌltɪtjuːd] n multitud f

**mum** [mʌm] (BRIT: inf) n mamá ♦ adj: **to keep** ~ mantener la boca cerrada

**mumble** ['mʌmbl] vt, vi hablar entre dientes, refunfuñar

**mummy** ['mʌmɪ] n (BRIT: mother) mamá; (embalmed) momia

**mumps** [mʌmps] n paperas fpl

**munch** [mʌntʃ] vt, vi mascar

**mundane** [mʌn'deɪn] adj trivial

**municipal** [mjuː'nɪsɪpl] adj municipal

**munitions** [mjuː'nɪʃənz] npl munición f

**murder** ['mɜːdə*] n asesinato; (in law) homicidio ♦ vt asesinar, matar; **~er/ess** n asesino/a; **~ous** adj homicida

**murky** ['mɜːkɪ] adj (water) turbio; (street, night) lóbrego

**murmur** ['mɜːmə*] n murmullo ♦ vt, vi murmurar

**muscle** ['mʌsl] n músculo; (fig: strength) garra, fuerza; ~ **in** vi entrometerse; **muscular** ['mʌskjulə*] adj musculoso; (person) musculoso

**muse** [mjuːz] vi meditar ♦ n musa

**museum** [mjuː'zɪəm] n museo

**mushroom** ['mʌʃrum] n seta, hongo; (CULIN) champiñón m ♦ vi crecer de la noche a la mañana

**music** ['mjuːzɪk] n música; **~al** adj musical; (sound) melodioso; (person) con talento musical ♦ n (show) comedia musical; **~al instrument** n instrumento musical; **~ hall** n teatro de variedades; **~ian** [-'zɪʃən] n músico/a

**musk** [mʌsk] n almizcle m

**Muslim** ['mʌzlɪm] adj, n musulmán/ana m/f

**muslin** ['mʌzlɪn] n muselina

**mussel** ['mʌsl] n mejillón m

**must** [mʌst] aux vb (obligation): **I** ~ **do it** debo hacerlo, tengo que hacerlo; (probability): **he** ~ **be there by**

now ya debe (de) estar allí ♦ n: it's a ~ es imprescindible

**mustache** ['mʌstæʃ] (US) n = moustache

**mustard** ['mʌstəd] n mostaza

**muster** ['mʌstə*] vt juntar, reunir

**mustn't** ['mʌsnt] = must not

**musty** ['mʌsti] adj mohoso, que huele a humedad

**mute** [mju:t] adj n mudo/a

**muted** ['mju:tɪd] adj callado; (colour) apagado

**mutilate** ['mju:tɪleɪt] vt (person) mutilar; (thing) destrozar

**mutiny** ['mju:tɪnɪ] n motín m ♦ vi amotinarse

**mutter** ['mʌtə*] vt, vi murmurar

**mutton** ['mʌtn] n carne f de cordero

**mutual** ['mju:tʃuəl] adj mutuo; (interest) común; ~ly adv mutuamente

**muzzle** ['mʌzl] n hocico; (for dog) bozal m; (of gun) boca ♦ vt (dog) poner un bozal a

**my** [maɪ] adj mi(s); ~ house/brother/sisters mi casa/mi hermano/mis hermanas; I've washed ~ hair/cut ~ finger me he lavado el pelo/cortado un dedo; is this ~ pen or yours? ¿es este bolígrafo mío o tuyo?

**myopic** [maɪ'ɔpɪk] adj miope

**myself** [maɪ'self] pron (reflexive) me; (emphatic) yo mismo; (after prep) mí (mismo); see also oneself

**mysterious** [mɪs'tɪərɪəs] adj misterioso

**mystery** ['mɪstərɪ] n misterio

**mystify** ['mɪstɪfaɪ] vt (perplex) dejar perplejo

**mystique** [mɪs'ti:k] n misterio (profesional etc)

**myth** [mɪθ] n mito

# N

**n/a** abbr (= not applicable) no interesa

**nag** [næg] vt (scold) regañar; **~ging**

adj (doubt) persistente; (pain) continuo

**nail** [neɪl] n (human) uña; (metal) clavo ♦ vt clavar; to ~ sth to sth clavar algo en algo; to ~ sb down to doing sth comprometer a uno a que haga algo; **~brush** n cepillo para las uñas; **~file** n lima para las uñas; **~ polish** n esmalte m or laca para las uñas; **~ polish remover** n quitaesmalte m; **~ scissors** npl tijeras fpl para las uñas; **~ varnish** (BRIT) n = ~ polish

**naïve** [naɪ'i:v] adj ingenuo

**naked** ['neɪkɪd] adj (nude) desnudo; (flame) expuesto al aire

**name** [neɪm] n nombre m; (surname) apellido; (reputation) fama, renombre m ♦ vt (child) poner nombre a; (criminal) identificar; (price, date etc) fijar; **what's your ~?** ¿cómo se llama?; **by ~** de nombre; **in the ~ of** en nombre de; to know one's ~ **and address** dar sus señas; **~less** adj (unknown) desconocido; (anonymous) anónimo, sin nombre; **~ly** adv a saber; **~sake** n tocayo/a

**nanny** ['nænɪ] n niñera

**nap** [næp] n (sleep) sueñecito, siesta; to be caught **~ping** estar desprevenido

**nape** [neɪp] n: **~ of the neck** nuca, cogote m

**napkin** ['næpkɪn] n (also: **table ~**) servilleta

**nappy** ['næpɪ] (BRIT) n pañal m; **~ rash** n prurito

**narcotic** [nɑː'kɔtɪk] adj, n narcótico

**narrow** ['nærəu] adj estrecho, angosto; (fig: majority etc) corto; (: ideas etc) estrecho ♦ vi (road) estrecharse; (diminish) reducirse; to have a **~ escape** escaparse por los pelos; to **~ sth down** reducir algo; **~ly** adv (miss) por poco; **~-minded** adj de miras estrechas

**nasty** ['nɑːstɪ] adj (remark) feo; (person) antipático; (revolting: taste, smell) asqueroso; (wound, disease etc) peligroso, grave

**nation** ['neɪʃən] n nación f

**national** ['næʃənl] adj, n nacional m/f; ~ **dress** n vestido nacional; **N~ Health Service** (BRIT) n servicio nacional de salud pública; ≈ Insalud m (SP); **N~ Insurance** (BRIT) n seguro social nacional; **~ism** n nacionalismo; **~ist** adj, n nacionalista m/f; **~ity** [-'nælɪtɪ] n nacionalidad f; **~ize** vt nacionalizar; **~ly** adv (nationwide) en escala nacional; (as a nation) nacionalmente, como nación

**nationwide** ['neɪʃənwaɪd] adj en escala or a nivel nacional

**native** ['neɪtɪv] n (local inhabitant) natural m/f, indígena m/f; (of tribe etc) indígena m/f, nativo/a ♦ adj (indigenous) indígena; (country) natal; (innate) natural, innato; a ~ of Russia un(a) natural m/f de Rusia; a ~ speaker of French un hablante nativo de francés; ~ **language** n lengua materna

**Nativity** [nə'tɪvɪtɪ] n: **the ~** Navidad f

**NATO** ['neɪtəu] n abbr (= North Atlantic Treaty Organization) OTAN f

**natural** ['nætʃrəl] adj natural; **~ize** vt: **to become ~ized** (person) naturalizarse; (plant) aclimatarse; **~ly** adv (speak etc) naturalmente; (of course) desde luego, por supuesto

**nature** ['neɪtʃə*] n (also: N~) naturaleza; (group, sort) género, clase f; (character) carácter m, genio; **by ~** por or de naturaleza

**naught** [nɔ:t] = **nought**

**naughty** ['nɔ:tɪ] adj (child) travieso

**nausea** ['nɔ:sɪə] n náuseas fpl; **~te** [-sɪeɪt] vt dar náuseas a; (fig) dar asco a

**nautical** ['nɔ:tɪkl] adj náutico, marítimo; (mile) marino

**naval** ['neɪvl] adj naval, de marina; **~ officer** n oficial m/f de marina

**nave** [neɪv] n nave f

**navel** ['neɪvl] n ombligo

**navigate** ['nævɪgeɪt] vt gobernar ♦ vi navegar; (AUT) ir de copiloto; **navigation** [-'geɪʃən] n (action) na-

vegación f; (science) náutica; **navigator** n navegador(a) m/f, navegante m/f; (AUT) copiloto m/f

**navvy** ['nævɪ] (BRIT) n peón m caminero

**navy** ['neɪvɪ] n marina de guerra; (ships) armada, flota; **~(-blue)** adj azul marino

**Nazi** ['nɑ:tsɪ] n nazi m/f

**NB** abbr (= nota bene) nótese

**near** [nɪə*] adj (place, relation) cercano; (time) próximo ♦ adv cerca ♦ prep (also: ~ to: space) cerca de, junto a; (: time) cerca de ♦ vt acercarse a, aproximarse a; **~by** [nɪə'baɪ] adj cercano, próximo ♦ adv cerca; **~ly** adv casi, por poco; **I ~ly fell** por poco me caigo; **~ miss** n tiro cercano; **~side** n (AUT: in Britain) lado izquierdo; (: in US, Europe etc) lado derecho; **~-sighted** adj miope, corto de vista

**neat** [ni:t] adj (place) ordenado, bien cuidado; (person) pulcro; (plan) ingenioso; (spirits) solo; **~ly** adv (tidily) con esmero; (skilfully) ingeniosamente

**necessarily** ['nesɪsrɪlɪ] adv necesariamente

**necessary** ['nesɪsrɪ] adj necesario, preciso

**necessitate** [nɪ'sesɪteɪt] vt hacer necesario

**necessity** [nɪ'sesɪtɪ] n necesidad f; **necessities** npl artículos mpl de primera necesidad

**neck** [nek] n (of person, garment, bottle) cuello; (of animal) pescuezo ♦ vi (inf) besuquearse; **~ and ~** parejos; **~lace** ['neklɪs] n collar m; **~line** n escote m; **~tie** ['nektaɪ] n corbata

**née** [neɪ] adj: **~ Scott** de soltera Scott

**need** [ni:d] n (lack) escasez f, falta; (necessity) necesidad f ♦ vt (require) necesitar; **I ~ to do it** tengo que or debo hacerlo; **you don't ~ to go** no hace falta que (te) vayas

**needle** ['ni:dl] n aguja ♦ vt (fig: inf)

picar, fastidiar

**needless** ['niːdlɪs] adj innecesario; ~ to say huelga decir que

**needlework** ['niːdlwɜːk] n (activity) costura, labor f de aguja

**needn't** ['niːdnt] = need not

**needy** ['niːdɪ] adj necesitado

**negative** ['nɛgətɪv] n (PHOT) negativo; (LING) negación f ♦ adj negativo

**neglect** [nɪ'glɛkt] vt (one's duty) faltar a, no cumplir con; (child) descuidar, desatender ♦ n (of house, garden etc) abandono; (of child) desatención f; (of duty) incumplimiento

**negligee** ['nɛglɪʒeɪ] n (nightgown) salto de cama

**negligence** ['nɛglɪdʒəns] n negligencia, descuido

**negligible** ['nɛglɪdʒɪbl] adj insignificante, despreciable

**negotiate** [nɪ'gəʊʃɪeɪt] vt (treaty, loan) negociar; (obstacle) franquear; (bend in road) tomar ♦ vi: to ~ (with) negociar (con); **negotiation** [-'eɪʃən] n negociación f, gestión f

**Negress** ['niːgrɪs] n negra

**Negro** ['niːgrəʊ] adj, n negro

**neigh** [neɪ] vi relinchar

**neighbour** ['neɪbə*] (US **neighbor**) n vecino/a; ~**hood** n (place) vecindad f, barrio; (people) vecindario; ~**ing** adj vecino; ~**ly** adj (person) amable; (attitude) de buen vecino

**neither** ['naɪðə*] adj si ♦ conj: I didn't move and ~ did John no me he movido, ni Juan tampoco ♦ pron ninguno; ~ is true ninguno/a de los/las dos es cierto/a ♦ adv: ~ good nor bad ni bueno ni malo

**neon** ['niːɒn] n neón m; ~ **light** n lámpara de neón

**nephew** ['nɛvjuː] n sobrino

**nerve** [nɜːv] n (ANAT) nervio; (courage) valor m; (impudence) descaro, frescura; a fit of ~s un ataque de nervios; ~**-racking** adj desquiciante

**nervous** ['nɜːvəs] adj (anxious, ANAT) nervioso; (timid) tímido, miedoso; ~ **breakdown** n crisis f nervio-

sa

**nest** [nɛst] n (of bird) nido; (wasps' ~) avispero ♦ vi anidar; ~ **egg** n (fig) ahorros mpl

**nestle** ['nɛsl] vi: to ~ down acurrucarse

**net** [nɛt] n (gen) red f; (fabric) tul m ♦ adj (COMM) neto, líquido ♦ vt coger (SP) or agarrar (AM) con red; (SPORT) marcar; ~**ball** n básquet m; ~ **curtains** npl visillos mpl

**Netherlands** ['nɛðələndz] npl: the ~ los Países Bajos

**nett** [nɛt] adj = **net**

**netting** ['nɛtɪŋ] n red f, redes fpl

**nettle** ['nɛtl] n ortiga

**network** ['nɛtwɜːk] n red f

**neurotic** [njʊ'rɒtɪk] adj, n neurótico/a m/f

**neuter** ['njuːtə*] adj (LING) neutro ♦ vt castrar, capar

**neutral** ['njuːtrəl] adj (person) neutral; (colour etc, ELEC) neutro ♦ n (AUT) punto muerto; ~**ize** vt neutralizar

**never** ['nɛvə*] adv nunca, jamás; I ~ went no fui nunca; ~ in my life jamás en la vida; see also **mind**; ~-**ending** adj interminable, sin fin; ~**theless** [nɛvəðə'lɛs] adv sin embargo, no obstante

**new** [njuː] adj nuevo; (brand new) a estrenar; (recent) reciente; ~**born** adj recién nacido; ~**comer** ['njuːkʌmə*] n recién venido/a or llegado/a; ~**-fangled** (pej) adj modernísimo; ~**-found** adj (friend) recién adquirido; ~**ly** adv nuevamente, recién; ~**ly-weds** npl recién casados mpl

**news** [njuːz] n noticias fpl; a piece of ~ una noticia; the ~ (RADIO, TV) las noticias fpl; ~ **agency** n agencia de noticias; ~**agent** (BRIT) n vendedor(a) m/f de periódicos; ~**caster** n presentador(a) m/f, locutor(a) m/f; ~ **dealer** (US) n ~**agent**; ~ **flash** n noticia de última hora; ~**letter** n hoja informativa, boletín m; ~**paper** n periódico, diario;

~**print** n papel m de periódico; ~**reader** n ~caster; ~**reel** n noticiario; ~ **stand** n quiosco or puesto de periódicos

**newt** [njuːt] n tritón m

**New Year** n Año Nuevo; ~'**s Day** n Día m de Año Nuevo; ~'**s Eve** n Nochevieja

**New York** ['njuː'jɔːk] n Nueva York

**New Zealand** [njuː'ziːlənd] n Nueva Zelanda; ~**er** n neozelandés/esa m/f

**next** [nɛkst] adj (house, room) vecino; (bus stop, meeting) próximo; (following: page etc) siguiente ♦ adv después; the ~ **day** el día siguiente; ~ **time** la próxima vez; ~ **year** el año próximo or que viene; the ~ junto a, al lado de; ~ **to nothing** casi nada; ~ **please!** ¡el siguiente! casi nada; ~ **please!** ¡el siguiente! adv en la casa de al lado ♦ adj vecino, de al lado; ~**-of-kin** n pariente m más cercano

**NHS** n abbr = **National Health Service**

**nib** [nɪb] n plumilla

**nibble** ['nɪbl] vt mordisquear, mordiscar

**Nicaragua** [nɪkə'ræɡjuə] n Nicaragua; ~**n** adj, n nicaragüense m/f

**nice** [naɪs] adj (likeable) simpático; (kind) amable; (pleasant) agradable; (attractive) bonito, mono, lindo (AM); ~**ly** adv amablemente; bien

**nick** [nɪk] n (wound) rasguño; (cut, indentation) mella, muesca ♦ vt (cut, steal) birlar, robar; in the ~ **of time** justo a tiempo

**nickel** ['nɪkl] n níquel m; (US) moneda de 5 centavos

**nickname** ['nɪkneɪm] n apodo, mote m ♦ vt apodar

**nicotine** ['nɪkətiːn] n nicotina

**niece** [niːs] n sobrina

**Nigeria** [naɪ'dʒɪərɪə] n Nigeria; ~**n** adj, n nigeriano/a m/f

**niggling** ['nɪɡlɪŋ] adj (trifling) nimio, insignificante; (annoying) molesto

**night** [naɪt] n (evening) tarde f; (after dark) noche f; the ~ **before last** anteanoche; at ~, by ~ de noche, por la noche

~**cap** n (drink) bebida que se toma antes de acostarse; n cabaret m; ~ **club** n cabaret m; ~**dress** (BRIT) n camisón m; ~**fall** n anochecer m; ~**gown** n = ~**dress**; ~**ie** ['naɪtɪ] n = ~**dress**

**nightingale** ['naɪtɪŋɡeɪl] n ruiseñor m

**nightlife** ['naɪtlaɪf] n vida nocturna

**nightly** ['naɪtlɪ] adj de todas las noches ♦ adv todas las noches, cada noche

**nightmare** ['naɪtmɛə*] n pesadilla

**night**: ~ **porter** n portero de noche; ~ **school** n clase(s) f(pl) nocturna(s); ~ **shift** n turno nocturno or de noche; ~**time** n noche f; ~ **watchman** n vigilante m nocturno

**nil** [nɪl] (BRIT) n (SPORT) cero, nada

**Nile** [naɪl] n: the ~ el Nilo

**nimble** ['nɪmbl] adj (agile) ágil, ligero; (skilful) diestro

**nine** [naɪn] num nueve; ~**teen** num diecinueve, diez y nueve; ~**ty** num noventa

**ninth** [naɪnθ] adj noveno

**nip** [nɪp] vt (pinch) pellizcar; (bite) morder

**nipple** ['nɪpl] n (ANAT) pezón m

**nitrogen** ['naɪtrədʒən] n nitrógeno

---

KEYWORD

**no** [nəʊ] (pl ~**es**) adv (opposite of "yes"): **are you coming?** — — (**I'm not**) ¿vienes? — no; **would you like some more?** — — **thank you** ¿quieres más? — no gracias ♦ adj (not any): **I have** ~ **money/time/books** no tengo dinero/tiempo/libros; ~ **other man** ningún otro or no hombre; **no other man would have done it** ningún otro lo hubiera hecho; "~ **entry**" "prohibido el paso"; "~ **smoking**" "prohibido fumar" ♦ n no m

---

**nobility** [nəʊ'bɪlɪtɪ] n nobleza

**noble** ['nəʊbl] adj noble

**nobody** ['nəʊbədɪ] pron nadie

**nod** [nɒd] vi saludar con la cabeza; (in agreement) decir que sí con la cabeza; (*doze*) dar cabezadas ♦ *vt*: **to ~ one's head** inclinar la cabeza ♦ *n* inclinación *f* de cabeza; **~ off** *vi* dar cabezadas

**noise** [nɔɪz] *n* ruido; (*din*) escándalo, estrépito; **noisy** *adj* ruidoso; (*child*) escandaloso

**nominate** ['nɔmɪneɪt] *vt* (*propose*) proponer; (*appoint*) nombrar; **nomination** [-'neɪʃən] *n* propuesta; nombramiento; **nominee** [-'niː] *n* candidato/a

**non...** [nɔn] *prefix* no, des..., in...; **~-alcoholic** *adj* no alcohólico; **~-aligned** *adj* no alineado

**nonchalant** ['nɔnʃələnt] *adj* indiferente

**non-committal** ['nɔnkə'mɪtl] *adj* evasivo

**nondescript** ['nɔndɪskrɪpt] *adj* soso

**none** [nʌn] *pron* ninguno/a ♦ *adv* de ninguna manera; **~ of you** ninguno de vosotros; **I've ~ left** no me queda ninguno/a; **he's ~ the worse for it** no le ha hecho ningún mal

**nonentity** [nɔ'nentɪtɪ] *n* cero a la izquierda, nulidad *f*

**nonetheless** [nʌnðə'les] *adv* sin embargo, no obstante

**non-existent** *adj* inexistente

**non-fiction** *n* literatura no novelesca

**nonplussed** [nɔn'plʌst] *adj* perplejo

**nonsense** ['nɔnsəns] *n* tonterías *fpl*, disparates *fpl*; **~!** ¡qué tonterías!

**non:** **~-smoker** *n* no fumador(a) *m/f*; **~-stick** *adj* (*pan, surface*) antiadherente; **~-stop** *adj* continuo; (*RAIL*) directo ♦ *adv* sin parar

**noodles** ['nuːdlz] *npl* tallarines *mpl*

**nook** [nuk] *n*: **~s and crannies** escondrijos *mpl*

**noon** [nuːn] *n* mediodía *m*

**no-one** *pron* = **nobody**

**noose** [nuːs] *n* (*hangman's*) dogal *m*

**nor** [nɔː] *conj* = **neither** ♦ *adv see* **neither**

**norm** [nɔːm] *n* norma

**normal** ['nɔːml] *adj* normal; **~ly** *adv* normalmente

**north** [nɔːθ] *n* norte *m* ♦ *adj* del norte, norteño ♦ *adv* al *or* hacia el norte; **N~ Africa** *n* África del Norte; **N~ America** *n* América del Norte; **~-east** *n* nor(d)este *m*; **~erly** ['nɔːðəlɪ] *adj* (*point, direction*) norteño; **~ern** ['nɔːðən] *adj* norteño, del norte; **N~ern Ireland** *n* Irlanda del Norte; **N~ Pole** *n* Polo Norte; **N~ Sea** *n* Mar *m* del Norte; **~ward(s)** ['nɔːθwəd(z)] *adv* hacia el norte; **~west** *n* nor(d)oeste *m*

**Norway** ['nɔːweɪ] *n* Noruega; **Norwegian** [-'wiːdʒən] *adj* noruego/a ♦ *n* noruego/a; (*LING*) noruego

**nose** [nəuz] *n* (*ANAT*) nariz *f*; (*ZOOL*) hocico; (*sense of smell*) olfato ♦ *vi*: **to ~** curiosear; **~bleed** *n* hemorragia nasal; **~dive** *n* (*of plane: deliberate*) picado vertical; (*: involuntary*) caída en picado; **~y** (*inf*) *adj* curioso, fisgón/ona

**nostalgia** [nɔs'tældʒɪə] *n* nostalgia

**nostril** ['nɔstrɪl] *n* ventana de la nariz

**nosy** ['nəuzɪ] (*inf*) *adj* = **nosey**

**not** [nɔt] *adv* no; **~ that ...** no es que ...; **it's too late, isn't it?** es demasiado tarde, ¿verdad *or* no?; **~ yet/ now** todavía/ahora no; **why ~?** ¿por qué no?; *see also* **all**; **only**

**notably** ['nəutəblɪ] *adv* especialmente

**notary** ['nəutərɪ] *n* notario/a

**notch** [nɔtʃ] *n* muesca, corte *m*

**note** [nəut] *n* (*MUS, record, letter*) nota; (*banknote*) billete *m*; (*tone*) tono ♦ *vt* (*observe*) notar, observar; (*write down*) apuntar, anotar; **~book** *n* libreta, cuaderno; **~d** ['nəutɪd] *adj* célebre, conocido; **~pad** *n* bloc *m*; **~paper** *n* papel *m* para cartas

**nothing** ['nʌθɪŋ] *n* nada; (*zero*) cero; **he does ~** no hace nada; **~ new** nada nuevo; **~ much** no mucho; **for ~** (*free*) gratis, sin pago; (*in vain*) en balde

**notice** ['nəutɪs] *n* (*announcement*) anuncio; (*warning*) aviso; (*dismissal*) despido; (*resignation*) dimisión *f*; (*period of time*) plazo ♦ *vt* (*observe*) notar, observar; **to bring sth to sb's ~** (*attention*) llamar la atención de uno sobre algo; **to take ~ of** tomar nota de, prestar atención a; **at short ~** con poca anticipación; **until further ~** hasta nuevo aviso; **to hand in one's ~** dimitir; **~able** *adj* evidente, obvio; **~ board** (BRIT) *n* tablón *m* de anuncios

**notify** ['nəʊtɪfaɪ] *vt*: **to ~ sb** (**of sth**) comunicar (algo) a uno

**notion** ['nəʊʃən] *n* idea; (*opinion*) opinión *f*

**notorious** [nəʊ'tɔːrɪəs] *adj* notorio

**notwithstanding** [nɒtwɪθ'stændɪŋ] *adv* no obstante, sin embargo ♦ *prep* a pesar de

**nougat** ['nuːgɑː] *n* turrón *m*

**nought** [nɔːt] *n* cero

**noun** [naʊn] *n* nombre *m*, sustantivo

**nourish** ['nʌrɪʃ] *vt* nutrir; (*fig*) alimentar; **~ing** *adj* nutritivo; **~ment** *n* alimento, sustento

**novel** ['nɒvl] *n* novela ♦ *adj* (*new*) nuevo, original; (*unexpected*) insólito; **~ist** *n* novelista *m/f*; **~ty** *n* novedad *f*

**November** [nəʊ'vembə*] *n* noviembre *m*

**novice** ['nɒvɪs] *n* principiante *m/f*, novato/a; (REL) novicio/a

**now** [naʊ] *adv* (*at the present time*) ahora; (*these days*) actualmente, hoy día ♦ *conj*: **~** (**that**) ya que, ahora que; **right ~** ahora mismo; **by ~** ya; **just ~** ahora mismo; **~ and then, ~ and again** de vez en cuando; **from ~ on** de ahora en adelante; **~adays** ['naʊədeɪz] *adv* hoy (en) día, actualmente

**nowhere** ['nəʊweə*] *adv* (*direction*) a ninguna parte; (*location*) en ninguna parte

**nozzle** ['nɒzl] *n* boquilla

**nuance** ['njuːɑːns] *n* matiz *m*

**nuclear** ['njuːklɪə*] *adj* nuclear

**nuclei** ['njuːklɪaɪ] *npl of* **nucleus**

**nucleus** ['njuːklɪəs] (*pl* **nuclei**) *n* núcleo

**nude** [njuːd] *adj*, *n* desnudo/a *m/f*; **in the ~** desnudo

**nudge** [nʌdʒ] *vt* dar un codazo a

**nudist** ['njuːdɪst] *n* nudista *m/f*

**nuisance** ['njuːsns] *n* molestia, fastidio; (*person*) pesado, latoso; **what a ~!** ¡qué lata!

**nuke** [njuːk] (*inf*) *n* bomba atómica ♦ *vt* atacar con arma nuclear

**null** [nʌl] *adj*: **~ and void** nulo y sin efecto

**numb** [nʌm] *adj*: **~ with cold/fear** entumecido por el frío/paralizado de miedo

**number** ['nʌmbə*] *n* número; (*quantity*) cantidad *f* ♦ *vt* (*pages etc*) numerar, poner número a; (*amount to*) sumar, ascender a; **to be ~ed among** figurar entre; **a ~ of** varios, algunos; **they were ten in ~** eran diez; **~ plate** (BRIT) *n* matrícula, placa

**numeral** ['njuːmərəl] *n* número, cifra

**numerate** ['njuːmərɪt] *adj* competente en la aritmética

**numerous** ['njuːmərəs] *adj* numeroso

**nun** [nʌn] *n* monja, religiosa

**nurse** [nɜːs] *n* enfermero/a; (*also*: **~maid**) niñera ♦ *vt* (*patient*) cuidar, atender

**nursery** ['nɜːsərɪ] *n* (*institution*) guardería infantil; (*room*) cuarto de los niños; (*for plants*) criadero, semillero; **~ rhyme** *n* canción *f* infantil; **~ school** *n* parvulario, escuela de párvulos; **~ slope** (BRIT) *n* (SKI) cuesta para principiantes

**nursing** ['nɜːsɪŋ] *n* (*profession*) profesión *f* de enfermera; (*care*) asistencia, cuidado; **~ home** *n* clínica de reposo; **~ mother** *n* madre *f* lactante

**nurture** ['nɜːtʃə*] *vt* (*child, plant*) alimentar, nutrir

**nut** [nʌt] *n* (TECH) tuerca; (BOT) nuez *f*; **~crackers** *npl* cascanueces *m inv*

**nutmeg** ['nʌtmeg] *n* nuez *f* moscada

**nutritious** [njuː'trɪʃəs] *adj* nutritivo,

alimenticio

**nuts** [nʌts] (inf) adj loco

**nutshell** ['nʌtʃel] n: **in a ~** en resumidas cuentas

**nylon** ['naɪlɔn] n nilón m ♦ adj de nilón

# O

**oak** [əuk] n roble m ♦ adj de roble

**O.A.P.** (BRIT) n abbr = **old-age pensioner**

**oar** [ɔː*] n remo

**oases** [əu'eɪsiːz] npl of **oasis**

**oasis** [əu'eɪsɪs] (pl **oases**) n oasis m inv

**oath** [əuθ] n juramento; (swear word) palabrota; **on** (BRIT) **or under ~** bajo juramento

**oatmeal** ['əutmiːl] n harina de avena

**oats** [əuts] n avena

**obedience** [ə'biːdɪəns] n obediencia

**obedient** [ə'biːdɪənt] adj obediente

**obey** [ə'beɪ] vt obedecer; (instructions, regulations) cumplir

**obituary** [ə'bɪtjuərɪ] n necrología

**object** [n 'ɔbdʒɪkt, vb əb'dʒekt] n objeto; (purpose) objeto, propósito; (LING) complemento ♦ vi: **to ~ to** estar en contra de; (proposal) oponerse a; **to ~ that** objetar que; **expense is no ~** no importa cuánto cuesta; **I ~!** ¡yo protesto!; **~ion** [əb'dʒekʃən] n protesta; **I have no ~ion to ...** no tengo inconveniente en que ...; **~ionable** [əb'dʒekʃənəbl] adj desagradable; (conduct) censurable; **~ive** adj, n objetivo

**obligation** [ɔblɪ'ɡeɪʃən] n obligación f; (debt) deber m; **without ~** sin compromiso

**oblige** [ə'blaɪdʒ] vt (do a favour for) complacer, hacer un favor a; **to ~ sb to do sth** forzar o obligar a uno a hacer algo; **to be ~d to sb for sth** estarle agradecido a uno por algo; **obliging** adj servicial, atento

**oblique** [ə'bliːk] adj oblicuo; (allusion) indirecto

**obliterate** [ə'blɪtəreɪt] vt borrar

**oblivion** [ə'blɪvɪən] n olvido; **oblivious** [-ɪəs] adj: **oblivious of** inconsciente de

**oblong** ['ɔblɔŋ] adj rectangular ♦ n rectángulo

**obnoxious** [əb'nɔkʃəs] adj odioso, detestable; (smell) nauseabundo

**oboe** ['əubəu] n oboe m

**obscene** [əb'siːn] adj obsceno

**obscure** [əb'skjuə*] adj oscuro ♦ vt oscurecer; (hide: view) esconder

**obsequious** [əb'siːkwɪəs] adj servil

**observance** [əb'zɔːvns] n observancia, cumplimiento

**observant** [əb'zɔːvnt] adj observador(a)

**observation** [ɔbzə'veɪʃən] n observación f; (MED) examen m

**observe** [əb'zɔːv] vt observar; (rule) cumplir; **~r** n observador(a) m/f

**obsess** [əb'ses] vt obsesionar; **~ive** adj obsesivo; obsesionante

**obsolete** ['ɔbsəliːt] adj: **to be ~** estar en desuso

**obstacle** ['ɔbstəkl] n obstáculo; (nuisance) estorbo; **~ race** n carrera de obstáculos

**obstinate** ['ɔbstɪnɪt] adj terco, porfiado; (determined) obstinado

**obstruct** [əb'strʌkt] vt obstruir; (hinder) estorbar, obstaculizar; **~ion** [əb'strʌkʃən] n (action) obstrucción f; (object) estorbo, obstáculo

**obtain** [əb'teɪn] vt obtener; (achieve) conseguir; **~able** adj asequible

**obvious** ['ɔbvɪəs] adj obvio, evidente; **~ly** adv evidentemente, naturalmente; **~ly not** por supuesto que no

**occasion** [ə'keɪʒən] n oportunidad f, ocasión f; (event) acontecimiento; **~al** adj poco frecuente, ocasional; **~ally** adv de vez en cuando

**occult** [ə'kʌlt] n: **the ~** lo sobrenatural, lo oculto

**occupant** ['ɔkjupənt] n (of house) inquilino/a; (of car) ocupante m/f

**occupation** [ɔkju'peɪʃən] n ocupación f; (job) trabajo; (pastime) ocupaciones fpl; **~al hazard** n riesgo profesional

**occupier** ['ɔkjupaɪə*] n inquilino/a

**occupy** ['ɔkjupaɪ] vt (seat, post, time) ocupar; (house) habitar; to ~ o.s. in doing pasar el tiempo haciendo

**occur** [ə'kə:*] vi pasar, suceder; to ~ to sb ocurrírsele a uno; **~rence** [ə'kʌrəns] n acontecimiento; (existence) existencia

**ocean** ['əuʃən] n océano; **~-going** adj de alta mar

**ochre** ['əukə*] (US ocher) n ocre m

**o'clock** [ə'klɔk] adv: it is 5 ~ son las 5

**OCR** n abbr = optical character recognition/reader

**octave** ['ɔktɪv] n octava

**October** [ɔk'təubə*] n octubre m

**octopus** ['ɔktəpəs] n pulpo

**odd** [ɔd] adj extraño, raro; (number) impar; (sock, shoe etc) suelto; 60-~ 60 y pico; at ~ times de vez en cuando; to be ~ the one out estar de más; **~ity** n rareza; (person) excéntrico; **~-job man** n chico para todo; **~ jobs** npl bricolaje m; **~s** npl (in betting) puntos mpl de ventaja; it makes no ~s da lo mismo; at ~s reñidos/as; **~s-and-ends** npl minucias fpl

**ode** [əud] n oda

**odometer** [ɔ'dɔmɪtə*] (US) n cuentakilómetros m inv

**odour** ['əudə*] (US odor) n olor m; (unpleasant) hedor m

---

KEYWORD

**of** [ɔv, əv] prep 1 (gen) de; a friend ~ ours un amigo nuestro; a boy ~ 10 un chico de 10 años; that was kind ~ you eso fue muy amable por or de tu parte

2 (expressing quantity, amount, dates etc) de; a kilo ~ flour un kilo de harina; there were 3 ~ them había tres; 3 ~ us went tres de nosotros fuimos; the 5th ~ July el 5 de julio

---

3 (from, out of) de; **made ~ wood** (hecho) de madera

**off** [ɔf] adj, adv (engine) desconectado; (light) apagado; (tap) cerrado; (BRIT: food: bad) pasado, malo; (: milk) cortado; (cancelled) cancelado ♦ prep de; to be ~ (to leave) irse, marcharse; to be ~ sick estar enfermo or de baja; a day ~ un día libre or sin trabajar; to have an ~ day tener un día malo; he had his coat ~ se había quitado el abrigo; 10% ~ (COMM) (con el) 10% de descuento; 5 km ~ (the road) a 5 km (de la carretera); ~ the coast frente a la costa; I'm ~ meat (no longer eat/like it) paso de la carne; on the ~ chance por si acaso; ~ and on de vez en cuando

**offal** ['ɔfl] (BRIT) n (CULIN) menudencias fpl

**off-colour** ['ɔf'kʌlə*] (BRIT) adj (ill) indispuesto

**offence** [ə'fɛns] (US offense) n (crime) delito; to take ~ at ofenderse por

**offend** [ə'fɛnd] vt (person) ofender; **~er** n delincuente m/f

**offensive** [ə'fɛnsɪv] adj ofensivo; (smell etc) repugnante ♦ n (MIL) ofensiva

**offer** ['ɔfə*] n oferta, ofrecimiento; (proposal) propuesta ♦ vt ofrecer; (opportunity) facilitar; "on ~" (COMM) "en oferta"; **~ing** n ofrenda

**offhand** [ɔf'hænd] adj informal ♦ adv de improviso

**office** ['ɔfɪs] n (place) oficina; (room) despacho; (position) carga, oficio; doctor's ~ (US) consultorio, to take ~ entrar en funciones; ~ **automation** n ofimática, buromática; ~ **block** (US ~ building) n bloque m de oficinas; (US: MED) horas fpl de consulta

**officer** ['ɔfɪsə*] n (MIL etc) oficial m/f; (also: police ~) agente m/f de policía; (*of organization*) director(a) m/f

**office worker** n oficinista m/f

**official** [ə'fɪʃl] adj oficial, autorizado ♦ n funcionario, oficial m; **~dom** n burocracia

**offing** ['ɔfɪŋ] n: **in the ~** (fig) en perspectiva

**off**: **~-licence** (BRIT) n (shop) bodega, tienda de vinos y bebidas alcohólicas; **~-line** adj, adv (COMPUT) fuera de línea; **~-peak** adj (electricity) de banda económica; (ticket) billete de precio reducido por viajar fuera de las horas punta; **~-putting** (BRIT) adj (person) asqueroso; (remark) desalentador(a); **~-season** adj, adv fuera de temporada

**offset** ['ɔfset] (irreg) vt contrarrestar, compensar

**offshoot** ['ɔfʃuːt] n (fig) ramificación f

**offshore** [ɔf'ʃɔː*] adj (breeze, island) costera; (fishing) de bajura

**offside** ['ɔf'saɪd] adj (SPORT) fuera de juego; (AUT: in Britain) del lado derecho; (: in US, Europe etc) del lado izquierdo

**offspring** ['ɔfsprɪŋ] n inv descendencia

**off**: **~-stage** adv entre bastidores; **~-the-peg** (US **~-the-rack**) adv confeccionado; **~-white** adj blanco grisáceo

**often** ['ɔfn] adv a menudo, con frecuencia; **how ~ do you go?** ¿cada cuánto vas?

**ogle** ['əugl] vt comerse con los ojos a

**oh** [əu] excl ¡ah!

**oil** [ɔɪl] n aceite m; (petroleum) petróleo; (for heating) aceite m combustible ♦ vt engrasar; **~can** n lata de aceite; **~field** n campo petrolífero; **~ filter** n (AUT) filtro de aceite; **~ painting** n pintura al óleo; **~ rig** n torre f de perforación; **~skins** npl impermeables mpl de hule, chubasquero; **~ tanker** n petrolero; (truck) camión m cisterna; **~ well** n pozo

(de petróleo); **~y** adj aceitoso; (food) grasiento

**ointment** ['ɔɪntmənt] n ungüento

**O.K., okay** ['əu'keɪ] excl O.K., ¡está bien!, ¡vale! (SP) ♦ adj bien ♦ vt dar el visto bueno a

**old** [əuld] adj viejo; (former) antiguo; **how ~ are you?** ¿cuántos años tienes?, ¿qué edad tienes?; **he's 10 years ~** tiene 10 años; **~er brother** hermano mayor; **~ age** n vejez f; **~-age pensioner** (BRIT) n jubilado/a; **~-fashioned** adj anticuado, pasado de moda

**olive** ['ɔlɪv] n (fruit) aceituna; (tree) olivo ♦ adj (also: **~-green**) verde oliva; **~ oil** n aceite m de oliva

**Olympic** [əu'lɪmpɪk] adj olímpico; **the ~ Games** npl las Olimpíadas; **the ~s** npl las Olimpíadas

**omelet(te)** ['ɔmlɪt] n tortilla (SP), tortilla de huevo (AM)

**omen** ['əumən] n presagio

**ominous** ['ɔmɪnəs] adj de mal agüero, amenazador(a)

**omit** [əu'mɪt] vt omitir

---

KEYWORD

---

**on** [ɔn] prep 1 (indicating position) en; sobre; **~ the wall** en la pared; **it's ~ the table** está sobre or en la mesa; **~ the left** a la izquierda

2 (indicating means, method, condition etc): **~ foot** a pie; **~ the train/plane** (go) en tren/avión; (be) en el tren/el avión; **~ the radio/television/telephone** por or en la radio/televisión/al teléfono; **to be ~ drugs** drogarse; (MED) estar a tratamiento; **to be ~ holiday/business** estar de vacaciones/en viaje de negocios

3 (referring to time): **~ Friday** el viernes; **~ Fridays** los viernes; **~ June 20th** el 20 de junio; **a week ~ Friday** del viernes en una semana; **~ arrival** al llegar; **~ seeing this** al ver esto

4 (about, concerning) sobre, acerca de; **a book ~ physics** un libro de or

sobre física

♦ *adv* **1** (*referring to dress*): **to have one's coat ~** tener *or* llevar el abrigo puesto; **she put her gloves ~** se puso los guantes

**2** (*referring to covering*): **"screw the lid ~ tightly"** "cerrar bien la tapa"

**3** (*further, continuously*): **to walk** *etc* **~** seguir caminando *etc*

♦ *adj* **1** (*functioning, in operation: machine, radio, TV, light*) encendido/a (*SP*), prendido/a (*AM*); (: *tap*) abierto/a; (: *brakes*) echado/a, puesto/a; **is the meeting still ~?** (*in progress*) ¿todavía continúa la reunión?; (*not cancelled*) ¿va a haber reunión al fin?; **there's a good film ~** at the cinema ponen una buena película en el cine

**2: that's not ~!** (*inf: not possible*) ¡eso ni hablar!; (: *not acceptable*) ¡eso no se hace!

**once** [wʌns] *adv* una vez; (*formerly*) antiguamente ♦ *conj* una vez que; **he had left/it was done** una vez que se había marchado/se hizo; **at ~** en seguida, inmediatamente; (*simultaneously*) a la vez; **~ a week** una vez por semana; **~ more** otra vez; **and for all** de una vez por todas; **~ upon a time** érase una vez

**oncoming** [ˈɒnkʌmɪŋ] *adj* (*traffic*) que viene de frente

**one** [wʌn] *num* un(o)/una; **~ hundred and fifty** ciento cincuenta; **~ by ~** uno a uno

♦ *adj* **1** (*sole*) único; **the ~ book which** el único libro que; **the ~ man who** el único que

**2** (*same*) mismo/a; **they came in the ~ car** vinieron en un solo coche

♦ *pron* **1:** **this ~** éste/ésta; **that ~** ése/ésa; (*more remote*) aquél/aquella; **I've already got a (red) ~** ya tengo una (roja); **~ by ~** uno/a por una/a

**2: ~ another** os (*SP*), se (+ *el uno al otro, unos a otros etc*); **do you two ever see ~ another?** ¿vosotros dos os veis alguna vez?; (*SP*), ¿se ven ustedes dos alguna vez?; **the boys didn't dare look at ~ another** los chicos no se atrevieron a mirarse (el uno al otro); **they all kissed ~ another** se besaron unos a otros

**3** (*impers*): **~ never knows** nunca se sabe; **to cut ~'s finger** cortarse el dedo; **~ needs to eat** hay que comer

**one: ~-day excursion** (*US*) *n* billete *m* de ida y vuelta en un día; **~-man** *adj* (*business*) individual; **~-man band** *n* hombre-orquesta *m*; **~-off** (*BRIT: inf*) *n* (*event*) acontecimiento único

**oneself** [wʌnˈsɛlf] *pron* (*reflexive*) se; (*after prep*) sí; (*emphatic*) uno/a mismo/a; **to hurt ~** hacerse daño; **to keep sth for ~** guardarse algo; **to talk to ~** hablar solo

**one: ~-sided** *adj* (*argument*) parcial; **~-to-~** *adj* (*relationship*) de dos; **~-upmanship** *n* arte *m* de aventajar a los demás; **~-way** *adj* (*street*) de sentido único

**ongoing** [ˈɒngəʊɪŋ] *adj* continuo

**onion** [ˈʌnjən] *n* cebolla

**on-line** *adj*, *adv* (*COMPUT*) en línea

**onlooker** [ˈɒnlʊkə*] *n* espectador(a) *m/f*

**only** [ˈəʊnlɪ] *adv* solamente, sólo ♦ *adj* único, solo ♦ *conj* solamente que, pero; **an ~ child** un hijo único; **not ~ ... but also ...** no sólo ... sino también ...

**onset** [ˈɒnsɛt] *n* comienzo

**onshore** [ˈɒnʃɔː*] *adj* (*wind*) que sopla del mar hacia la tierra

**onslaught** [ˈɒnslɔːt] *n* ataque *m*, embestida

**onto** [ˈɒntu] *prep* = **on to**

**onus** [ˈəʊnəs] *n* responsabilidad *f*

**onward(s)** [ˈɒnwəd(z)] *adj* (*move*) (hacia) adelante; **from that time ~** desde entonces en adelante

**onyx** ['ɔnɪks] n ónice m

**ooze** [uːz] vi rezumar

**opaque** [əu'peɪk] adj opaco

**OPEC** ['əupek] n abbr (= Organization of Petroleum-Exporting Countries) OPEP f

**open** ['əupn] adj abierto; (car) descubierto; (road, view) despejado; (meeting) público; (admiration) manifiesto ♦ vt abrir ♦ vi abrirse; (book etc: commence) comenzar; **in the ~ (air)** al aire libre; **~ on to** vi fus (subj: room, door) dar a; **~ up** vt abrir; (blocked road) despejar ♦ vi abrirse, empezar; **~ing** n abertura; (start) comienzo; (opportunity) oportunidad f; **~ly** adv abiertamente; **~-minded** adj imparcial; **~-necked** adj (shirt) desabrochado; sin corbata; **~-plan** adj: **~-plan office** gran oficina sin particiones

**opera** ['ɔpərə] n ópera; **~ house** n teatro de la ópera

**operate** ['ɔpəreɪt] vt (machine) hacer funcionar; (company) dirigir ♦ vi funcionar; **to ~ on sb** (MED) operar a uno

**operatic** [ɔpə'rætɪk] adj de ópera

**operating table** ['ɔpəreɪtɪŋ-] n mesa de operaciones

**operating theatre** n sala de operaciones

**operation** [ɔpə'reɪʃən] n operación f; (of machine) funcionamiento; **to be in ~** = estar funcionando o en funcionamiento; **to have an ~** (MED) ser operado; **~al** adj operacional, en buen estado

**operative** ['ɔpərətɪv] adj en vigor

**operator** ['ɔpəreɪtə*] n (of machine) maquinista m/f; operario/a; (TEL) operador(a) m/f, telefonista m/f

**opinion** [ə'pɪnjən] n opinión f; **in my ~** en mi opinión, a mi juicio; **~ated** adj testarudo; **~ poll** n encuesta, sondeo

**opponent** [ə'pəunənt] n adversario/a, contrincante m/f

**opportunist** [ɔpə'tjuːnɪst] n oportunista m/f

**opportunity** [ɔpə'tjuːnɪtɪ] n oportunidad f; **to take the ~ of doing** aprovechar la ocasión para hacer

**oppose** [ə'pəuz] vt oponerse a; **to ~d to sth** oponerse a algo; **as ~d to** a diferencia de; **opposing** adj opuesto, contrario

**opposite** ['ɔpəzɪt] adj opuesto, contrario a; (house etc) de enfrente ♦ adv en frente ♦ prep en frente de, frente a ♦ n lo contrario

**opposition** [ɔpə'zɪʃən] n oposición f

**oppress** [ə'prɛs] vt oprimir; **~ion** [ə'prɛʃən] n opresión f; **~ive** adj opresivo; (weather) agobiante

**opt** [ɔpt] vi: **to ~ for** optar por; **to ~ to do** optar por hacer; **~ out** vi: **to ~ out of** optar por no hacer

**optical** ['ɔptɪkl] adj óptico

**optician** [ɔp'tɪʃən] n óptico m/f

**optimist** ['ɔptɪmɪst] n optimista m/f; **~ic** [-'mɪstɪk] adj optimista

**optimum** ['ɔptɪməm] adj óptimo

**option** ['ɔpʃən] n opción f; **~al** adj facultativo, discrecional

**or** [ɔː*] conj o; (before o, ho) u; (with negative): **he hasn't seen ~ heard anything** no ha visto ni oído nada; **~ else** si no

**oracle** ['ɔrəkl] n oráculo

**oral** ['ɔːrəl] adj oral ♦ n examen m oral

**orange** ['ɔrɪndʒ] n (fruit) naranja ♦ adj color naranja

**orator** ['ɔrətə*] n orador(a) m/f

**orbit** ['ɔːbɪt] n órbita ♦ vt, vi orbitar

**orchard** ['ɔːtʃəd] n huerto

**orchestra** ['ɔːkɪstrə] n orquesta; (US: seating) platea

**orchid** ['ɔːkɪd] n orquídea

**ordain** [ɔː'deɪn] vt (REL) ordenar; decretar

**ordeal** [ɔː'diːl] n experiencia horrorosa

**order** ['ɔːdə*] n orden m; (command) orden f; (good ~) buen estado; (COMM) pedido ♦ vt (also: put in ~) arreglar, poner en orden; (COMM) pedir; (command) mandar, ordenar; **in ~** en orden; (of docu-

*ment*) en regla; **in (working)** ~ en funcionamiento; **in** ~ **to do/that** para hacer/que; **on** ~ (COMM) pedido; **to be out of** ~ estar desordenado; (*not working*) no funcionar; **to** ~ **sb to do sth** mandar a uno hacer algo; ~ **form** n hoja de pedido; **~ly** n (MIL) ordenanza m; (MED) enfermero/a (auxiliar) ♦ *adj* ordenado

**ordinary** ['ɔːdɪnrɪ] *adj* corriente, normal; (*pej*) común y corriente; **out of the** ~ fuera de lo común

**Ordnance Survey** ['ɔːdnəns-] (BRIT) n servicio oficial de topografía

**ore** [ɔː*] n mineral m

**organ** ['ɔːgən] n órgano; ~**ic** [ɔː'gænɪk] *adj* orgánico; ~**ism** n organismo

**organization** [ɔːgənaɪ'zeɪʃən] n organización f

**organize** ['ɔːgənaɪz] vt organizar; ~**r** n organizador(a) m/f

**orgasm** ['ɔːgæzəm] n orgasmo

**orgy** ['ɔːdʒɪ] n orgia

**Orient** ['ɔːrɪənt] n Oriente m; **oriental** [-'entl] *adj* oriental

**orientate** ['ɔːrɪənteɪt] vt: **to** ~ **o.s.** orientarse

**origin** ['ɔrɪdʒɪn] n origen m

**original** [ə'rɪdʒɪnl] *adj* original; (*first*) primero; (*earlier*) primitivo ♦ n original m; ~**ity** [-'nælɪtɪ] n originalidad f; ~**ly** *adv* al principio

**originate** [ə'rɪdʒɪneɪt] vi: **to** ~ **from, to** ~ **in** surgir de, tener su origen en

**Orkneys** ['ɔːknɪz] *npl*: **the** ~ (*also*: **the Orkney Islands**) las Órcadas

**ornament** ['ɔːnəmənt] n adorno; (*trinket*) chuchería; ~**al** [-'mentl] *adj* decorativo, de adorno

**ornate** [ɔː'neɪt] *adj* muy ornado, vistoso

**orphan** ['ɔːfn] n huérfano/a; ~**age** n orfanato

**orthodox** ['ɔːθədɒks] *adj* ortodoxo; ~**y** n ortodoxia

**orthopaedic** [ɔːθə'piːdɪk] (US

**orthopedic**) *adj* ortopédico

**oscillate** ['ɒsɪleɪt] vi oscilar; (*person*) vacilar

**ostensibly** [ɒs'tensɪblɪ] *adv* aparentemente

**ostentatious** [ɒsten'teɪʃəs] *adj* ostentoso

**osteopath** ['ɒstɪəpæθ] n osteópata m/f

**ostracize** ['ɒstrəsaɪz] vt hacer el vacío a

**ostrich** ['ɒstrɪtʃ] n avestruz m

**other** ['ʌðə*] *adj* otro ♦ *pron*: **the** ~ **(one)** el/la otro/a ♦ *adv*: ~ **than** aparte de; ~**s** (~ *people*) otros; **the** ~ **day** el otro día; ~**wise** *adv* de otra manera ♦ *conj* (*if not*) si no

**otter** ['ɒtə*] n nutria

**ouch** [autʃ] *excl* ¡ay!

**ought** [ɔːt] (*pt* ought) *aux vb*: **I** ~ **to do it** debería hacerlo; **this** ~ **to have been corrected** esto debiera haberse corregido; **he** ~ **to win** (*probability*) debe *or* debiera ganar

**ounce** [auns] n onza (28.35g)

**our** ['auə*] *adj* nuestro; *see also* **my**; ~**s** *pron* (el) nuestro/(la) nuestra *etc*; *see also* **mine**; ~**selves** *pron pl* (*reflexive*, *after prep*) nosotros; (*emphatic*) nosotros mismos; *see also* **oneself**

**oust** [aust] vt desalojar

**out** [aut] *adv* fuera, afuera; (*not at home*) fuera (de casa); (*light*, *fire*) apagado; ~ **there** allí (fuera); **he's** ~ (*absent*) no está, ha salido; **to be** ~ **in one's calculations** equivocarse (en sus cálculos); **to run** ~ salir corriendo; ~ **loud** en alta voz; ~ **of** (*outside*) fuera de; (*because of*: *anger etc*) por; ~ **of petrol** sin gasolina; "~ **of order**" "no funciona"

**out-and-out** *adj* (*liar*, *thief etc*) redomado, empedernido

**outback** ['autbæk] n interior m

**outboard** ['autbɔːd] *adj*: ~ **motor** (motor m) fuera borda m

**outbreak** ['autbreɪk] n (*of war*) comienzo; (*of disease*) epidemia; (*of violence etc*) ola

**outburst** ['autbə:st] n explosión f, arranque m

**outcast** ['autkɑːst] n paria m/f

**outcome** ['autkʌm] n resultado

**outcrop** ['autkrɔp] n (of rock) afloramiento

**outcry** ['autkraɪ] n protestas fpl

**outdated** [aut'deɪtɪd] adj anticuado, fuera de moda

**outdo** [aut'duː] (irreg) vt superar

**outdoor** [aut'dɔː*] adj exterior, de aire libre; (clothes) de calle; ~s adv al aire libre

**outer** [aut'ə*] adj exterior, externo; ~ space n espacio exterior

**outfit** ['autfɪt] n (clothes) conjunto

**outgoing** ['autgəʊɪŋ] adj (character) extrovertido; (retiring: president etc) saliente; ~s npl gastos mpl

**outgrow** [aut'grəʊ] (irreg) vt: he has ~n his clothes su ropa le queda pequeña ya

**outhouse** ['authaʊs] n dependencia

**outing** ['autɪŋ] n excursión f, paseo

**outlandish** [aut'lændɪʃ] adj estrafalario

**outlaw** ['autlɔː] n proscrito ♦ vt proscribir

**outlay** ['autleɪ] n inversión f

**outlet** ['autlɛt] n salida; (of pipe) desagüe m; (US: ELEC) toma de corriente; (also: retail ~) punto de venta

**outline** ['autlaɪn] n (shape) contorno, perfil m; (sketch, plan) esbozo ♦ vt (plan etc) esbozar; in ~ (fig) a grandes rasgos

**outlive** [aut'lɪv] vt sobrevivir a

**outlook** ['autlʊk] n (fig: prospects) perspectivas fpl; (: for weather) pronóstico

**outlying** ['autlaɪɪŋ] adj remoto, aislado

**outmoded** [aut'məʊdɪd] adj anticuado, pasado de moda

**outnumber** [aut'nʌmbə*] vt superar en número

**out-of-date** adj (passport) caducado; (clothes) pasado de moda

**out-of-the-way** adj apartado

**outpatient** ['autpeɪʃənt] n paciente m/f externo/a

**outpost** ['autpəʊst] n puesto avanzado

**output** ['autpʊt] n (volumen m de) producción f, rendimiento; (COMPUT) salida

**outrage** ['autreɪdʒ] n escándalo; (atrocity) atrocidad f ♦ vt ultrajar; ~ous [-'reɪdʒəs] adj monstruoso

**outright** [adv aut'raɪt, adj 'autraɪt] adv (ask, deny) francamente; (refuse) rotundamente; (win) de manera absoluta; (be killed) en el acto ♦ adj franco; rotundo

**outset** ['autsɛt] n principio

**outside** [aut'saɪd] n exterior m ♦ adj exterior, externo ♦ adv fuera ♦ prep fuera de; (beyond) más allá de; at the ~ (fig) a lo sumo; ~ lane n (AUT: in Britain) carril m de la derecha; (: in US, Europe etc) carril m de la izquierda; ~ line n (TEL) línea (exterior); ~r n (stranger) extraño, forastero

**outsize** ['autsaɪz] adj (clothes) de talla grande

**outskirts** ['autskə:ts] npl alrededores mpl, afueras fpl

**outspoken** [aut'spəʊkən] adj muy franco

**outstanding** [aut'stændɪŋ] adj excepcional, destacado; (remaining) pendiente

**outstay** [aut'steɪ] vt: to ~ one's welcome quedarse más de la cuenta

**outstretched** [aut'strɛtʃt] adj (hand) extendido

**outstrip** [aut'strɪp] vt (competitors, demand) dejar atrás, aventajar

**out-tray** [autwɔd] n bandeja de salida

**outward** ['autwəd] adj externo; (journey) de ida; ~ly adv por fuera

**outweigh** [aut'weɪ] vt pesar más que

**outwit** [aut'wɪt] vt ser más listo que

**oval** ['əʊvl] adj ovalado ♦ n óvalo

**ovary** ['əʊvərɪ] n ovario

**oven** ['ʌvn] n horno; ~proof adj resistente al horno

**over** ['əuvə*] adv encima, por encima ♦ adj (or adv) (finished) terminado; (surplus) de sobra ♦ prep (por) encima de; (above) sobre; (on the other side of) al otro lado de; (more than) más de; (during) durante; ~ **here** (por) aquí; ~ **there** (por) allí or allá; **all ~** (everywhere) por todas partes; ~ **and ~** (again) una y otra vez; ~ **and above** además de; **to ask sb** ~ invitar a uno a casa; **to bend** ~ inclinarse

**overall** [adj, n 'əuvərɔːl, adv əuvər'ɔːl] adj (length etc) total; (study) de conjunto ♦ adv en conjunto ♦ n (BRIT) guardapolvo; ~**s** npl mono (SP), overol m (AM)

**overawe** [əuvər'ɔː] vt: **to be** ~**d** (**by**) quedar impresionado (con)

**overbalance** [əuvə'bæləns] vi perder el equilibrio

**overbearing** [əuvə'bɛərɪŋ] adj autoritario, imperioso

**overboard** ['əuvəbɔːd] adv (NAUT) por la borda

**overbook** [əuvə'buk] vt sobrereservar

**overcast** ['əuvəkɑːst] adj encapotado

**overcharge** [əuvə'tʃɑːdʒ] vt: **to** ~ **sb** cobrar un precio excesivo a uno

**overcoat** ['əuvəkəut] n abrigo, sobretodo

**overcome** [əuvə'kʌm] (irreg) vt vencer; (difficulty) superar

**overcrowded** [əuvə'kraudɪd] adj atestado de gente; (city, country) superpoblado

**overdo** [əuvə'duː] (irreg) vt exagerar; (overcook) cocer demasiado; **to** ~ **it** (work etc) pasarse

**overdose** ['əuvədəus] n sobredosis f inv

**overdraft** ['əuvədrɑːft] n saldo deudor

**overdrawn** [əuvə'drɔːn] adj (account) en descubierto

**overdue** [əuvə'djuː] adj retrasado

**overestimate** [əuvər'ɛstɪmeɪt] vt sobreestimar

**overflow** [vb əuvə'fləu, n 'əuvəfləu] vi desbordarse ♦ n (also: ~ pipe) (cañería de) desagüe m

**overgrown** [əuvə'grəun] adj (garden) invadido por la vegetación

**overhaul** [vb əuvə'hɔːl, n 'əuvəhɔːl] vt revisar, repasar ♦ n revisión f

**overhead** [adv əuvə'hɛd, adj 'əuvəhɛd] adv por arriba or encima ♦ adj (cable) aéreo ♦ n (US) = ~**s**; ~**s** npl (expenses) gastos mpl generales

**overhear** [əuvə'hɪə*] (irreg) vt oír por casualidad

**overheat** [əuvə'hiːt] vi (engine) recalentarse

**overjoyed** [əuvə'dʒɔɪd] adj encantado, lleno de alegría

**overkill** ['əuvəkɪl] n excesos mpl

**overland** ['əuvəlænd] adj, adv por tierra

**overlap** [əuvə'læp] vi traslaparse

**overleaf** [əuvə'liːf] adv al dorso

**overload** [əuvə'ləud] vt sobrecargar

**overlook** [əuvə'luk] vt (have view of) dar a, tener vistas a; (miss: by mistake) pasar por alto; (excuse) perdonar

**overnight** [əuvə'naɪt] adv durante la noche; (fig) de la noche a la mañana ♦ adj de noche; **to stay** ~ pasar la noche

**overpass** ['əuvəpɑːs] (US) n paso superior

**overpower** [əuvə'pauə*] vt dominar; (fig) embargar; ~**ing** adj (heat) agobiante; (smell) penetrante

**overrate** [əuvə'reɪt] vt sobreestimar

**override** [əuvə'raɪd] (irreg) vt no hacer caso de; **overriding** adj predominante

**overrule** [əuvə'ruːl] vt (decision) anular; (claim) denegar

**overrun** [əuvə'rʌn] (irreg) vt (country) invadir; (time limit) rebasar, exceder

**overseas** [əuvə'siːz] adv (abroad: live) en el extranjero; (: travel) al extranjero ♦ adj (trade) exterior; (visitor) extranjero

**overshadow** [əuvə'ʃædəu] vt: **to be**

~ed by estar a la sombra de
**overshoot** [əuvəˈʃuːt] (irreg) vt excederse
**oversight** [ˈəuvəsaɪt] n descuido
**oversleep** [əuvəˈsliːp] (irreg) vi quedarse dormido
**overstate** [əuvəˈsteɪt] vt exagerar
**overstep** [əuvəˈstep] vt: to ~ the mark pasarse de la raya
**overt** [əuˈvɜːt] adj abierto
**overtake** [əuvəˈteɪk] (irreg) vt sobrepasar; (BRIT: AUT) adelantar
**overthrow** [əuvəˈθrəu] (irreg) vt (government) derrocar
**overtime** [ˈəuvətaɪm] n horas fpl extraordinarias
**overtone** [ˈəuvətəun] n (fig) tono
**overture** [ˈəuvətʃuə] n (MUS) obertura; (fig) preludio
**overturn** [əuvəˈtɜːn] vt volcar; (fig: plan) desbaratar; (: government) derrocar ♦ vi volcar
**overweight** [əuvəˈweɪt] adj demasiado gordo or pesado
**overwhelm** [əuvəˈwelm] vt aplastar; (subj: emotion) sobrecoger; ~ing adj (victory, defeat) arrollador(a); (feeling) irresistible
**overwork** [əuvəˈwɜːk] n trabajo excesivo ♦ vi trabajar demasiado
**overwrought** [əuvəˈrɔːt] adj sobreexcitado
**owe** [əu] vt: to ~ sb sth, to ~ sth to sb deber algo a uno; **owing to** prep debido a, por causa de
**owl** [aul] n búho, lechuza
**own** [əun] vt tener, poseer ♦ adj propio; a room of my ~ una habitación propia; to get one's ~ back tomar revancha; on one's ~ solo, a solas; ~ **up** vi confesar; ~**er** n dueño/a; ~**ership** n posesión f
**ox** [ɔks] (pl ~**en**) n buey m; ~**tail** n: ~ **soup** sopa de rabo de buey
**oxygen** [ˈɔksɪdʒən] n oxígeno; ~ **mask/tent** n máscara/tienda de oxígeno
**oyster** [ˈɔɪstə*] n ostra
**oz.** abbr = **ounce(s)**
**ozone hole** [ˈəuzəun-] n agujero m

de/en la capa de ozono
**ozone layer** [ˈəuzəun-] n capa f de ozono

# P

**p** [piː] abbr = **penny**; **pence**
**P.A.** n abbr = **personal assistant**; **public address system**
**p.a.** abbr = **per annum**
**pa** [pɑː] (inf) n papá m
**pace** [peɪs] n paso ♦ vi: to ~ up and down pasearse de un lado a otro; to **keep** ~ **with** llevar el mismo paso que; ~**maker** n (MED) regulador m cardíaco, marcapasos m inv; (SPORT: also: ~**setter**) liebre f
**Pacific** [pəˈsɪfɪk] n: the ~ (Ocean) el (Océano) Pacífico
**pacify** [ˈpæsɪfaɪ] vt apaciguar
**pack** [pæk] n (packet) paquete m; (of hounds) jauría; (of people) manada, bando; (of cards) baraja; (bundle) fardo; (US: of cigarettes) paquete m; (back ~) mochila ♦ vt (fill) llenar; (in suitcase etc) meter, poner; (cram) llenar, atestar; to ~ (one's bags) hacerse la maleta; to ~ **sb off** despachar a uno; ~ **it in!** (inf) ¡déjalo!
**package** [ˈpækɪdʒ] n paquete m; (bulky) bulto; (also: ~ **deal**) acuerdo global; ~ **holiday** n vacaciones fpl organizadas; ~ **tour** n viaje m organizado
**packed lunch** n almuerzo frío
**packet** [ˈpækɪt] n paquete m
**packing** [ˈpækɪŋ] n embalaje m; ~ **case** n cajón m de embalaje
**pact** [pækt] n pacto
**pad** [pæd] n (of paper) bloc m; (cushion) cojinete m; (inf: home) casa ♦ vt rellenar; ~**ding** (material) relleno
**paddle** [ˈpædl] n (oar) canalete m; (US: for table tennis) paleta ♦ vt impulsar con canalete ♦ vi (with feet) chapotear; ~ **steamer** n vapor m de ruedas; **paddling pool** (BRIT) n es-

tanque m de juegos

**paddock** ['pædək] n corral m

**paddy field** ['pædɪ-] n arrozal m

**padlock** ['pædlɔk] n candado

**paediatrics** [piːdɪ'ætrɪks] (US **pediatrics**) n pediatría

**pagan** ['peɪgən] adj, n pagano/a m/f

**page** [peɪdʒ] n (of book) página; (of newspaper) plana; (also: ~ **boy**) paje m ♦ vt (in hotel etc) llamar por altavoz a

**pageant** ['pædʒənt] n (procession) desfile m; (show) espectáculo; ~**ry** n pompa

**pager** ['peɪdʒə*] n (TEL) busca m

**paging device** ['peɪdʒɪŋ-] n (TEL) busca m

**paid** [peɪd] pt, pp of **pay** ♦ adj (work) remunerado; (holiday) pagado; (official etc) a sueldo; **to put ~ to** (BRIT) acabar con

**pail** [peɪl] n cubo, balde m

**pain** [peɪn] n dolor m; **to be in ~** sufrir; **to take ~s to do sth** tomarse grandes molestias en hacer algo; ~**ed** adj (expression) afligido; ~**ful** adj doloroso; (difficult) penoso; (disagreeable) desagradable; ~**fully** adv (fig: very) terriblemente; ~**killer** n analgésico; ~**less** adj que no causa dolor; ~**staking** ['peɪnzteɪkɪŋ] adj (person) concienzudo, esmerado

**paint** [peɪnt] n pintura ♦ vt pintar; **to ~ the door blue** pintar la puerta de azul; ~**brush** n (artist's) pincel m; (decorator's) brocha; ~**er** n pintor/a m/f; ~**ing** n pintura; ~**work** n pintura

**pair** [peə*] n (of shoes, gloves etc) par m; (of people) pareja; **a ~ of scissors** unas tijeras; **a ~ of trousers** unos pantalones, un pantalón

**pajamas** [pə'dʒɑːməz] (US) npl pijama m m

**Pakistan** [pɑːkɪ'stɑːn] n Paquistán m; ~**i** adj, n paquistaní m/f

**pal** [pæl] (inf) n compinche m/f, compañero/a

**palace** ['pæləs] n palacio

**palatable** ['pælɪtəbl] adj sabroso

**palate** ['pælɪt] n paladar m

**palatial** [pə'leɪʃəl] adj suntuoso, espléndido

**pale** [peɪl] adj (gen) pálido; (colour) claro ♦ n: **to be beyond the ~** pasarse de la raya

**Palestine** ['pælɪstaɪn] n Palestina; **Palestinian** [-'tɪnɪən] adj, n palestino/a m/f

**palette** ['pælɪt] n paleta

**pall** [pɔːl] n (of smoke) capa (de humo) ♦ vi perder el sabor

**pallet** ['pælɪt] n (for goods) pallet m

**pallid** ['pælɪd] adj pálido

**pallor** ['pælə*] n palidez f

**palm** [pɑːm] n (ANAT) palma; (also: ~ **tree**) palmera, palma ♦ vt: **to ~ sth off on sb** (inf) encajar algo a uno; **P~ Sunday** n Domingo de Ramos

**palpable** ['pælpəbl] adj palpable

**paltry** ['pɔːltrɪ] adj irrisorio

**pamper** ['pæmpə*] vt mimar

**pamphlet** ['pæmflət] n folleto

**pan** [pæn] n (also: **sauce~**) cacerola, cazuela, olla; (: also: **frying ~**) sartén f

**panache** [pə'næʃ] n: **with ~** con estilo

**Panama** ['pænəmɑː] n Panamá m; **the ~ Canal** el Canal de Panamá

**pancake** ['pænkeɪk] n crepe f

**panda** ['pændə] n panda m; ~ **car** (BRIT) n coche m Z (SP)

**pandemonium** [pændɪ'məunɪəm] n jaleo

**pander** ['pændə*] vi: **to ~ to** complacer a

**pane** [peɪn] n cristal m

**panel** ['pænl] n (of wood etc) panel m; (RADIO, TV) panel m de invitados; ~**ling** (US ~**ing**) n paneles mpl

**pang** [pæŋ] n: **a ~ of regret** (una punzada de) remordimiento; **hunger ~s** dolores mpl del hambre

**panic** ['pænɪk] n (terror m) pánico ♦ vi dejarse llevar por el pánico; ~**ky** adj (person) asustadizo; ~-**stricken** adj preso de pánico

**pansy** ['pænzɪ] n (BOT) pensamiento; (*inf: pej*) maricón *m*

**pant** [pænt] *vi* jadear

**panther** ['pænθə*] *n* pantera

**panties** ['pæntɪz] *npl* bragas *fpl*, pantis *mpl*

**pantihose** ['pæntɪhəuz] (*US*) *n* pantimedias *fpl*

**pantomime** ['pæntəmaɪm] (*BRIT*) *n* revista musical representada en Navidad, basada en cuentos de hadas

**pantry** ['pæntrɪ] *n* despensa

**pants** [pænts] *n* (*BRIT*: *underwear*: *woman's*) bragas *fpl*; (: *man's*) calzoncillos *mpl*; (*US*: *trousers*) pantalones *mpl*

**paper** ['peɪpə*] *n* papel *m*; (*also*: *news~*) periódico, diario; (*academic essay*) ensayo; (*exam*) examen *m* ♦ *adj* de papel ♦ *vt* (*wall*) empapelar, tapizar (*AM*); ~**s** *npl* (*also*: *identity ~s*) papeles *mpl*, documentos *mpl*; ~**back** *n* libro en rústica; ~ **bag** *n* bolsa de papel; ~ **clip** *n* clip *m*; ~ **hankie** *n* pañuelo de papel; ~**weight** *n* pisapapeles *m inv*; ~**work** *n* trabajo administrativo

**papier-mâché** ['pæpɪeɪ'mæʃeɪ] *n* cartón *m* piedra

**paprika** ['pæprɪkə] *n* pimentón *m*

**par** [pɑ:*] *n* par *f*; (*GOLF*) par *m*; to be on a ~ with estar a la par con

**parable** ['pærəbl] *n* parábola

**parachute** ['pærəʃu:t] *n* paracaídas *m inv*

**parade** [pə'reɪd] *n* desfile *m* ♦ *vt* (*show off*) hacer alarde de ♦ *vi* desfilar; (*MIL*) pasar revista

**paradise** ['pærədaɪs] *n* paraíso

**paradox** ['pærədɔks] *n* paradoja; ~**ically** [-'dɔksɪklɪ] *adv* paradójicamente

**paraffin** ['pærəfɪn] (*BRIT*) *n* (*also*: ~ *oil*) parafina

**paragon** ['pærəgən] *n* modelo

**paragraph** ['pærəgrɑ:f] *n* párrafo

**parallel** ['pærəlɛl] *adj* en paralelo; (*fig*) semejante ♦ *n* (*line*) paralela; (*fig, GEO*) paralelo

**paralyse** ['pærəlaɪz] *vt* paralizar

**paralysis** [pə'rælɪsɪs] *n* parálisis *f inv*

**paralyze** ['pærəlaɪz] (*US*) *vt* = **paralyse**

**paramount** ['pærəmaunt] *adj*: of ~ **importance** de suma importancia

**paranoid** ['pærənɔɪd] *adj* (*person, feeling*) paranoico

**paraphernalia** [pærəfə'neɪlɪə] *n* (*gear*) avíos *mpl*

**paraphrase** ['pærəfreɪz] *vt* parafrasear

**parasite** ['pærəsaɪt] *n* parásito/a

**parasol** ['pærəsɔl] *n* sombrilla, quitasol *m*

**paratrooper** ['pærətru:pə*] *n* paracaidista *m/f*

**parcel** ['pɑ:sl] *n* paquete *m* ♦ *vt* (*also*: ~ *up*) empaquetar, embalar

**parch** [pɑ:tʃ] *vt* secar, resecar; ~**ed** *adj* (*person*) muerto de sed

**parchment** ['pɑ:tʃmənt] *n* pergamino

**pardon** ['pɑ:dn] *n* (*LAW*) indulto ♦ *vt* perdonar; ~ **me!**, **I beg your ~!** (*I'm sorry!*) ¡perdone usted!; (**I beg your**) ~?, ~ **me?** (*what did you say?*) ¿cómo?

**parent** ['pɛərənt] *n* (*mother*) madre *f*; (*father*) padre *m*; ~**s** *npl* padres *mpl*; ~**al** [pə'rɛntl] *adj* paternal/maternal

**parentheses** [pə'rɛnθɪsi:z] *npl* of **parenthesis**

**parenthesis** [pə'rɛnθɪsɪs] (*pl* **parentheses**) *n* paréntesis *m inv*

**Paris** ['pærɪs] *n* París

**parish** ['pærɪʃ] *n* parroquia

**Parisian** [pə'rɪzɪən] *adj, n* parisiense *m/f*

**parity** ['pærɪtɪ] *n* paridad *f*, igualdad *f*

**park** [pɑ:k] *n* parque *m* ♦ *vt* aparcar, estacionar ♦ *vi* aparcar, estacionarse

**parka** ['pɑ:kə] *n* anorak *m*

**parking** ['pɑ:kɪŋ] *n* aparcamiento, estacionamiento; "**no** ~" "prohibido estacionarse"; ~ **lot** (*US*) *n* parking *m*; ~ **meter** *n* parquímetro; ~ **ticket** *n* multa de aparcamiento

**parlance** ['pɑ:ləns] *n* lenguaje *m*

**parliament** ['pɑ:ləmənt] *n* parlamento; (*Spanish*) Cortes *fpl*; ~**ary** [-'mentəri] *adj* parlamentario

**parlour** ['pɑ:lə*] (*US* **parlor**) *n* sala de recibo, salón *m*, living (*AM*)

**parochial** [pə'rəukiəl] (*pej*) *adj* de miras estrechas

**parody** ['pærədi] *n* parodia

**parole** [pə'rəul] *n*: **on** ~ libre bajo palabra

**parquet** ['pɑ:kei] *n*: ~ **floor(ing)** parquet *m*

**parrot** ['pærət] *n* loro, papagayo

**parry** ['pæri] *vt* parar

**parsimonious** [pɑ:si'məuniəs] *adj* tacaño

**parsley** ['pɑ:sli] *n* perejil *m*

**parsnip** ['pɑ:snip] *n* chirivía

**parson** ['pɑ:sn] *n* cura *m*

**part** [pɑ:t] *n* (*gen*, *MUS*) parte *f*; (*bit*) trozo; (*of machine*) pieza; (*THEATRE etc*) papel *m*; (*of serial*) entrega; (*US: in hair*) raya ♦ *adv* = **partly** ♦ *vt* separar ♦ *vi* (*people*) separarse; (*crowd*) apartarse; **to take** ~ **in** tomar parte o participar en; **to take sth in good** ~ tomar algo en buena parte; **to take sb's** ~ defender a uno; **for my** ~ por mi parte; **for the most** ~ en su mayor parte; **to** ~ **one's hair** hacerse la raya; ~ **with** *vt fus* ceder, entregar; (*money*) pagar; ~ **exchange** (*BRIT*) *n*: **in** ~ **exchange** como parte del pago

**partial** ['pɑ:ʃl] *adj* parcial; **to be** ~ **to** ser aficionado a

**participant** [pɑ:'tisipənt] *n* (*in competition*) concursante *m/f*; (*in campaign etc*) participante *m/f*

**participate** [pɑ:'tisipeit] *vi*: **to** ~ **in** participar en; **participation** [-'peiʃən] *n* participación *f*

**participle** ['pɑ:tisipl] *n* participio

**particle** ['pɑ:tikl] *n* partícula; (*of dust*) grano

**particular** [pə'tikjulə*] *adj* (*special*) particular; (*concrete*) concreto; (*given*) determinado; (*fussy*) quisquilloso; (*demanding*) exigente; ~ *npl* (*information*) datos *mpl*; (*details*) pormenores *mpl*; **in** ~ en particular;

~**ly** *adv* (*in particular*) sobre todo; (*difficult, good etc*) especialmente

**parting** ['pɑ:tiŋ] *n* (*act of*) separación *f*; (*farewell*) despedida; (*BRIT: in hair*) raya ♦ *adj* de despedida

**partisan** [pɑ:ti'zæn] *adj* partidista ♦ *n* partidario/a

**partition** [pɑ:'tiʃən] *n* (*POL*) división *f*; (*wall*) tabique *m*

**partly** ['pɑ:tli] *adv* en parte

**partner** ['pɑ:tnə*] *n* (*COMM*) socio/a; (*SPORT, at dance*) pareja; (*spouse*) cónyuge *m/f*; (*boy/girlfriend etc*) compañero/a; ~**ship** *n* asociación *f*; (*COMM*) sociedad *f*

**partridge** ['pɑ:trid3] *n* perdiz *f*

**part-time** *adj, adv* a tiempo parcial

**party** ['pɑ:ti] *n* (*POL*) partido; (*celebration*) fiesta; (*group*) grupo; (*LAW*) parte *f* interesada ♦ *cpd* (*POL*) de partido; ~ **dress** *n* vestido de fiesta; ~ **line** *n* (*TEL*) línea compartida

**pass** [pɑ:s] *vt* (*time, object*) pasar; (*place*) pasar por; (*overtake*) rebasar; (*exam*) aprobar; (*approve*) aprobar ♦ *vi* pasar; (*SCOL*) aprobar, ser aprobado ♦ *n* (*permit*) permiso; (*membership card*) carnet *m*; (*in mountains*) puerto, desfiladero; (*SPORT*) pase *m*; (*SCOL: also*: ~ **mark**): **to get a** ~ in aprobar en; **to** ~ **sth through sth** pasar algo por algo; **to make a** ~ **at sb** (*inf*) hacer proposiciones a uno; ~ **away** *vi* fallecer; ~ **by** *vi* pasar ♦ *vt* (*ignore*) pasar por alto; ~ **for** *vt fus* pasar por; ~ **on** *vt* transmitir; ~ **out** *vi* desmayarse; ~ **up** *vt* (*opportunity*) renunciar a; ~**able** *adj* (*road*) transitable; (*tolerable*) pasable

**passage** ['pæsid3] *n* (*also*: ~**way**) pasillo; (*act of passing*) tránsito; (*fare, in book*) pasaje *m*; (*by boat*) travesía; (*ANAT*) tubo

**passbook** ['pɑ:sbuk] *n* libreta de banco

**passenger** ['pæsind3ə*] *n* pasajero/a, viajero/a

**passer-by** [pɑ:sə'bai] *n* transeúnte

*m/f*

**passing** ['pɑːsɪŋ] *adj* pasajero; **in ~** de paso; **~ place** *n* (*AUT*) apartadero

**passion** ['pæʃən] *n* pasión *f*; **~ate** *adj* apasionado

**passive** ['pæsɪv] *adj* (*gen*, *also LING*) pasivo; **~ smoker** *n* fumador(a) *m/f* pasivo

**Passover** ['pɑːsəuvə*] *n* Pascua (de los judios)

**passport** ['pɑːspɔːt] *n* pasaporte *m*; **~ control** *n* control *m* de pasaporte

**password** ['pɑːswəːd] *n* contraseña

**past** [pɑːst] *prep* (*in front of*) por delante de; (*further than*) más allá de; (*later than*) después de ♦ *adj* pasado; (*president etc*) antiguo ♦ *n* (*time*) pasado; (*of person*) antecedentes *mpl*; **he's ~ forty** tiene más de cuarenta años; **ten/quarter ~ eight** las ocho y diez/cuarto; **for the ~ few/3 days** durante los últimos días/últimos 3 días; **to run ~ sb** pasar a uno corriendo

**pasta** ['pæstə] *n* pasta

**paste** [peɪst] *n* (*glue*) engrudo ♦ *vt* pegar

**pastel** ['pæstl] *adj* pastel

**pasteurized** ['pæstəraɪzd] *adj* pasteurizado

**pastille** ['pæstl] *n* pastilla

**pastime** ['pɑːstaɪm] *n* pasatiempo

**pastry** ['peɪstrɪ] *n* (*dough*) pasta; (*cake*) pastel *m*

**pasture** ['pɑːstʃə*] *n* pasto

**pasty**[1] ['pæstɪ] *n* empanada

**pasty**[2] ['peɪstɪ] *adj* (*complexion*) pálido

**pat** [pæt] *vt* dar una palmadita a; (*dog etc*) acariciar

**patch** [pætʃ] *n* (*of material, eye ~*) parche *m*; (*mended part*) remiendo; (*of land*) terreno ♦ *vt* remendar; (*to go through*) **a bad ~** (*pasar por*) una mala racha; **~ up** *vt* reparar; (*quarrel*) hacer las paces en; **~work** *n* labor *m* de retazos; **~y** *adj* desigual

**pâté** ['pæteɪ] *n* paté *m*

**patent** ['peɪtnt] *n* patente *f* ♦ *vt* patentar ♦ *adj* patente, evidente; **~ leather** *n* charol *m*

**paternal** [pə'təːnl] *adj* paternal; (*relation*) paterno

**path** [pɑːθ] *n* camino, sendero; (*trail, track*) pista; (*of missile*) trayectoria

**pathetic** [pə'θetɪk] *adj* patético, lastimoso; (*very bad*) malísimo

**pathological** [pæθə'lɔdʒɪkəl] *adj* patológico

**pathos** ['peɪθɔs] *n* patetismo

**pathway** ['pɑːθweɪ] *n* sendero, vereda

**patience** ['peɪʃns] *n* paciencia; (*BRIT: CARDS*) solitario

**patient** ['peɪʃnt] *n* paciente *m/f* ♦ *adj* paciente, sufrido

**patio** ['pætɪəu] *n* patio

**patriot** ['peɪtrɪət] *n* patriota *m/f*; **~ic** [pætrɪ'ɔtɪk] *adj* patriótico

**patrol** [pə'trəul] *n* patrulla ♦ *vt* patrullar por; **~ car** *n* coche *m* patrulla; **~man** (*US*) *n* policía *m*

**patron** ['peɪtrən] *n* (*in shop*) cliente *m/f*; (*of charity*) patrocinador(a) *m/f*; **~ of the arts** mecenas *m*; **~age** ['pætrənɪdʒ] *n* patrocinio; **~ize** ['pætrənaɪz] *vt* (*shop*) ser cliente de; (*artist etc*) proteger; (*look down on*) condescender con; **~ saint** *n* santo/a patrón/ona *m/f*

**patter** ['pætə*] *n* golpeteo; (*sales talk*) labia ♦ *vi* (*rain*) tamborilear

**pattern** ['pætən] *n* (*SEWING*) patrón *m*; (*design*) dibujo

**paunch** [pɔːntʃ] *n* panza, barriga

**pauper** ['pɔːpə*] *n* pobre *m/f*

**pause** [pɔːz] *n* pausa ♦ *vi* hacer una pausa

**pave** [peɪv] *vt* pavimentar; **to ~ the way for** preparar el terreno para

**pavement** ['peɪvmənt] (*BRIT*) *n* acera (*SP*), vereda (*AM*)

**pavilion** [pə'vɪlɪən] *n* (*SPORT*) caseta

**paving** ['peɪvɪŋ] *n* pavimento, enlosado; **~ stone** *n* losa

**paw** [pɔː] *n* pata

**pawn** [pɔːn] *n* (*CHESS*) peón *m*;

*(fig)* instrumento ♦ *vt* empeñar; ~ **broker** *n* prestamista *m/f*; ~**shop** *n* monte *m* de piedad

**pay** [peɪ] *(pt, pp* **paid)** *n (wage etc)* sueldo, salario ♦ *vt* pagar ♦ *vi (be profitable)* rendir; **to ~ attention (to)** prestar atención (a); **to ~ sb a visit** hacer una visita a uno; **to ~ one's respects to sb** presentar sus respetos a uno; **to ~ back** *(money)* reembolsar; *(person)* pagar; **~ for** *vt fus* pagar; **~ in** *vt* ingresar; **~ off** *vt* saldar ♦ *vi (scheme, decision)* dar resultado; **~ up** *vt* pagar (de mala gana); **~able** *adj:* **~able to** pagadero a; **~ day** *n* día *m* de paga; **~ee** *n* portador(a) *m/f;* **~ envelope** *(US) n* = **~ packet;** **~ment** *n* pago; **monthly ~ment** mensualidad *f;* **~ packet** *(BRIT) n* sobre *m* de paga); **~ phone** *n* teléfono público; **~roll** *n* nómina; **~ slip** *n* recibo de sueldo; **~ television** *n* televisión *f* de pago

**PC** *n abbr* = **personal computer;** *(BRIT)* = **police constable**

**p.c.** *abbr* = **per cent**

**pea** [piː] *n* guisante *m (SP),* chícharo *(AM),* arveja *(AM)*

**peace** [piːs] *n* paz *f; (calm)* paz *f,* tranquilidad *f;* **~ful** *adj (gentle)* pacífico; *(calm)* tranquilo, sosegado

**peach** [piːtʃ] *n* melocotón *m (SP),* durazno *(AM)*

**peacock** ['piːkɔk] *n* pavo real

**peak** [piːk] *n (of mountain)* cumbre *f,* cima; *(of cap)* visera; *(fig)* cumbre *f;* **~ hours** *npl* = **~ period;** **~ period** *n* horas *fpl* punta

**peal** [piːl] *n (of bells)* repique *m;* **~ of laughter** carcajada

**peanut** ['piːnʌt] *n* cacahuete *m (SP),* maní *m (AM);* **~ butter** manteca *f* de cacahuete *or* maní

**pear** [pɛə*] *n* pera

**pearl** [pəːl] *n* perla

**peasant** ['peznt] *n* campesino/a

**peat** [piːt] *n* turba

**pebble** ['pebl] *n* guijarro

**peck** [pek] *vt (also:* ~ **at)** picotear ♦ *n* picotazo; *(kiss)* besito; **~ing order**

*n* orden *m* de jerarquía; **~ish** *(BRIT: inf) adj:* **I feel ~ish** tengo ganas de picar algo

**peculiar** [pɪ'kjuːlɪə*] *adj (odd)* extraño, raro; *(typical)* propio, característico; **~ to** propio de; **~ity** [pɪkjuːlɪ'æɪtɪ] *n* peculiaridad *f,* característica

**pedal** ['pedl] *n* pedal *m* ♦ *vi* pedalear

**pedantic** [pɪ'dæntɪk] *adj* pedante

**peddler** ['pedlə*] *n:* **drugs ~** traficante *m/f;* camello

**pedestrian** [pɪ'destrɪən] *n* peatón/ona *m/f* ♦ *adj* pedestre; **~ crossing** *(BRIT) n* paso de peatones

**pediatrics** [piːdɪ'ætrɪks] *(US) n* = **paediatrics**

**pedigree** ['pedɪgriː] *n* genealogía; *(of animal)* raza, pedigrí *m* ♦ *cpd (animal)* de raza, de casta

**pee** [piː] *(inf) vi* mear

**peek** [piːk] *vi* mirar a hurtadillas

**peel** [piːl] *n (of orange, lemon)* cáscara; *(: removed)* peladuras *fpl* ♦ *vt* pelar ♦ *vi (paint etc)* desconcharse; *(wallpaper)* despegarse, desprenderse; *(skin)* pelar

**peep** [piːp] *n (BRIT: look)* mirada furtiva; *(sound)* pío ♦ *vi (BRIT: look)* mirar furtivamente; **~ out** *vi* salir (un poco); **~hole** *n* mirilla

**peer** [pɪə*] *vi:* **to ~ at** esdurfir ♦ *n (noble)* par *m; (equal)* igual *m; (contemporary)* contemporáneo/a; **~age** *n* nobleza

**peeved** [piːvd] *adj* enojado

**peg** [peg] *n (for coat etc)* gancho, colgadero; *(BRIT: also:* **clothes ~)** pinza

**Pekingese** [piːkɪ'niːz] *n (dog)* pequinés/esa *m/f*

**pelican** ['pelɪkən] *n* pelícano; **~ crossing** *(BRIT) n (AUT)* paso de peatones señalizado

**pellet** ['pelɪt] *n* bolita; *(bullet)* perdigón *m*

**pelt** [pelt] *vt:* **to ~ sb with sth** arrojarle algo a uno ♦ *vi (rain)* llover a cántaros; *(inf: run)* correr ♦ *n* pellejo

**pen** [pɛn] n (fountain ~) pluma; (ballpoint ~) bolígrafo; (for sheep) redil m

**penal** ['pi:nl] adj penal; **~ize** vt castigar

**penalty** ['pɛnltɪ] n (gen) pena; (fine) multa; **~ (kick)** n (FOOTBALL) penalty m; (RUGBY) golpe m de castigo

**penance** ['pɛnəns] n penitencia

**pence** [pɛns] npl of **penny**

**pencil** ['pɛnsl] n lápiz m, lapicero m (AM); **~ case** n estuche m; **~ sharpener** n sacapuntas m inv

**pendant** ['pɛndnt] n pendiente m

**pending** ['pɛndɪŋ] prep antes de ♦ adj pendiente

**pendulum** ['pɛndjuləm] n péndulo

**penetrate** ['pɛnɪtreɪt] vt penetrar; **penetrating** adj penetrante

**penfriend** ['pɛnfrɛnd] (BRIT) n amigo/a por carta

**penguin** ['pɛŋgwɪn] n pingüino

**penicillin** [pɛnɪ'sɪlɪn] n penicilina

**peninsula** [pə'nɪnsjulə] n península

**penis** ['pi:nɪs] n pene m

**penitent** ['pɛnɪtnt] adj arrepentido

**penitentiary** [pɛnɪ'tɛnʃərɪ] (US) n cárcel f, presidio

**penknife** ['pɛnnaɪf] n navaja

**pen name** n seudónimo

**penniless** ['pɛnɪlɪs] adj sin dinero

**penny** ['pɛnɪ] (pl **pennies** or (BRIT) **pence**) n penique m; (US) centavo

**penpal** ['pɛnpæl] n amigo/a por carta

**pension** ['pɛnʃən] n (state benefit) jubilación f; **~er** (BRIT) n jubilado/a; **~fund** n caja or fondo de pensiones

**pensive** ['pɛnsɪv] adj pensativo; (withdrawn) preocupado

**pentagon** ['pɛntəgən] n: **the P~** (US: POL) el Pentágono

**Pentecost** ['pɛntɪkɔst] n Pentecostés m

**penthouse** ['pɛnthaus] n ático de lujo

**pent-up** ['pɛntʌp] adj reprimido

**people** ['pi:pl] npl gente f; (citizens) pueblo, ciudadanos mpl; (POL): **the** ~ el pueblo ♦ n (nation, race) pueblo, nación f; **several** ~ came vinieron varias personas; ~ **say that** ... dice la gente que ...

**pep** [pɛp] (inf) n energía; **~ up** vt animar

**pepper** ['pɛpə*] n (spice) pimienta; (vegetable) pimiento ♦ vt: **to ~ with** (fig) salpicar de; **~mint** n (sweet) pastilla de menta

**peptalk** ['pɛptɔːk] n: **to give sb a ~** darle a uno una inyección de ánimo

**per** [pə:*] prep por; **~ day/person** por día/persona; **~ annum** al año; **~ capita** adj, adv per cápita

**perceive** [pə'si:v] vt percibir; (realize) darse cuenta de

**per cent** n por ciento

**percentage** [pə'sɛntɪdʒ] n porcentaje m

**perception** [pə'sɛpʃən] n percepción f; (insight) perspicacia; (opinion etc) opinión f; **perceptive** [-'sɛptɪv] adj perspicaz

**perch** [pə:tʃ] n (fish) perca; (for bird) percha ♦ vi: **to ~ (on)** (bird) posarse (en); (person) encaramarse (en)

**percolator** ['pə:kəleɪtə*] n (also: coffee ~) cafetera de filtro

**peremptory** [pə'rɛmptərɪ] adj perentorio; (person) autoritario

**perennial** [pə'rɛnɪəl] adj perenne

**perfect** [adj, n 'pə:fɪkt, vb pə'fɛkt] adj perfecto ♦ n (also: ~ tense) perfecto ♦ vt perfeccionar; **~ly** ['pə:fɪktlɪ] adv perfectamente

**perforate** ['pə:fəreɪt] vt perforar

**perform** [pə'fɔ:m] vt (carry out) realizar, llevar a cabo; (THEATRE) representar; (piece of music) interpretar ♦ vi (well, badly) funcionar; **~ance** n (of a play) representación f; (of actor, athlete etc) actuación f; (of car, engine, company) rendimiento m; (of economy) resultados mpl; **~er** n (actor) actor m, actriz f

**perfume** ['pə:fju:m] n perfume m

**perfunctory** [pə'fʌŋktərɪ] adj superficial

**perhaps** [pə'hæps] *adv* quizá(s), tal vez

**peril** ['perɪl] *n* peligro, riesgo

**perimeter** [pə'rɪmɪtə*] *n* perímetro

**period** ['pɪərɪəd] *n* período; (*SCOL*) clase *f*; (*full stop*) punto; (*MED*) regla ♦ *adj* (*costume, furniture*) de época; **~ic(al)** [-'ɒdɪk(l)] *adj* periódico; **~ical** [-'ɒdɪkl] *n* periódico; **~ically** [-'ɒdɪklɪ] *adv* de vez en cuando, cada cierto tiempo

**peripheral** [pə'rɪfərəl] *adj* periférico ♦ *n* (*COMPUT*) periférico, unidad *f* periférica

**perish** ['perɪʃ] *vi* perecer; (*decay*) echarse a perder; **~able** *adj* perecedero

**perjury** ['pɜːdʒərɪ] *n* (*LAW*) perjurio

**perk** [pɜːk] *n* extra ·*m*; **~ up** *vi* (*cheer up*) animarse; **~y** *adj* alegre, despabilado

**perm** [pɜːm] *n* permanente *f*

**permanent** ['pɜːmənənt] *adj* permanente

**permeate** ['pɜːmɪeɪt] *vi* penetrar, trascender ♦ *vt* penetrar, trascender a

**permissible** [pə'mɪsɪbl] *adj* permisible, lícito

**permission** [pə'mɪʃən] *n* permiso

**permissive** [pə'mɪsɪv] *adj* permisivo

**permit** [*n* 'pɜːmɪt, *vt* pə'mɪt] *n* permiso, licencia ♦ *vt* permitir

**pernicious** [pɜː'nɪʃəs] *adj* nocivo; (*MED*) pernicioso

**perpetrate** ['pɜːpɪtreɪt] *vt* cometer

**perpetual** [pə'petjuəl] *adj* perpetuo

**perpetuate** [pə'petjueɪt] *vt* perpetuar

**perplex** [pə'pleks] *vt* dejar perplejo

**persecute** ['pɜːsɪkjuːt] *vt* perseguir

**perseverance** [pɜːsɪ'vɪərəns] *n* perseverancia

**persevere** [pɜːsɪ'vɪə*] *vi* persistir

**Persian** ['pɜːʃən] *adj, n* persa *m/f*; **the (~) Gulf** *n* el Golfo Pérsico

**persist** [pə'sɪst] *vi*: **to ~ (in doing sth)** persistir (en hacer algo); **~ence** *n* empeño; **~ent** *adj* persistente; (*determined*) porfiado

**person** ['pɜːsn] *n* persona; **in ~** en persona; **~al** *adj* personal; individual; (*visit*) en persona; **~al assistant** *n* ayudante *m/f* personal; **~al call** *n* (*TEL*) llamada persona a persona; **~al column** *n* anuncios *mpl* personales; **~al computer** *n* ordenador *m* personal; **~ality** [-'nælɪtɪ] *n* personalidad *f*; **~ally** *adv* personalmente; (*in person*) en persona; **to take sth ~ally** tomarse algo a mal; **~al organizer** *n* agenda; **~al stereo** *n* walkman *m* ®; **~ify** [-'sɒnɪfaɪ] *vt* encarnar

**personnel** [pɜːsə'nel] *n* personal *m*

**perspective** [pə'spektɪv] *n* perspectiva

**Perspex** ['pɜːspeks] ® *n* plexiglás *m*

**perspiration** [pɜːspɪ'reɪʃən] *n* transpiración *f*

**persuade** [pə'sweɪd] *vt*: **to ~ sb to do sth** persuadir a uno para que haga algo

**pertaining** [pə'teɪnɪŋ]: **~ to** *prep* relacionado con

**pertinent** ['pɜːtɪnənt] *adj* pertinente, a propósito

**Peru** [pə'ruː] *n* el Perú

**peruse** [pə'ruːz] *vt* leer con detención, examinar

**Peruvian** [pə'ruːvɪən] *adj, n* peruano/a *m/f*

**pervade** [pə'veɪd] *vt* impregnar, infundirse en

**perverse** [pə'vɜːs] *adj* perverso; (*wayward*) travieso

**pervert** [*n* 'pɜːvɜːt, *vb* pə'vɜːt] *n* pervertido/a ♦ *vt* pervertir; (*truth, sb's words*) tergiversar

**pessimist** ['pesɪmɪst] *n* pesimista *m/f*; **~ic** [-'mɪstɪk] *adj* pesimista

**pest** [pest] *n* (*insect*) insecto nocivo; (*fig*) lata, molestia

**pester** ['pestə*] *vt* molestar, acosar

**pesticide** ['pestɪsaɪd] *n* pesticida *m*

**pet** [pet] *n* animal *m* doméstico ♦ *cpd* favorito ♦ *vt* acariciar ♦ *vi* (*inf*) besuquearse; **teacher's ~** favorito/a (del profesor); **~ hate** manía

**petal** ['petl] *n* pétalo

**peter** ['pi:tə*]: to ~ out *vi* agotarse, acabarse

**petite** [pə'ti:t] *adj* chiquita

**petition** [pə'tɪʃən] *n* petición *f*

**petrified** ['petrɪfaɪd] *adj* horrorizado

**petrol** ['petrəl] (*BRIT*) *n* gasolina; **two/four-star** ~ gasolina normal/súper; ~ **can** *n* bidón *m* de gasolina

**petroleum** [pə'trəʊlɪəm] *n* petróleo

**petrol**: ~ **pump** (*BRIT*) *n* (*in garage*) surtidor *m* de gasolina; ~ **station** (*BRIT*) *n* gasolinera; ~ **tank** (*BRIT*) *n* depósito (de gasolina)

**petticoat** ['petɪkəʊt] *n* enaguas *fpl*

**petty** ['petɪ] *adj* (*mean*) mezquino; (*unimportant*) insignificante; ~ **cash** *n* dinero para gastos menores; ~ **officer** *n* contramaestre *m*

**petulant** ['petjʊlənt] *adj* malhumorado

**pew** [pju:] *n* banco

**pewter** ['pju:tə*] *n* peltre *m*

**phantom** ['fæntəm] *n* fantasma *m*

**pharmacist** ['fɑ:məsɪst] *n* farmacéutico/a

**pharmacy** ['fɑ:məsɪ] *n* farmacia

**phase** [feɪz] *n* fase *f* ♦ *vt*: to ~ **sth in/out** introducir/retirar algo por etapas

**Ph.D.** *abbr* = **Doctor of Philosophy**

**pheasant** ['feznt] *n* faisán *m*

**phenomenon** [fə'nɒmɪnən] (*pl* **phenomena**) *n* fenómeno

**philanthropist** [fɪ'lænθrəpɪst] *n* filántropo/a

**Philippines** ['fɪlɪpi:nz] *npl*: **the ~** las Filipinas

**philosopher** [fɪ'lɒsəfə*] *n* filósofo/a

**philosophy** [fɪ'lɒsəfɪ] *n* filosofía

**phlegm** [flem] *n* flema; ~**atic** [fleg-'mætɪk] *adj* flemático

**phobia** ['fəʊbjə] *n* fobia

**phone** [fəʊn] *n* teléfono ♦ *vt* telefonear, llamar por teléfono; to **be on the ~** tener teléfono; (*be calling*) estar hablando por teléfono; ~ **back** *vt, vi* volver a llamar; ~ **up** *vt, vi* llamar por teléfono; ~ **book** *n* guía telefónica; ~ **box** (*BRIT*) *n* = ~ **booth**; ~ **booth** *n* cabina telefónica;

~ **call** *n* llamada (telefónica); ~**card** *n* teletarjeta; ~**-in** (*BRIT*) *n* (*RADIO, TV*) programa *m* de participación (telefónica)

**phonetics** [fə'netɪks] *n* fonética

**phoney** ['fəʊnɪ] *adj* falso

**photo** ['fəʊtəʊ] *n* foto *f*

**photo...** ['fəʊtəʊ] *prefix*: ~**copier** *n* fotocopiadora; ~**copy** *n* fotocopia ♦ *vt* fotocopiar

**photograph** ['fəʊtəgrɑ:f] *n* fotografía ♦ *vt* fotografiar; ~**er** [fə'tɒgrəfə*] *n* fotógrafo; ~**y** [fə'tɒgrəfɪ] *n* fotografía

**phrase** [freɪz] *n* frase *f* ♦ *vt* expresar; ~ **book** *n* libro de frases

**physical** ['fɪzɪkl] *adj* físico; ~ **education** *n* educación *f* física; ~**ly** *adv* físicamente

**physician** [fɪ'zɪʃən] *n* médico/a

**physicist** ['fɪzɪsɪst] *n* físico/a

**physics** ['fɪzɪks] *n* física

**physiotherapy** [fɪzɪəʊ'θerəpɪ] *n* fisioterapia

**physique** [fɪ'zi:k] *n* físico

**pianist** ['pi:ənɪst] *n* pianista *m/f*

**piano** [pɪ'ænəʊ] *n* piano

**piccolo** ['pɪkələʊ] *n* (*MUS*) flautín *m*

**pick** [pɪk] *n* (*tool*: *also*: ~*axe*) pico, piqueta ♦ *vt* (*select*) elegir, escoger; (*gather*) coger (*SP*), recoger; (*remove, take out*) sacar, quitar; (*lock*) abrir con ganzúa; **take your** ~ escoja lo que quiera; **the** ~ **of** lo mejor de; to ~ **one's nose/teeth** hurgarse las narices/limpiarse los dientes; to ~ **a quarrel with sb** meterse con alguien; ~ **at** *vt fus*: to ~ **at one's food** comer con poco apetito; ~ **on** *vt fus* (*person*) meterse con; ~ **out** *vt escoger*; (*distinguish*) identificar; ~ **up** *vi* (*improve*: *sales*) ir mejor; (*: patient*) reponerse; (*: FINANCE*) recobrarse ♦ *vt* recoger; (*learn*) aprender; (*POLICE*: *arrest*) detener; (*person*: *for sex*) ligar; (*RADIO*) captar; to ~ **up speed** acelerarse; to ~ **o.s. up** levantarse

**picket** ['pɪkɪt] *n* piquete *m* ♦ *vt* piquetear

**pickle** ['pɪkl] n (also: ~s: as condiment) escabeche m; (fig: mess) apuro ♦ vt encurtir

**pickpocket** ['pɪkpɔkɪt] n carterista m/f

**pickup** ['pɪkʌp] n (small truck) furgoneta

**picnic** ['pɪknɪk] n merienda ♦ vi ir de merienda

**picture** ['pɪktʃə*] n cuadro; (painting) pintura; (photograph) fotografía; (TV) imagen f; (film) película; (fig: description) descripción f; (: situation) situación f ♦ vt (imagine) imaginar; ~s npl: the ~s (BRIT) el cine; ~ book n libro de dibujos

**picturesque** [pɪktʃə'rɛsk] adj pintoresco

**pie** [paɪ] n pastel m; (open) tarta; (small: of meat) empanada

**piece** [piːs] n pedazo, trozo m; (of cake) trozo; (item): a ~ of clothing/furniture/advice una prenda (de vestir)/un mueble/un consejo ♦ vt: to ~ together juntar; (TECH) armar; to take to ~s desmontar; ~meal adv poco a poco; ~work n trabajo a destajo

**pie chart** n gráfico de sectores or tarta

**pier** [pɪə*] n muelle m, embarcadero

**pierce** [pɪəs] vt perforar

**piercing** ['pɪəsɪŋ] adj penetrante

**piety** ['paɪətɪ] n piedad f

**pig** [pɪg] n cerdo (SP), puerco (SP), chancho (AM); (pej: unkind person) asqueroso; (: greedy person) glotón/ona m/f

**pigeon** ['pɪdʒən] n paloma; (as food) pichón m; ~hole n casilla

**piggy bank** ['pɪgɪ-] n hucha (en forma de cerdito)

**pig: ~headed** ['pɪg'hɛdɪd] adj terco, testarudo; **~let** ['pɪglɪt] n cochinillo; **~skin** n piel f de cerdo; **~sty** ['pɪgstaɪ] n pocilga, chiquero; **~tail** n (girl's) trenza; (Chinese, TAUR) coleta

**pike** [paɪk] n (fish) lucio

**pilchard** ['pɪltʃəd] n sardina

**pile** [paɪl] n montón m; (of carpet,

cloth) pelo ♦ vt (also: ~ up) amontonar; (fig) acumular ♦ vi (also: ~ up) amontonarse; acumularse; ~ into n fus (car) meterse en; ~s [paɪlz] npl (MED) almorranas fpl, hemorroides mpl; **~-up** n (AUT) accidente m múltiple

**pilfering** ['pɪlfərɪŋ] n ratería

**pilgrim** ['pɪlgrɪm] n peregrino/a; **~age** n peregrinación f, romería

**pill** [pɪl] n píldora; the ~ la píldora

**pillage** ['pɪlɪdʒ] vt pillar, saquear

**pillar** ['pɪlə*] n pilar m; ~ box (BRIT) n buzón m

**pillion** ['pɪljən] n (of motorcycle) asiento trasero

**pillory** ['pɪlərɪ] vt poner en la picota, criticar con dureza

**pillow** ['pɪləʊ] n almohada; **~case** n funda

**pilot** ['paɪlət] n piloto ♦ cpd (scheme etc) piloto ♦ vt pilotar; ~ light n piloto

**pimp** [pɪmp] n chulo (SP), cafiche m (AM)

**pimple** ['pɪmpl] n grano

**PIN** n abbr (= personal identification number) número personal

**pin** [pɪn] n alfiler m ♦ vt prender (con alfiler); ~s and needles hormigueo; to ~ sb down (fig) hacer que uno concrete; to ~ sth on sb (fig) colgarle a uno el sambenito de algo

**pinafore** ['pɪnəfɔː*] n delantal m; **~dress** (BRIT) n mandil m

**pinball** ['pɪnbɔːl] n mesa americana

**pincers** ['pɪnsəz] npl pinzas fpl, tenazas fpl

**pinch** [pɪntʃ] n (of salt etc) pizca ♦ vt pellizcar; (inf: steal) birlar; at a ~ en caso de apuro

**pincushion** ['pɪnkʊʃən] n acerico

**pine** [paɪn] n (also: ~ tree, wood) pino ♦ vi: to ~ for suspirar por; ~ away vi morirse de pena

**pineapple** ['paɪnæpl] n piña, ananás m

**ping** [pɪŋ] n (noise) sonido agudo; **~pong** ® n pingpong m ®

**pink** [pɪŋk] adj rosado, (color de)

rosa ♦ n (colour) rosa; (BOT) clavel m, clavellina

**pinnacle** ['pɪnəkl] n cumbre f

**pinpoint** ['pɪnpɔɪnt] vt precisar

**pint** [paɪnt] n pinta (BRIT = 568cc; US = 473cc); (BRIT: inf: of beer) pinta de cerveza, ≈ jarra (SP)

**pin-up** n fotografía erótica

**pioneer** [paɪə'nɪə*] n pionero/a

**pious** ['paɪəs] adj piadoso, devoto

**pip** [pɪp] n (seed) pepita; the ~s (BRIT) la señal

**pipe** [paɪp] n tubo, caño; (for smoking) pipa ♦ vt conducir en cañerías; ~s npl (gen) cañería; (also: bag~s) gaita; ~ **down** (inf) vi callarse; ~ **cleaner** n limpiapipas m inv; ~ **dream** n sueño imposible; ~**line** n (for oil) oleoducto; (for gas) gasoducto; ~r n gaitero/a

**piping** ['paɪpɪŋ] adv: to be ~ hot estar que quema

**piquant** ['piːkənt] adj picante; (fig) agudo

**pique** [piːk] n pique m, resentimiento

**pirate** ['paɪərət] n pirata m/f ♦ vt (cassette, book) piratear; ~ **radio** n (BRIT) emisora pirata

**pirouette** [pɪru'ɛt] n pirueta

**Pisces** ['paɪsiːz] n Piscis m

**piss** [pɪs] (inf!) vi mear; ~ed (inf!) adj (drunk) borracho

**pistol** ['pɪstl] n pistola

**piston** ['pɪstən] n pistón m, émbolo

**pit** [pɪt] n hoyo; (also: coal ~) mina; (in garage) foso de inspección; (also: orchestra~) platea f ♦ vt: to ~ one's **wits against sb** medir fuerzas con uno; ~s npl (AUT) box m

**pitch** [pɪtʃ] n (MUS) tono; (BRIT: SPORT) campo, terreno; (fig) (tar) brea ♦ vt (throw) arrojar, lanzar ♦ vi (fall) caer(se); to ~ a **tent** montar una tienda (de campaña); ~**black** adj negro como boca de lobo; ~**ed battle** n batalla campal

**piteous** ['pɪtɪəs] adj lastimoso

**pitfall** ['pɪtfɔːl] n riesgo

**pith** [pɪθ] n (of orange) médula

**pithy** ['pɪθɪ] adj (fig) jugoso

**pitiful** ['pɪtɪful] adj (touching) lastimoso, conmovedor(a)

**pitiless** ['pɪtɪlɪs] adj despiadado

**pittance** ['pɪtns] n miseria

**pity** ['pɪtɪ] n compasión f, piedad f ♦ vt compadecer(se de); **what a ~!** ¡qué pena!

**pivot** ['pɪvət] n eje m

**pizza** ['piːtsə] n pizza

**placard** ['plækɑːd] n letrero; (in march etc) pancarta

**placate** [plə'keɪt] vt apaciguar

**place** [pleɪs] n lugar m, sitio; (seat) plaza, asiento; (post) puesto; (home): **at/to his** ~ en/a su casa; (role: in society etc) papel m ♦ vt (object) poner, colocar; (identify) reconocer; to **take** ~ tener lugar; to be ~d (in race, exam) colocarse; **out of** ~ (not suitable) fuera de lugar; **in the first** ~ en primer lugar; to **change** ~s **with sb** cambiarse de sitio con uno; ~ **of birth** n lugar m de nacimiento

**placid** ['plæsɪd] adj apacible

**plagiarism** ['pleɪdʒɪərɪzəm] n plagio

**plague** [pleɪg] n (also fig) plaga; (MED) peste f ♦ vt (fig) acosar, atormentar

**plaice** [pleɪs] n inv platija

**plaid** [plæd] n (material) tartán m

**plain** [pleɪn] adj (unpatterned) liso; (clear) claro, evidente; (simple) sencillo; (not handsome) poco atractivo ♦ adv claramente ♦ n llano, llanura; ~ **chocolate** n chocolate m amargo; ~**clothes** adj (police) vestido de paisano; ~**ly** adv claramente

**plaintiff** ['pleɪntɪf] n demandante m/f

**plaintive** ['pleɪntɪv] adj lastimero

**plait** [plæt] n trenza

**plan** [plæn] n (drawing) plano; (scheme) plan m, proyecto ♦ vt proyectar, planificar ♦ vi hacer proyectos; to ~ to do pensar hacer

**plane** [pleɪn] n (AVIAT) avión m; (MATH, fig) plano; (also: ~ tree) plátano; (tool) cepillo

**planet** ['plænɪt] n planeta m

**plank** [plæŋk] n tabla

**planner** ['plænə*] n planificador(a)

*m/f*

**planning** ['plænɪŋ] *n* planificación *f*; ~ **family** ~ planificación familiar; ~ **permission** *n* permiso para realizar obras

**plant** [plɑ:nt] *n* planta; (*machinery*) maquinaria; (*factory*) fábrica ♦ *vt* plantar; (*field*) sembrar; (*bomb*) colocar

**plaque** [plæk] *n* placa

**plaster** ['plɑ:stə*] *n* (*for walls*) yeso; (*also:* ~ *of Paris*) yeso mate; (*BRIT: also: sticking* ~) tirita (SP), esparadrapo, curita (AM) ♦ *vt* enyesar; (*cover*): **to** ~ **with** llenar o cubrir de; ~**ed** (*inf*) *adj* borracho; ~**er** *n* yesero

**plastic** ['plæstɪk] *n* plástico ♦ *adj* de plástico; ~ **bag** *n* bolsa de plástico

**plasticine** ['plæstɪsi:n] ® (BRIT) *n* plastilina ®

**plastic surgery** *n* cirugía plástica

**plate** [pleɪt] *n* (*dish*) plato; (*metal, in book*) lámina; (*dental* ~) placa de dentadura postiza

**plateau** ['plætəʊ] (*pl* ~**s** *or* ~**x**) *n* meseta, altiplanicie *f*

**plateaux** ['plætəʊz] *npl of* **plateau**

**plate glass** *n* vidrio cilindrado

**platform** ['plætfɔ:m] *n* (RAIL) andén *m*; (*stage, BRIT: on bus*) plataforma; (*at meeting*) tribuna; (POL) programa *m* (electoral)

**platinum** ['plætɪnəm] *adj,* *n* platino

**platitude** ['plætɪtju:d] *n* lugar *m* común, tópico

**platoon** [plə'tu:n] *n* pelotón *m*

**platter** ['plætə*] *n* fuente *f*

**plausible** ['plɔ:zɪbl] *adj* verosímil; (*person*) convincente

**play** [pleɪ] *n* (THEATRE) obra, comedia ♦ *vt* (*game*) jugar; (*compete against*) jugar contra; (*instrument*) tocar; (*part: in play etc*) hacer el papel de; (*tape, record*) poner ♦ *vi* jugar; (*band*) tocar; (*tape, record*) sonar; **to** ~ **safe** ir a lo seguro; ~ **down** *vt* quitar importancia a; ~ **up** *vi* (*cause trouble to*) dar guerra; ~**boy** *n* playboy *m*; ~**er** *n* juga-

dor(a) *m/f*; (THEATRE) actor/actriz *m/f*; (MUS) músico/a; ~**ful** *adj* juguetón/ona; ~**ground** *n* (*in school*) patio de recreo; (*in park*) parque *m* infantil; ~**group** *n* jardín *m* de niños; ~**ing card** *n* naipe *m*, carta; ~**ing field** *n* campo de deportes; ~**mate** *n* compañero/a de juego; ~**off** *n* (SPORT) (partido de) desempate *m*; ~**pen** *n* corral *m*; ~**time** *n* (SCOL) recreo; ~**wright** *n* dramaturgo/a

**plc** *abbr* (= *public limited company*) ≈ S.A

**plea** [pli:] *n* súplica, petición *f*; (LAW) alegato, defensa

**plead** [pli:d] *vt* (LAW): **to** ~ **sb's case** defender a uno; (*give as excuse*) poner como pretexto ♦ *vi* (LAW) declararse; (*beg*): **to** ~ **with sb** suplicar o rogar a uno

**pleasant** ['plɛznt] *adj* agradable; ~**ries** *npl* cortesías *fpl*

**please** [pli:z] *excl* ¡por favor! ♦ *vt* (*give pleasure to*) dar gusto a, agradar ♦ *vi* (*think fit*): **do as you** ~ haz lo que quieras; ~ **yourself!** (*inf*) ¡haz lo que quieras!, ¡como quieras!; ~**d** *adj* (*happy*) alegre, contento; ~**d** (**with**) satisfecho (de); ~**d to meet you** ¡encantado!, ¡tanto gusto!; **pleasing** *adj* agradable, grato

**pleasure** ['plɛʒə*] *n* placer *m*, gusto; "**it's a** ~" "el gusto es mío"; ~ **boat** *n* barco de recreo

**pleat** [pli:t] *n* pliegue *m*

**pledge** [plɛdʒ] *n* (*promise*) promesa, voto ♦ *vt* prometer

**plentiful** ['plɛntɪful] *adj* copioso, abundante

**plenty** ['plɛntɪ] *n*: ~ **of** mucho(s)/a(s)

**pliable** ['plaɪəbl] *adj* flexible

**pliant** ['plaɪənt] *adj* = **pliable**

**pliers** ['plaɪəz] *npl* alicates *mpl*, tenazas *fpl*

**plight** [plaɪt] *n* situación *f* difícil

**plimsolls** ['plɪmsəlz] (BRIT) *npl* zapatos *mpl* de tenis

**plinth** [plɪnθ] n plinto

**plod** [plɔd] vi caminar con paso pesado; (fig) trabajar laboriosamente

**plonk** [plɔŋk] (inf) n (BRIT: wine) vino peleón ♦ vt: to ~ sth down dejar caer algo

**plot** [plɔt] n (scheme) complot m, conjura; (of story, play) argumento; (of land) terreno, lote m (AM) ♦ vt (mark out) trazar; (conspire) tramar, urdir ♦ vi conspirar; ~ter n (instrument) trazador m de gráficos

**plough** [plau] (US **plow**) n arado m ♦ vt (earth) arar; to ~ money into invertir dinero en; ~ through vt fus (crowd) abrirse paso por la fuerza por; ~man's lunch (BRIT) n almuerzo de pub a base de pan, queso y encurtidos

**ploy** [plɔɪ] n truco, estratagema

**pluck** [plʌk] vt (fruit) coger (SP), recoger (AM); (musical instrument) puntear; (bird) desplumar; (eyebrows) depilar ♦ n valor m, ánimo; to ~ up courage hacer de tripas corazón

**plug** [plʌg] n tapón m; (ELEC) enchufe m, clavija; (AUT: also: spark(ing) ~) bujía ♦ vt (hole) tapar; (inf: advertise) dar publicidad a; ~ in vt (ELEC) enchufar

**plum** [plʌm] n (fruit) ciruela ♦ cpd: ~ job (inf) puesto (de trabajo) muy codiciado

**plumb** [plʌm] vt: to ~ the depths of alcanzar los mayores extremos de

**plumber** ['plʌmə*] n fontanero/a (SP), plomero/a (AM)

**plumbing** ['plʌmɪŋ] n (trade) fontanería, plomería; (piping) cañería

**plume** [plu:m] n pluma; (on helmet etc) penacho

**plummet** ['plʌmɪt] vi: to ~ (down) caer a plomo

**plump** [plʌmp] adj rechoncho, rollizo ♦ vi: to ~ for (inf: choose) optar por; ~ up vt mullir

**plunder** ['plʌndə*] n pillaje m; (loot) botín m ♦ vt pillar, saquear

**plunge** [plʌndʒ] n zambullida ♦ vt

sumergir, hundir ♦ vi (fall) caer; (dive) saltar; (person) arrojarse; to take the ~ lanzarse; ~r n (for drain) desatascador m; **plunging** adj: **plunging neckline** escote m pronunciado

**pluperfect** [plu:'pɜ:fɪkt] n pluscuamperfecto

**plural** ['pluərl] adj plural ♦ n plural m

**plus** [plʌs] n (also: ~ sign) signo más ♦ prep más, y, además de; ten/twenty ~ más de diez/veinte

**plush** [plʌʃ] adj lujoso

**plutonium** [plu:'təunɪəm] n plutonio

**ply** [plaɪ] vt (a trade) ejercer ♦ vi (ship) ir y venir ♦ n (of wool, rope) cabo; to ~ sb with drink insistir en ofrecer a uno muchas copas; ~wood n madera contrachapada

**P.M.** n abbr = **Prime Minister**

**p.m.** adv abbr (= post meridiem) de la tarde or noche

**pneumatic** [nju:'mætɪk] adj neumático; ~ **drill** n martillo neumático

**pneumonia** [nju:'məunɪə] n pulmonía

**poach** [pəutʃ] vt (cook) escalfar; (steal) cazar (or pescar) en vedado ♦ vi cazar (or pescar) en vedado; ~ed adj escalfado; ~er n cazador (a) m/f furtivo/a

**P.O. Box** n abbr = **Post Office Box**

**pocket** ['pɔkɪt] n bolsillo; (fig: small area) bolsa ♦ vt meter en el bolsillo; (steal) embolsar; to be out of ~ (BRIT) salir perdiendo; ~book (US) n cartera; ~ **calculator** n calculadora de bolsillo; ~ **knife** n navaja; ~ **money** n asignación f

**P.O. Box** n abbr = **Post Office Box**

**pod** [pɔd] n vaina

**podgy** ['pɔdʒɪ] adj gordinflón/ona

**podiatrist** [pɔ'di:ətrɪst] (US) n pedicuro/a

**poem** ['pəuɪm] n poema m

**poet** ['pəuɪt] n poeta m/f; ~**ic** [-'etɪk] adj poético; ~ **laureate** n poeta m laureado; ~**ry** n poesía

**poignant** ['pɔɪnjənt] adj conmovedor(a)

**point** [pɔɪnt] *n* punto; *(tip)* punta; *(purpose)* fin *m*, propósito; *(use)* utilidad *f*; *(significant part)* lo significativo; *(moment)* momento; *(ELEC)* toma (de corriente); *(also: decimal ~)*: 2 ~ 3 (2.3) dos coma tres (2.3) ♦ *vt* señalar; *(gun etc)*: **to ~ sth at sb** apuntar algo a uno ♦ *vi*: **to ~ at** señalar; **~s** *npl* (*AUT*) contactos *mpl*; (*RAIL*) agujas *fpl*; **to be on the ~ of doing sth** estar a punto de hacer algo; **to make a ~ of** poner empeño en; **to get/miss the ~** comprender/no comprender; **to come to the ~** ir al meollo; **there's no ~ (in doing)** no tiene sentido (hacer); **~ out** *vt* señalar; **~ to** *vt fus* (*fig*) indicar, señalar; **~-blank** *adv* (*also*: **at ~-blank range**) a quemarropa; **~ed** *adj* (*shape*) puntiagudo, afilado; (*remark*) intencionado; **~edly** *adv* intencionadamente; **~er** *n* (*needle*) aguja, indicador *m*; **~less** *adj* sin sentido; **~ of view** *n* punto de vista

**poise** [pɔɪz] *n* aplomo, elegancia

**poison** ['pɔɪzn] *n* veneno ♦ *vt* envenenar; **~ing** *n* envenenamiento; **~ous** *adj* venenoso; (*fumes etc*) tóxico

**poke** [pəuk] *vt* (*jab with finger, stick etc*) empujar; (*put*): **to ~ sth in(to)** introducir algo en; **~ about** *vi* fisgonnear

**poker** ['pəukə*] *n* atizador *m*; (*CARDS*) póker *m*; **~-faced** *adj* de cara impasible

**poky** ['pəukɪ] *adj* estrecho

**Poland** ['pəulənd] *n* Polonia

**polar** ['pəulə*] *adj* polar; **~ bear** *n* oso polar

**Pole** [pəul] *n* polaco/a

**pole** [pəul] *n* palo; (*fixed*) poste *m*; (*GEO*) polo; **~ bean** (*US*) *n* ≈ judía verde; **~ vault** *n* salto con pértiga

**police** [pə'liːs] *n* policía ♦ *vt* vigilar; **~ car** *n* coche-patrulla *m*; **~man** *n* policía *m*, guardia *m*; **~ state** *n* estado policial; **~ station** *n* comisaría; **~woman** *n* mujer *f* policía

**policy** ['pɔlɪsɪ] *n* política; (*also: insurance ~*) póliza

**polio** ['pəulɪəu] *n* polio *f*

**Polish** ['pəulɪʃ] *adj* polaco ♦ *n* (*LING*) polaco

**polish** ['pɔlɪʃ] *n* (*for shoes*) betún *m*; (*for floor*) cera (de lustrar); (*shine*) brillo, lustre *m*; (*fig: refinement*) educación *f* ♦ *vt* (*shoes*) limpiar; (*make shiny*) pulir, sacar brillo a; **~ off** *vt* (*work*) terminar; (*food*) despachar; **~ed** *adj* (*fig*) elegante

**polite** [pə'laɪt] *adj* cortés, atento; **~ness** *n* cortesía

**political** [pə'lɪtɪkl] *adj* político

**politician** [pɔlɪ'tɪʃən] *n* político/a

**politics** ['pɔlɪtɪks] *n* política

**poll** [pəul] *n* (*election*) votación *f*; (*also: opinion ~*) sondeo, encuesta ♦ *vt* (*votes*) obtener

**pollen** ['pɔlən] *n* polen *m*

**polling day** ['pəulɪŋ-] *n* día *m* de elecciones

**polling station** *n* centro electoral

**pollute** [pə'luːt] *vt* contaminar

**pollution** [pə'luːʃən] *n* polución *f*, contaminación *f* del medio ambiente

**polo** ['pəuləu] *n* (*sport*) polo; **~-necked** *adj* de cuello vuelto; **~ shirt** *n* polo, niqui *m*

**polyester** [pɔlɪ'estə*] *n* poliéster *m*

**polystyrene** [pɔlɪ'staɪriːn] *n* poliestireno

**polytechnic** [pɔlɪ'teknɪk] *n* politécnico

**polythene** ['pɔlɪθiːn] (*BRIT*) *n* politeno

**pomegranate** ['pɔmɪɡrænɪt] *n* granada

**pomp** [pɔmp] *n* pompa

**pompom** ['pɔmpɔm] *n* borla, pompón *m*

**pompous** ['pɔmpəs] *adj* pomposo

**pond** [pɔnd] *n* (*natural*) charca; (*artificial*) estanque *m*

**ponder** ['pɔndə*] *vt* meditar

**ponderous** ['pɔndərəs] *adj* pesado

**pong** [pɔŋ] (*BRIT: inf*) *n* hedor *m*

**pontoon** [pɔn'tuːn] *n* pontón *m*

**pony** ['pəunɪ] *n* poney *m*, jaca, potro

**poodle** ['pu:dl] n caniche m

**pool** [pu:l] n (natural) charca; (also: swimming ~) piscina (SP), alberca (AM); (fig: of light etc) charco; (SPORT) chapolín m ♦ vt juntar; ~s npl (football ~s) quinielas fpl; typing ~ servicio de mecanografía

**poor** [puə*] adj pobre; (bad) de mala calidad ♦ npl: the ~ los pobres; ~ly adj mal, enfermo ♦ adv mal

**pop** [pɔp] n (sound) ruido seco; (MUS) (música) pop m; (inf: father) papá m; (drink) gaseosa ♦ vt (put quickly) meter (de prisa) ♦ vi reventar; (cork) saltar; ~ in/out vi entrar/salir un momento; ~ up vi aparecer inesperadamente; ~corn n palomitas fpl

**pope** [pəup] n papa m

**poplar** ['pɔplə*] n álamo

**poplin** ['pɔplin] n popelina

**popper** ['pɔpə*] (BRIT) n automático

**poppy** ['pɔpi] n amapola

**popsicle** ['pɔpsikl] (US) n polo

**pop star** n estrella del pop

**populace** ['pɔpjuləs] n pueblo, plebe f

**popular** ['pɔpjulə*] adj popular; ~ize vt popularizar; (disseminate) vulgarizar

**population** [pɔpju'leiʃən] n población f

**porcelain** ['pɔ:slin] n porcelana

**porch** [pɔ:tʃ] n pórtico, entrada; (US) veranda

**porcupine** ['pɔ:kjupain] n puerco m espín

**pore** [pɔ:*] n poro ♦ vi: to ~ over engolfarse en

**pork** [pɔ:k] n carne f de cerdo (SP) or chancho (AM)

**pornography** [pɔ:'nɔgrəfi] n pornografía

**porpoise** ['pɔ:pəs] n marsopa

**porridge** ['pɔridʒ] n gachas fpl de avena

**port** [pɔ:t] n puerto (NAUT: left side) babor m; (wine) vino de Oporto; ~ of call puerto de escala

**portable** ['pɔ:təbl] adj portátil

**porter** ['pɔ:tə*] n (for luggage) maletero; (doorkeeper) portero/a, conserje m/f

**portfolio** [pɔ:t'fəuliəu] n cartera

**porthole** ['pɔ:θəul] n portilla

**portion** ['pɔ:ʃən] n porción f; (of food) ración f

**portly** ['pɔ:tli] adj corpulento

**portrait** ['pɔ:treit] n retrato

**portray** [pɔ:'trei] vt retratar; (subj: actor) representar; ~al n retrato; representación f

**Portugal** ['pɔ:tjugl] n Portugal m

**Portuguese** [pɔ:tju'gi:z] adj portugués/esa ♦ n inv portugués/esa m/f; (LING) portugués m

**pose** [pəuz] n postura, actitud f ♦ vi (pretend): to ~ as hacerse pasar por ♦ vt (question) plantear; to ~ for posar para

**posh** [pɔʃ] (inf) adj elegante, de lujo

**position** [pə'ziʃən] n posición f; (job) puesto; (situation) situación f ♦ vt colocar

**positive** ['pɔzitiv] adj positivo; (certain) seguro; (definite) definitivo

**possess** [pə'zes] vt poseer; ~ion [pə'zeʃən] n posesión f; ~ions npl (belongings) pertenencias fpl

**possibility** [pɔsi'biliti] n posibilidad f

**possible** ['pɔsibl] adj posible; as big as ~ lo más grande posible; **possibly** adv posiblemente; I cannot possibly come me es imposible venir

**post** [pəust] n (BRIT: system) correos mpl; (BRIT: letters, delivery) correo; (job, situation) puesto; (pole) poste m ♦ vt (BRIT: send by post) echar al correo; (BRIT: appoint): to ~ to enviar a; ~age n porte m, franqueo; ~age stamp n sello de correos; ~al adj postal, de correos; ~al order n giro postal; ~box (BRIT) n buzón m; ~card n tarjeta postal; ~**code** (BRIT) n código postal

**postdate** [pəust'deɪt] vt (cheque) poner fecha adelantada a

**poster** ['pəustə*] n cartel m

**poste restante** [pəust'rɛstɔ̃nt] (BRIT) n lista de correos

**postgraduate** [pəust'grædjuət] n posgraduado/a

**posthumous** ['pɔstjuməs] adj póstumo

**postman** ['pəustmən] n cartero

**postmark** ['pəustmɑːk] n matasellos m inv

**post-mortem** [-'mɔːtəm] n autopsia

**post office** n (building) (oficina de) correos m; (organization) the P~ O~ Administración f General de Correos; P~ O~ Box n apartado postal (SP), casilla de correos (AM)

**postpone** [pəs'pəun] vt aplazar

**postscript** ['pəustskrɪpt] n posdata

**posture** ['pɔstʃə*] n postura, actitud f

**postwar** [pəust'wɔː*] adj de la posguerra

**posy** ['pəuzɪ] n ramillete m (de flores)

**pot** [pɔt] n (for cooking) olla; (tea~) tetera; (coffee~) cafetera; (for flowers) maceta; (for jam) tarro, pote m; (inf: marijuana) chocolate m ♦ vt (plant) poner en tiesto; to go to ~ (inf) irse al traste

**potato** [pə'teɪtəu] (pl ~es) n patata (SP), papa (AM); ~ **peeler** n pelapatatas m inv

**potent** ['pəutnt] adj potente, poderoso; (drink) fuerte

**potential** [pə'tɛnʃl] adj potencial, posible ♦ n potencial m; ~**ly** adv en potencia

**pothole** ['pɔthəul] n (in road) bache m; (BRIT: underground) gruta; **potholing** (BRIT) n: to go potholing dedicarse a la espeleología

**potluck** [pɔt'lʌk] n: to take ~ to-mar lo que haya

**potted** ['pɔtɪd] adj (food) en conserva; (plant) en tiesto or maceta; (shortened) resumido

**potter** ['pɔtə*] n alfarero/a ♦ vi: to ~ around, ~ about (BRIT) hacer trabajitos; ~**y** n cerámica; (factory) alfarería

**potty** ['pɔtɪ] adj (inf: mad) chiflado ♦ n orinal m de niño

**pouch** [pautʃ] n (ZOOL) bolsa; (for tobacco) petaca

**poultry** ['pəultrɪ] n aves fpl de corral; (meat) pollo

**pounce** [pauns] vi: to ~ **on** precipitarse sobre

**pound** [paund] n libra (weight = 453g or 16oz; money = 100 pence) ♦ vt (beat) golpear; (crush) machacar ♦ vi (heart) latir; ~ **sterling** n libra esterlina

**pour** [pɔː*] vt echar; (tea etc) servir ♦ vi correr, fluir; to ~ **sb a drink** servirle a uno una copa; ~ **away** or **off** vt vaciar, verter; ~ **in** vi (people) entrar en tropel; ~ **out** vi salir en tropel ♦ vt (drink) echar, servir; (fig): to ~ **out one's feelings** desahogarse; ~**ing** adj: ~**ing rain** lluvia torrencial

**pout** [paut] vi hacer pucheros

**poverty** ['pɔvətɪ] n pobreza, miseria; ~**-stricken** adj necesitado

**powder** ['paudə*] n polvo; (face ~) polvos mpl ♦ vt polvorear; to ~ **one's face** empolvarse la cara; ~ **compact** n polvera; ~**ed milk** n leche f en polvo; ~ **puff** n borla; ~ **room** n aseos mpl

**power** ['pauə*] n poder m; (strength) fuerza; (nation, TECH) potencia; (drive) empuje m; (ELEC) fuerza, energía ♦ vt impulsar; to be in ~ (POL) estar en el poder; ~ **cut** (BRIT) n apagón m; ~**ed** adj: ~**ed by** impulsado por; ~ **failure** n = ~ **cut**; ~**ful** adj poderoso; (engine) potente; (speech etc) convincente; ~**less** adj: ~**less (to do)** incapaz (de hacer); ~ **point** (BRIT) n enchufe m; ~ **station** n central f eléctrica

**p.p.** abbr (= per procurationem): ~ **J. Smith** p.p. (por poder de) J.

Smith; (= *pages*) págs

**PR** *n abbr* = **public relations**

**practicable** ['præktikəbl] *adj* factible

**practical** ['præktikl] *adj* práctico; **~ity** [-'kæliti] *n* factibilidad *f*; ~ **joke** *n* broma pesada; **~ly** *adv* (*almost*) casi

**practice** ['præktis] *n* (*habit*) costumbre *f*; (*exercise*) práctica, ejercicio; (*training*) adiestramiento; (*MED: of profession*) práctica, ejercicio; (*MED, LAW: business*) consulta *f* ♦ *vt, vi* (*US*) = **practise**; **in** ~ (*in reality*) en la práctica; **out of** ~ desentrenado

**practise** ['præktis] (*US* **practice**) *vt* (*carry out*) practicar; (*profession*) ejercer; (*train at*) practicar ♦ *vi* ejercer; (*train*) practicar; **practising** *adj* (*Christian etc*) practicante; (*lawyer*) en ejercicio

**practitioner** [præk'tiʃənə*] *n* (*MED*) médico/a

**prairie** ['preəri] *n* pampa

**praise** [preiz] *n* alabanza(s) *f(pl)*, elogio(s) *m(pl)* ♦ *vt* alabar, elogiar; **~worthy** *adj* loable

**pram** [præm] *n* (*BRIT*) cochecito de niño

**prance** [praːns] *vi* (*person*) contonearse

**prank** [præŋk] *n* travesura

**prawn** [prɔːn] *n* gamba

**pray** [prei] *vi* rezar

**prayer** [preə*] *n* oración *f*, rezo; (*entreaty*) ruego, súplica

**preach** [priːtʃ] *vi* (*also fig*) predicar; **~er** *n* predicador(a) *m/f*

**precaution** [pri'kɔːʃən] *n* precaución *f*

**precede** [pri'siːd] *vt, vi* preceder

**precedent** ['presidənt] *n* precedente *m*

**preceding** [pri'siːdiŋ] *adj* anterior

**precinct** ['priːsiŋkt] *n* recinto; **~s** *npl* contornos *mpl*; **pedestrian** ~ (*BRIT*) zona peatonal; **shopping** ~ (*BRIT*) centro comercial

**precious** ['preʃəs] *adj* precioso

**precipice** ['presipis] *n* precipicio

**precipitate** [pri'sipiteit] *vt* precipitar

**precise** [pri'sais] *adj* preciso, exacto; **~ly** *adv* precisamente, exactamente

**preclude** [pri'kluːd] *vt* excluir

**precocious** [pri'kəuʃəs] *adj* precoz

**preconceived** [priːkən'siːvd] *adj* preconcebido

**precondition** [priːkən'diʃən] *n* condición *f* previa

**predator** ['predətə*] *n* animal *m* de rapiña, depredador *m*

**predecessor** ['priːdisesə*] *n* antecesor(a) *m/f*

**predicament** [pri'dikəmənt] *n* apuro

**predict** [pri'dikt] *vt* pronosticar; **~able** *adj* previsible; **~ion** [-'dikʃən] *n* predicción *f*

**predominantly** [pri'dominəntli] *adv* en su mayoría

**predominate** [pri'domineit] *vi* predominar

**pre-empt** [priː'emt] *vt* adelantarse a

**preen** [priːn] *vt*: **to** ~ **itself** (*bird*) limpiarse (las plumas); **to** ~ **o.s.** pavonearse

**prefab** ['priːfæb] *n* casa prefabricada

**preface** ['prefəs] *n* prefacio

**prefect** ['priːfekt] *n* (*BRIT*: *in school*) monitor(a) *m/f*

**prefer** [pri'fəː*] *vt* preferir; **to** ~ **doing** *or* **to do** preferir hacer; **~able** ['prefərəbl] *adj* preferible; **~ably** ['prefərəbli] *adv* de preferencia; **~ence** ['prefərəns] *n* preferencia; (*priority*) prioridad *f*; **~ential** [prefə'renʃəl] *adj* preferente

**prefix** ['priːfiks] *n* prefijo

**pregnancy** ['pregnənsi] *n* (*of woman*) embarazo; (*of animal*) preñez *f*

**pregnant** ['pregnənt] *adj* (*woman*) embarazada; (*animal*) preñada

**prehistoric** ['priːhis'tɔrik] *adj* prehistórico

**prejudice** ['predʒudis] *n* prejuicio; **~d** *adj* (*person*) predispuesto

**preliminary** [pri'liminəri] *adj* preliminar

**prelude** ['preljuːd] *n* preludio

**premarital** ['priː'mæritl] *adj* premarital

**premature** ['prɛmətʃuə*] adj prematuro

**premier** ['prɛmɪə*] adj primero, principal ♦ n (POL) primer(a) ministro/a

**première** ['prɛmɪeə*] n estreno

**premise** ['prɛmɪs] n premisa; ~s npl (of business etc) local m; on the ~s en el lugar mismo

**premium** ['pri:mɪəm] n premio; (insurance) prima; to be at a ~ ser muy solicitado; ~ **bond** (BRIT) n bono del estado que participa en una lotería nacional

**premonition** [prɛmə'nɪʃən] n presentimiento

**preoccupied** [pri:'ɔkjupaɪd] adj ensimismado

**prep** [prɛp] n (SCOL: study) deberes mpl

**prepaid** [pri:'peɪd] adj porte pagado

**preparation** [prɛpə'reɪʃən] n preparación f; ~s npl preparativos mpl

**preparatory** [prɪ'pærətərɪ] adj preparatorio, preliminar; ~ **school** n escuela preparatoria

**prepare** [prɪ'pɛə*] vt preparar, disponer; (CULIN) preparar ♦ vi: to ~ **for** (action) prepararse or disponerse para; (event) hacer preparativos para; ~**d** to dispuesto a; ~**d for** listo para

**preponderance** [prɪ'pɔndərns] n predominio

**preposition** [prɛpə'zɪʃən] n preposición f

**preposterous** [prɪ'pɔstərəs] adj absurdo, ridículo

**prep school** n = preparatory school

**prerequisite** [pri:'rɛkwɪzɪt] n requisito

**prerogative** [prɪ'rɔgətɪv] n prerrogativa

**Presbyterian** [prɛzbɪ'tɪərɪən] adj, n presbiteriano/a m/f

**preschool** ['pri:'sku:l] adj preescolar

**prescribe** [prɪ'skraɪb] vt (MED) recetar

**prescription** [prɪ'skrɪpʃən] n (MED) receta

**presence** ['prɛzns] n presencia; **in sb's** ~ en presencia de uno; ~ **of mind** aplomo

**present** [adj, n 'prɛznt, vb prɪ'zɛnt] adj (in attendance) presente; (current) actual ♦ n (gift) regalo; (actuality): **the** ~ la actualidad, el presente ♦ vt (introduce, describe) presentar; (expound) exponer; (give) presentar, dar, ofrecer; (THEATRE) representar; **to give sb a** ~ regalar algo a uno; **at** ~ actualmente; ~**able** [prɪ'zɛntəbl] adj: **to make o.s.** ~**able** arreglarse; ~**ation** [-'teɪʃən] n presentación f; (of report etc) exposición f; (formal ceremony) entrega de un regalo; ~**-day** adj actual; ~**er** [prɪ'zɛntə*] n (RADIO, TV) locutor(a) m/f; ~**ly** adv (soon) dentro de poco; (now) ahora

**preservation** [prɛzə'veɪʃən] n conservación f

**preservative** [prɪ'zɜ:vətɪv] n conservante m

**preserve** [prɪ'zɜ:v] vt (keep safe) preservar, proteger; (maintain) mantener; (food) conservar ♦ n (for game) coto, vedado; (often pl: jam) conserva, confitura

**preside** [prɪ'zaɪd] vi: to ~ **over** presidir

**president** ['prɛzɪdənt] n presidente m/f; ~**ial** [-'dɛnʃl] adj presidencial

**press** [prɛs] n (newspapers): **the P**~ la prensa; (printer's) imprenta; (of button) pulsación f ♦ vt empujar; (button etc) apretar; (clothes: iron) planchar; (put pressure on: person) presionar; (insist): **to** ~ **sth on sb** insistir en que uno acepte algo ♦ vi (squeeze) apretar; (pressurize): **to** ~ **for** presionar por; **we are** ~**ed for time/money** estamos apurados de tiempo/dinero; ~ **on** vi avanzar; (hurry) apretar el paso; ~ **agency** n agencia de prensa; ~ **conference** n rueda de prensa; ~**ing** adj apremiante; ~ **stud** (BRIT) n botón m de pre-

**pressure** 210 **print**

sión; ~-up (BRIT) n plancha

**pressure** ['preʃə*] n presión f; to put ~ on sb presionar a uni; ~ cooker n olla a presión; ~ gauge n manómetro; ~ group n grupo de presión; **pressurized** adj (container) a presión

**prestige** [pres'tiːʒ] n prestigio

**presumably** [prɪ'zjuːməblɪ] adv es de suponer que, cabe presumir que

**presume** [prɪ'zjuːm] vt: to ~ (that) presumir (que), suponer (que)

**presumption** [prɪ'zʌmpʃən] n suposición f

**presumptuous** [prɪ'zʌmptjuəs] adj presumido

**presuppose** [prɪːsə'pəuz] vt presuponer

**pretence** [prɪ'tens] (US pretense) n fingimiento; **under false ~s** con engaños

**pretend** [prɪ'tend] vt, vi (feign) fingir

**pretense** [prɪ'tens] (US) n = pretence

**pretentious** [prɪ'tenʃəs] adj presumido; (ostentatious) ostentoso, aparatoso

**pretext** ['priːtekst] n pretexto

**pretty** ['prɪtɪ] adj bonito (SP), lindo (AM) ♦ adv bastante

**prevail** [prɪ'veɪl] vi (gain mastery) prevalecer; (be current) predominar; ~ing adj (dominant) predominante

**prevalent** ['prevələnt] adj (widespread) extendido

**prevent** [prɪ'vent] vt: to ~ sb from doing sth impedir a uno hacer algo; to ~ sth from happening evitar que ocurra algo; ~ative adj = preventive; ~ive adj preventivo

**preview** ['priːvjuː] n (of film) preestreno

**previous** ['priːvɪəs] adj previo, anterior; ~ly adv antes

**prewar** [priː'wɔː*] adj de antes de la guerra

**prey** [preɪ] n presa ♦ vi: to ~ on (feed on) alimentarse de; **it was ~ing on his mind** le preocupaba, le

obsesionaba

**price** [praɪs] n precio ♦ vt (goods) fijar el precio de; ~**less** adj que no tiene precio; ~ **list** n tarifa

**prick** [prɪk] n (sting) picadura ♦ vt pinchar; (hurt) picar; to ~ **up one's ears** aguzar el oído

**prickle** ['prɪkl] n (sensation) picor m; (BOT) espina; **prickly** adj espinoso; (fig: person) enojadizo; **prickly heat** n sarpullido causado por exceso de calor

**pride** [praɪd] n orgullo; (pej) soberbia ♦ vt: to ~ **o.s. on** enorgullecerse de

**priest** [priːst] n sacerdote m; ~**ess** n sacerdotisa; ~**hood** n sacerdocio

**prig** [prɪg] n gazmoño/a

**prim** [prɪm] adj (demure) remilgado; (prudish) gazmoño

**primarily** ['praɪmərɪlɪ] adv ante todo

**primary** ['praɪmərɪ] adj (first in importance) principal ♦ n (US: POL) (elección f) primaria; ~ **school** (BRIT) n escuela primaria

**primate** ['praɪmeɪt] n (ZOOL) primate m

**prime** [praɪm] adj primero, principal; (excellent) selecto, de primera clase ♦ n: in the ~ of life en la flor de la vida ♦ vt (wood, fig) preparar; ~ **example** ejemplo típico; **P~ Minister** n primer(a) ministro/a

**primeval** [praɪ'miːvəl] adj primitivo

**primitive** ['prɪmɪtɪv] adj primitivo; (crude) rudimentario

**primrose** ['prɪmrəuz] n primavera, prímula

**primus (stove)** ['praɪməs-] (BRIT) n hornillo de camping ®

**prince** [prɪns] n príncipe m

**princess** [prɪn'ses] n princesa

**principal** ['prɪnsɪpl] adj principal, mayor ♦ n director(a) m/f; ~**ity** [-'pælɪtɪ] n principado

**principle** ['prɪnsɪpl] n principio; in ~ en principio; on ~ por principio

**print** [prɪnt] n (foot~) huella; (finger~) huella dactilar; (letters) letra de molde; (fabric) estampado;

(ART) grabado; (PHOT) impresión f ♦ vt imprimir; (cloth) estampar; (write in capitals) escribir en letras de molde; **out of** ~ agotado; **~ed matter** n impresos mpl; **~er** n (person) impresor(a) m/f; (machine) impresora; **~ing** n (art) imprenta; (act) impresión f; **~out** n (COMPUT) impresión f

**prior** ['praɪə*] adj anterior, previo; (more important) más importante; ~ **to** antes de

**priority** [praɪ'ɔrɪtɪ] n prioridad f; **to have ~ (over)** tener prioridad (sobre)

**prise** [praɪz] vt: **to ~ open** abrir con palanca

**prison** ['prɪzn] n cárcel f, prisión f ♦ cpd carcelario; **~er** n (in prison) preso/a; (captured person) prisionero; **~er-of-war** n prisionero de guerra

**pristine** ['prɪstiːn] adj inmaculado

**privacy** ['prɪvəsɪ] n intimidad f

**private** ['praɪvɪt] adj (personal) particular; (property, industry, discussion etc) privado; (place) tranquilo ♦ n soldado raso; **"~"** (on envelope) "confidencial"; (on door) "prohibido el paso"; **in ~** en privado; **~ enterprise** n empresa privada; **~ eye** n detective m/f privado/a; **~ property** n propiedad f privada; **~ school** n colegio particular

**privet** ['prɪvɪt] n alheña

**privilege** ['prɪvɪlɪdʒ] n privilegio; (prerogative) prerrogativa

**privy** ['prɪvɪ] adj: **to be ~ to** estar enterado de

**prize** [praɪz] n premio ♦ adj de primera clase ♦ vt apreciar, estimar; **~-giving** n distribución f de premios; **~winner** n premiado/a

**pro** [prəu] n (SPORT) profesional m/f ♦ prep a favor de; **the ~s and cons** los pros y los contras

**probability** [prɔbə'bɪlɪtɪ] n probabilidad f; **in all ~** con toda probabilidad

**probable** ['prɔbəbl] adj probable

**probably** ['prɔbəblɪ] adv probablemente

**probation** [prə'beɪʃən] n: **on ~** (employee) a prueba; (LAW) en libertad condicional

**probe** [prəub] n (MED, SPACE) sonda; (enquiry) encuesta, investigación f ♦ vt sondar; (investigate) investigar

**problem** ['prɔbləm] n problema m

**procedure** [prə'siːdʒə*] n procedimiento; (bureaucratic) trámites mpl

**proceed** [prə'siːd] vi (do afterwards): **to ~ to do sth** proceder a hacer algo; (continue): **to ~ (with)** continuar or seguir (con); **~ings** npl acto(s) (pl); (LAW) proceso; **~s** ['prəusiːdz] npl (money) ganancias fpl, ingresos mpl

**process** ['prəuses] n proceso ♦ vt tratar, elaborar; **~ing** n tratamiento, elaboración f; (PHOT) revelado

**procession** [prə'seʃən] n desfile m; **funeral ~** cortejo fúnebre

**proclaim** [prə'kleɪm] vt (announce) anunciar; **proclamation** [prɔklə'meɪʃən] n proclamación f; (written) proclama

**procrastinate** [prəu'kræstɪneɪt] vi demorarse

**procure** [prə'kjuə*] vt conseguir

**prod** [prɔd] vt empujar ♦ n empujón m

**prodigal** ['prɔdɪgl] adj pródigo

**prodigy** ['prɔdɪdʒɪ] n prodigio

**produce** [n 'prɔdjuːs, vt prə'djuːs] n (AGR) productos mpl agrícolas ♦ vt producir; (play, film, programme) presentar; **~r** n (of play, film, programme) productor(a) m/f; (of film, programme) director(a) m/ (of record) productor(a) m/f

**product** ['prɔdʌkt] n producto

**production** [prə'dʌkʃən] n producción f; (THEATRE) presentación f; **~ line** n línea de producción

**productive** [prə'dʌktɪv] adj productivo; **productivity** [prɔdʌk'tɪvɪtɪ] n productividad f

**profane** [prə'feɪn] adj profano

**profession** [prə'feʃən] n profesión f; **~al** adj profesional ♦ n profesional *m/f*; *(skilled person)* perito

**professor** [prə'fesə\*] *n* (BRIT) catedrático/a; *(US, Canada)* profesor(a) *m/f*

**proficiency** [prə'fıʃənsı] *n* capacidad *f*, habilidad *f*

**proficient** [prə'fıʃənt] *adj* experto, hábil

**profile** ['prəufaıl] *n* perfil *m*

**profit** ['prɒfıt] *n* (COMM) ganancia *f* ♦ *vi*: **to ~ by** or **from** aprovechar or sacar provecho de; **~eering** [-ə'tıərıŋ] *n* rentabilidad *f*; **~able** *adj* (ECON) rentable

**profound** [prə'faund] *adj* profundo

**profusely** [prə'fju:slı] *adv* profusamente

**profusion** [prə'fju:ʒən] *n* profusión *f*, abundancia *f*

**programme** ['prəugræm] (US **program**) *n* programa *m* ♦ *vt* programar; **~r** (US **programer**) *n* programador(a) *m/f*; **programming** (US **programing**) *n* programación *f*

**progress** [*n* 'prəugres, *vi* prə'gres] *n* progreso; *(development)* desarrollo ♦ *vi* progresar, avanzar; **in ~** en curso; **~ive** [-'gresıv] *adj* progresivo; *(person)* progresista

**prohibit** [prə'hıbıt] *vt* prohibir; **to ~ sb from doing sth** prohibir a uno hacer algo; **~ion** [-'bıʃən] *n* prohibición *f*; (US): **P~ion** Ley *f* Seca

**project** [*n* 'prɒdʒekt, *vb* prə'dʒekt] *n* proyecto ♦ *vt* proyectar ♦ *vi* (stick out) salir, sobresalir; **projectile** [prə'dʒektaıl] *n* proyectil *m*; **projection** [prə'dʒekʃən] *n* proyección *f*; *(overhang)* saliente *m*; **projector** [prə'dʒektə\*] *n* proyector *m*

**proletarian** [prəulı'tεərıən] *n* proletario/a

**proletariat** [prəulı'tεərıət] *n* proletariado

**prologue** ['prəulɒg] *n* prólogo

**prolong** [prə'lɒŋ] *vt* prolongar, extender

**prom** [prɒm] *n* *abbr* = **promenade**; (US: *ball*) baile *m* de gala

**promenade** [prɒmə'nɑːd] *n* (by sea)

paseo marítimo; **~ concert** (BRIT) *n* concierto (en que parte del público permanece de pie)

**prominence** ['prɒmınəns] *n* importancia

**prominent** ['prɒmınənt] *adj* (standing out) saliente; *(important)* eminente, importante

**promiscuous** [prə'mıskjuəs] *adj* (sexually) promiscuo

**promise** ['prɒmıs] *n* promesa ♦ *vt, vi* prometer; **promising** *adj* prometedor(a)

**promote** [prə'məut] *vt* (employee) ascender; *(product, pop star)* hacer propaganda por; *(ideas)* fomentar; **~r** *n* (of event) promotor(a) *m/f*; (of cause etc) impulsor(a) *m/f*; **promotion** [-'məuʃən] *n* (advertising campaign) campaña de promoción *f*; (in rank) ascenso

**prompt** [prɒmpt] *adj* rápido ♦ *adv*: **at 6 o'clock ~** a las seis en punto ♦ *n* (COMPUT) aviso ♦ *vt* (urge) mover, incitar; *(when talking)* instar; (THEATRE) apuntar; **to ~ sb to do sth** instar a uno a hacer algo; **~ly** *adv* rápidamente; *(exactly)* puntualmente

**prone** [prəun] *adj* (lying) postrado; **~ to** propenso a

**prong** [prɒŋ] *n* diente *m*, punta

**pronoun** ['prəunaun] *n* pronombre *m*

**pronounce** [prə'nauns] *vt* pronunciar; **~d** *adj* (marked) marcado

**pronunciation** [prənʌnsı'eıʃən] *n* pronunciación *f*

**proof** [pruːf] *n* prueba ♦ *adj*: **~ against** a prueba de

**prop** [prɒp] *n* apoyo; *(fig)* sostén *m* ♦ *vt* (also: **~ up**) apoyar; *(lean)*: **to ~ sth against** apoyar algo contra

**propaganda** [prɒpə'gændə] *n* propaganda

**propagate** ['prɒpəgeıt] *vt* (idea, information) difundir

**propel** [prə'pel] *vt* impulsar, propulsar; **~ler** *n* hélice *f*

**propensity** [prə'pensıtı] *n* propensión *f*

**proper** ['prɒpə*] adj (suited, right) propio; (exact) justo; (seemly) correcto, decente; (authentic) verdadero; (referring to place): **the village ~** el pueblo mismo; **~ly** adv (adequately) correctamente; (decently) decentemente; **~ noun** n nombre m propio

**property** ['prɒpətɪ] n propiedad f; (personal) bienes mpl muebles; **~ owner** n dueño/a de propiedades

**prophecy** ['prɒfɪsɪ] n profecía

**prophesy** ['prɒfɪsaɪ] vt (fig) predecir

**prophet** ['prɒfɪt] n profeta m

**proportion** [prə'pɔ:ʃən] n proporción f; (share) parte f; **~al** adj: **~al (to)** en proporción (con); **~al representation** n representación f proporcional; **~ate** adj: **~ate (to)** en proporción (con)

**proposal** [prə'pəuzl] n (offer of marriage) oferta de matrimonio; (plan) proyecto

**propose** [prə'pəuz] vt proponer ♦ vi declararse; **to ~ to do** tener intención de hacer

**proposition** [prɒpə'zɪʃən] n propuesta

**proprietor** [prə'praɪətə*] n propietario/a, dueño/a

**propriety** [prə'praɪətɪ] n decoro

**pro rata** [-'rɑːtə] adv a prorrateo

**prose** [prəuz] n prosa

**prosecute** ['prɒsɪkjuːt] vt (LAW) procesar; **prosecution** [-'kjuːʃən] n proceso, causa; (accusing side) acusación f; **prosecutor** n acusador/a m/f; (also: **public prosecutor**) fiscal m

**prospect** [n 'prɒspekt, vb prə'spekt] n (possibility) perspectiva ♦ vi: **to ~ for** buscar; **~s** npl (for work etc) perspectivas fpl; **~ing** n prospección f; **~ive** [prə'spektɪv] adj futuro

**prospectus** [prə'spektəs] n prospecto

**prosper** ['prɒspə*] vi prosperar; **~ity** [-'sperɪtɪ] n prosperidad f; **~ous** adj próspero

**prostitute** ['prɒstɪtjuːt] n prostituta;

(male) hombre que se dedica a la prostitución

**prostrate** ['prɒstreɪt] adj postrado

**protagonist** [prə'tægənɪst] n protagonista m/f

**protect** [prə'tekt] vt proteger; **~ion** [-'tekʃən] n protección f; **~ive** adj protector(a)

**protégé** ['prəuteʒeɪ] n protegido/a

**protein** ['prəutiːn] n proteína

**protest** [n 'prəutest, vb prə'test] n protesta ♦ vi: **to ~ about** or **at/against** protestar de/contra ♦ vt (insist): **to ~ (that)** insistir en (que)

**Protestant** ['prɒtɪstənt] adj, n protestante m/f

**protester** [prə'testə*] n manifestante m/f

**protracted** [prə'træktɪd] adj prolongado

**protrude** [prə'truːd] vi salir, sobresalir

**proud** [praud] adj orgulloso; (pej) soberbio, altanero

**prove** [pruːv] vt probar; (show) demostrar ♦ vi: **to ~ (to be) correct** resultar correcto; **to ~ o.s.** probar su valía

**proverb** ['prɒvɜːb] n refrán m

**provide** [prə'vaɪd] vt proporcionar, dar; **to ~ sb with sth** proveer a uno de algo; **~d (that)** conj con tal de que, a condición de que; **~ for** vt fus (person) mantener a; (problem etc) tener en cuenta; **providing** [prə'vaɪdɪŋ] conj: **~ (that)** a condición de que, con tal de que

**province** ['prɒvɪns] n provincia; (fig) esfera; **provincial** [prə'vɪnʃəl] adj provincial; (pej) provinciano

**provision** [prə'vɪʒən] n (supplying) suministro, abastecimiento; (of contract etc) disposición f; **~s** npl (food) comestibles mpl; **~al** adj provisional

**proviso** [prə'vaɪzəu] n condición f, estipulación f

**provocative** [prə'vɒkətɪv] adj provocativo

**provoke** [prə'vəuk] vt (cause) provocar, incitar; (*anger*) enojar

**prow** [prau] *n* proa

**prowess** ['praus] *n* destreza

**prowl** [praul] *vi* (*also*: ~ *about*, ~ *around*) merodear ♦ *n*: **on the** ~ **de merodeo;** ~**er** *n* merodeador(a) *m/f*

**proxy** ['prɔksi] *n*: **by** ~ **por poderes**

**prude** [pruːd] *n* remilgado/a

**prudent** ['pruːdənt] *adj* prudente

**prune** [pruːn] *n* ciruela pasa ♦ *vt* podar

**pry** [prai] *vi*: **to** ~ (**into**) entrometerse (en)

**PS** *n abbr* (= *postscript*) P.D.

**psalm** [sɑːm] *n* salmo

**pseudo-** [sjuːdəu] *prefix* seudo-; **pseudonym** *n* seudónimo

**psyche** ['saiki] *n* psique

**psychiatric** [saiki'ætrik] *adj* psiquiátrico

**psychiatrist** [sai'kaiətrist] *n* psiquiatra *m/f*

**psychic** ['saikik] *adj* (*also*: ~**al**) psíquico

**psychoanalyse** [saikəu'ænəlaiz] *vt* psicoanalizar; **psychoanalysis** [-ə'næləsis] *n* psicoanálisis *m inv*

**psychological** [saikə'lɔdʒikl] *adj* psicológico

**psychologist** [sai'kɔlədʒist] *n* psicólogo/a

**psychology** [sai'kɔlədʒi] *n* psicología

**PTO** *abbr* (= *please turn over*) sigue

**pub** [pʌb] *n abbr* (= *public house*) pub *m*, taberna

**puberty** ['pjuːbəti] *n* pubertad *f*

**public** ['pʌblik] *adj* público ♦ *n*: **the** ~ **el público; in** ~ **en público; to make** ~ **hacer público; to** ~ **address system** *n* megafonía

**publican** ['pʌblikən] *n* tabernero/a

**publication** [pʌbli'keiʃən] *n* publicación *f*

**public:** ~ **company** *n* sociedad *f* anónima; ~ **convenience** (*BRIT*) *n* aseos *mpl* públicos (*SP*), sanitarios *mpl* (*AM*); ~ **holiday** *n* día de fiesta (*SP*), (día) feriado (*AM*); ~ **house** (*BRIT*) *n* bar *m*, pub *m*

**publicity** [pʌb'lisiti] *n* publicidad *f*

**publicize** ['pʌblisaiz] *vt* publicitar

**publicly** ['pʌblikli] *adv* públicamente, en público

**public:** ~ **opinion** *n* opinión *f* pública; ~ **relations** *n* relaciones *fpl* públicas; ~ **school** *n* (*BRIT*) escuela privada; (*US*) instituto; ~-**spirited** *adj* que tiene sentido del deber ciudadano; ~ **transport** *n* transporte *m* público

**publish** ['pʌbliʃ] *vt* publicar; ~**er** *n* (*person*) editor(a) *m/f*; (*firm*) editorial *f*; ~**ing** *n* (*industry*) industria del libro

**puce** [pjuːs] *adj* de color pardo rojizo

**pucker** ['pʌkə*] *vt* (*pleat*) arrugar; (*brow etc*) fruncir

**pudding** ['pudiŋ] *n* pudín *m*; (*BRIT*: *dessert*) postre *m*; **black** ~ morcilla

**puddle** ['pʌdl] *n* charco

**puff** [pʌf] *n* soplo; (*of smoke, air*) bocanada; (*of breathing*) resoplido ♦ *vt*: **to** ~ **one's pipe** chupar la pipa ♦ *vi* (*pant*) jadear; ~ **out** *vi* hinchar; ~**ed** (*inf*) *adj* (*out of breath*) sin aliento; ~ **pastry** *n* hojaldre *m*; ~**y** *adj* hinchado

**pull** [pul] *n* (*tug*): **to give sth a** ~ dar un tirón a algo ♦ *vt* tirar de; (*press: trigger*) apretar; (*haul*) tirar, arrastrar; (*close: curtain*) echar ♦ *vi* tirar; **to** ~ **to pieces** hacer pedazos; **to not** ~ **one's punches** no andarse con bromas; **to** ~ **one's weight** hacer su parte; **to** ~ **o.s. together** sobreponerse; **to** ~ **sb's leg** tomar el pelo a uno; ~ **apart** *vt* (*break*) romper; ~ **down** *vt* (*building*) derribar; ~ **in** *vi* (*car etc*) parar (junto a la acera); (*train*) llegar a la estación; ~ **off** *vt* (*deal etc*) cerrar; ~ **out** *vi* (*car, train etc*) salir ♦ *vt* sacar, arrancar; ~ **over** *vi* (*AUT*) hacerse a un lado; ~ **through** *vi* (*MED*) reponerse; ~ **up** *vi* (*stop*) parar ♦ *vt* (*raise*) levantar; (*uproot*) arrancar, desarraigar

**pulley** ['puli] *n* polea

**pullover** ['puləuvə*] *n* jersey *m*, suéter *m*

**pulp** [pʌlp] *n* (*of fruit*) pulpa
**pulpit** ['pulpɪt] *n* púlpito *m*
**pulsate** [pʌl'seɪt] *vi* pulsar, latir
**pulse** [pʌls] *n* (ANAT) pulso; (*rhythm*) pulsación *f*; (BOT) legumbre *f*
**pummel** ['pʌml] *vt* aporrear
**pump** [pʌmp] *n* bomba; (*shoe*) zapatilla ♦ *vt* sacar con una bomba; ~ **up** *vt* inflar
**pumpkin** ['pʌmpkɪn] *n* calabaza
**pun** [pʌn] *n* juego de palabras
**punch** [pʌntʃ] *n* (*blow*) golpe *m*, puñetazo; (*tool*) punzón *m*; (*drink*) ponche *m* ♦ *vt* (*hit*): **to ~ sb/sth** dar un puñetazo or golpear a uno/algo; ~**line** *n* palabras que rematan un chiste; ~**-up** (BRIT: *inf*) *n* riña
**punctual** ['pʌŋktjuəl] *adj* puntual
**punctuation** [pʌŋktju'eɪʃən] *n* puntuación *f*
**puncture** ['pʌŋktʃə*] (BRIT) *n* pinchazo ♦ *vt* pinchar
**pundit** ['pʌndɪt] *n* experto/a
**pungent** ['pʌndʒənt] *adj* acre
**punish** ['pʌnɪʃ] *vt* castigar; ~**ment** *n* castigo
**punk** [pʌŋk] *n* (*also:* ~ *rocker*) punki *m/f*; (*also:* ~ *rock*) música punk; (US: *inf*: *hoodlum*) rufián *m*
**punt** [pʌnt] *n* (*boat*) batea
**punter** ['pʌntə*] (BRIT) *n* (*gambler*) jugador(a) *m/f*; (: *inf*) cliente *m/f*
**puny** ['pjuːnɪ] *adj* débil
**pup** [pʌp] *n* cachorro
**pupil** ['pjuːpl] *n* alumno/a; (*of eye*) pupila
**puppet** ['pʌpɪt] *n* títere *m*
**puppy** ['pʌpɪ] *n* cachorro, perrito
**purchase** ['pəːtʃɪs] *n* compra ♦ *vt* comprar; ~**r** *n* comprador(a) *m/f*
**pure** [pjuə*] *adj* puro
**purée** ['pjuəreɪ] *n* puré *m*
**purely** ['pjuəlɪ] *adv* puramente
**purge** [pəːdʒ] *n* (MED, POL) purga ♦ *vt* purgar
**purify** ['pjuərɪfaɪ] *vt* purificar, depurar
**puritan** ['pjuərɪtən] *n* puritano/a

**purity** ['pjuərɪtɪ] *n* pureza
**purple** ['pəːpl] *adj* purpúreo; morado
**purport** [pəː'pɔːt] *vi*: **to ~ to be/do** dar a entender que es/hace
**purpose** ['pəːpəs] *n* propósito; **on ~** a propósito, adrede; (*t*) ~**ful** *adj* resuelto, determinado
**purr** [pəː*] *vi* ronronear
**purse** [pəːs] *n* monedero; (US) bolsa (SP), cartera (AM) ♦ *vt* fruncir
**purser** ['pəːsə*] *n* (NAUT) comisario/a
**pursue** [pə'sjuː] *vt* seguir; ~**r** *n* perseguidor(a) *m/f*
**pursuit** [pə'sjuːt] *n* (*chase*) caza; (*occupation*) actividad *f*
**push** [puʃ] *n* empuje *m*, empujón *m*; (*of button*) presión *f*; (*drive*) empuje *m* ♦ *vt* empujar; (*button*) apretar; (*promote*) promover ♦ *vi* empujar; (*demand*): **to ~ for** luchar por; ~ **aside** *vt* apartar con la mano; ~ **off** (*inf*) *vi* largarse; ~ **on** *vi* seguir adelante; ~ **through** (*crowd*) abrirse paso a empujones ♦ *vt* (*measure*) despachar; ~ **up** *vt* (*total, prices*) hacer subir; ~**chair** (BRIT) *n* sillita de ruedas; ~**er** *n* (*drug* ~*er*) traficante *m/f* de drogas; ~**over** (*inf*) *n*: **it's a ~over** está tirado; ~**up** (US) *n* plancha; ~**y** (*pej*) *adj* agresivo
**puss** [pus] (*inf*) *n* minino
**pussy(-cat)** ['pusɪ-] (*inf*) *n* = **puss**
**put** [put] (*pt, pp* **put**) *vt* (*place*) poner, colocar; (~ *into*) meter; (*say*) expresar; (*a question*) hacer; (*estimate*) estimar; ~ **about or around** *vt* (*rumour*) diseminar; ~ **across** (*ideas etc*) comunicar; ~ **away** *vt* (*store*) guardar; ~ **back** (*replace*) devolver a su lugar; (*postpone*) aplazar; ~ **by** (*money*) guardar; ~ **down** *vt* (*on ground*) poner en el suelo; (*animal*) sacrificar; (*in writing*) apuntar; (*revolt etc*) sofocar; (*attribute*): **to ~ sth down to** atribuir algo a; ~ **forward** *vt* (*ideas*) presentar, proponer; ~ **in** *vt* (*complaint*) presentar; (*time*) dedicar; ~ **off** *vt* (*postpone*) aplazar; (*discourage*) des-

animar; ~ **on** vt ponerse; (light etc) encender; (play etc) presentar; (gain): to ~ **on** weight engordar; (brake) echar; ~ **out** vt (record, kettle etc) poner; (assume) adoptar; ~ **out** vt (fire, light) apagar; (rubbish etc) sacar; (cat etc) echar; (one's hand) alargar; (inf: person): to be ~ **out** alterarse; ~ **through** vt (TEL) poner; (plan etc) hacer aprobar; ~ **up** vt (raise) levantar, alzar; (hang) colgar; (build) construir; (increase) aumentar; (accommodate) alojar; ~ **up with** vt fus aguantar

**putrid** ['pju:trɪd] adj podrido

**putt** [pʌt] n putt m, golpe m corto; **~ing green** n green m; minigolf m

**putty** ['pʌtɪ] n masilla

**put-up** [' ] : ~ **job** (BRIT) n amaño

**puzzle** ['pʌzl] n rompecabezas m inv; (also: crossword ~) crucigrama m; (mystery) misterio ♦ vt dejar perplejo, confundir ♦ vi: to ~ **over** sth devanarse los sesos con algo; **puzzling** adj misterioso, extraño

**pyjamas** [pɪ'dʒɑ:məz] (BRIT) npl pijama m

**pylon** ['paɪlən] n torre f de conducción eléctrica

**pyramid** ['pɪrəmɪd] n pirámide f

**Pyrenees** [pɪrə'ni:z] npl: the ~ los Pirineos

**python** ['paɪθən] n pitón m

## Q

**quack** [kwæk] n graznido; (pej: doctor) curandero/a

**quad** [kwɒd] n abbr = **quadrangle**; **quadruplet**

**quadrangle** ['kwɒdræŋgl] n patio

**quadruple** [kwɒ'drupl] vt, vi cuadruplicar

**quadruplets** [kwɔ:'dru:plɪts] npl cuatrillizos/as

**quagmire** ['kwægmaɪə*] n lodazal m, cenegal m

**quail** [kweɪl] n codorniz f ♦ vi: to ~ **at** or **before** amedrentarse ante

**quaint** [kweɪnt] adj extraño; (picturesque) pintoresco

**quake** [kweɪk] vi temblar ♦ n abbr = **earthquake**

**Quaker** ['kweɪkə*] n cuáquero/a

**qualification** [kwɔlɪfɪ'keɪʃən] n (ability) capacidad f; (often pl: diploma etc) título; (reservation) salvedad f

**qualified** ['kwɔlɪfaɪd] adj capacitado; (professionally) titulado; (limited) limitado

**qualify** ['kwɔlɪfaɪ] vt (make competent) capacitar; (modify) modificar ♦ vi (in competition): to ~ **(for)** calificarse (para); (pass examination(s)): to ~ **(as)** calificarse (de), graduarse (en); (be eligible): to ~ **(for)** reunir los requisitos (para)

**quality** ['kwɔlɪtɪ] n calidad f; (of person) cualidad f

**qualm** [kwɑ:m] n escrúpulo

**quandary** ['kwɔndrɪ] n: to be in a ~ tener dudas

**quantity** ['kwɔntɪtɪ] n cantidad f; in ~ en grandes cantidades; ~ **surveyor** n aparejador/a m/f

**quarantine** ['kwɔrntɪn] n cuarentena

**quarrel** ['kwɔrəl] n riña, pelea ♦ vi reñir, pelearse; **~some** adj pendenciero

**quarry** ['kwɔrɪ] n cantera; (animal) presa

**quart** [kwɔ:t] n ≈ litro

**quarter** ['kwɔ:tə*] n cuarto, cuarta parte f; (US: coin) moneda de 25 centavos; (of year) trimestre m; (district) barrio ♦ vt dividir en cuartos; (MIL: lodge) alojar; ~**s** (barracks) cuartel m; (living ~s) alojamiento; a ~ **of an hour** un cuarto de hora; ~ **final** n cuarto de final; **~ly** adj trimestral ♦ adv cada 3 meses, trimestralmente

**quartet(te)** [kwɔ:'tet] n cuarteto

**quartz** [kwɔ:ts] n cuarzo

**quash** [kwɔʃ] vt (verdict) anular

**quasi-** ['kweɪzaɪ] prefix cuasi

**quaver** ['kweɪvə*] (BRIT) n (MUS) corchea ♦ vi temblar

**quay** [ki:] n (also: ~side) muelle m

**queasy** ['kwi:zı] adj: **to feel ~** tener náuseas

**queen** [kwi:n] n reina; (CARDS etc) dama; ~ **mother** n reina madre

**queer** [kwıə*] adj raro, extraño ♦ n (inf: highly offensive) maricón m

**quell** [kwel] vt (feeling) calmar; (rebellion etc) sofocar

**quench** [kwentʃ] vt: **to ~ one's thirst** apagar la sed

**querulous** ['kwerυləs] adj quejumbroso

**query** ['kwıərı] n (question) pregunta ♦ vt dudar de

**quest** [kwest] n busca, búsqueda

**question** ['kwestʃən] n pregunta; (doubt) duda; (matter) asunto, cuestión f ♦ vt (doubt) dudar de; (interrogate) interrogar, hacer preguntas a; **beyond ~** fuera de toda duda; **out of the ~** imposible; ni hablar; ~**able** adj dudoso; ~ **mark** n punto de interrogación; ~**naire** [-'nεə*] n cuestionario

**queue** [kju:] (BRIT) n cola ♦ vi (also: ~ up) hacer cola

**quibble** ['kwıbl] vi sutilizar

**quick** [kwık] adj rápido; (agile) ágil; (mind) listo ♦ n: **cut to the ~** (fig) herido en lo vivo ♦ excl: ~! ¡date prisa!; ~**en** vt apresurar ♦ vi apresurarse, darse prisa; ~**ly** adv rápidamente, de prisa; ~**sand** n arenas fpl movedizas; ~**witted** adj perspicaz

**quid** [kwıd] (BRIT: inf) n inv libra

**quiet** ['kwaıət] adj (voice, music etc) bajo; (person, place) tranquilo; (ceremony) íntimo ♦ n silencio; (calm) tranquilidad f ♦ vt, vi (US) = ~en; ~**en** (also: ~en down) vi (grow silent) callarse ♦ vt calmar; hacer callar; ~**ly** adv tranquilamente; (silently) silenciosamente; ~**ness** n silencio; tranquilidad f

**quilt** [kwılt] n edredón m

**quin** [kwın] n abbr = quintuplet

**quinine** [kwı'ni:n] n quinina

**quintet(te)** [kwın'tet] n quinteto

**quintuplets** [kwın'tju:plıts] npl quintillizos/as

**quip** [kwıp] n pulla

**quirk** [kwə:k] n peculiaridad f; (accident) capricho

**quit** [kwıt] (pt, pp quit or quitted) vt dejar, abandonar; (premises) desocupar ♦ vi (give up) renunciar; (resign) dimitir

**quite** [kwaıt] adv (rather) bastante; (entirely) completamente; **that's not ~ big enough** no acaba de ser lo bastante grande; **~ a few of them,** un buen número de ellos; ~ **(so)**! ¡así es!, ¡exactamente!

**quits** [kwıts] adj: ~ **(with)** en paz (con); **let's call it ~** dejémoslo en tablas

**quiver** ['kwıvə*] vi estremecerse

**quiz** [kwız] n concurso ♦ vt interrogar; ~**zical** adj burlón(ona)

**quota** ['kwəυtə] n cuota

**quotation** [kwəυ'teıʃən] n cita; (estimate) presupuesto; ~ **marks** npl comillas fpl

**quote** [kwəυt] n cita; (estimate) presupuesto ♦ vt citar; (price) cotizar ♦ vi: **to ~ from** citar de; ~**s** npl (inverted commas) comillas fpl

**quotient** ['kwəυʃənt] n cociente m

# R

**rabbi** ['ræbaı] n rabino

**rabbit** ['ræbıt] n conejo; ~ **hutch** n conejera

**rabble** ['ræbl] (pej) n chusma, populacho

**rabies** ['reıbi:z] n rabia

**RAC** (BRIT) n abbr = **Royal Automobile Club**

**rac(c)oon** [rə'ku:n] n mapache m

**race** [reıs] n carrera; (species) raza ♦ vt (horse) hacer correr; (engine) acelerar ♦ vi (compete) competir; (run) correr; (pulse) latir a ritmo acelerado; ~ **car** (US) n = **racing car;** ~ **car driver** (US) n = **racing driver;** ~**course** n hipódromo; ~**horse** n caballo de carreras;

~**track** n pista; (for cars) autódromo

**racial** ['reɪʃl] adj racial

**racing** ['reɪsɪŋ] n carreras fpl; ~ **car** (BRIT) n coche m de carreras; ~ **driver** (BRIT) n corredor(a) m/f de coches

**racism** ['reɪsɪzəm] n racismo; **racist** [-sɪst] adj, n racista m/f

**rack** [ræk] n (also: luggage ~) rejilla; (shelf) estante m; (also: roof ~) baca, portaequipajes m inv; (dish ~) escurreplatos m inv; (clothes ~) percha ♦ vt atormentar; **to ~ one's brains** devanarse los sesos

**racket** ['rækɪt] n (for tennis) raqueta; (noise) ruido, estrépito; (swindle) estafa, timo

**racquet** ['rækɪt] n raqueta

**racy** ['reɪsɪ] adj picante, salado

**radar** ['reɪdɑː*] n radar m

**radiance** ['reɪdɪəns] n brillantez f, resplandor m

**radiant** ['reɪdɪənt] adj radiante (de felicidad)

**radiate** ['reɪdɪeɪt] vt (heat) radiar; (emotion) irradiar ♦ vi (lines) extenderse

**radiation** [reɪdɪ'eɪʃən] n radiación f

**radiator** ['reɪdɪeɪtə*] n radiador m

**radical** ['rædɪkl] adj radical

**radii** ['reɪdɪaɪ] npl of **radius**

**radio** ['reɪdɪəu] n radio f; **on the ~** por radio

**radio...** [reɪdɪəu] prefix: ~**active** adj radioactivo; **radiography** [-'ɔgrəfɪ] n radiografía; **radiology** [-'ɔlədʒɪ] n radiología; **radio station** n emisora; **radiotherapy** [-'θerəpɪ] n radioterapia

**radish** ['rædɪʃ] n rábano

**radius** ['reɪdɪəs] (pl **radii**) n radio

**RAF** n abbr = **Royal Air Force**

**raffle** ['ræfl] n rifa, sorteo

**raft** [rɑːft] n balsa; (also: life ~) balsa salvavidas

**rafter** ['rɑːftə*] n viga

**rag** [ræg] n (piece of cloth) trapo; (torn cloth) harapo; (pej: newspaper) periodicucho; (for charity) actividades estudiantiles benéficas; ~**s** npl (torn clothes) harapos mpl;

~**-and-bone man** (BRIT) n = ~**man**; ~ **doll** n muñeca de trapo

**rage** [reɪdʒ] n rabia, furor m ♦ vi (person) rabiar, estar furioso; (storm) bramar; **it's all the ~** (very fashionable) está muy de moda

**ragged** ['rægɪd] adj (edge) desigual, mellado; (appearance) andrajoso, harapiento

**ragman** ['rægmæn] n trapero

**raid** [reɪd] n (MIL) incursión f; (criminal) asalto; (by police) redada ♦ vt invadir, atacar; asaltar

**rail** [reɪl] n (on stair) barandilla, pasamanos m inv; (on bridge, balcony) pretil m; (of ship) barandilla; (pour towel ~) toallero; ~**s** npl (RAIL) vía; **by ~** por ferrocarril; ~**ing(s)** n(pl) vallado; ~**road** (US) n = ~**way**; ~**way** (BRIT) n ferrocarril m, vía férrea; ~**way line** (BRIT) n línea (de ferrocarril); ~**wayman** (BRIT) n ferroviario; ~**way station** (BRIT) n estación f de ferrocarril

**rain** [reɪn] n lluvia ♦ vi llover; **in the ~** bajo la lluvia; **it's ~ing** llueve, está lloviendo; ~**bow** n arco iris; ~**coat** n impermeable m; ~**drop** n gota de lluvia; ~**fall** n lluvia; ~**forest** n selvas fpl tropicales; ~**y** adj lluvioso

**raise** [reɪz] n aumento ♦ vt levantar; (increase) aumentar; (improve: morale) subir; (: standards) mejorar; (doubts) suscitar; (a question) plantear; (cattle, family) criar; (crop) cultivar; (army) reclutar; (loan) obtener; **to ~ one's voice** alzar la voz

**raisin** ['reɪzn] n pasa de Corinto

**rake** [reɪk] n (tool) rastrillo; (person) libertino ♦ vt (garden) rastrillar; (with machine gun) barrer

**rally** ['rælɪ] n (POL etc) reunión f, mitin m; (AUT) rallye m; (TENNIS) peloteo ♦ vt reunir ♦ vi recuperarse; ~ **round** vt fus agruparse ♦ vt dar apoyo a

**RAM** [ræm] n abbr (= random access memory) RAM f

**ram** [ræm] n carnero; (also: battering ~) ariete m ♦ vt (crash into) dar contra, chócar con; (push: fist etc) empujar con fuerza

**ramble** ['ræmbl] n caminata, excursión f en el campo ♦ vi (pej: also: ~ on) divagar; **~r** n excursionista m/f; (BOT) trepadera; **rambling** adj (speech) inconexo; (house) laberíntico; (BOT) trepador(a)

**ramp** [ræmp] n rampa; **on/off ~** (US: AUT) vía de acceso/salida

**rampage** [ræm'peidʒ] n: to be on the **~** desmandarse ♦ vi: they went rampaging through the town recorrieron la ciudad armando alboroto

**rampant** ['ræmpənt] adj (disease etc): to be **~** estar extendiéndose mucho

**rampart** ['ræmpɑːt] n (fortification) baluarte m

**ramshackle** ['ræmʃækl] adj destartalado

**ran** [ræn] pt of **run**

**ranch** [rɑːntʃ] n hacienda, estancia; **~er** n ganadero

**rancid** ['rænsid] adj rancio

**rancour** ['ræŋkə*] (US **rancor**) n rencor m

**random** ['rændəm] adj fortuito, sin orden; (COMPUT, MATH) aleatorio ♦ n: **at ~** al azar

**randy** ['rændi] (BRIT: inf) adj cachondo

**rang** [ræŋ] pt of **ring**

**range** [reindʒ] n (of mountains) cadena de montañas, cordillera; (of missile) alcance m; (of voice) registro; (series) serie f; (of products) surtido; (MIL: also: shooting **~**) campo de tiro; (also: kitchen **~**) fogón m ♦ vt (place) colocar; (arrange) arreglar ♦ vi: to **~ over** (extend) extenderse por; to **~ from ... to ...** oscilar entre ... y ...

**ranger** [reindʒə*] n guardabosques m inv

**rank** [ræŋk] n (row) fila; (MIL) rango; (status) categoría; (BRIT: also: taxi **~**) parada de taxis ♦ vi: to **~ among** figurar entre ♦ adj fétido, rancio; **the ~ and file** (fig) la base

**rankle** ['ræŋkl] vi doler

**ransack** ['rænsæk] vt (search) registrar; (plunder) saquear

**ransom** ['rænsəm] n rescate m; to hold to **~** (fig) hacer chantaje a

**rant** [rænt] vi divagar, desvariar

**rap** [ræp] vt golpear, dar un golpecito en ♦ n (music) rap m

**rape** [reip] n violación f; (BOT) colza ♦ vt violar; **~ (seed) oil** n aceite m de colza

**rapid** ['ræpid] adj rápido; **~ity** [rə'piditi] n rapidez f; **~ly** adv rápidamente; **~s** npl (GEO) rápidos mpl

**rapist** ['reipist] n violador m

**rapport** [ræ'pɔː*] n simpatía

**rapture** ['ræptʃə*] n éxtasis m; **rapturous** adj extático

**rare** [rɛə*] adj raro, poco común; (CULIN: steak) poco hecho

**rarely** ['rɛəli] adv pocas veces

**raring** ['rɛəriŋ] adj: to be **~** to go (inf) tener muchas ganas de empezar

**rarity** ['rɛəriti] n rareza, escasez f

**rascal** ['rɑːskl] n pillo, pícaro

**rash** [ræʃ] adj imprudente, precipitado ♦ n (MED) sarpullido, erupción f (cutánea); (of events) serie f

**rasher** ['ræʃə*] n lonja

**raspberry** ['rɑːzbəri] n frambuesa

**rasping** ['rɑːspiŋ] adj: a **~** noise un ruido áspero

**rat** [ræt] n rata

**rate** [reit] n (ratio) razón f; (price) precio; (: of hotel etc) tarifa; (of interest) tipo; (speed) velocidad f ♦ vt (value) tasar; (estimate) estimar; **~s** npl (BRIT: property tax) impuesto municipal; (fees) tarifa; to **~ sth/sb** as considerar algo/a uno como; **~able value** (BRIT) n valor m impuesto; **~payer** (BRIT) n contribuyente m/f

**rather** ['rɑːðə*] adv: it's **~** expensive es algo caro; (too much) es demasiado caro; (to some extent) más bien; **there's ~ a lot** hay bastante; **I would** or **I'd ~ go** preferiría ir; or **~** mejor dicho

**ratify** ['rætifai] vt ratificar

**rating** ['reɪtɪŋ] n tasación f; (score) índice m; (BRIT: NAUT: sailor) marinero; (of ship) clase f; ~s npl (RADIO, TV) niveles mpl de audiencia

**ratio** ['reɪʃɪəu] n razón f; in the ~ of 100 to 1 a razón de 100 a 1

**ration** ['ræʃən] n ración f ♦ vt racionar; ~s npl víveres mpl

**rational** ['ræʃənl] adj (solution, reasoning) lógico, razonable; (person) cuerdo, sensato; ~e [-'nɑ:l] n razón f fundamental; ~ize vt justificar

**rationing** ['ræʃnɪŋ] n racionamiento

**rat race** n lucha incesante por la supervivencia

**rattle** ['rætl] n golpeteo; (of train etc) traqueteo; (for baby) sonaja, sonajero ♦ vi castañear; (car, bus): to ~ along traquetear ♦ vt hacer sonar agitando; ~snake n serpiente f de cascabel

**raucous** ['rɔːkəs] adj estridente, ronco

**ravage** ['rævɪdʒ] vt hacer estragos en, destrozar; ~s npl estragos mpl

**rave** [reɪv] vi (in anger) encolerizarse; (with enthusiasm) entusiasmarse; (MED) delirar, desvariar

**raven** ['reɪvən] n cuervo

**ravenous** ['rævənəs] adj hambriento

**ravine** [rə'viːn] n barranco

**raving** ['reɪvɪŋ] adj: ~ lunatic loco/a de atar

**ravishing** ['rævɪʃɪŋ] adj encantador(a)

**raw** [rɔː] adj crudo; (not processed) bruto; (sore) vivo; (inexperienced) novato, inexperto; ~ deal (inf) n injusticia; ~ material n materia prima

**ray** [reɪ] n rayo; ~ of hope (rayo de) esperanza

**rayon** ['reɪən] n rayón m

**raze** [reɪz] vt arrasar

**razor** ['reɪzə*] n (open) navaja; (safety ~) máquina de afeitar; (electric ~) máquina (eléctrica) de afeitar; ~ blade n hoja de afeitar

**Rd** abbr = road

**re** [riː] prep con referencia a

**reach** [riːtʃ] n alcance m; (of river etc) extensión f entre dos recodos ♦ vt alcanzar, llegar a; (achieve) lograr ♦ vi extenderse; within ~ al alcance (de la mano); out of ~ fuera del alcance; ~ out vt (hand) tender ♦ vi: to ~ out for sth alargar or tender la mano para tomar algo

**react** [riː'ækt] vi reaccionar; ~ion [-'ækʃən] n reacción f

**reactor** [riː'æktə*] n (also: nuclear ~) reactor m (nuclear)

**read** [riːd, pt, pp red] (pt, pp read) vi leer ♦ vt leer; (understand) entender; (study) estudiar; ~ out vt leer en alta voz; ~able adj (writing) legible; (book) leíble; ~er n lector/a m/f; (book) libro de lecturas; (BRIT: at university) profesor(a) m/f adjunto/a; ~ership n (of paper etc) (número de) lectores mpl

**readily** ['redɪlɪ] adv (willingly) de buena gana; (easily) fácilmente; (quickly) en seguida

**readiness** ['redɪnɪs] n buena voluntad f; (preparedness) preparación f; in ~ (prepared) listo, preparado

**reading** ['riːdɪŋ] n lectura; (on instrument) indicación f

**readjust** [riːə'dʒʌst] vt reajustar ♦ vi (adapt): to ~ (to) reajustarse (a)

**ready** ['redɪ] adj listo, preparado; (willing) dispuesto; (available) disponible ♦ adv: ~-cooked listo para comer ♦ n: at the ~ (MIL) listo para tirar; to get ~ vi prepararse ♦ vt preparar; ~-made adj confeccionado; ~ money n dinero contante; ~reckoner n libro de cálculos hechos; ~-to-wear adj confeccionado

**real** [rɪəl] adj verdadero, auténtico; in ~ terms en términos reales; ~ estate n bienes mpl raíces; ~istic [-'lɪstɪk] adj realista

**reality** [riː'ælɪtɪ] n realidad f

**realization** [rɪələ'zeɪʃən] n comprensión f; (fulfilment, COMM) realización f

**realize** ['rɪəlaɪz] vt (understand) darse cuenta de; (fulfil, COMM: asset realizar

**really** ['riəli] adv realmente; (for emphasis) verdaderamente; (actually): what ~ happened lo que pasó en realidad; ~? ¿de veras?; ~! (annoyance) ¡vamos!, ¡por favor!

**realm** [relm] n reino; (fig) esfera

**realtor** ['riəltɔ:*] (US) n corredor(a) m/f de bienes raíces

**reap** [ri:p] vt segar; (fig) cosechar, recoger

**reappear** [ri:ə'piə*] vi reaparecer

**rear** [riə*] adj trasero ♦ n parte f trasera ♦ vt (cattle, family) criar ♦ vi (also: ~ up) (animal) encabritarse; **~guard** n retaguardia

**rearmament** [ri:'ɑ:məmənt] n rearme m

**rearrange** [ri:ə'reɪndʒ] vt ordenar or arreglar de nuevo

**rear-view** : ~ **mirror** n (AUT) (espejo) retrovisor m

**reason** ['ri:zn] n razón f ♦ vi: to ~ with sb tratar de que uno entre en razón; it stands to ~ that es lógico que; **~able** adj razonable; (sensible) sensato; **~ably** adv razonablemente; **~ed** adj (argument) razonado; **~ing** n razonamiento, argumentos mpl

**reassurance** [ri:ə'ʃuərəns] n consuelo

**reassure** [ri:ə'ʃuə*] vt tranquilizar, alentar; to ~ sb that tranquilizar a uno asegurando que; **reassuring** adj alentador(a)

**rebate** ['ri:beɪt] n (on tax etc) desgravación f

**rebel** [n 'rɛbl, vi ri'bɛl] n rebelde m/f ♦ vi rebelarse, sublevarse; **~lion** [ri'beljən] n rebelión f, sublevación f; **~lious** [ri'beljəs] adj rebelde; (child) revoltoso

**rebirth** ['ri:bə:θ] n renacimiento

**rebound** [vi ri'baund, n 'ri:baund] vi (ball) rebotar ♦ n rebote m; on the ~ (also fig) de rebote

**rebuff** [ri'bʌf] n desaire m, rechazo

**rebuild** [ri:'bɪld] (irreg) vt reconstruir

**rebuke** [ri'bju:k] n reprimenda ♦ vt

reprender

**rebut** [ri'bʌt] vt rebatir

**recall** [ri'kɔ:l] vt (remember) recordar; (ambassador etc) retirar ♦ n recuerdo; retirada

**recant** [ri'kænt] vi retractarse

**recap** ['ri:kæp] vt, vi recapitular

**recapitulate** [ri:kə'pɪtjuleɪt] vt, vi = recap

**recapture** [ri:'kæptʃə*] vt recobrar

**rec'd** abbr (= received) rbdo

**recede** [ri'si:d] vi (memory) ir borrándose; (hair) retroceder; **receding** adj (forehead, chin) huidizo; (hair): **to have a receding hairline** tener entradas

**receipt** [ri'si:t] n (document) recibo; (for parcel etc) acuse m de recibo; (act of receiving) recepción f; **~s** npl (COMM) ingresos mpl

**receive** [ri'si:v] vt recibir; (guest) acoger; (wound) sufrir; **~r** n (TEL) auricular m; (RADIO) receptor m; (of stolen goods) perista m/f; (COMM) administrador m jurídico

**recent** ['ri:snt] adj reciente; **~ly** adv recientemente; **~ly arrived** recién llegado

**receptacle** [ri'septikl] n receptáculo

**reception** [ri'sepʃən] n recepción f; (welcome) acogida; **~ desk** n recepción f; **~ist** n recepcionista m/f

**recess** [ri'ses] n (in room) hueco; (for bed) nicho; (secret place) escondrijo; (POL etc: holiday) clausura; **~ion** [-'seʃən] n recesión f

**recharge** [ri:'tʃɑ:dʒ] vt (battery) recargar

**recipe** ['resɪpɪ] n receta; (for disaster, success) fórmula

**recipient** [ri'sɪpɪənt] n recibidor(a) m/f; (of letter) destinatario(a)

**recital** [ri'saɪtl] n recital m

**recite** [ri'saɪt] vt (poem) recitar

**reckless** ['rɛkləs] adj temerario, imprudente; (driving, driver) peligroso; **~ly** adv imprudentemente; de modo peligroso

**reckon** ['rɛkən] vt calcular; (consider) considerar; (think): **I ~ that** ...

me parece que ...; ~ **on** vt fus contar con; ~l) en m cálculo

**reclaim** [rɪ'kleɪm] vt (land, waste) recuperar; (land: from sea) rescatar; (demand back) reclamar

**reclamation** [reklə'meɪʃən] n (of land) acondicionamiento de tierras

**recline** [rɪ'klaɪn] vi reclinarse; **reclining** adj (seat) reclinable

**recluse** [rɪ'kluːs] n recluso/a

**recognition** [rekəg'nɪʃən] n reconocimiento; **transformed beyond ~** irreconocible

**recognizable** ['rekəgnaɪzəbl] adj: ~ (by) reconocible (por)

**recognize** ['rekəgnaɪz] vt: to ~ (by/as) reconocer (por/como)

**recoil** [rɪ'kɔɪl, n 'riːkɔɪl] vi (person): to ~ **from doing sth** retraerse de hacer algo ♦ n (of gun) retroceso

**recollect** [rekə'lekt] vt recordar, acordarse de; **~ion** [-'lekʃən] n recuerdo

**recommend** [rekə'mend] vt recomendar

**reconcile** ['rekənsaɪl] vt (two people) reconciliar; (two facts) compaginar; **to ~ o.s. to sth** conformarse a algo

**recondition** [riːkən'dɪʃən] vt (machine) reacondicionar

**reconnaissance** [rɪ'kɔnɪsns] n (MIL) reconocimiento

**reconnoitre** [rekə'nɔɪtə*] (US **reconnoiter**) vt, vi (MIL) reconocer

**reconsider** [riːkən'sɪdə*] vt repensar

**reconstruct** [riːkən'strʌkt] vt reconstruir

**record** [n 'rekɔːd, vt rɪ'kɔːd] n (MUS) disco; (of meeting etc) acta; (register) registro, partida; (file) archivo; (also: criminal ~) antecedentes mpl; (written) expediente m; (SPORT, COMPUT) récord m ♦ vt registrar; (MUS: song etc) grabar; **in ~ time** en un tiempo récord; **off the ~** adj no oficial ♦ adv confidencialmente; ~ **card** n (in file) ficha; **~ed delivery** (BRIT) n (POST) entrega con acuse de recibo; **~er** n (MUS) flauta de pico; ~ **holder** n

(SPORT) actual poseedor(a) m/f del récord; **~ing** n (MUS) grabación f; ~ **player** n tocadiscos m inv

**recount** [rɪ'kaunt] vt contar

**re-count** [n 'riːkaunt, vb rɪ'kaunt] n (POL: of votes) segundo escrutinio ♦ vt volver a contar

**recoup** [rɪ'kuːp] vt: to ~ **one's losses** recuperar las pérdidas

**recourse** [rɪ'kɔːs] n: to **have ~ to** recurrir a

**recover** [rɪ'kʌvə*] vt recuperar ♦ vi (from illness, shock) recuperarse; **~y** n recuperación f

**recreation** [rekrɪ'eɪʃən] n recreo; **~al** adj de recreo

**recruit** [rɪ'kruːt] n recluta m/f ♦ vt reclutar; (staff) contratar (personal); **~ment** n reclutamiento

**rectangle** ['rektæŋgl] n rectángulo; **rectangular** [-'tæŋgjulə*] adj rectangular

**rectify** ['rektɪfaɪ] vt rectificar

**rector** ['rektə*] n (REL) párroco; **~y** n casa del párroco

**recuperate** [rɪ'kuːpəreɪt] vi reponerse, restablecerse

**recur** [rɪ'kɜː*] vi repetirse; (pain, illness) producirse de nuevo; **~rence** [rɪ'kʌrəns] n repetición f; **~rent** [rɪ'kʌrənt] adj repetido

**recycle** [riː'saɪkl] vt reciclar

**red** [red] n rojo ♦ adj rojo; (hair) pelirrojo; (wine) tinto; **to be in the ~** (account) estar en números rojos; (business) tener un saldo negativo; **to give sb the ~ carpet treatment** recibir a uno con todos los honores; **R~ Cross** n Cruz f Roja; **~currant** n grosella roja; **~den** vt enrojecer ♦ vi enrojecerse; **~dish** adj rojizo

**redeem** [rɪ'diːm] vt redimir; (promises) cumplir; (sth in pawn) desempeñar; (fig, also REL) rescatar; **~ing** adj: **~ing feature** rasgo bueno or favorable

**redeploy** [riːdɪ'plɔɪ] vt (resources) reorganizar

**red:** **~-haired** adj pelirrojo; **~-handed** adj: **to be caught ~-**

handed cogerse (SP) o pillarse (AM) con las manos en la masa; ~**head** n pelirrojo/a; ~ **herring** n (fig) pista falsa; ~-**hot** adj candente

**redirect** [ri:dai'rekt] vt (mail) reexpedir

**red light** n: to go through a ~ (AUT) pasar la luz roja; **red-light district** n barrio chino

**redo** [ri:'du:] (irreg) vt rehacer

**redolent** ['rɛdələnt] adj: ~ of (smell) con fragancia a; to be ~ of (fig) recordar

**redouble** [ri:'dʌbl] vt: to ~ one's efforts intensificar los esfuerzos

**redress** [ri'drɛs] n reparación f ♦ vt reparar

**Red Sea** n: the ~ el mar Rojo

**redskin** ['rɛdskin] n piel roja m/f

**red tape** n (fig) trámites mpl

**reduce** [ri'dju:s] vt reducir; to ~ sb to tears hacer llorar a uno; to be ~d to begging no quedarle a uno otro remedio que pedir limosna; "~ speed now" (AUT) "reduzca la velocidad"; at a ~d price (of goods) (a precio) rebajado; **reduction** [ri'dʌkʃən] n reducción f; (of price) rebaja; (discount) descuento; (smaller-scale copy) copia reducida

**redundancy** [ri'dʌndənsı] n (dismissal) despido; (unemployment) desempleo

**redundant** [ri'dʌndnt] adj (BRIT: worker) parado, sin trabajo; (detail, object) superfluo; to be made ~ quedar(se) sin trabajo

**reed** [ri:d] n (BOT) junco, caña; (MUS) lengüeta

**reef** [ri:f] n (at sea) arrecife m

**reek** [ri:k] vi: to ~ (of) apestar a

**reel** [ri:l] n carrete m, bobina; (of film) rollo; (dance) baile m escocés ♦ vt (also: ~ up) devanar; (also: ~ in) sacar ♦ vi (sway) tambalear(se)

**ref** [rɛf] (inf) n abbr = referee

**refectory** [ri'fɛktərı] n comedor m

**refer** [ri'fə:*] vt (send: patient) referir; (: matter) remitir ♦ vi: to ~ to (allude to) referirse a, aludir a;

(apply to) relacionarse con; (consult) consultar

**referee** [rɛfə'ri:] n árbitro; (BRIT: for job application): to be a ~ for sb proporcionar referencias a uno ♦ vt (match) arbitrar en

**reference** ['rɛfrəns] n referencia; (for job application: letter) carta de recomendación; with ~ to (COMM: in letter) me remito a; ~ **book** n libro de consulta; ~ **number** n número de referencia

**refill** [vt ri:'fıl, n 'ri:fıl] vt rellenar ♦ n repuesto, recambio

**refine** [ri'faın] vt refinar; ~**d** adj (person) fino; ~**ment** n cultura, educación f; (of system) refinamiento

**reflect** [ri'flekt] vt reflejar ♦ vi (think) reflexionar, pensar; it ~s badly/well on him le perjudica/le hace honor; ~**ion** [-'flekʃən] n (act) reflexión f; (image) reflejo; (criticism) crítica; on ~**ion** pensándolo bien; ~**or** n (AUT) captafaros m inv; (of light, heat) reflector m

**reflex** ['ri:flɛks] adj, n reflejo; ~**ive** [ri'flɛksıv] adj (LING) reflexivo

**reform** [ri'fɔ:m] n reforma ♦ vt reformar; the R~**ation** [rɛfə'meıʃən] n la Reforma; ~**atory** (US) n reformatorio

**refrain** [ri'freın] vi: to ~ from doing abstenerse de hacer ♦ n estribillo

**refresh** [ri'frɛʃ] vt refrescar; ~**er course** (BRIT) n curso de repaso; ~**ing** adj refrescante; ~**ments** npl refrescos mpl

**refrigerator** [ri'frıdʒəreıtə*] n nevera (SP), refrigeradora (AM)

**refuel** [ri:'fjuəl] vi repostar (combustible)

**refuge** ['rɛfju:dʒ] n refugio, asilo; to take ~ in refugiarse en

**refugee** [rɛfju'dʒi:] n refugiado/a

**refund** [n 'ri:fʌnd, vb ri'fʌnd] n reembolso ♦ vt devolver, reembolsar

**refurbish** [ri:'fə:bıʃ] vt restaurar, renovar

**refusal** [ri'fju:zəl] n negativa; to

have first ~ on tener la primera opción a

**refuse** [n 'refju:s, vb rɪ'fju:z] n basura ♦ vt rechazar; (invitation) declinar; (permission) denegar ♦ vi: to ~ to do sth negarse a hacer algo; (horse) rehusar; ~ collection n recolección f de basuras

**regain** [rɪ'geɪn] vt recobrar, recuperar

**regal** ['ri:gl] adj regio, real

**regalia** [rɪ'geɪlɪə] n insignias fpl

**regard** [rɪ'gɑːd] n mirada; (esteem) respeto; (attention) consideración f ♦ vt (consider) considerar; to give one's ~s to saludar de su parte; "with kindest ~s" "con muchos recuerdos"; ~ing, as ~s, with ~ to con respecto a, en cuanto a; ~less adv a pesar de todo; ~less of sin reparar en

**régime** [reɪ'ʒi:m] n régimen m

**regiment** ['redʒɪmənt] n regimiento; ~al [-'mentl] adj militar

**region** ['ri:dʒən] n región f; in the ~ of (fig) alrededor de; ~al adj regional

**register** ['redʒɪstə*] n registro ♦ vt registrar; (birth) declarar; (car) matricular; (letter) certificar; (subj: instrument) marcar, indicar ♦ vi (at hotel) registrarse; (as student) matricularse; (make impression) producir impresión; ~ed adj (letter, parcel) certificado; ~ed trademark n marca registrada

**registrar** ['redʒɪstrɑ:*] n secretario/a (del registro civil)

**registration** [redʒɪs'treɪʃən] n (act) declaración f; (AUT: also: ~ number) matrícula

**registry** ['redʒɪstrɪ] n registro; ~ office (BRIT) n registro; to get married in a ~ office casarse por lo civil

**regret** [rɪ'gret] n sentimiento, pesar m ♦ vt sentir, lamentar; ~fully adv con pesar; ~table adj lamentable

**regular** ['regjulə*] adj regular; (soldier) profesional; (usual) habitual;

(: doctor) de cabecera ♦ n (client etc) cliente/a m/f habitual; ~ity [-'lærɪtɪ] n regularidad f; ~ly adv con regularidad; (often) repetidas veces

**regulate** ['regjuleɪt] vt controlar; **regulation** [-'leɪʃən] n (rule) regla, reglamento

**rehearsal** [rɪ'hə:səl] n ensayo

**rehearse** [rɪ'hə:s] vt ensayar

**reign** [reɪn] n reinado; (fig) predominio ♦ vi reinar; (fig) imperar

**reimburse** [ri:ɪm'bə:s] vt reembolsar

**rein** [reɪn] n (for horse) rienda

**reindeer** ['reɪndɪə*] n inv reno

**reinforce** [ri:ɪn'fɔ:s] vt reforzar; ~d concrete n hormigón m armado; ~ment n (action) refuerzo; ~ments npl (MIL) refuerzos mpl

**reinstate** [ri:ɪn'steɪt] vt reintegrar; (tax, law) restaurar

**reiterate** [ri:'ɪtəreɪt] vt reiterar, repetir

**reject** [n 'ri:dʒekt, vb rɪ'dʒekt] n (thing) desecho ♦ vt rechazar; (suggestion) descartar; (coin) expulsar; ~ion [rɪ'dʒekʃən] n rechazo

**rejoice** [rɪ'dʒɔɪs] vi: to ~ at or over regocijarse or alegrarse de

**rejuvenate** [rɪ'dʒu:vəneɪt] vt rejuvenecer

**relapse** [rɪ'læps] n recaída

**relate** [rɪ'leɪt] vt (tell) contar, relatar; (connect) relacionar ♦ vi relacionarse; ~d adj afín; (person) emparentado; ~d to (subject) relacionado con; **relating to** referente a

**relation** [rɪ'leɪʃən] n (person) familiar m/f, pariente/a m/f; (link) relación f; ~s npl (relatives) familiares mpl; ~ship n relación f; (personal) relaciones fpl; (also: family ~ship) parentesco

**relative** [relətɪv] n pariente/a m/f, familiar m/f ♦ adj relativo; ~ly adv (comparatively) relativamente

**relax** [rɪ'læks] vi descansar; (unwind) relajarse ♦ vt (one's grip) soltar, aflojar; (control) relajar; (mind, person) descansar; ~ation [ri:læk'seɪʃən] n descanso; (of rule, *control*) relajamiento; (*entertainment*) diversión *f*; **~ed** *adj* relajado; (*tranquil*) tranquilo; **~ing** *adj* relajante

**relay** ['ri:leɪ] *n* (*race*) carrera de relevos ♦ *vt* (*RADIO, TV*) retransmitir

**release** [rɪ'li:s] *n* (*liberation*) liberación *f*; (*from prison*) puesta en libertad; (*of gas etc*) escape *m*; (*of film etc*) estreno; (*of record*) lanzamiento ♦ *vt* (*prisoner*) poner en libertad; (*gas*) despedir, arrojar; (*free*: *wreckage*) soltar; (*catch, spring etc*) desenganchar; (*film*) estrenar; (*book*) publicar; (*news*) difundir

**relegate** ['relǝgeɪt] *vt* relegar; (*BRIT: SPORT*): **to be ~d** to bajar a

**relent** [rɪ'lent] *vi* ablandarse; **~less** *adj* implacable

**relevant** ['relǝvǝnt] *adj* (*fact*) pertinente; **~ to** relacionado con

**reliability** [rɪlaɪǝ'bɪlɪtɪ] *n* fiabilidad *f*; seguridad *f*; veracidad *f*

**reliable** [rɪ'laɪǝbl] *adj* (*person, firm*) de confianza, de fiar; (*method, machine*) seguro; (*source*) fidedigno; **reliably** *adv*: **to be reliably informed that** ... saber de fuente fidedigna que ...

**reliance** [rɪ'laɪǝns] *n*: **~ (on)** dependencia (de)

**relic** ['relɪk] *n* (*REL*) reliquia *f*; (*of the past*) vestigio

**relief** [rɪ'li:f] *n* (*from pain, anxiety*) alivio; (*help, supplies*) socorro, ayuda; (*ART, GEO*) relieve *m*

**relieve** [rɪ'li:v] *vt* (*pain*) aliviar; (*bring help to*) ayudar, socorrer; (*take over from*) sustituir; (: *guard*) relevar; **to ~ sb of sth** quitar algo a uno; **to ~ o.s.** hacer sus necesidades

**religion** [rɪ'lɪdʒǝn] *n* religión *f*; **religious** *adj* religioso

**relinquish** [rɪ'lɪŋkwɪʃ] *vt* abandonar; (*plan, habit*) renunciar a

**relish** ['relɪʃ] *n* (*CULIN*) salsa; (*enjoyment*) entusiasmo *m* ♦ *vt* (*food etc*) saborear; (*enjoy*): **to ~ sth** hacerle mucha ilusión a uno algo

**relocate** [ri:lǝu'keɪt] *vt* cambiar de lugar, mudar ♦ *vi* mudarse

**reluctance** [rɪ'lʌktǝns] *n* renuncia; **reluctant** *adj* renuente; **reluctantly** *adv* de mala gana

**rely** [rɪ'laɪ]: **~ on** *vt fus* depender de; (*trust*) contar con

**remain** [rɪ'meɪn] *vi* (*survive*) quedar; (*be left*) sobrar; (*continue*) quedar(se), permanecer; **~der** *n* resto; **~ing** *adj* que queda(n); (*surviving*) restante(s); **~s** *npl* restos *mpl*

**remand** [rɪ'mɑ:nd] *n*: **on ~** detenido (bajo custodia) ♦ *vt*: **to be ~ed in custody** quedar detenido bajo custodia; **~ home** (*BRIT*) *n* reformatorio

**remark** [rɪ'mɑ:k] *n* comentario ♦ *vt* comentar; **~able** *adj* (*outstanding*) extraordinario

**remarry** [ri:'mærɪ] *vi* volver a casarse

**remedial** [rɪ'mi:dɪǝl] *adj* de recuperación

**remedy** ['remǝdɪ] *n* remedio ♦ *vt* remediar, curar

**remember** [rɪ'membǝ*] *vt* recordar, acordarse de; (*bear in mind*) tener presente; (*send greetings to*): **~ me to him** dale muchos recuerdos de mi parte; **remembrance** *n* recuerdo

**remind** [rɪ'maɪnd] *vt*: **to ~ sb to do sth** recordar a uno que haga algo; **to ~ sb of sth** (*of fact*) recordar algo a uno; **she ~s me of her mother** me recuerda a su madre; **~er** *n* notificación *f*; (*memento*) recuerdo

**reminisce** [remɪ'nɪs] *vi* recordar (viejas historias); **~nt** *adj*: **to be ~nt of sth** recordar algo

**remiss** [rɪ'mɪs] *adj* descuidado; **it was ~ of him** fue un descuido de su parte

**remission** [rɪ'mɪʃǝn] *n* remisión *f*; (*of prison sentence*) disminución *f* de pena; (*REL*) perdón *m*

**remit** [rɪ'mɪt] *vt* (*send: money*) remitir, enviar; **~tance** *n* remesa, envío

**remnant** ['remnǝnt] *n* resto; (*of cloth*) retal *m*; **~s** *npl* (*COMM*) restos *mpl* de serie

**remorse** [rɪ'mɔːs] n remordimiento mpl; ~**ful** adj arrepentido; ~**less** adj (fig) implacable, inexorable

**remote** [rɪ'məut] adj (distant) lejano; (person) distante; ~ **control** n telecontrol m; ~**ly** adv remotamente; (slightly) levemente

**remould** ['riːməuld] (BRIT) n (tyre) neumático or llanta (AM) recauchutado/a

**removable** [rɪ'muːvəbl] adj (detachable) separable

**removal** [rɪ'muːvəl] n (taking away) el quitar; (BRIT: from house) mudanza; (from office: dismissal) destitución f; (MED) extirpación f; ~ **van** (BRIT) n camión m de mudanzas

**remove** [rɪ'muːv] vt quitar; (employee) destituir; (name: from list) tachar, borrar; (doubt) disipar; (abuse) suprimir, acabar con; (MED) extirpar; ~**rs** (BRIT) npl (company) agencia de mudanzas

**Renaissance** [rɪ'neɪsɒ̃s] n: the ~ el Renacimiento

**render** ['rɛndə*] vt (thanks) dar; (aid) proporcionar, prestar; (make): to ~ **sth useless** hacer algo inútil; ~**ing** n (MUS etc) interpretación f

**rendez-vous** ['rɒndɪvuː] n cita

**renew** [rɪ'njuː] vt renovar; (resume) reanudar; (loan etc) prorrogar; ~**able** adj renovable; ~**al** n reanudación f; prórroga f

**renounce** [rɪ'nauns] vt renunciar a; (right, inheritance) renunciar

**renovate** ['rɛnəveɪt] vt renovar

**renown** [rɪ'naun] n renombre m; ~**ed** adj renombrado

**rent** [rɛnt] n (for house) arriendo, renta ♦ vt alquilar; ~**al** n (for television, car) alquiler m

**renunciation** [rɪnʌnsɪ'eɪʃən] n renuncia

**rep** [rɛp] n abbr = **representative**; **repertory**

**repair** [rɪ'pɛə*] n reparación f, compostura ♦ vt reparar, componer; (shoes) remendar; **in good/bad** ~ en

buen/mal estado; ~ **kit** n caja de herramientas

**repatriate** [riː'pætrɪeɪt] vt repatriar

**repay** [riː'peɪ] (irreg) vt (money) devolver, reembolsar; (person) pagar; (debt) liquidar; (sb's efforts) devolver, corresponder a; ~**ment** n reembolso, devolución f; (sum of money) recompensa

**repeal** [rɪ'piːl] n revocación f ♦ vt revocar

**repeat** [rɪ'piːt] n (RADIO, TV) reposición f ♦ vt repetir ♦ vi repetirse; ~**edly** adv repetidas veces

**repel** [rɪ'pɛl] vt (drive away) rechazar; (disgust) repugnar; ~**lent** adj repugnante ♦ n: **insect** ~**lent** crema (or loción f) anti-insectos

**repent** [rɪ'pɛnt] vi: **to** ~ (**of**) arrepentirse (de); ~**ance** n arrepentimiento

**repercussions** [riːpə'kʌʃənz] npl consecuencias fpl

**repertoire** ['rɛpətwɑː*] n repertorio

**repertory** ['rɛpətərɪ] n (also: ~ theatre) teatro de repertorio

**repetition** [rɛpɪ'tɪʃən] n repetición f

**repetitive** [rɪ'pɛtɪtɪv] adj repetitivo

**replace** [rɪ'pleɪs] vt (put back) devolver a su sitio; (take the place of) reemplazar, sustituir; ~**ment** n (act) reposición f; (thing) recambio; (person) suplente m/f

**replay** [rɪ'pleɪ] n (SPORT) desempate m; (of tape, film) repetición f

**replenish** [rɪ'plɛnɪʃ] vt rellenar; (stock etc) reponer

**replica** ['rɛplɪkə] n copia, reproducción f (exacta)

**reply** [rɪ'plaɪ] n respuesta, contestación f ♦ vi contestar, responder; ~ **coupon** n cupón-respuesta f

**report** [rɪ'pɔːt] n informe m; (PRESS etc) reportaje m; (BRIT: also: school ~) boletín m escolar; (of gun) estallido ♦ vt informar de; (PRESS etc) hacer un reportaje sobre; (notify: accident, culprit) denunciar ♦ vi (make a report) presentar un informe; (present o.s.): **to** ~ (**to sb**) presentarse (ante uno); ~ **card** n (US, Scottish) cartilla escolar; ~**edly** adv según se dice; ~**er** n periodista m/f

**repose** [rɪ'pəuz] n: **in** ~ (face, mouth) en reposo

**reprehensible** [reprɪ'hensɪbl] adj reprensible, censurable

**represent** [reprɪ'zent] vt representar; (COMM) ser agente de; (describe) to ~ sth as describir algo como; ~**ation** [-'teɪʃən] n representación f; ~**ations** npl (protest) quejas fpl; ~**ative** n representante m/f; (US: POL) diputado/a m/f ♦ adj representativo

**repress** [rɪ'pres] vt reprimir; ~**ion** [-'preʃən] n represión f

**reprieve** [rɪ'priːv] n (LAW) indulto; (fig) alivio

**reprimand** [repri'mɑːnd] n reprimenda ♦ vt reprender

**reprint** ['riːprɪnt] n reimpresión f ♦ vt reimprimir

**reprisals** [rɪ'praɪzlz] npl represalias fpl

**reproach** [rɪ'prəutʃ] n reproche m ♦ vt: to ~ sb for sth reprochar algo a uno; ~**ful** adj de reproche, de acusación

**reproduce** [riːprə'djuːs] vt reproducir ♦ vi reproducirse; **reproduction** [-'dʌkʃən] n reproducción f

**reproof** [rɪ'pruːf] n reproche m

**reprove** [rɪ'pruːv] vt: to ~ sb for sth reprochar algo a uno

**reptile** ['reptaɪl] n reptil m

**republic** [rɪ'pʌblɪk] n república f; ~**an** adj, n republicano/a m/f

**repudiate** [rɪ'pjuːdɪeɪt] vt rechazar; (violence etc) repudiar

**repulse** [rɪ'pʌls] vt rechazar; **repulsive** adj repulsivo

**reputable** ['repjutəbl] adj (make etc) de renombre

**reputation** [repju'teɪʃən] n reputación f

**reputed** [rɪ'pjuːtɪd] adj supuesto; ~**ly** adv según dicen or se dice

**request** [rɪ'kwest] n petición f; (for-mal) solicitud f ♦ vt: to ~ sth of or from sb solicitar algo a uno; ~ **stop** n (BRIT) parada discrecional

**require** [rɪ'kwaɪə*] vt (need: subj: person) necesitar, tener necesidad de; (: thing, situation) exigir; (want) pedir; to ~ sb to do sth pedir a uno que haga algo; ~**ment** n requisito; (need) necesidad f

**requisite** ['rekwɪzɪt] n requisito ♦ adj necesario

**requisition** [rekwɪ'zɪʃən] n: ~ (for) solicitud f (de) ♦ vt (MIL) requisar

**resale** ['riːseɪl] n reventa

**rescind** [rɪ'sɪnd] vt (law) abrogar; (contract, order etc) anular

**rescue** ['reskjuː] n rescate m ♦ vt rescatar; ~ **party** n expedición f de salvamento; ~**r** n salvador(a) m/f

**research** [rɪ'səːtʃ] n investigaciones fpl ♦ vt investigar; ~**er** n investigador(a) m/f

**resemblance** [rɪ'zembləns] n parecido

**resemble** [rɪ'zembl] vt parecerse a

**resent** [rɪ'zent] vt tomar a mal; ~**ful** adj resentido; ~**ment** n resentimiento

**reservation** [rezə'veɪʃən] n reserva

**reserve** [rɪ'zəːv] n reserva; (SPORT) suplente m/f ♦ vt (seats etc) reservar; ~**s** npl (MIL) reserva; **in** ~ de reserva; ~**d** adj reservado

**reservoir** ['rezəvwɑː*] n embalse m

**reshuffle** [riː'ʃʌfl] n: **Cabinet** ~ (POL) remodelación f del Gabinete

**reside** [rɪ'zaɪd] vi residir, vivir

**residence** ['rezɪdəns] n (formal: home) domicilio; (length of stay) permanencia; ~ **permit** n (BRIT) permiso de permanencia

**resident** ['rezɪdənt] n (of area) vecino/a; (in hotel) huésped(a) m/f ♦ adj (population) permanente; (doctor) residente; ~**ial** [-'denʃəl] adj residencial

**residue** ['rezɪdjuː] n resto

**resign** [rɪ'zaɪn] vt renunciar a ♦ vi dimitir; to ~ o.s. to (situation) resignarse a; ~**ation** [rezɪg'neɪʃən] n dimisión f; (state of mind) resignación f; **~ed** adj resignado

**resilient** [rɪ'zɪlɪənt] adj (material) elástico; (person) resistente

**resin** ['rɛzɪn] n resina

**resist** [rɪ'zɪst] vt resistir, oponerse a; **~ance** n resistencia

**resolute** ['rɛzəluːt] adj resuelto; (refusal) tajante

**resolution** [rɛzə'luːʃən] n (gen) resolución f

**resolve** [rɪ'zɔlv] n resolución f ♦ vt resolver ♦ vi: **to ~ to do** resolver hacer; **~d** adj resuelto

**resort** [rɪ'zɔːt] n (town) centro turístico; (recourse) recurso ♦ vi: **to ~** recurrir a; **in the last ~** como último recurso

**resound** [rɪ'zaund] vi: **to ~ (with)** resonar (con); **~ing** adj sonoro; (fig) clamoroso

**resource** [rɪ'sɔːs] n recurso; **~s** npl recursos mpl; **~ful** adj despabilado, ingenioso

**respect** [rɪs'pɛkt] n respeto ♦ vt respetar; **~s** npl recuerdos mpl, saludos mpl; **with ~ to** con respecto a; **in this ~** en cuanto a eso; **~able** adj respetable; (large: amount) apreciable; (passable) tolerable; **~ful** adj respetuoso

**respective** [rɪs'pɛktɪv] adj respectivo; **~ly** adv respectivamente

**respite** ['rɛspaɪt] n respiro

**resplendent** [rɪs'plɛndənt] adj resplandeciente

**respond** [rɪs'pɔnd] vi responder; (react) reaccionar; **response** [-'pɔns] n respuesta; reacción f

**responsibility** [rɪspɔnsɪ'bɪlɪtɪ] n responsabilidad f

**responsible** [rɪs'pɔnsɪbl] adj (character) serio, formal; (job) de confianza; (liable): **~ (for)** responsable (de)

**responsive** [rɪs'pɔnsɪv] adj sensible

**rest** [rɛst] n descanso, reposo; (MUS, pause) pausa, silencio; (support) apoyo; (remainder) resto ♦ vi descansar; (be supported): **to ~ on** descansar sobre ♦ vt (lean): **to ~ sth on/against** apoyar algo en o sobre/contra; **the ~ of them** (people, objects) los demás; **it ~s with him to ...** depende de él el que ....

**restaurant** ['rɛstərɔŋ] n restaurante m; **~ car** (BRIT) n (RAIL) cochecomedor m

**restful** ['rɛstful] adj descansado, tranquilo

**rest home** n residencia para jubilados

**restive** ['rɛstɪv] adj inquieto; (horse) rebelón(ona)

**restless** ['rɛstlɪs] adj inquieto

**restoration** [rɛstə'reɪʃən] n restauración f; devolución f

**restore** [rɪ'stɔː] vt (building) restaurar; (sth stolen) devolver; (health) restablecer; (to power) volver a poner a

**restrain** [rɪs'treɪn] vt (feeling) contener, refrenar; (person): **to ~ (from doing)** disuadir (de hacer); **~ed** adj reservado; **~t** n (restriction) restricción f; (moderation) moderación f; (of manner) reserva

**restrict** [rɪs'trɪkt] vt restringir, limitar; **~ion** [-kʃən] n restricción f, limitación f; **~ive** adj restrictivo

**rest room** n (US) n aseos mpl

**result** [rɪ'zʌlt] n resultado ♦ vi: **to ~** in terminar en, tener por resultado; **as a ~ of** a consecuencia de

**resume** [rɪ'zjuːm] vt reanudar ♦ vi comenzar de nuevo

**résumé** ['reɪzjuːmeɪ] n resumen m; (US) currículum m

**resumption** [rɪ'zʌmpʃən] n reanudación f

**resurgence** [rɪ'səːdʒəns] n resurgimiento

**resurrection** [rɛzə'rɛkʃən] n resurrección f

**resuscitate** [rɪ'sʌsɪteɪt] vt (MED) resucitar

**retail** ['riːteɪl] adj, adv al por menor; **~er** n detallista m/f ~ **price** n precio de venta al público

**retain** [rɪ'teɪn] vt (keep) retener, conservar; ~**er** n (*fee*) anticipo

**retaliate** [rɪ'tælɪeɪt] vi: to ~ (**against**) tomar represalias (contra); **retaliation** [-'eɪʃən] n represalias fpl

**retarded** [rɪ'tɑːdɪd] adj retrasado

**retch** [retʃ] vi dársele a uno arcadas

**retentive** [rɪ'tentɪv] adj (*memory*) retentivo

**reticent** ['retɪsnt] adj reservado

**retire** [rɪ'taɪə*] vi (*give up work*) jubilarse; (*withdraw*) retirarse; (*go to bed*) acostarse; ~**d** adj (*person*) jubilado; ~**ment** n (*giving up work: state*) retiro; (: *act*) jubilación f; **retiring** adj (*leaving*) saliente; (*shy*) retraído

**retort** [rɪ'tɔːt] vi contestar

**retrace** [riː'treɪs] vt: to ~ **one's steps** volver sobre sus pasos, desandar lo andado

**retract** [rɪ'trækt] vt (*statement*) retirar; (*claws*) retraer; (*undercarriage, aerial*) replegar

**retrain** [riː'treɪn] vt reciclar; ~**ing** n readaptación f profesional

**retread** ['riːtred] n neumático (SP) or llanta (AM) recauchutado/a

**retreat** [rɪ'triːt] n (*place*) retiro; (MIL) retirada ♦ vi retirarse

**retribution** [retrɪ'bjuːʃən] n desquite m

**retrieval** [rɪ'triːvəl] n recuperación f

**retrieve** [rɪ'triːv] vt recobrar; (*situation, honour*) salvar; (COMPUT) recuperar; (*error*) reparar; ~**r** n perro cobrador

**retrograde** ['retrəgreɪd] adj retrógrado

**retrospect** ['retrəspekt] n: **in** ~ retrospectivamente; ~**ive** [-'spektɪv] adj retrospectivo; (*law*) retroactivo

**return** [rɪ'tɜːn] n (*going or coming back*) vuelta, regreso; (*of sth stolen etc*) devolución f; (FINANCE: *from land, shares*) ganancia, ingresos mpl ♦ cpd (*journey*) de regreso; (BRIT: *ticket*) de ida y vuelta; (*match*) de vuelta ♦ vi (*person etc: come or go back*) volver, regresar; (*symptoms*

*etc*) reaparecer; (*regain*): to ~ **to** recuperar ♦ vt devolver; (*favour, love etc*) corresponder a; (*verdict*) pronunciar; (POL: *candidate*) elegir; ~**s** npl (COMM) ingresos mpl; **in** ~ (**for**) a cambio (de); **by** ~ **of post** a vuelta de correo; **many happy** ~**s (of the day)** ! ¡feliz cumpleaños!

**reunion** [riː'juːnɪən] n (*of family*) reunión f; (*of two people, school*) reencuentro

**reunite** [riːju'naɪt] vt reunir; (*reconcile*) reconciliar

**rev** [rev] (AUT) n abbr (= revolution) revolución f ♦ vt (*also*: ~ **up**) acelerar

**revamp** [riː'væmp] vt (*company etc*) reorganizar

**reveal** [rɪ'viːl] vt revelar; ~**ing** adj revelador/a

**reveille** [rɪ'vælɪ] n (MIL) diana

**revel** ['revl] vi: to ~ **in sth/in doing sth** gozar de algo/con hacer algo

**revelry** ['revlrɪ] n jarana, juerga

**revenge** [rɪ'vendʒ] n venganza; to **take** ~ **on** vengarse de

**revenue** ['revənjuː] n ingresos mpl, rentas fpl

**reverberate** [rɪ'vɜːbəreɪt] vi (*sound*) resonar, retumbar; (*fig: shock*) repercutir; **reverberation** [-'reɪʃən] n retumbo, eco; repercusión f

**revere** [rɪ'vɪə*] vt venerar; ~**nce** ['revərəns] n reverencia

**Reverend** ['revərənd] adj (*in titles*): the ~ **John Smith** (*Anglican*) el Reverendo John Smith; (*Catholic*) el Padre John Smith; (*Protestant*) el Pastor John Smith

**reversal** [rɪ'vɜːsl] n (*of order*) inversión f; (*of direction, policy*) cambio; (*of decision*) revocación f

**reverse** [rɪ'vɜːs] n (*opposite*) contrario; (*back: of cloth*) revés m; (: *of coin*) reverso; (: *of paper*) dorso; (AUT: *also*: ~ **gear**) marcha atrás; (*setback*) revés m ♦ adj (*order*) inverso; (*direction*) contrario; (*process*) opuesto ♦ vt (*decision, AUT*) dar marcha atrás a; (*position, func-*

*tion*) invertir ♦ *vi* (BRIT: AUT) dar marcha atrás; **~charge call** (BRIT) *n* llamada a cobro revertido; **reversing lights** (BRIT) *npl* (AUT) luces *fpl* de retroceso

**revert** [rɪ'vɜːt] *vi*: **to ~ to** volver a

**review** [rɪ'vjuː] *n* (*magazine, MIL*) revista; (*of book, film*) reseña *n* (US: *examination*) repaso, examen *m* ♦ *vt* repasar, examinar; (*MIL*) pasar revista a; (*book, film*) reseñar; **~er** *n* crítico/a

**revile** [rɪ'vaɪl] *vt* injuriar, vilipendiar

**revise** [rɪ'vaɪz] *vt* (*manuscript*) corregir; (*opinion*) modificar; (*price, procedure*) revisar ♦ *vi* (*study*) repasar; **revision** [rɪ'vɪʒən] *n* corrección *f*; modificación *f*; (*for exam*) repaso

**revitalize** [riː'vaɪtəlaɪz] *vt* revivificar

**revival** [rɪ'vaɪvəl] *n* (*recovery*) reanimación *f*; (*of interest*) renacimiento; (*THEATRE*) reestreno; (*of faith*) despertar *m*

**revive** [rɪ'vaɪv] *vt* resucitar; (*custom*) restablecer; (*hope*) despertar; (*play*) reestrenar ♦ *vi* (*person*) volver en sí; (*business*) reactivarse

**revolt** [rɪ'vəʊlt] *n* rebelión *f* ♦ *vi* rebelarse, sublevarse ♦ *vt* dar asco a, repugnar; **~ing** *adj* asqueroso, repugnante

**revolution** [revə'luːʃən] *n* revolución *f*; **~ary** *adj*, *n* revolucionario/a *m/f*; **~ize** *vt* revolucionar

**revolve** [rɪ'vɒlv] *vi* dar vueltas, girar; **(life, discussion): to ~ (a)round** girar en torno a

**revolver** [rɪ'vɒlvə*] *n* revólver *m*

**revolving** [rɪ'vɒlvɪŋ] *adj* (*chair, door etc*) giratorio

**revue** [rɪ'vjuː] *n* (*THEATRE*) revista

**revulsion** [rɪ'vʌlʃən] *n* asco, repugnancia

**reward** [rɪ'wɔːd] *n* premio, recompensa ♦ *vt*: **to ~ (for)** recompensar or premiar (por); **~ing** *adj* (*fig*) valioso

**rewind** [riː'waɪnd] *vt* rebobinar

**rewire** [riː'waɪə*] *vt* (*house*) renovar la instalación eléctrica de

**rewrite** [riː'raɪt] (*irreg*) *vt* reescribir

**rhapsody** ['ræpsədɪ] *n* (MUS) rapsodia

**rhetorical** [rɪ'tɒrɪkl] *adj* retórico

**rheumatism** ['ruːmətɪzəm] *n* reumatismo, reúma *m*

**Rhine** [raɪn] *n*: **the ~** el (río) Rin

**rhinoceros** [raɪ'nɒsərəs] *n* rinoceronte *m*

**rhododendron** [rəʊdə'dendrn] *n* rododendro

**Rhone** [rəʊn] *n*: **the ~** el (río) Ródano

**rhubarb** ['ruːbɑːb] *n* ruibarbo

**rhyme** [raɪm] *n* rima; (*verse*) poesía

**rhythm** ['rɪðm] *n* ritmo

**rib** [rɪb] *n* (ANAT) costilla ♦ *vt* (*mock*) tomar el pelo a

**ribbon** ['rɪbən] *n* cinta; **in ~s** (*torn*) hecho trizas

**rice** [raɪs] *n* arroz *m*; **~ pudding** *n* arroz *m* con leche

**rich** [rɪtʃ] *adj* rico; (*soil*) fértil; (*food*) pesado; (: *sweet*) empalagoso; (*abundant*): **in** (*minerals etc*) rico en; **the ~** *npl* los ricos; **~es** *npl* riqueza; **~ly** *adv* ricamente; (*deserved, earned*) bien

**rickets** ['rɪkɪts] *n* raquitismo

**rickety** ['rɪkɪtɪ] *adj* tambaleante

**rickshaw** ['rɪkʃɔː] *n* carro de culi

**ricochet** ['rɪkəʃeɪ] *vi* rebotar

**rid** [rɪd] (*pt, pp* **rid**) *vt*: **to ~ sb of sth** librar a uno de algo; **to get ~ of** deshacerse or desembarazarse de

**ridden** ['rɪdn] *pp of* **ride**

**riddle** ['rɪdl] *n* (*puzzle*) acertijo; (*mystery*) enigma *n*, misterio ♦ *vt*: **to be ~d with** ser lleno *or* plagado de

**ride** [raɪd] (*pt* **rode**, *pp* **ridden**) *n* paseo; (*distance covered*) viaje *m*, recorrido ♦ *vi* (*as sport*) montar; (*go somewhere: on horse, bicycle*) dar un paseo, pasearse; (*travel: on bicycle, motorcycle, bus*) viajar ♦ *vt* (*a horse*) montar a; (*a bicycle, motorcycle*) andar en; (*distance*) recorrer; **to take sb for a ~** (*fig*) engañar a uno; **~r** *n* (*on horse*) jinete/a *m/f*; (*on bicycle*) ciclista *m/f*; (*on motorcycle*) motociclista *m/f*

**ridge** [rɪdʒ] *n* (*of hill*) cresta *f*; (*of roof*) caballete *m*; (*wrinkle*) arruga *f*

**ridicule** [ˈrɪdɪkjuːl] *n* irrisión *f*, burla *f* ♦ *vt* poner en ridículo, burlarse de; **ridiculous** [-ˈdɪkjuləs] *adj* ridículo

**riding** [ˈraɪdɪŋ] *n* equitación *f*; **I like ~** me gusta montar a caballo; **~ school** *n* escuela de equitación

**rife** [raɪf] *adj*: **to be ~** ser muy común; **to be ~ with** abundar en

**riffraff** [ˈrɪfræf] *n* gentuza *f*

**rifle** [ˈraɪfl] *n* rifle *m*, fusil *m* ♦ *vt* saquear; **~ through** *vt* (*papers*) registrar; **~ range** *n* campo de tiro; (*at fair*) tiro al blanco

**rift** [rɪft] *n* (*in clouds*) claro; (*fig: disagreement*) desavenencia

**rig** [rɪg] *n* (*also: oil ~: at sea*) plataforma petrolera ♦ *vt* (*election etc*) amañar; **~ out** *vt* (*BRIT*) disfrazar; **~ up** *vt* improvisar; **~ging** *n* (*NAUT*) aparejo

**right** [raɪt] *adj* (*correct*) correcto, exacto; (*suitable*) indicado, debido; (*proper*) apropiado; (*just*) justo; (*morally good*) bueno; (*not left*) derecho ♦ *n* bueno; (*title, claim*) derecho; (*not left*) derecha ♦ *adv* bien, correctamente; (*not left*) a la derecha; (*exactly*): **~ now** ahora mismo ♦ *vt* enderezar; (*correct*) corregir ♦ *excl* ¡bueno!, ¡está bien!; **to be ~** (*person*) tener razón; (*answer*) ser correcto; (*of clock*): **is that the ~ time?** ¿es esa la hora buena?; **by ~s** en justicia; **on the ~** a la derecha; **to be in the ~** tener razón; **~ away** en seguida; **~ in the middle** exactamente en el centro; **~ angle** *n* ángulo recto; **~eous** [ˈraɪtʃəs] *adj* justado, honrado; (*anger*) justificado; **~ful** *adj* legítimo; **~handed** *adj* diestro; **~-hand man** *n* brazo derecho; **~-hand side** *n* derecha; **~ly** *adv* correctamente, debidamente; (*with reason*) con razón; **~ of way** *n* (*on path etc*) derecho de paso; (*AUT*) prioridad *f*; **~-wing** *adj*

(*POL*) derechista

**rigid** [ˈrɪdʒɪd] *adj* rígido; (*person, ideas*) inflexible

**rigmarole** [ˈrɪgmərəʊl] *n* galimatías *m inv*

**rigorous** [ˈrɪgərəs] *adj* riguroso

**rigour** [ˈrɪgəʳ] (*US* **rigor**) *n* rigor *m*, severidad *f*

**rile** [raɪl] *vt* irritar

**rim** [rɪm] *n* borde *m*; (*of spectacles*) aro; (*of wheel*) llanta

**rind** [raɪnd] *n* (*of bacon*) corteza; (*of lemon etc*) cáscara; (*of cheese*) costra

**ring** [rɪŋ] (*pt* **rang**, *pp* **rung**) *n* (*of metal*) aro; (*on finger*) anillo; (*of people*) corro; (*of objects*) círculo; (*gang*) banda; (*for boxing*) cuadrilátero; (*of circus*) pista; (*bull ~*) ruedo, plaza; (*sound of bell*) toque *m* ♦ *vi* (*on telephone*) llamar por teléfono; (*bell*) repicar; (*doorbell, phone*) sonar; (*also: ~ out*) sonar; (*ears*) zumbar ♦ *vt* (*BRIT: TEL*) llamar, telefonear; (*bell etc*) hacer sonar; (*doorbell*) tocar; **to give sb a ~** (*BRIT: TEL*) llamar or telefonear a alguien; **~ back** (*BRIT*) *vt, vi* (*TEL*) devolver la llamada; **~ off** (*BRIT*) *vi* (*TEL*) colgar, cortar la comunicación; **~ up** (*BRIT*) *vt* (*TEL*) llamar, telefonear; **~ing** *n* (*of bell*) repique *m*; (*of phone*) el sonar; (*in ears*) zumbido; **~ing tone** *n* (*TEL*) tono de llamada; **~leader** *n* (*of gang*) cabecilla *m*; **~lets** [ˈrɪŋlɪts] *npl* rizos *mpl*, bucles *mpl*; **~ road** (*BRIT*) *n* carretera periférica or de circunvalación

**rink** [rɪŋk] *n* (*also: ice ~*) pista de hielo

**rinse** [rɪns] *n* aclarado; (*dye*) tinte *m* ♦ *vt* aclarar; (*mouth*) enjuagar

**riot** [ˈraɪət] *n* motín *m*, disturbio ♦ *vi* amotinarse; **to run ~** desmandarse; **~ous** *adj* alborotado; (*party*) bullicioso

**rip** [rɪp] *n* rasgón *m*, rasgadura *f* ♦ *vt* rasgar, desgarrar ♦ *vi* rasgarse, desgarrarse; **~cord** *n* cabo de desgarre

**ripe** [raɪp] *adj* maduro; **~n** *vt* madurar; (*cheese*) curar ♦ *vi* madurar

**ripple** ['rɪpl] *n* onda, rizo; (*sound*) murmullo ♦ *vi* rizarse

**rise** [raɪz] (*pt* **rose**, *pp* **risen**) *n* (*slope*) cuesta, pendiente *f*; (*hill*) altura; (BRIT: *in wages*) aumento; (*in prices, temperature*) subida; (*fig: to power etc*) ascenso ♦ *vi* subir; (*waters*) crecer; (*sun, moon*) salir; (*person: from bed etc*) levantarse; (*also*: ~ **up**: *rebel*) sublevarse; (*in rank*) ascender; **to give** ~ **to** dar lugar or origen a; **to** ~ **to the occasion** ponerse a la altura de las circunstancias; **risen** ['rɪzn] *pp* of **rise**; **rising** *adj* (*increasing*: *number*) creciente; (: *prices*) en aumento or alza; (*tide*) creciente; (*sun, moon*) naciente

**risk** [rɪsk] *n* riesgo, peligro ♦ *vt* arriesgar; (*run the* ~ *of*) exponerse a; **to take** or **run the** ~ **of doing** correr el riesgo de hacer; **at** ~ **in** peligro; **at one's own** ~ bajo su propia responsabilidad; ~**y** *adj* arriesgado, peligroso

**risqué** ['riːskeɪ] *adj* verde

**rissole** ['rɪsəul] *n* croqueta

**rite** [raɪt] *n* rito; **last** ~**s** exequias *fpl*

**ritual** ['rɪtjuəl] *adj* ritual ♦ *n* ritual *m*, rito

**rival** ['raɪvl] *n* rival *m/f*; (*in business*) competidor(a) *m/f* ♦ *adj* rival, opuesto ♦ *vt* competir con; ~**ry** *n* competencia

**river** ['rɪvə*] *n* río ♦ *cpd* (*port*) de río; (*traffic*) fluvial; **up/down** ~ río arriba/abajo; ~**bank** *n* orilla (del río); ~**bed** *n* lecho, cauce *m*

**rivet** ['rɪvɪt] *n* roblón *m*, remache *m* ♦ *vt* (*fig*) captar

**Riviera** [rɪvɪ'eərə] *n*: **the (French)** ~ la Costa Azul (francesa)

**road** [rəud] *n* camino; (*motorway etc*) carretera; (*in town*) calle *f* ♦ *cpd* (*accident*) de tráfico; **major/minor** ~ carretera principal/secundaria; ~**block** *n* barricada; ~**hog** *n* loco/a del volante; ~ **map** *n* mapa *m* de carreteras; ~ **safety** *n* seguridad *f* vial; ~**side** *n* borde *m*

(del camino); ~**sign** *n* señal *f* de tráfico; ~ **user** *n* usuario/a de la vía pública; ~**way** *n* calzada; ~**works** *npl* obras *fpl*; ~**worthy** *adj* (*car*) en buen estado para circular

**roam** [rəum] *vi* vagar

**roar** [rɔː*] *n* rugido; (*of vehicle, storm*) estruendo; (*of laughter*) carcajada ♦ *vi* rugir; hacer estruendo; **to** ~ **with laughter** reírse a carcajadas; **to do a** ~**ing trade** hacer buen negocio

**roast** [rəust] *n* carne *f* asada, asado ♦ *vt* asar; (*coffee*) tostar; ~ **beef** *n* rosbif *m*

**rob** [rɔb] *vt* robar; **to** ~ **sb of sth** robar algo a uno; (*fig: deprive*) quitar algo a uno; ~**ber** *n* ladrón/ona *m/f*; ~**bery** *n* robo

**robe** [rəub] *n* (*for ceremony etc*) toga; (*also*: *bath* ~, US) albornoz *m*

**robin** ['rɔbɪn] *n* petirrojo

**robot** ['rəubɔt] *n* robot *m*

**robust** [rəu'bʌst] *adj* robusto, fuerte

**rock** [rɔk] *n* (*boulder*) peña, peñasco; (US: *small stone*) piedrecita; (BRIT: *sweet*) ≈ piruli ♦ *vt* (*swing gently: cradle*) balancear, mecer; (: *child*) arrullar; (*shake*) sacudir ♦ *vi* mecerse, balancearse; sacudirse; **on the** ~**s** (*drink*) con hielo; (*marriage etc*) en ruinas; ~ **and roll** *n* rocanrol *m*; ~**-bottom** *n* (*fig*) punto más bajo; ~**ery** *n* cuadro alpino

**rocket** ['rɔkɪt] *n* cohete *m*

**rocking** ['rɔkɪŋ]: ~ **chair** *n* mecedora; ~ **horse** *n* caballo de balancín

**rocky** ['rɔkɪ] *adj* rocoso

**rod** [rɔd] *n* vara, varilla; (*also*: *fishing* ~) caña

**rode** [rəud] *pt* of **ride**

**rodent** ['rəudnt] *n* roedor *m*

**roe** [rəu] *n* (*species*: *also*: ~ *deer*) corzo; (*of fish*): **hard/soft** ~ hueva/lecha

**rogue** [rəug] *n* pícaro, pillo

**role** [rəul] *n* papel *m*

**roll** [rəul] *n* rollo; (*of bank notes*) fajo; (*also*: *bread* ~) panecillo; (*register, list*) lista, nómina; (*sound of* *drums etc)* redoble *m* ♦ *vt* hacer rodar; *(also: ~ up: string)* enrollar; *(: sleeves)* arremangar; *(cigarette)* liar; *(also: ~ out: pastry)* aplanar; *(flatten: road, lawn)* apisonar ♦ *vi* rodar; *(drum)* redoblar; *(ship)* balancearse; ~ **about** *or* **around** *vi (person)* revolcarse; *(object)* rodar (por); ~ **by** *vi (time)* pasar; ~ **in** *vi (mail, cash)* entrar a raudales; ~ **over** *vi* dar una vuelta; ~ **up** *vi (inf: arrive)* aparecer ♦ *vt (carpet)* arrollar; ~ **call** *n*: **to take a** ~ **call** pasar lista; ~**er** *n* rodillo *m*; *(wheel)* rueda; *(for road)* apisonadora *f*; *(for hair)* rulo; ~**er coaster** *n* montaña rusa; ~**er skates** *npl* patines *mpl* de rueda

**rolling** ['rəʊlɪŋ] *adj (landscape)* ondulado; ~ **pin** *n* rodillo (de cocina); ~ **stock** *n (RAIL)* material *m* rodante

**ROM** [rɔm] *n abbr (COMPUT: = read only memory)* ROM *f*

**Roman** ['rəʊmən] *adj* romano/a; ~ **Catholic** *adj, n* católico/a *m/f* (romano/a)

**romance** [rə'mæns] *n (love affair)* amor *m*; *(charm)* lo romántico; *(novel)* novela de amor

**Romania** [ruː'meɪnɪə] *n* = **Rumania**

**Roman numeral** *n* número romano

**romantic** [rə'mæntɪk] *adj* romántico

**Rome** [rəʊm] *n* Roma

**romp** [rɔmp] *n* retozo, juego ♦ *vi (also: ~ about)* jugar, brincar

**rompers** ['rɔmpəz] *npl* pelele *m*

**roof** [ruːf] *(pl* ~**s)** *n (gen)* techo; *(of house)* techo, tejado ♦ *vt* techar, poner techo a; **the** ~ **of the mouth** el paladar; ~**ing** *n* techumbre *f*; ~ **rack** *n (AUT)* baca, portaequipajes *m inv*

**rook** [rʊk] *n (bird)* graja; *(CHESS)* torre *f*

**room** [ruːm] *n* cuarto, habitación *f*, pieza *(esp AM)*; *(also: bed~)* dormitorio; *(in school etc)* sala; *(space, scope)* sitio, cabida; ~**s** *npl (lodging)* alojamiento; "~**s to let**", "~**s for rent**" *(US)* "se alquilan cuartos";

**single/double** ~ habitación individual/doble *or* para dos personas; ~**ing house** *(US)* *n* pensión *f*; ~**mate** *n* compañero/a de cuarto; ~ **service** *n* servicio de habitaciones; ~**y** *adj* espacioso; *(garment)* amplio

**roost** [ruːst] *vi* pasar la noche

**rooster** ['ruːstə*] *n* gallo

**root** [ruːt] *n* raíz *f* ♦ *vi* arraigarse; ~ **about** *vi (fig)* buscar y rebuscar; ~ **for** *vt fus (support)* apoyar a; ~ **out** *vt* desarraigar

**rope** [rəʊp] *n* cuerda; *(NAUT)* cable *m* ♦ *vt (tie)* atar *or* amarrar con *(una)* cuerda; *(climbers: also: ~ to-gether)* encordarse; *(an area: also: ~ off)* acordonar; **to know the** ~**s** *(fig)* conocer los trucos *(del oficio)*; ~ **in** *vt (fig)*: **to** ~ **sb in** persuadir a uno a tomar parte; ~ **ladder** *n* escala de cuerda

**rosary** ['rəʊzərɪ] *n* rosario

**rose** [rəʊz] *pt of* **rise** ♦ *n* rosa; *(shrub)* rosal *m*; *(on watering can)* roseta

**rosé** ['rəʊzeɪ] *n* vino rosado

**rosebud** ['rəʊzbʌd] *n* capullo de rosa

**rosebush** ['rəʊzbʊʃ] *n* rosal *m*

**rosemary** ['rəʊzmərɪ] *n* romero

**rosette** [rəʊ'zɛt] *n* escarapela

**roster** ['rɔstə*] *n*: **duty** ~ lista de deberes

**rostrum** ['rɔstrəm] *n* tribuna

**rosy** ['rəʊzɪ] *adj* rosado, sonrosado; **a** ~ **future** un futuro prometedor

**rot** [rɔt] *n* podredumbre *f*; *(fig: pej)* tonterías *fpl* ♦ *vt* pudrir ♦ *vi* pudrirse

**rota** ['rəʊtə] *n (sistema m de)* turnos *mpl*

**rotary** ['rəʊtərɪ] *adj* rotativo

**rotate** [rəʊ'teɪt] *vt (revolve)* hacer girar, dar vueltas a; *(jobs)* alternar ♦ *vi* girar, dar vueltas; **rotating** *adj* rotativo; **rotation** [-'teɪʃən] *n* rotación *f*

**rote** [rəʊt] *n*: **by** ~ maquinalmente, de memoria

**rotten** ['rɔtn] *adj* podrido; *(dishonest)* corrompido; *(inf: bad)* pocho;

# rotund · 234 · rpm

to feel ~ (ill) sentirse fatal

**rotund** [rəʊˈtʌnd] adj regordete

**rouble** [ˈruːbl] (US **ruble**) n rublo

**rouge** [ruːʒ] n colorete m

**rough** [rʌf] adj (skin, surface) áspero; (terrain) quebrado; (road) desigual; (voice) bronco; (person, manner) tosco, grosero; (weather) borrascoso; (treatment) brutal; (sea) picado; (town, area) peligroso; (cloth) basto; (plan) preliminar; (guess) aproximado ♦ n (GOLF): in the ~ en las hierbas altas; ~ to it vivir sin comodidades; to sleep ~ (BRIT) pasar la noche al raso; ~age n fibra(s) f(pl); ~-and-ready adj improvisado; ~ copy n borrador m; ~ draft n = ~ copy; ~en vt (a surface) poner áspero; ~ly adv (handle) torpemente; (make) toscamente; (speak) groseramente; (approximately) aproximadamente; ~ness n (of surface) aspereza; (of person) rudeza

**roulette** [ruːˈlet] n ruleta

**Roumania** [ruːˈmeɪnɪə] n = **Rumania**

**round** [raʊnd] adj redondo ♦ n círculo; (BRIT: of toast) rebanada; (of policeman) ronda; (of milkman) recorrido; (of doctor) visitas fpl; (game: of cards, in competition) partida; (of ammunition) cartucho; (BOXING) asalto; (of talks) ronda ♦ vt (corner) doblar ♦ prep alrededor de ♦ prep (surrounding): ~ his neck/the table en su cuello/alrededor de la mesa; (in a circular movement): to move ~ the room/sail ~ the world dar una vuelta a la habitación/circunnavigar el mundo; (in various directions): to move ~ a room/house moverse por toda la habitación/casa; (approximately): all ~ all sos por todos lados; the long way ~ por el camino menos directo; all the year ~ durante todo el año; it's just ~ the corner (fig) está a la vuelta de la esquina; ~ the clock adv las 24 horas;

to go ~ to sb's (house) ir a casa de uno; to go ~ the back pasar por atrás; to go ~ a house visitar una casa; enough to go ~ bastante (para todos); a ~ of applause una salva de aplausos; a ~ of drinks/sandwiches una ronda de bebidas/bocadillos; ~ off vt (speech etc) acabar, poner término a; ~ up vt (cattle) acorralar; (people) reunir; (price) redondear; ~about (BRIT) n (AUT) isleta; (at fair) tiovivo ♦ adj (route, means) indirecto; ~ers n (game) juego similar al béisbol; ~ly adv (fig) rotundamente; ~shouldered adj cargado de espaldas; ~ trip n viaje m de ida y vuelta; ~up n rodeo; (of criminals) redada; (of news) resumen m

**rouse** [raʊz] vt (wake up) despertar; (stir up) suscitar; **rousing** (cheer, welcome) caluroso

**rout** [raʊt] n (MIL) derrota ♦ vt derrotar

**route** [ruːt] n ruta, camino; (of bus) recorrido; (of shipping) derrota; ~ **map** (BRIT) (for journey) mapa m de carreteras

**routine** [ruːˈtiːn] adj rutinario ♦ n rutina; (THEATRE) número

**rove** [rəʊv] vt vagar or errar por

**row**[1] [rəʊ] n (line) fila, hilera; (KNITTING) pasada ♦ vi (in boat) remar ♦ vt conducir remando; 4 **days in a ~** 4 días seguidos

**row**[2] [raʊ] n (racket) escándalo; (dispute) bronca, pelea; (scolding) regaño ♦ vi pelearse

**rowboat** [ˈrəʊbəʊt] (US) n bote m de remos

**rowdy** [ˈraʊdɪ] adj (person: noisy) ruidoso; (occasion) alborotado

**rowing** [ˈrəʊɪŋ] n remo; ~ **boat** (BRIT) n bote m de remos

**royal** [ˈrɔɪəl] adj real; R~ **Air Force** n Fuerzas fpl Aéreas Británicas; ~ty n (~ persons) familia real; (payment to author) derechos mpl de autor

**rpm** abbr (= revs per minute) r.p.m.

**R.S.V.P.** *abbr* (= *répondez s'il vous plaît*) SRC

**Rt.Hon.** *abbr* (BRIT: = *Right Honourable*) título honorífico de diputado

**rub** [rʌb] *vt* frotar; (*scrub*) restregar ♦ *n*: to give sth a ~ frotar algo; to ~ sb up *or* ~ sb (US) the wrong way entrarle uno por mal ojo; ~ off *vi* borrarse; ~ off on *vt fus* influir en; ~ out *vt* borrar

**rubber** ['rʌbə*] *n* caucho, goma; (BRIT: *eraser*) goma de borrar; ~ **band** *n* goma, gomita; ~ **plant** *n* ficus *m*; ~y *adj* elástico; (*meat*) gomoso

**rubbish** ['rʌbɪʃ] *n* basura; (*waste*) desperdicios *mpl*; (*fig: pej*) tonterías *fpl*; (*junk*) pacotilla; ~ **bin** (BRIT) *n* cubo (SP) *or* bote *m* (AM) de la basura; ~ **dump** *n* vertedero, basurero

**rubble** ['rʌbl] *n* escombros *mpl*

**ruble** ['ru:bl] (US) *n* = **rouble**

**ruby** ['ru:bɪ] *n* rubí *m*

**rucksack** ['rʌksæk] *n* mochila

**rudder** ['rʌdə*] *n* timón *m*

**ruddy** ['rʌdɪ] *adj* (*face*) rubicundo; (*inf: damned*) condenado

**rude** [ru:d] *adj* (*impolite: person*) mal educado; (*: word, manners*) grosero; (*crude*) crudo; (*indecent*) indecente; ~**ness** *n* descortesía

**rueful** ['ru:ful] *adj* arrepentido

**ruffian** ['rʌfɪən] *n* matón *m*, criminal *m*

**ruffle** ['rʌfl] *vt* (*hair*) despeinar; (*clothes*) arrugar; to get ~d (*fig: person*) alterarse

**rug** [rʌg] *n* alfombra; (BRIT: *blanket*) manta

**rugby** ['rʌgbɪ] *n* (*also:* ~ *football*) rugby *m*

**rugged** ['rʌgɪd] *adj* (*landscape*) accidentado; (*features*) robusto

**rugger** ['rʌgə*] (BRIT: *inf*) rugby *m*

**ruin** ['ru:ɪn] *n* ruina ♦ *vt* arruinar; (*spoil*) estropear; ~s *npl* ruinas *fpl*, restos *mpl*; ~**ous** *adj* desastroso

**rule** [ru:l] *n* (*norm*) norma, costum-

bre *f*; (*regulation, ruler*) regla; (*government*) dominio ♦ *vt* (*country, person*) gobernar ♦ *vi* gobernar; (LAW) fallar; as a ~ por regla general; ~ **out** *vt* excluir; ~**d** *adj* (*paper*) rayado; ~**r** *n* (*sovereign*) soberano; (*for measuring*) regla; **ruling** *adj* (*party*) gobernante; (*class*) dirigente ♦ *n* (LAW) fallo, decisión *f*

**rum** [rʌm] *n* ron *m*

**Rumania** [ru:'meɪnɪə] *n* Rumania; ~**n** *adj* rumano/a ♦ *n* rumano/a *m/f*; (LING) rumano

**rumble** ['rʌmbl] *n* (*noise*) ruido sordo ♦ *vi* retumbar, hacer un ruido sordo; (*stomach, pipe*) sonar

**rummage** ['rʌmɪdʒ] *vi* (*search*) hurgar

**rumour** ['ru:mə*] (US **rumor**) *n* rumor *m* ♦ *vt*: it is ~ed that ... se rumorea que ....

**rump** [rʌmp] *n* (*of animal*) ancas *fpl*, grupa; ~ **steak** *n* filete *m* de lomo

**rumpus** ['rʌmpəs] *n* lío, jaleo

**run** [rʌn] (*pt* **ran**, *pp* **run**) *n* (*fast pace*): at a ~ corriendo; (SPORT, *in tights*) carrera; (*outing*) paseo, excursión *f*; (*distance travelled*) trayecto; (*series*) serie *f*; (THEATRE) temporada; (SKI) pista ♦ *vt* correr; (*operate: business*) dirigir; (*: competition, course*) organizar; (*: hotel, house*) administrar, llevar; (COMPUT) ejecutar; (*pass: hand*) pasar; (PRESS: *feature*) publicar ♦ *vi* correr; (*work: machine*) funcionar, marchar; (*bus, train: operate*) circular, ir; (*: travel*) ir; (*continue: play*) seguir; (*: contract*) ser válido; (*flow: river*) fluir; (*colours, washing*) desteñirse; (*in election*) ser candidato; there was a ~ on (*meat, tickets*) hubo mucha demanda de; **in the long** ~ a la larga; **on the** ~ en fuga; I'll ~ you to the station te llevaré a la estación (en coche); to ~ a risk correr un riesgo; to ~ a bath llenar la bañera; ~ **about** *or* **around** *vi* (*children*) correr por todos lados; ~ **across** *vt fus* (*find*) dar *or* topar con; **~ away** vi huir; **~ down** vt (production) ir reduciendo; (factory) ir restringiendo la producción en; (subj: car) atropellar; (criticize) criticar; **to be ~ down** (person: tired) estar debilitado; **~ in** (BRIT) vt (car) rodar; **~ into** vt fus (meet: person, trouble) tropezar con; (collide with) chocar con; **~ off** vt (water) dejar correr; (copies) sacar ♦ vi huir corriendo; **~ out** vi (person) salir corriendo; (liquid) irse; (lease) caducar, vencer; (money etc) acabarse; **~ out of** vt fus quedar sin; **~ over** vt (AUT) atropellar ♦ vt fus (revise) repasar; **~ through** vt fus (instructions) repasar; **~ up** vt (debt) contraer; **to ~ up against** (difficulties) tropezar con; **~away** adj (horse) desbocado; (truck) sin frenos; (child) escapado de casa

**rung** [rʌŋ] pp of **ring** ♦ n (of ladder) escalón m, peldaño

**runner** ['rʌnə*] n (in race: person) corredor(a) m/f; (: horse) caballo; (on sledge) patín m; **~ bean** (BRIT) n judía verde; **~-up** n subcampeón/ona m/f

**running** ['rʌnɪŋ] n (sport) atletismo; (business) administración f ♦ adj (water, costs) corriente; (commentary) continuo; **to be in/out of the ~ for** sth tener/no tener posibilidades de ganar algo; **6 days ~** 6 días seguidos; **~ commentary** n (TV, RADIO) comentario en directo; (on guided tour etc) comentario detallado; **~ costs** npl gastos mpl corrientes

**runny** ['rʌnɪ] adj fluido; (nose, eyes) gastante

**run-of-the-mill** adj común y corriente

**runt** [rʌnt] n (also pej) redrojo, enano

**run-up** n: **~ to** (election etc) período previo a

**runway** ['rʌnweɪ] n (AVIAT) pista de aterrizaje

**rupee** [ru:'pi:] n rupia

**rupture** ['rʌptʃə*] n (MED) hernia

**rural** ['ruərl] adj rural

**ruse** [ru:z] n ardid m

**rush** [rʌʃ] n ímpetu m; (hurry) prisa; (COMM) demanda repentina; (current) corriente f fuerte; (of feeling) torrente; (BOT) junco ♦ vt apresurar; (work) hacer de prisa ♦ vi correr, precipitarse; **~ hour** n horas fpl punta

**rusk** [rʌsk] n bizcocho tostado

**Russia** ['rʌʃə] n Rusia; **~n** adj ruso/a ♦ n ruso/a m/f; (LING) ruso

**rust** [rʌst] n herrumbre f, moho ♦ vi oxidarse

**rustic** ['rʌstɪk] adj rústico

**rustle** ['rʌsl] vi susurrar ♦ vt (paper) hacer crujir; (US: cattle) hurtar, robar

**rustproof** ['rʌstpru:f] adj inoxidable

**rusty** ['rʌstɪ] adj oxidado

**rut** [rʌt] n surco; (ZOOL) celo; **to be in a ~** ser esclavo de la rutina

**ruthless** ['ru:θlɪs] adj despiadado

**rye** [raɪ] n centeno; **~ bread** n pan de centeno

# S

**Sabbath** ['sæbəθ] n domingo; (Jewish) sábado

**sabotage** ['sæbətɑ:ʒ] n sabotaje m ♦ vt sabotear

**saccharin(e)** ['sækərɪn] n sacarina

**sachet** ['sæʃeɪ] n sobrecito

**sack** [sæk] n (bag) saco, costal m ♦ vt (dismiss) despedir; (plunder) saquear; **to get the ~** ser despedido; **~ing** n (dismissal); (material) arpillera

**sacred** ['seɪkrɪd] adj sagrado, santo

**sacrifice** ['sækrɪfaɪs] n sacrificio ♦ vt sacrificar

**sacrilege** ['sækrɪlɪdʒ] n sacrilegio

**sad** [sæd] adj (unhappy) triste; (deplorable) lamentable

**saddle** ['sædl] n silla (de montar); (of cycle) sillín m ♦ vt (horse) ensillar; **to be ~d with sth** (inf) quedar cargado con algo; **~bag** n alforja

**sadistic** [sə'dɪstɪk] adj sádico

**sadly** ['sædlɪ] adv lamentablemente; **to be ~ lacking** in estar por desgracia carente de

**sadness** ['sædnɪs] n tristeza

**s.a.e.** abbr (= stamped addressed envelope) sobre con las propias señas de uno y con sello

**safari** [sə'fɑ:rɪ] n safari m

**safe** [seɪf] adj (out of danger) fuera de peligro; (not dangerous, sure) seguro; (unharmed) ileso ♦ n caja de caudales, caja fuerte; **~ and sound** sano y salvo; (just) **to be on the ~ side** para mayor seguridad; **~conduct** n salvoconducto; **~deposit** n (vault) cámara acorazada; (box) caja de seguridad; **~guard** n protección f, garantía f ♦ vt proteger, defender; **~keeping** n custodia; **~ly** adv seguramente, con seguridad; **to arrive ~ly** llegar bien; **~ sex** n sexo seguro

**safety** ['seɪftɪ] n seguridad f; **~ belt** n cinturón m (de seguridad); **~ pin** n imperdible m (SP), seguro (AM); **~ valve** n válvula de seguridad

**saffron** ['sæfrən] n azafrán m

**sag** [sæg] vi aflojarse

**sage** [seɪdʒ] n (herb) salvia; (man) sabio

**Sagittarius** [sædʒɪ'tɛərɪəs] n Sagitario

**Sahara** [sə'hɑ:rə] n: **the ~ (Desert)** el (desierto del) Sáhara

**said** [sed] pt, pp of **say**

**sail** [seɪl] n (on boat) vela; (trip): **to go for a ~** dar un paseo en barco ♦ vt (boat) gobernar ♦ vi (travel: ship) navegar; (SPORT) hacer vela; (begin voyage) salir; **they ~ed into Copenhagen** arribaron a Copenhague; **~ through** vt fus (exam) aprobar sin ningún problema; **~boat** (US) n velero, barco de vela; **~ing** n (SPORT) vela; **to go ~ing** hacer vela; **~ing boat** n barco de vela; **~ing ship** n velero; **~or** n marinero, marino

**saint** [seɪnt] n santo; **~ly** adj santo

**sake** [seɪk] n: **for the ~ of** por

**salad** ['sæləd] n ensalada; **~ bowl** n ensaladera; **~ cream** (BRIT) n (especie f de) mayonesa; **~ dressing** n aliño

**salary** ['sælərɪ] n sueldo

**sale** [seɪl] n venta; (at reduced prices) liquidación f, saldo; (auction) subasta; **~s** npl (total amount sold) ventas fpl, facturación f; **"for ~"** "se vende"; **on ~** en venta; **on ~ or return** (goods) venta por reposición; **~room** n sala de subastas; **~s assistant** (US **~s clerk**) n dependiente/a m/f; **salesman/woman** n (in shop) dependiente/a m/f; (representative) viajante m/f

**salient** ['seɪlɪənt] adj sobresaliente

**saliva** [sə'laɪvə] n saliva

**sallow** ['sæləʊ] adj cetrino

**salmon** ['sæmən] n inv salmón m

**salon** ['sælɔn] n (hairdressing ~) peluquería; (beauty ~) salón m de belleza

**saloon** [sə'lu:n] n (US) bar m, taberna; (BRIT: AUT) (coche m de) turismo; (ship's lounge) cámara, salón m

**salt** [sɔlt] n sal f ♦ vt salar; (put ~ on) poner sal en; **~ away** (inf) vt (money) ahorrar; **~ cellar** n salero; **~water** adj de agua salada; **~y** adj salado

**salutary** ['sæljʊtərɪ] adj saludable

**salute** [sə'lu:t] n saludo; (of guns) salva ♦ vt saludar

**salvage** ['sælvɪdʒ] n (saving) salvamento, recuperación f; (things saved) objetos mpl salvados ♦ vt salvar

**salvation** [sæl'veɪʃən] n salvación f; **S~ Army** n Ejército de Salvación

**salvo** ['sælvəʊ] n (MIL) salva

**same** [seɪm] adj mismo ♦ pron: **the ~** el/la mismo/la, los/las mismos/as; **the ~ book** as el mismo libro que; **at the ~ time** (at the ~ moment) al mismo tiempo; (yet) sin embargo; **all** or **just the ~** sin embargo, aun así; **to do the ~** (as sb) hacer lo mismo (que uno); **the ~ to you!** ¡igualmente!

**sample** ['sɑːmpl] n muestra ♦ vt (food) probar; (wine) catar

**sanatorium** [sænə'tɔːrɪəm] (pl **sanatoria**) (BRIT) n sanatorio

**sanctimonious** [sæŋktɪ'məʊnɪəs] adj mojigato

**sanction** ['sæŋkʃən] n aprobación f ♦ vt sancionar; aprobar; ~s npl (POL) sanciones fpl

**sanctity** ['sæŋktɪtɪ] n santidad f; (inviolability) inviolabilidad f

**sanctuary** ['sæŋktjʊərɪ] n santuario; (refuge) asilo, refugio; (for wildlife) reserva

**sand** [sænd] n arena; (beach) playa ♦ vt (also: ~ down) lijar

**sandal** ['sændl] n sandalia

**sand:** ~**box** (US) n = ~**pit**; ~**castle** n castillo de arena; ~ **dune** n duna; ~**paper** n papel m de lija; ~**pit** n (for children) cajón m de arena; ~**stone** n piedra arenisca

**sandwich** ['sændwɪtʃ] n bocadillo (SP), sandwich m, emparedado (AM) ♦ vt intercalar; ~**ed between** apretujado entre; **cheese/ham** ~ **sandwich** de queso/jamón; ~ **course** (BRIT) n curso de medio tiempo

**sandy** ['sændɪ] adj arenoso; (colour) rojizo

**sane** [seɪn] adj cuerdo; (sensible) sensato

**sang** [sæŋ] pt of sing

**sanitarium** [sænɪ'tɛərɪəm] (US) n = **sanatorium**

**sanitary** ['sænɪtərɪ] adj sanitario; (clean) higiénico; ~ **towel** (US ~ **napkin**) n paño higiénico, compresa

**sanitation** [sænɪ'teɪʃən] n (in house) servicios mpl higiénicos; (in town) servicio de desinfección; ~ **department** (US) n departamento de limpieza y recogida de basuras

**sanity** ['sænɪtɪ] n cordura; (of judgment) sensatez f

**sank** [sæŋk] pt of sink

**Santa Claus** [sæntə'klɔːz] n San Nicolás, Papá Noel

**sap** [sæp] n (of plants) savia ♦ vt (strength) minar, agotar

**sapling** ['sæplɪŋ] n árbol nuevo or joven

**sapphire** ['sæfaɪə*] n zafiro

**sarcasm** ['sɑːkæzm] n sarcasmo

**sardine** [sɑː'diːn] n sardina

**Sardinia** [sɑː'dɪnɪə] n Cerdeña

**sash** [sæʃ] n faja

**sat** [sæt] pt, pp of sit

**Satan** ['seɪtn] n Satanás m

**satchel** ['sætʃl] n (child's) cartera (SP), mochila (AM)

**satellite** ['sætəlaɪt] n satélite m; ~ **dish** n antena de televisión por satélite; ~ **television** n televisión f vía satélite

**satin** ['sætɪn] n raso ♦ adj de raso

**satire** ['sætaɪə*] n sátira

**satisfaction** [sætɪs'fækʃən] n satisfacción f

**satisfactory** [sætɪs'fæktərɪ] adj satisfactorio

**satisfy** ['sætɪsfaɪ] vt satisfacer; (convince) convencer; ~**ing** adj satisfactorio

**saturate** ['sætʃəreɪt] vt: **to** ~ **(with)** empapar or saturar (de)

**Saturday** ['sætədɪ] n sábado

**sauce** [sɔːs] n salsa; (sweet) crema; jarabe m; ~**pan** n cacerola, olla

**saucer** ['sɔːsə*] n platillo

**saucy** ['sɔːsɪ] adj fresco, descarado

**Saudi** ['saʊdɪ]: ~ **Arabia** n Arabia Saudí or Saudita; ~ **(Arabian)** adj, n saudí m/f, saudita m/f

**sauna** ['sɔːnə] n sauna

**saunter** ['sɔːntə*] vi: **to** ~ **in/out** entrar/salir sin prisa

**sausage** ['sɔsɪdʒ] n salchicha; ~ **roll** n empanadita de salchicha

**sauté** ['səʊteɪ] adj salteado

**savage** ['sævɪdʒ] adj (cruel, fierce) feroz, furioso; (primitive) salvaje ♦ n salvaje m/f ♦ vt (attack) embestir; ~**ry** n salvajismo, salvajería

**save** [seɪv] vt (rescue) salvar, rescatar; (money, time) ahorrar; (put by, keep: seat) guardar; (COMPUT) salvar (y guardar); (avoid: trouble) evitar; (SPORT) parar ♦ vi (also: ~ up) ahorrar ♦ n (SPORT) parada ♦

*prep* salvo, excepto

**saving** ['seɪvɪŋ] *n* (*on price etc*) economía ♦ *adj*: **the ~ grace** of el único mérito de; **~s** *npl* ahorros *mpl*; **~s account** *n* cuenta de ahorros; **~s bank** *n* caja de ahorros

**saviour** ['seɪvjə*] (*US* **savior**) *n* salvador(a) *m/f*

**savour** ['seɪvə*] (*US* **savor**) *vt* saborear; **~y** *adj* sabroso; (*dish: not sweet*) salado

**saw** [sɔ:] (*pt* **sawed**, *pp* **sawed** or **sawn**) *pt of* **see** ♦ *n* (*tool*) sierra ♦ *vt* serrar; **~dust** *n* serrín *m*; **~mill** *n* aserradero *m*; **~n-off shotgun** *n* escopeta de cañones recortados

**saxophone** ['sæksəfəun] *n* saxófono *m*

**say** [seɪ] (*pt, pp* **said**) *n*: **to have one's ~** expresar su opinión; **to have a ~ or some ~** in sth tener voz or tener que ver en algo ♦ *vt* decir; **to ~ yes/no** decir que sí/no; **could you ~ that again?** ¿podría repetir eso?; **that is to ~** es decir; **that goes without ~ing** ni que decir tiene; **~ing** *n* dicho, refrán *m*

**scab** [skæb] *n* costra; (*pej*) esquirol *m*

**scaffold** ['skæfəuld] *n* cadalso *m*; **~ing** *n* andamio, andamiaje *m*

**scald** [skɔ:ld] *n* escaldadura ♦ *vt* escaldar

**scale** [skeɪl] *n* (*gen, MUS*) escala; (*of fish*) escama; (*of salaries, fees etc*) escalafón *m* ♦ *vt* (*mountain*) escalar; (*tree*) trepar; **~s** *npl* (*for weighing: small*) balanza; (: *large*) báscula; **on a large ~** en gran escala; **~ of charges** tarifa, lista de precios; **~ down** *vt* reducir a escala

**scallop** ['skɔləp] *n* (*ZOOL*) venera; (*SEWING*) festón *m*

**scalp** [skælp] *n* cabellera ♦ *vt* escalpar

**scalpel** ['skælpl] *n* bisturí *m*

**scamper** ['skæmpə*] *vi*: **to ~ away or off** irse corriendo

**scampi** ['skæmpɪ] *npl* gambas *fpl*

**scan** [skæn] *vt* (*examine*) escudriñar; (*glance at quickly*) dar un vistazo a;

(*TV, RADAR*) explorar, registrar ♦ *n* (*MED*): **to have a ~** pasar por el escáner

**scandal** ['skændl] *n* escándalo; (*gossip*) chismes *mpl*

**Scandinavia** [skændɪ'neɪvɪə] *n* Escandinavia; **~n** *adj, n* escandinavo/a *m/f*

**scant** [skænt] *adj* escaso; **~y** *adj* (*meal*) insuficiente; (*clothes*) ligero

**scapegoat** ['skeɪpgəut] *n* cabeza de turco, chivo expiatorio

**scar** [skɑ:] *n* cicatriz *f*; (*fig*) señal *f* ♦ *vt* dejar señales en

**scarce** [skɛəs] *adj* escaso; **to make o.s. ~** (*inf*) esfumarse; **~ly** *adv* apenas; **scarcity** *n* escasez *f*

**scare** [skɛə*] *n* susto, sobresalto; (*panic*) pánico ♦ *vt* asustar, espantar; **to ~ sb stiff** dar a uno un susto de muerte; **bomb ~** amenaza de bomba; **~ off** or **away** *vt* ahuyentar; **~crow** *n* espantapájaros *m inv*; **~d** *adj*: **to be ~d** estar asustado

**scarf** [skɑ:f] (*pl* **~s** or **scarves**) *n* (*long*) bufanda; (*square*) pañuelo

**scarlet** ['skɑ:lɪt] *adj* escarlata; **~ fever** *n* escarlatina

**scarves** [skɑ:vz] *npl of* **scarf**

**scary** ['skɛərɪ] (*inf*) *adj* espeluznante

**scathing** ['skeɪðɪŋ] *adj* mordaz

**scatter** ['skætə*] *vt* (*spread*) esparcir, desparramar; (*put to flight*) dispersar ♦ *vi* desparramarse; dispersarse; **~brained** *adj* ligero de cascos

**scavenger** ['skævɪndʒə*] *n* (*person*) basurero/a

**scenario** [sɪ'nɑ:rɪəu] *n* (*THEATRE*) argumento; (*CINEMA*) guión *m*; (*fig*) escenario

**scene** [si:n] *n* (*THEATRE, fig etc*) escena; (*of crime etc*) escenario; (*view*) panorama *m*; (*fuss*) escándalo; **~ry** *n* (*THEATRE*) decorado; (*landscape*) paisaje *m*; **scenic** *adj* pintoresco

**scent** [sɛnt] *n* perfume *m*, olor *m*; (*fig: track*) rastro, pista

**sceptic** ['skɛptɪk] (*US* **skeptic**) *n* escéptico/a; **~al** *adj* escéptico; **~ism**

['skeptɪsɪzm] n escepticismo

**sceptre** ['sɛptə*] (US **scepter**) n cetro

**schedule** ['fedjuːl, (US) 'skedjuːl] n (timetable) horario; (of events) programa m; (list) lista ♦ vt (visit) fijar la hora de; **to arrive on ~** llegar a la hora debida; **to be ahead of/behind ~** estar adelantado/en retraso; **~d flight** n vuelo regular

**schematic** [skɪ'mætɪk] adj (diagram etc) esquemático

**scheme** [skiːm] n (plan) plan m, proyecto; (plot) intriga; (arrangement) disposición f; (pension ~ etc) sistema m ♦ vi (intrigue) intrigar; **scheming** adj intrigante ♦ n intrigas fpl

**schism** ['skɪzəm] n cisma m

**schizophrenic** [skɪtsə'frɛnɪk] adj esquizofrénico

**scholar** ['skɔlə*] n (pupil) alumno/a; (learned person) sabio/a, erudito/a; **~ly** adj erudito; **~ship** n erudición f; (grant) beca

**school** [skuːl] n escuela, colegio; (in university) facultad f ♦ cpd escolar; **~ age** n edad f escolar; **~book** n libro de texto; **~boy** n alumno; **~children** npl alumnos mpl; **~days** npl años mpl del colegio; **~girl** n alumna; **~ing** n enseñanza; **~master/mistress** n (primary) maestro/a; (secondary) profesor(a) m/f; **~teacher** n (primary) maestro/a; (secondary) profesor(a) m/f

**schooner** ['skuːnə*] n (ship) goleta

**sciatica** [saɪ'ætɪkə] n ciática

**science** ['saɪəns] n ciencia; **~ fiction** n ciencia-ficción f; **scientific** [-'tɪfɪk] adj científico; **scientist** n científico/a m/f

**scintillating** ['sɪntɪleɪtɪŋ] adj brillante, ingenioso

**scissors** ['sɪzəz] npl tijeras fpl; a **pair of ~** unas tijeras

**scoff** [skɔf] n (BRIT: inf: eat) engullir ♦ vi: **to ~ (at)** (mock) mofarse (de)

**scold** [skəuld] vt regañar

**scone** [skɔn] n pastel de pan

**scoop** [skuːp] n (for flour etc) pala; (PRESS) exclusiva; **~ out** vt excavar; **~ up** vt recoger

**scooter** ['skuːtə*] n (motor cycle) moto f; (toy) patinete m

**scope** [skəup] n (of plan) ámbito; (of person) competencia; (opportunity) libertad f (de acción)

**scorch** [skɔːtʃ] vt (clothes) chamuscar; (earth, grass) quemar, secar

**score** [skɔː*] n (points etc) puntuación f; (MUS) partitura; (twenty) veintena ♦ vt (goal, point) ganar; (mark) rayar; (achieve: success) conseguir ♦ vi marcar un tanto; (FOOTBALL) marcar (un) gol; (keep score) llevar el tanteo; **~s of** (very many) decenas de; **on that ~** en lo que se refiere a eso; **to ~ 6 out of 10** obtener una puntuación de 6 sobre 10; **~ out** vt tachar; **~ over** vt fus obtener una victoria sobre; **~board** n marcador m

**scorn** [skɔːn] n desprecio ♦ vt despreciar; **~ful** adj desdeñoso, despreciativo

**Scorpio** ['skɔːpɪəu] n Escorpión m

**scorpion** ['skɔːpɪən] n alacrán m

**Scot** [skɔt] n escocés/esa m/f

**scotch** [skɔtʃ] vt (rumour) desmentir; (plan) abandonar; **S~** n whisky m escocés

**scot-free** adv: **to get off ~** (unpunished) salir impune

**Scotland** ['skɔtlənd] n Escocia

**Scots** [skɔts] adj escocés/esa m/f; **~man/woman** n escocés/esa m/f; **Scottish** ['skɔtɪʃ] adj escocés/esa

**scoundrel** ['skaundrl] n canalla m/f, sinvergüenza m/f

**scour** ['skauə*] vt (search) recorrer, registrar

**scourge** [skɔːdʒ] n azote m

**scout** [skaut] n (MIL, also: boy ~) explorador m; **girl ~** (US) niña exploradora; **~ around** vi reconocer el terreno

**scowl** [skaul] vi fruncir el ceño; **to ~ at sb** mirar con ceño a uno

**scrabble** ['skræbl] vi (claw): **to ~ (at)** arañar; (also: **to ~ around:**

_search_) revolver todo buscando ♦ _n:_ S~ ® Scrabble _m_ ®

**scraggy** ['skrægɪ] _adj_ descarnado

**scram** [skræm] (_inf_) _vi_ largarse

**scramble** ['skræmbl] _n_ (_climb_) subida (difícil); (_struggle_) pelea ♦ _vi:_ **to ~ through/out** abrirse paso/salir con dificultad; **to ~ for** pelear por; **~d eggs** _npl_ huevos _mpl_ revueltos

**scrap** [skræp] _n_ (_bit_) pedacito; (_fig_) pizca; (_fight_) riña, bronca; (_also:_ ~ **iron**) chatarra, hierro viejo ♦ _vt_ (_discard_) desechar, descartar ♦ _vi_ reñir, armar (una) bronca; **~s** _npl_ (_waste_) sobras _fpl_, desperdicios _mpl;_ **~book** _n_ álbum _m_ de recortes; **~ dealer** _n_ chatarrero/a

**scrape** [skreɪp] _n:_ **to get into a ~** meterse en un lío ♦ _vt_ raspar; (_skin etc_) rasguñar; (~ _against_) rozar ♦ _vi:_ **to ~ through** (_exam_) aprobar por los pelos; **~ together** _vt_ (_money_) juntar

**scrap:** **~ heap** _n_ (_fig_): **to be on the ~ heap** estar acabado; **~ merchant** (_BRIT_) _n_ chatarrero/a; **~ paper** _n_ pedazos _mpl_ de papel; **~py** _adj_ (_work_) imperfecto

**scratch** [skrætʃ] _n_ rasguño; (_from claw_) arañazo ♦ _cpd:_ **~ team** equipo improvisado ♦ _vt_ (_paint, car_) rayar; (_with claw, nail_) rasguñar, arañar; (_rub: nose etc_) rascarse ♦ _vi_ rascarse; **to start from ~** partir de cero; **to be up to ~** cumplir con los requisitos

**scrawl** [skrɔːl] _n_ garabatos _mpl_ ♦ _vi_ hacer garabatos

**scrawny** ['skrɔːnɪ] _adj_ flaco

**scream** [skriːm] _n_ chillido ♦ _vi_ chillar

**screech** [skriːtʃ] _vi_ chirriar

**screen** [skriːn] _n_ (_CINEMA, TV_) pantalla; (_movable barrier_) biombo ♦ _vt_ (_conceal_) tapar; (_from the wind etc_) proteger; (_film_) proyectar; (_candidates etc_) investigar ♦ **~ing** _n_ (_MED_) investigación _f_ médica; **~play** _n_ guión _m_

**screw** [skruː] _n_ tornillo ♦ _vt_ (_also:_ ~

_in_) atornillar; **~ up** _vt_ (_paper etc_) arrugar; **to ~ up one's eyes** arrugar el entrecejo; **~driver** _n_ destornillador _m_

**scribble** ['skrɪbl] _n_ garabatos _mpl_ ♦ _vt, vi_ garabatear

**script** [skrɪpt] _n_ (_CINEMA etc_) guión _m;_ (_writing_) escritura, letra

**scripture(s)** ['skrɪptʃə*(z)] _n(pl)_ Sagrada Escritura

**scroll** [skrəʊl] _n_ rollo

**scrounge** [skraʊndʒ] (_inf_) _vt:_ **to ~ sth off** _or_ **from sb** obtener algo de uno de gorra ♦ _n:_ **on the ~** de gorra; **~r** _n_ gorrón/ona _m/f_

**scrub** [skrʌb] _n_ (_land_) maleza ♦ _vt_ fregar, restregar; (_inf: reject_) cancelar, anular

**scruff** [skrʌf] _n:_ **by the ~ of the neck** por el pescuezo

**scruffy** ['skrʌfɪ] _adj_ desaliñado, piojoso

**scrum(mage)** ['skrʌm(mɪdʒ)] _n_ (_RUGBY_) melée _f_

**scruple** ['skruːpl] _n_ (_gen pl_) escrúpulo

**scrutinize** ['skruːtɪnaɪz] _vt_ escudriñar; (_votes_) escrutar; **scrutiny** ['skruːtɪnɪ] _n_ escrutinio, examen _m_

**scuff** [skʌf] _vt_ (_shoes, floor_) rayar

**scuffle** ['skʌfl] _n_ refriega

**sculptor** ['skʌlptə*] _n_ escultor(a) _m/f_

**sculpture** ['skʌlptʃə*] _n_ escultura

**scum** [skʌm] _n_ (_on liquid_) espuma; (_pej: people_) escoria

**scupper** ['skʌpə*] (_BRIT: inf_) _vt_ (_plans_) dar al traste con

**scurrilous** ['skʌrɪləs] _adj_ difamatorio, calumnioso

**scurry** ['skʌrɪ] _vi_ correr; **to ~ off** escabullirse

**scuttle** ['skʌtl] _n_ (_also: coal ~_) cubo, carbonera ♦ _vt_ (_ship_) barrenar ♦ _vi_ (_scamper_): **to ~ away,** **~ off** escabullirse

**scythe** [saɪð] _n_ guadaña

**SDP** (_BRIT_) _n abbr_ = Social Democratic Party

**sea** [siː] _n_ mar _m_ ♦ _cpd_ de mar, marítimo; **by ~** (_travel_) en barco; **on**

the ~ (*boat*) en el mar; (*town*) junto al mar; **to be all at** ~ (*fig*) estar despistado; **out to** ~, **at** ~ en alta mar; ~**board** n litoral m; ~**food** n mariscos *mpl*; ~ **front** n paseo marítimo; ~**going** adj de altura; ~**gull** n gaviota

**seal** [si:l] n (*animal*) foca; (*stamp*) sello ♦ vt (*close*) cerrar; ~ **off** vt (*area*) acordonar

**sea level** n nivel m del mar

**sea lion** n león m marino

**seam** [si:m] n costura; (*of metal*) juntura; (*of coal*) veta, filón m

**seaman** ['si:mən] n marinero

**seamy** ['si:mɪ] adj sórdido

**seance** ['seɪɒns] n sesión f de espiritismo

**seaplane** ['si:pleɪn] n hidroavión m

**seaport** ['si:pɔ:t] n puerto de mar

**search** [sə:tʃ] n (*for person, thing*) busca, búsqueda; (*COMPUT*) búsqueda; (*inspection: of sb's home*) registro ♦ vt (*look in*) buscar en; (*examine*) examinar; (*person, place*) registrar ♦ vi: **to** ~ **for** buscar; **in** ~ **of** en busca de; ~ **through** vt fus registrar; ~**ing** adj penetrante; ~**light** n reflector m; ~ **party** n pelotón m de salvamento; ~ **warrant** n mandamiento (judicial)

**sea:** ~**shore** n playa, orilla del mar; ~**sick** adj mareado; ~**side** n playa, orilla del mar; ~**side resort** n centro turístico costero

**season** ['si:zn] n (*of year*) estación f; (*sporting etc*) temporada; (*of films etc*) ciclo ♦ vt (*food*) sazonar; **in/out of** ~ en sazón/fuera de temporada; ~**al** adj estacional; ~**ed** adj (*fig*) experimentado; ~**ing** n condimento, aderezo; ~ **ticket** n abono

**seat** [si:t] n (*in bus, train*) asiento; (*chair*) silla; (*PARLIAMENT*) escaño; (*buttocks*) culo, trasero; (*of trousers*) culera ♦ vt sentar; (*have room for*) tener cabida para; **to be** ~**ed** sentarse; ~ **belt** n cinturón m de seguridad

**sea:** ~ **water** n agua del mar;

~**weed** n alga marina; ~**worthy** adj en condiciones de navegar

**sec.** abbr = **second(s)**

**secluded** [sɪ'klu:dɪd] adj retirado

**seclusion** [sɪ'klu:ʒən] n reclusión f

**second** ['sɛkənd] adj segundo ♦ adv en segundo lugar ♦ n segundo; (*AUT: also:* ~ *gear*) segunda; (*COMM*) artículo con algún desperfecto; (*BRIT: SCOL: degree*) título de licenciado con calificación de notable ♦ vt (*motion*) apoyar; (*BRIT: worker*) transferir; ~**ary** adj secundario; ~**ary school** n escuela secundaria; ~**-class** adj de segunda clase ♦ adv (*RAIL*) en segunda; ~**hand** adj de segunda mano, usado; ~ **hand** n (*on clock*) segundero; ~**ly** adv en segundo lugar; ~**ment** [sɪ'kɒndmənt] (*BRIT*) n traslado temporal; ~**-rate** adj de segunda categoría; ~ **thoughts** npl: **to have** ~ **thoughts** cambiar de opinión; **on** ~ **thoughts** or **thought** (*US*) pensándolo bien

**secrecy** ['si:krəsɪ] n secreto

**secret** ['si:krɪt] adj, n secreto; **in** ~ en secreto

**secretarial** [sɛkrɪ'tɛərɪəl] adj de secretario; (*course, staff*) de secretariado

**secretary** [sɛkrɪ'tɛərɪət] n secretaría

**secretary** ['sɛkrətərɪ] n secretario/a; **S~ of State (for)** (*BRIT: POL*) Ministro (de)

**secretive** ['si:krətɪv] adj reservado, sigiloso

**secretly** ['si:krɪtlɪ] adv en secreto

**sect** [sɛkt] n secta; ~**arian** [-'tɛərɪən] adj sectario

**section** ['sɛkʃən] n sección f; (*part*) parte f; (*of document*) artículo; (*of opinion*) sector m; (*cross-*) corte m transversal

**sector** ['sɛktə] n sector m

**secular** ['sɛkjulə] adj secular, seglar

**secure** [sɪ'kjuə] adj seguro; (*firmly fixed*) firme, fijo ♦ vt (*fix*) asegurar, afianzar; (*get*) conseguir

**security** [sɪ'kjuərɪtɪ] n seguridad f; (for loan) fianza; (: object) prenda

**sedan** [sɪ'dæn] (US) n (AUT) sedán m

**sedate** [sɪ'deɪt] adj tranquilo; ♦ vt tratar con sedantes

**sedation** [sɪ'deɪʃən] n (MED) sedación f

**sedative** ['sɛdɪtɪv] n sedante m, sedativo

**seduce** [sɪ'dju:s] vt seducir; **seduction** [-'dʌkʃən] n seducción f; **seductive** [-'dʌktɪv] adj seductor(a)

**see** [si:] (pt saw, pp seen) vt ver; (accompany): to ~ sb to the door acompañar a uno a la puerta; (understand) ver, comprender ♦ vi ver ♦ n (arz)obispado; to ~ that (ensure) asegurar que; ~ you soon! ¡hasta pronto!; ~ **about** vt fus atender a, encargarse de; ~ **off** vt despedir; ~ **through** vt fus (fig) calar ♦ vt (plan) llevar a cabo; ~ **to** vt fus atender a, encargarse de

**seed** [si:d] n semilla; (in fruit) pepita; (fig: gen pl) germen m; (TENNIS) preseleccionado/a; to go to ~ (plant) granar; (fig) descuidarse; ~**ling** n planta de semillero; ~**y** adj (shabby) desaseado, raído

**seeing** ['si:ɪŋ] conj: ~ (that) visto que, en vista de que

**seek** [si:k] (pt, pp sought) vt buscar; (post) solicitar

**seem** [si:m] vi parecer; **there seems to be ...** parece que hay ...; ~**ingly** adv aparentemente, según parece

**seen** [si:n] pp of **see**

**seep** [si:p] vi filtrarse

**seesaw** ['si:sɔ:] n subibaja

**seethe** [si:ð] vi hervir; to ~ **with anger** estar furioso

**see-through** ['si:θru:] adj transparente

**segment** ['sɛgmənt] n (part) sección f; (of orange) gajo

**segregate** ['sɛgrɪgeɪt] vt segregar

**seismic** ['saɪzmɪk] adj sísmico

**seize** [si:z] vt (grasp) agarrar, asir; (take possession of) secuestrar; (: territory) apoderarse de; (opportu-

nity) aprovecharse de; ~ **(up)on** vt fus aprovechar; ~ **up** vi (TECH) agarrotarse

**seizure** ['si:ʒə*] n (MED) ataque m; (LAW, of power) incautación f

**seldom** ['sɛldəm] adv rara vez

**select** [sɪ'lɛkt] adj selecto, escogido ♦ vt escoger, elegir; (SPORT) seleccionar; ~**ion** [-'lɛkʃən] n selección f, elección f; (COMM) surtido

**self** [sɛlf] (pl **selves**) n uno mismo; the ~ el yo ♦ prefix auto...; ~-**assured** adj seguro de sí mismo; ~-**catering** (BRIT) adj (flat etc) con cocina; ~-**centred** (US ~-**centered**) adj egocéntrico; ~-**confidence** n confianza en sí mismo; ~-**conscious** adj cohibido; ~-**contained** (BRIT) (flat) con entrada particular; ~-**control** n autodominio; ~-**defence** (US ~-**defense**) n defensa propia; ~-**discipline** n autodisciplina; ~-**employed** adj que trabaja por cuenta propia; ~-**evident** adj patente; ~-**governing** adj autónomo; ~-**indulgent** adj autocomplaciente; ~-**interest** n egoísmo; ~-**ish** adj egoísta; ~-**ishness** n egoísmo; ~-**less** adj desinteresado; ~-**made** adj: ~-**made man** hombre m que se ha hecho a sí mismo; ~-**pity** n lástima de sí mismo; ~-**portrait** n autorretrato; ~-**possessed** adj sereno, dueño de sí mismo; ~-**preservation** n propia conservación f; ~-**respect** n amor m propio; ~-**righteous** adj santurrón/ona; ~-**sacrifice** n abnegación f; ~-**satisfied** adj satisfecho de sí mismo; ~-**service** adj de autoservicio; ~-**sufficient** adj autosuficiente; ~-**taught** adj autodidacta

**sell** [sɛl] (pt, pp **sold**) vt vender ♦ vi venderse; to ~ **at** or **for £10** venderse a 10 libras; ~ **off** vt liquidar; ~ **out** vi: to ~ **out of tickets/milk** vender todas las entradas/toda la leche; ~-**by date** n fecha de caducidad; ~-**er** n vendedor(a) m/f; ~-**ing price** n precio de venta

**sellotape** ['sɛləuteɪp] ® (BRIT) n

cinta adhesiva, celo (SP), scotch m (AM)

**selves** [sɛlvz] npl of **self**
**semaphore** ['sɛməfɔ:*] n semáforo
**semblance** ['sɛmbləns] n apariencia f
**semen** ['si:mən] n semen m
**semester** [sɪ'mɛstə*] n (US) semestre m
**semi...** [sɛmɪ] prefix semi..., medio...; **~circle** n semicírculo; **~colon** n punto y coma; **~conductor** n semiconductor m; **~detached (house)** n (casa) semiseparada; **~final** n semi-final m
**seminar** ['sɛmɪnɑ:*] n seminario
**seminary** ['sɛmɪnərɪ] n (REL) seminario
**semiskilled** ['sɛmɪskɪld] adj (work, worker) semi-cualificado
**senate** ['sɛnɪt] n senado; **senator** n senador(a) m/f
**send** [sɛnd] (pt, pp sent) vt mandar, enviar; (signal) transmitir; **~ away** vt despachar; **~ away for** vt fus pedir; **~ back** vt devolver; **~ for** vt fus mandar traer; **~ off** vt (goods) despachar; (BRIT: SPORT: player) expulsar; **~ out** vt (invitation) mandar; (signal) emitir; **~ up** vt (person, price) hacer subir; (BRIT: parody) parodiar; **~er** n remitente m/f; **~-off** n: **a good ~-off** una buena despedida
**senior** ['si:nɪə*] adj (older) mayor, más viejo; (: on staff) de más antigüedad; (of higher rank) superior; **~ citizen** n persona de la tercera edad; **~ity** [-'ɒrɪtɪ] n antigüedad f
**sensation** [sɛn'seɪʃən] n sensación f; **~al** adj sensacional
**sense** [sɛns] n (faculty, meaning) sentido; (feeling) sensación f; (good ~) sentido común, juicio ♦ vt sentir, percibir; **it makes ~** tiene sentido; **~less** adj estúpido, insensato; (unconscious) sin conocimiento; **~ of humour** n sentido del humor
**sensible** ['sɛnsɪbl] adj sensato; (reasonable) razonable, lógico
**sensitive** ['sɛnsɪtɪv] adj sensible;

(touchy) susceptible
**sensual** ['sɛnsjuəl] adj sensual
**sensuous** ['sɛnsjuəs] adj sensual
**sent** [sɛnt] pt, pp of **send**
**sentence** ['sɛntns] n (LING) oración f; (LAW) sentencia, fallo ♦ vt: to **~ sb to death/to 5 years (in prison)** condenar a uno a muerte/a 5 años de cárcel
**sentiment** ['sɛntɪmənt] n sentimiento; (opinion) opinión f; **~al** [-'mɛntl] adj sentimental
**sentry** ['sɛntrɪ] n centinela m
**separate** [adj 'sɛprɪt, vb 'sɛpəreɪt] adj separado; (distinct) distinto ♦ vt separar; (part) dividir ♦ vi separarse; **~s** npl (clothes) coordinados mpl; **~ly** adv por separado; **separation** [-'reɪʃən] n separación f
**September** [sɛp'tɛmbə*] n se(p)tiembre m
**septic** ['sɛptɪk] adj séptico; **~ tank** n fosa séptica
**sequel** ['si:kwl] n consecuencia, resultado; (of story) continuación f
**sequence** ['si:kwəns] n sucesión f, serie f; (CINEMA) secuencia
**sequin** ['si:kwɪn] n lentejuela
**serene** [sɪ'ri:n] adj sereno, tranquilo
**sergeant** ['sɑ:dʒənt] n sargento
**serial** ['sɪərɪəl] n (TV) telenovela, serie f televisiva; (BOOK) serie f; **~ize** vt emitir como serial; **~ number** n número de serie
**series** ['sɪəri:z] n inv serie f
**serious** ['sɪərɪəs] adj serio; (grave) grave; **~ly** adv en serio; (ill, wounded etc) gravemente; **~ness** n seriedad f; gravedad f
**sermon** ['sɜ:mən] n sermón m
**serrated** [sɪ'reɪtɪd] adj serrado, dentellado
**serum** ['sɪərəm] n suero
**servant** ['sɜ:vənt] n servidor(a) m/f; (house ~) criado/a
**serve** [sɜ:v] vt servir; (customer) atender; (subj: train) pasar por; (apprenticeship) hacer; (prison term) cumplir ♦ vi (at table) servir; (TENNIS) sacar; to **~ as/for/to do**

servir de/para/para hacer ♦ *n* (TEN-
NIS) saque *m*; **it ~s him right** se lo
tiene merecido; **~ out** *vt* (food) servir; **~ up** *vt* = **~ out**

**service** ['sɔːvɪs] *n* servicio; (REL)
misa; (AUT) mantenimiento; (dishes
etc) juego ♦ *vt* (car etc) revisar; (:
repair) reparar; **the S~s** *npl* las
fuerzas armadas; **to be of ~ to sb**
ser útil a uno; **~able** *adj* servible,
utilizable; **~ area** *n* (on motorway)
area de servicio; **~ charge** (BRIT) *n*
servicio; **~man** *n* militar *m*; **~ station** *n* estación *f* de servicio

**serviette** [sɔːvɪ'et] (BRIT) *n* servilleta

**session** ['sɛʃən] *n* sesión *f*; **to be in
~** estar en sesión

**set** [sɛt] (*pt, pp* set) *n* juego; (RA-
DIO) aparato; (TV) televisor *m*; (of
utensils) batería *f*; (of cutlery) cubierto; (of books) colección *f*; (TENNIS)
set *m*; (group of people) grupo; (CIN-
EMA) plató *m*; (THEATRE) decorado; (HAIRDRESSING) marcado ♦
*adj* (fixed) fijo; (ready) listo ♦ *vt*
(place) poner, colocar; (fix) fijar;
(adjust) ajustar, arreglar; (decide:
rules etc) establecer, decidir ♦ *vi*
(sun) ponerse; (jam, jelly) cuajarse;
(concrete) fraguar; (bone) componerse; **to be ~ on doing sth** estar
empeñado en hacer algo; **to ~ to
music** poner música a; **to ~ on fire**
incendiar, poner fuego a; **to ~ free**
poner en libertad; **to ~ sth going**
poner algo en marcha; **to ~ sail** zarpar, hacerse a la vela; **~ about** *vt
fus* ponerse a; **~ aside** *vt* poner
aparte, dejar de lado; (money, time)
reservar; **~ back** *vt* (cost): **to ~ sb
back £5** costar a uno cinco libras; (:
in time): **to ~ back (by)** retrasar
(por); **~ off** *vi* partir ♦ *vt* (bomb)
hacer estallar; (events) poner en
marcha; (show up well) hacer resaltar; **~ out** *vi* partir ♦ *vt* (arrange)
disponer; (state) exponer; **to ~ out
to do sth** proponerse hacer algo;
**~ up** *vt* establecer; **~back** *n* revés *m*,

contratiempo; **~ menu** *n* menú *m*

**settee** [sɛ'tiː] *n* sofá *m*

**setting** ['sɛtɪŋ] *n* (scenery) marco;
(position) disposición *f*; (of sun)
puesta; (of jewel) engaste *m*, monta-
dura

**settle** ['sɛtl] *vt* (argument) resolver;
(accounts) ajustar, liquidar; (MED:
calm) calmar, sosegar ♦ *vi* (dust
etc) depositarse; (weather) serenarse; (also: **~ down**) instalarse; tranquilizarse; **to ~ for sth** convenir en
aceptar algo; **to ~ on sth** decidirse
por algo; **~ in** *vi* instalarse; **~ up**
*vi*: **to ~ up with sb** ajustar cuentas
con uno; **~ment** (payment) liquidación *f*; (agreement) acuerdo, convenio; (village etc) pueblo; **~r** *n*
colono/a, colonizador/a *m/f*

**setup** ['sɛtʌp] *n* sistema *m*; (situation) situación *f*

**seven** ['sɛvn] *num* siete; **~teen** *num*
diez y siete, diecisiete; **~th** *num* séptimo; **~ty** *num* setenta

**sever** ['sɛvə*] *vt* cortar; (relations)
romper

**several** ['sɛvərl] *adj, pron* varios/as
*m/fpl*, algunos/as *mpl/fpl*; **~ of us**
varios de nosotros

**severance** ['sɛvərəns] *n* (of relations) ruptura; **~ pay** *n* indemnización *f* por despido

**severe** [sɪ'vɪə*] *vt* cortar; (serious)
grave; (hard) duro; (pain) intenso;
**severity** [sɪ'vɛrɪtɪ] *n* severidad *f*; gravedad *f*; intensidad *f*

**sew** [səu] (*pt* sewed, *pp* sewn) *vt, vi*
coser; **~ up** *vt* coser, zurcir

**sewage** ['suːɪdʒ] *n* aguas *fpl* residua-
les

**sewer** ['suːə*] *n* alcantarilla, cloaca

**sewing** ['səuɪŋ] *n* costura; **~
machine** *n* máquina de coser

**sewn** [səun] *pp* of **sew**

**sex** [sɛks] *n* sexo; (lovemaking) **to
have ~** hacer el amor; **~ist** *adj, n*
sexista *m/f*; **sexual** ['sɛksjuəl] *adj*
sexual; **sexy** *adj* sexy

**shabby** ['ʃæbɪ] *adj* (person) desharrapado; (clothes) raído, gastado;

(*behaviour*) ruin *inv*
**shack** [ʃæk] *n* choza, chabola
**shackles** ['ʃæklz] *npl* grillos *mpl*, grilletes *mpl*
**shade** [ʃeɪd] *n* sombra; (*for lamp*) pantalla; (*for eyes*) visera; (*of colour*) matiz *m*, tonalidad *f*; (*small quantity*): **a ~** (**too big/more**) un poquitín (grande/más) ♦ *vt* dar sombra a; (*eyes*) proteger del sol; **in the ~** en la sombra
**shadow** ['ʃædəʊ] *n* sombra ♦ *vt* (*follow*) seguir y vigilar; **~ cabinet** (*BRIT*) *n* (*POL*) gabinete paralelo formado por el partido de oposición; **~y** *adj* oscuro; (*dim*) indistinto
**shady** ['ʃeɪdɪ] *adj* sombreado; (*fig: dishonest*) sospechoso; (*: deal*) turbio
**shaft** [ʃɑːft] *n* (*of arrow, spear*) astil *m*; (*AUT, TECH*) eje *m*, árbol *m*; (*of mine*) pozo; (*of lift*) hueco, caja; (*of light*) rayo
**shaggy** ['ʃægɪ] *adj* peludo
**shake** [ʃeɪk] (*pt* **shook**, *pp* **shaken**) *vt* sacudir; (*building*) hacer temblar; (*bottle, cocktail*) agitar ♦ *vi* (*tremble*) temblar; **to ~ one's head** (*in refusal*) negar con la cabeza; (*in dismay*) mover o menear la cabeza, incrédulo; **to ~ hands with sb** estrechar la mano a uno; **~ off** *vt* sacudirse; (*fig*) deshacerse de; **~ up** *vt* agitar; (*fig*) reorganizar; **shaky** *adj* (*hand, voice*) trémulo; (*building*) inestable
**shall** [ʃæl] *aux vb*: **~ I help you?** ¿quieres que te ayude?; **I'll buy three, ~ I?** compro tres, ¿no te parece?
**shallow** ['ʃæləʊ] *adj* poco profundo; (*fig*) superficial
**sham** [ʃæm] *n* fraude *m*, engaño ♦ *vt* fingir, simular
**shambles** ['ʃæmblz] *n* confusión *f*
**shame** [ʃeɪm] *n* vergüenza *f ♦ vt* avergonzar; **it is a ~ that/to do es una** lástima que/hacer; **what a ~!** ¡qué lástima!; **~faced** *adj* avergonzado; **~ful** *adj* vergonzoso; **~less** *adj* desvergonzado

**shampoo** [ʃæm'puː] *n* champú *m ♦ vt* lavar con champú; **~ and set** *n* lavado y marcado
**shamrock** ['ʃæmrɔk] *n* trébol *m* (*emblema nacional irlandés*)
**shandy** ['ʃændɪ] *n* mezcla de cerveza con gaseosa
**shan't** [ʃɑːnt] = **shall not**
**shanty town** ['ʃæntɪ-] *n* barrio de chabolas
**shape** [ʃeɪp] *n* forma ♦ *vt* formar, dar forma a; (*sb's ideas*) formar; (*sb's life*) determinar; **to take ~** tomar forma; **~ up** *vi* (*events*) desarrollarse; (*person*) formarse; **~d suffix: heart~d** en forma de corazón; **~less** *adj* informe, sin forma definida; **~ly** *adj* bien formado *etc*, esbelto
**share** [ʃeə*] *n* (*part*) parte *f*, porción *f*; (*contribution*) cuota; (*COMM*) acción *f ♦ vt* dividir; (*have in common*) compartir; **to ~ out** (*among or between*) repartir (entre); **~holder** (*BRIT*) *n* accionista *m/f*
**shark** [ʃɑːk] *n* tiburón *m*
**sharp** [ʃɑːp] *adj* (*blade, nose*) afilado; (*point*) puntiagudo; (*outline*) definido; (*pain*) intenso; (*MUS*) desafinado; (*contrast*) marcado; (*voice*) agudo; (*person: quick-witted*) astuto; (*: dishonest*) poco escrupuloso ♦ *n* (*MUS*) sostenido ♦ *adv*: **at 2 o'clock ~** a las 2 en punto; **~en** *vt* (*pencil*) sacar punta a; (*fig*) agudizar; **~ener** *n* (*also*: **pencil ~ener**) sacapuntas *m inv*; **~eyed** *adj* de vista aguda; **~ly** *adv* (*turn, stop*) bruscamente; (*stand out, contrast*) claramente; (*criticize, retort*) severamente
**shatter** ['ʃætə*] *vt* hacer añicos *o* pedazos; (*fig: ruin*) destruir, acabar con ♦ *vi* hacerse añicos
**shave** [ʃeɪv] *vt* afeitar, rasurar ♦ *vi* afeitarse, rasurarse ♦ *n*: **to have a ~** afeitarse; **~r** *n* (*also*: **electric ~r**) máquina de afeitar (*eléctrica*)
**shaving** ['ʃeɪvɪŋ] *n* (*action*) el afeitarse, rasurado; **~s** *npl* (*of wood etc*) virutas *fpl*; **~ brush** *n* brocha (de

afeitar); ~ **foam** n espuma de afeitar

**shawl** [ʃɔːl] n chal m

**she** [ʃiː] pron ella; ~**-cat** n gata

**sheaf** [ʃiːf] (pl **sheaves**) n (of corn) gavilla; (of papers) fajo

**shear** [ʃɪə*] (pt **sheared**, pp **sheared** or **shorn**) vt esquilar, trasquilar; ~**s** npl (for hedge) tijeras fpl de jardín; ~ **off** vi romperse

**sheath** [ʃiːθ] n vaina; (contraceptive) preservativo

**sheaves** [ʃiːvz] npl of **sheaf**

**shed** [ʃed] (pt, pp **shed**) n cobertizo ♦ vt (skin) mudar; (tears, blood) derramar; (load) derramar; (workers) despedir

**she'd** [ʃiːd] = **she had; she would**

**sheen** [ʃiːn] n brillo, lustre m

**sheep** [ʃiːp] n inv oveja; ~**dog** n perro pastor; ~**ish** adj tímido, vergonzoso; ~**skin** n piel f de carnero

**sheer** [ʃɪə*] adj (utter) puro, completo; (steep) escarpado; (material) diáfano ♦ adv verticalmente

**sheet** [ʃiːt] n (on bed) sábana; (of paper) hoja; (of glass, metal) lámina; (of ice) capa

**sheik(h)** [ʃeɪk] n jeque m

**shelf** [ʃelf] (pl **shelves**) n estante m

**shell** [ʃel] n (on beach) concha; (of egg, nut etc) cáscara; (explosive) proyectil m, obús m; (of building) armazón f ♦ vt (peas) desenvainar; (MIL) bombardear

**she'll** [ʃiːl] = **she will; she shall**

**shellfish** [ʃelfɪʃ] n inv crustáceo; (as food) mariscos mpl

**shell suit** n chándal m de calle

**shelter** [ʃeltə*] n abrigo, refugio ♦ vt (aid) amparar, proteger; (give lodging to) abrigar ♦ vi abrigarse, refugiarse; ~**ed** adj (life) protegido; (spot) abrigado; ~**ed housing** n viviendas vigiladas para ancianos y minusválidos

**shelve** [ʃelv] vt (fig) aplazar; ~**s** npl of **shelf**

**shepherd** [ʃepəd] n pastor m ♦ vt (guide) guiar, conducir; ~**'s pie**

**sherry** [ʃerɪ] n jerez m

**she's** [ʃiːz] = **she is; she has**

**Shetland** [ʃetlənd] n (also: the ~**s**, the ~ **Isles**) las Islas de Zetlandia

**shield** [ʃiːld] n escudo; (protection) blindaje m ♦ vt: **to ~ (from)** proteger (de)

**shift** [ʃɪft] n (change) cambio; (at work) turno ♦ vt trasladar; (remove) quitar ♦ vi moverse; ~**less** adj (person) perezoso; ~ **work** n trabajo a turnos; ~**y** adj tramposo; (eyes) furtivo

**shilling** [ʃɪlɪŋ] (BRIT) n chelín m

**shilly-shally** [ʃɪlɪʃælɪ] vi titubear, vacilar

**shimmer** [ʃɪmə*] n reflejo trémulo

**shin** [ʃɪn] n espinilla

**shine** [ʃaɪn] (pt, pp **shone**) n brillo, lustre m ♦ vi brillar, relucir ♦ vt (shoes) lustrar, sacar brillo a; **to ~ a torch on sth** dirigir una linterna hacia algo

**shingle** [ʃɪŋgl] n (on beach) guijarros mpl; ~**s** n (MED) herpes mpl or fpl

**shiny** [ʃaɪnɪ] adj brillante, lustroso

**ship** [ʃɪp] n buque m, barco ♦ vt (goods) embarcar; (send) transportar or enviar por vía marítima; ~**building** n construcción f de buques; ~**ment** n (goods) envío; ~**per** n exportador(a) m/f; ~**ping** n (act) embarque m; (traffic) buques mpl; ~**wreck** n naufragio ♦ vt: **to be ~wrecked** naufragar; ~**yard** n astillero

**shire** [ʃaɪə*] (BRIT) n condado

**shirk** [ʃəːk] vt (obligations) faltar a

**shirt** [ʃəːt] n camisa; **in (one's)** ~ **sleeves** en mangas de camisa

**shit** [ʃɪt] (inf!) excl ¡mierda! (!)

**shiver** [ʃɪvə*] n escalofrío ♦ vi temblar, estremecerse; (with cold) tiritar

**shoal** [ʃəʊl] n (of fish) banco; (fig: also: ~**s**) tropel m

**shock** [ʃɔk] n (impact) choque m; (ELEC) descarga (eléctrica);

(*emotional*) conmoción f; (*start*) sobresalto, susto; (*MED*) postración f nerviosa ♦ *vt* dar un susto a; (*offend*) escandalizar; ~ **absorber** n amortiguador m; ~**ing** adj (*awful*) espantoso; (*outrageous*) escandaloso

**shod** [ʃɔd] pt, pp of **shoe**

**shoddy** ['ʃɔdɪ] adj de pacotilla

**shoe** [ʃuː] (pt, pp **shod**) n zapato; (*for horse*) herradura ♦ *vt* (*horse*) herrar; ~**brush** n cepillo para zapatos; ~**lace** n cordón m; ~ **polish** n betún m; ~**shop** n zapatería; ~**string** n (*fig*): on a ~**string** con muy poco dinero

**shone** [ʃɔn] pt, pp of **shine**

**shoo** [ʃuː] excl ¡fuera!

**shook** [ʃuk] pt of **shake**

**shoot** [ʃuːt] (pt, pp **shot**) n (*on branch, seedling*) retoño, vástago ♦ *vt* disparar; (*kill*) matar a tiros; (*wound*) pegar un tiro; (*execute*) fusilar; (*film*) rodar, filmar ♦ *vi* (*FOOTBALL*) chutar; ~ **down** *vt* (*plane*) derribar; ~ **in/out** *vi* entrar corriendo/salir disparado; ~ **up** *vi* (*prices*) dispararse; ~**ing** n (*shots*) tiros *mpl*; (*HUNTING*) caza con escopeta; ~**ing star** n estrella fugaz

**shop** [ʃɔp] n tienda; (*workshop*) taller m ♦ *vi* (*also*: go ~**ping**) ir de compras; ~ **assistant** (*BRIT*) n dependiente/a m/f; ~ **floor** (*BRIT*) n (*fig*) taller m, fábrica; ~**keeper** n tendero/a m/f; ~**lifting** n mechería; ~**per** n comprador(a) m/f; ~**ping** n (*goods*) compras *fpl*; ~**ping bag** n bolsa (de compras); ~**ping centre** (*US* ~**ping center**) n centro comercial; ~**soiled** adj usado; ~ **steward** (*BRIT*) n (*INDUSTRY*) enlace m sindical; ~ **window** n escaparate n (*SP*), vidriera (*AM*)

**shore** [ʃɔː*] n orilla ♦ *vt*: to ~ (**up**) reforzar; **on** ~ en tierra

**shorn** [ʃɔːn] pp of **shear**

**short** [ʃɔːt] adj corto; (*in time*) de corta duración; (*person*) bajo; (*curt*) brusco, seco; (*insufficient*) insuficiente; to be ~ of sth estar falto

de algo; **in** ~ en pocas palabras; ~ **of doing** ... fuera de hacer ...; **it is** ~ **for** es la forma abreviada de; **to cut** ~ (*speech, visit*) interrumpir, terminar inesperadamente; **everything** ~ **of** ... todo menos ...; **to fall** ~ **of** no alcanzar; **to run** ~ **of** quedarle a uno poco; **to stop** ~ parar en seco; **to stop** ~ **of** detenerse antes de; ~**age** n: a ~**age** of una falta de; ~**bread** n especie de mantecada; ~**change** *vt* no dar el cambio completo a; ~**circuit** n cortocircuito; ~**coming** n defecto, deficiencia; ~**(crust) pastry** (*BRIT*) n pasta quebradiza; ~**cut** n atajo; ~**en** *vt* acortar; (*visit*) interrumpir; ~**fall** n déficit m; ~**hand** (*BRIT*) n taquigrafía; ~**hand typist** (*BRIT*) n taquimecanógrafo/a; ~ **list** (*BRIT*) n (*for job*) lista de candidatos escogidos; ~**lived** adj efímero; ~**ly** adv en breve, dentro de poco; ~**sighted** (*BRIT*) adj miope; (*fig*) imprudente; ~**staffed** adj: to be ~**staffed** estar falto de personal; ~**story** n cuento; ~**tempered** adj enojadizo; ~**term** adj (*effect*) a corto plazo; ~**wave** n (*RADIO*) onda corta

**shot** [ʃɔt] pt, pp of **shoot** ♦ n (*sound*) tiro, disparo; (*try*) tentativa; (*injection*) inyección f; (*PHOT*) toma, fotografía; to be a **good/poor** ~ (*person*) tener buena/mala puntería; **like a** ~ (*without any delay*) como un rayo; ~**gun** n escopeta

**should** [ʃud] *aux vb*: I ~ **go now** debo irme ahora; **he** ~ **be there now** debe de haber llegado (ya); I ~ **go if I were you** yo en tu lugar me iría; I ~ **like to** me gustaría

**shoulder** ['ʃəuldə*] n hombro ♦ *vt* (*fig*) cargar con; ~ **bag** n cartera de bandolera; ~ **blade** n omóplato; ~ **strap** n tirante m

**shouldn't** ['ʃudnt] = **should not**

**shout** [ʃaut] n grito ♦ *vt* gritar ♦ *vi* gritar, dar voces; ~ **down** *vt* acallar a gritos; ~**ing** n griterío

**shove** [ʃʌv] n empujón m ♦ *vt* empujar; (inf: put): to ~ sth in meter algo a empellones; ~ off (inf) vi largarse

**shovel** ['ʃʌvl] n pala; (mechanical) excavadora ♦ vt mover con pala

**show** [ʃəu] (pt showed, pp shown) n (of emotion) demostración f; (semblance) apariencia; (exhibition) exposición f; (THEATRE) función f, espectáculo; (TV) show m ♦ vt mostrar, enseñar; (courage etc) mostrar, manifestar; (exhibit) exponer; (film) proyectar ♦ vi mostrarse; (appear) aparecer; for ~ para impresionar; on ~ (exhibits etc) expuesto; ~ in vt hacer pasar; ~ off vi (pej) vi presumir ♦ vt (display) lucir; ~ out vt: to ~ sb out acompañar a uno a la puerta; ~ up vi (stand out) destacar; (inf: turn up) aparecer ♦ vt (unmask) desenmascarar; ~ business n mundo del espectáculo; ~down n enfrentamiento (final)

**shower** ['ʃauə*] n (rain) chaparrón m, chubasco; (of stones etc) lluvia; (for bathing) ducha (SP), regadera (AM) ♦ vi llover ♦ vt (fig): to ~ sb with sth colmar a uno de algo; to have a ~ ducharse; ~proof adj impermeable

**showing** ['ʃəuɪŋ] n (of film) proyección f

**show jumping** n hípica

**shown** [ʃəun] pp of show

**show**: ~-off (inf) n (person) presumido/a; ~piece n (of exhibition etc) objeto cumbre; ~room n sala de muestras

**shrank** [ʃræŋk] pt of shrink

**shrapnel** ['ʃræpnl] n metralla

**shred** [ʃred] n (gen pl) triza, jirón m ♦ vt hacer trizas; (CULIN) desmenuzar; ~der n (vegetable ~der) picadora; (document ~der) trituradora (de papel)

**shrewd** [ʃru:d] adj astuto

**shriek** [ʃri:k] n chillido ♦ vi chillar

**shrill** [ʃrɪl] adj agudo, estridente

**shrimp** [ʃrɪmp] n camarón m

**shrine** [ʃraɪn] n santuario, sepulcro

**shrink** [ʃrɪŋk] (pt shrank, pp shrunk) vi encogerse; (be reduced) reducirse; (also: ~ away) retroceder ♦ vt encoger ♦ n (inf: pej) loquero/a; to ~ from (doing) sth no atreverse a hacer algo; ~age n encogimiento; reducción f; ~wrap vt embalar con película de plástico

**shrivel** ['ʃrɪvl] (also: ~ up) vt (dry) secar ♦ vi secarse

**shroud** [ʃraud] n sudario ♦ vt: ~ed in mystery envuelto en el misterio

**Shrove Tuesday** ['ʃrəuv-] n martes de carnaval

**shrub** [ʃrʌb] n arbusto; ~bery n arbustos mpl

**shrug** [ʃrʌg] n encogimiento de hombros ♦ vt, vi: to ~ (one's shoulders) encogerse de hombros; ~ off vt negar importancia a

**shrunk** [ʃrʌŋk] pp of shrink

**shudder** ['ʃʌdə*] n estremecimiento, escalofrío ♦ vi estremecerse

**shuffle** ['ʃʌfl] vt (cards) barajar ♦ vi: to ~ (one's feet) arrastrar los pies

**shun** [ʃʌn] vt rehuir, esquivar

**shunt** [ʃʌnt] vt (train) maniobrar; (object) empujar

**shut** [ʃʌt] (pt, pp shut) vt cerrar ♦ vi cerrarse; ~ down vt, vi cerrar; ~ off vt (supply etc) cortar; ~ up vi (inf: keep quiet) callarse ♦ vt (close) cerrar; (silence) hacer callar; ~ter n contraventana; (PHOT) obturador m

**shuttle** ['ʃʌtl] n lanzadera; (also: ~ service) servicio rápido y continuo entre dos puntos: (: AER) puente m aéreo

**shuttlecock** ['ʃʌtlkɔk] n volante m

**shy** [ʃaɪ] adj tímido; ~ness n timidez f

**sibling** ['sɪblɪŋ] n hermano/a

**Sicily** ['sɪsɪlɪ] n Sicilia

**sick** [sɪk] adj (ill) enfermo; (nauseated) mareado; (humour) negro; (vomiting): to be ~ (BRIT) vomitar; to feel ~ tener náuseas; to be ~ of (fig) estar harto de; ~ bay n enfermería; ~**en** vt dar asco a; ~**ening** adj (fig) asqueroso

**sickle** ['sɪkl] n hoz f

**sick:** ~ **leave** n baja por enfermedad; ~**ly** adj enfermizo; (smell) nauseabundo; ~**ness** n enfermedad f, mal m; (vomiting) náuseas fpl; ~**pay** n subsidio de enfermedad

**side** [saɪd] n (gen) lado; (of body) costado; (of lake) orilla; (of hill) ladera; (team) equipo; ♦ adj (door, entrance) lateral ♦ vi: **to** ~ **with** sb tomar el partido de uno; **by the** ~ **of** al lado de; ~ **by** ~ juntos/as; **from** ~ **to** ~ de un lado para otro; **from all** ~**s** de todos lados; **to take** ~**s (with)** tomar partido (con); ~**board** n aparador m; ~**boards** (BRIT) npl = **sideburns**; ~**burns** npl patillas fpl; ~ **drum** n tambor m; ~ **effect** n efecto secundario; ~**light** n (AUT) luz f lateral; ~**line** n (SPORT) línea de banda; (fig) empleo suplementario; ~**long** adj de soslayo; ~**saddle** adv a mujeriegas, a la inglesa; ~**show** n (stall) caseta; ~**step** n (fig) esquivar; ~**track** vt calle f lateral; ~**track** vt (fig) desviar (de su propósito); ~**walk** (US) n acera; ~**ways** adv de lado

**siding** ['saɪdɪŋ] n (RAIL) apartadero, vía muerta

**sidle** ['saɪdl] vi: **to** ~ **up (to)** acercarse furtivamente (a)

**siege** [siːdʒ] n cerco, sitio

**sieve** [sɪv] n colador m ♦ vt cribar

**sift** [sɪft] vt cribar; (fig: information) escudriñar

**sigh** [saɪ] n suspiro ♦ vi suspirar

**sight** [saɪt] n (faculty) vista; (spectacle) espectáculo; (on gun) mira, alza ♦ vt divisar; **in** ~ a la vista; **out of** ~ fuera de (la) vista; **on** ~ (shoot) sin previo aviso; ~**seeing** n excursionismo, turismo; **to go** ~**seeing** hacer turismo

**sign** [saɪn] n (with hand) señal f, seña; (trace) huella, rastro; (notice) letrero; (written) signo ♦ vt firmar; (SPORT) fichar; **to** ~ **sth over to**

sb firmar el traspaso de algo a uno; ~ **on** vi (MIL) alistarse; (BRIT: as unemployed) registrarse como desempleado; (for course) inscribirse ♦ vt (MIL) alistar; (employee) contratar; ~ **up** vi (MIL) alistarse; (for course) inscribirse ♦ vt (player) fichar

**signal** ['sɪgnl] n señal f ♦ vi señalizar ♦ vt (person) hacer señas a; (message) comunicar por señales; ~**man** n (RAIL) guardavía m

**signature** ['sɪgnətʃə] n firma; ~ **tune** n sintonía de apertura de un programa

**signet ring** ['sɪgnət-] n anillo de sello

**significance** [sɪg'nɪfɪkəns] n (importance) trascendencia

**significant** [sɪg'nɪfɪkənt] adj significativo; (important) trascendente

**signify** ['sɪgnɪfaɪ] vt significar

**sign language** n lenguaje m para sordomudos

**signpost** ['saɪnpəust] n indicador m

**silence** ['saɪləns] n silencio ♦ vt acallar; (guns) reducir al silencio; ~**r** n (on gun, BRIT: AUT) silenciador m

**silent** ['saɪlnt] adj silencioso; (not speaking) callado; (film) mudo; **to remain** ~ guardar silencio; ~ **partner** n (COMM) socio/a comanditario/a

**silhouette** [sɪlu'et] n silueta

**silicon chip** ['sɪlɪkən-] n plaqueta de silicio

**silk** [sɪlk] n seda ♦ adj de seda; ~**y** adj sedoso

**silly** ['sɪlɪ] adj (person) tonto; (idea) absurdo

**silt** [sɪlt] n sedimento

**silver** ['sɪlvə] n plata; (money) moneda suelta ♦ adj de plata; (colour) plateado; ~ **paper** (BRIT) n papel m de plata; ~**plated** adj plateado; ~**smith** n platero/a; ~**ware** n plata; ~**y** adj argentino

**similar** ['sɪmɪlə] adj: ~ **(to)** parecido o semejante (a); ~**ity** [-'lærɪt] n semejanza; ~**ly** adv del mismo modo

**simile** ['sɪmɪlɪ] n símil m

**simmer** ['sɪmə*] vi hervir a fuego lento

**simpering** ['sɪmpərɪŋ] adj (foolish) bobo

**simple** ['sɪmpl] adj (easy) sencillo; (foolish, COMM: interest) simple; **simplicity** [-'plɪsɪtɪ] n sencillez f; **simplify** ['sɪmplɪfaɪ] vt simplificar

**simply** ['sɪmplɪ] adv (live, talk) sencillamente; (just, merely) sólo

**simulate** ['sɪmjʊleɪt] vt fingir, simular; ~d adj simulado; (fur) de imitación

**simultaneous** [sɪməl'teɪnɪəs] adj simultáneo; ~**ly** adv simultáneamente

**sin** [sɪn] n pecado ♦ vi pecar

**since** [sɪns] adv desde entonces, después ♦ prep desde ♦ conj (time) desde que; (because) ya que, puesto que; ~ **then**, **ever** ~ desde entonces

**sincere** [sɪn'sɪə*] adj sincero; ~**ly** adv: **yours** ~**ly** (in letters) le saluda atentamente; **sincerity** [-'sɛrɪtɪ] n sinceridad f

**sinew** ['sɪnju:] n tendón m

**sinful** ['sɪnful] adj (thought) pecaminoso; (person) pecador(a)

**sing** [sɪŋ] (pt sang, pp sung) vt, vi cantar

**Singapore** [sɪŋə'pɔ:*] n Singapur m

**singe** [sɪndʒ] vt chamuscar

**singer** ['sɪŋə*] n cantante m/f

**singing** ['sɪŋɪŋ] n canto

**single** ['sɪŋgl] adj único, solo; (unmarried) soltero; (not double) simple, sencillo ♦ n (BRIT: also: ~ ticket) billete m sencillo; (record) sencillo, single m; ~s npl (TENNIS) individual m; ~ **bed** cama individual; ~ **out** vt (choose) escoger; ~-**breasted** adj recto; ~ **file** n: **in** ~ **file** en fila de uno; ~-**handed** adv sin ayuda; ~-**minded** adj resuelto, firme; ~ **room** n cuarto individual

**singly** ['sɪŋglɪ] adv uno por uno

**singular** ['sɪŋgjʊlə*] adj (odd) raro, extraño; (outstanding) excepcional; (LING) singular ♦ n (LING) singular m

**sinister** ['sɪnɪstə*] adj siniestro

**sink** [sɪŋk] (pt sank, pp sunk) n fregadero ♦ vt (ship) hundir, echar a pique; (foundations) excavar ♦ vi (gen) hundirse; **to** ~ **sth into** hundir algo en; ~ **in** vi (fig) penetrar, calar

**sinner** ['sɪnə*] n pecador(a) m/f

**sinus** ['saɪnəs] n (ANAT) seno

**sip** [sɪp] n sorbo ♦ vt sorber, beber a sorbitos

**siphon** ['saɪfən] n sifón m; ~ **off** vt desviar

**sir** [sə*] n señor m; S~ **John Smith** Sir John Smith; **yes** ~ sí, señor

**siren** ['saɪərn] n sirena

**sirloin** ['sə:lɔɪn] n (also: ~ **steak**) solomillo

**sissy** ['sɪsɪ] (inf) n marica m

**sister** ['sɪstə*] n hermana; (BRIT: nurse) enfermera jefe; ~-**in-law** n cuñada

**sit** [sɪt] (pt, pp sat) vi sentarse; (be sitting) estar sentado; (assembly) reunirse; (for painter) posar ♦ vt (exam) presentarse a; ~ **down** vi sentarse; ~ **in on** vt fus asistir a; ~ **up** vi incorporarse; (not go to bed) velar

**sitcom** ['sɪtkɒm] n abbr (= situation comedy) comedia de situación

**site** [saɪt] n sitio; (also: **building** ~) solar m ♦ vt situar

**sit-in** n (demonstration) sentada

**sitting** ['sɪtɪŋ] n (of assembly etc) sesión f; (in canteen) turno; ~ **room** n sala de estar

**situated** ['sɪtjʊeɪtɪd] adj situado

**situation** [sɪtjʊ'eɪʃən] n situación f; **"~s vacant"** (BRIT) "ofrecen trabajo"

**six** [sɪks] num seis; ~**teen** num diez y seis, dieciséis; ~**th** num sexto; ~**ty** num sesenta

**size** [saɪz] n tamaño; (extent) extensión f; (of clothing) talla; (of shoes) número; ~ **up** vt formarse una idea de; ~**able** adj importante, considerable

**sizzle** ['sɪzl] vi crepitar

**skate** [skeɪt] n patín m; (fish: pl inv)

raya ♦ vi patinar; ~**board** n monopatín m; ~**r** n patinador(a) m/f;
**skating** n patinaje m; **skating rink** n pista de patinaje

**skeleton** ['skelɪtn] n esqueleto; (TECH) armazón f; (outline) esquema m; ~ **staff** n personal m reducido

**skeptic** etc ['skeptɪk] (US) = **sceptic**

**sketch** [sketʃ] n (drawing) dibujo; (outline) esbozo, bosquejo; (THEATRE) sketch m ♦ vt dibujar; (plan etc: also: ~ **out**) esbozar; ~**book** n libro de dibujos; ~**y** adj incompleto

**skewer** ['skjuːə*] n broqueta

**ski** [skiː] n esquí m ♦ vi esquiar; ~ **boot** n bota de esquí

**skid** [skɪd] n patinazo ♦ vi patinar

**ski:** ~**er** n esquiador(a) m/f; ~**ing** n esquí m; ~ **jump** n salto con esquís

**skilful** ['skɪlful] (BRIT) adj diestro, experto

**ski lift** n telesilla m, telesquí m

**skill** [skɪl] n destreza, pericia, técnica; ~**ed** adj hábil, diestro; (worker) cualificado; ~**full** (US) adj = **skilful**

**skim** [skɪm] vt (milk) desnatar; (glide over) rozar, rasar ♦ vi: to ~ **through** (book) hojear; ~**med milk** n leche f desnatada

**skimp** [skɪmp] vt (also: ~ **on:** work) chapucear; (cloth etc) escatimar; ~**y** adj escaso; (skirt) muy corto

**skin** [skɪn] n piel f; (complexion) cutis m ♦ vt (fruit etc) pelar; (animal) despellejar; ~ **cancer** n cáncer m de piel; ~**deep** adj superficial; ~ **diving** n buceo; ~**ny** adj flaco; ~**tight** adj (dress etc) muy ajustado

**skip** [skɪp] n brinco, salto; (BRIT: container) contenedor m ♦ vi brincar; (with rope) saltar a la comba ♦ vt saltarse

**ski pants** npl pantalones mpl de esquí

**ski pole** n bastón m de esquí

**skipper** ['skɪpə*] n (NAUT, SPORT) capitán m

**skipping rope** ['skɪpɪŋ-] (BRIT) n comba

**skirmish** ['skɜːmɪʃ] n escaramuza

**skirt** [skɜːt] n falda (SP), pollera (AM) ♦ vt (go round) ladear; ~**ing board** n rodapié m

**ski slope** n pista de esquí

**ski suit** n traje m de esquiar

**skittle** ['skɪtl] n bolo; ~**s** n (game) boliche m

**skive** [skaɪv] (BRIT: inf) vi gandulear

**skulk** [skʌlk] vi esconderse

**skull** [skʌl] n calavera; (ANAT) cráneo

**skunk** [skʌŋk] n mofeta

**sky** [skaɪ] n cielo; ~**light** n tragaluz m, claraboya; ~**scraper** n rascacielos m inv

**slab** [slæb] n (stone) bloque m; (flat) losa; (of cake) trozo

**slack** [slæk] adj (loose) flojo; (slow) de poca actividad; (careless) descuidado; ~**s** npl pantalones mpl; ~**en** (also: ~**en off**) vi aflojarse ♦ vt aflojar; (speed) disminuir

**slag heap** ['slæg-] n escorial m, escombrera

**slag off** (BRIT: inf) vt poner como un trapo

**slain** [sleɪn] pp of slay

**slam** [slæm] vt (throw) arrojar (violentamente); (criticize) criticar duramente ♦ vi (door) cerrarse de golpe; to ~ **the door** dar un portazo

**slander** ['slɑːndə*] n calumnia, difamación f

**slang** [slæŋ] n argot m; (jargon) jerga

**slant** [slɑːnt] n sesgo, inclinación f; (fig) interpretación f; ~**ed** adj; ~**ing** adj inclinado; (eyes) rasgado

**slap** [slæp] n palmada; (in face) bofetada ♦ vt dar una palmada or bofetada a; (paint etc): to ~ **sth on sth** embadurnar algo con algo ♦ adv (directly) exactamente, directamente; ~**dash** adj descuidado; ~**stick** n comedia de golpe y porrazo; ~**up** adj: a ~**up meal** (BRIT) un banquetazo, una comilona

**slash** [slæʃ] vt acuchillar; (fig: prices) fulminar

**slat** [slæt] n tablilla, listón m

**slate** [sleit] n pizarra ♦ vt (fig: criticize) criticar duramente

**slaughter** ['slɔːtə*] n (of animals) matanza; (of people) carnicería ♦ vt matar; **~house** n matadero

**Slav** [slɑːv] adj eslavo

**slave** [sleiv] n esclavo/a ♦ vi (also: ~ away) sudar tinta; **~ry** n esclavitud f

**slay** [slei] (pt slew, pp slain) vt matar

**sleazy** ['sliːzɪ] adj de mala fama

**sledge** [sledʒ] n trineo; **~hammer** n mazo

**sleek** [sliːk] adj (shiny) lustroso; (car etc) elegante

**sleep** [sliːp] (pt, pp slept) n sueño ♦ vi dormir; **to go to ~** quedarse dormido; **~ around** vi acostarse con cualquiera; **~ in** vi (oversleep) quedarse dormido; **~er** n (person) durmiente m/f; (BRIT: RAIL: on track) traviesa; (: train) coche-cama m; **~ing bag** n saco de dormir; **~ing car** n coche-cama m; **~ing partner** (BRIT) n (COMM) socio comanditario; **~ing pill** n somnífero; **~less** adj: a **~less night** una noche en blanco; **~walker** n sonámbulo/a; **~y** adj soñoliento; (place) soporífero

**sleet** [sliːt] n aguanieve f

**sleeve** [sliːv] n manga; (TECH) manguito; (of record) portada; **~less** adj sin mangas

**sleigh** [slei] n trineo

**sleight** [slait] n: **~ of hand** escamoteo

**slender** ['slendə*] adj delgado; (means) escaso

**slept** [slept] pt, pp of sleep

**slew** [sluː] pt of slay ♦ vi (BRIT: veer) torcerse

**slice** [slais] n (of meat) tajada; (of bread) rebanada; (of lemon) rodaja; (utensil) pala ♦ vt cortar (en tajos); rebanar

**slick** [slik] adj (skilful) hábil, diestro; (clever) astuto ♦ n (also: oil ~) marea negra

**slide** [slaid] (pt, pp slid) n (movement) descenso, desprendimiento; (in playground) tobogán m; (PHOT) diapositiva; (BRIT: also: hair ~) pasador m ♦ vt correr, deslizar ♦ vi (slip) resbalarse; (glide) deslizarse; **sliding** adj (door) corredizo; **sliding scale** n escala móvil

**slight** [slait] adj (slim) delgado; (frail) delicado; (pain etc) leve; (trivial) insignificante; (small) pequeño ♦ n desaire m (insult) ofender, desairar; **not in the ~est** en absoluto; **~ly** adv ligeramente, un poco

**slim** [slim] adj delgado, esbelto; (fig: chance) remoto ♦ vi adelgazar

**slime** [slaim] n limo, cieno; **slimy** adj cenagoso

**slimming** ['slimiŋ] n adelgazamiento

**sling** [sliŋ] (pt, pp slung) n (MED) cabestrillo; (weapon) honda ♦ vt tirar, arrojar

**slip** [slip] n (slide) resbalón m; (mistake) descuido; (underskirt) combinación f; (of paper) papelito ♦ vt (slide) deslizar ♦ vi deslizarse; (stumble) resbalar(se); (decline) decaer; (move smoothly) ir; **to ~ into/out of** (room etc) introducirse en/ salirse de (room etc); **to give sb the ~** eludir a uno; a **~ of the tongue** un lapsus; **to ~ with sth off/on** ponerse/quitarse algo; **~ away** vi escabullirse; **~ in** vt meter ♦ vi meterse; **~ out** vi (go out) salir (un momento); **~ up** vi (make mistake) equivocarse; meter la pata; **~ped disc** n vértebra dislocada

**slipper** ['slipə*] n zapatilla, pantufla

**slippery** ['slipəri] adj resbaladizo

**slip**: **~ road** (BRIT) n carretera de acceso; **~shod** adj descuidado; **~-up** n (error) desliz m; **~way** n grada, gradas fpl

**slit** [slit] (pt, pp slit) n raja; (cut) corte m ♦ vt rajar; cortar

**slither** ['sliðə*] vi deslizarse

**sliver** ['slivə*] n (of glass, wood) astilla; (of cheese etc) raja

**slob** [slɔb] (inf) n abandonado/a

**slog** [slɔg] (BRIT) vi sudar tinta; **it was a ~** costó trabajo (hacerlo)

**slogan** ['sləugən] n eslogan m, lema m

**slop** [slɔp] vi (also: **~ over**) derramarse, desbordarse ♦ vt derramar, verter

**slope** [sləup] n (up) cuesta, pendiente f; (down) declive m; (side of mountain) falda, vertiente m ♦ vi: **to ~ down** estar en declive; **to ~ up** inclinarse; **sloping** adj en pendiente; en declive; (writing) inclinado

**sloppy** ['slɔpɪ] adj (work) descuidado; (appearance) desaliñado

**slot** [slɔt] n ranura ♦ vt: **to ~ into** encajar en

**sloth** [sləuθ] n (laziness) pereza

**slot machine** n (BRIT: vending machine) distribuidor m automático; (for gambling) tragaperras m inv

**slouch** [slautʃ] vi andar etc con los hombros caídos

**Slovenia** [sləu'viːnɪə] n Eslovenia

**slovenly** ['slʌvənlɪ] adj desaliñado, desaseado; (careless) descuidado

**slow** [sləu] adj lento; (not clever) lerdo; (watch): **to be ~** atrasar ♦ adv lentamente, despacio ♦ vt, vi (also: **~ down, ~ up**) retardar; **"~"** (road sign) "disminuir velocidad"; **~down** (US) n huelga de manos caídas; **~ly** adv lentamente, despacio; **~ motion** n: **in ~ motion** a cámara lenta

**sludge** [slʌdʒ] n lodo, fango

**slue** [sluː] (US) vi = slew

**slug** [slʌg] n babosa; (bullet) posta; **~gish** adj lento; (person) perezoso

**sluice** [sluːs] n (gate) esclusa; (channel) canal m

**slum** [slʌm] n casucha

**slump** [slʌmp] n (economic) depresión f ♦ vi hundirse; (prices) caer en picado

**slung** [slʌŋ] pt, pp de sling

**slur** [slɜː*] n: **to cast a ~ on** insultar ♦ vt (speech) pronunciar mal

**slush** [slʌʃ] n nieve f a medio derre-

tir; **~ fund** n caja negra (fondos para sobornar)

**slut** [slʌt] n putona

**sly** [slaɪ] adj astuto; (smile) taimado

**smack** [smæk] n bofetada ♦ vt dar con la mano a; (child, on face) abofetear ♦ vi: **to ~ of** saber a, oler a

**small** [smɔːl] adj pequeño; **~ ads** (BRIT) npl anuncios mpl por palabras; **~ change** n suelto, cambio; **~ fry** npl gente f del montón; **~holder** (BRIT) n granjero/a, parcelero/a; **~ hours** npl: **in the ~ hours** a las altas horas (de la noche); **~pox** n viruela; **~ talk** n cháchara

**smart** [smɑːt] adj elegante; (clever) listo, inteligente; (quick) rápido, vivo ♦ vi escocer, picar; **~en up** vi arreglarse ♦ vt arreglar

**smash** [smæʃ] n (also: **~-up**) choque m; (MUS) exitazo ♦ vt (break) hacer pedazos; (car etc) estrellar; (SPORT: record) batir ♦ vi hacerse pedazos; (against wall etc) estrellarse; **~ing** (inf) adj estupendo

**smattering** ['smætərɪŋ] n: **a ~ of** algo de

**smear** [smɪə*] n mancha; (MED) frotis m inv ♦ vt untar; **~ campaign** n campaña de desprestigio

**smell** [smel] (pt, pp **smelt** or **smelled**) n olor m; (sense) olfato ♦ vt, vi oler; **~y** adj maloliente

**smile** [smaɪl] n sonrisa ♦ vi sonreír

**smirk** [smɜːk] n sonrisa falsa or afectada

**smith** [smɪθ] n herrero; **~y** ['smɪðɪ] n herrería

**smock** [smɔk] n blusa; (children's) mandilón m; (US: overall) guardapolvo

**smog** [smɔg] n esmog m

**smoke** [sməuk] n humo ♦ vi fumar; (chimney) echar humo ♦ vt (cigarettes) fumar; **~d** adj (bacon, glass) ahumado; **~r** n fumador(a) m/f; (RAIL) coche m fumador; **~ screen** n cortina de humo; **~ shop** (US) n estanco (SP), tabaquería (AM)

**smoking** n: **"no smoking"** "prohibido fumar"; **smoky** *adj (room)* lleno de humo; *(taste)* ahumado

**smolder** ['sməuldə\*] *(US)* vi = smoulder

**smooth** [smuːð] *adj* liso; *(sea)* tranquilo; *(flavour, movement)* suave; *(sauce)* fino; *(person: pej)* meloso ♦ *vt (also: ~ out)* alisar; *(creases, difficulties)* allanar

**smother** ['smʌðə\*] *vt* sofocar; *(repress)* contener

**smoulder** ['sməuldə\*] *(US* **smolder)** *vi* arder sin llama

**smudge** [smʌdʒ] *n* mancha ♦ *vt* manchar

**smug** [smʌg] *adj* presumido; orondo

**smuggle** ['smʌgl] *vt* pasar de contrabando; **~r** *n* contrabandista *m/f*; **smuggling** *n* contrabando

**smutty** ['smʌtɪ] *adj (fig)* verde, obsceno

**snack** [snæk] *n* bocado; **~ bar** *n* cafetería

**snag** [snæg] *n* problema *m*

**snail** [sneɪl] *n* caracol *m*

**snake** [sneɪk] *n* serpiente *f*

**snap** [snæp] *n (sound)* chasquido; *(photograph)* foto *f* ♦ *adj (decision)* instantáneo ♦ *vt (break)* quebrar; *(fingers)* castañetear ♦ *vi* quebrarse; *(fig: speak sharply)* contestar bruscamente; **to ~ shut** cerrarse de golpe; **~ at** *vt fus (subj: dog)* intentar morder; **~ off** *vi* partirse; **~ up** *vt* agarrar; **~ fastener** *(US)* *n* botón de presión; **~py** *(inf) adj (answer)* instantáneo; *(slogan)* conciso; **make it ~py!** *(hurry up)* ¡date prisa!; **~shot** *n* foto *f (instantánea)*

**snare** [snɛə\*] *n* trampa

**snarl** [snɑːl] *vi* gruñir

**snatch** [snætʃ] *n (small piece)* fragmento ♦ *vt (~ away)* arrebatar; *(fig)* agarrar; **to ~ some sleep** encontrar tiempo para dormir

**sneak** [sniːk] *(pt (US)* **snuck)** *vi:* **to ~ in/out** entrar/salir a hurtadillas ♦ *n (inf)* soplón/ona *m/f*; **~ up on sb** aparecérsele de improviso a uno; **~ers** *npl* zapatos *mpl* de lona; **~y**

*adj* furtivo

**sneer** [snɪə\*] *vi* reír con sarcasmo; *(mock):* **to ~ at** burlarse de

**sneeze** [sniːz] *vi* estornudar

**sniff** [snɪf] *vi* sollozar ♦ *vt* husmear, oler; *(drugs)* esnifar

**snigger** ['snɪgə\*] *vi* reírse con disimulo

**snip** [snɪp] *n* tijeretazo; *(BRIT: inf: bargain)* ganga ♦ *vt* tijeretear

**sniper** ['snaɪpə\*] *n* francotirador(a) *m/f*

**snippet** ['snɪpɪt] *n* retazo

**snivelling** ['snɪvlɪŋ] *adj* llorón/ona

**snob** [snɔb] *n* (e)snob *m/f*; **~bery** *n* (e)snobismo; **~bish** *adj* (e)snob

**snooker** ['snuːkə\*] *n* especie de billar

**snoop** [snuːp] *vi:* **to ~ about** fisgonear

**snooty** ['snuːtɪ] *adj* (e)snob

**snooze** [snuːz] *n* siesta ♦ *vi* echar una siesta

**snore** [snɔː\*] *n* ronquido ♦ *vi* roncar

**snorkel** ['snɔːkl] *n (tubo)* respirador *m*

**snort** [snɔːt] *n* bufido ♦ *vi* bufar

**snout** [snaut] *n* hocico, morro

**snow** [snəu] *n* nieve *f* ♦ *vi* nevar; **~ball** *n* bola de nieve ♦ *vi (fig)* agrandirse, ampliarse; **~bound** *adj* bloqueado por la nieve; **~drift** *n* ventisquero; **~drop** *n* campanilla; **~fall** *n* nevada; **~flake** *n* copo de nieve; **~man** *n* figura de nieves; **~plough** *(US* **~plow)** *n* quitanieves *m inv*; **~shoe** *n* raqueta (de nieve); **~storm** *n* nevada, nevasca

**snub** [snʌb] *vt (person)* desairar ♦ *n* desaire *m*, repulsa; **~-nosed** *adj* chato

**snuff** [snʌf] *n* rapé *m*

**snug** [snʌg] *adj (cosy)* cómodo; *(fitted)* ajustado

**snuggle** ['snʌgl] *vi:* **to ~ up to sb** arrimarse a uno

┌─────────────┐
│ **KEYWORD** │
└─────────────┘

**so** [səu] *adv* **1** *(thus, likewise)* así, de este modo; **if ~** de ser así; **I like**

swimming — ~ **do** I a mí me gusta nadar — a mí también; **I've got work to do** — ~ **has** Paul tengo trabajo que hacer — Paul también; **it's 5 o'clock** — ~ **it is!** son las cinco — ¡pues es verdad!; **I think/think** ~ espero/creo que sí; ~ **far** hasta ahora; (*in past*) hasta este momento **2** (*in comparisons etc: to such a degree*) tan; ~ **quickly (that)** tan rápido (que); ~ **big (that)** tan grande (que); **she's not** ~ **clever as her brother** no es tan lista como su hermano; **we were** ~ **worried** estábamos preocupadísimos

**3**: ~ **much** *adj, adv* tanto; ~ **many** tantos/as

**4** (*phrases*): **10 or** ~ unos 10, 10 o así; ~ **long!** (*inf: goodbye*) ¡hasta luego!

♦ *conj* **1** (*expressing purpose*): ~ **as to do** para hacer; ~ (**that**) para que + *sub*

**2** (*expressing result*) así que; ~ **you see, I could have gone** así que ya ves, (yo) podría haber ido

**soak** [səʊk] *vt* (*drench*) empapar; (*steep in water*) remojar ♦ *vi* remojarse, estar a remojo; ~ **in** *vi* penetrar; ~ **up** *vt* absorber

**soap** [səʊp] *n* jabón *m*; ~ **flakes** *npl* escamas *fpl* de jabón; ~ **opera** *n* telenovela; ~ **powder** *n* jabón *m* en polvo; ~**y** *adj* jabonoso

**soar** [sɔː*] *vi* (*on wings*) remontarse; (*rocket, prices*) dispararse; (*building etc*) elevarse

**sob** [sɒb] *n* sollozo ♦ *vi* sollozar

**sober** [ˈsəʊbə*] *adj* (*serious*) serio; (*not drunk*) sobrio; (*colour, style*) discreto; ~ **up** *vt* quitar la borrachera

**so-called** *adj* así llamado

**soccer** [ˈsɒkə*] *n* fútbol *m*

**social** [ˈsəʊʃl] *adj* social ♦ *n* velada, fiesta; ~ **club** *n* club *m*; ~**ism** *n* socialismo; ~**ist** *adj, n* socialista *m/f*; ~**ize** *vi*: **to** ~**ize (with)** alternar (con); ~**ly** *adv* socialmente; ~ **se-**

**curity** *n* seguridad *f* social; ~ **work** *n* asistencia social; ~ **worker** *n* asistente/a *m/f* social

**society** [səˈsaɪətɪ] *n* sociedad *f*; (*club*) asociación *f*; (*also:* **high** ~) alta sociedad

**sociology** [səʊsɪˈɒlədʒɪ] *n* sociología

**sock** [sɒk] *n* calcetín *m* (*SP*), media (*AM*)

**socket** [ˈsɒkɪt] *n* cavidad *f*; (*BRIT: ELEC*) enchufe *m*

**sod** [sɒd] *n* (*of earth*) césped *m*; (*BRIT: inf!*) cabrón/ona *m/f* (!)

**soda** [ˈsəʊdə] *n* (*CHEM*) sosa; (*also:* ~ **water**) soda; (*US: also:* ~ **pop**) gaseosa

**sodden** [ˈsɒdn] *adj* empapado

**sodium** [ˈsəʊdɪəm] *n* sodio

**sofa** [ˈsəʊfə] *n* sofá *m*

**soft** [sɒft] *adj* (*lenient, not hard*) blando; (*gentle, not bright*) suave; ~ **drink** *n* bebida no alcohólica; ~**en** [ˈsɒfn] *vt* ablandar; suavizar; (*effect*) amortiguar ♦ *vi* ablandarse; suavizarse; ~**ly** *adv* suavemente; (*gently*) delicadamente, con delicadeza; ~**ness** *n* blandura; suavidad *f*; ~ **spot** *n*: **to have a** ~ **spot for sb** tener debilidad por uno; ~**ware** *n* (*COMPUT*) software *m*

**soggy** [ˈsɒgɪ] *adj* empapado

**soil** [sɔɪl] *n* (*earth*) tierra, suelo ♦ *vt* ensuciar; ~**ed** *adj* sucio

**solace** [ˈsɒlɪs] *n* consuelo

**solar** [ˈsəʊlə*] *adj*; ~ **panel** *n* panel *m* solar; ~ **energy** *n* energía solar

**sold** [səʊld] *pt, pp* **of sell**; ~ **out** *adj* (*COMM*) agotado

**solder** [ˈsəʊldə*] *vt* soldar ♦ *n* soldadura

**soldier** [ˈsəʊldʒə*] *n* soldado; (*army man*) militar *m*

**sole** [səʊl] *n* (*of foot*) planta; (*of shoe*) suela; (*fish: pl inv*) lenguado ♦ *adj* único

**solemn** [ˈsɒləm] *adj* solemne

**sole trader** *n* (*COMM*) comerciante *m* exclusivo

**solicit** [səˈlɪsɪt] *vt* (*request*) solicitar ♦ *vi* (*prostitute*) importunar

**solicitor** [sə'lɪsɪtə*] (*BRIT*) n (*for wills etc*) ≈ notario/a; (*in court*) ≈ abogado/a

**solid** ['sɒlɪd] adj sólido; (*gold etc*) macizo ♦ n sólido; ~s npl (*food*) alimentos mpl sólidos

**solidarity** [sɒlɪ'dærɪtɪ] n solidaridad f

**solitaire** [sɒlɪ'tɛə*] n (*game, gem*) solitario

**solitary** ['sɒlɪtərɪ] adj solitario, solo; ~ **confinement** n incomunicación f

**solitude** ['sɒlɪtjuːd] n soledad f

**solo** ['səʊləʊ] n solo ♦ adv (*fly*) en solitario; ~**ist** n solista m/f

**soluble** ['sɒljʊbl] adj soluble

**solution** [sə'luːʃən] n solución f

**solve** [sɒlv] vt resolver, solucionar

**solvent** ['sɒlvənt] adj (*COMM*) solvente ♦ n (*CHEM*) solvente m

**sombre**, (*US* **somber**) ['sɒmbə*] adj sombrío

---

KEYWORD

---

**some** [sʌm] adj **1** (*a certain amount or number of*): ~ **tea/water/biscuits** té/agua/(unas) galletas; **there's ~ milk in the fridge** hay leche en el frigo; **there were ~ people outside** había algunas personas fuera; **I've got ~ money, but not much** tengo algo de dinero, pero no mucho

**2** (*certain: in contrasts*) algunos/as; ~ **people say that ...** hay quien dice que ...; ~ **films were excellent, but most were mediocre** hubo películas excelentes, pero la mayoría fueron mediocres

**3** (*unspecified*): ~ **woman was asking for you** una mujer estuvo preguntando por ti; **he was asking for ~ book (or other)** pedía un libro; ~ **day** algún día; ~ **day next week** un día de la semana que viene

♦ pron **1** (*a certain number*): **I've got ~ (books etc)** tengo algunos/as

**2** (*a certain amount*) algo; **I've got ~** (*money, milk*) tengo algo; **could I have ~ of that cheese?** ¿me puede dar un poco de ese queso?; **I've read ~ of the book** he leído parte

del libro
♦ adv: ~ **10 people** unas 10 personas, una decena de personas

---

**somebody** ['sʌmbədɪ] pron = **someone**

**somehow** ['sʌmhaʊ] adv de alguna manera; (*for some reason*) por una u otra razón

**someone** ['sʌmwʌn] pron alguien

**someplace** ['sʌmpleɪs] (*US*) adv = **somewhere**

**somersault** ['sʌməsɔːlt] n (*deliberate*) salto mortal; (*accidental*) vuelco ♦ vi dar un salto mortal; dar vuelcos

**something** ['sʌmθɪŋ] pron algo; **would you like ~ to eat/drink?** ¿te gustaría cenar/tomar algo?

**sometime** ['sʌmtaɪm] adv (*in future*) algún día, un día; (*in past*): ~ **last month** durante el mes pasado

**sometimes** ['sʌmtaɪmz] adv a veces

**somewhat** ['sʌmwɒt] adv algo

**somewhere** ['sʌmwɛə*] adv (*be*) en alguna parte; (*go*) a alguna parte; ~ **else** (*be*) en otra parte; (*go*) a otra parte

**son** [sʌn] n hijo

**song** [sɒŋ] n canción f

**son-in-law** ['sʌnɪnlɔː] n yerno

**sonnet** ['sɒnɪt] n soneto

**sonny** ['sʌnɪ] (*inf*) n hijo

**soon** [suːn] adv pronto, dentro de poco; ~ **afterwards** poco después; *see also* **as**; ~**er** adv (*time*) antes, más temprano; (*preference*): **I would ~er do that** preferiría hacer eso; ~**er or later** tarde o temprano

**soot** [sʊt] n hollín m

**soothe** [suːð] vt tranquilizar; (*pain*) aliviar

**sophisticated** [sə'fɪstɪkeɪtɪd] adj sofisticado

**sophomore** ['sɒfəmɔː*] (*US*) n estudiante m/f de segundo año

**sopping** ['sɒpɪŋ] adj: ~ (*wet*) empapado

**soppy** ['sɒpɪ] (*pej*) adj tonto

**soprano** [sə'prɑːnəu] n soprano f
**sorcerer** ['sɔːsərə*] n hechicero
**sore** [sɔː*] adj (painful) doloroso, que
duele ♦ n llaga; **~ly** adv: **I am ~ly
tempted to** estoy muy tentado a
**sorrow** ['sɔrəu] n pena, dolor m; **~s**
npl pesares mpl; **~ful** adj triste
**sorry** ['sɔrɪ] adj (regretful) arrepentido; (condition, excuse) lastimoso; ~!
¡perdón!, ¡perdone!; **~?** ¿cómo?; **to
feel ~ for sb** tener lástima a uno; **I
feel ~ for him** me da lástima
**sort** [sɔːt] n clase f, género, tipo ♦ vt
(also: ~ out: papers) clasificar; (:
problems) arreglar, solucionar; **~ing
office** n sala de batalla
**SOS** n abbr (= save our souls) SOS
m
**so-so** adv regular, así así
**soufflé** ['suːfleɪ] n suflé m
**sought** [sɔːt] pt, pp of **seek**
**soul** [soul] n alma; **~-destroying** adj
(work) deprimente; **~ful** adj lleno de
sentimiento
**sound** [saund] n (noise) sonido, ruido; (volume: on TV etc) volumen m;
(GEO) estrecho ♦ adj (healthy)
sano; (safe, not damaged) en buen
estado; (reliable: person) digno de
confianza; (sensible) sensato, razonable; (secure: investment) seguro ♦
adv: **~ asleep** profundamente dormido ♦ vt (alarm) sonar ♦ vi sonar,
resonar; (fig: seem) parecer; **to ~
like** sonar a; **~ out** vt sondear; **~
barrier** n barrera del sonido; **~ effects** npl efectos mpl sonoros; **~ly**
adv (sleep) profundamente; (defeated) completamente; **~proof** adj insonorizado; **~track** n (of film) banda
sonora
**soup** [suːp] n (thick) sopa; (thin) caldo; **in the ~** (fig) en apuros; **~
plate** n plato sopero; **~spoon** n cuchara sopera
**sour** [sauə*] adj agrio; (milk) cortado; **it's ~ grapes** (fig) están verdes
**source** [sɔːs] n fuente f
**south** [sauθ] n sur m ♦ adj del sur,
sureño ♦ adv al sur, hacia el sur;

**S~ Africa** n África del Sur; **S~ African** adj, n sudafricano/a m/f; **S~
America** n América del Sur, Sudamérica; **S~ American** adj, n
sudamericano/a m/f; **~-east** n sudeste m; **southerly** ['sʌðəlɪ] adj (from
the ~) del sur; **~ern** ['sʌðən] adj del
sur, meridional; **S~ Pole** n Polo Sur;
**~ward(s)** adv hacia el sur; **~-west**
n suroeste m
**souvenir** [suːvə'nɪə*] n recuerdo
**sovereign** ['sɔvrɪn] adj, n soberano/a
m/f; **~ty** n soberanía
**soviet** ['səuviət] adj soviético: the
**S~ Union** la Unión Soviética
**sow¹** [sou] (pt sowed, pp sown) ♦
vt sembrar
**sow²** [sau] n cerda (SP), puerca
(SP), chancha (AM)
**soy** [sɔɪ] (US) n = soya
**soya** ['sɔɪə] (BRIT) n soja; **~ bean** n
haba de soja; **~ sauce** n salsa de
soja
**spa** [spɑː] n balneario
**space** [speɪs] n espacio; (room) sitio
♦ cpd espacial ♦ vt (also: ~ out) espaciar; **~craft** n nave f espacial;
**~man/woman** n astronauta m/f, cosmonauta m/f; **~ship** n = **~craft**;
**spacing** n espaciado
**spacious** ['speɪʃəs] adj amplio
**spade** [speɪd] n (tool) pala, laya; **~s**
npl (CARDS: British) picas fpl; (:
Spanish) espadas fpl
**spaghetti** [spə'getɪ] n espaguetis
mpl, fideos npl
**Spain** [speɪn] n España
**span** [spæn] n (of bird, plane) envergadura; (of arch) luz f; (in time)
lapso ♦ vt extenderse sobre, cruzar;
(fig) abarcar
**Spaniard** ['spænjəd] n español/a m/f
**spaniel** ['spænjəl] n perro de aguas
**Spanish** ['spænɪʃ] adj español(a) ♦ n
(LING) español m, castellano; the ~
npl los españoles
**spank** [spæŋk] vt zurrar
**spanner** ['spænə*] (BRIT) n llave f
(inglesa)
**spar** [spɑː*] n palo, verga ♦ vi (BOX-

*ING)* entrenarse

**spare** [spɛə*] *adj* de reserva; *(surplus)* sobrante, de más ♦ *n* = ~ **part** ♦ *vt (do without)* pasarse sin; *(refrain from hurting)* perdonar; to ~ *(surplus)* sobrante, de sobra; ~ **part** *n* pieza de repuesto; ~ **time** *n* tiempo libre; ~ **wheel** *n (AUT)* rueda de recambio

**sparing** [ˈspɛərɪŋ] *adj*: to be ~ with ser parco en; ~**ly** *adv* con moderación

**spark** [spɑːk] *n* chispa; *(fig)* chispazo; ~**(ing) plug** *n* bujía

**sparkle** [ˈspɑːkl] *n* centelleo, destello ♦ *vi (shine)* relucir, brillar; **sparkling** *adj (eyes, conversation)* brillante; *(wine)* espumoso; *(mineral water)* con gas

**sparrow** [ˈspærəʊ] *n* gorrión *m*

**sparse** [spɑːs] *adj* esparcido, escaso

**spartan** [ˈspɑːtən] *adj (fig)* espartano

**spasm** [ˈspæzəm] *n (MED)* espasmo

**spastic** [ˈspæstɪk] *n* espástico/a

**spat** [spæt] *pt, pp of* **spit**

**spate** [speɪt] *n (fig)*: a ~ of un torrente de

**spatter** [ˈspætə*] *vt*: to ~ with salpicar de

**spawn** [spɔːn] *vi* desovar, frezar ♦ *n* huevas *fpl*

**speak** [spiːk] *(pt* **spoke**, *pp* **spoken)** *vt (language)* hablar; *(truth)* decir ♦ *vi* hablar; *(make a speech)* intervenir; to ~ to sb/of *or* about sth hablar con uno/de *or* sobre algo; ~ **up!** ¡habla fuerte!; ~**er** *n (in public)* orador(a) *m/f*; *(also: loud~er)* altavoz *m*; *(for stereo etc)* bafle *m*; *(POL)*: **the S~er** *(BRIT)* el Presidente de la *Cámara de los Comunes*; *(US)* el Presidente del Congreso

**spear** [spɪə*] *n* lanza ♦ *vt* alancear; ~**head** *vt (attack etc)* encabezar

**spec** [spɛk] *(inf)* n: on ~ como especulación

**special** [ˈspɛʃl] *adj* especial; *(edition etc)* extraordinario; *(delivery)* urgente; ~**ist** *n* especialista *m/f*; ~**ity** [spɛʃɪˈælɪtɪ] *(BRIT)* n especialidad *f*;

~**ize** *vi*: to ~**ize (in)** especializarse (en); ~**ly** *adv* sobre todo, en particular; ~**ty** *(US)* n = ~**ity**

**species** [ˈspiːʃiːz] *n inv* especie *f*

**specific** [spəˈsɪfɪk] *adj* específico; ~**ally** *adv* específicamente

**specify** [ˈspɛsɪfaɪ] *vt, vi* especificar, precisar

**specimen** [ˈspɛsɪmən] *n* ejemplar *m*; *(MED: of urine)* espécimen *m* (: *of blood)* muestra

**speck** [spɛk] *n* grano, mota

**speckled** [ˈspɛkld] *adj* moteado

**specs** [spɛks] *(inf)* npl gafas *fpl* (SP), anteojos *mpl*

**spectacle** [ˈspɛktəkl] *n* espectáculo; ~**s** *npl (BRIT: glasses)* gafas *fpl* (SP), anteojos *mpl*; **spectacular** [-ˈtækjʊlə*] *adj* espectacular; *(success)* impresionante

**spectator** [spɛkˈteɪtə*] *n* espectador(a) *m/f*

**spectre** [ˈspɛktə*] *(US* **specter**) *n* espectro, fantasma *m*

**spectrum** [ˈspɛktrəm] *(pl* **spectra**) *n* espectro

**speculate** [ˈspɛkjʊleɪt] *vi*: to ~ **(on)** especular (en)

**speculation** [spɛkjʊˈleɪʃən] *n* especulación *f*

**speech** [spiːtʃ] *n (faculty)* habla; *(formal talk)* discurso; *(spoken language)* lenguaje *m*; ~**less** *adj* mudo, estupefacto; ~ **therapist** *n* especialista que corrige defectos de pronunciación en los niños

**speed** [spiːd] *n* velocidad *f*; *(haste)* prisa; *(promptness)* rapidez *f*; **at full** *or* **top** ~ a máxima velocidad; ~ **up** *vi* acelerarse ♦ *vt* acelerar; ~**boat** *n* lancha motora; ~**ily** *adv* rápido, rápidamente; ~**ing** *n (AUT)* exceso de velocidad; ~ **limit** *n* límite *m* de velocidad, velocidad *f* máxima; ~**ometer** [spɪˈdɔmɪtə*] *n* velocímetro; ~**way** *n (sport)* pista de carrera; ~**y** *adj (fast)* veloz, rápido; *(prompt)* pronto

**spell** [spɛl] *(pt, pp* **spelt** *(BRIT)* or **spelled)** *n (also: magic* ~) encanto, hechizo; (period of time) rato, período ♦ vt deletrear; (fig) anunciar, presagiar; **to cast a ~ on sb** hechizar a uno; **he can't ~** pone faltas de ortografía; **~bound** adj embelesado, hechizado; **~ing** n ortografía

**spend** [spend] (pt, pp **spent**) vt (money) gastar; (time) pasar; (life) dedicar; **~thrift** n derrochador/a m/f, pródigo/a

**sperm** [spə:m] n esperma

**spew** [spju:] vt vomitar, arrojar

**sphere** [sfɪə*] n esfera

**sphinx** [sfɪŋks] n esfinge f

**spice** [spaɪs] n especia ♦ vt condimentar

**spick-and-span** ['spɪkən'spæn] adj aseado, (bien) arreglado

**spicy** ['spaɪsɪ] adj picante

**spider** ['spaɪdə*] n araña

**spike** [spaɪk] n (point) punta; (BOT) espiga

**spill** [spɪl] (pt, pp **spilt** or **spilled**) vt derramar, verter ♦ vi derramarse; **to ~ over** desbordarse

**spin** [spɪn] (pt, pp **spun**) n (AVIAT) barrena; (trip in car) paseo (en coche); (on ball) efecto ♦ vt (wool etc) hilar; (ball etc) hacer girar ♦ vi girar, dar vueltas; **~ out** vt alargar, prolongar

**spinach** ['spɪnɪtʃ] n espinaca; (as food) espinacas fpl

**spinal** ['spaɪnl] adj espinal; **~ cord** n columna vertebral

**spindly** ['spɪndlɪ] adj (leg) zanquivano

**spin-dryer** (BRIT) n secador m centrífugo

**spine** [spaɪn] n espinazo, columna vertebral; (thorn) espina; **~less** adj (fig) débil, pusilánime

**spinning** ['spɪnɪŋ] n hilandería; **~ top** n peonza; **~ wheel** n torno de hilar

**spin-off** n derivado, producto secundario

**spinster** ['spɪnstə*] n soltera

**spiral** ['spaɪərl] n espiral f ♦ vi (fig: prices) subir desorbitadamente; **~**

**staircase** n escalera de caracol

**spire** ['spaɪə*] n aguja, chapitel m

**spirit** ['spɪrɪt] n (soul) alma f; (ghost) fantasma m; (attitude, sense) espíritu m; (courage) valor m, ánimo; **~s** npl (drink) licor(es) m(pl); **in good ~s** alegre, de buen ánimo; **~ed** adj enérgico, vigoroso; **~ level** n nivel m de aire

**spiritual** ['spɪrɪtjuəl] adj espiritual ♦ n espiritual n

**spit** [spɪt] n (for roasting) asador m, espetón m; (saliva) saliva ♦ vi escupir; (sound) chisporrotear; (rain) lloviznar

**spite** [spaɪt] n rencor m, ojeriza ♦ vt causar pena a, mortificar; **in ~ of** a pesar de, pese a; **~ful** adj rencoroso, malévolo

**spittle** ['spɪtl] n saliva, baba

**splash** [splæʃ] n (sound) chapoteo; (of colour) mancha ♦ vt salpicar ♦ vi (also: **~ about**) chapotear

**spleen** [spli:n] n (ANAT) bazo

**splendid** ['splendɪd] adj espléndido

**splint** [splɪnt] n tablilla

**splinter** ['splɪntə*] n (of wood etc) astilla; (in finger) espigón m ♦ vi astillarse, hacer astillas

**split** [splɪt] (pt, pp **split**) n hendedura; (fig) división f; (POL) escisión f ♦ vt partir, rajar; (party) dividir; (share) repartir ♦ vi dividirse, escindirse; **~ up** vi (couple) separarse; (meeting) acabarse

**splutter** ['splʌtə*] vi chisporrotear; (person) balbucear

**spoil** [spɔɪl] (pt, pp **spoilt** or **spoiled**) vt (damage) dañar; (mar) estropear; (child) mimar, consentir; **~s** npl despojo, botín m; **~sport** n aguafiestas m inv

**spoke** [spəuk] pt of **speak** ♦ n rayo, radio

**spoken** ['spəukn] pp of **speak**

**spokesman** ['spəuksmən] n portavoz m; **spokeswoman** ['spəukswumən] n portavoz f

**sponge** [spʌndʒ] n esponja; (also: **~ cake**) bizcocho ♦ vt (wash) lavar con esponja ♦ vi: **to ~ off** or **on sb** vivir a costa de uno; **~ bag** (BRIT) n esponjera

**sponsor** ['spɔnsə*] n patrocinador(a) m/f ♦ vt (applicant, proposal etc) proponer; **~ship** n patrocinio

**spontaneous** [spɔn'teɪnɪəs] adj espontáneo

**spooky** ['spuːkɪ] (inf) adj espeluznante, horripilante

**spool** [spuːl] n carrete m

**spoon** [spuːn] n cuchara f; **~feed** vt dar de comer con cuchara a; (fig) tratar como un niño a; **~ful** n cucharada

**sport** [spɔːt] n deporte m; (person): **to be a good ~** ser muy majo ♦ vt (wear) lucir, ostentar; **~ing** adj deportivo; (generous) caballeroso; **to give sb a ~ing chance** darle a uno una (buena) oportunidad; **~ jacket** (US) n = **~s jacket**; **~s car** n coche m deportivo; **~s jacket** (BRIT) n chaqueta deportiva; **~sman** n deportista m; **~smanship** n espíritu deportivo f; **~swear** n trajes mpl de deporte or sport; **~swoman** n deportista f; **~y** adj deportista

**spot** [spɔt] n sitio, lugar m; (dot: on pattern) punto, mancha f; (pimple) grano; (RADIO) cuña publicitaria; (TV) espacio publicitario; (small amount): **a ~ of** un poquito de ♦ vt (notice) notar, observar; **on the ~** allí mismo; **~ check** n reconocimiento rápido; **~less** adj perfectamente limpio; **~light** n foco, reflector m; (AUT) faro auxiliar; **~ted** adj (pattern) de puntos; **~ty** adj (face) con granos

**spouse** [spauz] n cónyuge m/f

**spout** [spaut] n (of jug) pico; (of pipe) caño ♦ vi salir en chorro

**sprain** [spreɪn] n torcedura ♦ vt: **to ~ one's ankle/wrist** torcerse el tobillo/la muñeca

**sprang** [spræŋ] pt of **spring**

**sprawl** [sprɔːl] vi tumbarse

**spray** [spreɪ] n rociada; (of sea) espuma; (container) atomizador m; (for paint etc) pistola rociadora; (of flowers) ramita ♦ vt rociar; (crops) regar

**spread** [spred] (pt, pp **spread**) n extensión f; (for bread etc) pasta para untar; (inf: food) comilona ♦ vt extender; (butter) untar; (wings, sails) desplegar; (work, wealth) repartir; (scatter) esparcir ♦ vi (also: **~ out**: stain) extenderse; (news) diseminarse; **~ out** vi (move apart) separarse; **~-eagled** adj a pata tendida; **~sheet** n (COMPUT) hoja electrónica or de cálculo

**spree** [sprɪː] n: **to go on a ~** ir de juerga

**sprightly** ['spraɪtlɪ] adj vivo, enérgico

**spring** [sprɪŋ] (pt **sprang**, pp **sprung**) n (season) primavera f; (leap) salto, brinco; (coiled metal) resorte m; (of water) fuente f, manantial m ♦ vi saltar, brincar; **~ up** vi (thing: appear) aparecer; (problem) surgir; **~board** n trampolín m; **~-clean(ing)** n limpieza general; **~time** n primavera

**sprinkle** ['sprɪŋkl] vt (pour: liquid) rociar; (: salt, sugar) espolvorear; **to ~ water etc on, ~ with water** etc rociar or salpicar de agua etc; **~r** n (for lawn) rociadera; (to put out fire) aparato de rociadura automática

**sprint** [sprɪnt] n esprint m ♦ vi esprintar

**sprout** [spraut] vi brotar, retoñar; **(Brussels) ~s** npl coles fpl de Bruselas

**spruce** [spruːs] n inv (BOT) pícea ♦ adj aseado, pulcro

**sprung** [sprʌŋ] pp of **spring**

**spry** [spraɪ] adj ágil, activo

**spun** [spʌn] pt, pp of **spin**

**spur** [spəː*] n espuela; (fig) estímulo, aguijón m ♦ vt (also: **~ on**) estimular, incitar; **on the ~ of the moment** de improviso

**spurious** ['spjuərɪəs] adj falso

**spurn** [spəːn] vt desdeñar, rechazar

**spurt** [spəːt] n chorro; (of energy)

arrebato ♦ *vi* chorrear

**spy** [spaɪ] *n* espía *m/f* ♦ *vi*: **to ~ on** espiar a ♦ *vt* (*see*) divisar, lograr ver; **~ing** *n* espionaje *m*

**sq.** *abbr* = **square**

**squabble** ['skwɔbl] *vi* reñir, pelear

**squad** [skwɔd] *n* (*MIL*) pelotón *m*; (*POLICE*) brigada; (*SPORT*) equipo

**squadron** ['skwɔdrn] *n* (*MIL*) escuadrón *m*; (*AVIAT, NAUT*) escuadra

**squalid** ['skwɔlɪd] *adj* vil; (*fig: sordid*) sórdido

**squall** [skwɔːl] *n* (*storm*) chubasco; (*wind*) ráfaga

**squalor** ['skwɔlə*] *n* miseria

**squander** ['skwɔndə*] *vt* (*money*) derrochar, despilfarrar; (*chances*) desperdiciar

**square** [skwɛə*] *n* cuadro; (*in town*) plaza; (*inf: person*) carca *m/f* ♦ *adj* cuadrado; (*inf: ideas, tastes*) trasnochado ♦ *vt* (*arrange*) arreglar; (*MATH*) cuadrar; (*reconcile*) compaginar; **all ~** igual(es); **to have a ~ meal** comer caliente; **2 metres ~** 2 metros en cuadro; **2 ~ metres** 2 metros cuadrados; **~ly** *adv* de lleno

**squash** [skwɔʃ] *n* (*BRIT: drink*): **lemon/orange ~** zumo (*SP*) or jugo (*AM*) de limón/naranja; (*US: BOT*) calabacín *m*; (*SPORT*) squash *m*, frontenis *m* ♦ *vt* aplastar

**squat** [skwɔt] *adj* achaparrado ♦ *vi* (*also: ~ down*) agacharse, sentarse en cuclillas; **~ter** *n* persona *que ocupa ilegalmente una casa*

**squawk** [skwɔːk] *vi* graznar

**squeak** [skwiːk] *vi* (*hinge*) chirriar, rechinar; (*mouse*) chillar

**squeal** [skwiːl] *vi* chillar, dar gritos agudos

**squeamish** ['skwiːmɪʃ] *adj* delicado, remilgado

**squeeze** [skwiːz] *n* presión *f*; (*of hand*) apretón *m*; (*COMM*) restricción *f* ♦ *vt* (*hand, arm*) apretar; **~ out** *vt* exprimir

**squelch** [skweltʃ] *vi* chapotear

**squid** [skwɪd] *n inv* calamar *m*; (*CULIN*) calamares *mpl*

**squiggle** ['skwɪgl] *n* garabato

**squint** [skwɪnt] *vi* bizquear, ser bizco ♦ *n* (*MED*) estrabismo

**squire** [skwaɪə*] *n* (*BRIT*) terrateniente *m*

**squirm** [skwəːm] *vi* retorcerse, revolverse

**squirrel** ['skwɪrəl] *n* ardilla

**squirt** [skwəːt] *vi* salir a chorros ♦ *vt* chiscar

**Sr** *abbr* = **senior**

**St** *abbr* = **saint**; **street**

**stab** [stæb] *n* (*with knife*) puñalada; (*of pain*) pinchazo; (*inf: try*): **to have a ~ at (doing) sth** intentar (hacer) algo ♦ *vt* apuñalar

**stable** ['steɪbl] *adj* estable ♦ *n* cuadra, caballeriza

**stack** [stæk] *n* montón *m*, pila ♦ *vt* amontonar, apilar

**stadium** ['steɪdɪəm] *n* estadio

**staff** [stɑːf] *n* (*work force*) personal *m*, plantilla; (*BRIT: SCOL*) cuerpo docente ♦ *vt* proveer de personal

**stag** [stæg] *n* ciervo, venado

**stage** [steɪdʒ] *n* escena; (*point*) etapa; (*platform*) plataforma; (*profession*): **the ~** el teatro ♦ *vt* (*play*) poner en escena, representar; (*organize*) montar, organizar; **in ~s** por etapas; **~coach** *n* diligencia; **~ manager** *n* director(a) *m/f* de escena

**stagger** ['stægə*] *vi* tambalearse ♦ *vt* (*amaze*) asombrar; (*hours, holidays*) escalonar; **~ing** *adj* asombroso

**stagnant** ['stægnənt] *adj* estancado

**stagnate** [stæg'neɪt] *vi* estancarse

**stag party** *n* despedida de soltero

**staid** [steɪd] *adj* serio, formal

**stain** [steɪn] *n* mancha; (*colouring*) tintura ♦ *vt* manchar; (*wood*) teñir; **~ed glass window** *n* vidriera de colores; **~less steel** *n* acero inoxidable; **~ remover** *n* quitamanchas *m inv*

**stair** [stɛə*] *n* (*step*) peldaño, escalón *m*; **~s** *npl* escaleras *fpl*; **~case** *n* ~**way**; **~way** *n* escalera

**stake** [steɪk] *n* estaca, poste *m*;

(COMM) interés m; (BETTING) apuesta ♦ vt (money) apostar; (life) arriesgar; (reputation) poner en juego; (claim) presentar una reclamación; **to be at** ~ estar en juego

**stale** [steɪl] adj (bread) duro; (food) pasado; (smell) rancio; (beer) agrio

**stalemate** ['steɪlmeɪt] n tablas fpl (por ahogado), (fig) estancamiento

**stalk** [stɔːk] n tallo, caña ♦ vt acechar, cazar al acecho; ~ **off** vi irse airado

**stall** [stɔːl] n (in market) puesto; (in stable) casilla (de establo) ♦ vt (AUT) calar; (fig) dar largas a ♦ vi (AUT) calarse; (fig) andarse con rodeos; ~s npl (BRIT: in cinema, theatre) butacas fpl

**stallion** ['stælɪən] n semental m

**stalwart** ['stɔːlwət] n leal

**stamina** ['stæmɪnə] n resistencia

**stammer** ['stæmə*] n tartamudeo ♦ vi tartamudear

**stamp** [stæmp] n sello (SP), estampilla (AM); (mark, also fig) marca, huella; (on document) timbre m ♦ vi (also: ~ one's foot) patear ♦ vt (mark) marcar; (letter) poner sellos or estampillas en; (with rubber ~) sellar; ~ **album** n álbum m para sellos or estampillas; ~ **collecting** n filatelia

**stampede** [stæm'piːd] n estampida

**stance** [stæns] n postura

**stand** [stænd] (pt, pp stood) n (position) posición f, postura; (for taxis) parada; (hall ~) perchero; (music ~) atril m; (SPORT) tribuna; (at exhibition) stand m ♦ vi (be) estar, encontrarse; (be on foot) estar de pie; (rise) levantarse; (remain) quedar en pie; (in election) presentar candidatura ♦ vt (place) poner, colocar; (withstand) aguantar, soportar; (invite) invitar; **to make a** ~ (fig) mantener una postura firme; **to** ~ **for parliament** (BRIT) presentarse (como candidato) a las elecciones; ~ **by** vi (be ready) estar listo ♦ vt fus (opinion) aferrarse a; (person) apo-

yar; ~ **down** vi (withdraw) ceder el puesto; ~ **for** vt fus (signify) significar; (tolerate) aguantar, permitir; ~ **in for** vt fus suplir a; ~ **out** vi destacarse; ~ **up** vi levantarse, ponerse de pie; ~ **up for** vt fus defender; ~ **up to** vt fus hacer frente a

**standard** ['stændəd] n patrón m, norma; (level) nivel m; (flag) estandarte m ♦ adj (size etc) normal, corriente; (text) básico; ~s npl (morals) valores mpl morales; ~**ize** vt normalizar; ~ **lamp** (BRIT) n lámpara de pie; ~ **of living** n nivel m de vida

**stand-by** ['stændbaɪ] n (reserve) recurso seguro; **to be on** ~ estar sobre aviso; ~ **ticket** n (AVIAT) (billete m) standby m

**stand-in** ['stændɪn] n suplente m/f

**standing** ['stændɪŋ] adj (on foot) de pie, en pie; (permanent) permanente ♦ n reputación f; **of many years'** ~ que lleva muchos años; ~ **joke** n broma permanente; ~ **order** (BRIT) n (at bank) orden f de pago permanente; ~ **room** n sitio para estar de pie

**stand-: ~offish** adj reservado, poco afable; ~**point** n punto de vista; ~**still** n: **at a** ~**still** (industry, traffic) paralizado; (car) parado; **to come to a** ~**still** quedar paralizado; pararse

**stank** [stæŋk] pt of **stink**

**staple** ['steɪpl] n (for papers) grapa (SP, plug etc) básico ♦ vt grapar; ~**r** n grapadora

**star** [stɑː*] n estrella; (celebrity) estrella, astro ♦ vi (THEATRE, CINEMA) ser el/la protagonista de; the ~s npl (ASTROLOGY) el horóscopo

**starboard** ['stɑːbəd] n estribor m

**starch** [stɑːtʃ] n almidón m

**stardom** ['stɑːdəm] n estrellato

**stare** [stɛə*] n mirada fija ♦ vi: **to** ~ **at** mirar fijo

**starfish** ['stɑːfɪʃ] n estrella de mar

**stark** [stɑːk] adj (bleak) severo, escueto ♦ adv: ~ **naked** en cueros

**starling** ['stɑːlɪŋ] n estornino

**starry** ['stɑːrɪ] adj estrellado; **~-eyed** adj (innocent) inocentón/ona, ingenuo

**start** [stɑːt] n principio, comienzo; (departure) salida; (sudden movement) salto, sobresalto; (advantage) ventaja ♦ vt empezar, comenzar; (cause) causar; (found) fundar; (engine) poner en marcha ♦ vi comenzar, empezar; (with fright) asustarse, sobresaltarse; (train etc) salir; **to ~ doing** or **to do sth** empezar a hacer algo; **~ off** vi empezar, comenzar; (leave) salir, ponerse en camino; **~ up** vi comenzar; (car) ponerse en marcha ♦ vt comenzar; poner en marcha; **~er** n (AUT) botón m de arranque; (SPORT: official) juez m/f de salida; (BRIT: CULIN) entrada; **~ing point** n punto de partida

**startle** ['stɑːtl] vt asustar, sobrecoger; **startling** adj alarmante

**starvation** [stɑːˈveɪʃən] n hambre f

**starve** [stɑːv] vi tener mucha hambre; (to death) morir de hambre ♦ vt hacer pasar hambre

**state** [steɪt] n estado ♦ vt (say, declare) afirmar; **the S~s** los Estados Unidos; **to be in a ~** estar agitado; **~ly** adj majestuoso, imponente; **~ment** n afirmación f; **~sman** n estadista m

**static** ['stætɪk] n (RADIO) parásitos mpl ♦ adj estático; **~ electricity** n estática

**station** ['steɪʃən] n (gen) estación f; (RADIO) emisora; (rank) posición f social ♦ vt colocar, situar; (MIL) apostar

**stationary** ['steɪʃənrɪ] adj estacionario, fijo

**stationer** ['steɪʃənə*] n papelero/a; **~'s (shop)** (BRIT) n papelería; **~** [-nərɪ] n papel m de escribir, artículos mpl de escritorio

**station master** n (RAIL) jefe m de estación

**station wagon** (US) n ranchera

**statistic** [stəˈtɪstɪk] n estadística; **~al** adj estadístico; **~s** n (science) esta-

dística

**statue** ['stætjuː] n estatua

**status** ['steɪtəs] n estado; (reputation) estatus m; **~ symbol** n símbolo de prestigio

**statute** ['stætjuːt] n estatuto, ley f; **statutory** adj estatutario

**staunch** [stɔːntʃ] adj leal, incondicional

**stave** [steɪv] vt: **to ~ off** (attack) rechazar; (threat) evitar

**stay** [steɪ] n estancia ♦ vi quedar(se); (as guest) hospedarse; **to ~ put** seguir en el mismo sitio; **to ~ the night/5 days** pasar la noche/estar 5 días; **~ behind** vi quedar atrás; **~ in** vi quedarse en casa; **~ on** vi quedarse; **~ out** vi (of house) no volver a casa; (on strike) permanecer en huelga; **~ up** vi (at night) velar, no acostarse; **~ing power** n aguante m

**stead** [sted] n: **in sb's ~** en lugar de uno; **to stand sb in good ~** ser muy útil a uno

**steadfast** ['stedfɑːst] adj firme, resuelto

**steadily** ['stedɪlɪ] adv constantemente; (firmly) firmemente; (work, walk) sin parar; (gaze) fijamente

**steady** ['stedɪ] adj (firm) firme; (regular) regular; (person, character) sensato, juicioso; (boyfriend) formal; (look, voice) tranquilo ♦ vt (stabilize) estabilizar; (nerves) calmar

**steak** [steɪk] n (gen) filete m; (beef) bistec m

**steal** [stiːl] (pt **stole**, pp **stolen**) vt robar ♦ vi robar; (move secretly) andar a hurtadillas

**stealth** [stelθ] n: **by ~** a escondidas, sigilosamente; **~y** adj cauteloso, sigiloso

**steam** [stiːm] n vapor m; (mist) vaho, humo ♦ vt (CULIN) cocer al vapor ♦ vi echar vapor; **~ engine** n máquina de vapor; **~er** n (buque m de) vapor m; **~roller** n apisonadora; **~ship** n = **~er**; **~y** adj (room) lleno de vapor; (window) empañado;

(heat, atmosphere) bochornoso

**steel** [stiːl] n acero ♦ adj de acero; **~works** n acería

**steep** [stiːp] adj escarpado, abrupto; (stair) empinado; (price) exorbitante, excesivo ♦ vt empapar, remojar

**steeple** ['stiːpl] n aguja; **~chase** n carrera de obstáculos

**steer** [stɪə\*] vt (car) conducir (SP), manejar (AM); (person) dirigir ♦ vi conducir, manejar; **~ing** n (AUT) dirección f; **~ing wheel** n volante m

**stem** [stem] n (of plant) tallo; (of glass) pie m ♦ vt detener; (blood) restañar; **~ from** vt fus ser consecuencia de

**stench** [stentʃ] n hedor m

**stencil** ['stensl] n (pattern) plantilla ♦ vt hacer un cliché de

**stenographer** [ste'nɔgrəfə\*] (US) n taquígrafo/a

**step** [step] n paso; (on stair) peldaño, escalón m ♦ vi: to ~ **forward/back** dar un paso adelante/hacia atrás; **~s** npl (BRIT) = **ladder**; **in/out** ♦ vi (with) acorde/en disonancia (con); ~ **down** vi (fig) retirarse; ~ **on** vt fus pisar; ~ **up** vt (increase) aumentar; **~brother** n hermanastro; **~daughter** n hijastra; **~father** n padrastro; **~ladder** n escalera doble or de tijera; **~mother** n madrastra; **~ping stone** n pasadera; **~sister** n hermanastra; **~son** n hijastro

**stereo** ['sterɪəu] n estéreo ♦ adj (also: **~phonic**) estéreo, estereofónico

**sterile** ['sterail] adj estéril; **sterilize** ['sterilaɪz] vt esterilizar

**sterling** ['stɜːlɪŋ] adj (silver) de ley ♦ n (ECON) (libras fpl) esterlinas fpl; **one pound ~** una libra esterlina

**stern** [stɜːn] adj severo, austero ♦ n (NAUT) popa

**stethoscope** ['steθəskəup] n estetoscopio

**stew** [stjuː] n cocido (SP), estofado (SP), guisado (AM) ♦ vt estofar, guisar; (fruit) cocer

**steward** ['stjuːəd] n camarero; **~ess** n (esp on plane) azafata

**stick** [stɪk] (pt, pp **stuck**) n palo; (of dynamite) barreno; (as weapon) porra; (walking ~) bastón m ♦ vt (glue) pegar; (inf: put) meter; (: tolerate) aguantar, soportar; (thrust): to ~ **sth into** clavar or hincar algo en ♦ vi pegarse; (be unmoveable) quedarse parado; (in mind) quedarse grabado; ~ **out** vi sobresalir; ~ **up** vi sobresalir; ~ **up for** vt fus defender; **~er** n (label) etiqueta engomada; (with slogan) pegatina; **~ing plaster** n esparadrapo

**stickler** ['stɪklə\*] n: **to be a ~ for** insistir mucho en

**stick-up** (inf) n asalto, atraco

**sticky** ['stɪkɪ] adj pegajoso; (label) engomado; (fig) difícil

**stiff** [stɪf] adj rígido, tieso; (hard) duro; (manner) estirado; (difficult) difícil; (person) inflexible; (price) exorbitante ♦ adv: **scared/bored ~** muerto de miedo/aburrimiento; **~en** vi (muscles etc) agarrotarse; ~ **neck** n torticolis m inv; **~ness** n rigidez f, tiesura

**stifle** ['staɪfl] vt ahogar, sofocar; **stifling** adj (heat) sofocante, bochornoso

**stigma** ['stɪgmə] n (fig) estigma m

**stile** [staɪl] n portillo, portilla

**stiletto** [stɪ'letəu] (BRIT) n (also: ~ **heel**) tacón m de aguja

**still** [stɪl] adj inmóvil, quieto ♦ adv todavía; (even) aun; (nonetheless) sin embargo, aun así; **~born** adj nacido muerto; ~ **life** n naturaleza muerta

**stilt** [stɪlt] n zanco; (pile) pilar m, soporte m

**stilted** ['stɪltɪd] adj afectado

**stimulate** ['stɪmjuleɪt] vt estimular

**stimuli** ['stɪmjulaɪ] npl of **stimulus**

**stimulus** ['stɪmjuləs] (pl **stimuli**) n estímulo, incentivo

**sting** [stɪŋ] (pt, pp **stung**) n picadura; (pain) escozor m, picazón f; (organ) aguijón m ♦ vt, vi picar

**stingy** ['stɪndʒɪ] adj tacaño

**stink** [stɪŋk] (pt **stank**, pp **stunk**) n

hedor *m*, tufo ♦ *vi* heder, apestar;
**~ing** *adj* hediondo, fétido; (*fig: inf*)
horrible

**stint** [stɪnt] *n* tarea, trabajo ♦ *vi*: to
~ on escatimar

**stir** [stə:*]* *n* (*fig: agitation*) conmoción ♦ *vt* (*tea etc*) remover; (*fig:
emotions*) provocar ♦ *vi* moverse; ~
**up** *vt* (*trouble*) fomentar

**stirrup** [ˈstɪrəp] *n* estribo

**stitch** [stɪtʃ] *n* (*SEWING*) puntada, (*KNITTING*) punto; (*MED*) punto
(de sutura); (*pain*) punzada ♦ *vt* coser; (*MED*) suturar

**stoat** [stəut] *n* armiño

**stock** [stɔk] *n* (*COMM: reserves*)
existencias *fpl*, stock *m*; (*: selection*)
surtido; (*AGR*) ganado, ganadería,
(*CULIN*) caldo; (*descent*) raza, estirpe *f*; (*FINANCE*) capital *m* ♦ *adj*
(*fig: reply etc*) clásico ♦ *vt* (*have in
~*) tener existencias de; **~s and
shares** acciones y valores; **in ~** en
existencia or almacén; **out of ~** agotado; **to take ~ of** (*fig*) asesorar,
examinar; **~ up with** *vi fus* abastecerse de; **~broker** [ˈstɔkbrəukə*]* *n*
agente *m/f or* corredor(a) *m/f* de bolsa; **~ cube** (*BRIT*) *n* pastilla de caldo; **~ exchange** *n* bolsa

**stocking** [ˈstɔkɪŋ] *n* media

**stock**: **~ist** (*BRIT*) *n* distribuidor(a)
*m/f*; **~ market** *n* bolsa (de valores);
**~ phrase** *n* cliché *m*; **~pile** *n* reserva ♦ *vt* acumular, almacenar; **~taking** (*BRIT*) *n* (*COMM*) inventario

**stocky** [ˈstɔkɪ] *adj* (*strong*) robusto,
(*short*) achaparrado

**stodgy** [ˈstɔdʒɪ] *adj* indigesto, pesado

**stoke** [stəuk] *vt* atizar

**stole** [stəul] *pt of* **steal** ♦ *n* estola

**stolen** [ˈstəuln] *pp of* **steal**

**stolid** [ˈstɔlɪd] *adj* impertubable, impasible

**stomach** [ˈstʌmək] *n* (*ANAT*) estómago; (*belly*) vientre *m* ♦ *vt* tragar,
aguantar; **~ache** *n* dolor *m* de estómago

**stone** [stəun] *n* piedra; (*in fruit*) hueso; (*BRIT: weight*) = 6.348kg; 14 li-

bras ♦ *adj* de piedra ♦ *vt* apedrear
(*fruit*) deshuesar; **~-cold** *adj* helado
**~-deaf** *adj* sordo como una tapia
**~work** *n* (*art*) cantería; **stony** *ad*
pedregoso; (*fig*) frío

**stood** [stud] *pt, pp of* **stand**

**stool** [stu:l] *n* taburete *m*

**stoop** [stu:p] *vi* (*also: ~ down*) doblarse, agacharse; (*also: have a ~*)
ser cargado de espaldas

**stop** [stɔp] *n* parada; (*in punctuation*) punto ♦ *vt* parar, detener;
(*break off*) suspender; (*block: pay*)
suspender; (*: cheque*) invalidar;
(*also: put a ~ to*) poner término a ♦
*vi* pararse, detenerse; (*end*) acabarse; **to ~ doing sth** dejar de hacer
algo; **~ dead** *vi* pararse en seco; **~
off** *vi* interrumpir el viaje; **~ up** *vt*
(*hole*) tapar; **~gap** *n* (*person*)
interino/a; (*thing*) recurso provisional; **~over** *n* parada; (*AVIAT*) escala

**stoppage** [ˈstɔpɪdʒ] *n* (*strike*) paro;
(*blockage*) obstrucción *f*

**stopper** [ˈstɔpə*]* *n* tapón *m*

**stop press** *n* noticias *fpl* de última
hora

**stopwatch** [ˈstɔpwɔtʃ] *n* cronómetro

**storage** [ˈstɔ:rɪdʒ] *n* almacenaje *m*;
**~ heater** *n* acumulador *m*

**store** [stɔ:*]* *n* (*stock*) provisión *f*;
(*depot: BRIT, large shop*) almacén
*m*; (*US*) tienda; (*reserve*) reserva,
repuesto ♦ *vt* almacenar; **~s** *npl* víveres *mpl*; **in ~** (*fig*): to be in ~
**for sb** esperarle a uno; **~ up** *vt* acumular; **~room** *n* despensa

**storey** [ˈstɔ:rɪ] (*US* **story**) *n* piso

**stork** [stɔ:k] *n* cigüeña

**storm** [stɔ:m] *n* tormenta; (*fig: of
applause*) salva; (*: of criticism*)
nube *f* ♦ *vi* (*fig*) rabiar ♦ *vt* tomar
por asalto; **~y** *adj* tempestuoso

**story** [ˈstɔ:rɪ] *n* historia; (*lie*) mentira; (*US*) = **storey**; **~book** *n* libro de
cuentos

**stout** [staut] *adj* (*strong*) sólido;
(*fat*) gordo, corpulento; (*resolute*) resuelto ♦ *n* cerveza negra

**stove** [stəuv] n (for cooking) cocina; (for heating) estufa

**stow** [stəu] vt (also: ~ away) meter, poner; (NAUT) estibar; **~away** n polizón/ona m/f

**straddle** ['strædl] vt montar a horcajadas; (fig) abarcar

**straggle** ['strægl] vi (houses etc) extenderse; (lag behind) rezagarse; **straggly** adj (hair) desordenado

**straight** [streɪt] adj recto, derecho; (frank) franco, directo; (simple) sencillo ♦ adv derecho, directamente; (drink) sin mezcla; **to put** or **get sth ~** dejar algo en claro; **~ away**, **~ off** en seguida; **~en** vt (also: **~en out**) enderezar, poner derecho; **~-faced** adj serio; **~forward** adj (simple) sencillo; (honest) honrado, franco

**strain** [streɪn] n tensión f; (TECH) presión f; (MED) torcedura; (breed) tipo, variedad f ♦ vt (back etc) torcerse; (resources) agotar; (stretch) estirar; (food, tea) colar; **~s** npl (MUS) son m; **~ed** adj (muscle) torcido; (laugh) forzado; (relations) tenso; **~er** n colador m

**strait** [streɪt] n (GEO) estrecho; **to be in dire ~s** pasar grandes apuros; **~jacket** n camisa de fuerza; **~laced** adj mojigato, gazmoño

**strand** [strænd] n (of thread) hebra; (of hair) trenza; (of rope) ramal m; **~ed** adj (holidaymakers) colgado

**strange** [streɪndʒ] adj (not known) desconocido; (odd) extraño, raro; **~ly** adv de un modo raro; see also **enough**; **~r** n desconocido/a; (from another area) forastero/a

**strangle** ['stræŋgl] vt estrangular; **~hold** n (fig) dominio completo

**strap** [stræp] n correa; (of slip, dress) tirante m

**strapping** ['stræpɪŋ] adj robusto, fornido

**strategic** [strə'tiːdʒɪk] adj estratégico

**strategy** ['strætɪdʒɪ] n estrategia

**straw** [strɔː] n paja; (drinking ~) caña, pajita; **that's the last ~!** ¡eso es el colmo!

**strawberry** ['strɔːbərɪ] n fresa (SP), frutilla (AM)

**stray** [streɪ] adj (animal) extraviado; (bullet) perdido; (scattered) disperso ♦ vi extraviarse, perderse; (thoughts) vagar

**streak** [striːk] n raya; (in hair) raya ♦ vt rayar ♦ vi: **to ~ past** pasar como un rayo

**stream** [striːm] n riachuelo, arroyo; (of people, vehicles) riada, caravana; (of smoke, insults etc) chorro ♦ vt (SCOL) dividir en grupos por habilidad ♦ vi correr, fluir; **to ~ in/out** (people) entrar/salir en tropel

**streamer** ['striːmə*] n serpentina

**streamlined** ['striːmlaɪnd] adj aerodinámico

**street** [striːt] n calle f; **~car** (US) n tranvía m; **~ lamp** n farol m; **~ plan** n plano; **~wise** (inf) adj que tiene mucha calle

**strength** [streŋθ] n fuerza; (of girder, knot etc) resistencia; (fig: power) poder m; **~en** vt fortalecer, reforzar

**strenuous** ['strenjuəs] adj (energetic, determined) enérgico

**stress** [stres] n presión f; (mental strain) estrés m; (accent) acento ♦ vt subrayar, recalcar; (syllable) acentuar

**stretch** [stretʃ] n (of sand etc) trecho ♦ vi estirarse; (extend): **to ~ to** or **as far as** extenderse hasta ♦ vt extender, estirar; (make demands of): **to ~ to** exigir el máximo esfuerzo a; **to ~ out** or **as far as** extenderse hasta; **~ out** vi tenderse ♦ vt (arm etc) extender; (spread) estirar

**stretcher** ['stretʃə*] n camilla

**strewn** [struːn] adj: **~ with** cubierto or sembrado de

**stricken** ['strɪkən] adj (person) herido; (city, industry etc) condenado; **~ with** (disease) afectado por

**strict** [strɪkt] adj severo; (exact) estricto; **~ly** adv estrictamente, estrictamente

**stride** [straɪd] (pt **strode**, pp **stridden**) n zancada, tranco ♦ vi dar zancadas, andar a trancos

**strident** ['straɪdnt] adj estridente

**strife** [straɪf] n lucha

**strike** [straɪk] (pt, pp **struck**) n huelga; (of oil etc) descubrimiento; (attack) ataque m ♦ vt golpear, pegar; (oil etc) descubrir; (bargain, deal) cerrar ♦ vi declarar la huelga; (attack) atacar; (clock) dar la hora; **on ~** (workers) en huelga; **to ~ a match** encender un fósforo; **~ down** vt derribar; **~ up** vt (MUS) empezar a tocar; (conversation) entablar; (friendship) trabar; **~r** n huelgista m/f; (SPORT) delantero; **striking** adj llamativo

**string** [strɪŋ] (pt, pp **strung**) n (gen) cuerda; (row) hilera ♦ vt: **to ~ together** ensartar; **to ~ out** extenderse; the **~s** npl (MUS) los instrumentos de cuerda; **to pull ~s** (fig) mover palancas; **~ bean** n judía verde, habichuela; **~(ed) instrument** n (MUS) instrumento de cuerda

**stringent** ['strɪndʒənt] adj riguroso, severo

**strip** [strɪp] n tira; (of land) franja; (of metal) cinta, lámina ♦ vt desnudar; (paint) quitar; (also: **~ down:** machine) desmontar ♦ vi desnudarse; **~ cartoon** n tira cómica (SP), historieta (AM)

**stripe** [straɪp] n raya; (MIL) galón m; **~d** adj a rayas, rayado

**strip lighting** n alumbrado fluorescente

**stripper** ['strɪpə*] n artista m/f de striptease

**strive** [straɪv] (pt **strove**, pp **striven**) vi: **to ~ for sth/to do sth** luchar por conseguir/hacer algo; **striven** ['strɪvn] pp of **strive**

**strode** [strəud] pt of **stride**

**stroke** [strəuk] n (blow) golpe m; (SWIMMING) brazada; (MED) apoplejía; (of paintbrush) toque m ♦ vt acariciar; **at a ~** en un solo golpe

**stroll** [strəul] n paseo, vuelta ♦ vi dar

un paseo or una vuelta; **~er** (US) n (for child) sillita de ruedas

**strong** [strɒŋ] adj fuerte; **they are 50 ~** son 50; **~hold** n fortaleza; (fig) baluarte m; **~ly** adv fuertemente, con fuerza; (believe) firmemente; **~room** n cámara acorazada

**strove** [strəuv] pt of **strive**

**struck** [strʌk] pt, pp of **strike**

**structure** ['strʌktʃə*] n estructura; (building) construcción f

**struggle** ['strʌgl] n lucha ♦ vi luchar

**strum** [strʌm] vt (guitar) rasguear

**strung** [strʌŋ] pt, pp of **string**

**strut** [strʌt] n puntal m ♦ vi pavonearse

**stub** [stʌb] n (of ticket etc) talón m; (of cigarette) colilla; **to ~ one's toe on sth** dar con el dedo (del pie) contra algo; **~ out** vt apagar

**stubble** ['stʌbl] n rastrojo; (on chin) barba (incipiente)

**stubborn** ['stʌbən] adj terco, testarudo

**stuck** [stʌk] pt, pp of **stick** ♦ adj (jammed) atascado; **~up** adj engreído, presumido

**stud** [stʌd] n (shirt ~) corchete m; (of boot) taco; (earring) pendiente m (de bolita); (also: **~ farm**) caballeriza; (also: **~ horse**) caballo semental ♦ vt (fig): **~ded with** salpicado de

**student** ['stjuːdənt] n estudiante m/f ♦ adj estudiantil; **~ driver** (US) n aprendiz(a) m/f

**studio** ['stjuːdɪəu] n estudio; (artist's) taller m; **~ flat** (US **~ apartment**) n estudio

**studious** ['stjuːdɪəs] adj estudioso; (studied) calculado; **~ly** adv (carefully) con esmero

**study** ['stʌdɪ] n estudio ♦ vt estudiar; (examine) examinar, investigar ♦ vi estudiar

**stuff** [stʌf] n materia; (substance) material m, sustancia; (things) cosas fpl ♦ vt llenar; (CULIN) rellenar; (animals) disecar; (inf: push) meter; **~ing** n relleno; **~y** adj (room) mal ventilado; (person) de miras estrechas

**stumble** ['stʌmbl] vi tropezar, dar un traspié; **to ~ across, ~ on** (fig) tropezar con; **stumbling block** n tropiezo, obstáculo

**stump** [stʌmp] n (of tree) tocón m; (of limb) muñón m ♦ vt: **to be ~ed for an answer** no saber qué contestar

**stun** [stʌn] vt dejar sin sentido

**stung** [stʌŋ] pt, pp of **sting**

**stunk** [stʌŋk] pp of **stink**

**stunning** ['stʌnɪŋ] adj (fig: news) pasmoso; (: outfit etc) sensacional

**stunt** [stʌnt] n (in film) escena peligrosa; (publicity) truco publicitario; **~ed** adj enano, achaparrado; **~man** n doble m

**stupefy** ['stju:pɪfaɪ] vt dejar estupefacto

**stupendous** [stju:'pɛndəs] adj estupendo, asombroso

**stupid** ['stju:pɪd] adj estúpido, tonto; **~ity** [-'pɪdɪtɪ] n estupidez f

**sturdy** ['stɜːdɪ] adj robusto, fuerte

**stutter** ['stʌtə*] n tartamudeo ♦ vi tartamudear

**sty** [staɪ] n (for pigs) pocilga

**stye** [staɪ] n (MED) orzuelo

**style** [staɪl] n estilo; **stylish** adj elegante, a la moda

**stylus** ['staɪləs] n aguja

**suave** [swɑːv] adj cortés

**sub...** [sʌb] prefix sub...; **~conscious** adj subconsciente; **~contract** vt subcontratar; **~divide** vt subdividir

**subdue** [səb'dju:] vt sojuzgar; (passions) dominar; **~d** adj (light) tenue; (person) sumiso, manso

**subject** [n 'sʌbdʒɛkt, vb səb'dʒɛkt] n súbdito; (SCOL) asignatura; (matter) tema m; (GRAMMAR) sujeto ♦ vt: **to ~ sb to sth** someter a uno a algo; **to be ~ to** (law) estar sujeto a; (subj: person) ser propenso a; **~ive** [-'dʒɛktɪv] adj subjetivo; **~ matter** n (content) contenido

**subjunctive** [səb'dʒʌŋktɪv] adj, n subjuntivo

**sublet** [sʌb'lɛt] vt subarrendar

**submachine gun** [sʌbmə'ʃiːn-] n metralleta

**submarine** [sʌbmə'riːn] n submarino

**submerge** [səb'mɜːdʒ] vt sumergir ♦ vi sumergirse

**submissive** [səb'mɪsɪv] adj sumiso

**submit** [səb'mɪt] vt someter ♦ vi: **to ~ to sth** someterse a algo

**subnormal** [sʌb'nɔːməl] adj anormal

**subordinate** [sə'bɔːdɪnət] adj, n subordinado/a m/f

**subpoena** [səb'piːnə] n (LAW) citación f

**subscribe** [səb'skraɪb] vi suscribir; **to ~ to** (opinion, fund) suscribir, aprobar; (newspaper) suscribirse a; **~r** n (to periodical) subscriptor(a) m/f; (to telephone) abonado/a

**subscription** [səb'skrɪpʃən] n abono; (to magazine) subscripción f

**subsequent** ['sʌbsɪkwənt] adj subsiguiente, posterior; **~ly** adv posteriormente, más tarde

**subside** [səb'saɪd] vi hundirse; (flood) bajar; (wind) amainar; **~nce** [-'saɪdns] n hundimiento; (in road) socavón m

**subsidiary** [səb'sɪdɪərɪ] adj secundario ♦ n (also: ~ company) sucursal f, filial f

**subsidize** ['sʌbsɪdaɪz] vt subvencionar

**subsidy** ['sʌbsɪdɪ] n subvención f

**subsistence** [səb'sɪstəns] n subsistencia; **~ allowance** n salario mínimo

**substance** ['sʌbstəns] n sustancia

**substantial** [səb'stænʃl] adj sustancial, sustancioso; (fig) importante

**substantiate** [səb'stænʃɪeɪt] vt comprobar

**substitute** ['sʌbstɪtjuːt] n (person) suplente m/f; (thing) sustituto ♦ vt: **to ~ A for B** sustituir A por B, reemplazar B por A

**subtitle** ['sʌbtaɪtl] n subtítulo

**subtle** ['sʌtl] adj sutil; **~ty** n sutileza

**subtotal** [sʌb'təutl] n total m parcial

**subtract** [səb'trækt] vt restar, sustraer; **~ion** [-'trækʃən] n resta, sustracción f

**suburb** ['sʌbə:b] n barrio residencial; **the ~s** las afueras (de la ciudad); **~an** [sə'bə:bən] adj suburbano; (*train etc*) de cercanías; **~ia** [sə'bə:biə] n barrios mpl residenciales

**subway** ['sʌbwei] n (*BRIT*) paso subterráneo or inferior; (*US*) metro

**succeed** [sək'si:d] vi (*person*) tener éxito; (*plan*) salir bien ♦ vt suceder a; **to ~ in doing** lograr hacer; **~ing** adj (*following*) sucesivo

**success** [sək'ses] n éxito; **~ful** adj exitoso; (*business*) próspero; **to be ~ful (in doing)** lograr (hacer); **~fully** adv con éxito

**succession** [sək'seʃən] n sucesión f, serie f

**successive** [sək'sesiv] adj sucesivo, consecutivo

**succinct** [sək'sɪŋkt] adj sucinto

**succumb** [sə'kʌm] vi: **to ~ to** sucumbir a; (*illness*) ser víctima de

**such** [sʌtʃ] adj tal, semejante; (*of that kind*): **~ a book** tal libro; (*so much*): **~ courage** tanto valor ♦ adv tan; **~ a long trip** un viaje tan largo; **~ a lot of** tanto(s)/a(s); **~ as** (*like*) tal como; **as ~** como tal; **~-and-~** tal o cual

**suck** [sʌk] vt chupar; (*bottle*) sorber; (*breast*) mamar; **~er** n (*ZOOL*) ventosa; (*inf*) bobo, primo

**suction** ['sʌkʃən] n succión f

**Sudan** [su'dæn] n Sudán m

**sudden** ['sʌdn] adj (*rapid*) repentino, súbito; (*unexpected*) imprevisto; **all of a ~** de repente; **~ly** adv de repente

**suds** [sʌdz] npl espuma de jabón

**sue** [su:] vt demandar

**suede** [sweid] n ante m (*SP*), gamuza (*AM*)

**suet** ['suɪt] n sebo

**Suez** ['su:ɪz] n: **the ~ Canal** el Canal de Suez

**suffer** ['sʌfə*] vt sufrir, padecer; (*tolerate*) aguantar, soportar ♦ vi sufrir; **to ~ from** (*illness etc*) pade-

cer; **~er** n víctima; (*MED*) enfermo/a; **~ing** n sufrimiento

**suffice** [sə'fais] vi bastar, ser suficiente

**sufficient** [sə'fiʃənt] adj suficiente, bastante; **~ly** adv suficientemente, bastante

**suffix** ['sʌfiks] n sufijo

**suffocate** ['sʌfəkeit] vi ahogarse, asfixiarse; **suffocation** [-'keiʃən] n asfixia

**suffrage** ['sʌfridʒ] n sufragio

**suffused** [sə'fju:zd] adj: **~ with** bañado de

**sugar** ['ʃugə*] n azúcar m ♦ vt echar azúcar a, azucarar; **~ beet** n remolacha; **~ cane** n caña de azúcar

**suggest** [sə'dʒest] vt sugerir; **~ion** [-'dʒestʃən] n sugerencia; **~ive** (*pej*) adj indecente

**suicide** ['suɪsaɪd] n suicidio; (*person*) suicida m/f; *see also* **commit**

**suit** [su:t] n (*man's*) traje m; (*woman's*) conjunto; (*LAW*) pleito; (*CARDS*) palo ♦ vt convenir; (*clothes*) sentar a, ir bien a; (*adapt*): **to ~ sth to** adaptar or ajustar algo a; **well ~ed** (*well matched: couple*) hecho el uno para el otro; **~able** adj conveniente; (*apt*) indicado; **~ably** adv convenientemente; (*impressed*) apropiadamente

**suitcase** ['su:tkeis] n maleta (*SP*), valija (*AM*)

**suite** [swi:t] n (*of rooms, MUS*) suite f; (*furniture*): **bedroom/dining room ~** (juego de) dormitorio/ comedor

**suitor** ['su:tə*] n pretendiente m

**sulfur** ['sʌlfə*] (*US*) n = **sulphur**

**sulk** [sʌlk] vi estar de mal humor; **~y** adj malhumorado

**sullen** ['sʌlən] adj hosco, malhumorado

**sulphur** ['sʌlfə*] (*US* **sulfur**) n azufre m

**sultana** [sʌl'tɑ:nə] n (*fruit*) pasa de Esmirna

**sultry** ['sʌltri] adj (*weather*) bochornoso

**sum** [sʌm] n suma; (total) total m;
~ **up** vt resumir ♦ vi hacer un resumen

**summarize** ['sʌməraɪz] vt resumir

**summary** ['sʌmərɪ] n resumen m ♦
adj (justice) sumario

**summer** ['sʌmə*] n verano ♦ cpd de
verano; **in** ~ en verano; ~ **holidays**
npl vacaciones fpl de verano;
~**house** n (in garden) cenador m,
glorieta; ~**time** n (season) verano;
~ **time** n (by clock) hora de verano

**summit** ['sʌmɪt] n cima, cumbre f;
(also: ~ **conference**, ~ **meeting**)
(conferencia) cumbre f

**summon** ['sʌmən] vt (person) llamar; (meeting) convocar; (LAW) citar; ~ **up** vt (courage) armarse de;
~**s** n llamamiento, llamada ♦ vt
(LAW) citar

**sump** [sʌmp] n (BRIT) (AUT) cárter
m

**sumptuous** ['sʌmptjuəs] adj suntuoso

**sun** [sʌn] n sol m

**sunbathe** ['sʌnbeɪð] vi tomar el sol

**sunburn** ['sʌnbəːn] n (painful) quemadura; (tan) bronceado

**Sunday** ['sʌndɪ] n domingo; ~
**school** n catequesis f dominical

**sundial** ['sʌndaɪəl] n reloj m de sol

**sundown** ['sʌndaʊn] n anochecer m

**sundry** ['sʌndrɪ] adj varios/as,
diversos/as; **all and** ~ todos sin excepción; **sundries** npl géneros mpl
diversos

**sunflower** ['sʌnflaʊə*] n girasol m

**sung** [sʌŋ] pp of **sing**

**sunglasses** ['sʌnglɑːsɪz] npl gafas
fpl (SP) or anteojos mpl de sol

**sunk** [sʌŋk] pp of **sink**

**sun:** ~**light** n luz f del sol; ~**lit** adj
iluminado por el sol; ~**ny** adj soleado; (day) de sol; (fig) alegre; ~**rise**
n salida del sol; ~**roof** n (AUT) techo corredizo; ~**set** n puesta del sol;
~**shade** n (over table) sombrilla;
~**shine** n sol m; ~**stroke** n insolación f; ~**tan** n bronceado; ~**tan oil** n
aceite m bronceador

**super** ['suːpə*] (inf) adj genial

**superannuation** [suːpərænjuˈeɪʃən]
n cuota de jubilación

**superb** [suːˈpəːb] adj magnífico, espléndido

**supercilious** [suːpəˈsɪlɪəs] adj altanero

**superfluous** [suˈpəːfluəs] adj superfluo, de sobra

**superhuman** [suːpəˈhjuːmən] adj sobrehumano

**superimpose** [suːpərɪmˈpəuz] vt sobreponer

**superintendent** [suːpərɪnˈtɛndənt] n
director(a) m/f; (POLICE) subjefe/a
m/f

**superior** [suˈpɪərɪə*] adj superior;
(smug) desdeñoso ♦ n superior m;
~**ity** [-ˈɔrɪtɪ] n superioridad f

**superlative** [suˈpəːlətɪv] n superlativo

**superman** ['suːpəmæn] n superhom-
bre m

**supermarket** ['suːpəmɑːkɪt] n supermercado

**supernatural** [suːpəˈnætʃərəl] adj
sobrenatural ♦ n: **the** ~ lo sobrenatural

**superpower** ['suːpəpauə*] n (POL)
superpotencia

**supersede** [suːpəˈsiːd] vt suplantar

**superstar** ['suːpəstɑː*] n gran estrella

**superstitious** [suːpəˈstɪʃəs] adj
supersticioso

**supertanker** ['suːpətæŋkə*] n super-
petrolero

**supervise** ['suːpəvaɪz] vt supervisar;
**supervision** [-ˈvɪʒən] n supervisión f;
**supervisor** n supervisor(a) m/f

**supper** ['sʌpə*] n cena

**supplant** [səˈplɑːnt] vt suplantar

**supple** ['sʌpl] adj flexible

**supplement** [n 'sʌplɪmənt, vb
sʌplɪ'mɛnt] n suplemento ♦ vt suplir;
~**ary** [-'mɛntərɪ] adj suplementario;
~**ary benefit** (BRIT) n subsidio suplementario de la seguridad social

**supplier** [səˈplaɪə*] n (COMM) distri-
buidor(a) m/f

**supply** [sə'plaɪ] vt (provide) suministrar; (supply to ~ with) proveer (de) ♦ n provisión f; (gas, water etc) suministro; **supplies** npl (food) víveres mpl; (MIL) pertrechos mpl; ~**teacher** n profesor/a m/f suplente

**support** [sə'pɔːt] n apoyo; (TECH) soporte m ♦ vt apoyar; (financially) mantener; (uphold, TECH) sostener; ~**er** n (POL etc) partidario/a; (SPORT) aficionado/a

**suppose** [sə'pəuz] vt suponer; (imagine) imaginar; (duty): to be ~d to do sth deber hacer algo; ~**dly** [sə'pəuzɪdlɪ] adv según cabe suponer; **supposing** conj en caso de que

**suppress** [sə'prɛs] vt suprimir; (yawn) ahogar

**supreme** [su'priːm] adj supremo

**surcharge** ['sə:tʃɑːdʒ] n sobretasa, recargo

**sure** [ʃuə*] adj seguro; (definite, convinced) cierto; **to make** ~ **of sth/that** asegurarse de algo/asegurar que; ~! (of course) ¡claro!, ¡por supuesto!; ~ **enough** efectivamente; ~**footed** adj ágil y seguro; ~**ly** adv (certainly) seguramente

**surety** ['ʃuərətɪ] n fianza

**surf** [sə:f] n olas fpl

**surface** ['sə:fɪs] n superficie f ♦ vt (road) revestir ♦ vi (also fig) salir a la superficie; ~ **mail** n vía terrestre

**surfboard** ['sə:fbɔːd] n tabla (de surf)

**surfeit** ['sə:fɪt] n: **a** ~ **of** un exceso de

**surfing** ['sə:fɪŋ] n surf m

**surge** [sə:dʒ] n oleada, oleaje m ♦ vi (wave) romper; (people) avanzar en tropel

**surgeon** ['sə:dʒən] n cirujano/a

**surgery** ['sə:dʒərɪ] n cirugía; (BRIT: room) consultorio; ~ **hours** (BRIT) npl horas fpl de consulta

**surgical** ['sə:dʒɪkl] adj quirúrgico; ~ **spirit** (BRIT) n alcohol m de 90°

**surly** ['sə:lɪ] adj hosco, malhumorado

**surmount** [sə:'maunt] vt superar, vencer

**surname** ['sə:neɪm] n apellido

**surpass** [sə:'pɑːs] vt superar, exceder

**surplus** ['sə:pləs] n excedente m; (COMM) superávit m ♦ adj excedente, sobrante

**surprise** [sə'praɪz] n sorpresa ♦ vt sorprender; **surprising** adj sorprendente; **surprisingly** adv: **it was surprisingly easy** me etc sorprendió lo fácil que fue

**surrender** [sə'rɛndə*] n rendición f, entrega ♦ vi rendirse, entregarse

**surreptitious** [sʌrəp'tɪʃəs] adj subrepticio

**surrogate** ['sʌrəgɪt] n sucedáneo; ~**mother** n madre f portadora

**surround** [sə'raund] vt rodear, circundar; (MIL etc) cercar; ~**ing** adj circundante; ~**ings** npl alrededores mpl, cercanías fpl

**surveillance** [sə:'veɪləns] n vigilancia

**survey** [n 'sə:veɪ, vb sə:'veɪ] n inspección f, reconocimiento; (inquiry) encuesta ♦ vt examinar, inspeccionar; (look at) mirar, contemplar; ~**or** n agrimensor/a m/f

**survival** [sə'vaɪvl] n supervivencia

**survive** [sə'vaɪv] vi sobrevivir; (custom etc) perdurar ♦ vt sobrevivir a; **survivor** n superviviente m/f

**susceptible** [sə'sɛptəbl] adj: ~ (**to**) (disease) susceptible a; (flattery) sensible a

**suspect** [adj, n 'sʌspɛkt, vb səs'pɛkt] adj, n sospechoso/a m/f ♦ vt (person) sospechar de; (think) sospechar

**suspend** [səs'pɛnd] vt suspender; ~**ed sentence** n (LAW) libertad f condicional; ~**er belt** n portaligas m inv; ~**ers** npl (BRIT) ligas fpl; (US) tirantes mpl

**suspense** [səs'pɛns] n incertidumbre f, duda; (in film etc) suspense m; **to keep sb in** ~ mantener a uno en suspense

**suspension** [səs'pɛnʃən] n (gen, AUT) suspensión f; (of driving licence) privación f; ~ **bridge** n puente *m* colgante

**suspicion** [səs'pɪʃən] *n* sospecha; (*distrust*) recelo; **suspicious** [-ʃəs] *adj* receloso; (*causing* ~) sospechoso

**sustain** [səs'teɪn] *vt* sostener, apoyar; (*suffer*) sufrir, padecer; **~able** *adj* sostenible; **~ed** (*effort*) sostenido

**sustenance** ['sʌstɪnəns] *n* sustento

**swab** [swɔb] *n* (MED) algodón *m*

**swagger** ['swægə*] *vi* pavonearse

**swallow** ['swɔləu] *n* (*bird*) golondrina ♦ *vt* tragar; (*fig, pride*) tragarse; ~ **up** *vt* (*savings etc*) consumir

**swam** [swæm] *pt of* **swim**

**swamp** [swɔmp] *n* pantano, ciénaga ♦ *vt* (*with water etc*) inundar; (*fig*) abrumar, agobiar; **~y** *adj* pantanoso

**swan** [swɔn] *n* cisne *m*

**swap** [swɔp] *n* canje *m*, intercambio ♦ *vt*: **to** ~ (**for**) cambiar (por)

**swarm** [swɔːm] *n* (*of bees*) enjambre *m*; (*fig*) multitud *f* ♦ *vi* (*bees*) formar un enjambre; (*people*) pulular; **to be ~ing with** ser un hervidero de

**swarthy** ['swɔːðɪ] *adj* moreno

**swastika** ['swɔstɪkə] *n* esvástika

**swat** [swɔt] *vt* aplastar

**sway** [sweɪ] *vi* mecerse, balancearse ♦ *vt* (*influence*) mover, influir en

**swear** [swɛə*] *vt* (*pt* **swore**, *pp* **sworn**) *vi* (*curse*) maldecir; (*promise*) jurar ♦ *vt* jurar; **~word** *n* taco, palabrota

**sweat** [swɛt] *n* sudor *m* ♦ *vi* sudar

**sweater** ['swɛtə*] *n* suéter *m*

**sweatshirt** ['swɛtʃəːt] *n* suéter *m*

**sweaty** ['swɛtɪ] *adj* sudoroso

**Swede** [swiːd] *n* sueco/a

**swede** [swiːd] *n* (BRIT) nabo

**Sweden** ['swiːdn] *n* Suecia; **Swedish** ['swiːdɪʃ] *adj* sueco ♦ *n* (LING) sueco

**sweep** [swiːp] (*pt, pp* **swept**) *n* (*act*) barrido; (*also: chimney* ~) deshollinador/a *m/f* ♦ *vt* barrer; (*with arm*) empujar; (*subj: current*) arrastrar ♦ *vi* barrer; (*arm etc*) moverse rápidamente; (*wind*) soplar con violencia; ~ **away** *vt* barrer; ~ **past** *vi* pasar majestuosamente; ~ **up** *vi* barrer; **~ing** *adj* (*gesture*) dramático;

(*generalized: statement*) generalizado

**sweet** [swiːt] *n* (*candy*) dulce *m*, caramelo; (BRIT: *pudding*) postre *m* ♦ *adj* dulce; (*fig: kind*) dulce, amable; (: *attractive*) mono; **~corn** *n* maíz *m*; **~en** *vt* (*add sugar to*) poner azúcar a; (*person*) endulzar; **~heart** *n* novio/a; **~ness** *n* dulzura; ~ **pea** *n* guisante *m* de olor

**swell** [swɛl] (*pt* **swelled**, *pp* **swollen** *or* **swelled**) *n* (*of sea*) marejada, oleaje *m* ♦ *adj* (US: *inf: excellent*) estupendo, fenomenal ♦ *vt* hinchar, inflar ♦ *vi* (*also*: ~ **up**) hincharse; (*numbers*) aumentar; (*sound, feeling*) ir aumentando; **~ing** *n* (MED) hinchazón *f*

**sweltering** ['swɛltərɪŋ] *adj* sofocante, de mucho calor

**swept** [swɛpt] *pt, pp of* **sweep**

**swerve** [swɔːv] *vi* desviarse bruscamente

**swift** [swɪft] *n* (*bird*) vencejo ♦ *adj* rápido, veloz; **~ly** *adv* rápidamente

**swig** [swɪg] (*inf*) *n* (*drink*) trago

**swill** [swɪl] *vt* (*also*: ~ **out**, ~ **down**) lavar, limpiar con agua

**swim** [swɪm] (*pt* **swam**, *pp* **swum**) *n*: **to go for a** ~ ir a nadar *or* a bañarse ♦ *vi* nadar; (*head, room*) dar vueltas ♦ *vt* nadar; (*the Channel etc*) cruzar a nado; **~mer** *n* nadador/a *m/f*; **~ming** *n* natación *f*; **~ming cap** *n* gorro de baño; **~ming costume** (BRIT) *n* bañador *m*, traje *m* de baño; **~ming pool** *n* piscina (SP), alberca (AM); **~ming trunks** *n* bañador *m* (de hombre); **~suit** *n* = **~ming costume**

**swindle** ['swɪndl] *n* estafa ♦ *vt* estafar

**swine** [swaɪn] (*inf!*) *n* canalla (!)

**swing** [swɪŋ] (*pt, pp* **swung**) *n* (*in playground*) columpio; (*movement*) balanceo, vaivén *m*; (*change of direction*) viraje *m*; (*rhythm*) ritmo ♦ *vt* balancear; (*also*: ~ **round**) voltear, girar ♦ *vi* balancearse, columpiarse; (*also*: ~ **round**) dar media vuelta; **to be in full ~** estar en plena marcha; **~ bridge** n puente m giratorio; **~ door** (US **~ing door**) n puerta giratoria

**swingeing** ['swɪndʒɪŋ] (BRIT) adj (blow) abrumador(a); (cuts) atroz

**swipe** [swaɪp] vt (hit) golpear fuerte; (inf: steal) guindar

**swirl** [swəːl] vi arremolinarse

**swish** [swɪʃ] vi chasquear

**Swiss** [swɪs] adj, n inv suizo/a m/f

**switch** [swɪtʃ] n (for light etc) interruptor m; (change) cambio ♦ vt (change) cambiar de; **~ off** vt apagar; (engine) parar; **~ on** vt encender (SP), prender (AM); (engine, machine) arrancar; **~board** n (TEL) centralita de teléfonos (SP), conmutador m (AM)

**Switzerland** ['swɪtsələnd] n Suiza

**swivel** ['swɪvl] vi (also: ~ round) girar

**swollen** ['swəʊlən] pp of swell

**swoon** [swuːn] vi desmayarse

**swoop** [swuːp] n (by police etc) redada ♦ vi (also: ~ down) calarse

**swop** [swɔp] = swap

**sword** [sɔːd] n espada; **~fish** n pez m espada

**swore** [swɔː*] pt of swear

**sworn** [swɔːn] pp of swear ♦ adj (statement) bajo juramento; (enemy) implacable

**swot** [swɔt] (BRIT) vt, vi empollar

**swum** [swʌm] pp of swim

**swung** [swʌŋ] pt, pp of swing

**sycamore** ['sɪkəmɔː*] n sicomoro

**syllable** ['sɪləbl] n sílaba

**syllabus** ['sɪləbəs] n programa m de estudios

**symbol** ['sɪmbl] n símbolo

**symmetry** ['sɪmɪtrɪ] n simetría

**sympathetic** [sɪmpə'θetɪk] adj (understanding) comprensivo; (likeable) simpático; (showing support): **~ to(wards)** bien dispuesto hacia

**sympathize** ['sɪmpəθaɪz] vi: **to ~ with** (person) compadecerse de; (feelings) comprender; (cause) apoyar; **~r** n (POL) simpatizante m/f

**sympathy** ['sɪmpəθɪ] n (pity) compasión f; **sympathies** npl (tendencies) tendencias fpl; **with our deepest ~** en solidaridad

**symphony** ['sɪmfənɪ] n sinfonía

**symptom** ['sɪmptəm] n síntoma m, indicio

**synagogue** ['sɪnəgɒg] n sinagoga

**syndicate** ['sɪndɪkɪt] n (gen) sindicato; (of newspapers) agencia de noticias

**syndrome** ['sɪndrəʊm] n síndrome m

**synonym** ['sɪnənɪm] n sinónimo

**synopses** [sɪ'nɒpsiːz] npl of synopsis

**synopsis** [sɪ'nɒpsɪs] (pl synopses) n sinopsis f inv

**syntax** ['sɪntæks] n sintaxis f inv

**syntheses** ['sɪnθəsiːz] npl of synthesis

**synthesis** ['sɪnθəsɪs] (pl syntheses) n síntesis f inv

**synthetic** [sɪn'θetɪk] adj sintético

**syphilis** ['sɪfɪlɪs] n sífilis f

**syphon** ['saɪfən] = siphon

**Syria** ['sɪrɪə] n Siria; **~n** adj, n sirio/a

**syringe** [sɪ'rɪndʒ] n jeringa

**syrup** ['sɪrəp] n jarabe m; (also: golden ~) almíbar m

**system** ['sɪstəm] n sistema m; (ANAT) organismo; **~atic** [-'mætɪk] adj sistemático, metódico; **~ disk** n (COMPUT) disco del sistema; **~s analyst** n analista m/f de sistemas

# T

**ta** [tɑː] (BRIT: inf) excl ¡gracias!

**tab** [tæb] n lengüeta; (label) etiqueta; **to keep ~s on** (fig) vigilar

**tabby** ['tæbɪ] n (also: ~ cat) gato atigrado

**table** ['teɪbl] n mesa; (of statistics etc) cuadro, tabla ♦ vt (BRIT: motion etc) presentar; **to lay** or **set the ~** poner la mesa; **~cloth** n mantel m; **~ of contents** n índice m de materias; ~ **d'hôte** [tɑːblˈdəʊt] *adj* del menú; ~ **lamp** *n* lámpara de mesa; ~**mat** *n* (*for plate*) posaplatos *m inv*; (*for hot dish*) salvamantel *m*; ~**spoon** *n* cuchara de servir; (*also:* ~*spoonful: as measurement*) cucharada

**tablet** ['tæblɪt] *n* (*MED*) pastilla, comprimido *m*; (*of stone*) lápida

**table tennis** *n* ping-pong *m*, tenis *m* de mesa

**table wine** *n* vino de mesa

**tabloid** ['tæblɔɪd] *n* periódico popular sensacionalista

**tabulate** ['tæbjʊleɪt] *vt* disponer en tablas

**tack** [tæk] *n* (*nail*) tachuela; (*fig*) rumbo ♦ *vt* (*nail*) clavar con tachuelas; (*stitch*) hilvanar ♦ *vi* virar

**tackle** ['tækl] *n* (*fishing*) ~ aparejo (de pescar); (*for lifting*) aparejo *m* ♦ *vt* (*difficulty*) enfrentarse con; (*challenge: person*) hacer frente a; (*grapple with*) agarrar; (*FOOTBALL*) cargar; (*RUGBY*) placar

**tacky** ['tækɪ] *adj* pegajoso; (*pej*) cutre

**tact** [tækt] *n* tacto, discreción *f*; ~**ful** *adj* discreto, diplomático

**tactics** ['tæktɪks] *n, npl* táctica

**tactless** ['tæktlɪs] *adj* indiscreto

**tadpole** ['tædpəʊl] *n* renacuajo

**taffy** ['tæfɪ] (*US*) *n* toffee *m*

**tag** [tæg] *n* (*label*) etiqueta; ~ **along** *vi* ir (*or* venir) también

**tail** [teɪl] *n* cola; (*of shirt, coat*) faldón *m* ♦ *vt* (*follow*) vigilar a; ~**s** *npl* (*formal suit*) levita; ~ **away** *vi* (*in size, quality etc*) ir disminuyendo; ~**off** *vi* = ~ **away**; ~**back** (*BRIT*) *n* (*AUT*) cola; ~ **end** *n* cola, parte *f* final; ~**gate** *n* (*AUT*) puerta trasera

**tailor** ['teɪlə*] *n* sastre *m*; ~**ing** *n* (*cut*) corte *m*; (*craft*) sastrería; ~**made** *adj* (*also fig*) hecho a la medida

**tailwind** ['teɪlwɪnd] *n* viento de cola

**tainted** ['teɪntɪd] *adj* (*food*) pasado; (*water, air*) contaminado; (*fig*) manchado

**take** [teɪk] (*pt* **took**, *pp* **taken**) *vt* tomar; (*grab*) coger (*SP*), agarrar (*AM*); (*gain: prize*) ganar; (*require: effort, courage*) exigir; (*tolerate: pain etc*) aguantar; (*hold: passengers etc*) tener cabida para; (*accompany, bring, carry*) llevar; (*exam*) presentarse a; **to** ~ **sth from** (*drawer etc*) sacar algo de; (*person*) quitar algo a; **I** ~ **it that ...** supongo que ...; ~ **after** *vt fus* parecerse a; ~ **apart** *vt* desmontar; ~ **away** *vt* (*remove*) quitar; (*carry off*) llevar; (*MATH*) restar; ~ **back** *vt* (*return*) devolver; (*one's words*) retractarse de; ~ **down** *vt* (*building*) derribar; (*letter etc*) apuntar; ~ **in** *vt* (*deceive*) engañar; (*understand*) entender; (*include*) abarcar; (*lodger*) acoger, recibir; ~ **off** *vi* (*AVIAT*) despegar ♦ *vt* (*remove*) quitar; ~ **on** *vt* (*work*) aceptar; (*employee*) contratar; (*opponent*) desafiar; ~ **out** *vt* sacar; ~ **over** *vt* (*business*) tomar / posesión de; (*country*) tomar el poder ♦ *vi*: **to** ~ **over from sb** reemplazar a uno; ~ **to** *vt fus* (*person*) coger cariño a, encariñarse con; (*activity*) aficionarse a; ~ **up** *vt* (*a dress*) acortar; (*occupy: time, space*) ocupar; (*engage in: hobby etc*) dedicarse a; (*accept*): **to** ~ **sb up on** aceptar; ~**away** (*BRIT*) *adj* (*food*) para llevar ♦ *n* tienda (*or* restaurante *m*) de comida para llevar; ~**off** *n* (*AVIAT*) despegue *m*; ~**over** *n* (*COMM*) absorción *f*; ~**out** (*US*) *n* = ~**away**

**takings** ['teɪkɪŋz] *npl* (*COMM*) ingresos *mpl*

**talc** [tælk] *n* (*also:* ~**um powder**) (polvos de) talco

**tale** [teɪl] *n* (*story*) cuento; (*account*) relación *f*; **to tell** ~**s** (*fig*) chivarse

**talent** ['tælnt] *n* talento; ~**ed** *adj* de talento

**talk** [tɔːk] *n* charla; (*conversation*) conversación *f*; (*gossip*) habladurías *fpl*, chismes *mpl* ♦ *vi* hablar; ~**s** *npl* (*POL etc*) conversaciones *fpl*; **to** ~

about hablar de; **to ~ sb into doing sth** convencer a uno para que haga algo; **to ~ sb out of doing sth** disuadir a uno de que haga algo; **to ~ shop** hablar del trabajo; **~ over** *vt* discutir; **~ative** *adj* hablador(a); **~ show** *n* programa de entrevistas

**tall** [tɔ:l] *adj* alto; (*object*) grande; **to be 6 feet ~** (*person*) medir 1 metro 80

**tally** ['tælɪ] *n* cuenta ♦ *vi*: **to ~ (with)** corresponder (con)

**talon** ['tælən] *n* garra

**tambourine** [tæmbə'ri:n] *n* pandereta

**tame** [teɪm] *adj* domesticado; (*fig*) mediocre

**tamper** ['tæmpə*] *vi*: **to ~ with** tocar, andar con

**tampon** ['tæmpən] *n* tampón *m*

**tan** [tæn] *n* (*also: sun~*) bronceado *m* ♦ *vi* ponerse moreno ♦ *adj* (*colour*) marrón

**tang** [tæŋ] *n* sabor *m* fuerte

**tangent** ['tændʒənt] *n* (MATH) tangente *f*; **to go off at a ~** (*fig*) salirse por la tangente

**tangerine** [tændʒə'ri:n] *n* mandarina

**tangle** ['tæŋgl] *n* enredo; **to get in(to) a ~** enredarse

**tank** [tæŋk] *n* (*water* ~) depósito, tanque *m*; (*for fish*) acuario; (MIL) tanque *m*

**tanker** ['tæŋkə*] *n* (*ship*) buque *m* cisterna; (*truck*) camión *m* cisterna

**tanned** [tænd] *adj* (*skin*) moreno

**tantalizing** ['tæntəlaɪzɪŋ] *adj* tentador(a)

**tantamount** ['tæntəmaunt] *adj*: **~ to** equivalente a

**tantrum** ['tæntrəm] *n* rabieta

**tap** [tæp] *n* (BRIT: *on sink etc*) grifo (SP), canilla (AM); (*gas* ~) llave *f*; (*gentle blow*) golpecito ♦ *vt* (*hit gently*) dar golpecitos en; (*resources*) utilizar, explotar; (*telephone*) intervenir; **on ~** (*fig: resources*) a mano; **~-dancing** *n* claqué

**tape** [teɪp] *n* (*also: magnetic* ~) cinta magnética; (*cassette*) cassette *f*,

cinta; (*sticky* ~) cinta adhesiva; (*for tying*) cinta ♦ *vt* (*record*) grabar (en cinta); (*stick with* ~) pegar con cinta adhesiva; **~ deck** *n* grabadora; **~ measure** *n* cinta métrica, metro

**taper** ['teɪpə*] *n* cirio ♦ *vi* afilarse

**tape recorder** *n* grabadora

**tapestry** ['tæpɪstrɪ] *n* (*object*) tapiz *m*; (*art*) tapicería

**tar** [tɑ:] *n* alquitrán *m*, brea

**target** ['tɑ:gɪt] *n* (*gen*) blanco

**tariff** ['tærɪf] *n* (*on goods*) arancel *m*; (BRIT: *in hotels etc*) tarifa

**tarmac** ['tɑ:mæk] *n* (BRIT: *on road*) asfaltado; (AVIAT) pista (de aterrizaje)

**tarnish** ['tɑ:nɪʃ] *vt* deslustrar

**tarpaulin** [tɑ:'pɔ:lɪn] *n* lona impermeabilizada

**tarragon** ['tærəgən] *n* estragón *m*

**tart** [tɑ:t] *n* (CULIN) tarta; (BRIT: *inf: prostitute*) puta ♦ *adj* agrio, ácido; **~ up** *vt* (BRIT: *inf*) (*building*) remozar; **~ o.s. up** acicalarse

**tartan** ['tɑ:tn] *n* tejido escocés *m*

**tartar** ['tɑ:tə*] *n* (*on teeth*) sarro; **~(e) sauce** *n* salsa tártara

**task** [tɑ:sk] *n* tarea; **to take to ~** reprender; **~ force** *n* (MIL, POLICE) grupo de operaciones

**taste** [teɪst] *n* (*sense*) gusto; (*flavour*) sabor *m*; (*also: after~*) sabor *m*, dejo; (*sample*): **have a ~!** ¡prueba un poquito!; (*fig*: muestra, idea ♦ *vt* (*also: fig*) probar ♦ *vi*: **to ~ of** or **like** (*fish, garlic etc*) saber a; **you can ~ the garlic** (**in it**) se nota el sabor a ajo; **in good/bad ~** de buen/mal gusto; **~ful** *adj* de buen gusto; **~less** *adj* (*food*) soso; (*remark etc*) de mal gusto; **tasty** *adj* sabroso, rico

**tatters** ['tætəz] *npl*: **in ~** hecho jirones

**tattoo** [tə'tu:] *n* tatuaje *m*; (*spectacle*) espectáculo militar ♦ *vt* tatuar

**tatty** ['tætɪ] (BRIT: *inf*) *adj* cochambroso

**taught** [tɔ:t] *pt*, *pp* of **teach**

**taunt** [tɔ:nt] *n* burla ♦ *vt* burlarse de

**Taurus** ['tɔ:rəs] n Tauro

**taut** [tɔ:t] adj tirante, tenso

**tax** [tæks] n impuesto ♦ vt gravar (con un impuesto); (fig: memory) poner a prueba a: (: patience) agotar; **~able** adj (income) gravable; **~ation** [-'seɪʃən] n impuestos mpl; **~ avoidance** n evasión f de impuestos; **~ disc** (BRIT) n (AUT) pegatina del impuesto de circulación; **~ evasion** n evasión f fiscal; **~-free** adj libre de impuestos

**taxi** ['tæksɪ] n taxi m ♦ vi (AVIAT) rodar por la pista; **~ driver** n taxista m/f; **~ rank** (BRIT) n = **~ stand**; **~ stand** n parada de taxis

**tax: ~ payer** n contribuyente m/f; **~ relief** n desgravación f fiscal; **~ return** n declaración f de ingresos

**TB** n abbr = **tuberculosis**

**tea** [ti:] n té m; (BRIT: meal) ≈ merienda (SP); cena; **high ~** (BRIT) ≈ merienda-cena (SP); **~ bag** n bolsita de té; **~ break** (BRIT) n descanso para el té

**teach** [ti:tʃ] (pt, pp taught) vt: **to ~ sb sth, ~ sth to sb** enseñar algo a uno ♦ vi (be a teacher) ser profesor(a), enseñar; **~er** n (in secondary school) profesor(a) m/f; (in primary school) maestro (a), profesor(a) de EGB; **~ing** n enseñanza

**tea cosy** n cubretetera m

**teacup** ['ti:kʌp] n taza para el té

**teak** [ti:k] n (madera de) teca

**team** [ti:m] n equipo; (of horses) tiro; **~work** n trabajo en equipo

**teapot** ['ti:pɔt] n tetera

**tear¹** [tɪə*] n lágrima; **in ~s** llorando

**tear²** [tɛə*] (pt tore, pp torn) n rasgón m, desgarrón m ♦ vt romper, rasgar ♦ vi rasgarse; **~ along** vi (rush) precipitarse; **~ up** vt (sheet of paper etc) romper

**tearful** ['tɪəful] adj lloroso

**tear gas** n gas m lacrimógeno

**tearoom** ['ti:ru:m] n salón m de té

**tease** [ti:z] vt tomar el pelo a

**tea: ~ set** n servicio de té; **~spoon** n cucharita; (also: **~spoonful**: as

measurement) cucharadita

**teat** [ti:t] n (of bottle) tetina

**teatime** ['ti:taɪm] n hora del té

**tea towel** (BRIT) n paño de cocina

**technical** ['tɛknɪkl] adj técnico; **~ college** (BRIT) n ≈ escuela de artes y oficios (SP); **~ity** [-'kælɪtɪ] n (point of law) formalismo; (detail) detalle m técnico; **~ly** adv en teoría; (regarding technique) técnicamente

**technician** [tɛk'nɪʃn] n técnico/a

**technique** [tɛk'ni:k] n técnica

**technology** [tɛk'nɔlədʒɪ] n tecnología

**teddy (bear)** ['tɛdɪ-] n osito de felpa

**tedious** ['ti:dɪəs] adj pesado, aburrido

**teem** [ti:m] vi: **to ~ with** rebosar de; **it is ~ing (with rain)** llueve a cántaros

**teenage** ['ti:neɪdʒ] adj (fashions etc) juvenil; (children) quinceañero; **~r** n quinceañero/a

**teens** [ti:nz] npl: **to be in one's ~** ser adolescente

**tee-shirt** ['ti:ʃə:t] n = **T-shirt**

**teeter** ['ti:tə*] vi balancearse; (fig): **to ~ on the edge of ...** estar al borde de ...

**teeth** [ti:θ] npl of **tooth**

**teethe** [ti:ð] vi echar los dientes

**teething** ['ti:ðɪŋ]: **~ ring** n mordedor m; **~ troubles** npl (fig) dificultades fpl iniciales

**teetotal** ['ti:'təutl] adj abstemio

**telegram** ['tɛlɪgræm] n telegrama m

**telegraph** ['tɛlɪgrɑ:f] n telégrafo; **~ pole** n poste m telegráfico

**telepathy** [tə'lɛpəθɪ] n telepatía

**telephone** ['tɛlɪfəun] n teléfono ♦ vt llamar por teléfono, telefonear; (message) dar por teléfono; **to be on the ~** (talking) hablar por teléfono; (possessing ~) tener teléfono; **~ booth** n cabina telefónica; **~ box** (BRIT) n = **~ booth**; **~ call** n llamada (telefónica); **~ directory** n guía (telefónica); **~ number** n número de teléfono; **telephonist** [tə'lɛfənɪst] (BRIT) n telefonista m/f

**telescope** ['teliskəup] n telescopio

**television** [teli'viʒən] n televisión f; **on** ~ en la televisión; ~ **set** n televisor m

**telex** ['teleks] n télex m ♦ vt enviar un télex a

**tell** [tel] (pt, pp **told**) vt decir; (relate: story) contar; (distinguish): **to** ~ **sth from** distinguir algo de ♦ vi (talk): **to** ~ (**of**) contar; (have effect) tener efecto; **to** ~ **sb to do sth** mandar a uno hacer algo; ~ **off** vt: **to** ~ **sb off** regañar a uno; ~**er** n (in bank) cajero/a; ~**ing** adj (remark, detail) revelador(a); ~**tale** adj (sign) indicador(a)

**telly** ['teli] (BRIT: inf) n abbr (= television) tele f

**temp** [temp] n abbr (BRIT: = temporary) temporero/a

**temper** ['tempə*] n (nature) carácter m; (mood) humor m; (bad ~) (mal) genio; (fit of anger) acceso de ira ♦ vt (moderate) moderar; **to be in a** ~ estar furioso; **to lose one's** ~ enfadarse, enojarse

**temperament** ['tempromənt] n (nature) temperamento

**temperate** ['temprət] adj (climate etc) templado

**temperature** ['temprətʃə*] n temperatura; **to have** o **run a** ~ tener fiebre

**temple** ['templ] n (building) templo; (ANAT) sien f

**tempo** ['tempəu] (pl **tempos** or **tempi**) n (MUS) tempo, tiempo; (fig) ritmo

**temporarily** ['tempərərili] adv temporalmente

**temporary** ['tempərəri] adj provisional; (passing) transitorio; (worker) temporero; (job) temporal

**tempt** [tempt] vt tentar; **to** ~ **sb into doing sth** tentar o inducir a uno a hacer algo; ~**ation** [-'teiʃən] n tentación f; ~**ing** adj tentador(a); (food) apetitoso/a

**ten** [ten] num diez

**tenacity** [tə'næsiti] n tenacidad f

**tenancy** ['tenənsi] n arrendamiento, alquiler m

**tenant** ['tenənt] n inquilino/a

**tend** [tend] vt cuidar ♦ vi: **to** ~ **to do sth** tener tendencia a hacer algo

**tendency** ['tendənsi] n tendencia

**tender** ['tendə*] adj (person, care) tierno, cariñoso; (meat) tierno; (sore) sensible ♦ n (COMM: offer) oferta; (money): **legal** ~ moneda de curso legal ♦ vt ofrecer; ~**ness** n ternura; (of meat) blandura

**tenement** ['tenəmənt] n casa de pisos (SP)

**tenet** ['tenət] n principio

**tennis** ['tenis] n tenis m; ~ **ball** n pelota de tenis; ~ **court** n cancha de tenis; ~ **player** n tenista m/f; ~ **racket** n raqueta de tenis

**tenor** ['tenə*] n (MUS) tenor m

**tenpin bowling** ['tenpin-] n (juego de) los bolos

**tense** [tens] adj (person) nervioso; (moment, atmosphere) tenso; (muscle) tenso, en tensión ♦ n (LING) tiempo

**tension** ['tenʃən] n tensión f

**tent** [tent] n tienda (de campaña) (SP), carpa (AM)

**tentative** ['tentətiv] adj (person, smile) indeciso; (conclusion, plans) provisional

**tenterhooks** ['tentəhuks] npl: **on** ~ sobre ascuas

**tenth** [tenθ] num décimo

**tent peg** n clavija, estaca

**tent pole** n mástil m

**tenuous** ['tenjuəs] adj tenue

**tenure** ['tenjuə*] n (of land etc) tenencia; (of office) ejercicio

**tepid** ['tepid] adj tibio

**term** [tə:m] n (word) término; (period) período; (SCOL) trimestre m ♦ vt llamar; ~**s** npl (conditions, COMM) condiciones fpl; **in the short/long** ~ a corto/largo plazo; **to be on good** ~**s with sb** llevarse bien con uno; **to come to** ~**s with** (problem) aceptar

**terminal** ['tə:minl] adj (disease)

mortal; (patient) terminal ♦ n (ELEC) borne m; (COMPUT) terminal m; (also: air ~) terminal f; (BRIT: also: coach ~) terminal f

**terminate** ['tɜ:mɪneɪt] vt terminar

**terminus** ['tɜ:mɪnəs] (pl termini) n término, (estación f) terminal f

**terrace** ['terəs] n terraza; (BRIT: row of houses) hilera de casas adosadas; **the ~s** (BRIT: SPORT) las gradas fpl; **~d** adj (garden) en terrazas; (house) adosado

**terrain** [tɛ'reɪn] n terreno

**terrible** ['terɪbl] adj terrible, horrible; (inf) atroz; **terribly** adv terriblemente; (very badly) malísimamente

**terrier** ['terɪə'] n terrier m

**terrific** [tə'rɪfɪk] adj (very great) tremendo; (wonderful) fantástico, fenomenal

**terrify** ['terɪfaɪ] vt aterrorizar

**territory** ['terɪtəri] n (also fig) territorio

**terror** ['terə'] n terror m; **~ism** n terrorismo; **~ist** n terrorista m/f

**terse** [tɜ:s] adj brusco, lacónico

**test** [test] n (gen, CHEM) prueba; (MED) examen m; (SCOL) examen m, test m; (also: driving ~) examen m de conducir ♦ vt probar, poner a prueba; (MED, SCOL) examinar

**testament** ['testəmənt] n testamento; **the Old/New T~** el Antiguo/Nuevo Testamento

**testicle** ['testɪkl] n testículo

**testify** ['testɪfaɪ] vi (LAW) prestar declaración; **to ~ to sth** atestiguar algo

**testimony** ['testɪmənɪ] n (LAW) testimonio

**test**: **~ match** n (CRICKET, RUGBY) partido internacional; **~ pilot** n piloto/mujer piloto m/f de pruebas; **~ tube** n probeta

**tetanus** ['tetənəs] n tétano

**tether** ['teðə'] vt atar (con una cuerda) ♦ n: **to be at the end of one's ~** no aguantar más

**text** [tekst] n texto; **~book** n libro de texto

**textiles** ['tekstaɪlz] npl textiles mpl; (textile industry) industria textil

**texture** ['tekstʃə'] n textura

**Thailand** ['taɪlænd] n Tailandia

**Thames** [temz] n: **the ~** el (río) Támesis

**than** [ðæn] conj (in comparisons): more ~ 10/once más de 10/una vez; I have more/less ~ you/Paul tengo más/menos que tú/Paul; she is older ~ you think es mayor de lo que piensas

**thank** [θæŋk] vt dar las gracias a, agradecer; **~ you (very much)** muchas gracias; **~ God!** ¡gracias a Dios!; **~s** npl gracias fpl ♦ excl (also: many ~s, ~s a lot) ¡gracias!; **~s to** prep gracias a; **~ful** adj: **~ful (for)** agradecido (por); **~less** adj ingrato; **T~sgiving (Day)** n día m de Acción de Gracias

**KEYWORD**

**that** [ðæt] (pl those) adj (demonstrative) ese/a, pl esos/as; (more remote) aquel/aquella, pl aquellos/as; **leave those books on the table** deja esos libros sobre la mesa; **~ one** ése/ésa; (more remote) aquél/aquélla; **~ one over there** ése/ésa de ahí; aquél/aquélla de allí

♦ pron 1 (demonstrative) ése/a, pl ésos/as; (neuter) eso; (more remote) aquél/aquélla, pl aquéllos/as; (neuter) aquello; **what's ~?** ¿qué es eso (or aquello)?; **who's ~?** ¿quién es ése/a (or aquél/aquélla)?; **is ~ you?** ¿eres tú?; **will you eat all ~?** ¿vas a comer todo eso?; **~'s my house** ésa es mi casa; **~'s what he said** eso es lo que dijo; **~ is (to say)** es decir

2 (relative: subject, object) que; (with preposition) (el/la) que etc, el/la cual etc; **the book (~) I read** el libro que leí; **the books ~ are in the library** los libros que están en la biblioteca; **all (~) I have** todo lo que tengo; **the box (~) I put it in** la caja en la que or donde lo puse;

the people (~) I spoke to la gente
con la que hablé
**3** *(relative: of time)* que; **the day
(~) he came** el día (en) que vino
♦ *conj* que; **he thought ~ I was ill**
creyó que yo estaba enfermo
♦ *adv (demonstrative)*: **I can't
work ~ much** no puedo trabajar
tanto; **I didn't realise it was ~
bad** no creí que fuera tan malo; **~
high** así de alto

**thatched** [θætʃt] *adj (roof)* de paja;
*(cottage)* con tejado de paja
**thaw** [θɔː] *n* deshielo ♦ *vi (ice)* derretirse; *(food)* descongelarse ♦ *vt
(food)* descongelar

---

*KEYWORD*

**the** [ðiː, ðə] *def art* **1** *(gen)* el, *f* la,
*pl* los, *fpl* las (NB = el **immediately**
**before** *f* *n* **beginning with stressed**
*(h)a*; *a+el* = al; *de+el* = del); **to ~
boy/girl** el chico/la chica; **~ books/
flowers** los libros/las flores; **to ~
postman/from ~ drawer** al
cartero/del cajón; **I haven't ~
time/money** no tengo tiempo/dinero
**2** *(+ adj to form n)* los; lo; **~ rich
and ~ poor** los ricos y los pobres;
**to attempt ~ impossible** intentar lo
imposible
**3** *(in titles)*: **Elizabeth ~ First** Isabel primera; **Peter ~ Great** Pedro
el Grande
**4** *(in comparisons)*: **~ more he
works ~ more he earns** cuanto
más trabaja más gana

---

**theatre** ['θɪətə*] *(US* **theater)** *n* teatro; *(also: lecture ~)* aula; *(MED:
also: operating ~)* quirófano; **~-goer**
*n* aficionado/a al teatro
**theatrical** [θɪ'ætrɪkl] *adj* teatral
**theft** [θɛft] *n* robo
**their** [ðɛə*] *adj* su; **~s** *pron* suyo/(la) suya *etc*; *see also* **my;
mine**
**them** [ðɛm, ðəm] *pron (direct)* los/
las; *(indirect)* les; *(stressed, after*

*prep)* ellos/ellas; *see also* **me**
**theme** [θiːm] *n* tema *m*; **~ park** *n*
parque de atracciones *(en torno a un
tema central)*; **~ song** *n* tema *n*
(musical)
**themselves** [ðəm'sɛlvz] *pl pron
(subject)* ellos mismos/ellas mismas;
*(complement)* se; *(after prep)* sí
(mismos/as); *see also* **oneself**
**then** [ðɛn] *adv (at that time)* entonces; *(next)* después; *(later)* luego
después; *(and also)* además ♦ *conj
(therefore)* en ese caso, entonces ♦
*adj*: **the ~ president** el entonces
presidente; **by ~** para entonces;
**from ~ on** desde entonces
**theology** [θɪ'ɔlədʒɪ] *n* teología
**theoretical** [θɪə'rɛtɪkl] *adj* teórico
**theory** ['θɪərɪ] *n* teoría
**therapist** ['θɛrəpɪst] *n* terapeuta *m/f*
**therapy** ['θɛrəpɪ] *n* terapia

---

*KEYWORD*

**there** ['ðɛə*] *adv* **1**: **~ is, ~ are**
hay; **~ is no-one here/no bread
left** no hay nadie aquí/no queda pan;
**~ has been an accident** ha habido
un accidente
**2** *(referring to place)* ahí; *(distant)*
allí; **it's ~** está ahí; **put it in/on/
up/down ~** ponlo ahí dentro/encima/
arriba/abajo; **I want that book ~**
quiero ese libro de ahí; **~ he is!**
¡ahí está!
**3**: **~, ~** *(esp to child)* ea, ea

---

**there: ~abouts** *adv* por ahí; **~after**
*adv* después; **~by** *adv* así, de ese
modo; **~fore** *adv* por lo tanto; **~'s =
there is; there has**
**thermal** ['θəːml] *adj* termal; *(paper)*
térmico
**thermometer** [θə'mɔmɪtə*] *n* termómetro
**Thermos** ['θəːməs] ® *n (also: ~
flask)* termo
**thermostat** ['θəːməustæt] *n* termostato
**thesaurus** [θɪ'sɔːrəs] *n* tesoro
**these** [ðiːz] *pl adj* estos/as ♦ *pl pron*

éstos/as

**theses** ['θi:si:z] *npl of* thesis

**thesis** ['θi:sis] (*pl* **theses**) *n* tesis *f inv*

**they** [ðeɪ] *pl pron* ellos/ellas; (*stressed*) ellos (mismos)/ellas (mismas); ~ **say that...** (*it is said that*) se dice que...; ~'**d** = they had; they would; ~'**ll** = they shall; they will; ~'**re** = they are; ~'**ve** = they have

**thick** [θɪk] *adj* (*in consistency*) espeso; (*in size*) grueso; (*stupid*) torpe ♦ *n*: **in the ~ of the battle** en lo más reñido de la batalla; **it's 20 cm ~** tiene 20 cm de espesor; ~**en** *vi* espesarse ♦ *vt* (*sauce etc*) espesar; ~**ness** *n* espesor *m*; grueso; ~**set** *adj* fornido; ~**skinned** *adj* (*fig*) insensible

**thief** [θi:f] (*pl* **thieves**) *n* ladrón/ona *m/f*

**thieves** [θi:vz] *npl of* thief

**thigh** [θaɪ] *n* muslo

**thimble** ['θɪmbl] *n* dedal *m*

**thin** [θɪn] *adj* (*person, animal*) flaco; (*in size*) delgado; (*in consistency*) poco espeso; (*hair, crowd*) escaso ♦ *vt*: **to ~ (down)** diluir

**thing** [θɪŋ] *n* cosa; (*object*) objeto, artículo; (*matter*) asunto; (*mania*): **to have a ~ about sb/sth** estar obsesionado con uno/algo; ~**s** *npl* (*belongings*) efectos *mpl* (*personales*); **the best ~ would be to ...** lo mejor sería ...; **how are ~s?** ¿qué tal?

**think** [θɪŋk] (*pt, pp* **thought**) *vi* pensar ♦ *vt* pensar, creer; **what did you ~ of them?** ¿qué te pareceron?; **to ~ about sth/sb** pensar en algo/uno; **I'll ~ about it** lo pensaré; **to ~ of doing sth** pensar en hacer algo; **I ~ so/not** creo que sí/no; **to ~ well of sb** tener buen concepto de uno; ~ **over** *vt* reflexionar sobre, meditar; ~ **up** *vt* (*plan etc*) idear; ~ **tank** *n* gabinete *m* de estrategia

**thinly** ['θɪnlɪ] *adv* (*cut*) fino; (*spread*) ligeramente

**third** [θə:d] *adj* (*before n*) tercer(a); (*following n*) tercero/a ♦ *n* tercero/a; (*fraction*) tercio; (*BRIT: SCOL: degree*) título de licenciado con calificación de aprobado; ~**ly** *adv* en tercer lugar; ~ **party insurance** (*BRIT*) *n* seguro contra terceros; ~-**rate** *adj* (*de calidad*) mediocre; **T~ World** *n* Tercer Mundo

**thirst** [θə:st] *n* sed *f*; ~**y** *adj* (*person, animal*) sediento; (*work*) que da sed; **to be ~y** tener sed

**thirteen** [θə:'ti:n] *num* trece

**thirty** ['θə:tɪ] *num* treinta

KEYWORD

**this** [ðɪs] (*pl* **these**) *adj* (*demonstrative*) este/a; *pl* estos/as; (*neuter*) esto; ~ **man/woman** este hombre/esta mujer; **these children/flowers** estos chicos/estas flores; ~ **one** (*here*) éste/a, esto (de aquí)

♦ *pron* (*demonstrative*) éste/a; *pl* éstos/as; (*neuter*) esto; **who is ~?** ¿quién es éste/ésta?; **what is ~?** ¿qué es esto?; ~ **is where I live** aquí vivo; ~ **is what he said** esto es lo que dijo; ~ **is Mr Brown** (*in introductions*) le presento al Sr. Brown; (*photo*) éste es el Sr. Brown; (*on telephone*) habla el Sr. Brown

♦ *adv* (*demonstrative*): ~ **high/long** *etc* así de alto/largo *etc*; ~ **far** hasta aquí

**thistle** ['θɪsl] *n* cardo

**thorn** [θɔ:n] *n* espina

**thorough** ['θʌrə] *adj* (*search*) minucioso; (*wash*) a fondo; (*knowledge, research*) profundo; (*person*) meticuloso; ~**bred** *adj* (*horse*) de pura sangre; ~**fare** *n* calle *f*; "**no ~fare**" "prohibido el paso"; ~**ly** *adv* (*search*) minuciosamente; (*study*) profundamente; (*wash*) a fondo; (*utterly: bad, wet etc*) completamente, totalmente

**those** [ðəʊz] *pl adj* esos/esas; (*more remote*) aquellos/as

**though** [ðəʊ] *conj* aunque ♦ *adv* sin embargo

**thought** [θɔːt] *pt, pp of* **think** ♦ *n* pensamiento; *(opinion)* opinión *f*; **~ful** *adj* pensativo; *(serious)* serio; *(considerate)* atento; **~less** *adj* descuidado

**thousand** ['θauzənd] *num* mil; **two ~ dos mil**; **~s of** miles de; **~th** *num* milésimo

**thrash** [θræʃ] *vt* azotar; *(defeat)* derrotar; **~ about** *or* **around** *vi* debatirse; **~ out** *vt* discutir a fondo

**thread** [θrɛd] *n* hilo; *(of screw)* rosca *f* ♦ *vt (needle)* enhebrar; **~bare** *adj* raído

**threat** [θrɛt] *n* amenaza; **~en** *vi* amenazar ♦ *vt*: **to ~en sb with/to do** amenazar a uno con/con hacer

**three** [θriː] *num* tres; **~-dimensional** *adj* tridimensional; **~-piece suit** *n* traje *m* de tres piezas; **~-piece suite** *n* tresillo; **~-ply** *adj (wool)* de tres cabos

**thresh** [θrɛʃ] *vt (AGR)* trillar

**threshold** ['θrɛʃhəuld] *n* umbral *m*

**threw** [θruː] *pt of* **throw**

**thrifty** ['θrɪftɪ] *adj* económico

**thrill** [θrɪl] *n (excitement)* emoción *f*; *(shudder)* estremecimiento ♦ *vt* emocionar; **to be ~ed** *(with gift etc)* estar encantado; **~er** *n* novela *f* (*or obra or película*) de suspense; **~ing** *adj* emocionante

**thrive** [θraɪv] *(pt* **thrived** *or* **throve**, *pp* **thrived** *or* **thriven)** *vi (grow)* crecer; *(do well)*: **to ~ on sth** sentarle muy bien a uno algo; **thriven** ['θrɪvn] *pp of* **thrive**; **thriving** *adj* próspero

**throat** [θrəut] *n* garganta; **to have a sore ~** tener dolor de garganta

**throb** [θrɔb] *n (of heart)* latido; *(of wound)* punzada; *(of engine)* vibración *f* ♦ *vi* latir; *(pain)* dar punzadas; vibrar

**throes** [θrəuz] *npl*: **in the ~ of** en medio de

**throne** [θrəun] *n* trono

**throng** [θrɔŋ] *n* multitud *f*, muchedumbre *f* ♦ *vt* agolparse en

**throttle** ['θrɔtl] *n (AUT)* acelerador

*m* ♦ *vt* estrangular

**through** [θruː] *prep* por, a través de; *(time)* durante; *(by means of)* por medio de, mediante; *(owing to)* gracias a ♦ *adj (ticket, train)* directo ♦ *adv* completamente, de parte a parte; **de principio a fin**; **to put sb ~ to sb** *(TEL)* poner o pasar a uno con uno; **to be ~** *(TEL)* tener comunicación; *(have finished)* haber terminado; **"no ~ road"** *(BRIT)* "calle sin salida"; **~out** *prep (place)* por todas partes de, por todo; *(time)* durante todo ♦ *adv* por o en todas partes

**throve** [θrəuv] *pt of* **thrive**

**throw** [θrəu] *(pt* **threw**, *pp* **thrown)** *n* tiro; *(SPORT)* lanzamiento ♦ *vt* tirar, echar; *(SPORT)* lanzar; *(rider)* derribar; *(fig)* desconcertar; **to ~ a party** dar una fiesta; **~ away** *vt* tirar; *(money)* derrochar; **~ off** *vt* deshacerse de; **~ out** *vt* tirar; *(person)* echar; expulsar; **~ up** *vi* vomitar; **~away** *adj* para tirar, desechable; *(remark)* hecho de paso; **~-in** *n (SPORT)* saque *m*

**thru** [θruː] *(US)* = **through**

**thrush** [θrʌʃ] *n* zorzal *m*, tordo

**thrust** [θrʌst] *(pt, pp* **thrust**) *n (TECH)* empuje *m* ♦ *vt* empujar (con fuerza)

**thud** [θʌd] *n* golpe *m* sordo

**thug** [θʌg] *n* gamberro/a

**thumb** [θʌm] *n (ANAT)* pulgar *m*; **to ~ a lift** hacer autostop; **~ through** *vt fus (book)* hojear; **~tack** *(US)* *n* chincheta *(SP)*

**thump** [θʌmp] *n* golpe *m*; *(sound)* ruido seco *or* sordo ♦ *vt* golpear ♦ *vi (heart etc)* palpitar

**thunder** ['θʌndə*] *n* trueno ♦ *vi* tronar; *(train etc)*: **to ~ past** pasar como un trueno; **~bolt** *n* rayo; **~clap** *n* trueno; **~storm** *n* tormenta; **~y** *adj* tormentoso

**Thursday** ['θəːzdɪ] *n* jueves *m inv*

**thus** [ðʌs] *adv* así, de este modo

**thwart** [θwɔːt] *vt* frustrar

**thyme** [taɪm] *n* tomillo

**thyroid** ['θaɪrɔɪd] *n (also:* **~ gland)**

tiroides m inv

**tic** [tɪk] n tic m

**tick** [tɪk] n (sound: of clock) tictac m; (mark) palomita; (ZOOL) garrapata; (BRIT: inf): **in a** ~ en un instante ♦ vi hacer tictac ♦ vt marcar; ~ **off** vt marcar; (person) reñir; ~ **over** vi (engine) girar en marcha lenta; (fig) ir tirando

**ticket** ['tɪkɪt] n billete m (SP), tíquet m, boleto (AM); (for cinema etc) entrada (SP), boleto (AM); (in shop: on goods) etiqueta; (for raffle) papeleta; (for library) tarjeta; (parking ~) multa por estacionamiento ilegal; ~ **collector** n revisor(a) m/f; ~ **office** n (THEATRE) taquilla (SP), boletería (AM); (RAIL) despacho de billetes (SP) or boletos (AM)

**tickle** ['tɪkl] vt hacer cosquillas a ♦ vi hacer cosquillas; **ticklish** adj (person) cosquilloso; (problem) delicado

**tidal** ['taɪdl] adj de marea; ~ **wave** n maremoto

**tidbit** ['tɪdbɪt] (US) n = titbit

**tiddlywinks** ['tɪdlɪwɪŋks] n juego infantil con fichas de plástico

**tide** [taɪd] n marea; (fig: of events etc) curso, marcha; ~ **over** vt (help out) ayudar a salir del apuro

**tidy** ['taɪdɪ] adj (room etc) ordenado; (dress, work) limpio; (person) (bien) arreglado ♦ vt (also: ~ **up**) poner en orden

**tie** [taɪ] n (string etc) atadura; (BRIT: also: **neck**~) corbata; (fig: link) vínculo, lazo; (SPORT: match: draw) empate m ♦ vt atar ♦ vi (SPORT etc) empatar; **to** ~ **in a bow** atar con un lazo; **to** ~ **a knot in sth** hacer un nudo en algo; ~ **down** vt (fig: person: restrict) atar; (: to price, date etc) obligar a; ~ **up** vt (parcel) envolver; (dog, person) atar; (arrangements) concluir; **to be** ~**d up** (busy) estar ocupado

**tier** [tɪə*] n grada; (of cake) piso

**tiger** ['taɪgə*] n tigre m

**tight** [taɪt] adj (rope) tirante; (money) escaso; (clothes) ajustado;

(bend) cerrado; (shoes, schedule) apretado; (budget) ajustado; (security) estricto; (inf: drunk) borracho ♦ adv (squeeze) muy fuerte; (shut) bien; ~**s** (BRIT) npl panti mpl; ~**en** vt (rope) estirar; (screw, grip) apretar; (security) reforzar ♦ vi estirarse; apretarse; ~**fisted** adj tacaño; ~**ly** adv (grasp) muy fuerte; ~**rope** n cuerda floja

**tile** [taɪl] n (on roof) teja; (on floor) baldosa; (on wall) azulejo; ~**d** adj de tejas; embaldosado; (wall) alicatado

**till** [tɪl] n caja (registradora) ♦ vt (land) cultivar ♦ prep, conj = **until**

**tilt** [tɪlt] vt inclinar ♦ vi inclinarse

**timber** ['tɪmbə*] n (material) madera; (trees) árboles mpl

**time** [taɪm] n tiempo; (epoch: often pl) época; (by clock) hora; (moment) momento; (occasion) vez f; (MUS) compás m ♦ vt calcular or medir el tiempo de; (race) cronometrar; (remark, visit etc) elegir el momento para; **a long** ~ mucho tiempo; **4 at a** ~ de 4 en 4; 4 a la vez; **for the** ~ **being** de momento, por ahora; **from** ~ **to** ~ de vez en cuando; **at** ~**s** a veces; **in** ~ (soon enough) a tiempo; (after some time) con el tiempo; (MUS) al compás; **in a week's** ~ dentro de una semana; **in no** ~ en un abrir y cerrar de ojos; **any** ~ cuando sea; **on** ~ a la hora; **5** ~**s 5** 5 por 5; **what** ~ **is it?** ¿qué hora es?; **to have a good** ~ pasarlo bien, divertirse; ~ **bomb** n bomba de efecto retardado; ~**less** adj eterno; ~ **limit** n plazo; ~**ly** adj oportuno; ~ **off** n tiempo libre; ~**r** n (in kitchen etc) programador m horario; ~ **scale** (BRIT) n escala de tiempo; ~ **share** n apartamento (or casa) a tiempo compartido; ~ **switch** (BRIT) n interruptor m (horario); ~**table** n horario; ~ **zone** n huso horario

**timid** ['tɪmɪd] adj tímido

**timing** ['taɪmɪŋ] n (SPORT) cronometraje *m*; **the ~ of his resignation** el momento que eligió para dimitir

**timpani** ['tɪmpənɪ] *npl* tímpanos *mpl*

**tin** [tɪn] *n* estaño; (*also:* ~ **plate**) hojalata; (*BRIT: can*) lata; **~foil** *n* papel *m* de estaño

**tinge** [tɪndʒ] *n* matiz *m* ♦ *vt*: **~d with** teñido de

**tingle** ['tɪŋgl] *vi* (*person*): **to ~ (with)** estremecerse (de); (*hands etc*) hormiguear

**tinker** ['tɪŋkə*]: **~ with** *vt fus* jugar con, tocar

**tinned** [tɪnd] (*BRIT*) *adj* (*food*) en lata, en conserva

**tin opener** [-'əupnə*] (*BRIT*) *n* abrelatas *m inv*

**tinsel** ['tɪnsl] *n* (guirnalda de) espumillón *m*

**tint** [tɪnt] *n* matiz *m*; (*for hair*) tinte *m*; **~ed** *adj* (*hair*) teñido; (*glass, spectacles*) ahumado

**tiny** ['taɪnɪ] *adj* minúsculo, pequeñito

**tip** [tɪp] *n* (*end*) punta; (*gratuity*) propina; (*BRIT: for rubbish*) vertedero; (*advice*) consejo ♦ *vt* (*waiter*) dar una propina a; (*tilt*) inclinar; (*empty: also:* ~ **out**) vaciar, echar; (*overturn: also:* ~ **over**) volcar; **~ off** *n* (*hint*) advertencia; **~ped** (*BRIT*) *adj* (*cigarette*) con filtro

**Tipp-Ex** ['tɪpɛks] ® *n* Tipp-Ex ® *m*

**tipsy** ['tɪpsɪ] (*inf*) *adj* alegre, mareado

**tiptoe** ['tɪptəu] *n*: **on ~** de puntillas

**tiptop** ['tɪp'tɒp] *adj*: **in ~ condition** en perfectas condiciones

**tire** ['taɪə*] *n* (*US*) = **tyre** ♦ *vt* cansar ♦ *vi* (*gen*) cansarse; (*become bored*) aburrirse; **to be ~d of sth** estar harto de algo; **~less** *adj* incansable; **~some** *adj* aburrido; **tiring** *adj* cansado

**tissue** ['tɪʃu:] *n* tejido; (*paper handkerchief*) pañuelo de papel, kleenex ® *m*; **~ paper** *n* papel *m* de seda

**tit** [tɪt] *n* (*bird*) herrerillo común; **to give ~ for tat** dar ojo por ojo

**titbit** ['tɪtbɪt] (*US* **tidbit**) *n* (*food*) go-

losina; (*news*) noticia sabrosa

**titillate** ['tɪtɪleɪt] *vt* estimular, excitar

**title** ['taɪtl] *n* título; **~ deed** *n* (*LAW*) título de propiedad; **~ role** *n* papel *m* principal

**titter** ['tɪtə*] *vi* reírse entre dientes

**TM** *abbr* = **trademark**

*KEYWORD*

**to** [tu:, tə] *prep* **1** (*direction*) a; **to go ~ France/London/school/the station** ir a Francia/Londres/al colegio/a la estación; **to go ~ Claude's/the doctor's** ir a casa de Claude/al médico; **the road ~ Edinburgh** la carretera de Edimburgo

**2** (*as far as*) hasta, a; **from here ~ London** de aquí a or hasta Londres; **to count ~ 10** contar hasta 10; **from 40 ~ 50 people** entre 40 y 50 personas

**3** (*with expressions of time*) **a quarter/twenty ~ 5** las 5 menos cuarto/veinte

**4** (*for, of*): **the key ~ the front door** la llave de la puerta principal; **she is secretary ~ the director** es la secretaria del director; **a letter ~ his wife** una carta a or para su mujer

**5** (*expressing indirect object*) a; **to give sth ~ sb** darle algo a alguien; **to talk ~ sb** hablar con alguien; **to be a danger ~ sb** ser un peligro para alguien; **to carry out repairs ~ sth** hacer reparaciones en algo

**6** (*in relation to*): **3 goals ~ 2** 3 goles a 2; **30 miles ~ the gallon** = 9,4 litros a los cien (kms)

**7** (*purpose, result*): **to come ~ sb's aid** venir en auxilio or ayuda de alguien; **to sentence sb ~ death** condenar a uno a muerte; **~ my great surprise** con gran sorpresa mía

♦ *with vb* **1** (*simple infin*): ~ **go/eat** ir/comer

**2** (*following another vb*): **to want/try/start ~ do** querer/intentar/empezar a hacer; *see also relevant*

*vb*
**3** (*with vb omitted*): **I don't want ~** no quiero
**4** (*purpose, result*) para; **I did it ~ help you** lo hice para ayudarte; **he came ~ see you** vino a verte
**5** (*equivalent to relative clause*): **I have things ~ do** tengo cosas que hacer; **the main thing is ~ try** lo principal es intentarlo
**6** (*after adj etc*): **ready ~ go** listo para irse; **too old ~ ...** demasiado viejo (como) para ...
♦ *adv*: **pull/push the door ~** tirar de/empujar la puerta

**toad** [təud] *n* sapo; **~stool** *n* hongo venenoso

**toast** [təust] *n* (*CULIN*) tostada; (*drink, speech*) brindis *m* ♦ *vt* (*CULIN*) tostar; (*drink to*) brindar por; **~er** *n* tostador *m*

**tobacco** [təˈbækəu] *n* tabaco; **~nist** *n* estanquero/a (*SP*), tabaquero/a (*AM*); **~nist's (shop)** (*BRIT*) *n* estanco (*SP*), tabaquería (*AM*)

**toboggan** [təˈbɒgən] *n* tobogán *m*

**today** [təˈdeɪ] *adv*, *n* (*also fig*) hoy *m*

**toddler** [ˈtɒdlə*] *n* niño/a (que empieza a andar)

**to-do** *n* (*fuss*) lío

**toe** [təu] *n* dedo (del pie); (*of shoe*) punta; **to ~ the line** (*fig*) conformarse; **~nail** *n* uña del pie

**toffee** [ˈtɒfɪ] *n* toffee *m*; **~ apple** (*BRIT*) *n* manzana acaramelada

**together** [təˈgeðə*] *adv* juntos; (*at same time*) al mismo tiempo, a la vez; **~ with** junto con

**toil** [tɔɪl] *n* trabajo duro, labor *f* ♦ *vi* trabajar duramente

**toilet** [ˈtɔɪlət] *n* retrete *m*; (*BRIT: room*) servicios *mpl* (*SP*), wáter *m* (*SP*), sanitario (*AM*) ♦ *cpd* (*soap etc*) de aseo; **~ paper** *n* papel *m* higiénico; **~ries** *npl* artículos *mpl* de tocador; **~ roll** *n* rollo de papel higiénico; **~ water** *n* (agua de) colonia

**token** [ˈtəukən] *n* (*sign*) señal *f*, muestra; (*souvenir*) recuerdo; (*disc*)

**ficha** ♦ *adj* (*strike, payment etc*) simbólico; **book/record/gift ~** (*BRIT*) vale *m* para comprar libros/ discos/vale-regalo

**Tokyo** [ˈtəukjəu] *n* Tokio, Tokío

**told** [təuld] *pt, pp* of **tell**

**tolerable** [ˈtɒlərəbl] *adj* (*bearable*) soportable; (*fairly good*) pasable

**tolerant** [ˈtɒlərnt] *adj*: **~ of** tolerante con

**tolerate** [ˈtɒləreɪt] *vt* tolerar

**toll** [təul] *n* (*of casualties*) número de víctimas; (*tax, charge*) peaje *m* ♦ *vi* (*bell*) doblar

**tomato** [təˈmɑːtəu] (*pl* **~es**) *n* tomate *m*

**tomb** [tuːm] *n* tumba

**tomboy** [ˈtɒmbɔɪ] *n* marimacho

**tombstone** [ˈtuːmstəun] *n* lápida

**tomcat** [ˈtɒmkæt] *n* gato (macho)

**tomorrow** [təˈmɒrəu] *adv*, *n* (*also: fig*) mañana; **the day after ~** pasado mañana; **~ morning** mañana por la mañana

**ton** [tʌn] *n* tonelada (*BRIT* = 1016 *kg*; *US* = 907 *kg*); (*metric ~*) tonelada métrica; **~s of** (*inf*) montones de

**tone** [təun] *n* tono ♦ *vi* (*also: ~ in*) armonizar; **~ down** *vt* (*criticism*) suavizar; (*colour*) atenuar; **~ up** *vt* (*muscles*) tonificar; **~-deaf** *adj* con mal oído

**tongs** [tɒŋz] *npl* (*for coal*) tenazas *fpl*; (*curling ~*) tenacillas *fpl*

**tongue** [tʌŋ] *n* lengua; **~ in cheek** irónicamente; **~-tied** *adj* (*fig*) mudo; **~-twister** *n* trabalenguas *m inv*

**tonic** [ˈtɒnɪk] *n* (*MED, also fig*) tónico; (*also: ~ water*) (agua) tónica

**tonight** [təˈnaɪt] *adv*, *n* esta noche; esta tarde

**tonnage** [ˈtʌnɪdʒ] *n* (*NAUT*) tonelaje *m*

**tonsil** [ˈtɒnsl] *n* amígdala; **~litis** [-ˈlaɪtɪs] *n* amigdalitis *f*

**too** [tuː] *adv* (*excessively*) demasiado; (*also*) también; **~ much** demasiado; **~ many** demasiados/as

**took** [tuk] *pt* of **take**

**tool** [tuːl] *n* herramienta; **~ box** *n*

caja de herramientas

**toot** [tuːt] n pitido ♦ vi tocar el pito

**tooth** [tuːθ] (pl **teeth**) n (ANAT, TECH) diente m; (molar) muela; **~ache** n dolor m de muelas; **~brush** n cepillo de dientes; **~paste** n pasta de dientes; **~pick** n palillo

**top** [tɔp] n (of mountain) cumbre f, cima; (of tree) copa; (of head) coronilla; (of ladder, page) lo alto; (of table) superficie f; (of cupboard) parte f de arriba; (lid: of box) tapa; (: of bottle, jar) tapón m; (of list etc) cabeza; (toy) peonza; (garment) blusa; camiseta ♦ adj de arriba; (in rank) principal, primero; (best) mejor ♦ vt (exceed) exceder; (be first in) encabezar; **on ~ of** (above) sobre, encima de; (in addition to) además de; **from ~ to bottom** de pies a cabeza; **~ off** (US) vt = **~ up**; **~ up** vt llenar; **~ floor** n último piso; **~ hat** n sombrero de copa; **~-heavy** adj (object) mal equilibrado

**topic** ['tɔpɪk] n tema m; **~al** adj actual

**top:** **~less** adj (bather, bikini) topless inv; **~less** adj (talks) al más altonivel; **~most** adj más alto

**topple** ['tɔpl] vt derribar ♦ vi caerse

**top-secret** adj de alto secreto

**topsy-turvy** ['tɔpsɪ'tɜːvɪ] adj al revés ♦ adv patas arriba

**torch** [tɔːtʃ] n antorcha; (BRIT: electric) linterna

**tore** [tɔː*] pt of **tear**

**torment** [n 'tɔːment, vt tɔː'ment] n tormento ♦ vt atormentar; (fig: annoy) fastidiar

**torn** [tɔːn] pp of **tear**

**torrent** ['tɔrnt] n torrente m

**torrid** ['tɔrɪd] adj (fig) apasionado

**tortoise** ['tɔːtəs] n tortuga; **~shell** ['tɔːtəʃel] adj de carey

**torture** ['tɔːtʃə*] n tortura ♦ vt torturar; (fig) atormentar

**Tory** ['tɔːrɪ] (BRIT) adj, n (POL) conservador/a m/f

**toss** [tɔs] vt tirar, echar; (one's head) sacudir; **to ~ a coin** echar a

cara o cruz; **to ~ up for sth** jugar a cara o cruz algo; **to ~ and turn** (in bed) dar vueltas

**tot** [tɔt] n (BRIT: drink) copita; (child) nene/a m/f

**total** ['təʊtl] adj total, entero; (emphatic: failure etc) completo, total ♦ n total m, suma ♦ vt (add up) sumar; (amount to) ascender a

**totalitarian** [təʊtælɪ'tɛərɪən] adj totalitario

**totally** ['təʊtəlɪ] adv totalmente

**totter** ['tɔtə*] vi tambalearse

**touch** [tʌtʃ] n tacto; (contact) contacto ♦ vt tocar; (emotionally) conmover; **a ~ of** (fig) un poquito de; **to get in ~ with sb** ponerse en contacto con uno; **to lose ~** (friends) perder contacto; **~ on** vt fus (topic) aludir (brevemente) a; **~ up** vt (paint) retocar; **~-and-go** adj arriesgado; **~down** n aterrizaje m; (on sea) amerizaje m; (US: FOOTBALL) ensayo; **~ed** adj (moved) conmovido; **~ing** adj (moving) conmovedor(a); **~line** n (SPORT) línea de banda; **~y** adj (person) quisquilloso

**tough** [tʌf] adj (material) resistente; (meat) duro; (problem etc) difícil; (policy, stance) inflexible; (person) fuerte; **~en** vt endurecer

**toupée** ['tuːpeɪ] n peluca

**tour** [tʊə*] n viaje m, vuelta; (also: package ~) viaje m todo comprendido; (of town, museum) visita; (by band etc) gira ♦ vt recorrer, visitar

**tourism** ['tʊərɪzm] n turismo

**tourist** ['tʊərɪst] n turista m/f ♦ adj turístico; **~ office** n oficina de turismo

**tournament** ['tʊənəmənt] n torneo

**tousled** ['tauzld] adj (hair) despeinado

**tout** [taut] vi: **to ~ for business** solicitar clientes ♦ n (also: ticket ~) revendedor/a m/f

**tow** [təʊ] vt remolcar; **"on** or **in ~"** (AUT) "a remolque"

**toward(s)** [tə'wɔːd(z)] prep hacia; (attitude) respecto a, con; (purpose) para

**towel** ['tauəl] n toalla; ~**ling** n (fabric) felpa; ~ **rail** (US = **rack**) n toallero

**tower** ['tauə*] n torre f; ~ **block** (BRIT) n torre f (de pisos); ~**ing** adj muy alto, imponente

**town** [taun] n ciudad f; **to go to** ~ ir a la ciudad; (fig) echar la casa por la ventana; ~ **centre** n centro de la ciudad; ~ **council** n ayuntamiento, consejo municipal; ~ **hall** n ayuntamiento; ~ **plan** n plano de la ciudad; ~ **planning** n urbanismo

**towrope** ['tourəup] n cable m de remolque

**tow truck** n camión m grúa

**toy** [tɔɪ] n juguete m; ~ **with** vt fus jugar con; (idea) acariciar; ~**shop** n juguetería

**trace** [treɪs] n rastro ♦ vt (draw) trazar, delinear; (locate) encontrar; (follow) seguir la pista de; **tracing paper** n papel m de calco

**track** [træk] n (mark) huella, pista; (path: gen) camino, senda; (: of bullet etc) trayectoria; (: of suspect, animal) pista, rastro; (RAIL) vía; (SPORT) pista; (on tape, record) canción f ♦ vt seguir la pista de; **to keep** ~ **of** mantenerse al tanto de, seguir; ~ **down** vt (prey) seguir el rastro de; (sth lost) encontrar; ~**suit** n chandal m

**tract** [trækt] n (GEO) región f; (pamphlet) folleto

**traction** ['trækʃən] n (power) tracción f; **in** ~ (MED) en tracción

**tractor** ['træktə*] n tractor m

**trade** [treɪd] n comercio; (skill, job) oficio ♦ vi negociar, comerciar ♦ vt (exchange) cambiar; **to** ~ **sth** (**for sth**) cambiar algo (por algo); ~ **in** vt (old car etc) ofrecer como parte del pago; ~ **fair** n feria comercial; ~**mark** n marca de fábrica; ~ **name** n marca registrada; ~**r** n comerciante m/f; ~**sman** n (shopkeeper) tendero; ~ **union** n sindicato; ~ **unionist** n sindicalista m/f

**tradition** [trə'dɪʃən] n tradición f; ~**al** adj tradicional

**traffic** ['træfɪk] n (gen, AUT) tráfico, circulación f, tránsito (AM) ♦ vi: **to** ~ **in** (pej: liquor, drugs) traficar en; ~ **circle** (US) n isleta; ~ **jam** n embotellamiento; ~ **lights** npl semáforo; ~ **warden** n guardia m/f de tráfico

**tragedy** ['trædʒədɪ] n tragedia

**tragic** ['trædʒɪk] adj trágico

**trail** [treɪl] n (tracks) rastro, pista; (path) camino, sendero; (dust, smoke) estela ♦ vt (drag) arrastrar; (follow) seguir la pista de ♦ vi arrastrar; (in contest etc) ir perdiendo; ~ **behind** vi quedar a la zaga; ~**er** n (AUT) remolque m; (caravan) caravana; (CINEMA) trailer m, avance m; ~**er truck** (US) n trailer m

**train** [treɪn] n tren m; (of dress) cola; (series) serie f ♦ vt (educate, teach skills to) formar; (sportsman) entrenar; (dog) adiestrar; (point: gun etc): **to** ~ **on** apuntar a ♦ vi (SPORT) entrenarse; (learn a skill): **to** ~ **as a teacher** etc estudiar para profesor etc; **one's** ~ **of thought** el razonamiento de uno; ~**ed** adj (worker) cualificado; (animal) amaestrado; ~**ee** [treɪ'ni:] n aprendiz/a m/f; ~**er** n (SPORT: coach) entrenador(a) m/f; (: shoe): ~**ers** zapatillas fpl (de deporte); (of animals) domador(a) m/f; ~**ing** n formación f; entrenamiento; **to be in** ~**ing** (SPORT) estar entrenando; ~**ing college** n (gen) colegio de formación profesional; (for teachers) escuela de formación del profesorado; ~**ing shoes** npl zapatillas fpl (de deporte)

**traipse** [treɪps] vi andar penosamente

**trait** [treɪt] n rasgo

**traitor** ['treɪtə*] n traidor(a) m/f

**tram** [træm] n (BRIT) n (also: ~**car**) tranvía m

**tramp** [træmp] n (person) vagabundo/a m/f; (inf: pej: woman) puta ♦ vi andar con pasos pesados

**trample** ['træmpl] vt: **to** ~ (underfoot) pisotear

**trampoline** ['træmpəli:n] n trampolín m

**tranquil** ['træŋkwıl] adj tranquilo; **~lizer** n (MED) tranquilizante m

**transact** [træn'zækt] vt (business) despachar; **~ion** [-'zækʃən] n transacción f, operación f

**transcend** [træn'send] vt rebasar

**transcript** ['trænskrıpt] n copia

**transfer** [n 'trænsfə:*, vb træns'fə:*] n (of employees) traslado; (of money, power) transferencia; (SPORT) traspaso; (picture, design) calcomanía ♦ vt trasladar; transferir; **to ~ the charges** (BRIT: TEL) llamar a cobro revertido

**transform** [træns'fɔ:m] vt transformar

**transfusion** [træns'fju:ʒən] n transfusión f

**transient** ['trænzıənt] adj transitorio

**transistor** [træn'zıstə*] n (ELEC) transistor m; **~ radio** n transistor m

**transit** ['trænzıt] n: **in ~** en tránsito

**transitional** [træn'zıʃənl] adj de transición

**transitive** ['trænzıtıv] adj (LING) transitivo

**transit lounge** n sala de tránsito

**translate** [trænz'leıt] vt traducir; **translation** [-'leıʃən] n traducción f; **translator** n traductor(a) m/f

**transmit** [trænz'mıt] vt transmitir; **~ter** n transmisor m

**transparency** [træns'pɛərnsı] n transparencia; (BRIT: PHOT) diapositiva

**transparent** [træns'pærnt] adj transparente

**transpire** [træns'paıə*] vi (turn out) resultar; (happen) ocurrir, suceder; it **~d that …** se supo que …

**transplant** [n 'trænsplɑ:nt, vt træns'plɑ:nt] vt transplantar ♦ n (MED) transplante m

**transport** [n 'trænspɔ:t, vt træns'pɔ:t] n transporte m; (car) coche (SP), carro (AM), automóvil m ♦ vt transportar; **~ation** [-'teıʃən] n transporte m; **~ café** (BRIT) n bar-restaurant

m de carretera

**transvestite** [trænz'vestaıt] n travestí m/f

**trap** [træp] n (snare, trick) trampa; (carriage) cabriolé m ♦ vt coger (SP) or agarrar (AM) en una trampa; (trick) engañar; (confine) atrapar; **~ door** n escotilla

**trapeze** [trə'pi:z] n trapecio

**trappings** ['træpıŋz] npl adornos mpl

**trash** [træʃ] n (rubbish) basura; (pej): **the book/film is ~** el libro/la película no vale nada; (nonsense) tonterías fpl; **~ can** (US) n cubo (SP) or balde m (AM) de la basura

**travel** ['trævl] n el viajar ♦ vi viajar ♦ vt (distance) recorrer; **~s** npl (journeys) viajes mpl; **~ agent** n agente m/f de viajes; **~ler** (US ~er) n viajero/a; **~ler's cheque** (US **~er's check**) n cheque m de viaje; **~ling** (US **~ing**) n los viajes, el viajar; **~ sickness** n mareo

**travesty** ['trævəstı] n parodia

**trawler** ['trɔ:lə*] n pesquero de arrastre

**tray** [treı] n bandeja; (on desk) cajón m

**treacherous** ['tretʃərəs] adj traidor, traicionero; (dangerous) peligroso

**treacle** ['tri:kl] n melaza

**tread** [tred] (pt trod, pp trodden) n (step) paso, pisada; (sound) ruido de pasos; (of stair) escalón m; (of tyre) banda de rodadura ♦ vi pisar; **~ on** vt fus pisar

**treason** ['tri:zn] n traición f

**treasure** ['treʒə*] n (also fig) tesoro ♦ vt (value: object, friendship) apreciar; (: memory) guardar

**treasurer** ['treʒərə*] n tesorero/a

**treasury** ['treʒərı] n: **the T~** el Ministerio de Hacienda

**treat** [tri:t] n (present) regalo ♦ vt tratar; **to ~ sb to sth** invitar a uno a algo

**treatment** ['tri:tmənt] n tratamiento

**treaty** ['tri:tı] n tratado

**treble** ['trebl] adj triple ♦ vt triplicar ♦ vi triplicarse; **~ clef** n (MUS) clave f de sol

**tree** [triː] n árbol m; ~ **trunk** tronco (de árbol)

**trek** [trek] n (long journey) viaje m largo y difícil; (tiring walk) caminata

**trellis** ['trelɪs] n enrejado

**tremble** ['trembl] vi temblar

**tremendous** [trɪ'mendəs] adj tremendo, enorme; (excellent) estupendo

**tremor** ['tremə*] n temblor m; (also: earth ~) temblor m de tierra

**trench** [trentʃ] n zanja

**trend** [trend] n (tendency) tendencia; (of events) curso; (fashion) moda; ~**y** adj de moda

**trepidation** [trepɪ'deɪʃən] n inquietud f

**trespass** ['trespəs] vi: to ~ on entrar sin permiso en; "no ~ing" "prohibido el paso"

**trestle** ['tresl] n caballete m

**trial** ['traɪəl] n (LAW) juicio, proceso; (test: of machine etc) prueba; ~s npl (hardships) dificultades fpl; by ~ **and error** a fuerza de probar

**triangle** ['traɪæŋgl] n (MATH, MUS) triángulo

**tribe** [traɪb] n tribu f

**tribulations** [trɪbju'leɪʃənz] npl dificultades fpl, sufrimientos

**tribunal** [traɪ'bjuːnl] n tribunal m

**tributary** ['trɪbjutərɪ] n (river) afluente m

**tribute** ['trɪbjuːt] n homenaje m, tributo; to pay ~ to rendir homenaje a

**trick** [trɪk] n (skill, knack) tino, truco; (conjuring ~) truco; (joke) broma; (CARDS) baza ♦ vt engañar; to play a ~ on sb gastar una broma a uno; that should do the ~ a ver si funciona así; ~**ery** n engaño

**trickle** ['trɪkl] n (of water etc) goteo ♦ vi gotear

**tricky** ['trɪkɪ] adj difícil; delicado

**tricycle** ['traɪsɪkl] n triciclo

**trifle** ['traɪfl] n bagatela; (CULIN) dulce de bizcocho borracho, gelatina, fruta y natillas ♦ adv: a ~ long un

poquito largo; **trifling** adj insignificante

**trigger** ['trɪgə*] n (of gun) gatillo; ~ **off** vt desencadenar

**trill** [trɪl] vi trinar, gorjear

**trim** [trɪm] adj (house, garden) en buen estado; (person, figure) esbelto ♦ n (haircut etc) recorte m; (on car) guarnición f ♦ vt (neaten) arreglar; (cut) recortar; (decorate) adornar; (NAUT: a sail) orientar; ~**mings** npl (CULIN) guarnición f

**trinket** ['trɪŋkɪt] n chuchería

**trip** [trɪp] n viaje m; (excursion) excursión f; (stumble) traspié m ♦ vi (stumble) tropezar; (go lightly) andar a paso ligero; on a ~ de viaje; ~ **up** vi tropezar, caerse ♦ vt hacer tropezar or caer

**tripe** [traɪp] n (CULIN) callos mpl; (pej: rubbish) tonterías fpl

**triple** ['trɪpl] adj triple; **triplets** ['trɪplɪts] npl trillizos/as mpl/fpl; **triplicate** ['trɪplɪkət] n: in ~ por triplicado

**trite** [traɪt] adj trillado

**triumph** ['traɪʌmf] n triunfo ♦ vi: to ~ (over) vencer; ~**ant** [traɪ'ʌmfənt] adj (team etc) vencedor(a); (wave, return) triunfal

**trivia** ['trɪvɪə] npl trivialidades fpl

**trivial** ['trɪvɪəl] adj insignificante; (commonplace) banal

**trod** [trɒd] pt of **tread**

**trodden** ['trɒdn] pp of **tread**

**trolley** ['trɒlɪ] n carrito; (also: bus) trolebús m

**trombone** [trɒm'bəʊn] n trombón m

**troop** [truːp] n grupo, banda; ~s npl (MIL) tropas fpl; ~ **in/out** vi entrar/salir en tropel; ~**ing the colour** n (ceremony) presentación f de la bandera

**trophy** ['trəʊfɪ] n trofeo

**tropical** ['trɒpɪkl] adj tropical

**trot** [trɒt] n trote m ♦ vi trotar; on **the** ~ (BRIT: fig) seguidos/as

**trouble** ['trʌbl] n problema m, dificultad f; (worry) preocupación f; (bother, effort) molestia, esfuerzo;

(*unrest*) inquietud *f*; (*MED*): stomach *etc* ~ problemas *mpl* gástricos *etc* ♦ *vt* (*disturb*) molestar; (*worry*) preocupar, inquietar ♦ *vi*: **to ~ to do sth** molestarse en hacer algo; **~s** *npl* (*POL etc*) conflictos *mpl*; (*personal*) problemas *mpl*; **to be in ~** estar en un apuro; **it's no ~!** ¡no es molestia (ninguna)!; **what's the ~?** (*with broken TV etc*) ¿cuál es el problema?; (*doctor to patient*) ¿qué pasa?; ~**d** *adj* (*person*) preocupado; (*country, epoch, life*) agitado; ~**maker** *n* agitador(a) *m/f*; (*child*) alborotador *m*; ~**shooter** *n* (*in conflict*) conciliador(a) *m/f*; ~**some** *adj* molesto

**trough** [trɔf] *n* (*also: drinking ~*) abrevadero; (*also: feeding ~*) comedero; (*depression*) depresión *f*

**troupe** [truːp] *n* grupo

**trousers** ['trauzəz] *npl* pantalones *mpl*; **short ~** pantalones *mpl* cortos

**trousseau** ['truːsəu] (*pl* **~x** *or* **~s**) *n* ajuar *m*

**trout** [traut] *n inv* trucha

**trowel** ['trauəl] *n* (*of gardener*) palita; (*of builder*) paleta

**truant** ['truənt] *n*: **to play ~** (*BRIT*) hacer novillos

**truce** [truːs] *n* tregua

**truck** [trʌk] *n* (*lorry*) camión *m*; (*RAIL*) vagón *m*; ~ **driver** *n* camionero; ~ **farm** (*US*) *n* huerto

**trudge** [trʌdʒ] *vi* (*also: ~ along*) caminar penosamente

**true** [truː] *adj* verdadero; (*accurate*) exacto; (*genuine*) auténtico; (*faithful*) fiel; **to come ~** realizarse

**truffle** ['trʌfl] *n* trufa

**truly** ['truːlɪ] *adv* (*really*) realmente; (*truthfully*) verdaderamente; (*faithfully*): **yours ~** (*in letter*) le saluda atentamente

**trump** [trʌmp] *n* triunfo; ~**ed-up** *adj* inventado

**trumpet** ['trʌmpɪt] *n* trompeta

**truncheon** ['trʌntʃən] *n* porra

**trundle** ['trʌndl] *vt* (*pushchair etc*) empujar; hacer rodar ♦ *vi*: **to ~**

**along** ir sin prisas

**trunk** [trʌŋk] *n* (*of tree, person*) tronco; (*of elephant*) trompa; (*case*) baúl *m*; (*US: AUT*) maletero; ~**s** *npl* (*also: swimming ~s*) bañador *m* (de hombre)

**truss** [trʌs] *n* (*MED*) braguero; ~ (**up**) *vt* atar

**trust** [trʌst] *n* confianza *f*; (*responsibility*) responsabilidad *f*; (*LAW*) fideicomiso ♦ *vt* (*rely on*) tener confianza en; (*hope*) esperar; (*entrust*): **to ~ sth to sb** confiar algo a uno; **to take sth on ~** aceptar algo a ojos cerrados; ~**ed** *adj* de confianza; ~**ee** [trʌs'tiː] *n* (*LAW*) fideicomisario; (*of school*) administrador *m*; ~**ful** *adj* confiado; ~**ing** *adj* confiado; ~**worthy** *adj* digno de confianza

**truth** [truːθ] *pl* **~s** [truːðz] *n* verdad *f*; ~**ful** *adj* veraz

**try** [traɪ] *n* tentativa, intento; (*RUGBY*) ensayo ♦ *vt* (*attempt*) intentar; (*test: also: ~ out*) probar, someter a prueba; (*LAW*) juzgar, procesar; (*strain: patience*) hacer perder ♦ *vi* probar; **to have a ~** probar suerte; **to ~ to do sth** intentar hacer algo; ~ **again!** ¡vuelve a probar!; ~ **harder!** ¡esfuérzate más!; **well, I tried** al menos lo intenté; ~ **on** *vt* (*clothes*) probarse; ~**ing** *adj* (*experience*) cansado; (*person*) pesado

**tsar** [zɑː] *n* zar *m*

**T-shirt** ['tiːʃəːt] *n* camiseta

**T-square** *n* regla en T

**tub** [tʌb] *n* cubo (*SP*), balde *m* (*AM*); (*bath*) tina, bañera

**tubby** ['tʌbɪ] *adj* regordete

**tube** [tjuːb] *n* tubo; (*BRIT: underground*) metro; (*for tyre*) cámara de aire

**tuberculosis** [tjubəːkjuˈləusɪs] *n* tuberculosis *f inv*

**tube station** (*BRIT*) *n* estación *f* de metro

**tubular** ['tjuːbjulə*] *adj* tubular

**TUC** (*BRIT*) *n abbr* (= Trades Union Congress) federación nacional de sin-

*dicatos*

**tuck** [tʌk] *vt* (*put*) poner; ~ **away** *vt* (*money*) guardar; (*building*): **to be ~ed away** esconderse, ocultarse; ~ **in** *vt* meter dentro; (*child*) arropar ♦ *vi* (*eat*) comer con apetito; ~ **up** *vt* (*child*) arropar; ~ **shop** *n* (SCOL) tienda; ≈ **bar** *m* (del colegio) (SP)

**Tuesday** ['tjuːzdɪ] *n* martes *m inv*

**tuft** [tʌft] *n* mechón *m*; (*of grass etc*) manojo

**tug** [tʌg] *n* (*ship*) remolcador *m*, tirar de; ~**-of-war** *n* lucha de tiro de cuerda; (*fig*) tira y afloja *m*

**tuition** [tjuː'ɪʃən] *n* (BRIT) enseñanza; (: *private* ~) clases *fpl* particulares; (US: *school fees*) matrícula

**tulip** ['tjuːlɪp] *n* tulipán *m*

**tumble** ['tʌmbl] *n* (*fall*) caída ♦ *vi* caer; **to ~ to sth** (*inf*) caer en la cuenta de algo; ~**-down** *adj* destartalado; ~ **dryer** (BRIT) *n* secadora

**tumbler** ['tʌmblə*] *n* (*glass*) vaso

**tummy** ['tʌmɪ] (*inf*) *n* barriga, tripa

**tumour** ['tjuːmə*] (US **tumor**) *n* tumor *m*

**tuna** ['tjuːnə] *n inv* (*also*: ~ *fish*) atún *m*

**tune** [tjuːn] *n* (*melody*) melodía ♦ *vt* (MUS) afinar; (RADIO, TV, AUT) sintonizar; **to be in/out of ~** (*instrument*) estar afinado/desafinado; (*singer*) cantar afinadamente/desafinar; **to be in/out of ~ with** (*fig*) estar de acuerdo/en desacuerdo con; ~ **in** *vi* (to) (RADIO, TV) sintonizar (con); ~ **up** *vi* (*musician*) afinar (su instrumento); ~**ful** *adj* melodioso; ~**r** *n*: **piano** ~**r** afinador(a) *m/f* de pianos

**tunic** ['tjuːnɪk] *n* túnica

**Tunisia** [tjuː'nɪzɪə] *n* Túnez *m*

**tunnel** ['tʌnl] *n* túnel *m*; (*in mine*) galería ♦ *vi* construir un túnel/una galería

**turban** ['təːbən] *n* turbante *m*

**turbine** ['təːbaɪn] *n* turbina

**turbulent** ['təːbjulənt] *adj* turbulento

**tureen** [tə'riːn] *n* sopera

**turf** [təːf] *n* césped *m*; (*clod*) tepe *m*

♦ *vt* cubrir con césped; ~ **out** (*inf*) *vt* echar a la calle

**turgid** ['təːdʒɪd] *adj* (*prose*) pesado

**Turk** [təːk] *n* turco/a

**Turkey** ['təːkɪ] *n* Turquía

**turkey** ['təːkɪ] *n* pavo

**Turkish** ['təːkɪʃ] *adj*, *n* turco

**turmoil** ['təːmɔɪl] *n* desorden *m*, alboroto; ~ **in ~** revuelto

**turn** [təːn] *n* turno; (*in road*) curva; (*of mind, events*) rumbo; (THEATRE) número; (MED) ataque *m* ♦ *vt* girar, volver; (*collar, steak*) dar la vuelta a; (*page*) pasar; (*change*): **to ~ sth into** convertir algo en ♦ *vi* volver; (*person: look back*) volverse; (*reverse direction*) dar la vuelta; (*milk*) cortarse; (*become*): **to ~ nasty/forty** ponerse feo/cumplir los cuarenta; **a good ~** un favor; **it gave me quite a ~** me dio un susto; **"no left ~"** (AUT) "prohibido girar a la izquierda"; **it's your ~** te toca a ti; **in ~** por turnos; **to take ~s** (at) turnarse (en); ~ **away** *vi* apartar la vista ♦ *vi* rechazar; ~ **back** *vi* volverse atrás ♦ *vt* hacer retroceder; (*clock*) retrasar; ~ **down** *vt* (*refuse*) rechazar; (*reduce*) bajar; (*fold*) doblar; ~ **in** *vi* (*inf*: *go to bed*) acostarse ♦ *vt* (*fold*) doblar hacia dentro; ~ **off** *vi* (*from road*) desviarse ♦ *vt* (*light, radio etc*) apagar; (*tap*) cerrar; (*engine*) parar; ~ **on** *vt* (*light, radio etc*) encender (SP), prender (AM); (*tap*) abrir; (*engine*) poner en marcha; ~ **out** *vt* (*light, gas*) apagar; (*produce*) producir ♦ *vi* (*voters*) concurrir; **to ~ out to be ...** resultar ser ...; ~ **over** *vi* (*person*) volverse ♦ *vt* (*object*) dar la vuelta a; (*page*) volver; ~ **round** *vi* volverse; (*rotate*) girar; ~ **up** *vi* (*person*) llegar, presentarse; (*lost object*) aparecer ♦ *vt* (*gen*) subir; ~**ing** *n* (*in road*) vuelta; ~**ing point** *n* (*fig*) momento decisivo

**turnip** ['təːnɪp] *n* nabo

**turnout** ['təːnaut] *n* concurrencia

**turnover** ['təːnəuvə*] *n* (COMM:

*amount of money*) volumen *m* de ventas; (: *of goods*) movimiento

**turnpike** ['tə:npaɪk] (*US*) *n* autopista de peaje

**turnstile** ['tə:nstaɪl] *n* torniquete *m*

**turntable** ['tə:nteɪbl] *n* plato

**turn-up** (*BRIT*) *n* (*on trousers*) vuelta

**turpentine** ['tə:pəntaɪn] *n* (*also: turps*) trementina

**turquoise** ['tə:kwɔɪz] *n* (*stone*) turquesa ♦ *adj* color turquesa

**turret** ['tʌrɪt] *n* torreón *m*

**turtle** ['tə:tl] *n* galápago; **~neck (sweater)** *n* jersey *m* de cuello vuelto

**tusk** [tʌsk] *n* colmillo

**tussle** ['tʌsl] *n* pelea

**tutor** ['tju:tə*] *n* profesor(a) *m/f*; **~ial** [-'tɔ:rɪəl] *n* (*SCOL*) seminario

**tuxedo** [tʌk'si:dəu] (*US*) *n* smóking *m*, esmoquin *m*

**TV** [ti:'vi:] *n abbr* (= *television*) tele *f*

**twang** [twæŋ] *n* (*of instrument*) punteado; (*of voice*) timbre *m* nasal

**tweezers** ['twi:zəz] *npl* pinzas *fpl* (de depilar)

**twelfth** [twelfθ] *num* duodécimo

**twelve** [twelv] *num* doce; **at ~ o'clock** (*midday*) a mediodía; (*midnight*) a medianoche

**twentieth** ['twentɪɪθ] *adj* vigésimo

**twenty** ['twentɪ] *num* veinte

**twice** [twaɪs] *adv* dos veces; **~ as much** dos veces más

**twiddle** ['twɪdl] *vt* juguetear con ♦ *vi*: **to ~ (with)** sth dar vueltas a algo; **to ~ one's thumbs** (*fig*) estar mano sobre mano

**twig** [twɪg] *n* ramita ♦ *vi* (*inf*) caer en la cuenta

**twilight** ['twaɪlaɪt] *n* crepúsculo

**twin** [twɪn] *adj*, *n* gemelo/a *m/f* ♦ *vt* hermanar; **~-bedded room** *n* habitación *f* doble

**twine** [twaɪn] *n* bramante *m* ♦ *vi* (*plant*) enroscarse

**twinge** [twɪndʒ] *n* (*of pain*) punzada; (*of conscience*) remordimiento

**twinkle** ['twɪŋkl] *vi* centellear; (*eyes*) brillar

**twirl** [twə:l] *vt* dar vueltas a ♦ *vi* dar vueltas

**twist** [twɪst] *n* (*action*) torsión *f*; (*in road, coil*) vuelta; (*in wire, flex*) doblez *f*; (*in story*) giro ♦ *vt* torcer; (*weave*) trenzar; (*roll around*) enrollar; (*fig*) deformar ♦ *vi* serpentear

**twit** [twɪt] *n* (*inf*) *n* tonto

**twitch** [twɪtʃ] *n* (*pull*) tirón *m*; (*nervous*) tic *m* ♦ *vi* crisparse

**two** [tu:] *num* dos; **to put ~ and ~ together** (*fig*) atar cabos; **~-door** *adj* (*AUT*) de dos puertas; **~-faced** *adj* (*pej: person*) falso; **~fold** *adv*: **to increase ~fold** doblarse; **~-piece** (*suit*) *n* traje *m* de dos piezas; **~-piece** (*swimsuit*) *n* dos piezas *m inv*, bikini *m*; **~some** *n* (*people*) pareja; **~-way** *adj*: **~-way traffic** circulación *f* de dos sentidos

**tycoon** [taɪ'ku:n] *n*: (*business*) **~** magnate *m*

**type** [taɪp] *n* (*category*) tipo, género; (*model*) tipo; (*TYP*) tipo, letra ♦ *vt* (*letter etc*) escribir a máquina; **~-cast** *adj* (*actor*) encasillado; **~face** *n* letra; **~script** *n* texto mecanografiado; **~writer** *n* máquina de escribir; **~written** *adj* mecanografiado

**typhoid** ['taɪfɔɪd] *n* tifoidea

**typical** ['tɪpɪkl] *adj* típico

**typing** ['taɪpɪŋ] *n* mecanografía

**typist** ['taɪpɪst] *n* mecanógrafo/a

**tyranny** ['tɪrənɪ] *n* tiranía

**tyrant** ['taɪərnt] *n* tirano/a

**tyre** ['taɪə*] (*US* **tire**) *n* neumático (*SP*), llanta (*AM*); **~ pressure** *n* presión *f* de los neumáticos

**tzar** [za:*] *n* = tsar

# U

**U-bend** ['ju:'bend] *n* (*AUT, in pipe*) recodo

**udder** ['ʌdə*] *n* ubre *f*

**UFO** ['ju:fəu] *n abbr* = (*unidentified flying object*) OVNI *m*

**ugh** [ə:h] *excl* ¡uf!

**ugly** ['ʌglɪ] *adj* feo; (*dangerous*) peligroso

**UK** n abbr = **United Kingdom**

**ulcer** ['ʌlsə*] n úlcera; (mouth ~) llaga

**Ulster** ['ʌlstə*] n Ulster m

**ulterior** [ʌl'tɪərɪə*] adj: ~ **motive** segundas intenciones fpl

**ultimate** ['ʌltɪmət] adj último, final; (greatest) máximo; ~**ly** adv (in the end) por último, al final; (fundamentally) a or en fin de cuentas

**umbilical cord** [ʌm'bɪlɪkl-] n cordón m umbilical

**umbrella** [ʌm'brelə] n paraguas m inv; (for sun) sombrilla

**umpire** ['ʌmpaɪə*] n árbitro

**umpteen** [ʌmp'ti:n] adj enésimos/as; ~**th** adj: for the ~**th** time por enésima vez

**UN** n abbr (= United Nations) NN. UU.

**unable** [ʌn'eɪbl] adj: to be ~ to do sth no poder hacer algo

**unaccompanied** [ʌnə'kʌmpənɪd] adj no acompañado; (song) sin acompañamiento

**unaccountably** [ʌnə'kaʊntəblɪ] adv inexplicablemente

**unaccustomed** [ʌnə'kʌstəmd] adj: to be ~ to no estar acostumbrado a

**unanimous** [juː'nænɪməs] adj unánime

**unarmed** [ʌn'ɑːmd] adj (defenceless) inerme; (without weapon) desarmado

**unashamed** [ʌnə'ʃeɪmd] adj descarado

**unassuming** [ʌnə'sjuːmɪŋ] adj modesto, sin pretensiones

**unattached** [ʌnə'tætʃt] adj (person) soltero y sin compromiso; (part etc) suelto

**unattended** [ʌnə'tendɪd] adj desatendido

**unattractive** [ʌnə'træktɪv] adj poco atractivo

**unauthorized** [ʌn'ɔːθəraɪzd] adj no autorizado

**unavoidable** [ʌnə'vɔɪdəbl] adj inevitable

**unaware** [ʌnə'weə*] adj: to be ~ of ignorar; ~**s** adv de improviso

**unbalanced** [ʌn'bælənst] adj (report) poco objetivo; (mentally) trastornado

**unbearable** [ʌn'beərəbl] adj insoportable

**unbeatable** [ʌn'biːtəbl] adj (team) invencible; (price) inmejorable; (quality) insuperable

**unbelievable** [ʌnbɪ'liːvəbl] adj increíble

**unbend** [ʌn'bend] (irreg) vi (relax) relajarse ♦ vt (wire) enderezar

**unbiased** [ʌn'baɪəst] adj imparcial

**unborn** [ʌn'bɔːn] adj que va a nacer

**unbroken** [ʌn'brəʊkən] adj (seal) intacto; (series) continuo; (record) no batido; (spirit) indómito

**unbutton** [ʌn'bʌtn] vt desabrochar

**uncalled-for** [ʌn'kɔːldfɔː*] adj gratuito, inmerecido

**uncanny** [ʌn'kænɪ] adj extraño

**unceremonious** ['ʌnserɪ'məʊnɪəs] adj (abrupt, rude) brusco, hosco

**uncertain** [ʌn'sɜːtn] adj incierto; (indecisive) indeciso

**unchanged** [ʌn'tʃeɪndʒd] adj igual, sin cambios

**unchecked** [ʌn'tʃekt] adv sin estorbo, sin restricción

**uncivilized** [ʌn'sɪvɪlaɪzd] adj inculto; (fig: behaviour etc) bárbaro; (hour) inoportuno

**uncle** ['ʌŋkl] n tío

**uncomfortable** [ʌn'kʌmfətəbl] adj incómodo; (uneasy) inquieto

**uncommon** [ʌn'kɒmən] adj poco común, raro

**uncompromising** [ʌn'kɒmprəmaɪzɪŋ] adj intransigente

**unconcerned** [ʌnkən'sɜːnd] adj indiferente, despreocupado

**unconditional** [ʌnkən'dɪʃənl] adj incondicional

**unconscious** [ʌn'kɒnʃəs] adj sin sentido; (unaware): to be ~ of no darse cuenta de ♦ n: the ~ el inconsciente

**uncontrollable** [ʌnkən'trəʊləbl] adj

(*child etc*) incontrolable; (*temper*) indomable; (*laughter*) incontenible

**unconventional** [ʌnkən'venʃənl] *adj* poco convencional

**uncouth** [ʌn'kuːθ] *adj* grosero, inculto

**uncover** [ʌn'kʌvə*] *vt* descubrir; (*take lid off*) destapar

**undecided** [ʌndɪ'saɪdɪd] *adj* (*character*) indeciso; (*question*) no resuelto

**under** ['ʌndə*] *prep* debajo de; (*less than*) menos de; (*according to*) según, de acuerdo con; (*sb's leadership*) bajo ♦ *adv* debajo, abajo; ~ **there** allí abajo; ~ **repair** en reparación

**under...** ['ʌndə*] *prefix* sub; ~**age** *adj* menor de edad; (*drinking etc*) de los menores de edad; ~**carriage** (*BRIT*) *n* (*AVIAT*) tren *m* de aterrizaje; ~**charge** *vt* cobrar menos de la cuenta; ~**clothes** *npl* ropa interior (*SP*) *or* íntima (*AM*); ~**coat** *n* (*paint*) primera mano; ~**cover** *adj* clandestino; ~**current** *n* (*fig*) corriente *f* oculta; ~**cut** *vt irreg* vender más barato que; ~**developed** *adj* subdesarrollado; ~**dog** *n* desvalido/a; ~**done** *adj* (*CULIN*) poco hecho; ~**estimate** *vt* subestimar; ~**exposed** *adj* (*PHOT*) subexpuesto; ~**fed** *adj* subalimentado; ~**foot** *adv* con los pies; ~**go** *vt irreg* sufrir; (*treatment*) recibir; ~**graduate** *n* estudiante *m/f*; ~**ground** *n* (*BRIT: railway*) metro; (*POL*) movimiento clandestino ♦ *adj* (*car park*) subterráneo ♦ *adv* (*work*) en la clandestinidad; ~**growth** *n* maleza; ~**hand(ed)** *adj* (*fig*) socarrón; ~**lie** *vt irreg* (*fig*) ser la razón fundamental de; ~**line** *vt* subrayar; ~**ling** ['ʌndəlɪŋ] (*pej*) *n* subalterno/a, inferior *m/f*; ~**mine** *vt* socavar, minar; ~**neath** [ʌndə'niːθ] *adv* debajo ♦ *prep* debajo de, bajo; ~**paid** *adj* mal pagado; ~**pants** *npl* calzoncillos *mpl*; ~**pass** (*BRIT*) *n* paso subterráneo; ~**privileged** *adj* desposeído; ~**rate** *vt* menospreciar, subestimar; ~**shirt** (*US*) *n* camiseta; ~**shorts**

(*US*) *npl* calzoncillos *mpl*; ~**side** *n* parte *f* inferior; ~**skirt** (*BRIT*) *n* enaguas *fpl*

**understand** [ʌndə'stænd] (*irreg*) *vt, vi* entender, comprender; (*assume*) tener entendido; ~**able** *adj* comprensible; ~**ing** *adj* comprensivo ♦ *n* comprensión *f*, entendimiento; (*agreement*) acuerdo

**understatement** ['ʌndəsteɪtmənt] *n* modestia (excesiva); **that's an** ~! ¡eso es decir poco!

**understood** [ʌndə'stud] *pt, pp de* **understand** ♦ *adj* (*agreed*) acordado; (*implied*): **it is** ~ **that** se sobreentiende que

**understudy** ['ʌndəstʌdɪ] *n* suplente *m/f*

**undertake** [ʌndə'teɪk] (*irreg*) *vt* emprender; **to** ~ **to do sth** comprometerse a hacer algo

**undertaker** ['ʌndəteɪkə*] *n* director(a) *m/f* de pompas fúnebres

**undertaking** ['ʌndəteɪkɪŋ] *n* empresa; (*promise*) promesa

**undertone** ['ʌndətəun] *n*: **in an** ~ en voz baja

**underwater** [ʌndə'wɔːtə*] *adv* bajo el agua ♦ *adj* submarino

**underwear** ['ʌndəweə*] *n* ropa interior (*SP*) *or* íntima (*AM*)

**underworld** ['ʌndəwəːld] *n* (*of crime*) hampa, inframundo

**underwriter** ['ʌndəraɪtə*] *n* (*INSURANCE*) asegurador(a) *m/f*

**undesirable** [ʌndɪ'zaɪrəbl] *adj* (*person*) indeseable; (*thing*) poco aconsejable

**undies** ['ʌndɪz] (*inf*) *npl* ropa interior (*SP*) *or* íntima (*AM*)

**undo** [ʌn'duː] (*irreg*) *vt* (*laces*) desatar; (*button etc*) desabrochar; (*spoil*) deshacer; ~**ing** *n* ruina, perdición *f*

**undoubted** [ʌn'dautɪd] *adj* indudable

**undress** [ʌn'dres] *vi* desnudarse

**undulating** ['ʌndjuleɪtɪŋ] *adj* ondulante

**unduly** [ʌn'djuːlɪ] *adv* excesivamente, demasiado

**unearth** [ʌn'ɔːθ] vt desenterrar

**unearthly** [ʌn'əːθlɪ] adj (hour) inverosímil

**uneasy** [ʌn'iːzɪ] adj intranquilo, preocupado; (feeling) desagradable; (peace) inseguro

**uneducated** [ʌn'edjukeɪtɪd] adj ignorante, inculto

**unemployed** [ʌnɪm'plɔɪd] adj parado, sin trabajo ♦ npl: the ~ los parados

**unemployment** [ʌnɪm'plɔɪmənt] n paro, desempleo

**unending** [ʌn'endɪŋ] adj interminable

**unerring** [ʌn'əːrɪŋ] adj infalible

**uneven** [ʌn'iːvn] adj desigual; (road etc) lleno de baches

**unexpected** [ʌnɪk'spɛktɪd] adj inesperado; ~ly adv inesperadamente

**unfailing** [ʌn'feɪlɪŋ] adj (support) indefectible; (energy) inagotable

**unfair** [ʌn'fɛə*] adj: ~ (to sb) injusto (con uno)

**unfaithful** [ʌn'feɪθful] adj infiel

**unfamiliar** [ʌnfə'mɪlɪə*] adj extraño, desconocido; to be ~ with desconocer

**unfashionable** [ʌn'fæʃnəbl] adj pasado or fuera de moda

**unfasten** [ʌn'fɑːsn] vt (knot) desatar; (dress) desabrochar; (open) abrir

**unfavourable** [ʌn'feɪvərəbl] (US unfavorable) adj desfavorable

**unfeeling** [ʌn'fiːlɪŋ] adj insensible

**unfinished** [ʌn'fɪnɪʃt] adj inacabado, sin terminar

**unfit** [ʌn'fɪt] adj bajo de forma; (incompetent): ~ (for) incapaz (de); ~ for work no apto para trabajar

**unfold** [ʌn'fəuld] vt desdoblar ♦ vi abrirse

**unforeseen** ['ʌnfɔː'siːn] adj imprevisto

**unforgettable** [ʌnfə'gɛtəbl] adj inolvidable

**unfortunate** [ʌn'fɔːtʃnət] adj desgraciado; (event, remark) inoportu-

no; ~ly adv desgraciadamente

**unfounded** [ʌn'faundɪd] adj infundado

**unfriendly** [ʌn'frendlɪ] adj antipático; (behaviour, remark) hostil, poco amigable

**ungainly** [ʌn'geɪnlɪ] adj desgarbado

**ungodly** [ʌn'gɔdlɪ] adj: at an ~ hour a una hora inverosímil

**ungrateful** [ʌn'greɪtful] adj ingrato

**unhappiness** [ʌn'hæpɪnɪs] n tristeza, desdicha

**unhappy** [ʌn'hæpɪ] adj (sad) triste; (unfortunate) desgraciado; (childhood) infeliz; ~ about/with (arrangements etc) poco contento con, descontento de

**unharmed** [ʌn'hɑːmd] adj ileso

**unhealthy** [ʌn'hɛlθɪ] adj (place) malsano; (person) enfermizo; (fig: interest) morboso

**unheard-of** [ʌn'həːdɔv] adj inaudito, sin precedente

**unhurt** [ʌn'həːt] adj ileso

**unidentified** [ʌnaɪ'dentɪfaɪd] adj no identificado, sin identificar; see also UFO

**uniform** ['juːnɪfɔːm] n uniforme m ♦ adj uniforme

**unify** ['juːnɪfaɪ] vt unificar, unir

**uninhabited** [ʌnɪn'hæbɪtɪd] adj desierto

**unintentional** [ʌnɪn'tenʃənəl] adj involuntario

**union** ['juːnjən] n unión f; (also: trade ~) sindicato ♦ cpd sindical; U~ Jack n bandera del Reino Unido

**unique** [juː'niːk] adj único

**unison** ['juːnɪsn] n: in ~ (speak, reply, sing) al unísono

**unit** ['juːnɪt] n unidad f; (section: of furniture etc) elemento; (team) grupo; kitchen ~ módulo de cocina

**unite** [juː'naɪt] vt unir ♦ vi unirse; ~d adj unido; (effort) conjunto; U~d Kingdom n Reino Unido; U~d Nations (Organization) n Naciones fpl Unidas; U~d States (of America) n Estados mpl Unidos

**unit trust** (BRIT) n bono fiduciario

**unity** [ˈjuːnɪtɪ] n unidad f
**universe** [ˈjuːnɪvəːs] n universo
**university** [juːnɪˈvəːsɪtɪ] n universidad f
**unjust** [ʌnˈdʒʌst] adj injusto
**unkempt** [ʌnˈkɛmpt] adj (appearance) descuidado; (hair) despeinado
**unkind** [ʌnˈkaɪnd] adj poco amable; (behaviour, comment) cruel
**unknown** [ʌnˈnəun] adj desconocido
**unlawful** [ʌnˈlɔːful] adj ilegal, ilícito
**unleaded** [ʌnˈlɛdɪd] adj (petrol, fuel) sin plombo
**unleash** [ʌnˈliːʃ] vt desatar
**unless** [ʌnˈlɛs] conj a menos que; ~ he comes a menos que venga; ~ otherwise stated salvo indicación contraria
**unlike** [ʌnˈlaɪk] adj (not alike) distinto de or a; (not like) poco propio de ♦ prep a diferencia de
**unlikely** [ʌnˈlaɪklɪ] adj improbable; (unexpected) inverosímil
**unlimited** [ʌnˈlɪmɪtɪd] adj ilimitado
**unlisted** [ʌnˈlɪstɪd] (US) adj (TEL) que no consta en la guía
**unload** [ʌnˈləud] vt descargar
**unlock** [ʌnˈlɔk] vt abrir (con llave)
**unlucky** [ʌnˈlʌkɪ] adj desgraciado; (object, number) que da mala suerte; to be ~ tener mala suerte
**unmarried** [ʌnˈmærɪd] adj soltero
**unmistakable** [ʌnmɪsˈteɪkəbl] adj inconfundible
**unnatural** [ʌnˈnætʃrəl] adj (gen) antinatural; (manner) afectado; (habit) perverso
**unnecessary** [ʌnˈnɛsəsərɪ] adj innecesario, inútil
**unnoticed** [ʌnˈnəutɪst] adj: to go or pass ~ pasar desapercibido
**UNO** [ˈjuːnəu] n abbr (= United Nations Organization) ONU f
**unobtainable** [ʌnəbˈteɪnəbl] adj inconseguible; (TEL) inexistente
**unobtrusive** [ʌnəbˈtruːsɪv] adj discreto
**unofficial** [ʌnəˈfɪʃl] adj no oficial; (news) sin confirmar
**unorthodox** [ʌnˈɔːθədɔks] adj poco

ortodoxo; (REL) heterodoxo
**unpack** [ʌnˈpæk] vi deshacer las maletas ♦ vt deshacer
**unpalatable** [ʌnˈpælətəbl] adj incomible; (truth) desagradable
**unparalleled** [ʌnˈpærəleld] adj (unequalled) incomparable
**unpleasant** [ʌnˈplɛznt] adj (disagreeable) desagradable; (person, manner) antipático
**unplug** [ʌnˈplʌg] vt desenchufar, desconectar
**unpopular** [ʌnˈpɔpjulə*] adj impopular, poco popular
**unprecedented** [ʌnˈprɛsɪdəntɪd] adj sin precedentes
**unpredictable** [ʌnprɪˈdɪktəbl] adj imprevisible
**unprofessional** [ʌnprəˈfɛʃənl] adj (attitude, conduct) poco ético
**unqualified** [ʌnˈkwɔlɪfaɪd] adj sin título, no cualificado; (success) total
**unquestionably** [ʌnˈkwɛstʃənəblɪ] adv indiscutiblemente
**unravel** [ʌnˈrævl] vt desenmarañar, (mystery) desentrañar
**unreal** [ʌnˈrɪəl] adj irreal; (extraordinary) increíble
**unrealistic** [ʌnrɪəˈlɪstɪk] adj poco realista
**unreasonable** [ʌnˈriːznəbl] adj irrazonable; (demand) excesivo
**unrelated** [ʌnrɪˈleɪtɪd] adj sin relación; (family) no emparentado
**unrelenting** [ʌnrɪˈlɛntɪŋ] adj inexorable
**unreliable** [ʌnrɪˈlaɪəbl] adj (person) informal; (machine) poco fiable
**unremitting** [ʌnrɪˈmɪtɪŋ] adj constante
**unreservedly** [ʌnrɪˈzəːvɪdlɪ] adv sin reserva
**unrest** [ʌnˈrɛst] n inquietud f, malestar m; (POL) disturbios mpl
**unroll** [ʌnˈrəul] vt desenrollar
**unruly** [ʌnˈruːlɪ] adj indisciplinado
**unsafe** [ʌnˈseɪf] adj peligroso
**unsaid** [ʌnˈsɛd] adj: to leave sth ~ dejar algo sin decir
**unsatisfactory** [ˈʌnsætɪsˈfæktərɪ] adj

poco satisfactorio

**unsavoury** [ʌnˈseɪvərɪ] (US **unsavory**) adj (fig) repugnante

**unscathed** [ʌnˈskeɪðd] adj ileso

**unscrew** [ʌnˈskruː] vt destornillar

**unscrupulous** [ʌnˈskruːpjələs] adj sin escrúpulos

**unsettled** [ʌnˈsetld] adj inquieto, intranquilo; (weather) variable

**unshaven** [ʌnˈʃeɪvn] adj sin afeitar

**unsightly** [ʌnˈsaɪtlɪ] adj feo

**unskilled** [ʌnˈskɪld] adj (work) no especializado; (worker) no cualificado

**unspeakable** [ʌnˈspiːkəbl] adj indecible; (awful) incalificable

**unstable** [ʌnˈsteɪbl] adj inestable

**unsteady** [ʌnˈstedɪ] adj inestable

**unstuck** [ʌnˈstʌk] adj: **to come ~** despegarse; (fig) fracasar

**unsuccessful** [ʌnsəkˈsɛsful] adj (attempt) infructuoso; (writer, proposal) sin éxito; **to be ~** (in attempting sth) no tener éxito, fracasar; **~ly** adv en vano, sin éxito

**unsuitable** [ʌnˈsuːtəbl] adj inapropiado; (time) inoportuno

**unsure** [ʌnˈʃuə*] adj inseguro, poco seguro

**unsuspecting** [ˈʌnsəˈpɛktɪŋ] adj desprevenido

**unsympathetic** [ʌnsɪmpəˈθɛtɪk] adj poco comprensivo; (unlikeable) antipático

**untapped** [ʌnˈtæpt] adj (resources) sin explotar

**unthinkable** [ʌnˈθɪŋkəbl] adj inconcebible, impensable

**untidy** [ʌnˈtaɪdɪ] adj (room) desordenado; (appearance) desaliñado

**untie** [ʌnˈtaɪ] vt desatar

**until** [ənˈtɪl] prep hasta ♦ conj hasta que; **~ he comes** hasta que venga; **~ now** hasta ahora; **~ then** hasta entonces

**untimely** [ʌnˈtaɪmlɪ] adj inoportuno; (death) prematuro

**untold** [ʌnˈtəʊld] adj (story) nunca contado; (suffering) indecible; (wealth) incalculable

**untoward** [ʌntəˈwɔːd] adj adverso

**unused** [ʌnˈjuːzd] adj sin usar

**unusual** [ʌnˈjuːʒuəl] adj insólito, poco común; (exceptional) inusitado

**unveil** [ʌnˈveɪl] vt (statue) descubrir

**unwanted** [ʌnˈwɒntɪd] adj (clothing) viejo; (pregnancy) no deseado

**unwelcome** [ʌnˈwɛlkəm] adj inoportuno; (news) desagradable

**unwell** [ʌnˈwel] adj: **to be/feel ~** estar indispuesto/sentirse mal

**unwieldy** [ʌnˈwiːldɪ] adj difícil de manejar

**unwilling** [ʌnˈwɪlɪŋ] adj: **to be ~ to do sth** estar poco dispuesto a hacer algo; **~ly** adv de mala gana

**unwind** [ʌnˈwaɪnd] (irg: like wind) vt desenvolver ♦ vi (relax) relajarse

**unwise** [ʌnˈwaɪz] adj imprudente

**unwitting** [ʌnˈwɪtɪŋ] adj inconsciente

**unworkable** [ʌnˈwɔːkəbl] adj (plan) impracticable

**unworthy** [ʌnˈwɔːðɪ] adj indigno

**unwrap** [ʌnˈræp] vt desenvolver

**unwritten** [ʌnˈrɪtn] adj (agreement) tácito; (rules, law) no escrito

---

KEYWORD

**up** [ʌp] prep: **to go/be ~ sth** subir/estar subido en algo; **he went ~ the stairs/the hill** subió las escaleras/la colina; **we walked/climbed ~ the hill** subimos la colina; **they live further ~ the street** viven más arriba en la calle; **go ~ that road and turn left** sigue por esa calle y gira a la izquierda

♦ adv **1** (upwards, higher) más arriba; **~ in the mountains** en lo alto (de la montaña); **put it a bit higher ~** ponlo un poco más arriba o alto; **~ there** ahí o allí arriba; **~ above** en lo alto, por encima, arriba

**2**: **to be ~** (out of bed) estar levantado; (prices, level) haber subido

**3**: **~ to** (as far as) hasta; **~ to now** hasta ahora o la fecha

**4**: **to be ~ to** (depending on): **it's ~ to you** depende de ti; **he's not ~ to**

it (job, task etc) no es capaz de hacerlo; **his work is not ~ to the required standard** su trabajo no da la talla; (inf: be doing): **what is he ~ to?** ¿que estará tramando?

♦ n: **~s and downs** altibajos mpl

**upbringing** ['ʌpbrɪŋɪŋ] n educación f
**update** [ʌp'deɪt] vt poner al día
**upgrade** [ʌp'greɪd] vt (house) modernizar; (employee) ascender
**upheaval** [ʌp'hiːvl] n trastornos mpl; (POL) agitación f
**uphill** [ʌp'hɪl] adj cuesta arriba; (fig: task) penoso, difícil ♦ adv: **to go ~** ir cuesta arriba
**uphold** [ʌp'həʊld] (irreg) vt defender
**upholstery** [ʌp'həʊlstərɪ] n tapicería f
**upkeep** ['ʌpkiːp] n mantenimiento m
**upon** [ə'pɒn] prep sobre
**upper** ['ʌpə*] adj superior, de arriba
♦ n (of shoe: also: ~s) empeine m; **~-class** adj de clase alta; **~ hand** n: **to have the ~ hand** tener la sartén por el mango; **~most** adj el más alto; **what was ~most in my mind** lo que me preocupaba más
**upright** ['ʌpraɪt] adj derecho; (vertical) vertical; (fig) honrado
**uprising** ['ʌpraɪzɪŋ] n sublevación f
**uproar** ['ʌprɔː*] n escándalo
**uproot** [ʌp'ruːt] vt (also fig) desarraigar
**upset** [n 'ʌpset, vb, adj ʌp'set] n (to plan etc) revés m, contratiempo; (MED) trastorno m (irreg) vt (glass etc) volcar; (plan) alterar; (person) molestar, disgustar ♦ adj molesto, disgustado; (stomach) revuelto
**upshot** ['ʌpʃɒt] n resultado
**upside-down** adv al revés; **to turn a place ~** (fig) revolverlo todo
**upstairs** [ʌp'steəz] adv arriba ♦ adj (room) de arriba ♦ n el piso superior
**upstart** ['ʌpstɑːt] n advenedizo/a
**upstream** [ʌp'striːm] adv río arriba
**uptake** ['ʌpteɪk] n: **to be quick/slow on the ~** ser muy listo/torpe
**uptight** [ʌp'taɪt] adj tenso, nervioso
**up-to-date** adj al día

**upturn** ['ʌptəːn] n (in luck) mejora (COMM: in market) resurgimiento económico
**upward** ['ʌpwəd] adj ascendente **~(s)** adv hacia arriba; (more than): **~(s) of** más de
**urban** ['əːbən] adj urbano
**urchin** ['əːtʃɪn] n pilluelo, golfillo
**urge** [əːdʒ] n (desire) deseo ♦ vt: **to ~ sb to do sth** animar a uno a hacer algo
**urgent** ['əːdʒənt] adj urgente; (voice) perentorio
**urinate** ['jʊərɪneɪt] vi orinar
**urine** ['jʊərɪn] n orina, orines mpl
**urn** [əːn] n urna; (also: tea ~) cacharro metálico grande para hacer té
**Uruguay** ['jʊərəgwaɪ] n (el) Uruguay; **~an** adj, n uruguayo/a m/f
**US** n abbr (= United States) EE. UU.
**us** [ʌs] pron nos; (after prep) nosotros/as; see also **me**
**USA** n abbr (= United States (of America)) EE. UU
**usage** ['juːzɪdʒ] n (LING) uso
**use** [n juːs, vb juːz] n uso, empleo; (usefulness) utilidad f ♦ vt usar, emplear; **she ~d to do it** (ella) solía or acostumbraba hacerlo; **in ~** en uso; **out of ~** en desuso; **to be of ~** servir; **it's no ~** (pointless) es inútil; (not useful) no sirve; **to be ~d to** estar acostumbrado a, acostumbrar; **~ up** vt (food) consumir; (money) gastar; **~d** adj (car) usado; **~ful** adj útil; **~fulness** n utilidad f; **~less** adj (unusable) inservible; (pointless) inútil; (person) inepto; **~r** n usuario/a; **~r-friendly** adj (computer) amistoso
**usher** ['ʌʃə*] n (at wedding) ujier m; **~ette** [-'ret] n (in cinema) acomodadora
**USSR** n: **the ~** la URSS
**usual** ['juːʒuəl] adj normal, corriente; **as ~** como de costumbre; **~ly** adv normalmente
**utensil** [juː'tensl] n utensilio; **kitchen ~s** batería de cocina
**uterus** ['juːtərəs] n útero
**utility** [juː'tɪlɪtɪ] n utilidad f; (public

~) (empresa de) servicio público; ~
**room** n ofis m

**utilize** ['ju:tɪlaɪz] vt utilizar

**utmost** ['ʌtməust] adj mayor ♦ n: to
do one's ~ hacer todo lo posible

**utter** ['ʌtə*] adj total, completo ♦ vt
pronunciar, proferir; **~ance** n palabras fpl, declaración f; **~ly** adv completamente, totalmente

**U-turn** ['ju:'tə:n] n viraje m en redondo

# V

**v.** abbr = **verse**; **versus**; (= volt) v;
(= vide) véase

**vacancy** ['veɪkənsɪ] n (BRIT: job)
vacante f; (room) habitación f libre

**vacant** ['veɪkənt] adj desocupado, libre; (expression) distraído; ~ **lot**
(US) n solar m

**vacate** [və'keɪt] vt (house, room)
desocupar; (job) dejar (vacante)

**vacation** [və'keɪʃən] n vacaciones fpl

**vaccinate** ['væksɪneɪt] vt vacunar

**vaccine** ['væksi:n] n vacuna

**vacuum** ['vækjum] n vacío; ~
**cleaner** n aspiradora; **~-packed** adj
empaquetado al vacío

**vagina** [və'dʒaɪnə] n vagina

**vagrant** ['veɪgrnt] n vagabundo/a

**vague** [veɪg] adj vago; (blurred:
memory) borroso; (ambiguous) impreciso; (person: absent-minded) distraído; (: evasive): to be ~ no decir
las cosas claramente; **~ly** adv vagamente; distraídamente; con evasivas

**vain** [veɪn] adj (conceited) presumido; (useless) vano, inútil; **in** ~ en
vano

**valentine** ['væləntaɪn] n (also: ~
card) tarjeta del Día de los Enamo-
rados

**valet** ['væleɪ] n ayuda m de cámara

**valid** ['vælɪd] adj válido; (ticket) valedero; (law) vigente

**valley** ['vælɪ] n valle m

**valuable** ['væljuəbl] adj (jewel) de
valor; (time) valioso; **~s** npl objetos

mpl de valor

**valuation** [vælju'eɪʃən] n tasación f,
valuación f; (judgement of quality)
valoración f

**value** ['vælju:] n valor m; (importance) importancia ♦ vt (fix price of)
tasar, valorar; (esteem) apreciar;
**~ added tax** (BRIT) n impuesto sobre
el valor añadido; **~d** adj (apprecia-
ted) apreciado

**valve** [vælv] n válvula

**van** [væn] n (AUT) furgoneta (SP),
camioneta (AM)

**vandal** ['vændl] n vándalo/a; **~ism**
n vandalismo; **~ize** vt dañar, destruir

**vanilla** [və'nɪlə] n vainilla

**vanish** ['vænɪʃ] vi desaparecer

**vanity** ['vænɪtɪ] n vanidad f

**vantage point** ['vɑ:ntɪdʒ-] n (for
viewing) punto panorámico

**vapour** ['veɪpə*] (US **vapor**) n vapor
m; (on breath, window) vaho

**variable** ['veərɪəbl] adj variable

**variance** ['veərɪəns] n: to be at ~
(with) estar en desacuerdo (con)

**variation** [veərɪ'eɪʃən] n variación f

**varicose** ['værɪkəus] adj: ~ **veins**
varices fpl

**varied** ['veərɪd] adj variado

**variety** [və'raɪətɪ] n (diversity) diversidad f; (type) variedad f; ~ **show** n
espectáculo de variedades

**various** ['veərɪəs] adj (several: people) varios/as; (reasons) diversos/as

**varnish** ['vɑ:nɪʃ] n barniz m; (nail
~) esmalte m ♦ vt barnizar; (nails)
pintar (con esmalte)

**vary** ['veərɪ] vt variar; (change)
cambiar ♦ vi variar

**vase** [vɑ:z] n florero

**Vaseline** ['væsɪli:n] ® n Vaselina ®

**vast** [vɑ:st] adj enorme

**VAT** [væt] (BRIT) n abbr (= Value
Added Tax) IVA m

**vat** [væt] n tina, tinaja

**Vatican** ['vætɪkən] n: the ~ el Vaticano

**vault** [vɔ:lt] n (of roof) bóveda;
(tomb) panteón m; (in bank) cámara

acorazada ♦ vt (also: ~ over) saltar (por encima de)

**vaunted** ['vɔːntɪd] adj: **much ~** cacareado, alardeado

**VCR** n abbr = video cassette recorder

**VD** n abbr = venereal disease

**VDU** n abbr (= visual display unit) UPV f

**veal** [viːl] n ternera

**veer** [vɪə*] vi (vehicle) virar; (wind) girar

**vegetable** ['vedʒtəbl] n (BOT) vegetal m; (edible plant) legumbre f, hortaliza f ♦ adj vegetal; ~s npl (cooked) verduras fpl

**vegetarian** [vedʒɪ'tɛəriən] adj, n vegetariano/a m/f

**vehement** ['viːɪmənt] adj vehemente, apasionado

**vehicle** ['viːɪkl] n vehículo; (fig) medio

**veil** [veɪl] n velo ♦ vt velar; ~ed adj (fig) velado

**vein** [veɪn] n vena; (of ore etc) veta

**velocity** [vɪ'lɒsɪtɪ] n velocidad f

**velvet** ['velvɪt] n terciopelo

**vending machine** ['vendɪŋ-] n distribuidor m automático

**vendor** ['vendə*] n vendedor(a) m/f

**veneer** [və'nɪə*] n chapa, enchapado; (fig) barniz m

**venereal disease** [vɪ'nɪərɪəl-] n enfermedad f venérea

**Venetian blind** [vɪ'niːʃən-] n persiana

**Venezuela** [venɪ'zweɪlə] n Venezuela; ~n adj, n venezolano/a m/f

**vengeance** ['vendʒəns] n venganza; **with a ~** (fig) con creces

**venison** ['venɪsn] n carne f de venado

**venom** ['venəm] n veneno; (bitterness) odio; ~ous adj venenoso; lleno de odio

**vent** [vent] n (in jacket) respiradero; (in wall) rejilla (de ventilación) ♦ vt (fig: feelings) desahogar

**ventilator** ['ventɪleɪtə*] n ventilador m

**venture** ['ventʃə*] n empresa ♦ vt (opinion) ofrecer ♦ vi arriesgarse, lanzarse; **business ~** empresa comercial

**venue** ['venjuː] n lugar m

**veranda(h)** [və'rændə] n terraza

**verb** [vɜːb] n verbo; **~al** adj verbal

**verbatim** [vɜː'beɪtɪm] adj, adv palabra por palabra

**verbose** [vɜː'bəus] adj prolijo

**verdict** ['vɜːdɪkt] n veredicto, fallo; (fig) opinión f, juicio

**verge** [vɜːdʒ] (BRIT) n borde m; **"soft ~s"** (AUT) "arcén m no asfaltado"; **to be on the ~ of doing sth** estar a punto de hacer algo; **~ on** vt fus rayar en

**verify** ['verɪfaɪ] vt comprobar, verificar

**veritable** ['verɪtəbl] adj verdadero, auténtico

**vermin** ['vɜːmɪn] npl (animals) alimañas fpl; (insects, children) parásitos mpl

**vermouth** ['vɜːməθ] n vermut m

**vernacular** [və'nækjulə*] n lengua vernácula

**versatile** ['vɜːsətaɪl] adj (person) polifacético; (machine, tool etc) versátil.

**verse** [vɜːs] n poesía; (stanza) estrofa; (in bible) versículo

**versed** [vɜːst] adj: **(well-)~ in** versado en

**version** ['vɜːʃən] n versión f

**versus** ['vɜːsəs] prep contra

**vertebra** ['vɜːtɪbrə] (pl ~e) n vértebra

**vertical** ['vɜːtɪkl] adj vertical

**verve** [vɜːv] n brío

**very** ['verɪ] adv muy ♦ adj: **the ~ book which** el mismo libro que; **the ~ last** el último de todos; **at the ~ least** al menos; **~ much** muchísimo

**vessel** ['vesl] n (ship) barco; (container) vasija; see **blood**

**vest** [vest] n (BRIT) camiseta; (US: waistcoat) chaleco; **~ed interests** npl (COMM) intereses mpl creados

**vestige** ['vestɪdʒ] n vestigio, rastro

**vet** [vet] vt (candidate) investigar ♦ n abbr (BRIT) = veterinary surgeon

**veteran** ['vetərn] n veterano

**veterinary surgeon** ['vetrinəri] (US **veterinarian**) n veterinario/a m/f

**veto** ['viːtəu] (pl ~es) n veto ♦ vt prohibir, poner el veto a

**vex** [veks] vt fastidiar; **~ed** adj (question) controvertido

**VHF** abbr (= very high frequency) muy alta frecuencia

**via** [vaɪə] prep por, por medio de

**vibrant** ['vaɪbrənt] adj (lively) animado; (bright) vivo; (voice) vibrante

**vibrate** [vaɪ'breɪt] vi vibrar

**vicar** ['vɪkə*] n párroco (de la Iglesia Anglicana); **~age** n parroquia

**vice** [vaɪs] n (evil) vicio; (TECH) torno de banco

**vice-** [vaɪs] prefix vice-; **~chairman** n vicepresidente m

**vice squad** n brigada antivicio

**vice versa** ['vaɪsɪ'vɜːsə] adv viceversa

**vicinity** [vɪ'sɪnɪtɪ] n: **in the ~ (of)** cercano a

**vicious** ['vɪʃəs] adj (attack) violento; (words) cruel; (horse, dog) resabido; **~ circle** n círculo vicioso

**victim** ['vɪktɪm] n víctima; **~ize** vt tomar represalias contra

**victor** ['vɪktə*] n vencedor(a) m/f

**victorious** [vɪk'tɔːrɪəs] adj (team) vencedor(a)

**victory** ['vɪktərɪ] n victoria

**video** ['vɪdɪəu] cpd video ♦ n (~ film) videofilm m; (also: ~ cassette) videocassette f; (also: ~ cassette recorder) magnetoscopio; **~ game** n videojuego; **~ tape** n cinta de vídeo

**vie** [vaɪ] vi: **to ~ (with sb for sth)** competir (con uno por algo)

**Vienna** [vɪ'enə] n Viena

**Vietnam** [vjet'næm] n Vietnam m; **~ese** [-nə'miːz] n inv, adj vietnamita m/f

**view** [vjuː] n vista; (outlook) perspectiva; (opinion) opinión f, criterio

♦ vt (look at) mirar; (fig) considerar; **on ~** (in museum etc) expuesto; **in full ~ (of)** en plena vista (de); **in ~ of the weather/the fact that** en vista del tiempo/del hecho de que; **in my ~** en mi opinión; **~er** n espectador(a) m/f; (TV) telespectador(a) m/f; **~finder** n visor m de imagen; **~point** n (attitude) punto de vista; (place) mirador m

**vigour** ['vɪgə*] (US **vigor**) n energía, vigor m

**vile** [vaɪl] adj vil, infame; (smell) asqueroso; (temper) endemoniado

**villa** ['vɪlə] n (country house) casa de campo; (suburban house) chalet m

**village** ['vɪlɪdʒ] n aldea; **~r** n aldeano/a

**villain** ['vɪlən] n (scoundrel) malvado/a; (in novel) malo; (BRIT: criminal) maleante m/f

**vindicate** ['vɪndɪkeɪt] vt vindicar, justificar

**vindictive** [vɪn'dɪktɪv] adj vengativo

**vine** [vaɪn] n vid f

**vinegar** ['vɪnɪgə*] n vinagre m

**vineyard** ['vɪnjɑːd] n viña, viñedo

**vintage** ['vɪntɪdʒ] n (year) vendimia, cosecha ♦ cpd de época; **~ wine** n vino añejo

**vinyl** ['vaɪnl] n vinilo

**viola** [vɪ'əulə] n (MUS) viola

**violate** ['vaɪəleɪt] vt violar

**violence** ['vaɪələns] n violencia

**violent** ['vaɪələnt] adj violento; (intense) intenso

**violet** ['vaɪələt] adj violado, violeta ♦ n (plant) violeta

**violin** [vaɪə'lɪn] n violín m; **~ist** n violinista m/f

**VIP** n abbr (= very important person) VIP m

**virgin** ['vɜːdʒɪn] n virgen f

**Virgo** ['vɜːgəu] n Virgo

**virtually** ['vɜːtjuəlɪ] adv prácticamente

**virtual reality** ['vɜːtjuəl-] n (COMPUT) mundo virtual

**virtue** ['vɜːtjuː] n virtud f; (advantage) ventaja; **by ~ of** en virtud de

**virtuous** ['vəːtjuəs] adj virtuoso

**virus** ['vaiərəs] n (also: COMPUT) virus m

**visa** ['viːzə] n visado (SP), visa (AM)

**vis-à-vis** [viːzəˈviː] prep con respecto a

**visible** ['vizəbl] adj visible

**vision** ['viʒən] n (sight) vista; (foresight, in dream) visión f

**visit** ['vizit] n visita ♦ vt (person: US: also: ~ with) visitar, hacer una visita a; (place) ir a, (ir a) conocer; **~ing hours** npl (in hospital etc) horas fpl de visita; **~or** n (in museum) visitante m/f; (invited to house) visita; (tourist) turista m/f

**visor** ['vaizə*] n visera

**vista** ['vistə] n vista, panorama m

**visual** ['vizjuəl] adj visual; ~ **aid** n medio visual; ~ **display unit** n unidad f de presentación visual; **~ize** vt imaginarse

**vital** ['vaitl] adj (essential) esencial, imprescindible; (dynamic) dinámico; (organ) vital; **~ly** adv: **~ly important** de primera importancia; ~ **statistics** npl (fig) medidas fpl vitales

**vitamin** ['vitəmin] n vitamina

**vivacious** [vi'veiʃəs] adj vivaz, alegre

**vivid** ['vivid] adj (account) gráfico; (light) intenso; (imagination, memory) vivo; **~ly** adv gráficamente; (remember) como si fuera hoy

**V-neck** ['viːnek] n cuello de pico

**vocabulary** [vəu'kæbjuləri] n vocabulario

**vocal** ['vəukl] adj vocal; (articulate) elocuente; ~ **chords** npl cuerdas fpl vocales

**vocation** [vəu'keiʃən] n vocación f; **~al** adj profesional

**vodka** ['vodkə] n vodka m

**vogue** [vəug] n: **in ~** en boga, de moda

**voice** [vois] n voz f ♦ vt expresar

**void** [void] n vacío; (hole) hueco ♦ adj (invalid) nulo, inválido; (empty): ~ **of** carente or desprovisto de

**volatile** ['volətail] adj (situation)

inestable; (person) voluble; (liquid) volátil

**volcano** [vol'keinəu] (pl **~es**) n volcán m

**volition** [və'liʃən] n: **of one's own** ~ de su propia voluntad

**volley** ['voli] n (of gunfire) descarga (of stones etc) lluvia; (fig) torrente m; (TENNIS etc) volea; **~ball** n vol(e)ibol m

**volt** [vəult] n voltio; **~age** n voltaje m

**volume** ['volju:m] n (gen) volumen m; (book) tomo

**voluminous** [və'lu:minəs] adj (clothes) amplio; (notes) prolijo

**voluntary** ['voləntəri] adj voluntario

**volunteer** [volən'tiə*] n voluntario/a ♦ vt (information) ofrecer ♦ vi ofrecerse (de voluntario); **to ~ to do** ofrecerse a hacer

**vomit** ['vomit] n vómito ♦ vt, vi vomitar

**vote** [vəut] n voto; (votes cast) votación f; (right to ~) derecho de votar; (franchise) sufragio ♦ vt (chairman) elegir; (propose): **to ~ that** proponer que ♦ vi votar, ir a votar; ~ **of thanks** voto de gracias; **~r** n votante m/f; **voting** n votación f

**vouch** [vautʃ]: **to ~ for** vt fus garantizar, responder de

**voucher** ['vautʃə*] n (for meal, petrol) vale m

**vow** [vau] n voto ♦ vt: **to ~ to do/ that** jurar hacer/que

**vowel** ['vauəl] n vocal f

**voyage** ['vɔiidʒ] n viaje m

**V-sign** (BRIT) n ≈ corte m de mangas

**vulgar** ['vʌlgə*] adj (rude) ordinario, grosero; (in bad taste) de mal gusto; **~ity** ['-'gæriti] n grosería; mal gusto

**vulnerable** ['vʌlnərəbl] adj vulnerable

**vulture** ['vʌltʃə*] n buitre m

# W

**wad** [wɔd] *n* bolita; (*of banknotes etc*) fajo

**waddle** ['wɔdl] *vi* anadear

**wade** [weid] *vi*: to ~ **through** (*water*) vadear; (*fig: book*) leer con dificultad; **wading pool** (*US*) *n* piscina para niños

**wafer** ['weifə*] *n* galleta, barquillo

**waffle** ['wɔfl] *n* (*CULIN*) gofre *m* ♦ *vi* dar el rollo

**waft** [wɔft] *vt* llevar por el aire ♦ *vi* flotar

**wag** [wæg] *vt* menear, agitar ♦ *vi* moverse, menearse

**wage** [weidʒ] *n* (*also:* ~s) sueldo, salario ♦ *vt*: to ~ **war** hacer la guerra; ~ **earner** *n* asalariado/a; ~ **packet** *n* sobre *m* de paga

**wager** ['weidʒə*] *n* apuesta

**waggle** ['wægl] *vt* menear, mover

**wag(g)on** ['wægən] *n* (*horse-drawn*) carro; (*BRIT: RAIL*) vagón *m*

**wail** [weil] *n* gemido ♦ *vi* gemir

**waist** [weist] *n* cintura, talle *m*; ~**coat** (*BRIT*) *n* chaleco; ~**line** *n* talle *m*

**wait** [weit] *n* (*interval*) pausa ♦ *vi* esperar; **to lie in** ~ acechar; **I can't** ~ **to** (*fig*) estoy deseando; **to** ~ **for** esperar (a); ~ **behind** *vi* quedarse; ~ **on** *vt fus* servir a; ~**er** *n* camarero; ~**ing** *n*: "**no ~ing**" (*BRIT: AUT*) "prohibido estacionarse"; ~**ing list** *n* lista de espera; ~**ing room** *n* sala de espera; ~**ress** *n* camarera

**waive** [weiv] *vt* suspender

**wake** [weik] (*pt* **woke** *or* **waked**, *pp* **woken** *or* **waked**) *vt* (*also:* ~ **up**) despertar ♦ *vi* (*also:* ~ **up**) despertarse ♦ *n* (*for dead person*) vela, velatorio; (*NAUT*) estela; **waken** *vt*, *vi* = **wake**

**Wales** [weilz] *n* País *m* de Gales; **the Prince of** ~ el príncipe de Gales

**walk** [wɔːk] *n* (*stroll*) paseo; (*hike*)

excursión *f* a pie, caminata; (*gait*) paso, andar *m*; (*in park etc*) paseo, alameda ♦ *vi* andar, caminar; (*for pleasure, exercise*) pasear ♦ *vt* (*distance*) recorrer a pie, andar; (*dog*) pasear; **10 minutes'** ~ **from here** a 10 minutos de aquí andando; **people from all** ~**s of life** gente de todas las esferas; ~ **out** *vi* (*audience*) salir; (*workers*) declararse en huelga; ~ **out on** (*inf*) *vt fus* abandonar; ~**er** *n* (*person*) paseante *m/f*, caminante *m/f*; ~**ie-talkie** *n* 'wɔːkiːˈtɔːki] *n* walkie-talkie *m*; ~**ing** *n* el andar; ~**ing shoes** *npl* zapatos *mpl* para andar; ~**ing stick** *n* bastón *m*; ~ **out** *n* huelga; ~**over** (*inf*) *n*: **it was a** ~**over** fue pan comido; ~**way** *n* paseo

**wall** [wɔːl] *n* pared *f*; (*exterior*) muro; (*city - etc*) muralla; ~**ed** *adj* amurallado; (*garden*) con tapia

**wallet** ['wɔlit] *n* cartera (*SP*), billetera (*AM*)

**wallflower** ['wɔːlflauə*] *n* alhelí *m*; **to be a** ~ (*fig*) comer pavo

**wallop** ['wɔləp] (*inf*) *vt* zurrar

**wallow** ['wɔləu] *vi* revolcarse

**wallpaper** ['wɔːlpeipə*] *n* papel *m* pintado ♦ *vt* empapelar

**walnut** ['wɔːlnʌt] *n* nuez *f*; (*tree*) nogal *m*

**walrus** ['wɔːlrəs] (*pl* ~ *or* ~**es**) *n* morsa

**waltz** [wɔːls] *n* vals *m* ♦ *vi* bailar el vals

**wan** [wɔn] *adj* pálido

**wand** [wɔnd] *n* (*also: magic* ~) varita (mágica)

**wander** ['wɔndə*] *vi* (*person*) vagar; deambular; (*thoughts*) divagar ♦ *vt* recorrer, vagar por

**wane** [wein] *vi* menguar

**wangle** ['wæŋgl] (*BRIT: inf*) *vt* agenciarse

**want** [wɔnt] *vt* querer, desear; (*need*) necesitar ♦ *n*: **for** ~ **of** por falta de; ~**s** *npl* (*needs*) necesidades *fpl*; **to** ~ **to do** querer hacer; **to** ~ **sb to do sth** querer que uno haga algo; **~ed** adj (criminal) buscado; "**~ed**" (in advertisements) "se busca"; **~ing** adj: to be found **~ing** no estar a la altura de las circunstancias

**wanton** ['wɒntn] adj (playful) juguetón/ona; (licentious) lascivo

**war** [wɔː*] n guerra f; **to make ~ (on)** (also fig) declarar la guerra (a)

**ward** [wɔːd] n (in hospital) sala; (POL) distrito electoral; (LAW: child: also: **~ of court**) pupilo/a; **~ off** vt (blow) desviar, parar; (attack) rechazar

**warden** ['wɔːdn] n (BRIT: of institution) director(a) m/f; (of park, game reserve) guardián/ana m/f; (BRIT: also: **traffic ~**) guardia m/f

**warder** ['wɔːdə*] (BRIT) n guardián/ana m/f, carcelero/a

**wardrobe** ['wɔːdrəub] n armario, guardarropa, ropero (esp LAm)

**warehouse** ['wɛəhaus] n almacén m, depósito

**wares** [wɛəz] npl mercancías fpl

**warfare** ['wɔːfɛə*] n guerra

**warhead** ['wɔːhed] n cabeza armada

**warily** ['wɛərɪlɪ] adv con cautela, cautelosamente

**warlike** ['wɔːlaɪk] adj guerrero; (appearance) belicoso

**warm** [wɔːm] adj caliente; (thanks) efusivo; (clothes etc) abrigado; (welcome, day) caluroso; **it's ~** hace calor; **I'm ~** tengo calor; **to ~ up** vi (room) calentarse; (person) entrar en calor; (athlete) hacer ejercicios de calentamiento ♦ vt calentar; **~-hearted** adj afectuoso; **~ly** adv afectuosamente; **~th** n calor m

**warn** [wɔːn] vt avisar, advertir; **~ing** n aviso, advertencia; **~ing light** n luz f de advertencia; **~ing triangle** n (AUT) triángulo señalizador

**warp** [wɔːp] vi (wood) combarse ♦ vt combar; (mind) pervertir

**warrant** ['wɒrənt] n autorización f; (LAW: to arrest) orden f de detención; (: to search) mandamiento de

registro

**warranty** ['wɒrəntɪ] n garantía

**warren** ['wɒrən] n (of rabbits) madriguera; (fig) laberinto

**warrior** ['wɒrɪə*] n guerrero/a

**Warsaw** ['wɔːsɔː] n Varsovia

**warship** ['wɔːʃɪp] n buque m o barco de guerra

**wart** [wɔːt] n verruga

**wartime** ['wɔːtaɪm] n: **in ~** en tiempos de guerra, en la guerra

**wary** ['wɛərɪ] adj cauteloso

**was** [wɒz] pt of **be**

**wash** [wɒʃ] vt lavar ♦ vi lavarse; (sea etc): **to ~ against/over sth** llegar hasta/cubrir algo ♦ n (clothes etc) lavado; (of ship) estela; **to have a ~** lavarse; **~ away** vt (stain) quitar lavando; (subj: river etc) llevarse; **~ off** vi quitarse (al lavar); **~ up** vi (BRIT) fregar los platos; (US) lavarse; **~able** adj lavable; **~basin** (US **~bowl**) n lavabo; **~ cloth** (US) n manopla; **~er** n (TECH) arandela; **~ing** n (dirty) ropa sucia; (clean) colada; **~ing machine** n lavadora; **~ing powder** (BRIT) n detergente m (en polvo)

**Washington** ['wɒʃɪŋtən] n Washington m

**wash: washing-up** n fregado, platos mpl (para fregar); **~ing-up liquid** n líquido lavavajillas; **~-out** (inf) n fracaso; **~room** (US) n servicios mpl

**wasn't** ['wɒznt] = **was not**

**wasp** [wɒsp] n avispa

**wastage** ['weɪstɪdʒ] n desgaste m; (loss) pérdida

**waste** [weɪst] n derroche m, despilfarro; (of time) pérdida; (food) sobras fpl; (rubbish) basura, desperdicios mpl ♦ adj (material) de desecho; (left over) sobrante; (land) baldío, descampado ♦ vt malgastar, derrochar; (time) perder; (opportunity) desperdiciar; **~s** npl (area of land) tierras fpl baldías; **~ away** vi consumirse; **~ disposal unit** (BRIT) n triturador m de basura; **~ful** adj derrochador(a); (*process*) antieconómico; **~ ground** (*BRIT*) *n* terreno baldío; **~paper basket** *n* papelera; **~ pipe** *n* tubo de desagüe

**watch** [wɒtʃ] *n* (*also*: **wrist ~**) reloj *m*; (*MIL*: *group of guards*) centinela *m*; (*act*) vigilancia *f*; (*NAUT*: *spell of duty*) guardia ♦ *vt* (*look at*) mirar, observar; (: *match, programme*) ver; (*spy on, guard*) vigilar; (*be careful of*) cuidarse de, tener cuidado de ♦ *vi* ver, mirar; (*keep guard*) montar guardia; **~ out** *vi* cuidarse, tener cuidado; **~dog** *n* perro guardián; (*fig*) persona u organismo encargado de asegurarse de que las empresas actúan dentro de la legalidad; **~ful** *adj* vigilante, sobre aviso; **~maker** *n* relojero/a; **~man** *n see* **night**; **~strap** *n* pulsera (de reloj)

**water** [ˈwɔːtə*] *n* agua ♦ *vt* (*plant*) regar ♦ *vi* (*eyes*) llorar; (*mouth*) hacerse la boca agua; **~ down** *vt* (*milk etc*) aguar; (*fig*: *story*) dulcificar, diluir; **~ closet** *n* wáter *m*; **~colour** *n* acuarela; **~cress** *n* berro; **~fall** *n* cascada, salto de agua; **~heater** *n* calentador de agua; **~ing can** *n* regadera; **~ lily** *n* nenúfar *m*; **~line** *n* (*NAUT*) línea de flotación; **~logged** *adj* (*ground*) inundado; **~ main** *n* cañería del agua; **~melon** *n* sandía; **~proof** *adj* impermeable; **~shed** *n* (*GEO*) cuenca; (*fig*) momento crítico; **~skiing** *n* esquí *m* acuático; **~tight** *adj* hermético; **~way** *n* vía fluvial o navegable; **~works** *n* central *f* depuradora; **~y** *adj* (*coffee etc*) aguado; (*eyes*) lloroso

**watt** [wɒt] *n* vatio

**wave** [weɪv] *n* (*of hand*) señal *f* con la mano; (*on water*) ola; (*RADIO, in hair*) onda; (*flag etc*) oleada ♦ *vi* agitar la mano; (*flag etc*) ondear ♦ *vt* (*handkerchief, gun*) agitar; **~length** *n* longitud *f* de onda

**waver** [ˈweɪvə*] *vi* (*voice, love etc*) flaquear; (*person*) vacilar

**wavy** [ˈweɪvɪ] *adj* ondulado

**wax** [wæks] *n* cera ♦ *vt* encerar ♦ *vi* (*moon*) crecer; **~ paper** (*US*) *n* papel *m* apergaminado; **~works** *n* museo de cera ♦ *npl* figuras *fpl* de cera

**way** [weɪ] *n* camino; (*distance*) trayecto, recorrido; (*direction*) dirección *f*, sentido; (*manner*) modo, manera; (*habit*) costumbre *f*; **which ~?** – **this ~** ¿por dónde?, ¿en qué dirección? – por aquí; **on the ~** (*en route*) en (el) camino; **to be on one's ~** estar en camino; **to be in the ~** bloquear el camino; (*fig*) estorbar; **to go out of one's ~ to do sth** desvivirse por hacer algo; **under ~** en marcha; **to lose one's ~** extraviarse; **in a ~** en cierto modo *o* sentido; **no ~!** (*inf*) ¡de eso nada!; **by the ~** ... a propósito ...; **"~ in"** (*BRIT*) "entrada"; **"~ out"** (*BRIT*) "salida"; **the ~ back** el camino de vuelta; **"give ~"** (*BRIT*: *AUT*) "ceda el paso"

**waylay** [weɪˈleɪ] (*irreg*) *vt* salir al paso a

**wayward** [ˈweɪwəd] *adj* díscolo

**W.C.** *n* (*BRIT*) wáter *m*

**we** [wiː] *pl pron* nosotros/as

**weak** [wiːk] *adj* débil, flojo; (*tea etc*) claro; **~en** *vi* debilitarse; (*give way*) ceder ♦ *vt* debilitar; **~ling** *n* debilucho/a; (*morally*) persona de poco carácter; **~ness** *n* debilidad *f*; (*fault*) punto débil; **to have a ~ness for** tener debilidad por

**wealth** [welθ] *n* riqueza; (*of details*) abundancia; **~y** *adj* rico

**wean** [wiːn] *vt* destetar

**weapon** [ˈwepən] *n* arma

**wear** [wɛə*] *n* (*pt* **wore**, *pp* **worn**) (*use*) uso; (*deterioration through use*) desgaste *m*; (*clothing*): **sports/baby~** ropa de deportes/de niños; **evening ~** ropa de etiqueta ♦ *vt* (*clothes*) llevar; (*shoes*) calzar; (*damage: through use*) gastar, usar ♦ *vi* (*last*) durar; (*rub through etc*) desgastarse; **~ away** *vt* gastar ♦ *vi* desgastarse; **~ down** *vt* gastar; (*strength*) agotar; **~ off** *vi* (*pain etc*) pasar, desaparecer; ~ **out** vt desgastar; (person, strength) agotar; ~ **and tear** n desgaste m

**weary** ['wɪərɪ] adj cansado; (dispirited) abatido ♦ vi: to ~ **of** cansarse de

**weasel** ['wiːzl] n (ZOOL) comadreja

**weather** ['weðə*] n tiempo ♦ vt (storm, crisis) hacer frente a; **under the** ~ (fig: ill) indispuesto, pachucho; ~**beaten** adj (skin) curtido; (building) deteriorado por la intemperie; ~**cock** n veleta; ~ **forecast** n boletín m meteorológico; ~**man** (inf) n hombre m del tiempo; ~ **vane** n = ~**cock**

**weave** [wiːv] (pt **wove**, pp **woven**) vt (cloth) tejer; (fig) entretejer; ~ **r** n tejedor(a) m/f; **weaving** n tejeduría

**web** [web] n (of spider) telaraña; (on duck's foot) membrana; (network) red f

**wed** [wed] (pt, pp **wedded**) vt casar ♦ vi casarse

**we'd** [wiːd] = **we had**; **we would**

**wedding** ['wedɪŋ] n boda, casamiento; **silver/golden** ~ (anniversary) bodas fpl de plata/de oro; ~ **day** n día m de la boda; ~ **dress** n traje m de novia; ~ **present** n regalo de boda; ~ **ring** n alianza

**wedge** [wedʒ] n (of wood etc) cuña; (of cake) trozo ♦ vt acuñar; (push) apretar

**Wednesday** ['wednzdɪ] n miércoles m inv

**wee** [wiː] (Scottish) adj pequeñito

**weed** [wiːd] n mala hierba, maleza ♦ vt escardar, desherbar; ~**killer** n herbicida m; ~**y** adj (person) mequetréfico

**week** [wiːk] n semana; **a** ~ **today/on Friday** de hoy/del viernes en ocho días; ~ **day** n día m laborable; ~**end** n fin de semana; ~**ly** adv semanalmente, cada semana ♦ adj semanal ♦ n semanario

**weep** [wiːp] (pt, pp **wept**) vi llorar; ~**ing willow** n sauce m llorón

**weigh** [weɪ] vt, vi pesar; **to** ~ **anchor** levar anclas; (fig: with worry) agobiar; ~ **down** vt sobrecargar; ~ **up** vt sopesar

**weight** [weɪt] n peso; (metal ~) pesa; **to lose/put on** ~ adelgazar/engordar; ~**ing** (allowance): (London) ~**ing** dietas (por residir en Londres); ~**lifter** n levantador m de pesas; ~**y** adj pesado; (matters) de relevancia or peso

**weir** [wɪə*] n presa

**weird** [wɪəd] adj raro, extraño

**welcome** ['welkəm] adj bienvenido ♦ n bienvenida ♦ vt dar la bienvenida a; (be glad of) alegrarse de; **thank you — you're** ~ gracias — de nada

**weld** [weld] n soldadura ♦ vt soldar

**welfare** ['welfeə*] n bienestar m; (social aid) asistencia social; ~ **state** n estado del bienestar; ~ **work** n asistencia social

**well** [wel] n fuente f, pozo ♦ adv bien ♦ adj: **to be** ~ estar bien (de salud) ♦ excl ¡vaya!, ¡bueno!; **as** ~ también; **as** ~ **as** además de; ~ **done!** ¡bien hecho!; **get** ~ **soon!** ¡que te mejores pronto!; **to do** ~ (business) ir bien; (person) tener éxito; ~ **up** vi (tears) saltar

**we'll** [wiːl] = **we will**; **we shall**

**well**: ~**behaved** adj bueno; ~**being** n bienestar m; ~**built** adj (person) fornido; ~**deserved** adj merecido; ~**dressed** adj bien vestido; ~**groomed** adj de buena presencia; ~**heeled** (inf) adj (wealthy) rico

**wellingtons** ['welɪŋtənz] npl (also: **wellington boots**) botas fpl de goma

**well**: ~**known** adj (person) conocido; ~**mannered** adj educado; ~**meaning** adj bienintencionado; ~**off** adj acomodado; ~**read** adj leído; ~**to-do** adj acomodado; ~**wisher** n admirador(a) m/f

**Welsh** [welʃ] adj galés/esa ♦ n (LING) galés m; **the** ~ npl los galeses; ~**man** n galés m; ~ **rarebit**

pan *m* con queso tostado; ~**woman** *n* galesa

**went** [wɛnt] *pt of* go

**wept** [wɛpt] *pt, pp of* weep

**were** [wəː*] *pt of* be

**we're** [wɪə*] = we are

**weren't** [wəːnt] = were not

**west** [wɛst] *n* oeste *m* ♦ *adj* occidental, del oeste ♦ *adv* al or hacia el oeste; **the W~** el Oeste, el Occidente; **W~ Country** (BRIT) *n*: **the W~ Country** el suroeste de Inglaterra; ~**erly** *adj* occidental; (*wind*) del oeste; ~**ern** *adj* occidental ♦ *n* (CINEMA) película del oeste; **W~ Germany** *n* Alemania Occidental; **W~ Indian** *adj, n* antillano/a *m/f*; **W~ Indies** *npl* Antillas *fpl*; ~**ward(s)** *adv* hacia el oeste

**wet** [wɛt] *adj* (*damp*) húmedo; (~ *through*) mojado; (*rainy*) lluvioso ♦ (BRIT) *n* (POL) conservador(a) *m/f* moderado/a; **to get** ~ mojarse; "~ **paint**" "recién pintado"; ~ **blanket** *n*: **to be a** ~ **blanket** (*fig*) ser un/ una aguafiestas; ~**suit** *n* traje *m* térmico

**we've** [wiːv] = we have

**whack** [wæk] *vt* dar un buen golpe a

**whale** [weɪl] *n* (ZOOL) ballena

**wharf** [wɔːf] *n* muelle *m*; **wharves** [wɔːvz] *npl of* wharf

┌─────────────┐
│ KEYWORD     │
└─────────────┘

**what** [wɔt] *adj* 1 (*in direct/indirect questions*) qué; ~ **size is** your talla usa?; ~ **colour/shape is it?** ¿de qué color/forma es?

2 (*in exclamations*): ~ **a mess!** ¡qué desastre!; ~ **a fool I am!** ¡qué tonto soy!

♦ *pron* 1 (*interrogative*) qué; ~ **are you doing?** ¿qué haces or estás haciendo?; ~ **is happening?** ¿qué pasa or está pasando?; ~ **is it called?** ¿cómo se llama?; ~ **about me?** ¿y yo qué?; ~ **about doing ...?** ¿qué tal si hacemos ...?

2 (*relative*) lo que; **I saw** ~ **you did/was on the table** vi lo que

hiciste/había en la mesa

♦ *excl* (*disbelieving*) ¡cómo!; ~, **no coffee!** ¡que no hay café!

**whatever** [wɔt'ɛvə*] *adj*: ~ **book you choose** cualquier libro que elijas ♦ *pron*: **do** ~ **is necessary** haga lo que sea necesario; ~ **happens** pase lo que pase; **no reason** ~ or **whatsoever** ninguna razón sea la que sea; **nothing** ~ nada en absoluto

**whatsoever** [wɔtsəu'ɛvə*] *adj* = whatever

**wheat** [wiːt] *n* trigo

**wheedle** [ˈwiːdl] *vt*: **to** ~ **sb into doing sth** engatusar a uno para que haga algo; **to** ~ **sth out of sb** sonsacar algo a uno

**wheel** [wiːl] *n* rueda; (AUT: *also*: **steering** ~) volante *m*; (NAUT) timón *m* ♦ *vt* (*pram etc*) empujar ♦ *vi* (*also*: ~ **round**) dar la vuelta, girar; ~**barrow** *n* carretilla; ~**chair** *n* silla de ruedas; ~ **clamp** *n* (AUT) cepo

**wheeze** [wiːz] *vi* resollar

┌─────────────┐
│ KEYWORD     │
└─────────────┘

**when** [wɛn] *adv* cuando; ~ **did it happen?** ¿cuándo ocurrió?; **I know** ~ **it happened** sé cuándo ocurrió

♦ *conj* 1 (*at, during, after the time that*) cuando; **be careful** ~ **you cross the road** ten cuidado al cruzar la calle; **that was** ~ **I needed you** fue entonces que te necesité

2 (*on, at which*): **on the day** ~ **I met him** el día en qué le conocí

3 (*whereas*) cuando

**whenever** [wɛn'ɛvə*] *conj* cuando; (*every time that*) cada vez que ♦ *adv* cuando sea

**where** [wɛə*] *adv* dónde ♦ *conj* donde; **this is** ~ aquí es donde; ~**abouts** *adv* dónde ♦ *n*: **nobody knows his** ~**abouts** nadie conoce su paradero; ~**as** *conj* visto que, mientras; ~**by** *pron* por lo cual; ~**upon** *conj* con lo cual, después de lo cual;

~**ver** [-'ɛvə*] *conj* dondequiera que; (*interrogative*) dónde; ~**withal** *n* recursos *mpl*

**whet** [wɛt] *vt* estimular

**whether** ['wɛðə*] *conj* si; I don't know ~ to accept or not no sé si aceptar o no; ~ **you go or not va**yas o no vayas

---

KEYWORD

---

**which** [wɪtʃ] *adj* **1** (*interrogative: direct, indirect*) qué; ~ **picture(s) do you want?** ¿qué cuadro(s) quieres?; ~ **one?** ¿cuál?
**2: in ~ case** en cuyo caso; **we got there at 8 pm, by ~ time the cinema was full** llegamos allí a las 8, cuando el cine estaba lleno
♦ *pron* **1** (*interrogative*) cuál; I don't mind ~ el/la que sea
**2** (*relative: replacing noun*) que; (: *replacing clause*) lo que; (: *after preposition*) el/la que *etc*, el/la cual *etc*; **the apple ~ you ate/~ is on the table** la manzana que comiste/que está en la mesa; **the chair on ~ you are sitting** la silla en la que estás sentado; **he said he knew, ~ is true/I feared** dijo que lo sabía, lo cual o lo que es cierto/me temía

---

**whichever** [wɪtʃ'ɛvə*] *adj*: take ~ **book you prefer** coja (SP) el libro que prefiera; ~ **book you take** cualquier libro que coja
**whiff** [wɪf] *n* vaharada
**while** [waɪl] *n* rato, momento ♦ *conj* mientras; (*although*) aunque; **for a ~** durante algún tiempo; ~ **away** *vt* pasar
**whim** [wɪm] *n* capricho
**whimper** ['wɪmpə*] *n* sollozo ♦ *vi* lloriquear
**whimsical** ['wɪmzɪkl] *adj* (*person*) caprichoso; (*look*) juguetón/ona
**whine** [waɪn] *n* (*of pain*) gemido; (*of engine*) zumbido; (*of siren*) aullido ♦ *vi* gemir; zumbar; (*fig: complain*) gimotear
**whip** [wɪp] *n* látigo; (*POL: person*)

encargado de la disciplina partidaria en el parlamento ♦ *vt* azotar; (*CULIN*) batir; (*move quickly*): **to ~ sth out/off** sacar/quitar algo de un tirón; ~**ped cream** *n* nata o crema montada; ~**round** (*BRIT*) *n* colecta
**whirl** [wəːl] *vt* hacer girar, dar vueltas a ♦ *vi* girar, dar vueltas; (*leaves etc*) arremolinarse; ~**pool** *n* remolino; ~**wind** *n* torbellino
**whirr** [wəː*] *vi* zumbar
**whisk** [wɪsk] *n* (*CULIN*) batidor *m* ♦ *vt* (*CULIN*) batir; **to ~ sb away** or **off** llevar volando a uno
**whiskers** ['wɪskəz] *npl* (*of animal*) bigotes *mpl*; (*of man*) patillas *fpl*
**whiskey** ['wɪskɪ] (US, Ireland) *n* = **whisky**
**whisky** ['wɪskɪ] *n* whisky *m*
**whisper** ['wɪspə*] *n* susurro ♦ *vi*, *vt* susurrar
**whist** [wɪst] (*BRIT*) *n* juego de naipes
**whistle** ['wɪsl] *n* (*sound*) silbido; (*object*) silbato ♦ *vt* silbar
**white** [waɪt] *adj* blanco; (*pale*) pálido ♦ *n* blanco; (*of egg*) clara; ~ **coffee** (*BRIT*) *n* café *m* con leche; ~ **collar worker** *n* oficinista *m/f*; ~ **elephant** *n* (*fig*) maula; ~ **lie** *n* mentirilla; ~**ness** *n* blancura; ~ **noise** *n* sonido blanco; ~ **paper** *n* (*POL*) libro rojo; ~**wash** *n* (*paint*) jalbegue *m*, cal *f* ♦ *vt* (*also fig*) blanquear
**whiting** ['waɪtɪŋ] *n* *inv* (*fish*) pescadilla
**Whitsun** [wɪtsn] *n* pentecostés *m*
**whittle** ['wɪtl] *vt*: **to ~ away**, ~ **down** ir reduciendo
**whizz** [wɪz] *vi*: **to ~ past** or **by** pasar a toda velocidad; ~ **kid** (*inf*) *n* prodigio

---

KEYWORD

---

**who** [huː] *pron* **1** (*interrogative*) quién; ~**s** it? ¿quién es?; ~**s there?** ¿quién es?; ~ **are you looking for?** ¿a quién buscas? I told her ~ I was le dije quién era yo
**2** (*relative*) que; **the man/woman**

spoke to me el hombre/la mujer que habló conmigo; **those ~ can swim** los que saben *or* sepan nadar

**whodun(n)it** [huːˈdʌnɪt] (*inf*) *n* novela policíaca

**whoever** [huːˈɛvə*] *pron*: **~ finds it** cualquiera *or* quienquiera que lo encuentre; **ask ~ you like** pregunta a quien quieras; **~ he marries** no importa con quién se case

**whole** [həʊl] *adj* (*entire*) todo, entero; (*not broken*) intacto ♦ *n* todo; (*all*): **the ~ of the town** toda la ciudad, la ciudad entera ♦ *n* (*total*) total *m*; (*sum*) conjunto; **on the ~, as a ~** en general; **~ food(s)** *n*(*pl*) alimento(s) *m*(*pl*) integral(es); **~hearted** *adj* sincero, cordial; **~meal** *adj* integral; **~sale** *n* venta al por mayor ♦ *adj* al por mayor; (*fig: destruction*) sistemático; **~saler** *n* mayorista *m/f*; **~some** *adj* sano; **~wheat** *adj* = **~meal**; **wholly** *adv* totalmente, enteramente

*KEYWORD*

**whom** [huːm] *pron* **1** (*interrogative*): **~ did you see?** ¿a quién viste?; **to ~ did you give it?** ¿a quién se lo diste?; **tell me from ~ you received it** dígame de quién lo recibió

**2** (*relative*) que; **to ~ a** quien(es); **of ~** de quien(es), del/de la que *etc*; **the man ~ I saw/to ~ I wrote** el hombre que vi/a quien escribí; **the lady about/with ~ I was talking** la señora de (la) que/con quien or (la) que hablaba

**whooping cough** [ˈhuːpɪŋ-] *n* tos *f* ferina

**whore** [hɔː*] (*inf: pej*) *n* puta

*KEYWORD*

**whose** [huːz] *adj* **1** (*possessive: interrogative*): **~ book is this?**, **~ is this book?** ¿de quién es este libro?; **~ pencil have you taken?**

¿de quién es el lápiz que has cogido?; **~ daughter are you?** ¿de quién eres hija?

**2** (*possessive: relative*) cuyo/a, *pl* cuyos/as; **the man ~ son you rescued** el hombre cuyo hijo rescataste; **those ~ passports I have** aquellas personas cuyos pasaportes tengo; **the woman ~ car was stolen** la mujer a quien le robaron el coche

♦ *pron* de quién; **~ is this?** ¿de quién es esto?; **I know ~ it is** sé de quién es

*KEYWORD*

**why** [waɪ] *adv* por qué; **~ not?** ¿por qué no?; **~ not do it now?** ¿por qué no lo haces (*or* hacemos *etc*) ahora?

♦ *conj*: **I wonder ~ he said that** me pregunto por qué dijo eso; **that's not ~ I'm here** no es por eso (por lo) que estoy aquí; **the reason ~** la razón por la que

♦ *excl* (*expressing surprise, shock, annoyance*) ¡hombre!, ¡vaya! (*explaining*): **~, it's you!** ¡hombre, eres tú!; **~, that's impossible** ¡pero si eso es imposible!

**wicked** [ˈwɪkɪd] *adj* malvado, cruel

**wickerwork** [ˈwɪkəwəːk] *n* artículos *mpl* de mimbre ♦ *adj* de mimbre

**wicket** [ˈwɪkɪt] *n* (*CRICKET: stumps*) palos *mpl*; (: *grass area*) terreno de juego

**wide** [waɪd] *adj* ancho; (*area, knowledge*) vasto, grande; (*choice*) amplio ♦ *adv*: **to open ~** abrir de par en par; **to shoot ~** errar el tiro; **~-angle lens** *n* objetivo de gran angular; **~awake** *adj* bien despierto; **~ly** *adv* (*travelled*) mucho; (*spaced*) muy; **it is ~ly believed/known that...** mucha gente piensa/sabe que...; **~n** *vt* ensanchar; (*experience*) ampliar ♦ *vi* ensancharse; **~open** *adj* abierto de par en par; **~spread** *adj* extendido, general

**widow** ['wɪdəu] n viuda; **~ed** adj
viudo; **~er** n viudo
**width** [wɪdθ] n anchura; (of cloth)
ancho
**wield** [wi:ld] vt (sword) blandir;
(power) ejercer
**wife** [waɪf] (pl **wives**) n mujer f, esposa
**wig** [wɪg] n peluca
**wiggle** ['wɪgl] vt menear
**wild** [waɪld] adj (animal) salvaje;
(plant) silvestre; (person) furioso,
violento; (idea) descabellado;
(rough: sea) bravo; (: land) agreste;
(: weather) muy revuelto; **~s** npl re-
giones fpl salvajes, tierras fpl vírge-
nes; **~erness** ['wɪldənɪs] n desierto;
**~-goose chase** n (fig) búsqueda inútil; **~life** n fauna; **~ly** adv (behave)
locamente; (lash out) a diestro y siniestro; (guess) a lo loco; (happy) a
más no poder
**wilful** ['wɪlful] (US **willful**) adj (action) deliberado; (obstinate) testarudo

KEYWORD

**will** [wɪl] aux vb **1** (forming future
tense): **I ~ finish** it tomorrow lo
terminaré o voy a terminar mañana; **I ~ have finished** it by tomorrow lo habré terminado para
mañana; **~ you do it? – yes I ~/
no I won't** ¿lo harás? – sí/no
**2** (in conjectures, predictions): **he ~**
or **he'll be there by now** ya habrá
or debe (de) haber llegado; **that ~
be the postman** será or debe ser el
cartero
**3** (in commands, requests, offers): **~
you be quiet!** ¡quieres callarte?; **~
you help me?** ¿quieres ayudarme?;
**~ you have a cup of tea?** ¿te apetece un té?; **I won't put up with it!**
¡no lo soporto!
♦ vt (pt, pp **willed**): **to ~ sb to do
sth** desear que alguien haga algo; **he
~ed himself to go on** con gran
fuerza de voluntad, continuó
♦ n voluntad f; (testament) testa-

mento
**willful** ['wɪlful] (US) adj = wilful
**willing** ['wɪlɪŋ] adj (with goodwill) de
buena voluntad; (enthusiastic) entusiasta; **he's ~ to do** it está dispuesto a hacerlo; **~ly** adv con mucho gusto; **~ness** n buena voluntad
**willow** ['wɪləu] n sauce m
**willpower** ['wɪlpauə*] n fuerza de
voluntad
**willy-nilly** [wɪlɪ'nɪlɪ] adv quiérase o
no
**wilt** [wɪlt] vi marchitarse
**wily** ['waɪlɪ] adj astuto
**win** [wɪn] (pt, pp **won**) n victoria,
triunfo ♦ vt ganar; (obtain) conseguir, lograr ♦ vi ganar; **~ over**
vt convencer a; **~ round** (BRIT) vt =
**~ over**
**wince** [wɪns] vi encogerse
**winch** [wɪntʃ] n torno
**wind¹** [wɪnd] n viento; (MED) gases mpl ♦ vt (take breath away
from) dejar sin aliento a
**wind²** [waɪnd] (pt, pp **wound**) vt
enrollar; (wrap) envolver; (clock,
toy) dar cuerda a ♦ vi (road, river)
serpentear; **~ up** vt (clock) dar
cuerda a; (debate, meeting) concluir,
terminar
**windfall** ['wɪndfɔ:l] n golpe m de
suerte
**winding** ['waɪndɪŋ] adj (road) tortuoso; (staircase) de caracol
**wind instrument** [wɪnd-] n (MUS)
instrumento de viento
**windmill** ['wɪndmɪl] n molino de
viento
**window** ['wɪndəu] n ventana; (in
car, train) ventanilla; (in shop etc)
escaparate m (SP), vitrina (AM); **~
box** n jardinera de ventana; **~
cleaner** n (person) limpiador de
cristales; **~ ledge** n alféizar m, repisa; **~ pane** n cristal m; **~shopping**
n: **to go ~shopping** ir de escapara-
tes; **~sill** n alféizar m, repisa
**windpipe** ['wɪndpaɪp] n tráquea
**wind power** n energía eólica

**windscreen** ['wɪndskriːn] (US **windshield**) n parabrisas m inv; ~ **washer** n lavaparabrisas m inv; ~ **wiper** n limpiaparabrisas m inv

**windswept** ['wɪndswept] adj azotado por el viento

**windy** ['wɪndɪ] adj de mucho viento; it's ~ hace viento

**wine** [waɪn] n vino; ~ **bar** n enoteca; ~ **cellar** n bodega; ~ **glass** n copa (para vino); ~ **list** n lista de vinos; ~ **merchant** n vinatero; ~ **waiter** n escanciador m

**wing** [wɪŋ] n ala; (AUT) aleta; ~s npl (THEATRE) bastidores mpl; ~**er** n (SPORT) extremo

**wink** [wɪŋk] n guiño, pestañeo ♦ vi guiñar, pestañear

**winner** ['wɪnə*] n ganador(a) m/f

**winning** ['wɪnɪŋ] adj (team) ganador(a); (goal) decisivo; (smile) encantador(a); ~s npl ganancias fpl

**winter** ['wɪntə*] n invierno ♦ vi invernar; **wintry** ['wɪntrɪ] adj invernal

**wipe** [waɪp] n: **to give sth a** ~ pasar un trapo sobre algo ♦ vt limpiar; (tape) borrar; ~ **off** vt limpiar con un trapo; (remove) quitar; ~ **out** vt (debt) liquidar; (memory) borrar; (destroy) destruir; ~ **up** vt limpiar

**wire** [waɪə*] n alambre m; (ELEC) cable m (eléctrico); (TEL) telegrama m ♦ vt (house) poner la instalación eléctrica en; (also: ~ up) conectar; (person) telegrafiar

**wireless** ['waɪəlɪs] (BRIT) n radio f

**wiring** ['waɪərɪŋ] n instalación f eléctrica

**wiry** ['waɪərɪ] adj (person) enjuto y fuerte; (hair) crespo

**wisdom** ['wɪzdəm] n sabiduría, saber m; (good sense) cordura; ~ **tooth** n muela del juicio

**wise** [waɪz] adj sabio; (sensible) juicioso

**...wise** [waɪz] suffix: **time**~ en cuanto a o respecto al tiempo

**wisecrack** ['waɪzkræk] n broma

**wish** [wɪʃ] n deseo ♦ vt querer; **best** ~**es** (on birthday etc) felicidades fpl;

**with best** ~**es** (in letter) saludos mpl, recuerdos mpl; ~ **sb good-bye** despedirse de uno; **he** ~**ed me well** me deseó mucha suerte; **to do/sb to do sth** querer hacer/que alguien haga algo; **to** ~ **for** desear; ~**ful** adj: **it's** ~**ful thinking** eso sería soñar

**wishy-washy** ['wɪʃɪwɒʃɪ] (inf) adj (colour, ideas) desvaído

**wisp** [wɪsp] n mechón m; (of smoke) voluta

**wistful** ['wɪstful] adj pensativo

**wit** [wɪt] n ingenio, gracia; (also: ~s) inteligencia; (person) chistoso/a

**witch** [wɪtʃ] n bruja; ~**craft** n brujería; ~-**hunt** n (fig) caza de brujas

---

KEYWORD

---

**with** [wɪð, wɪθ] prep **1** (accompanying, in the company of) con (con+ mí, ti, sí = conmigo, contigo, consigo); **I was** ~ **him** estaba con él; **we stayed** ~ **friends** nos hospedamos en casa de unos amigos; **I'm (not)** ~ **you** (understand) (no) te entiendo; **to be** ~ **it** (inf: person: up-to-date) estar al tanto; (: alert) ser despabilado

**2** (descriptive, indicating manner etc) con; de; **a room** ~ **a view** una habitación con vistas; **the man** ~ **the grey hat/blue eyes** el hombre del sombrero gris/de los ojos azules; **red** ~ **anger** rojo de ira; **to shake** ~ **fear** temblar de miedo; **to fill sth** ~ **water** llenar algo de agua

**withdraw** [wɪθ'drɔː] (irreg) vt retirar, sacar ♦ vi retirarse; **to** ~ **money (from the bank)** retirar fondos (del banco); ~**al** n retirada; (of money) reintegro; ~**al symptoms** npl (MED) síndrome m de abstinencia; ~**n** adj (person) reservado, introvertido

**wither** ['wɪðə*] vi marchitarse

**withhold** [wɪθ'həuld] (irreg) vt (money) retener; (decision) aplazar; (permission) negar; (information) ocultar

**within** [wið'ın] *prep* dentro de ♦ *adv*
dentro; ~ **reach (of)** al alcance
(de); ~ **sight (of)** a la vista (de); ~
**the week** antes de acabar la semana; ~ **a mile (of)** a menos de una
milla (de)

**without** [wið'aut] *prep* sin; **to go** ~
**sth** pasar sin algo

**withstand** [wið'stænd] *(irreg) vt* resistir a

**witness** ['wıtnıs] *n* testigo *m/f* ♦ *vt*
(*event*) presenciar; (*document*) atestiguar la veracidad de; **to bear** ~ **to**
(*fig*) ser testimonio de; ~ **box** *n* tribuna de los testigos; ~ **stand** (*US*) *n*
= ~ **box**

**witty** ['wıtı] *adj* ingenioso

**wives** [waıvz] *npl of* **wife**

**wizard** ['wızəd] *n* hechicero

**wk** *abbr* = **week**

**wobble** ['wɔbl] *vi* temblar; (*chair*)
cojear

**woe** [wəu] *n* desgracia

**woke** [wəuk] *pt of* **wake**

**woken** ['wəukən] *pp of* **wake**

**wolf** [wulf] *n* lobo; **wolves** [wulvz]
*npl of* **wolf**

**woman** ['wumən] (*pl* **women**) *n* mujer *f*; ~ **doctor** *n* médica; **women's
lib** (*inf: pej*) *n* liberación *f* de la mujer; ~**ly** *adj* femenino

**womb** [wu:m] *n* matriz *f*, útero

**women** ['wımın] *npl of* **woman**

**won** [wʌn] *pt, pp of* **win**

**wonder** ['wʌndə\*] *n* maravilla, prodigio; (*feeling*) asombro ♦ *vi*: **to** ~
**whether/why** preguntarse si/por
qué; **to** ~ **at** asombrarse de; **to** ~
**about** pensar sobre or en; **it's no** ~
(**that**) no es de extrañarse (que
+ *subjun*); ~**ful** *adj* maravilloso;
~**fully** *adv* maravillosamente, estupendamente

**won't** [wəunt] = **will not**

**woo** [wu:] *vt* (*woman*) cortejar

**wood** [wud] *n* (*timber*) madera;
(*forest*) bosque *m*; ~ **carving** *n* (*act*)
tallado en madera; (*object*) talla en
madera; ~**ed** *adj* arbolado; ~**en** *adj*

de madera; (*fig*) inexpresivo;
~**pecker** *n* pájaro carpintero; ~**wind**
*n* (*MUS*) instrumentos *mpl* de viento
de madera; ~**work** *n* carpintería; ~
**worm** *n* carcoma

**wool** [wul] *n* lana; **to pull the** ~
**over sb's eyes** (*fig*) engatusar a
uno; ~ **en** (*US*) *adj* ~**len**; ~**len**
*adj* de lana; ~**lens** *npl* géneros *mpl*
de lana; ~**ly** *adj* lanudo, de lana;
(*fig: ideas*) confuso; ~**y** (*US*) *adj* =
~**ly**

**word** [wə:d] *n* palabra; (*news*) noticia; (*promise*) palabra (de honor) ♦
*vt* redactar; **in other** ~**s** en otras
palabras; **to break/keep one's** ~
faltar a la palabra/cumplir la promesa; **to have** ~**s with sb** reñir con
uno; ~**ing** *n* redacción *f*; ~ **processing** *n* proceso de textos; ~ **processor**
*n* procesador *m* de textos

**wore** [wɔ:\*] *pt of* **wear**

**work** [wə:k] *n* trabajo; (*job*) empleo,
trabajo; (*ART, LITERATURE*) obra
♦ *vi* trabajar; (*mechanism*) funcionar, marchar; (*medicine*) ser eficaz,
surtir efecto ♦ *vt* (*shape*) trabajar;
(*stone etc*) tallar; (*mine etc*) explotar; (*machine*) manejar, hacer
funcionar; **to be out of** ~ estar parado, no tener trabajo; ~**s** *n* (*BRIT:
factory*) fábrica ♦ *npl* (*of clock, machine*) mecanismo; **to** ~ **loose**
(*part*) desprenderse; (*knot*) aflojarse; ~ **on** *vt fus* trabajar en, dedicarse a; (*principle*) basarse en; ~ **out**
*vi* (*plans etc*) salir bien, funcionar ♦
*vt* (*problem*) resolver; (*plan*) elaborar; **it** ~**s out at £100** suma 100 libras; ~ **up** *vt*: **to get** ~**ed up** excitarse; ~**able** *adj* (*solution*) práctico,
factible; ~**aholic** *n* trabajador-a
obsesivo/a *m/f*; ~**er** *n* trabajador-a
*m/f*, obrero/a; ~**force** *n* mano *f* de
obra; ~**ing class** *n* clase *f* obrera;
~**ing-class** *adj* obrero; ~**ing order**
*n*: **in** ~**ing order** en funcionamiento;
~**man** *n* obrero; ~**manship** *n* habilidad *f*, trabajo; ~**sheet** *n* hoja de trabajo; ~**shop** *n* taller *m*; ~ **station** *n*

puesto *or* estación *f* de trabajo; ~ **to-rule** (BRIT) *n* huelga de celo

**world** [wə:ld] *n* mundo ♦ *cpd* (*champion*) del mundo; (*power, war*) mundial; **to think the ~ of sb** (*fig*) tener un concepto muy alto de uno; **~ly** *adj* mundano; **~-wide** *adj* mundial, universal

**worm** [wə:m] *n* (*also*: *earth~*) lombriz *f*

**worn** [wɔ:n] *pp of* **wear** ♦ *adj* usado; **~-out** *adj* (*object*) gastado; (*person*) rendido, agotado

**worried** ['wʌrɪd] *adj* preocupado

**worry** ['wʌrɪ] *n* preocupación *f* ♦ *vt* preocupar, inquietar ♦ *vi* preocuparse; **~ing** *adj* inquietante

**worse** [wə:s] *adj, adv* peor ♦ *n* lo peor; **a change for the ~** un empeoramiento; **~n** *vt, vi* empeorar; **~ off** *adj* (*financially*) to be ~ off tener menos dinero; (*fig*): **you'll be ~ off this way** de esta forma estarás peor que nunca

**worship** ['wə:ʃɪp] *n* adoración *f* ♦ *vt* adorar; **Your W~** (BRIT: *to mayor*) señor alcalde; (: *to judge*) señor juez

**worst** [wə:st] *adj, adv* peor ♦ *n* lo peor; **at ~** en lo peor de los casos

**worth** [wə:θ] *n* valor *m* ♦ *adj*: **to be ~** valer; **it's ~ it** vale *or* merece la pena; **to be ~ one's while (to do)** merecer la pena (hacer); (: *useless*) inútil; **~while** *adj* (*activity*) que merece la pena; (*cause*) loable

**worthy** ['wə:ðɪ] *adj* respetable; (*motive*) honesto; **~ of** digno de

---

KEYWORD

**would** [wud] *aux vb* **1** (*conditional tense*): **if you asked him he ~** do it si se lo pidieras, lo haría; **if you had asked him he ~ have done it** si se lo hubieras pedido, lo habría *or* hubiera hecho

**2** (*in offers, invitations, requests*): **~ you like a biscuit?** ¿quieres una galleta?; (*formal*) ¿querría una galleta?; **~ you ask him to come in?** ¿quiere hacerle pasar?; **~ you open the window please?** ¿quiere *or* podría abrir la ventana, por favor?

**3** (*in indirect speech*): **I said I ~** do it dije que lo haría

**4** (*emphatic*): **it WOULD have to snow today!** ¡tenía que nevar precisamente hoy!

**5** (*insistence*): **she ~n't behave** no quiso comportarse bien

**6** (*conjecture*): **it ~ have been midnight** sería medianoche; **it ~ seem so** parece ser que sí

**7** (*indicating habit*): **he ~ go there on Mondays** iba allí los lunes

---

**would-be** (*pej*) *adj* presunto

**wouldn't** ['wudnt] = **would not**

**wound**[1] [wu:nd] *n* herida ♦ *vt* herir

**wound**[2] [waund] *pt, pp of* **wind**

**wove** [wəuv] *pt of* **weave**

**woven** ['wəuvən] *pp of* **weave**

**wrangle** ['ræŋgl] *n* riña

**wrap** [ræp] *n* (*stole*) chal *m*; (*cape*) capa ♦ *vt* (*also*: ~ *up*) envolver; **~per** *n* (*on chocolate*) papel *m*; (BRIT: *of book*) sobrecubierta; **~ping paper** *n* papel *m* de envolver; (*fancy*) papel *m* de regalo

**wrath** [rɔθ] *n* cólera

**wreak** [ri:k] *vt*: **to ~ havoc (on)** hacer estragos (en); **to ~ vengeance (on)** vengarse de

**wreath** [ri:θ, *pl* ri:ðz] *n* (*funeral ~*) corona

**wreck** [rek] *n* (*ship*: *destruction*) naufragio; (: *remains*) restos *mpl* del barco; (*pej*: *person*) ruina *m* (*car etc*) destrozar; (*chances*) arruinar; **~age** *n* restos *mpl*; (*of building*) escombros *mpl*

**wren** [ren] *n* (ZOOL) reyezuelo

**wrench** [rentʃ] *n* (TECH) llave *f* inglesa; (*tug*) tirón *m*; (*fig*) dolor *m* ♦ *vt* arrancar; **to ~ sth from sb** arrebatar algo violentamente a uno

**wrestle** ['resl] *vi*: **to ~ (with sb)** luchar (con *or* contra uno); **~r** *n* luchador(a) *m/f* (de lucha libre); **wrestling** *n* lucha libre

**wretched** ['rɛtʃɪd] adj miserable

**wriggle** ['rɪgl] vi (also: ~ about) menearse, retorcerse

**wring** [rɪŋ] (pt, pp wrung) vt retorcer; (wet clothes) escurrir; (fig): to ~ sth out of sb sacar algo por la fuerza a uno

**wrinkle** ['rɪŋkl] n arruga ♦ vt arrugar ♦ vi arrugarse

**wrist** [rɪst] n muñeca; ~ watch n reloj m de pulsera

**writ** [rɪt] n mandato judicial

**write** [raɪt] (pt wrote, pp written) vt escribir; (cheque) extender ♦ vi escribir; ~ down vt escribir; (note) apuntar; ~ off vt (debt) borrar (como incobrable); (fig) desechar por inútil; ~ out vt escribir; ~ up vt redactar; ~-off n siniestro total; ~r n escritor(a) m/f

**writhe** [raɪð] vi retorcerse

**writing** ['raɪtɪŋ] n escritura; (hand-~) letra; (of author) obras fpl; in ~ por escrito; ~ paper n papel m de escribir

**written** ['rɪtn] pp of write

**wrong** [rɒŋ] adj (wicked) malo; (unfair) injusto; (incorrect) equivocado, incorrecto; (not suitable) inoportuno, inconveniente; (reverse) del revés ♦ adv equivocadamente ♦ n injusticia ♦ vt ser injusto con; you are ~ to do it hacer mal en hacerlo; you are ~ about that, you've got it ~ en eso estás equivocado; to be in the ~ no tener razón, tener la culpa; what's ~? ¿qué pasa?; to go ~ (person) equivocarse; (plan) salir mal; (machine) estropearse; ~ful adj injusto; ~ly adv mal, incorrectamente; (by mistake) por error

**wrote** [rəut] pt of write

**wrought** [rɔːt] adj: ~ iron hierro forjado

**wrung** [rʌŋ] pt, pp of wring

**wry** [raɪ] adj irónico

**wt.** abbr = weight

# X

**Xmas** ['ɛksməs] n abbr = Christmas

**X-ray** [ɛks'reɪ] vt radiografiar ♦ n radiografía; to ~ radiografiar, sacar radiografías de

**xylophone** ['zaɪləfəun] n xilófono

# Y

**yacht** [jɒt] n yate m; ~ing n (sport) balandrismo; ~sman/woman n balandrista m/f

**Yank** [jæŋk] (pej) n yanqui m/f

**Yankee** ['jæŋkɪ] (pej) n = Yank

**yap** [jæp] vi (dog) aullar

**yard** [jɑːd] n patio; (measure) yarda; ~stick n (fig) criterio, norma

**yarn** [jɑːn] n hilo; (tale) cuento, historia

**yawn** [jɔːn] n bostezo ♦ vi bostezar; ~ing adj (gap) muy abierto

**yd(s).** abbr = yard(s)

**yeah** [jɛə] (inf) adv sí

**year** [jɪə*] n año; to be 8 ~s old tener 8 años; an eight-~-old child un niño de ocho años (de edad); ~ly adj anual ♦ adv anualmente, cada año

**yearn** [jəːn] vi: to ~ for sth añorar algo, suspirar por algo; ~ing n ansia, añoranza

**yeast** [jiːst] n levadura

**yell** [jɛl] n grito, alarido ♦ vi gritar

**yellow** ['jɛləu] adj amarillo

**yelp** [jɛlp] n aullido ♦ vi aullar

**yeoman** ['jəumən] n: Y~ of the Guard alabardero de la Casa Real

**yes** [jɛs] adv sí ♦ n sí m; to say/answer ~ decir/contestar que sí

**yesterday** ['jɛstədɪ] adv ayer ♦ n ayer m; ~ morning/evening ayer por la mañana/tarde; all day ~ todo el día de ayer

**yet** [jɛt] adv aún; (negative) todavía ♦ conj sin embargo, a pesar de todo; it is not finished ~ todavía no está acabado; the best ~ el/la mejor hasta ahora; as ~ hasta ahora, todavía

**yew** [ju:] *n* tejo

**yield** [ji:ld] *n* (*AGR*) cosecha; (*COMM*) rendimiento ♦ *vt* ceder; (*results*) producir, dar; (*profit*) rendir ♦ *vi* rendirse, ceder; (*US: AUT*) ceder el paso

**YMCA** *n abbr* (= *Young Men's Christian Association*) Asociación *f* de Jóvenes Cristianos

**yog(h)ourt** ['jəugət] *n* yogur *m*

**yog(h)urt** ['jəugət] *n* = yog(h)ourt

**yoke** [jəuk] *n* yugo

**yolk** [jəuk] *n* yema (de huevo)

**yonder** ['jɔndə*] *adv* allá (a lo lejos)

KEYWORD

**you** [ju:] *pron* **1** (*subject: familiar*) tú, *pl* vosotros/as (*SP*), ustedes (*AM*); (*polite*) usted, *pl* ustedes; ~ **are very kind** eres/es *etc* muy amable; ~ **French enjoy your food** a vosotros (*or* ustedes) los franceses os (*or* les) gusta la comida; ~ **and I will go** iremos tú y yo

**2** (*object: direct: familiar*) te, *pl* os (*SP*), les (*AM*); (*polite*) le, *pl* les, *f* la, *pl* las; **I know** ~ te/le *etc* conozco

**3** (*object: indirect: familiar*) te, *pl* os (*SP*), les (*AM*); (*polite*) le, *pl* les; **I gave the letter to** ~ **yesterday** te/os *etc* di la carta ayer

**4** (*stressed*): **I told YOU to do it** te dije a ti que lo hicieras, esa a ti a quien dije que lo hicieras; *see also* **3, 5**

**5** (*after prep: NB:* con+*ti* = *contigo*): *familiar*) ti, *pl* vosotros/as (*SP*), ustedes (*AM*); (*: polite*) usted, *pl* ustedes; **it's for** ~ es para ti/vosotros *etc*

**6** (*comparisons: familiar*) tú, *pl* vosotros/as (*SP*), ustedes (*AM*); (*: polite*) usted, *pl* ustedes; **she's younger than** ~ es más joven que tú/vosotros *etc*

**7** (*impersonal: one*): **fresh air does** ~ **good** el aire puro (te) hace bien; ~ **never know** nunca se sabe; ~ **can't do that!** ¡eso no se hace!

**you'd** [ju:d] = **you had; you would**

**you'll** [ju:l] = **you will; you shall**

**young** [jʌŋ] *adj* joven ♦ *npl* (*of animal*) cría; (*people*): **the** ~ los jóvenes, la juventud; ~**er** *adj* (*brother etc*) menor; ~**ster** *n* joven *m/f*

**your** [jɔ:*] *adj* tu; (*pl*) vuestro; (*formal*) su; *see also* **my**

**you're** [juə*] = **you are**

**yours** [jɔ:z] *pron* tuyo; (*pl*) vuestro; (*formal*) suyo; *see also* **faithfully; mine; sincerely**

**yourself** [jɔ:'self] *pron* tú mismo; (*complement*) te; (*after prep*) ti (mismo); (*formal*) usted mismo; (: *complement*) se; (: *after prep*) sí (mismo); **yourselves** *pl pron* vosotros mismos; (*after prep*) vosotros (mismos); (*formal*) ustedes (mismos); (: *complement*) se; (: *after prep*) sí mismos; *see also* **oneself**

**youth** [ju:θ, *pl* ju:ðz] *n* juventud *f*; (*young man*) joven *m*; ~ **club** *n* club *m* juvenil; ~**ful** *adj* juvenil; ~ **hostel** *n* albergue *m* de juventud

**you've** [ju:v] = **you have**

**Yugoslav** ['ju:gəusləv] *adj*, *n* yugo(e)slavo/a *m/f*

**Yugoslavia** [ju:gəu'sla:vɪə] *n* Yugoslavia

**yuppie** ['jʌpɪ] (*inf*) *adj*, *n* yupi *m/f*, yupy *m/f*

**YWCA** *n abbr* (= *Young Women's Christian Association*) Asociación *f* de Jóvenes Cristianas

# Z

**zany** ['zeɪnɪ] *adj* estrafalario

**zap** [zæp] *vt* (*COMPUT*) borrar

**zeal** [zi:l] *n* celo, entusiasmo; ~**ous** ['zeləs] *adj* celoso, entusiasta

**zebra** ['zi:brə] *n* cebra; ~ **crossing** (*BRIT*) *n* paso de peatones

**zenith** ['zenɪθ] *n* cénit *m*

**zero** ['zɪərəu] *n* cero

**zest** [zest] *n* ánimo, vivacidad *f*; (*of orange*) piel *f*

**zigzag** ['zɪgzæg] *n* zigzag *m* ♦ *vi* zig-

zaguear, hacer eses
**zinc** [zɪŋk] n cinc m, zinc m
**zip** [zɪp] n (also: ~ fastener, (US) ~per) cremallera (SP), cierre m (AM) ♦ vt (also: ~ up) cerrar la cremallera de; ~ **code** (US) n código postal
**zodiac** ['zəudɪæk] n zodíaco

**zone** [zəun] n zona
**zoo** [zu:] n (jardín m) zoo m
**zoology** [zu'ɔlədʒɪ] n zoología
**zoom** [zu:m] vi: to ~ past pasar zumbando; ~ **lens** n zoom m
**zucchini** [zu:'ki:nɪ] (US) n(pl) calabacín(ines) m(pl)

# SPANISH VERB TABLES

*1* Gerund. *2* Imperative. *3* Present. *4* Preterite. *5* Future. *6* Present subjunctive. *7* Imperfect subjunctive. *8* Past participle. *9* Imperfect. *Etc* indicates that the irregular root is used for all persons of the tense, e.g. **oir**: *6* oiga, oigas, oigamos, oigáis, oigan.

**agradecer** *3* agradezco *6* agradezca *etc*

**aprobar** *2* aprueba *3* apruebo, apruebas, aprueba, aprueban *6* apruebe, apruebes, apruebe, aprueben

**atravesar** *2* atraviesa *3* atravieso, atraviesas, atraviesa, atraviesan *6* atraviese, atravieses, atraviese, atraviesen

**caber** *3* quepo *4* cupe, cupiste, cupo, cupimos, cupisteis, cupieron *5* cabré *etc* *6* quepa *etc* *7* cupiera *etc*

**caer** *1* cayendo *3* caigo *4* cayó, cayeron *6* caiga *etc* *7* cayera *etc*

**cerrar** *2* cierra *3* cierro, cierras, cierra, cierran *6* cierre, cierres, cierre, cierren

**COMER** *1* comiendo *2* come, comed *3* como, comes, come comemos, coméis, comen *4* comí, comiste, comió, comimos, comisteis, comieron *5* comeré, comerás, comerá, comeremos, comeréis, comerán *6* coma, comas, coma, comamos, comáis, coman *7* comiera, comieras, comiera, comiéramos, comierais, comieran *8* comido *9* comía, comías, comía, comíamos, comíais, comían

**conocer** *3* conozco *6* conozca *etc*

**contar** *2* cuenta *3* cuento, cuentas, cuenta, cuentan *6* cuente, cuentes, cuente, cuenten

**dar** *3* doy *4* di, diste, dio, dimos, disteis, dieron *7* diera *etc*

**decir** *2* di *3* digo *4* dije, dijiste, dijo, dijimos, dijisteis, dijeron *5* diré *etc* *6* diga *etc* *7* dijera *etc* *8* dicho

**despertar** *2* despierta *3* despierto, despiertas, despierta, despiertan *6* despierte, despiertes, despierte, despierten

**divertir** *1* divirtiendo *2* divierte *3* divierto, diviertes, divierte, divierten *4* divirtió, divirtieron *6* divierta, diviertas, divierta, divirtamos, divirtáis, diviertan *7* divirtiera *etc*

**dormir** *1* durmiendo *2* duerme *3* duermo, duermes, duerme, duermen *4* durmió, durmieron *6* duerma, duermas, duerma, durmamos, durmáis, duerman *7* durmiera *etc*

**empezar** *2* empieza *3* empiezo, empiezas, empieza, empiezan *4* empecé *6* empiece, empieces, empecemos, empecéis, empiecen

**entender** *2* entiende *3* entiendo, entiendes, entiende, entienden *6* entienda, entiendas, entienda, entiendan

**ESTAR** *2* está *3* estoy, estás, está, están *4* estuve, estuviste, estuvo, estuvimos, estuvis-

teis, estuvieron 6 esté, estés,
esté, estén 7 estuviera etc

**HABER** 3 he, has, ha, hemos,
han 4 hube, hubiste, hubo,
hubimos, hubisteis, hubieron5
habré etc 6 haya etc 7 hubiera
etc

**HABLAR** 1 hablando 2 habla,
hablad 3 hablo, hablas, habla,
hablamos, habláis, hablan 4
hablé, hablaste, habló, hablá-
mos, hablasteis, hablaron 5
hablaré, hablarás, hablará,
hablaremos, hablaréis, ha-
blarán 6 hable, hables, hable,
hablemos, habléis, hablen 7
hablara, hablaras, hablara,
habláramos, hablaras, ha-
blaran 8 hablado 9 hablaba,
hablabas, hablaba, hablába-
mos, hablabais, hablaban

**hacer** 2 haz 3 hago 4 hice,
hiciste, hizo, hicimos, hicis-
teis, hicieron 5 haré etc 6 haga
etc 7 hiciera etc 8 hecho

**instruir** 1 instruyendo 2 instruye 3 instruyo, instruyes,
instruye, instruyen 4 instruyó,
instruyeron 6 instruya etc 7
instruyera etc

**ir** 1 yendo 2 ve 3 voy, vas, va,
vamos, vais, van 4 fui, fuiste,
fue, fuimos, fuisteis, fueron 6
vaya, vayas, vaya, vayamos,
vayáis, vayan 7 fuera etc 8 iba,
ibas, iba, íbamos, ibais, iban

**jugar** 2 juega 3 juego, juegas,
juega, juegan 4 jugué 6 juegue
etc

**leer** 1 leyendo 4 leyó, leyeron 7
leyera etc

**morir** 1 muriendo 2 muere 3
muero, mueres, muere,
mueren 4 murió, murieron 6
muera, mueras, muera,

muramos, muráis, mueran 7
muriera etc 8 muerto

**mover** 2 mueve 3 muevo,
mueves, mueve, mueven 6
mueva, muevas, mueva,
muevan

**negar** 2 niega 3 niego, niegas,
niega, niegan 4 negué 6
niegue, niegues, niegue,
neguemos, neguéis, nieguen

**ofrecer** 3 ofrezco 6 ofrezca etc

**oír** 1 oyendo 2 oye 3 oigo, oyes,
oye, oyen 4 oyó, oyeron 6 oiga
etc 7 oyera etc

**oler** 2 huele 3 huelo, hueles,
huele, huelen 6 huela, huelas,
huela, huelan

**parecer** 3 parezco 6 parezca etc

**pedir** 1 pidiendo 2 pide 3 pido,
pides, pide, piden 4 pidió,
pidieron 6 pida etc 7 pidiera
etc

**pensar** 2 piensa 3 pienso, piensas, piensa, piensan 6 piense,
pienses, piense, piensen

**perder** 2 pierde 3 pierdo,
pierdes, pierde, pierden 6
pierda, pierdas, pierda,
pierdan

**poder** 1 pudiendo 2 puede 3
puedo, puedes, puede, pueden
4 pude, pudiste, pudo, pudi-
mos, pudisteis, pudieron 5
podré etc 6 pueda, puedas,
pueda, puedan 7 pudiera etc

**poner** 2 pon 3 pongo 4 puse,
pusiste, puso, pusimos, pusis-
teis, pusieron 5 pondré etc 6
ponga etc 7 pusiera etc 8
puesto

**preferir** 1 prefiriendo 2 prefiere
3 prefiero, prefieres, prefiere,
prefieren 4 prefirió, pre-
firieron 6 prefiera, prefieras,
prefiera, prefiramos, pre-

**firáis, prefieran** 7 **prefiriera** *etc*

**querer** 2 **quiere** 3 **quiero, quieres, quiere, quieren** 4 **quise, quisiste, quiso, quisimos, quisisteis, quisieron** 5 **querré** *etc* 6 **quiera, quieras, quiera, quieran** 7 **quiera** *etc*

**reír** 2 **ríe** 3 **río, ríes, ríe, ríen** 4 **río, rieron** 6 **ría, rías, ría, riamos, riáis, rían** 7 **riera** *etc*

**repetir** 1 **repitiendo** 2 **repite** 3 **repito, repites, repite, repiten** 4 **repitió, repitieron** 6 **repita** *etc* 7 **repitiera** *etc*

**rogar** 2 **ruega** 3 **ruego, ruegas, ruega, ruegan** 4 **rogué** 6 **ruegue, ruegues, ruegue, roguemos, roguéis, rueguen**

**saber** 3 **sé** 4 **supe, supiste, supo, supimos, supisteis, supieron** 5 **sabré** *etc* 6 **sepa** *etc* 7 **supiera** *etc*

**salir** 2 **sal** 3 **salgo** 5 **saldré** *etc* 6 **salga** *etc*

**seguir** 1 **siguiendo** 2 **sigue** 3 **sigo, sigues, sigue, siguen** 4 **siguió, siguieron** 6 **siga** *etc* 7 **siguiera** *etc*

**sentar** 2 **sienta** 3 **siento, sientas, sienta, sientan** 6 **siente, sientes, siente, sienten**

**sentir** 1 **sintiendo** 2 **siente** 3 **siento, sientes, siente, sienten** 4 **sintió, sintieron** 6 **sienta, sientas, sienta, sintamos, sintáis, sientan** 7 **sintiera** *etc*

**SER** 2 **sé** 3 **soy, eres, es, somos, sois, son** 4 **fui, fuiste, fue, fuimos, fuisteis, fueron** 6 **sea** *etc* 7 **fuera** *etc* 9 **era, eras, era, éramos, erais, eran**

**servir** 1 **sirviendo** 2 **sirve** 3 **sirvo, sirves, sirve, sirven** 4 **sirvió, sirvieron** 6 **sirva** *etc* 7 **sir-**

**viera** *etc*

**soñar** 2 **sueña** 3 **sueño, sueñas, sueña, sueñan** 6 **sueñe, sueñes, sueñe, sueñen**

**tener** 2 **ten** 3 **tengo, tienes, tiene, tienen** 4 **tuve, tuviste, tuvo, tuvimos, tuvisteis, tuvieron** 5 **tendré** *etc* 6 **tenga** *etc* 7 **tuviera** *etc*

**traer** 1 **trayendo** 3 **traigo** 4 **traje, trajiste, trajo, trajimos, trajisteis, trajeron** 6 **traiga** *etc* 7 **trajera** *etc*

**valer** 2 **val** 3 **valgo** 5 **valdré** *etc* 6 **valga** *etc*

**venir** 2 **ven** 3 **vengo, vienes, viene, vienen** 4 **vine, viniste, vino, vinimos, vinisteis, vinieron** 5 **vendré** *etc* 6 **venga** *etc* 7 **viniera** *etc*

**ver** 3 **veo** 6 **vea** *etc* 8 **visto** 9 **veía** *etc*

**vestir** 1 **vistiendo** 2 **viste** 3 **visto, vistes, viste, visten** 4 **vistió, vistieron** 6 **vista** *etc* 7 **vistiera** *etc*

**VIVIR** 1 **viviendo** 2 **vive, vivid** 3 **vivo, vives, vive, vivimos, vivís, viven** 4 **viví, viviste, vivió, vivimos, vivisteis, vivieron** 5 **viviré, vivirás, vivirá, viviremos, viviréis, vivirán** 6 **viva, vivas, viva, vivamos, viváis, vivan** 7 **viviera, vivieras, viviera, viviéramos, vivierais, vivieran** 8 **vivido** 9 **vivía, vivías, vivía, vivíamos, vivíais, vivían**

**volver** 2 **vuelve** 3 **vuelvo, vuelves, vuelve, vuelven** 6 **vuelva, vuelvas, vuelva, vuelvan** 8 **vuelto**

# VERBOS IRREGULARES EN INGLÉS

| present | pt | pp | present | pt | pp |
|---|---|---|---|---|---|
| arise | arose | arisen | **dig** | dug | dug |
| awake | awoke | awaked | **do** (3rd | did | done |
| be (am, is, | was, | been | person; | | |
| are; | were | | he/she/it/ | | |
| being) | | | does) | | |
| bear | bore | born(e) | **draw** | drew | drawn |
| beat | beat | beaten | **dream** | dreamed, | dreamed, |
| become | became | become | | dreamt | dreamt |
| begin | began | begun | **drink** | drank | drunk |
| behold | beheld | beheld | **drive** | drove | driven |
| bend | bent | bent | **dwell** | dwelt | dwelt |
| beset | beset | beset | **eat** | ate | eaten |
| bet | bet, | bet, | **fall** | fell | fallen |
| | betted | betted | **feed** | fed | fed |
| bid | bid, | bid, | **feel** | felt | felt |
| | bade | bidden | **fight** | fought | fought |
| bind | bound | bound | **find** | found | found |
| bite | bit | bitten | **flee** | fled | fled |
| bleed | bled | bled | **fling** | flung | flung |
| blow | blew | blown | **fly (flies)** | flew | flown |
| break | broke | broken | **forbid** | forbade | forbidden |
| breed | bred | bred | **forecast** | forecast | forecast |
| bring | brought | brought | **forget** | forgot | forgotten |
| build | built | built | **forgive** | forgave | forgiven |
| burn | burnt, | burnt, | **forsake** | forsook | forsaken |
| | burned | burned | **freeze** | froze | frozen |
| burst | burst | burst | **get** | got | got, (US) |
| buy | bought | bought | | | gotten |
| can | could | (been | **give** | gave | given |
| | | able) | **go (goes)** | went | gone |
| cast | cast | cast | **grind** | ground | ground |
| catch | caught | caught | **grow** | grew | grown |
| choose | chose | chosen | **hang** | hung, | hung, |
| cling | clung | clung | | hanged | hanged |
| come | came | come | **have (has;** | had | had |
| cost | cost | cost | having) | | |
| creep | crept | crept | **hear** | heard | heard |
| cut | cut | cut | **hide** | hid | hidden |
| deal | dealt | dealt | **hit** | hit | hit |

| present | pt | pp | present | pt | pp |
|---|---|---|---|---|---|
| hold | held | held | sell | sold | sold |
| hurt | hurt | hurt | send | sent | sent |
| keep | kept | kept | set | set | set |
| kneel | knelt, kneeled | knelt, kneeled | shake | shook | shaken |
|  |  |  | shall | should |  |
| know | knew | known | shear | sheared | shorn, sheared |
| lay | laid | laid |  |  |  |
| lead | led | led | shed | shed | shed |
| lean | leant, leaned | leant, leaned | shine | shone | shone |
|  |  |  | shoot | shot | shot |
| leap | leapt, leaped | leapt, leaped | show | showed | shown |
|  |  |  | shrink | shrank | shrunk |
| learn | learnt, learned | learnt, learned | shut | shut | shut |
|  |  |  | sing | sang | sung |
| leave | left | left | sink | sank | sunk |
| lend | lent | lent | sit | sat | sat |
| let | let | let | slay | slew | slain |
| lie (lying) | lay | lain | sleep | slept | slept |
| light | lit, lighted | lit, lighted | slide | slid | slid |
|  |  |  | sling | slung | slung |
| lose | lost | lost | slit | slit | slit |
| make | made | made | smell | smelt, smelled | smelt, smelled |
| may | might | — |  |  |  |
| mean | meant | meant | sow | sowed | sown, sowed |
| meet | met | met |  |  |  |
| mistake | mistook | mistaken | speak | spoke | spoken |
| mow | mowed | mown, mowed | speed | sped, speeded | sped, speeded |
| must | (had to) | (had to) | spell | spelt, spelled | spelt, spelled |
| pay | paid | paid |  |  |  |
| put | put | put | spend | spent | spent |
| quit | quit, quitted | quit, quitted | spill | spilt, spilled | spilt, spilled |
| read | read | read | spin | spun | spun |
| rid | rid | rid | spit | spat | spat |
| ride | rode | ridden | split | split | split |
| ring | rang | rung | spoil | spoiled, spoilt | spoiled, spoilt |
| rise | rose | risen |  |  |  |
| run | ran | run | spread | spread | spread |
| saw | sawed | sawn | spring | sprang | sprung |
| say | said | said | stand | stood | stood |
| see | saw | seen | steal | stole | stolen |
| seek | sought | sought | stick | stuck | stuck |

| present | pt | pp | present | pt | pp |
|---|---|---|---|---|---|
| sting | stung | stung | think | thought | thought |
| stink | stank | stunk | throw | threw | thrown |
| stride | strode | stridden | thrust | thrust | thrust |
| strike | struck | struck, stricken | tread | trod | trodden |
| | | | wake | woke, waked | woken, waked |
| strive | strove | striven | | | |
| swear | swore | sworn | wear | wore | worn |
| sweep | swept | swept | weave | wove, weaved | woven, weaved |
| swell | swelled | swollen, swelled | wed | wedded, wed | wedded, wed |
| swim | swam | swum | | | |
| swing | swung | swung | weep | wept | wept |
| take | took | taken | win | won | won |
| teach | taught | taught | wind | wound | wound |
| tear | tore | torn | wring | wrung | wrung |
| tell | told | told | write | wrote | written |

# LOS NÚMEROS

# NUMBERS

| | | |
|---|---|---|
| un, uno(a) | 1 | one |
| dos | 2 | two |
| tres | 3 | three |
| cuatro | 4 | four |
| cinco | 5 | five |
| seis | 6 | six |
| siete | 7 | seven |
| ocho | 8 | eight |
| nueve | 9 | nine |
| diez | 10 | ten |
| once | 11 | eleven |
| doce | 12 | twelve |
| trece | 13 | thirteen |
| catorce | 14 | fourteen |
| quince | 15 | fifteen |
| dieciséis | 16 | sixteen |
| diecisiete | 17 | seventeen |
| dieciocho | 18 | eighteen |
| diecinueve | 19 | nineteen |
| veinte | 20 | twenty |
| veintiuno | 21 | twenty-one |
| veintidós | 22 | twenty-two |
| treinta | 30 | thirty |
| treinta y uno(a) | 31 | thirty-one |
| treinta y dos | 32 | thirty-two |
| cuarenta | 40 | forty |
| cincuenta | 50 | fifty |
| sesenta | 60 | sixty |
| setenta | 70 | seventy |
| ochenta | 80 | eighty |
| noventa | 90 | ninety |
| cien, ciento | 100 | a hundred, one hundred |
| ciento uno(a) | 101 | a hundred and one |
| doscientos(as) | 200 | two hundred |
| doscientos(as) uno(a) | 201 | two hundred and one |
| trescientos(as) | 300 | three hundred |
| cuatrocientos(as) | 400 | four hundred |
| quinientos(as) | 500 | five hundred |
| seiscientos(as) | 600 | six hundred |
| setecientos(as) | 700 | seven hundred |
| ochocientos(as) | 800 | eight hundred |
| novecientos(as) | 900 | nine hundred |
| mil | 1 000 | a thousand |
| mil dos | 1 002 | a thousand and two |
| cinco mil | 5 000 | five thousand |
| un millón | 1 000 000 | a million |

# LOS NÚMEROS

# NUMBERS

| | |
|---|---|
| primer, primero(a), $1^o$, $1^{er}$ ($1^a$, $1^{era}$) | first, 1st |
| segundo(a) $2^o$ ($2^a$) | second, 2nd |
| tercer, tercero(a), $3^o$ ($3^a$) | third, 3rd |
| cuarto(a), $4^o$ ($4^a$) | fourth, 4th |
| quinto(a), $5^o$ ($5^a$) | fifth, 5th |
| sexto(a), $6^o$ ($6^a$) | sixth, 6th |
| séptimo(a) | seventh |
| octavo(a) | eighth |
| noveno(a) | ninth |
| décimo(a) | tenth |
| undécimo(a) | eleventh |
| duodécimo(a) | twelfth |
| decimotercio(a) | thirteenth |
| decimocuarto(a) | fourteenth |
| decimoquinto(a) | fifteenth |
| decimosexto(a) | sixteenth |
| vigésimo(a) | twentieth |
| vigésimo(a) primero(a) | twenty-first |
| trigésimo(a) | thirtieth |
| centésimo(a) | hundredth |
| centésimo(a) primero(a) | hundred-and-first |
| milésimo(a) | thousandth |

## Números Quebrados etc

## Fractions etc

| | |
|---|---|
| un medio | a half |
| un tercio | a third |
| un cuarto | a quarter |
| un quinto | a fifth |
| cero coma cinco, 0,5 | (nought) point five, 0.5 |
| diez por cien(to) | ten per cent |

**N.B.** In Spanish the ordinal numbers from 1 to 10 are commonly used; from 11 to 20 rather less; above 21 they are rarely written and almost never heard in speech. The custom is to replace the forms for 21 and above by the cardinal number.

# LA HORA

# THE TIME

¿qué hora es?

*what time is it?*

es/son

*it's o it is*

| | |
|---|---|
| medianoche, las doce (de la noche) | midnight, twelve p.m. |
| la una (de la madrugada) | one o'clock (in the morning), one (a.m.) |
| la una y cinco | five past one |
| la una y diez | ten past one |
| la una y cuarto *or* quince | a quarter past one, one fifteen |
| la una y veinticinco | twenty-five past one, one twenty-five |
| la una y media *or* treinta | half-past one, one thirty |
| las dos menos veinticinco, la una treinta y cinco | twenty-five to two, one thirty-five |
| las dos menos veinte, la una cuarenta | twenty to two, one forty |
| las dos menos cuarto, la una cuarenta y cinco | a quarter to two, one forty-five |
| las dos menos diez, la una cincuenta | ten to two, one fifty |
| mediodía, las doce (de la tarde) | twelve o'clock, midday, noon |
| la una (de la tarde) | one o'clock (in the afternoon), one (p.m.) |
| las siete (de la tarde) | seven o'clock (in the evening), seven (p.m.) |

¿a qué hora?

*(at) what time?*

| | |
|---|---|
| a medianoche | at midnight |
| a las siete | at seven o'clock |
| en veinte minutos | in twenty minutes |
| hace quince minutos | fifteen minutes ago |

# COLLINS

## *for your PC*

Collins Electronic Dictionaries
are now available for use with
your personal computer.

For details write to:
Collins Dictionaries: Dept. RDH
PO Box, Glasgow G4 0NB